COLLECTION

offices

büros

Imprint

The Deutsche Nationalbibliothek lists this publication in the Deutsche Nationalbibliografie; detailed bibliographical data are available on the internet at http://dnb.d-nb.de.

ISBN 978-3-03768-050-6
Copyright 2010 by Braun Publishing AG
www.braun-publishing.ch

The work is copyright protected. Any use outside of the close boundaries of the copyright law, which has not been granted permission by the publisher, is unauthorized and liable for prosecution. This especially applies to duplications, translations, microfilming, and any saving or processing in electronic systems.

1st edition 2010

Editorial coordination:
van Uffelen Editorial Office
Editorial staff:
Anika Burger, Chris van Uffelen
Translation into English:
Cosima Talhouni
Graphic design:
Michaela Prinz
Layout:
Natascha Saupe, Georgia van Uffelen

All of the information in this volume has been compiled to the best of the editors knowledge. It is based on the information provided to the publisher by the architects offices and excludes any liability. The publisher assumes no responsibility for its accuracy or completeness as well as copyright discrepancies and refers to the specified sources (architects offices). All rights to the photographs are property of the photographer (please refer to the picture).

Chris van Uffelen

offices

büros

CONTENTS
INHALT

8 Preface

ASIA

12 **LANDMARK EAST**_CHINA_HONG KONG
Arquitectonica

16 **77/32**_INDIA_GURGAON
Morphogenesis

18 **CORPORATE OFFICE FOR INDIA GLYCOLS**
INDIA_NOIDA
Morphogenesis

20 **MENARA KARYA**_INDONESIA_JAKARTA
Arquitectonica

22 **BENETTON GROUP**_IRAN_TEHRAN
8A Architects

24 **KAYAC**_JAPAN_KAMAKURA-SHI
Klein Dytham Architecture

26 **AIG BUILDING**_JAPAN_NAGASAKI
George Dasic Architects

28 **CBS BUILDING**_JAPAN_TOKYO
George Dasic Architects

30 **TV ASAHI**_JAPAN_MINATO-KU, TOKYO
Maki and Associates / Fumihiko Maki

32 **MEGURO OFFICE**_JAPAN_TOKYO
Nendo

34 **AKASAKA OFFICE**_JAPAN_TOKYO
Nendo

36 **DOHA HIGH RISE OFFICE BUILDING**
QATAR_DOHA
Ateliers Jean Nouvel

38 **FEDERATION COMPLEX**_RUSSIA_MOSCOW
Prof. Peter Schweger and Sergei Tchoban

42 **THE EDGE**_UAE_DUBAI
RCR Arquitectes

EUROPE

46 **OFFICE BUILDING GRABENSTRASSE**
AUSTRIA_GRAZ
Architektur Consult ZT GmbH with
Herfried Peyker

48 **FROG QUEEN**_AUSTRIA_GRAZ
Splitterwerk

50 **VOESTALPINE STAHL GMBH**
AUSTRIA_LINZ
Dietmar Feichtinger Architectes

54 **T-CENTER ST. MARX**_AUSTRIA_VIENNA
Architektur Consult ZT GmbH with
Günther Domenig

58 **ADMINISTRATIVE CENTER BONHEIDEN**
BELGIUM_BONHEIDEN
VBMarchitects

60 **EURO SPACE CENTER**
BELGIUM_LIBIN-TRANSINNE
Philippe Samyn and Partners

62 **HEAD OFFICE JOKER TOURISM**
BELGIUM_MECHELEN
META Architectuurbureau

66 **OFFICE VANHAERENTS TORHOUT**
BELGIUM_TORHOUT
Buro II

70 **C. F. MØLLER ARCHITECTS HEAD OFFICE**
DENMARK_AARHUS
C. F. Møller Architects

72 **O-ZONE, ORACLE HEADQUARTERS**
DENMARK_BALLERUP
Lars Gitz Architects

74 **WORLD HEALTH ORGANISATION**
DENMARK_COPENHAGEN
Lars Gitz Architects

76 **VITUS BERING INNOVATION PARK**
DENMARK_HORSENS
C. F. Møller Architects

78 **COMM2**
DENMARK_KOKKEDAL
Lars Gitz Architects

80 **ADVICE HOUSE**_DENMARK_VEJLE
C. F. Møller Architects

82 **MEISTRI OFFICE BUILDING**
ESTONIA_TALLINN
Palm-E Arhitektibüroo

84 **PORTAALI BUSINESS PARK**
FINLAND_HELSINKI
B&M Architects

88 **21 BOISSEAU**
FRANCE_CLICHY-LA-GARENNE
AW²

90 **GENNEVILLIERS LOGISTICS CENTER**
FRANCE_GENNEVILLIERS
Dietmar Feichtinger Architectes

94 **EXALTIS TOWER**_FRANCE_LA DÉFENSE
Arquitectonica

96 **PHARE TOWER**_FRANCE_LA DÉFENSE
Morphosis Architects

98 **GENERALI TOWER**_FRANCE_LA DÉFENSE
Valode & Pistre Architectes

100 **8 ROCHEFOUCAULD**_FRANCE_PARIS
AW²

102 **118 ELYSÉES**_FRANCE_PARIS
AW²

104 **CARDBOARD OFFICE**_FRANCE_PARIS
Paul Coudamy

106 **LABOBRAIN**_FRANCE_PARIS
Mathieu Lehanneur

108 **CINETIC OFFICE BUILDING**
FRANCE_PARIS
Valode & Pistre Architectes

110 **COMPANY HEADQUARTERS**
FRANCE_SAINT-MESMES
LAN Architecture

112 **BÖSL MEDIZINTECHNIK GMBH**
GERMANY_AACHEN
Fischerarchitekten GmbH & Co. KG

114 **MONASTERY ST. ALFONS**
GERMANY_AACHEN
Kaiser Schweitzer Architekten and
Glashaus Architekten PSG

116 **DAIMLER CHRYSLER MARKETING OFFICE**
GERMANY_BERLIN
Hemprich Tophof Architekten

118 **ABSPANNWERK BUCHHÄNDLER WEG**
GERMANY_BERLIN
HSH Hoyer Schindele Hirschmüller

120 **ORCO GERMANY**_GERMANY_BERLIN
Iris Steinbeck Architekten

124 **DEUTSCHER CARITASVERBAND E. V.**
GERMANY_BERLIN
Vonbock Architekten

126	**ENBW CENTER OBERSCHWABEN** GERMANY_BIBERACH A. D. RISS WMA Wöhr Mieslinger Architekten	
128	**Q-CELLS HEADQUARTERS** GERMANY_BITTERFELD-WOLFEN BHSS-Architekten GmbH / Behnisch Hermus Schinko Schumann	
132	**OFFICE BUILDING BONN-LENGSDORF** GERMANY_BONN Kohl: Fromme Architekten	
134	**T-HOME CAMPUS**_GERMANY_BONN van den Valentyn Architektur	
138	**ROMA FORUM**_GERMANY_BURGAU Ott Architekten	
142	**CONSTANTIN HÖFE**_GERMANY_COLOGNE JSWD Architekten	
144	**RHEINAU ART OFFICE** GERMANY_COLOGNE Kubalux Architekten GmbH	
148	**OFFICE BUILDING AT ST. KUNIBERT** GERMANY_COLOGNE van den Valentyn Architektur	
152	**LAMELLENHAUS**_GERMANY_CONSTANCE Thomas Pink	Petzinka Pink Architekten	
156	**FIVE BOATS**_GERMANY_DUISBURG Bahl + Partner Architekten BDA with Grimshaw Architects	
158	**HITACHI POWER OFFICE** GERMANY_DUISBURG Bahl + Partner Architekten	
160	**E-PLUS HEADQUARTERS** GERMANY_DÜSSELDORF NPS Tchoban Voss Architekten BDA / Sergei Tchoban with Stephan Lohre	
164	**FOUR ELEMENTS** GERMANY_DÜSSELDORF Thomas Pink	Petzinka Pink Architekten	
168	**IDEENBOTSCHAFT** GERMANY_DÜSSELDORF Thomas Pink	Petzinka Pink Architekten	
172	**DOCK 2.0**_GERMANY_FRANKFURT/MAIN Meixner Schlüter Wendt Architekten	
174	**PUBLIC ORDER OFFICE FRANKFURT** GERMANY_FRANKFURT/MAIN Meixner Schlüter Wendt Architekten	
178	**MAIN ADMINISTRATION GELSENWASSER AG**_GERMANY_GELSENKIRCHEN Anin · Jeromin · Fitilidis & Partner	
182	**HANS-SACHS-HAUS** GERMANY_GELSENKIRCHEN PASD Feldmeier + Wrede	
184	**ADMINISTRATION BUILDING THS** GERMANY_GELSENKIRCHEN THS / PASD Feldmeier + Wrede	
188	**RED RABBIT WERBEAGENTUR GMBH** GERMANY_HAMBURG BFGF Design Studios	
192	**MUTTER**_GERMANY_HAMBURG BFGF Design Studios	
196	**JOHANNISCONTOR** GERMANY_HAMBURG KBNK Architekten GmbH	
200	**OFFICE BUILDING GROSSE ELBSTRASSE**_GERMANY_HAMBURG SEHW Architekten Hamburg	
204	**NDR RADIO CONSTRUCTION PHASE 1+2** GERMANY_HAMBURG Schweger Associated Architects GmbH	
208	**VGH WARMBÜCHENQUARTIER** GERMANY_HANOVER ASP Architekten Schneider Meyer Partner	
212	**VOLKSBANK KARLSRUHE HEADQUARTERS**_GERMANY_KARLSRUHE Herrmann+Bosch Architekten	
214	**BINDER WOODCENTER** GERMANY_KOESCHING Matteo Thun & Partners	
216	**KROGMANN HEADQUARTERS** GERMANY_LOHNE Despang Architekten	
220	**WEISSLILIENGASSE 7** GERMANY_MAINZ CMA Cyrus Moser Architekten	
222	**HUGO BOSS HEADQUARTERS** GERMANY_METZINGEN Riehle+Partner Architekten und Stadtplaner	
226	**TECHNOLOGY CENTER MUNICH MTZ** GERMANY_MUNICH h4a Gessert+Randecker Architekten BDA	
228	**FRAUNHOFER BUILDING** GERMANY_MUNICH Henn Architekten	
232	**BMW OFFICE BUILDING** GERMANY_MUNICH Plajer & Franz Studio	
234	**REVITALIZATION BMW HIGH RISE PREMISES**_GERMANY_MUNICH Schweger Associated Architects GmbH	
236	**INTERNATIONAL CONSULTANCY** GERMANY_MUNICH Wagenknecht Architekten	
240	**SILO4PLUS5**_GERMANY_ROSTOCK Beyer Architekten & Tilo Ries	
242	**IMTECH HEADQUARTERS** GERMANY_STUTTGART Merz Objektbau	
246	**ADVERTISING AGENCY SCHWARZ-SPRINGER**_GERMANY_STUTTGART ZieglerBürg, Büro für Gestaltung	
250	**SCHATTDECOR AG HEADQUARTERS** GERMANY_THANSAU Obersteiner Architekten	
254	**RENOVATION STATISTISCHES BUNDESAMT**_GERMANY_WIESBADEN Sander.Hofrichter Architekten	
256	**SAMAS**_GERMANY_WORMS 100% Interior Sylvia Leydecker	
258	**JUWI HOLDING CORPORATE HEADQUARTERS**_GERMANY_WÖRRSTADT GriffnerHaus AG	
260	**LIMERICK COUNTY COUNCIL HEADQUARTERS**_IRELAND_DOORADOYLE Bucholz McEvoy Architects, Ltd	
262	**SAP BUILDING GALWAY** IRELAND_GALWAY Bucholz McEvoy Architects, Ltd	
264	**WESTMEATH COUNTY COUNCIL HEADQUARTERS**_IRELAND_MULLINGAR Bucholz McEvoy Architects, Ltd	
266	**BISAZZA HEADQUARTERS** ITALY_ALTE DI MONTECCHIO Carlo Dal Bianco	
268	**NAVILE TRE**_ITALY_BOLOGNA JSWD Architekten	

270 **BLAAS GENERAL PARTNERSHIP** ITALY_BOLZANO monovolume architecture + design	314 **DIFRAX HEAD OFFICE** THE NETHERLANDS_BILTHOVEN Smits + Ramaekers Interior Architects	356 **PARKING AND OFFICES DE COPE UTRECHT** THE NETHERLANDS_UTRECHT JHK Architecten
274 **ROTHO BLAAS LIMITED COMPANY** ITALY_KURTATSCH monovolume architecture + design	316 **RECYCLED OFFICE** THE NETHERLANDS_DUIVENDRECHT i29 Interior Architects	360 **DNB NOR HEADQUARTERS** NORWAY_OSLO MVRDV
278 **NEW HEADQUARTERS ERMENEGILDO ZEGNA** ITALY_MILAN Antonio Citterio, Patricia Viel and Partners	318 **CARDBOARD OFFICE FOR SCHERP-ONTWERP** THE NETHERLANDS_EINDHOVEN RO&AD Architecten	362 **URBAN ENERGY**_NORWAY_OSLO Transform with BSAA Architects
282 **TIZIANO 32 HEADQUARTERS**_ITALY_MILAN Park Associati and Zucchi & Partners	320 **NEDAP GROENLO** THE NETHERLANDS_GROENLO Bartijn Architecten	364 **CITY MUNICIPALITY** SLOVENIA_LJUBLJANA OFIS Arhitekti
286 **OFECOMES, SPANISH FOREIGN TRADE OFFICE**_ITALY_MILAN Francesc Rifé	324 **VISSER GROEN**_THE NETHERLANDS_HENDRIK-IDO-AMBACHT Nine Oaks / Ben Huygen	366 **PARCLOGISTIC ILLA-B1** SPAIN_BARCELONA Ricardo Bofill Taller De Arquitectura
288 **GLASS BOX IN THE COLUMNS BOX** ITALY_PALERMO Marco Viola and Filippo Saponaro	326 **OFFICE BRAINPARK III** THE NETHERLANDS_ROTTERDAM Broekbakema	368 **TORRE LAMINAR**_SPAIN_BARCELONA Soriano & Asociados Arquitectos
290 **CMB HEADQUARTERS OFFICE**_ITALY_ROME 3c+t Capolei Cavalli Architects, Molinari Landi architects	328 **SABIC EUROPE HEAD OFFICE** THE NETHERLANDS_ROTTERDAM Group A	370 **INDRET**_SPAIN_BARCELONA Francesc Rifé
292 **OFFICE CENTRE "1000"**_LITHUANIA_KAUNAS JSC "Ra Studija"	332 **CABALLERO FABRIEK** THE NETHERLANDS_ROTTERDAM Group A	374 **TORRES DE HÉRCULES**_SPAIN_CÁDIZ Rafael de La-Hoz Castanys
296 **MFT OFFICE**_LITHUANIA_VILNIUS Audrius Bucas & Marina Buciene	334 **DEBRUG / DEKADE UNILEVER ROTTERDAM** THE NETHERLANDS_ROTTERDAM JHK Architecten	376 **THE MYSTERIOUS STORY OF THE GARDEN THAT PRODUCES WATER**_SPAIN_CEHEGÍN Cómo Crear Historias
298 **OFFICES LA DEFENSE** THE NETHERLANDS_ALMERE UNStudio	338 **OFFICE VAN DER ZWAN & ZN.** THE NETHERLANDS_SCHEVENINGEN Meyer en Van Schooten Architecten	378 **TELEFONICA'S DISTRICT C** SPAIN_MADRID Rafael de La-Hoz Castanys
300 **ERICK VAN EGERAAT OFFICE TOWER** THE NETHERLANDS_AMSTERDAM Erick van Egeraat	342 **DE KUYPER ROYAL DISTILLERS** THE NETHERLANDS_SCHIEDAM Broekbakema	382 **STUDIO IN GREEN**_SPAIN_MADRID SelgasCano – Jose Selgas, Lucia Cano
302 **POST PANIC AMSTERDAM** THE NETHERLANDS_AMSTERDAM Maurice Mentjens	344 **THE OUTLOOK** THE NETHERLANDS_SCHIPHOL Cepezed Architects	384 **INNOVA**_SPAIN_PINEDA DE MAR Alcolea+Tárrago Arquitectos
306 **ATRADIUS HEADQUARTERS** THE NETHERLANDS_AMSTERDAM van den Oever, Zaaijer & Partners Architecten	348 **OFFICE KROPMAN** THE NETHERLANDS_UTRECHT Broekbakema	386 **SGAE CENTRAL OFFICE** SPAIN_SANTIAGO DE COMPOSTELA Antón García-Abril & Ensamble Studio
308 **KRAANSPOOR** THE NETHERLANDS_AMSTERDAM OTH Ontwerpgroep Trude Hooykaas	352 **WESTRAVEN** THE NETHERLANDS_UTRECHT Cepezed Architects	388 **ARCHITECTURAL ASSOCIATION GALICIA** SPAIN_VIGO Irisarri + Piñera
312 **MAHLER 4 OFFICE TOWER** THE NETHERLANDS_AMSTERDAM Rafael Viñoly Architects PC		392 **SAVINGS BANK HEADQUARTERS** SPAIN_VITORIA-GASTEIZ Mozas+Aguirre Arquitectos
		394 **PIONEN – WHITE MOUNTAIN** SWEDEN_STOCKHOLM Albert France-Lanord Architects

396	**MOBIMO VERWALTUNGS AG HEADQUARTERS**
SWITZERLAND_KÜSNACHT
Stücheli Architekten	

396 **MOBIMO VERWALTUNGS AG HEADQUARTERS**
SWITZERLAND_KÜSNACHT
Stücheli Architekten

398 **CLARIANT SPENGLER FLEXIBLE OFFICE**
SWITZERLAND_MÜNCHENSTEIN
Wirth+Wirth Architects

400 **COCOON – GOOGLE OFFICE HEADQUARTERS**
SWITZERLAND_ZURICH
Camenzind Evolution

404 **GOOGLE'S NEW EMEA ENGINEERING HUB**
SWITZERLAND_ZURICH
Camenzind Evolution

408 **SAM HEADQUARTERS**
SWITZERLAND_ZURICH
Andres Carosio Architekten

410 **BANK VONTOBEL HEADQUARTERS**
SWITZERLAND_ZURICH
Stücheli Architekten

412 **SUPERTANKER, ADDITION OF STORIES**
SWITZERLAND_ZURICH
Stücheli Architekten

414 **THE WELLCOME TRUST HEADQUARTERS**
UNITED KINGDOM_LONDON
Hopkins Architects

416 **LG EUROPEAN DESIGN CENTRE**
UNITED KINGDOM_LONDON
Jump studios

418 **10 HILLS PLACE**
UNITED KINGDOM_LONDON
Amanda Levete Architects

420 **FARRINGDON BUILDINGS**
UNITED KINGDOM_LONDON
Nissen Adams

422 **THE LONDON BRIDGE TOWER**
UNITED KINGDOM_LONDON
Renzo Piano Building Workshop with Adamson Associates

NORTH AMERICA

426 **GRIP LIMITED**_CANADA_TORONTO (ON)
Johnson Chou Inc.

430 **FALCON HEADQUARTERS**
MEXICO_MEXICO CITY
Rojkind Arquitectos with Derek Dellekamp

434 **CORPORATIVO FREXPORT**
MEXICO_ZAMORA MICHOACAN
CC Arquitectos / Manuel Cervantes Cespedes

438 **3ALITY DIGITAL**_USA_BURBANK (CA)
Fung + Blatt Architects, Inc.

440 **111 SOUTH WACKER**_USA_CHICAGO (IL)
Goettsch Partners

444 **LARCHMONT OFFICE**
USA_LOS ANGELES (CA)
Rios Clementi Hale Studios

448 **BARODA VENTURES**
USA_LOS ANGELES (CA)
Rios Clementi Hale Studios

450 **BRAND NEW SCHOOL**
USA_LOS ANGELES (CA)
Shubin + Donaldson Architects

454 **HEARST TOWER**
USA_NEW YORK CITY (NY)
Foster + Partners

456 **505 FIFTH AVENUE**
USA_NEW YORK CITY (NY)
KPF – Kohn Pedersen Fox Associates

460 **OFFICE MICHAEL NEUMANN ARCHITECTURE**_USA_NEW YORK CITY (NY)
Michael Neumann Architecture, LLC

464 **THE NEW YORK TIMES BUILDING**
USA_NEW YORK CITY (NY)
Renzo Piano Building Workshop with Fox & Fowle Architects

466 **GSC OFFICES**_USA_NEW YORK CITY (NY)
Skidmore, Owings & Merrill LLP

470 **FACEBOOK HEADQUARTERS**
USA_PALO ALTO (CA)
Studio O+A

474 **HYDRAULX**_USA_SANTA MONICA (CA)
Shubin + Donaldson Architects

476 **MOVING PICTURE COMPANY**
USA_SANTA MONICA (CA)
Patrick Tighe Architecture

480 **SARASOTA HERALD-TRIBUNE HEADQUARTERS**_USA_SARASOTA (FL)
Arquitectonica

SOUTH AMERICA

484 **AGÊNCIA DE PUBLICIDADE MPM**
BRAZIL_SÃO PAULO
Bernardes + Jacobsen Arquitetura

488 **SOUZA, CESCON, BARRIEU E FLESCH**_BRAZIL_SÃO PAULO
RMAA / Henrique Reinach and Mauricio Mendonça

492 **LODUCCA AGENCY**
BRAZIL_SÃO PAULO
Triptyque Architecture

494 **ARCHITECTS STUDIO**
BRAZIL_SÃO PAULO
Frederico Zanelato Arquitetos

496 **VAN DER LAAT & JIMÉNEZ OFFICE BUILDING**_COSTA RICA_SAN JOSÉ
Fournier-Rojas Arquitectos / FoRo

AUSTRALIA

502 **NATIONAL@DOCKLANDS**
AUSTRALIA_MELBOURNE
BVN Architecture

504 **STOCKLAND HEAD OFFICE**
AUSTRALIA_SYDNEY
BVN Architecture

506 **CHALLENGER WORKPLACE**
AUSTRALIA_SYDNEY
BVN Architecture

508 Architects Index

510 Projects Index

COLLECTION_OFFICES **PREFACE**

The focus of **Collection: Offices** is on buildings that primarily serve the handling and processing of data and methods. Their most frequently used production facility is the computer and their warehouses often only measure a few 3.5 inch hard drives, which can fit on a single shelf.

The rapidly advancing digital revolution, diversification of tasks, and heightened expectations towards office buildings in terms of building equipment and technology as well as an attractive building and work environment design have substantially changed the building process within the past few decades. Sophisticated ventilation technology and energy concepts nowadays go hand in hand with contemporary designs that usually serve as the flagships of a company or as part of its corporate design. New office concepts such as the combination office or even the lounge workspace have been introduced alongside the open space or cell office concepts that have basically been in use since antiquity. Psychology explained to market economy the economic added value of workplaces with wellness factors, while communication research taught Taylorism the advantages of flexibility and spontaneity. Ecology and high-technology have jointly dispelled the "office climate" described by German author Franz Kafka.

Office buildings have been found in all advanced cultures since Mesopotamia, but the work places of scribes were usually located in other buildings. It was not until the Renaissance era, that true office buildings were constructed, the most famous being the Uffizes ("offices") in Florence (Girogio Vasari, 1511–1574), a U-shaped section with group cells for thirteen administrative officers each. In the 19th century the number of urban and state administration offices once again increased rapidly and large office buildings were constructed also for the private sector with prestigious receptions and extensive hallway systems leading to the upstairs offices.

In the first quarter of the 20th century, the "employee" behind a Remington typewriter became a full-fledge mass phenomenon and office high rises began to conquer urban settings (Cass Gilberts Woolworth-Building, 1910–1913), until the 1960s/70s when new layout solutions that attempted to combine individual and open-plan offices were introduced – office landscapes, office islands, and combination offices overcame the discrepancy of individual and open-plan offices.

Starting in the 1990s, computerization enabled new office forms such as non-territorial offices with touchdown and desk sharing work places, business hubs and lounge workspaces. Competency centers and competency neighborhoods now structured areas according to their functions and reversible offices can be adjusted to any office style within a short period of time (just-in-time office). The realization that spontaneous meetings in informal zones or chance discussions can advance work processes cost-efficiently through "shorter connections" and spontaneous exchange of information, loosened up the fixed territorial character of work places. The cost factor of the newly developed spaces was turned into valuable social hubs, whose use is advanced by winding paths. All these tendencies are presented in many examples in **Collection: Offices**, in which even the presumably old office types appear totally changed with the glamour of a new modern design – as places in which it is a joy to work.

VORWORT

Im Mittelpunkt der **Collection: Offices** stehen Bauten, die in erster Linie dem Verwalten und Verarbeiten von Informationen und von Vorgängen dienen. Häufigstes Produktionsmittel ist der Computer, und das Archiv ist oft nur noch wenige 3,5-Zoll Festplatten groß und passt auf ein einziges Regalbrett.

Die rasant fortschreitende digitale Revolution, die Diversifizierung der Arbeiten und die zunehmend hohen Ansprüche an den Bürohausbau in Gebäudeausstattung und -technik sowie in ansprechender Gestaltung des Baukörpers und des Arbeitsumfelds haben die Bauaufgabe in den letzten Jahrzehnten grundlegend gewandelt. Ausgefeilte Belüftungstechniken und Energiekonzepte gehen heute mit zeitgemäßer Gestaltung – häufig Aushängeschild des Betriebes oder Teil eines Corporate Designs – einher. Neue Büroformen wie das Kombibüro oder gar der Lounge Workspace treten neben die im Prinzip seit dem Altertum bekannten Typen des Großraumes oder des Zellenbüros. Die Psychologie hat der Marktwirtschaft den ökonomischen Mehrwert eines Arbeitsplatzes mit Wohlfühlcharakter erklärt, die Kommunikationsforschung hat dem Taylorismus die Vorteile von Flexibilität und Spontanität beigebracht, Ökologie und High-Tech haben gemeinsam die „Büroluft" Franz Kafkas vertrieben.

Büroräume sind in jeder Hochkultur seit Mesopotamien nachzuweisen, doch als Arbeitsplätze dienten den Schreibern meist bestehende Bauten anderer Gattungen, echte Bürogebäude gab es nicht. Erst in der Renaissance entstanden echte Bürobauten, deren bekanntester sicher die Uffizien („offices") in Florenz (Girogio Vasari, 1511–1574) sind, ein U-förmiger Trakt mit Gruppenzellen für je dreizehn Verwaltungsangestellte. Im 19. Jahrhundert stieg die Anzahl städtischer und staatlicher Verwaltungsgebäude dann erneut rapide an und es entstanden auch für die Privatwirtschaft große Bürobauten mit repräsentativem Empfang und umfangreichen Korridorsystemen zu den Büros im Obergeschoss.

Im ersten Viertel des 20. Jahrhunderts wurde der „Büroangestellte" an einer Remington-Schreibschine endgültig ein Massenphänomen und Bürohochhäuser begannen ihren Siegeszug (Cass Gilberts Woolworth-Building, 1910–1913) als stadtprägende Bauform. Erst in den 1960er/1970er Jahren enstanden neue Grundrisslösungen, die das Einzel- und Großraumbüro zu verbinden suchten: Bürolandschaft, Büroinseln und Kombi-Büro überwinden den Gegensatz von Einzel- und Großraumbüro.

Die Computerisierung machte seit den 1990er Jahren weitere Typen wie non-territoriale Büros mit Touchdown- und Desk-sharing-Arbeitsplätzen, Business hubs und Lounge Workspace möglich. Kompetenzzentren und -nachbarschaften gliedern Bereiche nun aufgabenorientiert, und das reversible Büro ist jedem Bürotyp kurzfristig (just-in-time Büro) anzupassen. Die Erkenntnis, dass spontane Treffen in informellen Zonen oder sich zufällig ergebende Gespräche den Arbeitsprozess durch „kurze Dienstwege" und spontanen Wissensautausch kostengünstig voranbringen, lockerte den Arbeitsplatz als festes Territorium. Aus dem Kostenfaktor der Erschließungsräume wurden wertvolle social hubs, deren Nutzung durch gewundene Wege forciert wird. All diese Tendenzen finden sich in vielerlei Besipielen in der **Collection: Offices**, wobei auch die vermeintlich alten Büroraumtypologien sich im Glanz einer schicken modernen Gestaltung völlig gewandelt zeigen – als Orte, an denen Arbeit Spaß macht.

COLLECTION

asia

NDMARK EAST_CHINA_HONG KONG_77/32_INDIA_GURGAON_CORPORATE O
CE FOR INDIA GLYCOLS_INDIA_NOIDA_MENARA KARYA_INDONES
JAKARTA_BENETTONGROUP_IRAN_TEHRAN_KAYAC_JAPAN_KAMAKURA-SHI_AIGBUI
NG_JAPAN_NAGASAKI_CBS BUILDING_JAPAN_TOKYO_AKASAKA OFFICE_J
N_TOKYO_MEGURO OFFICE_JAPAN_TOKYO_TV ASAHI_JAPAN_TOKYO_DO
HIGH RISE OFFICE BUILDING_QATAR_DOHA_FEDERATION COM
X_RUSSIA_MOSCOW_THE EDGE_UAE_DUBAI_LANDMARK EAST_CHINA_HO
KONG_77/32_INDIA_GURGAON_CORPORATE OFFICE FOR INDIA GLYCOLS
DIA_NOIDA_MENARAKARYA_INDONESIA_JAKARTA_BENETTONGROUP_IRAN_T
AN_KAYAC_JAPAN_KAMAKURA-SHI_AIG BUILDING_JAPAN_NAGASAKI_CB
ILDING_JAPAN_TOKYO_AKASAKAOFFICE_JAPAN_TOKYO_MEGUROOFFICE_J
N_TOKYO_TV ASAHI_JAPAN_TOKYO_DOHA HIGH RISE OFFICE BUILDING_QA
DOHA_FEDERATIONCOMPLEX_RUSSIA_MOSCOW_THEEDGE_UAE_DUBAI_L
MARK EAST_CHINA_HONG KONG_77/32_INDIA_GURGAON_CORPORATE OF
FOR INDIA GLYCOLS_INDIA_NOIDA_MENARA KARYA_INDONESIA_JAKAR
BENETTONGROUP_IRAN_TEHRAN_KAYAC_JAPAN_KAMAKURA-SHI_AIGBUI
NG_JAPAN_NAGASAKI_CBS BUILDING_JAPAN_TOKYO_AKASAKA OFFICE_J
TOKYO_MEGURO OFFICE JAPAN_TOKYO_TV ASAHI_JAPAN_TOKYO

CHINA_HONG KONG **LANDMARK EAST**

ARCHITECTS: ARQUITECTONICA
SCULPTURE: POLO BOURIEAU_**COMPLETION:** 2008
NUMBER OF WORKPLACES: 7,300
GROSS FLOOR AREA: 110,000 M²_**COMMON AREA:** MEETING ROOMS, BREAKOUT AREAS
KIND OF WORKPLACES: COMBINATION
PHOTOS: WINSOR PROPERTY, HONG KONG (12), ARQUITECTONICA, HONG KONG (13, 14), CHINA TREND BUILDING PRESS LTD, HONG KONG (15)

Landmark East is a twin tower development located in Hong Kong's Kwun Tong area. Derived from the long narrow site, the rectilinear slab towers constitute a composition of slim, interlocking planes, slanted at varying angles to create a sense of movement and play. The cores and floor zones are arranged to take advantage of harbor views. The car park and loading area was restricted to the basement and a podium structure at the base of tower two. This allows the remainder of the site to open up to form a landscaped ground floor plaza, a unique feature for office developments in the area. The project received a platinum rating from HK-Beam, a voluntary initiative to promote the environmental efficiency of buildings in Hong Kong.

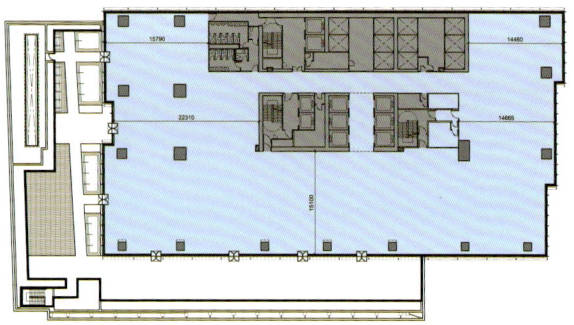

Die Zwillingstürme befinden sich im Kwun Tong-Bezirk Hong Kongs auf einem schmalen langgezogenen Grundstück. Dessen geradlinige Struktur wird vom Bau aufgegriffen und löst sich in einer Komposition von dünnen, ineinander greifenden Ebenen auf, die in verschiedenen Winkeln geneigt sind und ein Gefühl von Bewegung und Spiel hervorrufen. Kernbereiche und Korridore sind so angeordnet, dass man einen guten Blick auf den Hafen hat. Die Park- und Ladebereiche sind auf das Untergeschoss und eine Podiumstruktur im Fundament des zweiten Turms beschränkt, sodass der Rest des Gebietes einen ebenerdigen Freiraum bildet, der für die Entwicklung dieses Bürogebiets einzigartig ist. Das Projekt bekam ein Platinum Rating von HK-Beam, einem freiwilligen Programm, das die Umwelteffizienz von Gebäuden in Hong Kong bewertet.

left: Tower 2, third and sixth floor plan_Conference area of Winsor Properties Holdings Ltd._Breakout area. right: Polo Bourieaus "Man Walking East" in front of tower.
links: Turm 2, Grundrisse drittes und sechstes Obergeschoss_Konferenzbereich der Winsor Properties Holdings Ltd._Pausenbereich. rechts: Polo Bourieaus „Mann nach Osten gehend" vor dem Turm.

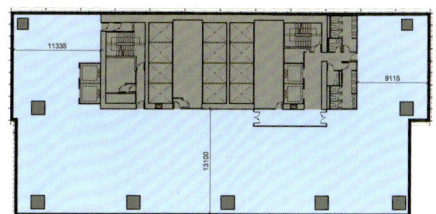
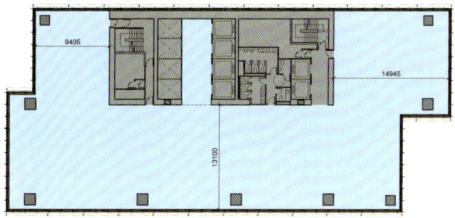

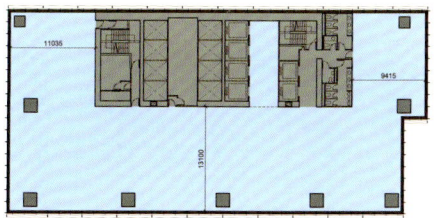
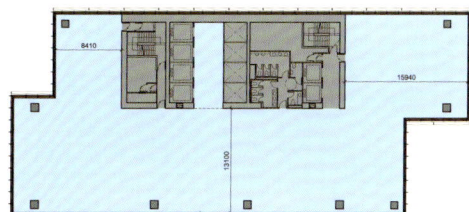

left: Exterior view. right: Floor plans, tower 1_South façade.
links: Außenansicht. rechts: Grundrisse, Turm 1_Südfassade.

INDIA_GURGAON **77/32**

ARCHITECTS: MORPHOGENESIS_**COMPLETION:** 2009
NUMBER OF WORKPLACES: 700_**GROSS FLOOR AREA:** 7,339 M²
COMMON AREA: CAFÉ_**KIND OF WORKPLACES:** OPEN-PLAN
PHOTOS: ANDRÉ J. FANTHOME

The office hub with rentable office spaces for a range of clients in the suburbs of New Delhi moves away from the typical office typology by providing alternating interweaving open social spaces, and closed workspaces. The ground floor with a cafe is designed to be a recreational, informal meeting space. A passive cooling strategy was implemented via bodies of water, and allowing for built mass only on two sides while the remaining two sides are left open to capture the wind movement. Each individual office was provided with a terrace garden as its private, informal zone. The East and West sun are blocked off with the help of solid stonewalls that act as a thermal buffer.

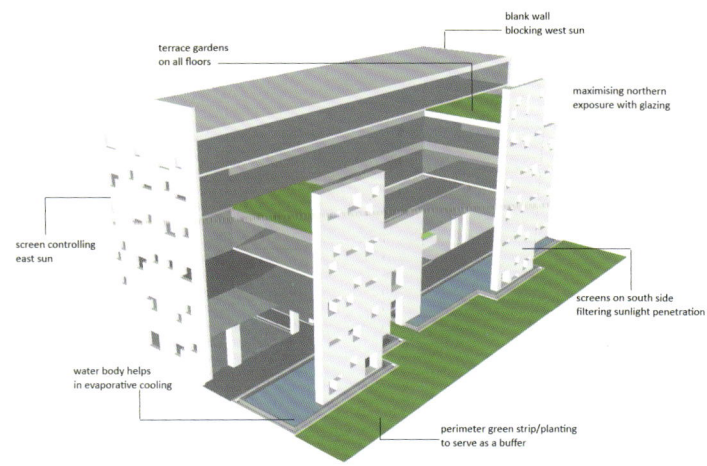

Das Gebäude mit Büros zur Vermietung an verschiedenste Kunden in einem Vorort New Delhis geht auf Distanz zur üblichen Typologie und stellt verwobene, offene Gemeinschaftsräume und geschlossene Arbeitsfläche zur Verfügung. Das Erdgeschoss mit Café dient als informeller Treffpunkt und der Entspannung. Eine passive Kühlung des Baues wurde einerseits durch Wasser, andererseits durch die beiden geschlossenen Seiten des Baues erreicht, während die beiden übrigen Seiten offen blieben um Wind hinein zu lassen. Jedes einzelne Büro hat einen Balkon als privaten informellern Rückzugsraum. Die Sonne wird im Osten und Westen mittels massiver Steinwände als thermische Puffer abgehalten.

left: Perspective_Reception_Entrance area. right: Roof gardens_Exterior by night_Glass façade_Stone façade.
links: Perspektive_Empfang_Eingangsbereich. rechts: Dachgärten_Außenansicht bei Nacht_Glasfassade_Steinfassade.

INDIA_NOIDA **CORPORATE OFFICE FOR INDIA GLYCOLS**

ARCHITECTS: MORPHOGENESIS
COMPLETION: 2009_**NUMBER OF WORKPLACES:** 200
GROSS FLOOR AREA: 36,389 M²_**COMMON AREA:**
MEETING ROOMS, INNER COURTYARDS, TERRACES, PATIO
KIND OF WORKPLACES: CELLULAR, OPEN-PLAN
PHOTOS: EDMUND SUMNER

The corporate office embodies issues concerning the today's workplace and the paradigm of the office space as a social activity location. Sited in a non-contextual suburban area of Delhi, the setting led to the development of an introverted scheme that addresses environmental and socio-economic issues. The building had to exemplify the brand identity and corporate ideology of equity and transparency in the workplace as an integral part of the architectural vocabulary. A stacking system was used to generate a variety of open spaces such as courtyards, verandahs, terraces, etc. A central spine traversing the built volume serves as the common activity zone from which the other departments branch out.

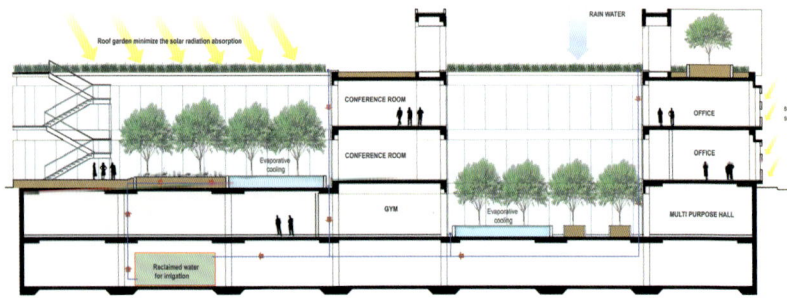

Der Firmensitz beschäftigt sich mit den aktuellen Fragen des Arbeitsumfeldes und der Organisaton des Büroraums als soziales Umfeld. Fast kontextfrei in einem Vorort Delhis gelegen, wurde von Beginn an eine nach Innen gerichtete Struktur mit Umwelt- und sozioökonomische Faktoren angestrebt. Das Gebäude sollte die Firmenidentität vergegenwärtigen und ihrer Auffassung von Gleichheit und Transparenz am Arbeitsplatz architektonischen Ausdruck verleihen. Durch Stapelung von Volumina wurden beispielsweise vielfältige Freiräume, Höfe, Veranden und Terrassen geschaffen. Ein Gemeinschaftsbereich, der das gesamte Bauvolumen durchzieht, bildet das Rückgrat, aus dem die Abteilungen abzweigen.

left: Environmental strategy_Reception_Meeting room. right: View into one of the offices_Inner courtyard_Exterior_Façade.
links: Ökologische Planung_Empfang_Besprechungszimmer. rechts: Blick in eines der Büros_ Innenhof_Außenansicht_Fassade.

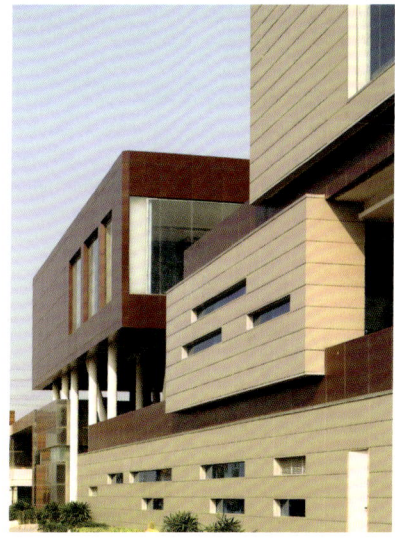

INDONESIA_JAKARTA **MENARA KARYA**

ARCHITECTS: ARQUITECTONICA
COMPLETION: 2006 **NUMBER OF WORKPLACES:** 3480
GROSS FLOOR AREA: 52,200 M² **COMMON AREA:** CONFERENCE ROOMS, GRAND LOBBY **KIND OF WORKPLACES:** COMBINATION
PHOTOS: RAY SUGIHARTO

This 26-story commercial office development is located in the prestigious business and embassy district of Jakarta. The project's design consists of an angular form that uses a simple curtain wall with a contrasting emphasis of vertical and horizontal mullions to achieve a striking balance. The building's purity is violated only once near its top, where a portion of the volume rotates to identify the anchor tenant's corporate board room, creating a terrace with spectacular views across the city. The randomly balanced forms extend to the interiors where natural stone is used in an elegant and spacious lobby. The building sits on landscaped grounds which isolate the 17,000-square-meters underground parking structure.

Das 26-stöckige Mietbürohaus liegt im angesehenen Geschäfts- und Botschaftsviertel Jakartas. Die mehrfach abgewinkelte Form nutzt eine übliche Vorhangfassade kontrastierend zu horizontalem und vertikalem Stabwerk, so dass ein ausgewogener Gesamteindruck entsteht. Lediglich kurz vor dem oberen Abschluss wird das Volumen an der Stelle, wo sich der Vorstandssitzungssaal des Mieters befindet, auffallend herausgerückt, um einen Balkon mit spektakulärer Aussicht über die Stadt zu schaffen. Die ausgewogene aber gebrochene Struktur setzt sich im Inneren, insbesondere in der geräumigen und eleganten Lobby mit Naturstein fort. Unterhalb der den Bau umgebenden, gestalteten Landschaft befinden sich 17.000 Quadratmeter Parkplatzfläche.

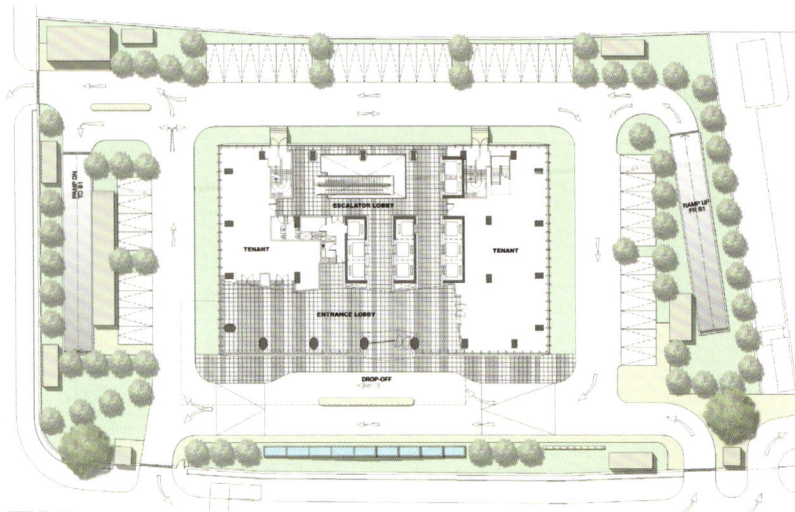

left: Ground floor plan_Lobby_Corridor. right: Façade, detail_Exterior by day_Vie from street_Exterior by night.
links:Grundriss Erdgeschoss_Lobby_Flur. rechts: Fassade, Detail_Ansicht bei Tag_Blick von der Straße_Nachtansicht.

IRAN_TEHRAN **BENETTON GROUP**

ARCHITECTS: 8A ARCHITECTS
COMPLETION: ONGOING_**NUMBER OF WORKPLACES:** 500
GROSS FLOOR AREA: 4,050 M²_**KIND OF WORKPLACES:** OPEN-PLAN, TEAM_**PHOTOS:** 8A ARCHITECTS (22, 23 B. R.), BMD3D, BELGIUM (23 A., B. L.)

An integral and pragmatic stance towards the local culture and climate, the given situation and the specific location requiring a reduction of the floor plan area from ground to top level, led to the utilization of the total plot space instead of horizontally progressive leveling floors. This created interconnected patios in the middle of the building, giving it a cool shadowed and quiet inner space that introduces a sustainable atmosphere into the building. The office spaces are positioned in a U-shaped layout around the patios and gradually reduced from 900 square meter to 675 square meter of floors space. The office spaces can be subdivided by glass partition walls into three or four offices per floor, resulting in maximum openness.

Eine eindeutige zugleich pragmatische Haltung bezüglich Lokalkultur und Klima sowie das Raumprogramm und der spezifische Bauplatz, der eine Reduktion der Grundfläche vom Erd- zum Obergeschoss verlangte, waren Ausgangspunkte zur Nutzung des geamten Geländes und zur Vermeidung einer gestafelten Bauweise. Es ergaben sich verbundene Patios im Herzen des Gebäudes und somit sowohl kühler, schattiger und ruhiger Innenraum als auch ein nachhaltiges Umfeld. Die Büroräume sind U-förmig um die Patios angeordnet und reduzieren deren Grundfläche allmählich von 900 auf 675 Quadratmeter. Der Büroraum kann geschossweise in drei bis vier Einheiten geteilt werden, wobei Glaswände die Offenheit gewährleisten.

left: Section_Floor plans. right: Façade seen from Vali Asr Avenue_Façade, detail_Interior workspace.
links: Schnitt_Grundrisse. rechts: Fassade, Ansicht von der Vali Asr Avenue_Fassade, Detail_Innenansicht Arbeitsbereich.

JAPAN_KAMAKURA-SHI **KAYAC**

ARCHITECTS: KLEIN DYTHAM ARCHITECTURE
COMPLETION: 2007_**NUMBER OF WORKPLACES:** 40
GROSS FLOOR AREA: 373 M²_**PHOTOS:** DAICI ANO

Mixing elements from traditional Japanese architecture together with the fluid nature of an innovative web design firm created a 21st century work environment. A raised floor of tatami mats, with cushions and low tables for meetings, and with a horigotatsu (dug out) conference table are very different from the web industry's typical style and offer a comfortable working environment. The tatami floor is surrounded by a continuous wooden desk that seats up to 40 staff members. A meeting and entertaining space on the upper floor makes a more explicitly contemporary interpretation of tatami mats, with a shoes-off raised floor of richly colored sofa-like mats, where staff can sit, brainstorm or unwind.

Traditionelle japanische Architekturelemente verschmelzen hier mit der Aura einer innovativen Web-Designfirma zu einem Arbeitsplatz des 21. Jahrhunderts. Ein erhöhter Boden aus Tatami Matten für Meetings mit Kissen und niedrigen Tischen und einem horigotatsu (freigelegter) Konferenztisch – bietet einen Ausweg aus dem Web-Industrie-Lebensstil und verwandelt Arbeits- in Lebenszeit. Der Tatami-Boden ist von einem ununterbrochenen hölzernen Schreibtisch für 40 Mitarbeiter eingefasst. Ein Treff- und Unterhaltungsraum im Obergeschoss setzt die zeitgenössische Interpretation von Tatami Matten mit einem Schuh-freien erhöhten Boden aus bunten sofaartigen Matten um, auf dem Mitarbeiter sitzen, brainstormen oder eine Pause einlegen können.

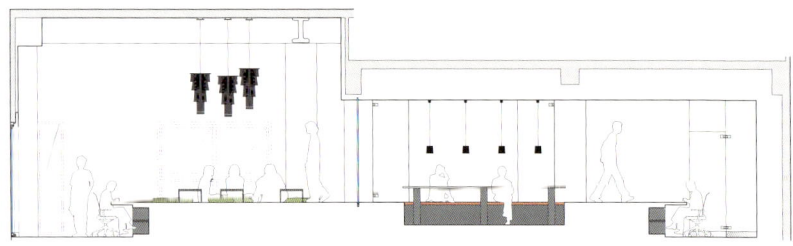

left: Section_The tatami floor has been enclosed with a continuous wooden desk_The wooden desk seats up to 40 staff. right: A horigotatsu (dug out) conference table_Tempered glass with white printed film walls_Elevation.
links: Schnitt_Tatami-Boden, umgeben von einem umlaufenden Holzarbeitstisch_Hölzerne Arbeitsplatte mit Arbeitsplätzen für bis zu 40 Mitarbeiter. rechts: horigotatsu Konferenztisch_Gläserne Trennwand mit aufgedrucktem weißen Dekor_Ansicht.

JAPAN_NAGASAKI **AIG BUILDING**

ARCHITECTS: GEORGE DASIC ARCHITECTS
PROJECT MANAGEMENT AND ENGINEERS: ARUP JAPAN / DUNCAN MACINTYRE, TEPPEI ISHIBASHI
CONSTRUCTION: TAISEI CONSTRUCTION_**COMPLETION:** 2006
NUMBER OF WORKPLACES: 2,000_**GROSS FLOOR AREA:** 20,000 M²
COMMON AREA: TRAINING ROOM, BREAK ROOM
KIND OF WORKPLACES: OPEN-PLAN_**PHOTOS:** PETER COOK

Because of hot summers and a scorching sun, the design had to provide openness and transparency to the east and west and protection on the south. The fifth floor space will not be used as a standard office floor like the other four, but will house a serious of training facilities. The roof was almost completely landscaped with a roof garden and a deck making this rather large structure "blend" with the surrounding park and hills. To protect from the direct sun, a system of louvers was installed within north and south wings. The two-meter-thick skin envelope offers additional sun shading. Nagasaki Civic Hall, which is a separate entity, is housed in the glass box extruding from the building block.

Aufgrund der heißen Sommer und der stechenden Sonne musste der Entwurf Offenheit und Transparenz auf der Ost- und Westseite sowie Schutz auf der Südseite gewährleisten. Das fünfte Stockwerk wird nicht als gewöhnliche Büroetage, sondern durch eine Reihe von Ausbildungseinrichtungen genutzt. Das Dach wurde fast vollständig als Dachgärten mit Sonnenterrasse ausgestaltet, die diese große Struktur in den umliegenden Park und die Hügel integrieren. Um die Büros vor der direkten Sonneneinstrahlung zu schützen, wurden im Nord- und Südflügel Sonnenblenden angebracht. Die zwei Meter dicke Außenwand sorgt für zusätzlichen Sonnenschutz. Die Nagasaki Civic Hall befindet sich als eigenständigen Einheit in einer Glasbox, die aus der Gebäudemasse hervortritt.

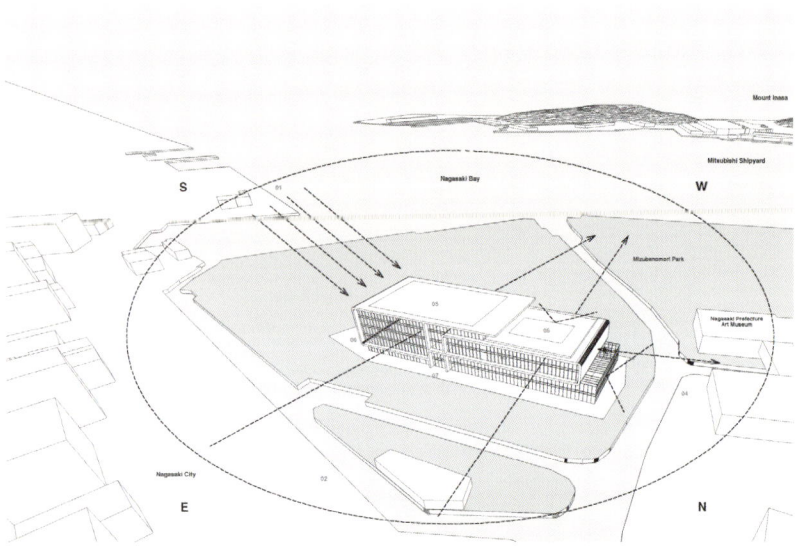

left: Concept drawing_Exterior view_Entrance. right: Bird's-eye view_Entrance hall with parking area_Civic hall.
links: Konzeptskizze_Außenansicht_Eingang. rechts: Vogelperspektive_Eingangshalle mit Parkplätzen_Civic Hall.

JAPAN_TOKYO **CBS BUILDING**

ARCHITECTS: GEORGE DASIC ARCHITECTS
STRUCTURE: ARUP JAPAN_**CONSTRUCTION:** EIGER SANGYOU
COMPLETION: 2009_**NUMBER OF WORKPLACES:** 4
GROSS FLOOR AREA: 196 M²_**COMMON AREA:** MEETING LOUNGE, TRAINING ROOM, GALLERY_**KIND OF WORKPLACES:** OPEN-PLAN, DESKSHARING, LOUNGE WORKSPACE_**PHOTOS:** PETER COOK

The building with its concept of three floating cubes stacked one above the other in a "programmatic hierarchy" offers the three different functions of work, rest, and play in the form of a gallery, office and seminar rooms, and a pod (lounge, kitchen and bathroom). The strip windows separating the cubes create a diffused light effect suitable for a gallery and seminars, while allowing maximum wall space for artwork and business charts. The pod is oriented upwards with a skylight flooding the area with natural light. The cubes are clad in steel panels, which create a structural skin. The services are concentrated in the vertical core allowing simple internal plumbing and an uncluttered exterior.

Das Gebäudekonzept mit drei schwebenden, in „programmatischer Hierarchie" gestapelten Würfeln entspricht den drei Funktionen Arbeit, Erholung und Vergnügen mit einer Galerie, Büro- und Seminarräumen und einem Sockel, der Küche, Aufenthalts- und Waschräume umfasst. Schmale Fenster zwischen den Würfeln schaffen eine indirekte, der Galerie und den Seminarräumen angemessene Beleuchtung und gewährleisten maximale Wandfläche für Kunstwerke und Business-Pläne. Durch ein Dachfenster wird der Raum im Sockel mit natürlichem Licht versorgt. Die Stahlverkleidung der Würfel schafft eine strukturelle Außenwand. Alle Service-Bereiche befinden sich im vertikalen Kern, um eine einfache interne Rohrverlegung und ein ungestörtes äußeres Erscheinungsbild zu ermöglichen.

left: Floor plans and elevations_Couch_Kitchenette and dining corner. right: Exterior_Meeting lounge_Workplaces.
links: Grundrisse und Ansichten_Sofa_Teeküche und Essecke. rechts: Außenansicht_Besprechungslounge_Arbeitsplätze.

JAPAN_MINATO-KU, TOKYO **TV ASAHI**

ARCHITECTS: MAKI AND ASSOCIATES / FUMIHIKO MAKI
COMPLETION: 2003_**NUMBER OF WORKPLACES:** 1,200
GROSS FLOOR AREA: 73,700 M²_**COMMON AREA:** ATRIUM, CAFETERIA, GALLERY_**KIND OF WORKPLACES:** COMBINATION, OPEN-PLAN, TEAM, TV STUDIO_**PHOTOS:** TOSHIHARU KITAJIMA (34 B. L., M., 35 A.), MAKI AND ASSOCIATES (34 B. R., 35 B. L., B. R.)

The building is located on the southern corner of the Roppongi Hills area, surrounded by a square and a garden. The glass-walled atrium, the icon of the project, marks an interface between the public and private domain. The 30-meter-high, 120-meter-long Vierendeel frames form a gentle curve following the adjacent streets. The building is organized around a central core of studio spaces with offices located along the perimeter. Their proximity to the broadcast-related facilities provides both work-flow efficiency and conserves energy. Exterior louvers provide sun shading for the office areas, while also creating an ephemeral silhouette in the evening, resembling a Japanese lantern.

Das Gebäude in der Südecke von Roppongi Hills, wird von zwei Hauptstraßen einem Platz und einem Garten umfasst. Das verglaste Atrium, Sinnbild des Projekts, bildet die Schnittstelle zwischen öffentlichem und privatem Raum. 30 Meter hohe und 120 Meter lange Vierendeel-Träger bilden dezente, dem Straßenverlauf folgende Kurven aus. Zentrum des Baus sind die Studioräume, während die Büros den Rand bilden, was sowohl den Arbeitsfluss effizienter macht und Energie einspart, als auch eine Abschirmung gegen Hitze und Lärm bildet. Eine Lamellenstruktur am Außenbau schützt die Büros vor Sonneneinstrahlung und ruft abends die Erinnerung an japanische Laternen wach.

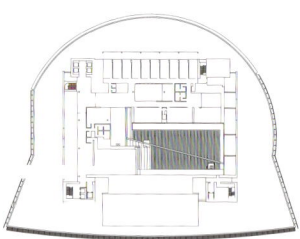

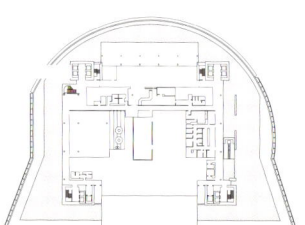

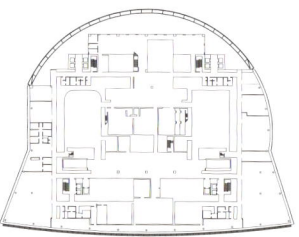

left: Floor plans_Evening view of digital wall_Interior of the atrium_View of the atrium from the second floor. right: Bird's-eye view from north_Glass reception counter at the atrium designed by Kazuko Fujie_Glass stairs and garden beyond seen from the reception lobby.
links: Grundrisse_Abendansicht der digitalen Wand_Innenansicht des Atriums_Atrium vom zweiten Obergeschoss aus gesehen. rechts: Vogelperspektive aus Norden_Empfangstresen aus Glas, entworfen von Kazuko Fujie_Glastreppe und Garten vom Enpfangsbereich her gesehen.

JAPAN_TOKYO **MEGURO OFFICE**

ARCHITECTS: NENDO_**COMPLETION:** 2007
NUMBER OF WORKPLACES: 4_**GROSS FLOOR AREA:** 140 M²
COMMON AREA: CONFERENCE ROOM
KIND OF WORKPLACES: CELLULAR, TEAM
PHOTOS: DAICI ANO

nendo's office is located near the Meguro River, on the fifth floor of an old office building. To create the common separate spaces and functions – meeting space, management, workspace and storage – on the one hand, but also a sense of connection between them on the other hand the space was divided with walls that seem to sag and flop. They enclose the various spaces more than the usual office dividers, but less than actual walls. Employees can move between spaces by walking over the parts of the walls that "sag" the most. Spaces that need more sound-proofing are enclosed with plastic curtains. Standing up and looking through the whole space, people, shelves and plants seem to appear and disappear as though floating between the waves.

Das eigene Büro von nendo liegt unweit des Flusses Meguro im fünften Obergeschoss eines alten Bürohauses. Es sollte die üblichen Räume für eigenständige Funktionen bieten – Konferenzraum, Geschäftsleitung, Arbeitsfläche und Lager – aber diese Bereiche auch miteinander verbinden. So wurde der Raum mit durchhangenden Wänden geteilt. Diese trennen die verschiedenen Bereiche zwar stärker als Stellwände, aber weniger als richtige Wände. Die Mitarbeiter können sich über die am stärksten durchhängenden Partien bewegen. Aufstehend und durch dem Raum schauend erscheinen und verschwinden Menschen, Schränke und Pflanzen, als befänden sie sich zwischen Wellenkämmen. Räume, die stärkere akustische Abschirmung benötigen, sind mit Kunststoffvorhängen umgeben..

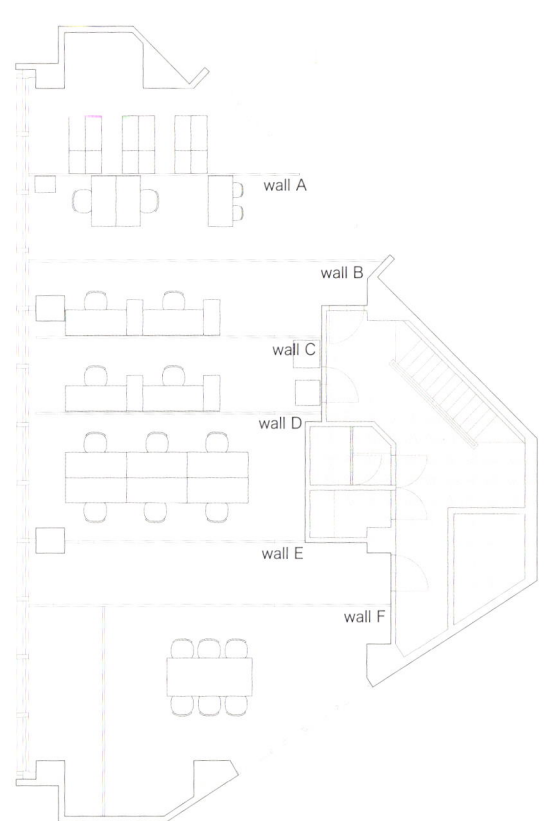

left: Floor plan_Office_Meeting room. right: Corridor_Overview_Walls, detail.
links: Grundriss_Büro_Besprechungszimmer. rechts: Flur_Überblick_Trennwände, Detail.

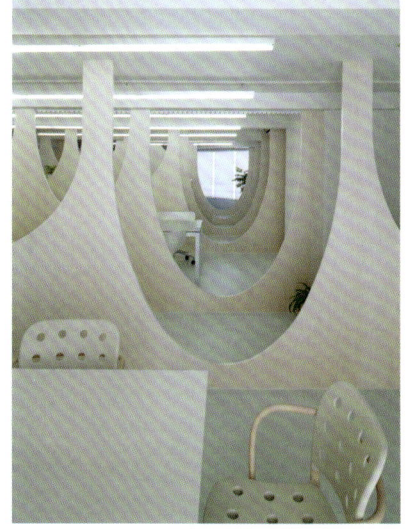

JAPAN_TOKYO **AKASAKA OFFICE**

ARCHITECTS: NENDO_**COMPLETION:** 2008
NUMBER OF WORKPLACES: 6_**GROSS FLOOR AREA:** 165 M²
COMMON AREA: TERRACE, MEETING ROOM_**KIND OF WORKPLACES:** CELLULAR, TEAM_**PHOTOS:** DAICI ANO

The advertising agency occupies a U-shaped space that wraps around a central terrace on the top floor of a small building in Akasaka in central Tokyo. The design keeps new walls and furnishings to a minimum to preserve the airy, comfortable feel that the space already possessed. Blinds were cut in loose waves for a gentle, draping three-dimensionality, halfway between blinds and curtains, giving the entire space a more relaxed feel. The wall have been clad with whiteboards and a bar-like opening was cut in the wall between the meeting room and the kitchen. A large desk and an adjustable tent on the terrace facilitate outdoor meetings and parties.

Die Werbeagentur befindet sich in U-förmig um eine Terrasse gelegten Räumlichkeiten eines kleinen Gebäudes in Akasaka im Zentrum von Tokio. Der Entwurf beschränkte neue Wände und die Möblierung auf ein Minimum, um die luftige, angenehme Atmosphäre des Raumes zu erhalten. Jalousien wurden in eine leichte Wellenform geschnitten, so dass eine dezente, dreidimensionale Draperie entstand, die dem Ganzen eine entspannte Atmosphäre verleiht. Die Wände wurden mit Whiteboards versehen und eine Bar-artige Öffnung verbinden den Konferenzraum mit der Küche. Ein großer Tisch und ein variables Zelt auf der Terrasse machen Meetings und Feste im Freien möglich.

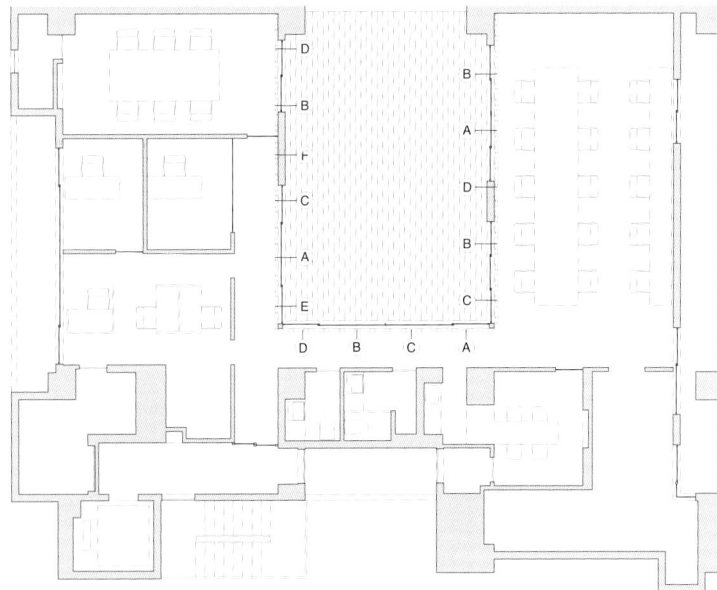

left: Floor plan_Corridor, detail_Corridor. right: Blind, detail_Meeting room_Blind.
links: Grundriss_Flur, Detail_Flur. rechts: Fensterrollo, Detail_Besprechungszimmer_ Fensterrollo.

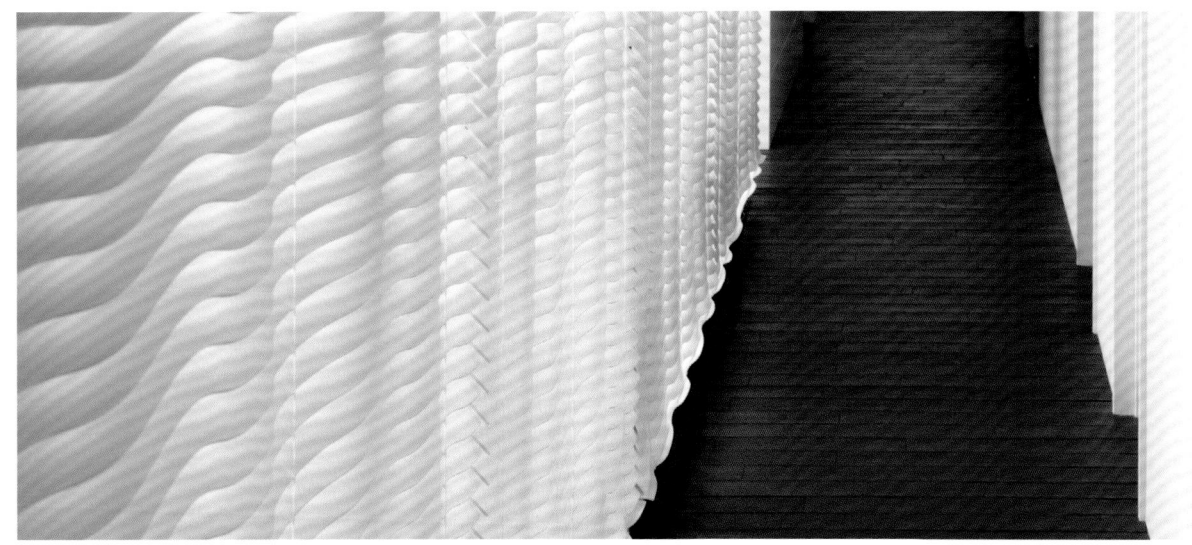

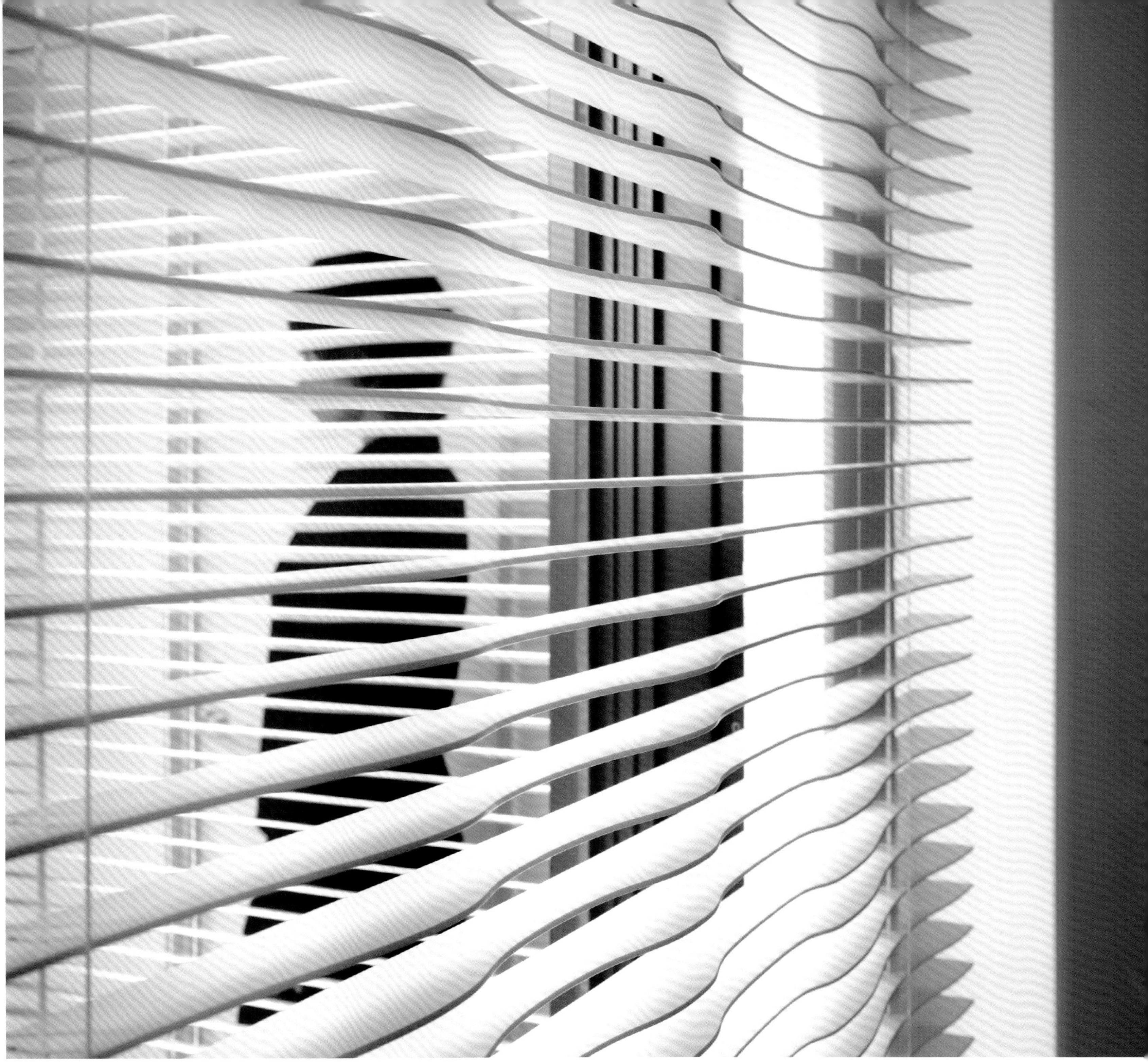

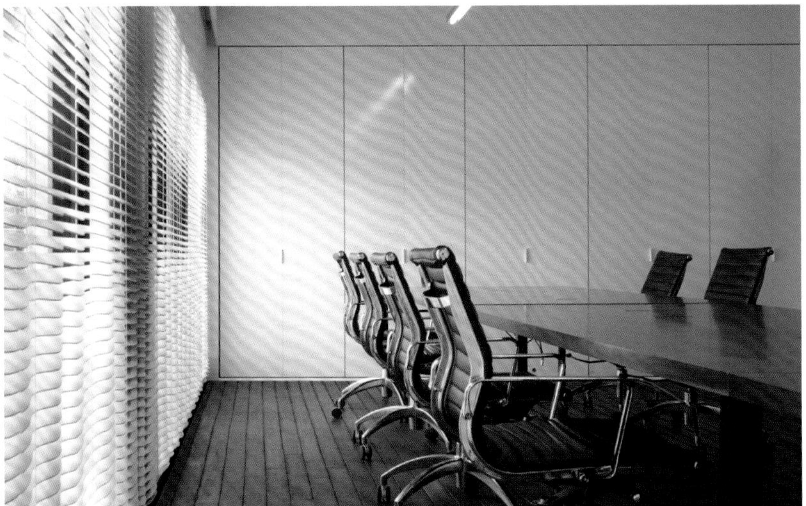

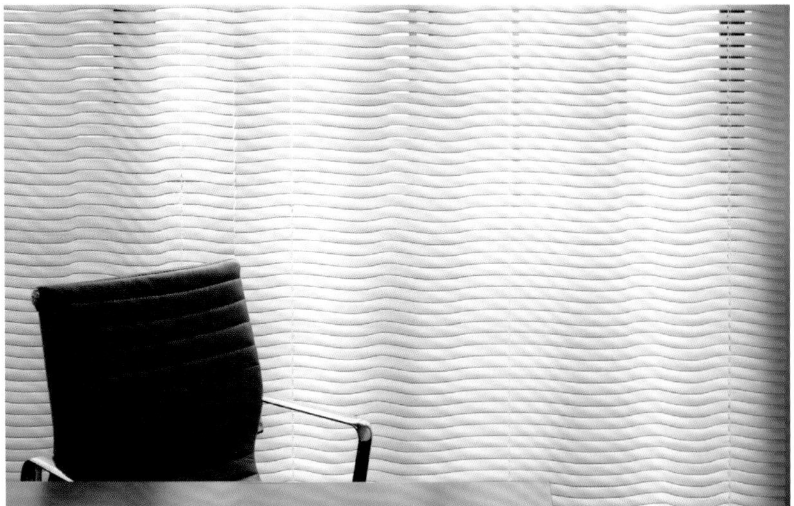

QATAR_DOHA DOHA HIGH RISE OFFICE BUILDING

ARCHITECTS: ATELIERS JEAN NOUVEL
COMPLETION: 2010_**GROSS FLOOR AREA:** 60,000 M²
COMMON AREA: RESTAURANT
PHOTOS: COURTESY OF THE ARCHITECTS

The office building will become one of the monuments of Doha, which not only wants to gain a high recognition value from buildings by famous architects, but also wants to establish itself as the cultural center of the Gulf states. Nouvel, who has for some time worked on high rises with a circular layout, designed a tower with a circumference of 45 meters and a height of roughly 230 meters. Its beveled double-glazed façade resembles cut diamonds as well as traditional Arabic Qamariah windows. The light permeability of the outer façade is adjusted to the sun's orbit (25 percent north and up to 40 percent south). The surrounding garden blends into a glass lobby that leads to a 27-floor atrium.

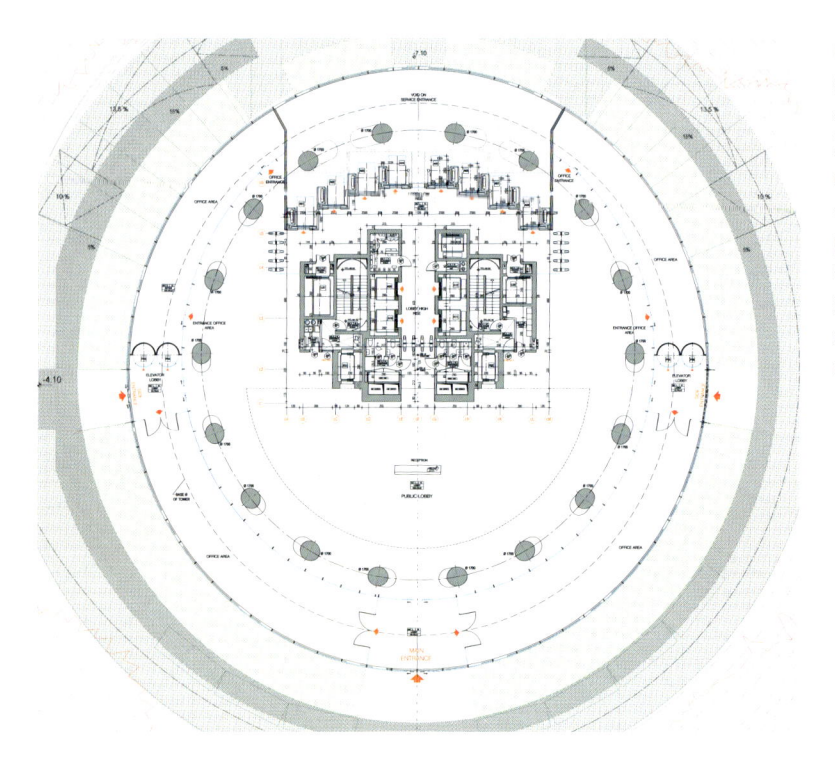

Das Bürogebäude wird eines der Wahrzeichen Dohas, das sich durch außergewöhnliche Bauten bekannter Architekten nicht nur einen hohen Wiedererkennbarkeitsgrad verleihen, sondern darüber hinaus als kulturelles Zentrum der Golfstaaten profilieren möchte. Nouvel, der sich schon lange mit Hochhäusern auf rundem Grundriss beschäftigt, entwarf einen Turm von 45 Metern Durchmesser und rund 230 Metern Höhe, dessen facettierte Doppelglasfassade sowohl an Diamantschnitt, als auch an traditionelle arabische Qamarya erinnert. Die Lichtdurchlässigkeit der äußeren Fassade ist der Sonnenbahn angepasst (25 Prozent im Norden bis 40 Prozent in Süden). Der umliegende Garten verschneidet sich mit einer gläsernen Lobby, von der aus man ein 27-stöckiges Atrium betritt.

left: Ground floor plan_Model_Qamariah. right: Exterior.
links: Grundriss Erdgeschoss_Modell_Qamarya. rechts: Außenansicht.

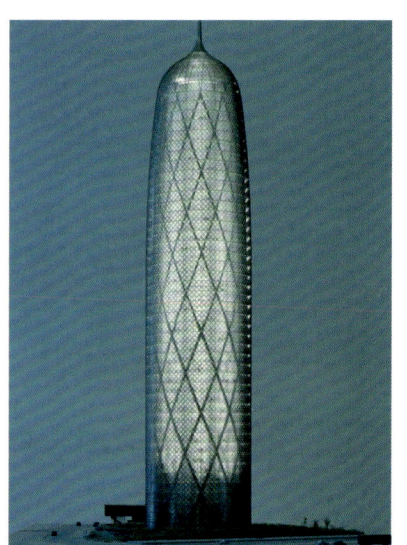

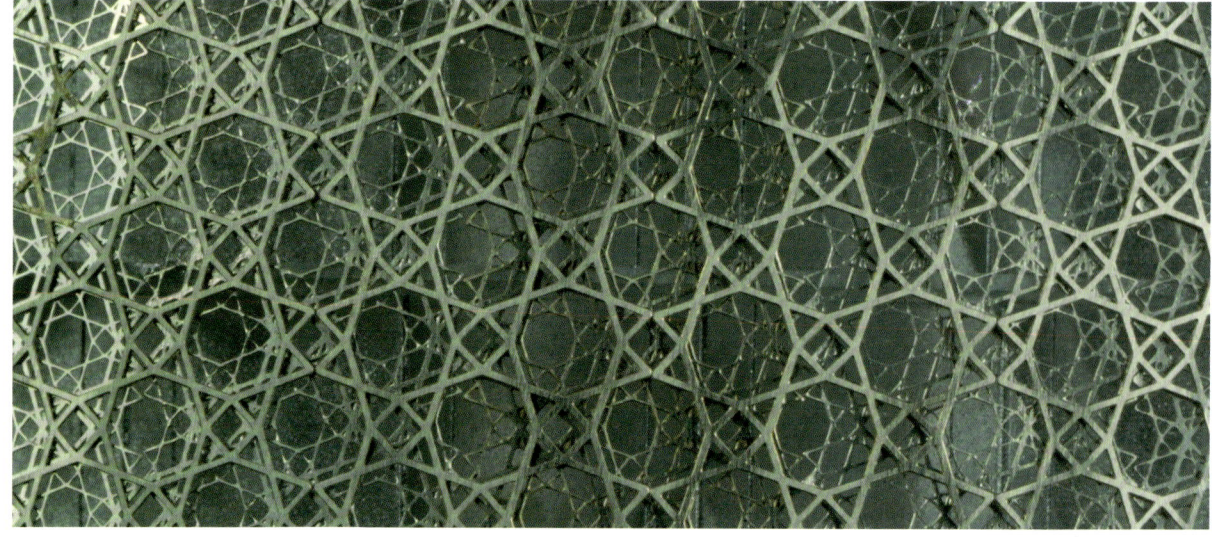

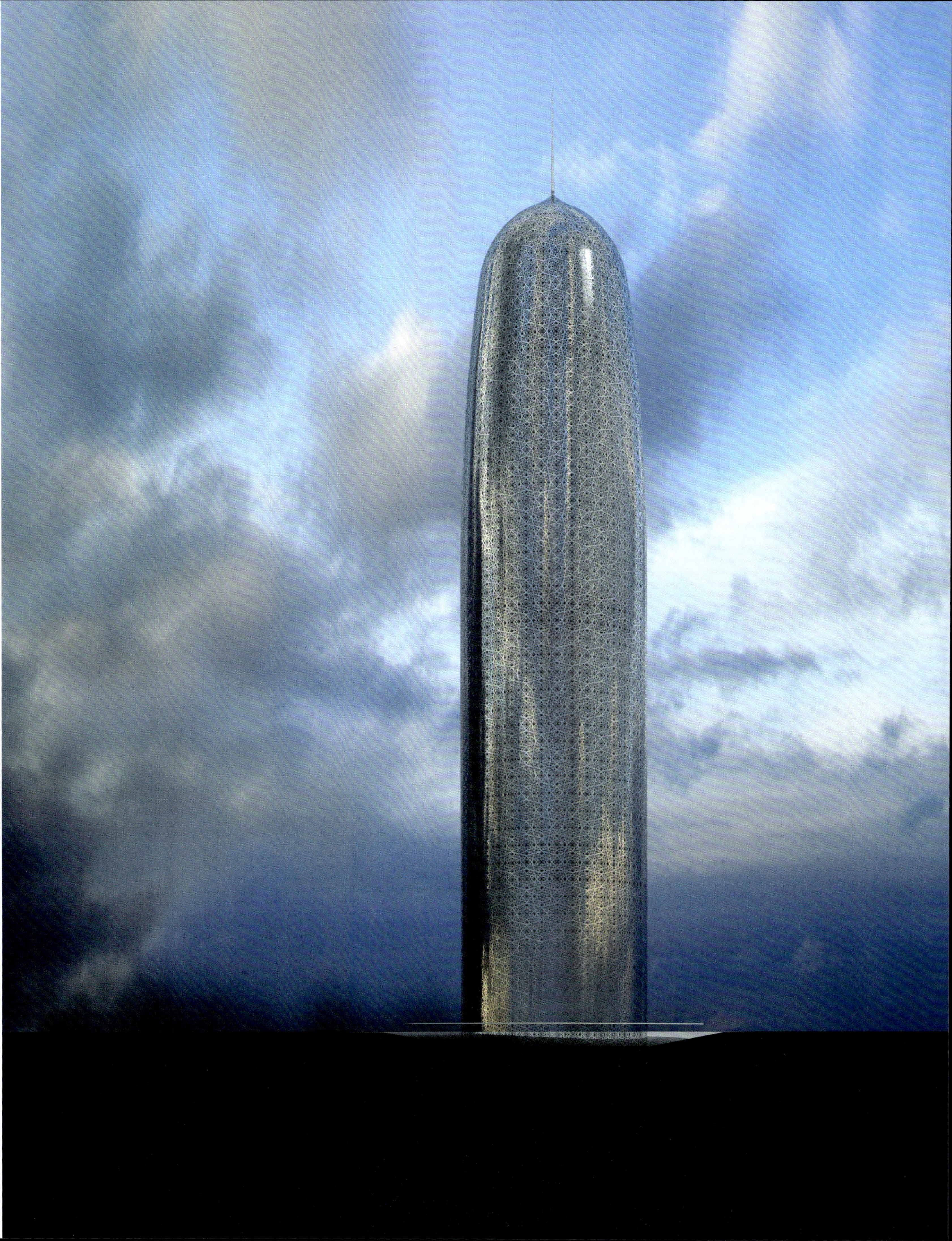

RUSSIA_MOSCOW **FEDERATION COMPLEX**

ARCHITECTS: PROF. PETER SCHWEGER (ASP SCHWEGER ASSOZIIERTE GESAMTPLANUNG GMBH, HAMBURG) AND SERGEI TCHOBAN (NPS TCHOBAN VOSS ARCHITEKTEN BDA)_**COMPLETION:** ONGOING
NUMBER OF WORKPLACES: 18,000_**GROSS FLOOR AREA:** 430,000 M²
COMMON AREA: CONFERENCE CENTER, BALLROOMS, CANTEENS, CAFÉS, FOOD COURT, BANKS, VIEWING PLATFORM
KIND OF WORKPLACES: CELLULAR, COMBINATION, OPEN-PLAN
PHOTOS: ALEKSEJ NARODIZKIJ

With its highest point located 448 meters above the streets of the new Moscow City business district, the Federation Complex will be Europe's highest building after its completion. It offers approximately 430,000 square meters of space across 93 above-ground floors (365 meters) with areas for offices, apartments, a luxury hotel with wellness and recreation areas, as well as a public view platform. A six-floor podium with retail areas serves as the above-ground basis of the building. Above the four story high lense are the tower structures in the shape of two spherical equilateral triangles. Including the technical floors, the façades are fully glazed with in part multiple curved and printed glass.

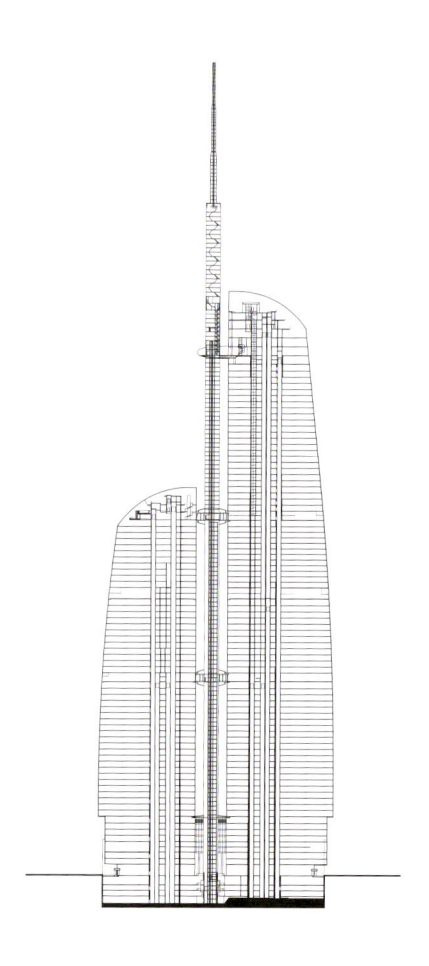

Mit dem höchsten Punkt 448 Meter über den Straßen des neuen Geschäftszentrums Moskau-City, wird der Federation Complex nach seiner Fertigstellung Europas höchstes Gebäude sein. Er bietet auf rund 430.000 Quadratmetern in den 93 oberirdischen Geschossen (365 Meter) Flächen für Büros, Appartements, einem Luxushotel mit Wellness- und Unterhaltungsbereichen sowie einer öffentlichen Aussichtsplattform. Ein sechsstöckiger Sockel mit Geschäftsflächen dient dem Gebäude als oberirdische Basis. Oberhalb der viergeschossigen Linse erheben sich die Turmbauten in Form zweier sphärischer, gleichseitiger Dreiecke. Einschließlich der Technikgeschosse sind die Fassaden vollflächig mit teils mehrfach gekrümmtem und bedrucktem Glas verkleidet.

left: Section_General view of the new business center Moskow City_Forecourt_Night view. right: West tower.
links: Schnitt_Gesamtübersicht des neuen Geschäftszentrums Moskau City_Vorplatz_Nachtansicht. rechts: Westturm.

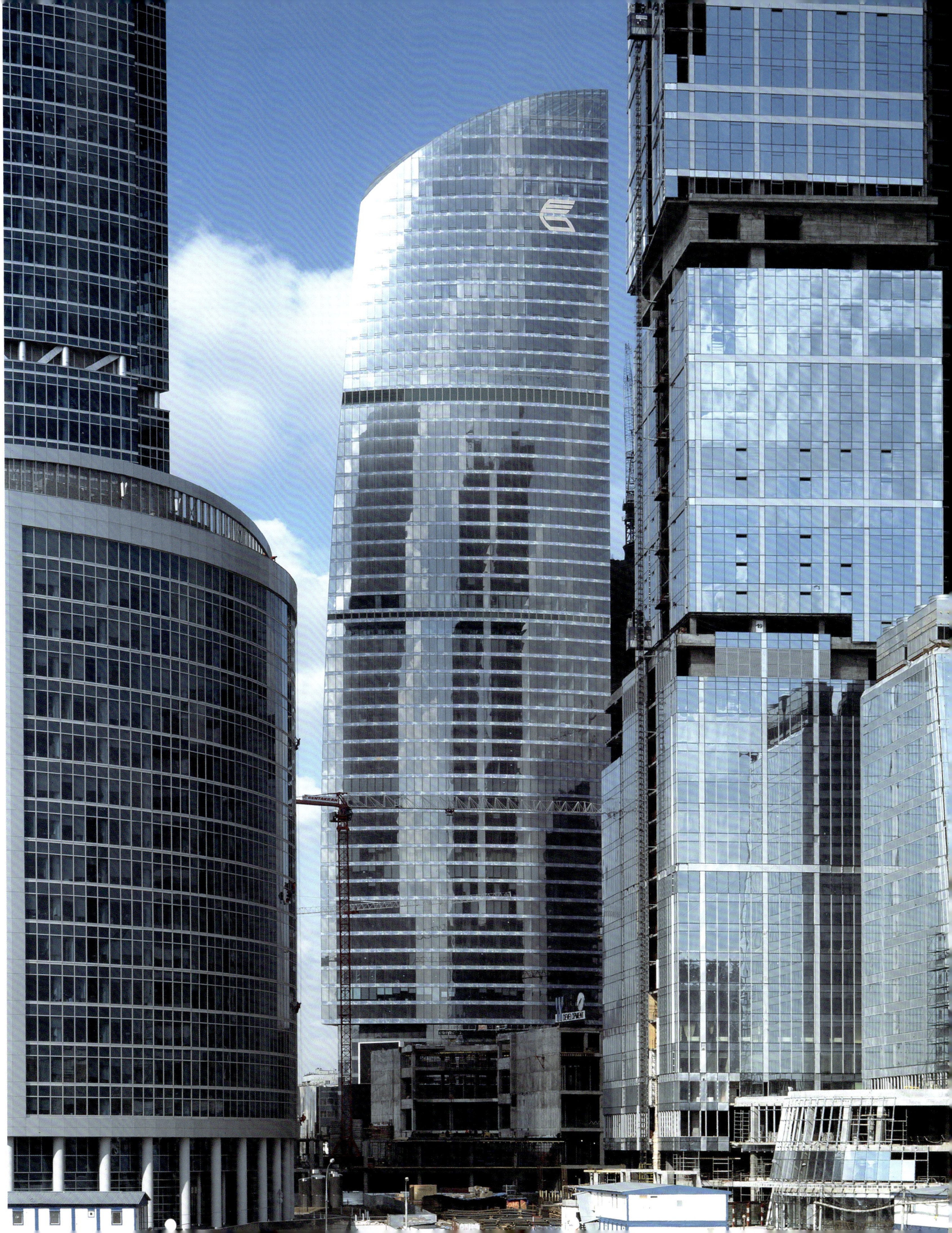

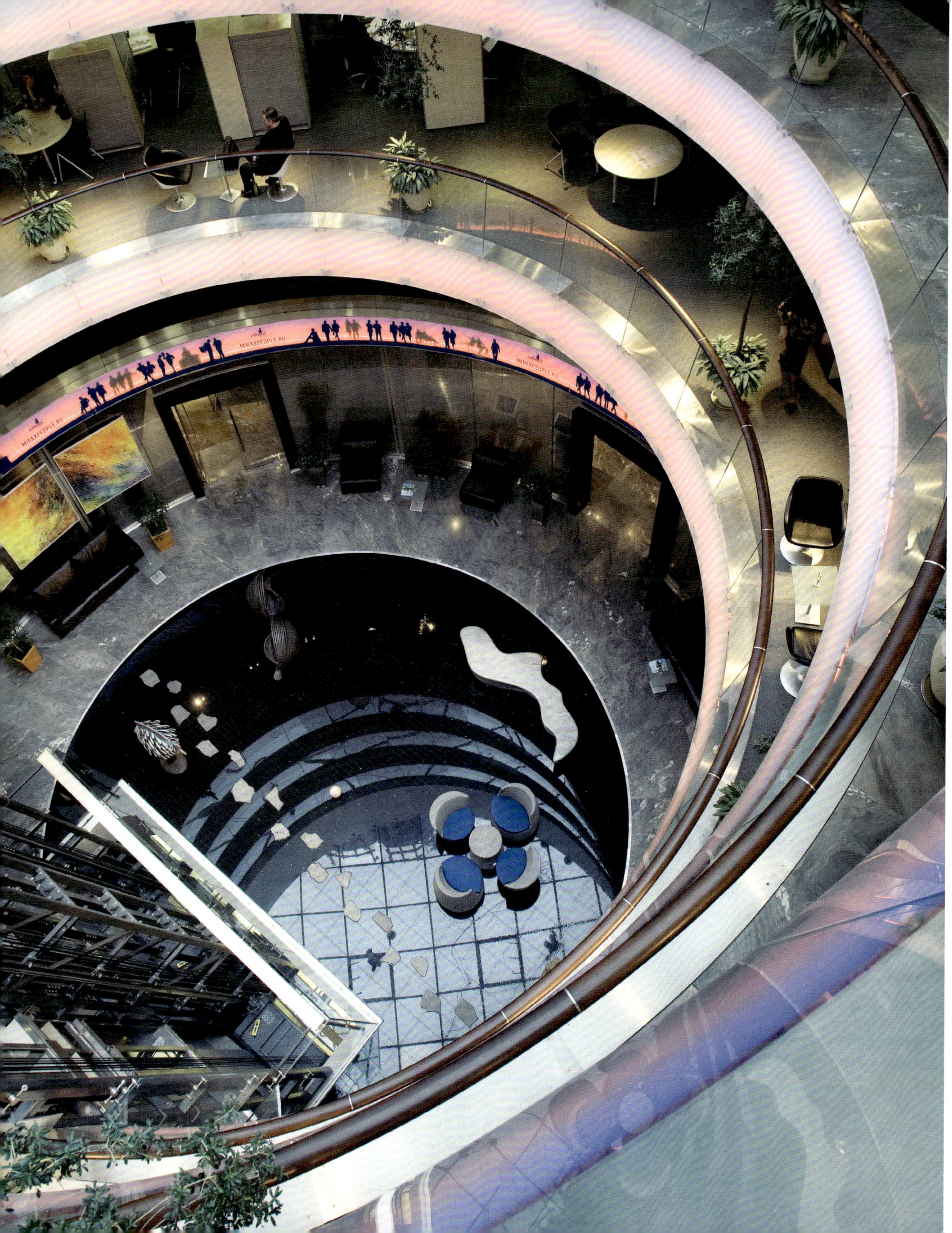
MIRAXPEOPLE.RU
MIRAXPEOPLE.RU
MIRAXPEOPLE.RU

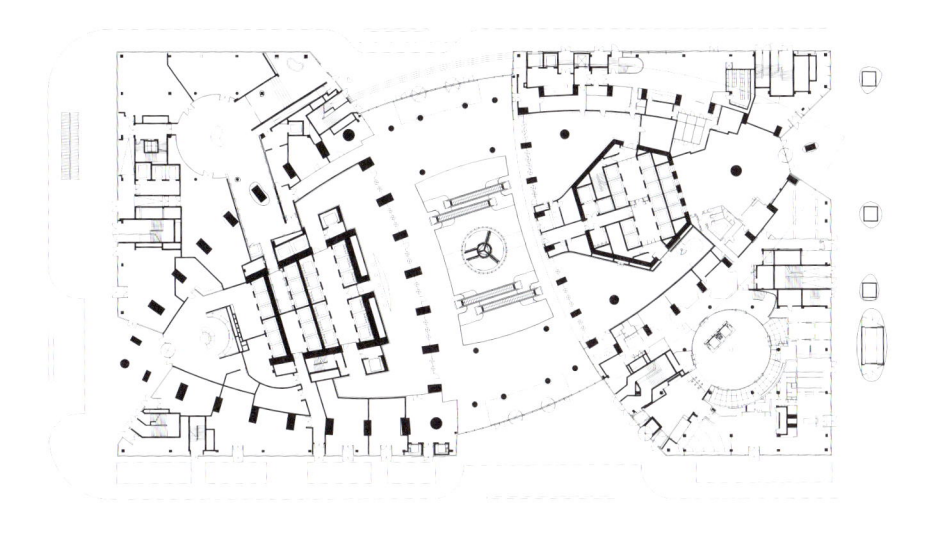

left: Atrium, view towards the ground floor. right: Ground floor plan_Atrium sixth floor, paramount basic floor_Atrium of one office abutter.
links: Atrium, Blick zum Erdgeschoss. rechts: Grundriss Erdgeschoss_Atrium im sechsten Obergeschoss, oberstes Basisgeschoss_Atrium eines der Büroanrainer.

UAE_DUBAI THE EDGE

ARCHITECTS: RCR ARQUITECTES_**PLANNING PARTNERS:** COUSSÉE&GORIS ARCHITECTEN _**COMPLETION:** 2007
NUMBER OF WORKPLACES: 65_**GROSS FLOOR AREA:** 344,000 M²
COMMON AREA: CONFERENCE CENTER, RETAIL, SPORT CENTER, HEALTH CENTER, RESTAURANTS, HOTEL, HOUSING_**KIND OF WORKPLACES:** OPEN-PLAN, BUSINESS CLUB, LOUNGE WORKSPACE_**PHOTOS:** COURTESY OF THE ARCHITECTS

The horizontal structure of the urban landscape with its public, social base, is gradually being replaced by a more fragmented, private vertical structure of skyscrapers. The design of this project wants to get back to the basic landscape of the Arab city, featuring plains, oases, dunes, microclimates and the sea, composed of light and shadows, and above all, filters that could well become the identifying symbol of Dubai. A recreated new landscape, a new city with new concepts, was proposed as a dune or an oasis (to view the horizon and the city) on top of the market or souk, created as an urban space (a social park or square) and sheltered by the foliage-like grid of the building.

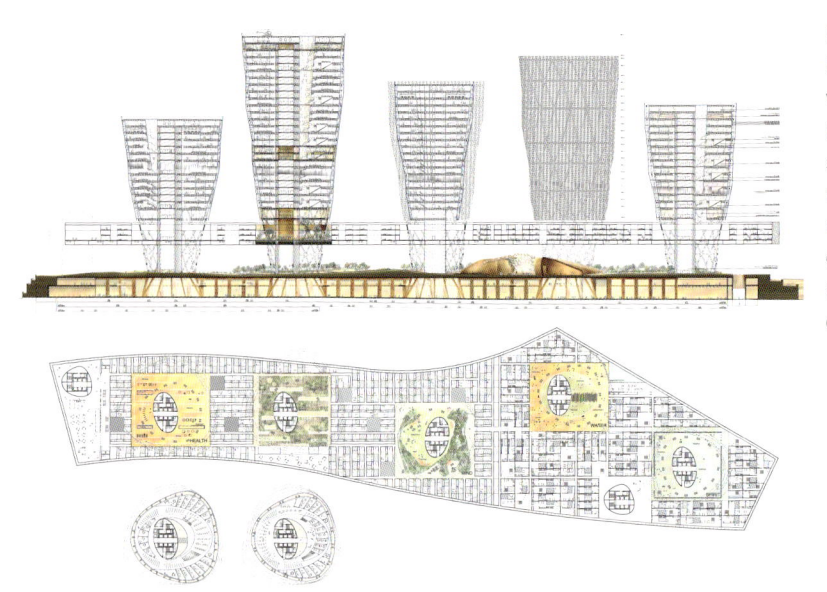

Die horizontale Struktur der Stadtlandschaft mit ihrer öffentlichen und sozialen Basis wird schrittweise durch eine fragmentiertere, vertikale Struktur von privaten Hochhäusern ersetzt. Das Design geht zurück zur Landschaft mit Flächen, Oasen, Dünen, Mikroklima und dem Meer der arabischen Stadt, setzt sich aus Lichtern und Schatten und insbesondere aus Filtern zusammen, die zum Symbol für Dubai werden könnten. Eine neue Landschaft, eine neue Stadt mit neuen Konzepten wurde auf dem Markt oder Suk als Düne oder Oase vorgeschlagen, die den Blick auf den Horizont und die Stadt freigeben, als öffentlicher Platz oder Park, geschützt von dem laubartigen Gerüst des Gebäudes.

left: Sections and floor plans_Conference center_Shopping mall. right: General view_Offices.
links: Ansichten und Grundrisse_Kongresszentrum_Einkaufsstraße. rechts: Gesamtansicht_Büros.

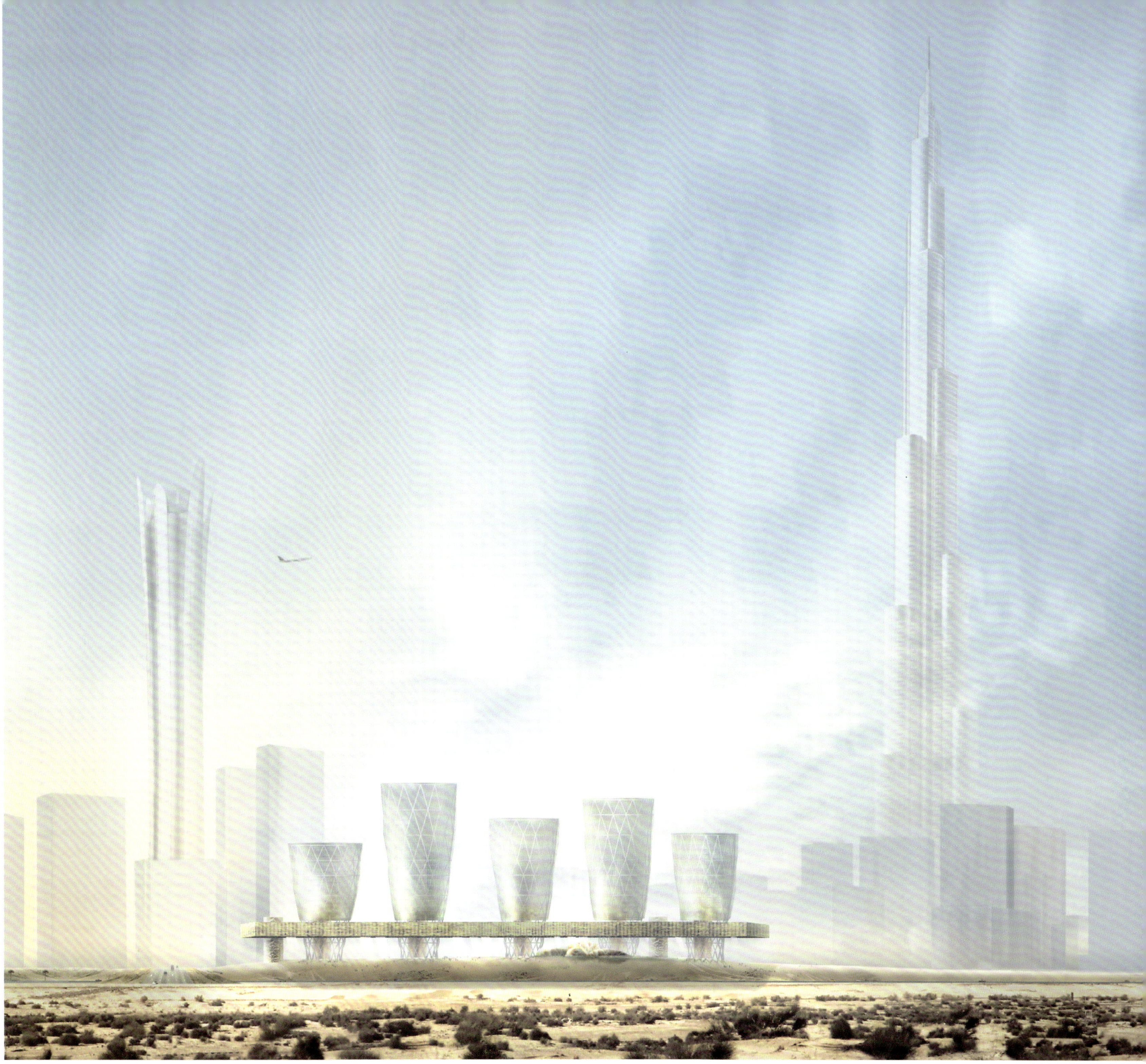

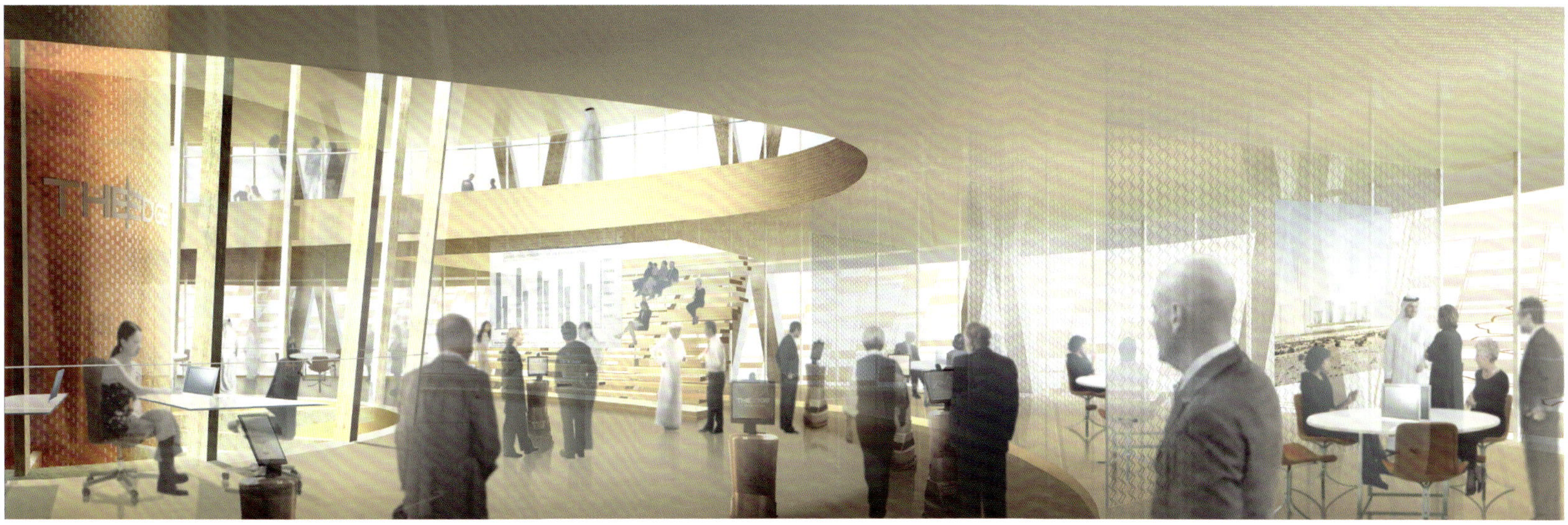

COLLECTION

europe

FICE BUILDING GRABENSTRASSE_AUSTRIA_GRAZ_FROG QUEEN_AUSTR
GRAZ_VOESTALPINE STAHL GMBH_AUSTRIA_LINZ_T-CENTER ST. MARX_AU
A_VIENNA_ADMINISTRATIVECENTERBONHEIDEN_BELGIUM_BONHEIDEN_E
SPACE CENTER AT LIBIN-TRANSINNE_BELGIUM_LIBIN-TRANSINNE_H
OFFICE JOKER TOURISM_BELGIUM_MECHELEN_OFFICE VANHAERE
TORHOUT_BELGIUM_TORHOUT_C. F. MØLLER ARCHITECTS HEAD OFFICE_D
ARK_AARHUS_O-ZONE,HEADQUARTERORACLE_DENMARK_BALLERUP_WO
HEALTH ORGANISATION_DENMARK_COPENHAGEN_VITUS BERING INNOV
PARK_DENMARK_HORSENS_COMM2_DENMARK_KOKKEDAL INDUSTR
RK_ADVICEHOUSE_DENMARK_VEJLE_MEISTRIOFFICEBUILDING_ESTONIA_T
NN_PORTAALI BUSINESS PARK_FINLAND_HELSINKI_21 BOISSEAU_FR
E_CLICHY-LA-GARENNE_GENNEVILLIERS LOGISTICS CENTER_FRANCE_GE
VILLIERS_PHARE TOWER_FRANCE_LA DÉFENSE_GENERALI TOWER FR
E_LADÉFENSE_EXALTISTOWER_FRANCE_LADÉFENSE_CINETICOFFICEBUILD
G_FRANCE_PARIS_CARDBOARD OFFICE_FRANCE_PARIS_LABOBRAIN_FR
E_PARIS_8 ROCHEFOUCAULD_FRANCE_PARIS_118 ELYSÉES_FRANCE_P
COMPANY HEADQUARTERS_FRANCE_SAINT-MESMES_MONASTERY ST. A
NS_GERMANY_AACHEN_BÖSLMEDIZINTECHNIKGMBH_GERMANY_AACHEN

AUSTRIA_GRAZ **OFFICE BUILDING GRABENSTRASSE**

ARCHITECTS: ARCHITEKTUR CONSULT ZT GMBH WITH HERFRIED PEYKER_**COMPLETION:** 2003
NUMBER OF WORKPLACES: 30_**GROSS FLOOR AREA:** 3,560 M²
COMMON AREA: ROOF TERRACE_**PHOTOS:** PAUL OTT, GRAZ

The location near the highly frequented Grabenstraße, as well as the different heights of the neighboring buildings were that basis of a distinctive design concept. The steel skeleton buildings opens towards the backyard via generous glass façades, while the street side presents a closed, yet dynamic impression. Only the showroom areas on the ground floor provide the greatest possible view inside. Terraces are situated in front of the offices on the upper floors. Their cascaded arrangement links the neighboring block constructions on the front to the mixed structures on the yard side. Concrete core activation eliminates the need for separate heating and cooling systems.

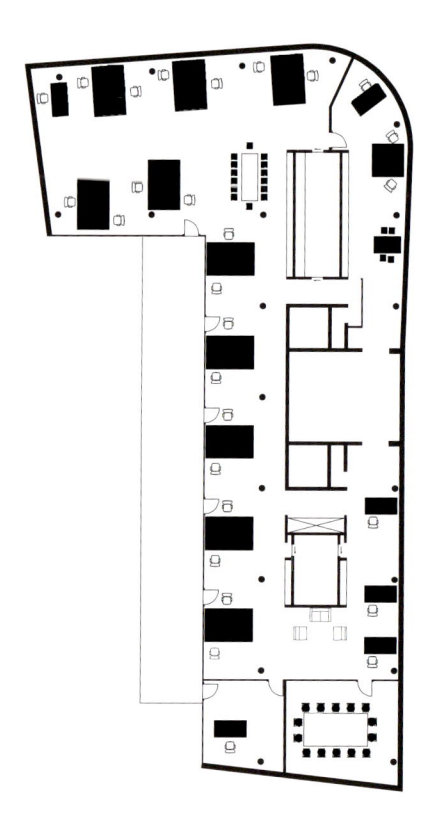

Die Lage an der stark befahrenen Grabenstraße sowie die unterschiedlichen Höhen der Nachbarbebauung wurden als Ausgangspunkt für eine markante Gestaltung herangezogen. An der Hofseite öffnet sich der Stahbetonskelettbau durch großzügige Glasfassaden, während an der Straßenseite ein verschlossener aber dynamischer Eindruck gesucht wurde. Hier gewähren lediglich die Ausstellungsflächen im Erdgeschoss größtmögliche Einsicht. Den Büros in den Obergeschossen sind Terrassen vorgelagert, deren stufenförmige Anordnung städtebaulich zwischen angrenzender Blockbebauung an der Vorder- und aufgelockerter Bebauung an der Hofseite vermittelt. Dank der Betonkernaktivierung sind keine gesonderten Heiz- und Kühlsysteme notwendig.

left: Floor plan with furniture_Corner, view from street_Perspective. right: Night view_Roof terrace_Interior view.
links: Grundriss mit Möblierung_Ecke, Straßenansicht_Perspektive. rechts: Nachtansicht_Dachterrasse_Innenansicht.

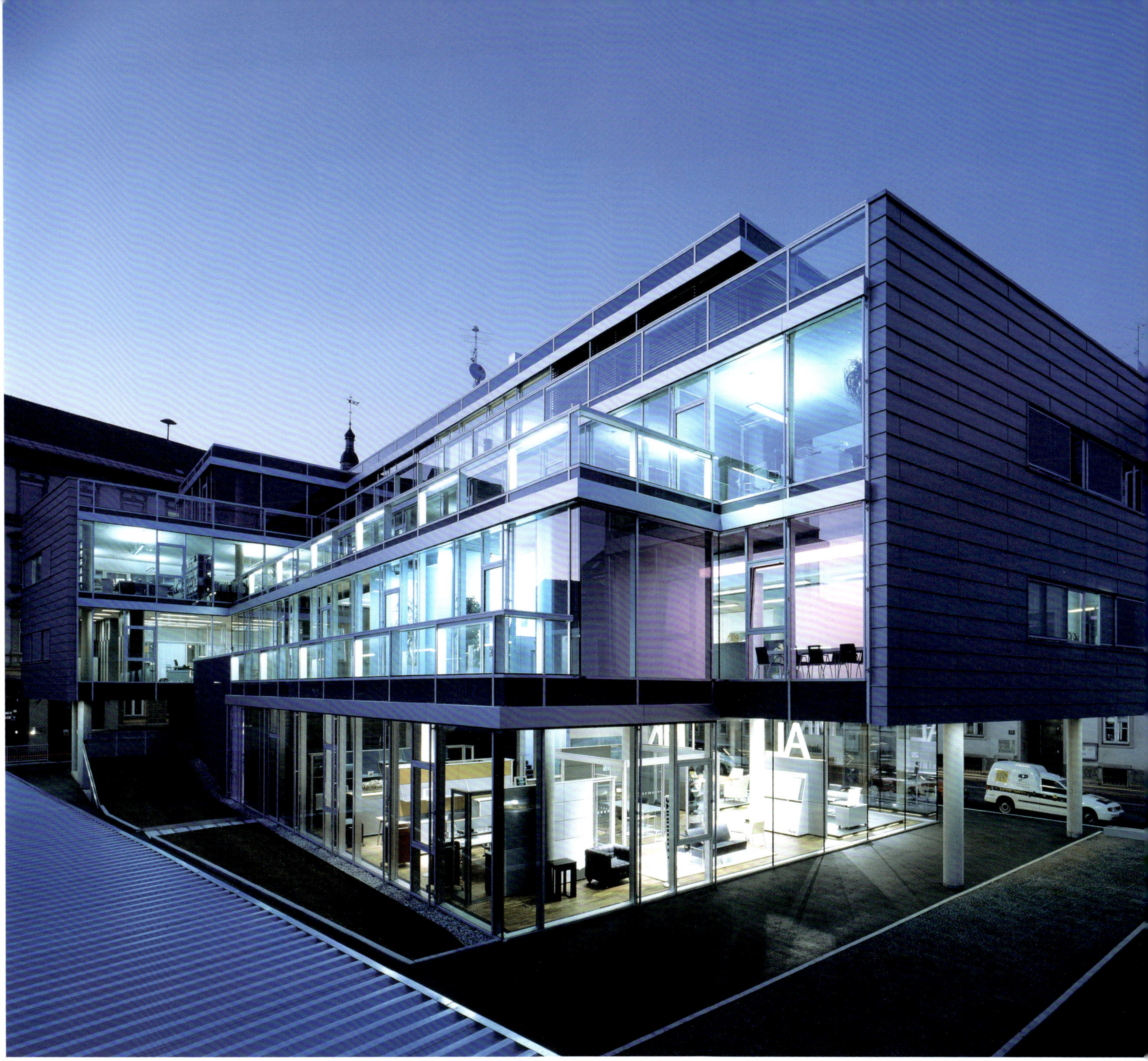

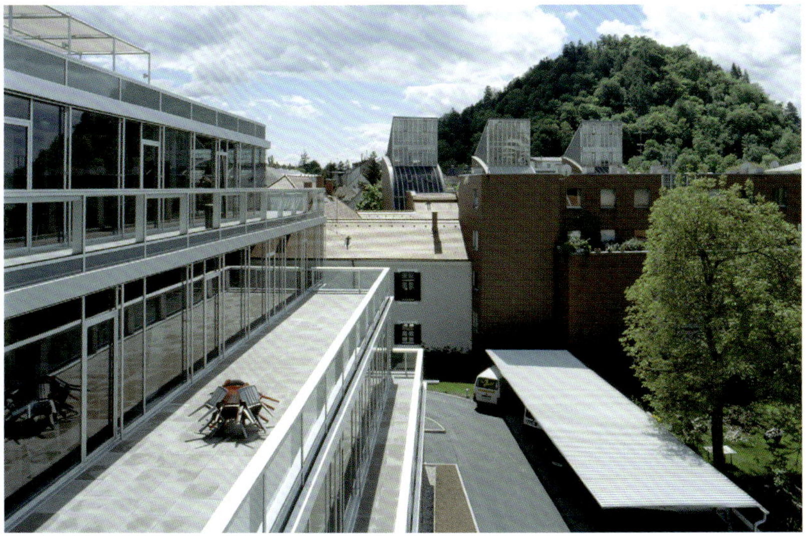

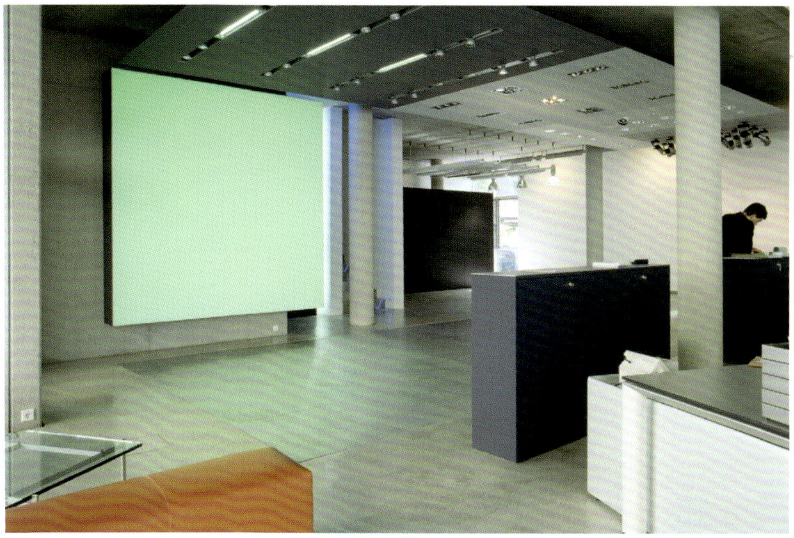

AUSTRIA_GRAZ **FROG QUEEN**

ARCHITECTS: SPLITTERWERK
COMPLETION: 2007_**NUMBER OF WORKPLACES:** 35
GROSS FLOOR AREA: 1,400 M²_**COMMON AREA:** MEETING ROOMS_**KIND OF WORKPLACES:** CELLULAR
PHOTOS: NIKOLAOS ZACHARIADIS, GRAZ (48, 49 B. L., B. R.), PAUL OTT, GRAZ (49 A.)

The architects dubbed the cubic structure "Frog Queen". It is the headquarters with engineering offices and test hall of Prisma Engineering Maschinen- und Motorentechnik GmbH in Graz. The distinctive building with its complex façade pattern in various shades of grey is already visible from a distance, but its ornamentation only appears upon closer inspection. As if pulled by a magic hand, a part of the façade opens slowly to reveal a mirrored room which is a lift that automatically moves up into the foyer located on the first floor. Individual work environments in the various offices represent a tension between the virtual and real view.

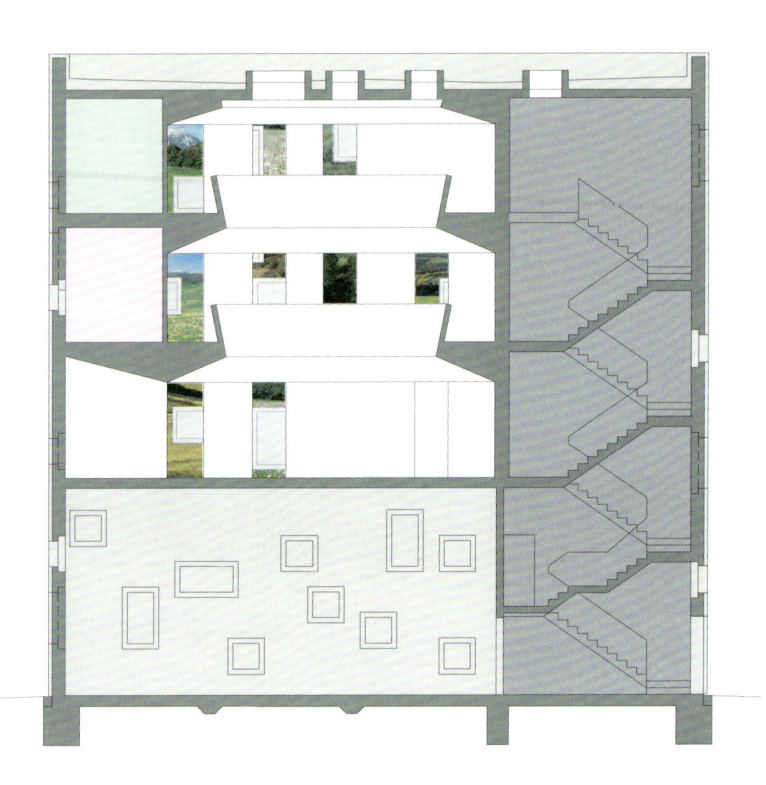

„Frog Queen" nennen die Architekten diesen würfelförmigen Baukörper, die Hauptverwaltung der Prisma Engineering Maschinen-und Motorentechnik GmbH mit Sitz in Graz mit Ingenieurbüros und einer Prüfhalle. Der markante Bau ist mit seiner komplexen Fassadenzeichnung in unterschiedlichsten Grautönen schon von weitem sichtbar, doch erst bei näherer Betrachtung zeigen sich Ornamente. Nähert man sich, öffnet sich wie von Zauberhand langsam ein Stück Fassade – dahinter befindet sich ein verspiegelter Raum, der als Lift automatisch in das im ersten Obergeschoss liegende Foyer fährt. Individuelle Arbeitswelten in den einzelnen Büroräumen thematisieren ein Spannungsverhältnis zwischen virtueller und realer Aussicht.

left: Section_South view_Small office. right: Foyer with atrium_Atrium, reception desk_Meeting room.
links: Schnitt_Blick von Süden_Kleines Büro. rechts: Foyer im Atrium_ Atrium, Empfangstresen_ Besprechungsraum.

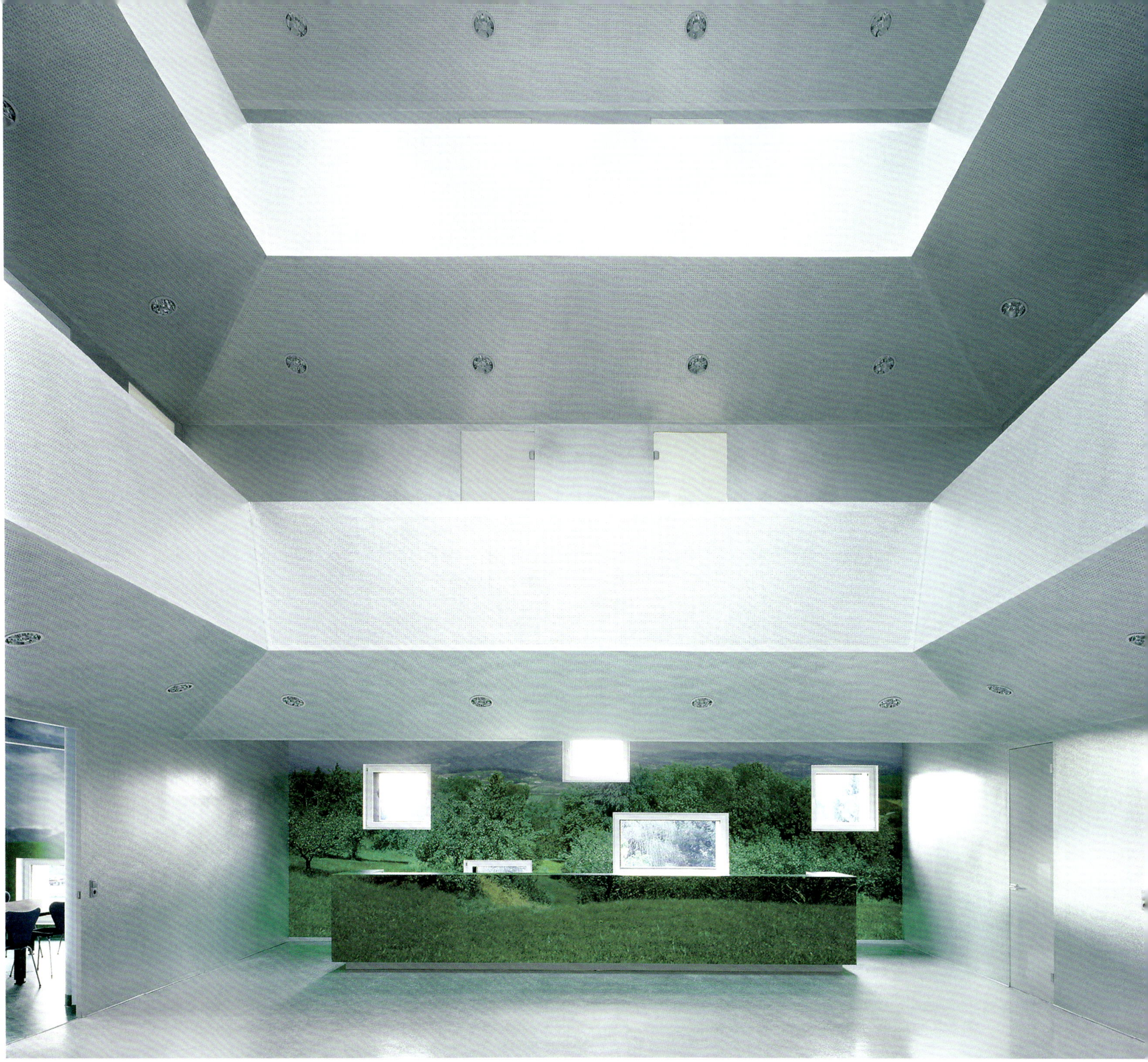
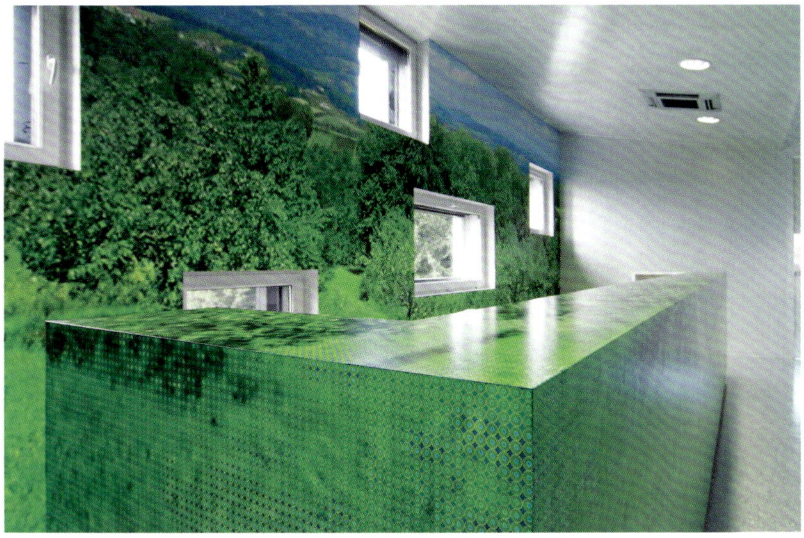
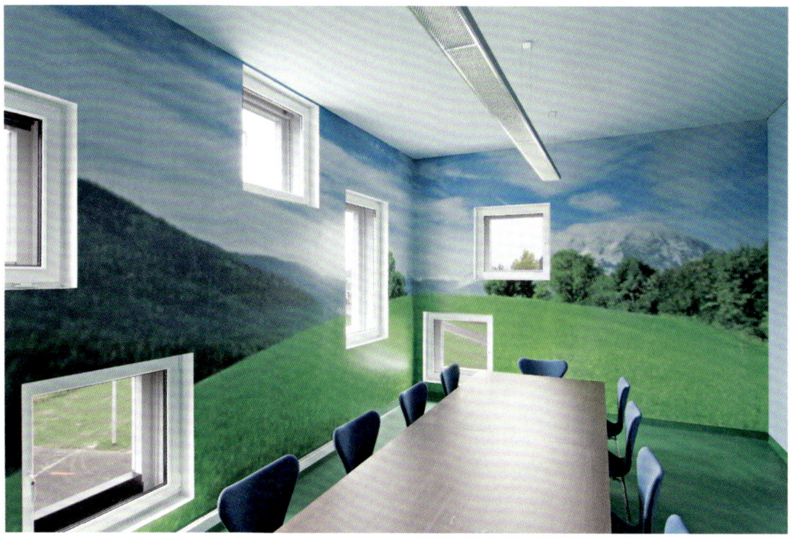

AUSTRIA_LINZ **VOESTALPINE STAHL GMBH**

ARCHITECTS: DIETMAR FEICHTINGER ARCHITECTES
COMPLETION: 2009_**NUMBER OF WORKPLACES:** 404
GROSS FLOOR AREA: 11,671 M²_**COMMON AREA:** COMMUNICATION AREAS, CONFERENCE ROOMS, TRAVEL AGENCY, BANK, GROCERY_**KIND OF WORKPLACES:** COMBINATION, TEAM
PHOTOS: JOSEF PAUSCH, BARBARA FEICHTINGER-FELBER (53 A. R.)

Together with the "Blue tower", the new corporate headquarters forms the entrance to the premises of the steel manufacturer. Between the old and new buildings extends a generous open space with 630 underground parking spaces. The new building defines the northern edge of the premises, its unusual, yet not overly dramatic, shape demonstrates the capacities of steel. The offices are located on a wide middle strip out of which four greened atriums are cut. The flexible shading elements made of frameless expanded metal on the outside and fabric glare protection on the inside of the façade ensure comfortable illumination.

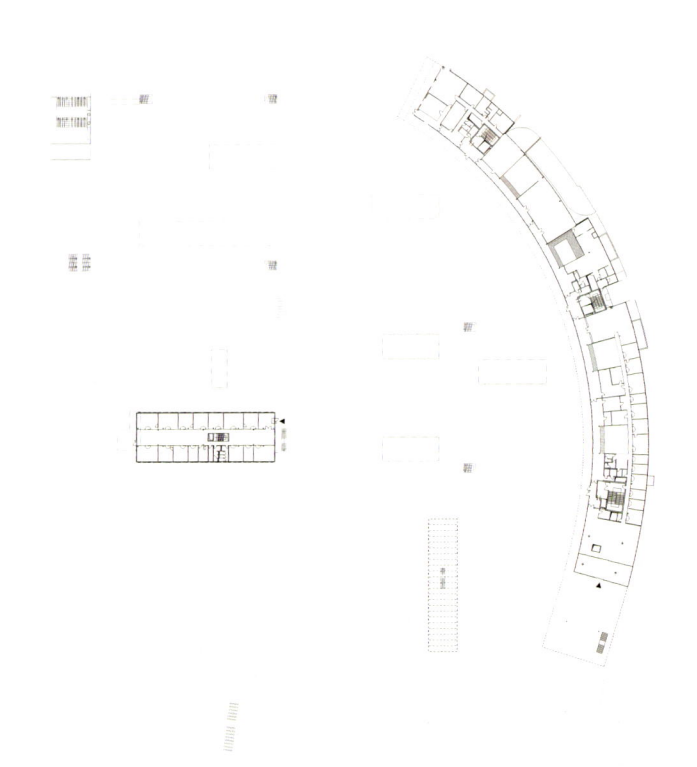

Die neue Unternehmenszentrale bildet gemeinsam mit dem „BlauenTurm" das Portal zum Betriebsgelände des Stahlherstellers. Zwischen Bestand und Neubauten spannt sich ein großzügiger Freiraum mit 630 unterirdischen Parkplätzen. Das neue Gebäude definiert den nördlichen Abschluss des Geländes und demonstriert in seiner ungewöhnlichen, aber nicht übertrieben dramatisierten Formgebung die Fähigkeiten des Stahls. Die Büros liegen an einer breiten Mittelzone, in welche vier begrunte Atrien eingeschnitten sind. Die verschiebbaren Beschattungselemente aus rahmenlosem Streckmetall an der Außen- und ein textiler Blendschutz an der Innenseite der Fassade gewährleisten komfortable Lichtverhältnisse.

left: Ground floor plan_General view with forecourt_Detail, façade. right: Entrance area in the gloaming.
links: Grundriss Erdgeschoss_Gesamtansicht mit Vorplatz_Detail, Fassade. rechts: Eingangsbereich in der Dämmerung.

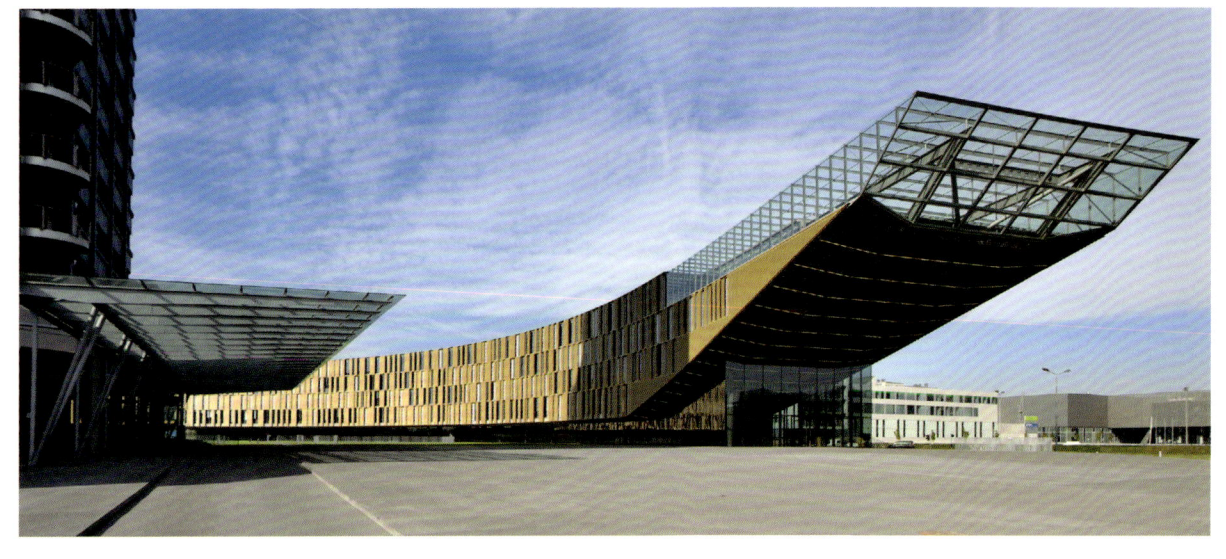

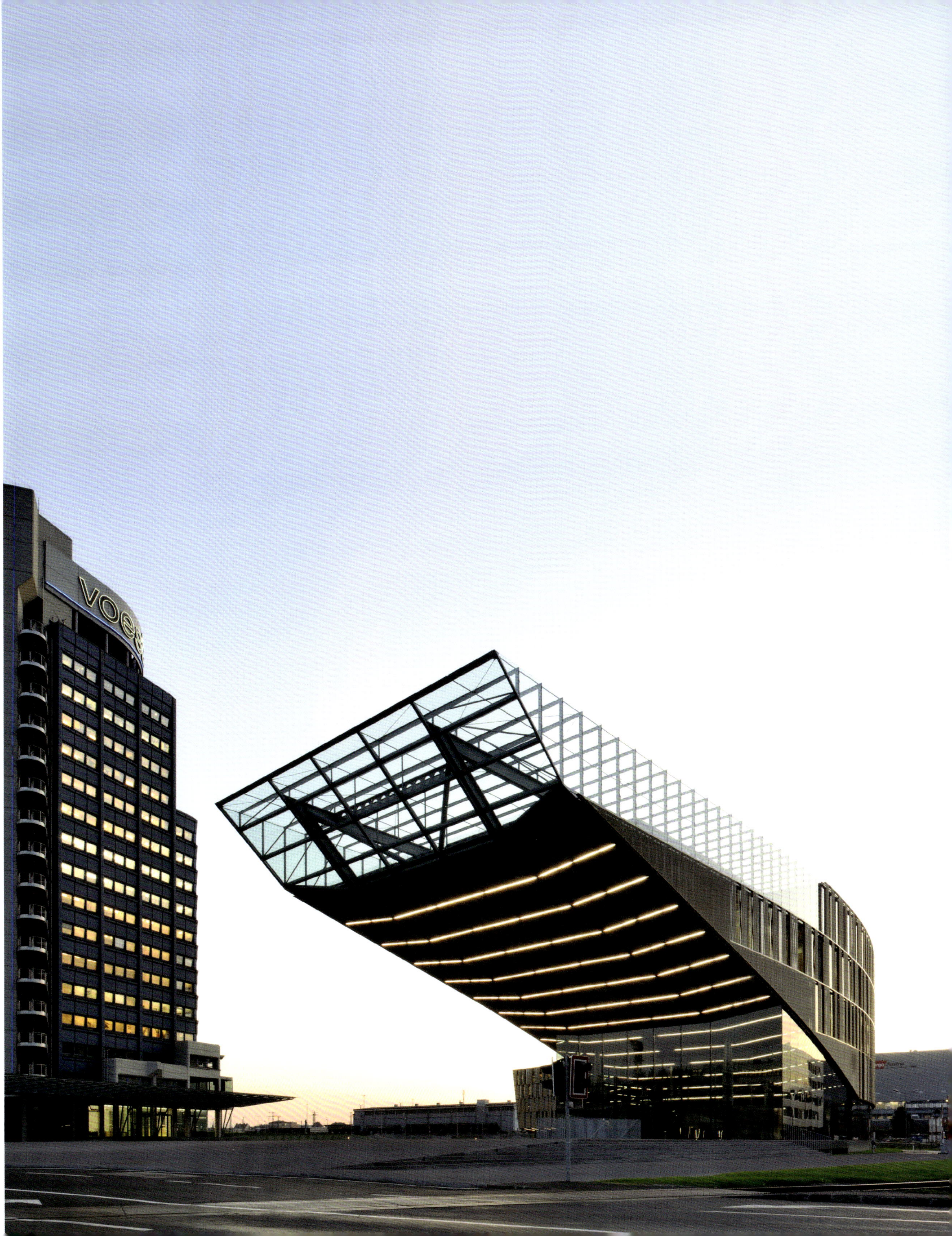

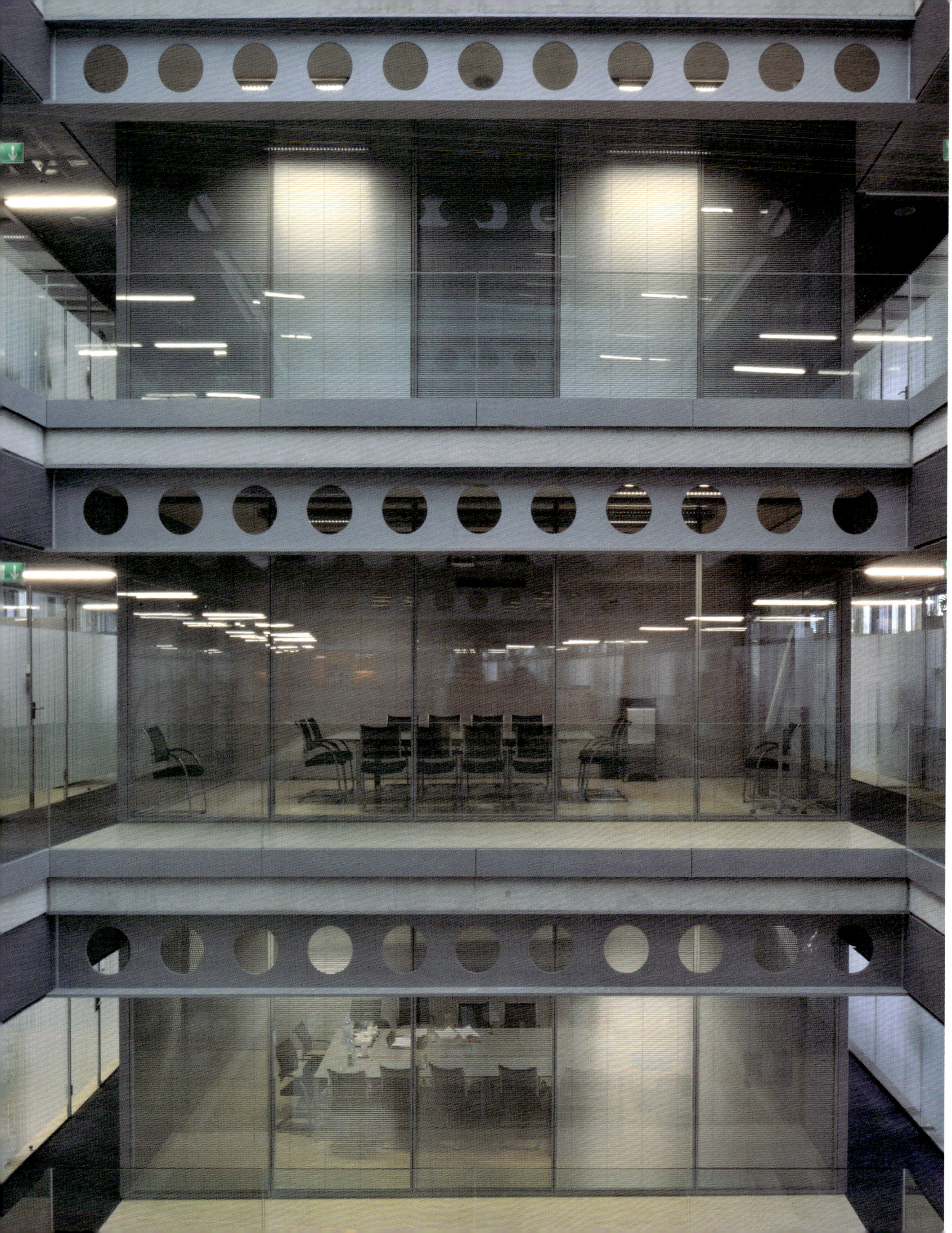

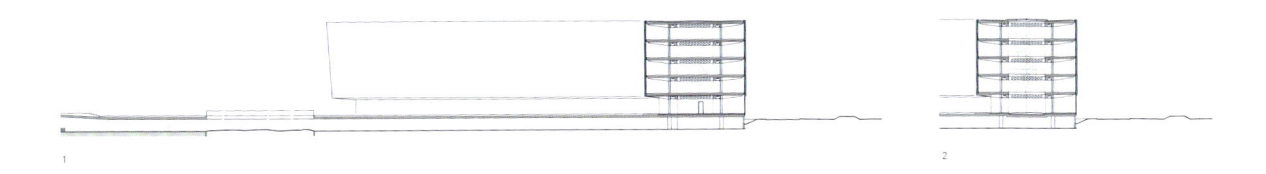

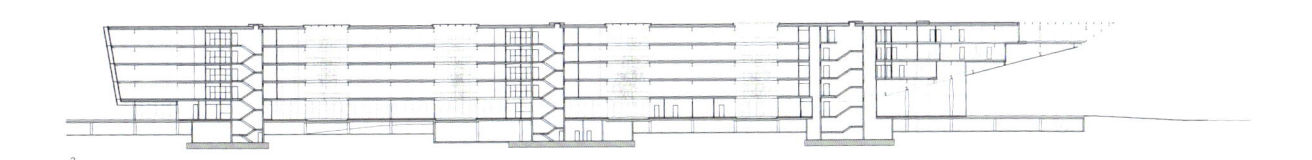

left: Atrium, meeting rooms. right: Sections_South elevation_Conference room_Office_Atrium with small kitchen.
links: Atrium, Besprechungsräume. rechts: Schnitte_Südfassade_Konferenzraum_Büroraum_ Atrium mit Teeküche.

AUSTRIA_VIENNA **T-CENTER ST. MARX**

ARCHITECTS: ARCHITEKTUR CONSULT ZT GMBH WITH GÜNTHER DOMENIG_**COMPLETION:** 2004
NUMBER OF WORKPLACES: 2,500
GROSS FLOOR AREA: 140,000 M²
PHOTOS: PAUL OTT, GRAZ

On the terrain of a communal slaughterhouse, crossed by an urban highway, a distinctive design was sought to initiate the conversion of the premises. The desired solution was a sculptural building shape whose basic architectural layout offered very large spaces at a price that was in line with the market. Prominent wings (core areas with a central up-station and internal distribution level) and fingers (modularly extendable for various office and other uses) were placed on top of a visually and physically open base with secondary uses (parking, utilities management, storage and logistics) and a public zone (business and service units that can be traversed).

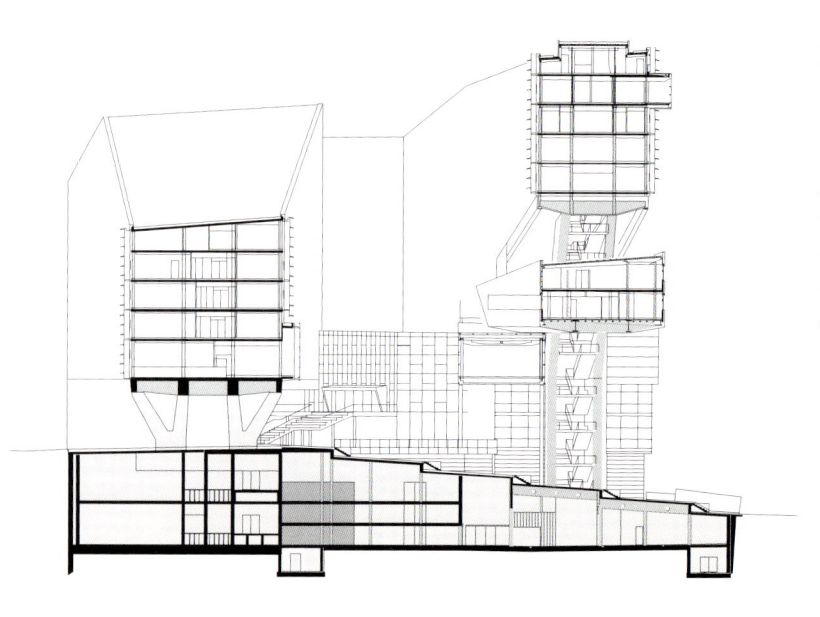

Auf dem von einer Stadtautobahn zerschnittenen Terrain eines kommunalen Schlachthofs sollte eine markante Formensprache den Auftakt zur Umnutzung des Areals bilden. Eine skulpturale Gebäudeausformung bei architektonischer Grundgestaltung wurde gesucht, die zudem ein riesiges Raumprogramm zu einem marktkonformen Preis erfüllen konnte. Über einem visuell wie physisch offenen Sockel mit Sekundärnutzungen (Parken, Haustechnik, Lager und Logistik) und öffentlicher Zone (Geschäfts-, Dienstleistungseinheiten als durchwanderbare Zone) entstanden markante Flügel (Kernbereich mit zentralem Hochpunkt und interner Verteilerebene) und Finger (modular erweiterbar für verschiedene Büro- oder andere Nutzer).

left: Section_General view_Detail. right: Entrance area.
links: Schnitt_Gesamtansicht_Detail. rechts: Eingangsbereich.

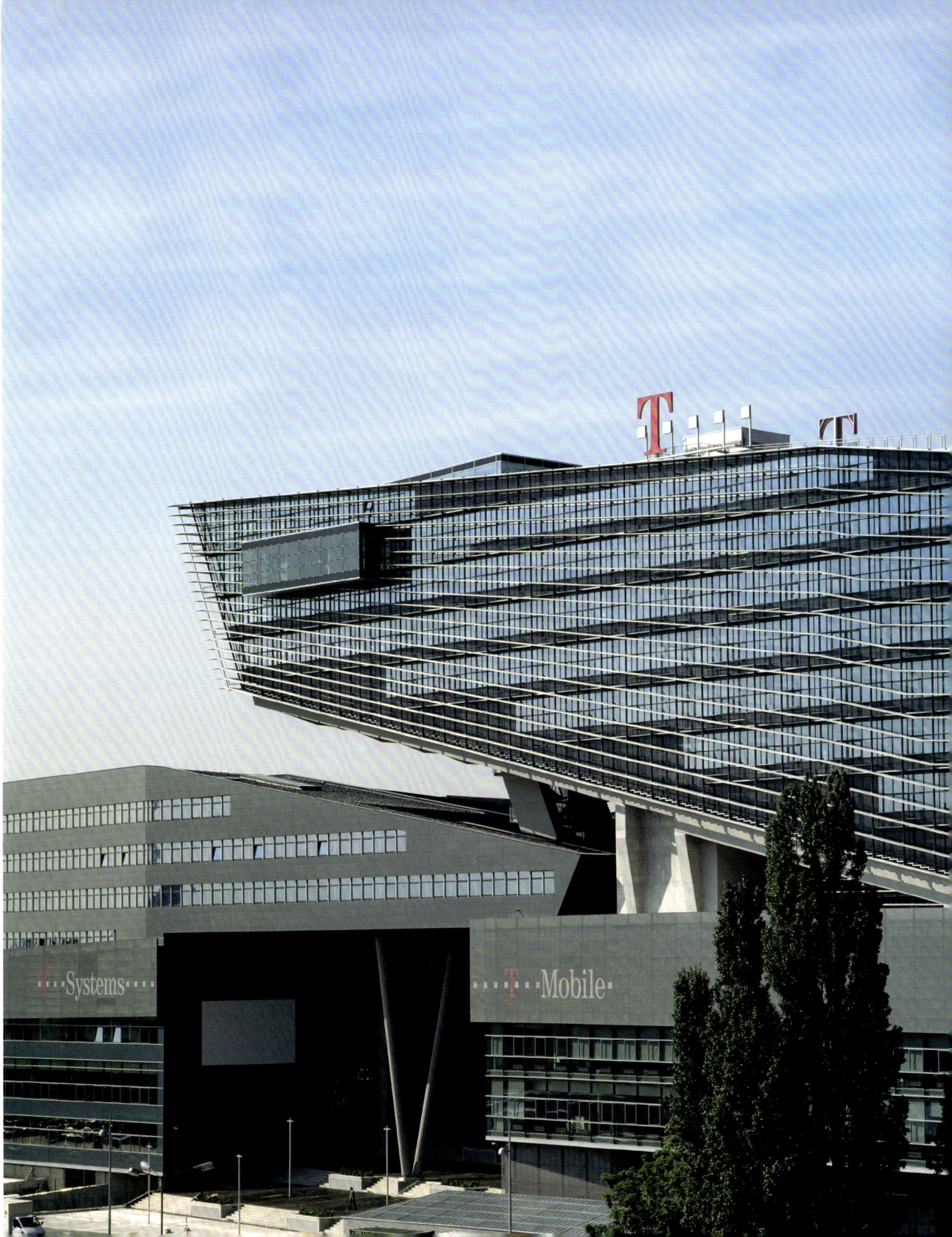
T · · Systems · ·
· · · T · · Mobile ·

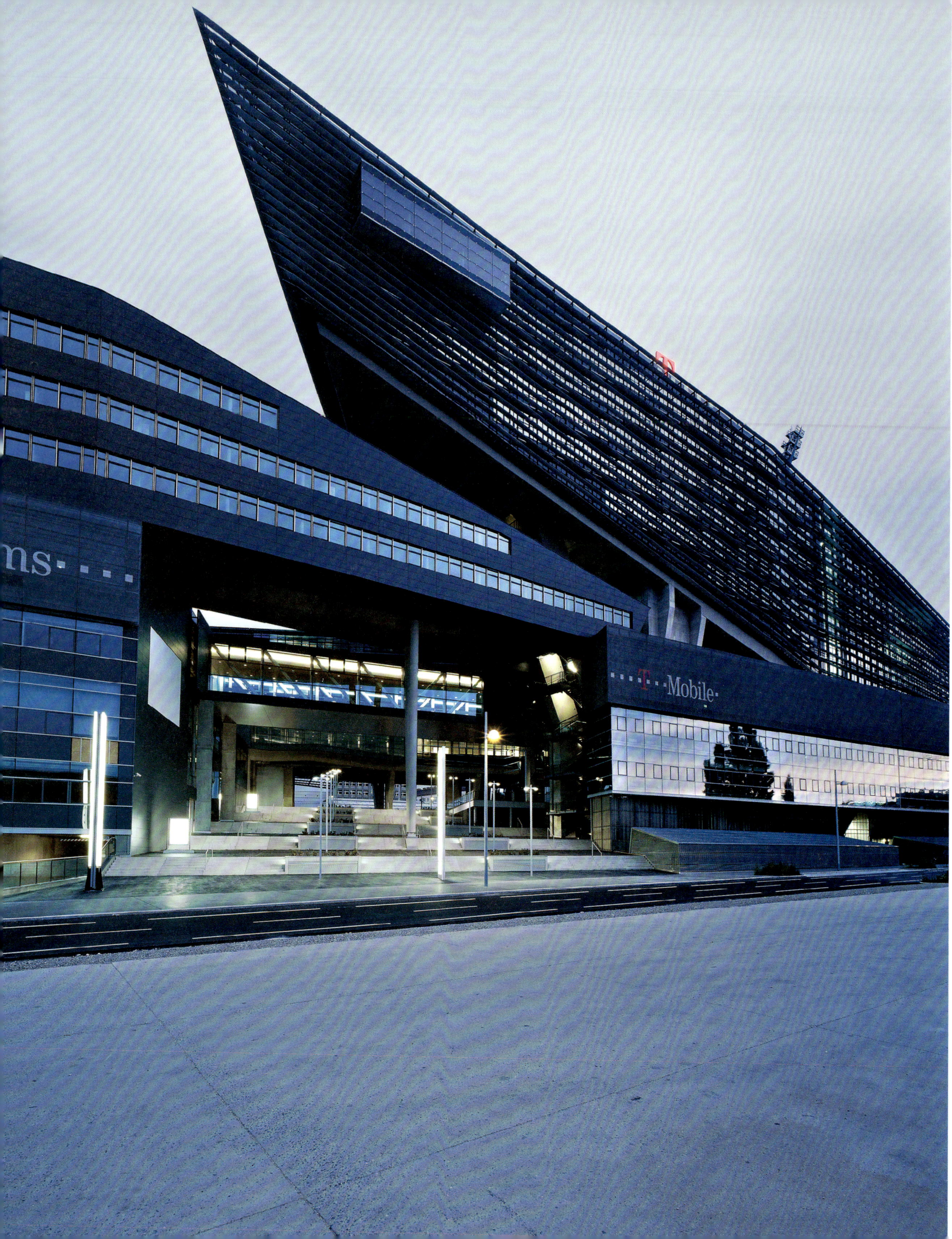
ms
T · · Mobile

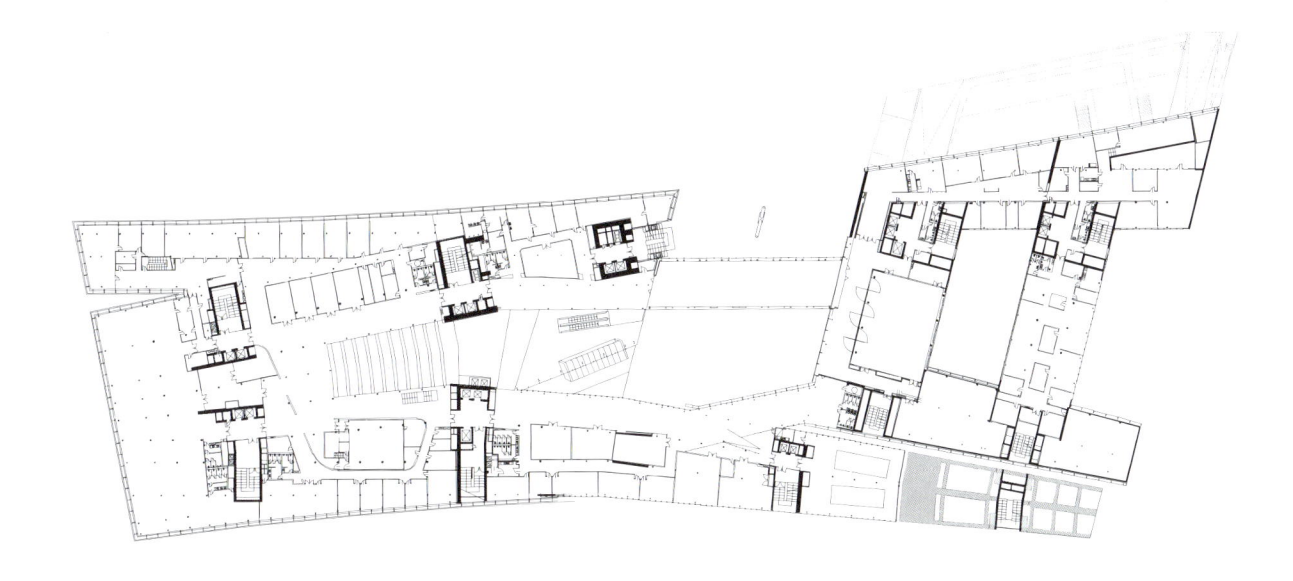

left: Entrance and forecourt by night. right: Second floor plan_Interior view_Entrance and mezzanine.
links: Eingang und Vorplatz bei Nacht. rechts: Grundriss zweites Obergeschoss_Innenansicht_Eingang und Zwischengeschoss.

BELGIUM_BONHEIDEN **ADMINISTRATIVE CENTER BONHEIDEN**

ARCHITECTS: VBMARCHITECTS (NOW BOGDAN & VAN BROECK ARCHITECTS AND LAVA ARCHITECTS)_**COMPLETION:** 2005
NUMBER OF WORKPLACES: 65_**GROSS FLOOR AREA:** 3,008 M²
COMMON AREA: LIBRARY_**KIND OF WORKPLACES:** CELLULAR, COMBINATION, OPEN-PLAN, TEAM
PHOTOS: TOON GROBET

This ecological town hall expresses open management, low thresholds and high accessibility with a communicative attitude towards citizens. Well-controlled transparency rules, not only between visitors and the political powers but also amongst the employees themselves. Moreover, without any muscular boasting, the building adds social control and a homely feeling of safety to its surroundings. Modular open-plan offices on concrete floor slabs without beams or false ceilings, maximize flexibility and allow free positioning of partition walls. Pluvial water from the roof is stored in concrete tanks in the basement, from where it can be recycled for toilet flushing, fire-fighting and cooling.

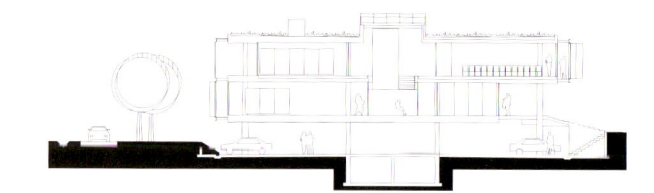

Dieses ökologische Rathaus steht für eine offene Verwaltung, einen niedrigen Schwellenwert, einen leichten Zugang sowie für kommunikative Offenheit gegenüber den Bürgern. Eine ausgewogene Transparenz herrscht nicht nur zwischen den Besuchern und den politischen Mächten, sondern auch unter dem Personal selbst. Zudem gewährleistet das Gebäude – ohne jedes Imponiergehabe – soziale Kontrolle und ein Gefühl von Heimat und Sicherheit. Modulare Großraumbüros auf Betonbodenplatten ohne Balken sowie abgehängte Decken maximieren die Flexibilität und ermöglichen die freie Einteilung durch Trennwände. Regenwasser vom Dach wird in Betontanks im Keller gesammelt und für Toilettenspülung, Brandschutz und Kühlung recycelt.

left: Section_General view_Between inner and outer skin. right: Central atrium_Inner view of council room_Façade with galvanised steel mesh.
links: Schnitt_Gesamtansicht_Zwischen innerer und äußerer Gebäudehülle. rechts: Zentrales Atrium_Innenansicht des Sitzungssaals_Fassade mit feuerverzinktem Stahlgitter.

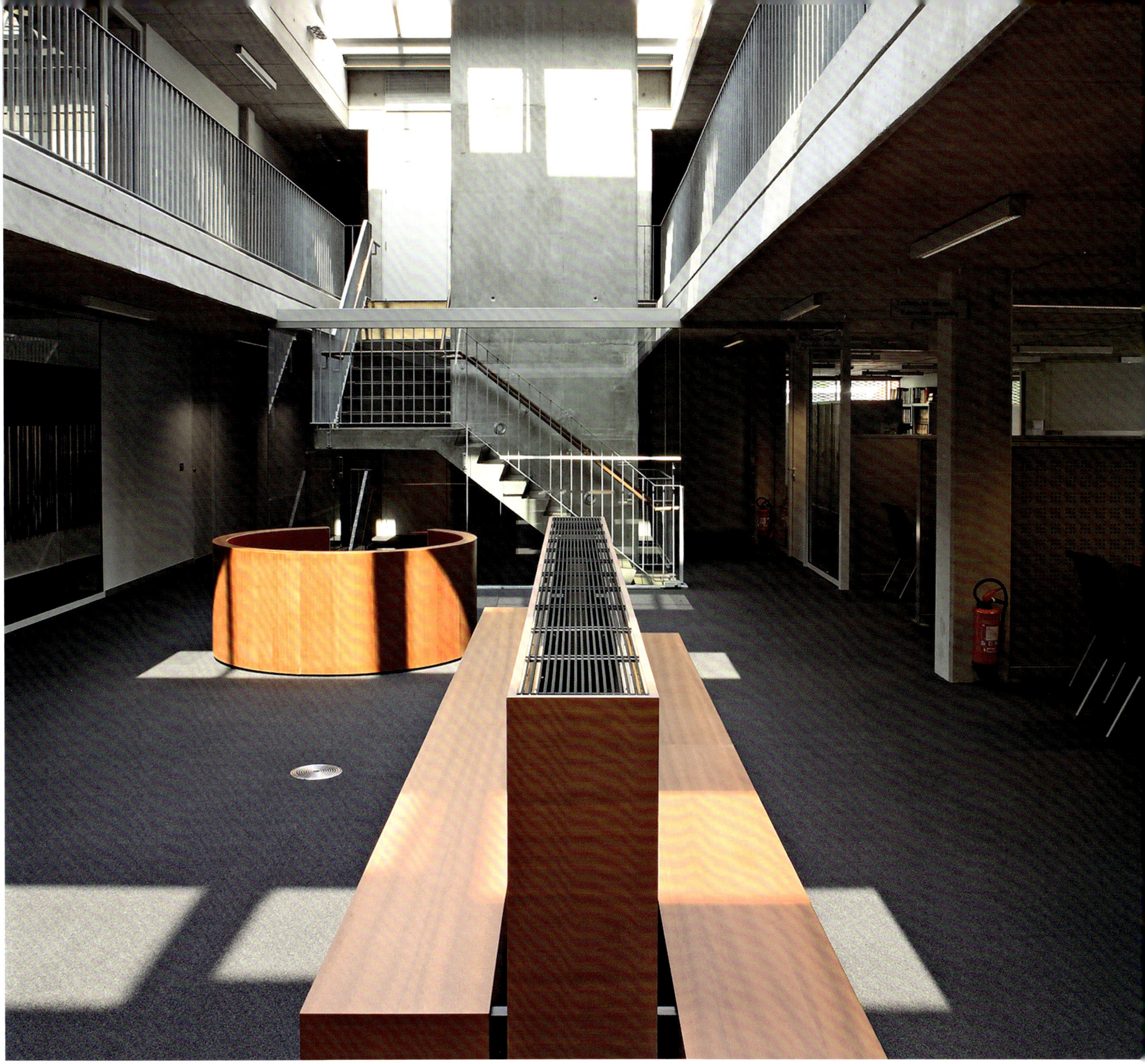

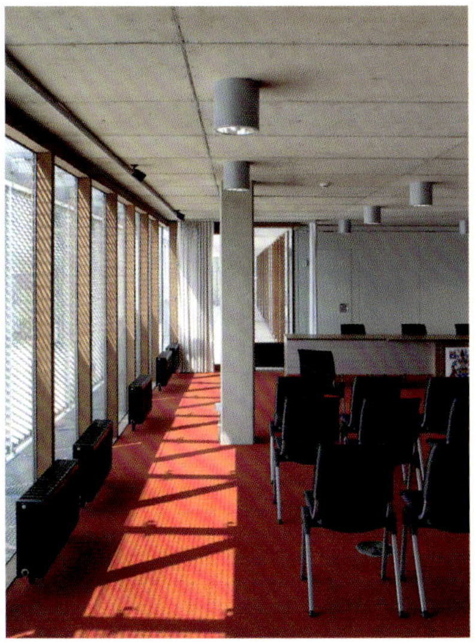

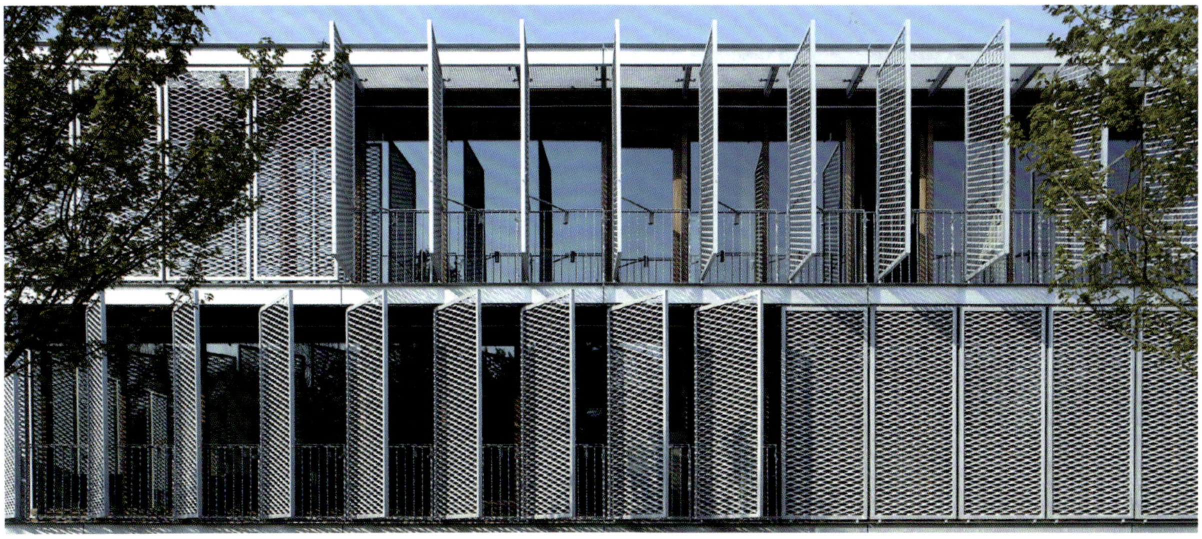

BELGIUM_LIBIN-TRANSINNE **EURO SPACE CENTER AT LIBIN-TRANSINNE**

ARCHITECTS: PHILIPPE SAMYN AND PARTNERS
COMPLETION: 2006_**NUMBER OF WORKPLACES:** 90
GROSS FLOOR AREA: 1,800 M²_**COMMON AREA:** KITCHEN, MEETING ROOM_**KIND OF WORKPLACES:** CELLULAR
PHOTOS: LA FIBRE COMM., FRANCE (60, 61 B. L., M.), MARIE-FRANÇOISE PLISSART, BRUSSELS (61 A., B. R.)

The Euro Space Center is responsible for providing information concerning space exploration activities and telecommunications. The project houses diverse enterprises active in these sectors, located in modules consisting of low-rise wooden constructions. A large parallelepiped, like a raised horticultural greenhouse, provides a common roof to the ensemble. The glass façade along the highway is prolonged by a 120-meter-long gallery that covers the existing building. The three-dimensional structure is the ideal support for large banners, signaling the nature of the activities of this center. The southern slopes of the roof and façade elements are equipped with photovoltaic panels.

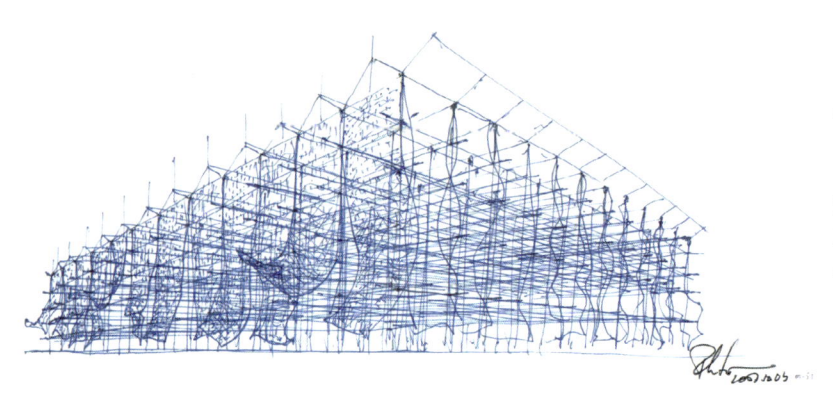

Das Euro Space Center dient der Verbreitung von Wissen über Weltraumforschung und Telekommunikation. Das Projekt beherbergt verschiedene Unternehmen, die in diesen Sektoren arbeiten, in Modulen, die aus niedrigen Holzkonstruktionen bestehen. In dem großen, wie ein hohes Gewächshaus aussehenden Quader befindet sich das Ensemble unter einem gemeinsamen Dach. Die Glasfassade entlang der Autobahn wurde um eine 120 Meter lange Galerie vor dem bestehenden Gebäude verlängert. Die dreidimensionale Struktur eignet sich sehr gut für große Plakate, die auf die Aktivitäten im Zentrum hinweisen. Die südliche Seite des Dachs und die Fassadenelemente sind mit Solarzellen ausgestattet.

left: Sketch_General view_Inner courtyard under photovoltaic roof. right: View from parking area_Perspective_Office space_Banners on the three-dimensional structure.
links: Skizze_Ansicht_Innenhof unter einem Dach mit Solarzellen. rechts: Blick vom Parkplatz_Büroraum_Plakat auf der dreidimensionalen Struktur.

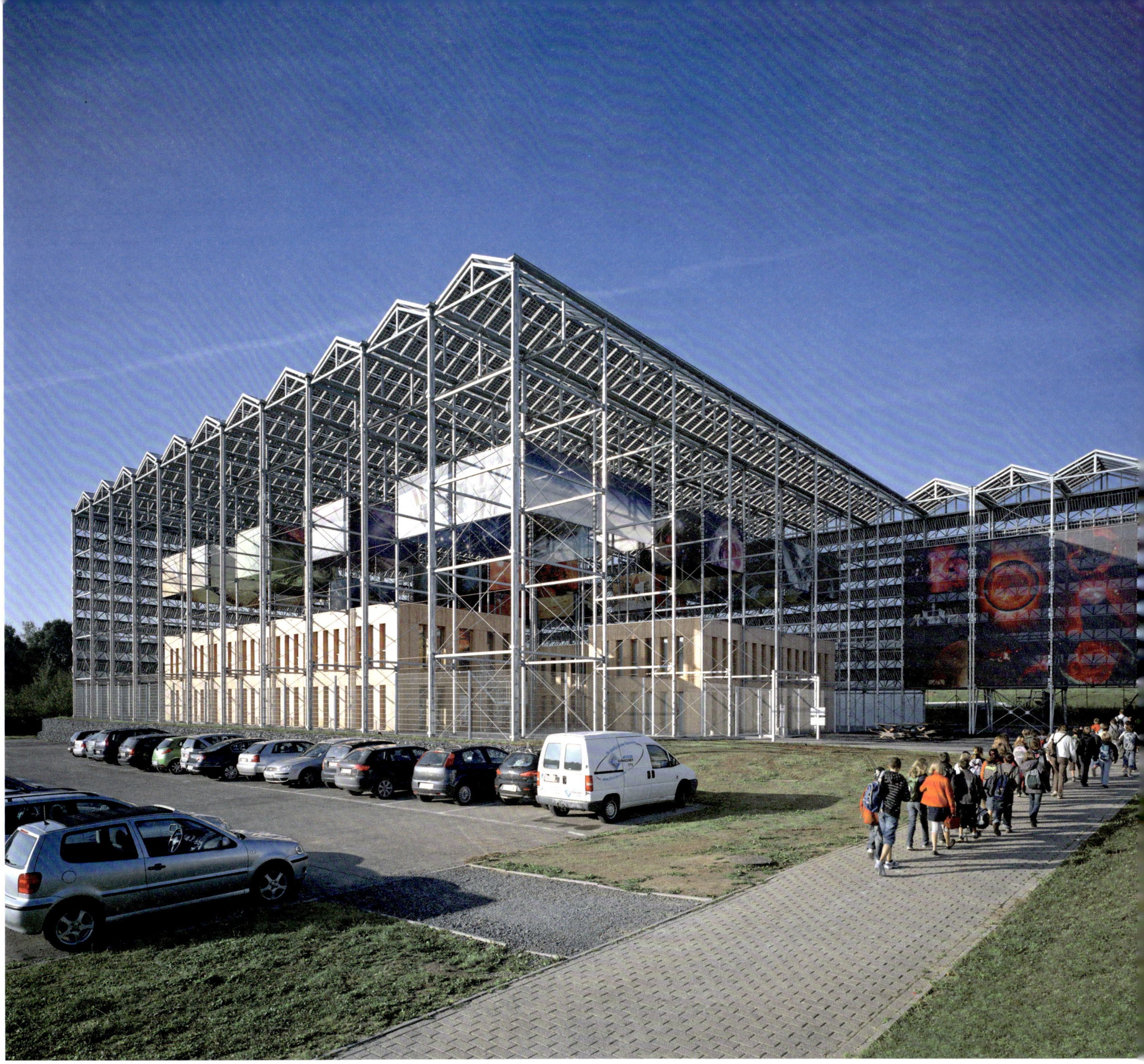
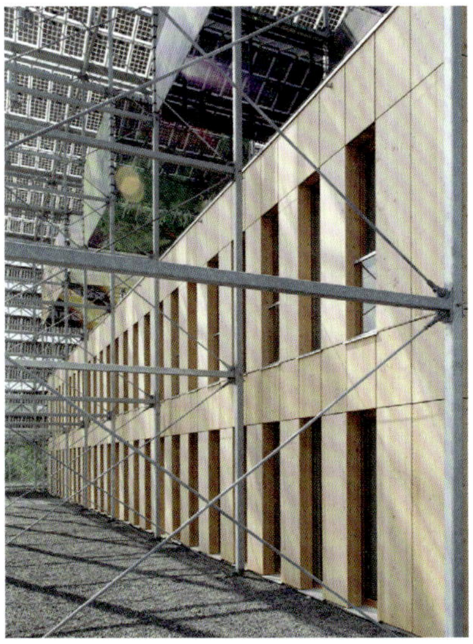
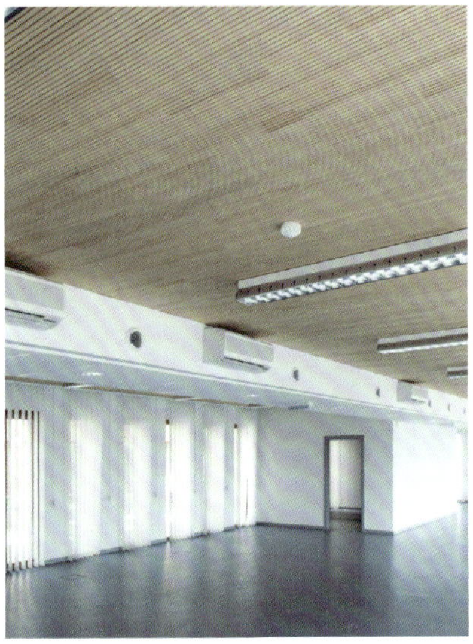
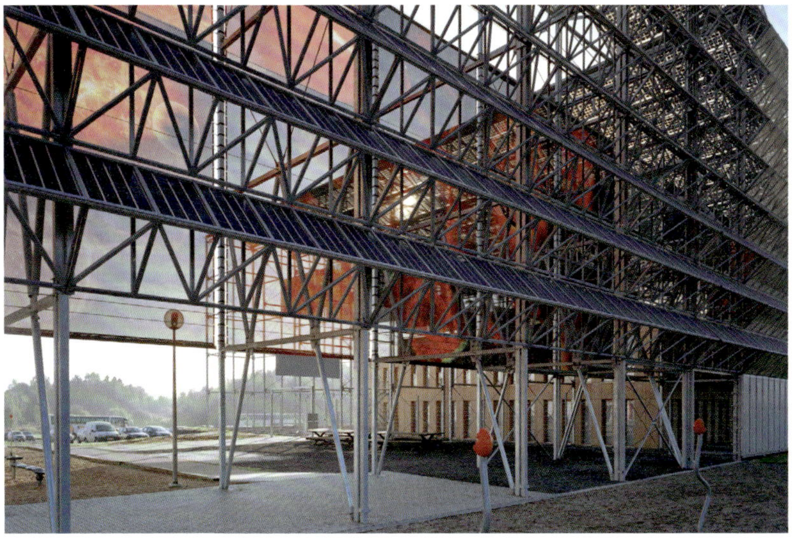

BELGIUM_MECHELEN **HEAD OFFICE JOKER TOURISM**

ARCHITECTS: META ARCHITECTUURBUREAU
COMPLETION: 2005_**NUMBER OF WORKPLACES:** 40
GROSS FLOOR AREA: 1,420 M²_**COMMON AREA:** CONFERENCE ROOM, CLASSROOM_**KIND OF WORKPLACES:** OPEN-PLAN, COCKPIT, TEAM_**PHOTOS:** TOON GROBET, ANTWERPEN

Of an existing building complex, only the rearmost building has been kept and renovated, its rational concrete structure providing a double height space. This was then linked to a new building that maintains the street-line. The use of a single façade material – both buildings are clad in gray shingles – formally unites the two volumes. Entrance and vertical circulation are strategically situated between the old and new buildings. The shell was conceived in such a way that it could also function as a finished state. This strategy saves both material and time, making the building more economical without affecting quality while enhancing flexibility and sustainability.

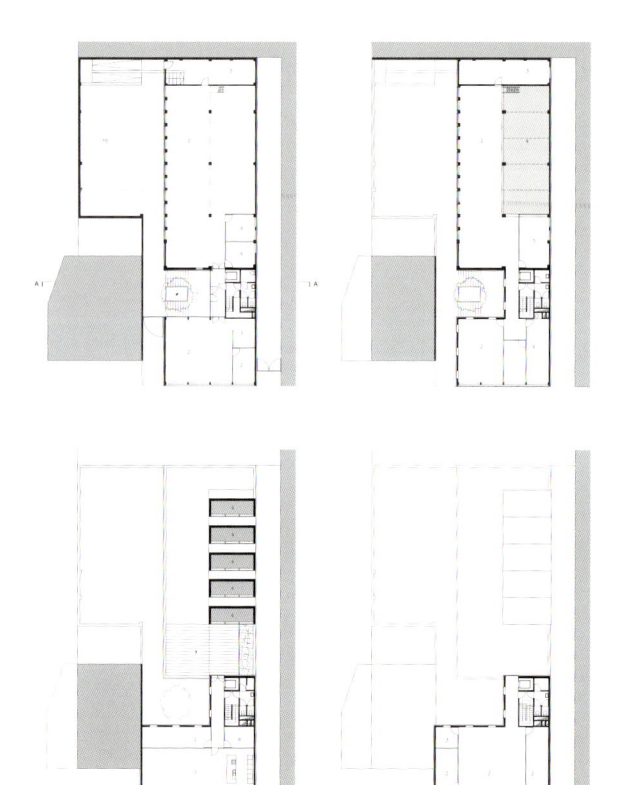

Vom bestehenden Gebäude wurde nur der hintere Teil erhalten und renoviert. Die Betonstruktur mit Räumen doppelter Höhe wurde mit dem neuen Gebäude verbunden, das die Straßenflucht einhält. Der Gebrauch von nur einem Fassadenmaterial – beide Gebäude sind mit grauen Schindeln verkleidet – verbindet die beiden Volumen äußerlich. Der Ein- und Durchgangsbereich ist strategisch zwischen dem alten und dem neuen Gebäude platziert. Der Rohbau wurde so konzipiert, dass die Mauern auch als fertige Außenwand fungieren können, was sowohl Material als auch Zeit spart. So ergibt sich ein ökonomischeres Gebäude mit gesteigerter Flexibilität und Nachhaltigkeit ohne Einfluss auf die Qualität.

left: Floor plans_Exterior elevation of patio_Exterior elevation from railway. right: Entrance area.
links: Grundrisse_Außenansicht des Innenhofs_Ansicht von der Bahnstrecke. rechts: Eingangsbereich.

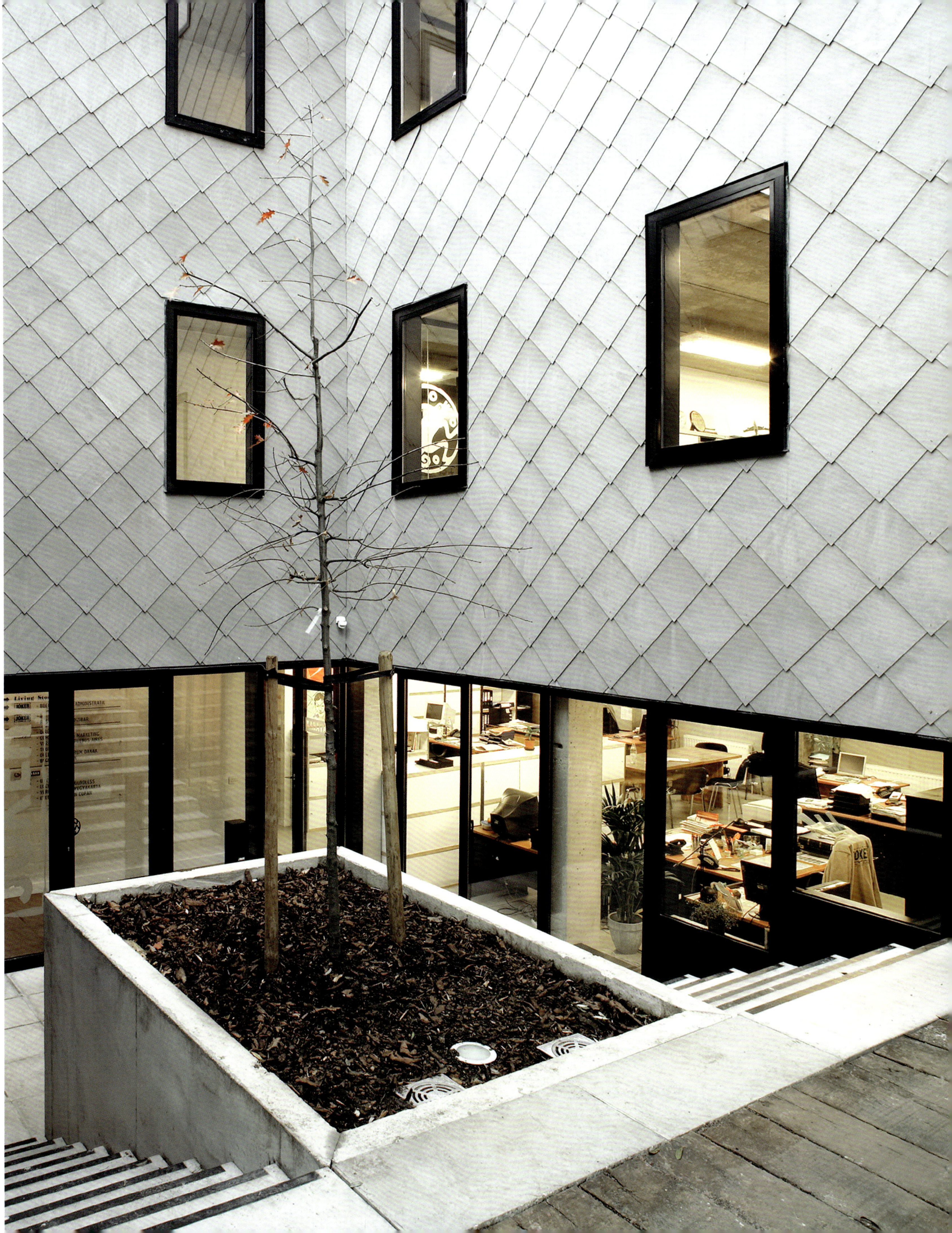

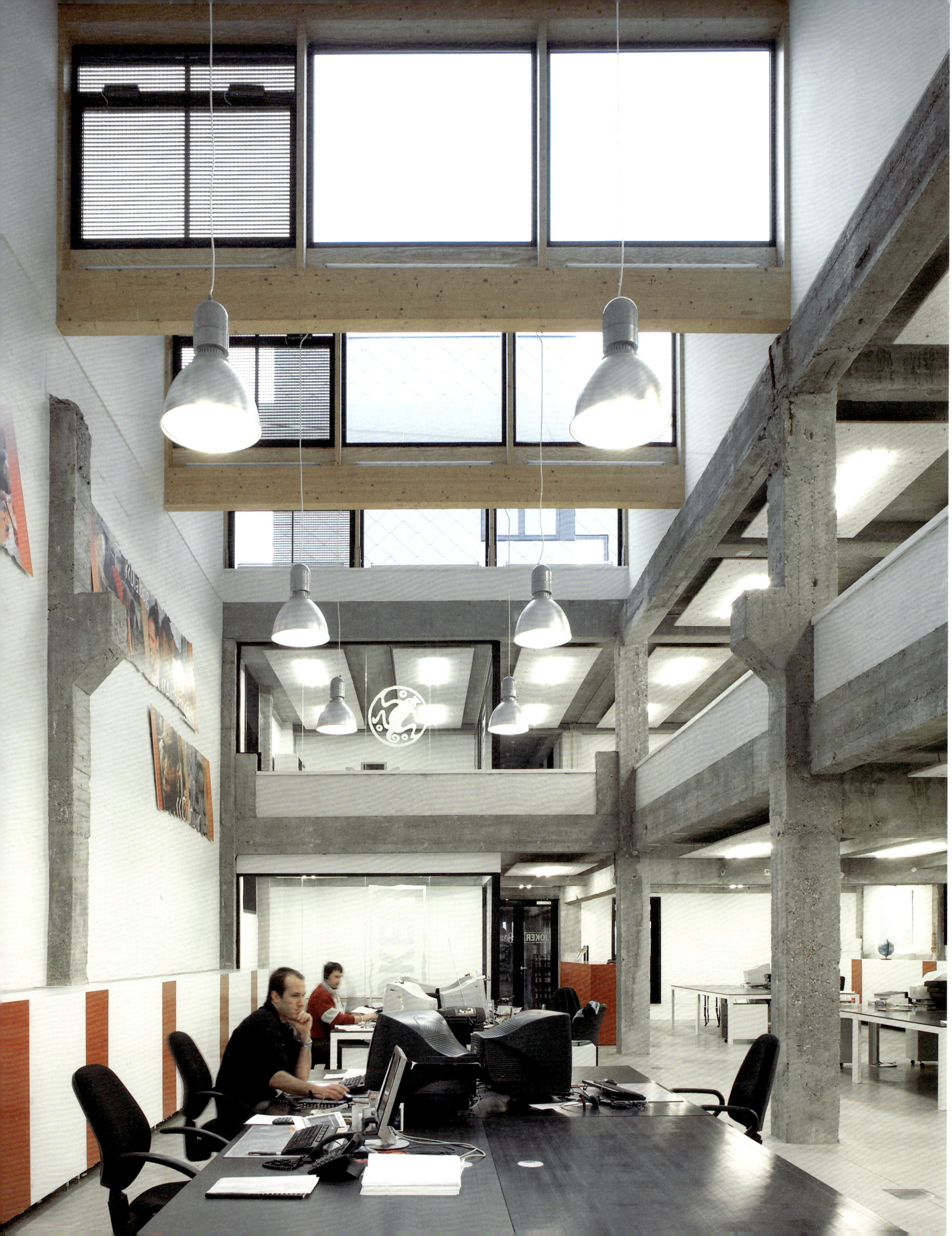

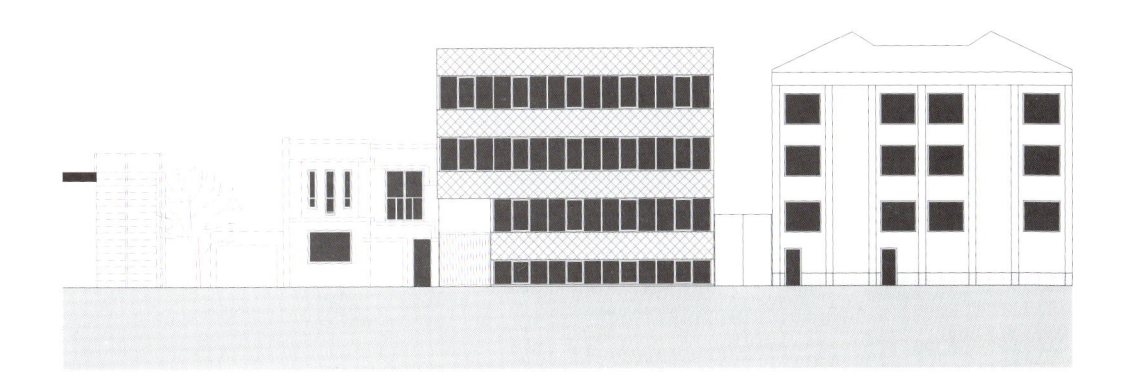

left: Office. right: Section_Night view_Interior view of offices_Conference room.
links: Office. rechts: Ansicht_Nachtansicht_Blick in eines der Büros_Konferenzraum.

BELGIUM_TORHOUT **OFFICE VANHAERENTS TORHOUT**

ARCHITECTS: BURO II_**COMPLETION:** 2008
NUMBER OF WORKPLACES: 15_**GROSS FLOOR AREA:** 1,400 M²
COMMON AREA: CONFERENCE SPACE_**KIND OF WORKPLACES:** COMBINATION_**PHOTOS:** JEAN GODECHARLE

This project is an extension of the existing offices of property developer Vanhaerents. It is an excellent example of collaboration between the architectural department and the interior design department of BURO II. The new building is conceived as a light, white box in steel and glass that floats over the existing building, which is painted black to create a contrast. The building is more than just a functional and flexible office. The interaction between old and new mirrors the image of the company Vanhaerents, which is founded on a strong tradition while at the same time maintaining a fresh vision of the future. A prime example of this is the public opening of the Vanhaerents Art Collection in Brussels.

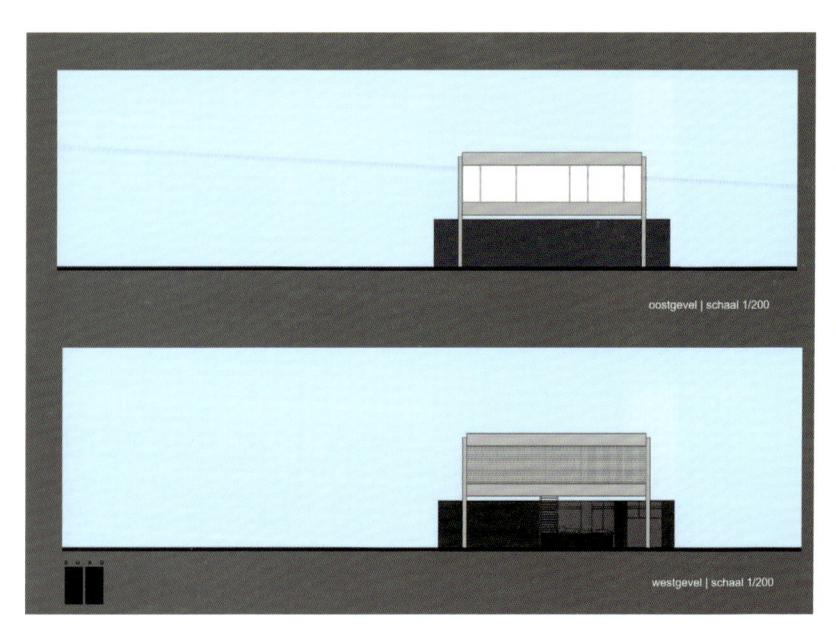

Dieser Ausbau der bestehenden Büros für den Bauträger Vanhaerents ist ein ausgezeichnetes Beispiel für die Zusammenarbeit zwischen der Architekturabteilung und der Innenarchitekturabteilung von BURO II. Das neue Gebäude ist eine helle Box aus Stahl und Glas, die als über dem bestehenden Gebäude schwebend wahrgenommen wird. Letzteres wurde schwarz angestrichen, um den Kontrast zu erhöhen. Das Gebäude ist mehr als nur ein funktionelles und flexibles Büro. Die Interaktion zwischen Altem und Neuem spiegelt das Image der Firma wieder, die stark in der Tradition verwurzelt ist, gleichzeitig aber eine klare Zukunftsvision hat. Dies zeigt sich auch in der öffentlich zugänglichen Vanhaerents Art Collection in Brüssel.

left: Cross section_Exterior perspective_View by night. right: Entrance area, reception by night.
links: Querschnitt_Außenperspektive_Ansicht bei Nacht. rechts: Eingang mit Empfang bei Nacht.

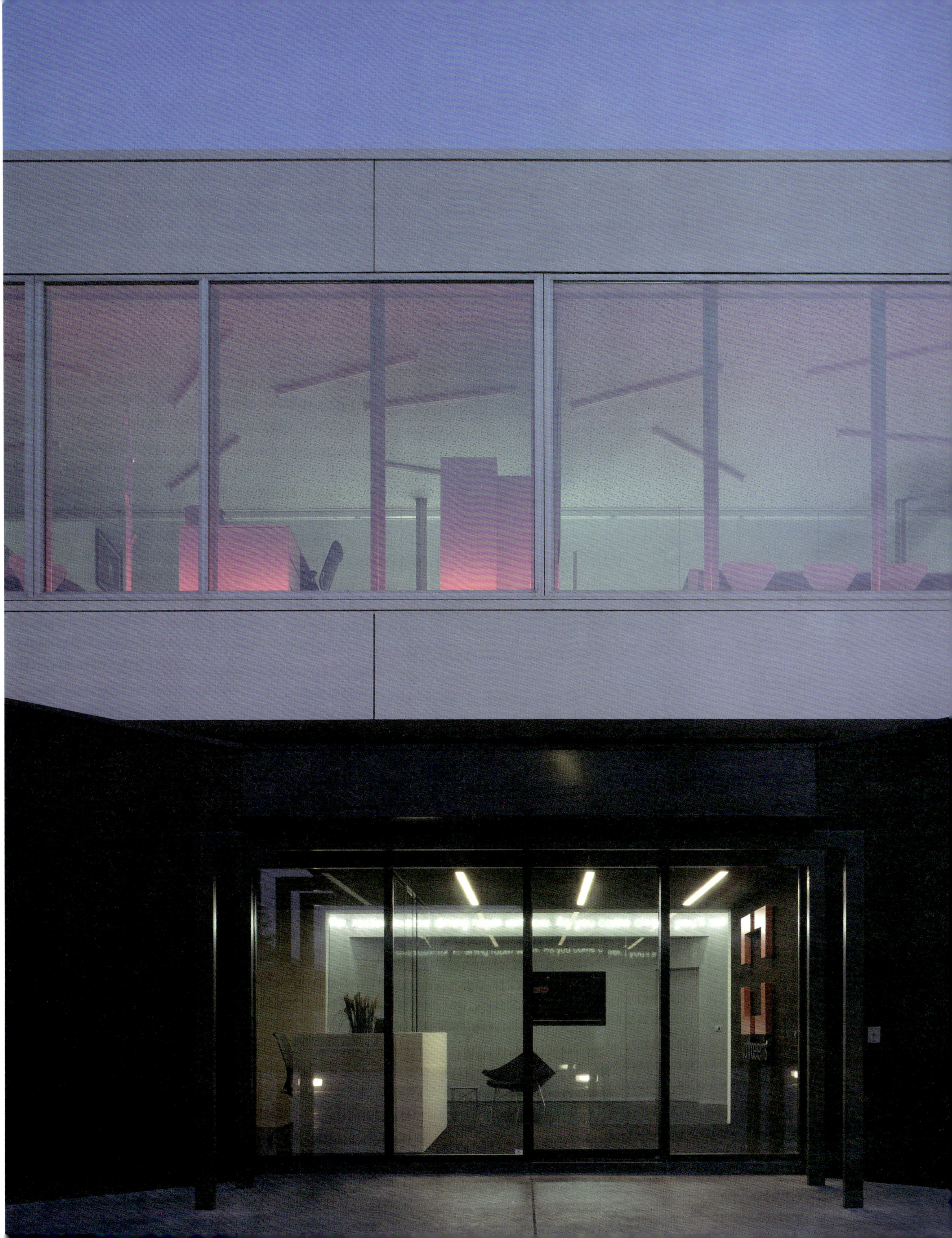

A blown glass vase

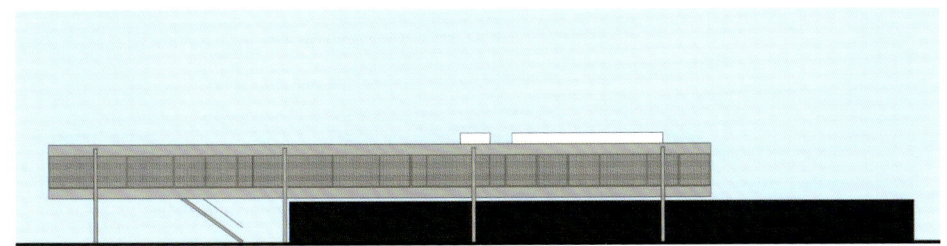

left: Office area. right: Longitudinal section_Workplace example.
links: Bürobereich. rechts: Längsschnitt_Arbeitsplatzbeispiel.

DENMARK_AARHUS C. F. MØLLER ARCHITECTS HEAD OFFICE

ARCHITECTS: C. F. MØLLER ARCHITECTS
COMPLETION: 2007_**ORIGINAL BUILDING:** 1957
NUMBER OF WORKPLACES: 120_**GROSS FLOOR AREA:** 3,500 M²
COMMON AREA: CANTEEN, MEETING, ROOF TERRACES
KIND OF WORKPLACES: OPEN-PLAN, TEAM
PHOTOS: JULIAN WEYER, AARHUS

On Europaplads, where the city meets the harbor, the Architects installed their new head offices in the top five floors of the Europahuset, constructed in 1957. They remodeled the floor plans and constructed a new penthouse story canteen, meeting facilities and several generous roof terraces. The design studio occupies three coherent open-plan floors, linked by a single long, sculptural stairway that passes through all the floors in openings cut out of the floor slabs. Meeting rooms with "sketchable" glass walls subdivide the plans. The superstructure is constructed of glass with a pre-patinated copper cladding, which refers to the nearby copper-clad spires of the Cathedral and other buildings.

Am Europaplads, wo die Stadt an den Hafen grenzt, bezogen die Architekten in den oberen fünf Stockwerken des Europahuset von 1957 ihr neues Hauptbüro. Die Raumverteilung wurde überarbeitet eine Kantine als neues Penthausgeschoss aufgesetzt, Besprechungsräume und großzügige Dachterrassen entstanden. Das Entwurfsbüro befindet sich in Großraumbüros auf drei Etagen und sind mit einer einzigen langen, skulptural aufgefassten und die alten Stockwerke durchstoßende Treppe verbunden. Konferenzräume mit bemalbaren Glaswänden teilen die Großraumbüros. Der Altbau mit Glas- und vorpatinierter Kupferfassade nimmt Bezug zu den benachbarten Türmen der Kathedrale.

left: Penthouse (12. floor) and typical floor (11. floor)_Penthouse meeting room_Penthouse, roof terrace. right: Sketchable partitions_ Connecting stairs_Office.
links: Penthouse (12. Obergeschoss) und typischer Grundriss (11. Obergeschoss)_Besprechungszimmer im Penthouse_Penthouse, Dachterrasse. rechts: Beschreibbare Zwischenwände_Verbindungstreppen_Büro.

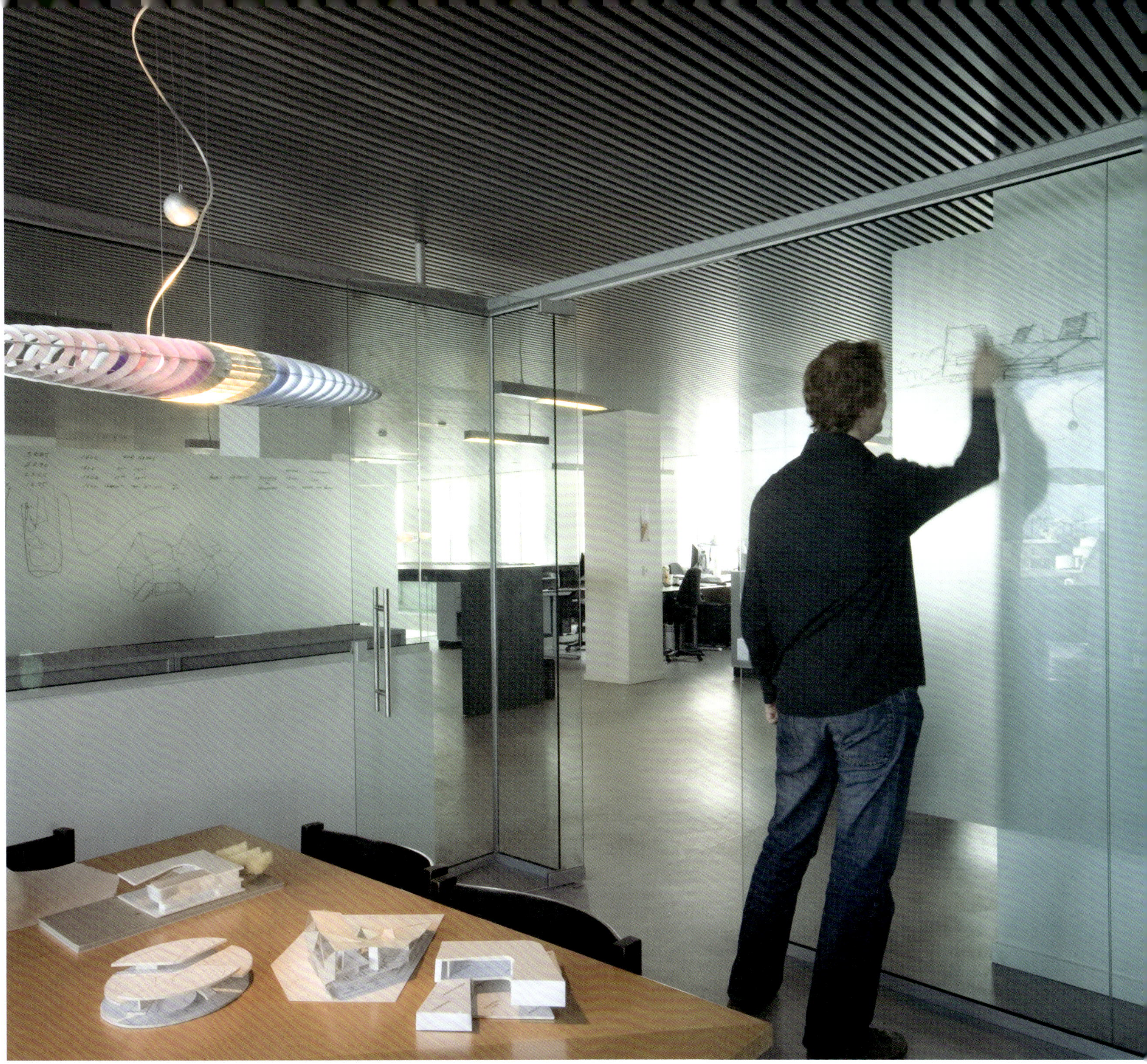

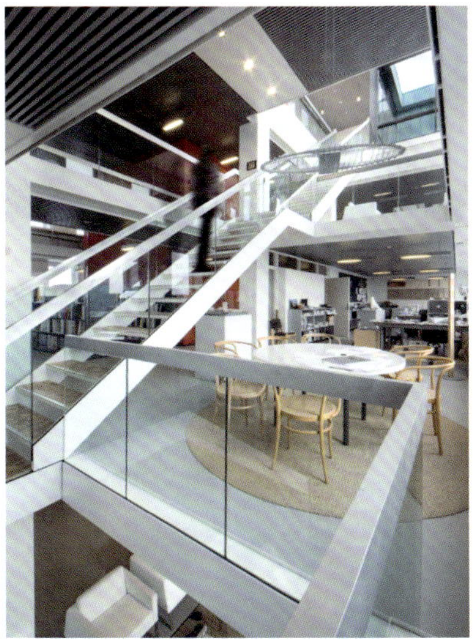

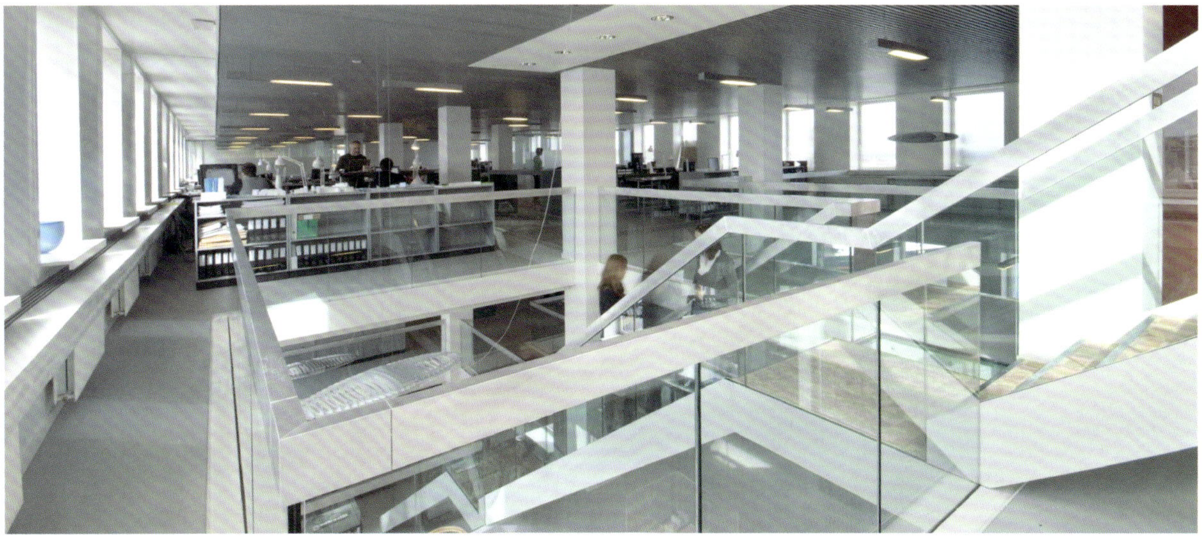

DENMARK_BALLERUP O-ZONE, ORACLE HEADQUARTERS

ARCHITECTS: LARS GITZ ARCHITECTS_**COMPLETION:** 2009
NUMBER OF WORKPLACES: 150_**GROSS FLOOR AREA:** 3,100 M²
COMMON AREA: LOUNGES, CONFERENCE ROOMS, FITNESS
KIND OF WORKPLACES: COMBINATION, OPEN-PLAN, TEAM, DESKSHARING, LOUNGE WORKSPACE AREA
PHOTOS: COURTESY OF THE ARCHITECTS

The architecture and the interior design are based on a vision offering inspiring and functional surroundings for the employees and on Scandinavian minimalism mixed with organic shapes. Oracle´s employees were involved in the design of O-Zone from an early stage. The office space is divided in to four areas suited for different types of work – the Call Zone, Dialog Zone, Project Zone and Quiet Zone. No employee has a permanent desk but instead a private locker and is welcome everywhere in the house. Based on the American high school model, this emphasizes the campus feel of the building. The day starts off in the locker area fetching one´s carrier, before deciding on today's workspace.

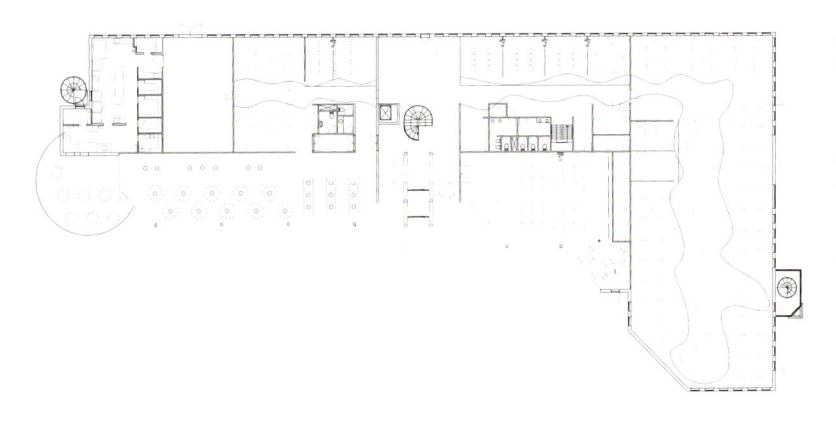

Architektur und Interieur beruhen auf den Ideen eines inspirierenden und funktionalen Arbeitsumfeldes und auf skandinavischem Minimalismus vereint mit organischen Formen. Die Mitarbeiter Oracles wurden schon in einem frühen Stadium in den Entwurf einbezogen. Es existieren vier Zonen entsprechend unterschiedlicher Arbeitsanforderungen: Anruf-Zone, Dialog-Zone, Projekt-Zone and Ruhe-Zone. Keiner der Angestellten hat einen eigenen Schreibtisch, jeder ist überall willkommen und jeder hat einen eigenen, privaten Spind. Dort beginnt der Arbeitstag, wenn man seinen Rollcontainer holt und sich für eine Zone entscheidet. Das Vorbild einer amerikanischen Highschool soll die Campus-Atmosphäre des Baues unterstreichen.

left: Ground floor plan_Reception and lobby. right: Main entrance_Call-Zone_Library-Zone.
links: Grundriss Erdgeschoss_Empfang und Lobby. rechts: Haupteingang_Telefonzone_Bibliothekszone.

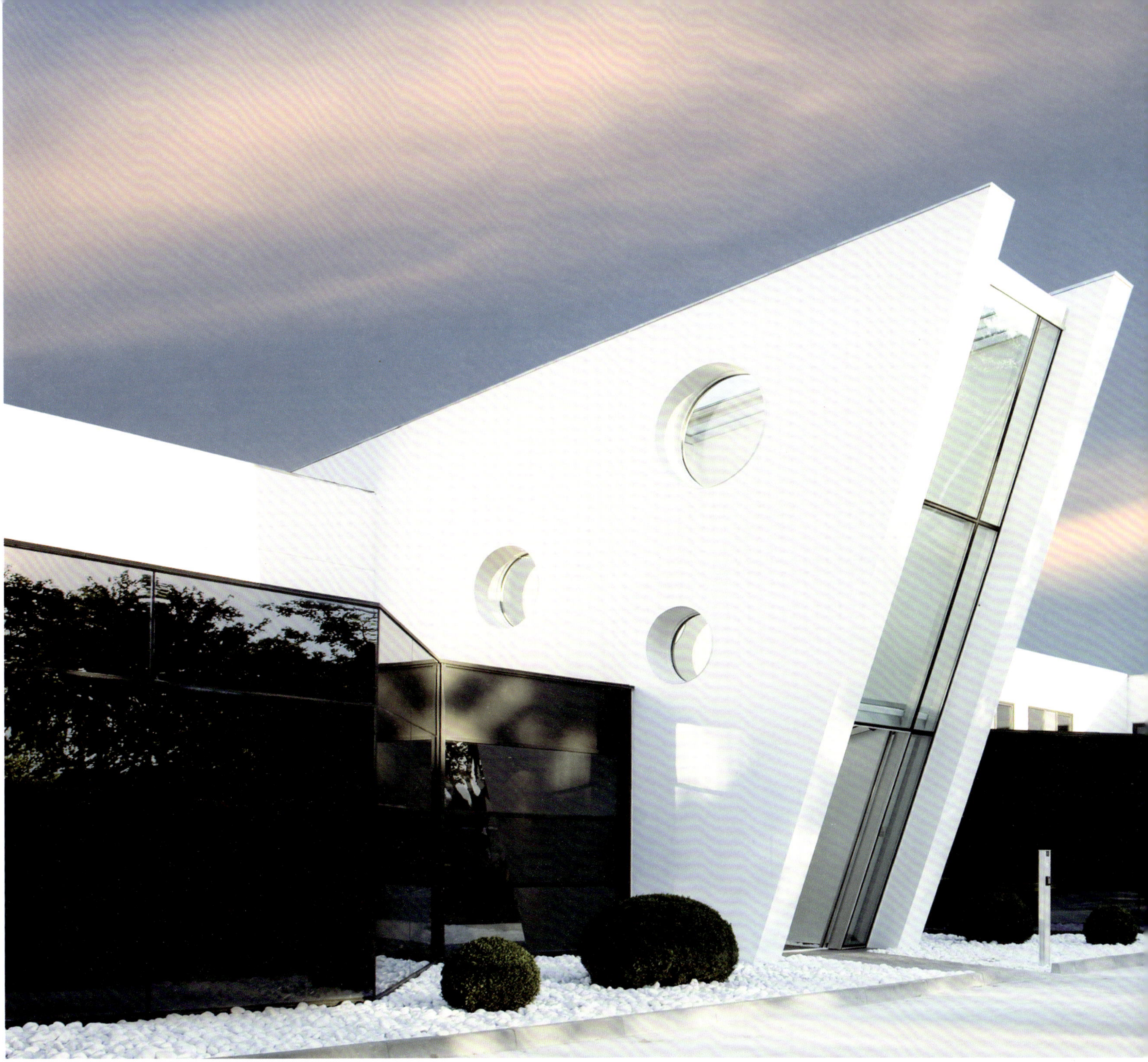

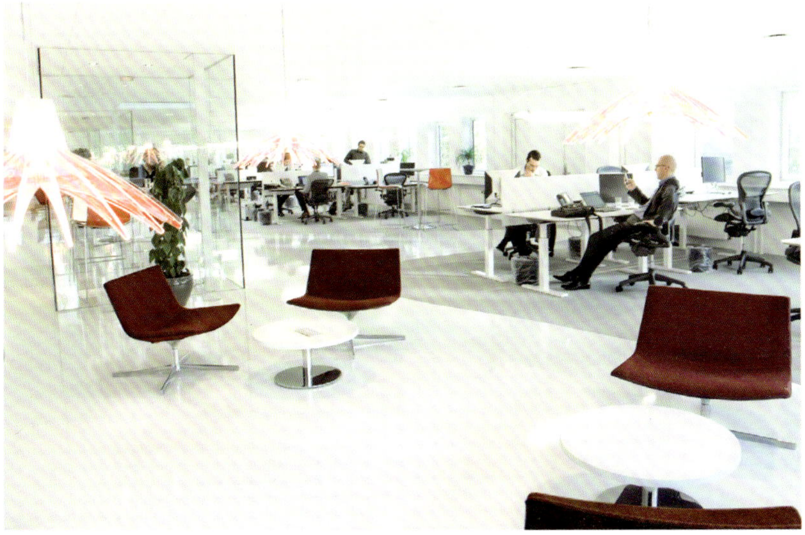

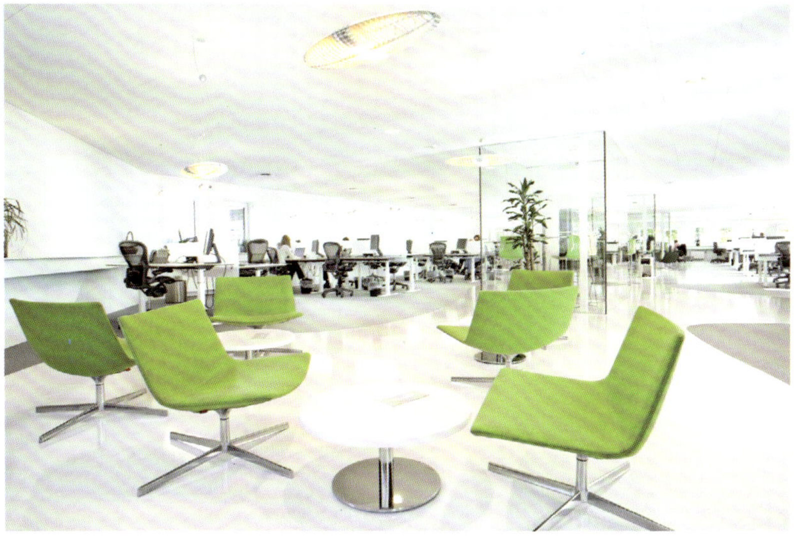

DENMARK_COPENHAGEN **WORLD HEALTH ORGANISATION**

ARCHITECTS: LARS GITZ ARCHITECTS_**COMPLETION:** 2006
NUMBER OF WORKPLACES: 144_**GROSS FLOOR AREA:** 2,026 M²
COMMON AREA: LOUNGES, CONFERENCE ROOMS, FITNESS AREA
KIND OF WORKPLACES: COMBINATION, LOUNGE WORKSPACE AREA
PHOTOS: COURTESY OF THE ARCHITECTS

This building tries to bring together man and architecture, humanism and minimalism in a kind of "huminalism". Functions, surfaces and volumes were split up into individual elements and then recombined in a composition without transitions, e.g. between the façades and roofs. The landscape and building volumes are perceived as coherent commensurate elements as well. A floating entrance bridge protrudes from the building, while inside the building the bridge sequence is a long concrete slab that is cut off and folded to produce stairs and landings. Around the atrium, the workplaces are located in open office landscapes and a new office system, "Flexus", was specially designed as an extension of the building's "huminalistic" architecture.

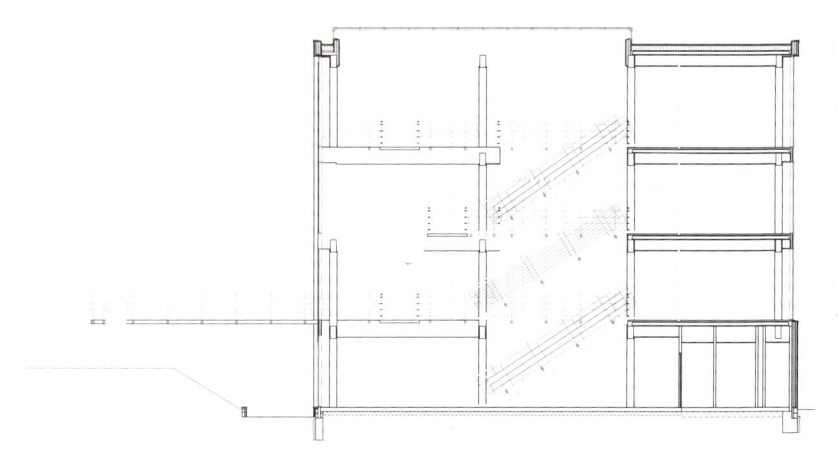

Das Gebäude versucht Menscheit und Architektur, Humanismus und Minimalismus in einer Art „Huminalismus" zu vereinen. Funktionen, Oberflächen und Volumen wurden in Einzelelemente zerlegt und zu einer neuen Komposition zusammengefügt, ohne dass Übergänge, beispielsweise zwischen Fassaden und Dächern, entstehen. Auch Landschaft und Bauvolumina werden als gleichgewichtige Elemente wahrgenommen. Eine Schwimmbrücke erstreckt sich aus dem Gebäude heraus und faltet sich im Inneren zu einer Abfolge abgeschnittener Betonstreifen auf, die Treppen und Absätze ausbildet. Die Arbeitsplätze liegen in Großraumbüros rund um das Atrium und ein neues Bürosystem, „Flexus" genannt, wurde speziell als Fortsetzung der Idee einer huminalistischen Architektur geschaffen.

left: Longitudinal section_Front elevation at night_Stairway. right: Workspaces_Bird's-eye view of entrance_Bridge and balcony at night.
links: Längsschnitt_Vorderansicht_Treppenhaus. rechts: Arbeitsplatz_Vogelperspektive auf den Eingang_Brücke und Balkon bei Nacht.

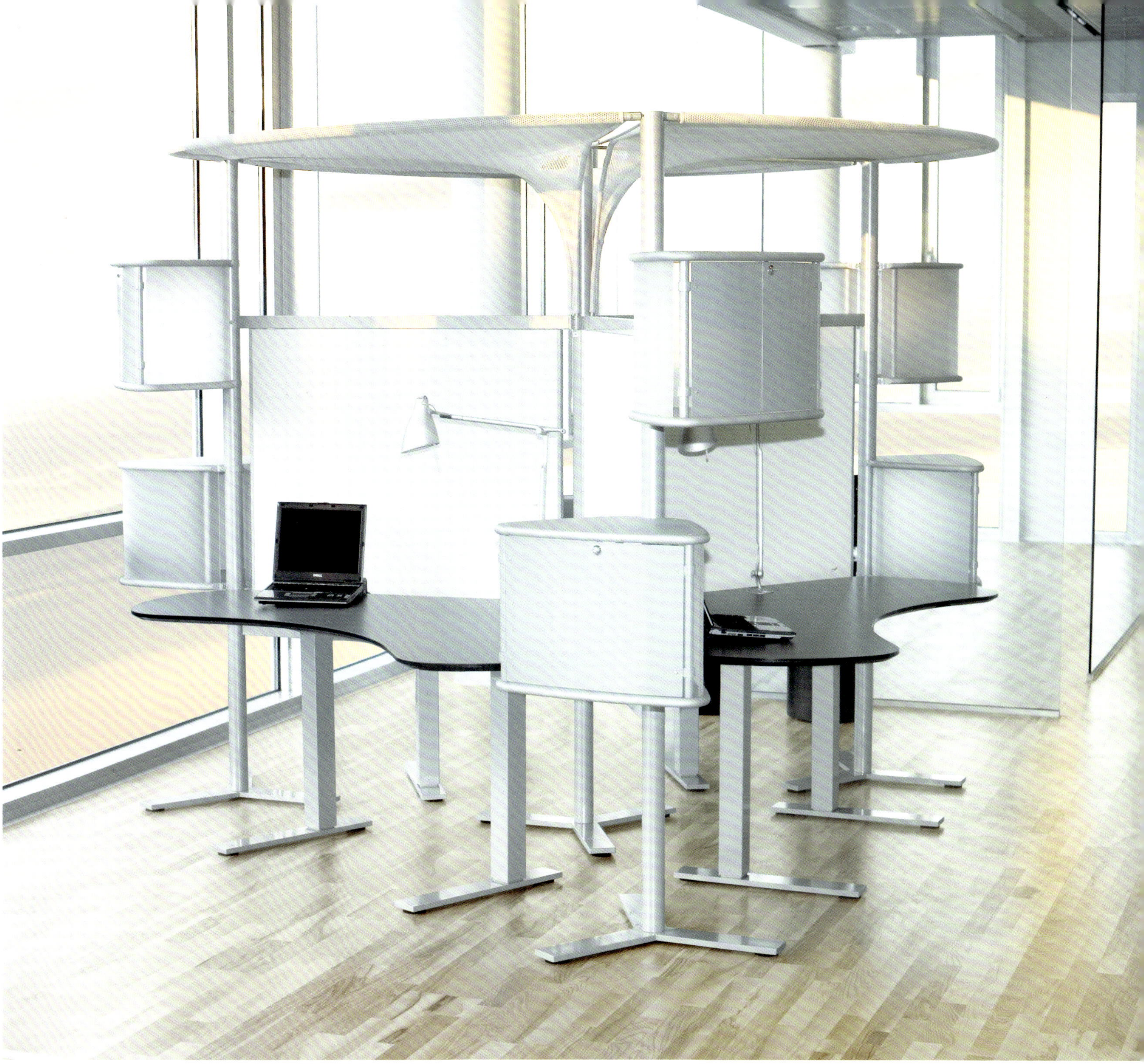

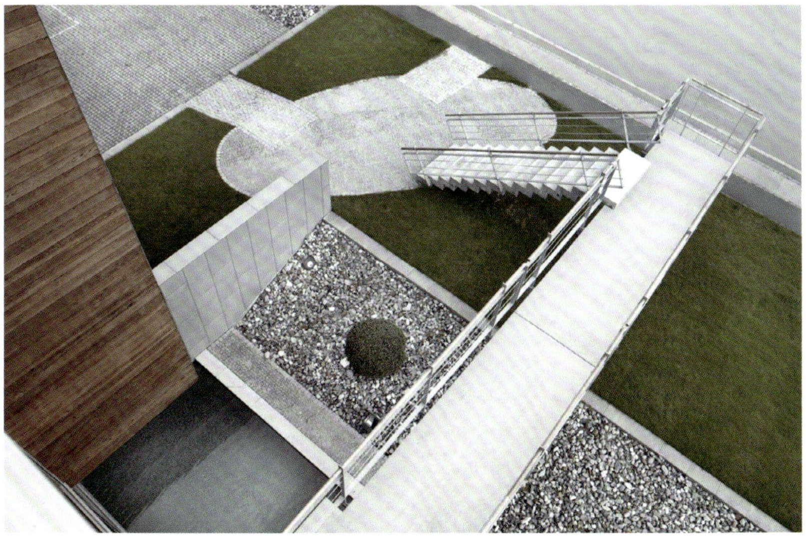

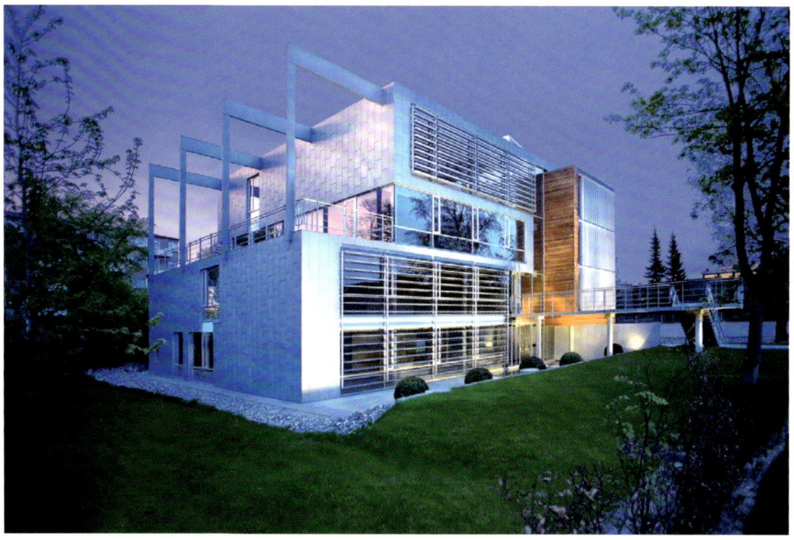

DENMARK_HORSENS **VITUS BERING INNOVATION PARK**

ARCHITECTS: C. F. MØLLER ARCHITECTS
COMPLETION: 2009_**NUMBER OF WORKPLACES:** 300
GROSS FLOOR AREA: 8,000 M²_**COMMON AREA:** CANTEEN, LOUNGES, ROOF TERRACE_**KIND OF WORKPLACES:** CELLULAR, COMBINATION, OPEN-PLAN, TEAM, COMBINATION, LOUNGE WORKSPACE AREA
PHOTOS: JULIAN WEYER, AARHUS

Teaching and business start-up office facilities side by side is the philosophy behind the extension of the existing 1970's University College Vitus Bering Denmark. The building's dynamic and innovative character is expressed in its spiral shape – on the façades, the movement is present in the glazing strips that stretch towards the sky, while internally it is expressed via the green staircase, which runs as a spiral between the floors of the common internal atrium up to the common meeting facilities and roof terrace. It is one of the first office complexes in Denmark to be classified as low-energy class 1 – double the minimum required by the Danish building regulations.

Die Lehre und Existenzgründer an einem Ort zu vereinen ist die Idee hinter dem markanten Erweiterungsbau des University College Vitus Bering Denmark. Der dynamische und innovative Charakter der Idee findet in dem Gebäude seinen Ausdruck im Motiv von Spiralen: an den Fassaden in Form gläserner sich himmelwärts windender Streifen; im Inneren als grüne Treppenanlage die geschossübergreifend vom Atrium zu den gemeinschaftlichen Konferenzräumen und der Dachterrasse strebt. Das Bürogebäude ist eines der ersten in Dänemark, das die Niedrigenergieklasse 1 erfüllt und so den hier einzuhaltenden Wert um die Hälfte unterbietet.

left: Floor plan top floor and roof terrace_Exterior view_Façade, detail. right: Spiral stair detail_ View down atrium_Interior elevation_ Atrium full view.
links: Grundriss Dachgeschoss und Dachterrasse_Außenansicht_Fassadendetail. rechts: Wendeltreppe, Detail_Blick nach unten ins Atrium_Innenansicht_Totale Atrium.

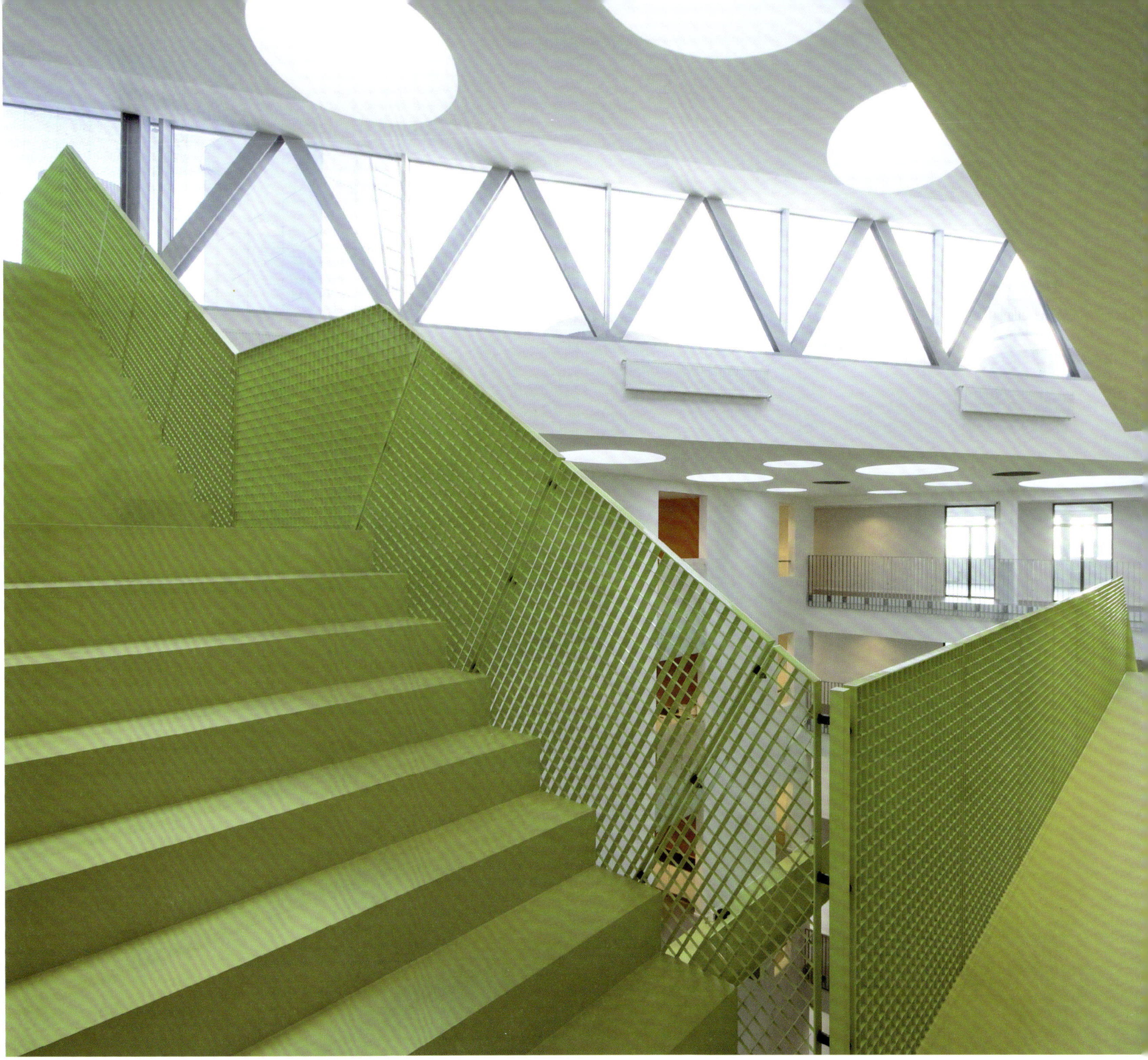
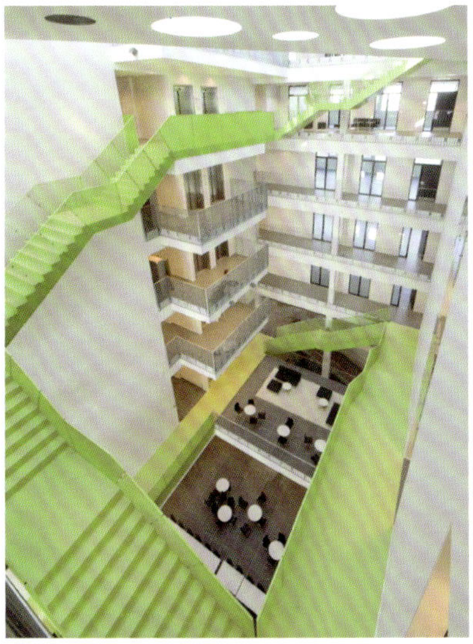
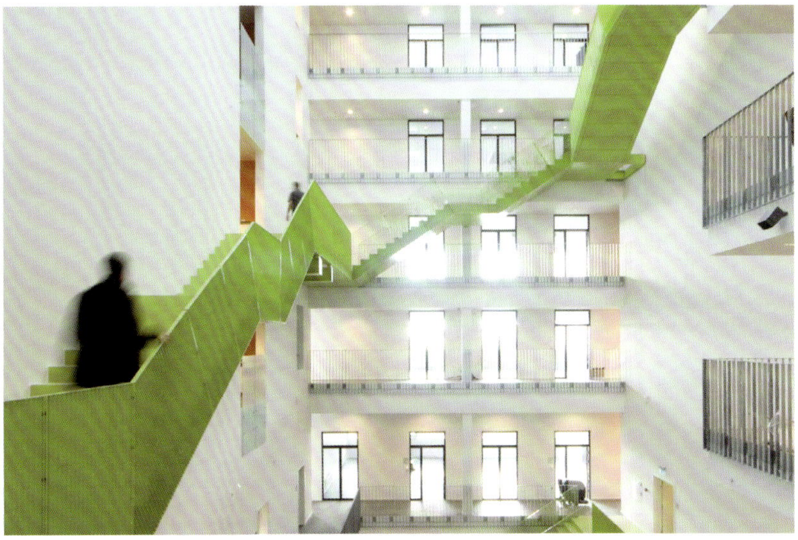
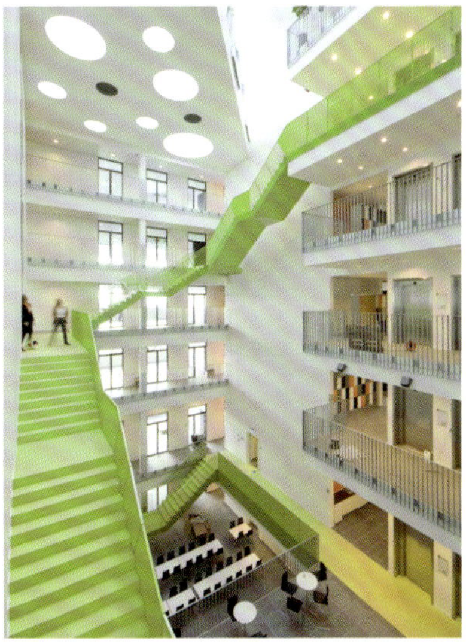

DENMARK_KOKKEDAL COMM2

ARCHITECTS: LARS GITZ ARCHITECTS **COMPLETION:** 2009_**NUMBER OF WORKPLACES:** 40_**GROSS FLOOR AREA:** 1,800 M²_**COMMON AREA:** LOUNGES, CONFERENCE ROOMS, RESTAURANT_**KIND OF WORKPLACES:** OPEN-PLAN, LOUNGE WORKSPACE_**PHOTOS:** COURTESY OF THE ARCHITECTS

Allowing the employees to experience the IT company's concern for long term investment in well-being and job satisfaction were keywords from early stages of the project along with the company's virtues – high quality, efficiency, innovation, and care for details. Structural concrete beams and heavy masonry pillars of the former industrial building were incorporated in the new design. Big white surfaces vertically divided by glazing from ground to roof create a homogeneous and simplistic backdrop for refined details in steel, glass and high gloss surfaces. A suspended bridge makes the arrival to the headquarters a special experience and divides the inner calmness of the house from the surrounding industrial area.

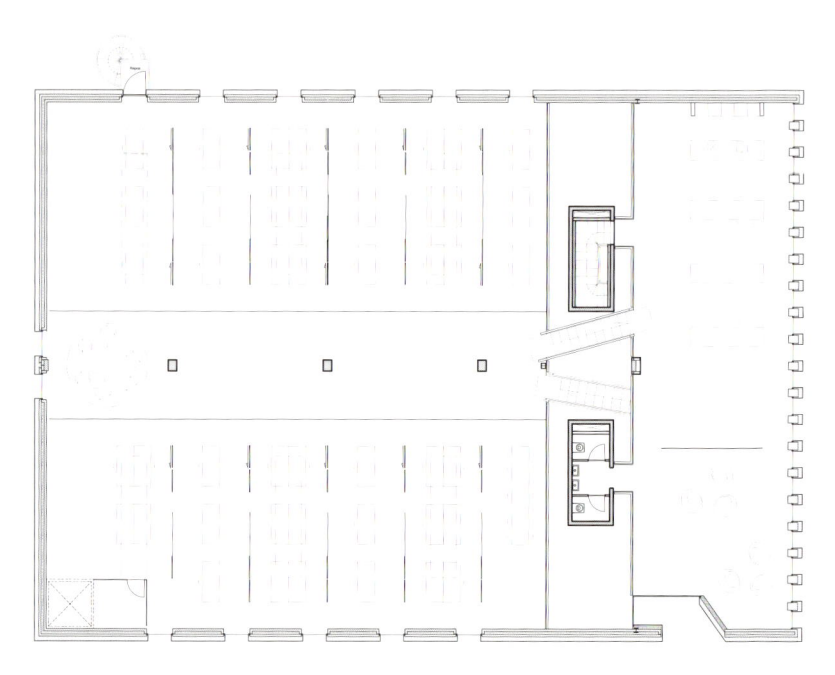

Der Eindruck eines sich langfristig um das Wohlergehen und die Arbeitszufriedenheit seiner Mitarbeiter bemühenden IT-Unternehmens war neben den Firmenwerten Qualität, Effizienz, Innovation und Detailinteresse der Ausgangspunkt der Gestaltung. Konstruktive Betonbalken und schwere gemauerte Pfeiler des ehemaligen Industriebaus wurden in die Gestaltung einbezogen. Große weiße Flächen vertikal von geschossübergreifenden Glasflächen durchschnitten bilden ein homogenes und schlichtes Umfeld für raffinierte Details aus Stahl, Glas und glänzenden Oberflächen. Die Ankunft in dem Hauptsitz der Firma wird durch eine abgehängte Brücke zum speziellen Erlebnis und schafft Distanz zwischen der Ruhe im Gebäude und der industriellen Umgebung.

left: Plan upper levels_Arrival, suspended bridge_Reception and lobby. right: Lobby lounge and meeting rooms_Extreme openness_Suspended stairs crossing the atrium_Black cores in the atrium.
links: Grundriss obere Stockwerke_Zugang über eine aufgehängte Brücke_Empfang und Lobby. rechts: Lobby und Besprechungszimmer_Extreme Großzügigkeit_Aufgehängte Treppen durchkreuzen das Atrium_Schwarze Grundpfeiler im Atrium.

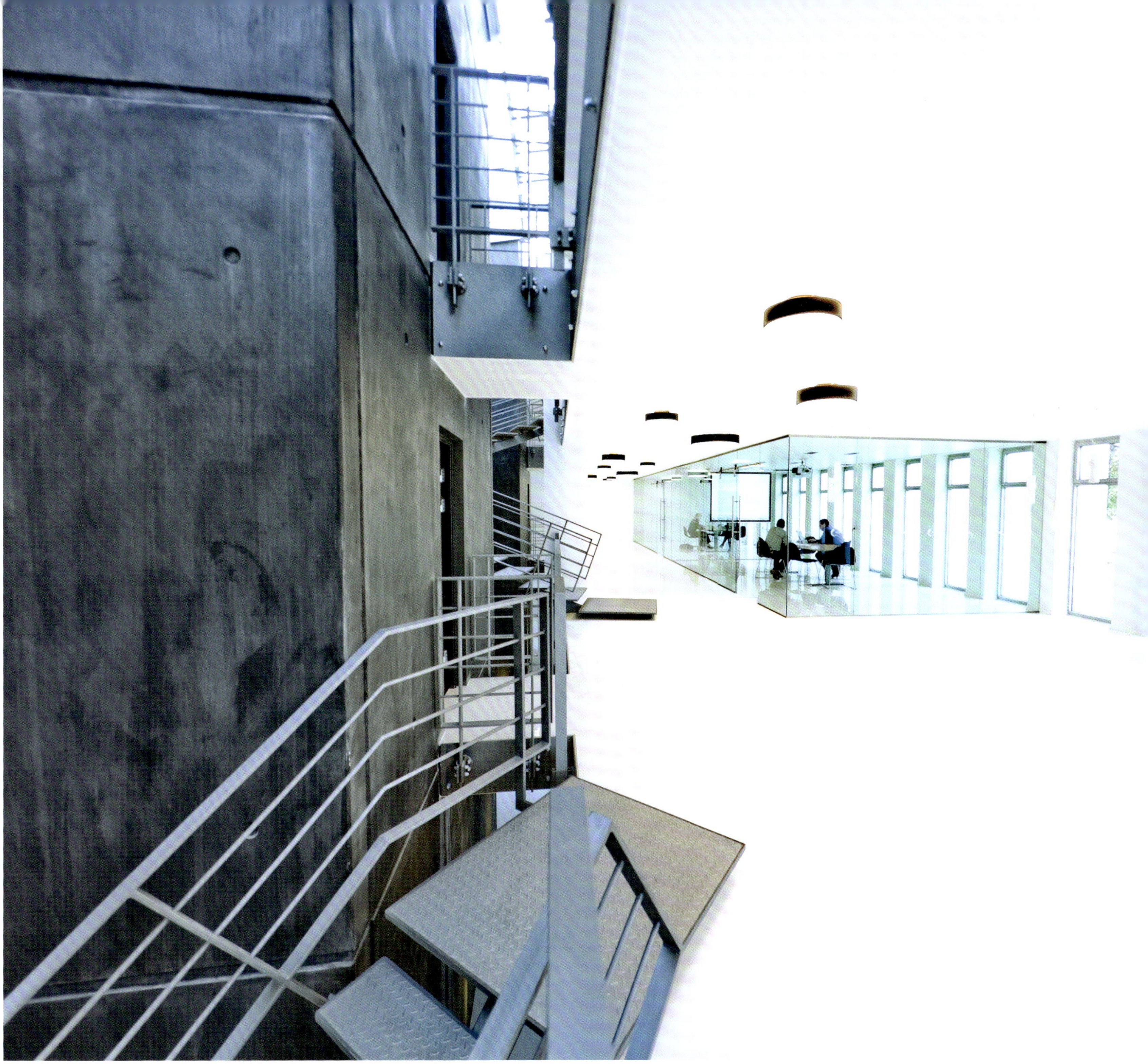

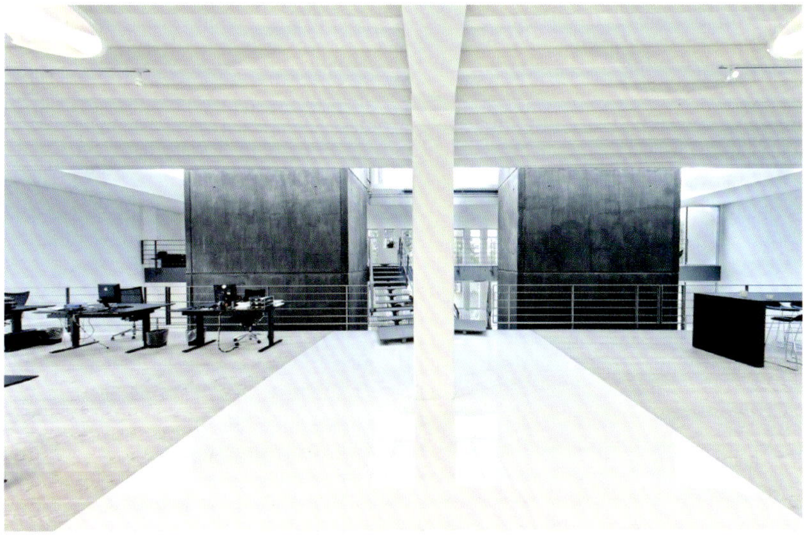

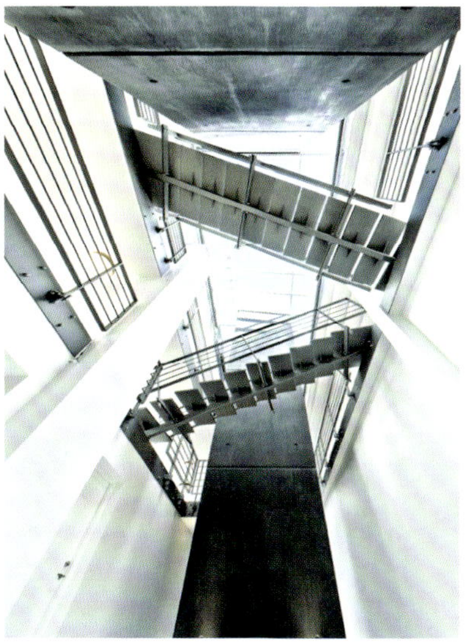

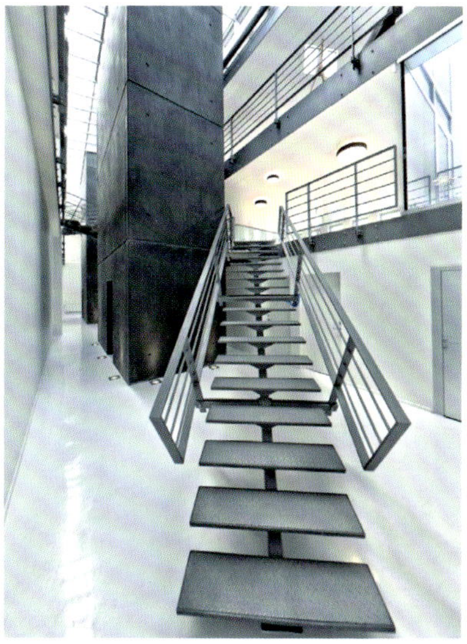

DENMARK_VEJLE **ADVICE HOUSE**

ARCHITECTS: C. F. MØLLER ARCHITECTS
COMPLETION: 2009_**NUMBER OF WORKPLACES:** 250
GROSS FLOOR AREA: 5,000 M²_**COMMON AREA:** CANTEEN, MEETING ROOMS, TERRACE
KIND OF WORKPLACES: CELLULAR, COMBINATION, OPEN-PLAN, LOUNGE WORKSPACE AREA
PHOTOS: JULIAN WEYER, AARHUS

The building has an open and flexible office layout, in which various tenants share the same large space, with dramatic perspectives and angles. The building is shaped around two angled office wings, separated by an equally angled atrium, resulting in a plan resembling a hexagon with one corner pushed inwards. The two wings are connected by walkways across the atrium, the floors' continuous window-bands great planning freedom, while the open and transparent interior is naturally ventilated. The building's unusual geometry offers passers-by a dramatic and changing appearance, enhanced by the special color-changing cladding and textures of the façades.

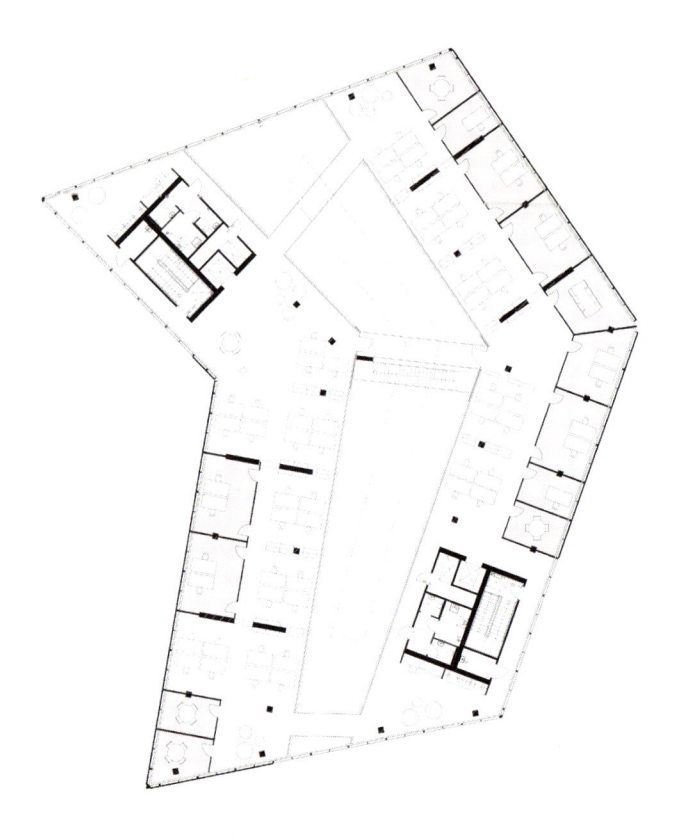

Das Gebäude mit offenen und flexiblen Räumlichkeiten, die von den Mietern gemeinsam genutzt werden, bietet dramatische Ansichten und Perspektiven. Es besteht aus zwei gewinkelten Flügeln, die ein entsprechendes Atrium flankieren, so dass der Grundriss wie ein Hexagon mit einer nach innen gedrückten Ecke erscheint. Die Flügel sind über das Atrium hinweg mit Rampen verbunden. Die durchgehenden Fensterbänder ermöglichen eine sehr freie Raumeinteilung. Die Räume sind natürlich belüftet. Die ungewöhnliche Geometrie des Baus beschert dem Vorbeifahrenden, verstärkt durch die sich farblich ändernde Verkleidung und Textur der Fassaden, dramatische und vielfältige Eindrücke.

left: Floor plan, typical floor_Staircase_View from canteen. right: Façade_ View from motorway.
links: Grundriss Regelgeschoss_Treppenhaus_Blick von der Kantine. rechts: Fassade_Ansicht von der Autobahn.

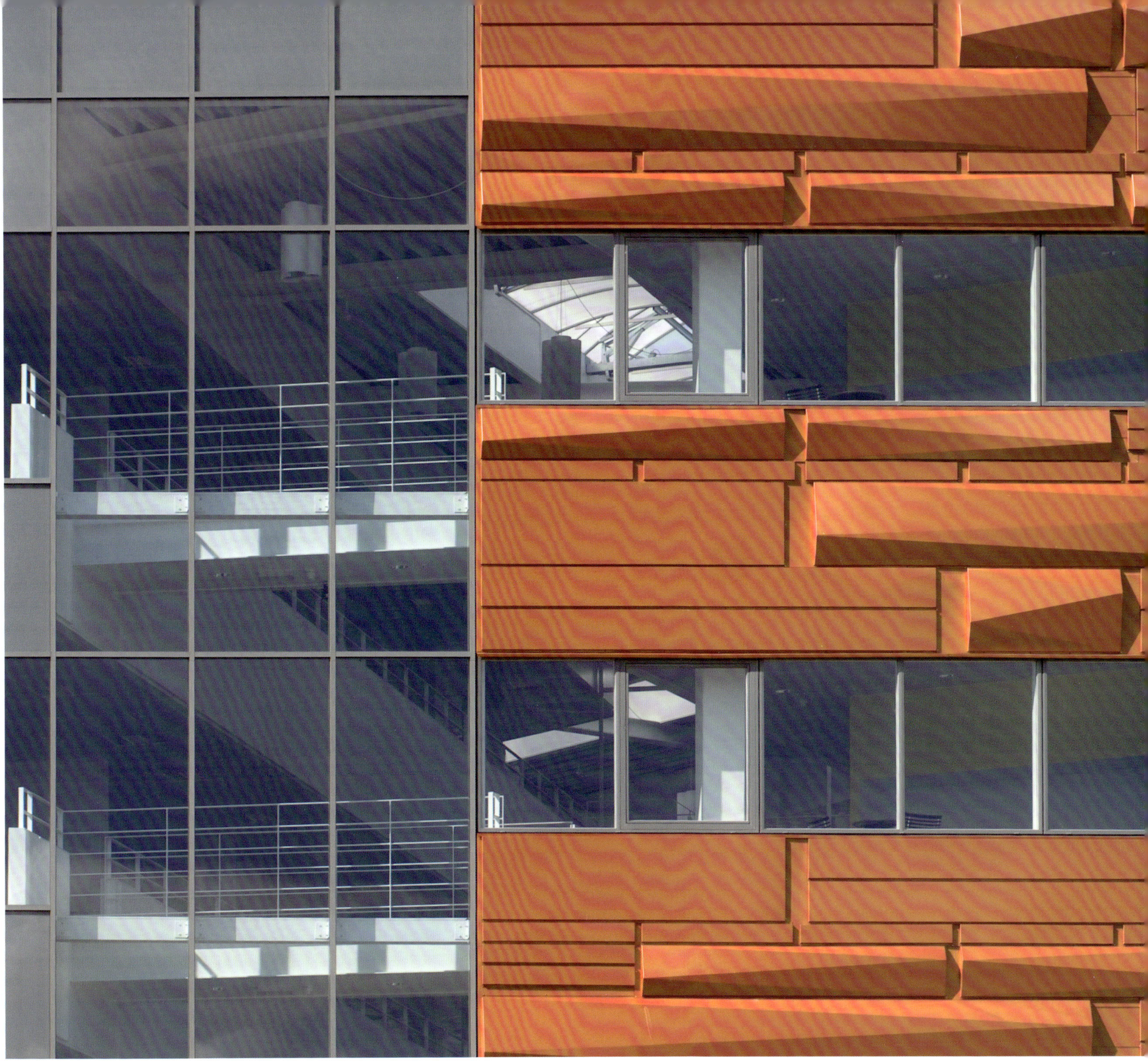
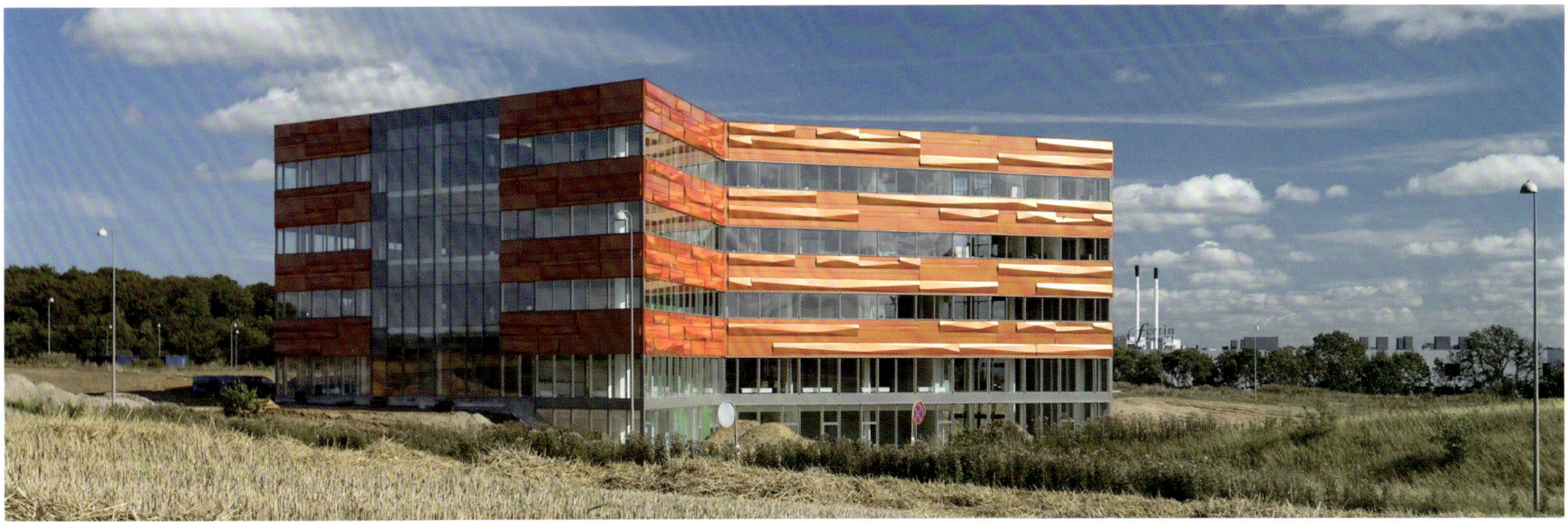

ESTONIA_TALLINN MEISTRI OFFICE BUILDING

ARCHITECTS: PALM-E ARHITEKTIBÜROO
COMPLETION: 2004_**NUMBER OF WORKPLACES:** 20
GROSS FLOOR AREA: 200 M²_**KIND OF WORKPLACES:** OPEN-PLAN_**PHOTOS:** ANU VAHTRA, TALLINN, EERO PALM, TALLIN (83 B. R.)

The building has four floors and a basement. According to the layout, each floor will contain large empty office areas, with either one or two offices, depending on the floor. All offices will have separate rest room facilities and kitchenettes. Spacious designs will allow tenants to partition the space with light walls as they see fit. A staggered modular system has been employed in designing the façade, which produces a kind of dancing rhythm. Since the building is cube-shaped, attractive walk-on balconies and expansive glass surfaces have been added. The primary materials are unfinished and rust-colored concrete and glass. A fire escape, that also functions as the way to the roof livens up the façade on the parking garage side.

Das Gebäude mit Erd- und vier Obergeschossen bietet je nach Stockwerk Platz für ein oder zwei großräumige Bürobereiche, die jeweils eigene Toilettenanlagen und Kochecken haben. Der großzügige Entwurf erlaubt Mietern eine individuelle Raumeinteilung. Ein modulares Wandsystem wurde an der Fassade asymmetrisch genutzt, um einen rhythmisch bewegten Eindruck zu erzielen. Das kubischen Volumen wurden durch Balkone und aufwendige Glasoberflächen bereichert. Bevorzugte Materialien sind unlegierter, rostiger Stahl und Glas. Die Fassade oberhalb der Garage wird durch eine Feuerleiter, die auch das Dach erschließt, belebt.

left: Section_Worm's-eye view_Façade. right: General view_Side elevation_Interior.
links: Schnitt_Froschperspektive_Fassade. rechts: Übersicht_Seitensicht_Innenansicht.

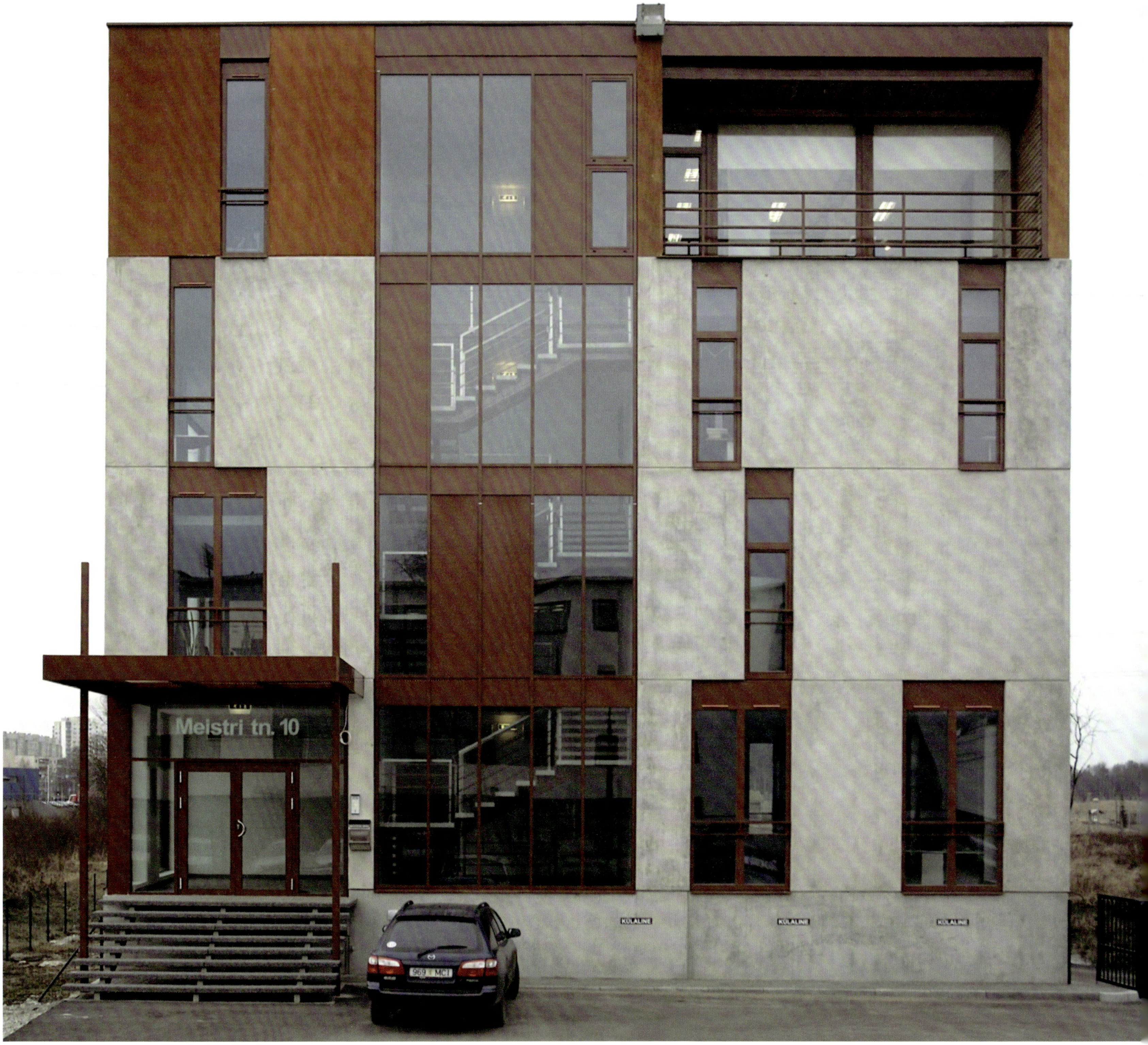
Meistri tn. 10
KÜLALINE
KÜLALINE
KÜLALINE

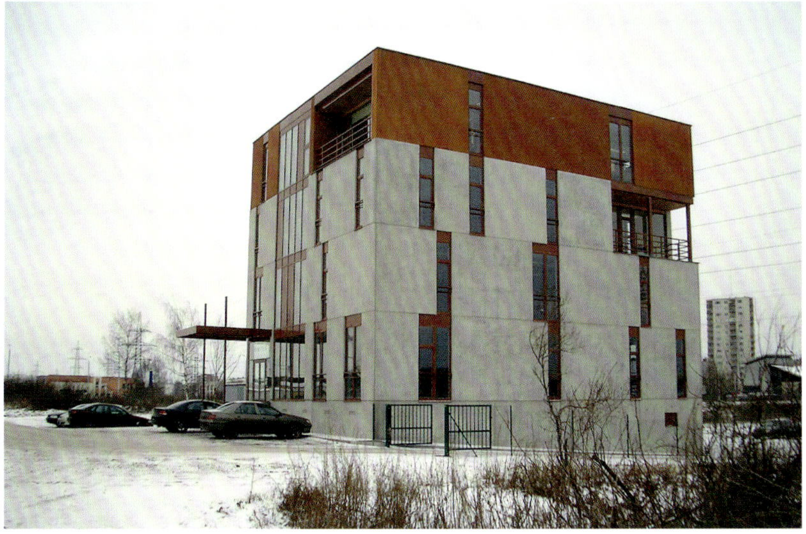

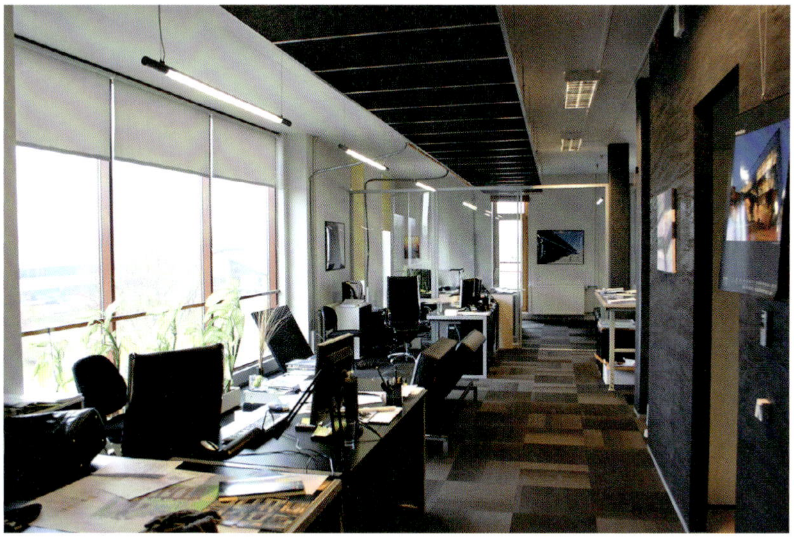

FINLAND_HELSINKI PORTAALI BUSINESS PARK

ARCHITECTS: B&M ARCHITECTS **COMPLETION:** 2002
NUMBER OF WORKPLACES: 450 **GROSS FLOOR AREA:** 13,000 M²
COMMON AREAS: CANTEEN, MEETING LOUNGE
KIND OF WORKPLACES: CELLULAR, COMBINATION, OPEN-PLAN, TEAM, CUBICAL, LOUNGE WORKSPACE
PHOTOS: JUSSI TIAINEN AND VOITTO NIEMELA

The Cromo building was designed to meet the needs of multiple end-users and to become a part of the newly constructed Business Park. Each floor provides approximately 1,300 square meters of modifiable and flexible space with a minimum of fixed structures and installations. Open views from one area to another as well as the open lobby facilitate internal communication. All common meeting facilities, restaurant, etc. have been situated onto two floors around the lobby in the heart of the building. The materials used for the building are fair-faced concrete, glass and steel. Perforated and profiled steel double façades protect the offices from direct sunlight and reduce the cooling need.

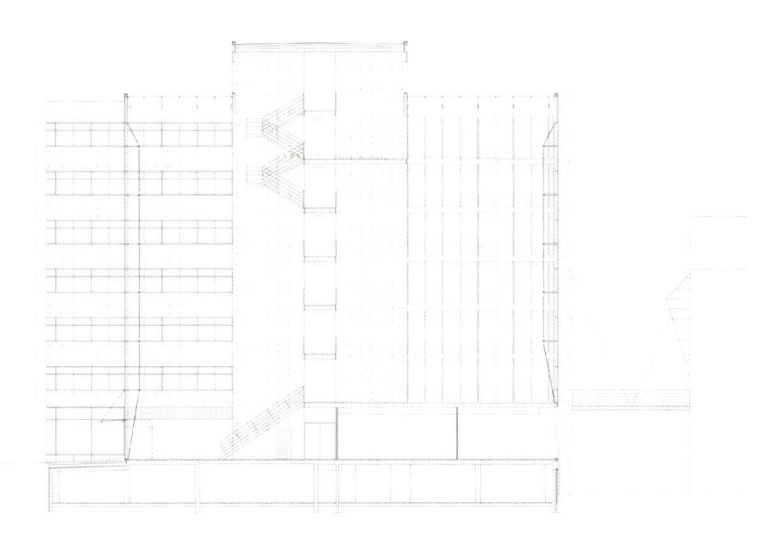

Das Cromo-Gebäude wurde als Teil eines im entstehen begriffenen Gewerbegebiets für verschiedene Nutzungen entworfen. In jedem Geschoss gibt es etwa 1.300 Quadratmeter flexibelen und modifizierbaren Raumes, der nur von einem Minimum an ortsfesten Installationen gestört wird. Der freie Durchblick von Raum zu Raum sowie ein offener Empfangsraum erleichtern die interne Kommunikation. Gemeinschaftseinrichtungen, wie Konferenzräume Restaurent usw. wurden auf zwei Stockwerken um die Lobby als Herz des Gebäudes zusammengeführt. Sichtbeton, Glas und Stahl dominieren und die Doppelfassade schützt mit perforiertem Loch- und Profilstahl vor Sonnen- und Wärmeeinstrahlung.

left: Section_Exterior view_Façade, detail. right: Entrance lobby.
links: Schnitt_Außenansicht_Fassade, Detail. rechts: Eingangshalle.

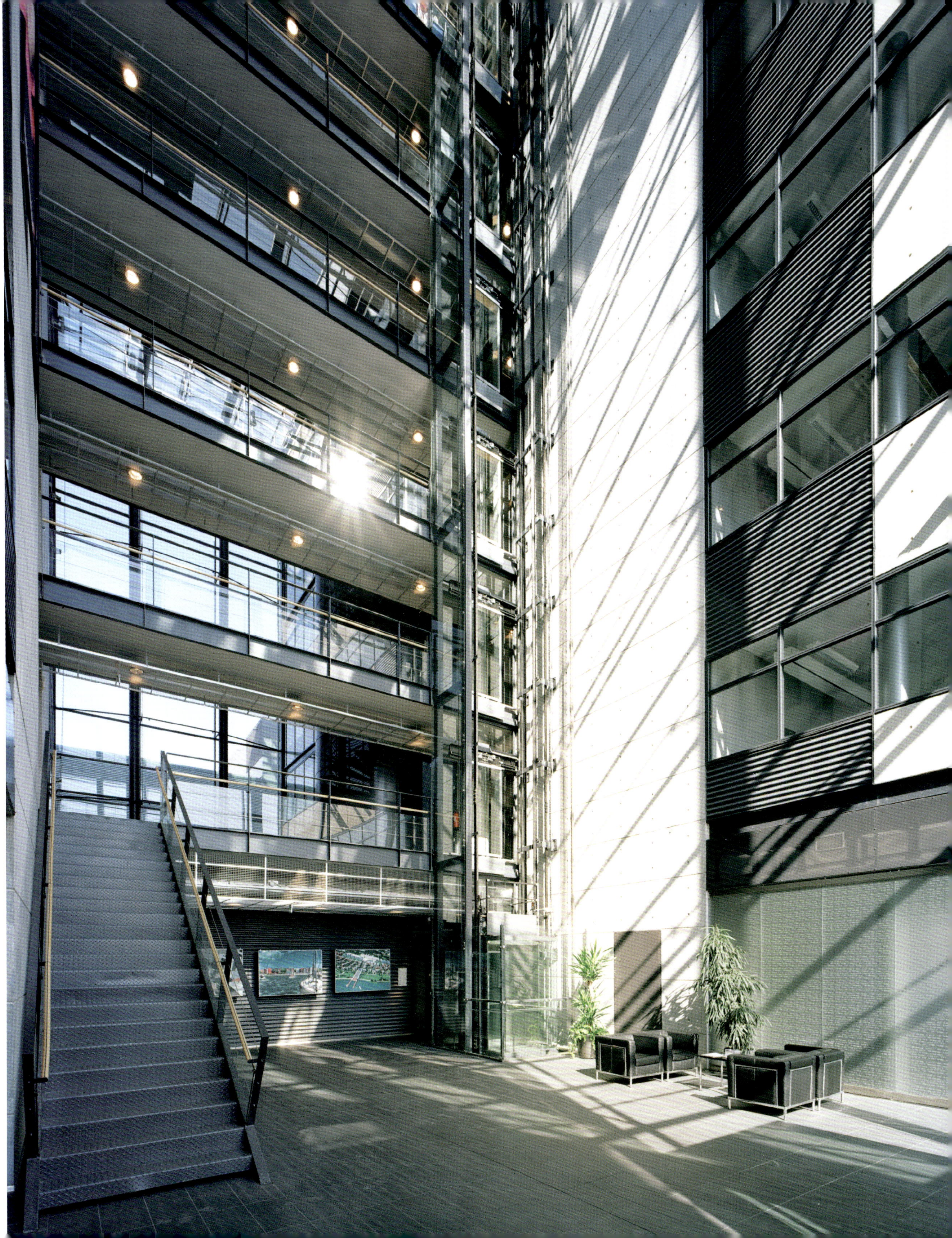

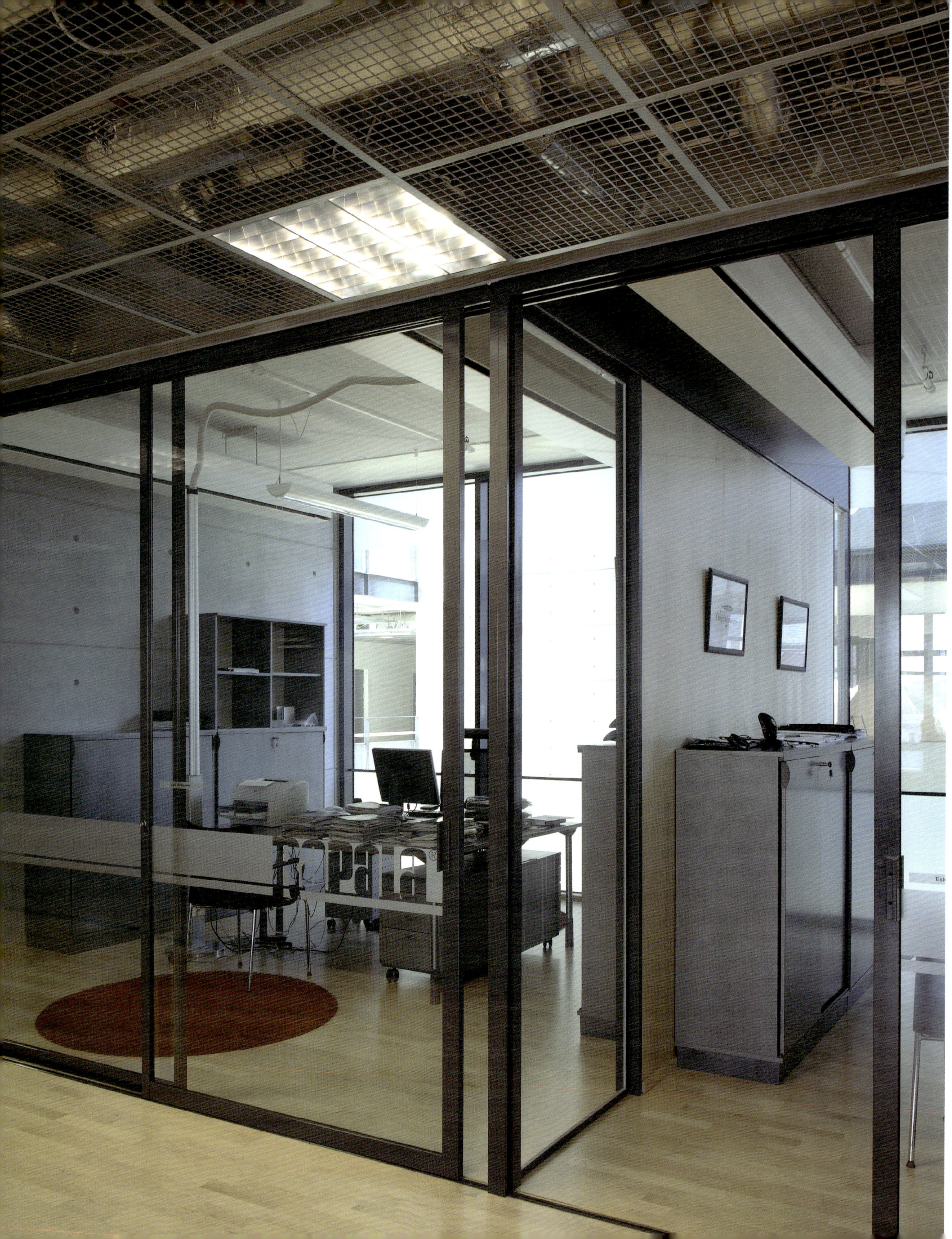

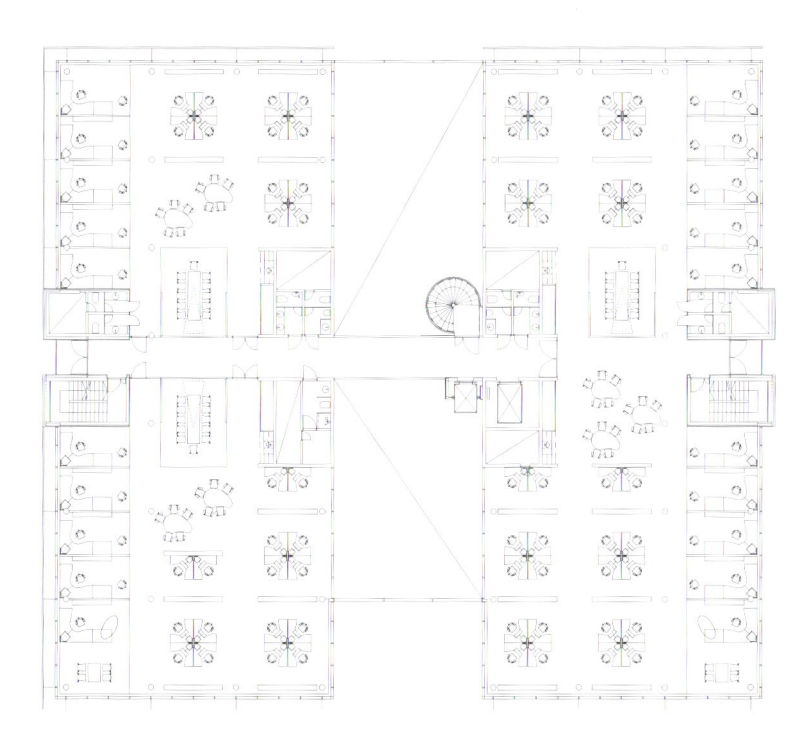

left: Flexible office space. right: Standard floor plan_Detail_Waiting area in front of an office_Restaurant, designed by interior design office Tuula Hägerström.
links: Flexibler Bürobereich. rechts: Grundriss Regelgeschoss_Detail_ Wartebereich vor einem Büro_Restaurant, eingerichtet durch das Innenarchitekturbüro Tuula Hägerström.

FRANCE_CLICHY-LA-GARENNE 21 BOISSEAU

ARCHITECTS: AW² **COMPLETION:** 2005
ORIGINAL BUILDING: 1950
NUMBER OF WORKPLACES: 200
GROSS FLOOR AREA: 2,600 M²
KIND OF WORKPLACES: OPEN-PLAN
PHOTOS: SÉBASTIEN LAVAL, PARIS

AW² was appointed for the conversion of an existing light industrial warehouse into a new office building at Clichy-La-Garenne. The refurbishment included building an additional floor and a mezzanine level to bring the building to the height of its neighbors. The façades were modified with a new brick facing and the existing windows were refurbished, while the existing basement was turned into a parking garage. A full redesign and new interior styling took advantage of the complete flexible floor plans to create different environments.

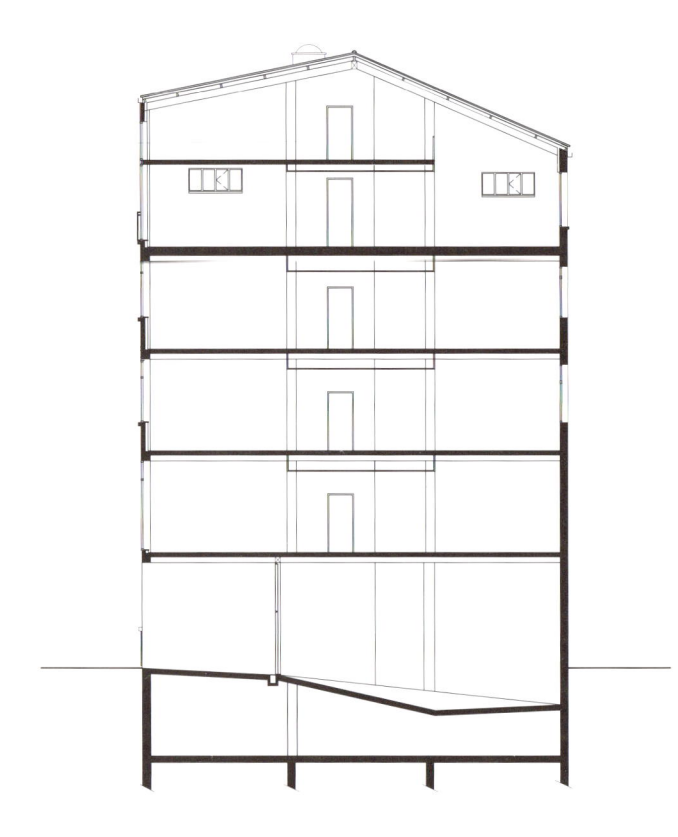

Für die Umgestaltung eines bestehenden Kleinlagers zu einem neuen Bürogebäude in Clichy-La-Garenne wurde AW² herangezogen. Die Renovierung beinhaltete auch den Bau eines zusätzlichen Stockwerks und eines Mezzanins, um das Gebäude auf die Höhe der Nachbarhäuser zu bringen. Die Fassaden sollten mit einer neuen Ziegelverkleidung verändert werden. Die bestehenden Fenster wurden saniert, aus dem vorhandenen Untergeschoss entstand eine Parkebene. Bei der vollständigen Umgestaltung und Ausstattung der Interieurs wurde der Vorteil der gänzlich flexiblen Stockwerkspläne genutzt, um unterschiedliche Umgebungen zu schaffen.

left: Section_Interior_Interior with balcony. right: View from the rue Georges Boisseau_Open-plan office_Red boxes.
links: Schnitt_Innenraum_Innenraum mit Gallerie. rechts: Blick von der rue Georges Boisseau_ Großraumbüro_Rote Büroboxen.

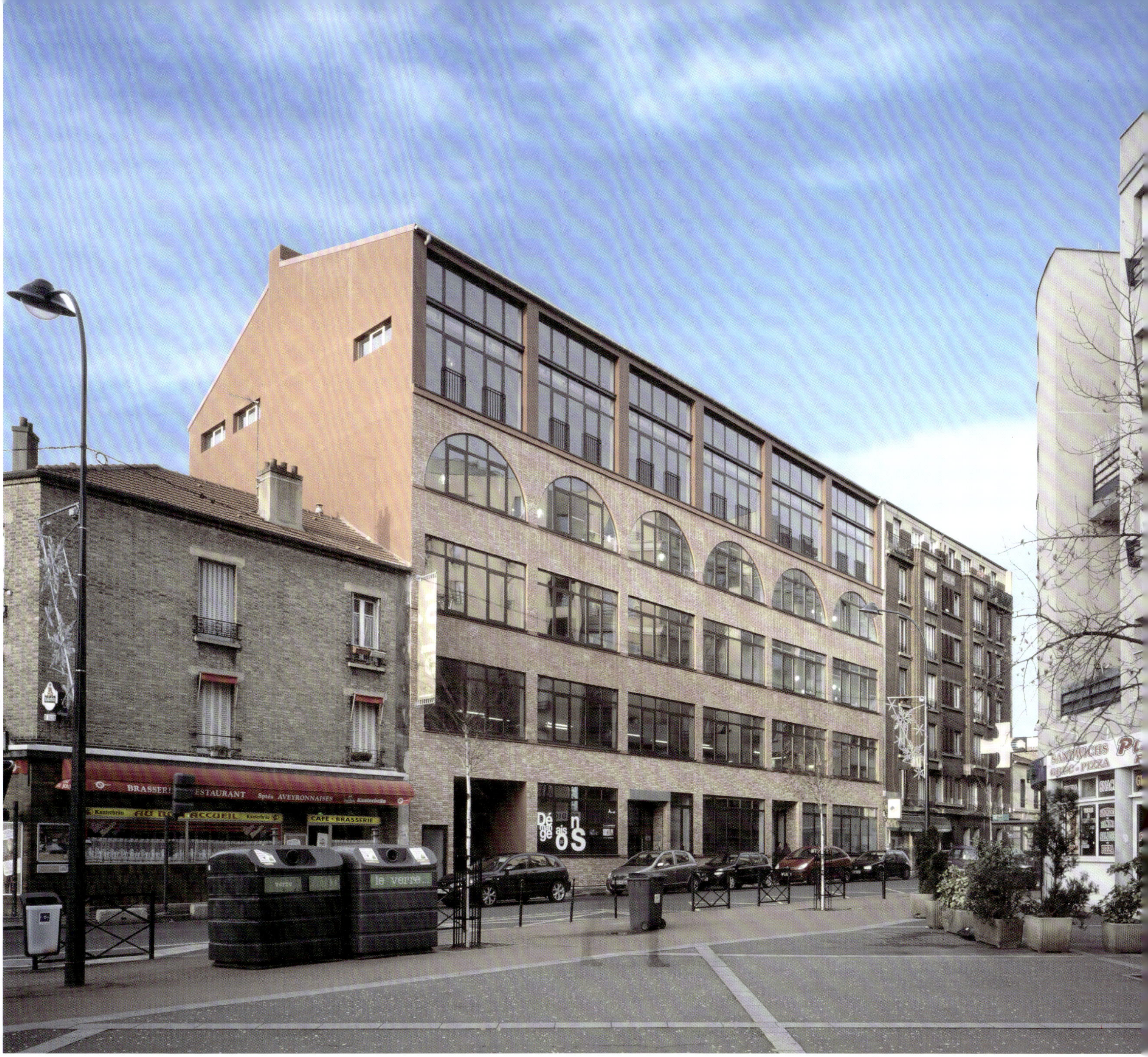
RESTAURANT
CAFE - BRASSERIE
le verre

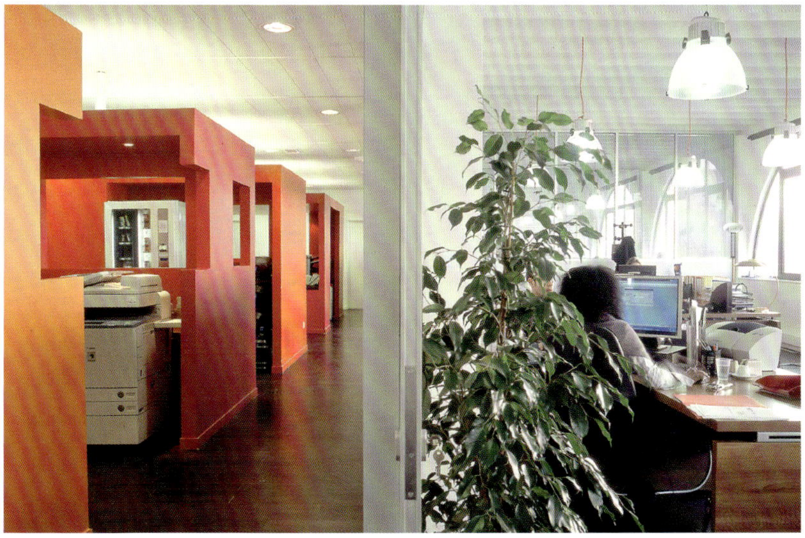

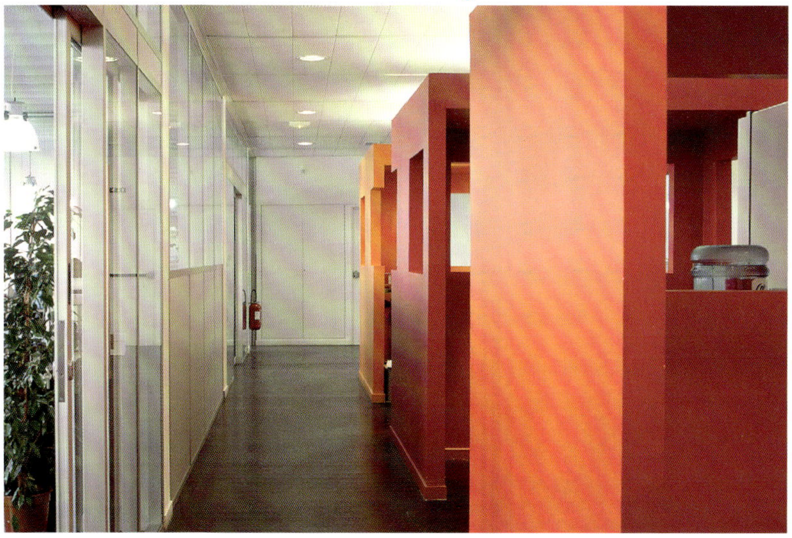

FRANCE_GENNEVILLIERS GENNEVILLIERS LOGISTICS CENTER

ARCHITECTS: DIETMAR FEICHTINGER ARCHITECTES
COMPLETION: 2005_**NUMBER OF WORKPLACES:** 180
GROSS FLOOR AREA: 1,980 M²_**COMMON AREA:** RECEPTION HALL, OUTDOOR AREAS, EMPLOYEES' LOUNGES_**KIND OF WORKPLACES:** CELLULAR, COMBINATION, OPEN-PLAN_**PHOTOS:** DAVID BOUREAU

The significant domestic harbor of Gennevilliers near Paris is connected to Rotterdam and Le Havre via the Seine and canals. The seat of the public authority for container management constitutes the connection between shipping and road haulage. The image of containers was incorporated into the design of the building. The ground floor houses the logistics area while the management and a large reception hall are found on the top floor. The floors in between have large outdoor areas, which are connected to the employees' lounges. The offices are glazed from roof to ceiling. Vertical rotating lamellas protect the building from direct sunlight and overheating.

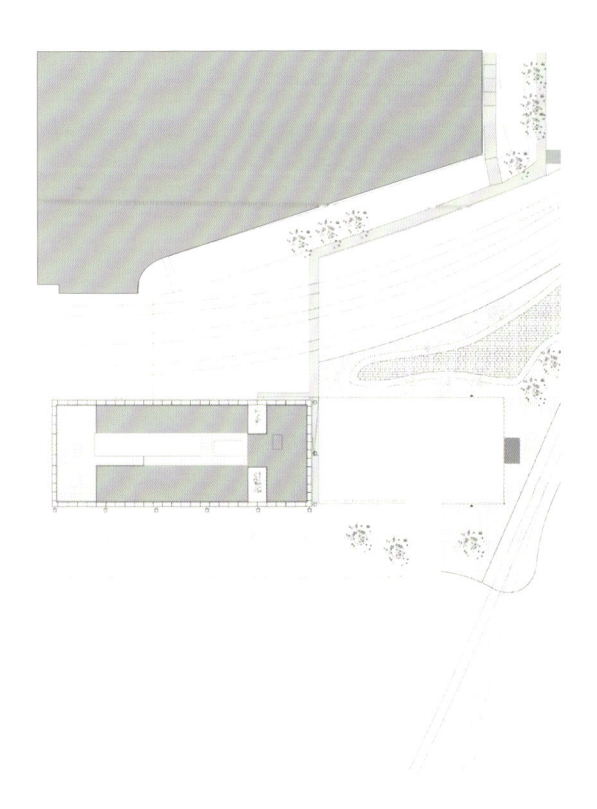

Der bedeutende Binnenhafen von Gennevilliers bei Paris ist durch die Seine und verschiedene Kanäle mit Rotterdam und Le Havre verbunden. Als Sitz der Behörde für die Containerverwaltung stellt das Gebäude eine Verbindung zwischen Schifffahrt und Straßentransport dar. Das Bild der Container wurde im Entwurf aufgenommen. Im Erdgeschoss befindet sich der Logistikbereich, im obersten Geschoss die Direktion und ein großer Empfangssaal. Die Zwischengeschosse verfügen über einen großen Freibereich, der mit den Aufenthaltsräumen des Personals verbunden ist. Die Büros sind raumhoch verglast. Vertikale drehbare Lamellen schützen das Gebäude vor direktem Sonnenlicht und übermäßiger Aufheizung.

left: Site plan_South elevation_Façade, detail. right: Interior view, building envelope.
links: Lageplan_Südfassade_Fassade, Detail. rechts: Innenansicht der Gebäudehülle.

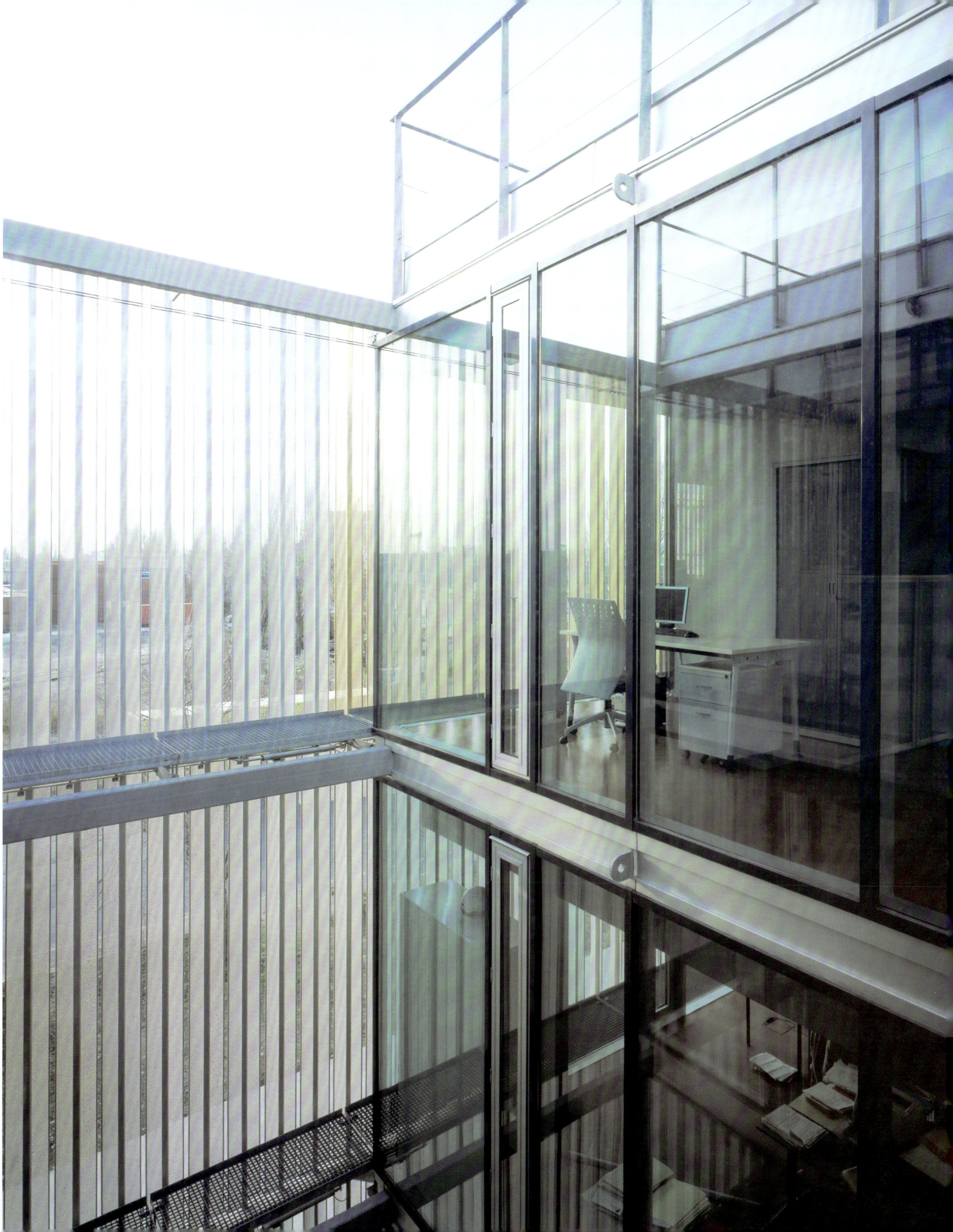

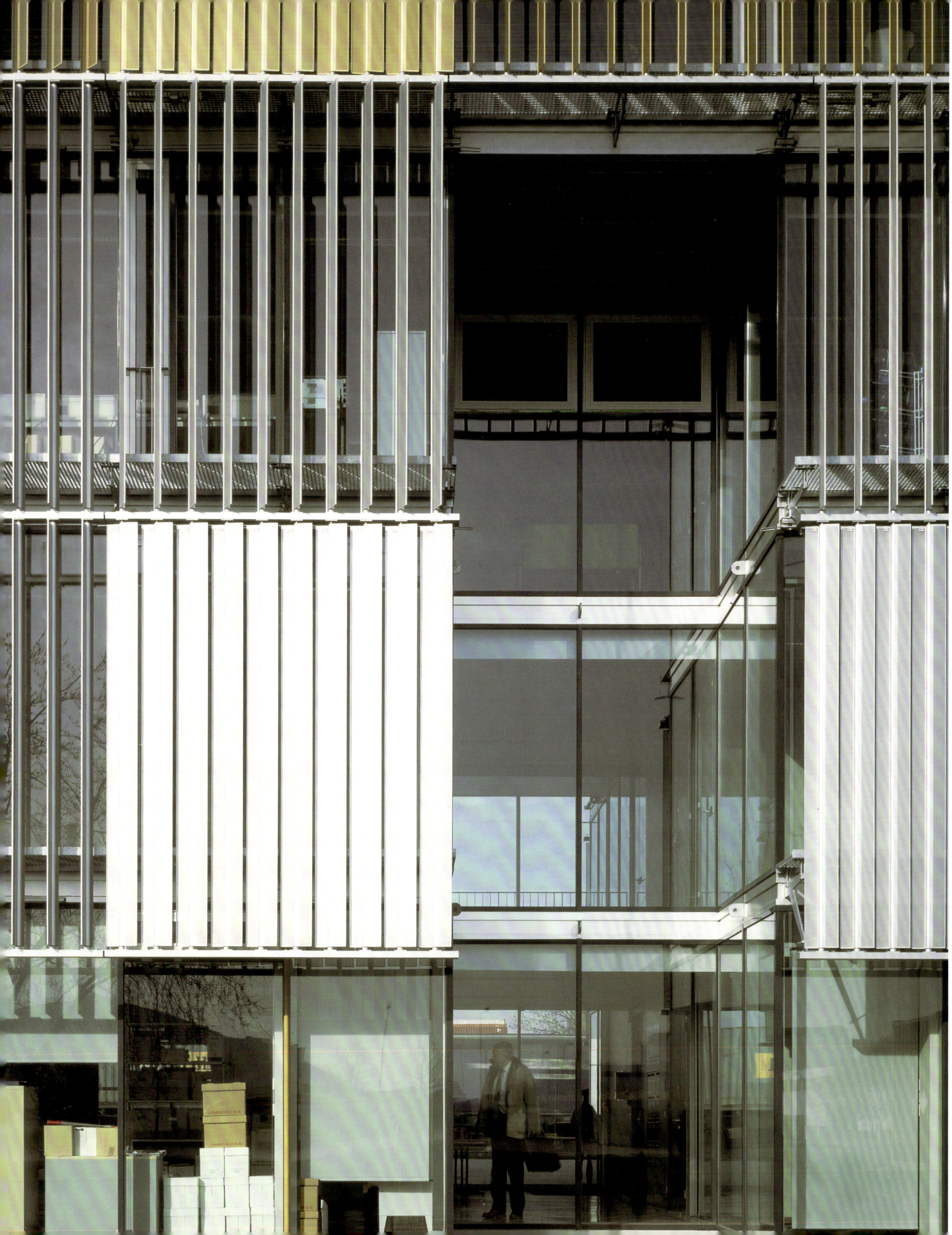

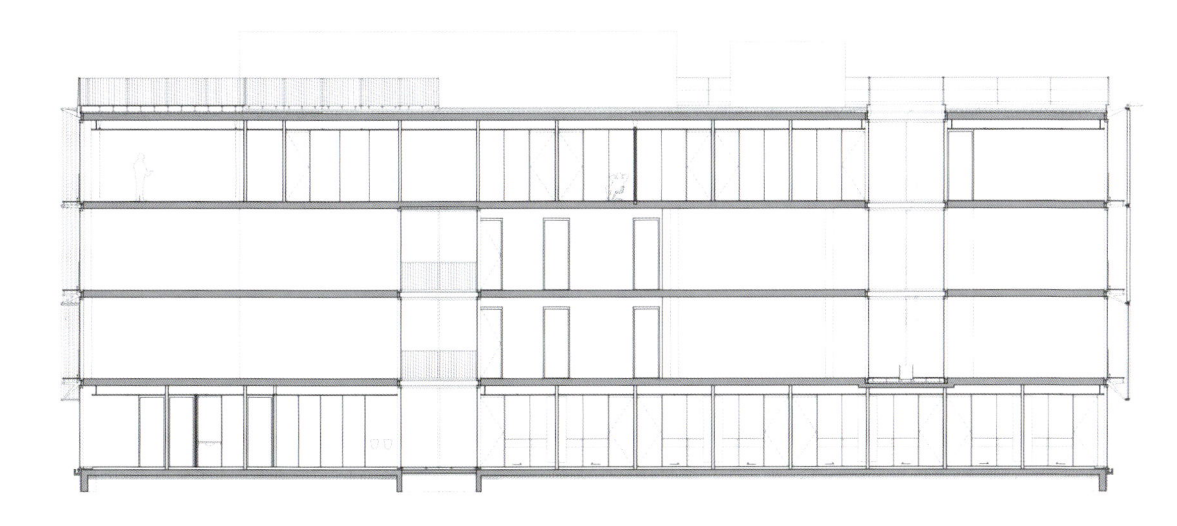

left: Entrance. right: Longitudinal section_Fins façade, detail_Conference room.
links: Eingang. rechts: Längsschnitt_Lamellenfassade, Detail_Konferenzraum.

FRANCE_LA DÉFENSE **EXALTIS TOWER**

ARCHITECTS: ARQUITECTONICA
COMPLETION: 2006_**NUMBER OF WORKPLACES:** 1,560
GROSS FLOOR AREA: 23,000 M²_**COMMON AREA:** RESTAURANT, CAFETERIA_**KIND OF WORKPLACES:** COMBINATION
PHOTOS: PAUL MAURER, PARIS

Exaltis is a new 15-floor 23,000-square-meter office building with three levels of underground parking in La Défense. Conceived as a tower of glistening glass, Exaltis defines the axis of the Avenue Gambetta. In form, the building is a rectangular prism that is modified and sculpted by the introduction of two curves along its short facades. These curving surfaces transform the rigid rectangles into fluid forms. The two curves radiate from different points somewhere below the ground and splay as they rise towards the sky. The two end walls present contrasting forms, one convex and the other concave. The result is a building with dynamic quality, implying horizontal movement along the axis of the avenue.

Exaltis ist ein 15-stöckiges Gebäude mit 23.000 Quadratmetern Bürofläche und drei unterirdischen Parkgeschossen in La Défense. Der funkelnde Glasturm markiert die Achse der Avenue Gambetta. Die Form ist die eines rechtwinkligen Prismas, das durch die beiden gekurvten Schmalseiten modifiziert wird und so skulptural erscheint. Sie verwandeln die strengen Rechtecke in eine fließende Form. Die beiden Kurven haben ihren Mittelpunkt an unterschiedlichen unterirdischen Stellen und entfernen sich, je weiter sie aufsteigen, voneinander. Die abschließenden Wände erscheinen als gegenläufige Formen: die eine konvex, die andere konkav. So ergibt sich ein Gebäude voller dynamischer Qualitäten, das eine horizontale Bewegung auf der Achse der Avenue impliziert.

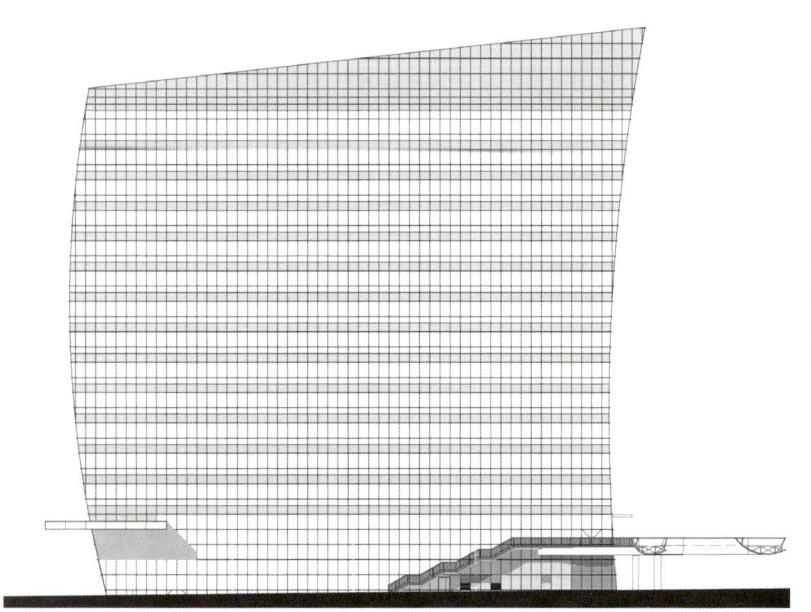

left: North elevation_View from plaza_Elevators_Reception. right: Exterior.
links: Nordansicht_Blick von der Plaza_Aufzüge_Empfang. rechts: Außenansicht.

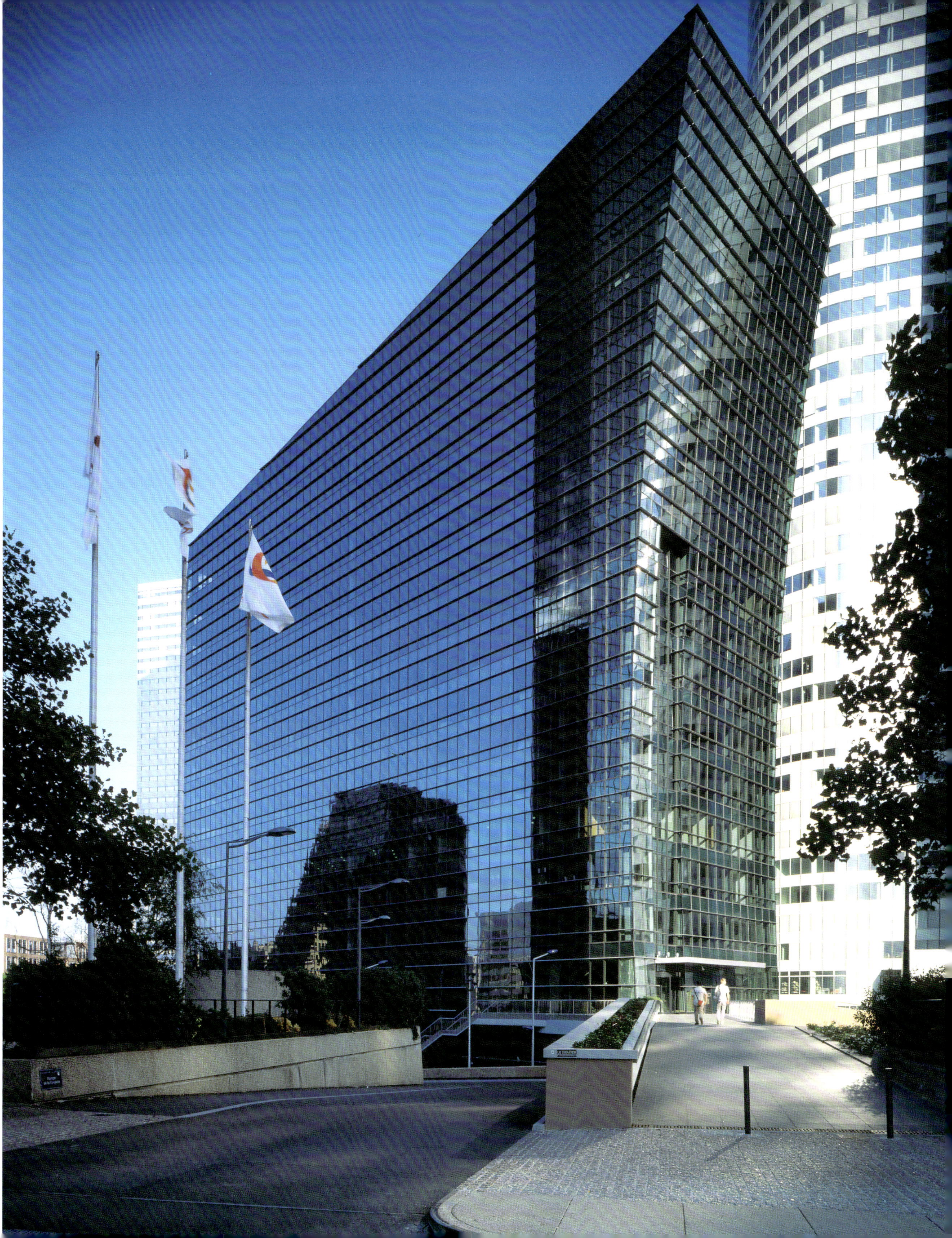

FRANCE_LA DÉFENSE **PHARE TOWER**

ARCHITECTS: MORPHOSIS ARCHITECTS
COMPLETION: 2014_**GROSS FLOOR AREA:** 185,494 M²
COMMON AREA: PUBLIC CAFE, AMENITIES_**KIND OF WORKPLACES:** MODULAR / FLEXIBLE ARRANGEMENT
RENDERINGS: COURTESY OF THE ARCHITECTS

Drawing on the power of parametric scripting, the design of the Phare Tower combines disparate programmatic, physical, and infrastructural elements from the givens of the building, and synthesizes them into a form that seamlessly integrates the building into the idiosyncrasies of its site. At the same time, it expresses multiple flows of movement. In the spirit of the Paris Exposition competition proposals, the tower embodies state-of-the-art technology, which turns it into a cultural landmark.

Auf die Fähigkeit von Programmierschnittstellen vertrauend, wurden für den Phare-Turm die unterschiedlichste Faktoren wie Raumanforderungen, physische Elemente und Infrastrukturmaßnahmen zusammengetragen und in einer Gebäudeform synthetisiert, die sich nahtlos in das eigenartige Grundstück einfügt und verschiedene Bewegungsmomente aufgreift und fortführt. Im Geiste der Entwürfe der Pariser Weltausstellungen nutzt der Turm den neuesten Stand der Technik, um zum Wahrzeichen seiner Kultur zu werden.

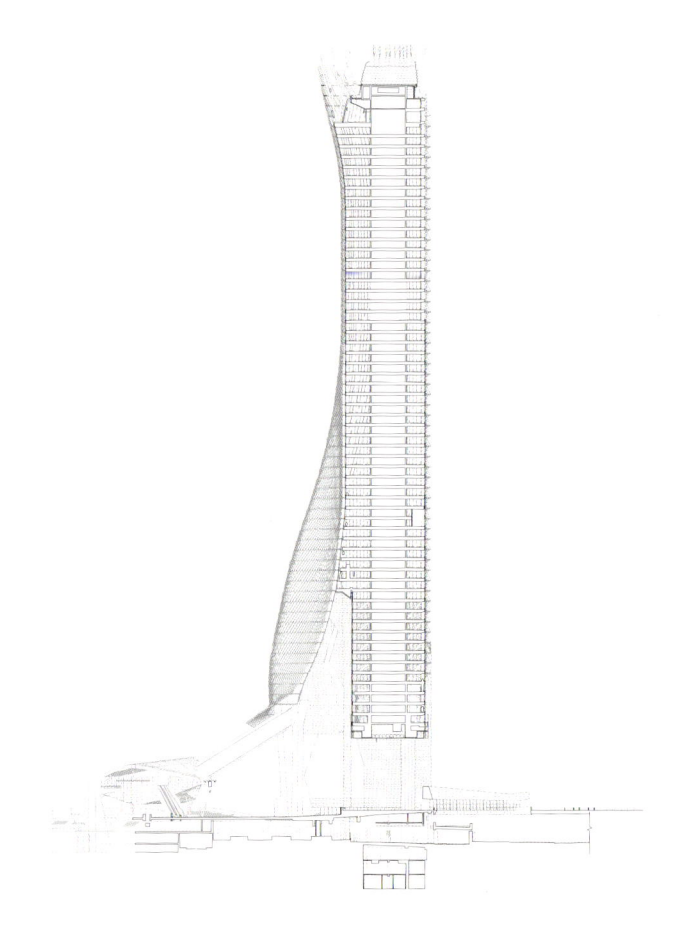

left: Elevation_Restaurant_Street level. right: Phare, next to Grande Arche and CNIT (Centre des Nouvelles Industries et Technologies)_Plaza_View on La Défense_Entrance area.
links: Ansicht_Restaurant_Straßenebene. rechts: Phare in Nachbarschaft zu Grande Arche und CNIT (Centre des Nouvelles Industries et Technologies)_Plaza_Blick über La Défense_Eingangsbereich.

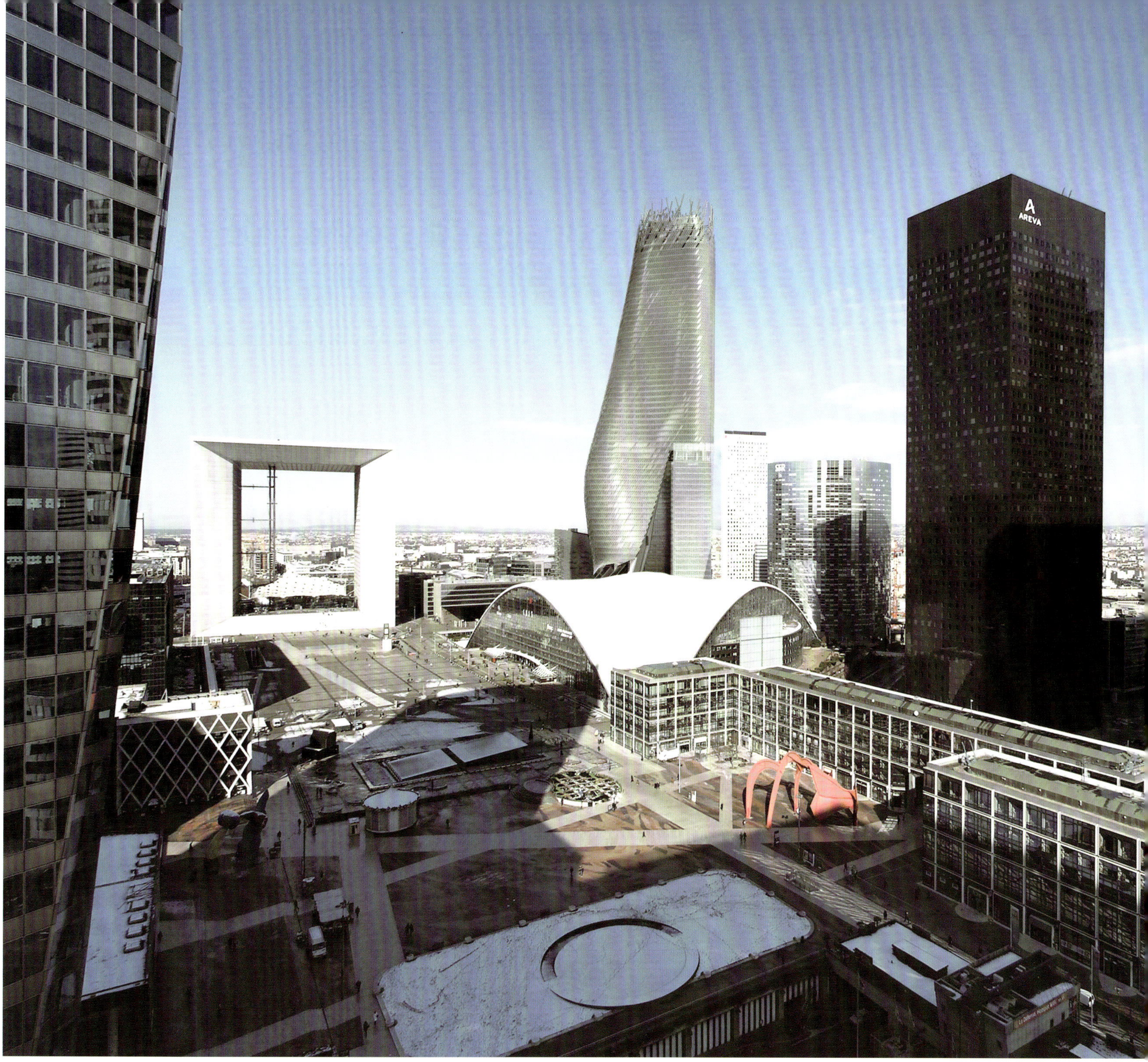
AREVA

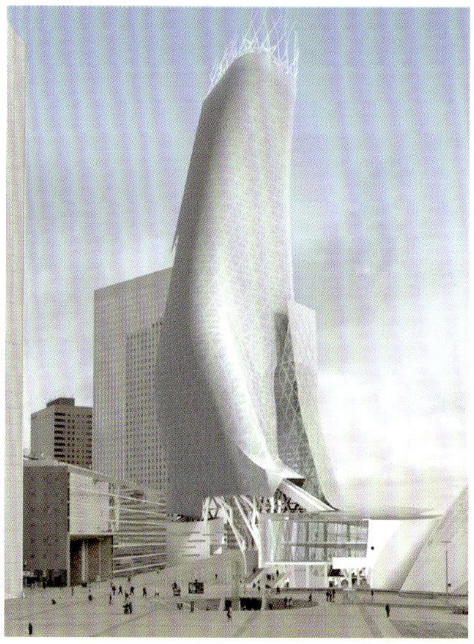

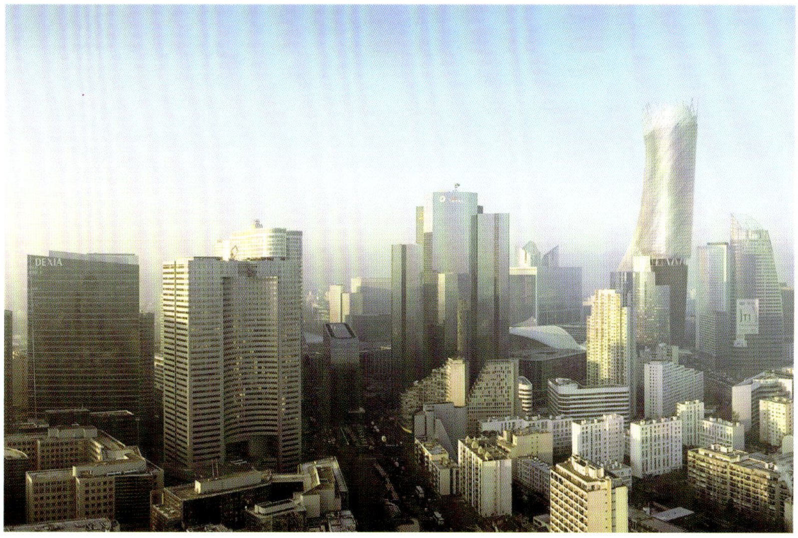

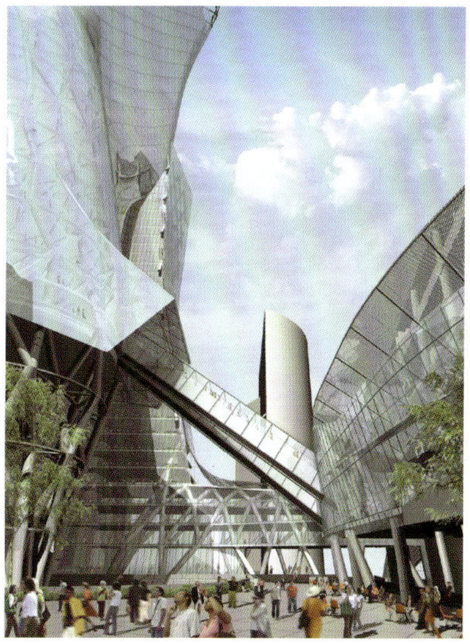

FRANCE_LA DÉFENSE **GENERALI TOWER**

ARCHITECTS: VALODE & PISTRE ARCHITECTES
MEP ENGINNERS: IOSIS_**COMPLETION:** 2013
GROSS FLOOR AREA: 90,000 M²
KIND OF WORKPLACES: OPEN-PLAN
PHOTOS: COURTESY OF THE ARCHITECTS

This almost 300-meter high tower is part of the urban renewal of the La Défense quarter. Its tall, futuristic silhouette constitutes a new signal in the skyline. Sustainability is at the heart of the architectural approach developed for this project, involving all components of its construction. The innovative envelope and equipment are all designed to reduce energy expenditures as much as possible. The tower also makes extensive use of renewable forms of energy. Exterior gardens set into the corners of the tower embellish each floor and connect the offices with nature providing a view of trees when looking out of the windows. This emphasizes the environmentally-friendly concept.

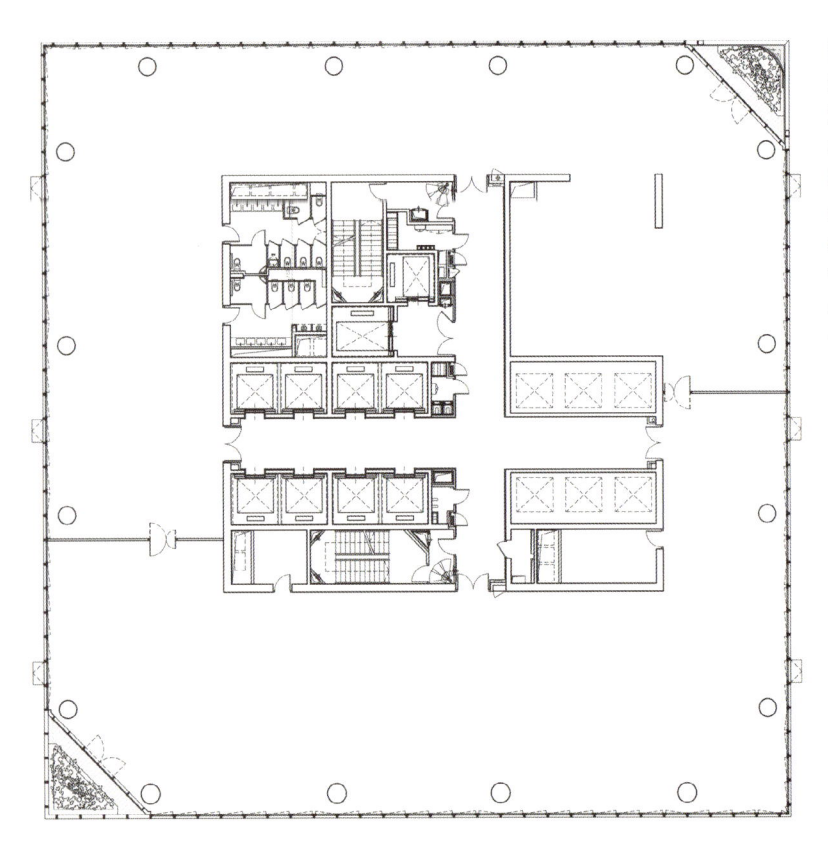

Dieser fast 300 Meter hohe Turm ist Teil der Stadterneuerung von La Défense. Seine hohe, futuristische Silhouette setzt einen neuen Akzent in der Skyline. Nachhaltigkeit steht im Zentrum des für dieses Projekt entwickelten, architektonischen Programms und umfasst alle Konstruktionskomponenten. Der Entwurf der innovativen Gebäudehülle und der Ausstattung zielt auf eine möglichst große Reduzierung des Energieaufwands. Der Turm nutzt intensiv erneuerbare Energien. Außen angebrachte Gärten in den Ecken des Turms verschönern die Stockwerke und verbinden die Büros mit der Natur, indem sie durch das Fenster einen Blick auf Bäume bieten. So wird das umweltfreundliche Konzept nochmals betont.

left: Typical floor plan_View on La Défense_Detail, façade. right: Suspended gardens_Entrance hall_Office.
links: Regelgeschoss_Blick auf La Défense_Ansicht. rechts: Eingeschobene Gärten_Eingangshalle_Büro.

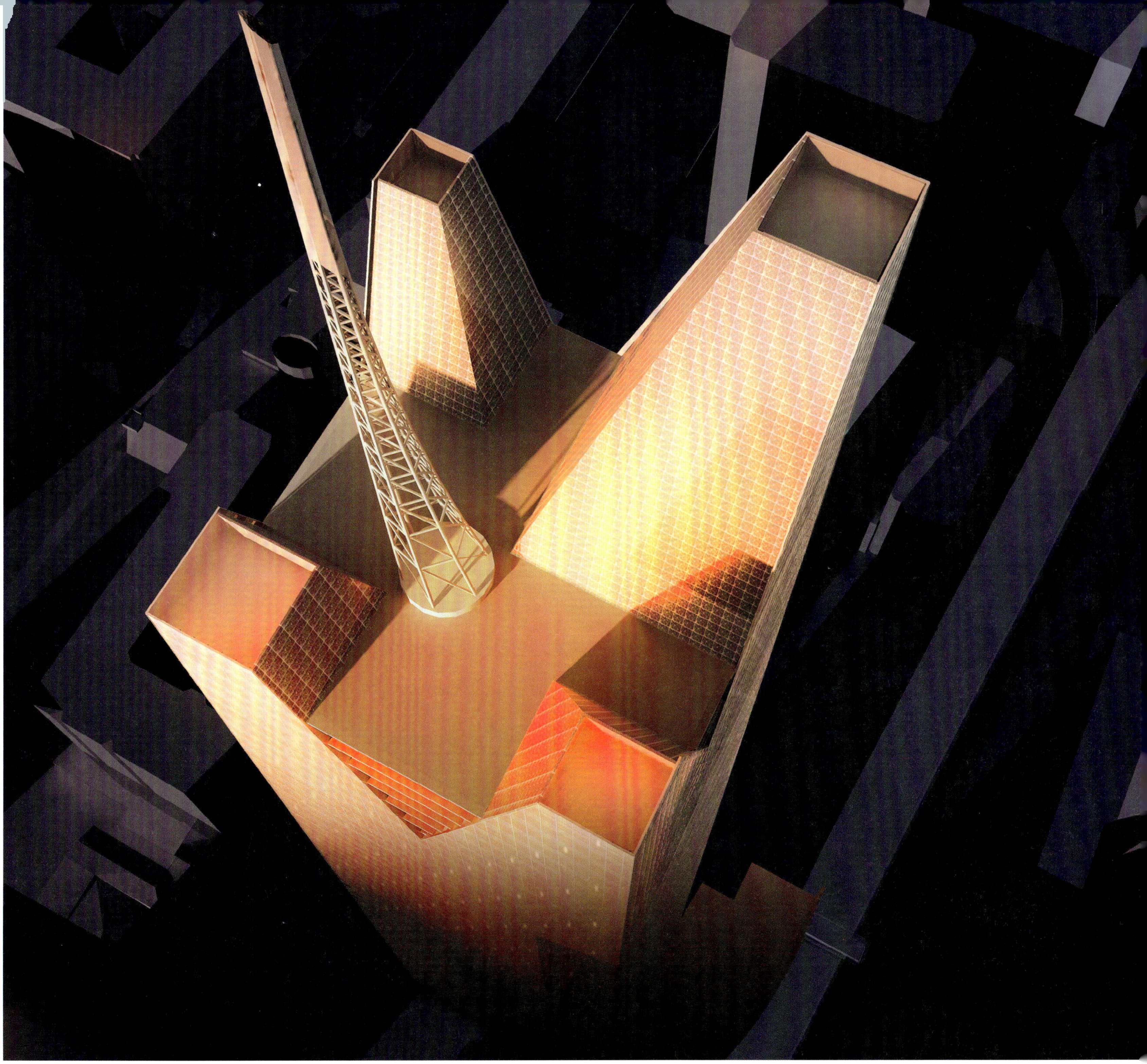

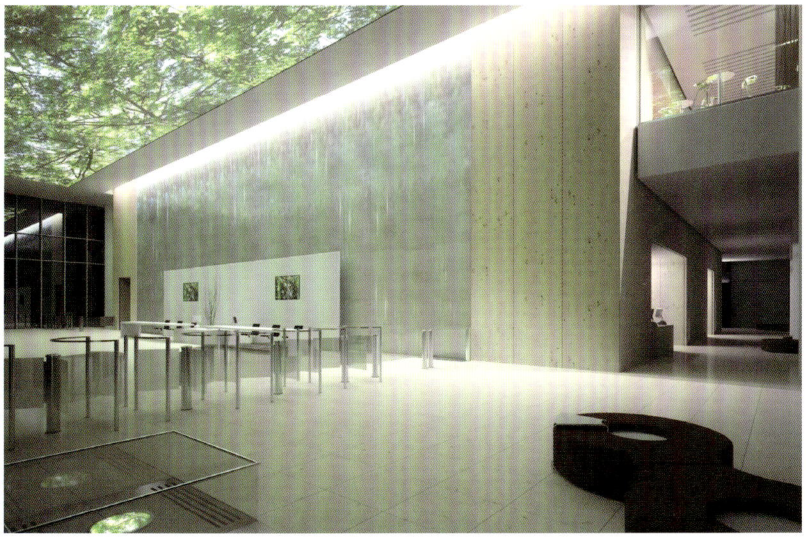

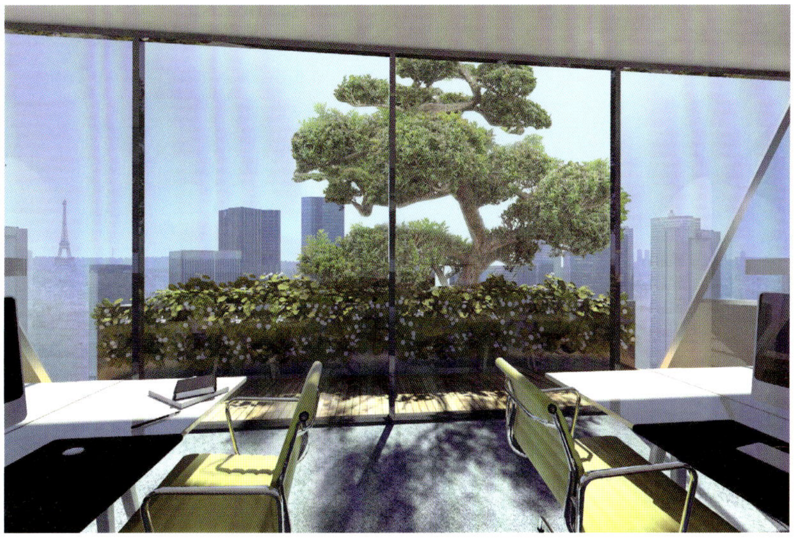

FRANCE_PARIS **8 ROCHEFOUCAULD**

ARCHITECTS: AW²_**COMPLETION:** 2006
ORIGINAL BUILDING: END 1960S_**NUMBER OF WORKPLACES:** 200_**GROSS FLOOR AREA:** 2,500 M²
COMMON AREA: RECEPTION, CAFETERIA_**KIND OF WORKPLACES:** OPEN-PLAN_**PHOTOS:** AW², PARIS (100), SÉBASTIEN LAVAL, PARIS (101)

The project consisted in gutting and refurbishing an existing building located in the 9th arrondissement of Paris. The fact that the plot is set back from the traditional street line gave the opportunity to create a contemporary building with a new façade organized in vertical layers of transparent glass and opaque timber panels. During daytime, the curtain wall creates a pattern of glass and wood, while at night the building becomes a patterned "light box" within a traditional stone building environment. The ground level is designed to allow pedestrian views into the urban block, while the glass walls and sloping street allow the user to enjoy stunning views over the roofscape of Paris.

Das bestehende Gebäude im neunten Arrondissement in Paris sollte entkernt und neu gestaltet werden. Die Einrückung von der traditionellen Straßenbegrenzungslinie ermöglichte die Erschaffung eines zeitgenössischen Gebäudes mit neuer Fassade, die in vertikalen Schichten aus transparentem Glas und blickdichten Holztafeln besteht. Diese Vorhangfassade zeigt sich tagsüber in einem Glas- und Holzmuster, während das Gebäude nachts zu einer gemusterten „Lichtbox" in einem traditionellen Viertel mit Steinbauten wird. Das Erdgeschoss ist so gestaltet, dass Passanten Einblick in den Häuserblock haben, während Glaswände und die abfallende Straße es den Nutzern ermöglichen, einen atemberaubenden Blick über Paris' Dächer zu genießen.

left: Section_New elevation_View from rue de la Rochefoucauld. right: Offices reception_Reception desk.
links: Schnitt_Neue Ansicht_Blick von der rue de la Rochefoucauld. rechts: Bürorezeption_Empfangstheke.

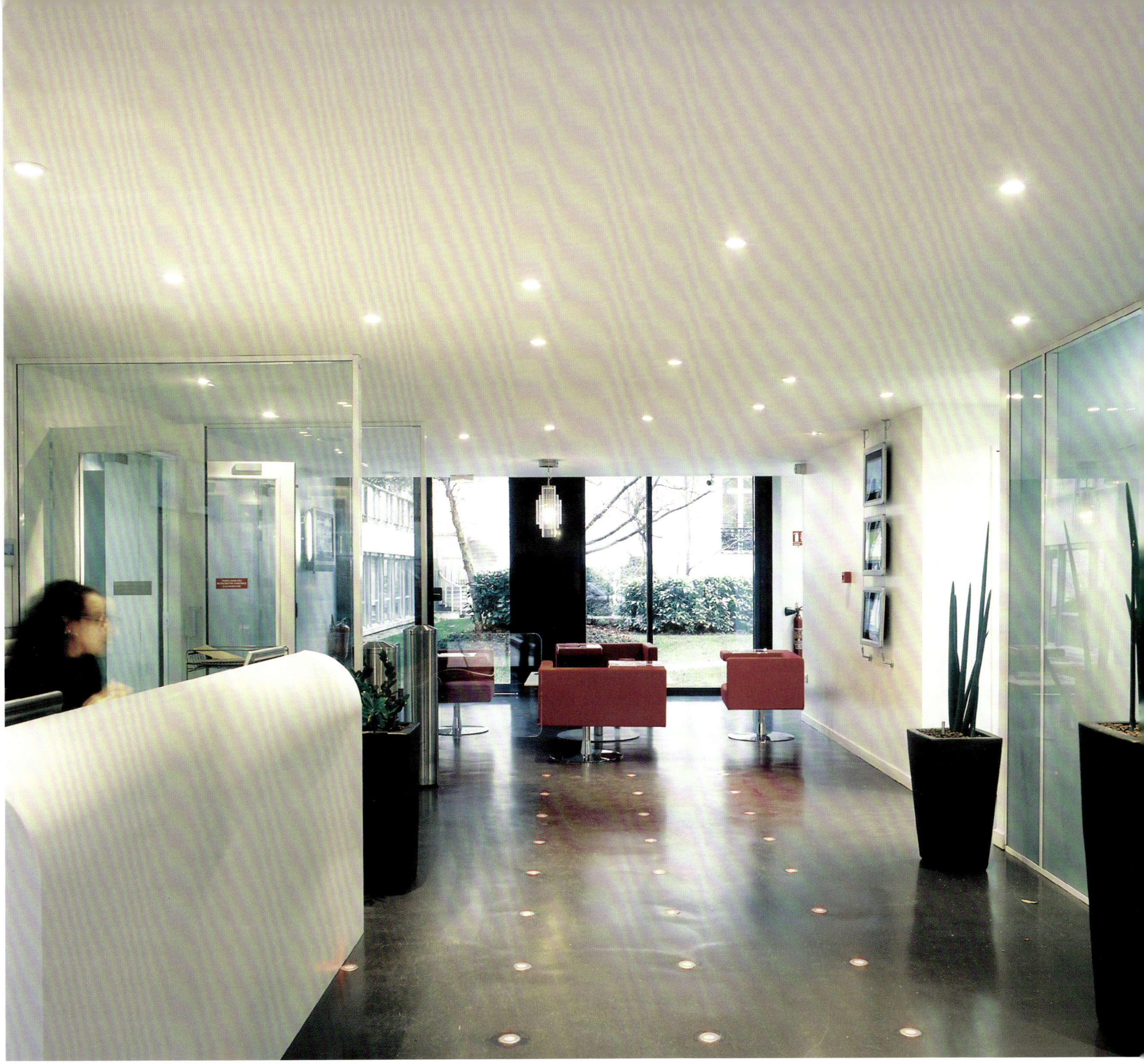

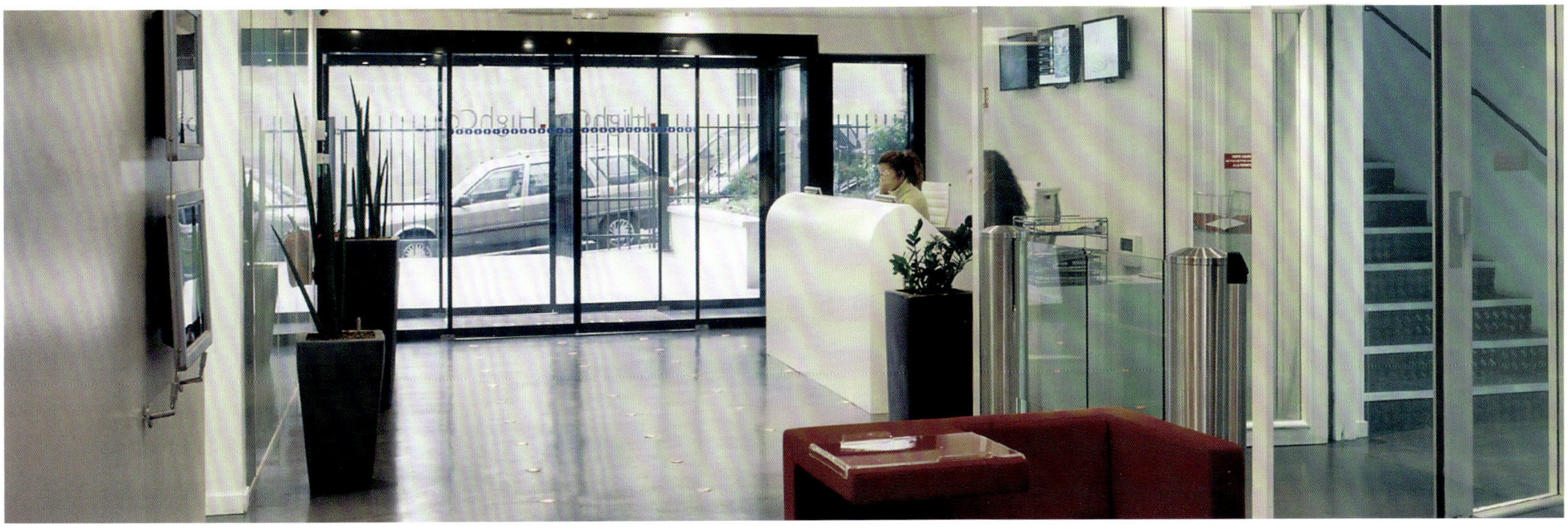

FRANCE_PARIS **118 ELYSÉES**

ARCHITECTS: AW² _ **ENGINEERS OFFICE:** SATO & ASSOCIÉS
COMPLETION: 2009_**ORIGINAL BUILDING:** END OF 19. CENTURY_**NUMBER OF WORKPLACES:** 200
GROSS FLOOR AREA: 2,500 M²_**COMMON AREA:** EXTERNAL COURT_**KIND OF WORKPLACES:** OPEN-PLAN
PHOTOS: TENDANCE FLOUE, PARIS

AW² was commissioned with the complete refurbishment of an existing office building on the Avenue des Champs Elysées in Paris. The existing façades were completely refurbished, along with all the interiors. The courtyard was modified by introducing a vertical garden, which, in the contrived allowed space, changes both the look and feel of the whole building. This is the strongest feature of the design, which will contribute to a renewed quality of the workspace for all users. The entrance hall was also totally redesigned by introducing a white Corian wall decorated with a backlit plant pattern, which recalls the vertical garden of the central courtyard. All office levels were entirely refurbished, allowing the workspaces to reflect a contemporary and luxurious environment.

Das bestehende Bürogebäude auf der Avenue des Champs Elysées wurde von AW² vollständig renoviert. Die bestehende Fassade und das gesamte Interieur wurden runderneuert. Der neue vertikale Garten verändert Aussehen und Ambiente des Hofes und des ganzen Baus völlig. Er ist das stärkste Merkmal, das zur neuen Qualität des Arbeitsbereichs aller Nutzer beiträgt. Die Eingangshalle wurde ebenfalls vollständig neu gestaltet. Eine weiße, mit hintergrundbeleuchteten Pflanzenmustern geschmückte Corian-Wand nimmt den Garten im Hof wieder auf. Alle Büroebenen wurden komplett renoviert, so dass die Arbeitsplätze ein zeitgenössisches und luxuriöses Ambiente bieten.

left: Section_ Entrance to the offices_Court with the vertical garden created by AW²_Inner court yard.
right: Offices_Reception of the offices_Perspective offices and corridor.
links: Schnitt_Eingang zu den Büros_Hof mit vertikalem Garten, entworfen von AW²_Innenhof.
rechts: Büro_Empfang_Perspektive, Büro und Flur.

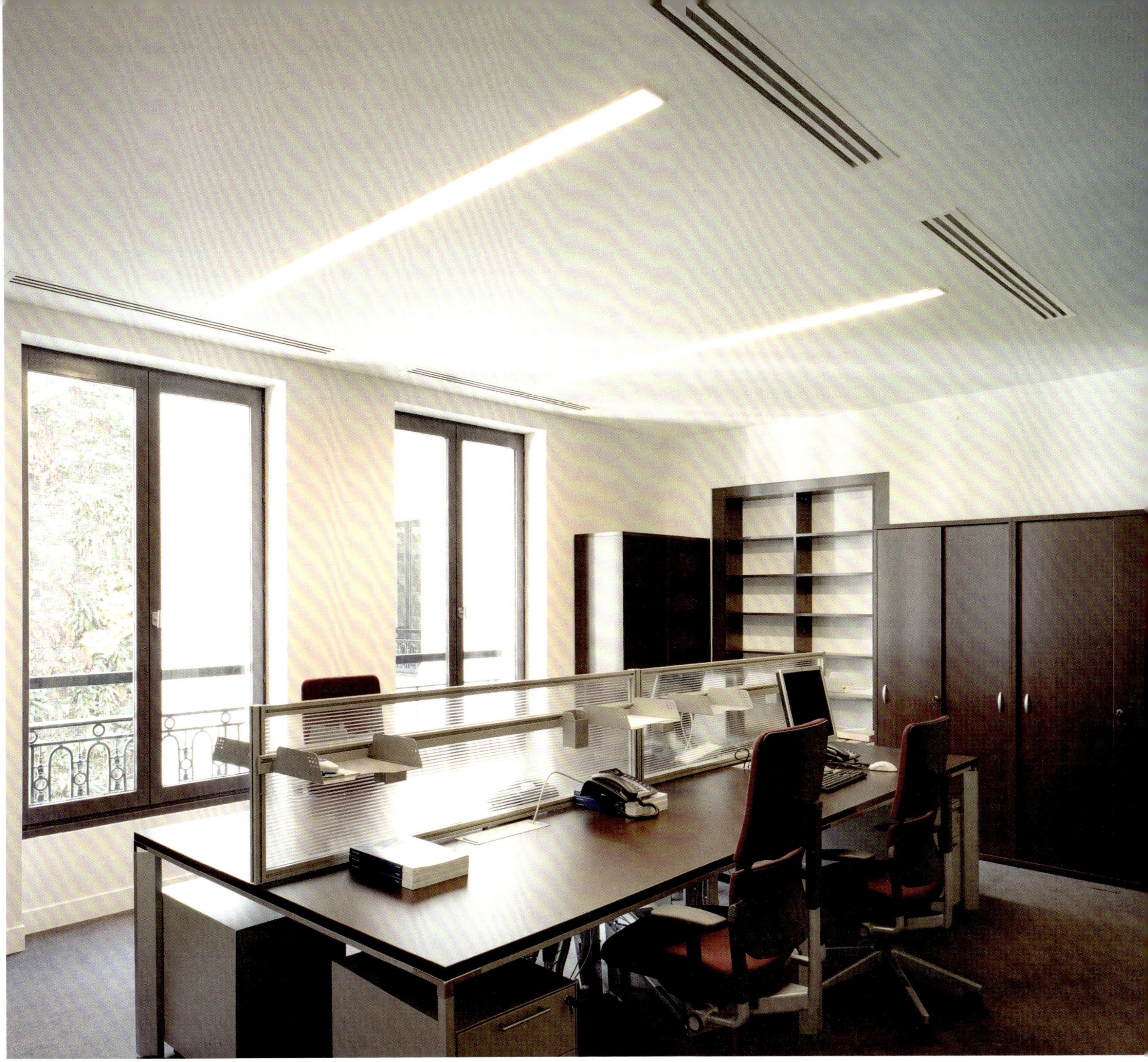
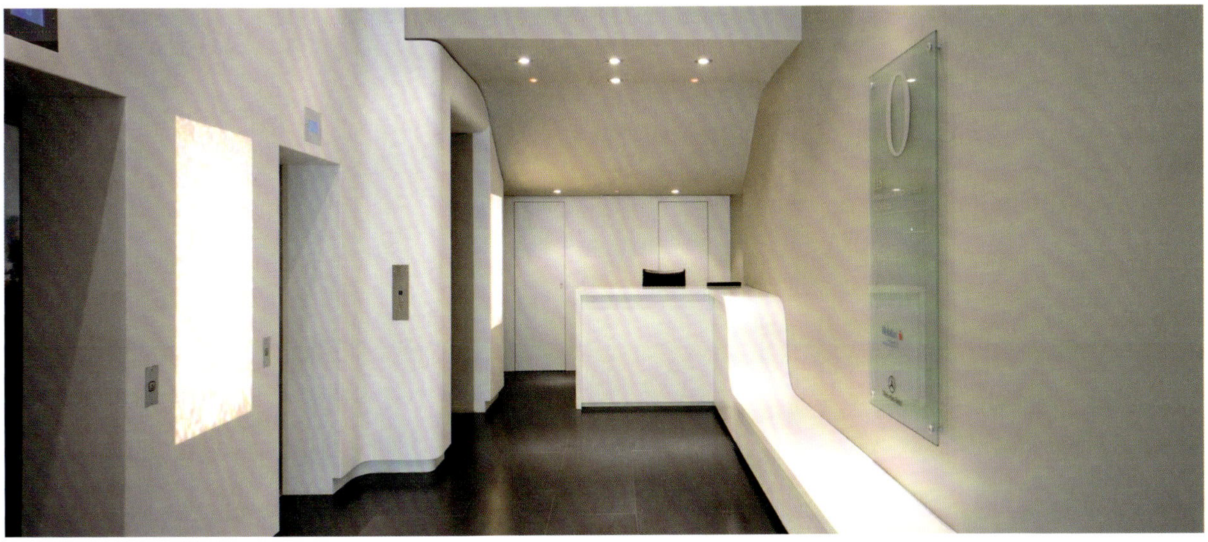
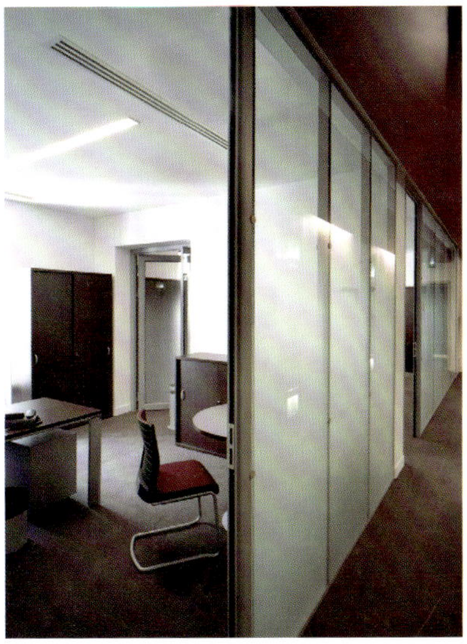

FRANCE_PARIS **CARDBOARD OFFICE**

ARCHITECTS: PAUL COUDAMY
COMPLETION: 2008_**NUMBER OF WORKPLACES:** 20
GROSS FLOOR AREA: 160 M²_**COMMON AREA:** MEETING ROOM_**KIND OF WORKPLACES:** OPEN-PLAN
PHOTOS: BENJAMIN BOCCAS

The project converts industrial space into a twenty-people office of the Elegangz company. The challenge was to provide the firm with a flexible space that would embrace its various activities such as advertising, internet, events and music. The client was interested in a solution with a life-span of a few months to several years rather than a fixed design. The entire design was implemented from water-resistant honeycomb cardboard that was folded, glued or taped into any type of furniture needed. Additional cardboard and umbrellas were used for acoustic comfort. This unusual interior design, with a recycling and low-tech approach, offers a functional and flexible space, which can be built in a very short time at a competitive price.

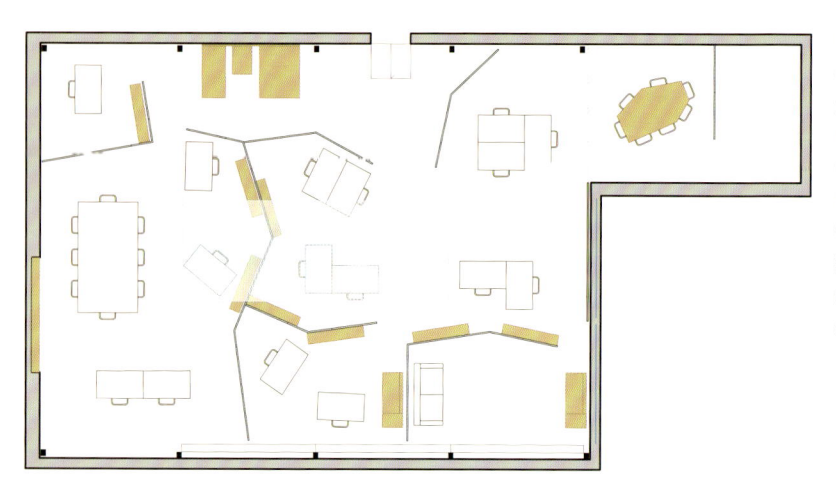

Das Projekt wandelt Industriefläche in ein Büro für die zwanzig Mitarbeiter der Firma Elegangz um. Die Herausforderung bestand darin, einen flexiblen Raum zu schaffen, der so verschiedene Arbeitsbereiche wie Werbung, Internet, Veranstaltungen und Musik vereint. Der Kunde wünschte keine unveränderliche Lösung, sondern eine, die wenige Monate oder einige Jahre halten konnte. Die gesamte Ausstattung und benötigte Möblierung wurde aus wasserfestem Wabenkarton gefaltet und geklebt. Zusätzlicher Karton sowie Schirme dienen der akustischen Optimierung. Das ungewöhnliche Recycling- und Low-tech-Interieur bietet funktionalen und flexiblen, schnell zu errichtenden und konkurrenzfähig günstigen Raum.

left: Floor plan_Desk partitions_Meeting room. right: Isolation cabine, detail_ Isolation cabine_ General view.
links: Grundriss_Schreibtische_Besprechungszimmer. rechts: Einzelkabine, Detail_Einzelkabine_ Gesamtansicht.

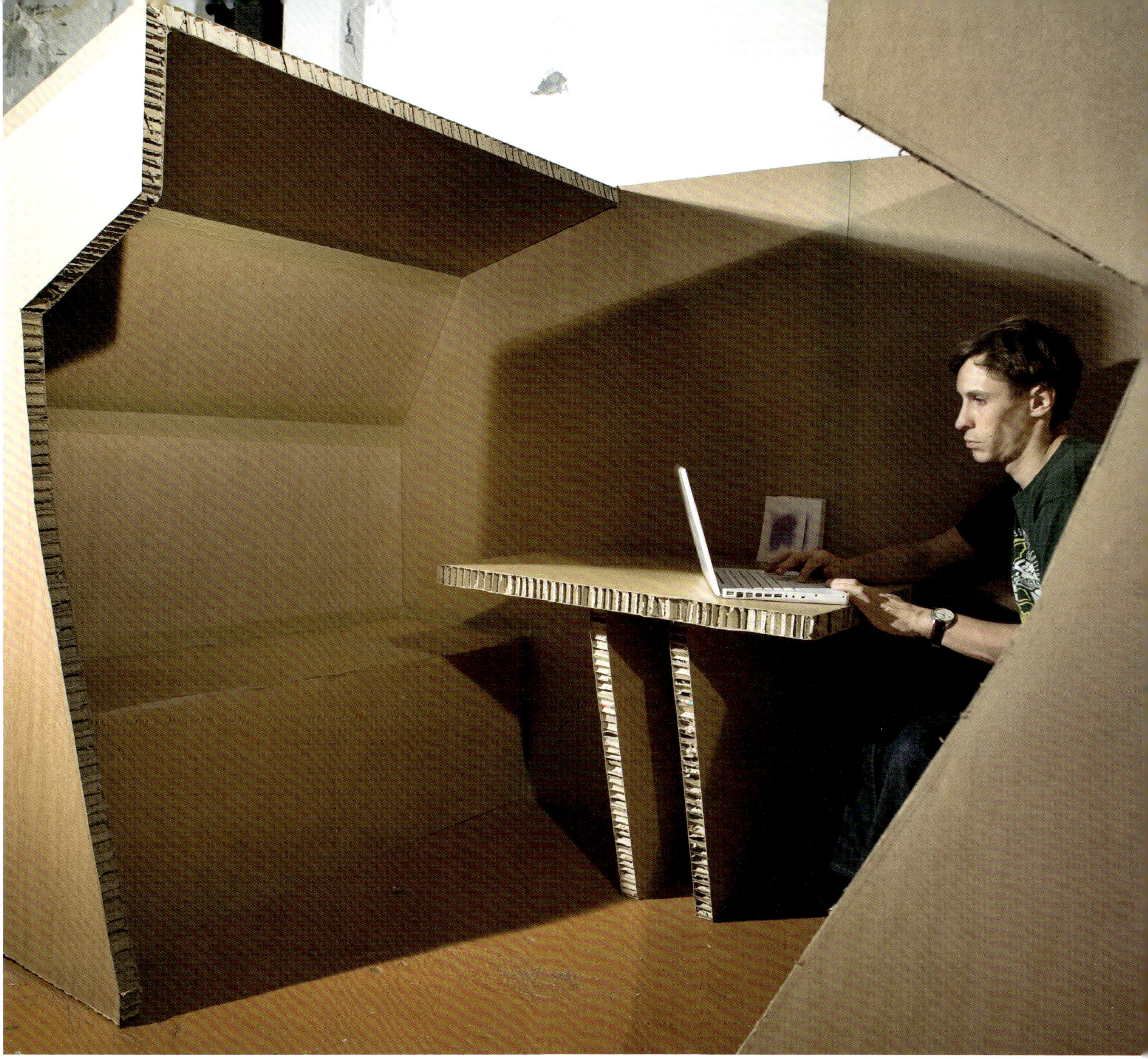
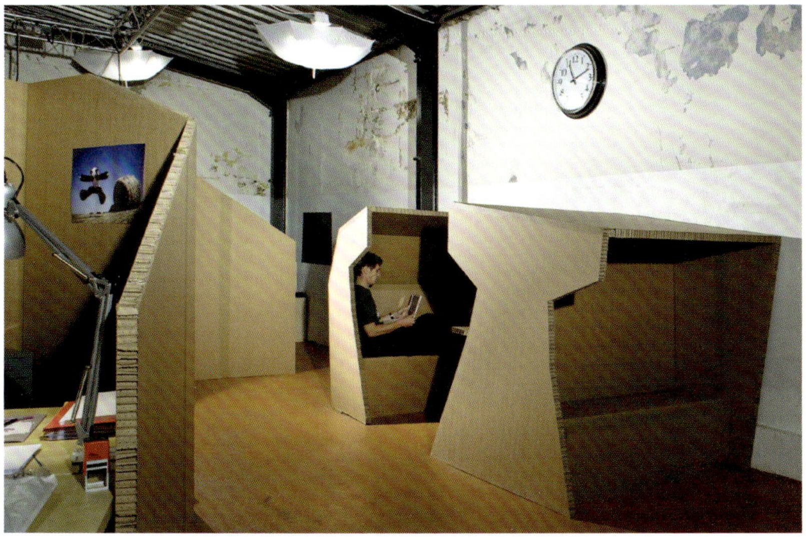
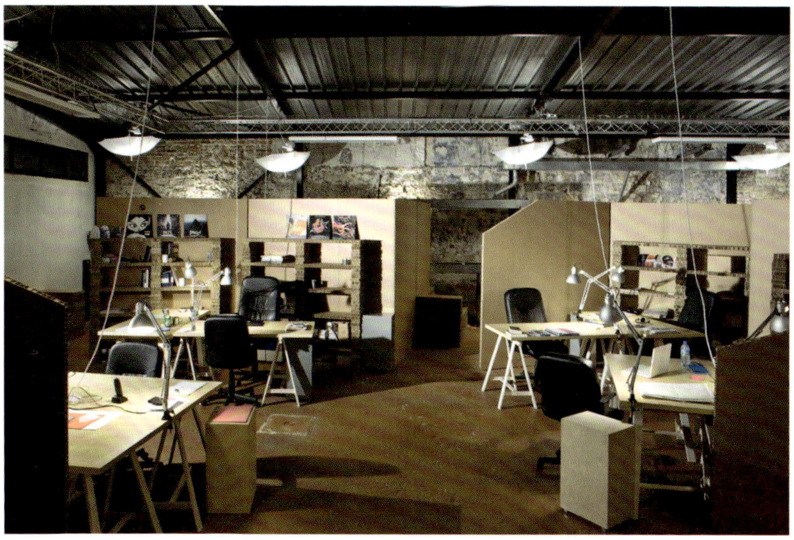

FRANCE_PARIS **LABOBRAIN**

ARCHITECTS: MATHIEU LEHANNEUR
COMPLETION: 2008_**NUMBER OF WORKPLACES:** 3
GROSS FLOOR AREA: 80 M²_**KIND OF WORKPLACES:**
THINK TANK, LOUNGE WORKSPACE
PHOTOS: FABIEN THOUVENIN

Labobrain is the office of the founder of Le Laboratoire, a Think Tank that links art and science. The room resembles a living room with distinguished designer furniture (Cork Chair by Jasper Morrison, Bentwood chair by Frank Gehry) and a geodetic cathedral transformed into an easy chair conceived by the interior designer, rather than a conventional work place. Lehanneur's "Delicious" boxes and plant-based room filter "Andrea" complete this section of the room that is enclosed in a large rounded delineable wall disc. In contrast to the emotional "frontal lobe" section of the room, the back section represents the rational memory with white drawers and a large work desk.

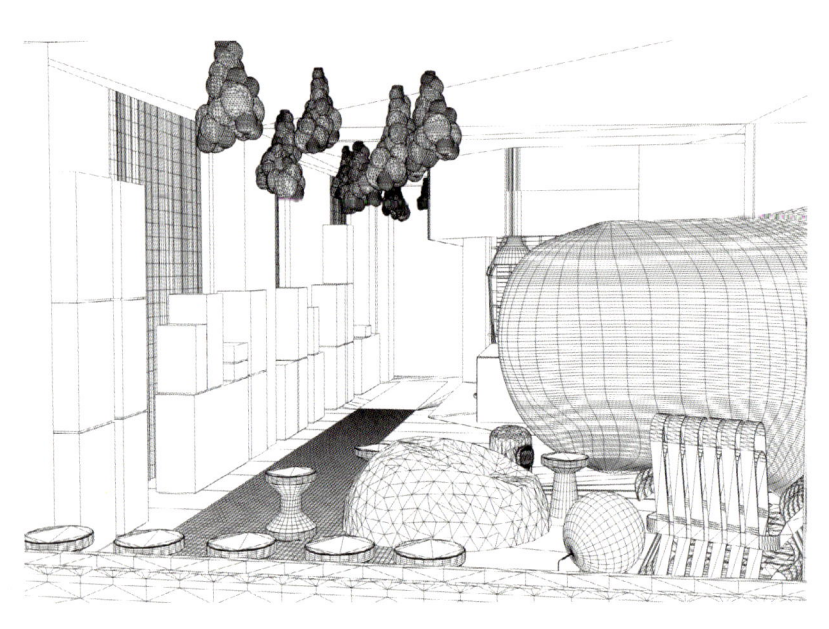

Labobrain ist das Büro des Gründer von Le Laboratoire, ein Think Tank, der Kunst und Wissenschaft zusammenbringt. Der Raum erscheint eher als Wohnzimmer mit bedeutenden Designermöbeln (Korkhocker von Jasper Morrison, Bugholzstuhl von Frank Gehry) und einem zum Sessel abgewandten geodätischen Dom nach Entwurf des Innenarchitekten denn als klassischer Arbeitsplatz. Lehanneurs Kästen „Delicious" und sein durch Pflanzen betriebener Raumluftfilter „Andrea" vervollständigen den durch eine große gerundete, beschreibbare Wandscheibe umfangenen Raumteil. Der hintere Raumteil hingegen versteht sich – im Gegensatz zur emotionalen Hirnhälfte des vorderen – als rationales Gedächtnis, mit weißen Schubladen und großem Arbeitstisch.

left: Sketch_Geodetic cathedral transformed into an easy chair and "Delicious" boxes_Easy chair_Easy chair in use. right: Back section_Easy chair and boxes_Delineable wall disc_At the work desk. links: Skizze_Abgewandelter geodätischer Dom als Sessel und Kästen „Delicious"_Sessel_Sessel in Benutzung. rechts: Hinterer Raumteil_Sessel und Kästen_Beschreibbare Wandscheibe_Am Arbeitstisch.

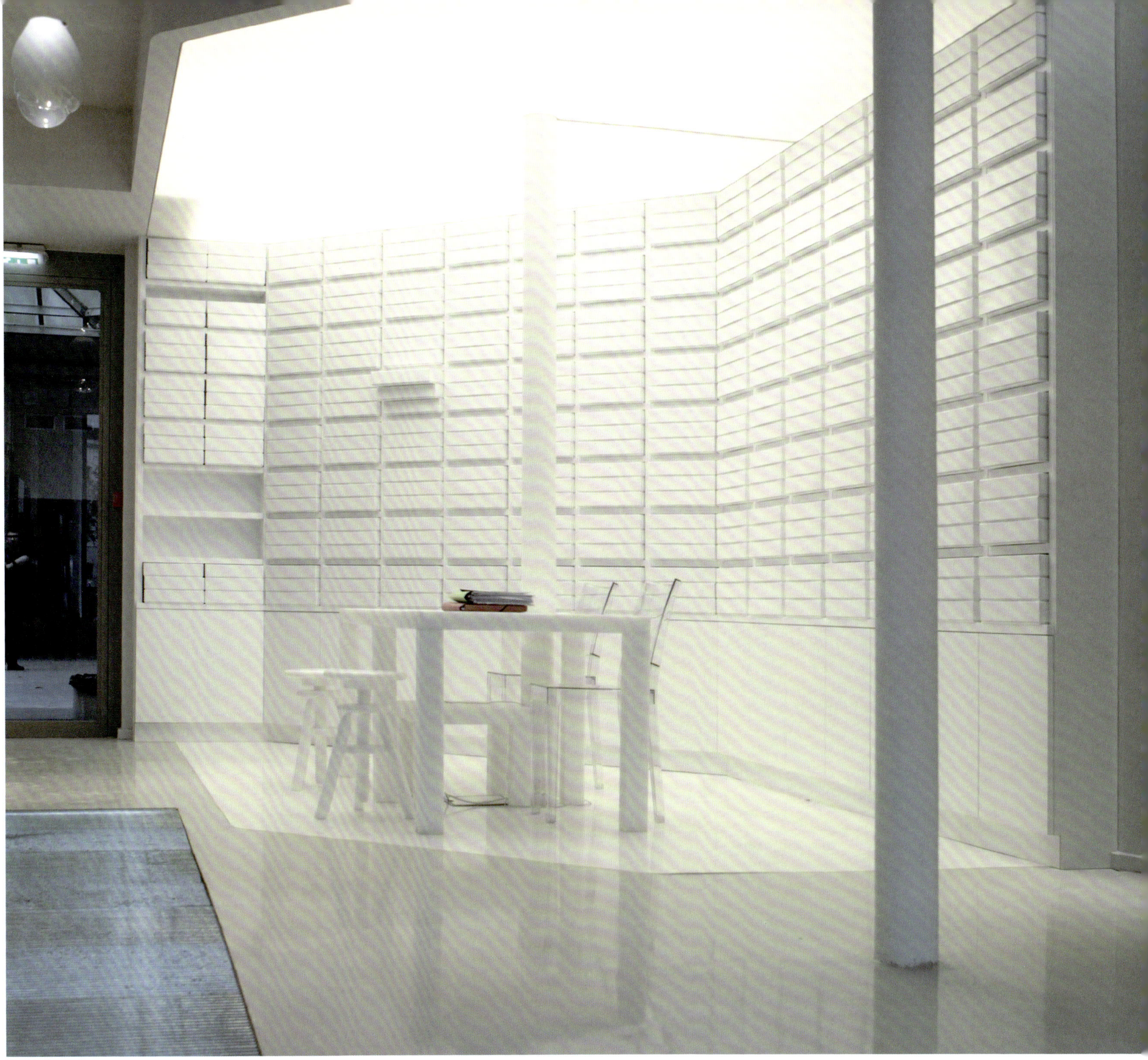
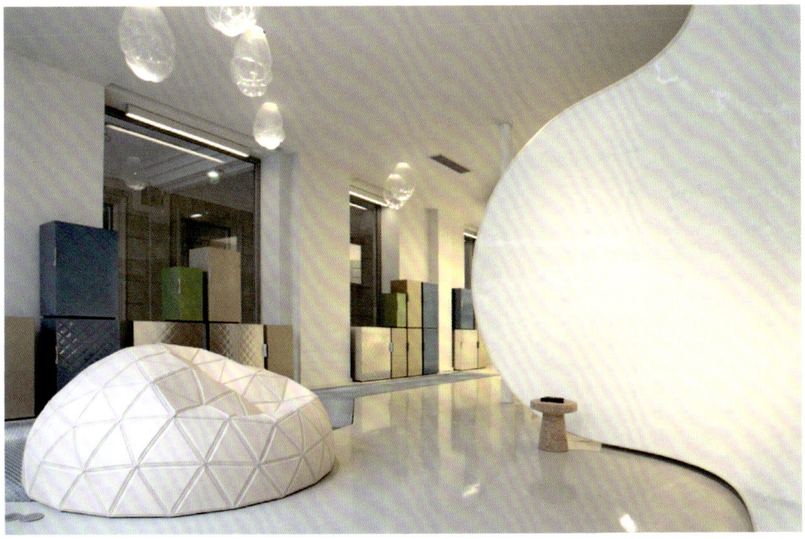
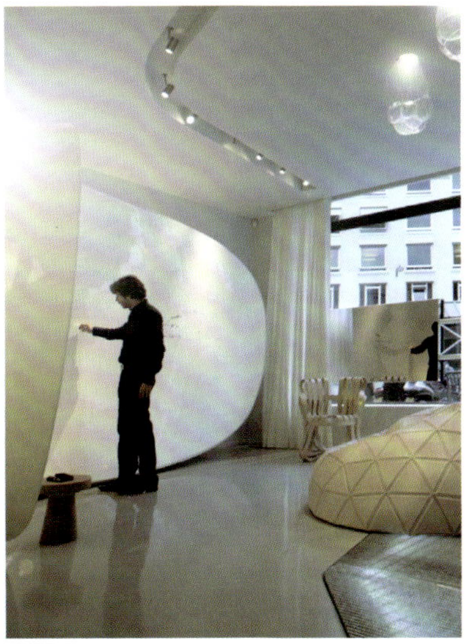
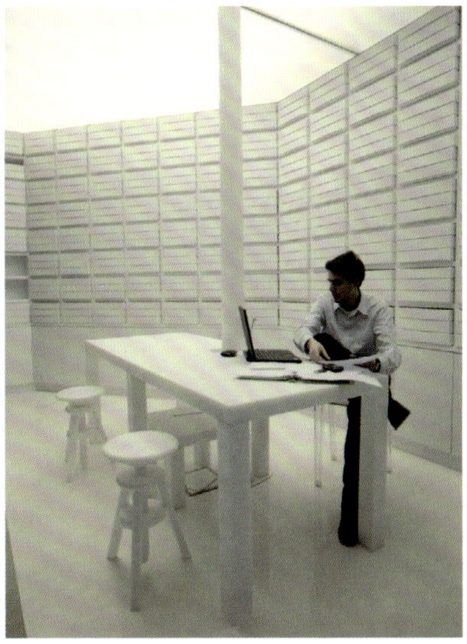

FRANCE_PARIS CINETIC OFFICE BUILDING

ARCHITECTS: VALODE & PISTRE ARCHITECTES
ENGINEERING: VP & GREEN_**ARTIST:** ELISABETH BALLET
COMPLETION: 2009_**GROSS FLOOR AREA:** 22,000 M²
COMMON AREA: RESTAURANT_**PHOTOS:** A. NARODITSKY, M. DENANCÉ (108 B. L., 109 B. R.)

A strategic link in the restructuring of Paris's Porte des Lilas, the Cinetic office building respects the area's symmetry effect and assumes the role of a gateway between Paris and the contiguous suburbs. The project presents different strongly identified façades matching the styles of the nearby buildings, in particular the north-west façade which is distinguished by its innovative, irregular folded patterns. The folds facing north on the suburban side are made of clear glass, while those facing west on the Paris side are made of silk-screened glass, serving as the medium for a work by artist Elisabeth Ballet, representing a close-up of a chestnut tree and its branches.

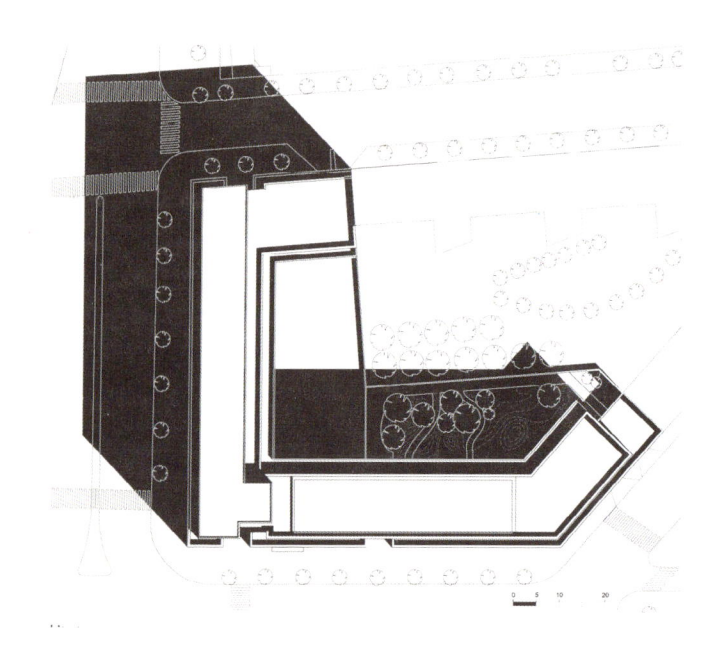

Das kinetische Bürogebäude respektiert als strategische Verbindung in der Restrukturierung der Pariser Porte de Lilas die Symmetrie der Umgebung und fungiert als Tor zwischen Paris und den angrenzenden Vorstädten. Der Bau hat verschiedene, charakteristische Fassaden, die sich jeweils auf die benachbarte Bebauung beziehen. Insbesonders die Nordwestfassade sticht mit ihrem innovativen, unregelmäßig verknickten Muster hervor. Die nördlich ausgerichteten Faltungen auf der Vorstadtseite bestehen aus Klarglas und jene westlichen auf der städtischen Seite aus Siebdruck-Glas. Dieses dient als Träger für ein Werk der Künstlerin Elisabeth Ballet, das eine Großaufnahme eines Kastanienbaums und dessen Zweigen zeigt.

left: Plan_General elevation_ Façade, detail. right: Silk screened glass detail by Elisabeth Ballet_ Corner_Façade_Interior view.
links: Plan_Gesamtansicht_Fassadendetail. rechts: Milchglasdetails von Elisabeth Ballet_Ecke_ Fassade_Innenansicht.

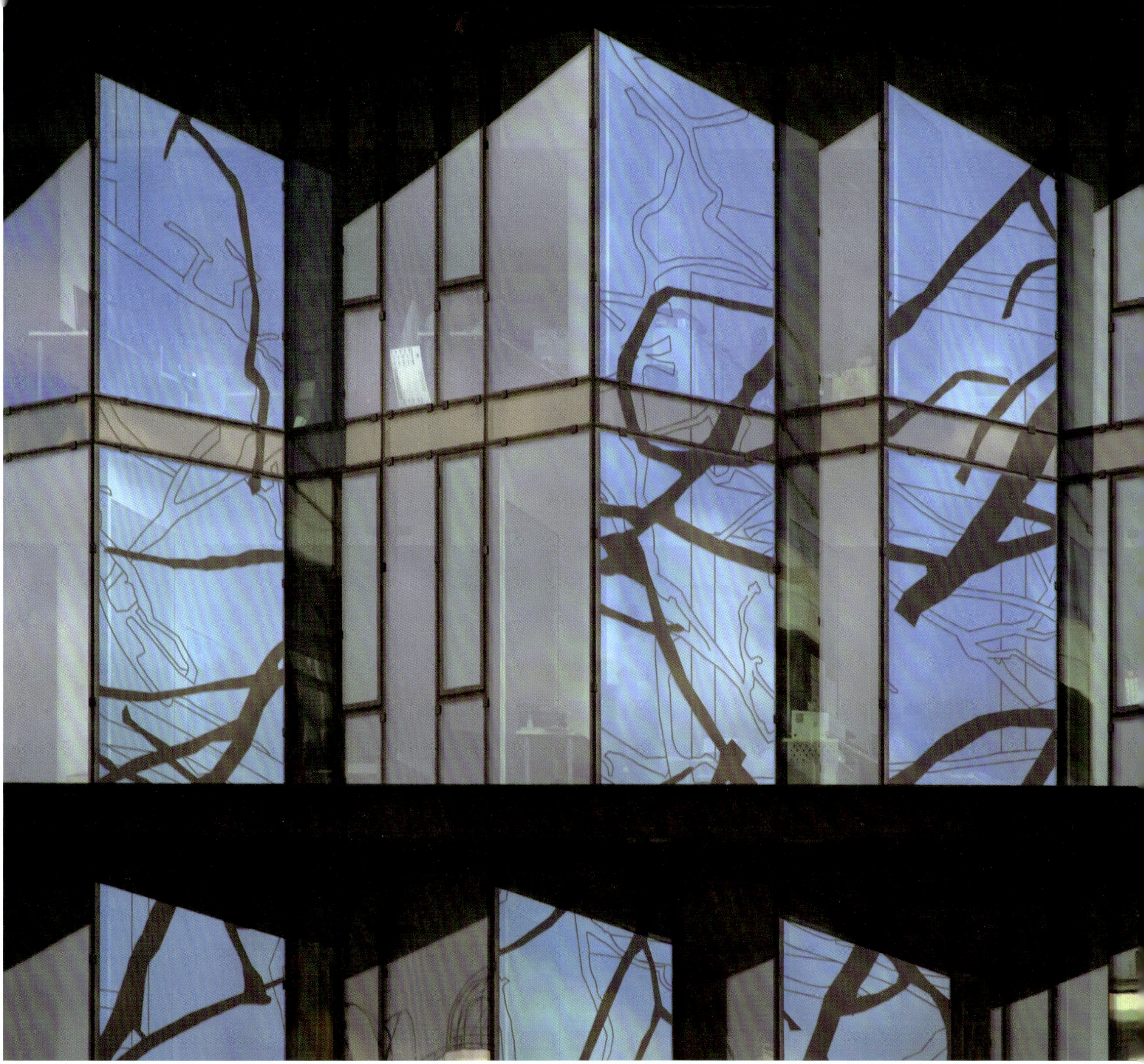
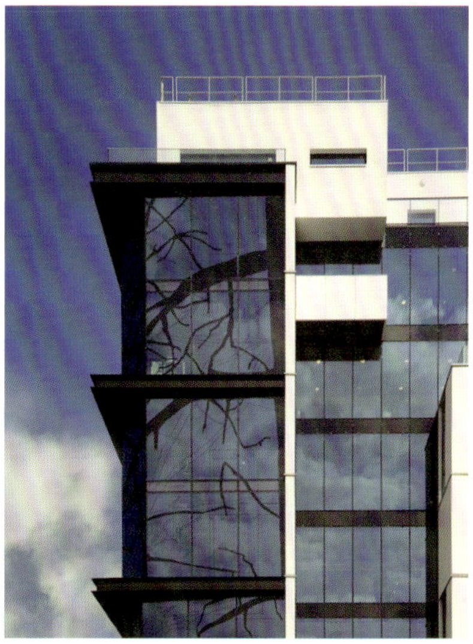
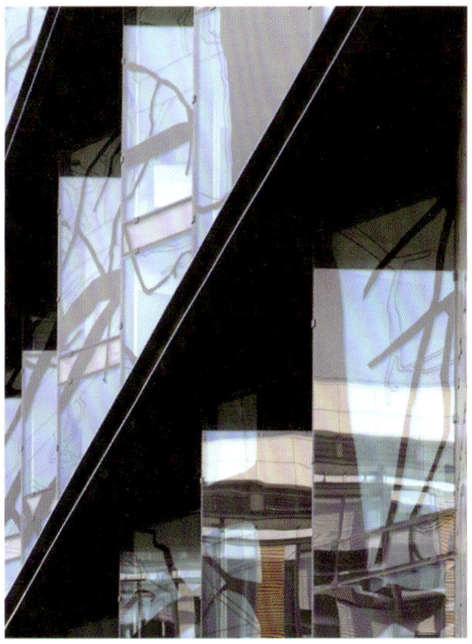
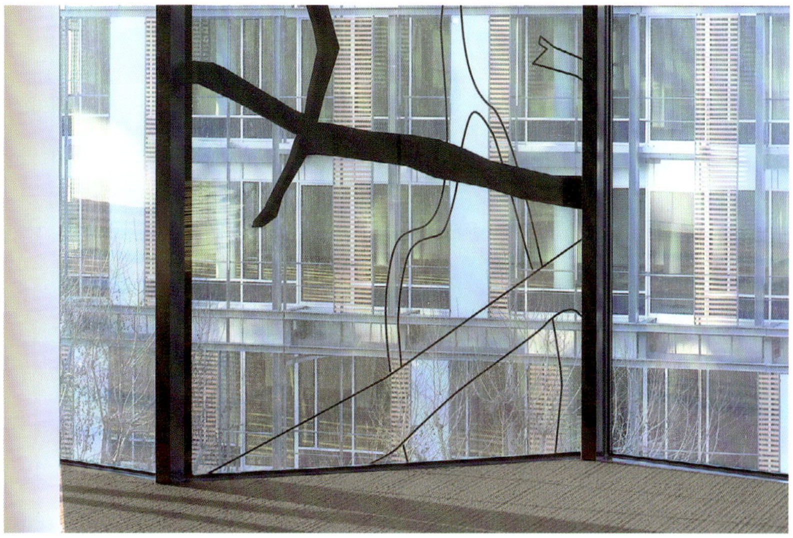

FRANCE_SAINT-MESMES **COMPANY HEADQUARTERS**

ARCHITECTS: LAN ARCHITECTURE
COMPLETION: 2008_**NUMBER OF WORKPLACES:** 25
GROSS FLOOR AREA: 1,000 M²
KIND OF WORKPLACES: CELLULAR, TEAM
PHOTOS: JEAN-MARIE MONTHIERS, PARIS

The primary intention of the project was to explore the relationship between the building and its surroundings. One of the main design concerns was the building's environmental adaptation and appropriation. Thus, the building was seen as a sort of line that simultaneously follows the skyline and the ground. The space was separated into two distinct volumes: one contains flexible work spaces, the other encloses a showroom, maintenance space and storage areas. The offices occupy the upper area of the site and are raised above ground level to provide an impression of lightness. The workshop volume is located at a lower level and gives the appearance of being solidly anchored to the ground.

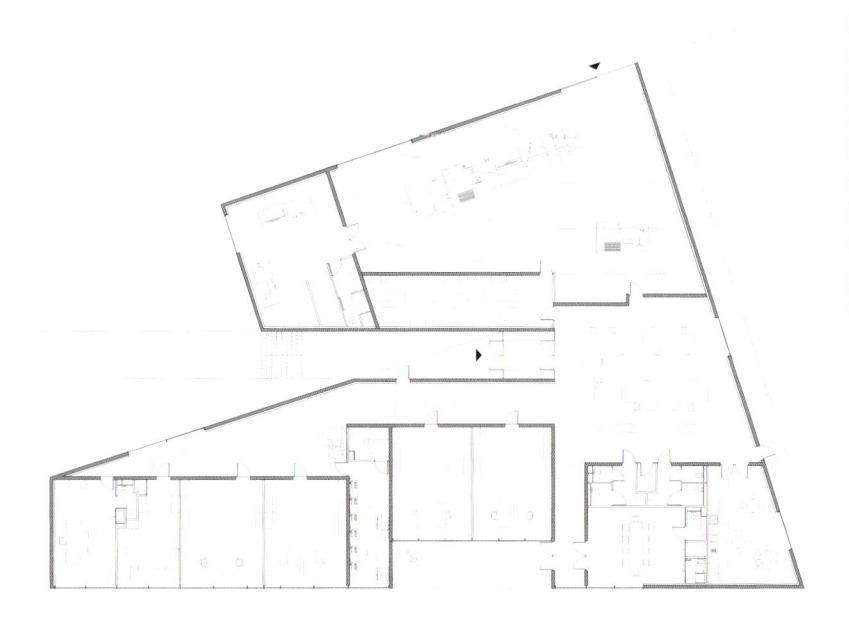

Dem Volumen liegt die Untersuchung des Verhältnisses zwischen Gebäude und Umgebung zugrunde. Eines der Hauptanliegen des Entwurfs war die Einpassung des Gebäudes in die Umgebung. Folglich wurde es als eine Art Linie ausgelegt, die gleichzeitig parallel zur Skyline und zum Boden verläuft. Der Raum wurde auf zwei verschiedene Bauteile verteilt: Der eine enthält flexible Arbeitsräume, der andere einen Ausstellungsraum, Verwaltungs- und Lagerräume. Die Büros befinden sich im oberen Bereich, der über einen Sockelbereich auskragend den Eindruck von Leichtigkeit vermittelt. Der gewerbliche Gebäudeteil liegt im Sockelgeschoss und scheint fest mit dem Boden verwachsen zu sein.

left: Ground floor plan_Office's volume view_Zoom of the cantilever. right: View to the entrance_Work spaces façade and the terrace_Working spaces open toward the landscape.
links: Grundriss Erdgeschoss_Ansicht Bürogebäude_Detail Ausleger. rechts: Blick zum Eingang_Fassade des Bürobereichs und der Terrasse_Büros mit freiem Blick in die Landschaft.

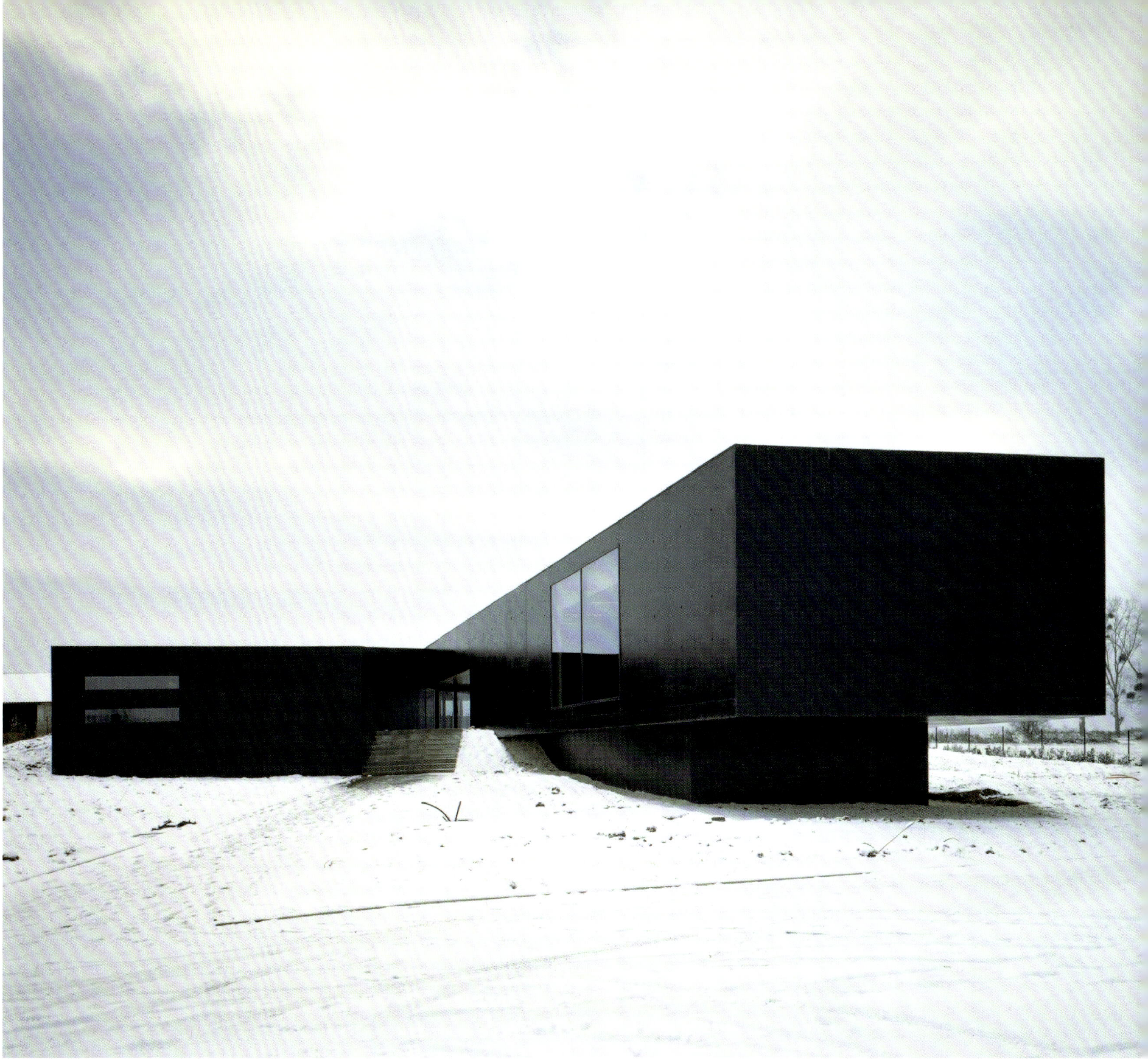

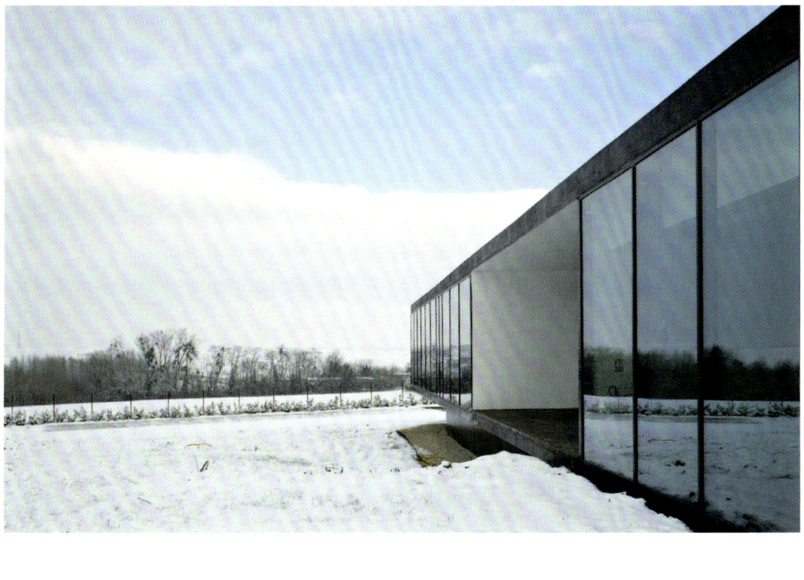

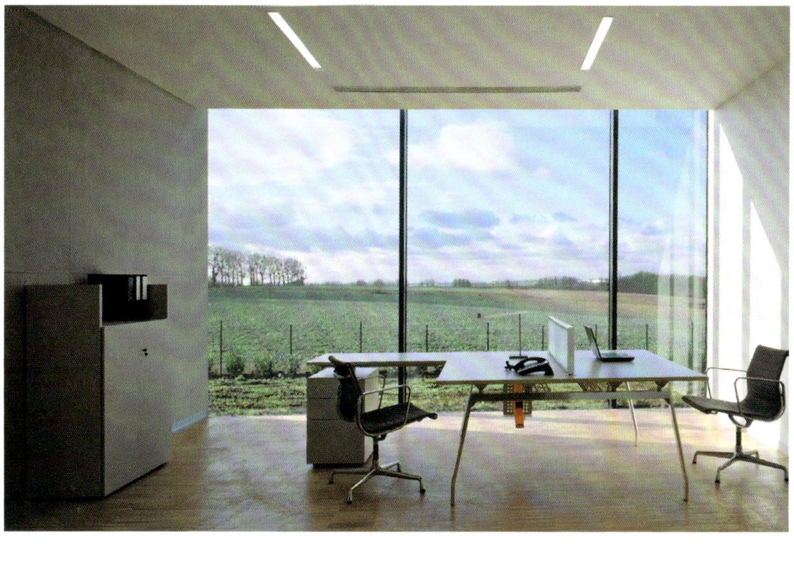

GERMANY_AACHEN BÖSL MEDIZINTECHNIK GMBH

ARCHITECTS: FISCHERARCHITEKTEN GMBH & CO. KG
COMPLETION: 2004_**NUMBER OF WORKPLACES:** 14
GROSS FLOOR AREA: 650 M²_**COMMON AREA:** TRAINING CENTER
KIND OF WORKPLACES: OPEN OFFICE AND PRODUCTION SPACE
PHOTOS: OLAF MAHLSTEDT, DÜSSELDORF, FISCHERARCHITEKTEN, AACHEN (114 R.)

An L-shaped facility with a steel-skeleton structure, the building encloses a development yard, which is used for parking and deliveries. The concept allows a subsequent modular extension into a U-shape. The ground floor of the administration section houses the sales department and the social room. The upper floor, with the training room and management office, can be reached via the entrée. The technical area and the sanitary facilities are located between the administration and production sections. The thermally insulated outer wall is constructed of sandwich elements with a ventilated metal façade, while generously applied glazing provides optimal natural illumination and attractive links to the free spaces.

Das Gebäude fasst als L-förmige Anlage in Stahlskelettbauweise einen Erschließungshof ein, der dem Parken und der Anlieferung dient. Das Konzept ermöglicht eine spätere modulare Erweiterung zur U-Form. Im Erdgeschoss des Verwaltungstraktes befinden sich die Verkaufsabteilung und der Sozialraum. Über das Entreé erreicht man das Obergeschoss mit Schulungsraum und Büro der Firmenleitung. Zwischen Verwaltungstrakt und Produktion befinden sich die Technikzone sowie Sanitäranlagen. Die hochwärmegedämmte Außenwand wurde aus Sandwichelementen mit hinterlüfteter Metallfassade errichtet, großzügige Verglasungen sorgen für optimale, natürliche Belichtung und angenehme Freiraumbezüge.

left: Ground floor plan_Entrance area_Lobby. right: West façade_Administration area_Production area.
links: Grundriss Erdgeschoss_Eingangsbereich_Eingangshalle. rechts: Westfassade_Verwaltungsbereich_Produktion.

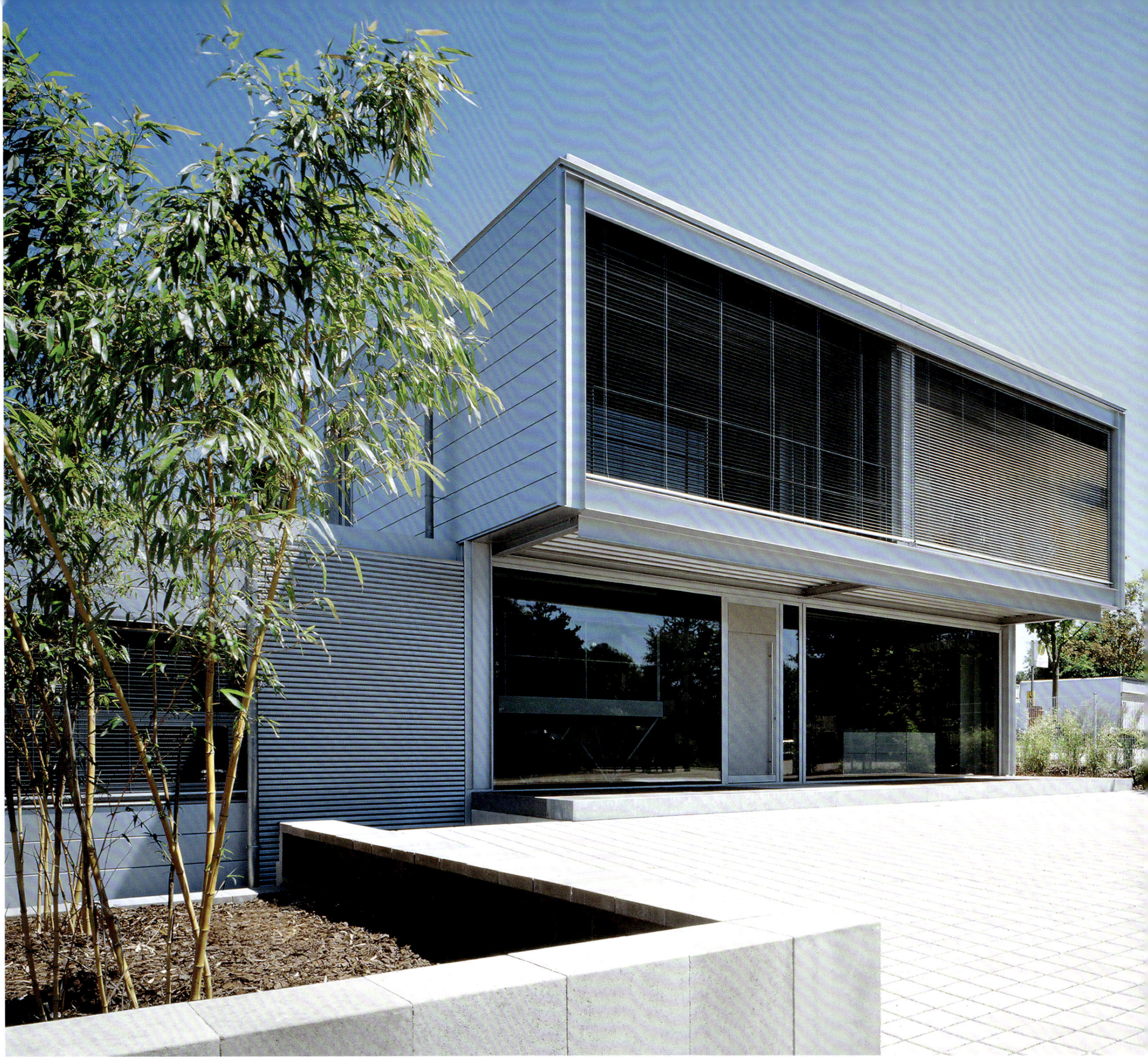
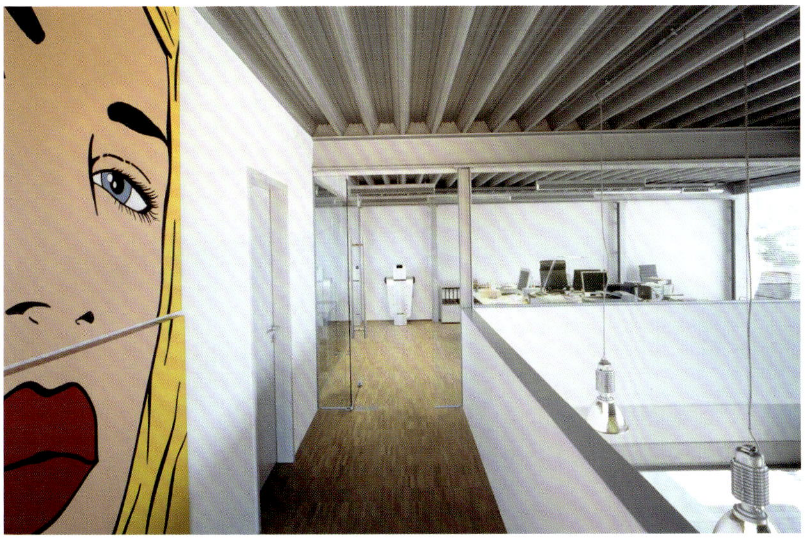
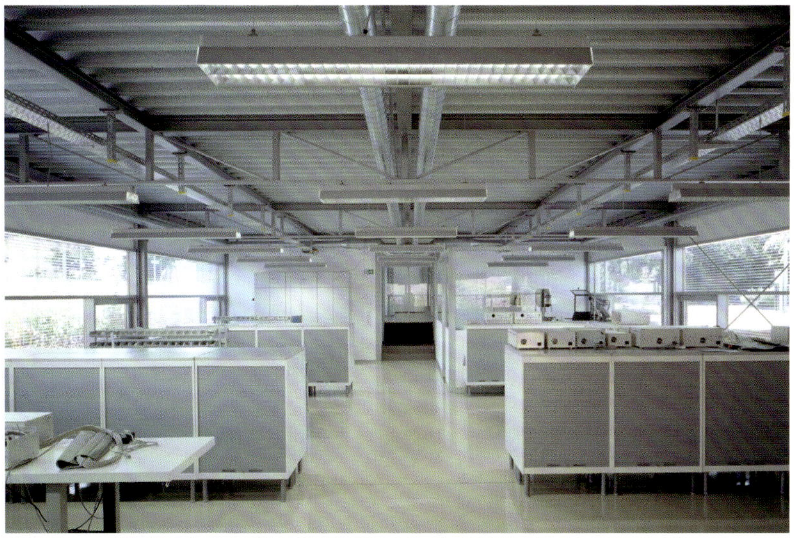

GERMANY_AACHEN MONASTERY ST. ALFONS

ARCHITECTS: ARGE KLOSTER ST. ALFONS: KAISER SCHWEITZER ARCHITEKTEN AND GLASHAUS ARCHITEKTEN PSG
PROJECT DEVELOPMENT: SCHLEIFF DENKMALENTWICKLUNG GMBH & CO KG, ERKELENZ_**ORIGINAL BUILDING:** H. J. WIETHASE, 1865_**COMPLETION:** 2009_**NUMBER OF WORKPLACES:** 100
NET FLOOR AREA: 3,700 M²_**COMMON AREA:** GARDEN, ATRIUM_**KIND OF WORKPLACES:** CELLULAR, COMBINATION
PHOTOS: LANDES FOTOGRAFIE, DORTMUND

After being rebuilt following destruction in the war, the monastery was converted several times. In 2005, the year it was sold by the diocese, the church room featured the minimalist style of the Society of Jesus. This character was preserved in the new use concept along with the monastery and church space as monuments. A 'glass case' positioned in front of the monastery provides access to all office floors. The reversible gallery level in the aisles created space for additional offices. The central nave is available to all employees as a multi-purpose communication zone and serves as a lecture, discussion or concert hall. Meeting rooms are located in the apse, the chapel, and on a new floor underneath the rose window.

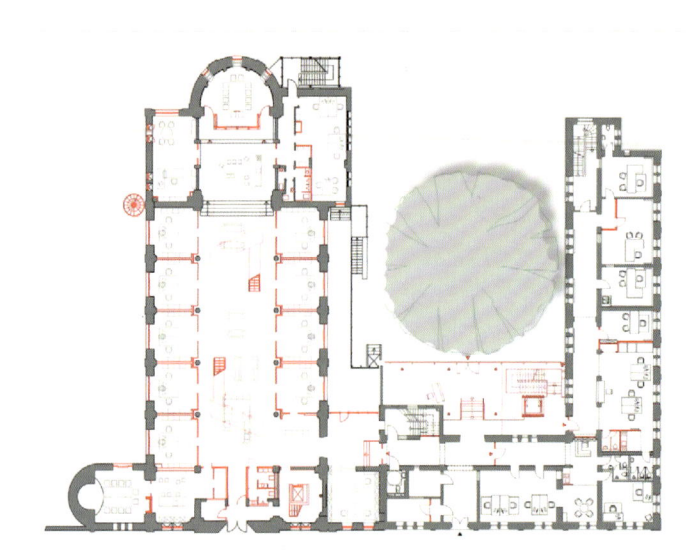

Das Kloster wurde nach Kriegzerstörung und Wiederaufbau mehrfach umgestaltet. 2005, im Jahr der Veräußerung durch das Bistum, war der Kirchenraum durch die karge Gestaltung des Jesuitenordens geprägt. Das neue Büronutzungskonzept erhält das gesamte Denkmal und den Charakter des Kloster- und Kirchenraum. Eine vor das Kloster gesetzte ‚Glasvitrine' erschließt alle Bürogeschosse. Die reversible Galerieebene in den Seitenschiffen bildet Raum für zusätzliche Büros. Das Mittelschiff steht als kommunikative Kombizone allen Mitarbeitern zur Verfügung und dient als Vortrags-, Diskussions- oder Konzertraum. Besprechungsräume sind in der Apsis, in der Kapelle und in einer neuen Ebene unterhalb des Rosenfensters untergebracht.

left: Ground floor plan_Meeting room rose window_Espresso bar chapell. right: Combination zone nave_Nave_Offices.
links: Grundriss Erdgeschoss_Besprechungsraum mit Rosenfenster_Espressobar Kapelle. rechts: Kombizone Mittelschiff_Mittelschiff_Büros.

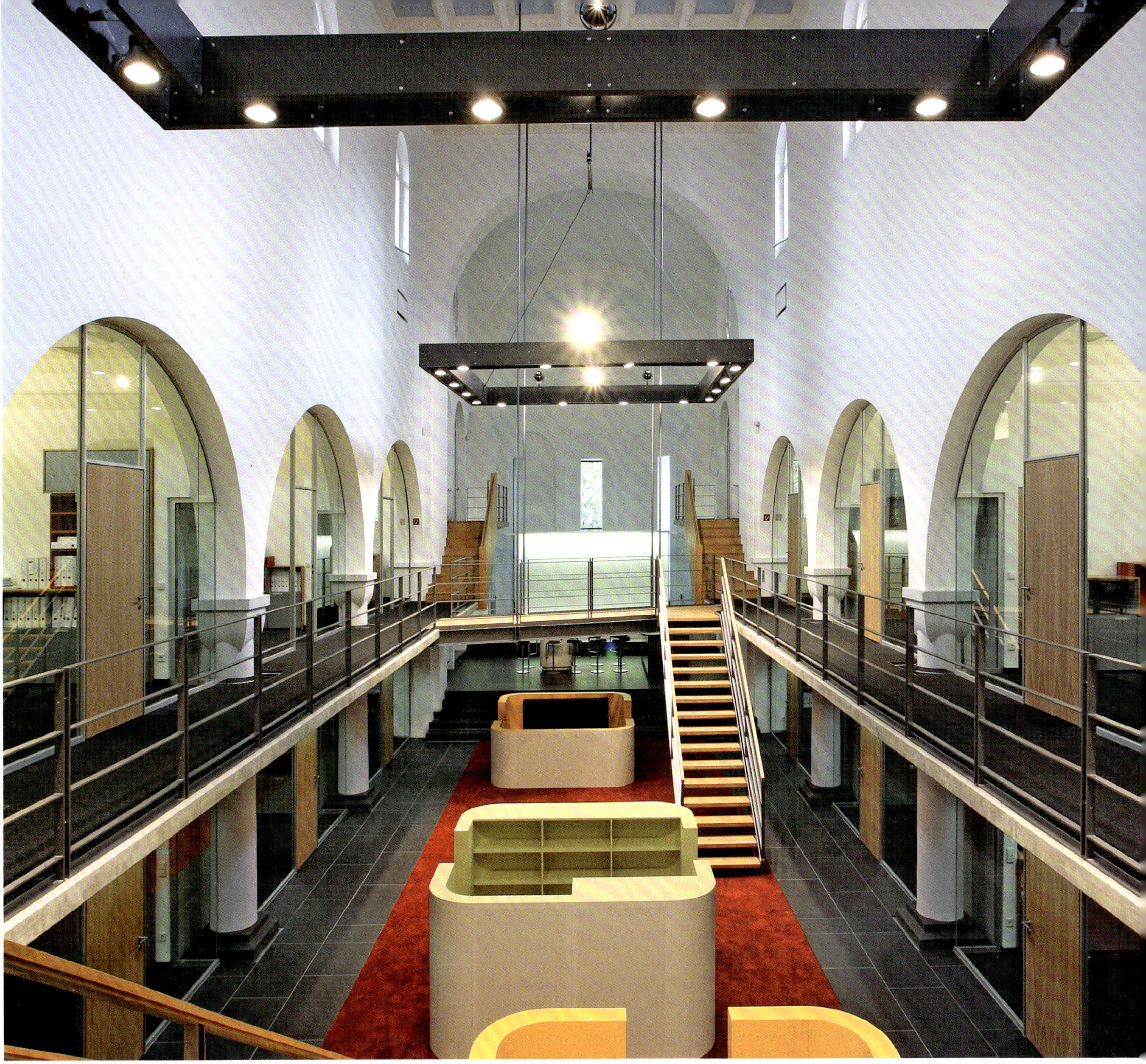

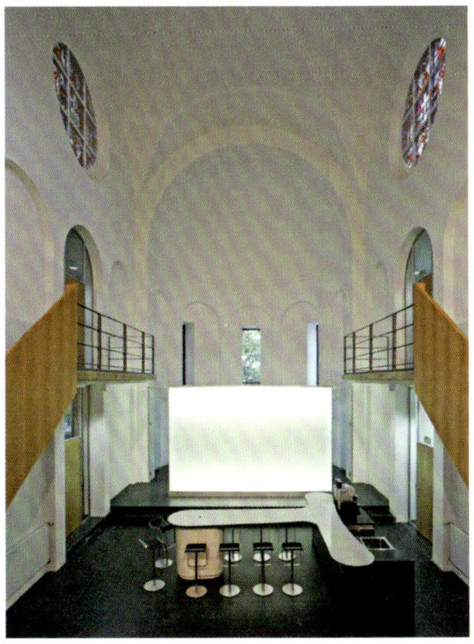

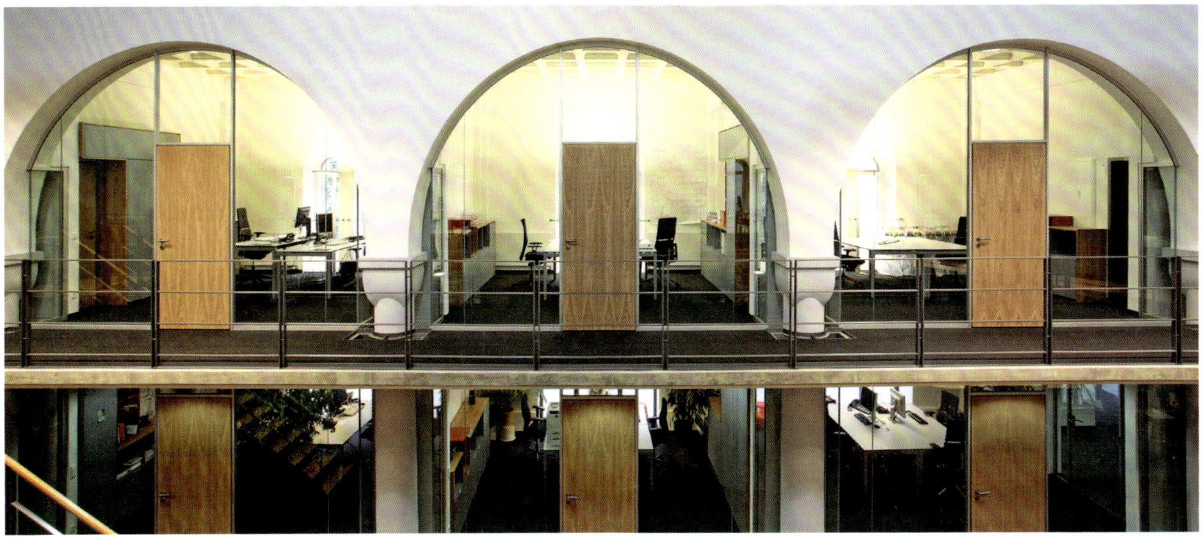

GERMANY_BERLIN **DAIMLER CHRYSLER MARKETING OFFICE**

ARCHITECTS: HEMPRICH TOPHOF ARCHITEKTEN
COMPLETION: 2004_**NUMBER OF WORKPLACES:** 800
GROSS FLOOR AREA: 21,000 M²_**COMMON AREA:** SHOWROOM, GARAGE, CONFERENCE ROOMS, CANTEEN_**KIND OF WORKPLACES:** CELLULAR, COMBINATION_**PHOTOS:** WILMAR KÖNIG, BERLIN, NORBERT MEISE, BERLIN (116 A.)

The office high rise of Daimler Sales Germany is a dominant urban structure near the Charlottenburg Tor that constitutes the entrance to a new city district. Its six-floor base building incorporates the entire building block. On its ground and first floor it includes Germany's largest Smart Center with a showroom and workshop, which are accented and illuminated by the inner courtyards. The various opening sizes and a portico of the dark and light natural stone façades are suited for current and future uses. The office areas on the upper floors can be flexibly laid out and contain conference areas on every floor.

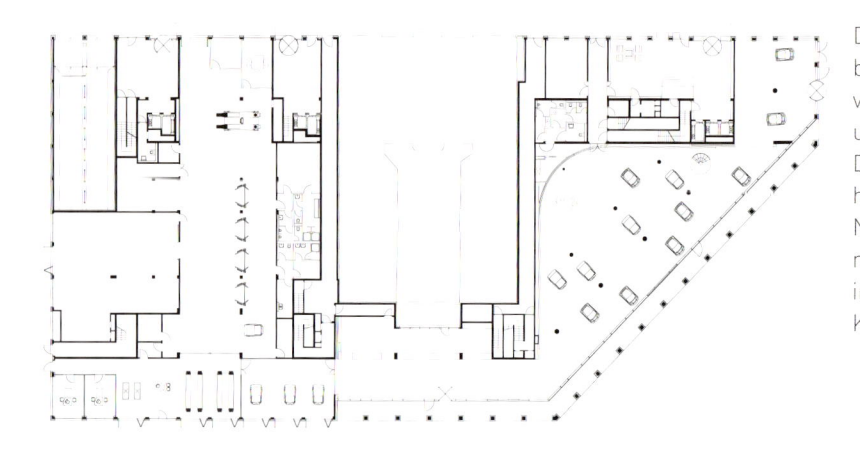

Das Bürohochhaus der Daimler Vertrieb Deutschland bildet am Charlottenburger Tor eine städtebauliche Dominate als Eingang in ein neues Stadtviertel. Seine sechsstöckige Fußbebauung umfasst den gesamten Baublock und integriert im Erd- und ersten Obergeschoss das größte Smart Center Deutschlands mit Showroom und Werkstatt, die durch die verglasten Innenhöfe akzentuiert und belichtet werden. Die Fassaden aus dunklem und hellen Naturstein reagieren mit unterschiedlichen Öffnungsgrößen und einer Kolonnade auf die heutigen und zukünftig geplanten Nutzungen. Die Büroflächen in den Obergeschossen sind flexibel aufteilbar und beinhalten etagenweise Konferenzbereiche.

left: Ground floor plan_Garage courtyard_Smart showroom. right: Exterior_View out of Smart showroom_North-east elevation.
links: Grundriss Erdgeschoss_Werkstatthof_Smart Showroom. rechts: Außenansicht_Blick aus dem Smart-Showroom_Nordostfassade.

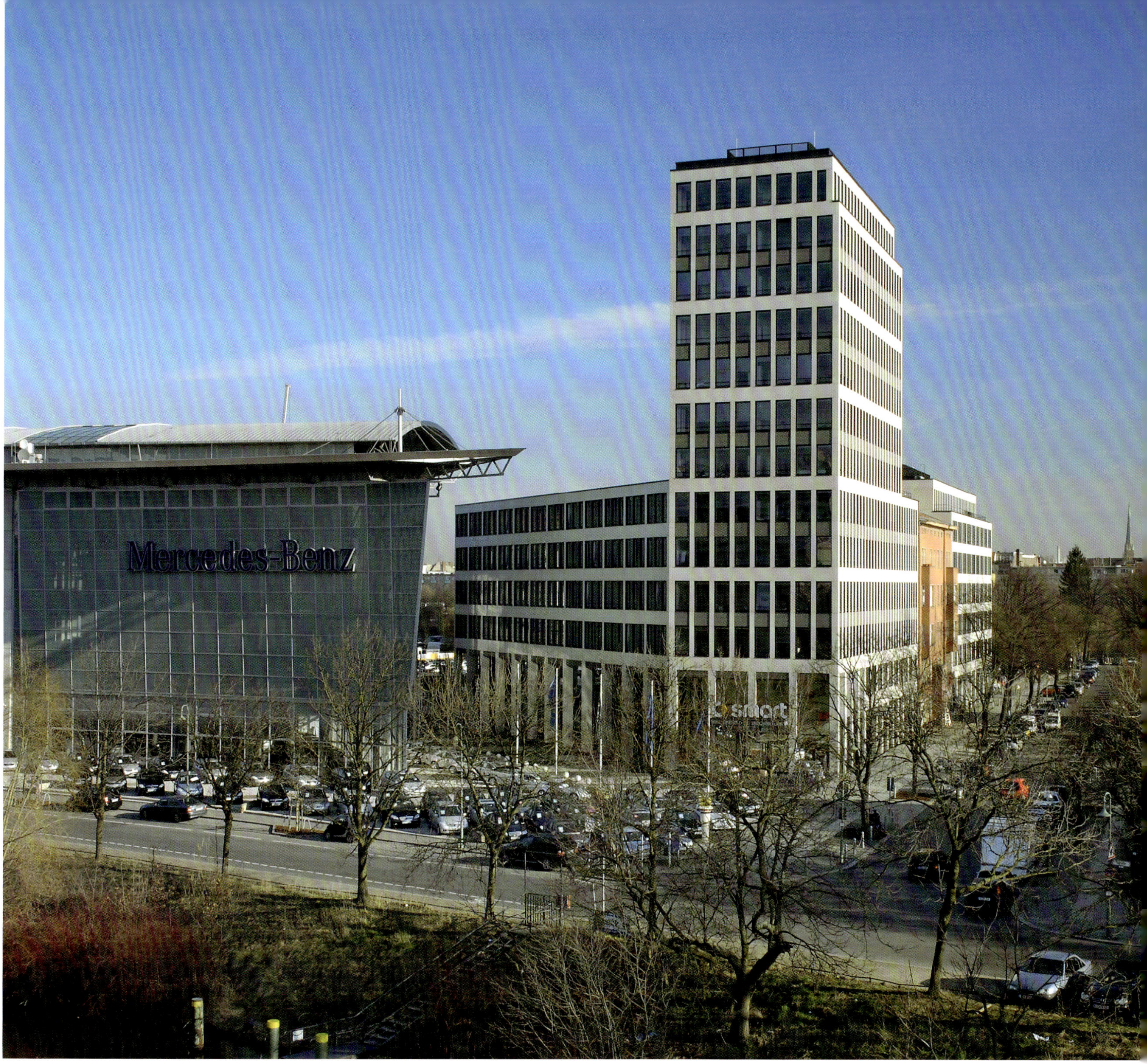
Mercedes-Benz
smart

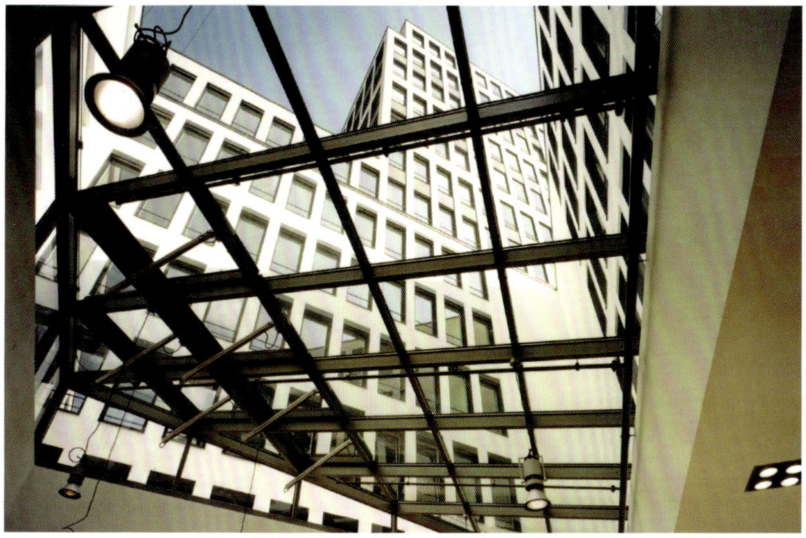

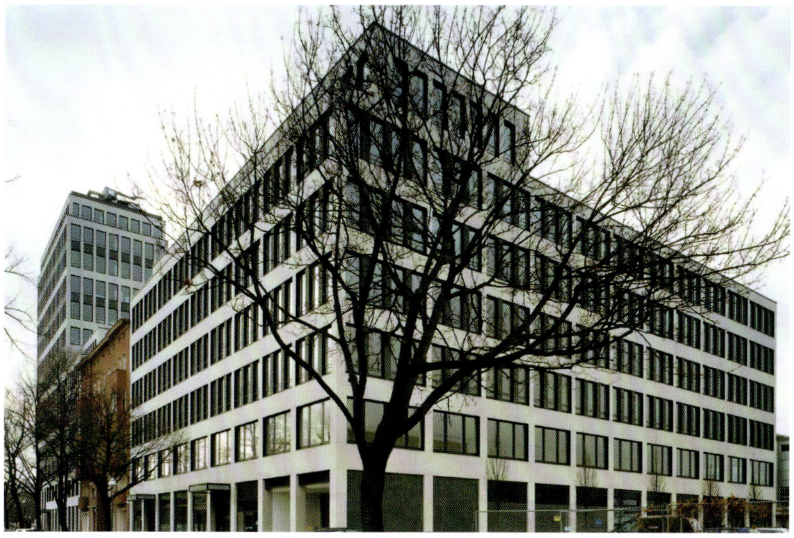

GERMANY_BERLIN ABSPANNWERK BUCHHÄNDLER WEG

ARCHITECTS: HSH HOYER SCHINDELE HIRSCHMÜLLER
ORIGINAL ARCHITECT: HANS HEINRICH MÜLLER
COMPLETION: 2005_**NUMBER OF WORKPLACES:** 320
GROSS FLOOR AREA: 13,000 M²_**COMMON AREA:** ROOF TERRACE
KIND OF WORKPLACES: CELLULAR, LOUNGE WORKSPACE
PHOTOS: ANNE KRIEGER (118 B. L., M.), NOSHE (118 B. R.), HSH ARCHITEKTEN (118 B. R., 119 A., B. M., B. R.), ELKE STAMM (119 B. L.)

The restructuring of this power plant reactivated a long since abandoned area near the former German wall. The traces of history remain visible on the building today. The existing building substance was restored in line with monument protection regulations. It continues to express the history of the site with contrasting shapes and materials. The landmarked halls have been preserved in their structure, the upper floors, however radically changed in order to adapt them to the office use. These changes to the façade can be seen through colored glass balustrades located in front of the windows. The softly shaped new staircase of anodized aluminum contrasts with the expressionist existing architecture.

Mit dem Umbau des E-Werks wurde ein lange verstummter Ort am ehemaligen Mauerstreifen reaktiviert. Die Spuren der Geschichte sind heute noch im Gebäude lesbar. Die bestehende Bausubstanz wurde denkmalgerecht wieder hergestellt und durch neue Bauteile ergänzt. In einer kontrastierenden Formen- und Materialsprache erzählen sie die Geschichte des Ortes weiter. Die denkmalgeschützten Hallen wurden in ihrer Struktur erhalten, die Obergeschosse hingegen tiefgreifend verändert, um sie an die Büronutzung anzupassen. Durch farbige Glasbrüstungen vor den Fenstern zeichnen sich diese Veränderungen in der Fassade ab. Das weich geformte neue Treppenhaus aus eloxiertem Aluminium kontrastiert mit der spätexpressionistischen Bestandsarchitektur.

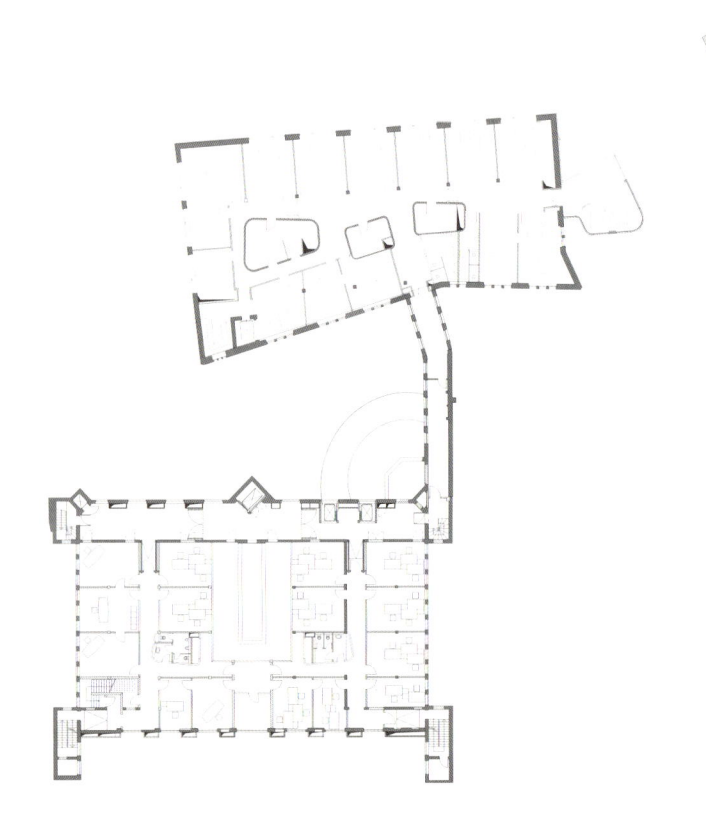

left: Floor plans, offices_New staircase, perspective_New staircase made of anodized aluminum, added on the northern section of the building_Access from corridor to office space. right: Exterior_Interior, corridor_Slightly narrowing aluminum gate, which marks the transition from the central corridor to the individual offices_Rest rooms in Hall F.
links: Grundrisse, Bürogeschosse_Neues Treppenhaus, Perspektive_Neues Treppenhaus aus eloxiertem Aluminium, hinzugefügt am nördlichen Gebäudetrakt_Zugang vom Flur zum Bürobereich. rechts: Außenansicht_Innenansicht, Flur. Sich leicht verengende Aluminiumschleuse, die den Übergang vom zentralen Flur zu den einzelnen Büros kennzeichnet_Sanitärtrakt in Halle F.

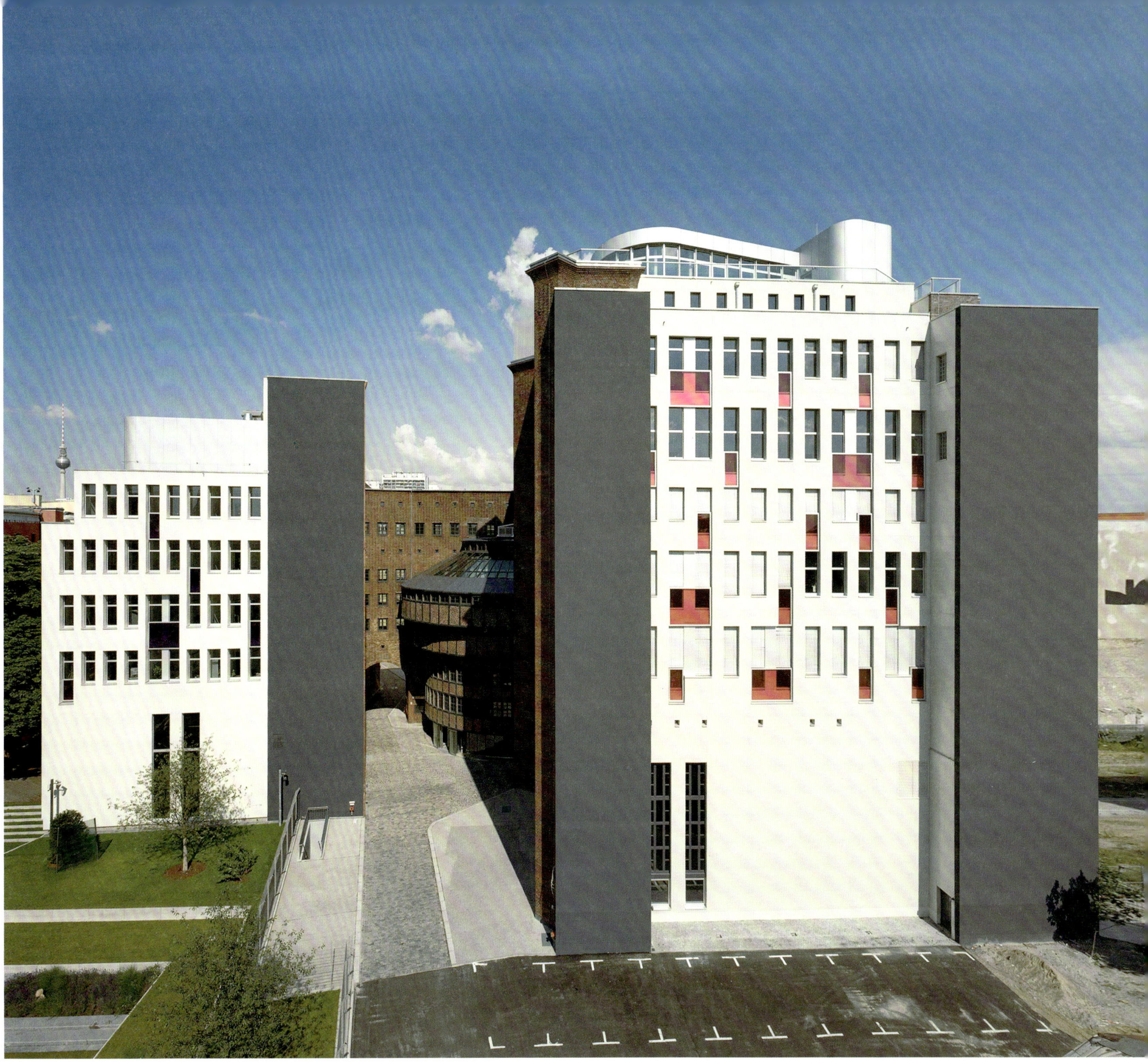

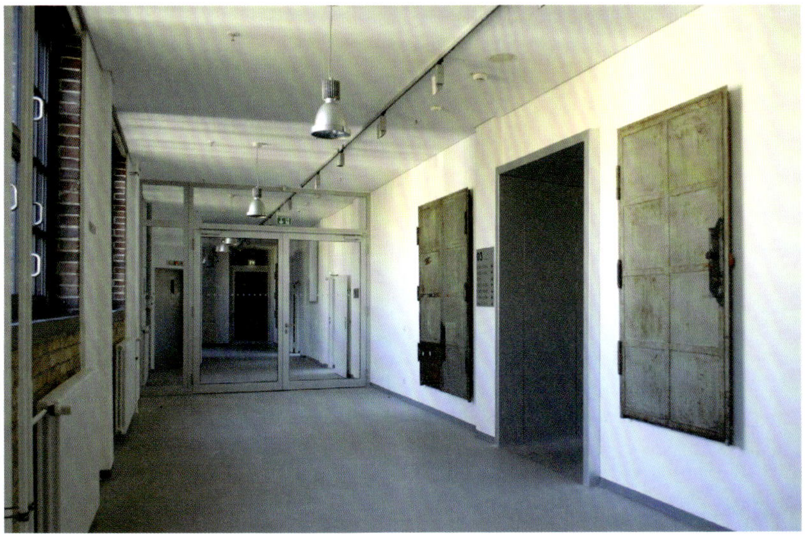

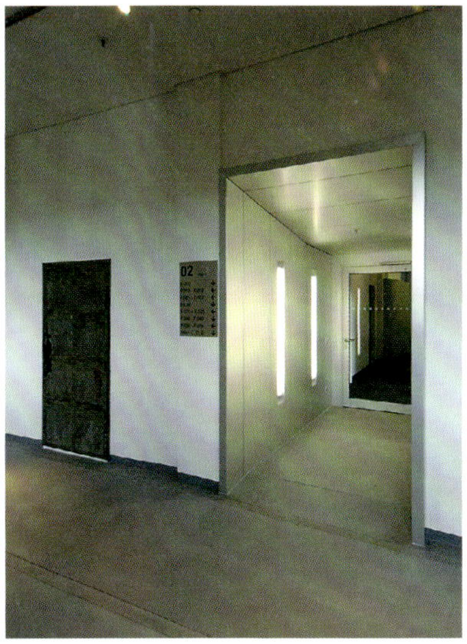

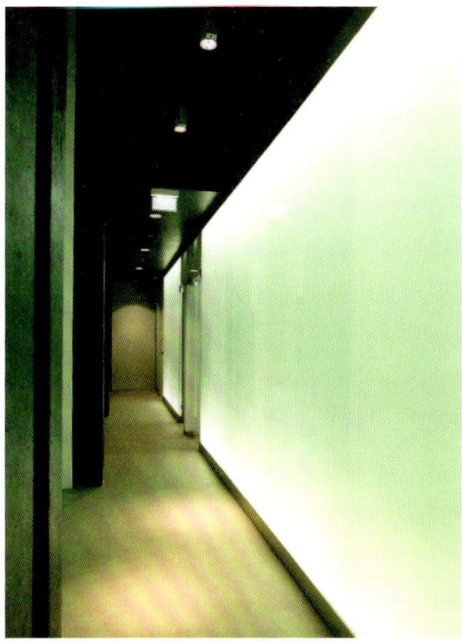

GERMANY_BERLIN ORCO GERMANY

ARCHITECTS: IRIS STEINBECK ARCHITEKTEN
COMPLETION: 2007_**ORIGINAL BUILDING:** 1908
NUMBER OF WORKPLACES: 45_**GROSS FLOOR AREA:** 1,500 M²
COMMON AREA: RECEPTION AND WAITING AREA INCLUDING KITCHEN AREA, PRASENTATIONS, MEETING ROOMS
KIND OF WORKPLACES: CELLULAR, TEAM, BUSINESS CLUB, LOUNGE WORKSPACE_**PHOTOS:** WERNER HUTHMACHER, BERLIN

The dissolving of segmented utilization areas created a consistent work environment. The reception area with levitating Corian counters, is connected to the kitchen area by a back-lit media wall, also made of Corian. In addition to the blue back-lit company logo, two plasma monitors are integrated into the wall and can be covered by a sliding door if required. The color white conveys an atmosphere of clarity and concentration. In addition to painted MDF, there are leather-covered wall areas with fold-out benches. The open kitchen area is used for presentations, working, eating, and team meetings.

Durch Auflösung segmentierter Nutzungsbereiche wurde ein konsistentes Arbeitsumfeld geschaffen. Der Empfangsbereich mit frei schwebenden Tresen aus Corian, ist über eine hinterleuchtete Medienwand, ebenfalls aus Corian, mit dem Küchenbereich verbunden. Neben dem blau hinterleuchteten Firmenlogo sind zwei Plasmabildschirme in die Wand integriert, welche auf Wunsch durch eine Gleittür verdeckt werden können. Die Farbe Weiß vermittelt in ihrer atmosphärischen Stimmung Klarheit und Konzentration. Neben lackiertem MDF finden sich in Leder bezogene Wandfelder mit ausklappbarer Sitzbank. In dem offenen Küchenbereich wird präsentiert, gearbeitet, gegessen und es finden Teammeetings statt.

left: Second floor plan_Team office_Corridor. right: Conference room.
links: Grundriss zweites Obergeschoss_Teambüro _Flur. rechts: Konferenzraum.

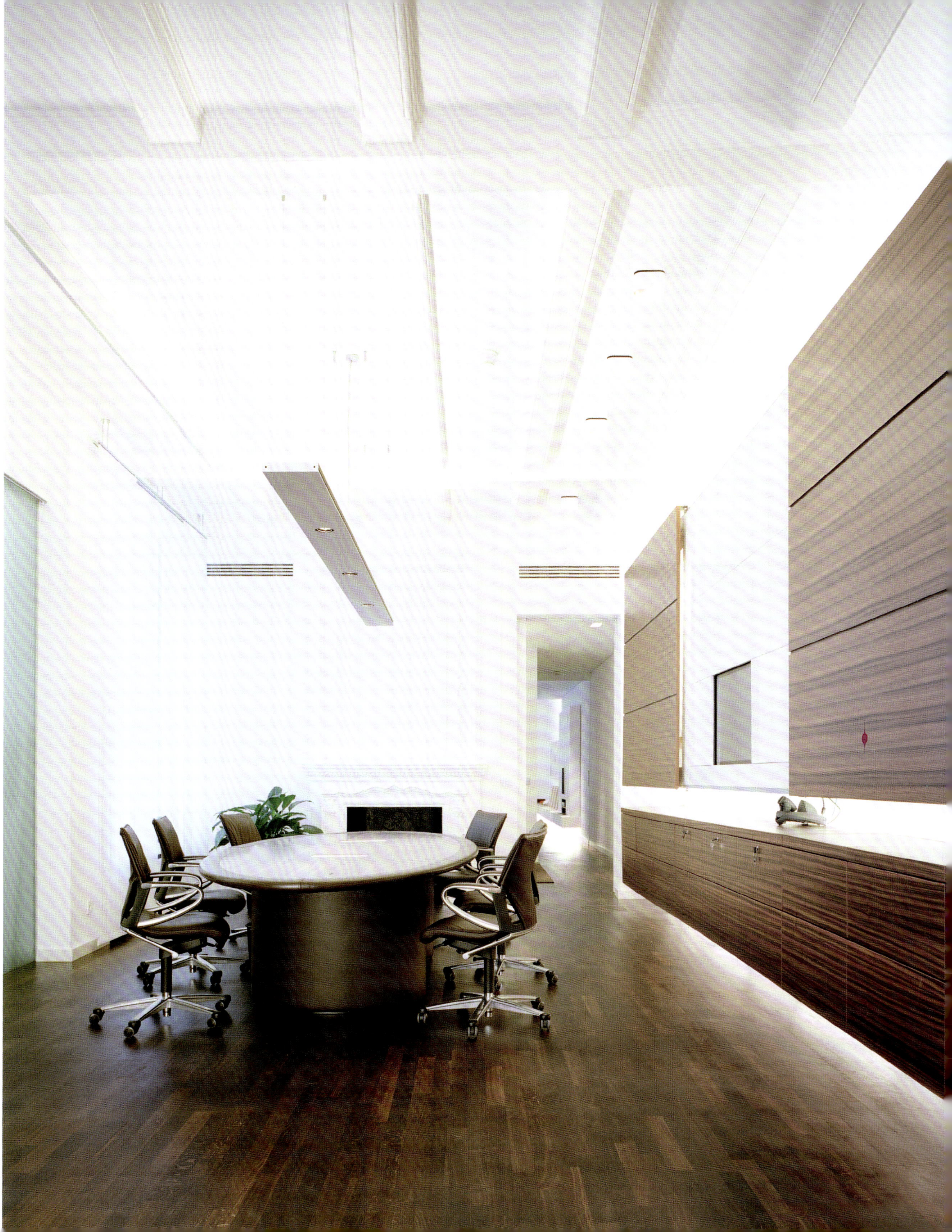

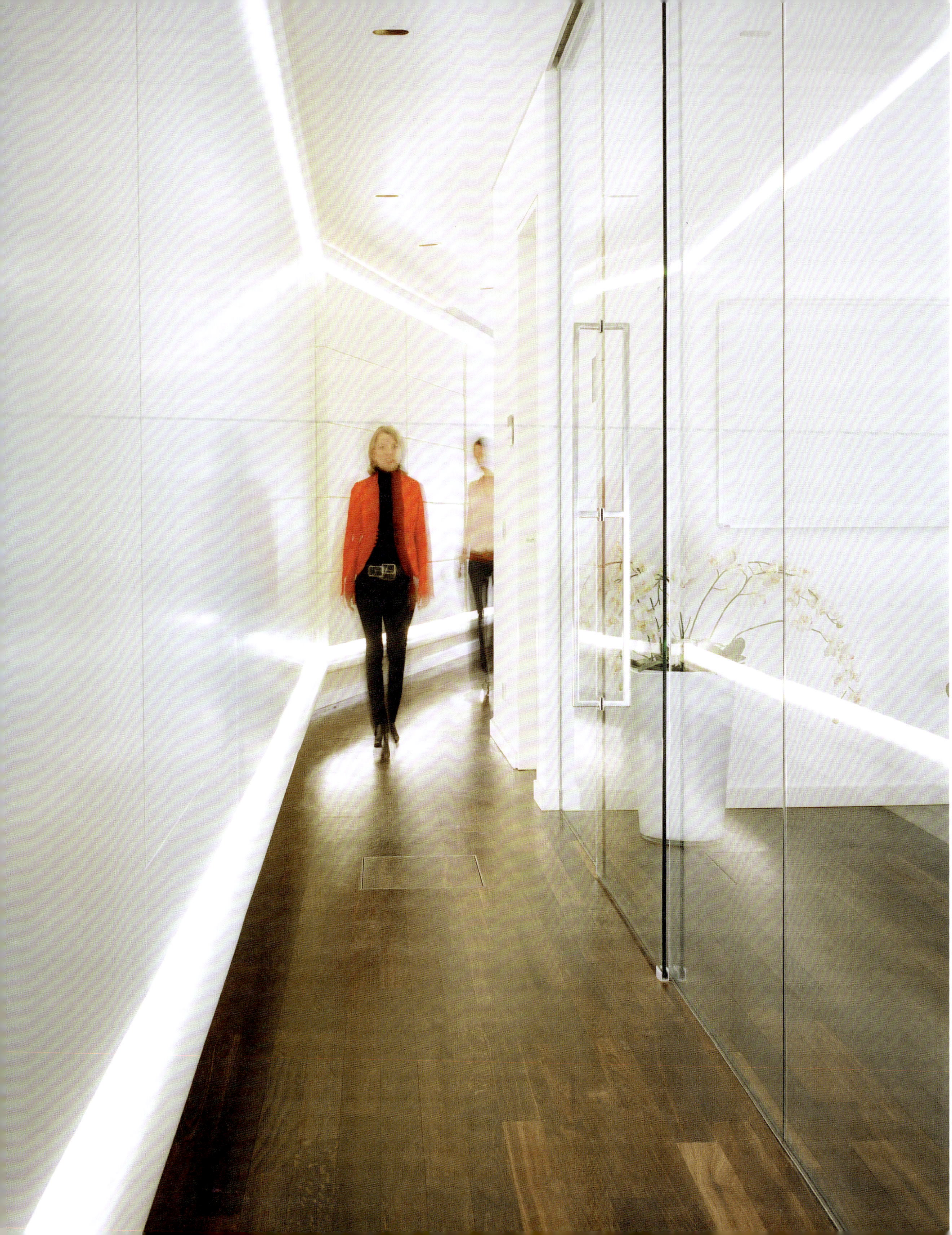

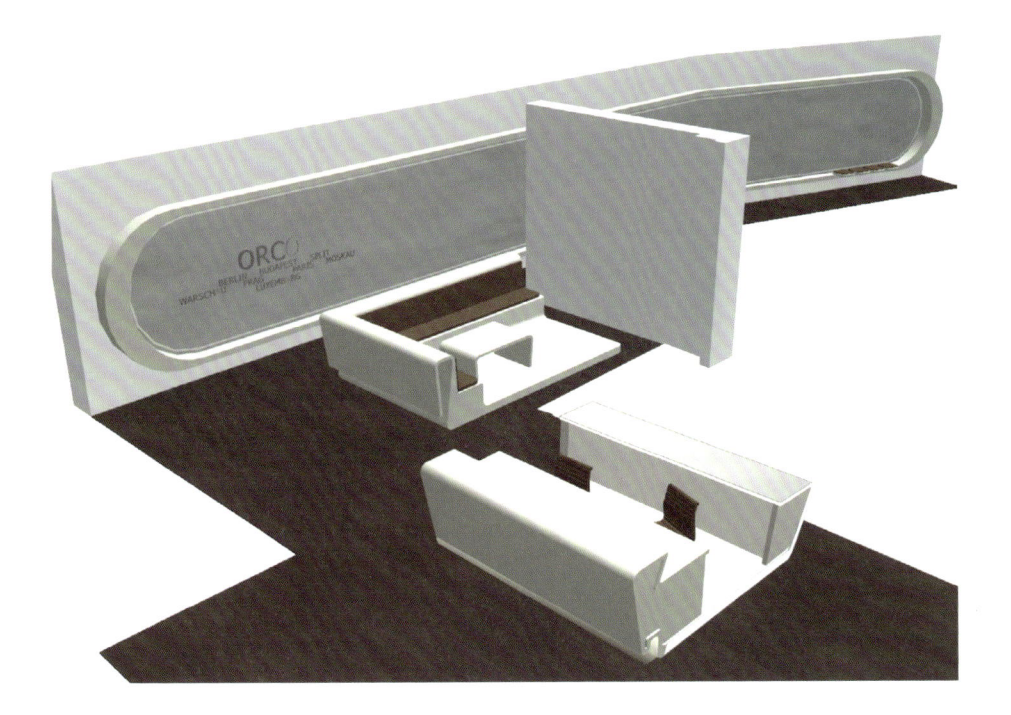

left: Media wall between reception and kitchen area. right: Design study reception_Reception and media wall_Kitchen.

links: Medienwand zwischen.Empfang und Küchenbereich. rechts: Vorentwurfsstudie Empfang_ Empfang und Medienwand_Corian-Tresen_Küche.

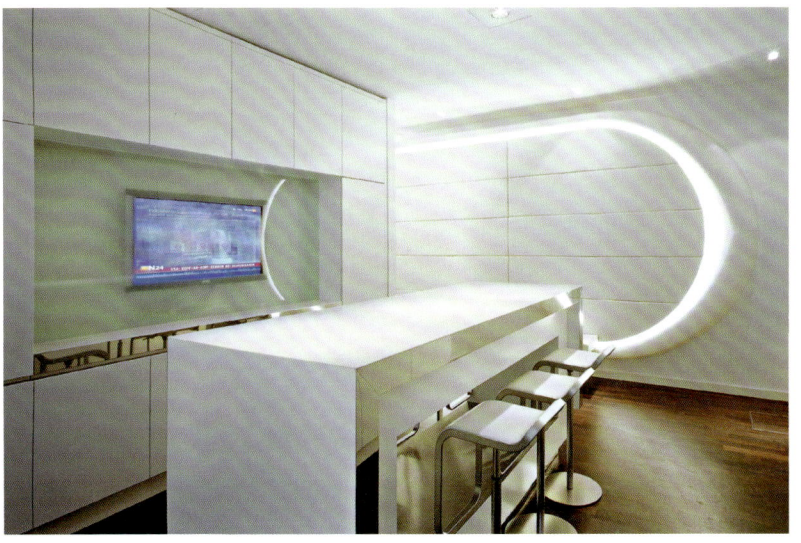

GERMANY_BERLIN DEUTSCHER CARITASVERBAND E.V.

ARCHITECTS: VONBOCK ARCHITEKTEN_**COMPLETION:** 2005
NUMBER OF WORKPLACES: 40_**GROSS FLOOR AREA:** 2,700 M²
COMMON AREA: CONFERENCE ROOMS, ORATORY, SMALL KITCHENS, SOCIAL ROOMS_**KIND OF WORKPLACES:** CELLULAR
PHOTOS: KLAUS VON BOCK

The new building is part of a landmarked ensemble near the Reinhardtstraße, the axle between Friedrichstadtpalast and Reichstag. The building incorporates the eaves height of the historical neighboring buildings, but with its own interpretation of their curb roofs in the shape of a classic Berlin stepped roof floor. The façade reflects the style of the neighboring older buildings, while the perfect curve of glass and natural rock incorporates the classic modernity style of Berlin. In the heart of the vibrant metropolitan life, the conference rooms and the chapel are located at eye level with passers-by. They are topped by four administrative floors, while the recessed roof floor offers apartments with a view of the city roofs.

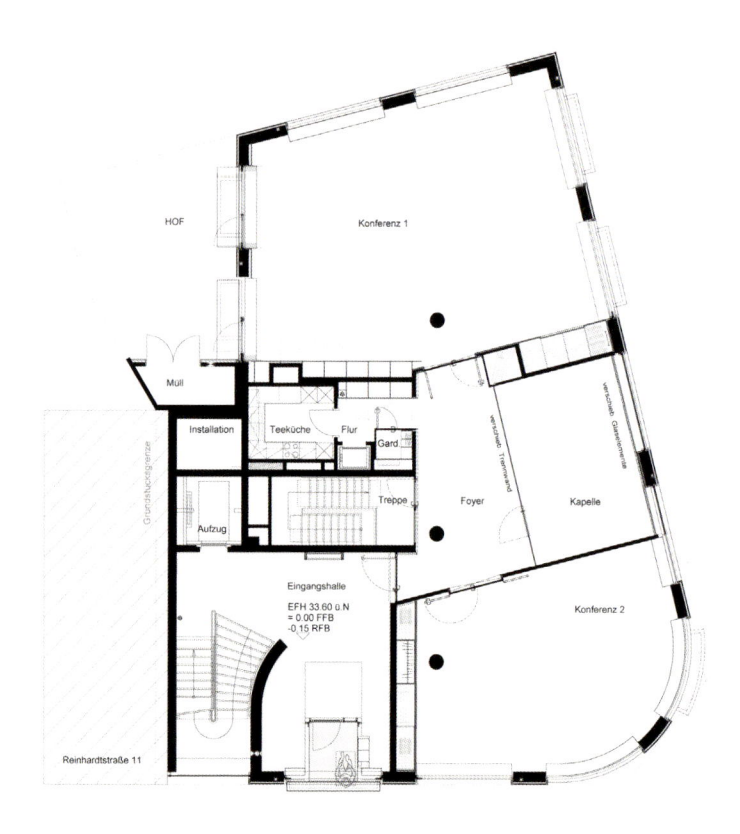

Der Neubau steht in einem denkmalgeschützten Ensemble an der Reinhardtstraße, in der Achse zwischen Friedrichstadtpalast und Reichstag. Das Gebäude nimmt die Trauflinie der historischen Nachbargebäude auf. An Stelle von deren Mansarddächern wurde hier jedoch eine Lösung mit klassischem Berliner Staffeldachgeschoss gewählt. Die Fassade nimmt Bezug auf angrenzende Altbauten, die perfekte Rundung aus Glas und Naturstein bezieht Berlins klassische Moderne ein. Inmitten des pulsierenden Großstadtlebens liegen Konferenzräume und eine Kapelle auf gleicher Augenhöhe mit den Passanten. Es folgen vier Verwaltungsgeschosse, während das zurückgesetzte Dachgeschoss Wohnungen mit Ausblick über die Dächer der Stadt bietet.

left: Ground floor plan_Entrance area_Conference room. right: North-west elevation_Oratory_Corridor, administration floor.
links: Grundriss Erdgeschoss_Eingangsbereich_Konferenzraum. rechts: Nordwestansicht_Hauskapelle_Flur Verwaltungsgeschoss.

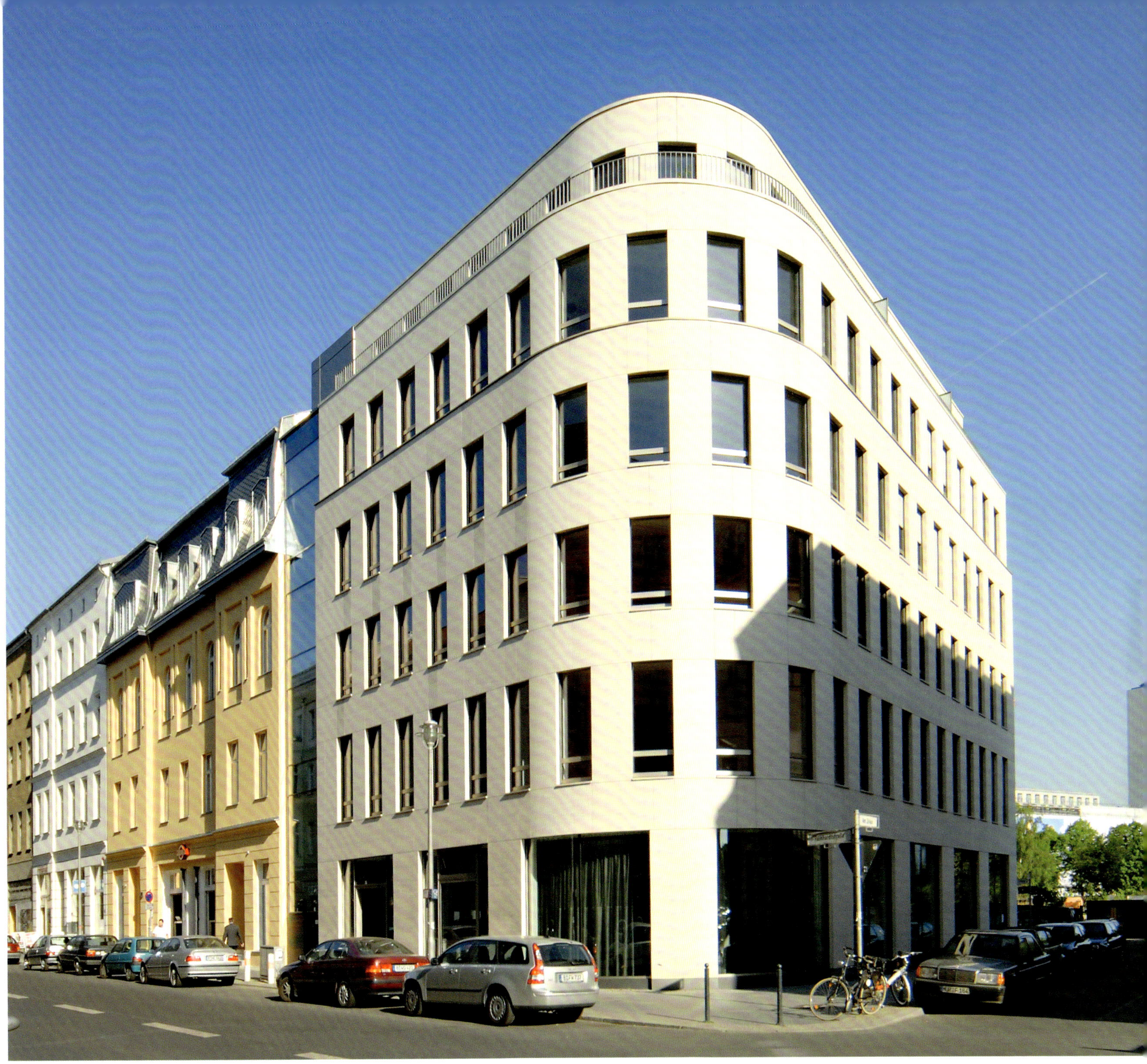

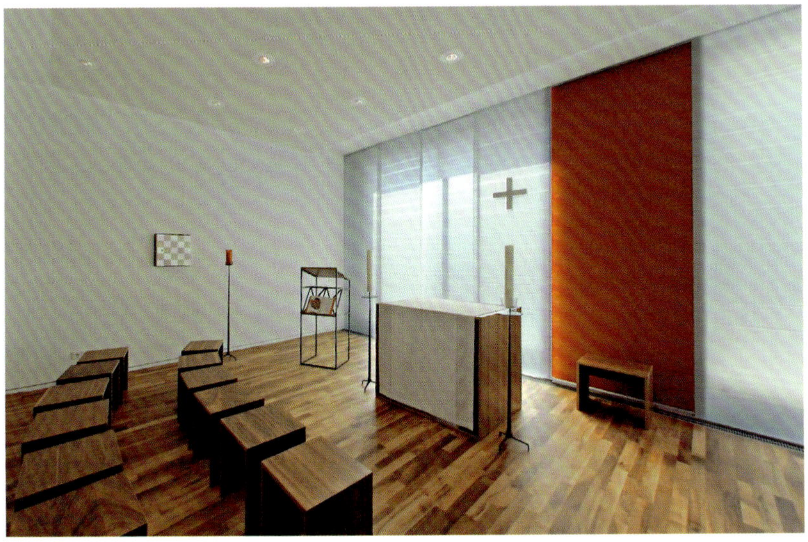

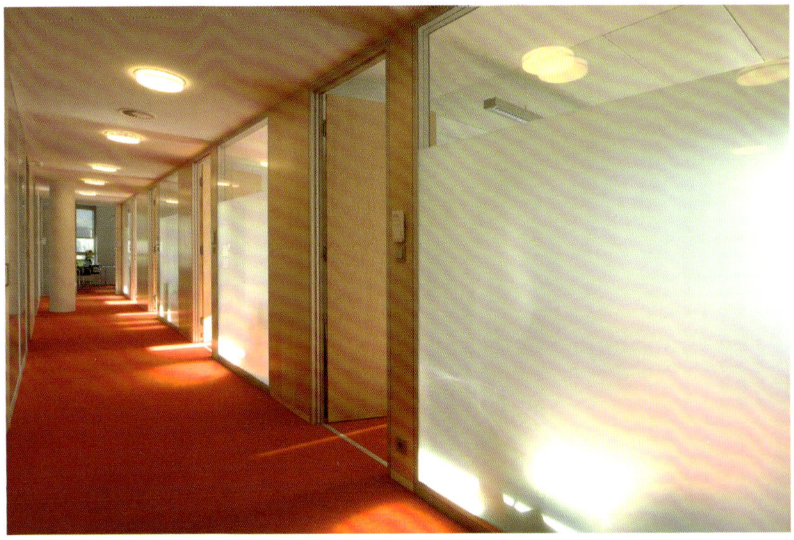

GERMANY_BIBERACH A. D. RISS ENBW CENTER OBERSCHWABEN

ARCHITECTS: WMA WÖHR MIESLINGER ARCHITEKTEN
OTHER CREATIVES: DREES & SOMMER, BDE BORNSCHEUER DREXLER EISELE, THURM UND DINGES, GÄNSSLE + HEHR
COMPLETION: 2008_**NUMBER OF WORKPLACES:** 550
GROSS FLOOR AREA: 20,876 M²_**COMMON AREA:** CASINO, CONFERENCE AREA_**KIND OF WORKPLACES:** OPEN-PLAN, BUSINESS CLUB_**PHOTOS:** WMA / THOMAS MÜLLER, STUTTGART

As a ring-shaped structure, the new building constitutes a distinguished entrance building to the new quarter. The southern longitudinal side is the background for a prestigious square in front of the main entrance. Inside, the building contains a greened inner courtyard with an outdoor terrace for the company restaurant. The façade consists of pre-fabricated timber-post-and-beam elements with fixed glazing, high format revolving leafs and sliding shutters. Horizontally, the facade is structured by distinctly molded aluminum aprons at the position of the ceiling fronts. Air conditioned via geothermal energy, the office areas are divided into different room zones via flexible system division walls.

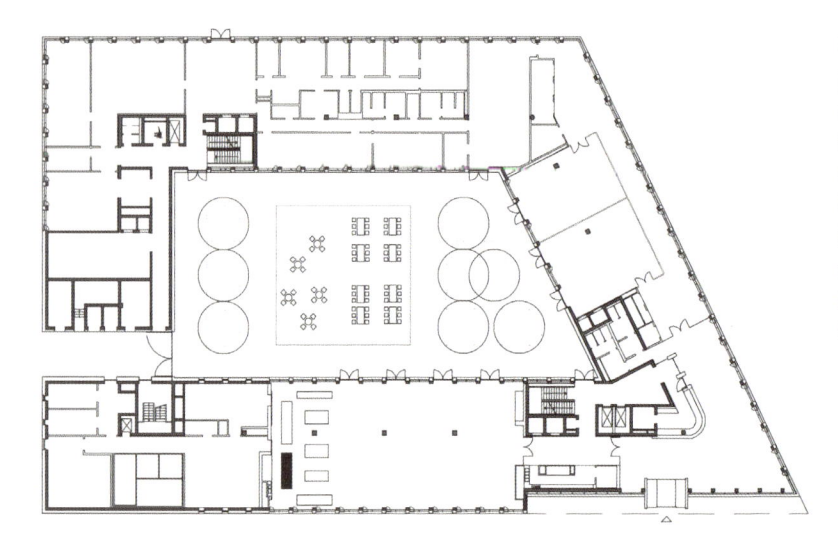

Der Neubau bildet als ringförmiger Baukörper ein prägnantes Eingangsgebäude in das neue Quartier. Die südliche Längsseite ist der Hintergrund für einen repräsentative Platz vor dem Haupteingang. Im Inneren des Gebäudes befindet sich ein begrünter Innenhof mit Außenterrasse für das Betriebsrestaurant. Die Fassade besteht aus vorgefertigten Holz-Pfosten-Riegel Elementen mit Festverglasung, hochformatigen Drehflügeln und Schiebeläden. Horizontal wird die Fassade durch stark profilierte Aluminiumbänder vor den Deckenstirnseiten gegliedert. Die mittels Geothermie klimatisierten Bürobereiche sind durch flexible Systemtrennwände in unterschiedliche Raumzonen unterteilt.

left: Ground floor plan_Casino_Open-space office. right: Main entrance interior_ Main entrance exterior_Inner yard.
links: Erdgeschoss Grundriss_Mitarbeiterrestaurant_Offene Bürozone. rechts: Haupteingang innen_Haupteingang außen_Innenhof.

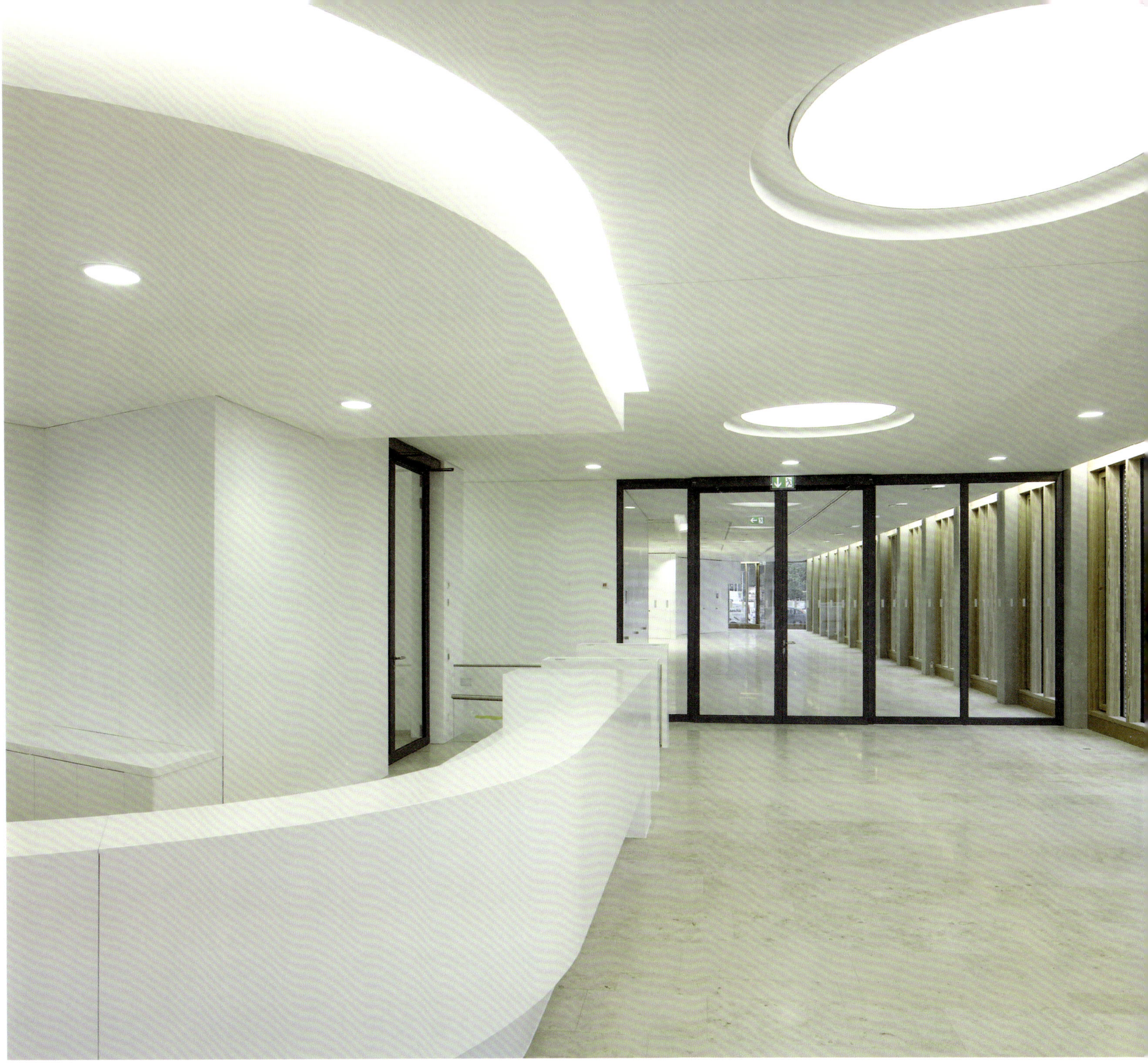

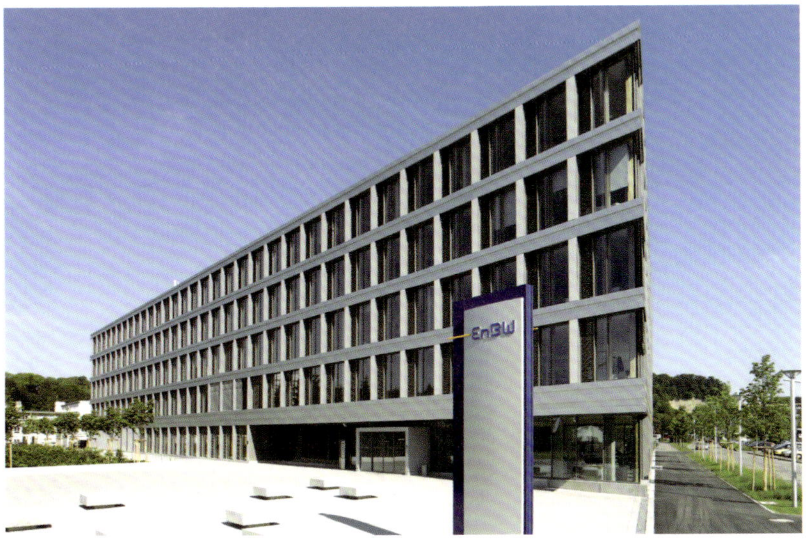
EnBW

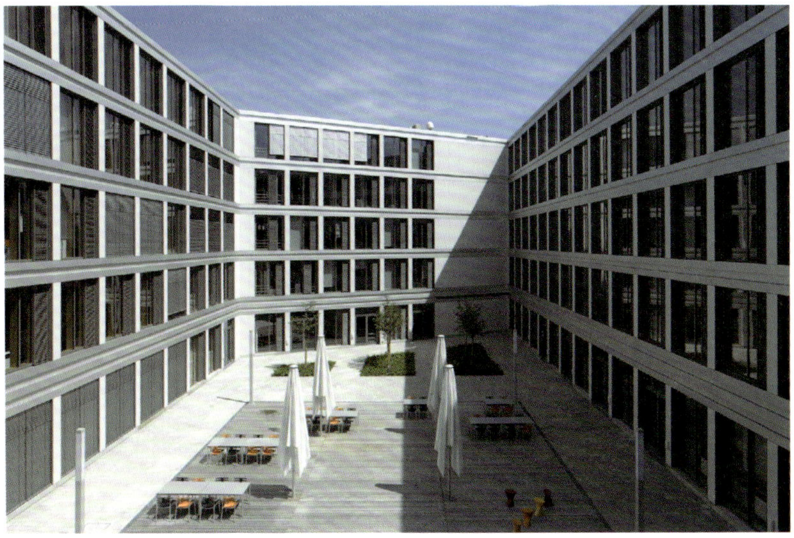

GERMANY_BITTERFELD-WOLFEN Q-CELLS HEADQUARTERS

ARCHITECTS: BHSS - ARCHITEKTEN GMBH / BEHNISCH HERMUS SCHINKO SCHUMANN_**GENERAL PLANNER:** HOCHTIEF CONSTRUCTION AG_**COMPLETION:** 2009_**NUMBER OF WORKPLACES:** 1,040_**GROSS FLOOR AREA:** 29,600 M²
COMMON AREA: INFORMATION-, LOBBY-, CONFERENCE SPACE, ESPRESSO BAR, LOUNGE_**KIND OF WORKPLACES:** CELLULAR, COMBINATION, TEAM, CUBICALS, BUSINESS CLUB, NON-TERRITORIAL, THINK TANKS, LOUNGE WORKSPACE
PHOTOS: STEFFEN JUNGHANS, LEIPZIG (128, 131 B. R.), UWE SCHUMANN, LEIPZIG (129, 130, 131 L., A. R.)

The headquarters of Q-Cells SE is located at Solar Valley – Europe's largest solar production site. Divided across three building modules on six levels, the premises include the research, marketing and sales departments, as well as the management section. An intensive meeting culture dominates the image of the flexible office landscape. The ring-shaped arrangement of the office sections into homogenous building parts from all sides creates short distances and flexible layouts for the individual zones. The project and teamwork areas are located in the outer ring, work places for focused individual work are arranged around a contemplative inner courtyard, and a multifunctional ring is situated in the middle, offering areas for communication and meetings, as well as tea kitchens.

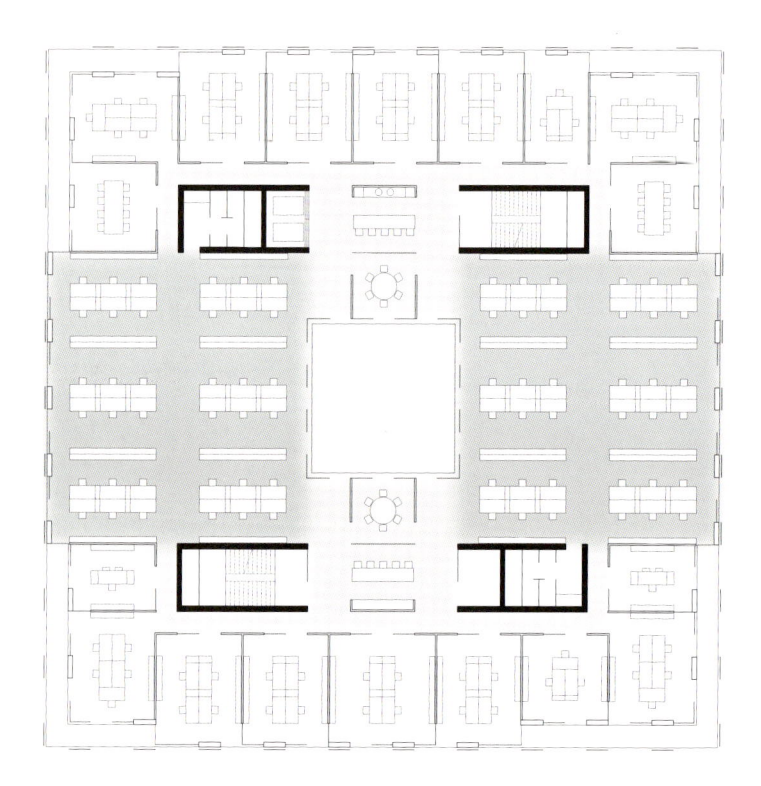

Im Solar Valley – Europas größter Solarproduktionsstätte – befindet sich die Hauptverwaltung der Q-Cells SE. In drei Gebäudemodulen auf sechs Ebenen sind die Abteilungen für Forschung, Marketing und Vertrieb sowie der Vorstandsbereich untergebracht. Eine intensive Besprechungskultur prägt das Bild einer flexiblen Bürolandschaft. Die ringförmige Anordnung der Bürobereiche zu allseitig homogenen Gebäudeteilen ermöglicht kurze Wege und flexible Flächenzuschnitte für die einzelnen Zonen: Projekt- und Teamarbeitsflächen im äußeren Ring, Arbeitsplätze für konzentrierte Einzelarbeit um einen kontemplativen Innenhof, dazwischen der multifunktionale Ring mit Flächen für Kommunikation, Meeting und Teeküchen.

left: Floor plan, open-plan office_General view_Circular balcony and solar collector. right: Common reception for the whole headquarters.
links: Grundriss, Großraumbüro_Ansicht_Umlaufender Balkon und Solaranlage. rechts: Zentraler Empfang für die gesamte Hauptverwaltung.

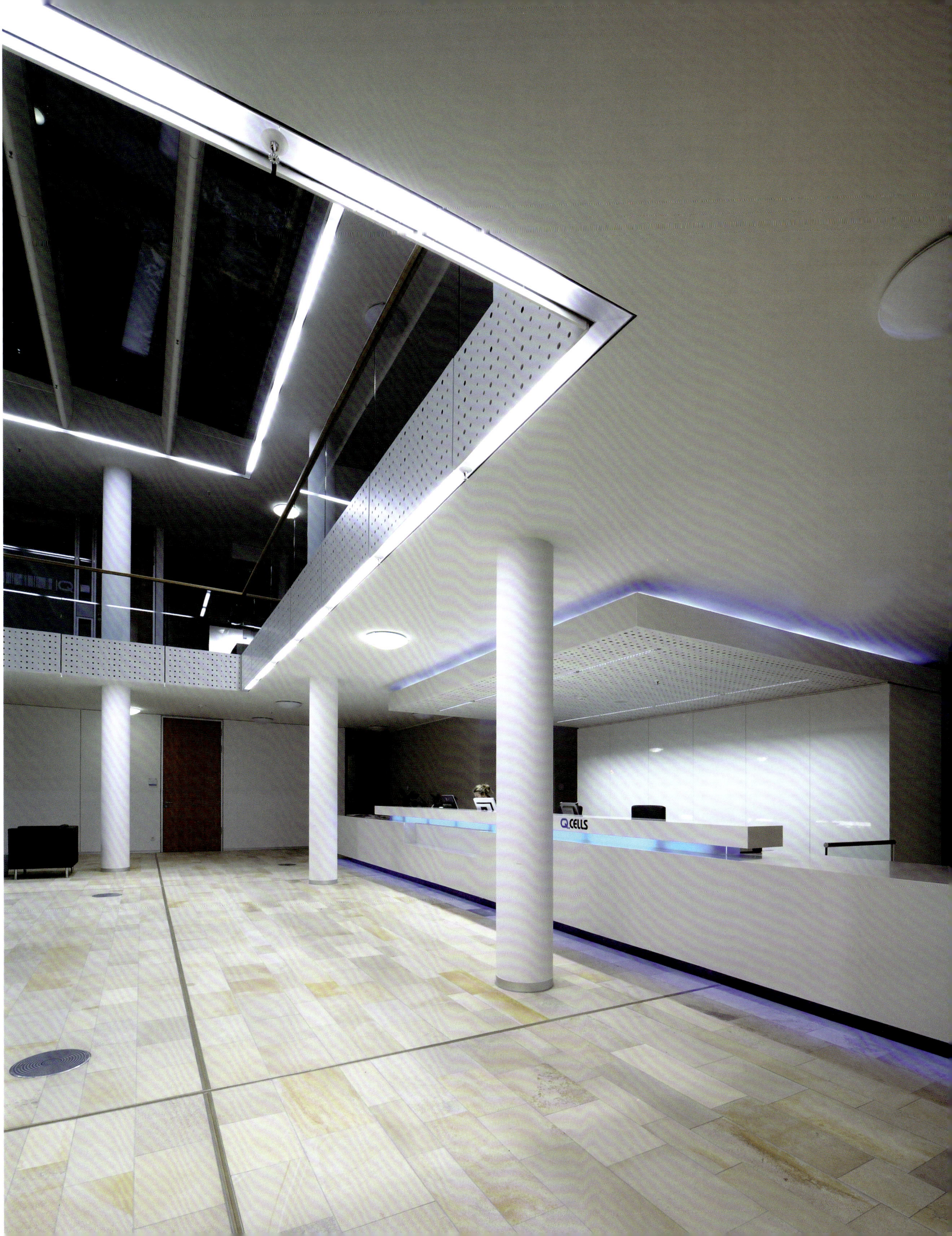
Q.CELLS

G01-E5-043

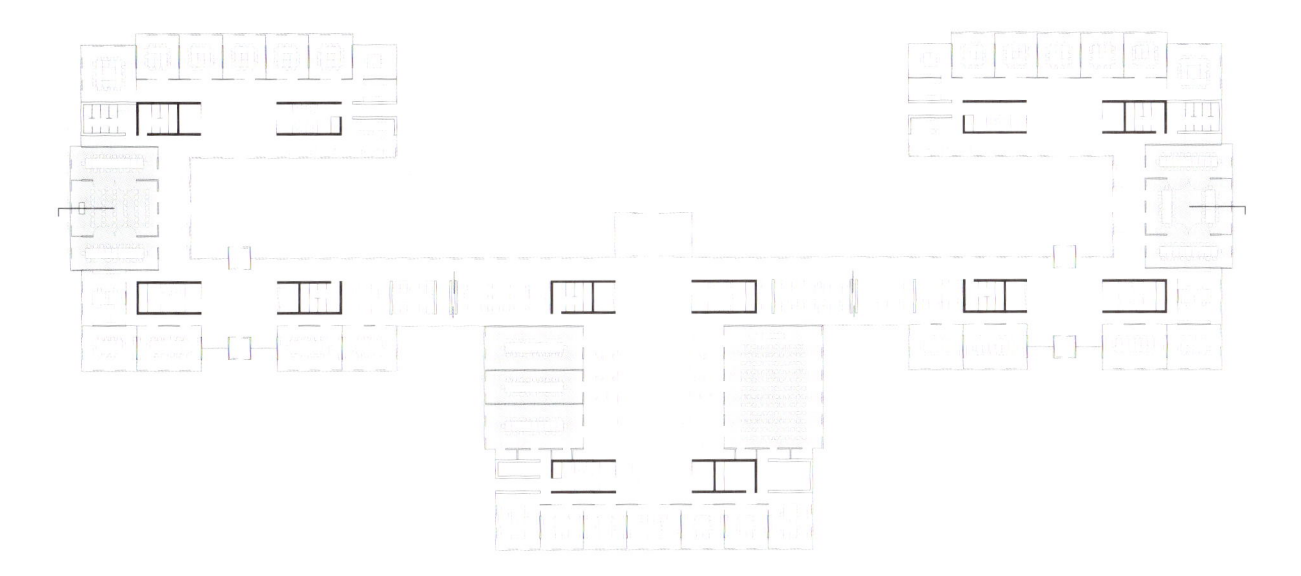

left: Meeting rooms and Think Tanks next to the inner courtyard. right: Ground floor plan, lobby and conference rooms_Team workplaces at the outer ring of the building_Meeting cabins and cubicals on the inner courtyard_Conference room.

links: Besprechungszimmer und Think Tanks am Innenhof. rechts: Grundriss Erdgeschoss, Foyer und Konferenzraum_Teamarbeitsplätze im Außenring des Gebäudes_Besprechungskojen und Cubicals am Innenhof_Konferenzraum.

GERMANY_BONN **OFFICE BUILDING BONN-LENGSDORF**

ARCHITECTS: KOHL:FROMME ARCHITEKTEN
ORIGINAL BUILDING: STAATSHOCHBAUAMT BONN, 1968
COMPLETION: 2006_**NUMBER OF WORKPLACES:** 450
GROSS FLOOR AREA: 22,500 M²_**COMMON AREA:** CAFETERIA, LIBRARY, CONFERENCE ROOMS, MEETING ROOMS
KIND OF WORKPLACES: CELLULAR, TEAM
PHOTOS: COURTESY OF THE ARCHITECTS

The former labor ministry building in Bonn-Lengsdorf can serve as a good example of the conversion of former federal administration buildings into economy-oriented office properties. The building ensemble consists of structures from the 1960s and 1990s. The older buildings required a complete core refurbishment with observation of the regulations concerning the renovation of contaminant-laden building elements. The revitalization of all buildings incorporated modernization of the energy supply system, handicap accessibility, and high-quality electronic equipment with self-sufficient redundancy. The room requirements of the tenant required the addition of floors and the construction of a new building with special functions.

Am Beispiel des ehemaligen Arbeitsministeriums in Bonn-Lengsdorf kann die Ertüchtigung ehemaliger Bundesbauten zur marktorientierten Nachnutzung als Büroliegenschaft dargestellt werden. Das Gebäudeensemble besteht aus Bauten der 1960er und 1990er Jahre. Bei den älteren Bauten war eine vollständige Kernsanierung erforderlich unter Beachtung der Anforderungen an die Sanierung von mit Schadstoffen belasteten Bauteilen. Die Revitalisierung aller Bauten umfasst die energetische Modernisierung, die barrierefreie Erschließung und eine hochwertige elektrotechnische Ausstattung mit autarker Redundanz. Das Raumprogramm des Nutzers erforderte sowohl eine Aufstockung als auch die Errichtung eines Neubaus mit Sonderfunktionen.

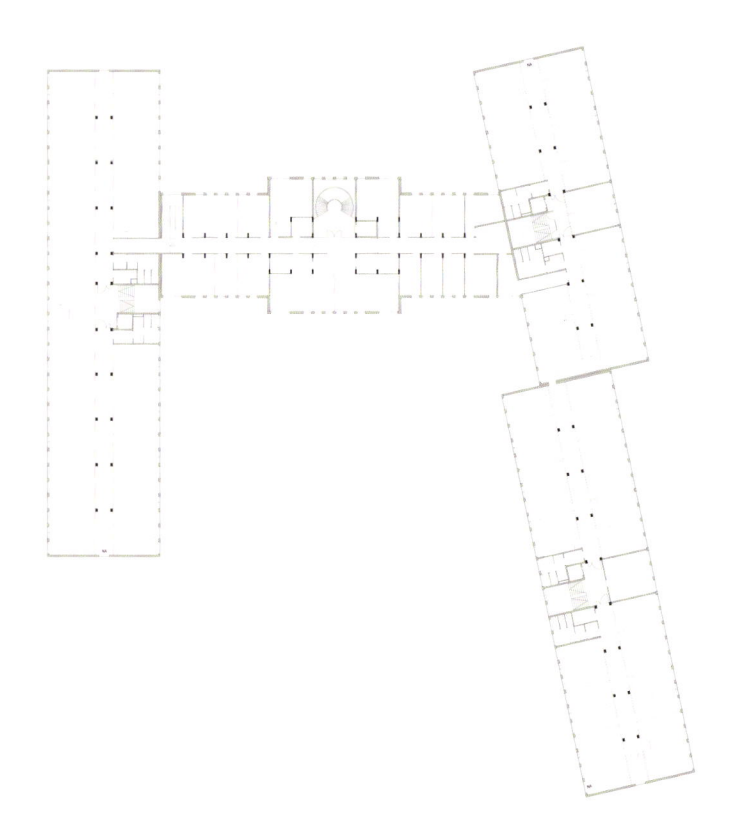

left: Typical floor plan_Perspective ensemble of buildings_Perspective inner courtyard. right: Main entrance with addition in stepped roof floor_Connecting footpathbetween the four buildings_Printed glass panel with wood grain.
links: Grundriss Regelgeschoss_Perspektive Gebäudeensemble_Perspektive Innenhof. rechts: Haupteingang mit Ergänzung im Staffelgeschoss_Wegebeziehung zwischen den vier Gebäudeteilen_Bedruckte Glaspanele mit Holzmaserung.

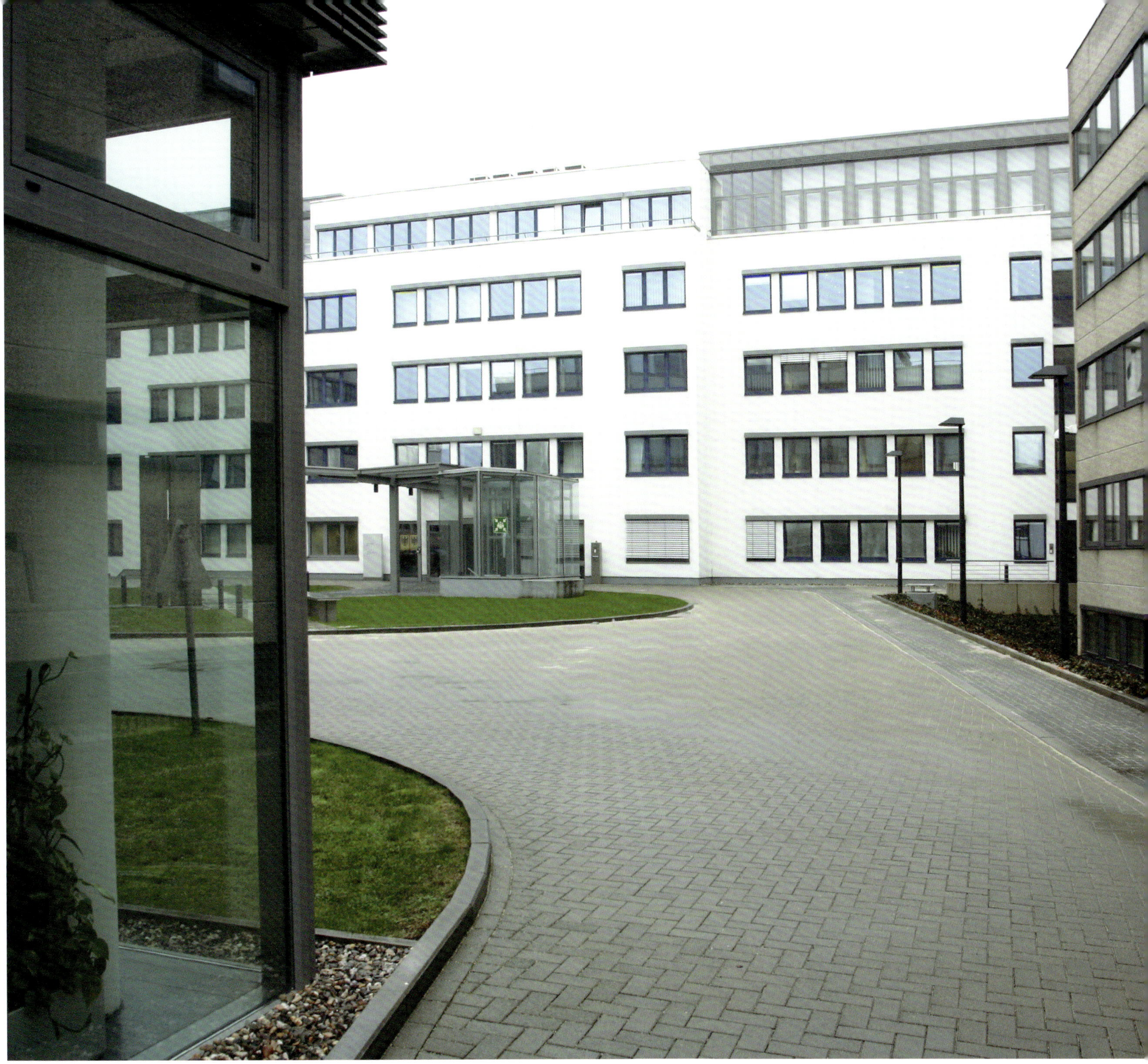

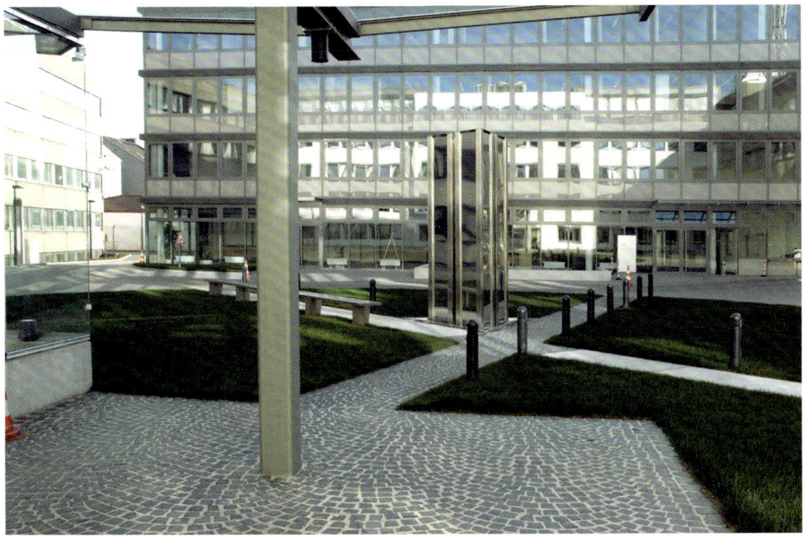

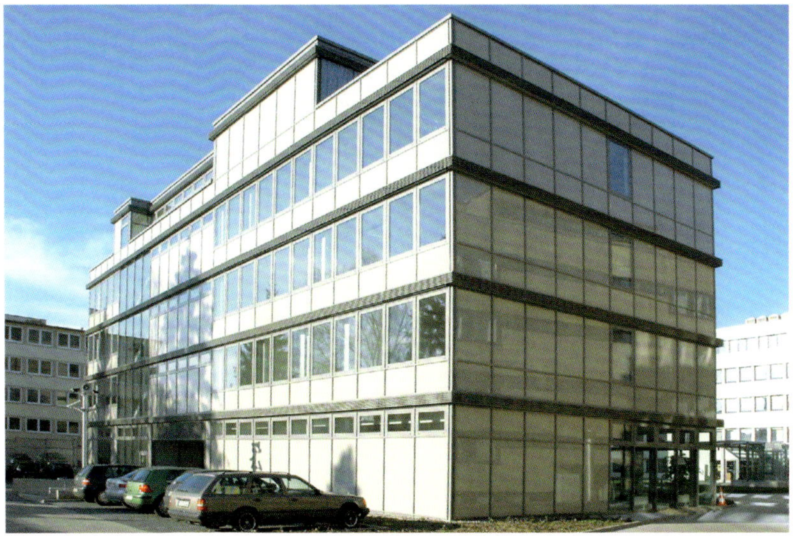

GERMANY_BONN T-HOME CAMPUS

ARCHITECTS: VAN DEN VALENTYN ARCHITEKTUR – THOMAS VAN DEN VALENTYN WITH TOM WIENTGEN AND BERND DRIESSEN
COMPLETION: 2008_**NUMBER OF WORKPLACES:** 1,500
GROSS FLOOR AREA: 61,000 M²_**COMMON AREA:** EMPLOYEE RESTAURANT (CASINO WITH LOUNGE), CONFERENCE CENTER, MANAGEMENT AREAS WITH BOARD ROOMS
KIND OF WORKPLACES: TEAM, LOUNGE WORKSPACE
PHOTOS: RAINER MADER, COLOGNE

Positioned as the terminal point of Bonn's major thoroughfare across from the Telekom headquarters, the four U-shaped buildings present an attractive variation with their alternating heights and create pleasant urban transitions via open, greened courtyards. The high-quality structured style of the buildings – white concrete pilaster strips, Tyrolean natural stone, highly efficient double-glazed windows – create a comfortable sense of calm. The blocks are connected via five glass vestibules – the serpentines. The interior design is warm, bright and complies with the high demands of networked work processes. The intricately structured open team areas and the generous cafeteria further enhance the project's quality.

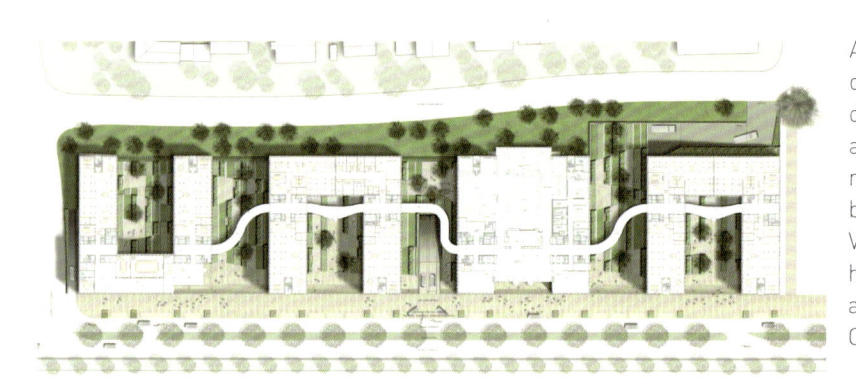

Als Schlussstein an die Bonner Magistrale gesetzt, schaffen die gegenüber der Telekomzentrale gelegenen vier U-förmigen Bauten in ihrer Höhenmodulation spannende Abwechslung und erzeugen über offene, begrünte Höfe angenehme stadträumliche Übergänge. Die wertige, strukturierte Erscheinung der Gebäude – Weißbetonlisenen, Tiroler Naturstein, hocheffiziente Verbundfenster – bewirkt wohltuende Ruhe. Die Karrees sind über fünf gläserne Verbindungsgänge – die Serpentinen – miteinander verknüpft. Die warme, helle und hohe Anforderungen an vernetzte Arbeitsprozesse erfüllende Innenarchitektur der kleingliedrigen, offenen Teambereiche sowie das großzügige Casino steigern die Qualität des Projektes.

left: Ground floor plan_View from the street_Outside area casino. right: Courtyard with serpentine.
links: Grundriss Erdgeschoss_Straßenansicht_Außenbereich Casino. rechts: Hof mit Serpentine.

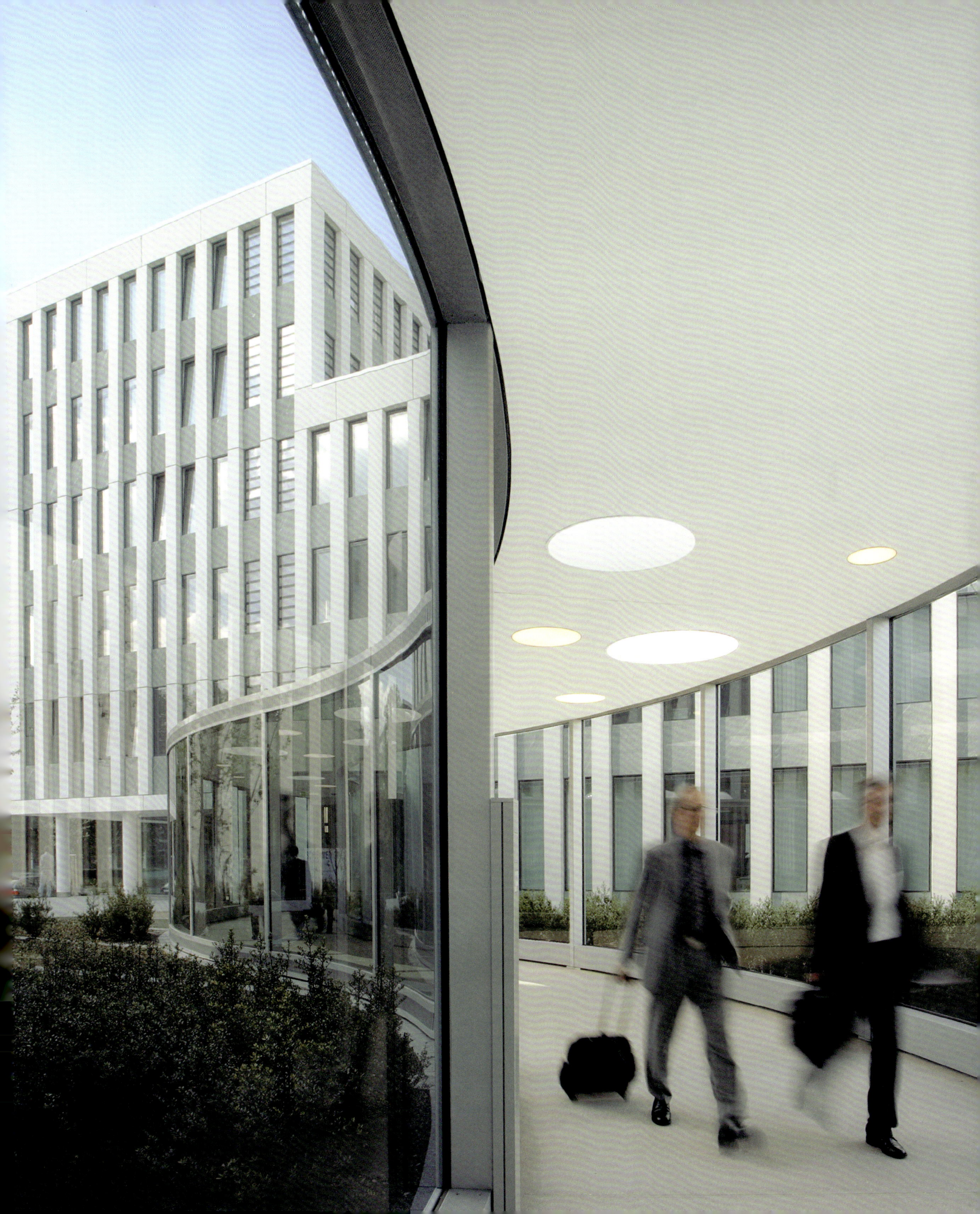

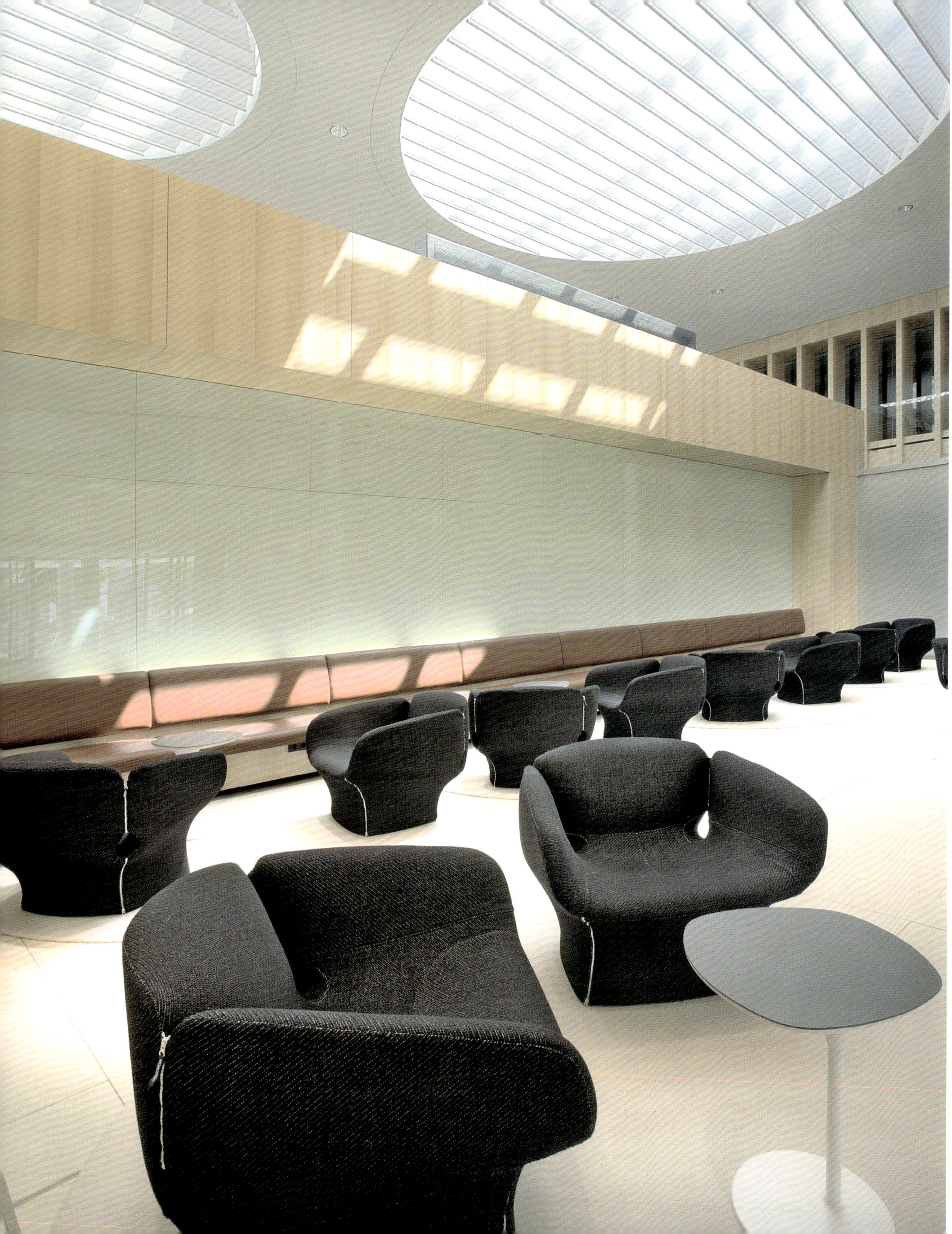

left: Lounge main entrance. right: Second floor plan_Interior view, casino_Team office with coffee point_Board room_Lounge meeting, management board.
links: Lounge Haupteingang. rechts: Grundriss zweites Obergeschoss_Innenansicht Casino_Teambüro mit Kaffeeecke_Sitzungsraum_Lounge meeting, Vorstandsbereich.

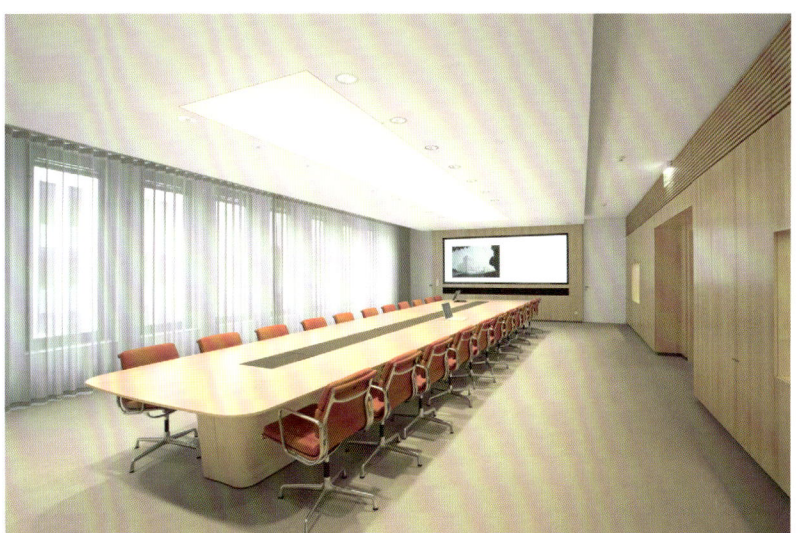

GERMANY_BURGAU **ROMA FORUM**

ARCHITECTS: OTT ARCHITEKTEN
INTERIOR DESIGN: ULRIKE SEEGER
COMPLETION: 2009_**NUMBER OF WORKPLACES:** 100
GROSS FLOOR AREA: 2,050 M²_**COMMON AREA:** TRAINING CLASSROOMS, EXHIBITION SPACE
KIND OF WORKPLACES: TRAINING DESKS
PHOTOS: ECKHART MATTHÄUS, AUGSBURG

In line with the corporate design of the globally leading rolling shutter manufacturer, the strictly arranged ensemble of buildings and outdoor areas was exclusively implemented in black-dyed exposed concrete. It serves as a multi-functional platform for the sophisticated interaction between customers, architects and manufacturer. An extensive lounge with an espresso bar and fireplace welcomes guest to the extended concrete bar-like building. Along both of its sides there are generous exhibition areas and offices, as well as a lecture hall and training rooms. In summer and winter the core-activated building is exclusively heated and air conditioned via energy-intensive ground water feed- in and heat pumps.

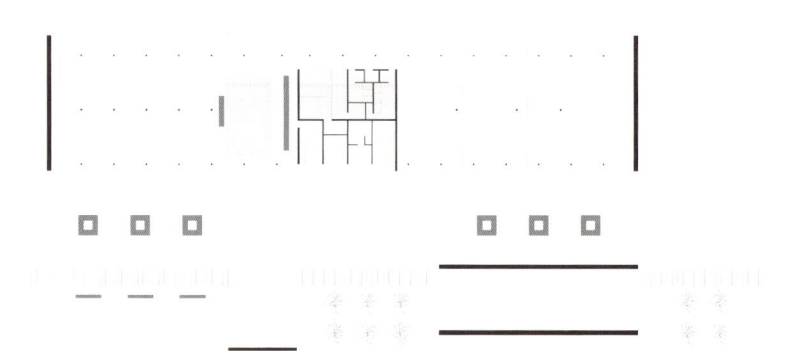

Dem Corporate Design des Marktführers im Rollladenbau entsprechend, wurde das streng geordnete Ensemble aus Gebäuden und Freianlagen ausschließlich in schwarz durchfärbtem Sichtbeton erbaut. Es dient als multifunktionale Plattform für den kultivierten Austausch zwischen Kunden, Architekten und Anbietern. Eine weitläufige Lounge mit Espressobar und Kamin empfängt den Gast des langgestreckten Betonbarrens. Zu beiden Seiten reihen sich großzügige Ausstellungsbereiche und Büros sowie Vortragssaal und Schulungsräume aneinander. Klimatisiert wird das baukernaktivierte Gebäude – Sommer wie Winter – ausschließlich über Grundwassereinspeisung und Wärmepumpen.

left: Ground floor plan_A nearly 100-meter-long bar made of black concrete. right: Entrance area_Waterfall in front of ornamented concrete wall.
links: Grundriss Erdgeschoss_Fast 100 Meter langer Gebäuderiegel aus schwarzem Beton_Wasserlounge. rechts: Eingangsbereich_ Wasserfall vor schwarzem Ornamentbeton.

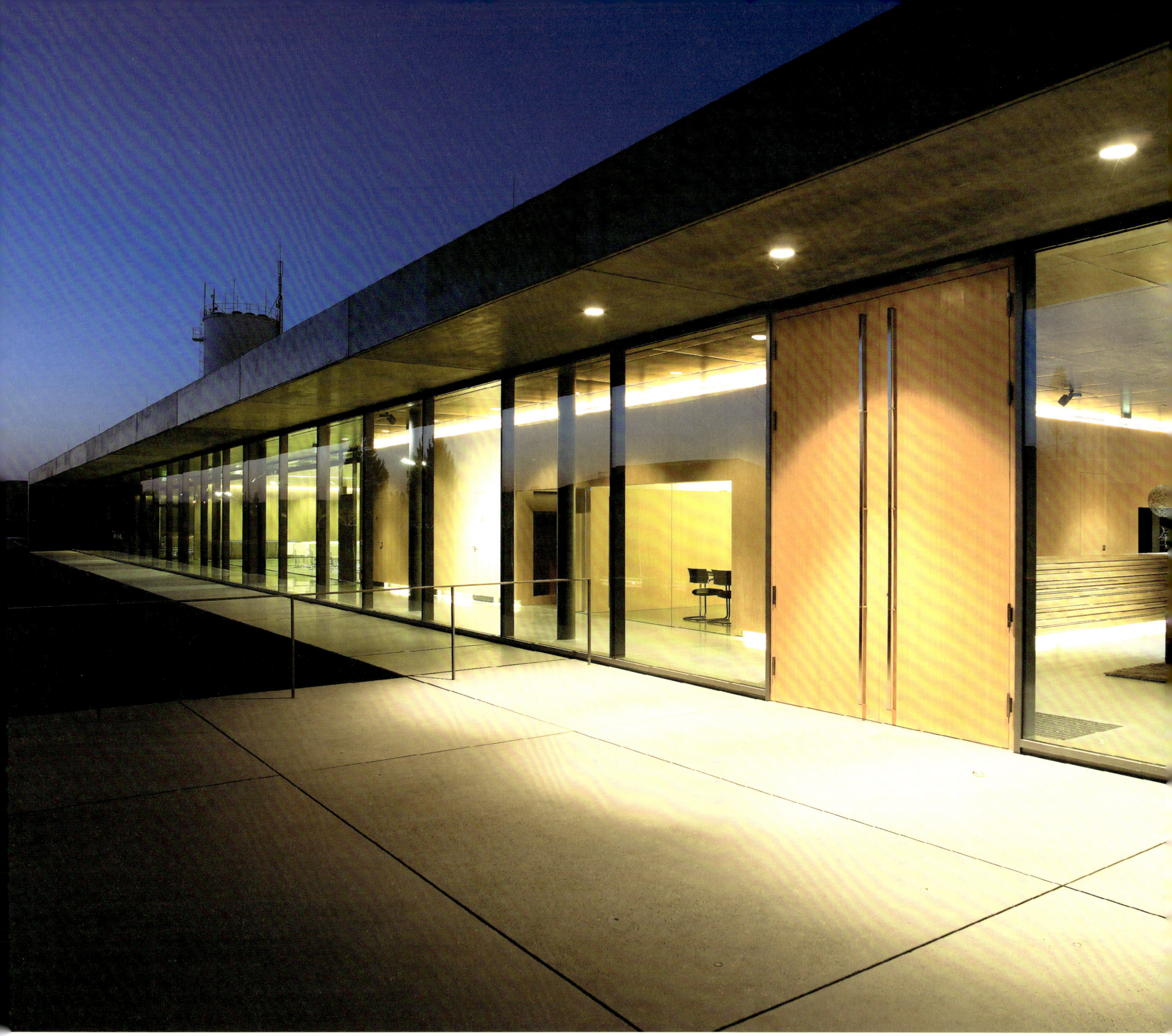
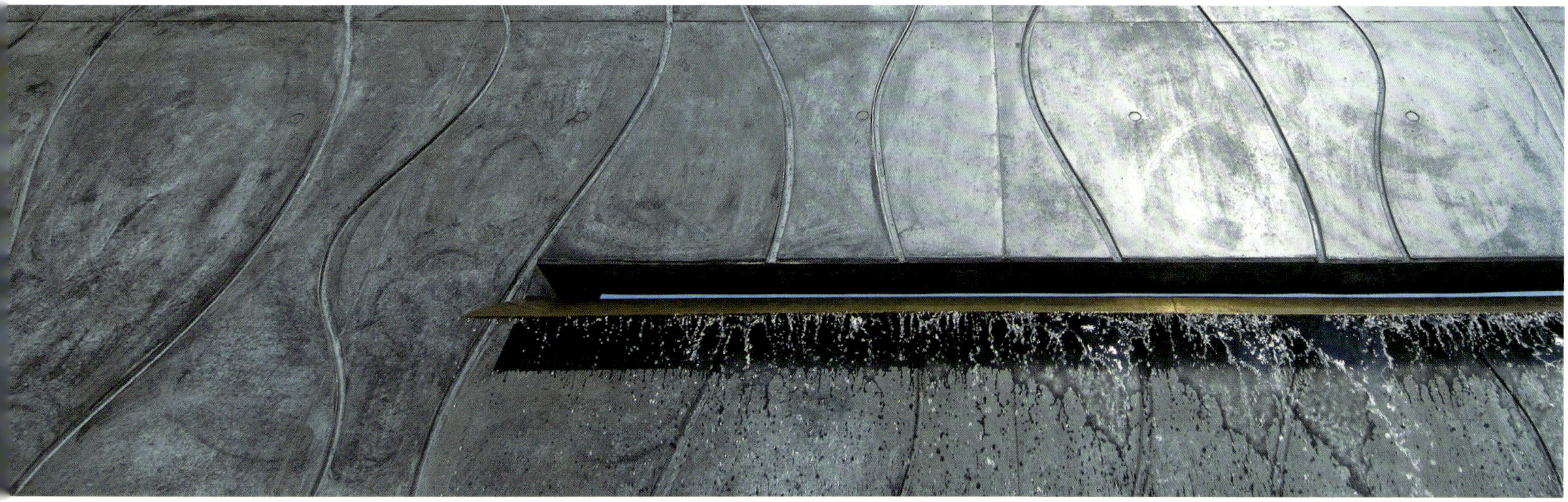

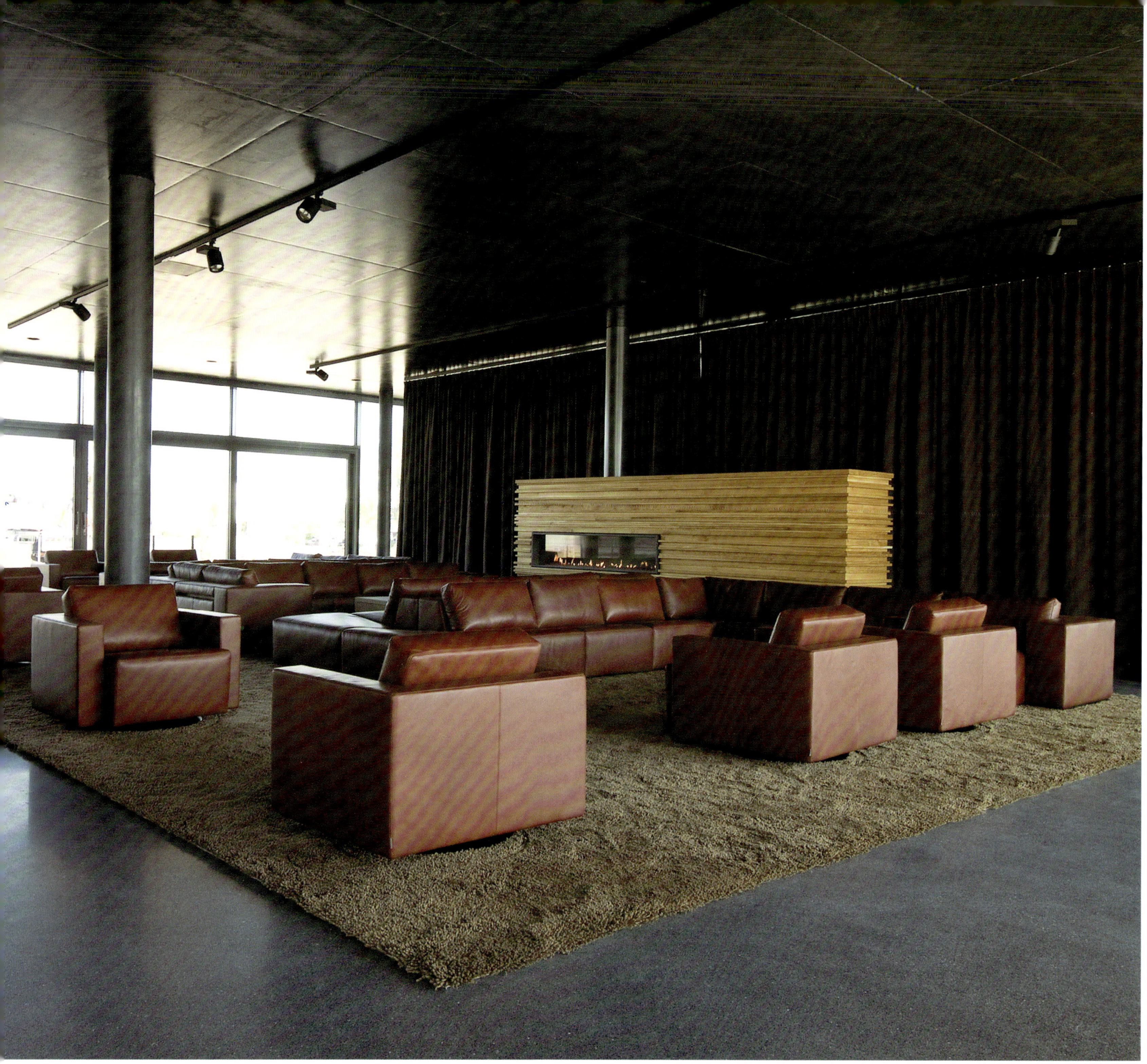

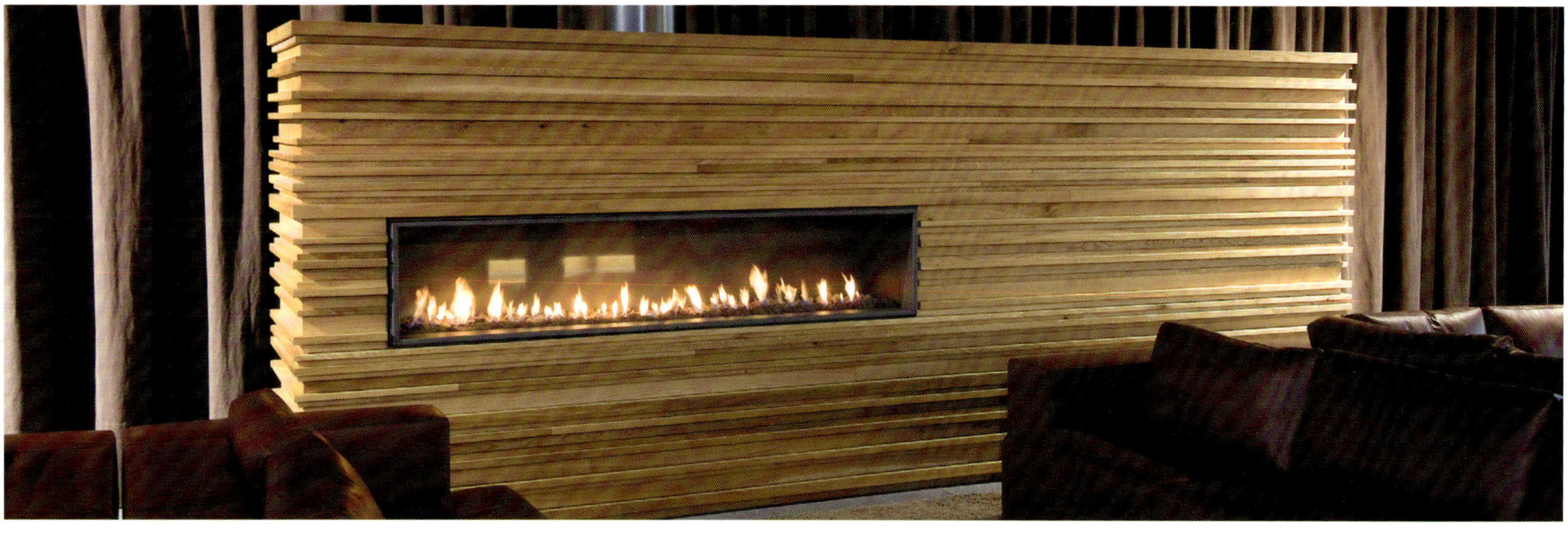

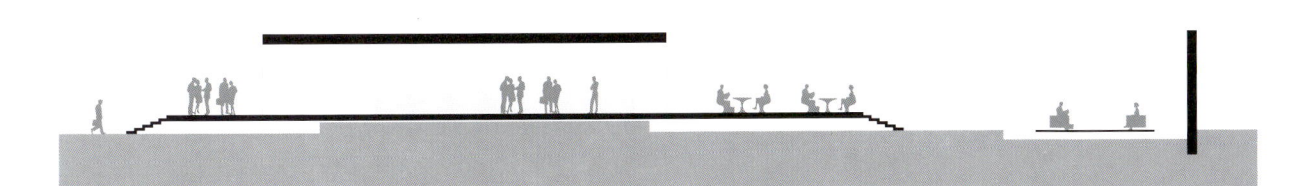

left: Leather lounge suite_fireplace. right: Lecture hall for 500 people located in the north wing of the building_Bar_Waterlounge.
links: Ledersitzlandschaft_Kamin. rechts: Schnitt_ Vortragssaal für 500 Personen im nördlichen Gebäudeflügel_Theke_Wasserlounge.

GERMANY_COLOGNE **CONSTANTIN HÖFE**

ARCHITECTS: JSWD ARCHITEKTEN
COMPLETION: 2006_**NUMBER OF WORKPLACES:** 600
GROSS FLOOR AREA: 22,000 M²_**COMMON AREA:** CASINO, CAFETERIA, LOUNGE, VARIABLE CONFERENCE ZONES, RESTAURANT_**KIND OF WORKPLACES:** CELLULAR, COMBINATION, OPEN-PLAN, OPEN SPACE ZONES_**PHOTOS:** JENS WILLEBRAND, NICOLE COMPÈRE (146 B. R.), HTP GMBH (146 B. L.)

The meander-shaped building occupies the transition zone between the small-structured construction of the residential districts of Deutz and the up-and-coming development area of the trade fair premises and ICE train terminal Köln-Deutz. The austere façade establishes a connecting pattern within this heterogeneous setting. Situated along the highly frequented arterial road in the north, the offices and apartments are grouped around two atriums whose glazing provides sound protection. To the south, in the direction of the residential district, the premises surround a city square that is bordered by restaurants and other public utilities.

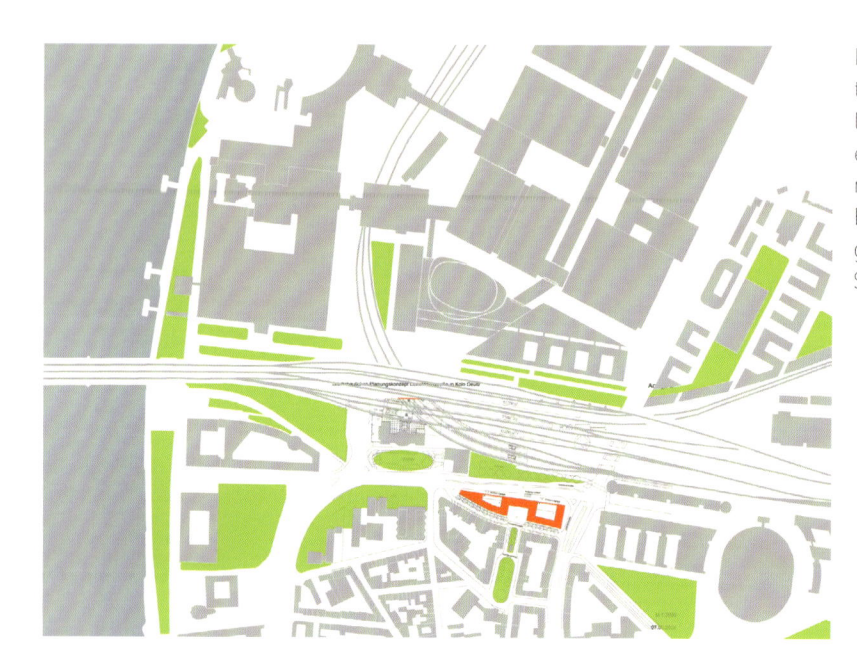

Das mäanderförmige Gebäude besetzt die Schnittstelle zwischen der kleinteiligen Bebauung der Deutzer Wohnviertel und dem aufstrebenden Entwicklungsgebiet von Messe und ICE-Terminal Köln-Deutz. Die strenge Fassade etabliert innerhalb des heterogenen Umfeldes ein verbindendes Ordnungsmuster. Entlang der lebhaften Verkehrsader im Norden gruppieren sich die Büros und Wohnungen um zwei Atrien, deren Verglasung den Schallschutz gewährleistet. Nach Süden zum Wohnquartier hin umschließt die Anlage einen Stadtplatz, an den die Gastronomie und andere öffentliche Nutzungen grenzen.

left: Site plan_Cafeteria_Lounge. right: Façade_North façade twilight_West view.
links: Lageplan_Cafeteria_Lounge. rechts: Fassade_Nordfassade in der Dämmerung_Ansicht West.

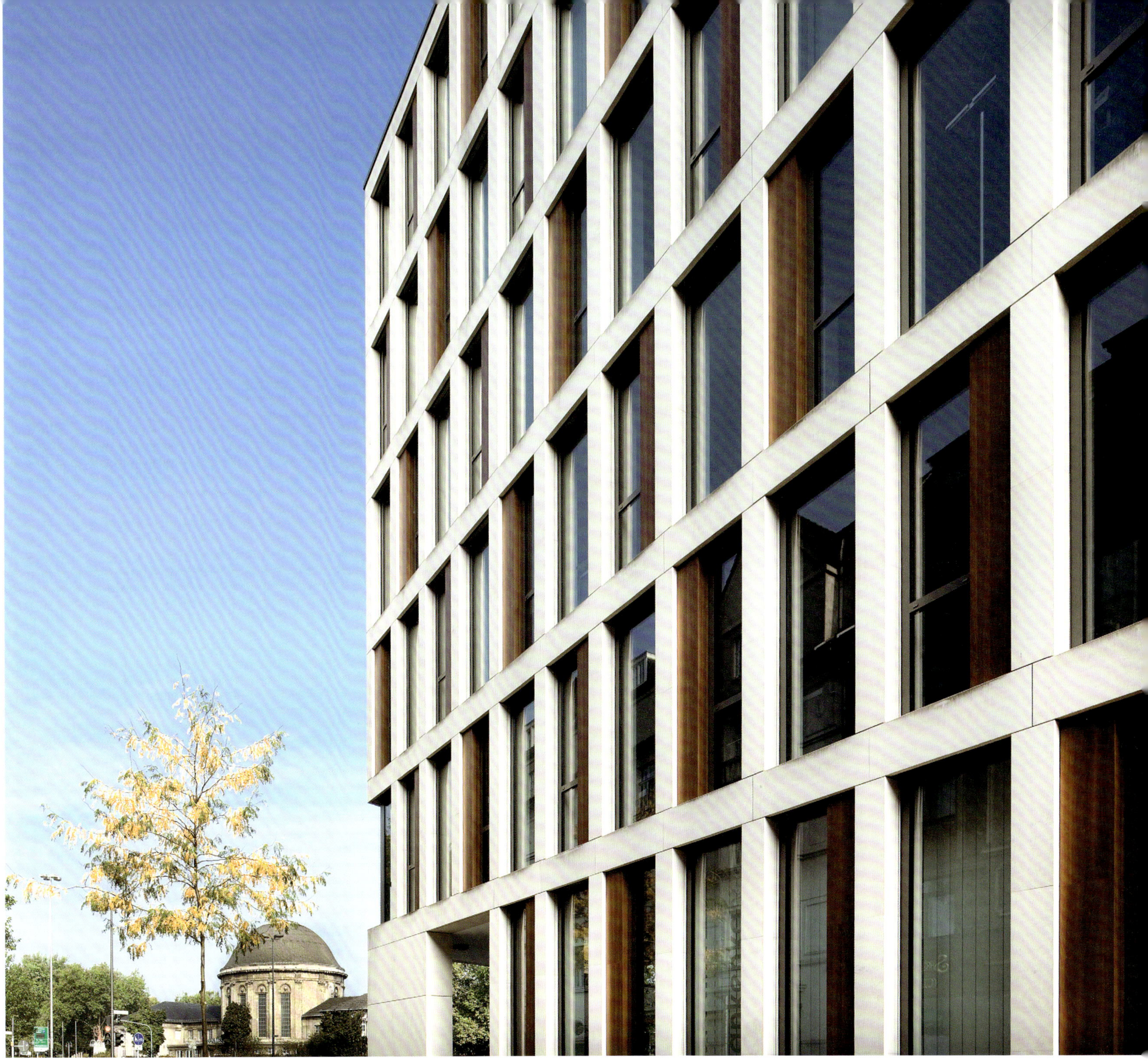

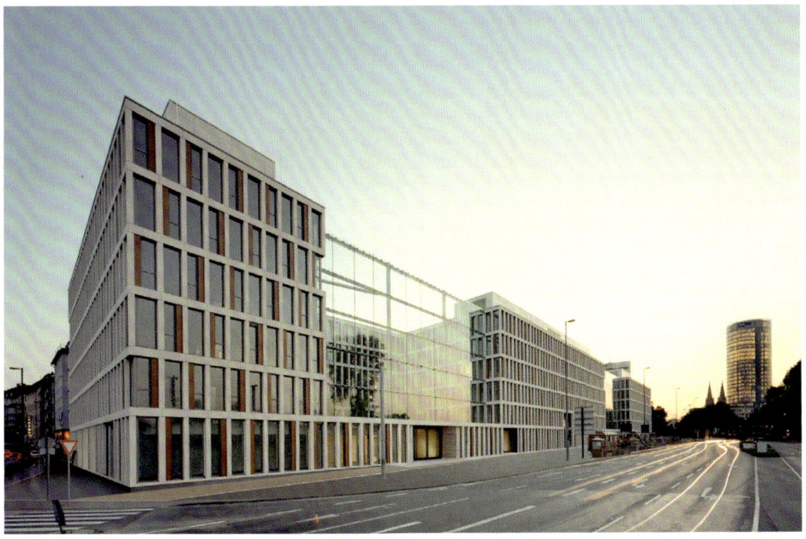

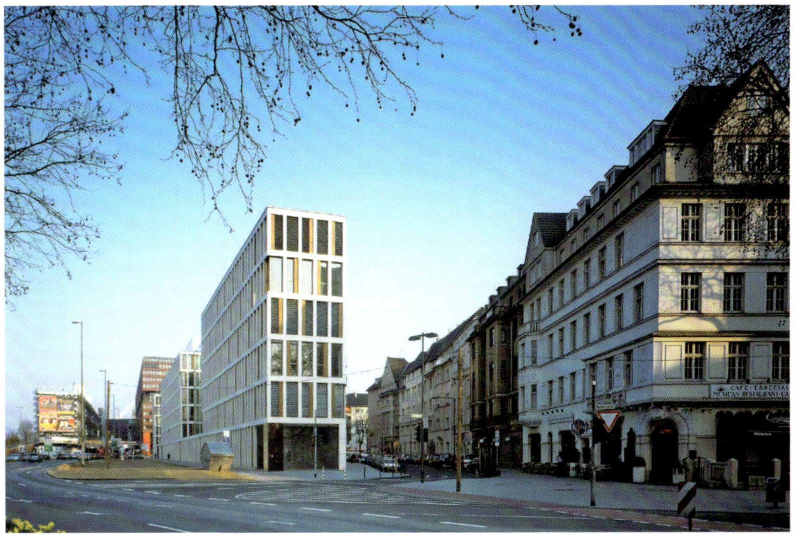

GERMANY_COLOGNE **RHEINAUARTOFFICE**

ARCHITECTS: KUBALUX ARCHITEKTEN GMBH
INTERIOR ARCHITECTS: BÜRO FÜR INNENARCHITEKTUR DANIELA STÖRZINGER_**COMPLETION:** 2009_**NUMBER OF WORKPLACES:** 200_**GROSS FLOOR AREA:** 8,000 M² OVERGROUND, 6,700 M² UNDERGROUND_**COMMON AREA:** CAFETERIA, CONFERENCE ROOMS, LOUNGE AREA, EXECUTIVE BRIEFING CENTER, TECHNOLOGY CENTER_**KIND OF WORKPLACES:** CELLULAR, COMBINATION, OPEN-PLAN, TEAM, DESKSHARING
PHOTOS: HARALD OPPERMANN

The distinctive shape of Microsoft's office in North-Rhine Westphalia is a prominent landmark at Cologne's docks. Essentially, the building volume consists of two supporting, asymmetrical 'belts' which, shifted against each other, loop through the whole edifice, thus connecting two individual rhomboid building units in a sculptural way. A two-storied bridge construction connects the volumes, which stand on a flood protection platform, to ensure maximum spatial efficiency. The open space under the bridge presents a stage-like view of the docks. Generous glass surfaces constitutes a transparent and dynamic architecture, through which both city and river remain perceptible.

Die unverwechselbare Form des Microsoft Office NRW setzt ein markantes Zeichen im Kölner Hafen. Leitbild sind zwei tragende Fassadenstränge, die sich – gegeneinander versetzt - durch das gesamte Bauwerk ziehen und so zwei rautenförmige Einzelgrundstücke auf skulpturale Weise miteinander verbinden. Eine zweistöckige Brückenkonstruktion zwischen den beiden auf einer dem Hochwasserschutz dienenden Plattform stehen Gebäudeteilen gewährleistet hohe Flächeneffizienz. Unterhalb der Brücke ist der Blick auf den Hafen bühnenhaft inszeniert. Auch im Inneren der transparenten und dynamischen Architektur sind Stadt und Fluss durch großflächige Verglasung erfahrbar.

left: Site plan_Port view_Street view. right: North tower.
links: Lageplan_Hafenansicht_Straßenansicht. rechts: Nordturm.

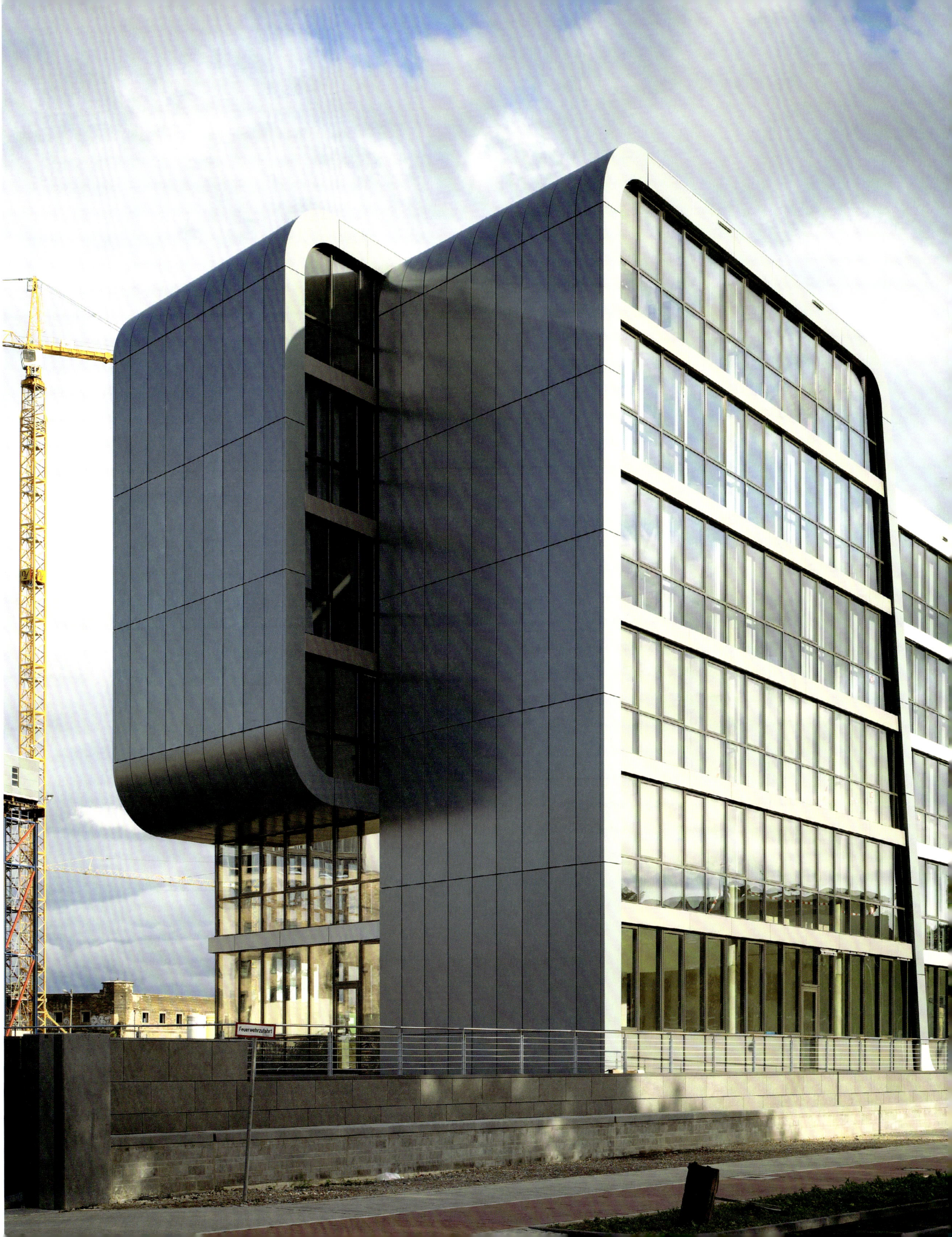

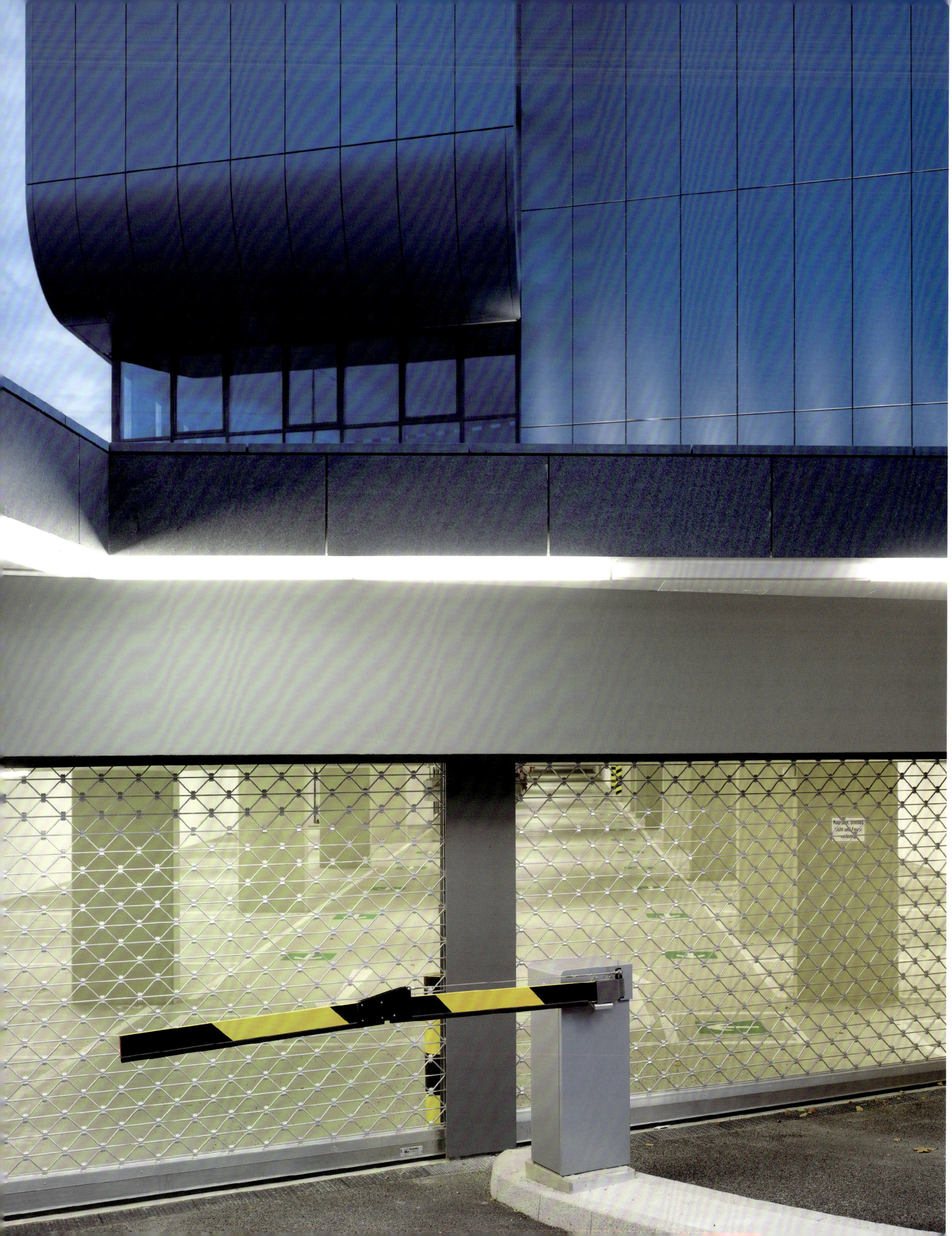

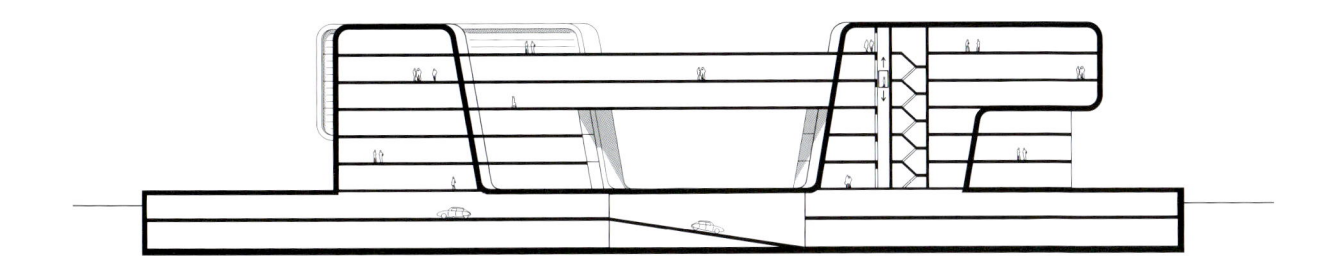

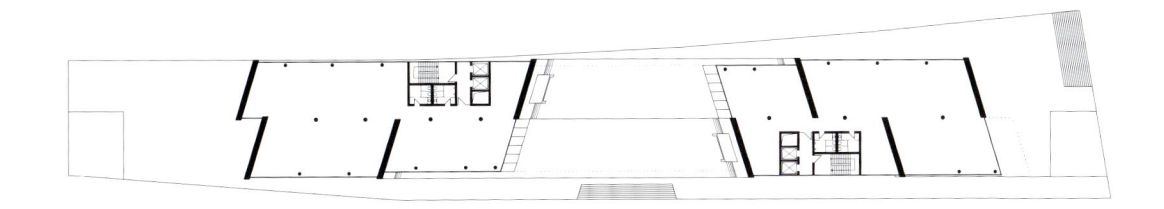

left: Underground parking driveway. right: Section and ground floor plan_Main entrance_Engineering room_Under the bridge_Open-plan office in the bridge floor.
links: Tiefgarageneinfahrt. rechts: Schnitt und Grundriss_Haupteingang_Technikraum_Unter der Brücke_Großraumbüro im Brückengeschoss.

GERMANY_COLOGNE OFFICE BUILDING AT ST. KUNIBERT

ARCHITECTS: VAN DEN VALENTYN ARCHITEKTUR – THOMAS VAN DEN VALENTYN WITH SUSANNE FALKE AND INGO HÜTTER
COMPLETION: 2009_**NUMBER OF WORKPLACES:** 500
GROSS FLOOR AREA: 23,700 M²_**COMMON AREA:** CONFERENCE AREA_**KIND OF WORKPLACES:** CELLULAR, COMBINATION, TEAM_**PHOTOS:** RAINER MADER, COLOGNE

The new building is located in the front row of the Rhine on the Konrad-Adenauer bank in Cologne in the immediate vicinity of the late Romanesque St. Kunibert church with its distinctive silhouette in the city panorama north of the Gothic Cologne cathedral. Understated, yet self-confident the six-floor office building with its slightly arched facades and rounded block corners fits into the Rhine panorama. Measuring approximately 45 x 80 meters, the building is structured by two inner courtyards around which the office units are grouped. Understatement and classic elegance define the dynamic façade in which pilaster strips of Roman travertine alternate with continuous aprons of natural Dorf green stone.

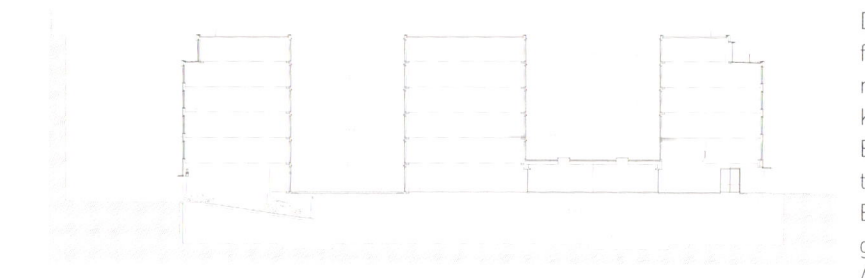

Der Neubau in vorderster Rheinfront am Konrad-Adenauer-Ufer in Köln befindet sich in direkter Nachbarschaft zur spätromanischen Kirche St. Kunibert mit ihrer markanten Silhouette im Stadtpanorama nördlich des gotischen Kölner Domes. Dezent aber selbstbewusst fügt sich das sechsgeschossige Bürogebäude mit seinen leicht gewölbten Fassaden und den abgerundeten Blockkanten in das Rheinpanorama ein. Der etwa 45 x 80 Meter große Baukörper ist durch zwei Innenhöfe gegliedert, um welche die Büroeinheiten gruppiert sind. Zurückhaltung und klassische Eleganz prägen die dynamische Außenfassade, bei der sich Lisenen aus römischem Travertin mit Brüstungsbändern aus Dorfer Grün abwechseln.

left: Longitudinal section_Konrad-Adenauer-Ufer with St. Kunibert_Perspective Konrad-Adenauer-Ufer. right: Konrad-Adenauer-Ufer with St. Kunibert.
links: Längsschnitt_Konrad-Adenauer-Ufer mit St. Kunibert_Perspektive Konrad-Adenauer-Ufer. rechts: Konrad-Adenauer-Ufer mit St. Kunibert.

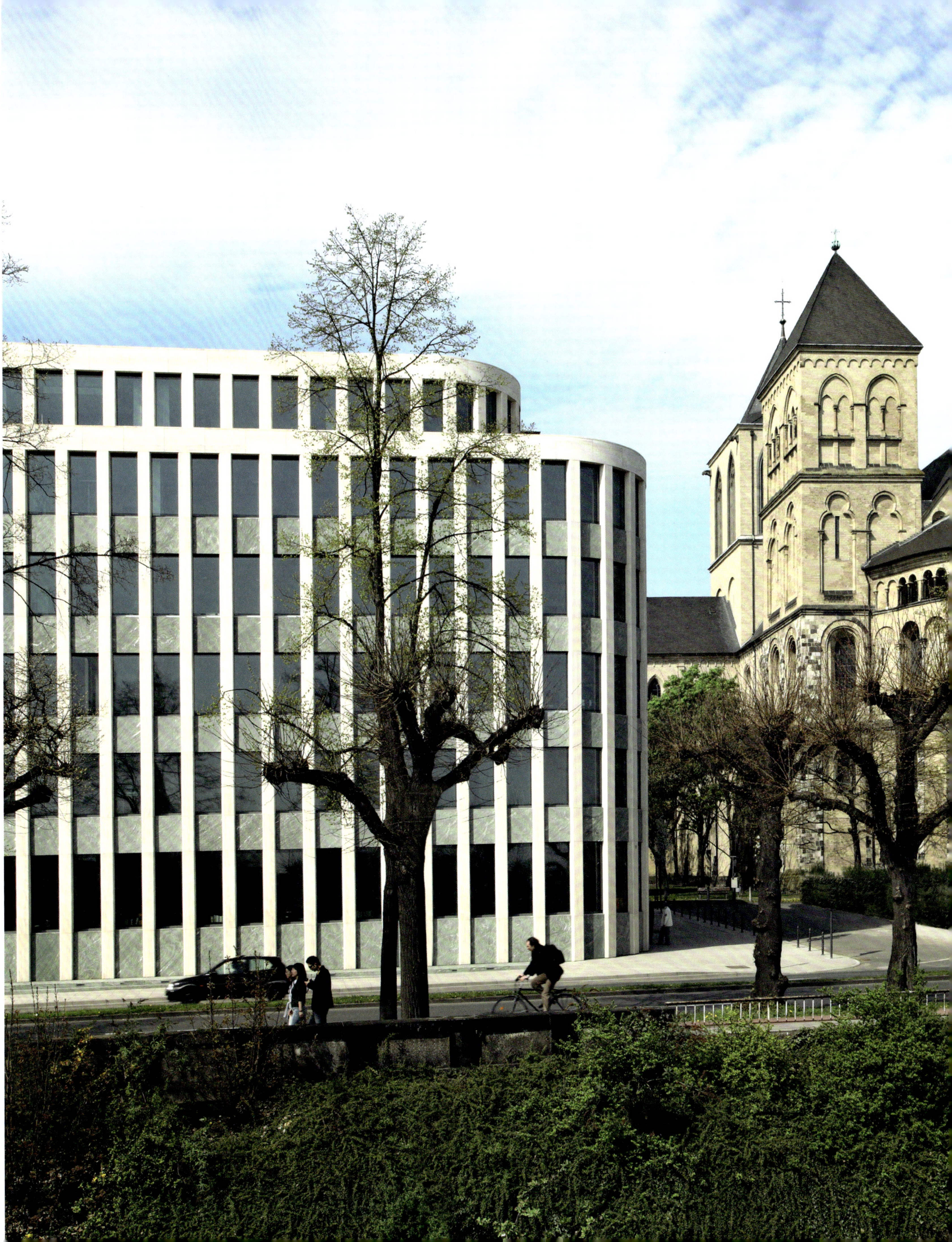

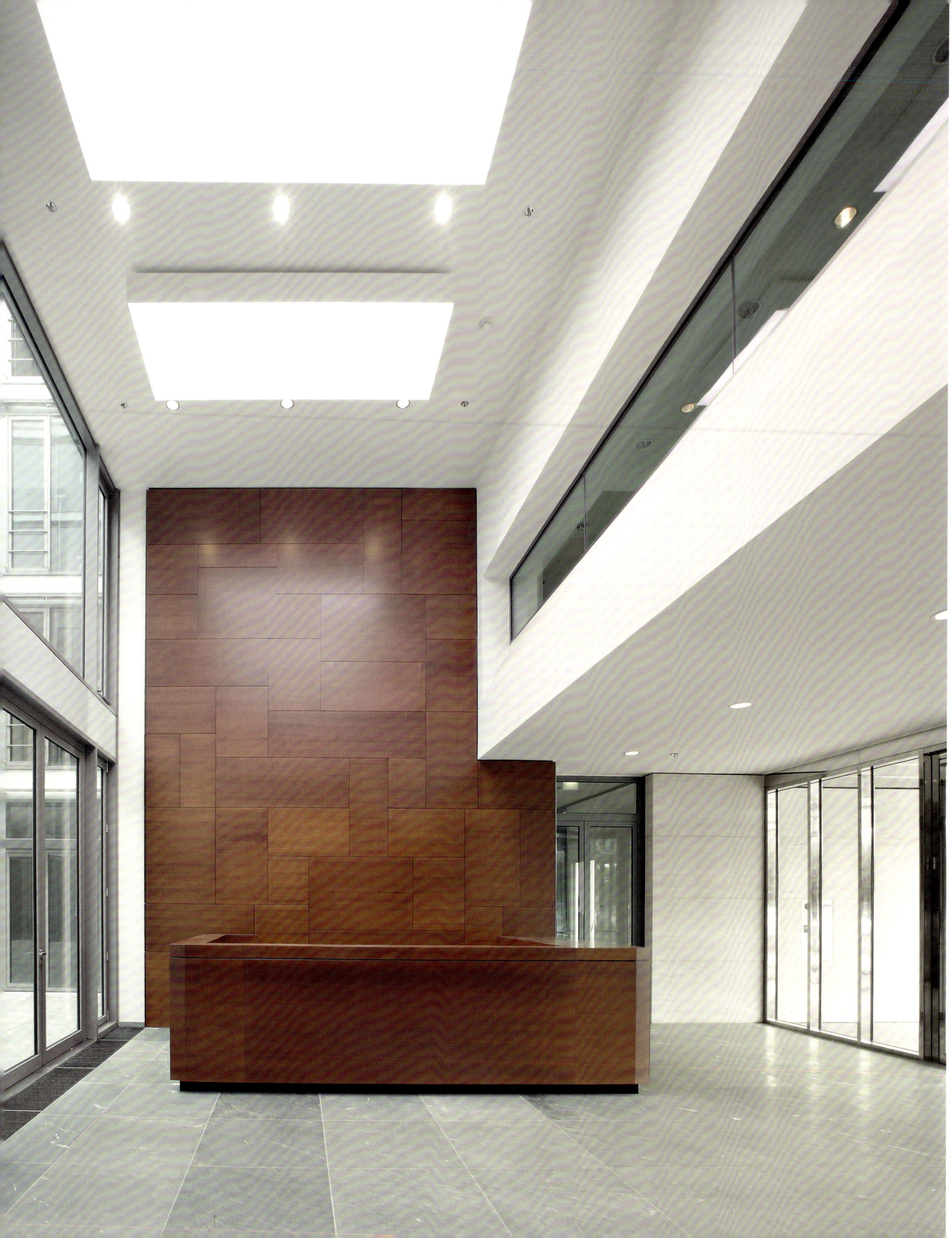

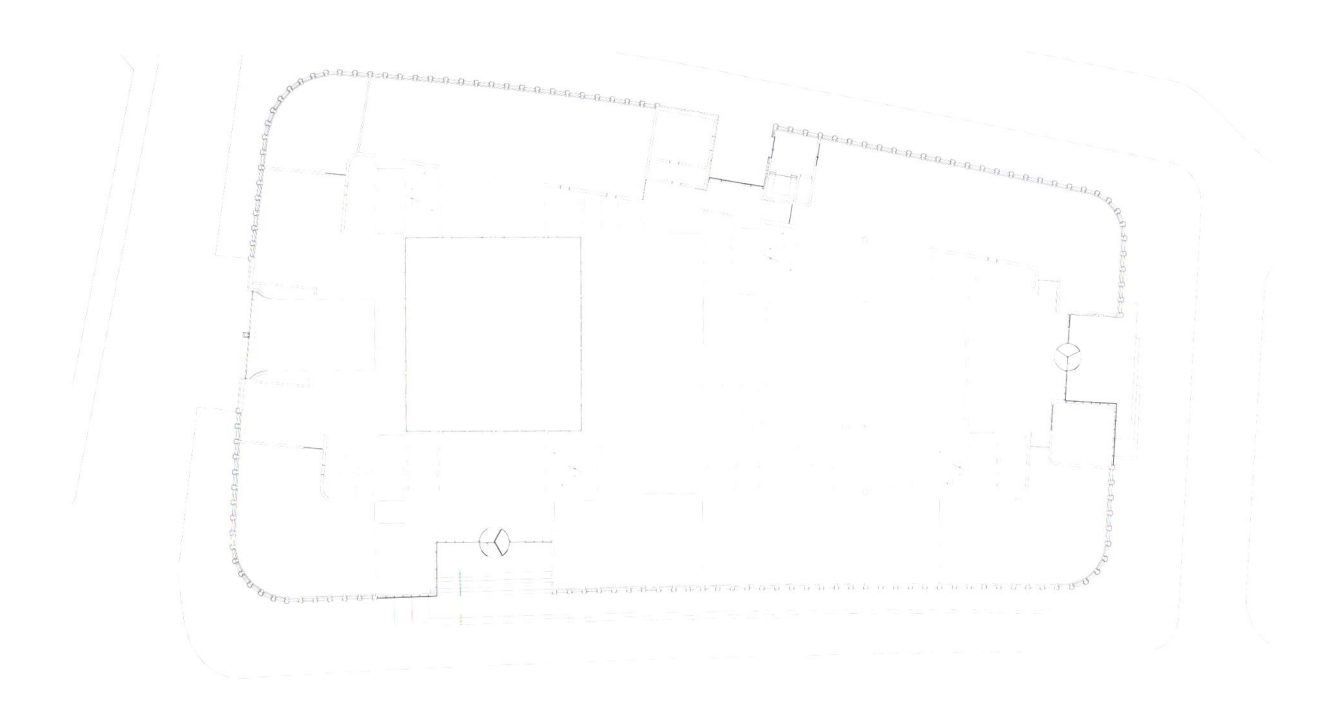

left: Entrance hall and reception. right: Ground floor plan_Inner courtyard_Conference room, fifth floor_Elevator vestibule.
links: Eingangshalle und Empfang. rechts: Grundriss Erdgeschoss_Innenhof_Konferenzraum, fünftes Obergeschoss_Aufzugvorraum.

GERMANY_CONSTANCE **LAMELLENHAUS**

ARCHITECTS: THOMAS PINK | PETZINKA PINK ARCHITEKTEN
OTHER CREATIVES: DS-PLAN, WHP, HHP, AG LICHT_**COMPLETION:** 2008_**NUMBER OF WORKPLACES:** 500_**GROSS FLOOR AREA:** 19,553 M²_**COMMON AREA:** CANTEEN, ATRIUM, MEETING AND PRESENTATION ROOMS_**KIND OF WORKPLACES:** CELLULAR, COMBINATION, OPEN-PLAN, DESKSHARING, NON-TERRITORIAL
PHOTOS: TAUFIK KENAN, BERLIN

In terms of both looks and energy consumption, the "lamella house" is the ideal location for a representative office. It was conceived as a holistic-integral design for a sustainable office building with an excellent wellness climate. The cubic structure sends a clear urban development message. The open façade links the building to the landscape. A significant and responsive fully glazed lamella façade operates as a type of "sun-dial" to provide sun and weather protection. The air conditioning and comfortable climate result in high user acceptance, while the optimized primary energy balance and reduced utilities management lead to sustainably lower costs. The environmentally friendly power generation ensures significant reductions to CO_2 emission.

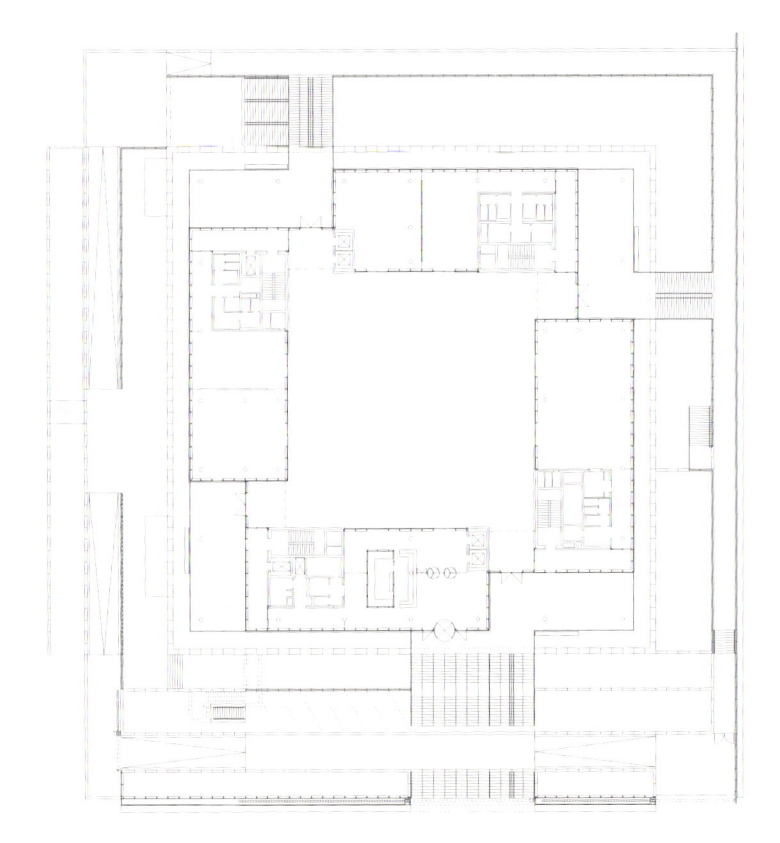

Optisch wie energetisch bietet das „Lamellenhaus" den idealen Rahmen für eine Firmenrepräsentanz. Es entstand als ganzheitlich-integraler Entwurf eines nachhaltigen Bürogebäudes mit bestem Wohlfühl-Klima, zugleich setzt der Kubus ein klares städtebauliches Zeichen. Die Offenheit der Fassade verbindet Landschaft und Gebäude. Eine signifikante und reagible Ganzglas-Lamellen-Fassade fungiert in Form einer Sonnenuhr als Sonnen- und Witterungsschutz. Klimatechnik und Klimakomfort erzeugen eine hohe Nutzerakzeptanz. Eine optimierte Primärenergiebilanz und schlanke Haustechnik minimieren nachhaltig die Kosten. Die klimaschützende Energieerzeugung sorgt für eine überzeugende CO_2-Einsparung.

left: Ground floor plan_General view, main entrance_Reception with view to the atrium. right: Main entrance, vertical louvers.
links: Grundriss, Erdgeschoss_Gesamtansicht mit Haupteingang_Empfang mit Blick zum Atrium.
rechts: Haupteingang, Vertikallamellen.

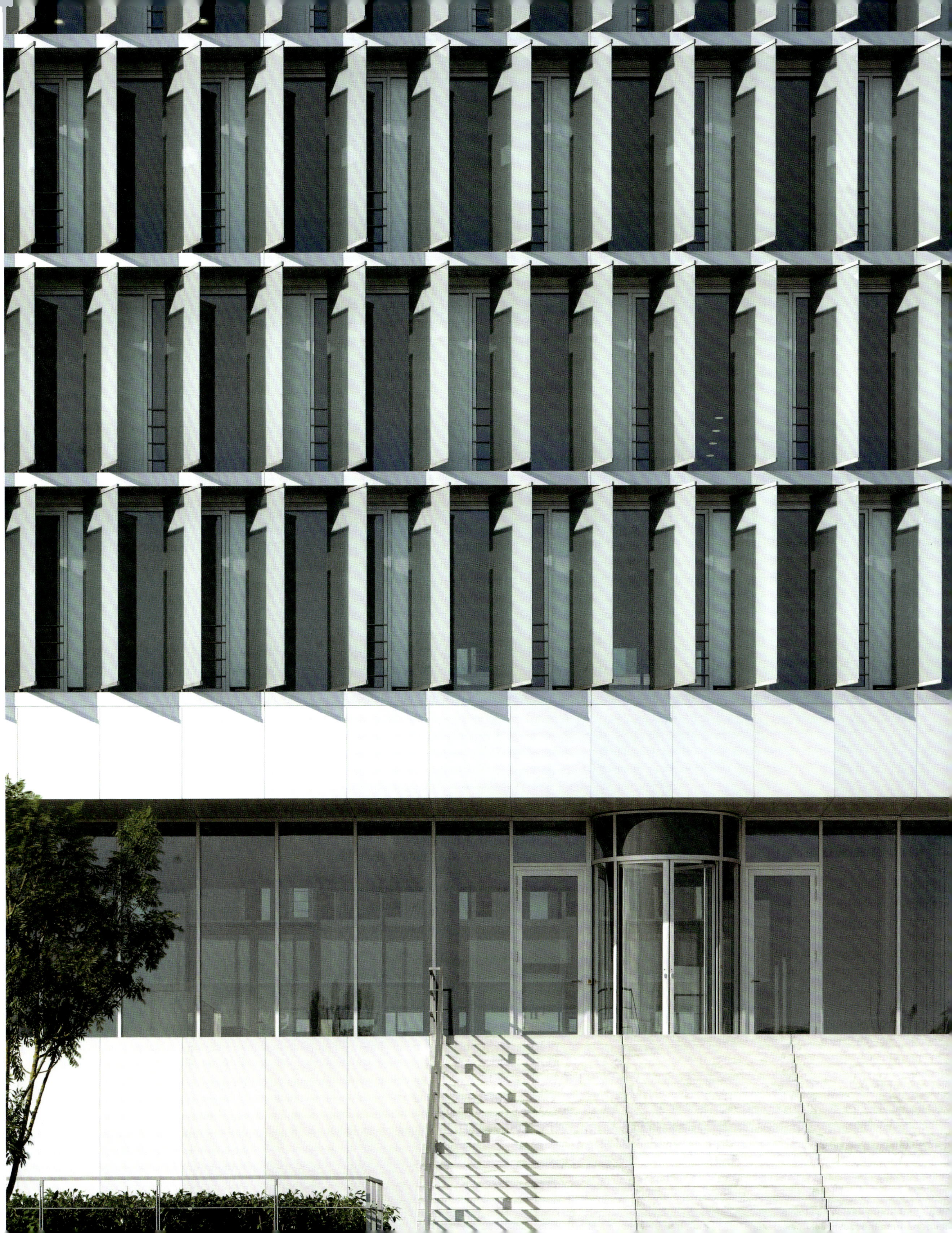

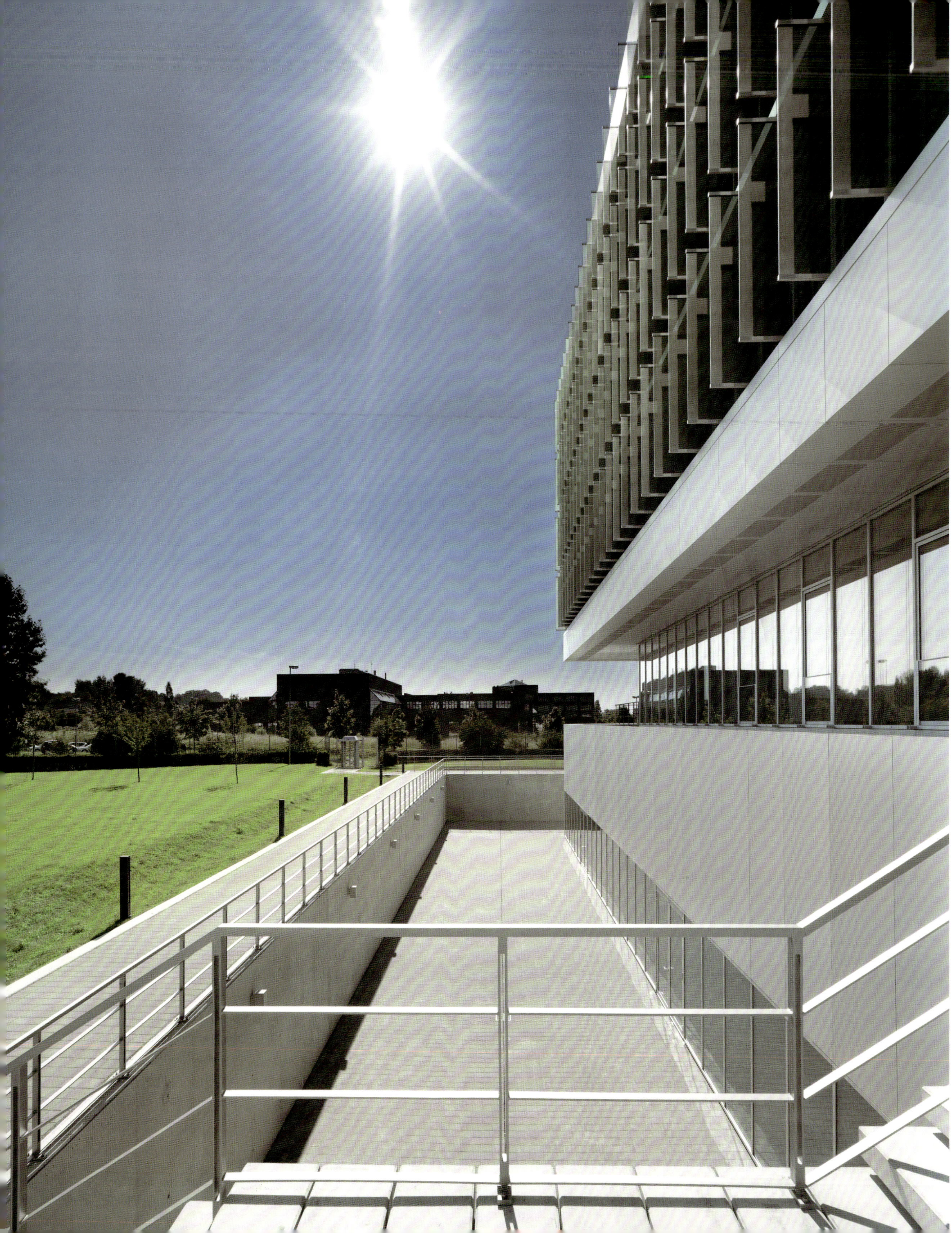

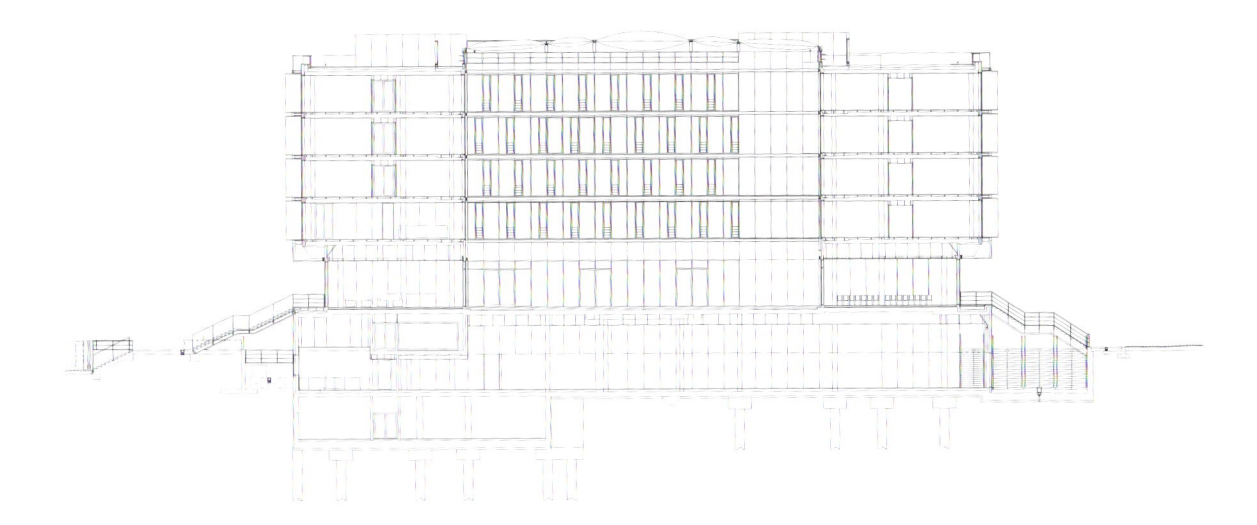

left: View to the circulating court, canteen. right: Section_Atrium with foil roof_Office view to Lake Constance_Canteen.
links: Blick in den umlaufenden Hof, Kantine. rechts: Schnitt_Atrium mit Foliendach_Büro-Ausblick zum Bodensee_Kantine.

GERMANY_DUISBURG **FIVE BOATS**

ARCHITECTS: BAHL + PARTNER ARCHITEKTEN BDA WITH GRIMSHAW ARCHITECTS_**OTHER CREATIVES:** LWS INGENIEURE, PGH, RACHE ENGINEERING_**COMPLETION:** 2005 **NUMBER OF WORKPLACES:** 700_**GROSS FLOOR AREA:** 25,800 M² **COMMON AREA:** GASTRONOMY, MEETING AREA, TV STUDIO **KIND OF WORKPLACES:** CELLULAR, COMBINATION, OPEN-PLAN, TEAM, LOUNGE WORKSPACE_**PHOTOS:** F. KRISCHER, DUISBURG

The building's plots' potential is fully utilized by a fan-shaped transparent crown structure, which fulfills urban planning as well as architectural requirements. The relation to the water and the equality of all work places are basic design concepts. The division of the program into the connection track with technical and supply areas, and the five office tracks allows the positioning of all work spaces towards the water and the linking of the departments on a horizontal and vertical level to create maximum flexibility. The twisting of the structures expands the peripheral spaces, which offer an unobstructed view of the harbor and the city of Duisburg.

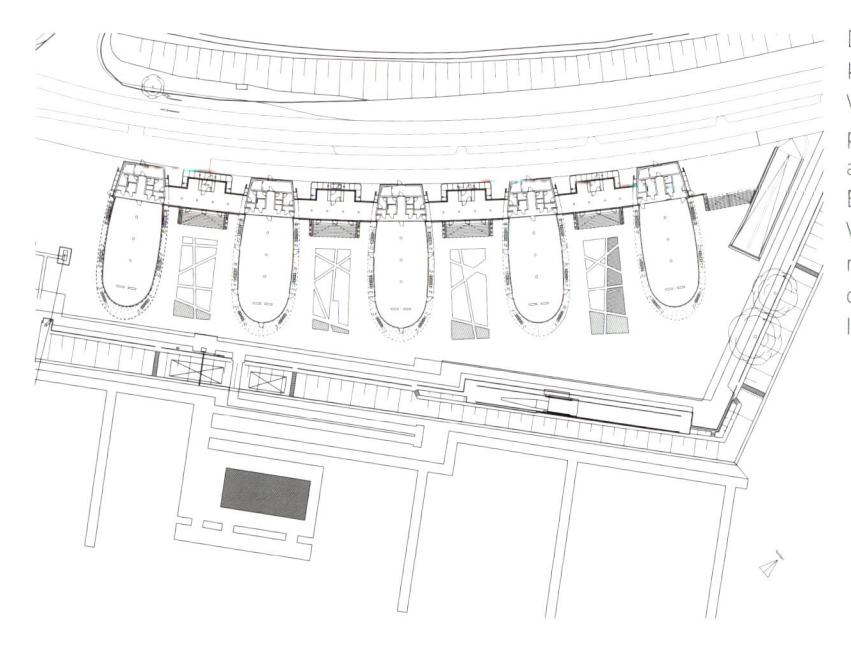

Das Potenzial des Grundstücks wird durch eine fächerförmige, transparente Kammstruktur genutzt, die sowohl städtebauliche als auch architektonische Vorgaben erfüllt. Der Bezug zum Wasser und die Gleichwertigkeit aller Arbeitsplätze sind elementare Entwurfsgedanken. Die Aufteilung des Programms auf einem Verbindungstrakt mit Technik- und Versorgungsräumen und fünf Bürotrakte ermöglicht die Orientierung aller Arbeitsplätze zum Wasser und die Vernetzung der Abteilungen in horizontaler und vertikaler Ebene, um maximale Flexibilität zu schaffen. Durch die Drehung der Baukörper weiten sich die Zwischenbereiche auf und bieten einen freien Blick auf den Hafen und die Innenstadt von Duisburg.

left: Site plan_Reception area_View office corridor. right: View by night_General view_Illuminated display.
links: Lageplan_Empfangsbereich_Einblick Büroflur. rechts: Nachtansicht_Gesamtansicht_Verbindungstrakt.

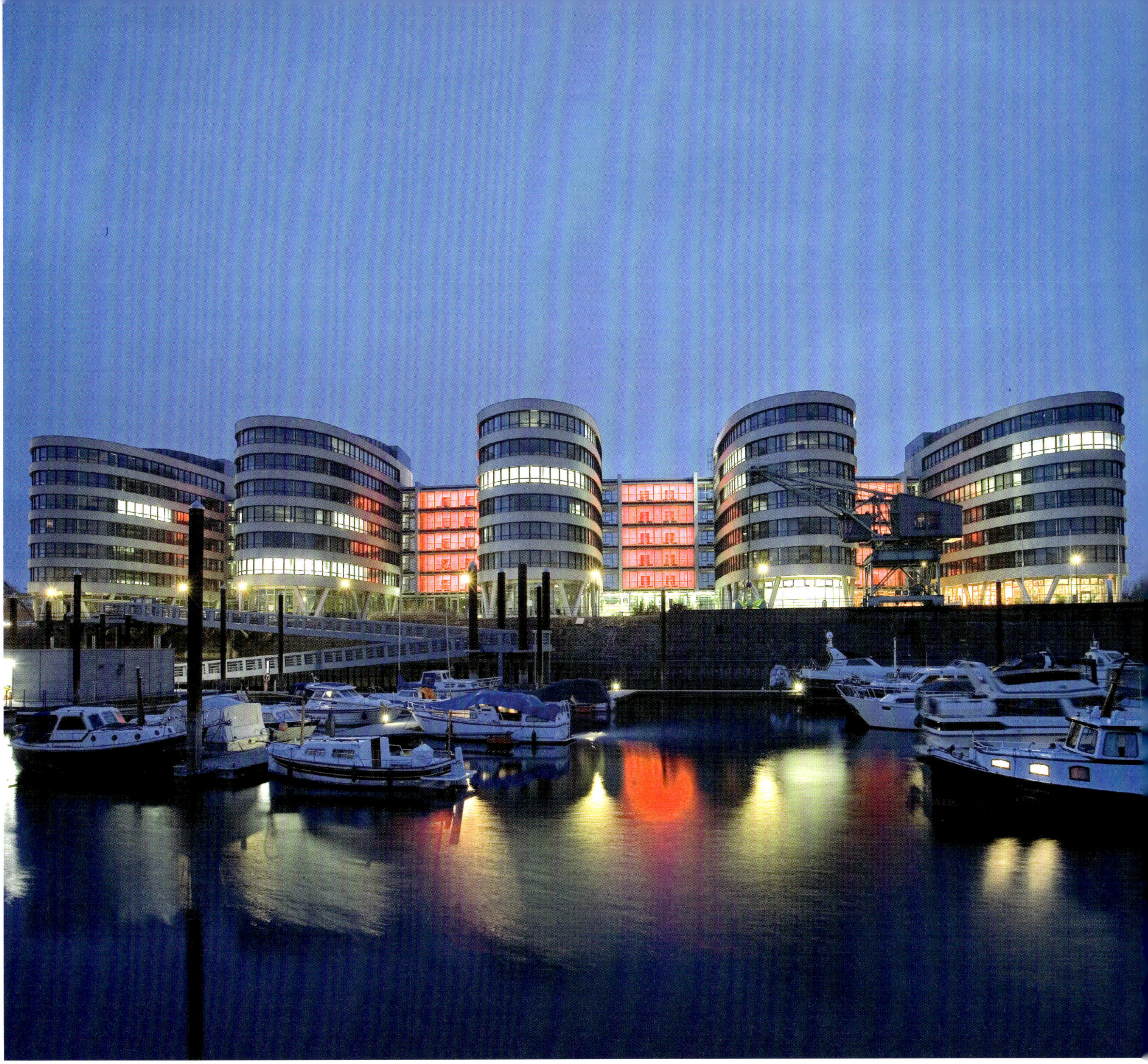

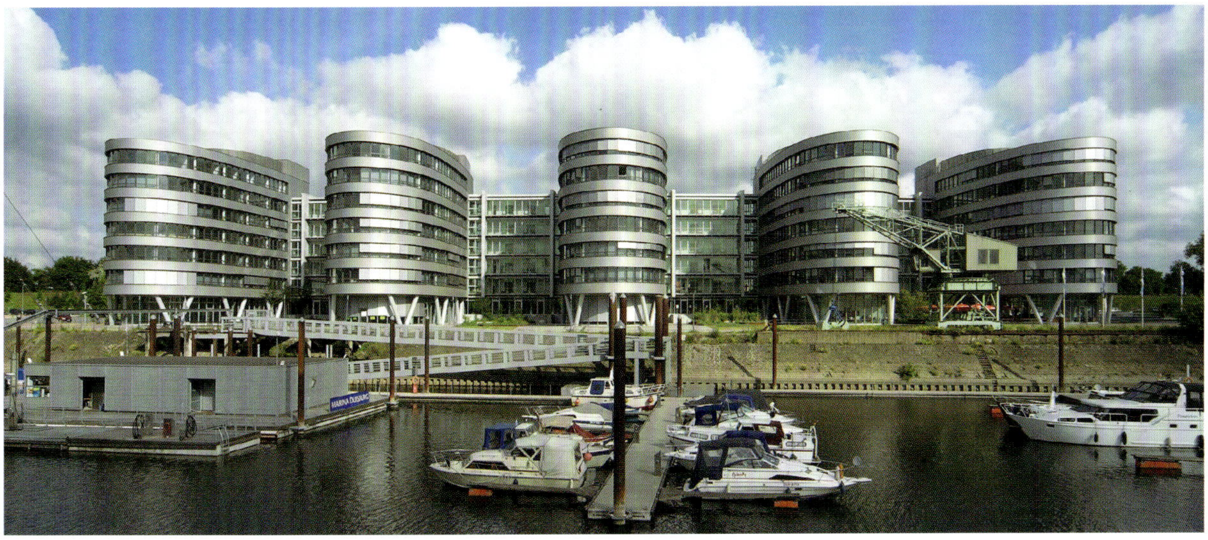

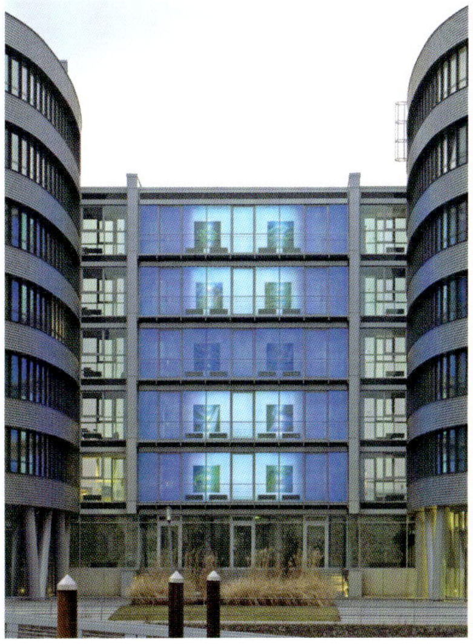

GERMANY_DUISBURG HITACHI POWER OFFICE

ARCHITECTS: BAHL + PARTNER ARCHITEKTEN_**OTHER CREATIVES:** LWS INGENIEURE, PGH, RACHE ENGINEERING **COMPLETION:** 2007_**NUMBER OF WORKPLACES:** 600 **GROSS FLOOR AREA:** 22,500 M² _**COMMON AREA:** PRINT FACTORY, LABORATORY, ARCHIVE, MEETING AREA **KIND OF WORKPLACES:** CELLULAR, COMBINATION, TEAM **PHOTOS:** F. KRISCHER, DUISBURG

The corporate headquarters of Hitachi Power Europe GmbH was completed in September 2007 in the Duisburg inner harbor area. The compact building volume is broken up by two atriums on the water side covered by foil roofs, a five-floor entrance hall, and roof terrace with a magnificent view of Duisburg. The generously proportioned outdoor areas and the sloped basic form offer most work places a view of the former inner harbor. In cooperation with the tenant, an office concept was developed that enables all types of uses from individual offices up to team spaces. The entire building is characterized by modifiable work environments as well as open and bright spaces.

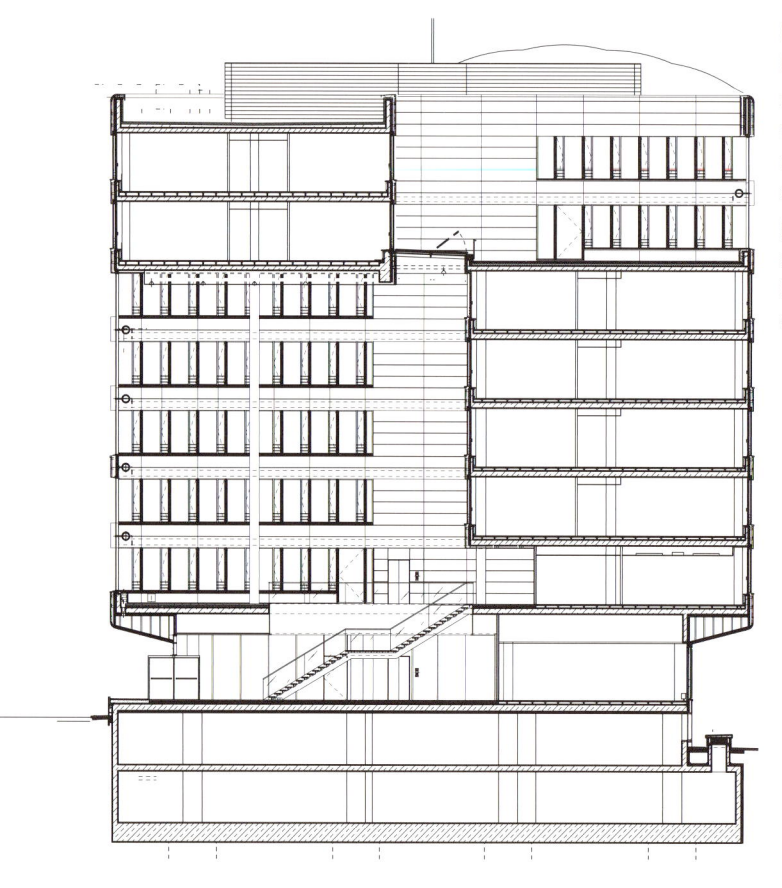

Im Duisburger Innenhafen wurde die Konzernzentrale für die Hitachi Power Europe GmbH im September 2007 fertiggestellt. Das kompakte Gebäudevolumen wird durch zwei zur Wasserseite orientierte, mit Foliendächern überspannte Atrien, eine fünfgeschossige Eingangshalle und eine Dachterrasse mit herrlichem Blick über Duisburg aufgelockert. Die großzügigen Freibereiche und die geschwungene Grundform ermöglichen den meisten Arbeitsplätzen einen Blick auf das ehemalige Hafenbecken. Mit dem Nutzer wurde ein Bürokonzept entwickelt, das von Einzelbüros bis hin zu Teamflächen alle Nutzungen ermöglicht. Veränderbare Arbeitswelten sind für dieses Gebäude ebenso charakteristisch wie offene und helle Flächen.

left: Cross section_View from the dock_Glass roof top. right: Night view_Entrance hall_Atrium.
links: Querschnitt_Blick vom Hafenbecken_Glasdach. rechts: Nachtansicht_Eingangshalle_Atrium.

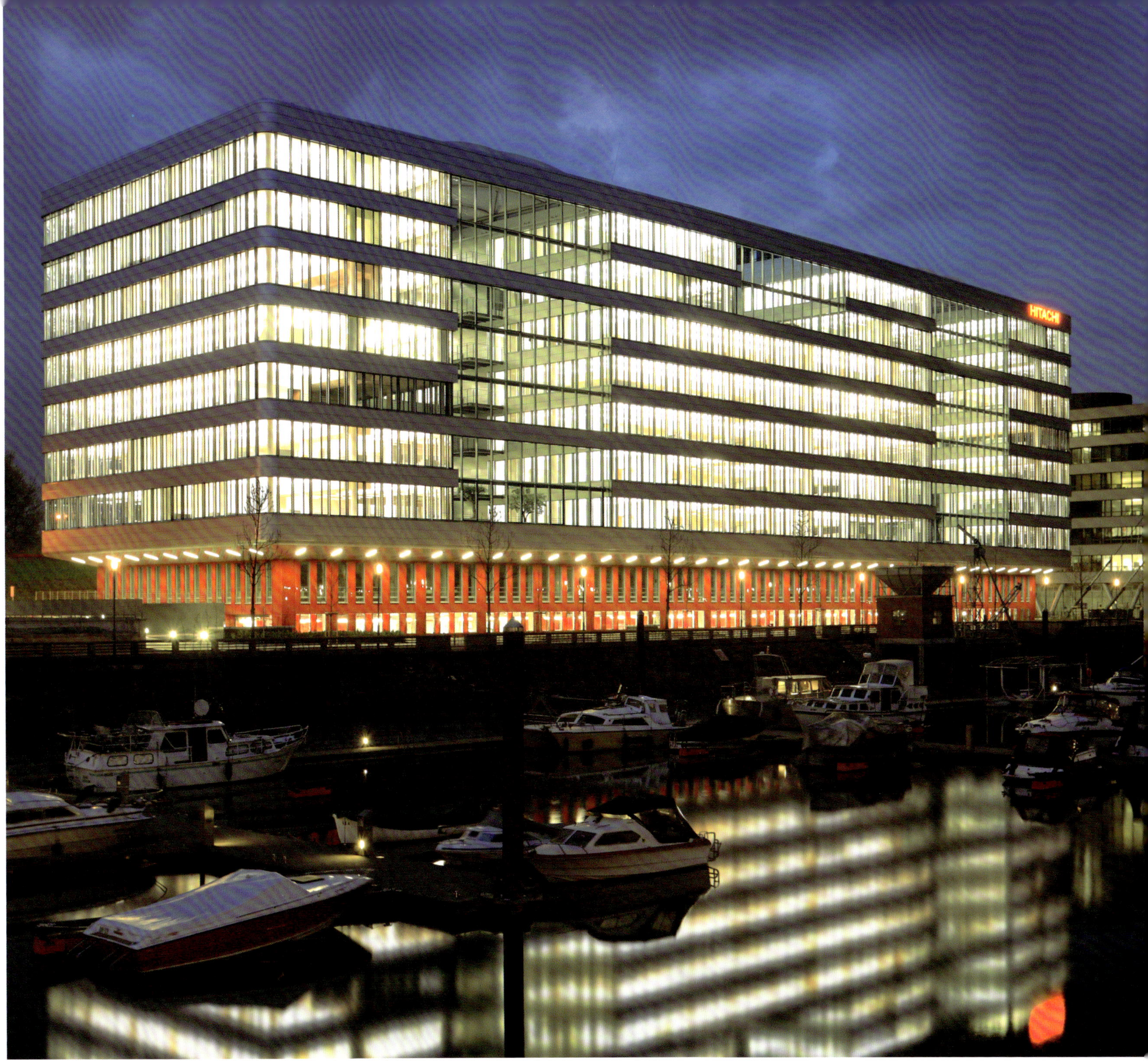
HITACHI

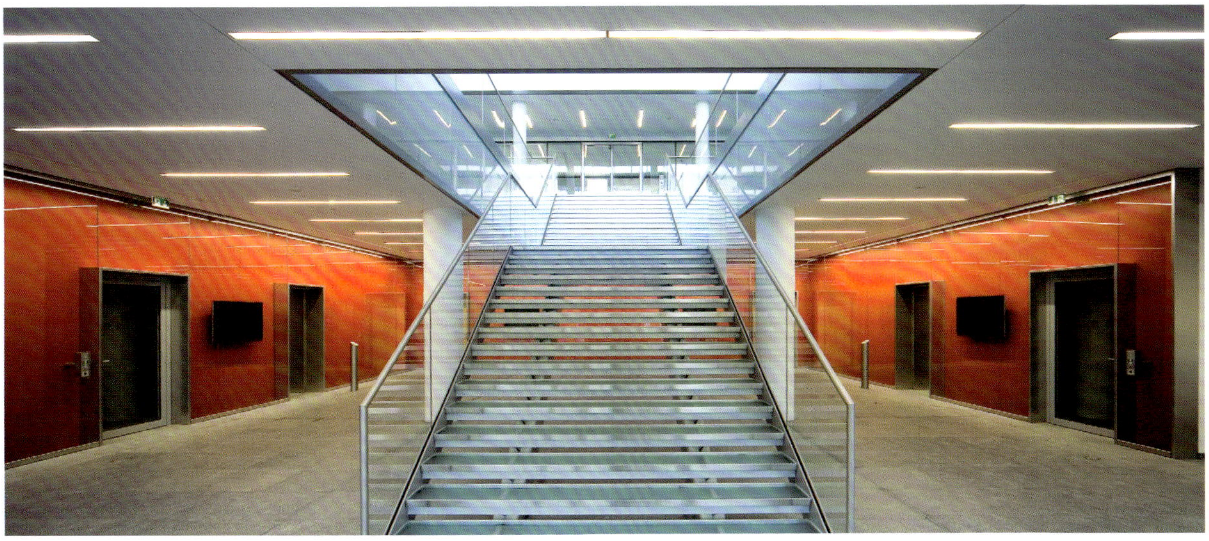

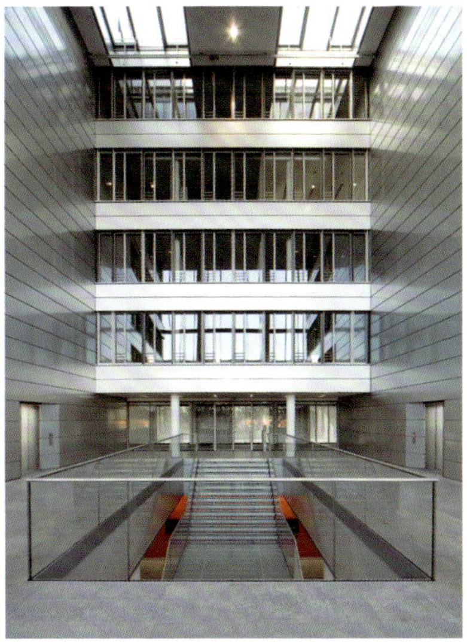

GERMANY_DÜSSELDORF E-PLUS HEADQUARTERS

ARCHITECTS: NPS TCHOBAN VOSS ARCHITEKTEN BDA / SERGEI TCHOBAN WITH STEPHAN LOHRE_**COLOR CONCEPT:** NPS TCHOBAN VOSS WITH FRIEDERIEKE TEBBE_**COMPLETION:** 2009_**NUMBER OF WORKPLACES:** 1,200_**GROSS FLOOR AREA:** 51,000 M²_**COMMON AREA:** MEETING POINTS, RESTAURANTS, CONFERENCE ROOMS, DATA CENTER, LOBBY_**KIND OF WORKPLACES:** OPEN-PLAN_**PHOTOS:** CLAUS GRAUBNER

The new headquarters of the mobile phone operator E-Plus on the former Kaufring premises presents itself as a hybrid structure consisting of the meander-shaped administration section, resting on a single-floor base and the directly attached parking garage, which is also underpinned by the basic floor. The design provides a highly promotionally effective presence near the neighboring highway with additional emblematic recognition from the air. The superimposition of the glass skywalks facing the highway on the meander ensures high sound insulation of the office areas coupled with internal connections with short distances and optimal utilization of the illuminated areas.

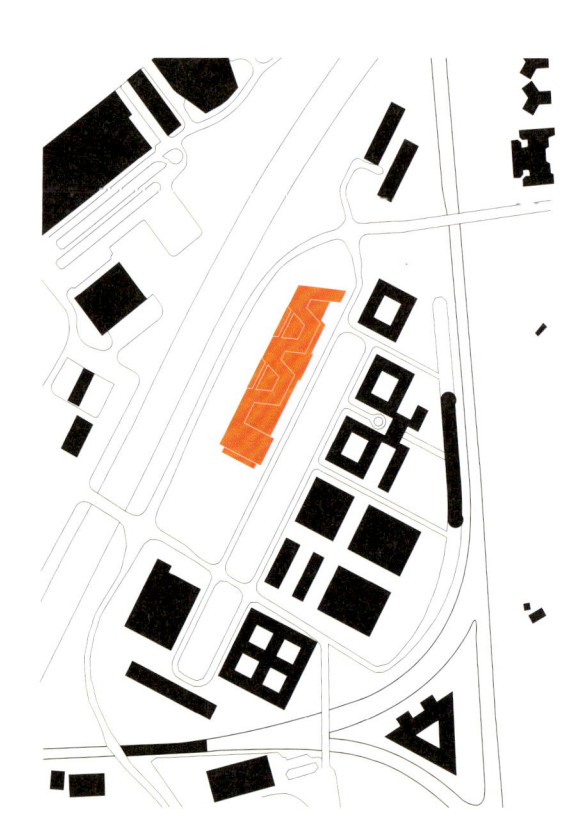

Die neue Hauptverwaltung des Mobilfunkbetreibers E-Plus auf dem ehemaligen Kaufring-Areal präsentiert sich als hybrider Baukörper, bestehend aus dem mäanderförmigen Verwaltungstrakt, der auf einer eingeschossigen Basis lagert sowie dem ebenfalls vom Basisgeschoss unterfangenen direkt angeschlossenen Parkhaus. Der Entwurf bietet maximale, werbewirksame Präsenz zur nahe gelegenen Autobahn mit zeichenhafter Erkennbarkeit aus der Luft. Die Überlagerung des Mäanders mit den zur Autobahn orientierten gläsernen Skywalks sorgt für einen hohen Schallschutz der Bürobereiche und eine Binnenerschließung mit kurzen Wegen bei optimaler Ausnutzung der belichteten Flächen.

left: Site plan_General view_Skywalk. right: Back view.
links: Lageplan_Hauptansicht_Skywalk. rechts: Rückansicht.

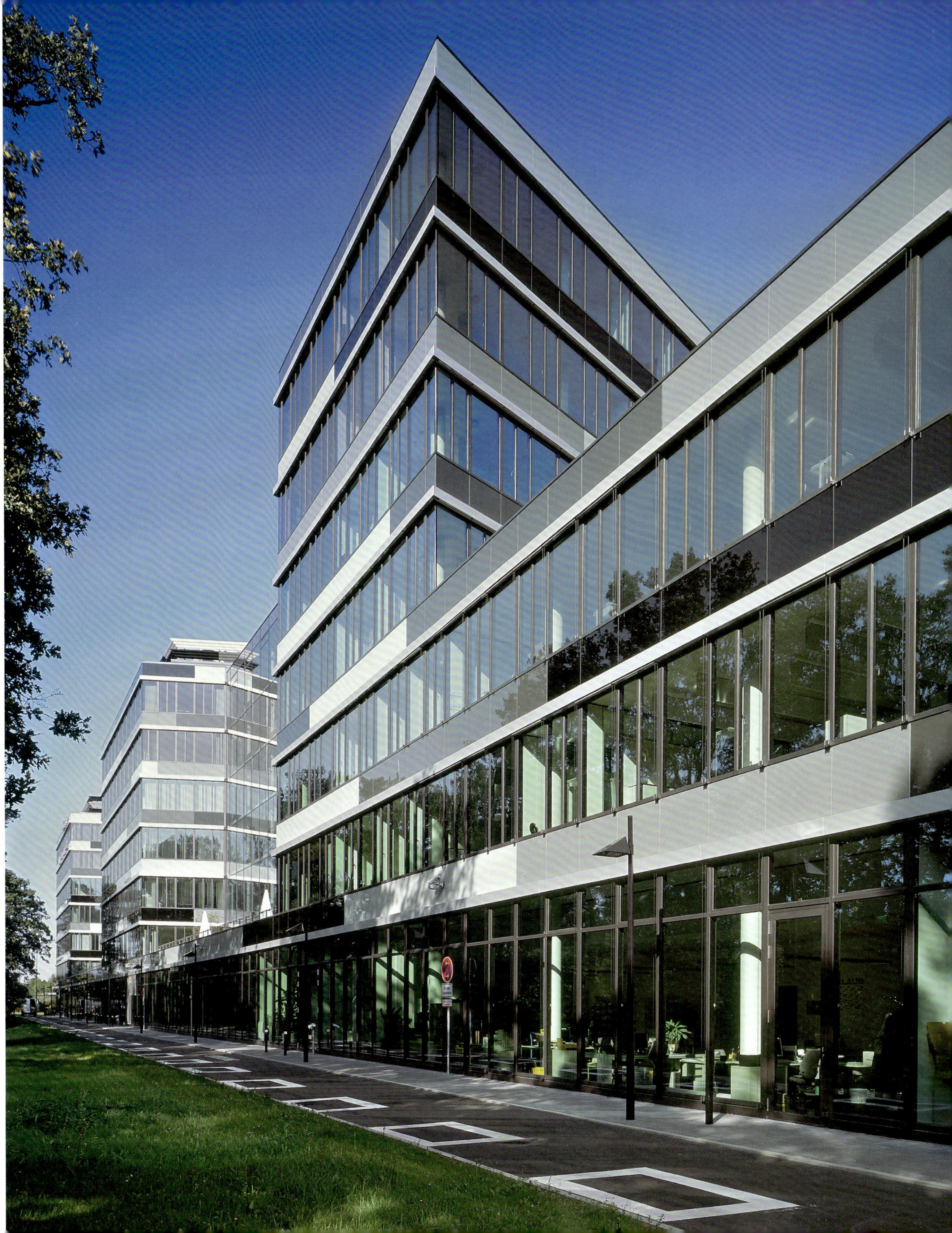

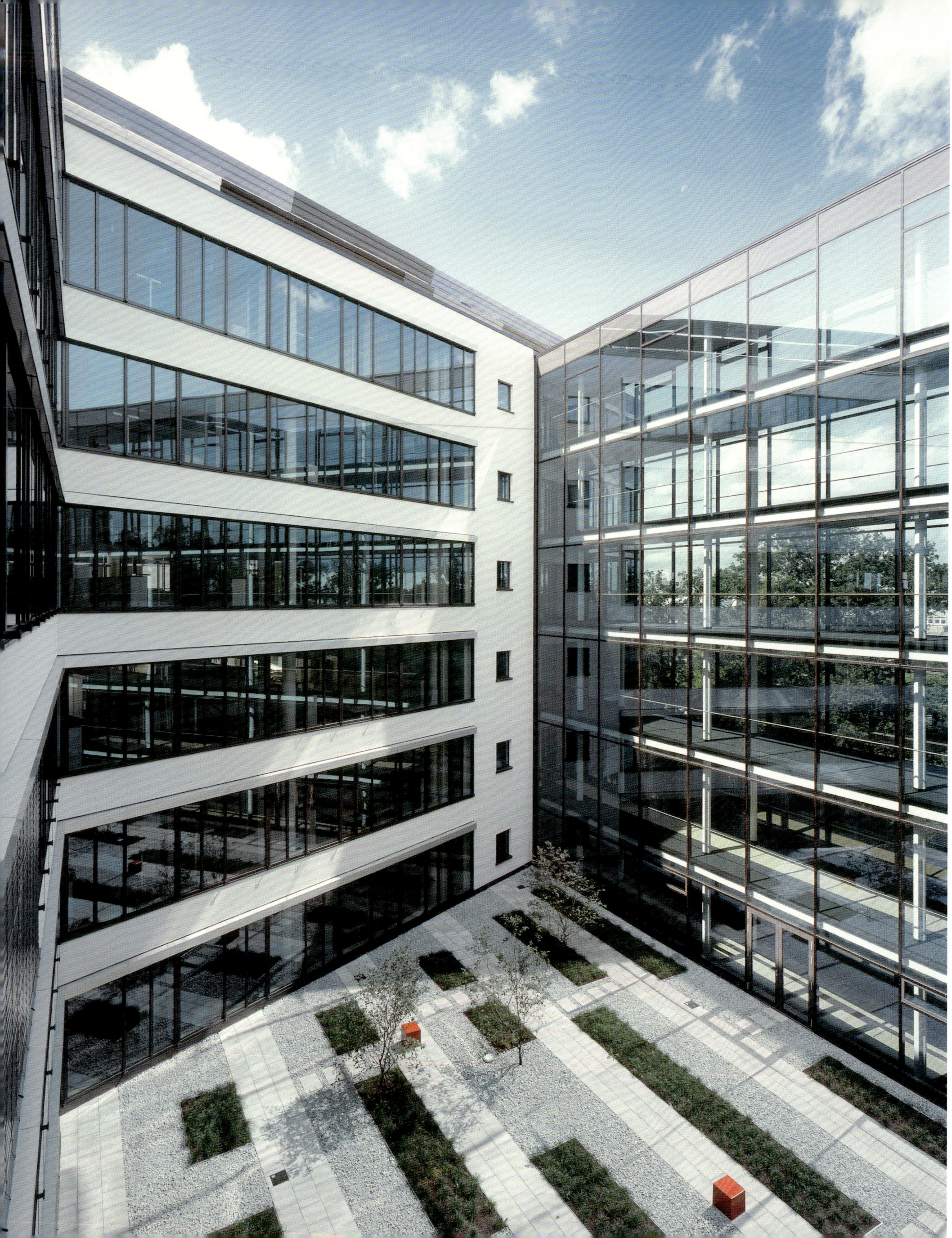

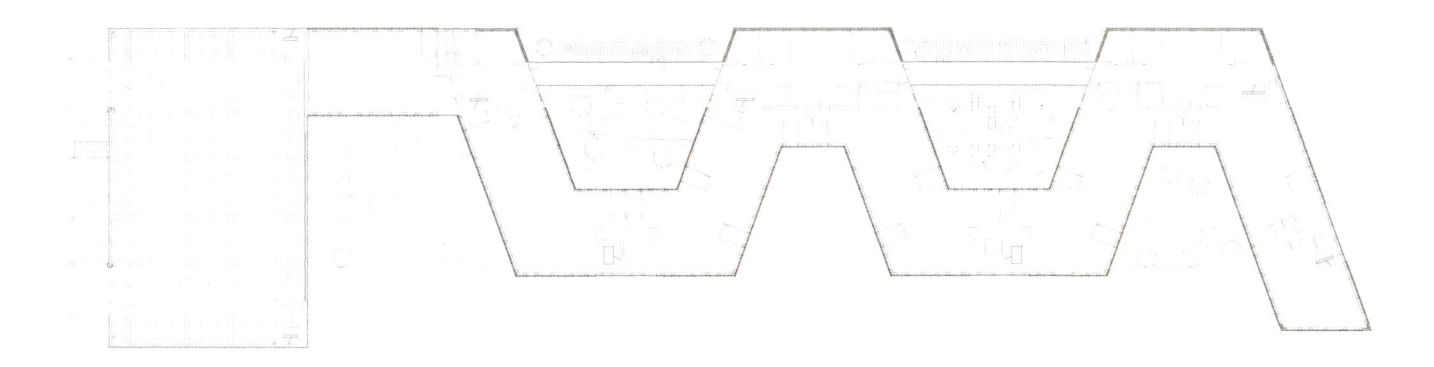

left: Granithof, one of the inner courtyards. right: First floor plan, standard floor_Canteen, detail_ Lobby and reception_View through the corridor to the elevator.
links: Granithof, einer der Innenhöfe. rechts: Grundriss erstes Obergeschoss, Regelgeschoss_ Mitarbeiterrestaurant, Detail_Lobby und Empfang_Blick durch den Flur zum Aufzug.

GERMANY_DÜSSELDORF **FOUR ELEMENTS**

ARCHITECTS: THOMAS PINK | PETZINKA PINK ARCHITEKTEN
COMPLETION: 2009_**NUMBER OF WORKPLACES:** 500–600
GROSS FLOOR AREA: 23,970 M²_**COMMON AREA:** RECEPTION, CONFERENCE ROOMS, MEETING ROOMS, GASTRONOMY
KIND OF WORKPLACES: CELLULAR, COMBINATION, TEAM
PHOTOS: TOMAS RIEHLE / © ARTURIMAGES

Four Elements adopted the basic concept of interruptions to the urban structure and it repairs the public space according to the original urban development plan. In harmony with the landmarked building across from it, the new building reacts to the successive spatial expansions and contractions of the street with variably positioned façade protrusions and different floor depths. The powerful ornamentation of the façade, resembling the designs by the Dutch cubists, coupled with the snow-white surfaces of the cubic frames, draw a full circle of 80 years of architectural history. Thus an office building with great visual power was established in northern Düsseldorf.

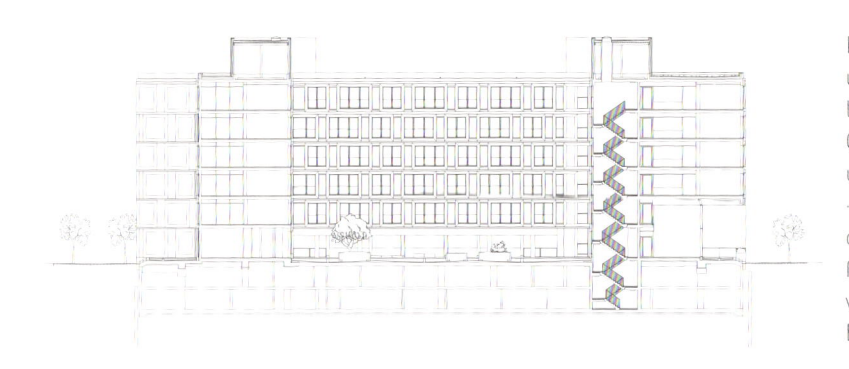

Four Elements greift die ursprüngliche Idee von Stadtraum-Zäsuren auf und repariert, im Sinne der ursprünglichen Stadtplanung, den öffentlichen Stadtraum. Im Zusammenklang mit seinem denkmalgeschützten Gegenüber reagiert der Neubau mit versetzten Fassadenvorsprüngen und unterschiedlichen Geschosstiefen auf sukzessive Raumaufweitungen und -verjüngungen des Straßenverlaufs. Die kraftvolle Ornamentik der Fassade, die an Entwürfe niederländischer Kubisten erinnert, sowie die schneeweißen Oberflächen der kubischen Rahmen schaffen einen Spannungsbogen von 80 Jahren Baugeschichte. So entstand im Düsseldorfer Norden ein Bürogebäude von großer visueller Kraft.

left: Section_Entrance Georg-Glock-Straße_Corner Uerdinger Straße / Kaiserswerther Straße. right: Detail, Façade.
links: Schnitt_Eingang Georg-Glock-Straße_Ecke Uerdinger Straße / Kaiserswerther Straße. rechts: Fassadendetail.

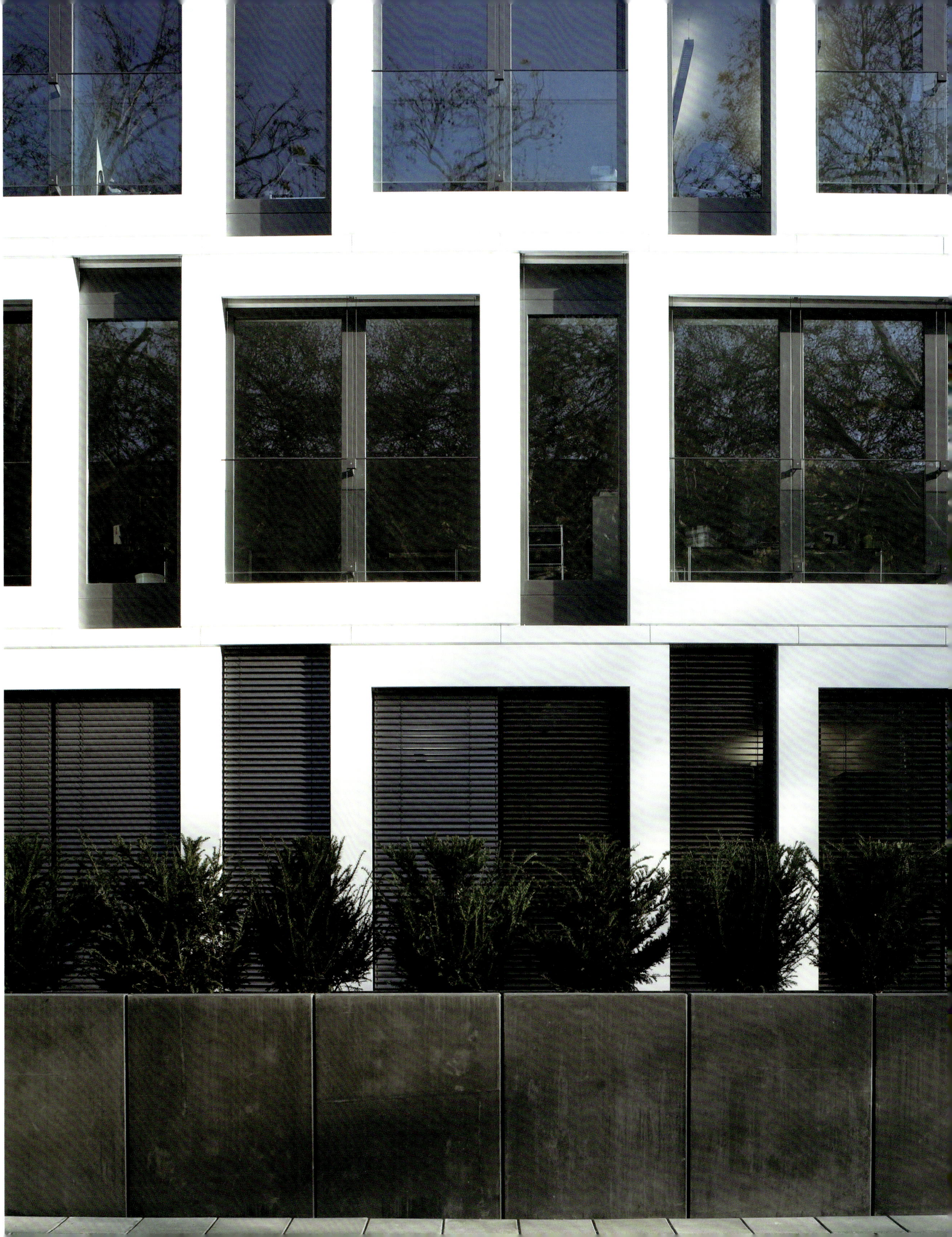

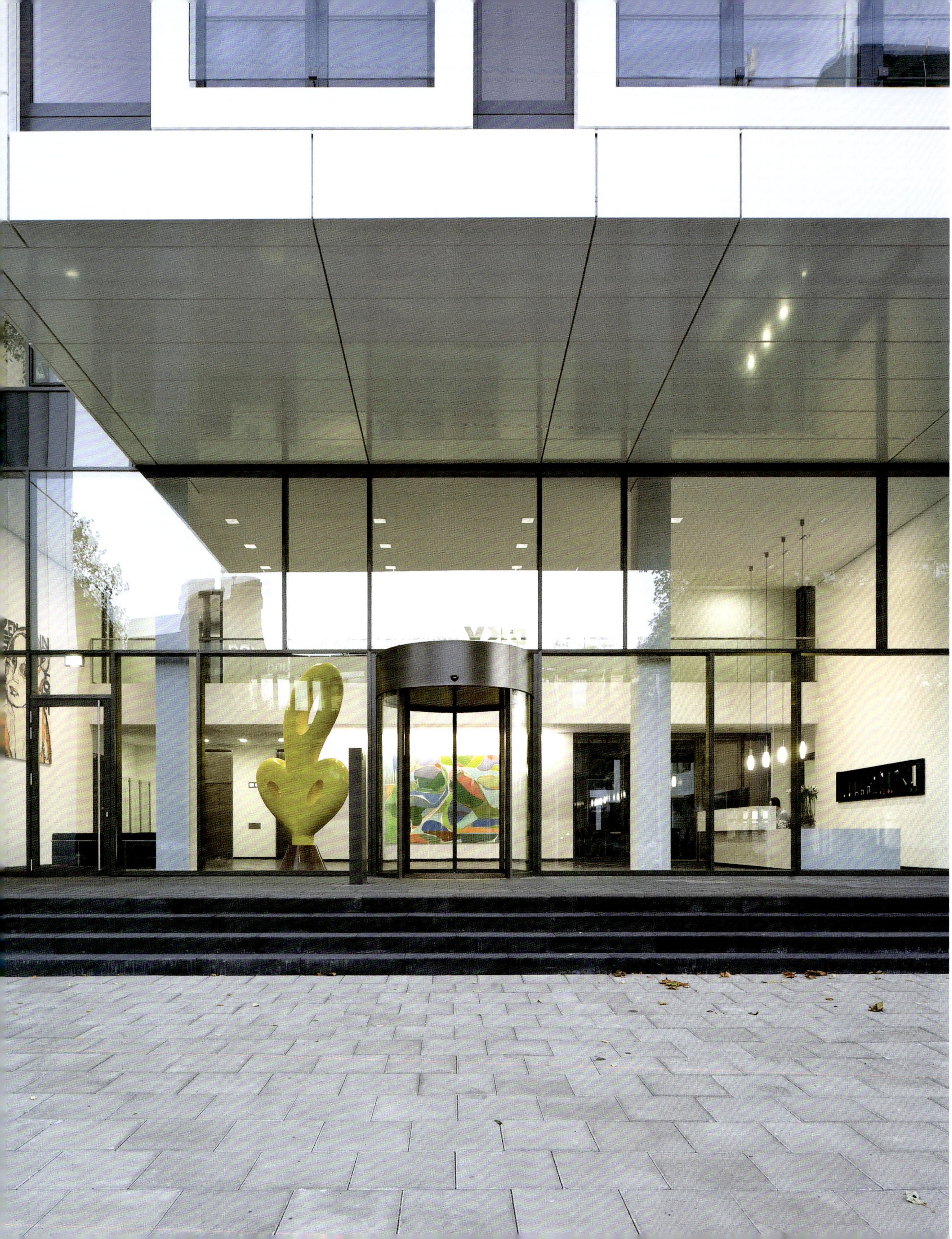

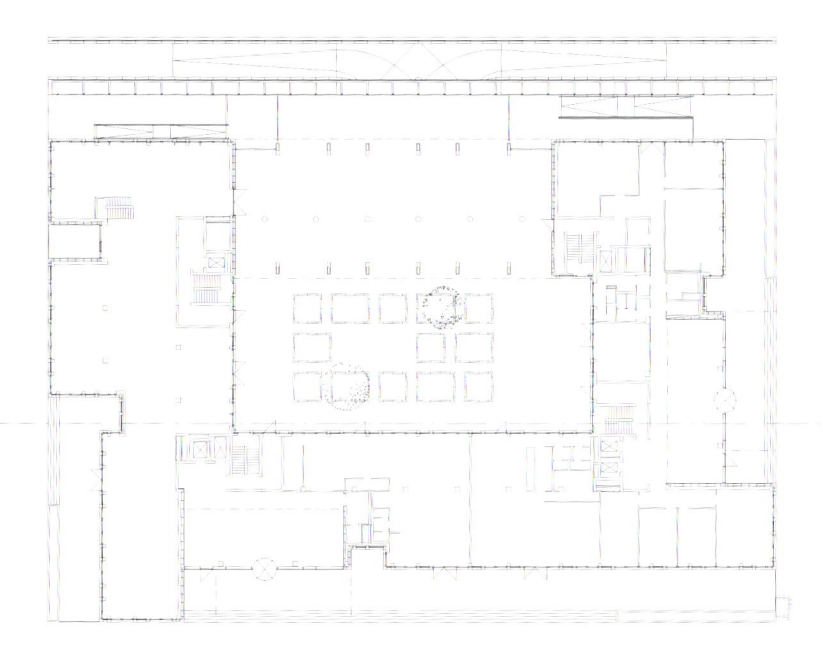

left: Entrance. right: Ground floor plan_Entrance area and reception_Office with meeting table in the foreground_Fifth floor, lobby / meeting floor.
links: Eingang. rechts: Grundriss Erdgeschoss_Eingangsbereich und Empfang_Büro mit Besprechungstisch im Vordergrund_Fünftes Obergeschoss, Foyer / Besprechungsetage.

GERMANY_DÜSSELDORF **IDEENBOTSCHAFT**

ARCHITECTS: THOMAS PINK | PETZINKA PINK ARCHITEKTEN
ORIGINAL BUILDING: GARNISONSBAUINSPEKTOR PETERS&KURING, 1893–1898_**COMPLETION:** 2008
NUMBER OF WORKPLACES: 600_**GROSS FLOOR AREA:** 20,841 M²
COMMON AREA: CONFERENCE AREAS, MEETING ROOMS, INFORMAL SEATING ARRANGEMENTS, RESTAURANT / CATERING
KIND OF WORKPLACES: CELLULAR, COMBINATION, OPEN-PLAN, TEAM, DESKSHARING, NON-TERRITORIAL, LOUNGE WORKSPACE
PHOTOS: MAX HAMPEL, DÜSSELDORF (168 B. L., 170, 171 B. L., R.), TAUFIK KENAN, BERLIN (168 B. R., 169, 171 A. L.)

The revitalization and expansion of the landmarked former Wilhelmian Uhlan casern was carried out within its overall urban context with the careful addition of new buildings and annexes. The special architectural attraction of the project stems from the interaction of historic and modern architectural elements and materials. The new building with its modern powerful interpretation of brick, encloses the "Platz der Ideen" ("Square of ideas") and combines the existing and the new buildings into an ensemble. Since summer 2008, seven agencies with approximately 600 employees took up their work on the campus of the so-called "Ideenbotschaft" ("Ideas embassy") of the Grey Global Group.

Die Revitalisierung und Erweiterung der denkmalgeschützten ehemaligen wilheminischen Ulanenkaserne erfolgte im stadthistorischen Gesamtkontext und unter umsichtiger Hinzufügung von Neu- und Anbauten. Der besondere architektonische Reiz des Projektes besteht im Zusammenspiel von historischen mit modernen Architekturelementen und Materialien. Der Neubau mit seiner modernen und grafisch kraftvollen Interpretation des Materials Ziegel schließt den „Platz der Ideen" ein und verbindet die Bestandsgebäude und den Neubau zu einem Ensemble. Auf dem Campus der so benannten „Ideenbotschaft" der Grey Global Group sind seit Sommer 2008 sieben Agenturen mit circa 600 Mitarbeitern tätig.

left: Site plan_Extension and heightening barracks_New building. right: Office barracks.
links: Lageplan_Anbau und Aufstockung Mannschaftsgebäude_Neubau. rechts: Büro Mannschaftsgebäude.

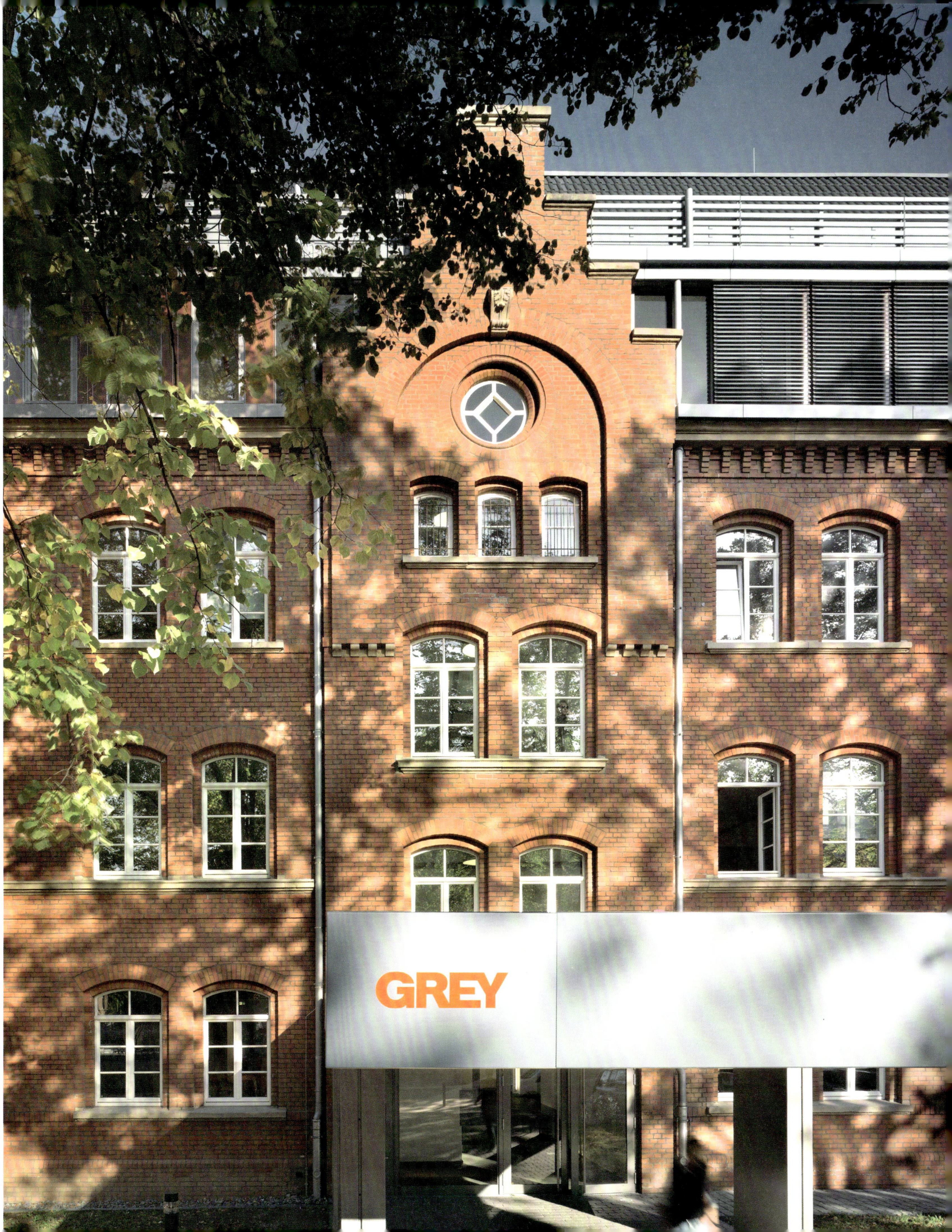
GREY

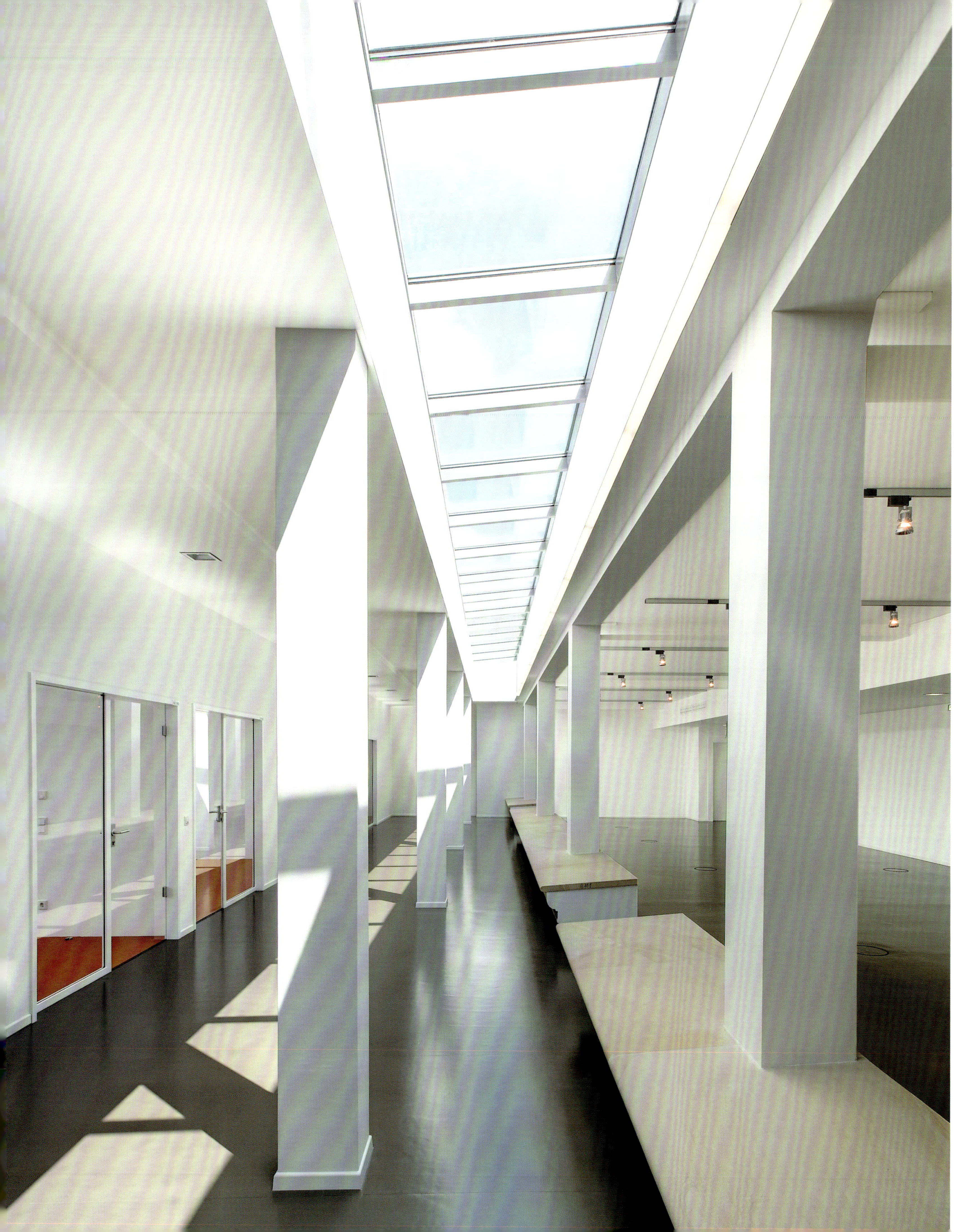

left: Roof floor, baracks. right: Section baracks_Office baracks_Conference room, extension baracks_Canteen, former building of the married_Reception, new building.
links: Dachgeschoss, Mannschaftsgebäude. rechts: Schnitt Mannschaftsgebäude_Büro Mannschaftsgebäude_Konferenzraum, Anbau Mannschaftsgebäude_Kantine, ehemaliges Verheiratetenhaus_Empfang, Neubau.

GERMANY_FRANKFURT/MAIN **DOCK 2.0**

ARCHITECTS: MEIXNER SCHLÜTER WENDT ARCHITEKTEN
COMPLETION: ONGOING_**GROSS FLOOR AREA:** 24,000 M²
KIND OF WORKPLACES: CELLULAR, COMBINATION, OPEN-PLAN
PHOTOS: COURTESY OF THE ARCHITECTS

The concept for the Lindleystraße 8–11 office building was developed from the setting and specific requirements. Based on the special harbor atmosphere, the image and modular functionality of container facilities were adopted. An associative connection was established through terms such as "storage", "stacking" and "moving", while the obvious efficiency of the harbor structures serves as a prototype for the clearly-structured functionality of the office building. Its expandable flexible building structure can incorporate the addition of various additional units beyond the normal use, including areas for special function or a division into several tracts.

Das Konzept für das Bürogebäude Lindleystraße 8–11 wurde aus den Vorgaben durch Ort und Aufgabe entwickelt. Von der besonderen Hafenatmosphäre ausgehend, wurde das Bild und die modulare Funktionalität von Containernanlagen aufgegriffen. Eine assoziative Verbindung wird durch Begriffe wie „lagern", „stapeln" und „verschieben" erreicht und die offensichtliche Effizenz der Hafenstrukturen ist Vorbild für die Funktionalität des Bürogebäudes. So kann eine additive flexible Gebäudestruktur über die üblichen Nutzungsanforderungen hinaus verschiede zuschaltbare Nutzungseinheiten, möglicherweise in Sondernutzung, und eine Gliederung in Bauabschnitte gewährleisten.

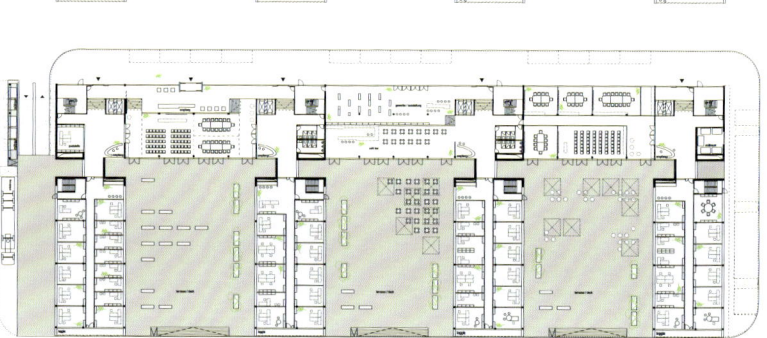

left: Ground and standard floor plan_3-D sketch_General view. right: North-west view_Top floor by night_Interior view.
links: Grundriss Erd- und Regelgeschoss_3-D Zeichnung_Gesamtansicht. rechts: Nordwestansicht_ Dachgeschoss in der Nacht_Innenansicht.

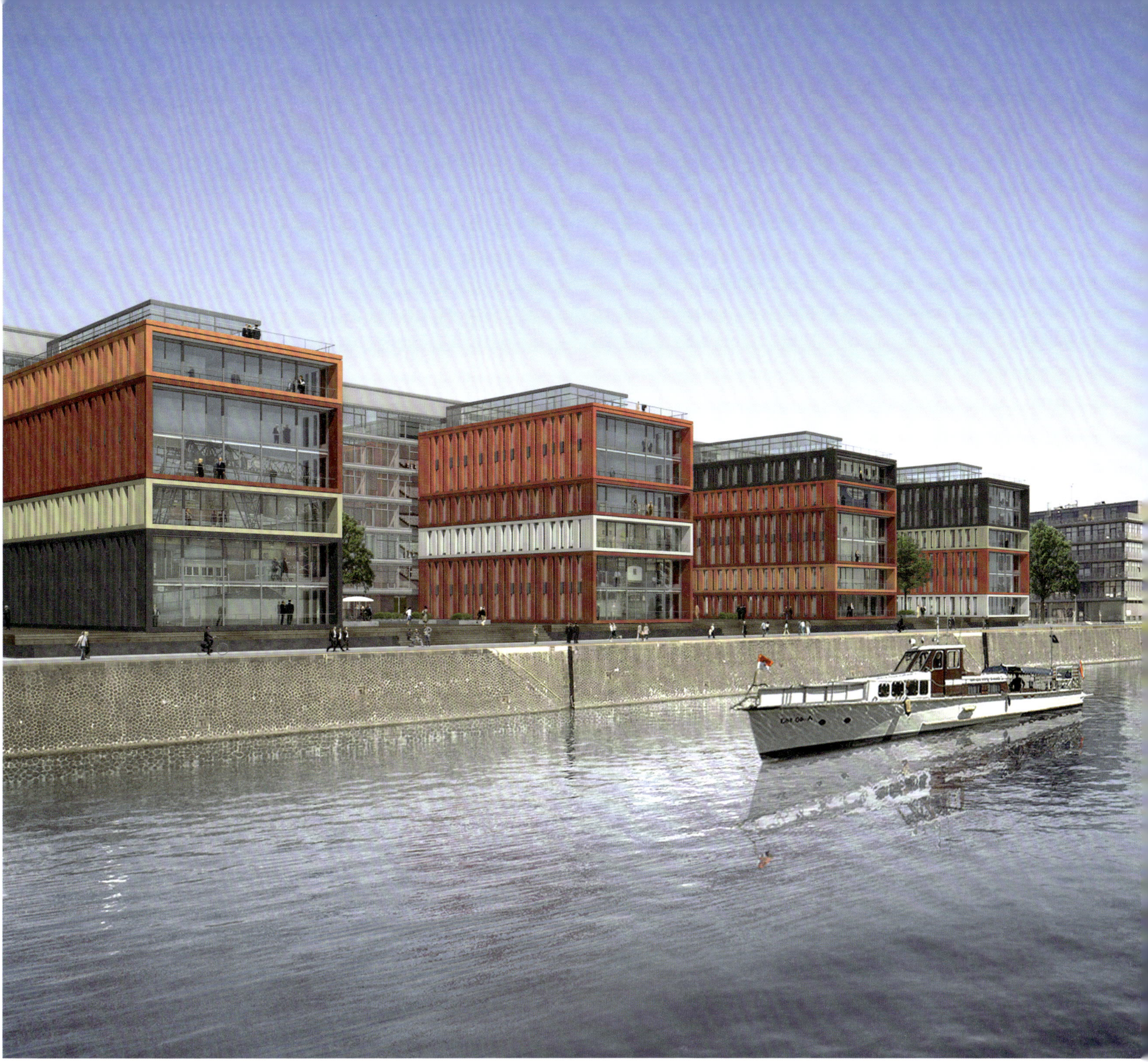

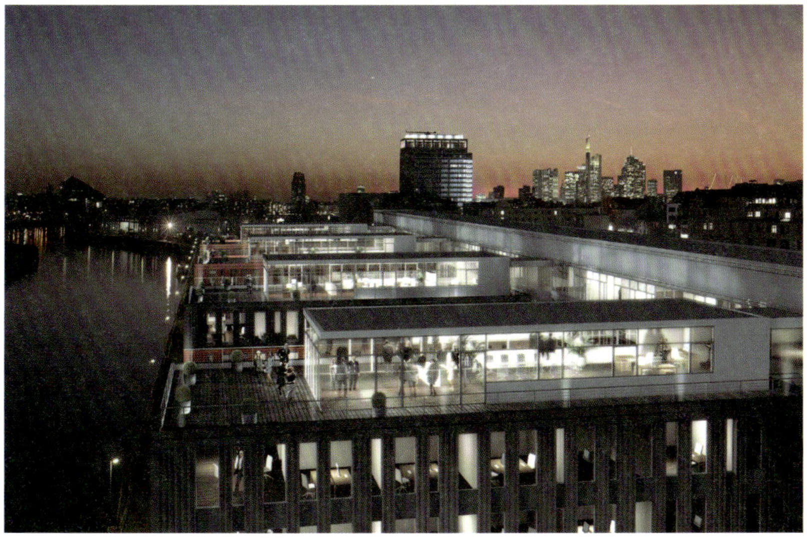

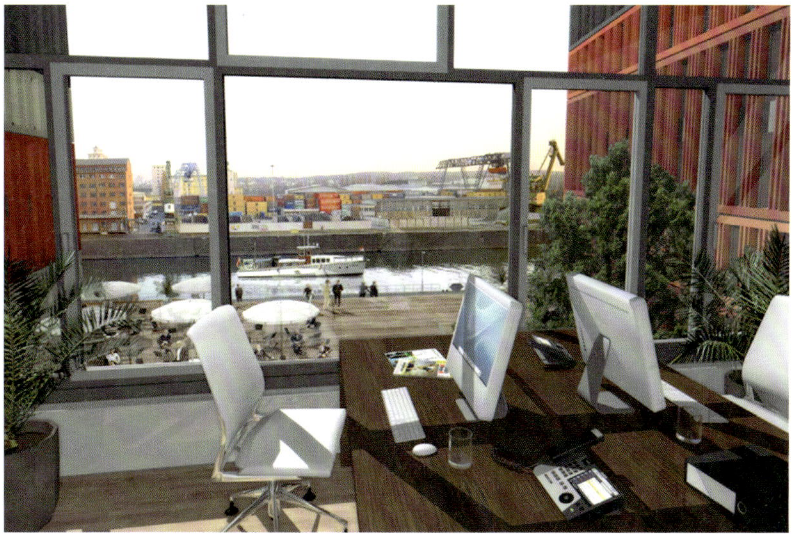

GERMANY_FRANKFURT/MAIN PUBLIC ORDER OFFICE FRANKFURT

ARCHITECTS: MEIXNER SCHLÜTER WENDT ARCHITEKTEN
COMPLETION: 2009_**NUMBER OF WORKPLACES:** 650
GROSS FLOOR AREA: 30,000 M²_**COMMON AREA:** CANTEEN, CAFETERIA, CONFERENCE ROOMS
KIND OF WORKPLACES: CELLULAR, OPEN-PLAN, TEAM
PHOTOS: CHRISTOPH KRANEBURG, COLOGNE

The design complements the urban block structure, while incorporating the curved movement of the adjacent railroad tracks. The shape of the basic layout, which does not differentiate the front and back side, i.e. the street and backyard façade, enables both urban aggregation as well as an open structure with the associated illumination quality. The layout presents the typical stacked floors of office buildings that are divided into horizontal layers. This is in line with the functional structure of the compilation of various administrative areas. The alteration and covering up of these layers provides an exceptional look. The complex shape of the layout and the floor plan provided the public affairs office with a significant building that has a high recognition value.

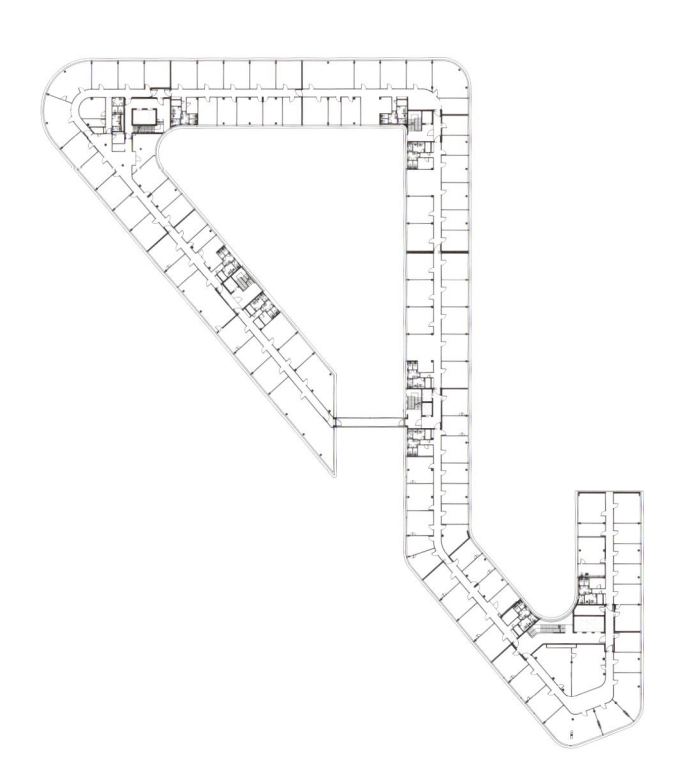

Der Entwurf ergänzt die städtebauliche Blockstruktur und greift zugleich die Kurvenbewegung der benachbarten Bahngleise auf. Die Grundrissform, ohne Unterscheidung von Vor- und Rückseite bzw. Straßen und Hoffassade, ermöglicht sowohl Stadtraumverdichtung als auch Offenheit mit entsprechender Belichtungsqualität. Der Aufriss thematisiert die spezifische, für Bürogebäude typische Geschossstapelung durch Differenzierung in horizontale Schichten, was funktional auch der Stapelung unterschiedlicher Behördenbereiche entspricht. Durch das Verfremden und Überspielen dieser Schichten wird ein ungewohnter Wahrnehmungsprozeß initiiert. Durch die komplexe Formgebung in Grund- und Aufriss ist das Ordnungsamt ein signifikantes Gebäude mit hohem Wiedererkennungswert.

left: Second floor plan_North-east elevation. right: Aerial view.
links: Grundriss zweites Obergeschoss_Nordostfassade. rechts: Luftaufnahme.

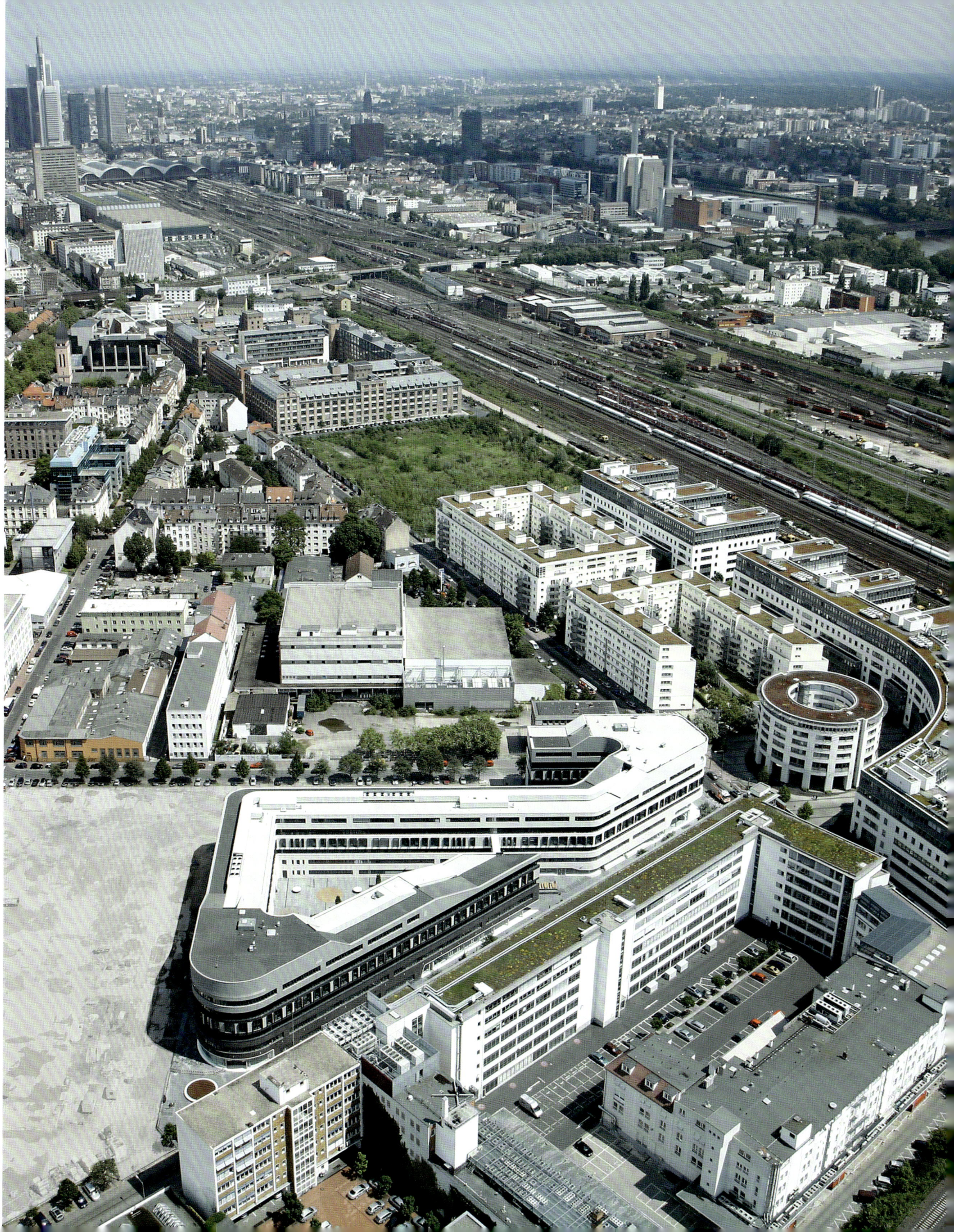

Servicezentrum

1

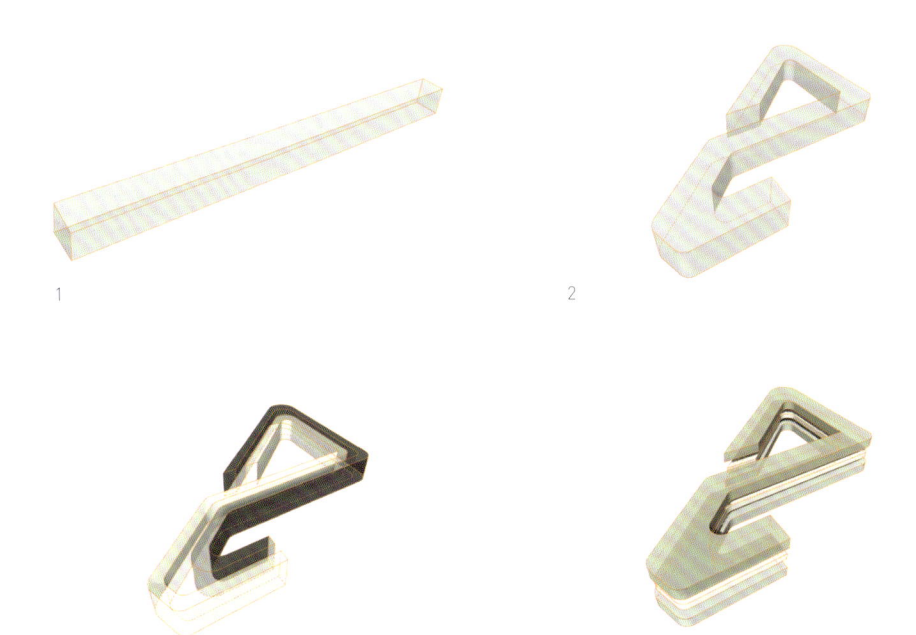

2

3

4

left: Entrance hall, counter. right: Volume, urban typology, vertical layers horizontal layers_Elevation Rebstöcker Straße_Inner courtyard.
links: Eingangshalle, Tresen. rechts: Volumen, städtebauliche Typologie, vertikale Schichtung, horizontal Schichtung_Teilansicht Rebstöcker Straße_Innenhof.

GERMANY_GELSENKIRCHEN **MAIN ADMINISTRATION GELSENWASSER AG**

ARCHITECTS: ANIN · JEROMIN · FITILIDIS & PARTNER
COMPLETION: 2004_**NUMBER OF WORKPLACES:** 200
GROSS FLOOR AREA: 7,130 M²_**COMMON AREA:** CONFERENCE ROOMS_**KIND OF WORKPLACES:** CELLULAR, COMBINATION, OPEN-PLAN_**PHOTOS:** HOLGER KNAUF, DÜSSELDORF, ANIN · JEROMIN · FITILIDIS & PARTNER (180, 181 A. R.)

The new building is located at the intersection of two federal highways, within sight of the Gelsenkirchen stadium. The transparent extension building is a clear commitment of the company to its open and communicative structure. The flexible layout plan of the individual floors and the open stairs that are integrated into the work space support communication among employees. With renewable energies constituting 63 percent of the building's total energy consumption, the new building of Gelsenwasser AG is exemplary across Europe. The centrally controlled sunscreen is integrated into the void between the panes of the double-glazed windows. The key detail of the façade, which has been reduced to a minimum, is the "aluminum gill". This new type of ventilation is integrated into the edge of the ceiling. The floor-to-ceiling façade elements provide extraordinary transparency throughout.

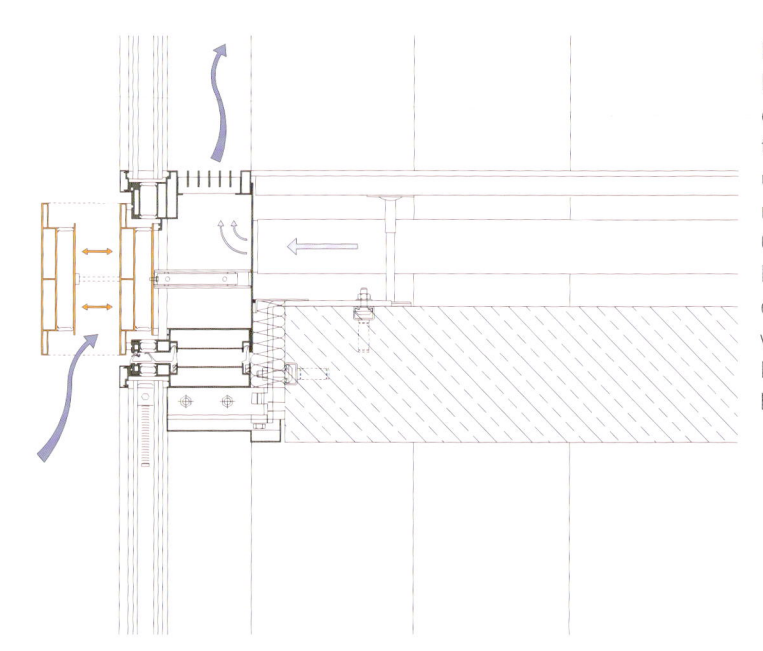

Der Neubau liegt am Kreuzungspunkt zweier Bundesstraßen, in sichtbarer Nähe zum Gelsenkirchener Stadion. Der transparente Erweiterungsbau ist ein klares Bekenntnis des Unternehmens zu seiner offenen und kommunikativen Struktur. Die flexible Grundrissaufteilung der einzelnen Geschossebenen und die offenen, in die Arbeitsfläche integrierten Treppen, fördern die Kommunikation der Mitarbeiter. Mit einem regenerativen Anteil von 63 Prozent am Gesamtenergieverbrauch ist der Neubau der Gelsenwasser AG vorbildlich in Europa. Der zentral gesteuerte Sonnenschutz ist im Scheibenzwischenraum der Isolierverglasung angeordnet. Das entscheidende Detail der auf das notwendigste reduzierten Fassade ist die im Deckenrand integrierte „Aluminium Kieme" – eine Neuinterpretation der herkömmlichen Lüftung. Die geschosshohen Fassadenelemente gewähren eine außerordentliche Transparenz.

left: Detail, "ventilation gill"_Double volumes_The "aluminum gill". right: Night view.
links: Detail, „Lüftungkieme"_Doppeltes Volumen_Die „Aluminium Kieme". rechts: Nachtansicht.

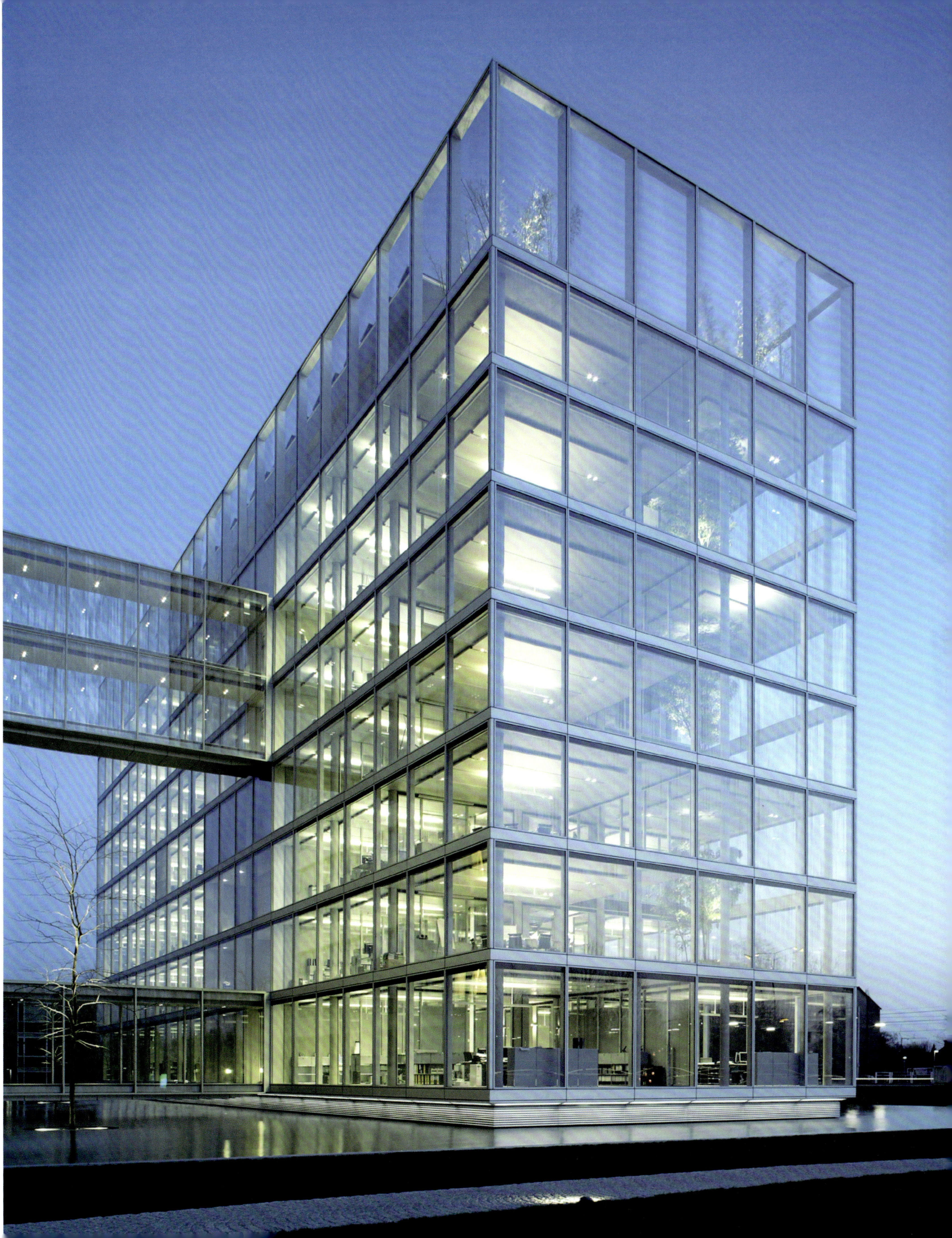

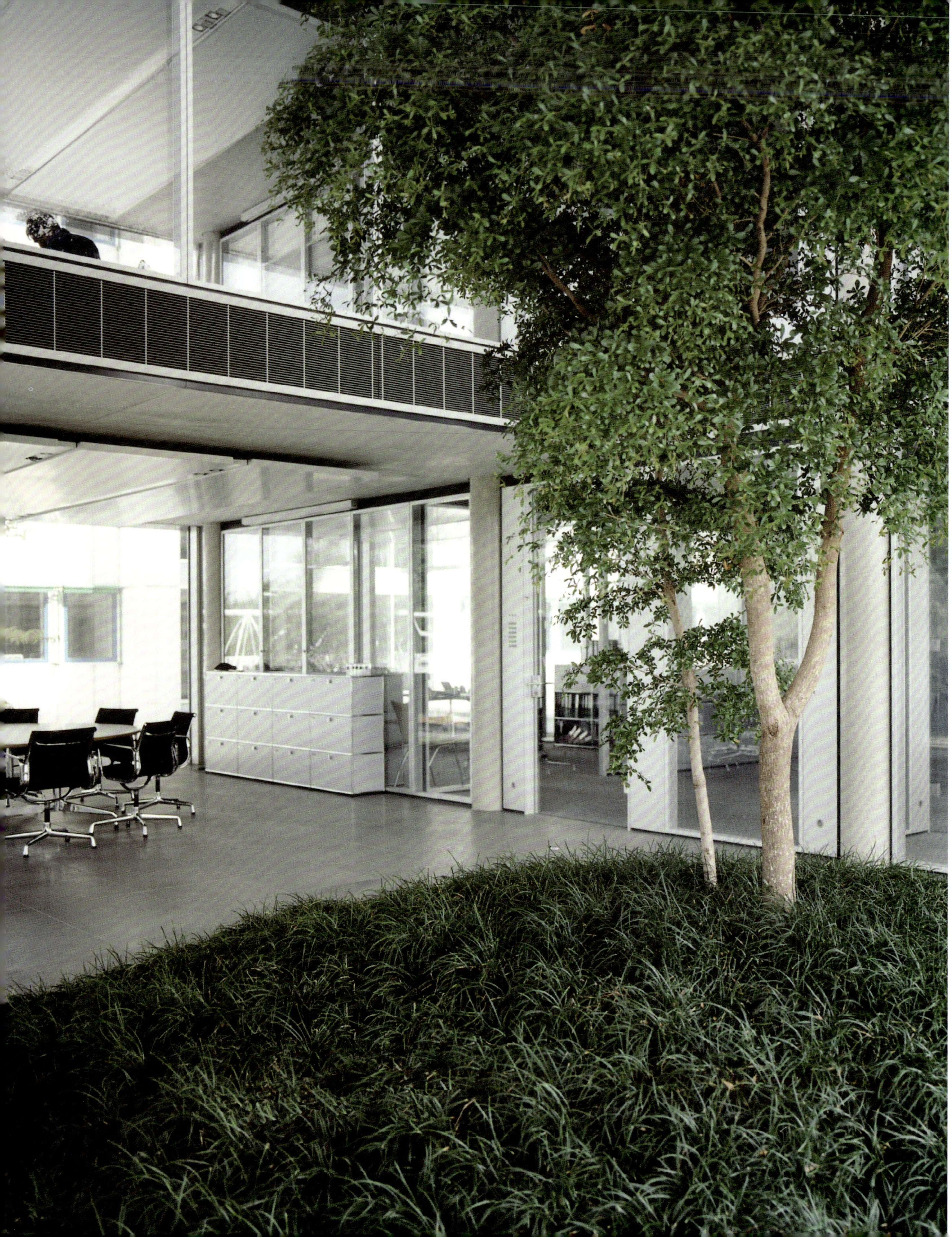

left: A green tree in front of the conference room. right: First floor plan_Staircase_Connecting stairs in the office corridor_Communication zone.
links: Grüner Baum vor dem Besprechungszimmer. rechts: Grundriss erstes Obergeschoss_Treppenhaus_Verbindungstreppe in der Büroflurzone_Kommunikationszone.

GERMANY_GELSENKIRCHEN HANS-SACHS-HAUS

ARCHITECTS: PASD FELDMEIER + WREDE
ORIGINAL ARCHITECT: ALFRED FISCHER_**COMPLETION:** ONGOING
NUMBER OF WORKPLACES: 450_**GROSS FLOOR AREA:** 21,456 M²
COMMON AREA: FORUM, LOBBY, CAFETERIA, ADVICE HALL, MEETING ROOMS, COMMUNAL GALLERY **KIND OF WORKPLACES:** CELLULAR, TEAM_**RENDERINGS:** COURTESY OF THE ARCHITECTS

On the one hand, the building ensemble was to be preserved as much as possible given its importance as a cultural monument. On the other hand, it was to be updated to meet the requirements of a modern administration, in accordance with building regulations and the responsibility towards the climate and the environment and with reasonable implementation costs. The design includes an old and a new wing. The new outer skin – an understated high-quality glass lamella construction with a 'new interpretation' of the rounded 'Fischer-corners' led to the emergence of an inner skin, which opens up towards the glass-covered inner courtyard as a simple post-and-beam construction.

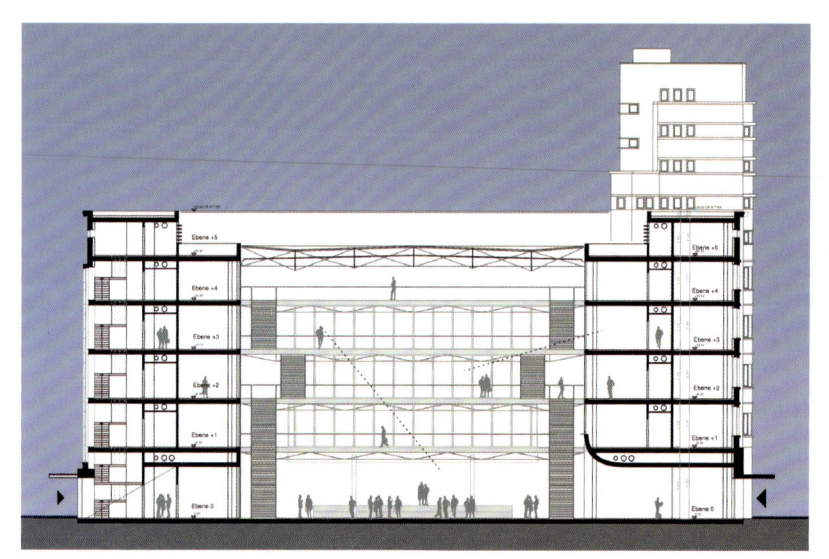

Das Gebäudeensemble sollte unter Berücksichtigung seiner Bedeutung als Kulturdenkmal soweit wie möglich erhalten bleiben, gleichzeitig aber entsprechend der Anforderungen eines modernen Verwaltungsbetriebes unter Beachtung der baurechtlichen Vorgaben und der Verantwortung für Klima und Umwelt in den Grenzen einer angemessenen finanziellen Realisierbarkeit aktualisiert werden. Der Entwurf gliedert sich in einen Altbau- und einen Neubautrakt. Aus der neuen äußeren Hülle – einer zurückhaltenden, hochwertigen Glaslamellen-Konstruktion, mit ‚Neuinterpretation' der gerundeten ‚Fischer-Ecken'- entwickelt sich in der Abwicklung eine innere Hülle, die sich als einfache Pfosten-Riegel-Fassade zum glasüberdachten Innenhof öffnet.

left: Cross section_Exterior view, corner Ebertstraße_Exterior view, interface historical and new façade. right: Entrance hall_Elevation Vattmannstraße.
links: Querschnitt_Außenansicht Ecke Ebertstraße_ Außenansicht, Schnittstelle zwischen historischer und neuer Fassade. rechts: Eingangshalle_Ansicht Vattmannstraße.

Schalke-Lounge

GERMANY_GELSENKIRCHEN ADMINISTRATION BUILDING THS

ARCHITECTS: THS / PASD FELDMEIER + WREDE_**ORIGINAL BUILDING:** SCHUPP UND KREMER_**COMPLETION:** 2003_**NUMBER OF WORKPLACES:** 350_**GROSS FLOOR AREA:** 17,100 M²_**COMMON AREA:** EVENT HALL, RESTAURANT / CAFETERIA, LIBRARY, MEETING CUBES, COMBINATION ZONE IN FRONT OF THE OFFICES **KIND OF WORKPLACES:** COMBINATION, OPEN-PLAN, TEAM **PHOTOS:** THOMAS RIEHLE / THS, WERNER HANNAPEL / THS (184)

The former coal mine was transformed into a contemporary building with an open structure that was preserved to accommodate open utilization. High-quality extension and fitted elements, often made of glass, such as front stairs and bridges that condense and liven up communication paths, were added to the existing structure. The contrast of old and new was highlighted, resulting in a unique work environment, which can nevertheless serve as a model for the conversion of other industrial plants. The original façades and roofs were preserved and renovated to comply with current construction and building regulations.

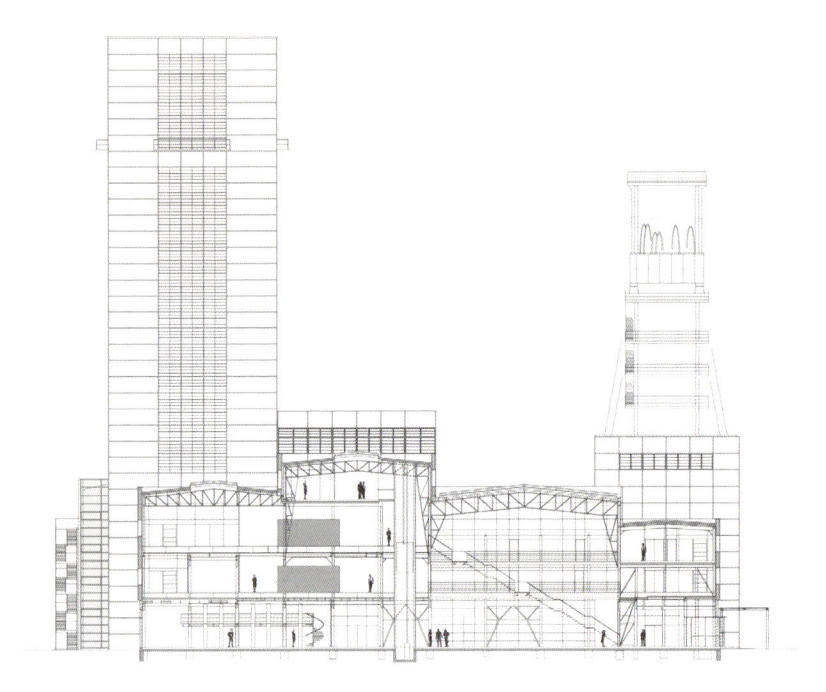

Die ehemalige Zeche wurde in ein zeitgemäßes Gebäude umgewandelt wobei die offene Struktur einer offenen Nutzung entsprechend erhalten blieb. Qualitativ hochwertige, oftmals gläserne Erweiterungs- und Einbauten, wie Freitreppen und Brücken, die verkürzte und interessante Kommunikationswege ermöglichen, ergänzen den Bestand. Der Kontrast von Altem und Neuem wurde herausgearbeitet, wodurch ein einmaliges Arbeitsumfeld entstand, das dennoch als Modell für die Umwandlung anderer Industrieanlagen dienen kann. Die überlieferte Konstruktion von Fassaden und Dächern wurde erhalten und renoviert, um aktuellen konstruktionstechnischen und gebäudetechnischen Anforderungen zu genügen.

left: Section_Bridges and stairs in the atrium_Entrance hall_View to shaft I. right: Atrium, elevator on the second floor.
links: Schnitt_Brücken und Treppen in der Eingangshalle_Blick auf Schacht I. rechts: Aufzug im zweiten Obergeschoss der Eingangshalle.

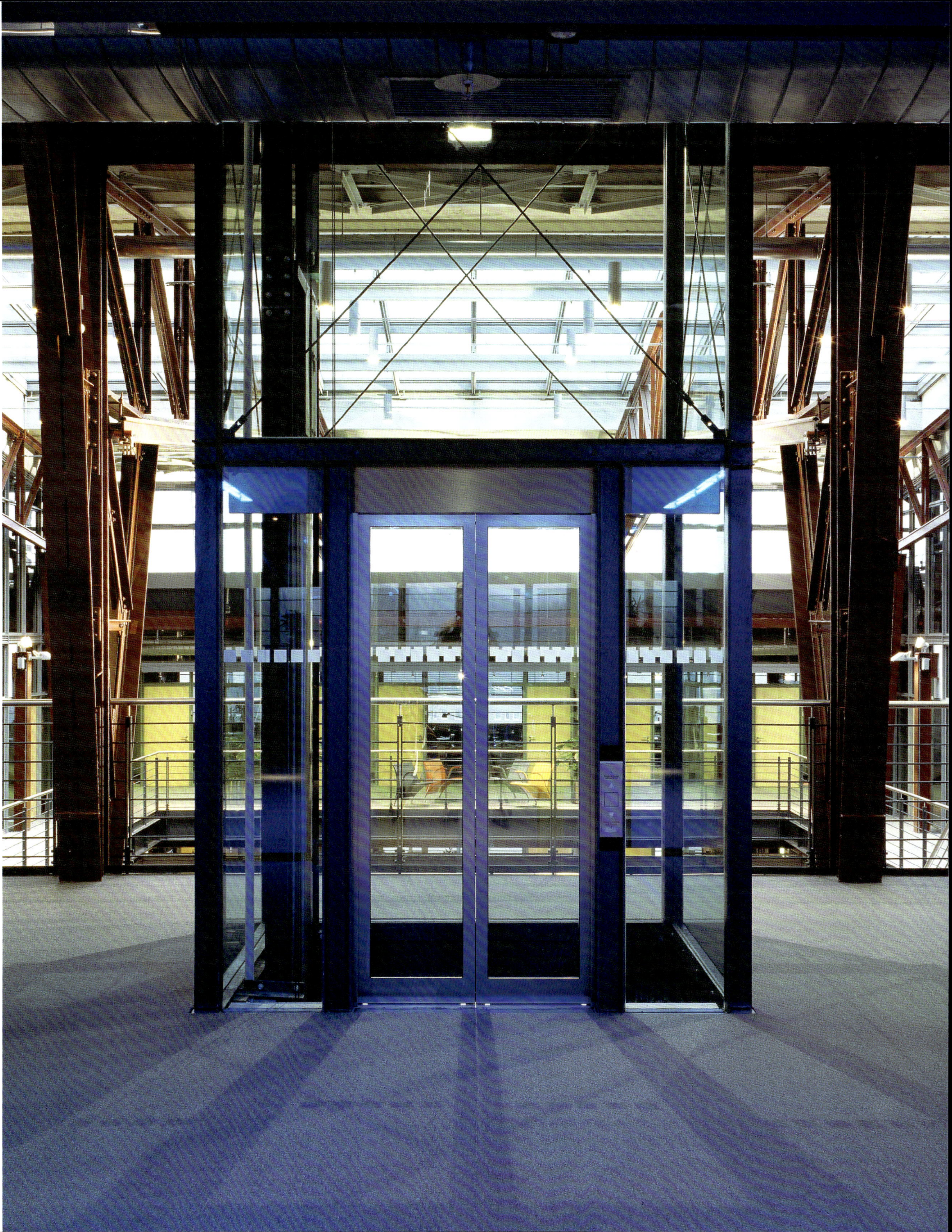

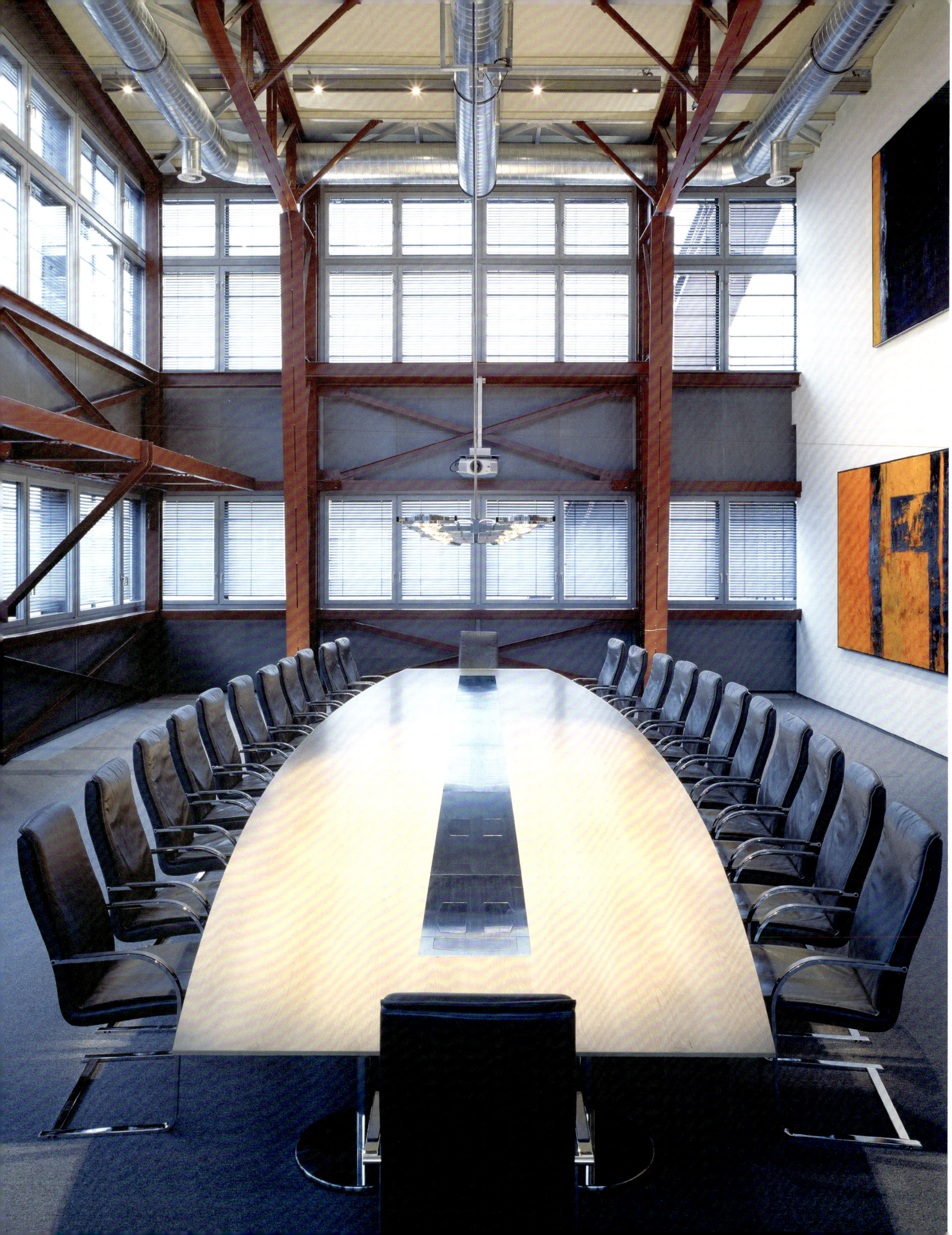

left: Conference room. right: Ground floor plan_Meeting cube_Meeting room with view towards the atrium_Meeting cube with combination zone_Meeting room, second floor.
links: Konferenzraum. rechts: Grundriss, Erdgeschoss_Besprechungsraumkubus_Besprechungsraum mit Blick zum Atrium_Besprechungsraumkuben mit Kombizonen_Besprechungsraum, zweites Obergeschoss.

GERMANY_HAMBURG **RED RABBIT WERBEAGENTUR GMBH**

ARCHITECTS: BFGF DESIGN STUDIOS_**OTHER CREATIVES:** PETER UNZEITIG, UNZEITIG ID_**COMPLETION:** 2009
NUMBER OF WORKPLACES: 30_**GROSS FLOOR AREA:** 650 M²
COMMON AREA: KITCHEN, MEETING ROOM
KIND OF WORKPLACES: COMBINATION, OPEN-PLAN
PHOTOS: DORFMÜLLER & KRÖGER, HAMBURG

The nationally and internationally award-winning advertising firm deliberately chose a location outside the stylish downtown area and close to the public in an area located between the Reeperbahn district and the Elbe in a David Chipperfield building. Based on the polygonal floor plan and the orthogonal room structure located around a rectangular inner courtyard, the previously divided office floor was given a creative design incorporating Feng shui principles, which visitors can experience as a creative unit. The entrance area is dominated by a red-rabbit colored wall segment that is tilted in two directions, whose diagonal location in the area alters predefined traffic ways and provides the area with a direction.

Die national und international ausgezeichnete Kreativagentur hat ihren Standort bewusst abseits der schicken Innenstadt und volksnah zwischen Reeperbahn und Elbe in einem David Chipperfield-Gebäude gewählt. Ausgehend von dem polygonalen Grundriss und der orthogonalen Raumaufteilung um einen längsrechteckigen Innenhof sollte die zuvor zweigeteilte Büroetage unter Einbeziehung von Feng-Shui-Prinzipien kreativ erschlossen und für den Besucher als eine gestalterische Einheit erlebbar gemacht werden. Den Eingangsbereich charakterisiert ein in zwei Richtungen geneigtes Wandsegment in Red-Rabbit-Rot, dessen diagonale Stellung im Grundriss die vorgegebenen Verkehrswege ändert und dem Raum eine Richtung gibt.

left: Furniture plan_Entrance Red Rabbit Lounge_Conference room with view. right: Conference room, central perspective.
links: Möblierungsplan_Eingang Red Rabbit Lounge_Konferenzraum mit Aussicht. rechts: Konferenzraum, Zentralperspektive.

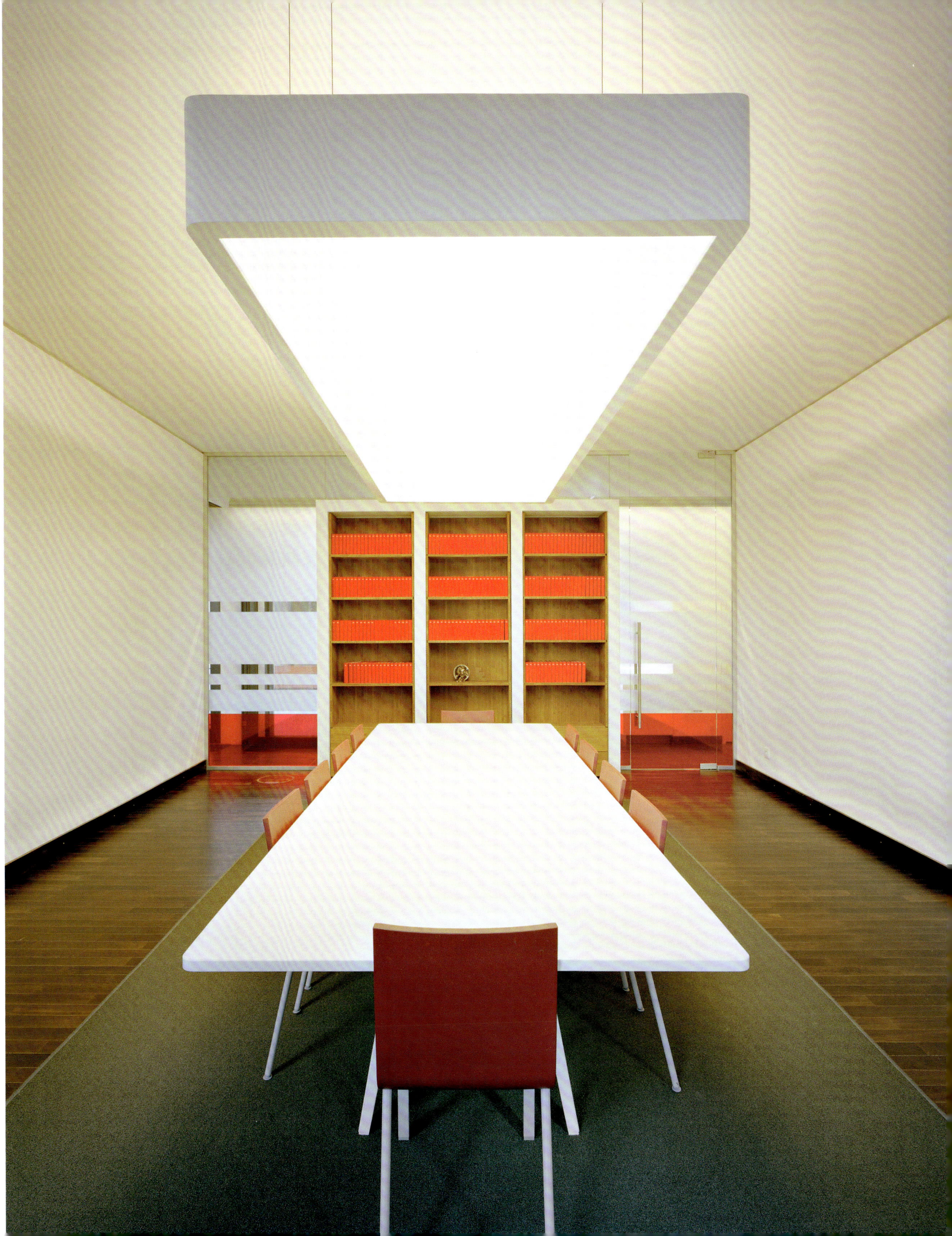

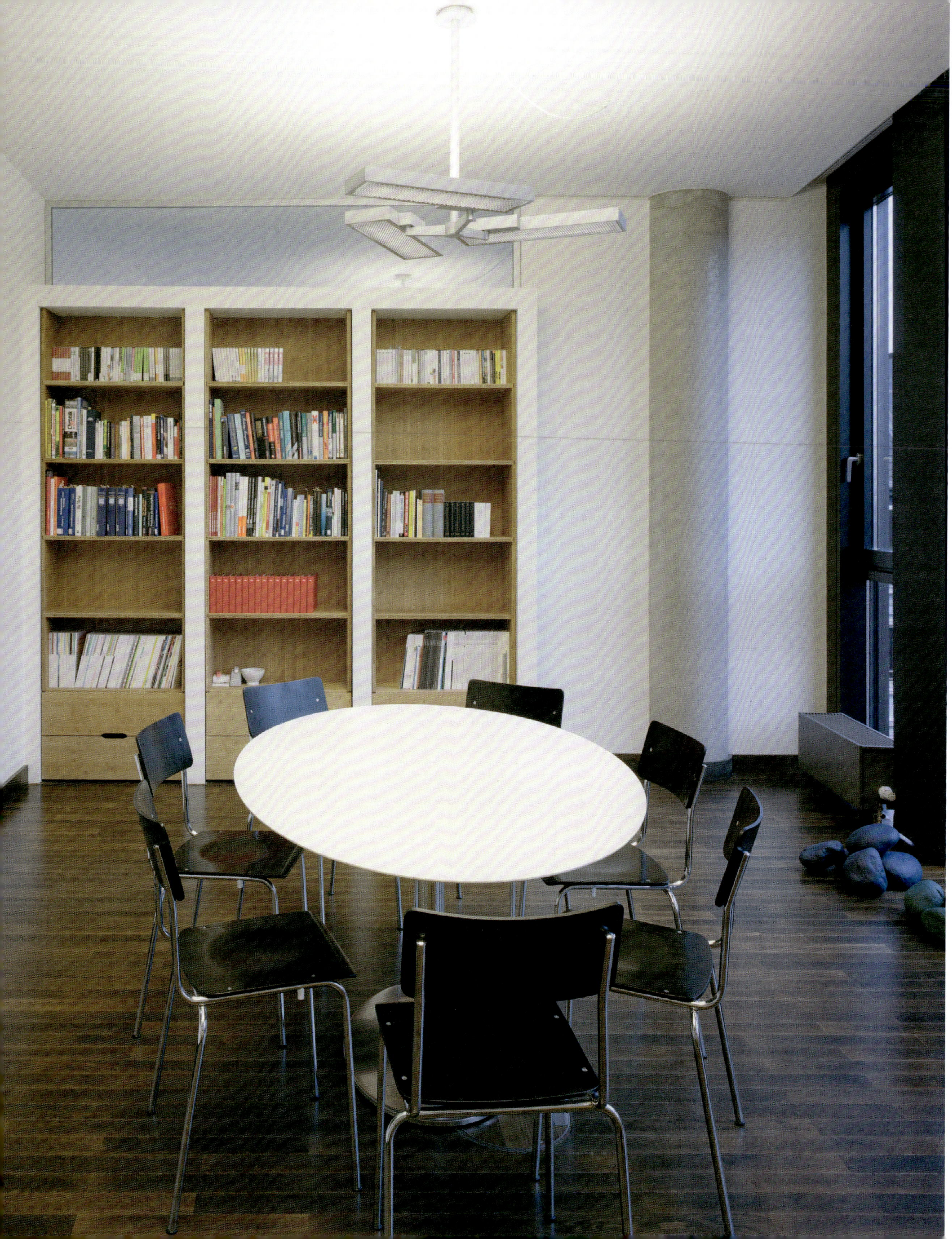

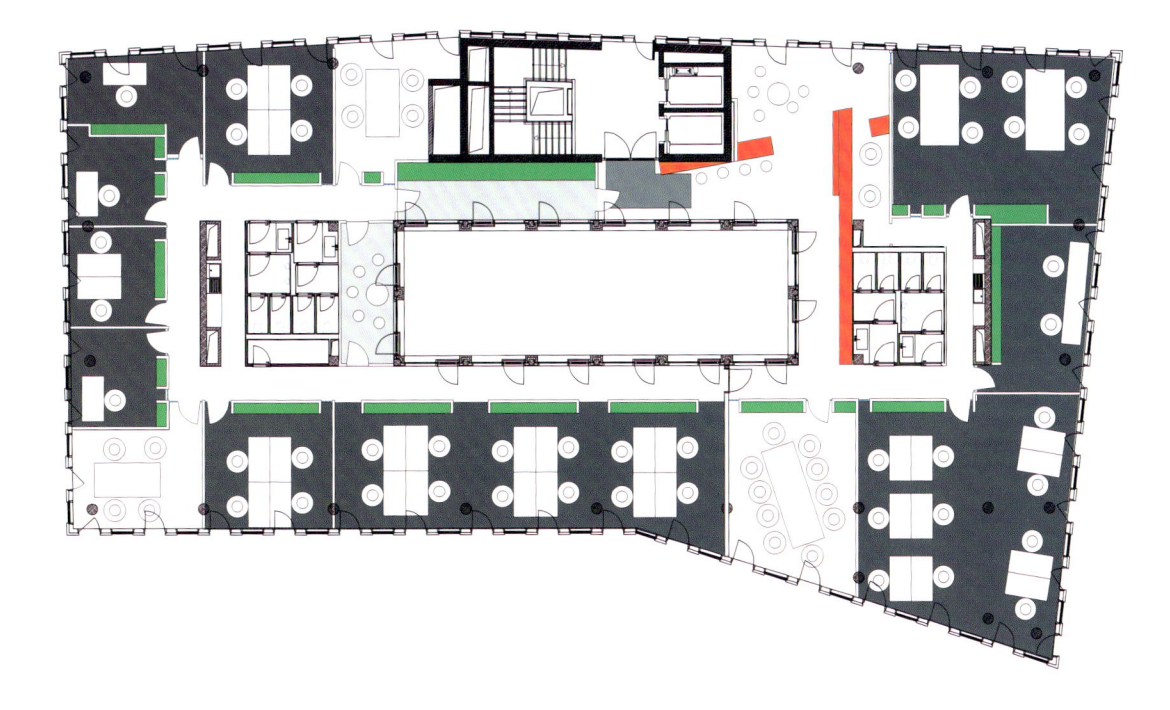

left: Meeting room. right: Floor plan_Glass partitions with built-in shelf wall_Open-plan office with sunlight_Konfiquarium.

links: Besprechungsraum. rechts: Grundriss_Glastrennwände mit integrierter Regalwand_Großraumbüro im Sonnenlicht_Konfiquarium.

GERMANY_HAMBURG **MUTTER**

ARCHITECTS: BFGF DESIGN STUDIOS
COMPLETION: 2009_**NUMBER OF WORKPLACES:** 6
GROSS FLOOR AREA: 70 M²_**COMMON AREA:** KITCHEN
KIND OF WORKPLACES: OPEN-PLAN
PHOTOS: DORFMÜLLER & KRÖGER, HAMBURG

The move of the design office in the vibrant St. Georg district was part of a concentration process that allowed the office owner to once again work as a designer instead of managing a design company. In an interactive process, the customer together with the architect conceived a design that combines a modern working atmosphere with the listed building structure. The previous spatial structure was highlighted, for example through a five-meter-long table that balances out different levels, existing structures were maintained and even complemented, and the old structures were incorporated into a functional office concept. An eat-in kitchen was established into a small basement thanks to custom-made furniture.

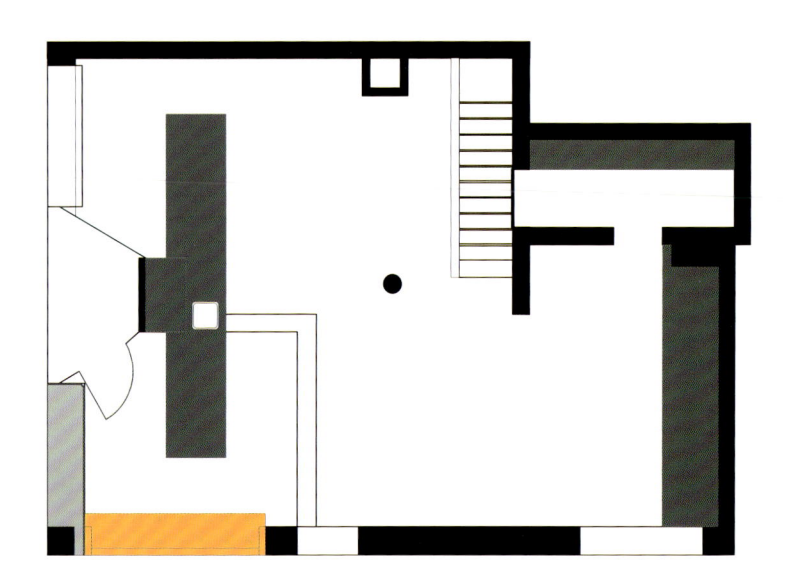

Der Umzug des Designbüros in den lebendigen Stadtteil St. Georg war Teil eines Konzentrationsprozesses, der es dem Büroinhaber ermöglichte, selbst wieder als Designer tätig zu sein statt eine gestaltende Firma zu leiten. In einem interaktiven Prozess erarbeiteten Auftraggeber und Architekt einen Entwurf, der moderne Arbeitsatmosphäre und denkmalgeschützte Bausubstanz verbindet. Die überlieferte räumliche Struktur wird betont, so durch einen Niveauunterschiede ausgleichenden, fünf Meter langen Tisch, Baubefunde wurden gesichert, sogar ergänzt und die alte Substanz einer funktionalen Büronutzung zugeführt. Eine Essküche konnte dank maßgefertigter Möbel in einem kleinen Kellerraum angelegt werden.

left: Ground floor plan_Working counter_Basement pantry. right: Stairs to the basement floor.
links: Grundriss Erdgeschoss_Arbeitstresen_Kellerpantry. rechts: Treppe zum Untergeschoss.

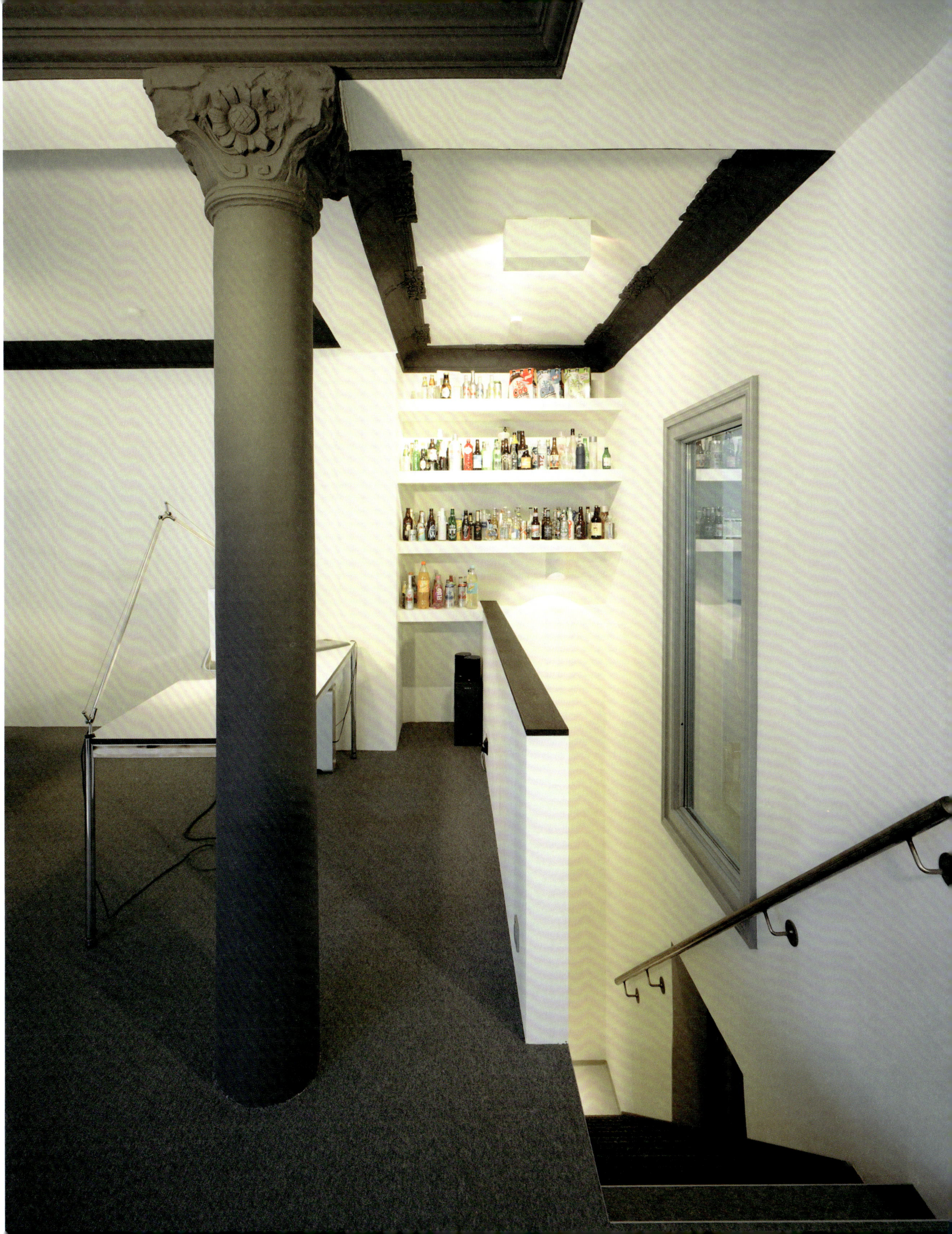

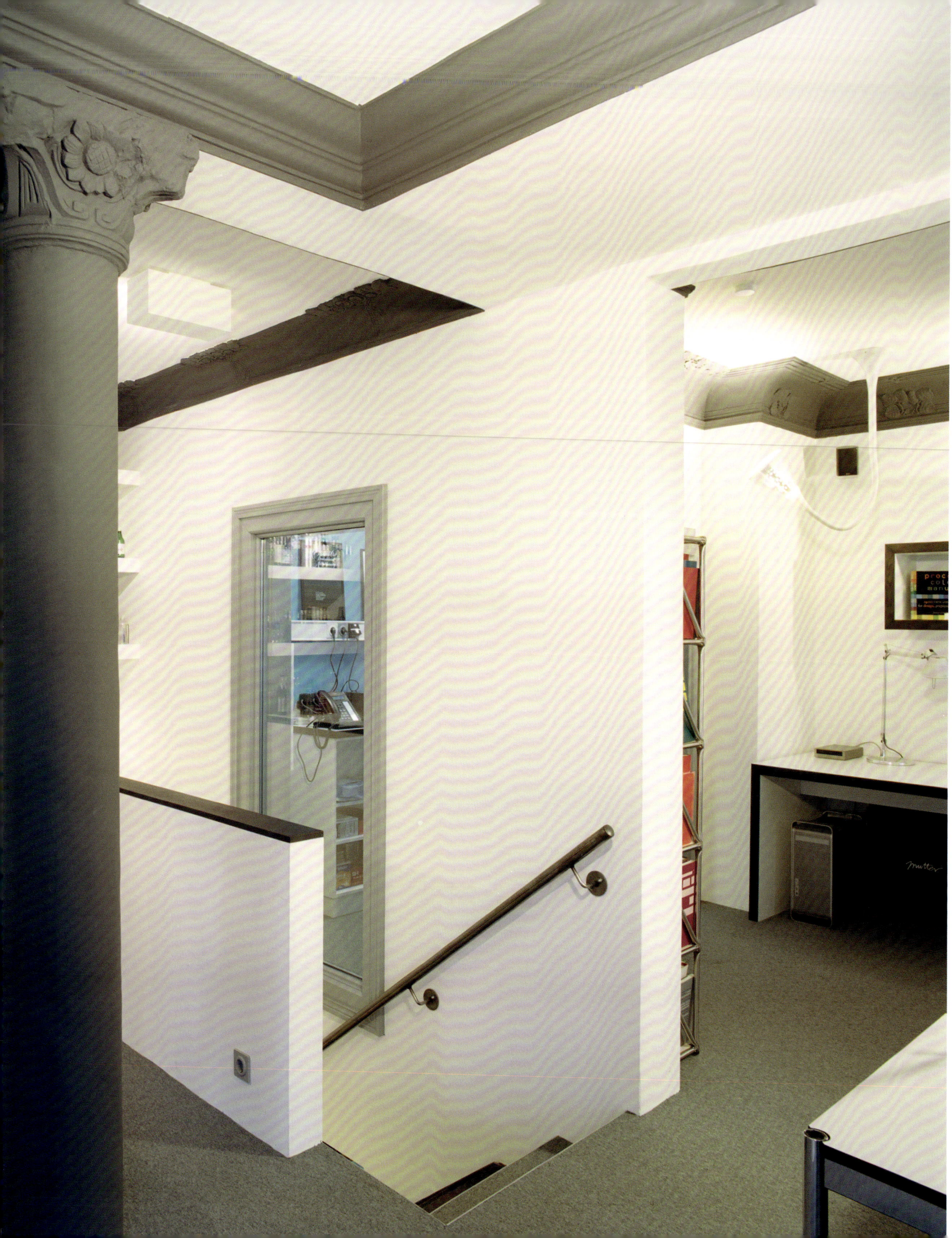

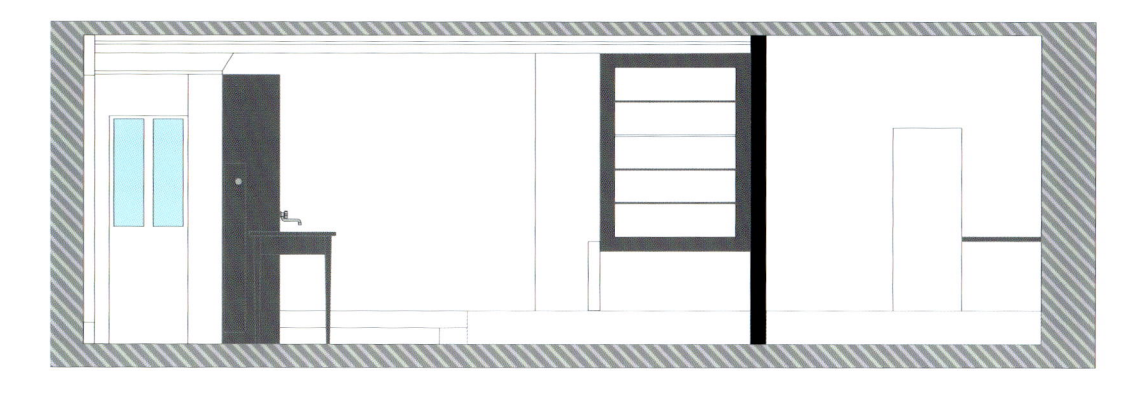

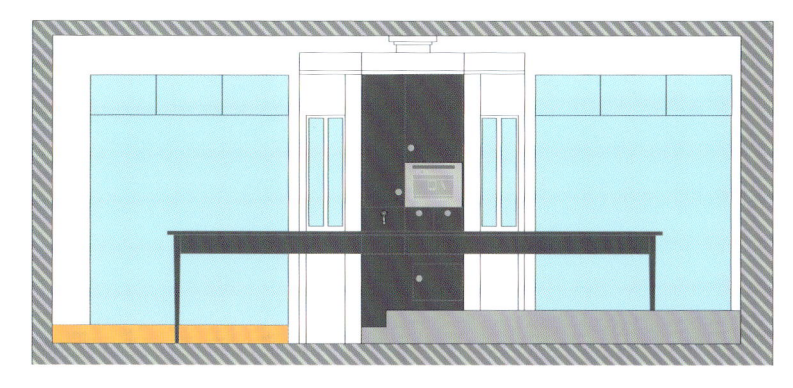

left: View to the blue copy room. right: Counter_Reception and workplaces in the background.
links: Blick zum blauen Kopierraum. rechts: Tresen_Empfang und Arbeitsplätze im Hintergrund.

GERMANY_HAMBURG JOHANNISCONTOR

ARCHITECTS: KBNK ARCHITEKTEN GMBH
STRUCTURAL ENGINEERS: WETZEL & VON SEHT
COMPLETION: 2009_**NUMBER OF WORKPLACES:** 70
GROSS FLOOR AREA: 3,000 M²_**KIND OF WORKPLACES:** INDIVIDUAL EXTENSION VARIATIONS_**PHOTOS:** MARCUS BREDT (196 B. L.), DORFMÜLLER & KRÖGER FOTOGRAFEN

The extension of the Johanniscontor blends in with its neighboring buildings. The interaction of a high-quality renovated façade with flexible building utilization as well as the modern addition of floors results in a contemporary and prestigious architecture with a high recognition value in the Hanseatic tradition. The building contains six office floors as well as two retail floors. Open, self-supporting areas allow individual layouts, while glass partitions present an unobstructed view across the entire building depth as well as breathtaking views of the chamber of commerce and the Hamburg town hall.

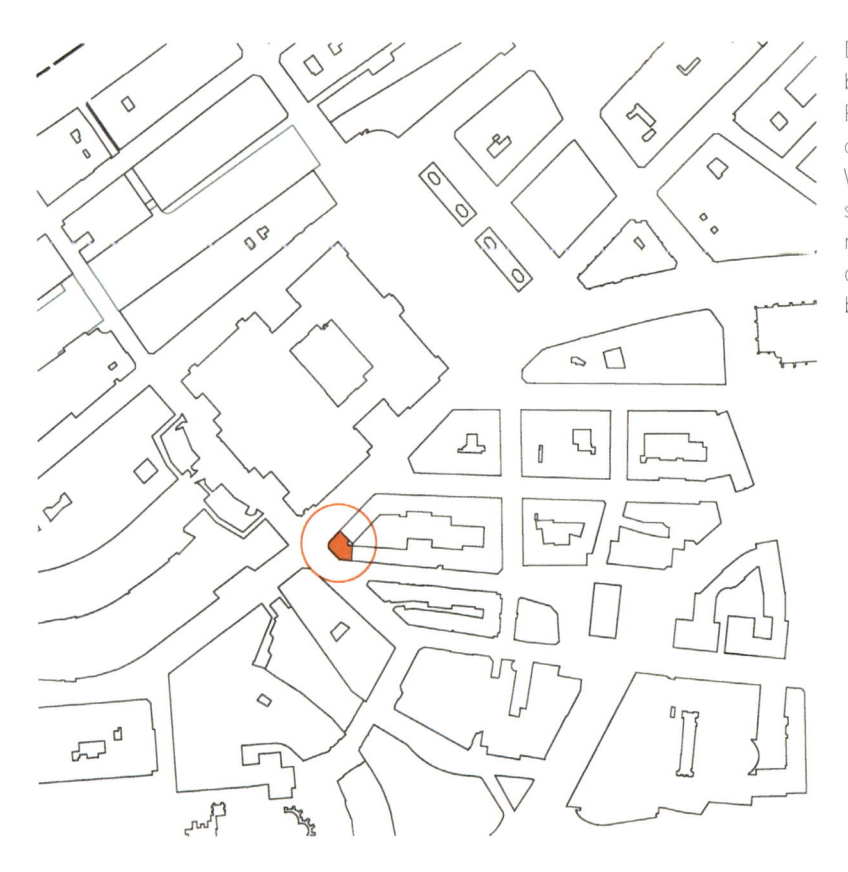

Der Weiterbau des Johanniscontors fügt sich stadträumlich in die Nachbarbebauung ein. Im Zusammenspiel von hochwertig restaurierter, historischer Fassade mit einer flexiblen Nutzung dahinter sowie der modernen Aufstockung ergibt sich eine zeitgemäße und repräsentative Architektur mit hohem Wiedererkennungswert in hanseatischer Tradition. Das Gebäude verfügt über sechs Bürogeschosse sowie zwei Ladennutzungen. Offene, stützenfreie Ebenen ermöglichen den individuellen Ausbau. Gläserne Trennwände gestatten den ungehinderten Blick durch die gesamte Gebäudetiefe und atemberaubende Ausblicke auf die Handelskammer und das Hamburger Rathaus.

left: Site plan_Demolition work_Façade, detail_Perspective, roof. right: View from Börsenbrücke.
links: Lageplan_Entkernung des historischen Gebäudes_Fassadendetail_Dachperspektive. rechts: Blick von der Börsenbrücke.

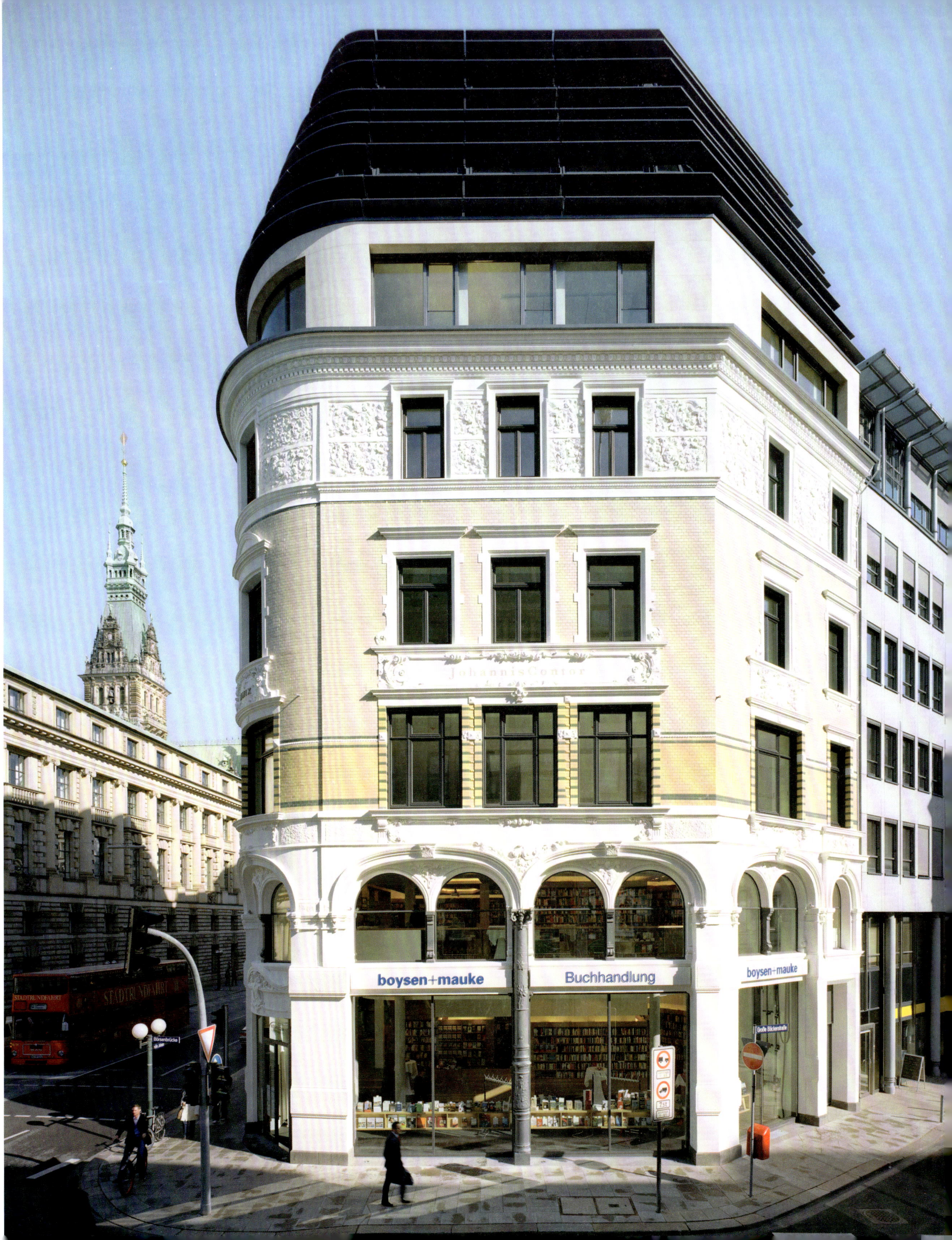
boysen+mauke
Buchhandlung
boysen+mauke

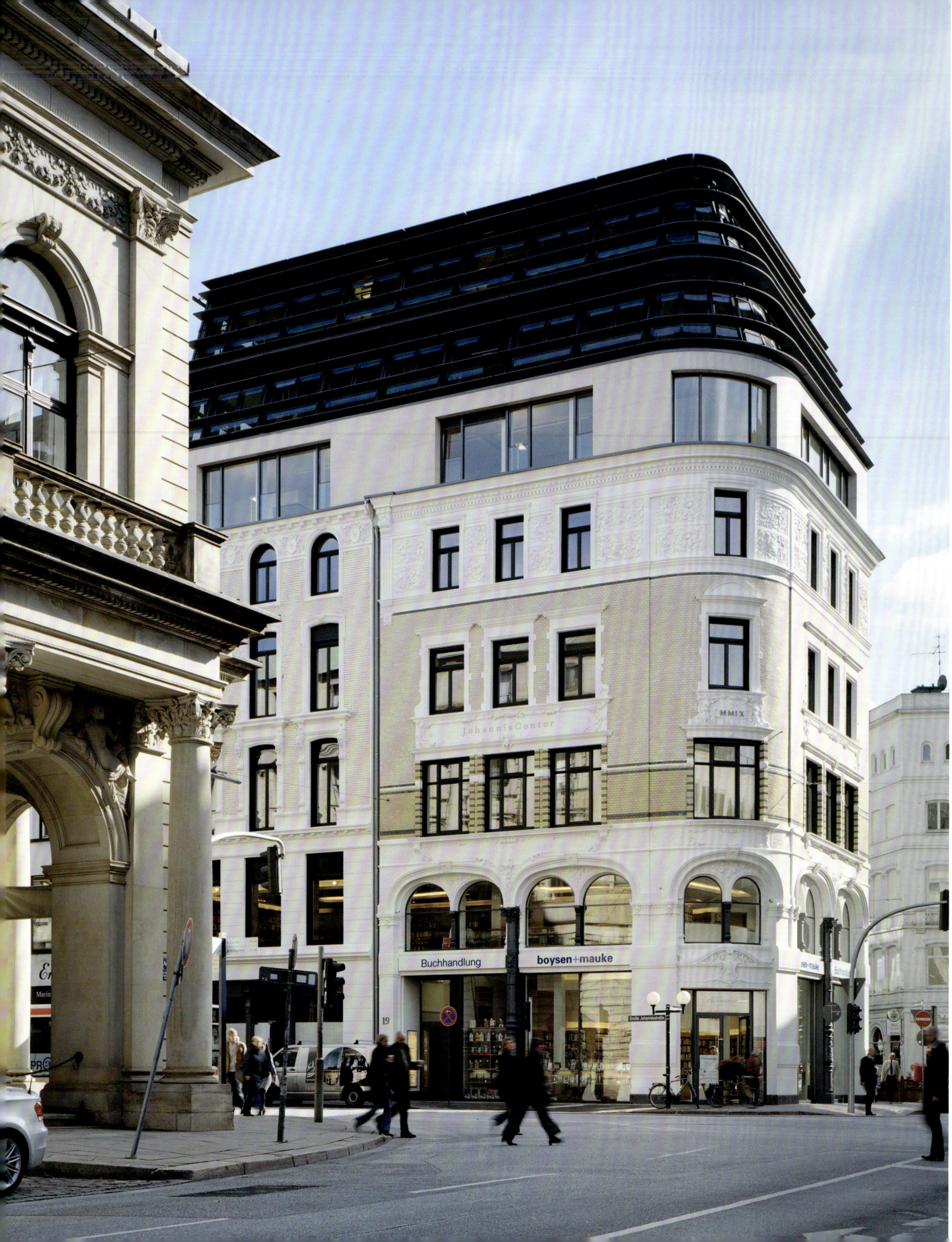
JohannisContor
MMIX
Buchhandlung
boysen+mauke
19

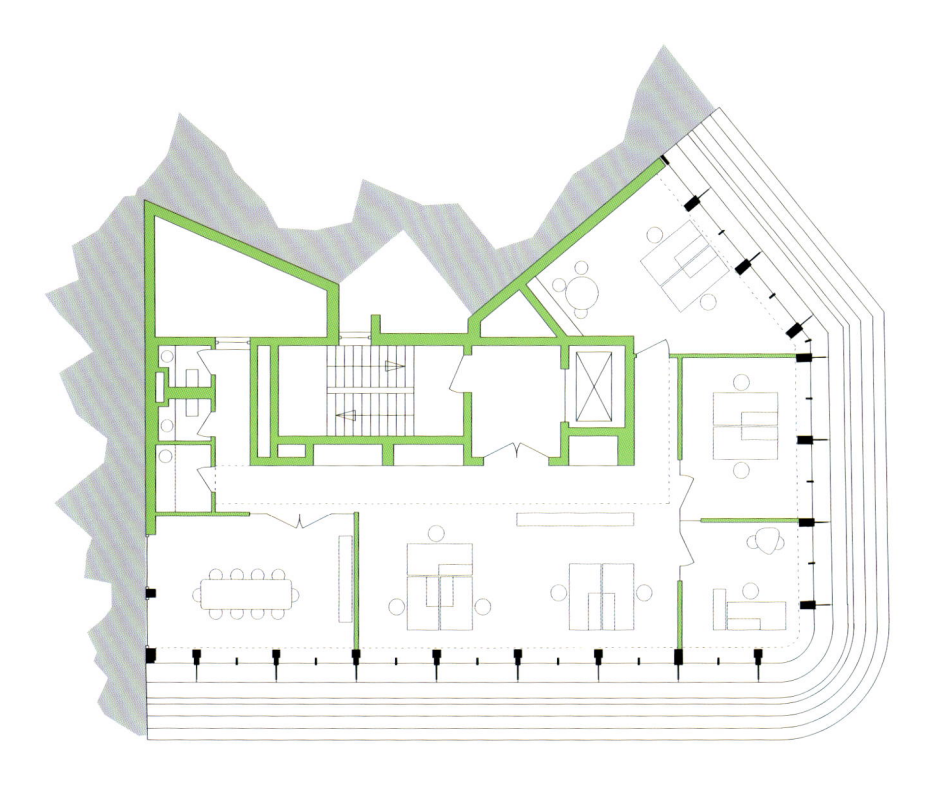

left: View from Adolfplatz. right: Sixth floor plan_Interior view, book store_Fifth floor, dentist practice_ Interior view, bookstore.
links: Blick vom Adolfplatz. rechts: Grundriss sechstes Obergeschoss_Innenansicht, Buchladen_ Fünftes Obergeschoss, Zahnarztpraxis_Innenansicht, Buchladen.

GERMANY_HAMBURG OFFICE BUILDING GROSSE ELBSTRASSE

ARCHITECTS: SEHW ARCHITEKTEN HAMBURG
COMPLETION: 2007_**NUMBER OF WORKPLACES:** 52
GROSS FLOOR AREA: 1,271 M²_**COMMON AREA:** CAFÉ WITH SEPARATE ENTRANCE_**KIND OF WORKPLACES:** OPEN-PLAN
PHOTOS: ANDREAS FROMM, HAMBURG

In the immediate vicinity of the Elbe in Hamburg's historical harbor district, a prominent administration office of a Hamburg shipping company was established on the hillside. The sculpted new office building is a reaction to the small-structured historic neighboring buildings near the Sandberg as well as the topography of the site in which three centuries constitute a natural ensemble. The innovative façade of the building with its large-scale stainless steel boards and blue sun-screen glazing, which attractively interacts with its surroundings through reflection, appears differently at the different times of the day. The colors range from a melancholy grey-blue during rain up to a brilliant copper red in the evening sun.

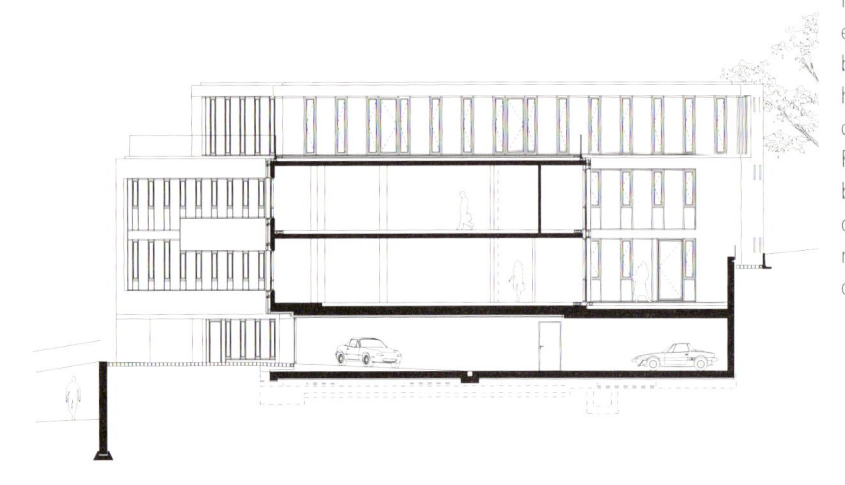

In unmittelbarer Nähe der Elbe, in Hamburgs historischem Hafengebiet, entstand an der Hangseite ein auffälliger Verwaltungsbau für eine Hamburger Reederei. Der skulpturale Büroneubau reagiert auf die kleinteilige, historische Nachbarbebauung am Sandberg und auf die Topografie des Ortes, drei Jahrhunderte bilden ein selbstverständliches Ensemble. Die innovative Fassade des Gebäudes mit ihren großformatigen Edelstahltafeln und einer blauen Sonnenschutzverglasung, die durch Reflexion ein reizvolles Spiel mit der Umgebung eingeht, erscheint zu jeder Tageszeit anders. Das Farbenspiel reicht von melancholischem grau-blau bei Regen, bis hin zu einem funkelnden Kupferrot in der Abendsonne.

left: Section_View from Große Elbstraße_Entrance courtyard between new and old building. right: Façade.
links: Schnitt_Blick von der Großen Elbstraße_Eingangshof zwischen Alt- und Neubau. rechts: Fassade.

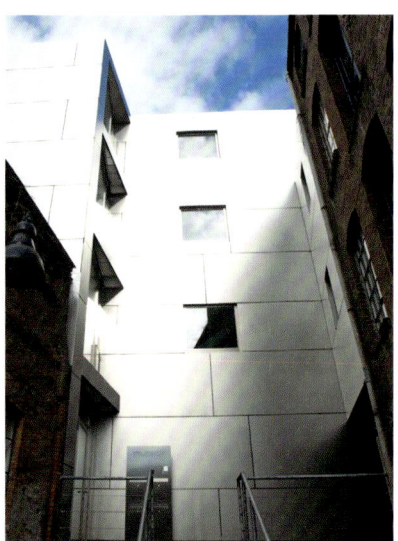

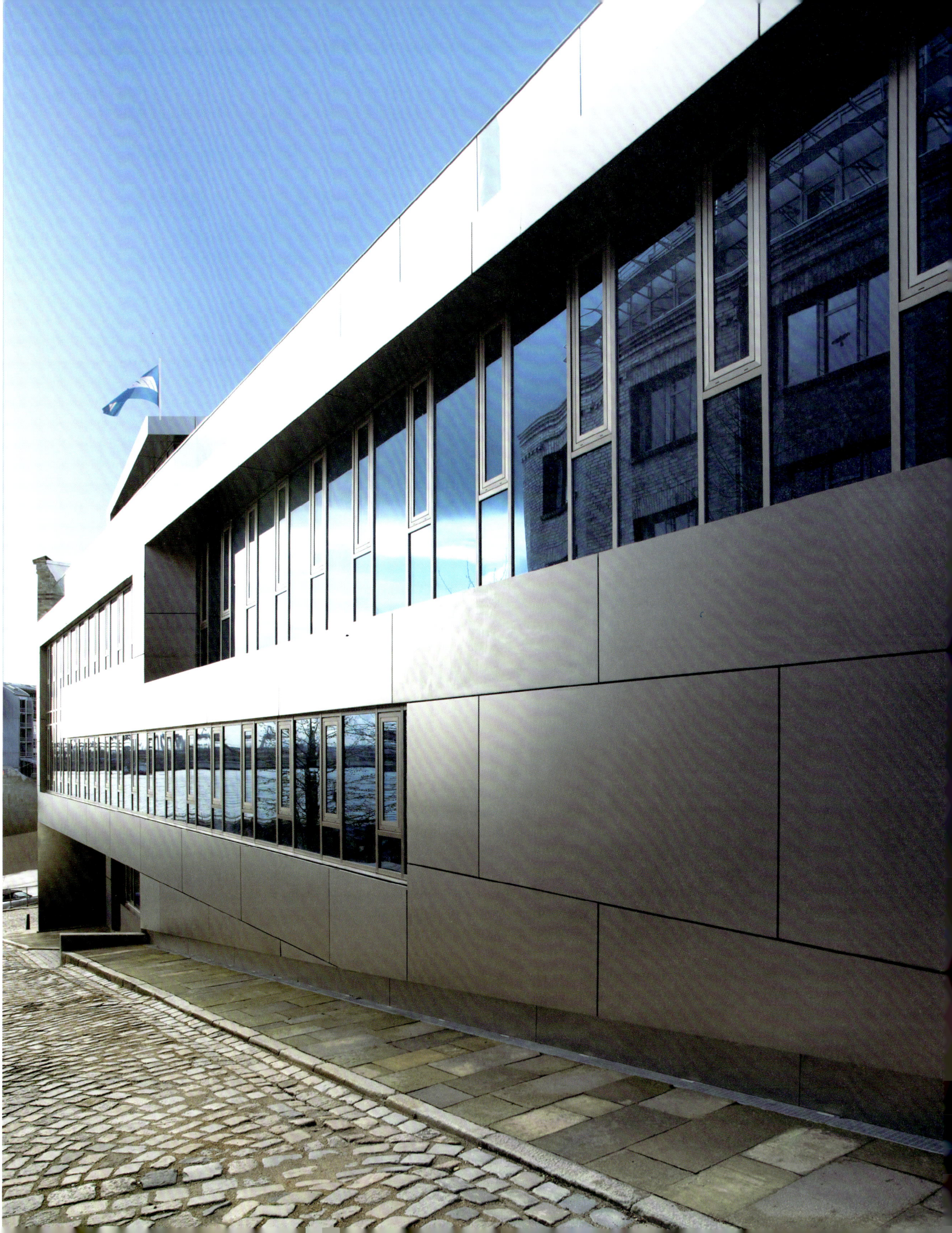

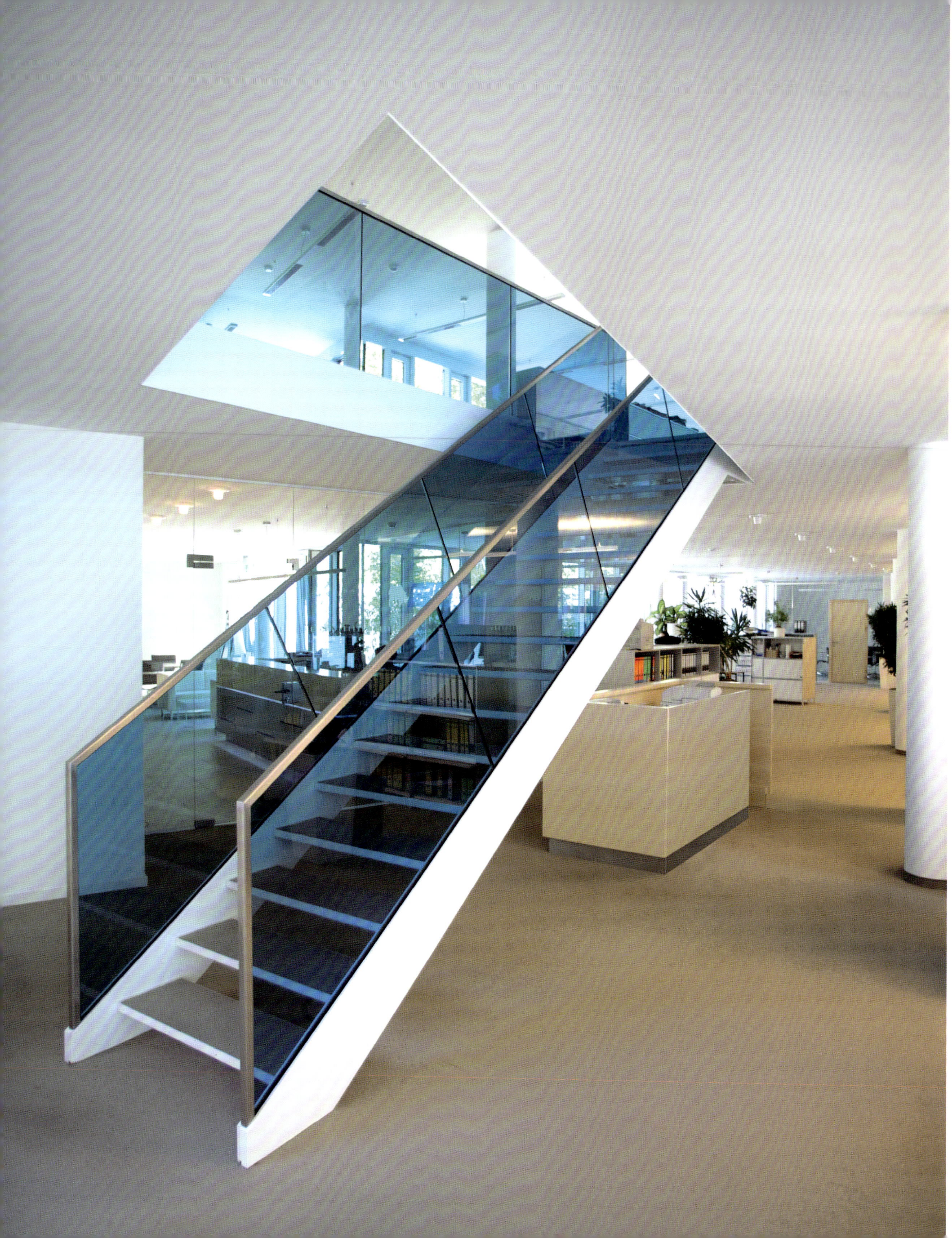

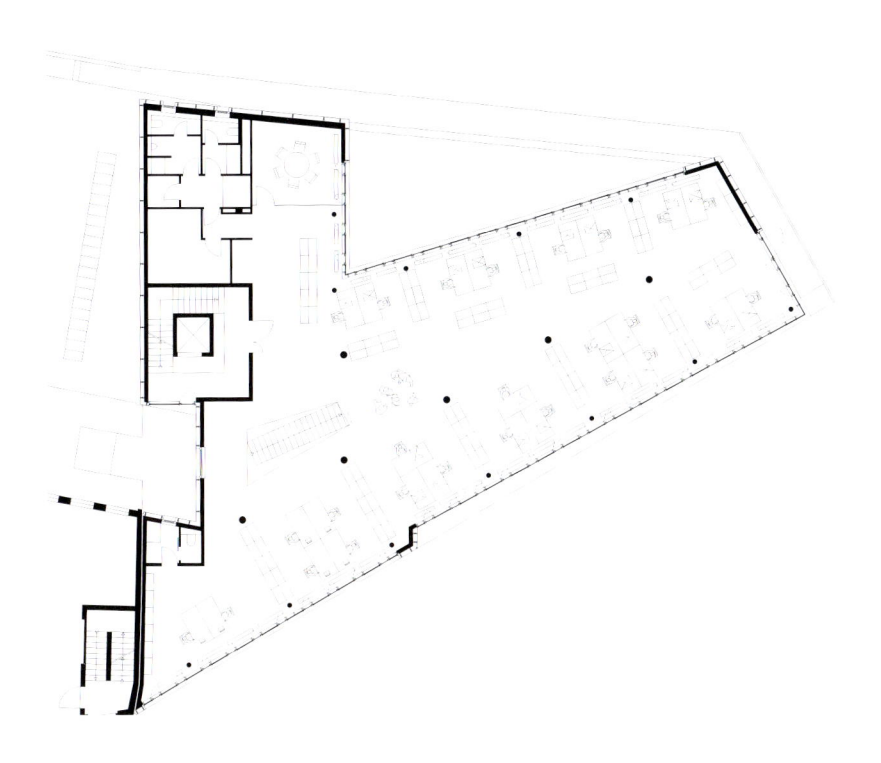

left: Stair in the office area. right: First floor plan_Elevator_Reception_Façade.
links: Verbindungstreppe zwischen den Büros. rechts: Grundriss Obergeschoss_Aufzug_Empfang_Fassade.

GERMANY_HAMBURG **NDR RADIO CONSTRUCTION PHASE 1 + 2**

ARCHITECTS: SCHWEGER ASSOCIATED ARCHITECTS GMBH
COMPETITION ARCHITECTS: ARCHITEKTEN SCHWEGER+PARTNER
COMPLETION: 2008_**NUMBER OF WORKPLACES:** 500_**GROSS FLOOR AREA:** 32,800 M²_**COMMON AREA:** CONFERENCE ROOM
KIND OF WORKPLACES: COMBINATION_**PHOTOS:** WERNER HUTHMACHER, BERLIN (204, 206, 207 R.), BERNHARD KROLL, GROSSHANSDORF (205), MARTIN WOLTER, HAMBURG (207 L.)

The new buildings had to fit in to the urban and landscape context while creating a new order with an independent architectural expression. The linear building structure adopts the layout and alignment of the existing buildings, respects the old trees surrounding them, and interprets the premises as a campus in a park. The high-tech rooms of the studios are arranged vertically across three levels and housed in different buildings according to broadcast and production areas. The functionally assigned office areas are positioned offset from the studios on four floors of two buildings.

Die Neubauten sollten sich sowohl in den städtebaulichen und landschaftlichen Kontext eingliedern als auch eine neue Ordnung mit einem eigenständigen architektonischen Ausdruck schaffen. Die lineare Baustruktur bezieht sich in Gliederung und Ausrichtung auf die bestehenden Gebäude, respektiert den alten Baumbestand und interpretiert das Areal als Campus im Park. Die hochtechnisierten Räume der Studios sind vertikal auf drei Ebenen organisiert und gegliedert und nach Sende- und Produktionsbereich in getrennten Baukörpern untergebracht. Jeweils versetzt zu den Studioeinheiten sind die funktional zugeordneten Büroflächen in zwei Baukörpern viergeschossig organisiert.

left: Site plan_Night view_Path through the buildings. right: Inner courtyard.
links: Lageplan_Nachtansicht_Weg zwischen den Gebäuden. rechts: Innenhof.

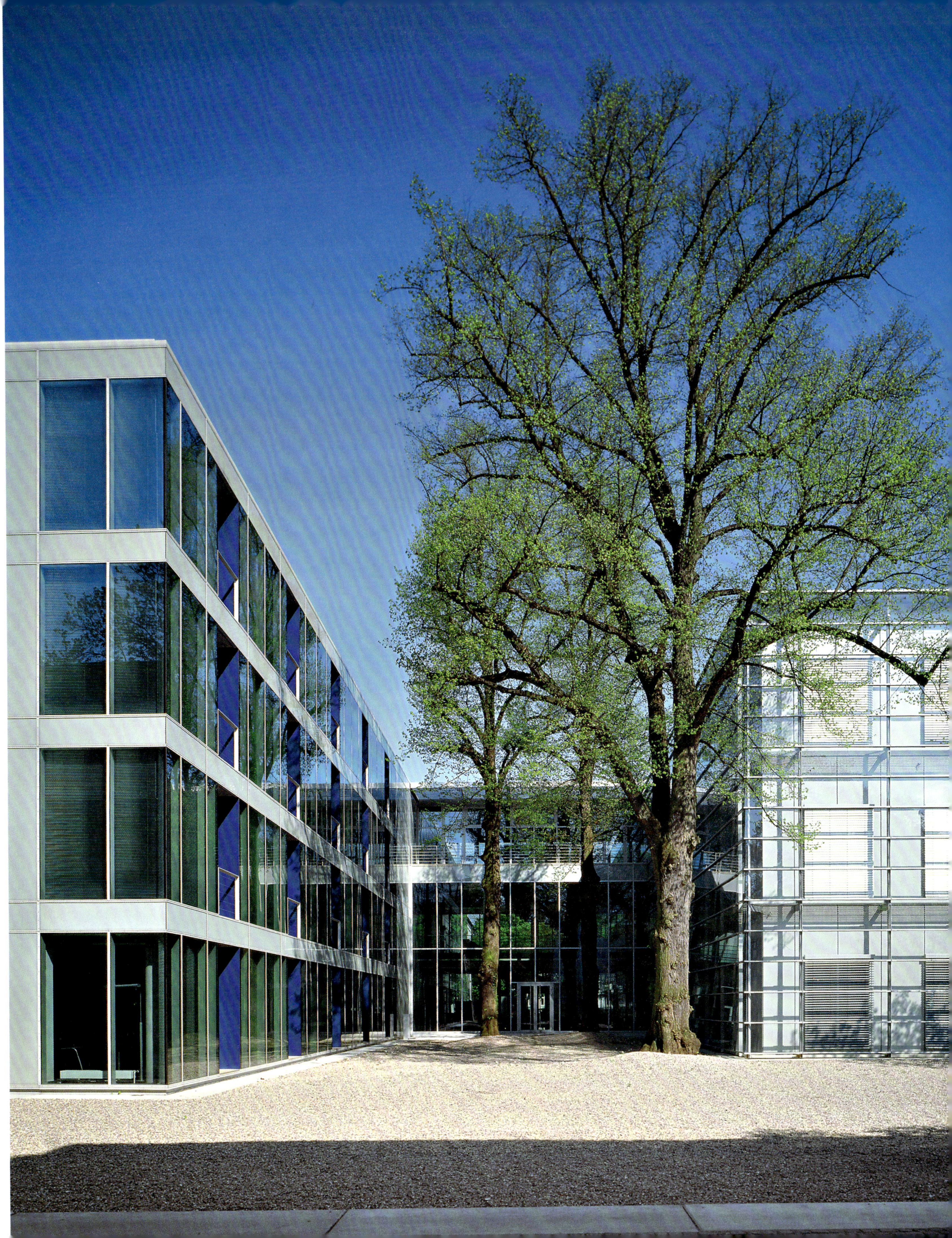

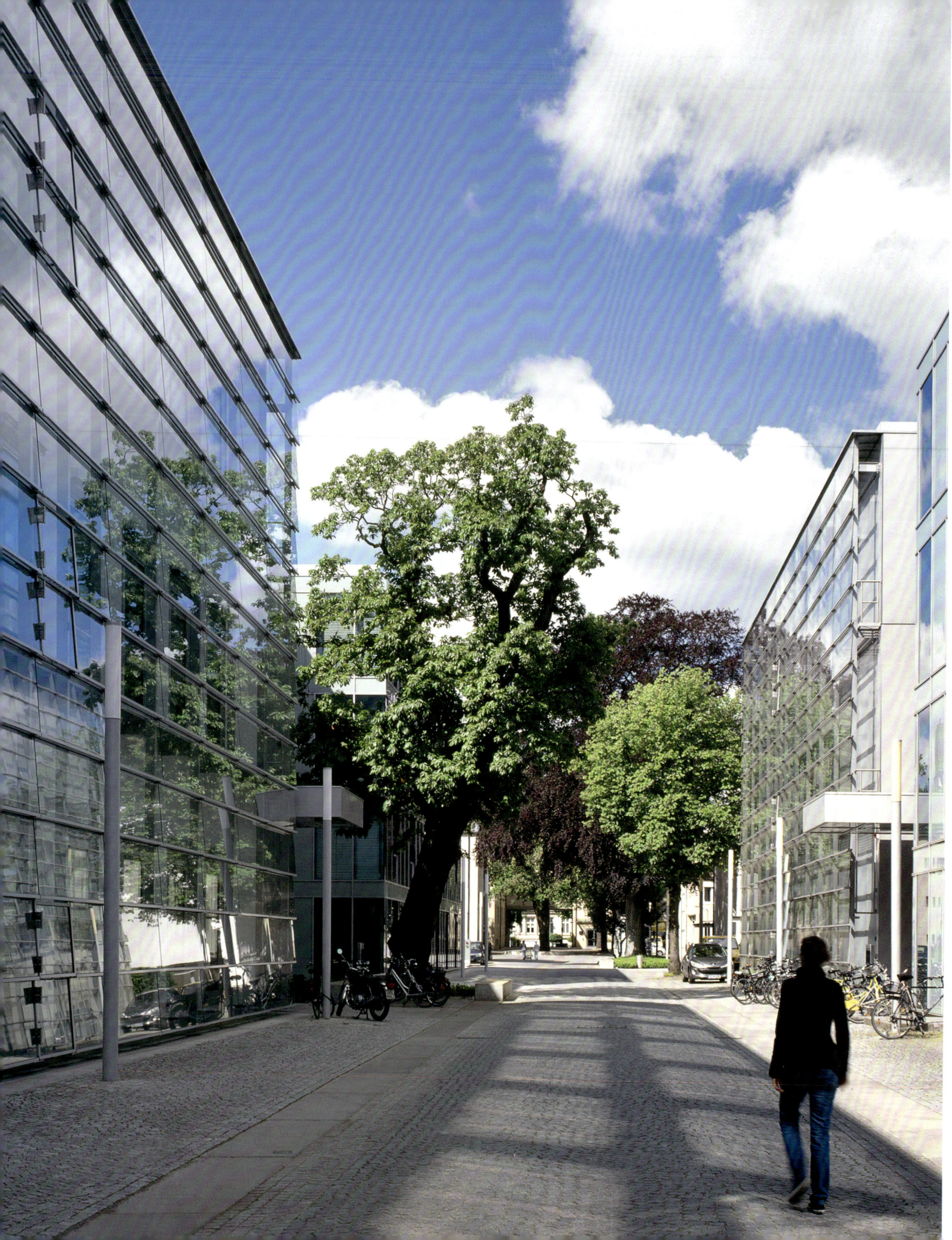

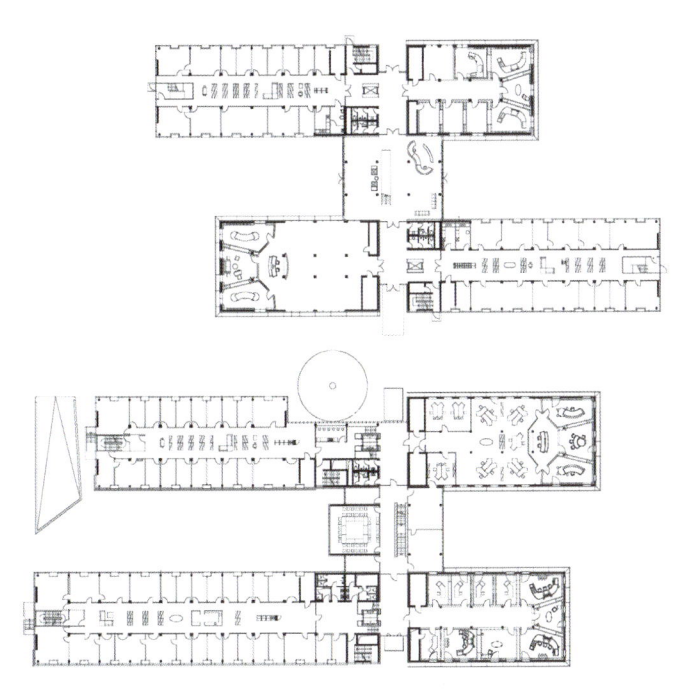

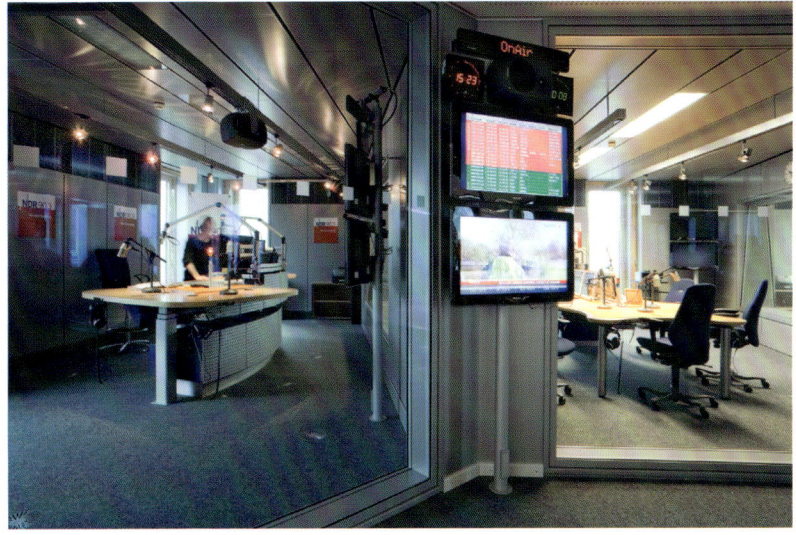

left: Exterior view. right: Ground floor plans, first and second construction phase_Corridor with meeting points_Corridor with frames and meeting points_Recording studio.
links: Außenansicht. rechts: Grundrisse, erster und zweiter Bauabschnitt_Flur mit Treffpunkten_Flur mit Regalen und Treffpunkten_Aufnahmestudio.

GERMANY_HANOVER VGH WARMBÜCHENQUARTIER

ARCHITECTS: ASP ARCHITEKTEN SCHNEIDER MEYER PARTNER / WOLFGANG SCHNEIDER, PROF. WILHELM MEYER
COMPLETION: 2009_**NUMBER OF WORKPLACES:** 500
GROSS FLOOR AREA: 27,000 M²_**COMMON AREA:** TRAINING, LOUNGE, CONFERENCE ROOM, EVENT_**KIND OF WORKPLACES:** TEAM, BUSINESS CLUB, LOUNGE WORKSPACE
PHOTOS: K.-D. WEISS, MINDEN

The VGH ensemble contains offices, classrooms, conference rooms, event areas and residential units. It is an extension of the VGH Insurance quarter, complementing the existing urban structure on the inner city's east perimeter. The three crystalline structures positioned on a common stone plateau form a unique composition. These buildings offer generous entrance halls – one with Timm Ulrich's 90 meter mosaic "The favorite colors of the lower Saxonians" – conference rooms, classroom areas with additional office spaces, business clubs or team working offices with lounge areas as well as two-story apartments in building 3. The project offers an abundance of rooms and room types for working, learning, and comfortable urban living.

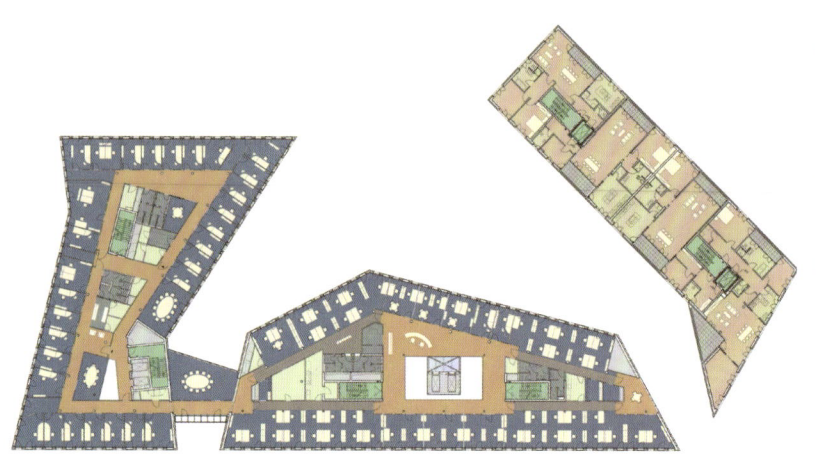

Das VGH Ensemble umfasst Büros, Klassenzimmer, Konferenzräume, Veranstaltungsräume sowie Wohneinheiten. Als Erweiterung des VGH Quartiers vervollständigt es die räumliche Struktur der Stadt im Osten. Drei kristallin gebrochene Volumen auf gemeinschaftlichem Sockel bilden eine ungewöhnliche Komposition. Im Inneren bieten sie großzügige Foyers – eines mit Timm Ulrichs 90 Meter langen Moasik „Die Lieblingsfarben der Niedersachsen" – Konferenzräume, Klassenzimmer mit zusätzlichem Büroraum, Business Clubs und Gruppenarbeitsplätze mit Loungebereichen, aber auch zweigeschossige Apartments in Gebäude 3. Viel Raum und viele Raumtypen für komfortables Arbeiten, Lernen und urbanes Leben.

left: Second floor plan_Atrium, building 1_Atrium, building 2. right: Building 1 and building 2.
links: Grundriss zweites Obergeschoss_Atrium, Haus 1_Atrium. Haus 2. rechts: Haus 1 und Haus 2.

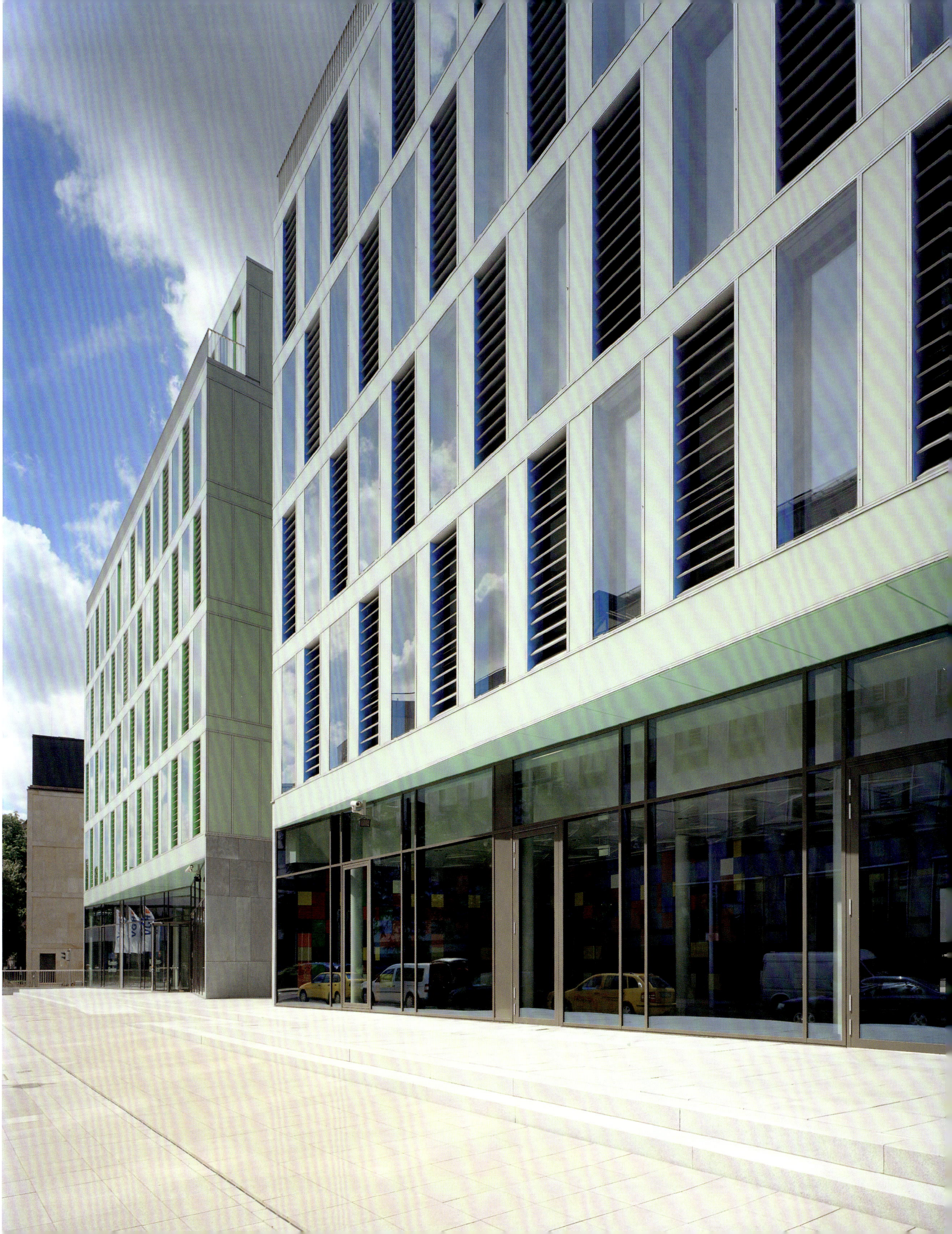

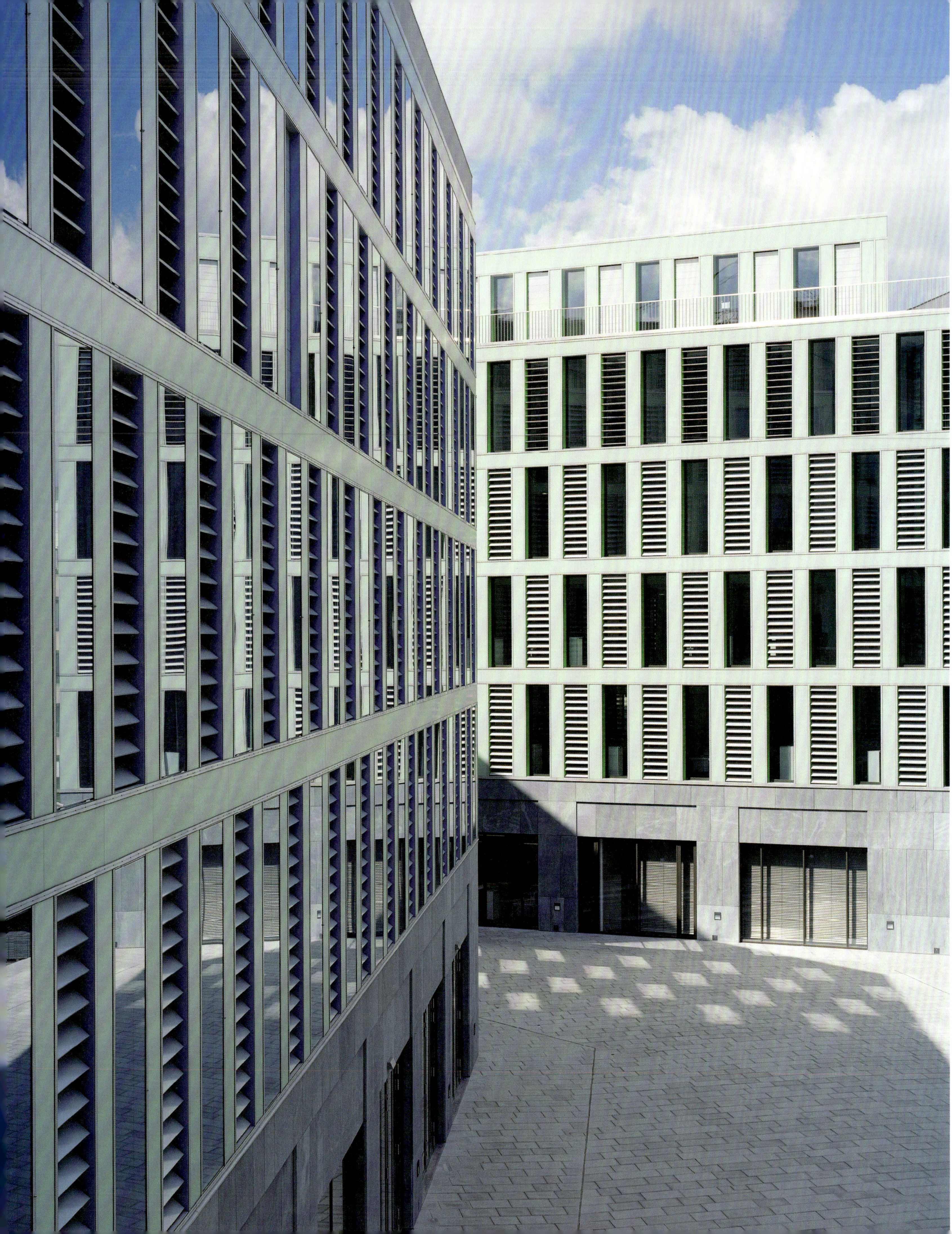

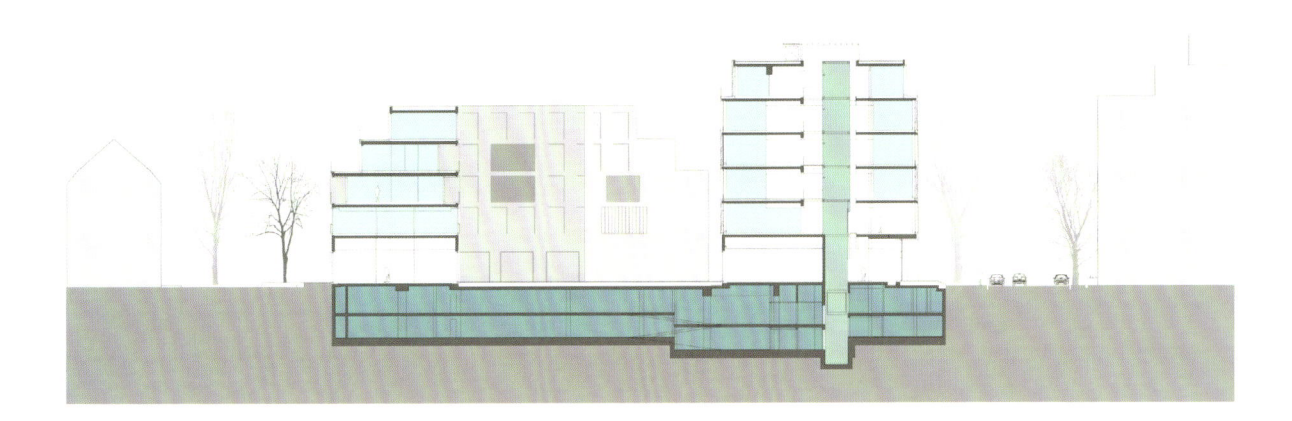

left: Courtyard. right: Section_Entrance area, building 2_Meeting room, connecting bridge, second floor_Conference room, office space.
links: Hof. rechts: Schnitt_Eingangsbereich, Haus 2_Konferenzraum, Bautenbrücke zweites Obergeschoss_Besprechungsraum Bürozone.

GERMANY_KARLSRUHE **VOLKSBANK KARLSRUHE HEADQUARTERS**

ARCHITECTS: HERRMANN+BOSCH ARCHITEKTEN
COMPLETION: 2008_**NUMBER OF WORKPLACES:** 250
GROSS FLOOR AREA: 7,400 M²_**COMMON AREA:** MEETING ROOMS, LOUNGES, EMPLOYEE BISTRO_**KIND OF WORKPLACES:** CELLULAR, TEAM, OPEN-PLAN, LOUNGE WORKSPACE, HOT DESKS
PHOTOS: WERNER HUTHMACHER (212 B. L.), ROLAND HALBE / © ARTURIMAGES (212 B. R., 213)

The working title of the project "3xL" describes the three workplace qualities of the project that were guaranteed by the introduction of three patios: Licht (light), Luft (air), and Lebensqualität (quality of life). These have a positive effect on the corporate culture, work processes, motivation, and productivity, in addition to supporting the corporate identity and corporate branding. To the north, the building unfolds towards an idyllic park, while to the south a protective wall shields it from a highly frequented road and the rays of the sun. The protective wall merges with the roof, catches the light and passes it onto the patios, which vertically connect the office floors and play an important role in the ecologic concept.

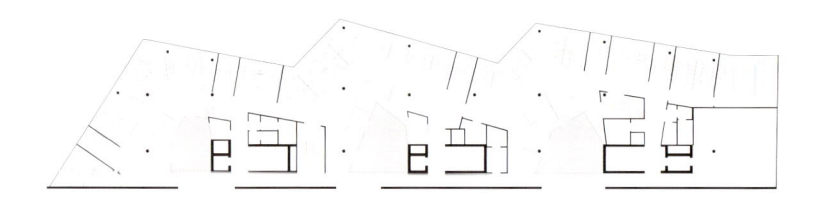

Der Arbeitstitel des Projekts „3xL" beschreibt die durch drei eingeschnittene Lichthöfe garantierten Qualitäten und Ziele des Projekts: Licht, Luft und Lebensqualität am Arbeitsplatz, die sich positiv auf Arbeitskultur, Arbeitsprozesse, Leistungsbereitschaft und Produktivität auswirken und sowohl der Corporate Identity als auch der Markenbildung zuträglich sind. Nach Norden faltet sich das Gebäude in den ruhigen idyllischen Park hin auf, während die Südseite mit einem Schild gegen die Beeinträchtigung durch eine stark befahrene Straße und Sonneneinstrahlung geschützt wird. Das Schild leitet ins Dach über, fängt das Licht ein und gibt es in die Lichthöfe ab, die die Büroebenen vertikal verbinden und im ökologischen Konzept eine wichtige Rolle spielen.

left: Second floor plan_Exterior_void. right: View down into atrium_Informal space_Meeting room.
links: Grundriss zweites Obergeschoss_Außenansicht_Lichthof. rechts: Blick nach unten ins Atrium_informeller Raum_Besprechungsraum.

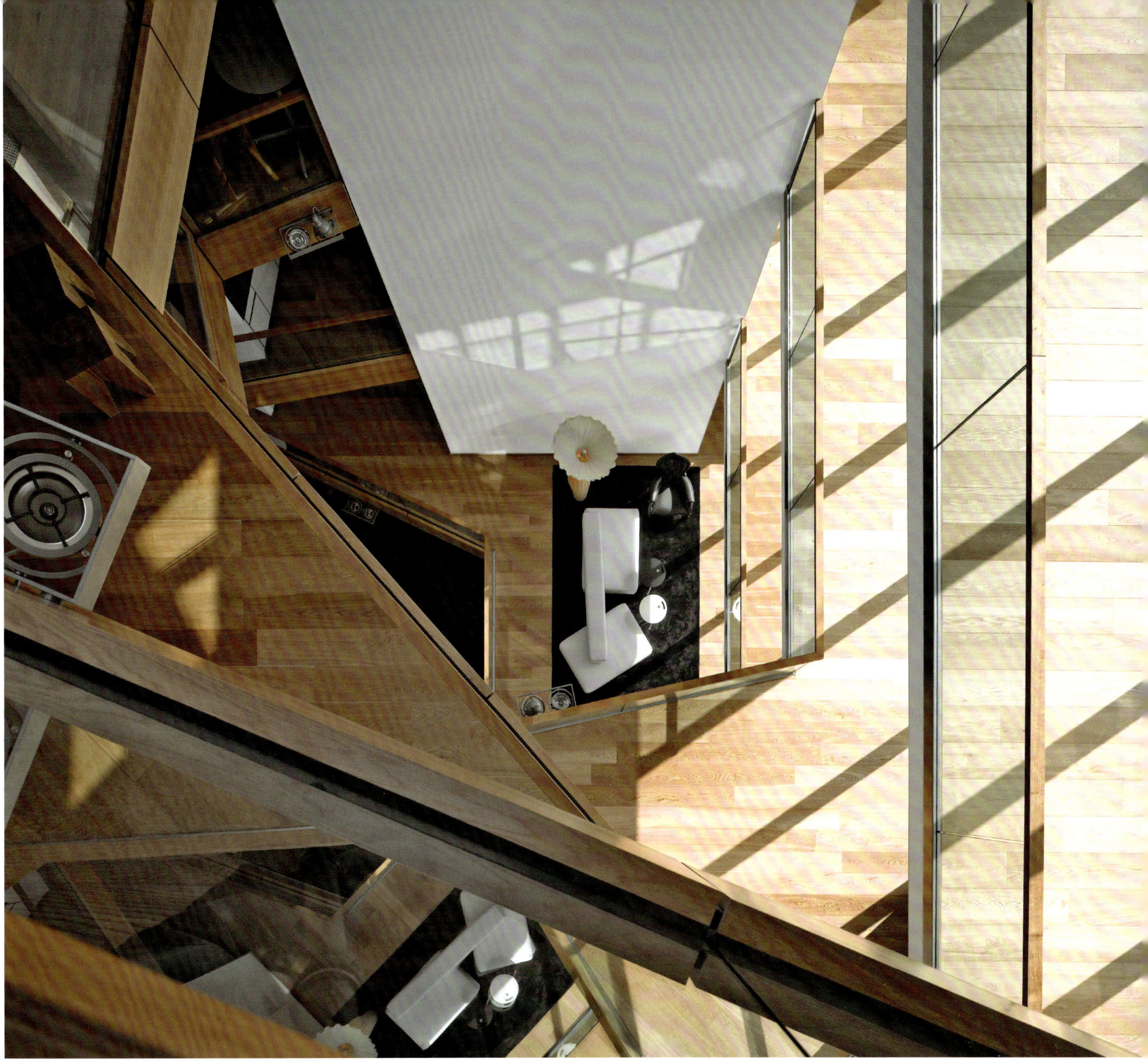

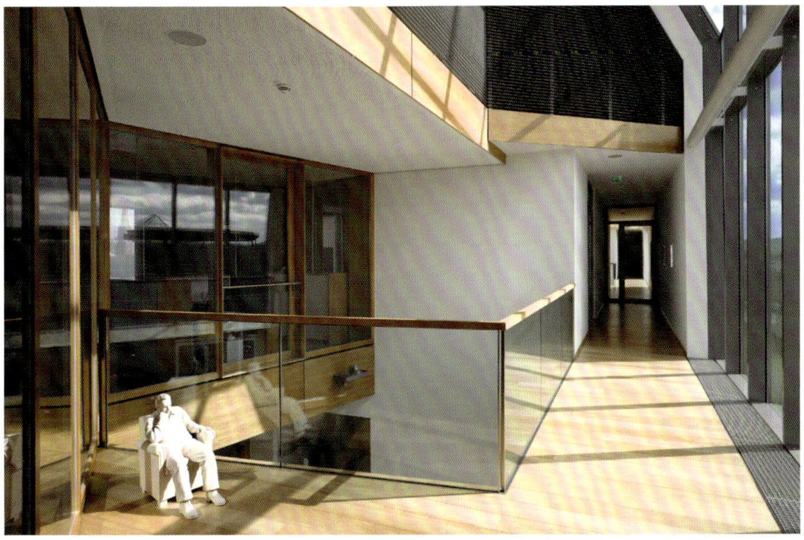

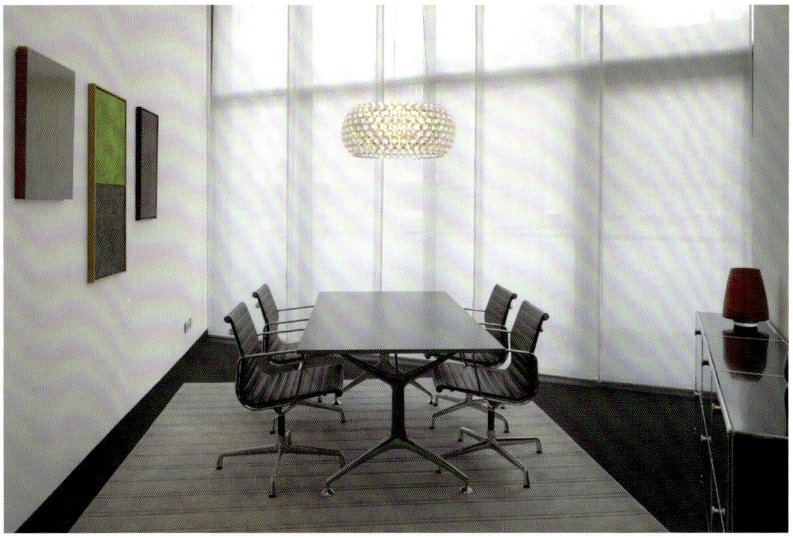

GERMANY_KOESCHING **BINDER WOODCENTER**

ARCHITECTS: MATTEO THUN & PARTNERS
COMPLETION: 2007_**NUMBER OF WORKPLACES:** 68
GROSS FLOOR AREA: 3,000 M²_**COMMON AREA:** CONFERENCE AREA, ENTRANCE HALL_**KIND OF WORKPLACES:** OPEN-PLAN_**PHOTOS:** © JENS WEBER, MUNICH

Creating a business card from architecture is the basic concept of this "Less is more" executive pavilion for one of the leading firms of the European wood industry. With classic modern proportions, the clean-cut and meticulously designed construction surrounded by warehouses is situated around two quiet courtyards. The building, containing offices as well as conference and seminar-rooms, benefits to the very last millimeter from the typical properties of a new material: BBS panels, which Binder manufactures of multi-layered structural plywood. Under a large flat wood roof that looks like a wide-brimmed hat, these panels alternate with full-height glass windows framing the landscape.

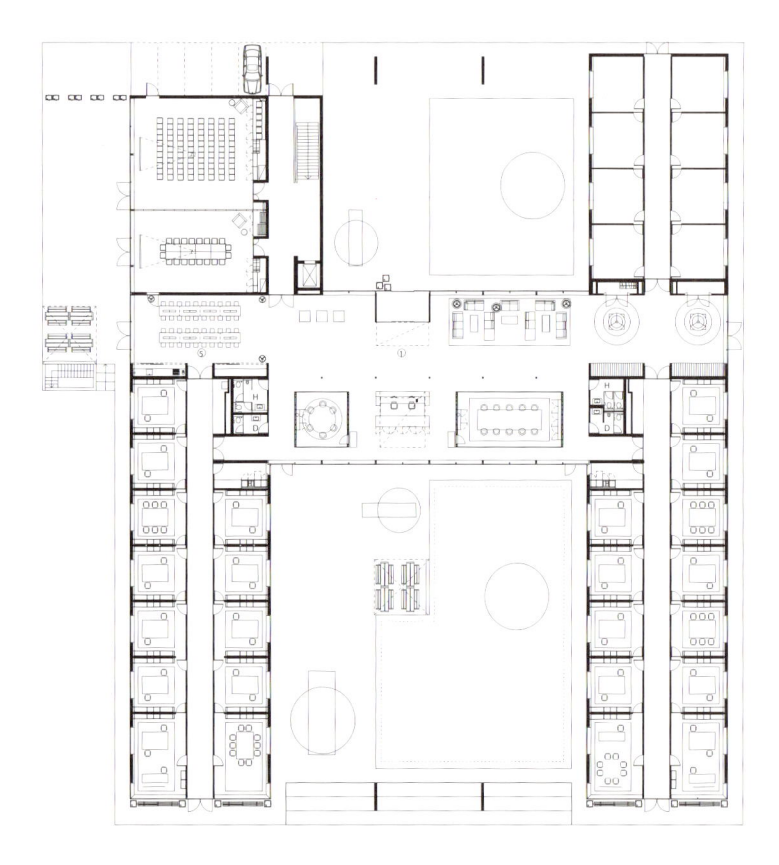

Eine architektonische Visitenkarte zu schaffen war der grundlegende Gedanke zu diesem „Less is more" Pavillon der Geschäftsleitung einer der im europäischen Holzmarkt führenden Firmen. Proportionen der klassischen Moderne folgend, ist die ausgeklügelt und minuziös entworfene Konstruktion von Lagern umgeben und zu zwei ruhigen Innenhöfen ausgerichtet. Das Büros, Konferenz- und Seminarräume umfassende Gebäude nutzt die Eigenschaften eines neuen Materials – BBS Paneele, ein mehrschichtiges Sperrholz, das von Binder produziert wird – bis zu den Grenzen aus. Mit geschosshoher Verglasung wechselnd, rahmen die BSS-Paneele unter dem breiten Überstand des hölzernen Flachdachs die Landschaft.

left: Ground floor plan_Inner courtyard by night_Lobby. right: Conference area_Outside.
links: Plan Erdgeschoss_Nachtaufnahme des Innenhofs_Lobby. rechts: Konferenzbereich_Außenansicht.

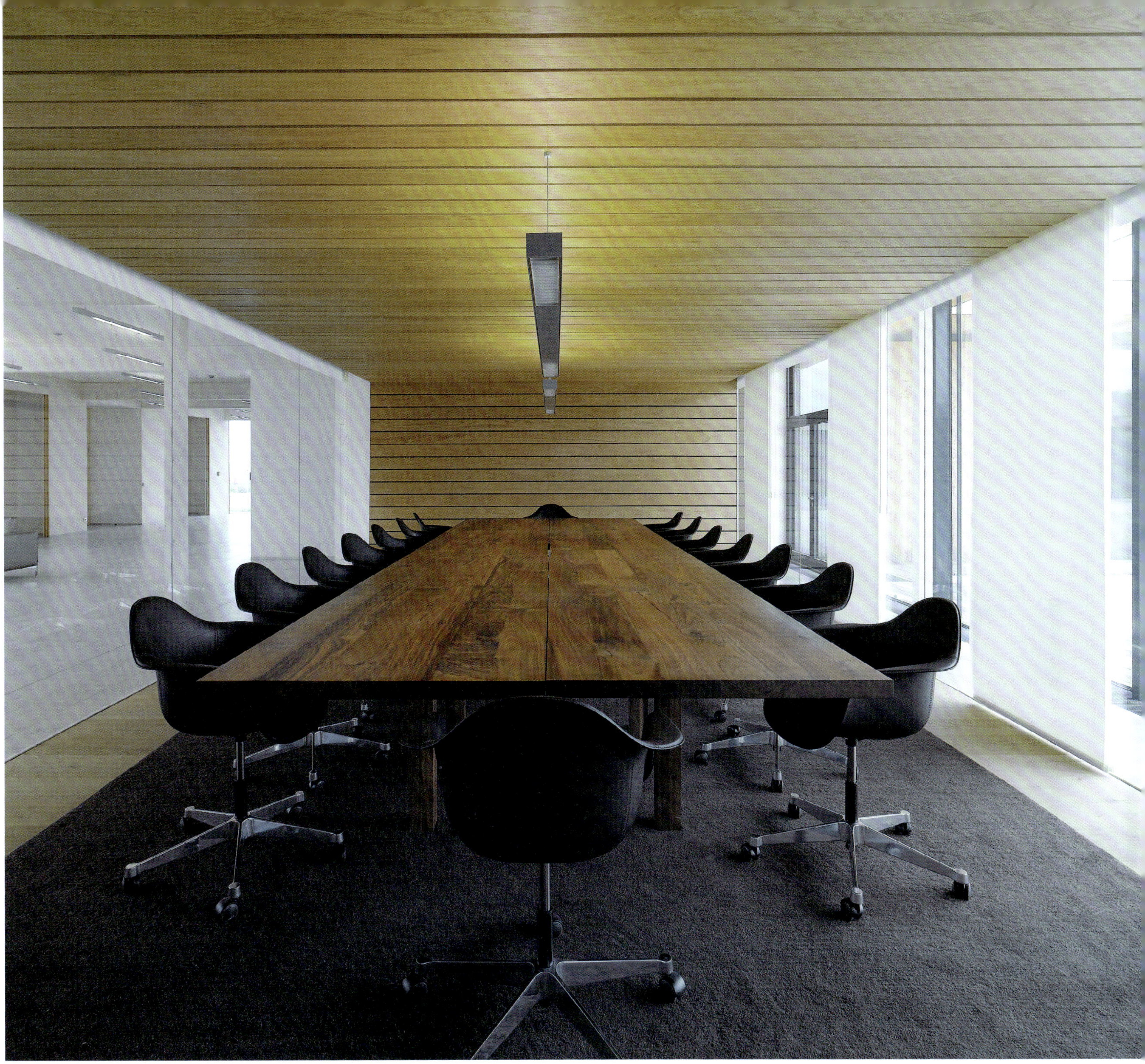

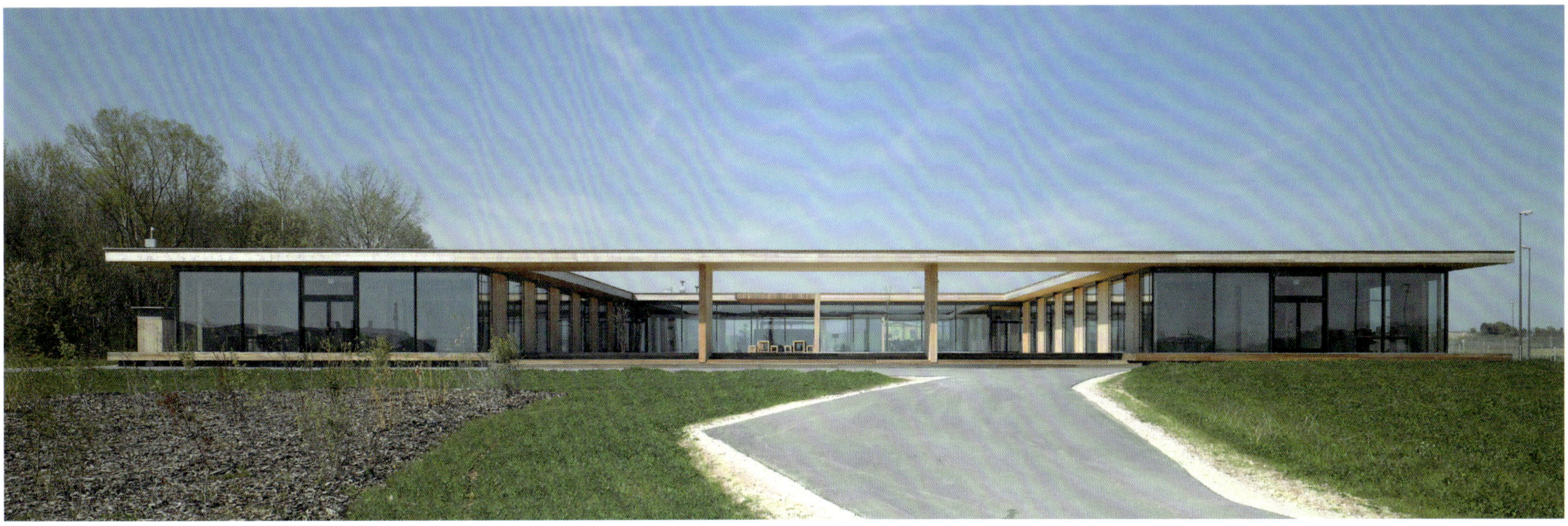

GERMANY_LOHNE **KROGMANN HEADQUARTERS**

ARCHITECTS: DESPANG ARCHITEKTEN_**COMPLETION:** 2009
NUMBER OF WORKPLACES: 5_**GROSS FLOOR AREA:** 300 M²
COMMON AREA: KITCHENETTE, CONFERENCE ROOM_**KIND OF WORKPLACES:** OPEN-PLAN_**PHOTOS:** OLAF BAUMANN, HANOVER

The woodworking company, which is well-known for its cooperation with architects, constructed the new corporate headquarters itself based upon a plan by an architect. Designed as an architectural résumé, the modern building not only demonstrates the characteristics of various woods – such as sound protection optimization, thermal storage capacity and humidity control, and their symbiotic interaction with concrete, glass, and fiber cement, but also symbolizes the generation change in the company management and the new status of the construction culture among medium-sized businesses. The distinctive trapezoid shape avoids the winter winds on the low northern side, while seeking daylight and passive solar optimization in its main façade.

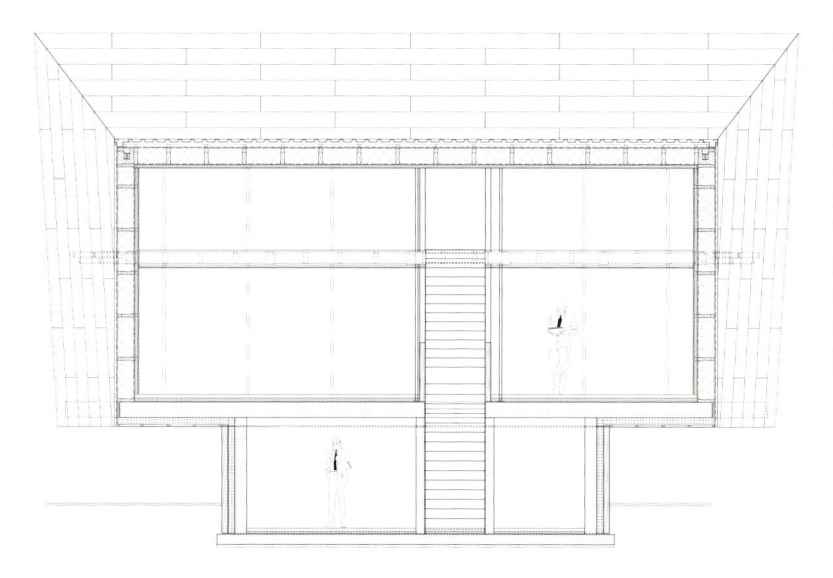

Das für die Zusammenarbeit mit Architekten bekannte Holzbauunternehmen errichtete seinen neuen Firmensitz in handwerklicher Eigenleistung nach gemeinsamer Planung mit den Architekten. Als architektonische Selbstdarstellung konzipiert, demonstriert der moderne Baukörper nicht allein die Fähigkeiten verschiedener Hölzer – schallakustische Optimierung, thermische Speicherkapazität und Feuchtigkeitsregulierung   und ihre symbiotische Verwendung mit Beton, Glas und Faserzement. Er symbolisiert zugleich den Generationenwechsel in der Firmenführung und die neue Wertschätzung, die Baukultur im Mittelstand genießt. Die markante, trapezoide Form meidet die Winterwinde an der niedrigen Nordseite und sucht in der Hauptansicht Tageslicht- und passive Solaroptimierung.

left: Section_Entrance_Detail corner. right: South elevation.
links: Schnitt_Eingang_Detail Gebäudekante. rechts: Südfassade.

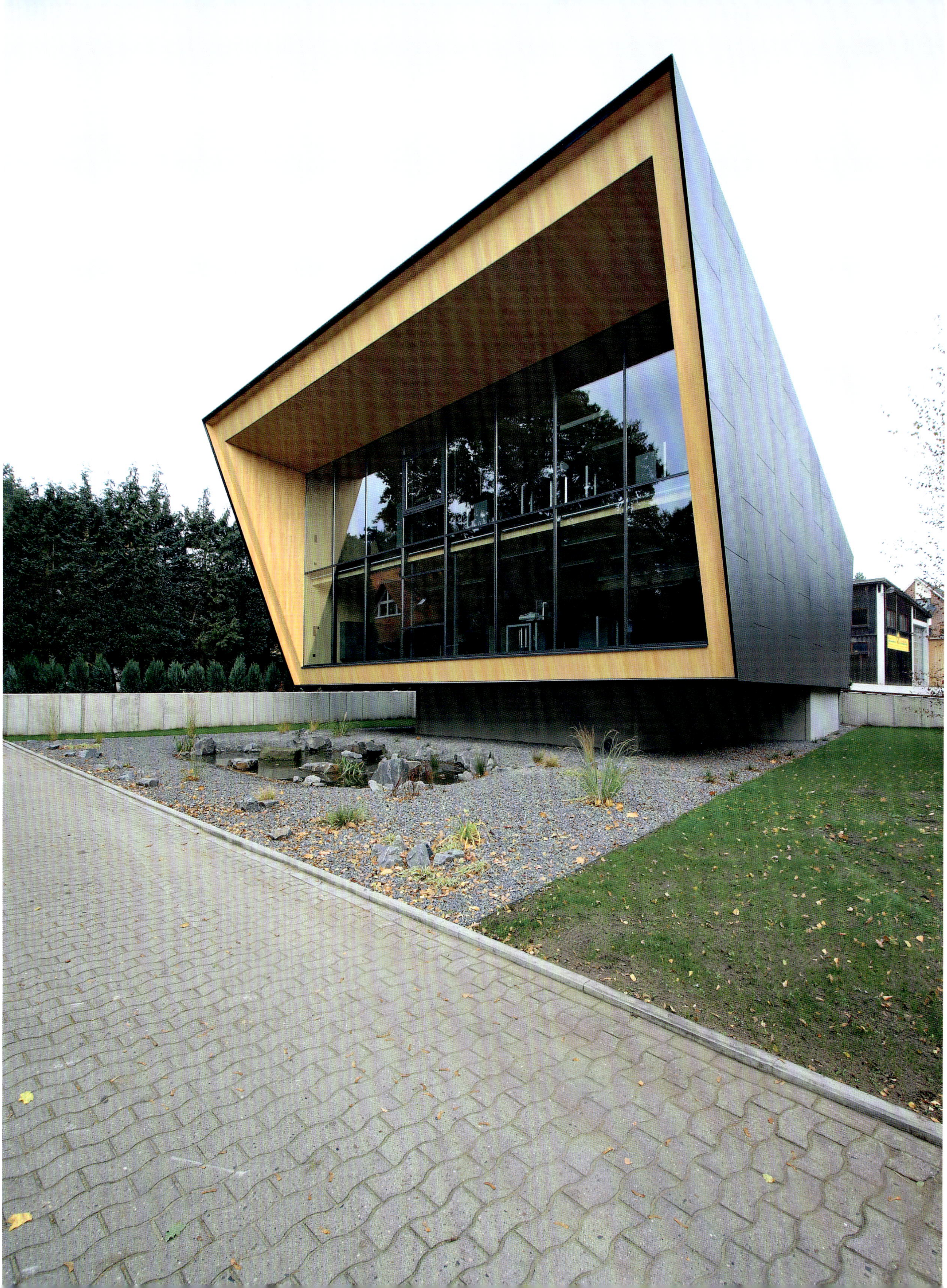

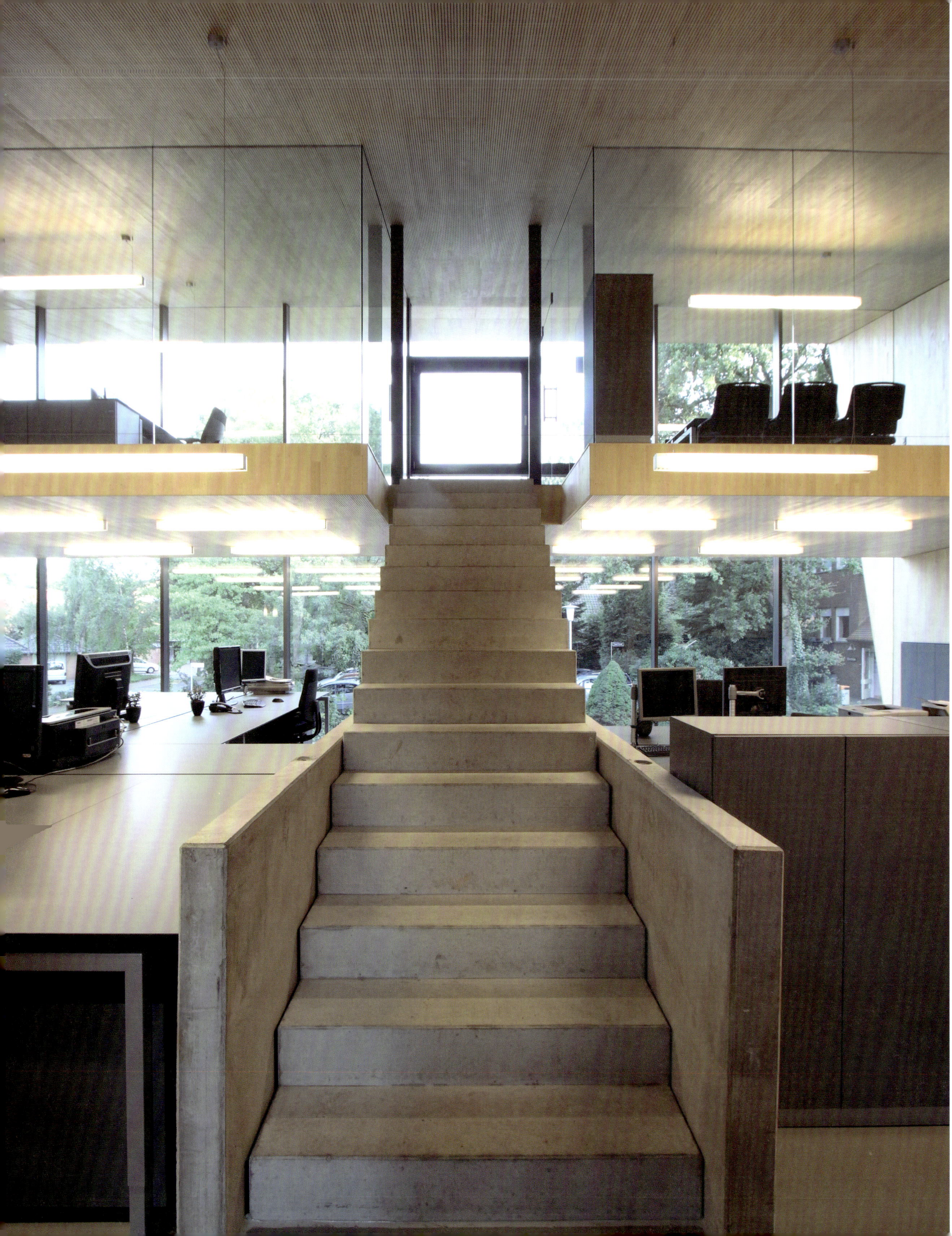

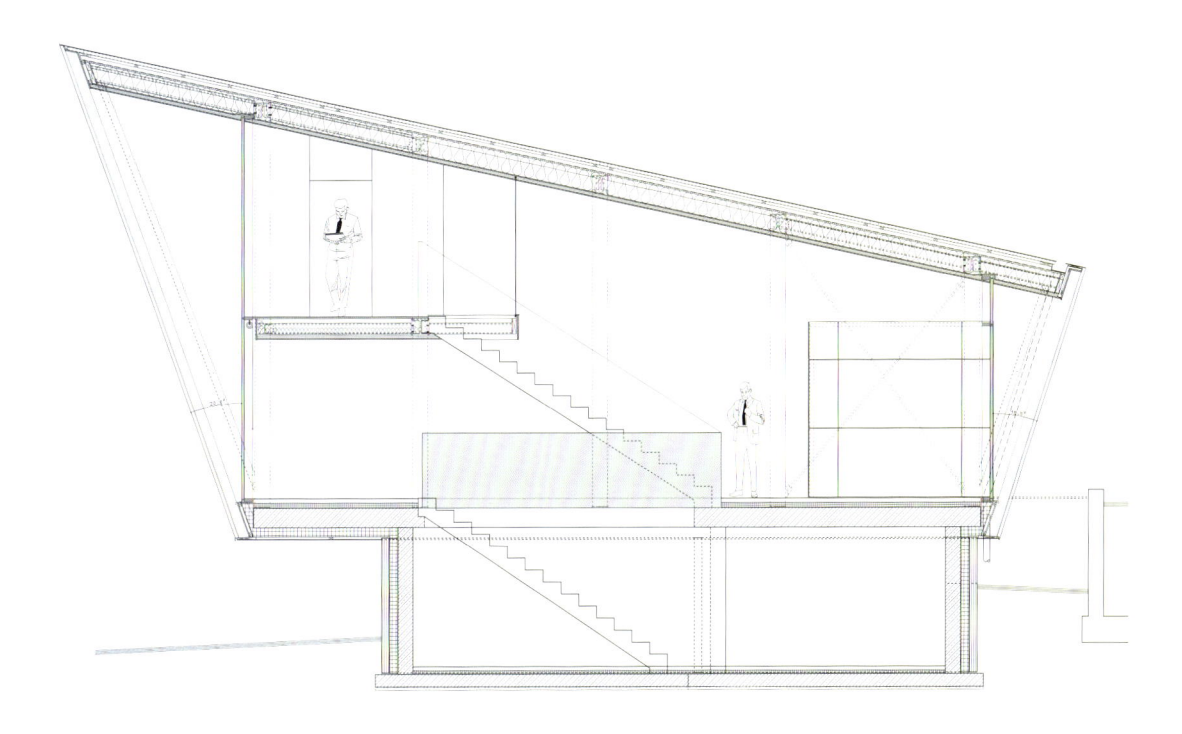

left: Stair in the center of the office. right: Longitudinal section_Workplaces upper floor_Detail_Workplaces lower floor.
links: Treppe im Zentrum Büros. rechts: Längsschnitt_Detail_Arbeitsplätze Obergeschoss_Arbeitsplätze Untergeschoss.

GERMANY_MAINZ **WEISSLILIENGASSE 7**

ARCHITECTS: CMA CYRUS I MOSER I ARCHITEKTEN
ORIGINAL BUILDING: EDUARD KREYSSLIGS, 1872
COMPLETION: 2005_**NUMBER OF WORKPLACES:** 18
GROSS FLOOR AREA: 1,586 M²_**COMMON AREA:** LECTURE HALL, TEA KITCHENS, CONFERENCE ROOMS_**KIND OF WORKPLACES:** CELLULAR, BUSINESS CLUB, LOUNGE WORKSPACE
PHOTOS: COURTESY OF THE ARCHITECTS

The three-floor former residential building was renovated for the Leoff Holding GmbH in its original form and expanded by a peripheral and yard building with deliberately contrasting modern, reduced shapes. The extensively glazed levels of the yard building are linked by a frame of dark-colored exposed concrete. The peripheral building with its quarry-faced silver quartzite façade creates a link between the main structure and the yard building. It creates a connection to the main building and contains service rooms such as warehouses, kitchenettes, sanitary areas. Rising 2.50 meters higher than the yard building, it serves the remaining roof apartment of the old building as a terrace.

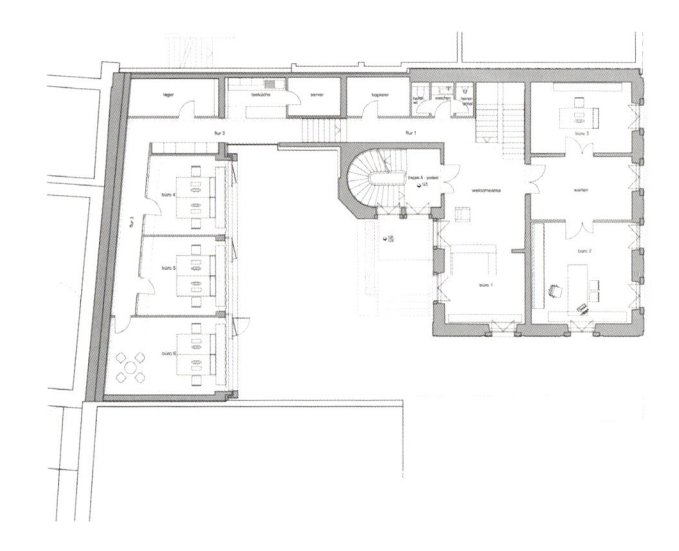

Das dreigeschossige, ehemalige Wohngebäude wurde in seiner ursprünglichen Form für die Leoff Holding GmbH saniert und durch ein Seiten- und Hofgebäude in bewusst kontrastierender moderner, reduzierter Formensprache erweitert. Die stark verglasten Geschosse des Hofgebäudes werden durch einen Rahmen aus dunkel eingefärbtem Sichtbeton zusammengezogen. Der Seitenbau mit bruchrauer Silberquarzithfassade vermittelt formal zwischen Haupt- und Hofgebäude. Er stellt die Verbindung zur Erschließung im Hauptbau her und nimmt dienende Räume wie Lager, Teeküchen, Sanitärbereiche auf. 2,50 Meter höher als das Hofgebäude, bietet er der verbliebenen Dachgeschosswohnung des Altbaus eine Terrasse.

left: First floor plan_Reception_Entrance_Rehabilitated staircase. right: Entrance area_Work place_Internal connection steps between ground floor and first floor_Window to the courtyard, tea kitchen.
links: Grundriss erstes Obergeschoss_Empfang_Eingang_Saniertes Bestandstreppenhaus. rechts: Eingangsbereich_Interne Verbindungstreppe zwischen Erdgeschoss und erstem Obergeschoss_Fenster zum Hof, Teeküche.

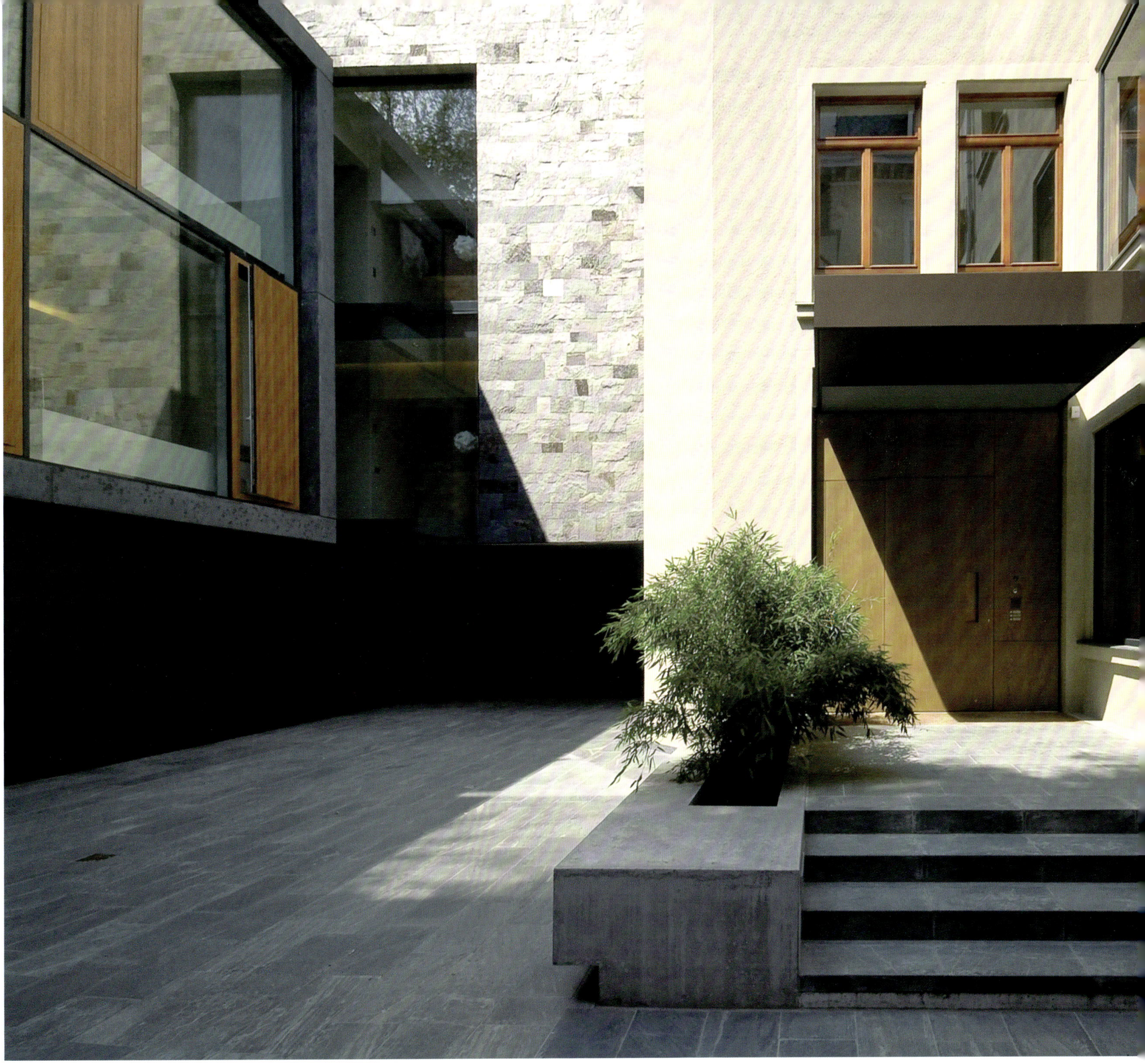

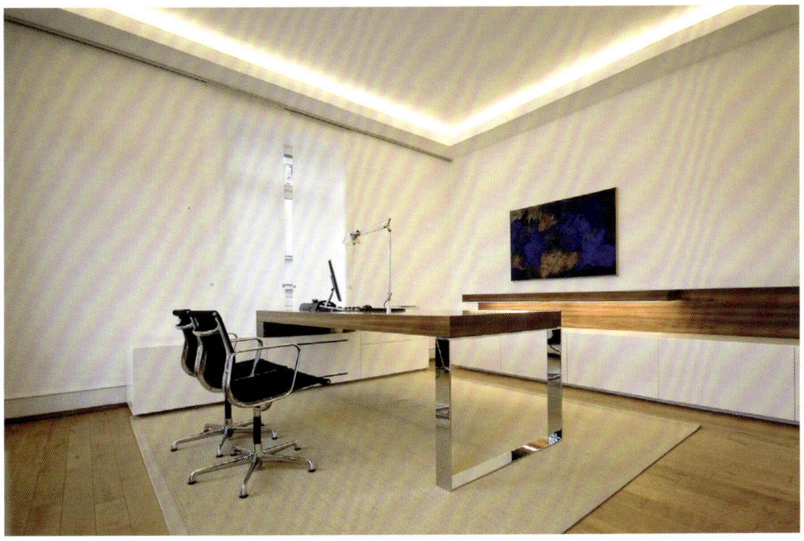

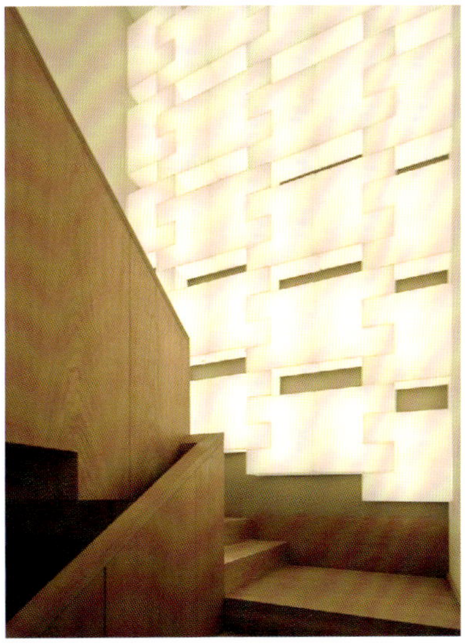

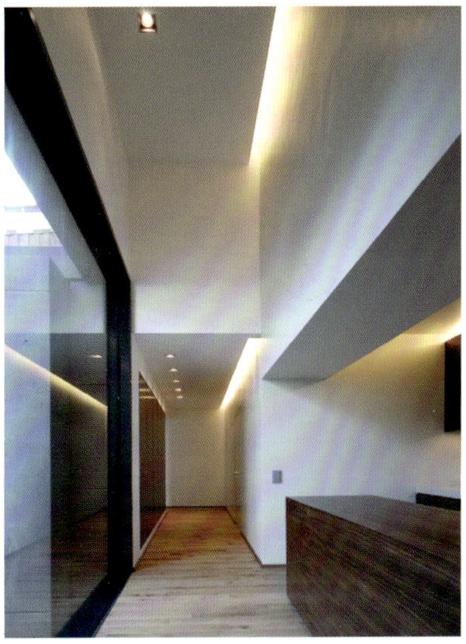

GERMANY_METZINGEN **HUGO BOSS HEADQUARTERS**

ARCHITECTS: RIEHLE + PARTNER ARCHITEKTEN UND STADT-PLANER_**OTHER CREATIVES:** DOMINO ARCHITEKTEN.INGENIEURE.DESIGNER_**COMPLETION:** 2007
NUMBER OF WORKPLACES: APPROX. 400_**GROSS FLOOR AREA:** 21,000 M²_**COMMON AREA:** CANTEEN, CONFERENCE ROOMS, EVENT ROOM_**KIND OF WORKPLACES:** OPEN-PLAN
PHOTOS: ANDREAS KELLER, ALTDORF

A four-story atrium office building with a simple cubic shape and an underground garage. It is a highly flexible skeleton construction that accommodates individual, group or open-plan offices, offering all work places daylight illumination and window ventilation. The architectural design focused on neutrality as a background for the changing design products of the fashion sector – through exposed concrete, honed cement flooring, glass, hot-dip galvanized steel profiles and doors. The ground floor incorporates showroom and presentation areas, as well as a restaurant with an outdoor area and a water pool.

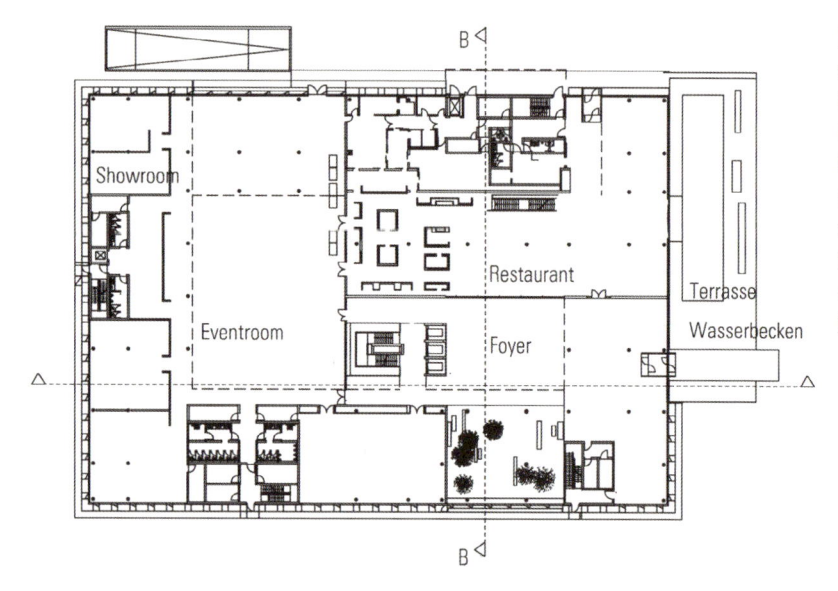

Das viergeschossige Atrium-Bürogebäude in einfacher, kubischer Bauform mit Tiefgarage ist die neueste Erweiterung der HUGO BOSS Hauptverwaltung in Metzingen. Es ist ein hochflexibler Skelettbau, der sowohl Einzel-, als auch Gruppen- oder Großraumbüros ermöglicht und allen Arbeitsplätzen Tagesbelichtung und Fensterlüftung bietet. In der architektonischen Gestaltung wurde Neutralität als Hintergrund für die wechselnden Design-Produkte der Modebranche gesucht: Sichtbeton, geschliffener Zementestrich, Glas, feuerverzinkte Stahlprofile und Türen gewährleisten dies. Das Erdgeschoss umfasst Ausstellungs- und Präsentationsflächen sowie ein Restaurant mit Freibereich und Wasserfläche.

left: Ground floor plan_Entrance area_Lobby. right: Atrium, indoor garden with café.
links: Grundriss, Erdgeschoss_Eingangsbereich_Lobby. rechts: Atrium, Innengarten mit Café.

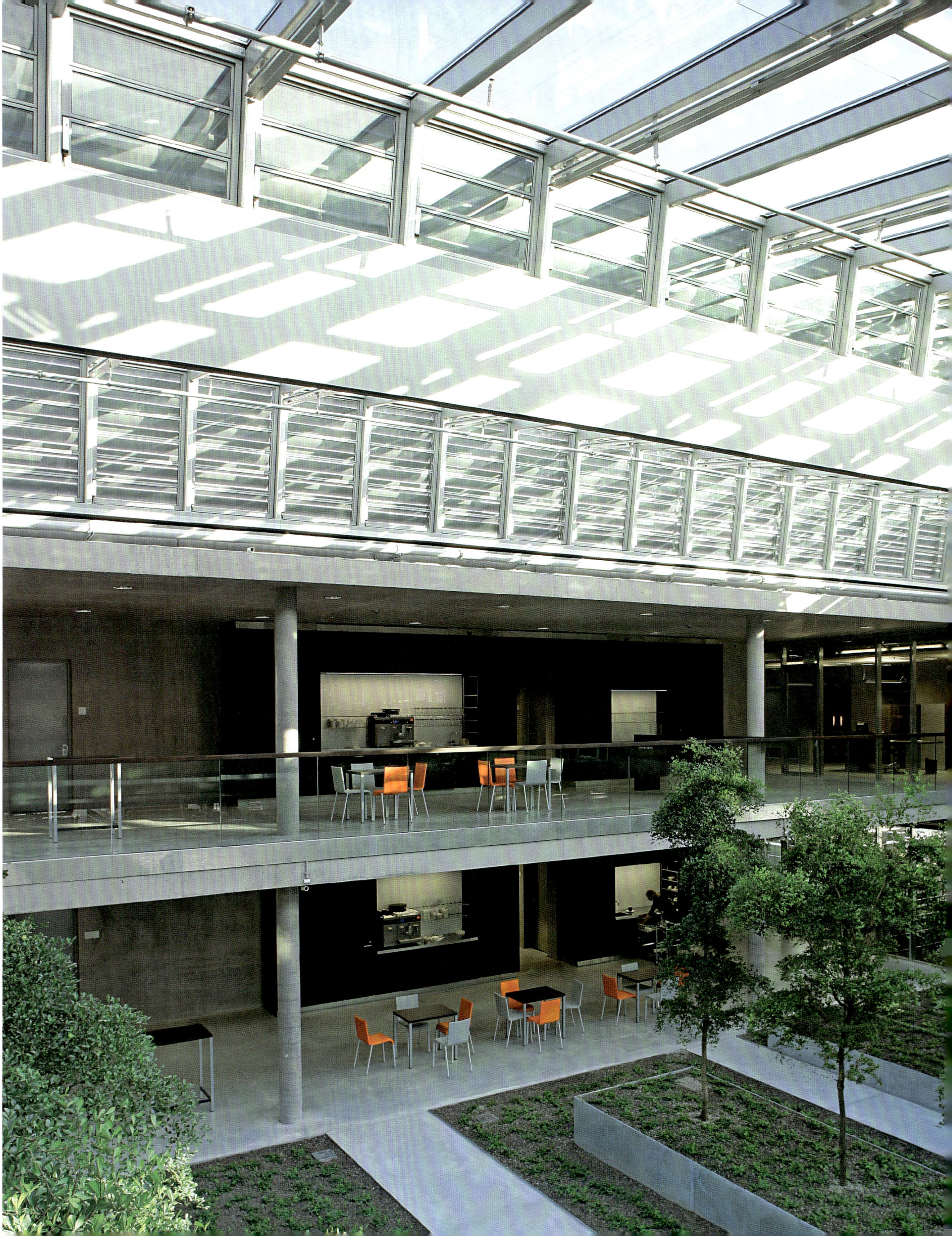

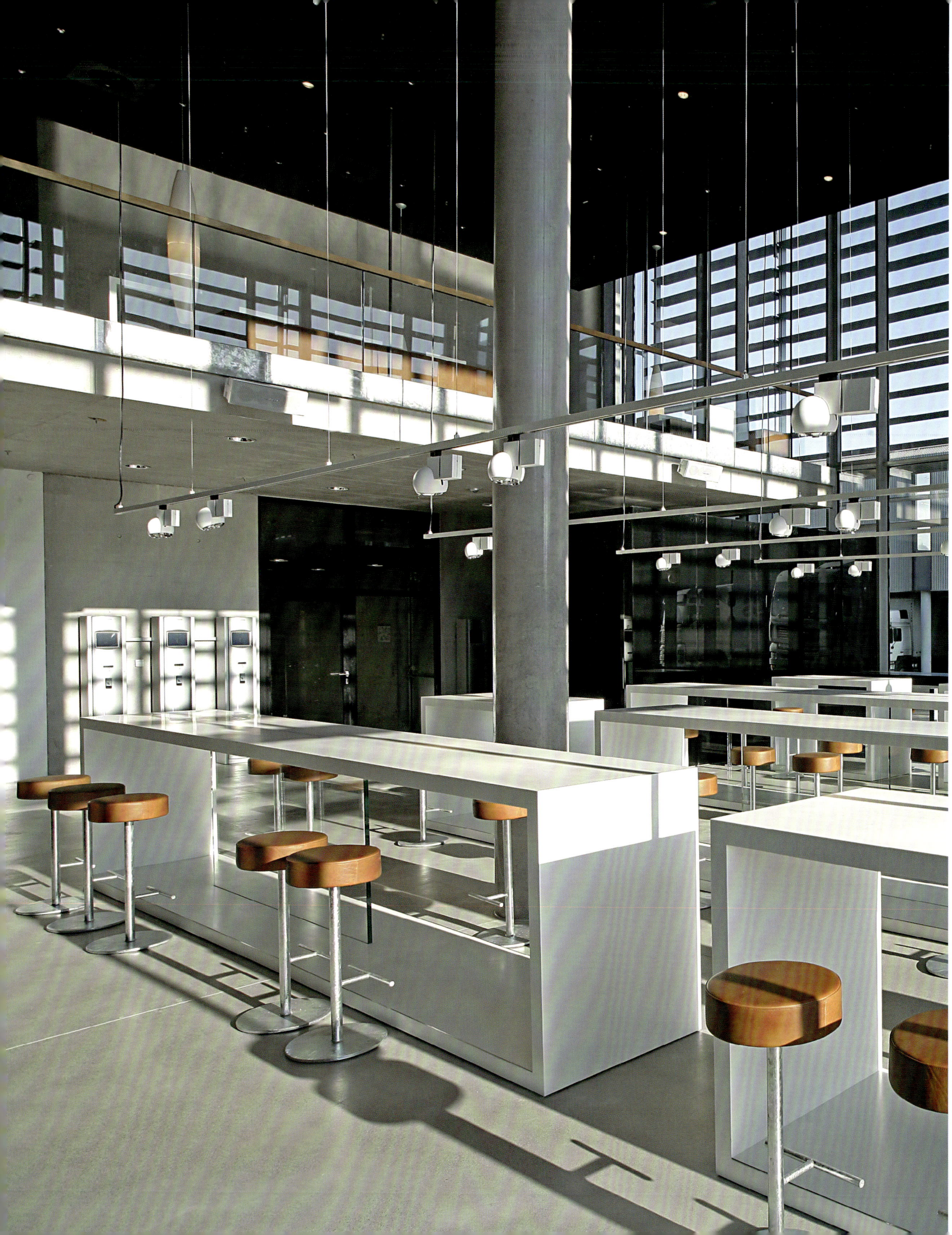

225

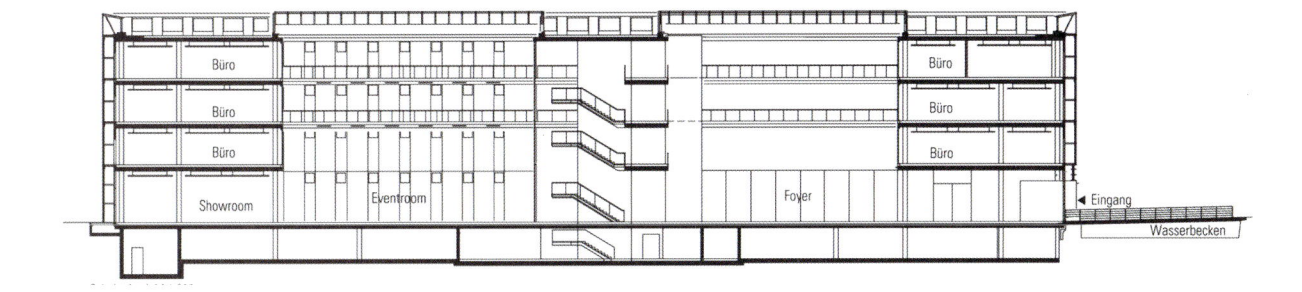

left: Canteen, internet café. right: Section_Meeting room.
links: Kantine, Internet café. rechts: Schnitt_Besprechungsraum.

GERMANY_MUNICH TECHNOLOGY CENTER MUNICH MTZ

ARCHITECTS: H4A GESSERT + RANDECKER ARCHITEKTEN BDA
LANDSCAPE ARCHITECTS: GLÜCK LANDSCHAFTSARCHITEKTUR
STRUCTURAL ENGINEERS: SAILER + STEPAN + PARTNER
COMPLETION: 2008_**NUMBER OF WORKPLACES:** 750
GROSS FLOOR AREA: 25,240 M²_**COMMON AREA:** CONSERVATORY FOR LOBBY, CAFÉ, MEETING BOXES WITH PRE-LOCATED SMALL KITCHENS_**KIND OF WORKPLACES:** CELLULAR, COMBINATION, OPEN-PLAN, DESKSHARING_**PHOTOS:** MÜLLER-NAUMANN, MUNICH

The MTZ technology center is the first project of the M-Campus technology park. The entrance hall is located in the intersection of the campus thoroughfare and the visual and road axes to the M-Tower and the Olympics premises. Designed as a winter garden, it is the central communicative center of the building. Eight modules are arranged as a "house within a house" system in a uniform building grid. They offer a total area of approximately 370 square meters on every level. A layer of flexible glass elements is suspended in front of the eastern and western façade. Together with the colored façade panels they constitute a sunscreen that automatically adjusts to the position of the sun.

Das Technologiezentrum MTZ bildet den Auftakt zum Technologiepark M-Campus. Die Eingangshalle liegt im Schnittpunkt von Campusmagistrale und den Sicht- und Wegeachsen zu M-Tower sowie Olympiagelände. Als Wintergarten konzipiert, ist sie der zentrale, kommunikative Ort im Gebäude. Acht Module besetzen als „Haus im Haus" ein einheitliches Gebäuderaster. Sie bieten auf jeder Ebene eine Fläche von zirka 370 Quadratmetern. Vor den Ost- und Westfassaden hängt eine Schicht aus beweglichen Glaselementen, die zusammen mit den farbigen Fassadenpaneelen den Sonnenschutz gewährleisten und in Abhängigkeit vom Sonnenstand automatisch nachgeführt werden.

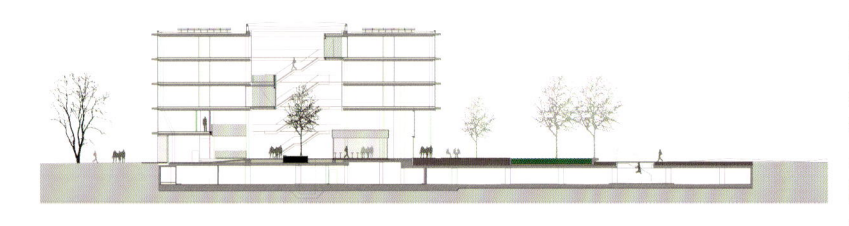

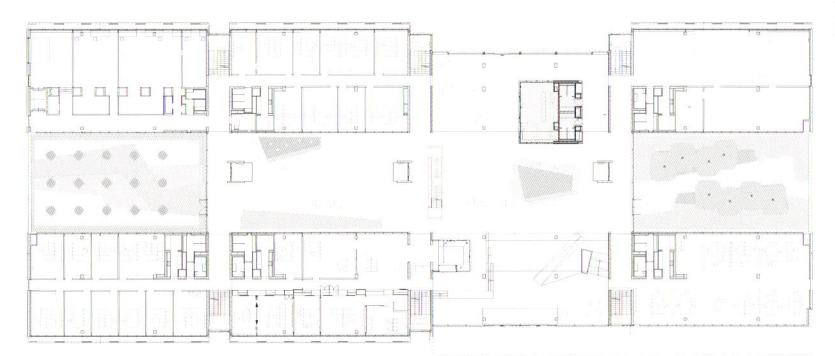

left: Section and ground floor plan_West elevation. right: Conservatory_Façade, detail_View into a inner courtyard_Corridor.
links: Schnitt, Grundriss Erdgeschoss_Westfassade. rechts: Wintergarten_Fassadendetail_Blick in einen Innenhof_Flur.

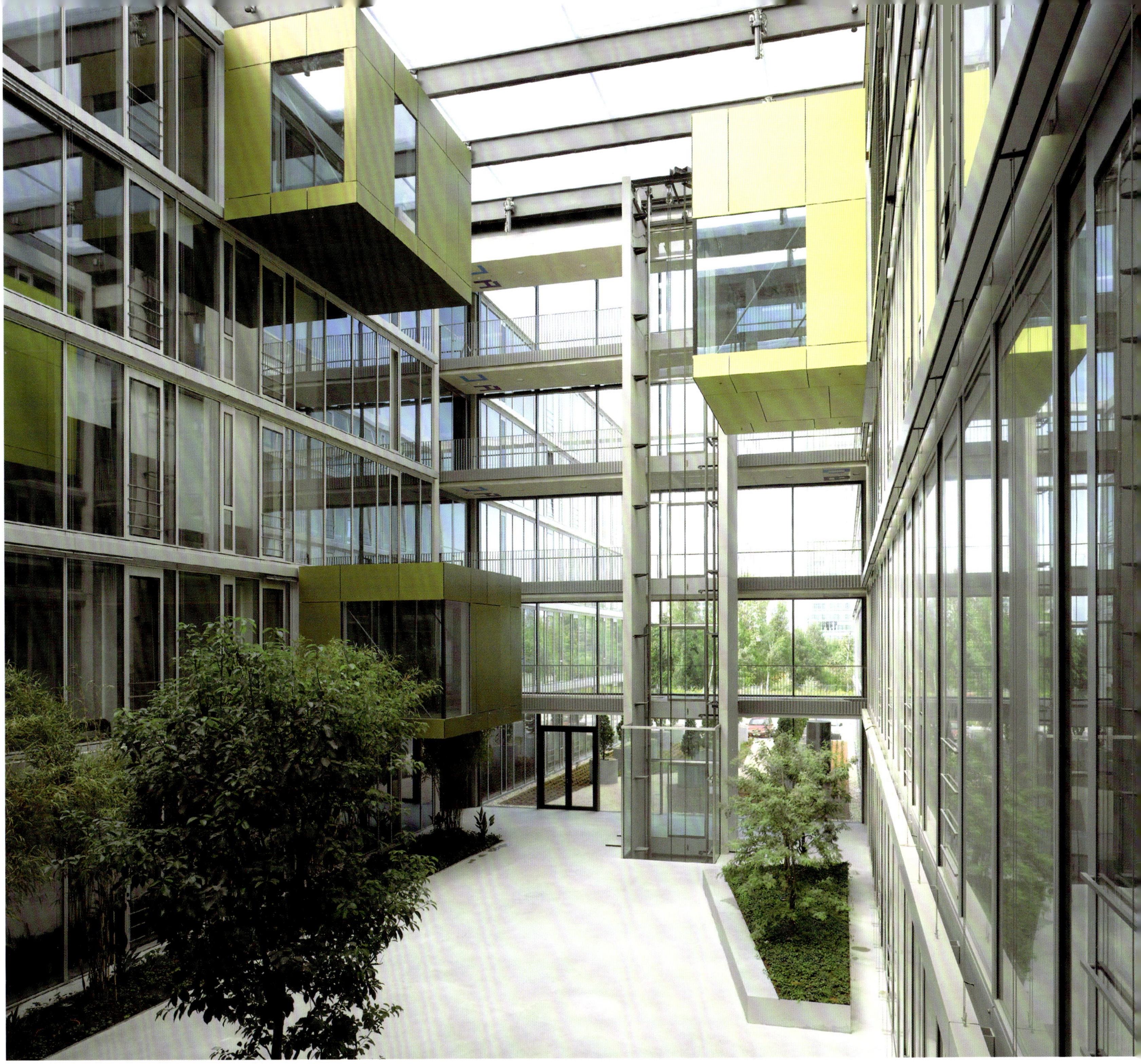

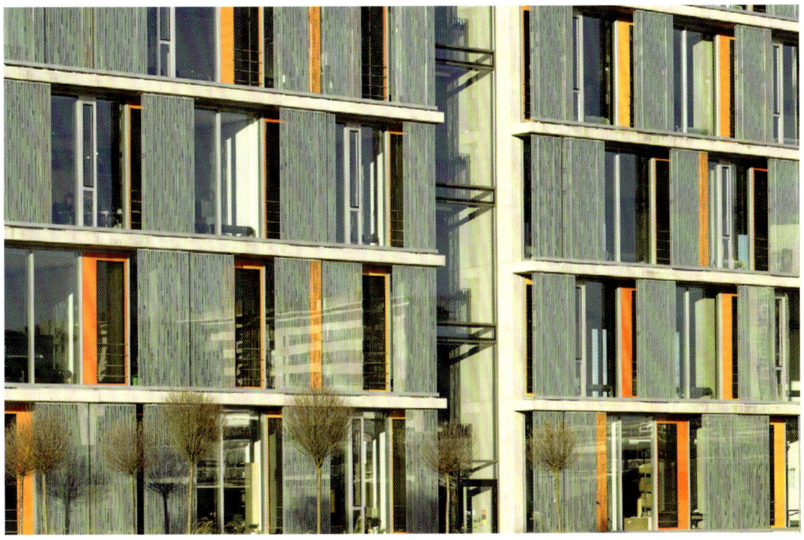

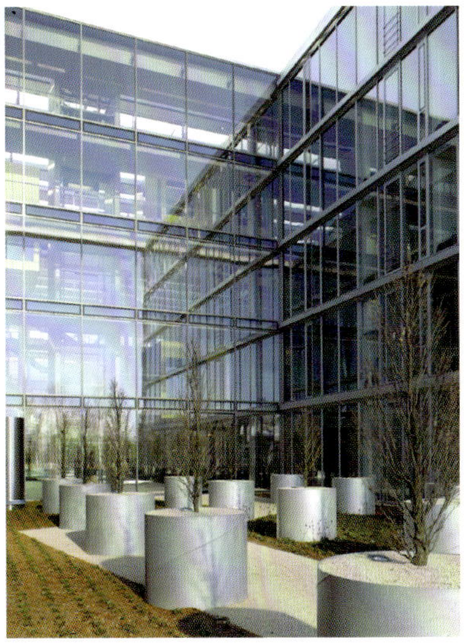

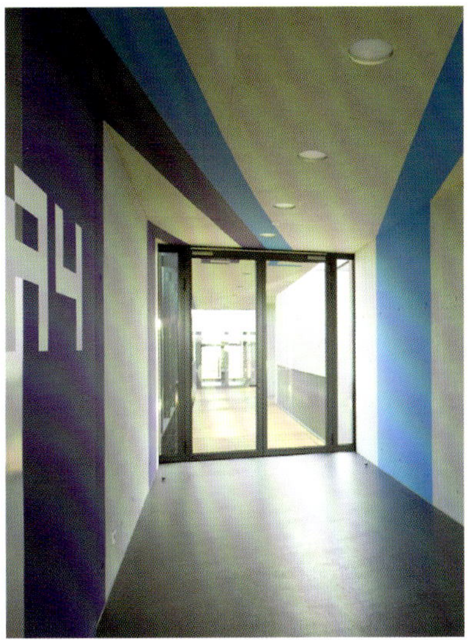

GERMANY_MUNICH FRAUNHOFER BUILDING

ARCHITECTS: HENN ARCHITEKTEN
COMPLETION: 2003_**NUMBER OF WORKPLACES:** 500
GROSS FLOOR AREA: 30,280 M²_**COMMON AREA:** SEMINAR ROOMS, MULITIMEDIA EVENT CENTER, CAFÉ_**KIND OF WORKPLACES:** CELLULAR, COMBINATION, OPEN-PLAN, TEAM, DESKSHARING
PHOTOS: H.G. ESCH / © HENN ARCHITEKTEN

Providing innovations for application-focused research is the core principle of Fraunhofer Gesellschaft, which it vividly demonstrates in its building. The building includes both simple conventional heating as well as centrally-controlled thermal building section activation, while ventilation flaps and sun screens are automatically controlled yet individually adjustable for energy optimization. The shape and function of the 17-floor new building demonstrates transparency and communication through the use of glass and bright offices that allow direct visual horizontal and vertical relations. Transparently designed open areas serve to condense the space and are meeting points for communication and balance.

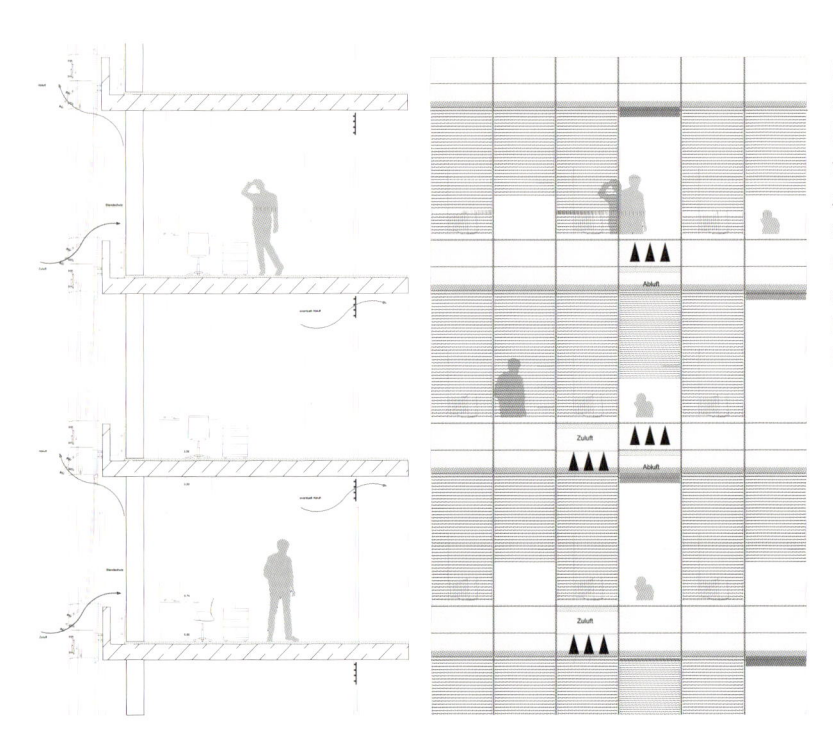

Innovation in anwendungsorientierter Forschung – das Prinzip der Fraunhofer Gesellschaft – wird in ihrem Gebäude exemplarisch vorgeführt. Es bietet neben einer individuellen, konventionellen Heizung auch eine zentral gesteuerte thermische Bauteilaktivierung. Lüftungsklappen und Sonnenschutz werden zur energetischen Optimierung automatisch gesteuert, sind aber individuell einstellbar. Der 17-geschossige Neubau demonstriert Transparenz und Kommunikation in Funktion und Form durch Glas und enthält lichte Büroräume, die direkten visuellen horizontalen und vertikalen Bezug zueinander ermöglichen. Transparent gestaltete Lufträume dienen als Verdichtung von Ort und Raum, als Treffpunkte für Kommunikation und Ausgleich.

left: Façade, section and elevation_Night view_Detail façade. right: Elevation tower.
links: Fassade, Schnitt und Ansicht_Nachtansicht_Fassadendetail. rechts: Ansicht Hochhaus.

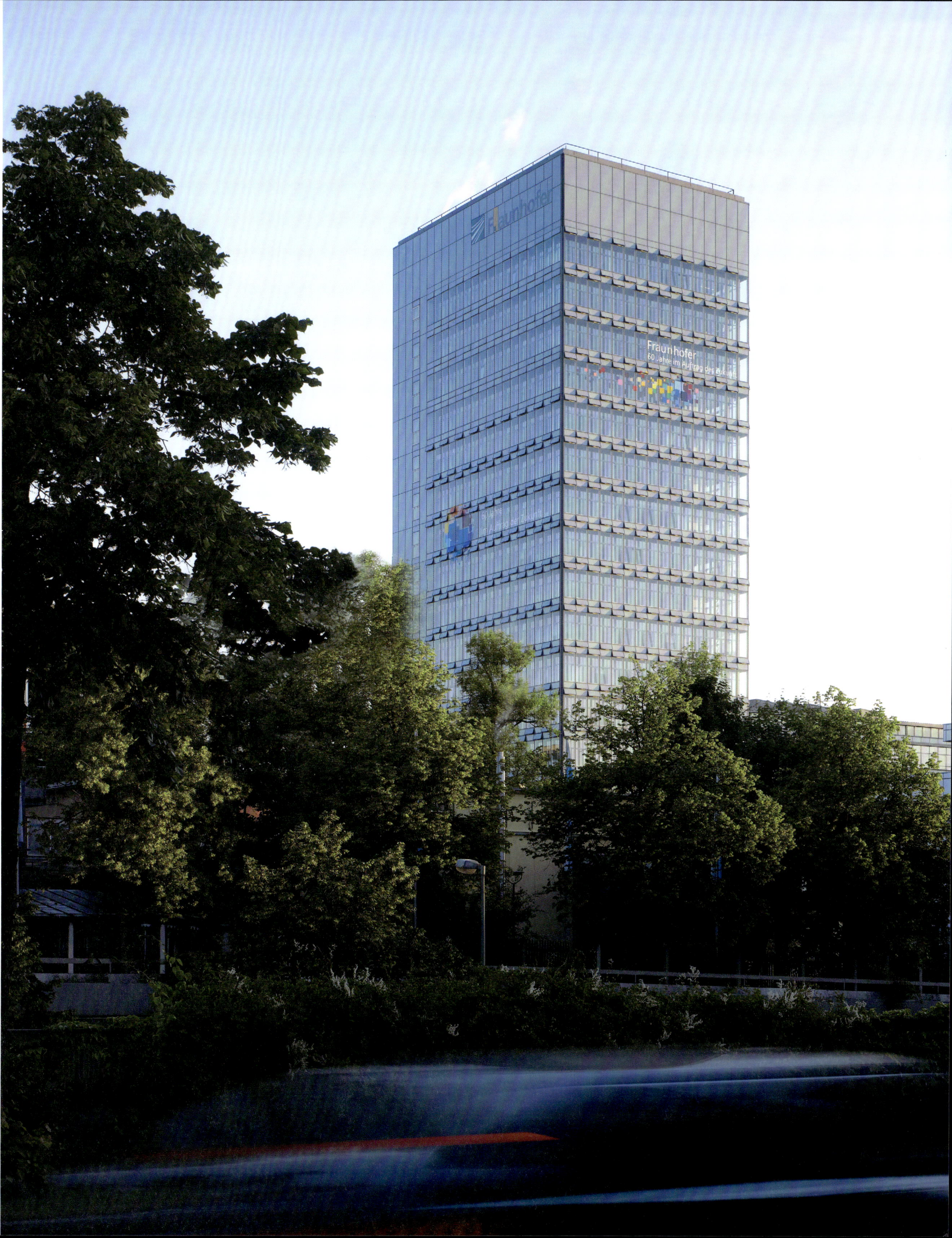
Fraunhofer
Fraunhofer

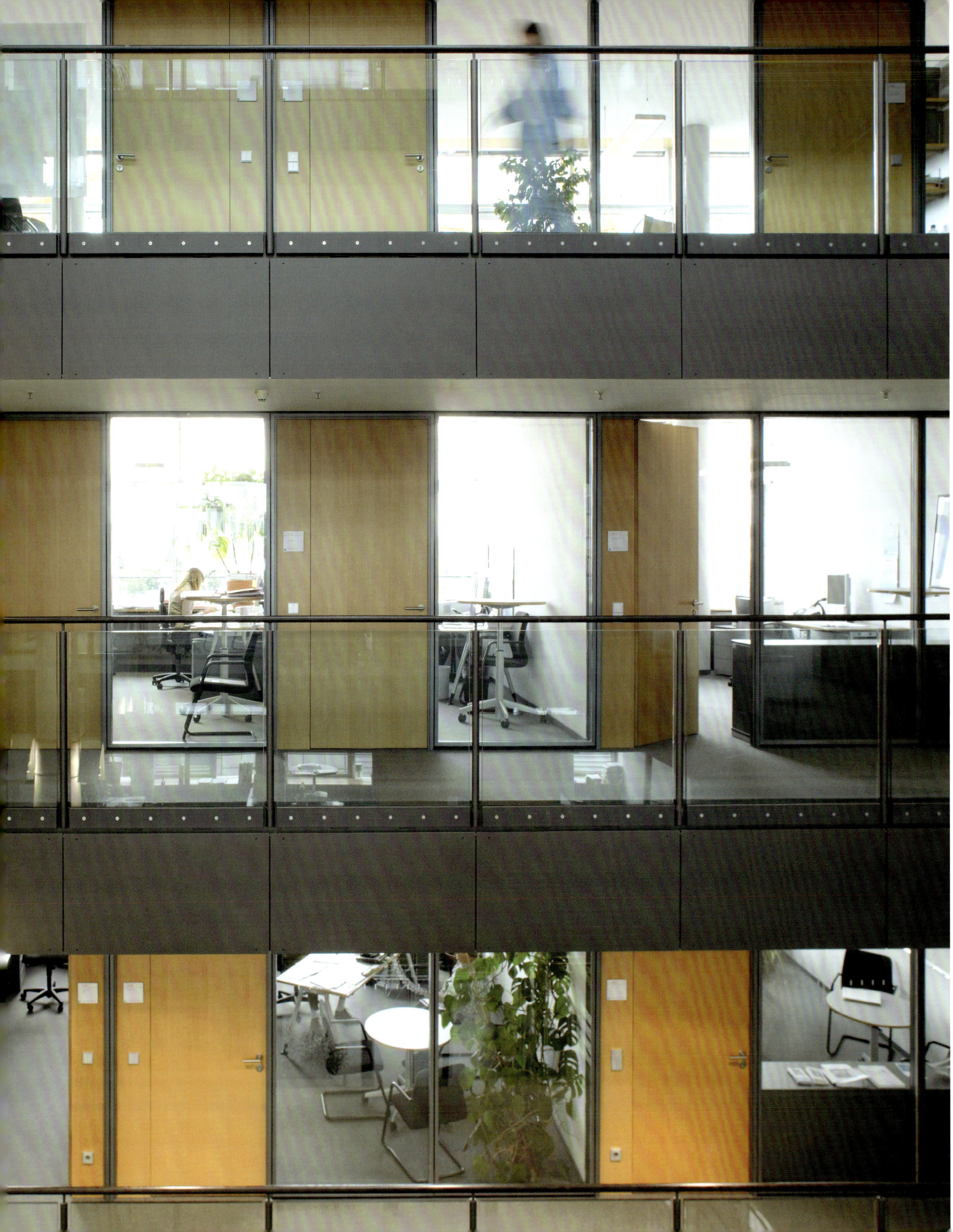

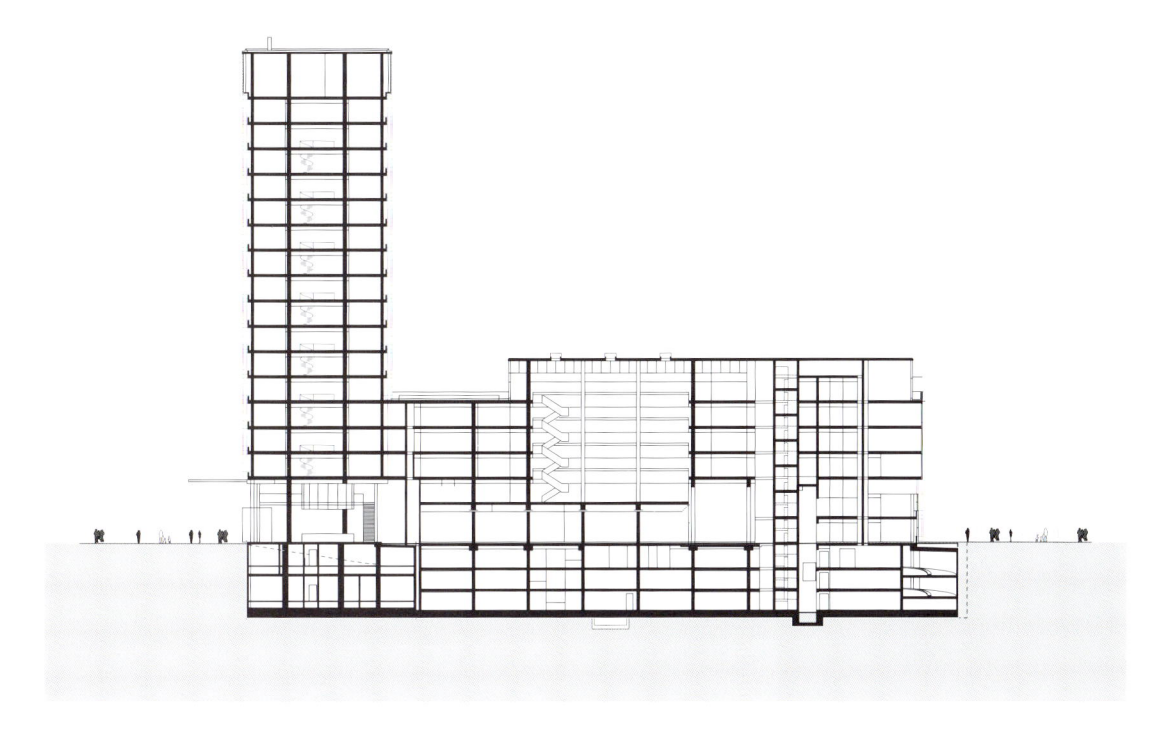

left: Offices. right: Section_Atrium_Communication area_Atrium.
links: Büros. rechts: Schnitt_Atrium_Kommunikationszone_Atrium.

GERMANY_MUNICH **BMW OFFICE BUILDING**

ARCHITECTS: PLAJER & FRANZ STUDIO
COMPLETION: 2008_**NUMBER OF WORKPLACES:** 144
GROSS FLOOR AREA: 15,650 M²_**KIND OF WORKPLACES:** CELLULAR, OPEN-PLAN, TEAM
PHOTOS: DIEPHOTODESIGNER.DE, KEN SCHLUCHTMANN, BERLIN

The new BMW office building combines creativity and high-tech elements. The architects created an intelligent ensemble of generous outdoor areas, inner courtyards and workshops, offering space for innovation and creativity in combination with loft-style office workplaces. The boundaries of the constructed space are made unobtrusive by transparent façades and the inner courtyard covered by membrane cushions. The open spaces and the transparent architecture is intended to promote creativity by appealing to the senses. It architecturally translates the slogan of the car maker "The joy of driving" into "The joy of creativity".

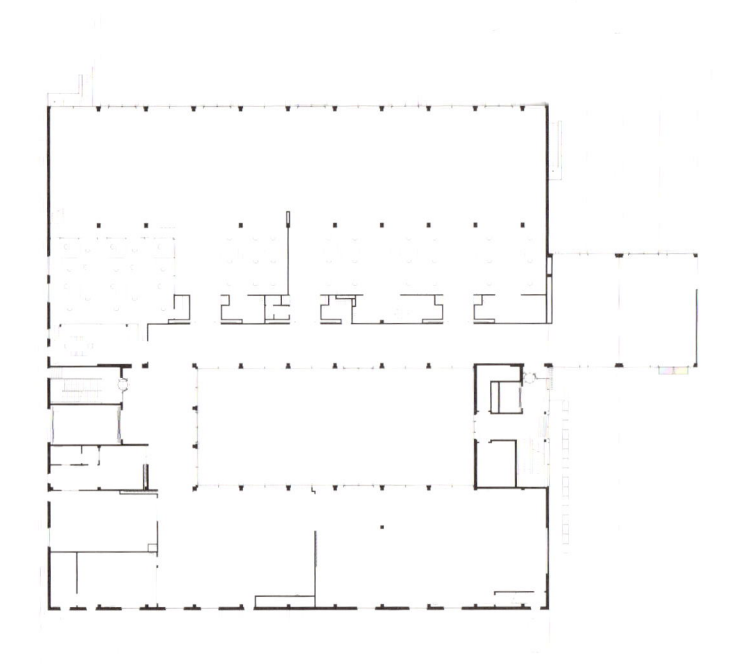

Das neue Bürogebäude für BMW verbindet Kreativität und High-Tech. Die Architekten schufen ein intelligentes Ensemble aus großzügigen Freiflächen, Innenhöfen und Werkstätten, das in Verbindung mit loftartigen Büroarbeitsplätzen einen Raum für Innovation und Kreativität bietet. Die Grenzen des umbauten Raumes werden durch transparente Fassaden und dem mit Membrankissen überdeckte Innenhof verwischt. Der offene Raum und die transparente Architektur sollen durch Reizung der Sinne der Kreativität Vorschub leisten. Der Slogan des Autobauers „Freude am Fahren" wurde architektonisch in „Freude am Kreativen" übertragen.

left: Ground floor plan_Entrance_Entrance area at night. right: Open-plan offices_Arched glass rooftop_Workplaces_Stairway.
links: Grundriss Erdgeschoss_Eingang_Eingangsbereich nachts. rechts: Gemeinschaftsbüros_ Gewölbtes Glasdach_Arbeitsplätze_Treppenaufgang.

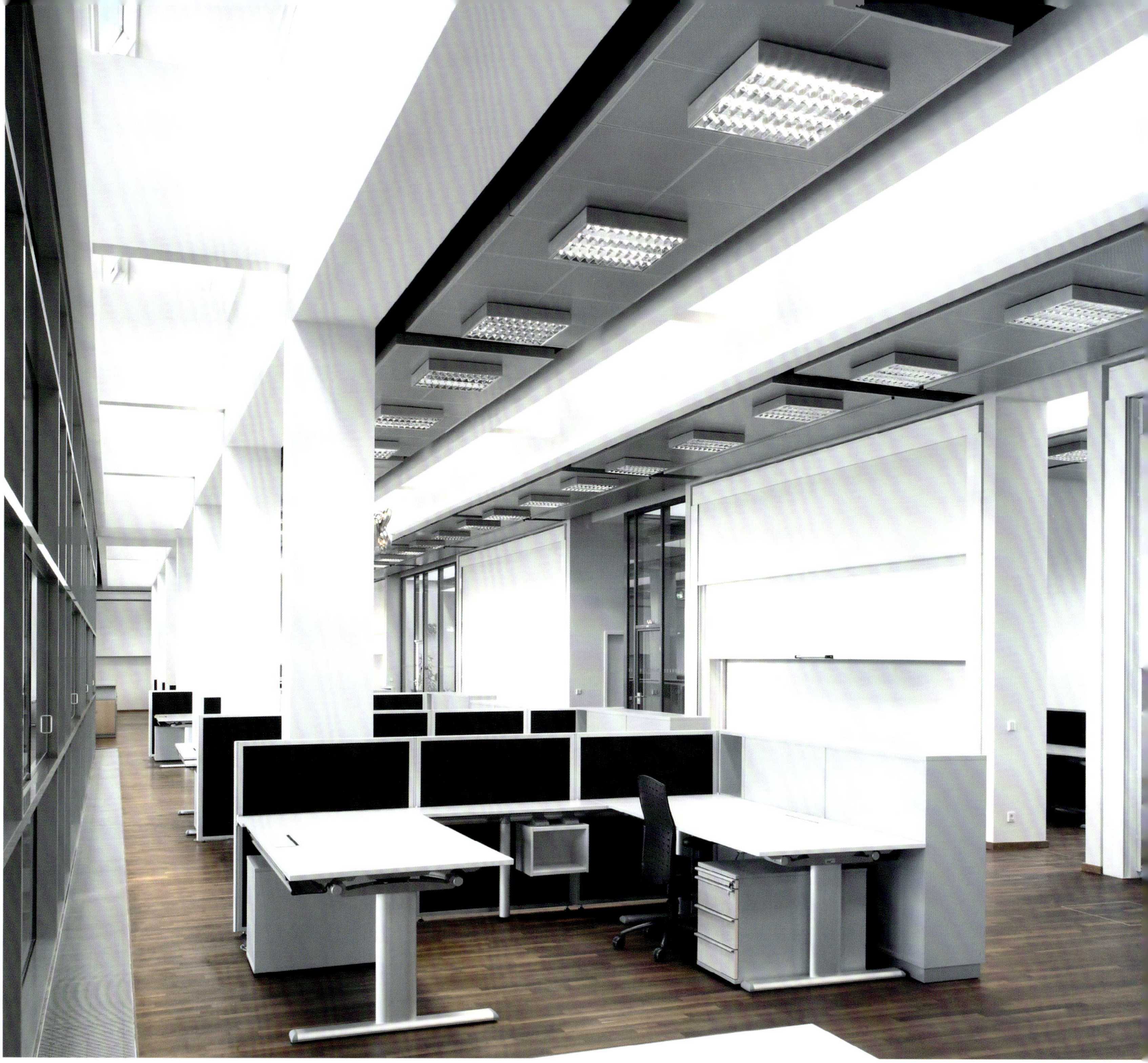
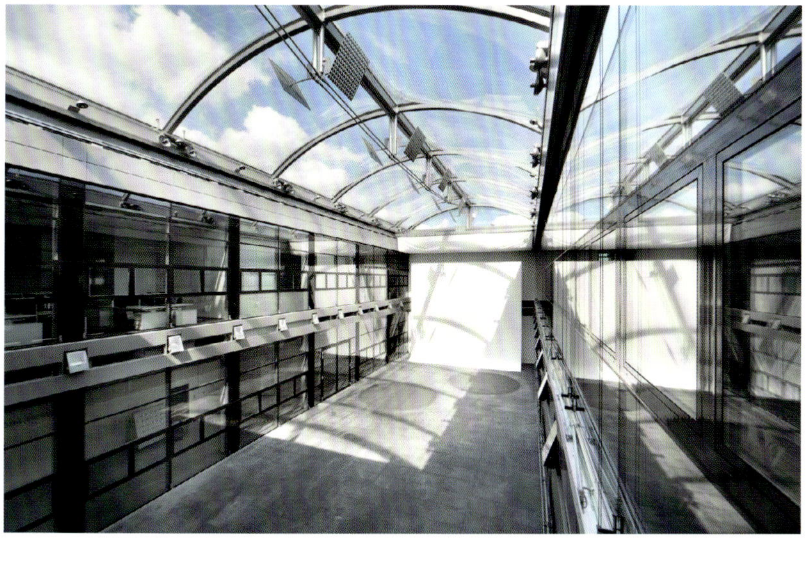
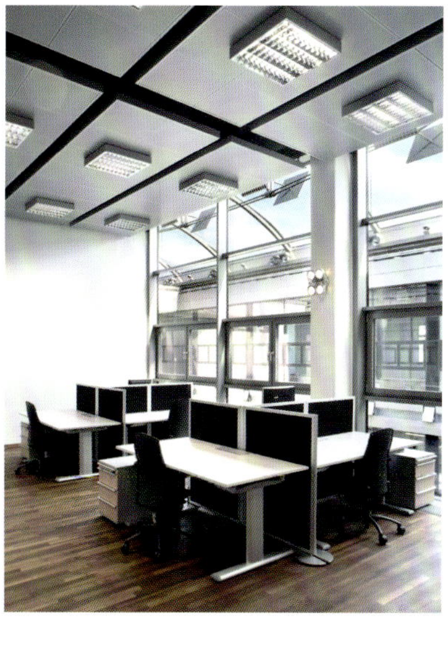
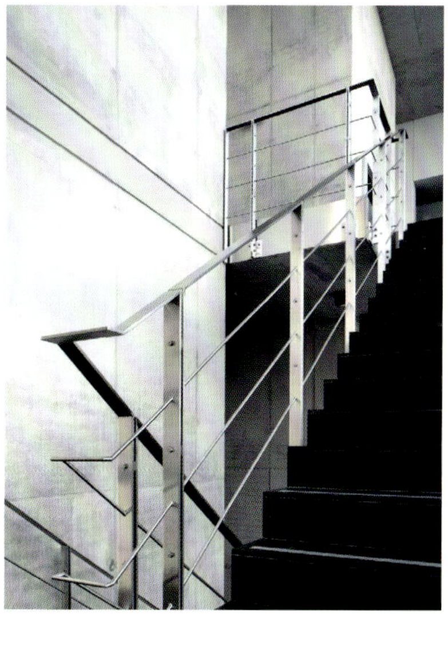

GERMANY_MUNICH REVITALIZATION BMW HIGH RISE PREMISES

ARCHITECTS: SCHWEGER ASSOCIATED ARCHITECTS GMBH
ORIGINAL BUILDING: PROF. KARL SCHWANZER, 1972
COMPLETION: 2006_ **NUMBER OF WORKPLACES:** 1,200
GROSS FLOOR AREA: 30,950 M² BMW HIGHRISE, 72,000 M² ENTIRE BUILDING PROJECT_**COMMON AREA:** CANTEEN, CONFERENCE CENTER_**KIND OF WORKPLACES:** CELLULAR, OPEN-PLAN, OFFICE LANDSCAPE_**PHOTOS:** BERNHARD KROLL, GROSSHANSDORF (235 B. L.), MARCUS BUCK, MUNICH (235 A.), ROLAND HALBE, MUNICH (234, 235 B. R.)

The revitalization was intended to carry on and further develop the self-image of the BMW Group and its current CI as well as the architectural work of Karl Schwanzer. Memory values were preserved while technical innovations were introduced. In addition, it had to provide the users with natural elements such as light, air, and greeners and function perfectly down to the most trivial details. These different aspects were combined in a clear structure, precision, technical perfection and beauty which does justice to both the "four-cylinders" assets, as well as the dynamic yet cultured image of the client.

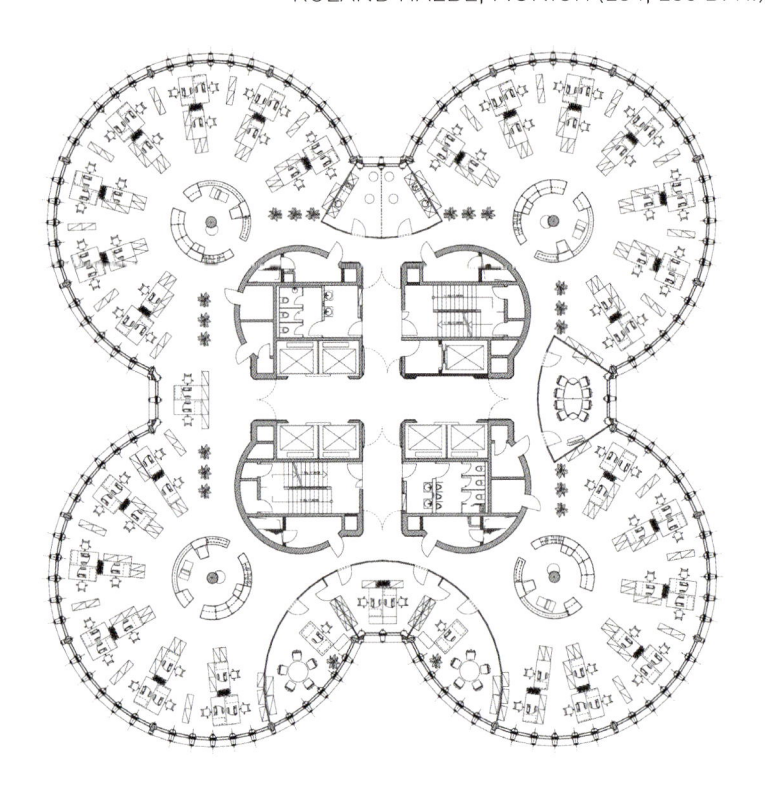

Die Revitalisierung sollte sowohl das Selbstverständnis der BMW Group und die aktuelle CI als auch das architektonische Werk von Karl Schwanzer fortführen beziehungsweise weiterentwickeln und somit den Erhalt von Erinnerungswerten ebenso wie technische Innovationen umfassen. Darüber hinaus musste es den Benutzern natürlichen Elemente wie Licht, Luft und Grün bringen und auch in den einfachsten Details gut funktionieren. Diese unterschiedlichen Aspekte fanden in einer klaren Gestaltung, Präzision, technische Vollkommenheit und Formschönheit zusammen, die sowohl dem Bestand des „Vierzylinders" als auch dem dynamischen zugleich kultivierten Image des Auftraggebers gerecht wird.

left: Ground floor plan with new work structure_Open-plan office, view to the middle zone_Workplaces in a new disposal. right: General view after revitalization_New lobby_Canteen.
links: Grundriss mit neuer Arbeitsplatzanordnung_Großraumbüro, Blick zur Mittelzone_Arbeitsplätze in neuer Anordnung. rechts: Gesamtansicht nach der Revitalisierung_Neues Foyer_Betriebsrestaurant.

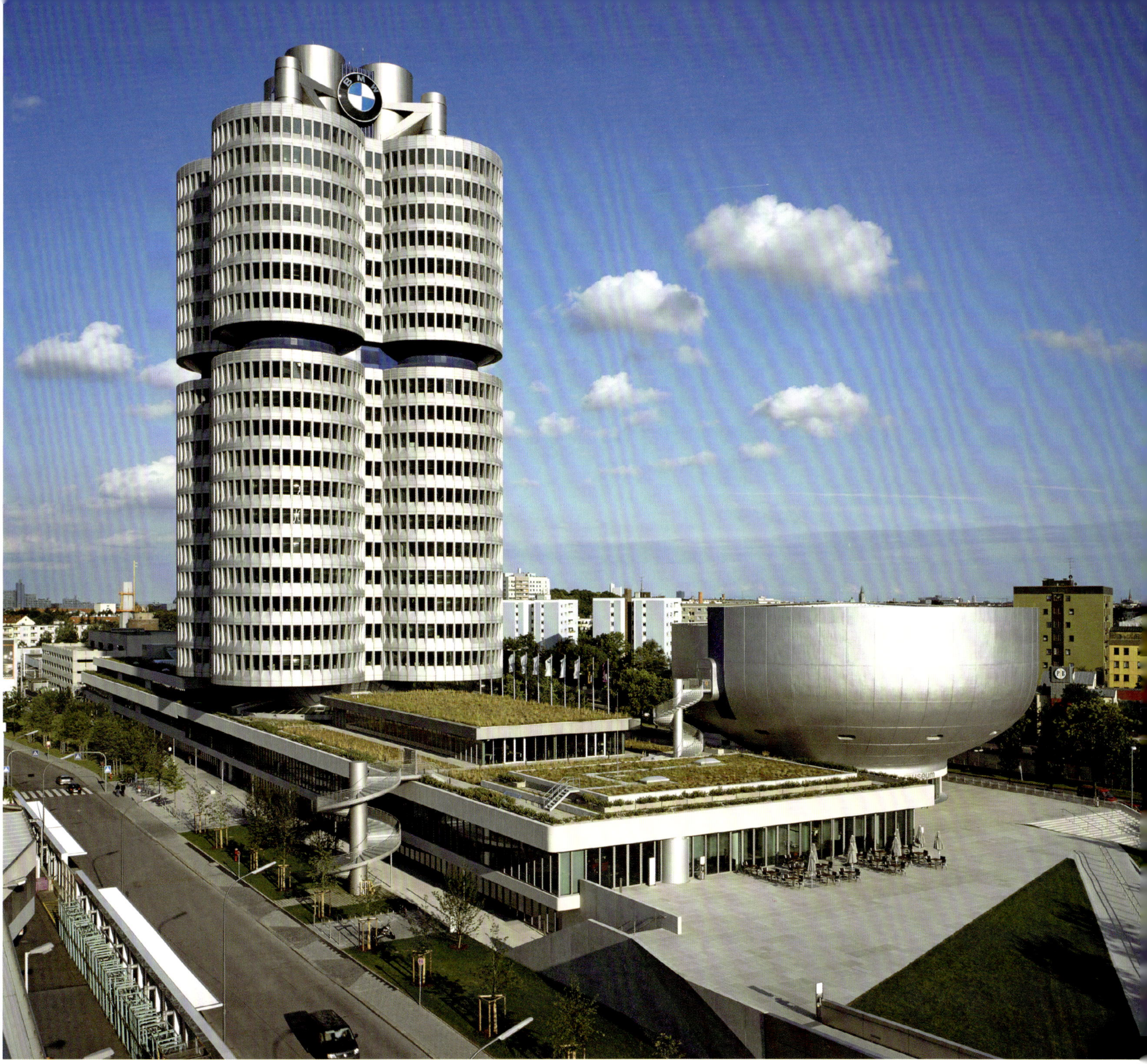

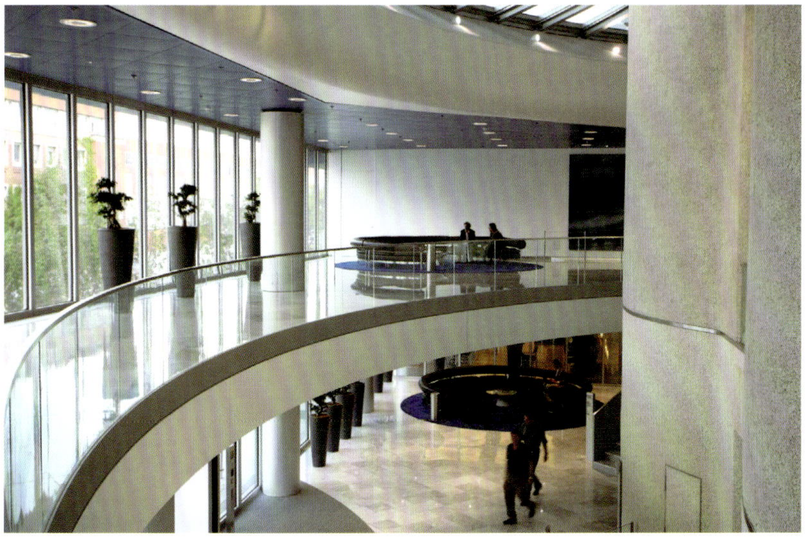

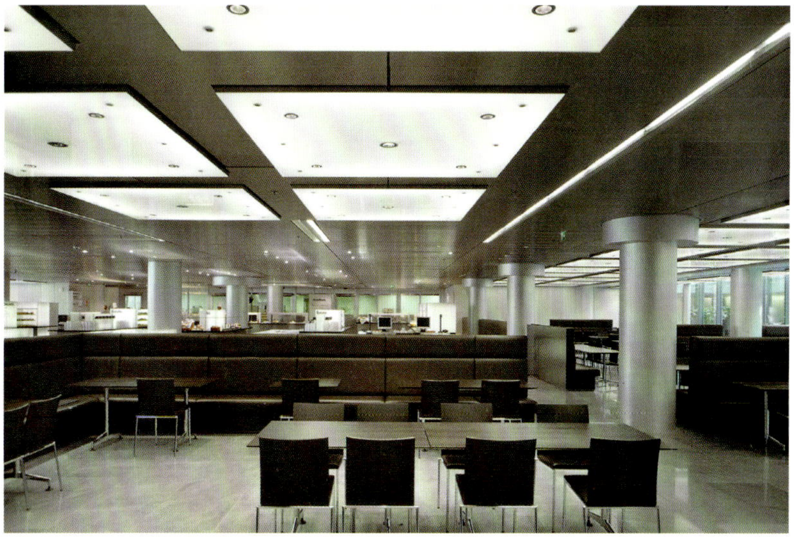

GERMANY_MUNICH **INTERNATIONAL CONSULTANCY**

ARCHITECTS: WAGENKNECHT ARCHITEKTEN
ORIGINAL ARCHITECTS: HILMER SATTLER UND ALBRECHT, 2006_**LIGHTING:** TROPP LIGHTING DESIGN_**COMPLETION:** 2007
NUMBER OF WORKPLACES: 450_**GROSS FLOOR AREA:** 15,000 M²
COMMON AREA: CONFERENCE ROOM, CAFETERIA
KIND OF WORKPLACES: CELLULAR, TEAM, BUSINESS CLUB, LOUNGE WORKSPACE_**PHOTOS:** FLORIAN HOLZHERR, MUNICH

Six floors, the administration service areas, are grouped around a central inner courtyard. Its design is incorporated into the "central core area". Serving orientation, it is constantly visible due to its surface design. The work places of the advisers surround this core. The generous application of glass establishes transparency towards the movement zones. Central meeting points with high amenity values function as orientation points within the room sequences. The conference area is immediately connected to the reception on the ground floor. In addition to fulfilling the highest acoustics, illumination, and conference technology, it complies with the required flexibly adjustable room units.

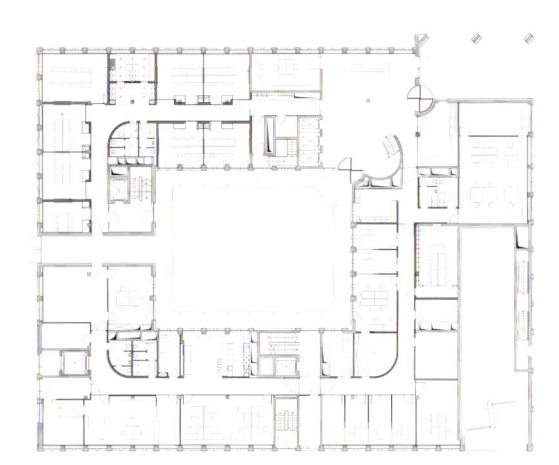

Um einen zentralen Innenhof gliedern sich über sechs Geschosse die Serviceflächen für die Verwaltung. Gestalterisch in den „zentralen Kernbereich" eingebunden, dient er der Orientierung und ist aufgrund der Oberflächengestaltung jederzeit erkennbar. Die Arbeitsbereiche der Berater umgeben diesen Kern. Durch überwiegende Verwendung von Glas wird Transparenz zu den Bewegungszonen erreicht. Zentrale Meetingpoints mit hoher Aufenthaltsqualität dienen als Orientierungszentren innerhalb des Raumkontinuums. Der Konferenzbereich ist im Erdgeschoss unmittelbar dem Empfang angegliedert und erfüllt, neben höchsten Ansprüchen an Akustik, Beleuchtung und Konferenztechnik, die Forderung nach flexibel koppelbaren Raumeinheiten.

left: Ground floor plan_Waiting area_Perspective. right: Corridor zone.
links: Grundriss_Wartebereich_Perspektive. rechts: Flurzone.

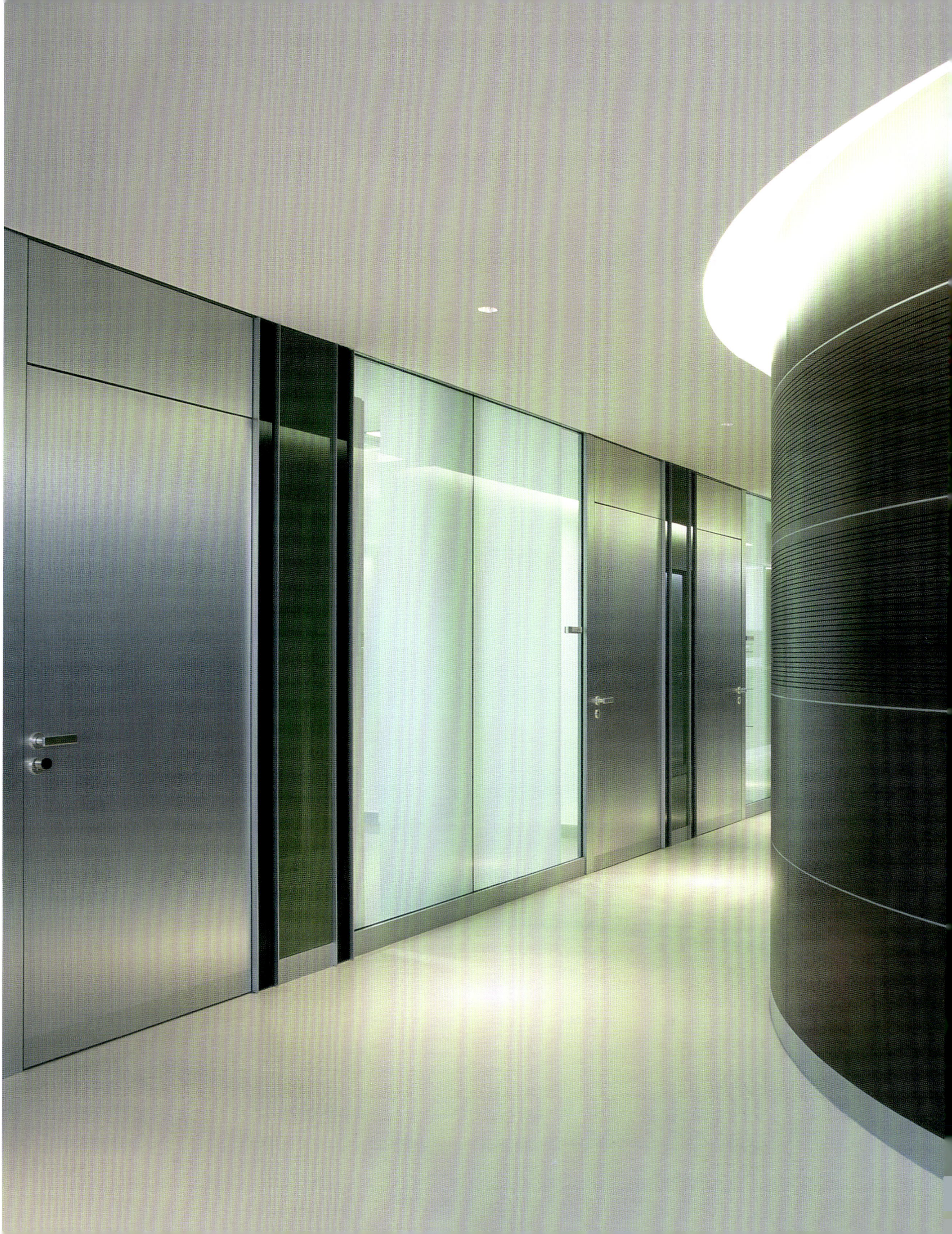

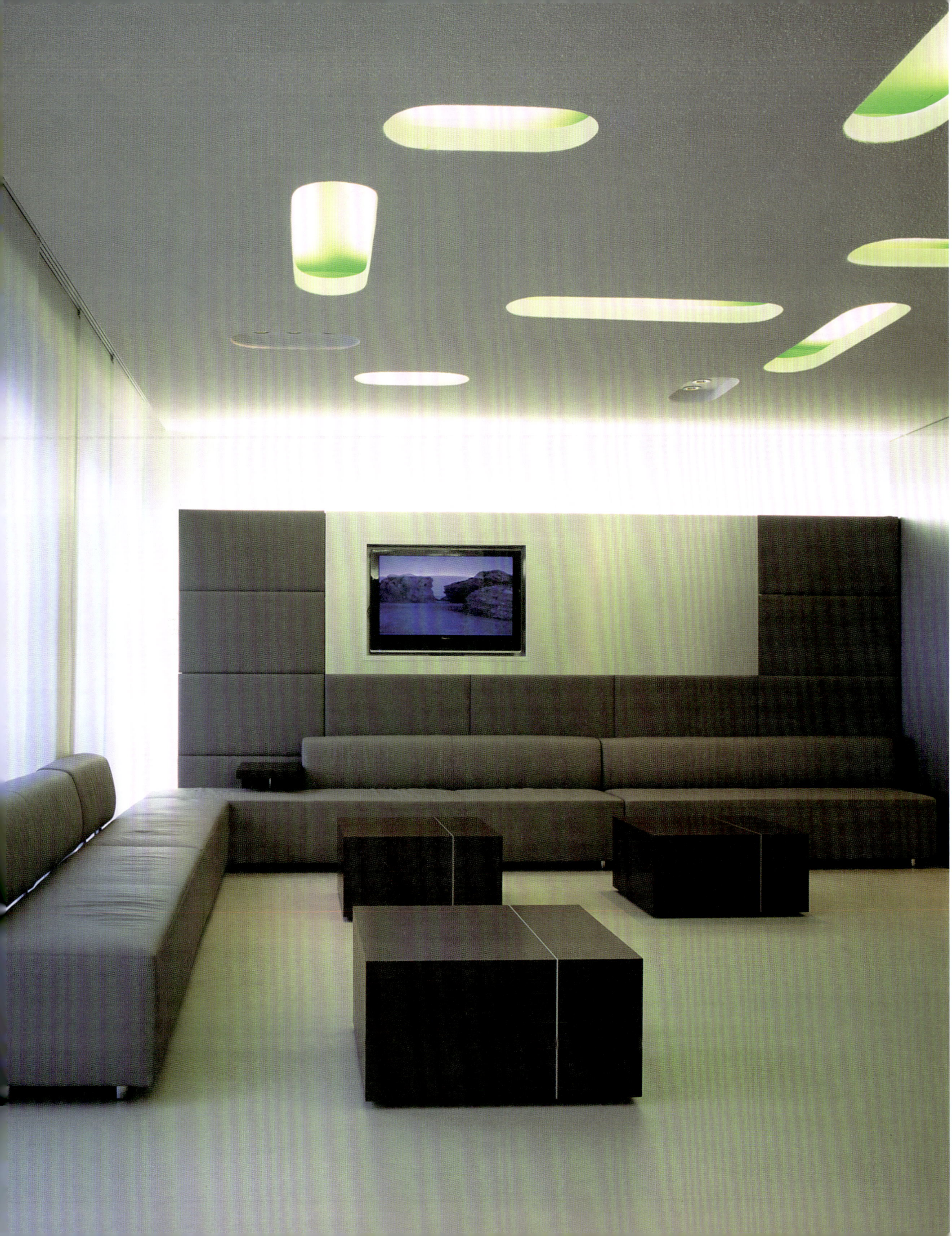

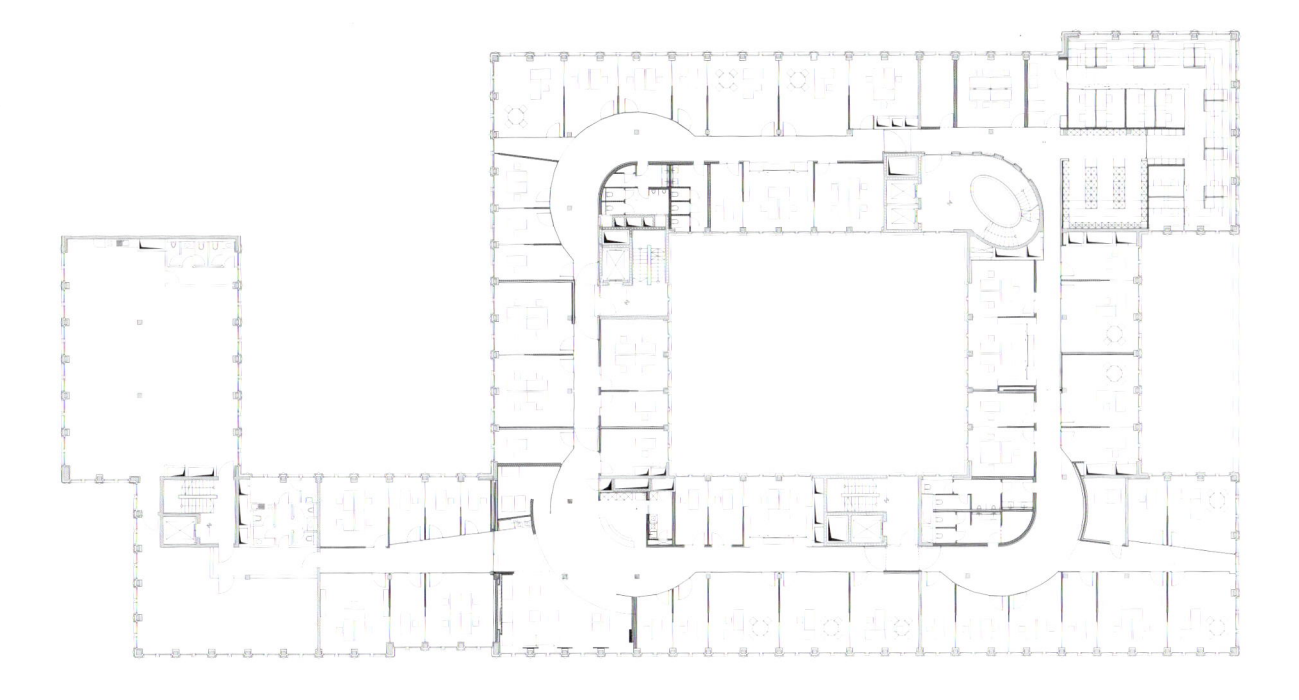

left: Lounge / meeting area. right: Second floor plan_Flexible area corridor / archive_Registry_ Flexible area workplace.
links: Lounge und Besprechungsbereich. rechts: Grundriss, zweites Obergeschoss_Flexibler Bereich Flur / Archiv_Sekretariat_Flexibler Bereich Arbeitsplatz.

GERMANY_ROSTOCK **SILO4PLUS5**

ARCHITECTS: BEYER ARCHITEKTEN
PLANNING PARTNER: TILO RIES_**COMPLETION:** 2004
NUMBER OF WORKPLACES: 345
GROSS FLOOR AREA: 15,100 M²_**COMMON AREA:** EMPLOYEE RESTAURANT (IN THE EVENING PUBLIC BAR), CONFERENCE ROOMS
KIND OF WORKPLACES: COMBINATION
PHOTOS: DEUTSCHE IMMOBILIEN ROSTOCK

The redesign of the Silo 4plus5 into an impressive headquarters of the DSR Group and AIDA Cruises in the city harbor of Rostock initiated the revitalization of the water edge in the historic town foundation area. Within the historic urban development plan, the prominent silo buildings from the 1930s were given a contemporary design, expanded towards the water with transparent elliptic façades, and connected by a bridge. Wall areas featuring intarsia were renovated. This interpretation of traditional Hanseatic construction with a new utilization concept provides the site with an unmistakable unique identity.

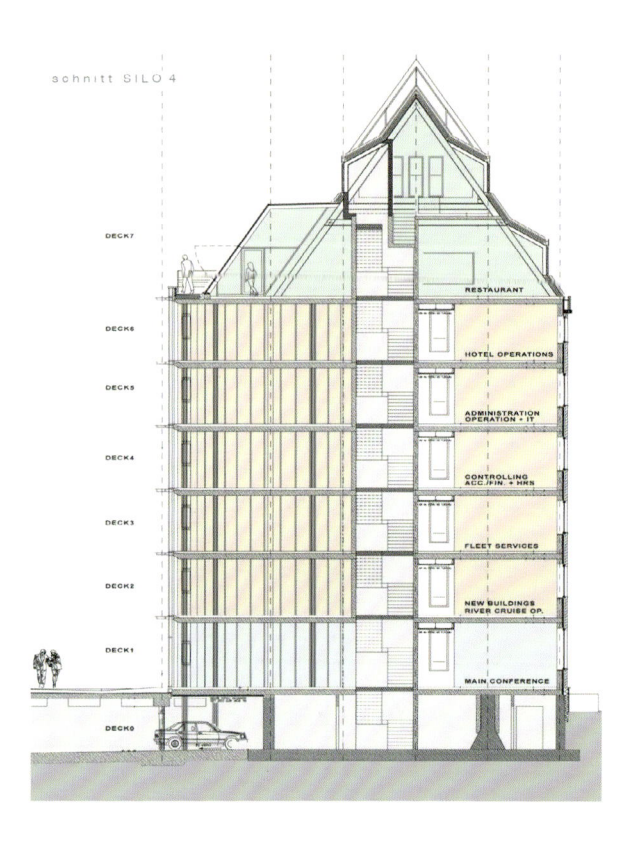

Die Neugestaltung der Silo 4plus5 zum repräsentativen Firmensitz der DSR-Gruppe sowie AIDA Cruises im Stadthafen von Rostock ist der Auftakt zur Revitalisierung der Wasserkante im Bereich der historischen Stadtgründung. Die markanten Silobauwerke aus den 1930ern wurden im historischen städtebaulichen Kontext zeitgemäß gestaltet, zum Wasser hin mit transparenten elyptischen Fassaden erweitert und brückenartig verbunden. Intarsiengeschmückte Wandbereiche wurden saniert. Diese Interpretation traditioneller hanseatischer Baukultur mit einem neuen Nutzungskonzept verleiht dem Platz eine einmalige und unverwechselbare Idenität.

left: Section_Marquetry walls and eclipse_Corridor combination offices_Corridor conference area.
right: View from water side_Corridor_Management office.
links: Schnitt_Intarsienwände und Elipse_Flur Kombibüros_Flur Konferenzbereich. rechts: Blick von der Wasserkante_Büroflur_Vorstandsbüro.

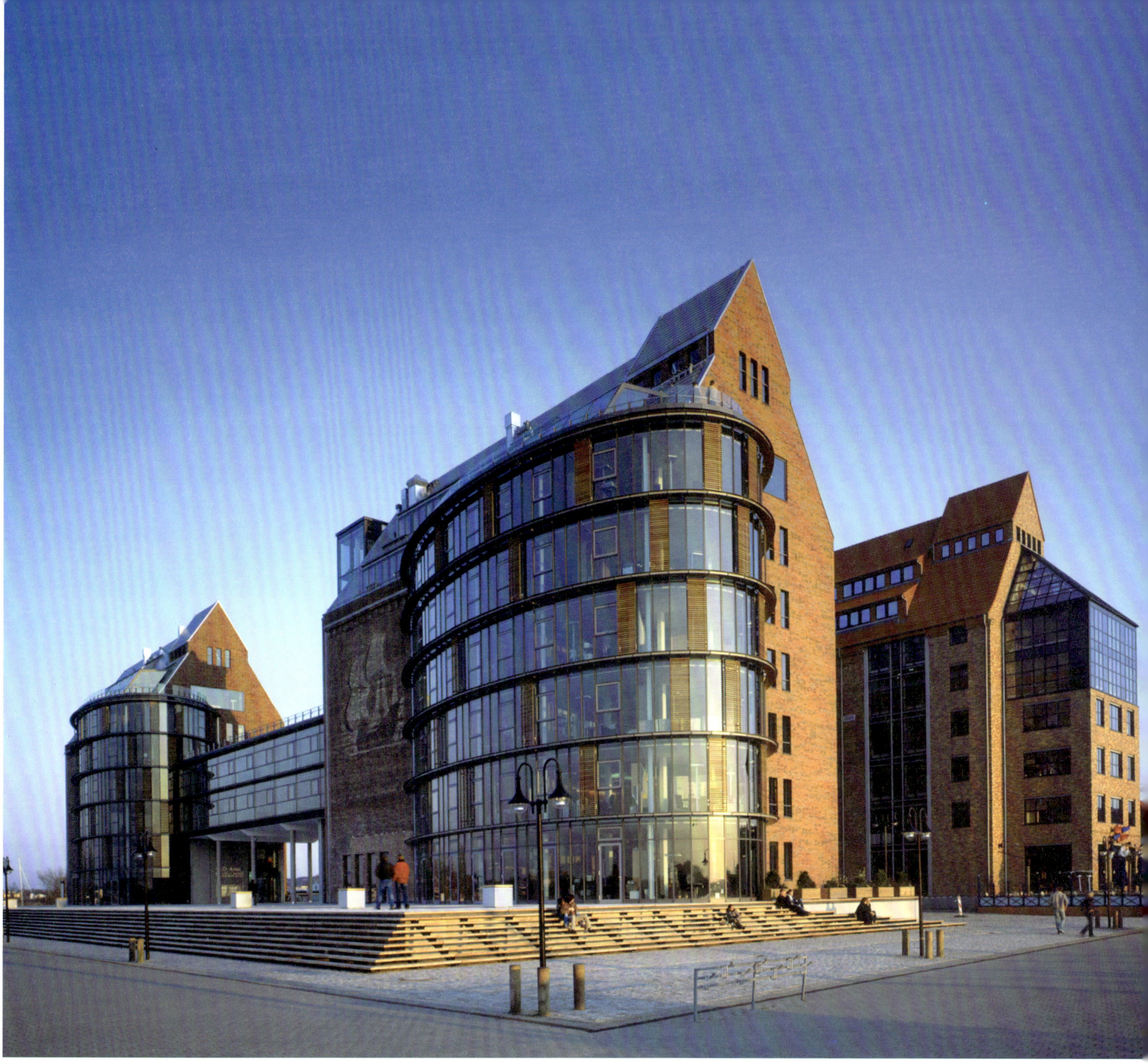

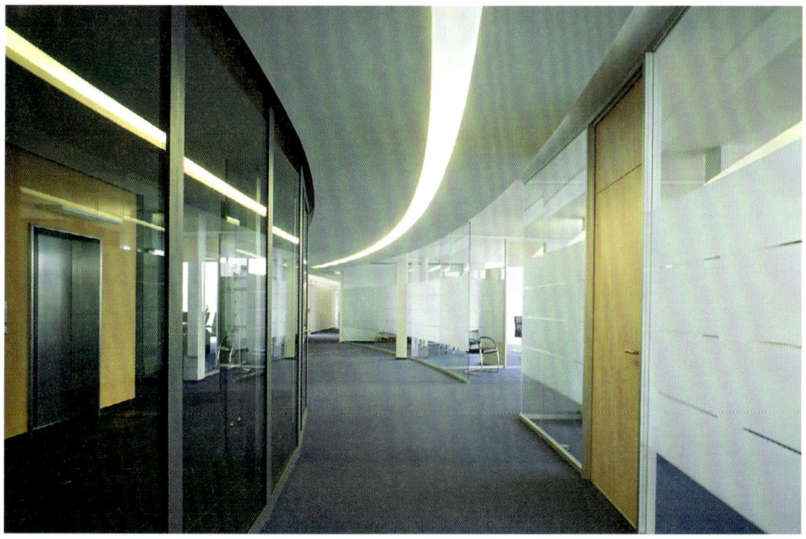

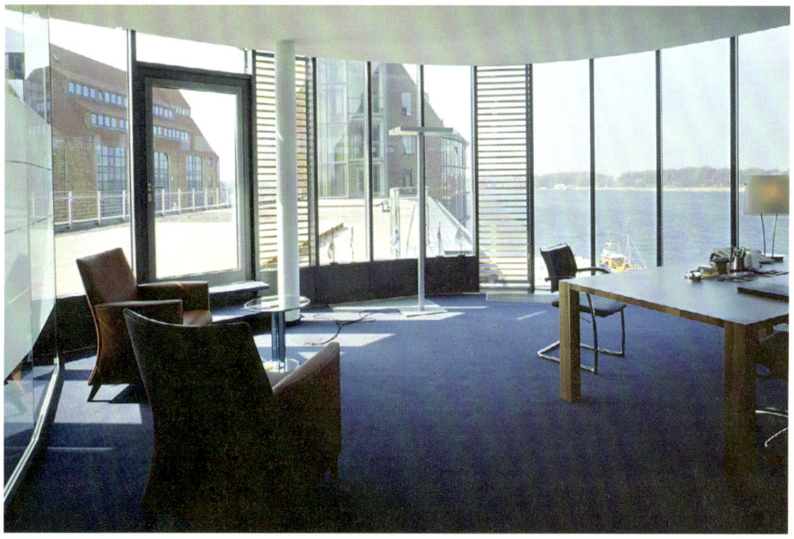

GERMANY_STUTTGART IMTECH HEADQUARTERS

ARCHITECTS: MERZ OBJEKTBAU
ARTIST: PROF. HELMUT SCHUSTER_**COMPLETION:** 2008
NUMBER OF WORKPLACES: 65_**GROSS FLOOR AREA:** 1,300 M²
COMMON AREA: CASINO, TRAINING CLASSROOM, CONFERENCE AND MEETING ROOM, SEMINAR AND INSTRUCTION ROOM_**KIND OF WORKPLACES:** TEAM
PHOTOS: MICHAEL SCHNELL

In the course of a comprehensive renovation, which was completed in only three months, the reception area with the conference and meeting rooms on the ground floor and the casino with the training area on the lower floor were totally transformed. The owner, a building equipment and appliances specialist, requested and implemented in cooperation with the architect many intricate details that were by no means limited to technical applications. Rather, Imtech wanted to create an inviting atmosphere in the highly technical rooms. The room layout plan with bright dominating colors transformed the circular layout into a more user-friendly oval and also incorporated the furniture design, especially counters and illuminated ceilings.

Nach einer umfassenden Sanierung in nur drei Monaten zeigen sich der Empfangsbereich mit Konferenz- und Besprechungsräumen im Erdgeschoss sowie das Casino mit Schulungsbereich im Untergeschoss vollkommen verwandelt. Der Bauherr, ein Spezialist für Haustechnik, forderte und realisierte in Absprache mit dem Architekten zahlreiche Raffinessen, die aber keinesfalls nur technisch angewandt werden sollten. Vielmehr wünschte Imtech einen einladenden Charakter für die hoch technisierten Räume. Die innenräumliche Planung mit starken Leitfarben wandelte den kreisförmigen Grundriss zum nutzungsfreundlicheren Oval und umfasste auch die Möbelplanung, insbesondere der Theken und Lichtdecken.

left: Ground floor plan_Illuminated counter_Conference room. right: Lobby with LED-ceiling.
links: Grundriss Erdgeschoss_Beleuchtete Theke_Konferenzraum. rechts: Foyer mit LED-Lichtdecke.

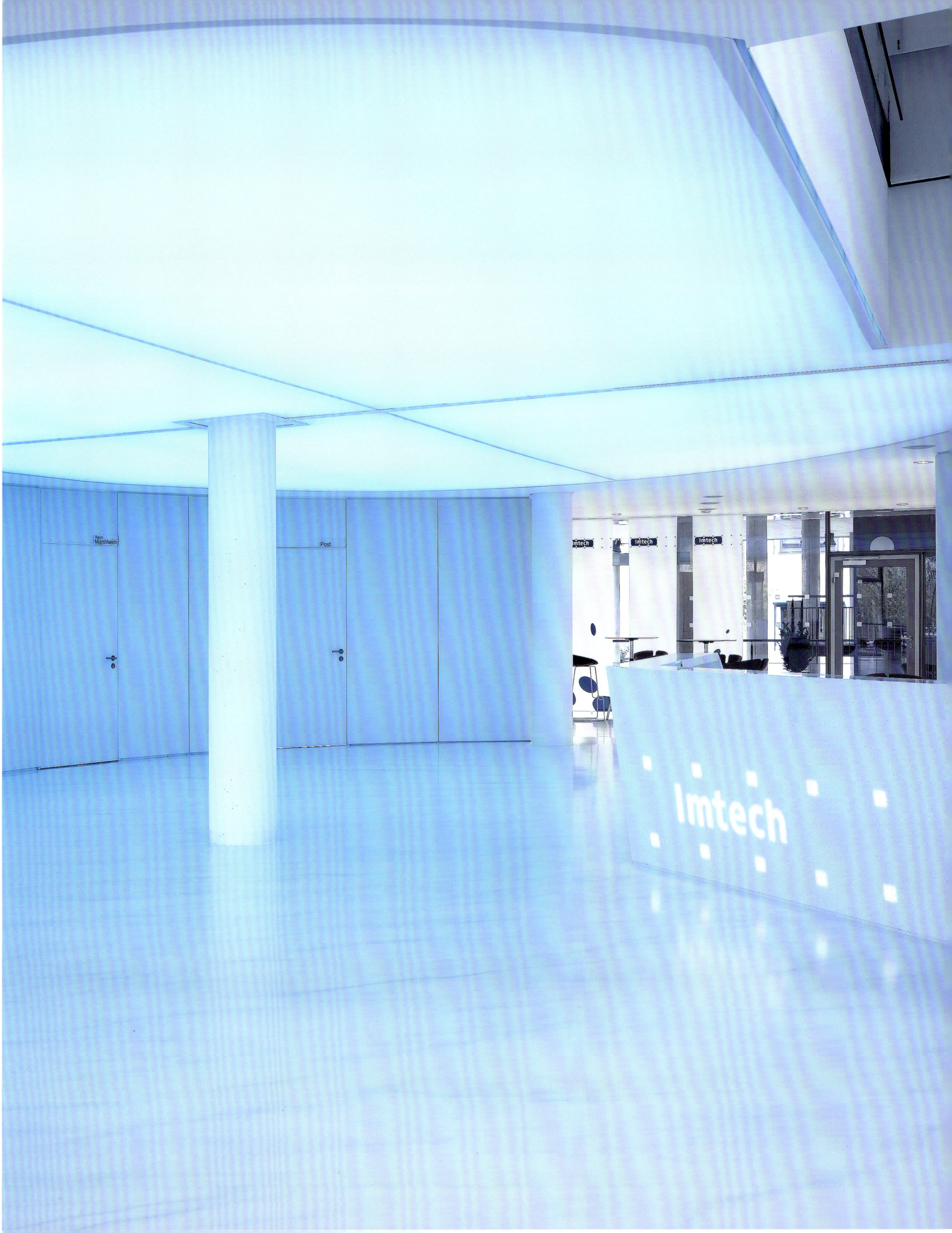
Imtech
Post

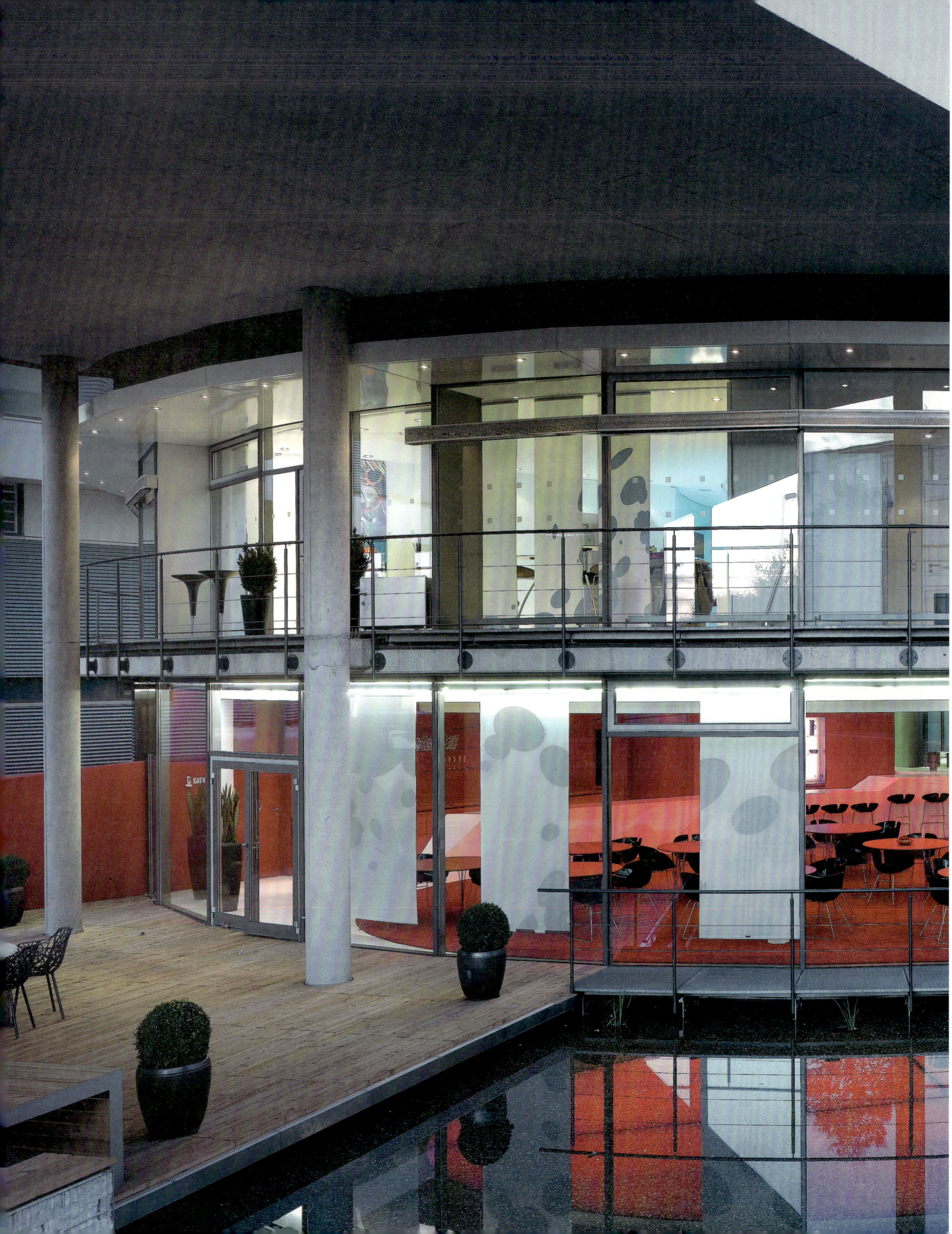

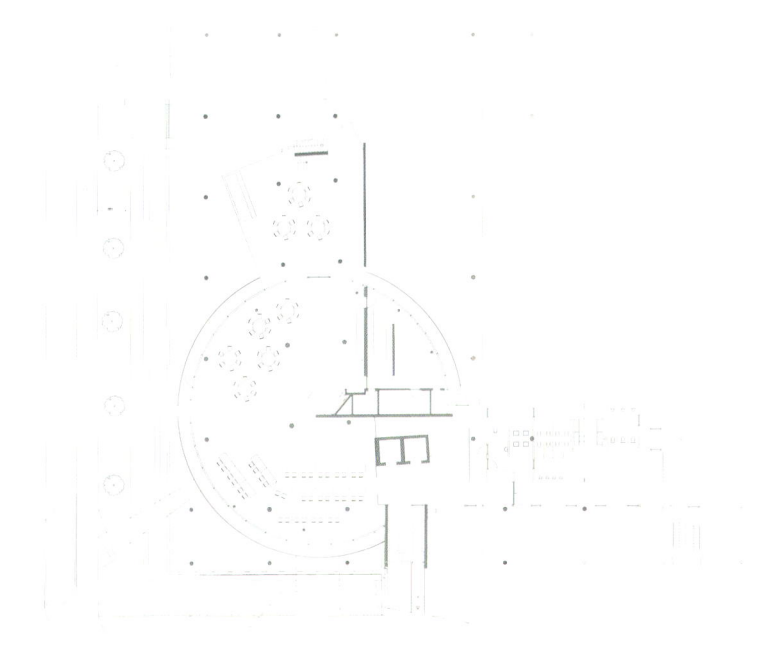

left: View into the new designed levels and the new outside area. right: Basement floor plan_Casino located on the basement_Corridor_LED-light ceiling and the created counter in the casino.
links: Einblick in die neu gestaltenen Ebenen und den neu angelegten Außenbereich. rechts: Grundriss Untergeschoss_Casino im Untergeschoss_Flur_LED-Lichtdecke und speziell angefertigte Theke im Casinobereich.

GERMANY_STUTTGART ADVERTISING AGENCY SCHWARZSPRINGER

ARCHITECTS: ZIEGLERBÜRG, BÜRO FÜR GESTALTUNG
COMPLETION: 2007_**NUMBER OF WORKPLACES:** 22
GROSS FLOOR AREA: 380 M²_**COMMON AREA:** TEA KITCHEN
KIND OF WORKPLACES: OPEN-PLAN, TEAM
PHOTOS: ANDREAS KÖRNER, SUSANNE WEGNER (246 B. L.)

In accordance with the slogan of the agency – "The one picture", the new company premises also present a clear and visual message. Located on the 12th floor of the Charlotte high rise with a 360° panorama view of Stuttgart, the magnificent view was turned into the image of the company through the all-round band window. Semi-transparent glass walls maintain the generous proportions also in areas in which some screening is required. Profiles and lamps were fitted flush into the ceilings that rise towards the façade. The black of the lettering was added to the pink / white color scheme of the company's CI. The furniture was designed specifically for the conceptual design.

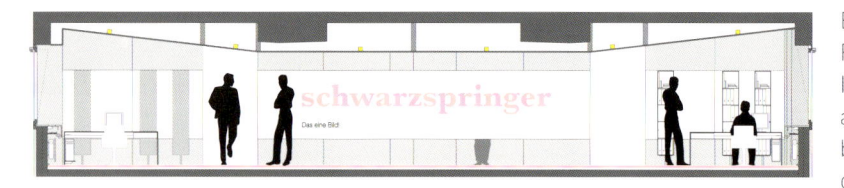

Entsprechend des Slogans der Agentur „Das eine Bild" sollten auch die neuen Räumlichkeiten mit einer klaren und optischen Botschaft gestaltet werden. Im zwölften Stockwerk des Charlottenhochhauses mit 360° Panoramablick auf Stuttgart sollte die grandiose Aussicht durch das umlaufende Fensterband zum Bild der Agentur werden. Teiltransparente Glaswände erhalten den großzügigen Raum auch in jenen Bereichen, in denen Sichtschutz erwünscht ist. Profile und Lampen wurden bündig in die zur Fassade ansteigenden Decken eingelassen. Das rosa / weiß der Firmen-CI wurde um das Schwarz von Schrift gut ergänzt. Die Möbel wurden speziell für die Agentur gefertigt.

left: Section_Entrance wall_Blinds. right: Night view.
links: Schnitt_Eingangswand_Sichtschutz. rechts: Nachtansicht.

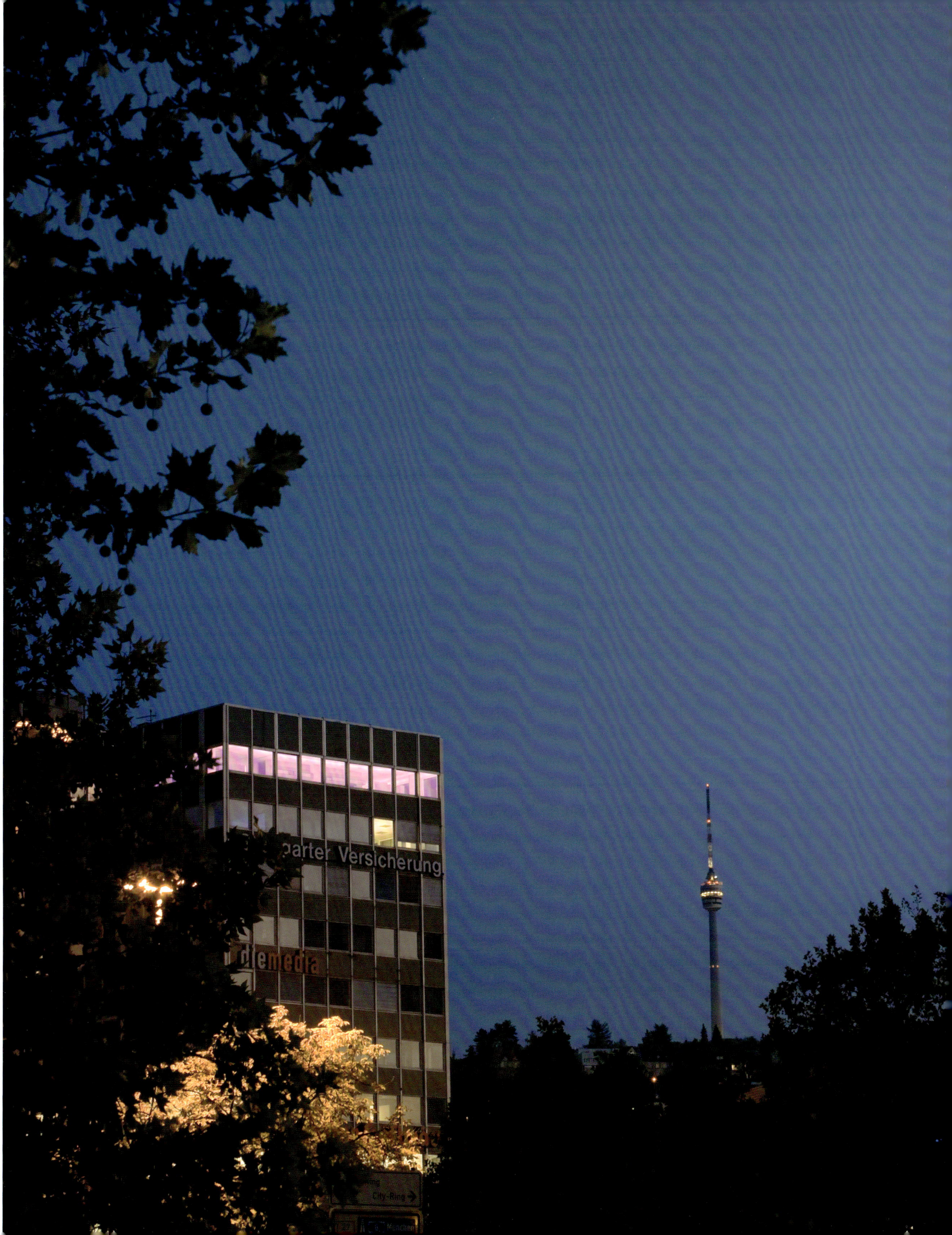
parter Versicherung
diemedia

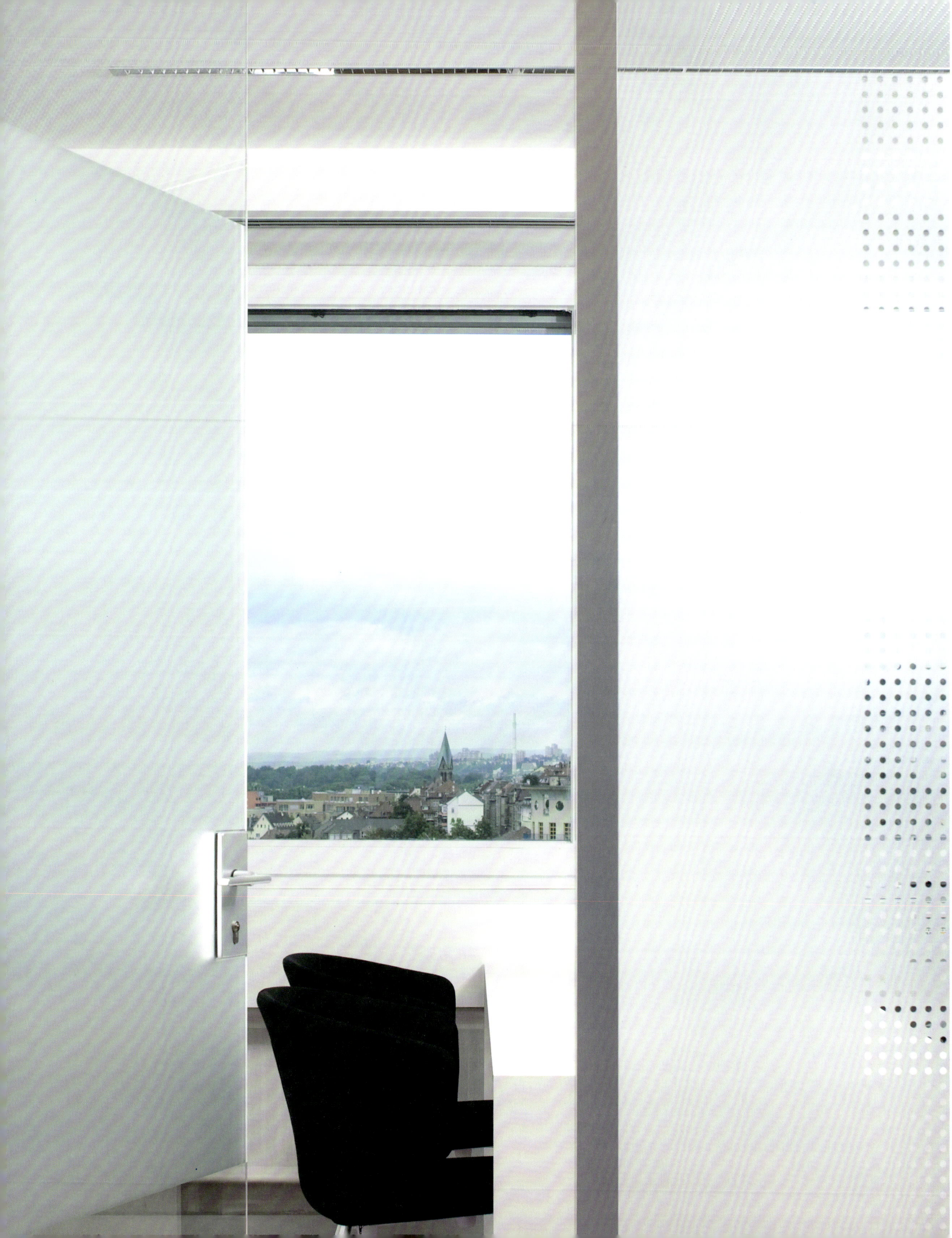

left: Office entrance. right: Floor plan_Workplace_Workspace with meeting point_Tea kitchen.
links: Büroeingang. rechts: Grundriss_Arbeitsplatz_Arbeitsraum mit Besprechungsecke_Teeküche.

GERMANY_THANSAU **SCHATTDECOR AG HEADQUARTERS**

ARCHITECTS: OBERSTEINER ARCHITEKTEN
COMPLETION: 2007_**NUMBER OF WORKPLACES:** 60
GROSS FLOOR AREA: 6,000 M²_**COMMON AREA:** EMPLOYEE RESTAURANT, CONFERENCE ROOMS, TRAINING ROOMS, SHOW ROOM, EVENT HALL, APARTMENTS
KIND OF WORKPLACES: CELLULAR, TEAM, LOUNGE WORKSPACE
PHOTOS: KEN LIU, PRIEN, JÖRG HEMPEL, AACHEN (253)

The restructuring and expansion of the company premises was implemented under the motto "The workplace is also living space". On an adjacent higher plot, the parking lot, warehouse, guest hostels, as well as the new main entrance were created. A 40-m aerial walkway, which bridges the gap in the terrain and crosses the old existing trees, constitutes the connection between the entrance hall and the first floor reception of the new cylindrical administration office building on the old company premises. The ground floor of the cylinder contains exhibition areas, while the offices are located on the upper floors. The individual offices are located in a radial shape along the exterior wall, while the building core includes technical rooms, toilets, and kitchenettes.

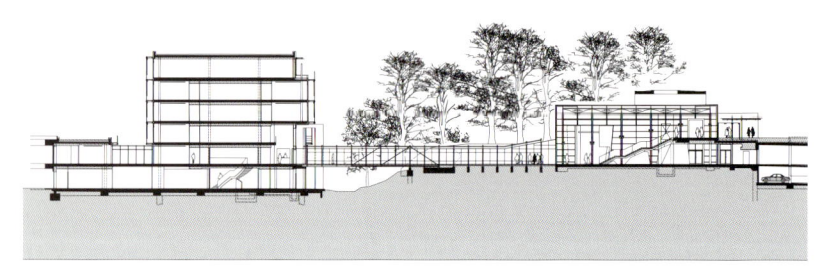

Die Restrukturierung und Erweiterung des Firmenareals wurde unter dem Motto „Arbeitsplatz ist auch Lebensraum" realisiert. Auf einem angrenzenden, höher liegenden Gelände entstanden Parkplätze, Lager, Gästehäuser sowie der neue Haupteingang. Eine 40 Meter lange Glaspasserelle, die den Geländesprung überbrückt und den alten Baumbestand quert, stellt die Verbindung zwischen der Eingangshalle und dem ersten Obergeschoss – Empfang – des neuen, zylindrischen Verwaltungsbaus auf dem alten Firmengelände her. Hier befinden sich im Erdgeschoss des Zylinders Ausstellungsflächen, während die Obergeschosse Büros beherbergen. Die einzelnen Büros liegen radial an der Außenwand, der Gebäudekern umfasst technische Räume, Toiletten und Teeküchen.

left: Section_Office building with acces via footbridge_Foyer. right: Stair tower office building.
links: Schnitt_Bürogebäude mit Zugang über Passerelle_Eingangshalle. rechts: Treppenturm, Bürogebäude.

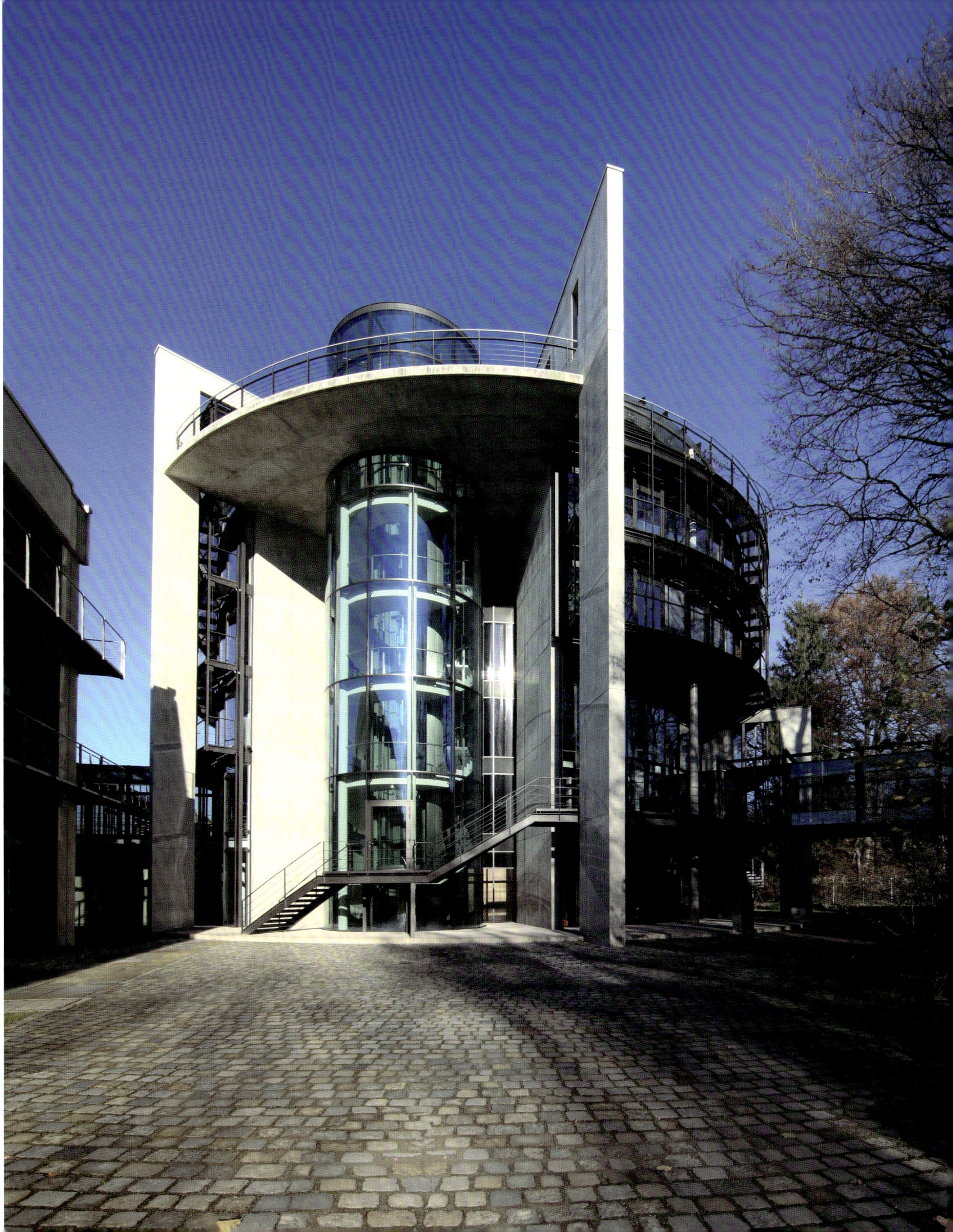

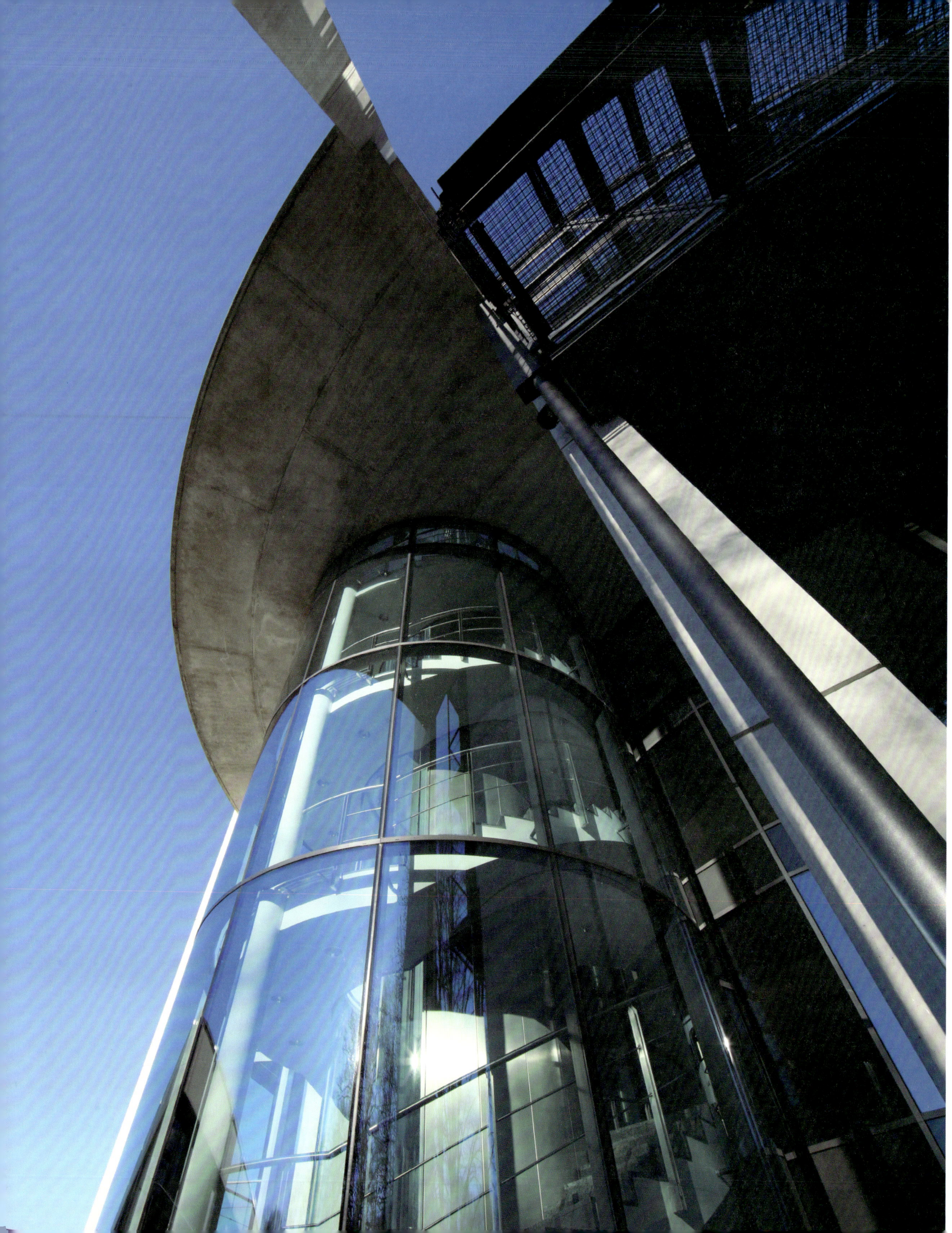

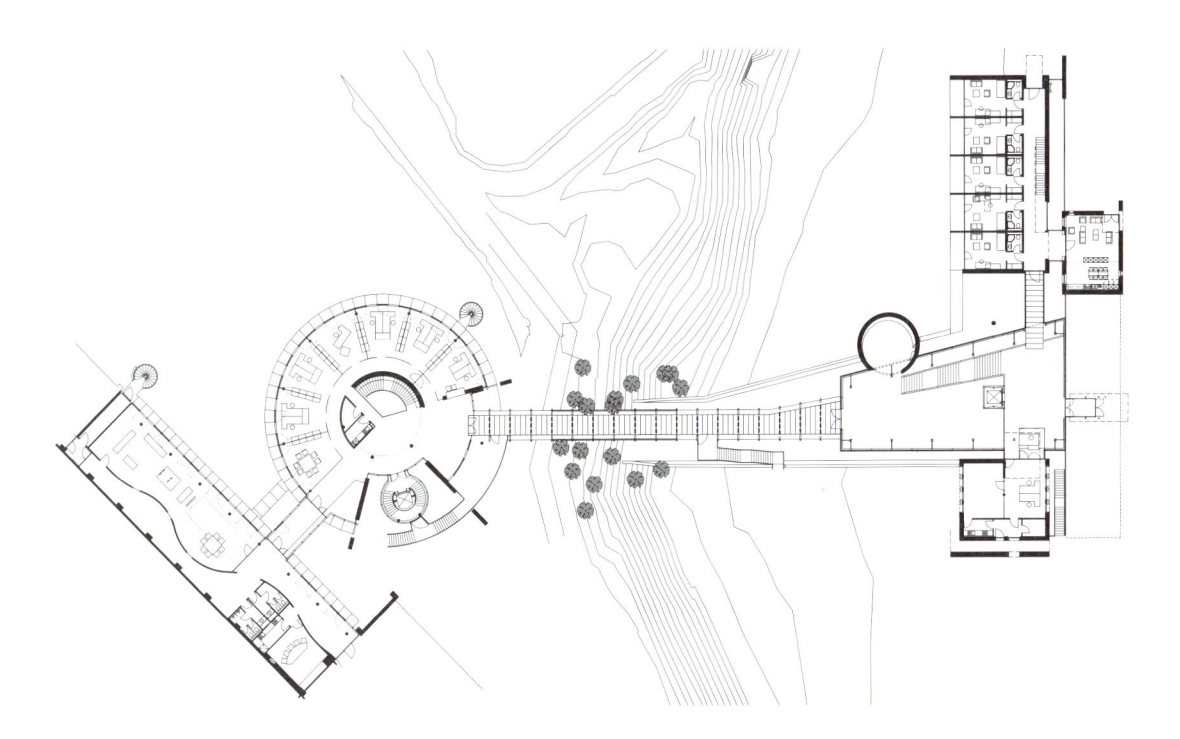

left: Glass façade, stair tower office building. right: First floor plan_Typical floor office units.
links: Glasfassade Treppenturm Bürogebäude. rechts: Grundriss erstes Obergeschoss_Büroeinheiten Regelgeschoss.

GERMANY_WIESBADEN RENOVATION STATISTISCHES BUNDESAMT

ARCHITECTS: SANDER.HOFRICHTER ARCHITEKTEN
COMPLETION: 2009_**ORIGINAL BUILDING:** PAUL SCHAEFFER-HEYROTHSBERGE,1956_**NUMBER OF WORKPLACES:** 1,850
GROSS FLOOR AREA: 47,769 M²_**COMMON AREA:** CONFERENCE ROOMS, MEETING ROOMS, COMMUNICATION AREAS, FOYER, LIBRARY_**KIND OF WORKPLACES:** COMBINATION
PHOTOS: COURTESY OF THE ARCHITECTS

The building of the German census bureau, which is landmarked as a typical high rise of the 1950s, had to be completely renovated due to faulty fire protection and contaminant-laden elements. The entrance hall and main hallways with functioning paternoster lifts remained unchanged. The improvement of the office quality and the hallways was the main focus of the project. Small, dark hallways were replaced by optimized zones with high comfort qualities. Room-high glazing created an almost daylight atmosphere. The building shell was updated with contemporary elements such as aluminum and glass. The proportions, patterns and colors of the 1950s were nevertheless integrated into the design.

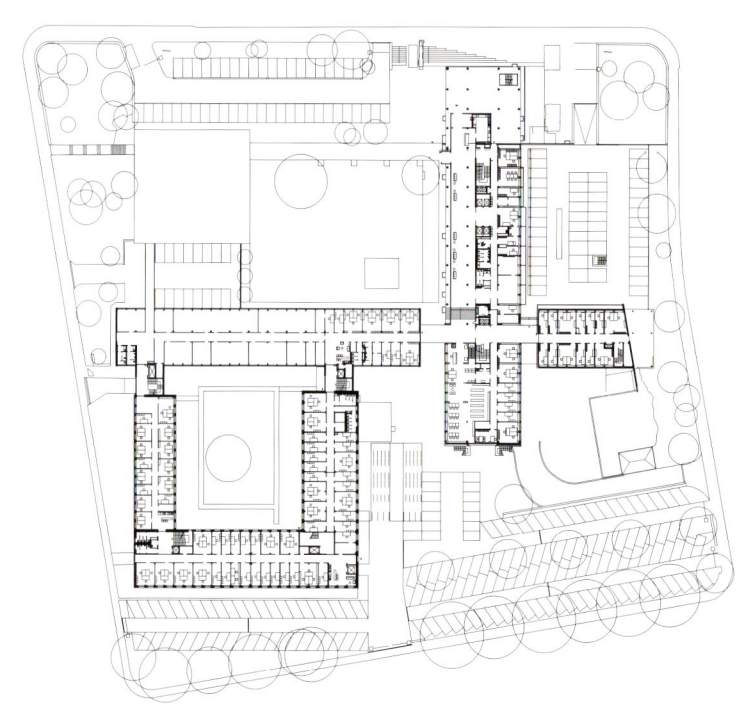

Das Statistische Bundesamt, das als typisches Hochhaus der 1950er Jahre unter Denkmalschutz steht, musste aufgrund mangelhaften Brandschutzes und schadstoffhaltiger Bauteile komplett saniert werden. Eingangshalle und Haupterschließungen mit funktionstüchtigen Pater-Noster-Aufzügen blieben unverändert. Die Verbesserung der Büroqualität und der Flure stand im Mittelpunkt. Schmale, dunkle Gänge sind optimierten Zonen mit hoher Aufenthaltsqualität gewichen. Raumhohe Verglasungen schaffen eine tageslichtähnliche Atmosphäre. Die Gebäudehülle wurde zeitgemäß mit Materialien wie Aluminium und Glas neu interpretiert. Proportionen, Profilierungen und Farben aus den 1950er Jahren wurden aufgenommen.

left: Ground floor plan_Façade north -east_Foyer. right: Corridor_Communication area_Conference room floor 13.
links: Grundriss Erdgeschoss_Fassadenansicht Nordost_Foyer. rechts: Flurzone_Kommunikationszone_Konferenzraum Ebene 13.

Konferenzra
A.12.208

GERMANY_WORMS **SAMAS**

ARCHITECTS: 100% INTERIOR SYLVIA LEYDECKER
COMPLETION: 2007_**NUMBER OF WORKPLACES:** 28
GROSS FLOOR AREA: 1,000 M²
COMMON AREA: MEETING ROOM, LOUNGE
KIND OF WORKPLACES: TEAM, OPEN-PLAN
PHOTOS: KARIN HESSMANN, DORTMUND

The German Samas headquarters required a new look. The new flowing design of the interior with its open structure corresponds to its garden architecture, and a continued axle connects the lobby with offices and the exterior. The warm natural colors of the reception and the lounge together with the gentle shapes and subtle materials create a pleasantly relaxed atmosphere. A main street extends through the open space, across informal meeting areas and bench-style workplaces, up to formally closed glass cubes, resulting a natural and relaxed office landscape for active office jobs. The toilets feature the 3-letter codes of international metropolises.

Der deutsche Samas Hauptsitz benötigte eine neue Erscheinung. Die fließenden Formen des offen strukturierten Interiors korrespondieren mit der Gartenarchitektur, eine durchlaufende Achse verbindet das Foyer mit Büros und Außenbereich. Empfang und Lounge in warmen, natürlichen Farben und die Formensprache und subtile Materialtextur erzeugen eine angenehm entspannte Atmosphäre. Eine Hauptstraße mäandert durch das Großraumbüro und führt zu Besprechungsbereichen in informeller Runde, über Bench-Arbeitsplätze hin zum formellen geschlossenen Glas-Cube: eine natürliche und entspannte Bürolandschaft für vitale Büroarbeit. In den Toiletten findet man 3-Letter-Codes internationaler Metropolen.

left: Ground floor plan_The "main street" within the open-space gives structure and connects_Interior and exterior in a harmonious interplay. right: Relaxed atmosphere in the lounge_Open-space workplaces_Official meeting in the conference room.
links: Grundriss Erdgeschoss_Die „Hauptstraße" im Großraumbüro strukturiert und verbindet_Innenraum und Außenraum in harmonischem Zusammenspiel. rechts: Entspannte Atmosphäre in der Lounge_Arbeitsplätze im Großraumbüro_Besprechungsraum für offizielle Meetings.

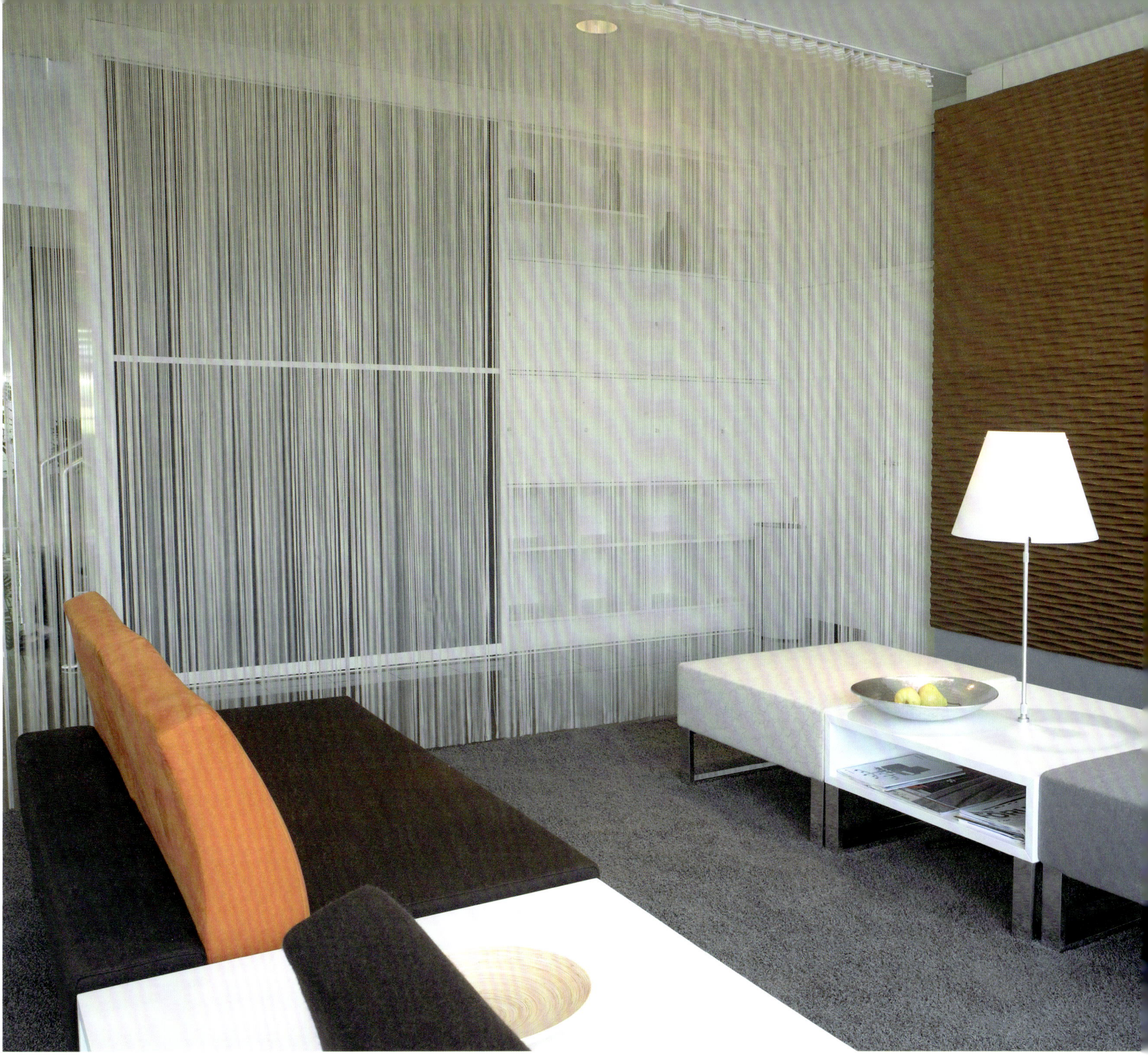
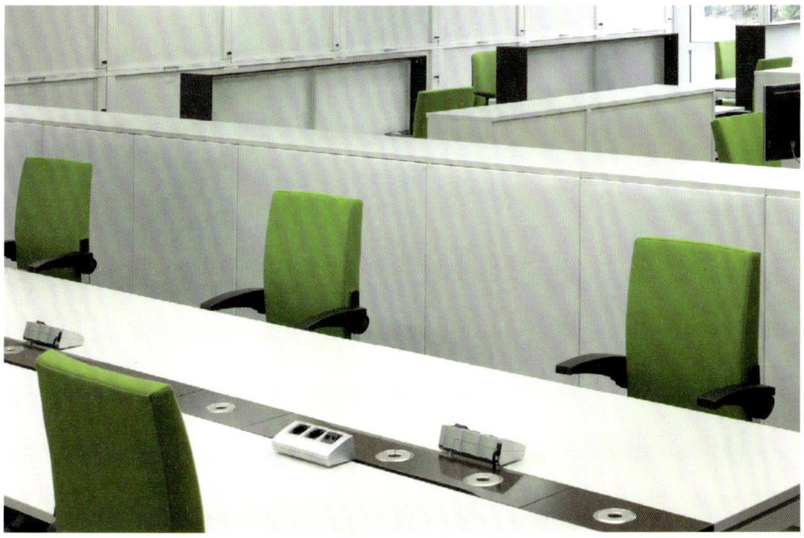
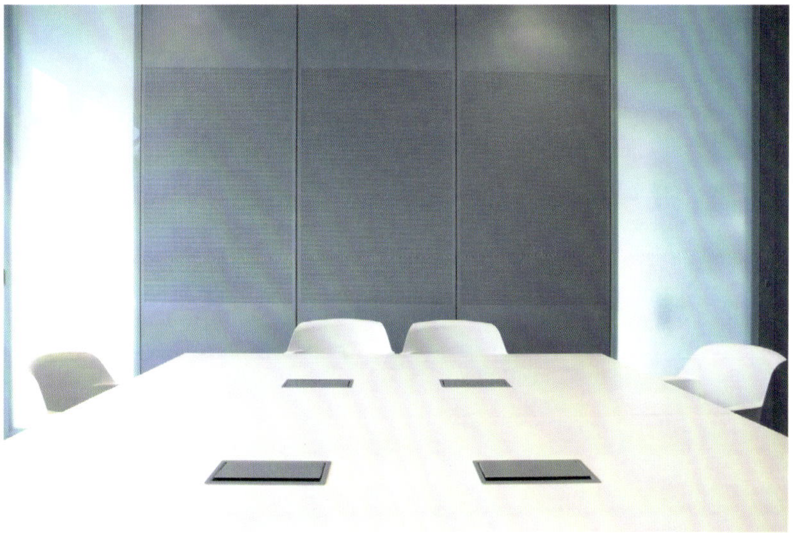

GERMANY_WÖRRSTADT **JUWI HOLDING CORPORATE HEADQUARTERS**

ARCHITECTS: GRIFFNERHAUS AG_**COMPLETION:** 2008
NUMBER OF WORKPLACES: 300_**GROSS FLOOR AREA:** 8,000 M^2
COMMON AREA: CANTEEN, FITNESS AERA, KITCHENETTES, CONFERENCE ROOMS, KINDERGARDEN, LOUNGE, COMMUNICATION ZONES, ORATORY_**KIND OF WORKPLACES:** CELLULAR, BUSINESS CLUB, LOUNGE WORKSPACE
PHOTOS: RÜDIGER MOSLER

According to the owner, a renewable energy specialist, this was the world's most energy-efficient office building in 2008. Conceived as an environmentally-friendly ecological wood construction, it utilizes photovoltaic cells and other alternative energy sources, to generate more energy than it consumes. With the use of ecological construction and insulation materials and industrial pre-constructed elements, the architects and wooden construction specialists of Griffner were able to construct the basic building for 300 employees in only six months. A wood skeleton construction with suspended pre-fabricated wall elements and visible solid wood ceilings helped the construction to proceed quickly. For example, a second building complex with room for more than 100 workplaces has been implemented in the meantime.

Das Bürogebäude war nach Aussage des im Bereich erneuerbare Energie tätigen Bauherrn 2008 das energieeffizienteste Bürogebäude der Welt. In naturschonender, ökologischer Holzbauweise errichtet, erzeugt es mit Solarzellen und anderen alternativen Energiequellen mehr Energie als es verbraucht. Durch die Verwendung ökologischer Bau- und Dämmmaterialien und industrieller Vorfertigung konnten Architekten und Holzbauspezialisten von Griffner das Gebäude für 300 Mitarbeiter errichten. Eine Holzskelettkonstruktion mit vorgehängten, vorgefertigten Wandelementen und mit sichtbaren Massivholzdecken ermöglichte den schnellen Baufortschritt. Inzwischen wurde ein zweiter Gebäudekomplex mit Platz für über 100 Arbeitsplätze realisiert.

left: Sketch_South façade_Staircase. right: Lounge area_Canteen_Main entrance.
links: Skizze_Südfassade_Treppenhaus. rechts: Loungebereich_Kantine_Haupteingang.

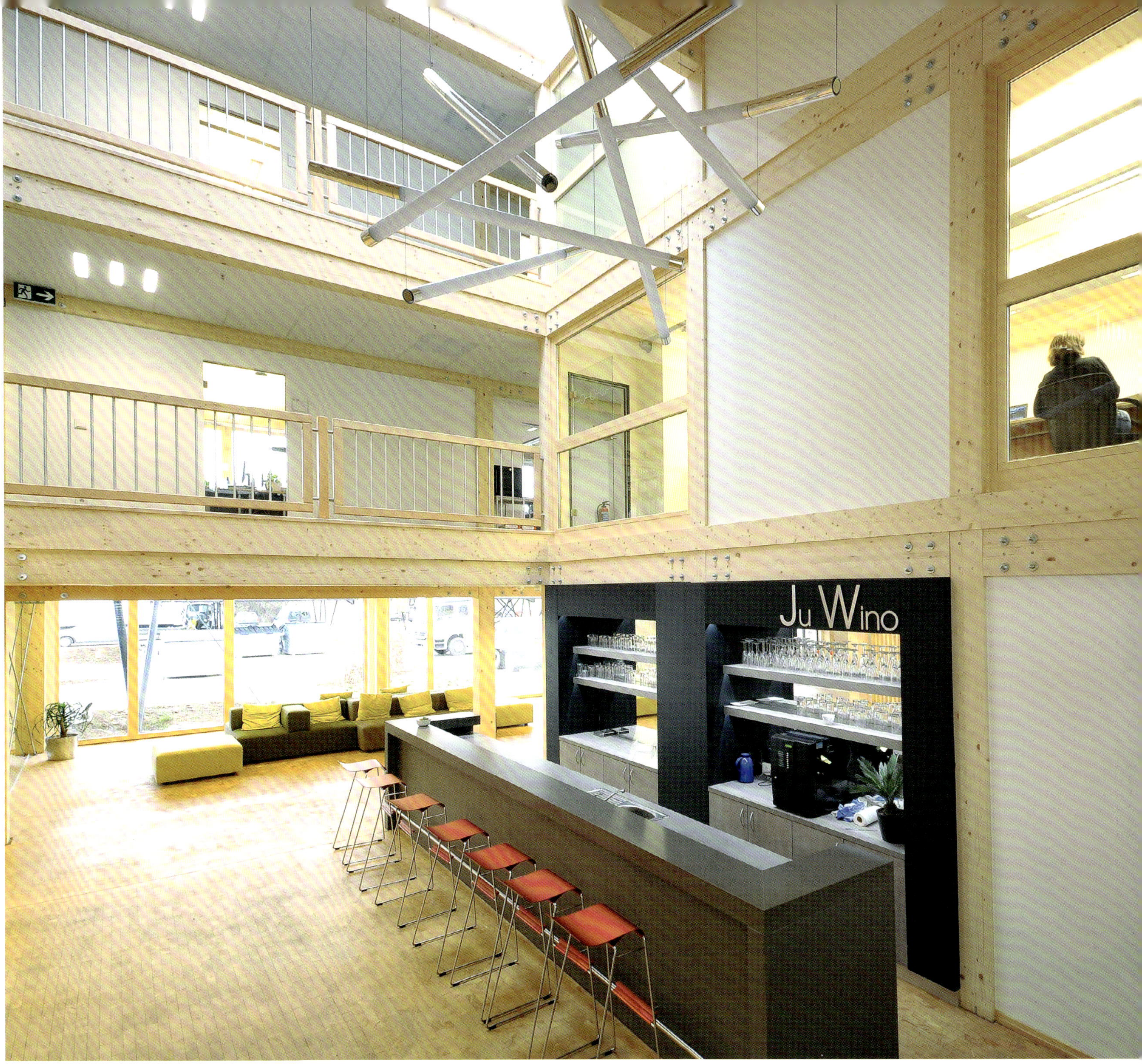
Ju Wino

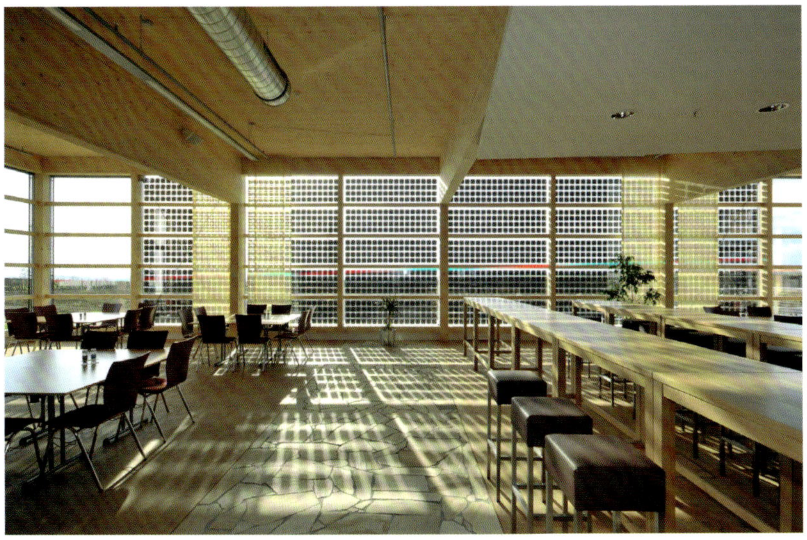

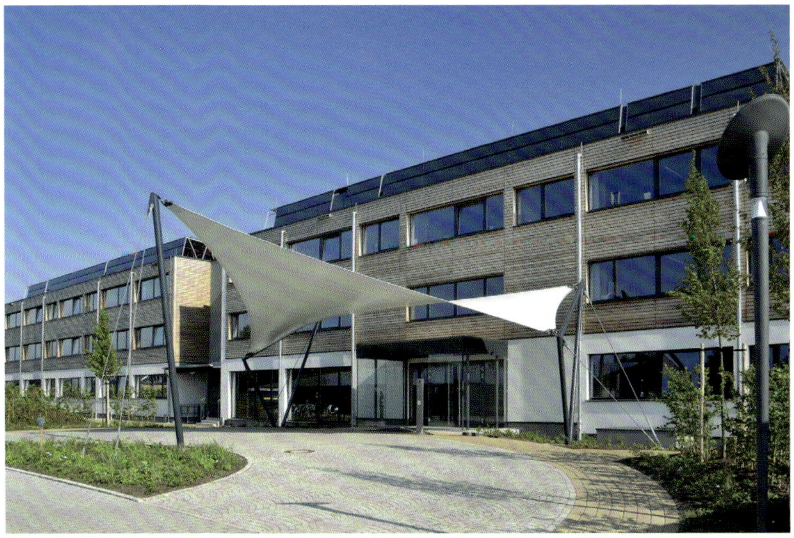

IRELAND_DOORADOYLE **LIMERICK COUNTY COUNCIL HEADQUARTERS**

ARCHITECTS: BUCHOLZ MCEVOY ARCHITECTS, LTD
COMPLETION: 2003_**NUMBER OF WORKPLACES:** 280
GROSS FLOOR AREA: 7,000 M²_**COMMON AREA:** ATRIUM, CONFERENCE ROOMS_**KIND OF WORKPLACES:** COMBINATION
PHOTOS: MICHAEL MORAN, NY

The principal objective of the new headquarters was to provide an environment conducive to the tasks of a county council. These include the effective delivery of a wider range of public services, public accessibility, and accountability. The building consists of a 75-meter-long block with an equally long atrium facing west that serves as the main public space. It is a lung that ventilates and illuminates the office spaces and a meeting place for the general public. This civic office building is fully naturally ventilated with a bespoke structural timber brise soliel, combining both environmental control and structural stability to the south-west façade.

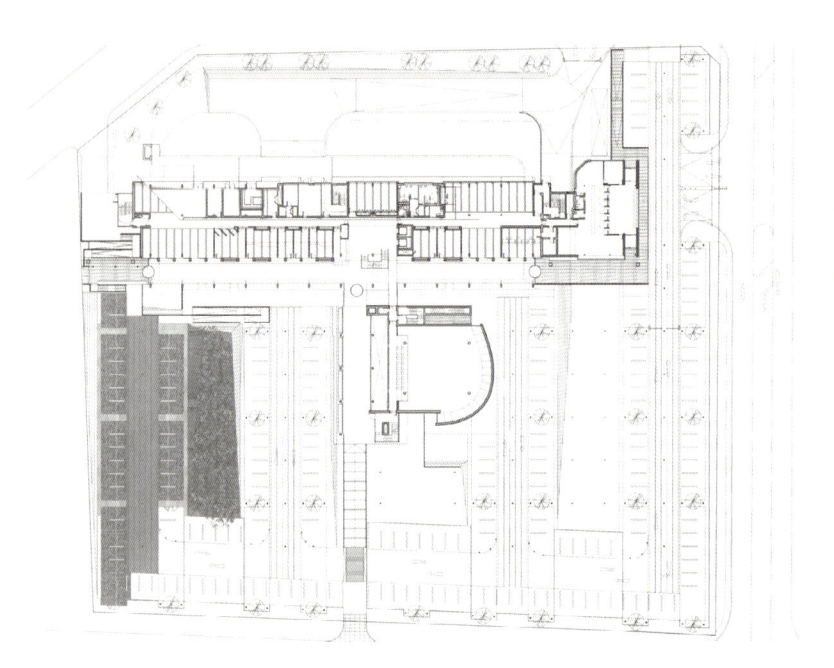

Die neue Hauptverwaltung wurde entwickelt, um ein optimales Umfeld für die Abläufe in einer Kreisverwaltung zu schaffen. Zu den Zielen gehören die effiziente Durchführung einer großen Bandbreite von Dienstleistungen für Bürger, Zugang zu öffentlichen Gebäuden und die Transparenz von öffentlichen Dienstleistungen. Das Gebäude ist 75 Meter lang und hat ein ebenso langes, nach Westen ausgerichtetes Foyer, das der größte öffentliche Raum des Gebäudes ist und zur Belüftung und natürlichen Beleuchtung der Büroräume sowie als öffentlicher Platz für Bürger dient. Das Gebäude wird durch eine Holzlamellenkonstuktion entlang der Südwestfassade komplett natürlich belüftet. Sie dient dem klimatischen Gleichgewicht und stabilisiert gleichzeitig die Konstruktion der Glasfassade.

left: Site plan_Exterior_Atrium north view. right: Detail of shading screen_Workspace_Atrium looking south.
links: Lageplan_Außenansicht_Atrium von Norden. rechts: Schattenpaneel, Detail_Arbeitsplatz_Blick durch das Atrium Richtung Süden.

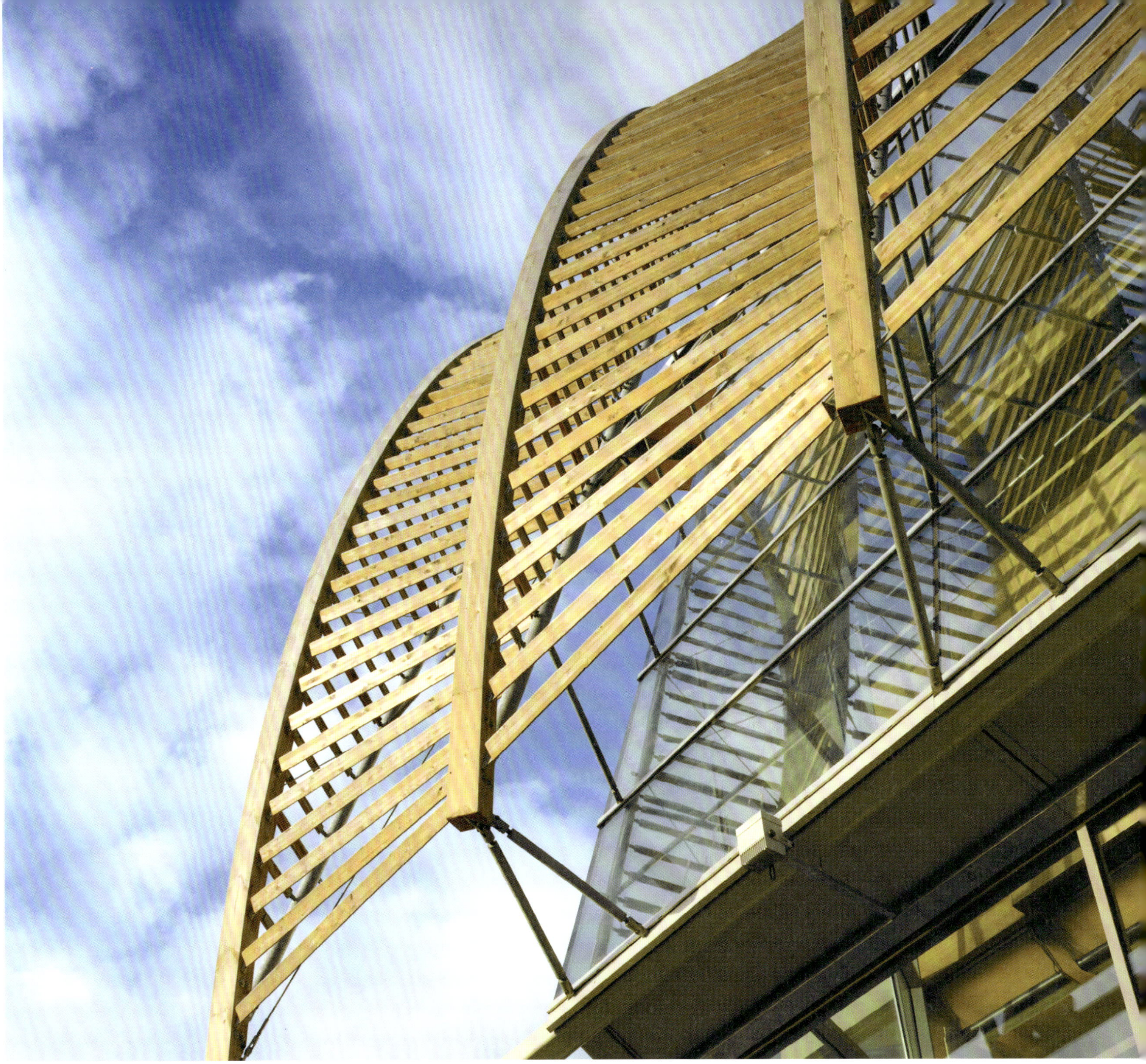

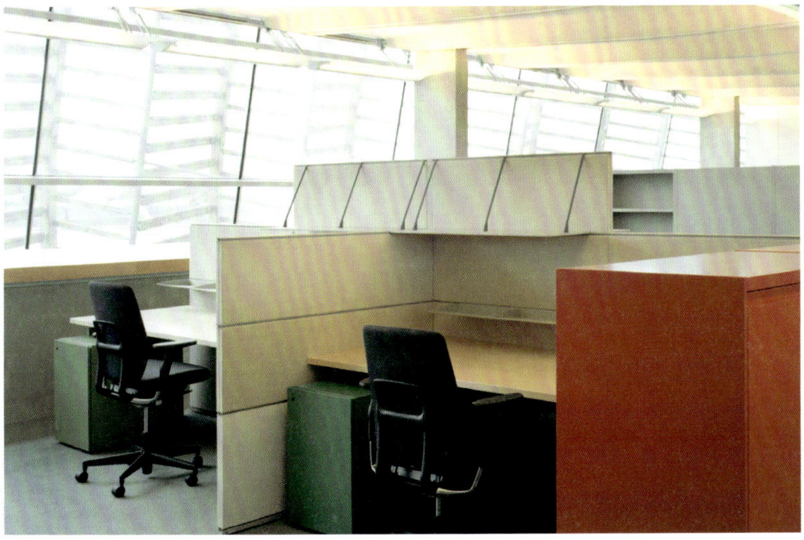

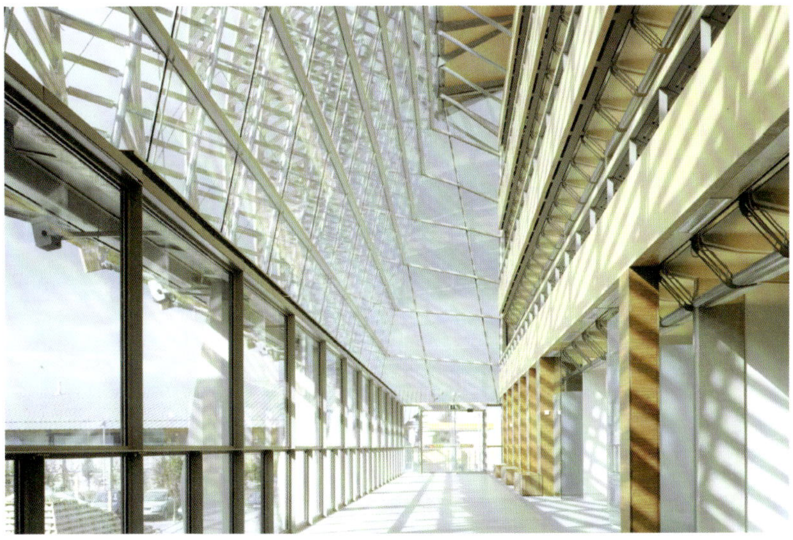

IRELAND_GALWAY **SAP BUILDING GALWAY**

ARCHITECTS: BUCHOLZ MCEVOY ARCHITECTS, LTD
COMPLETION: 2004_**NUMBER OF WORKPLACES:** 380
GROSS FLOOR AREA: 6,000 M²_**COMMON AREA:** ATRIUM, CONFERENCE ROOMS_**KIND OF WORKPLACES:** COMBINATION
PHOTOS: MICHAEL MORAN, NY

The contact center of the German software company SAP is located in a business park to the east of Galway, on an exposed site elevated from the surrounding landscape. The building was designed before its final location was decided. Therefore, the only calculable factors were internal functions and external environmental aspects, allowing a flexible choice of the location. The building is designed to offer employees a balanced and comfortable working environment while minimizing the use of non-renewable energy resources. The building is cooled with fresh outside air as its only cooling source. An atrium separates the office floors, which are connected by bridge structures.

Das Support-Zentrum für das deutsche Software-Unternehmen SAP befindet sich in einem Business-Park östlich von Galway auf einem Grundstück, das sich über die umliegende Landschaft erhebt. Der Entwurf für das Gebäude wurde konzipiert, bevor der endgültige Standort festlag. Daher waren die einzigen kalkulierbaren Faktoren die internen Funktionen und die äußeren Umweltaspekte, so dass die Umgebung nahezu austauschbar bleibt. Das Design schafft ein angenehmes Arbeitsumfeld für die Mitarbeiter, gleichzeitig verbraucht das Gebäude nur ein Minimum an Energie aus nicht erneuerbaren Ressourcen. Kühlung erfolgt ausschließlich durch Frischluft. Ein Atrium erhebt sich zwischen den Büros, welche über Brückenkonstruktionen verbunden sind.

left: Site plan_External view_Workspace sample. right: Interior garden, atrium_Internal façade detail_Lighting detail.
links: Lageplan_Außenansicht_Beispiel eines Arbeitsplatzes. rechts: Garten im Atrium_Innenfassade_Beleuchtung, Detail.

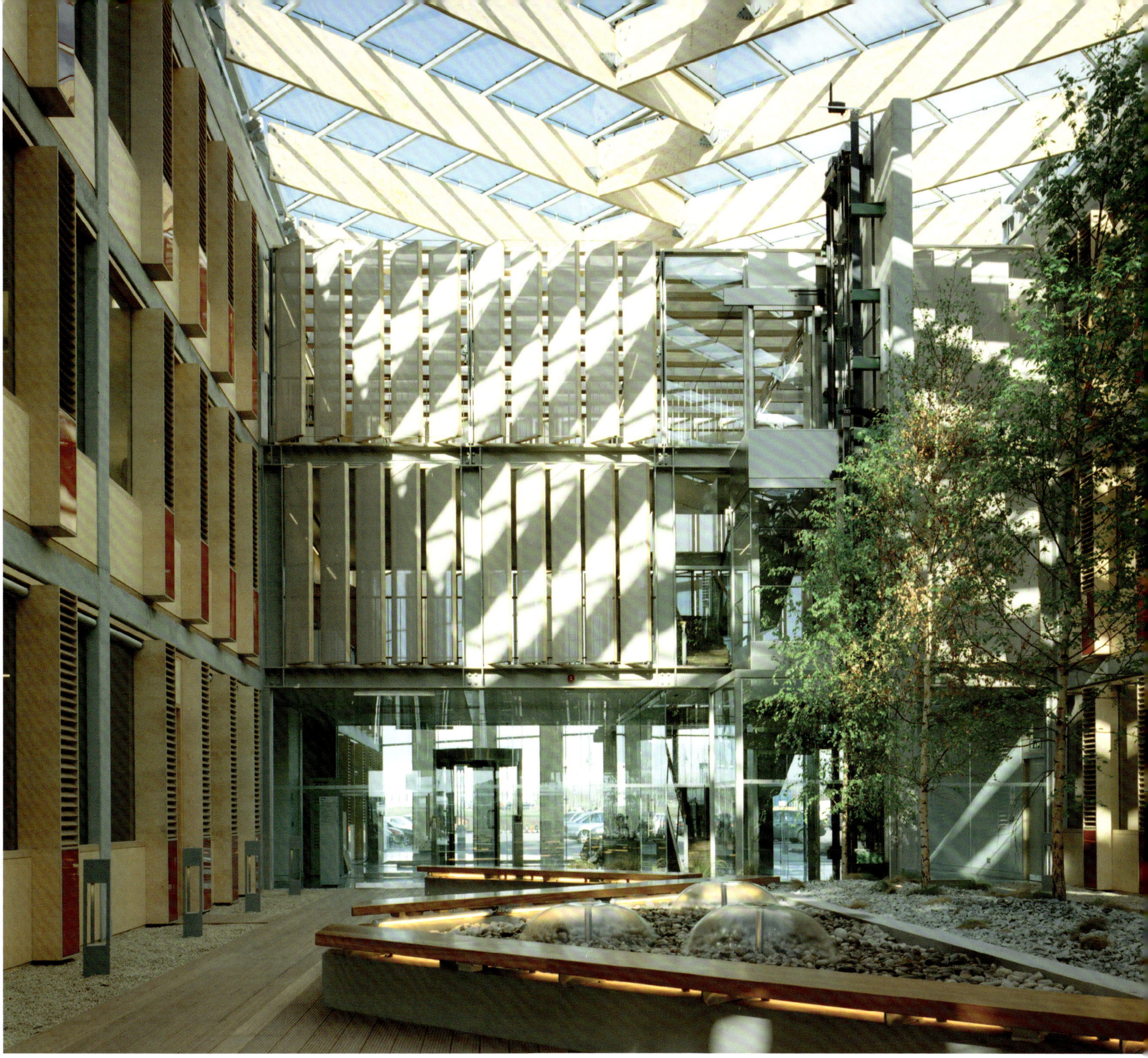
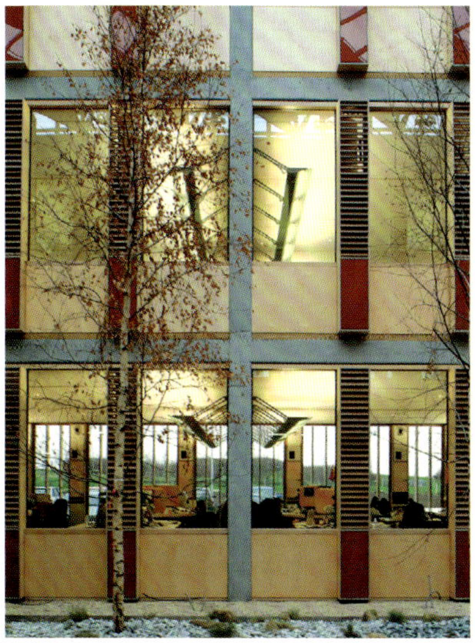
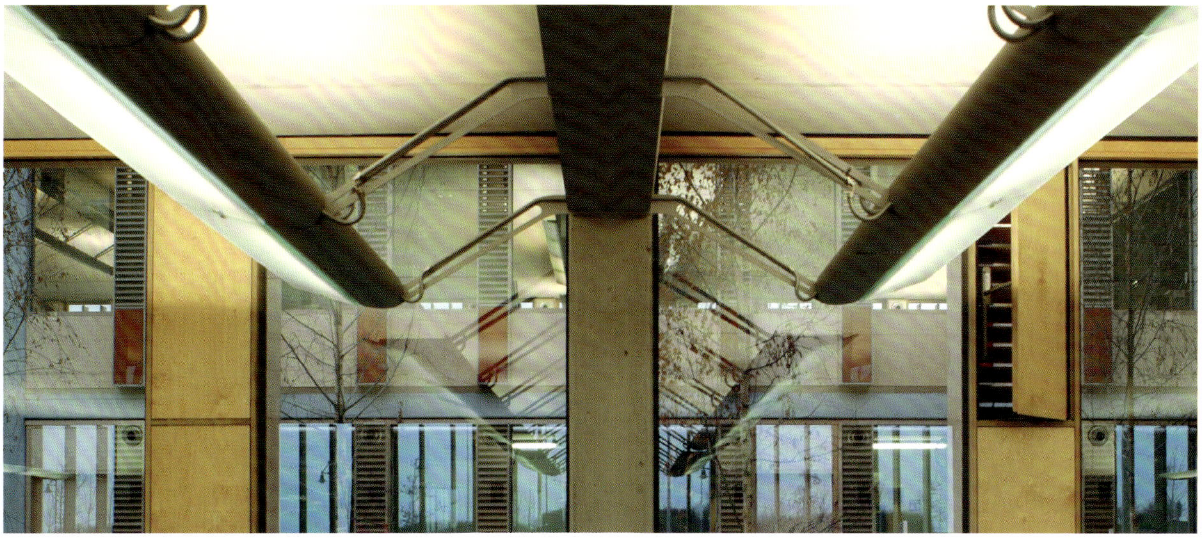

IRELAND_MULLINGAR **WESTMEATH COUNTY COUNCIL HEADQUARTERS**

ARCHITECTS: BUCHOLZ MCEVOY ARCHITECTS, LTD
COMPLETION: 2009_**NUMBER OF WORKPLACES:** 220
GROSS FLOOR AREA: NEW BUILDING 7,750 M², RENOVATION 1,550 M²_**COMMON AREA:** ATRIUM, RESTAURANT, CONFERENCE ROOMS, LIBRARY_**KIND OF WORKPLACES:** COMBINATION_**PHOTOS:** MICHAEL MORAN, NY, VERENA HILGENFELD, HAMBURG (264 B. L., 265 B. L.)

Westmeath County Council headquarters is a low-energy civil services office building located at the heart of an important archaeological site. The open and transparent building was carefully woven into the historic context, creating an ensemble of new and old buildings around this civic site. On the inside, the new building is a sculpture of light, created primarily with glass, timber and concrete, while on the outside it represents an open and transparent expression of local government. The building form is principally organized in two axes and two buildings; one north-south which contains the library and cafe and the other an east-west curved office block. The entirely naturally ventilated building has a double façade combined with an atrium lung serve to effect all of the ventilation in the office building.

Das Rathaus von Westmeath ist ein Niedrigenergie-Gebäude im Herzen einer bedeutenden archäologischen Grabungsstätte. Die offene und transparente Architektur ist sorgfältig in den historischen Kontext eingebettet und formt ein spannendes Ensemble aus Alt und Neu um einen städtischen Platz. Der Neubau wirkt innen wie eine Lichtskulptur, die aus Glas, Holz und Beton geformt wurde; nach außen drückt er die Offenheit und Transparenz der Gemeindeverwaltung aus. Der Komplex ist in zwei Achsen und zwei Gebäude aufgeteilt; Bibliothek und Mensa bilden die Nordsüd- und das Bürogebäude die Ostwestachse. Das ausschließlich natürlich belüftete Gebäude kombiniert eine Doppelfassade mit einem Atrium, um die Frischluftversorgung des gesamten Bürokomplexes sicherzustellen.

left: Site plan_Reading room_Library with view. right: Urban composition_Main buidling entrance_Double façade south.
links: Lageplan_Lesebereich_Bibliothek mit Aussicht. rechts: Urbane Komposition_Haupterschließung des Gebäudes_Doppelte Südfassade.

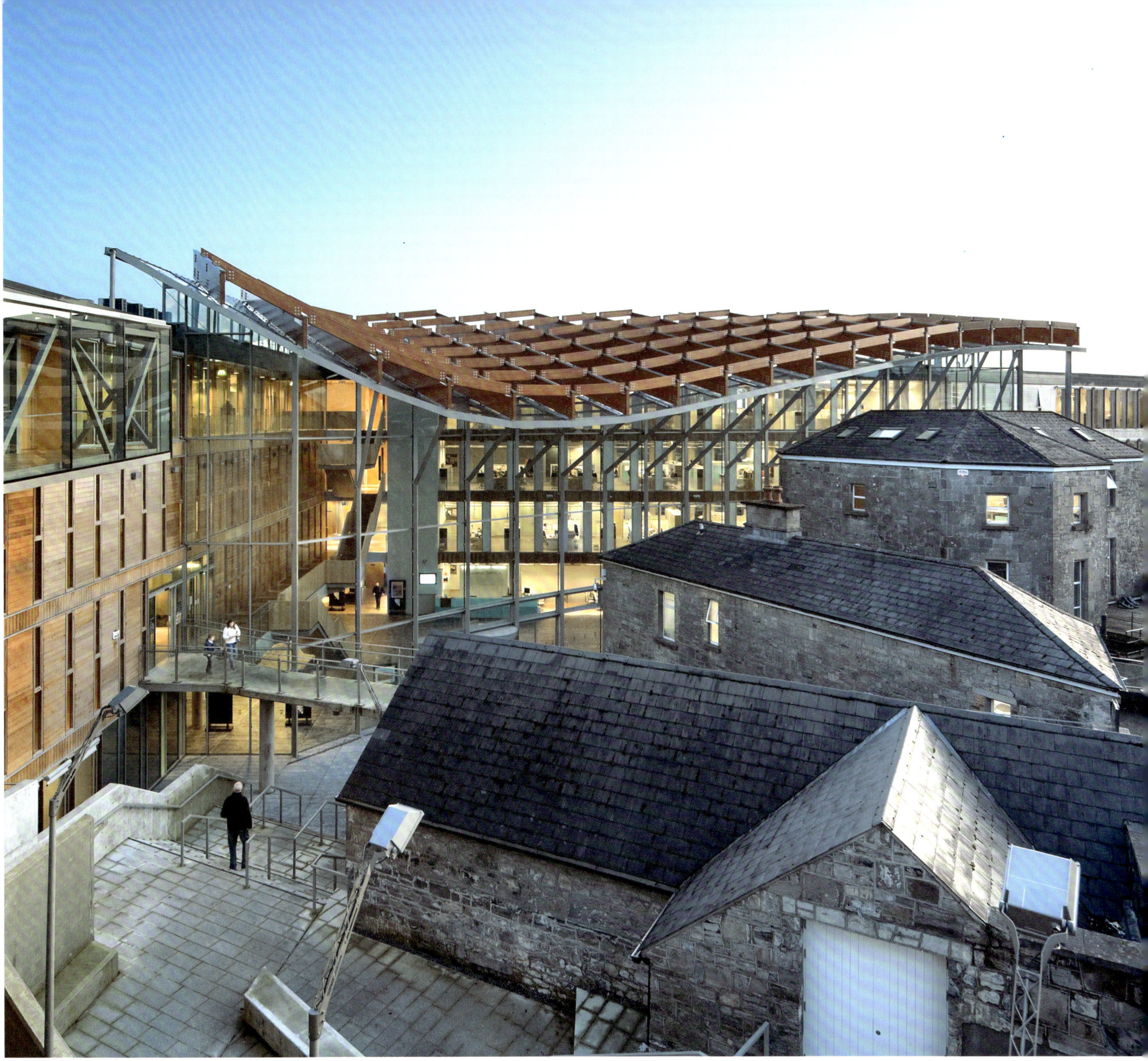
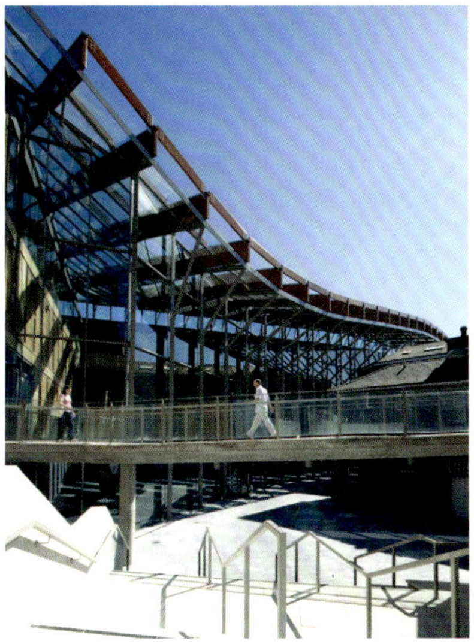
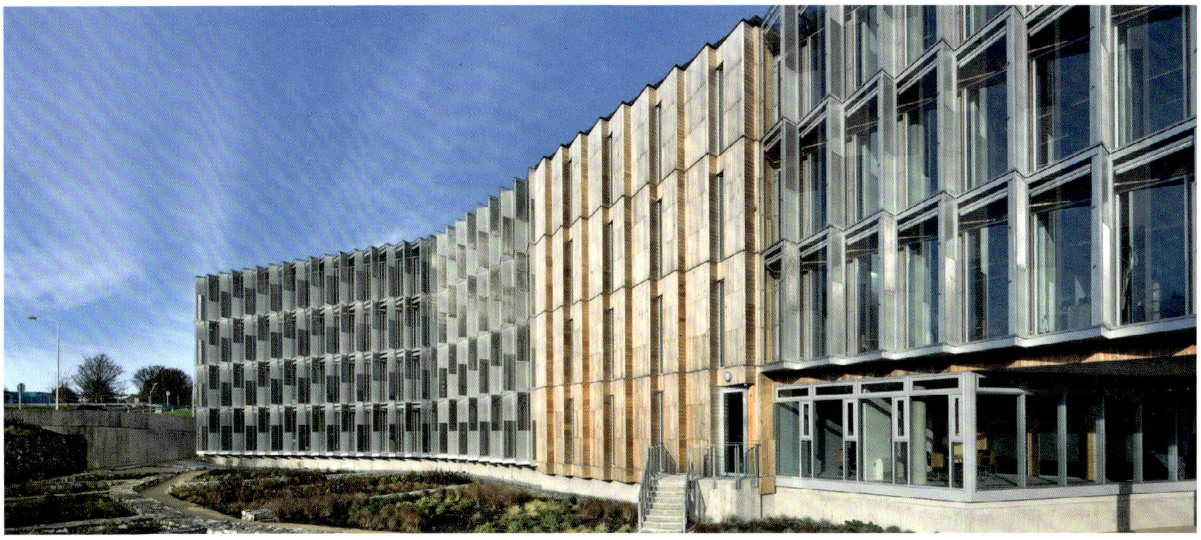

ITALY_ALTE DI MONTECCHIO BISAZZA HEADQUARTES

ARCHITECTS: CARLO DAL BIANCO_**COMPLETION:** 2002
NUMBER OF WORKPLACES: 140_**GROSS FLOOR AREA:** 2,000 M²_**COMMON AREA:** CONFERENCE ROOMS, MEETING ROOMS, LIBRARY_**KIND OF WORKPLACES:** CELLULAR, OPEN-PLAN, TEAM_**PHOTOS:** OTTAVIO TOMASINI (266 B. R., 267 A.), ALBERTO FERRERO (266 B. L., 267 B. L., B. R.)

The renovation project for the Bisazza headquarters is headed up by architect Carlo Dal Bianco, current director of the Bisazza Design Studio, who was first assigned the task in 2002. Bisazza's aim with this restyling is to convey a new image, to be reiterated in the homogenous Bisazza stores in the main design capitals of the world. Entire areas, previously used for mosaic production, have been reclaimed and set up for exhibiting works, objects, sculptures, furnishing accessories and installations created together with internationally recognised architects and designers. In the headquarters are located big exhibition rooms which are up-dated with the latest mosaic installations.

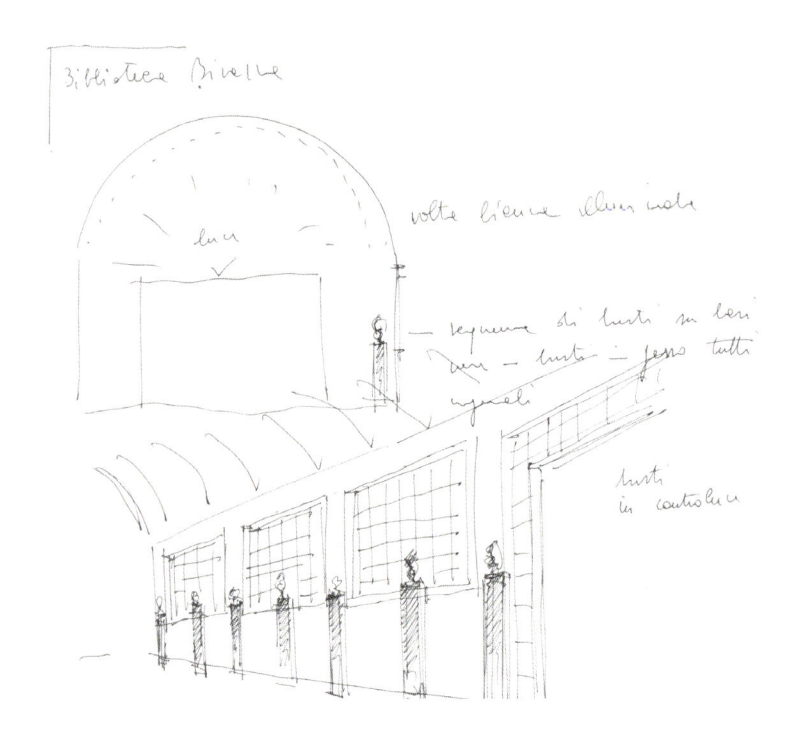

Die Renovierung des Bisazza-Hauptsitzes wird seit 2002 von dem Architekten Carlo Dal Bianco, dem derzeitigen Direktor der Bisazza Design Studios, geleitet. Bisazzas Ziel in dieser Neugestaltung ist, ein neues Firmenimage zu vermitteln, das sich in den gleichartigen Bisazza-Geschäften in den Designerhauptstädten der Welt wiederholt. Ganze Bereiche, die früher für Mosaikproduktionen genutzt wurden, wurden zusammen mit international anerkannten Architekten und Designern aufgearbeitet und für Ausstellungsstücke, Objekte, Skulpturen, Einrichtungsaccesoires und Installationen eingerichtet. Im Hauptsitz befinden sich große Ausstellungsräume, die mit Mosaik-Installationen modernisiert wurden.

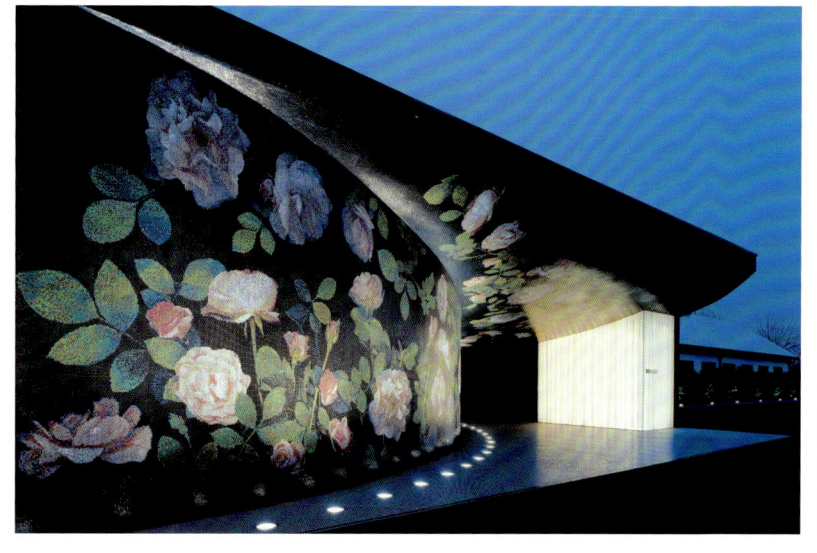

left: Sketch_Exterior view_Entrance hall. right: Meeting room_Reception_Exhibition hall.
links: Skizze_Außenansicht_Eingangshalle. rechts: Besprechungsraum_Empfang_Austellungshalle.

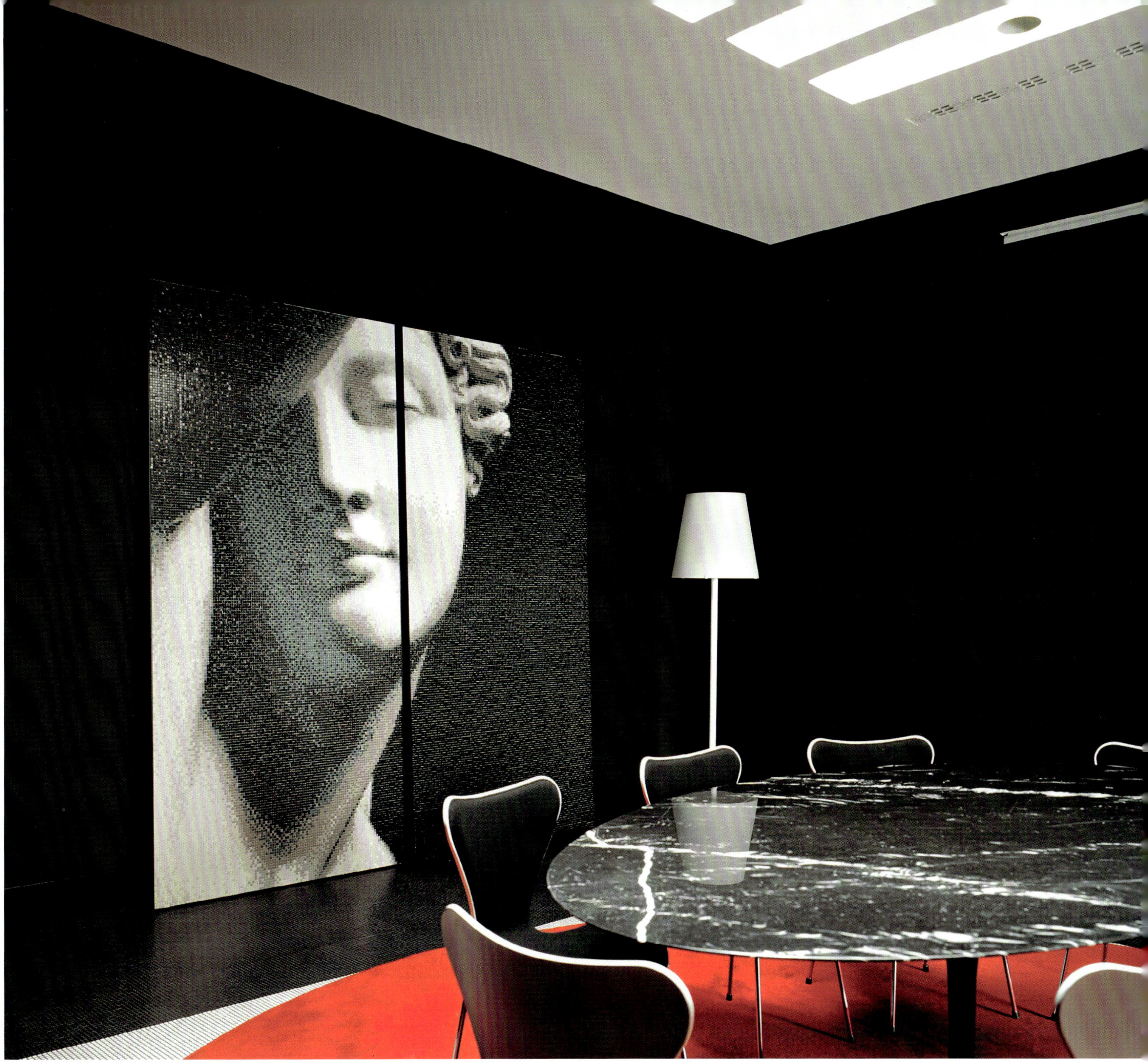

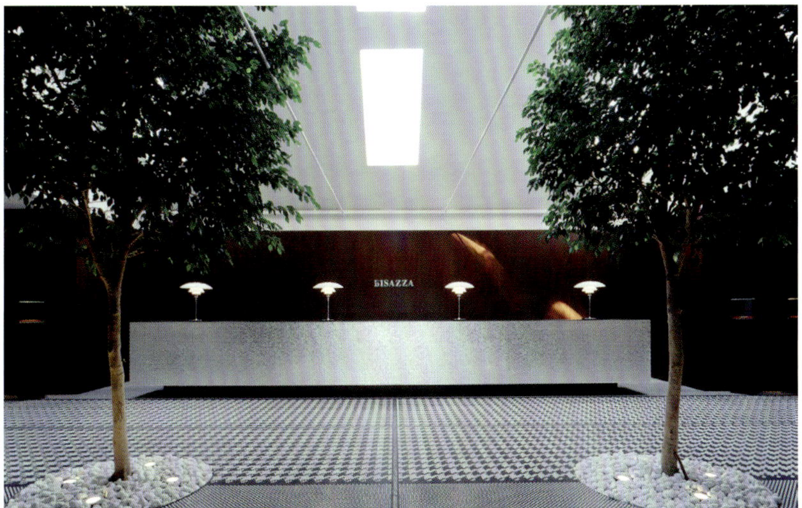
BISAZZA

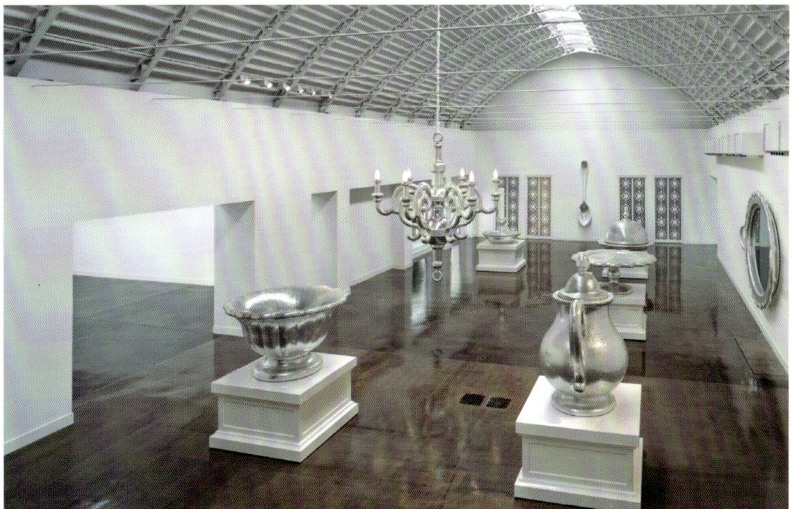

ITALY_BOLOGNA **NAVILE TRE**

ARCHITECTS: JSWD ARCHITEKTEN
COMPLETION: 2012_ **NUMBER OF WORKPLACES:** 100
GROSS FLOOR AREA: 11,900 M² _**COMMON AREA:** ATRIUM, LIBRARY, FITNESS AREA _**KIND OF WORKPLACES:** CELLULAR, OPEN-SPACE
PHOTOS: COURTESY OF THE ARCHITECTS

In the northwestern part of downtown Bologna, the new city district "Mercato Navile" is emerging in the location of the former central market. This ensemble of an office building and a boardinghouse is the new district's first project. It is positioned slightly elevated on a base that unites both sections into a spatial unit. In the center of the square office building there is an atrium hall with a glass roof that gives the impression of a weatherproof piazetta. An austere natural stone façade constitutes the outer shell of the cube. On the city side, a three-floor gate-shaped opening has been introduced to the building through which the atrium opens up horizontally and towards the new town square.

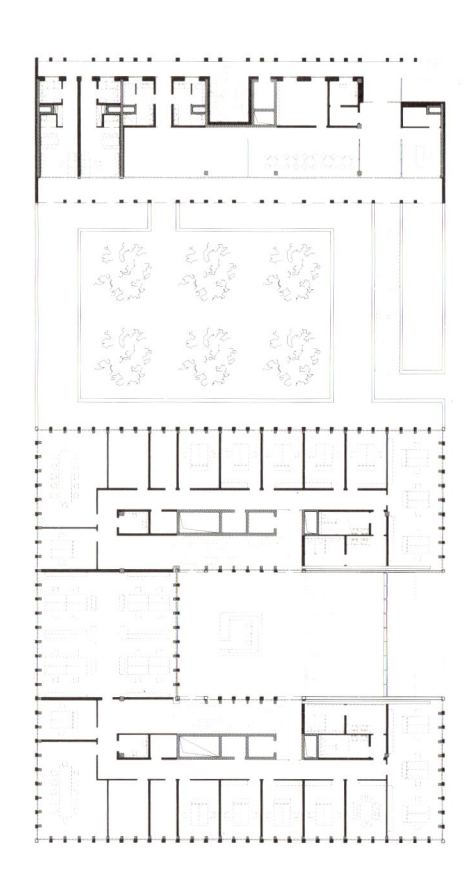

Im Nordwesten der Innenstadt von Bologna entsteht anstelle des früheren Großmarkts das neue Stadtquartier „Mercato Navile". Das Ensemble aus Büro- und Boardinghaus bildet den Auftakt. Es steht leicht erhöht auf einem Sockel, der beide Bauteile zu einer räumlichen Einheit zusammenfasst. Im Zentrum des im Grundriss quadratischen Bürohauses befindet sich eine Atriumhalle mit Glasdach, die den Eindruck einer wettergeschützten Piazetta entstehen lässt. Eine strenge Natursteinfassade bildet die äußere Schale des Kubus. Auf der Stadtseite ist eine dreigeschossige torförmige Öffnung in das Gebäude eingeschnitten, mit der sich das Atrium in die Horizontale und auf den neuen Stadtplatz öffnet.

left: Ground floor plan_Section. right: Atrium_Exterior_ Boardinghouse.
links: Grundriss Erdgeschoss_Schnitt. rechts: Atrium_Außenansicht_Wohngebäude.

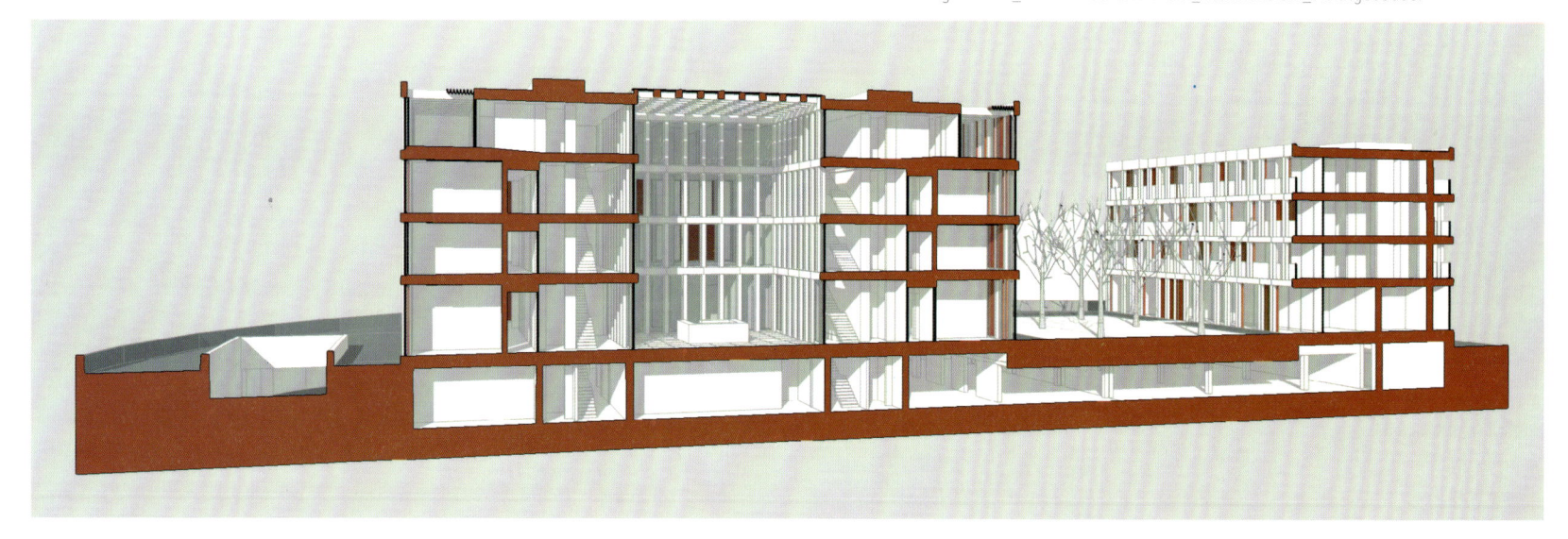

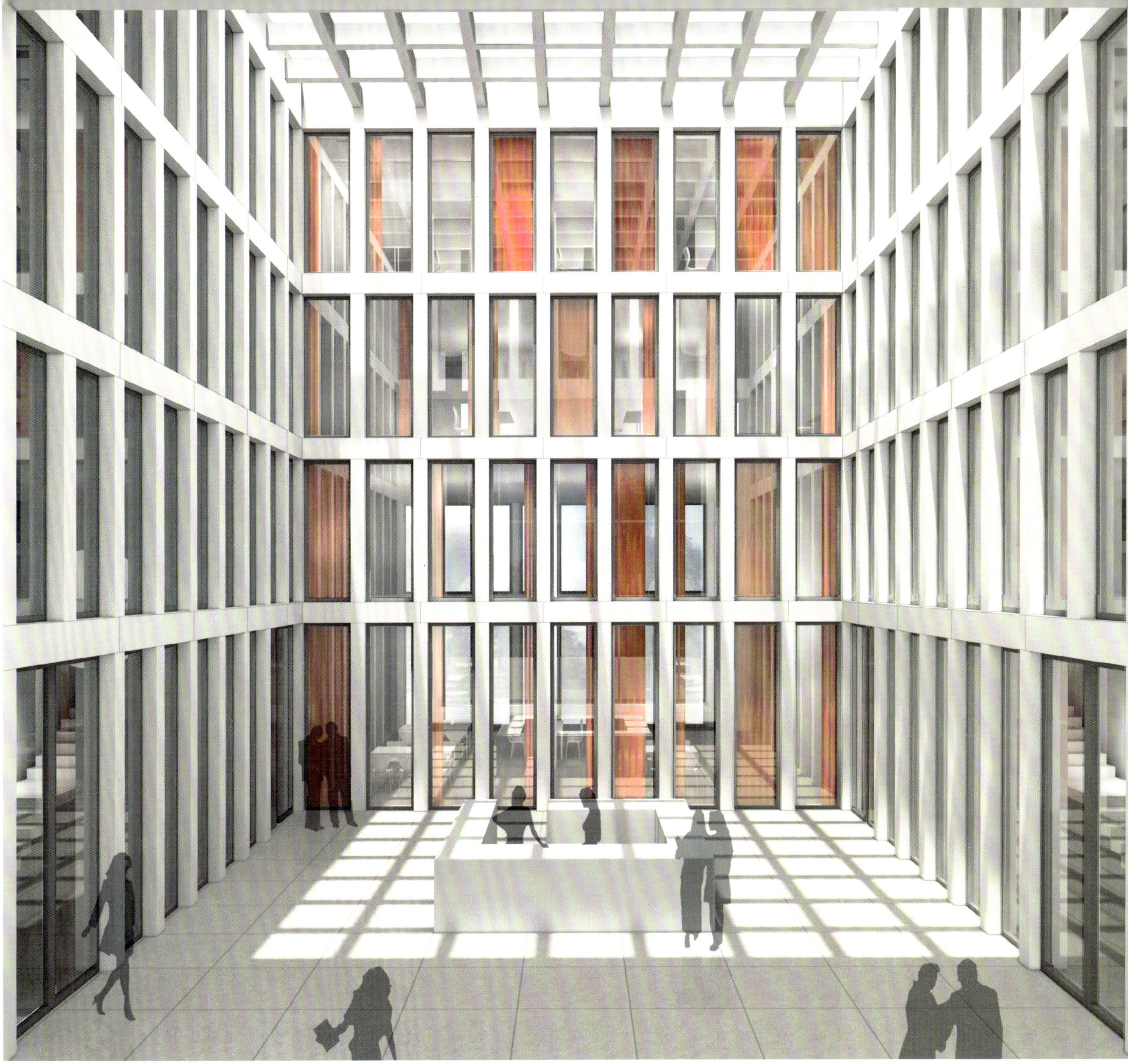

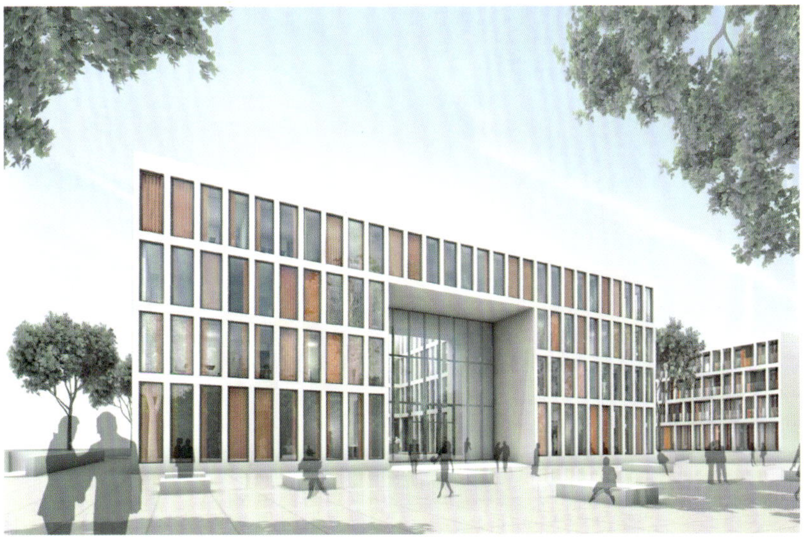

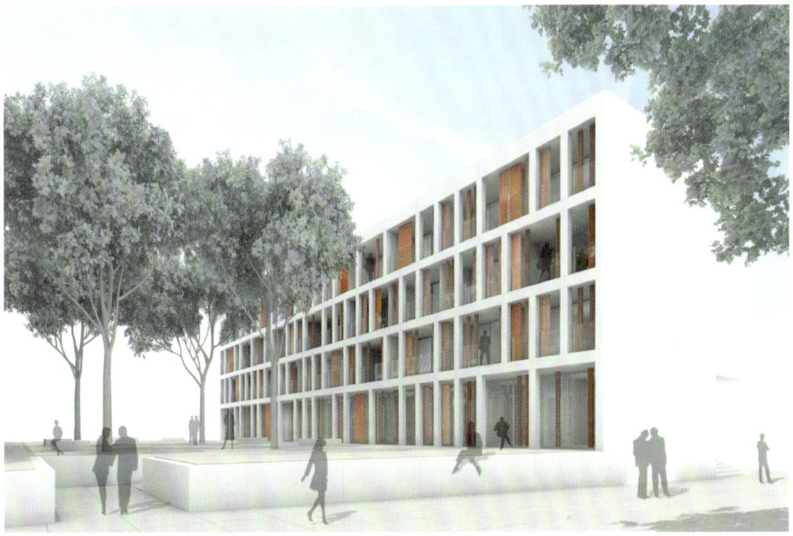

ITALY_BOLZANO **BLAAS GENERAL PARTNERSHIP**

ARCHITECTS: MONOVOLUME ARCHITECTURE + DESIGN
COMPLETION: 2007_**NUMBER OF WORKPLACES:** 16
GROSS FLOOR AREA: 1,250 M²_**COMMON AREA:** CONFERENCE ROOM_**KIND OF WORKPLACES:** COMBINATION, TEAM
PHOTOS: OSKAR DA RIZ, BOZEN

The company Blaas in Bolzano is specialized in electro-mechanics. At its new head office, the company presents its new product range and offers repair services. On the ground floor of the building there is the sales division, with the showroom and the repair shop located on the first floor. All administration offices are situated on the second floor. The overall impression of the structure is a homogenous and closed building. Nevertheless, there is a clear and formal separation between the public and the private sector which can be perceived already from the outside. The glass façade on the northern side provides maximum visibility and transparency to the exhibition and sales area.

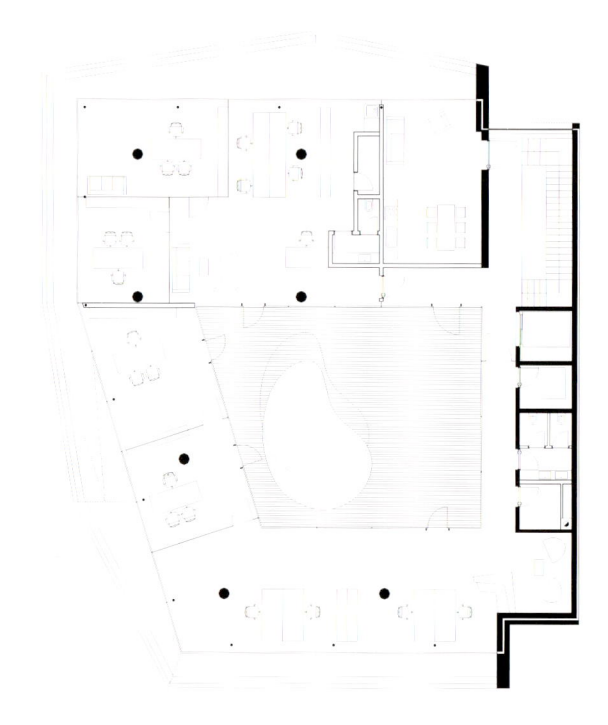

Die Firma Blaas in Bozen ist auf Elektro-Mechanik spezialisiert. Im Erdgeschoss des neuen Hauptsitzes, in dem das Unternehmen seine neuen Produktreihen präsentiert, befindet sich die Verkaufsabteilung, im ersten Stock die Ausstellungsräume und der Reparaturservice und im zweiten Stock alle Verwaltungsbüros. Der Gesamteindruck der Struktur ist ein homogenes und in sich schlüssiges Gebäude. Dennoch besteht eine klare formale Trennung zwischen den öffentlichen und den nicht-öffentlichen Bereichen, die schon von außen ersichtlich ist. Die Glasfassade auf der Nordseite sorgt für maximale Einblicke und Transparenz zu den Ausstellungs- und Verkaufsräumen.

left: Third floor plan_Main stair with rooflight_Main stair. right: Detail main stair.
links: Grundriss drittes Obergeschoss_Haupttreppe mit Oberlicht_Haupttreppe. rechts: Detail Haupttreppe.

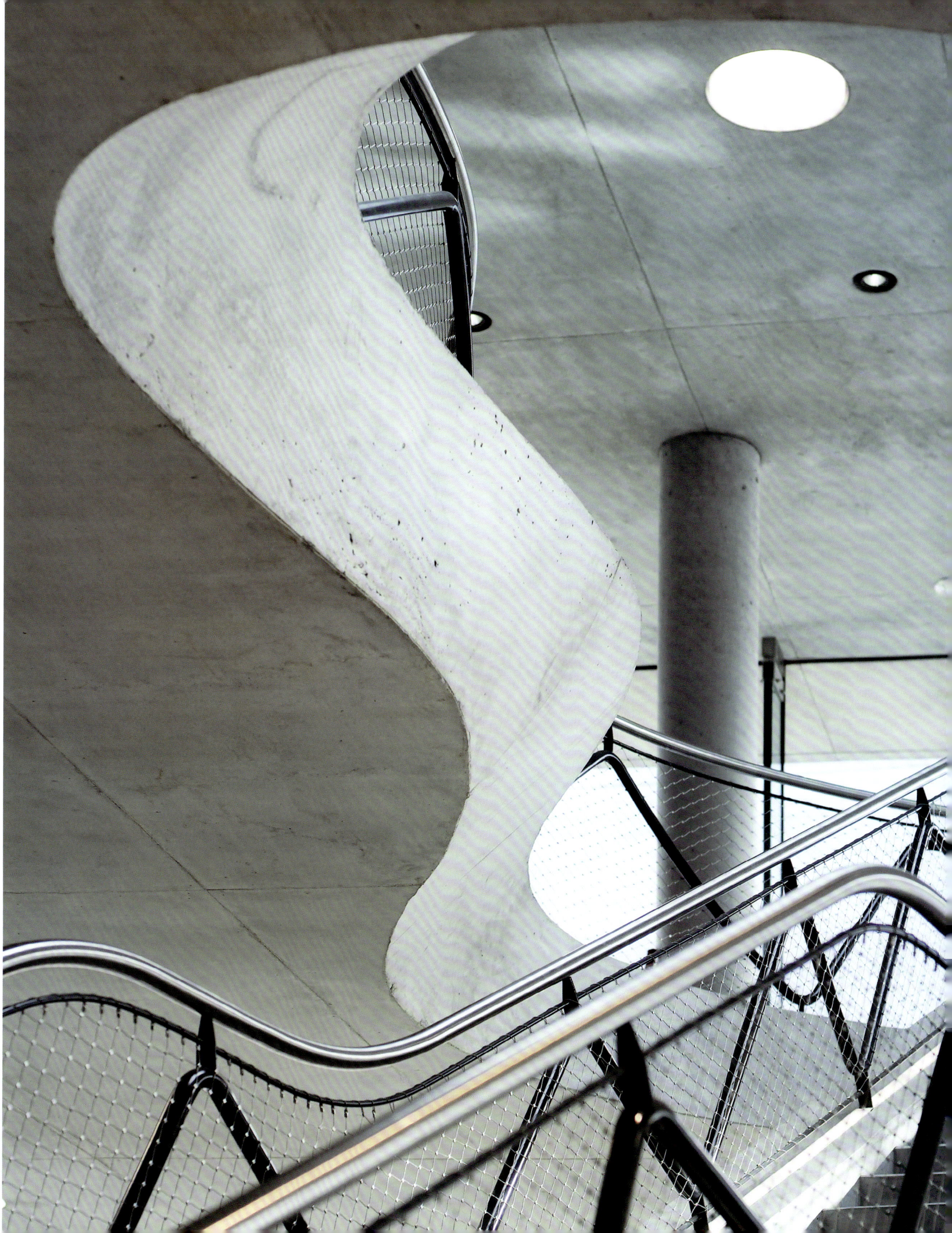

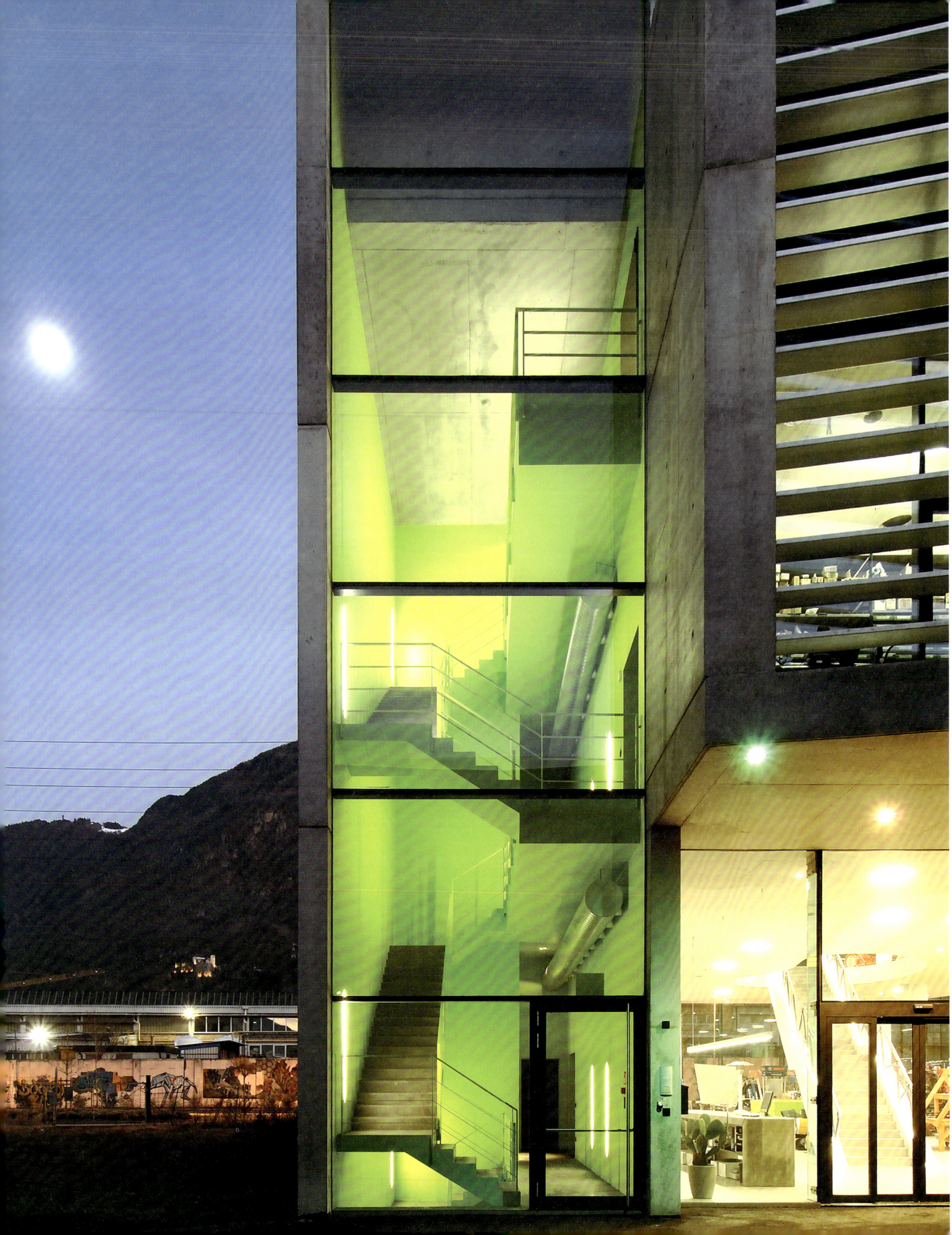

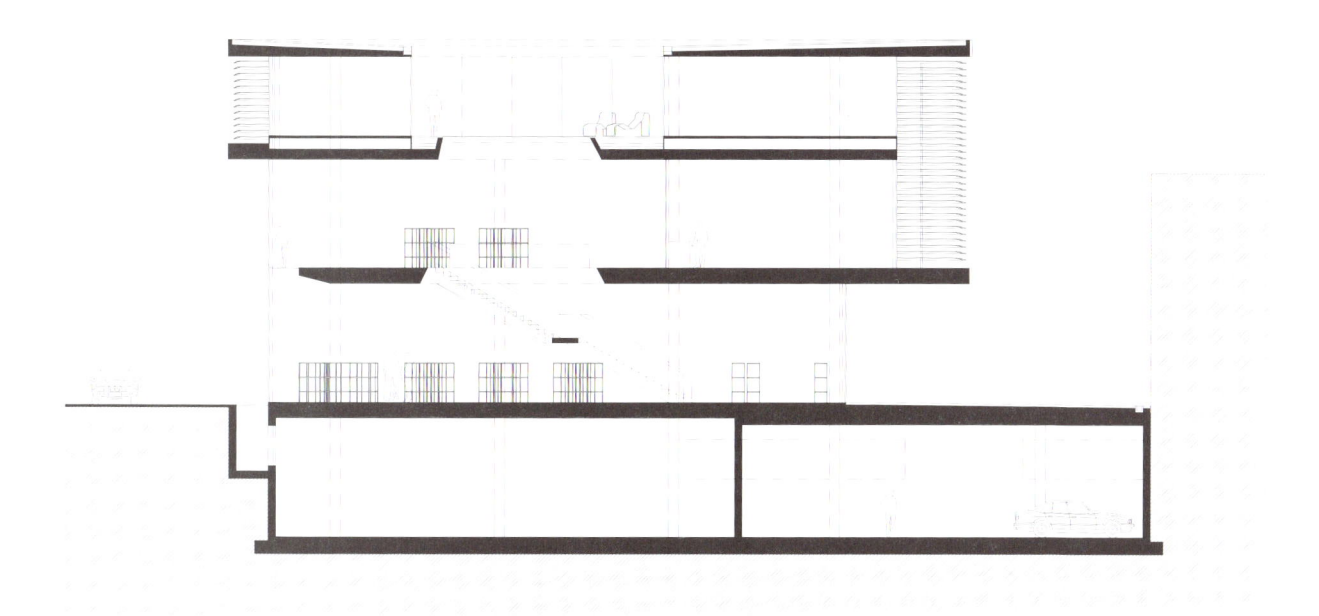

left: West elevation with entrance and staircase. right: Section_South elevation_Workplace_Roof garden with skylight_Third floor office.
links: Westfassade mit Eingang und Treppenhaus. rechts: Schnitt_Südfassade_Arbeitsplatz_Dachgarten mit Oberlicht_Büro im dritten Obergeschoss.

ITALY_KURTATSCH **ROTHO BLAAS LIMITED COMPANY**

ARCHITECTS: MONOVOLUME ARCHITECTURE + DESIGN
COMPLETION: 2005_**NUMBER OF WORKPLACES:** 27
GROSS FLOOR AREA: 3,700 M²_**COMMON AREA:** CONFERENCE ROOM, BAR, LOUNGE
KIND OF WORKPLACES: OPEN-PLAN, TEAM
PHOTOS: OSKAR DA RIZ, BOZEN

Rotho Blaas is a large-scale commercial operation specializing in assembling systems and power tools for the woodworking industry. Warehouse and commissioning are situated on the ground floor whereas administration, a meeting room and a showroom can be found on the upper floor. The aim of the project was to create a compact building with a high recognition value, a building that serves as an embodiment of the enterprise's contemporary corporate identity. This has lead to a functional, compact structural shell, provided with a glass envelope. The main building material employed is wood to showcase the company's own products.

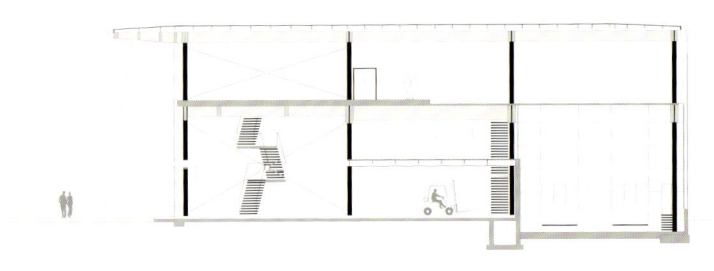

Rotho Blaas ist ein großes auf Elektrowerkzeuge und Montagesysteme für die Holzindustrie spezialisiertes Handelsunternehmen. Lager und Versand befinden sich im Erdgeschoss, die Verwaltung sowie ein Konferenzzimmer und ein Ausstellungsraum im Obergeschoss. Ziel des Projekts war, ein kompaktes Gebäude mit hohem Wiedererkennungswert zu schaffen. Das Gebäude sollte die zeitgemäße und repräsentative CI des Unternehmens darstellen, was zu einer funktionalen, kompakten Struktur und gläsernen Hülle führte. Hauptmaterial ist jedoch das auf das Tätigkeitsfeld verweisende Holz.

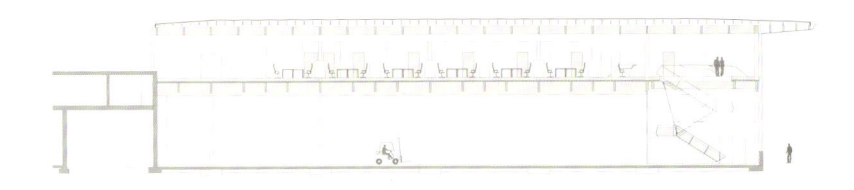

left: Cross and longitudinal section_Reception and lounge_West elevation. right: West elevation.
links: Quer- und Längsschnitt_Empfang und Lounge_Westfassade. rechts: Westfassade.

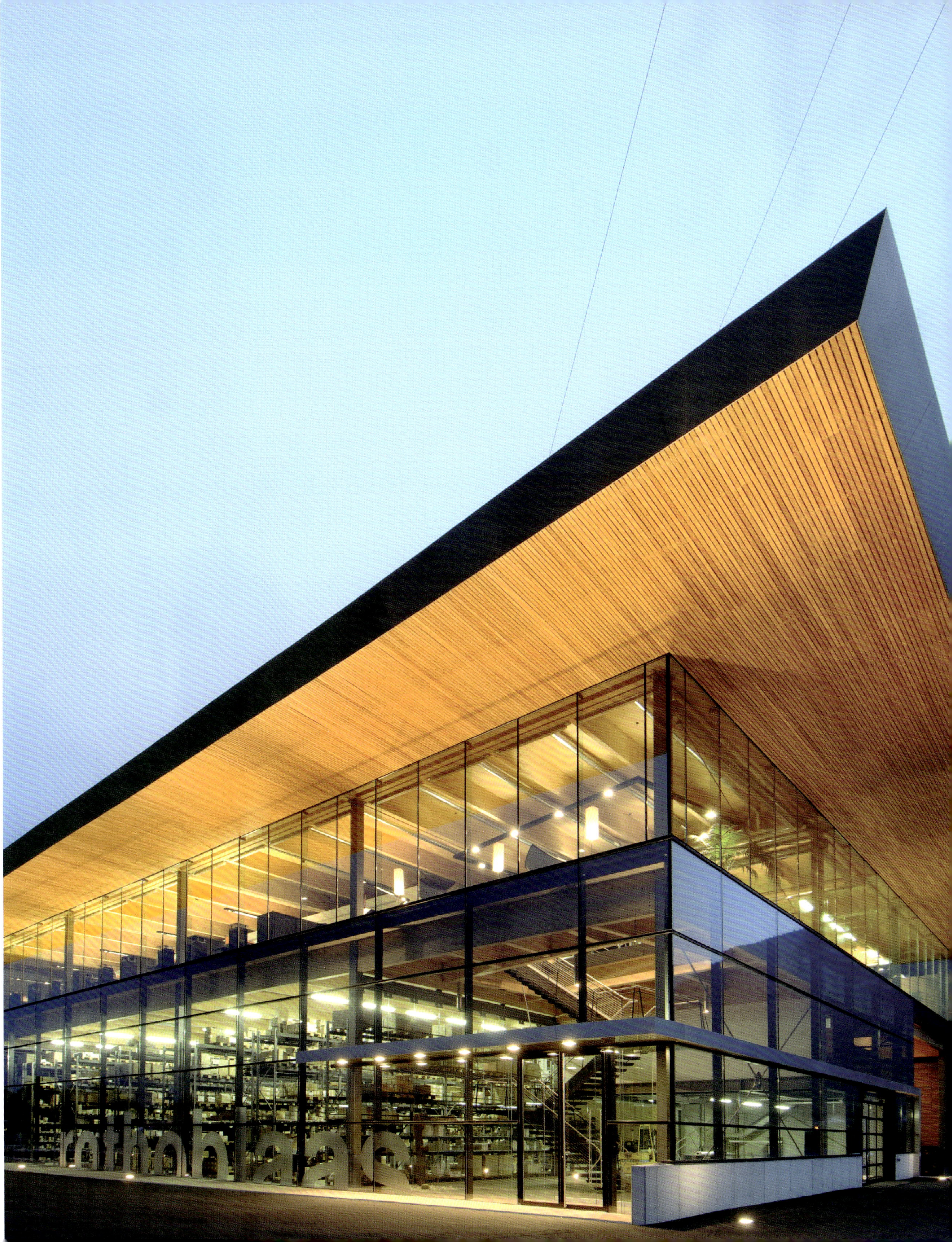

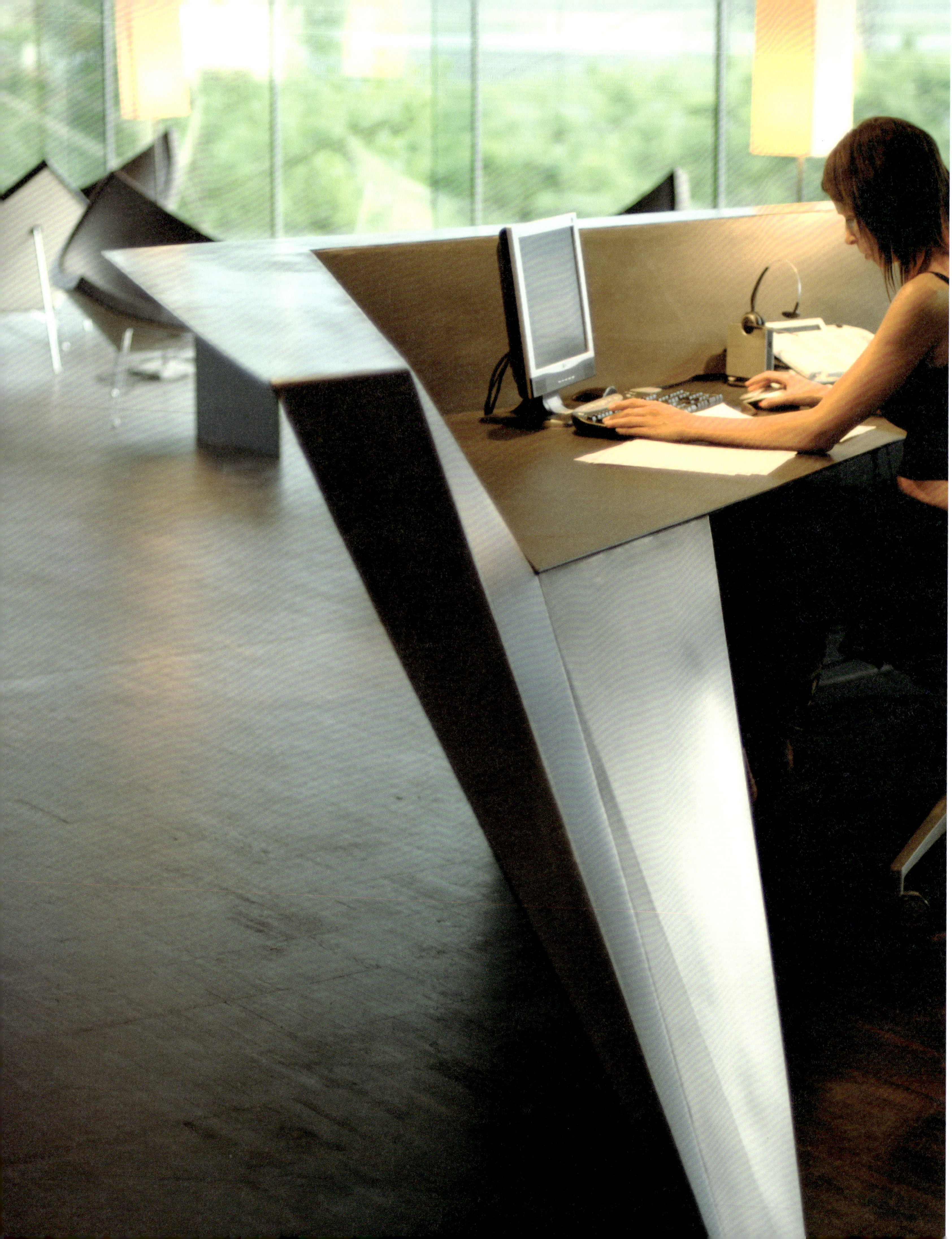

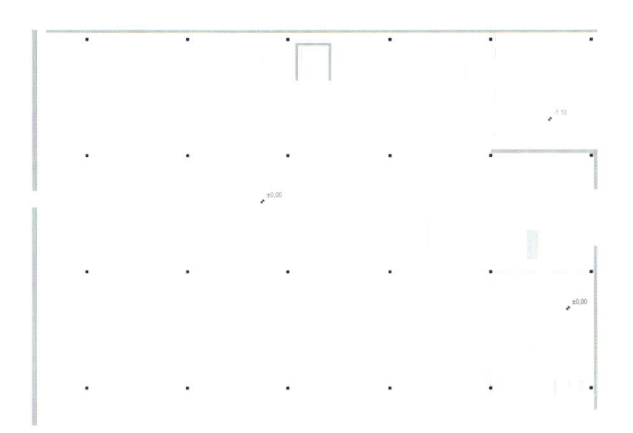

left: Reception desk. right: Ground floor plan_Roof garden_View from storage across roof garden into the office_Reception_Open-space office.
links: Empfangstresen. rechts: Grundriss Erdgeschoss_Dachgarten_Blick vom Lager durch das Büro Richtung Dachgarten_Empfang_Großraumbüro.

ITALY_MILAN **NEW HEADQUARTERS ERMENEGILDO ZEGNA**

ARCHITECTS: ANTONIO CITTERIO, PATRICIA VIEL AND PARTNERS
COMPLETION: 2007_**NUMBER OF WORKPLACES:** 200_**GROSS FLOOR AREA:** 2,020 M² (OFFICES); 4,232 M² (PRODUCTION)_**COMMON AREA:** SHOWROOMS, AUDITORIUM AND THEATER_**KIND OF WORKPLACES:** CELLULAR, OPEN-PLAN_**PHOTOS:** LEO TORRI, MILAN

The structure overlooks the street from a long glass tunnel which opens into Via Stendhal through a narrow foyer. The long tunnel has four levels with footbridges connecting the showroom area to the office building. Zegna's headquarters has a showroom for each of its collections, the commercial and public relations offices, and a presentation area on the ground floor. All the functional spaces are grouped around an inside courtyard terrace, which is shaped like the ceiling and presents an inside view of the building's different activities. The external front is only partly glazed and treated with reflecting materials. It utilizes the inclined plane shapes to reflect the surrounding industrial scenery.

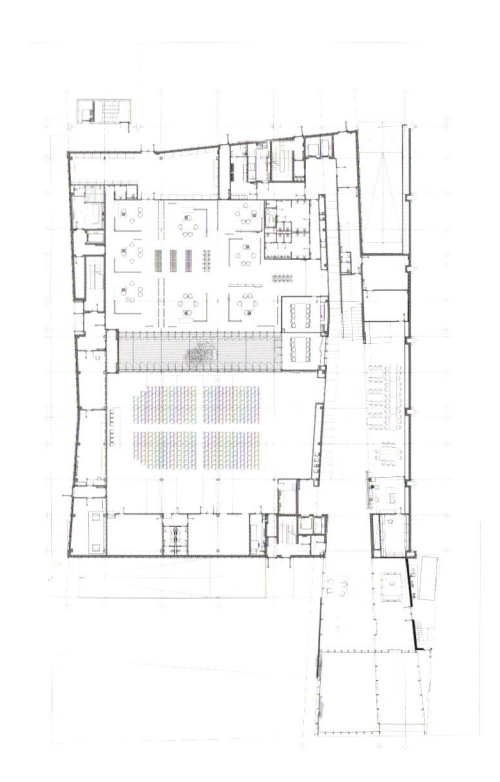

Das Gebäude öffnet sich zur Straße lediglich durch einen langen Glastunnel, der sich zur Via Stendhal zu einem schmelan Foyer ausweitet. Der Tunnel erstreckt sich über vier Etagen, Brücken verbinden den Austellungsbereich mit den Büroräumen. Es gibt einen Ausstellungsraum für jede von Zengas Kollektionen, Büros für Werbung und Öffentlichkeitsarbeit sowie einen Vortragsraum im Erdgeschoss. Die Funktionsbereiche sind um einen Innenhof gruppiert, der sich der Fassade anpasst und einen Einblick in die verschiedenen Abläufe gibt. Die Außenfassade ist nur zum Teil verglast und mit reflektierenden Materialien behandelt. Sie nutzt die schrägen Flächen aus, um die umliegende Industriekulisse wiederzuspiegeln.

left: Ground floor plan_Main entrance_Inner courtyard terrace. right: Stair case.
links: Grundriss, Erdgeschoss_Haupteingang_Innenhofterasse. rechts: Treppenhaus.

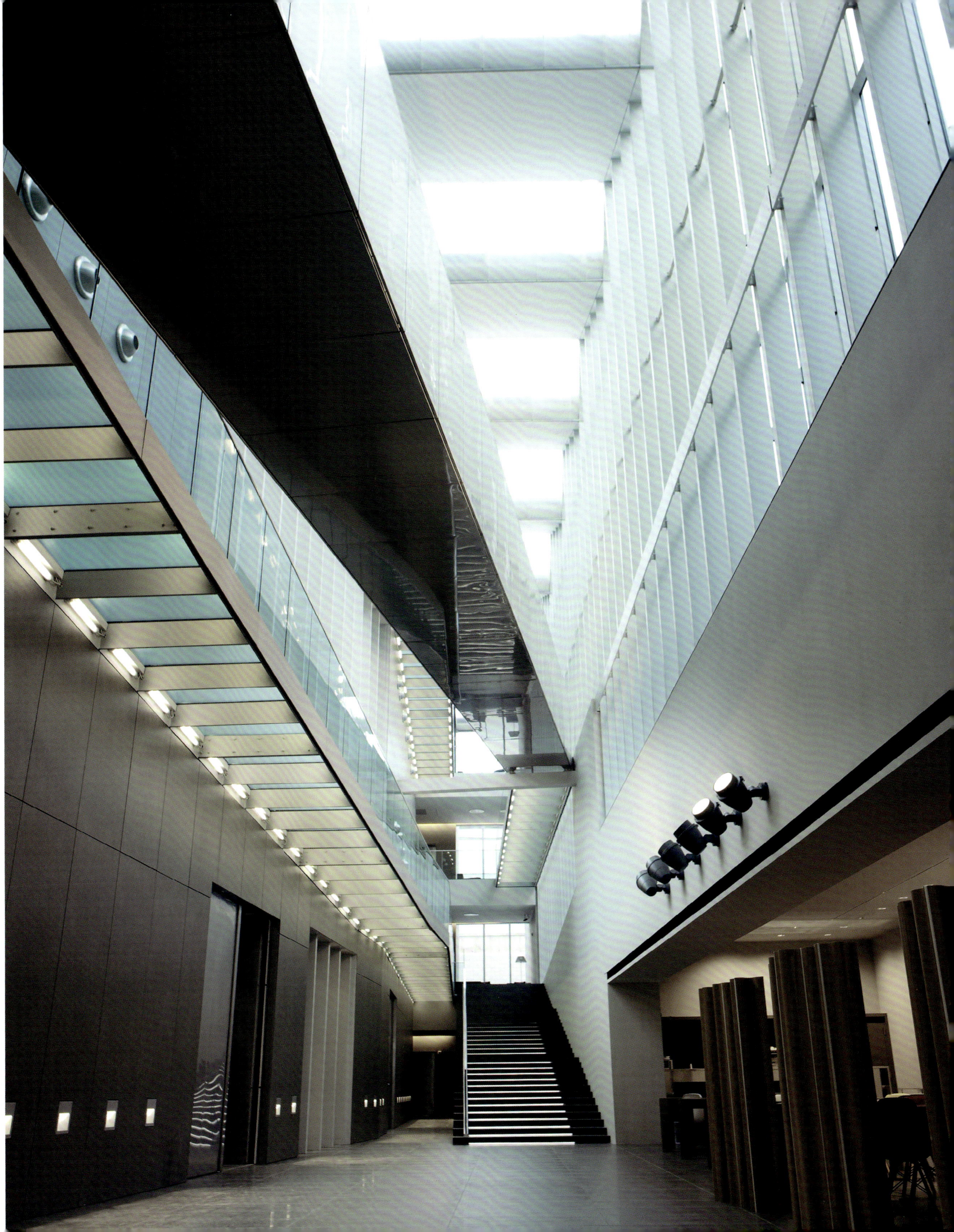

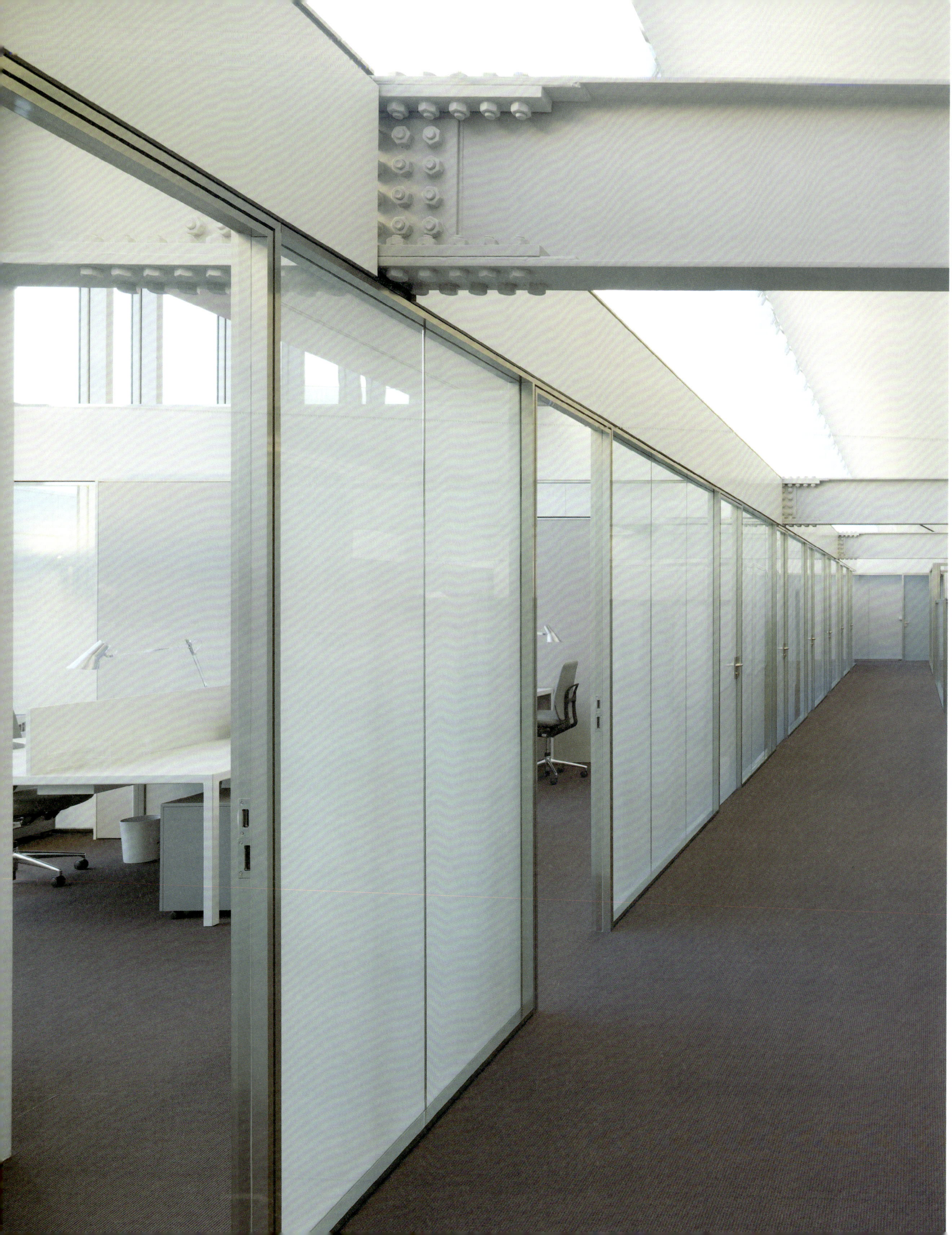

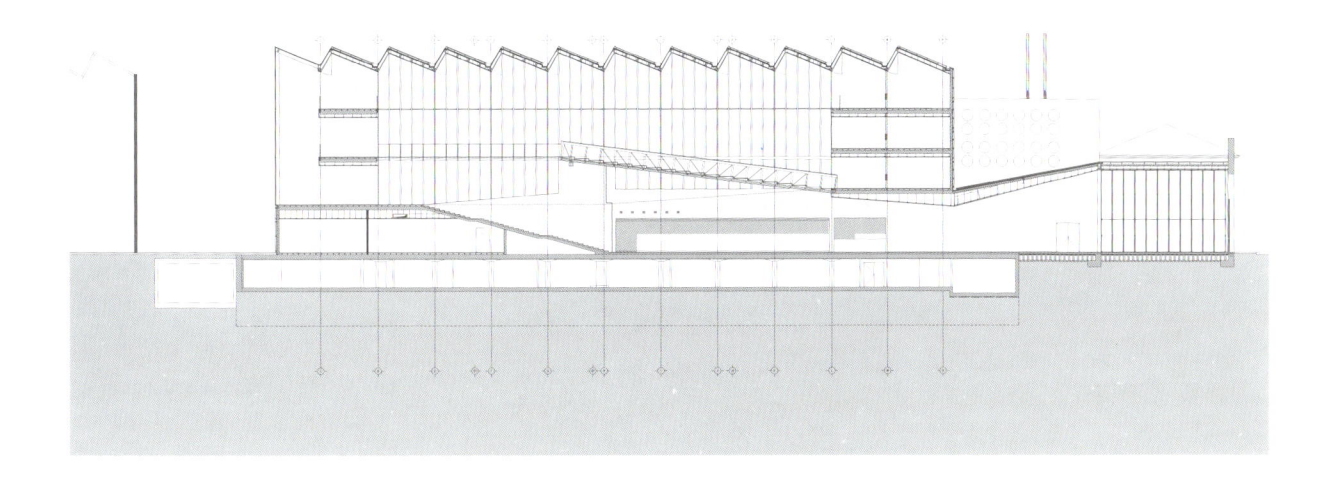

left: Offices seen from the corridor. right: Longitudinal section_Lobby_Showroom and the main stairs_Meeting room_Showroom.
links: Büros, vom Gang aus gesehen. rechts: Längsschnitt_Foyer_Showroom und Haupttreppe_ Besprechungsraum_Showroom.

ITALY_MILAN TIZIANO 32 HEADQUARTERS

ARCHITECTS: PARK ASSOCIATI AND ZUCCHI & PARTNERS
COMPLETION: 2009_**NUMBER OF WORKPLACES:** 520
GROSS FLOOR AREA: 1,550 M²_**KIND OF WORKPLACES:** COMBINATION, OPEN-PLAN, TEAM
PHOTOS: LEO TORRI

The renovation of the common areas of the 1950s-building in Via Tiziano involved moving the building's entrance to the basement to redistribute previously unused spaces and to provide the whole complex with a new image. A new entrance canopy serves as the access to the new entrance hall. It is covered in a skin of expanded metal panels that appear to be cut out of the surrounding lawn. The project also involves a general revision of the distribution of the spaces on all the floors, as well as the recuperation of the building's attic. Finally, the general refurbishment of the volume's front is now enhanced by a series of thin continuous vertical wings of micro-perforated aluminum sheets.

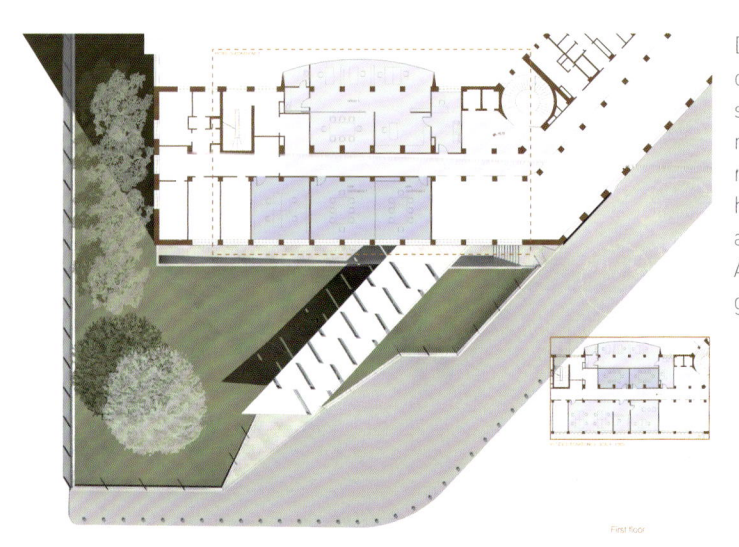

Die Renovierung der Gemeinschaftsflächen des 1950er-Jahre Gebäudes in der Via Tiziano umfasste auch die Verlegung des Eingangs ins Untergeschoss, so dass ein neuer Gesamteindruck entstand und zuvor ungenutzte Fläche nutzbar wurde. Ein neues Vordach führt in das neue Foyer. Es ist mit Streckmetallplatten verkleidet und scheint sich aus dem umgebenden Rasen zu erheben. Das Projekt bezieht die Überarbeitung der gesamten Raumverteilung aller Geschosse ebenso ein, wie die Wiederherstellung des Dachgeschosses. Auch die Fassade wurde mit filigranen mikroperforierten Aluminiumblechen geschossübergreifend vertikal gegliedert.

left: Ground floor plan_Façade and canopy_Entrance hall. right: Façade and canopy.
links: Grundriss Erdgeschoss_Fassade und Vordach_Eingangshalle. rechts: Fassade und Vordach.

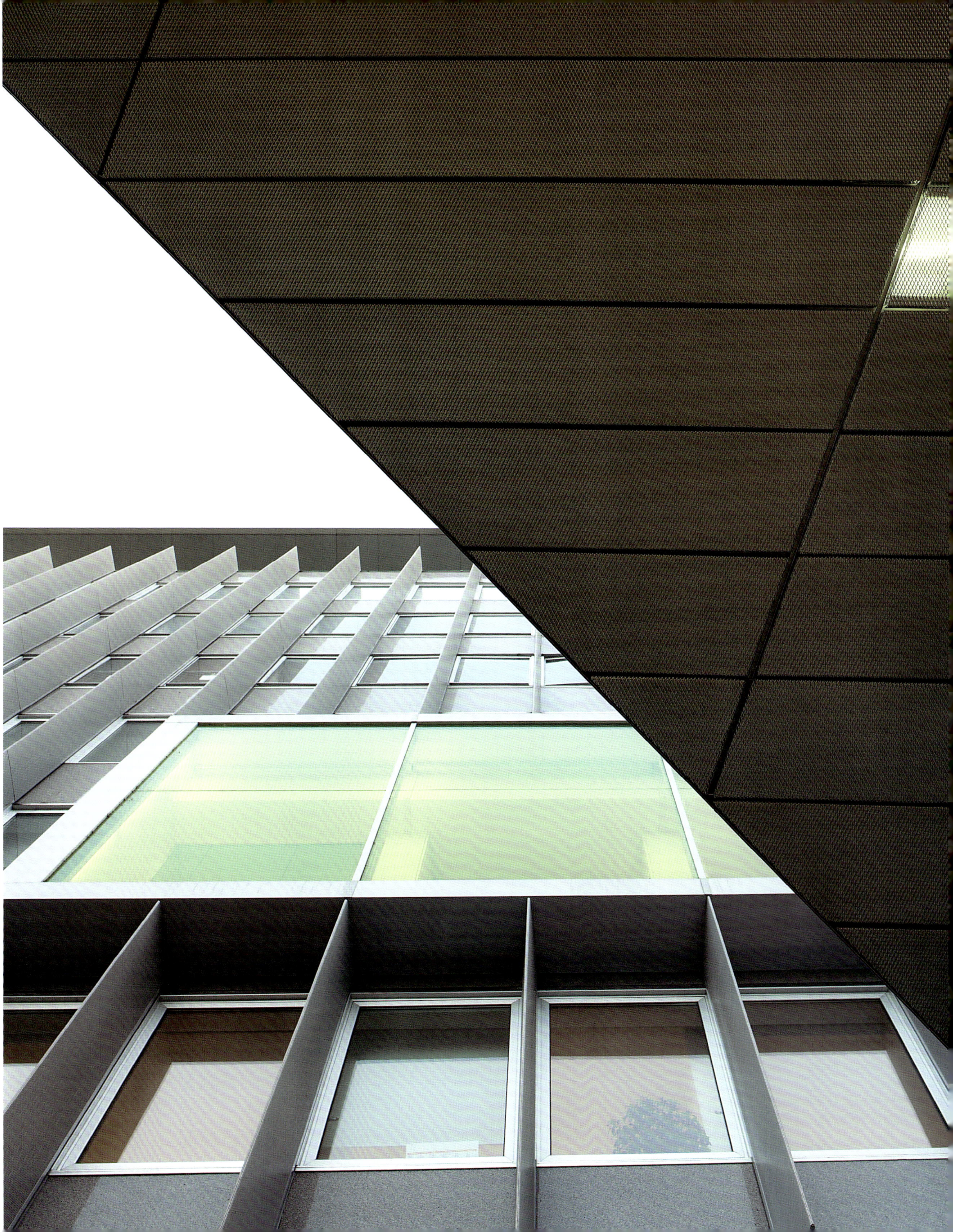

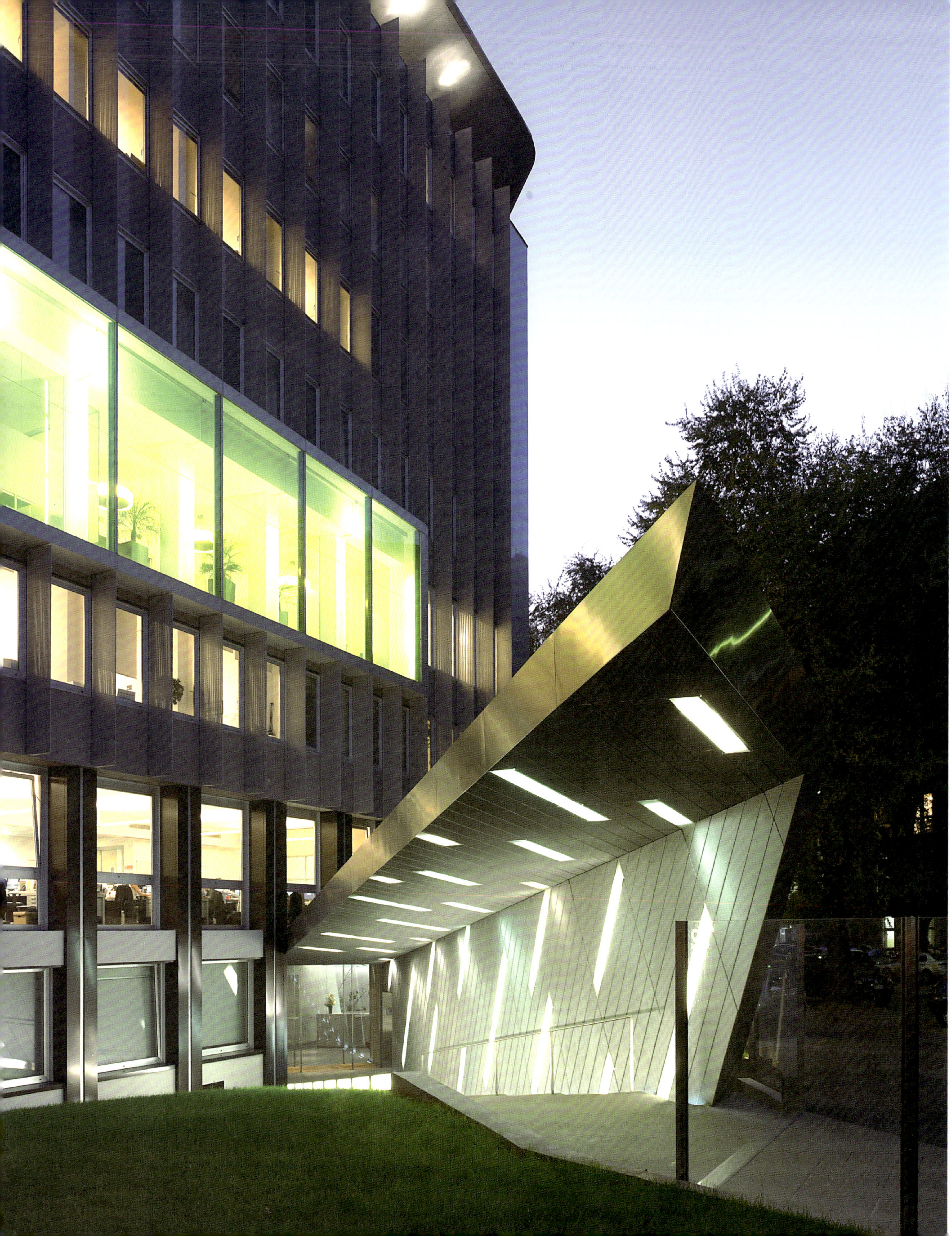

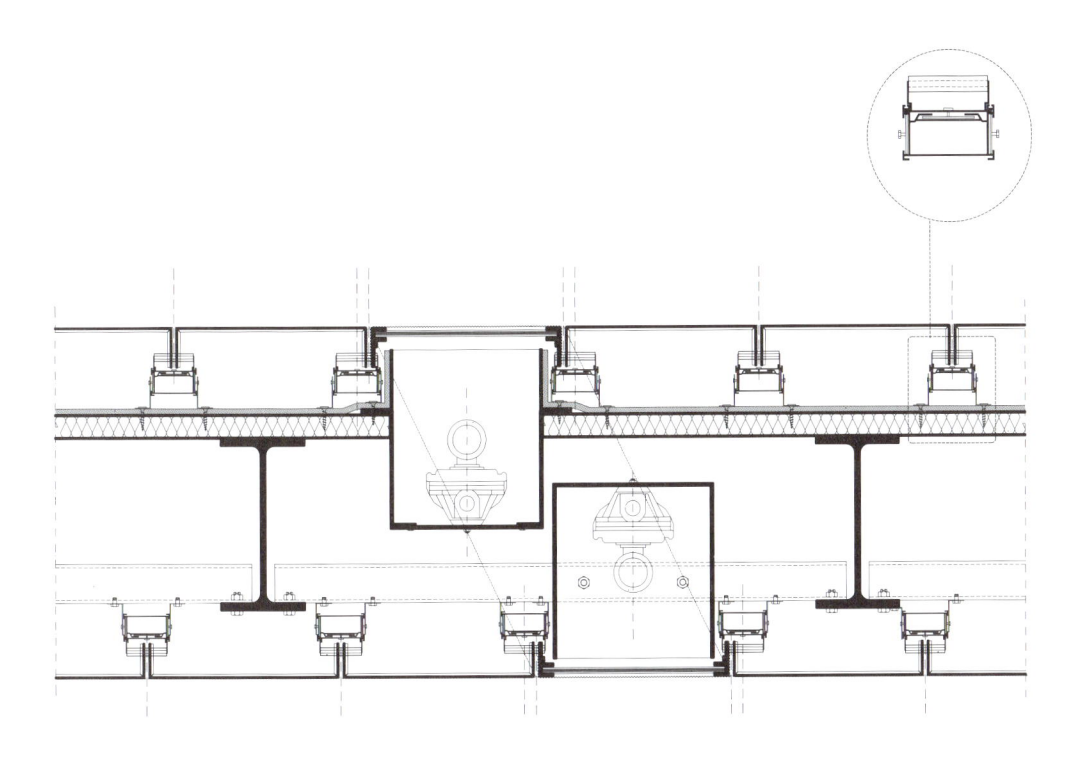

left: Entrance area. right: Canopy, detail_Entrance at night_Façade.
links: Eingangsbereich. rechts: Vordach, Detail_Eingang bei Nacht_Fassade.

ITALY_MILAN **OFECOMES, SPANISH FOREIGN TRADE OFFICE**

INTERIOR DESIGNER: FRANCESC RIFÉ_**COMPLETION:** 2008
NUMBER OF WORKPLACES: 16_**GROSS FLOOR AREA:** 350 M²
COMMON AREA: LUNCH CORNER_**KIND OF WORKPLACES:** COMBINATION, CUBICAL_**PHOTOS:** EUGENI PONS, GIRONA

The comprehensive, stringent design concept fulfills the customer's representation needs coupled with optimal space utilization, while offering employees ultimate functionality and comfort. Strict geometry, hard edges and thinned out volumes define the individual components of the concept. To control the abundant illumination, a lamella system, made of wood for the windows and of PVC for internal dividers, was developed to allow the individual control of privacy and public access of the offices.

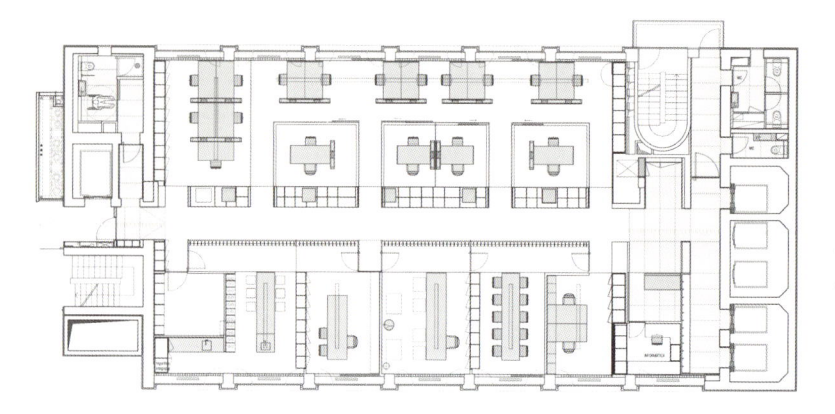

Das übergreifende, stringente Designkonzept erfüllt sowohl repräsentative Bedürfnisse des Auftraggebers als auch dessen Interesse an optimaler Flächennutzung. Darüber hinaus bietet es den Arbeitnehmern aber auch ein Höchstmaß an Funktionalität und Komfort. Strenge Geometrie, harte Kanten und ausgedünnte Volumen vereinheitlichen die einzelnen Teile des Konzepts. Zur Regulierung des reichlich vorhandenen Lichts wurde ein Lamellensystem – aus Holz für die Fenster, aus PVC für die Inneren Abtrennungen – entworfen, so dass Privatheit und Öffentlichkeit der Büros individuell geregelt werden können.

left: Floor plan_Reception_Conference and meeting hall. right: Corridor_Workplaces_ Area for lunch.
links: Grundriss_Empfang_Konferenz- und Besprechungszimmer. rechts: Flur_Arbeitsplätze_Essecke.

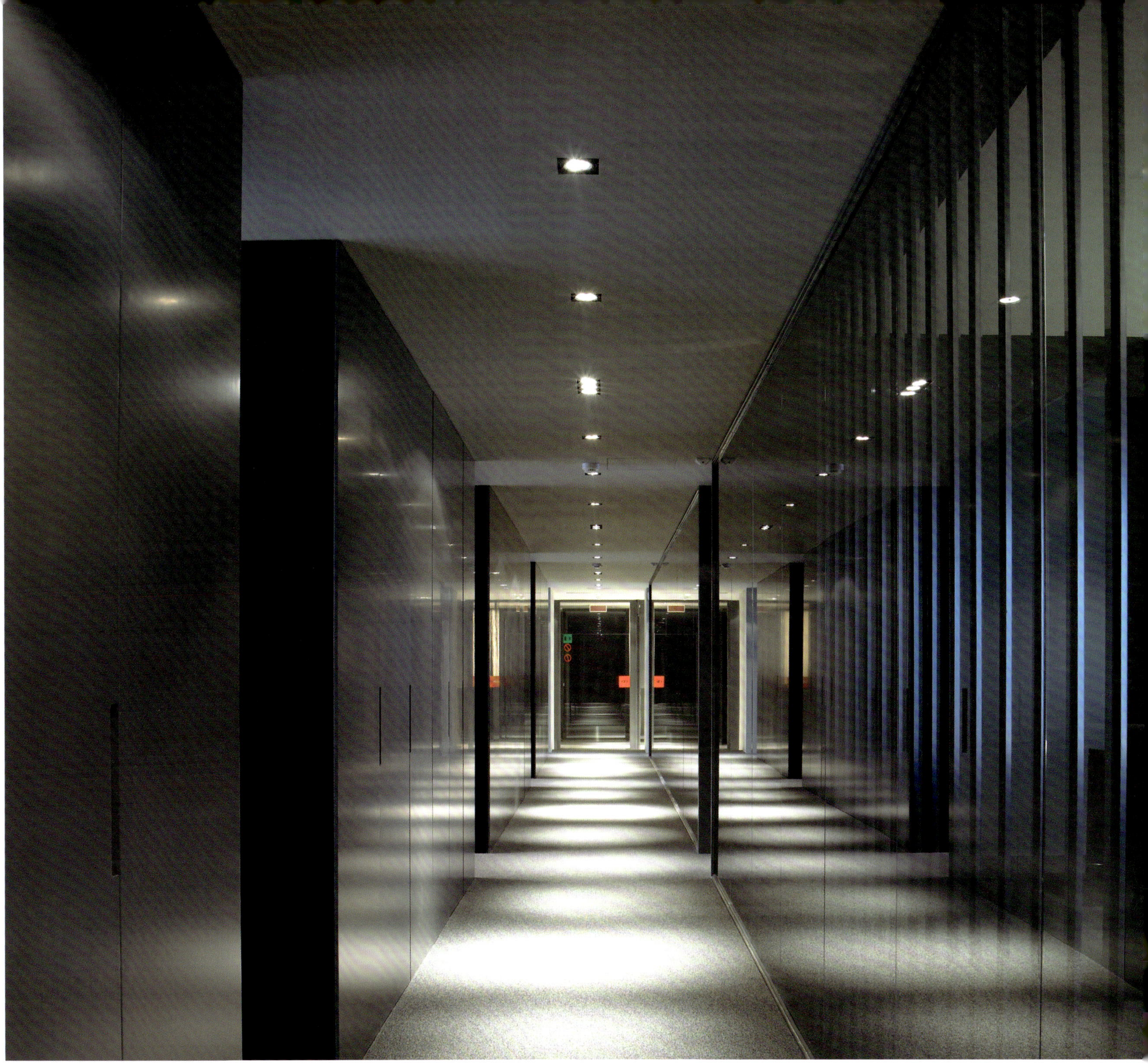

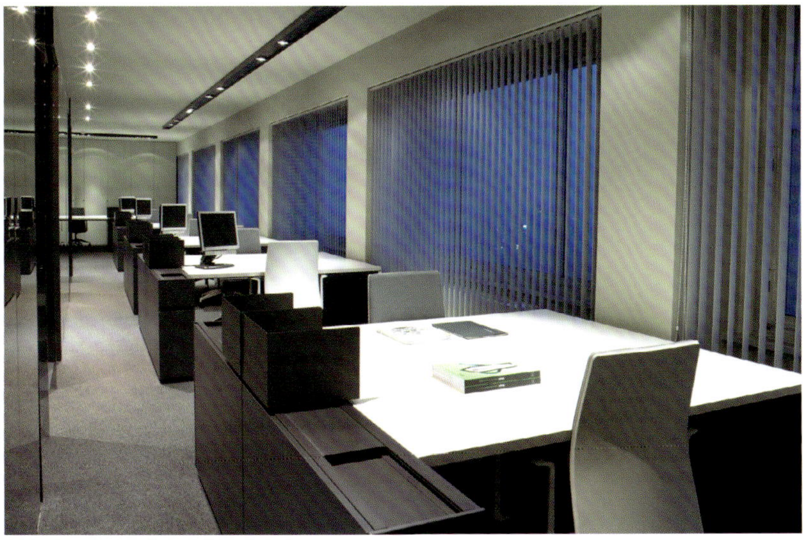

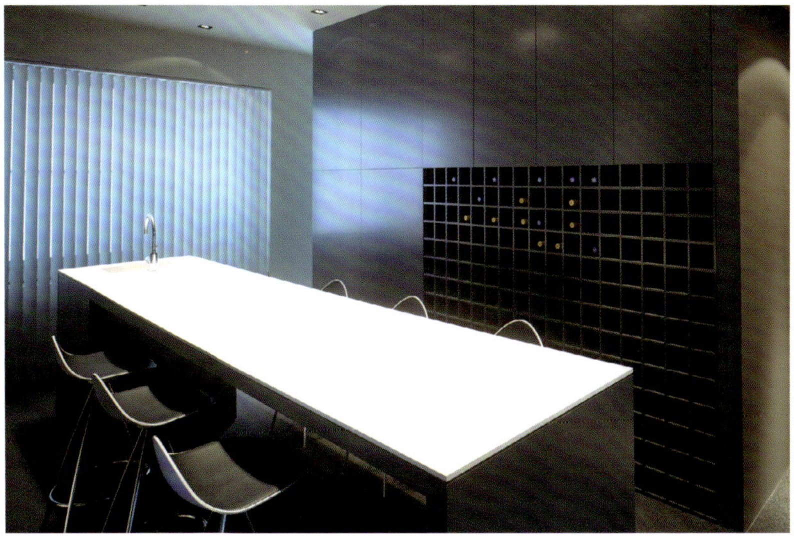

ITALY_PALERMO GLASS BOX IN THE COLUMNS BOX

ARCHITECTS: MARCO VIOLA AND FILIPPO SAPONARO
COMPLETION: 2008_**NUMBER OF WORKPLACES:** 8
GROSS FLOOR AREA: 450 M²_**COMMON AREA:** MEETING ROOMS, SHOWROOM_**KIND OF WORKPLACES:** TEAM
PHOTOS: ADRIANO FERRARA, PALERMO

The construction lot at the edge of Palermo was to be used in such a way as to distinguish it from the industrial building. For this purpose, the existing structure was to be altered as little as possible and the available elements utilized. The project was implemented as two interlaced "boxes". One of them is a grey cement building with beams and columns that creates a neutral space. The second glass box contains the offices and was positioned in the center of the other box. The main element is light – warm and focused on products in the building, and white and technical in the offices. The surprise factor is thus guaranteed.

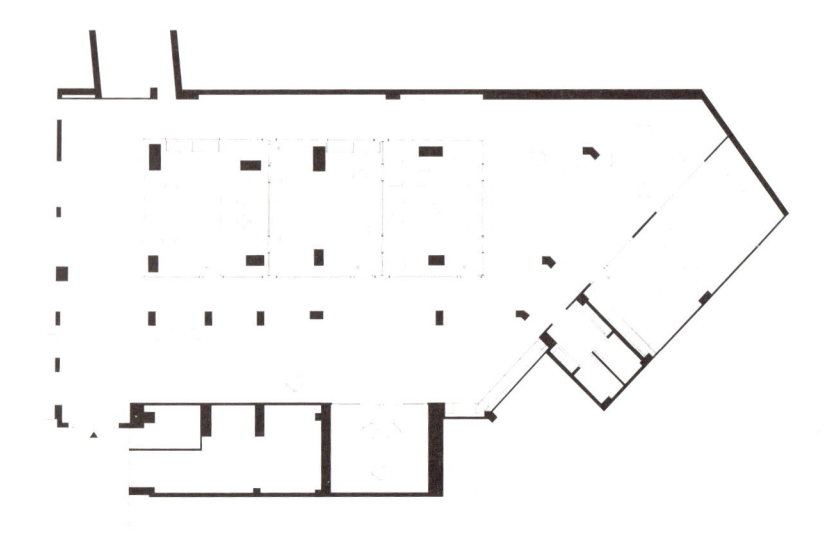

Der Befund am Stadtrand von Palermo sollte so genutzt werden, dass er sich von einem üblichen Industriegebäude abhebt. Dennoch sollte die bestehende Struktur so wenig wie möglich verändert und die zur Verfügung stehenden Elemente genutzt werden. Das Projekt wurde in Form zweier verschachtelter „Kästen" realisiert. Einer davon ist ein Gebäude aus grauem Zement mit Balken und Säulen, das einen neutralen Raum schafft. Der zweite, gläserne Kasten dient den Büroräumen und wurde in der Mitte des anderen Kastens platziert. Das wichtigste Gestaltungsmerkmal ist Licht; im Gebäude warmes und auf die Produkte gerichtetes, in den Büros weißes und technisches, sodass ein Moment der Verwunderung entsteht.

left: Floor plan_Panoramic view_Entrance with metal doors. right: Light box_Offices_Exterior.
links: Grundriss_Gesamtansicht_Eingang mit Metalltüren. rechts: Lichtbox_Büros_Außenansicht.

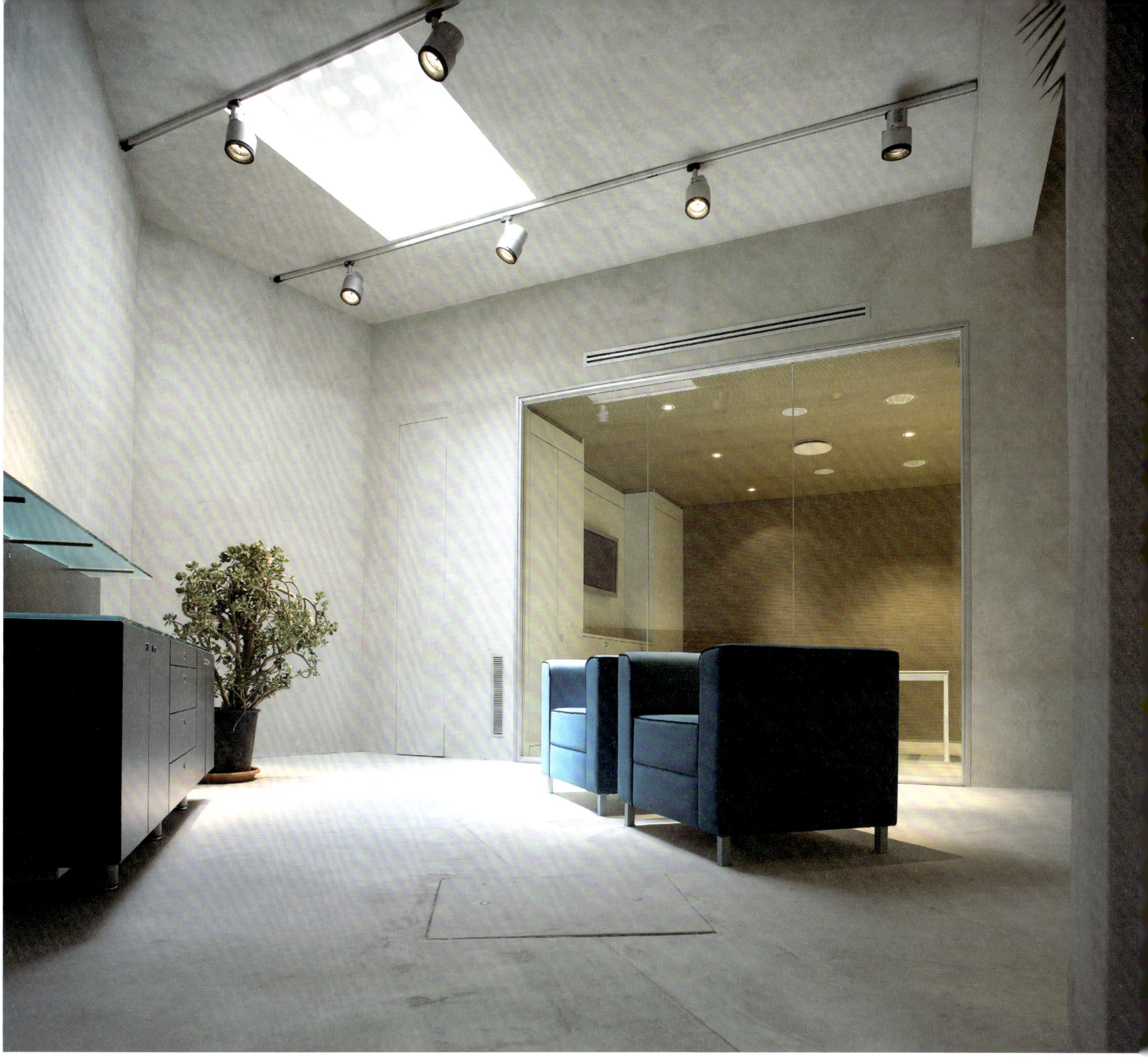

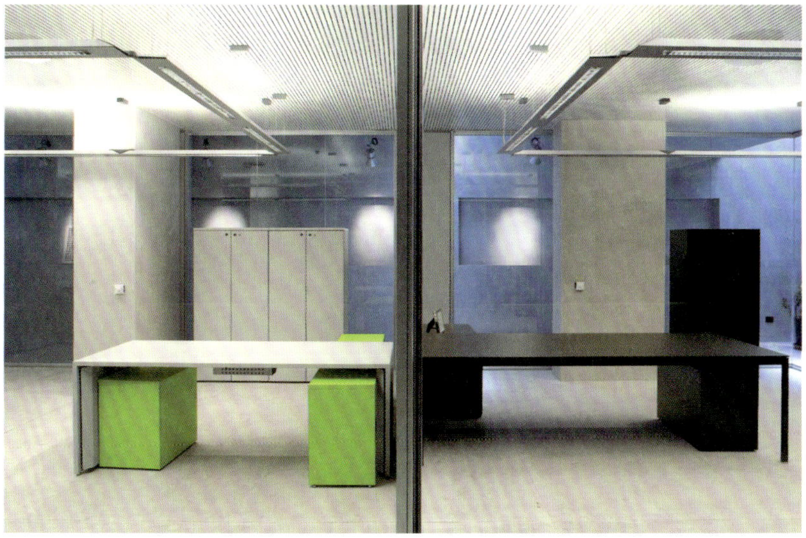

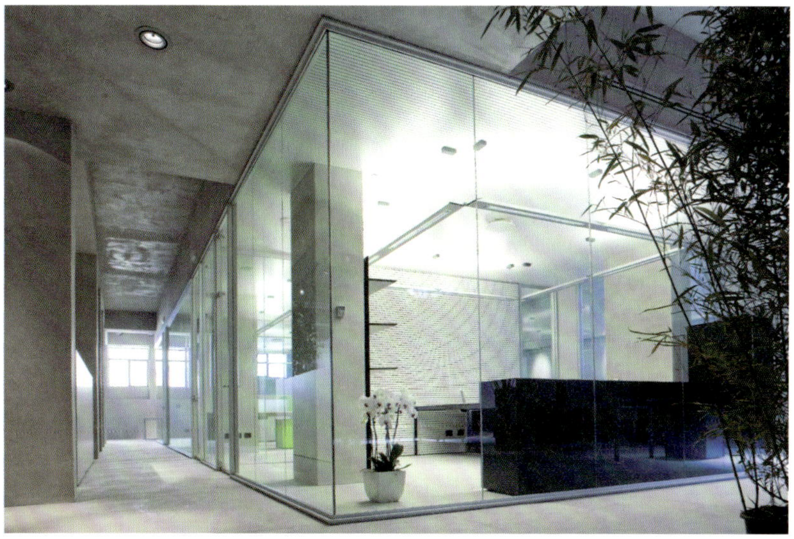

ITALY_ROME **CMB HEADQUARTERS OFFICE**

ARCHITECTS: 3C+T CAPOLEI CAVALLI ARCHITECTS, MOLINARI LANDI ARCHITECTS_**COMPLETION:** 2006
NUMBER OF WORKPLACES: 100_**GROSS FLOOR AREA:** 3,000 M²
COMMON AREA: STAFF CAFÉ, CONFERENCE ROOM, MEETING ROOMS_**KIND OF WORKPLACES:** CELLULAR, COMBINATION, OPEN-PLAN_**PHOTOS:** FABRIZIO CAPOLEI, ROME

The design of the building of one of Italy's most important construction firms is based on the original design of the main structure, combining large windows with integrated Schüco photovoltaic cells and a ventilated façade in brick, a construction material rooted in the Italian tradition. The large structural windows with integrated photovoltaic cells open towards the central part, allowing the sun to permeate the interior and emphasizing the volume towards the outside. CMB's new Rome office is therefore a communication structure on an urban scale, projecting the innovative language and sophisticated energy-saving technology used in its construction.

Im Entwurf des Gesamtbaus für eine der wichtigsten italienischen Baufirmen dominiert das Hauptgeschoss, das mit großen Fenstern mit Schüco Photovoltaikzellen und einer hinterlüfteten Backsteinfassade ausgestattet ist, also einem in Italien tradierten Baumaterial. Das große Fenster mit integrierter Photovoltaic öffnet den mittleren Teil des Gebäudes und ermöglicht das Eindringen von Sonnenlicht ins Innere, betont aber das Volumen am Außenbau. Das neue Büro von CMB in Rom kommuniziert mit seinem innovativen Erscheinungsbild raffinierte Energieeinsparung in den Stadtraum.

left: Site plan_Front elevation_Entrance_Detail, façade. right: East elevation_Façade_Building angle_Office with photovoltaic detail.
links: Lageplan_Hauptfassade_Eingang_Detail, Fassade. rechts: Ostfassade_Fassadendetail_Gebäude-ecke_Büro mit Photovoltaik Detail.

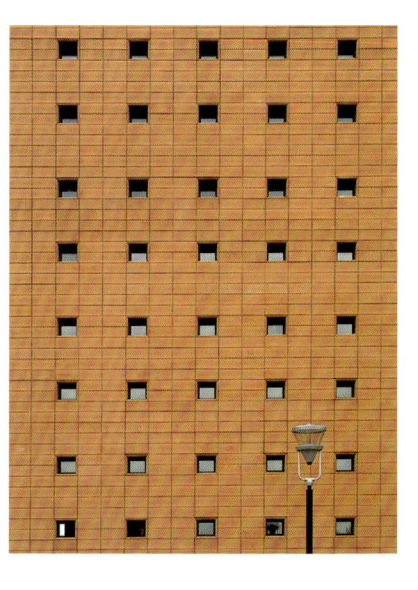

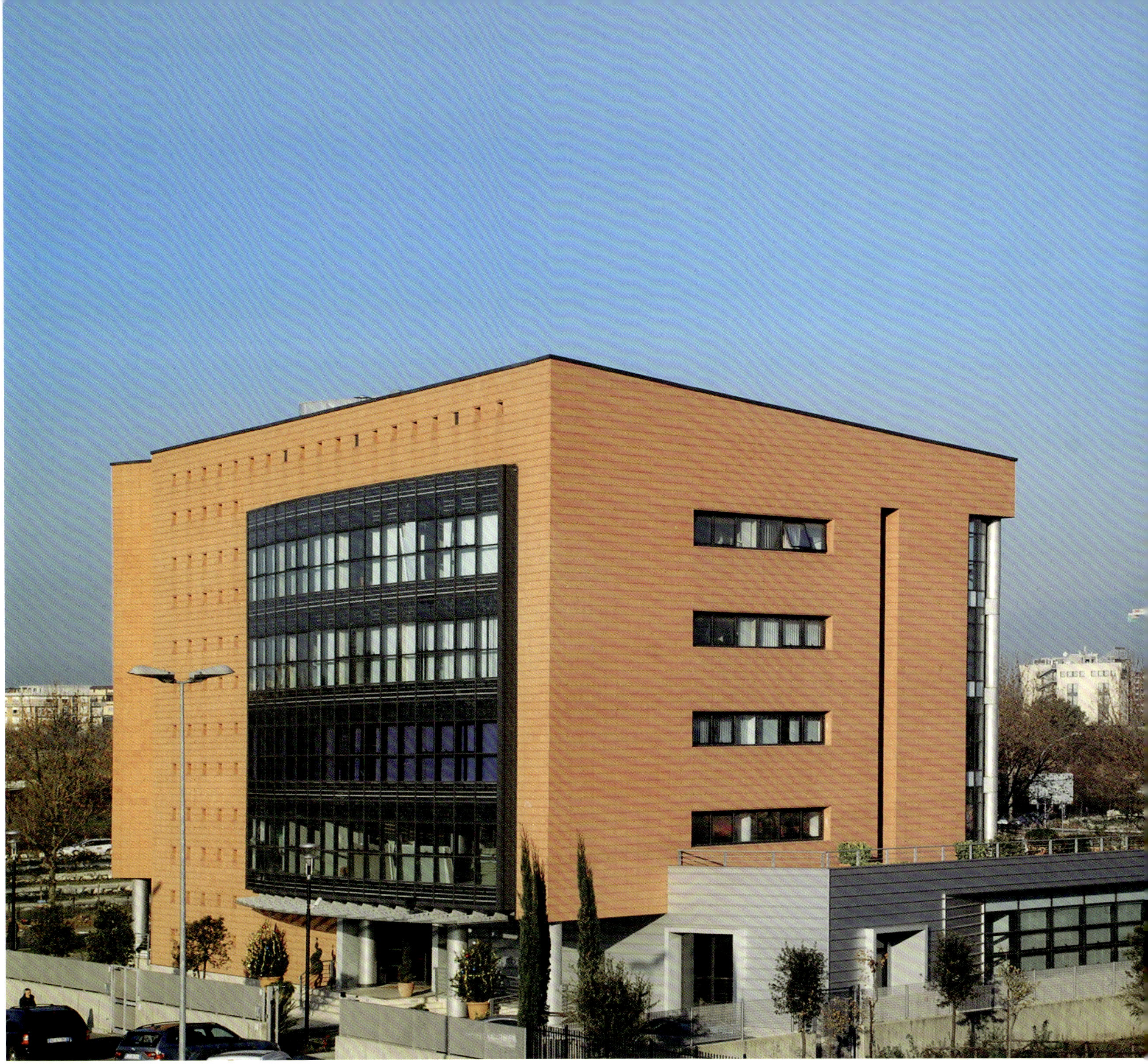
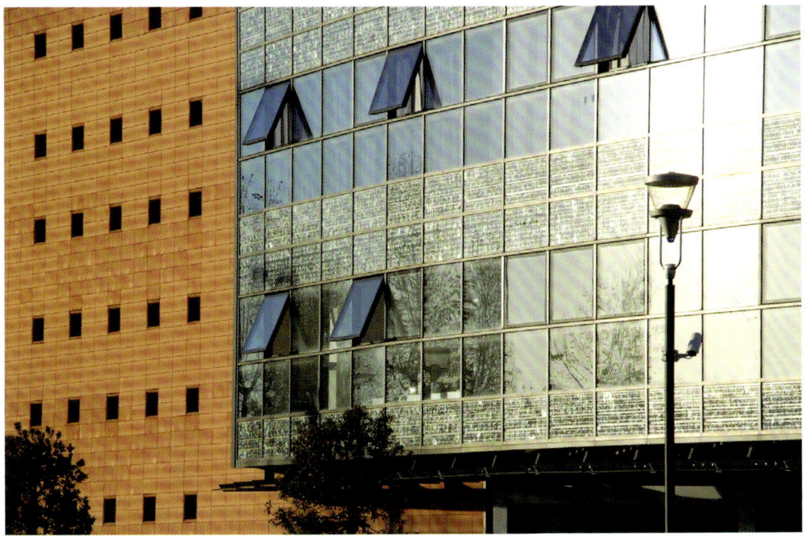
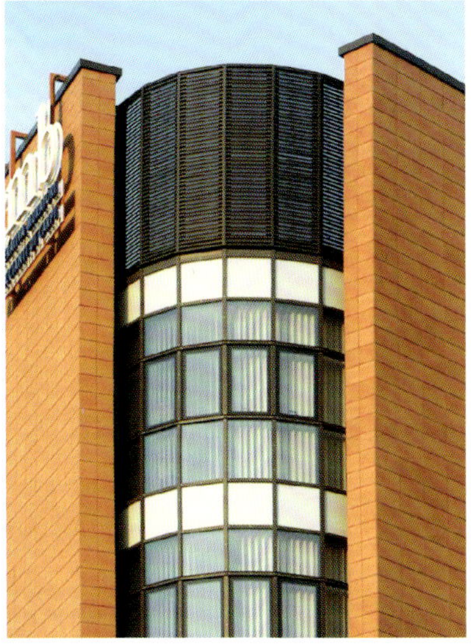
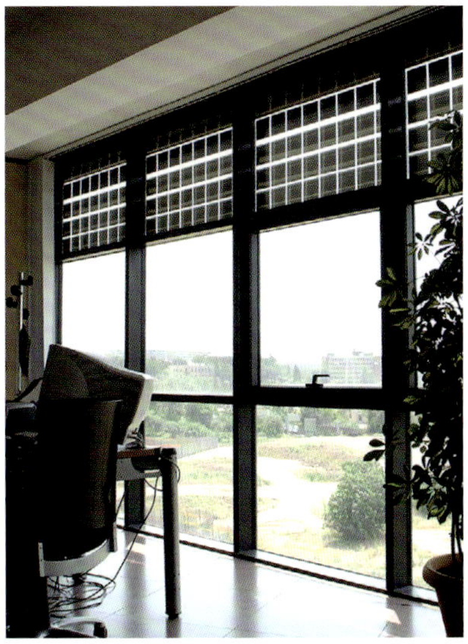

LITHUANIA_KAUNAS OFFICE CENTRE 1000

ARCHITECTS: JSC RA STUDIJA_**COMPLETION:** 2008
NUMBER OF WORKPLACES: 300_**GROSS FLOOR AREA:** 440 M²
COMMON AREA: 10TH FLOOR CONFERENCE CENTER
KIND OF WORKPLACES: CELLULAR
PHOTOS: COURTESY OF THE ARCHITECTS

This class A office and service center represents a 1,000 Lithuanian litas banknote from 1925, the period of Lithuania's independence between the two devastating world wars. The façade is covered with a striking illustration, consisting of 4,500 different pieces of glass that were assembled like a puzzle. Complicated "silk graphic" technology was chosen to paint the ornament on the glass using special enamel, which later becomes ceramic. To depict the original banknote image, the building façade lights up with white, green and blue lights in the evening. During the day it reflects white and dark grey colors. Shadows falling indoors leave watermark reflections, creating a lively atmosphere inside.

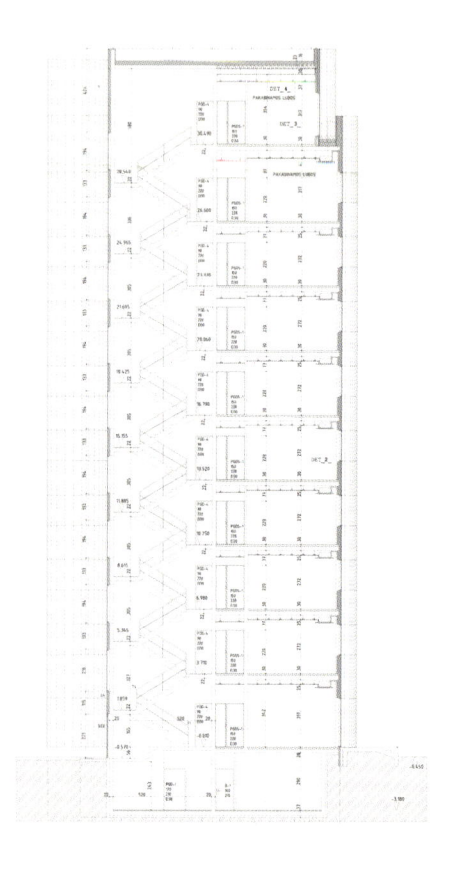

Dieses Büro und Servicecenter stellt einen 1.000-litauische-Litas-Schein von 1925 dar, der Zeit von Litauens Unabhängigkeit zwischen den beiden verheerenden Weltkriegen. Die Fassade bietet eine eindrucksvolle Illustration, die aus 4.500, wie in einem Puzzle zusammengefügten, Glasteilen besteht. Aufwendige Seidengrafik-Technologie wurde gewählt, um die Verzierung mit einer speziellen Glasur auf das Glas aufzutragen, die sich später im Prozess zu Keramik wandelt. Um das Originalbild des Scheins zu komplettieren, leuchten abends weiße, grüne und blaue Lichter an der Fassade. Tagsüber spiegelt sie weiße und dunkelgraue Farbtöne wider. Hineinfallende Schatten hinterlassen Reflexionen wie Wasserzeichen, die im Inneren für eine lebhafte Atmosphäre sorgen.

left: Section_General view_Façade by night. right: General view.
links: Schnitt_Gesamtansicht_Fassade bei Nacht. rechts: Gesamtansicht.

1000
Taikos pr. 88A
SEB
SNORAS
EASY OFFICE
1000
1000
TUKSTANTIS
1000

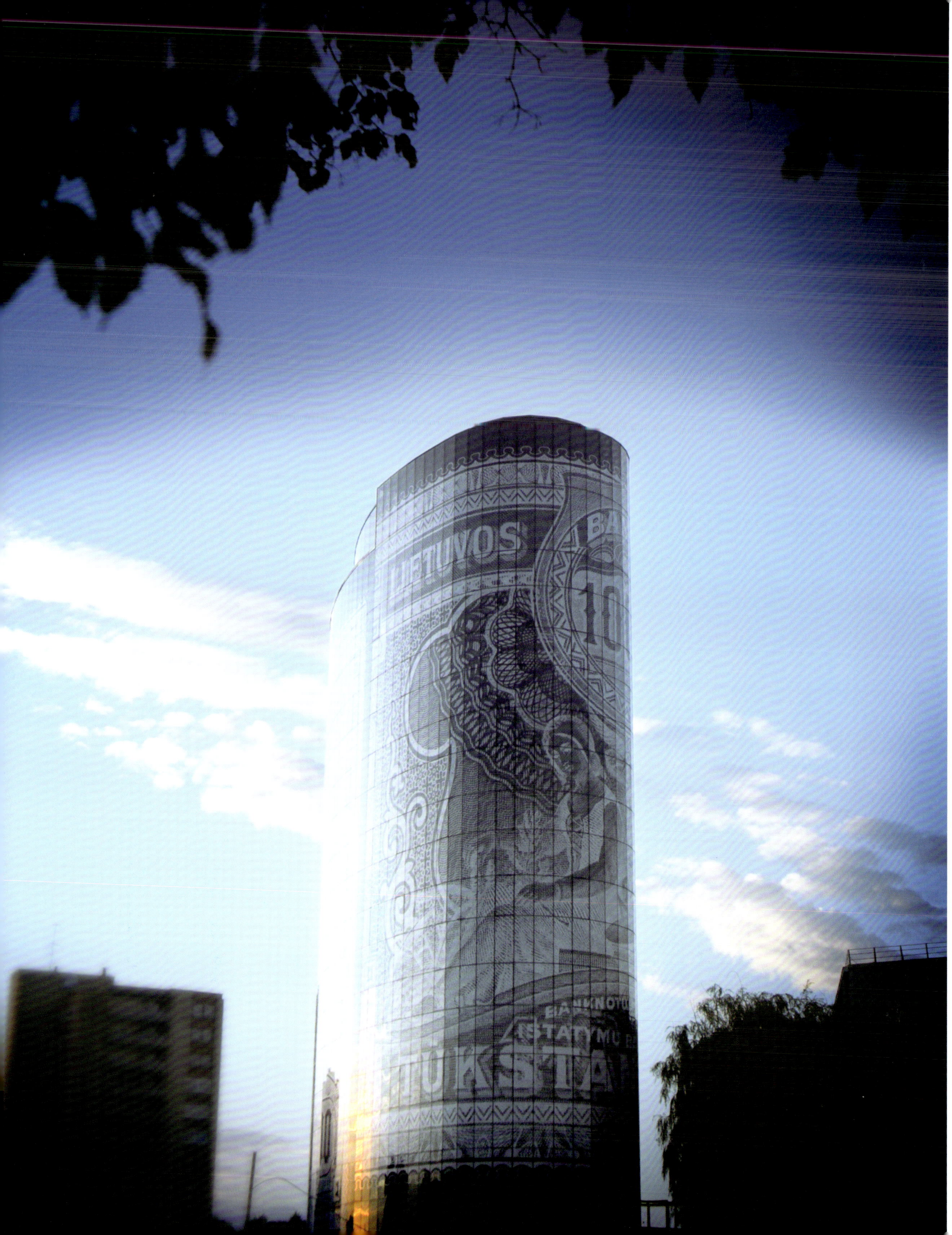
LIETUVOS

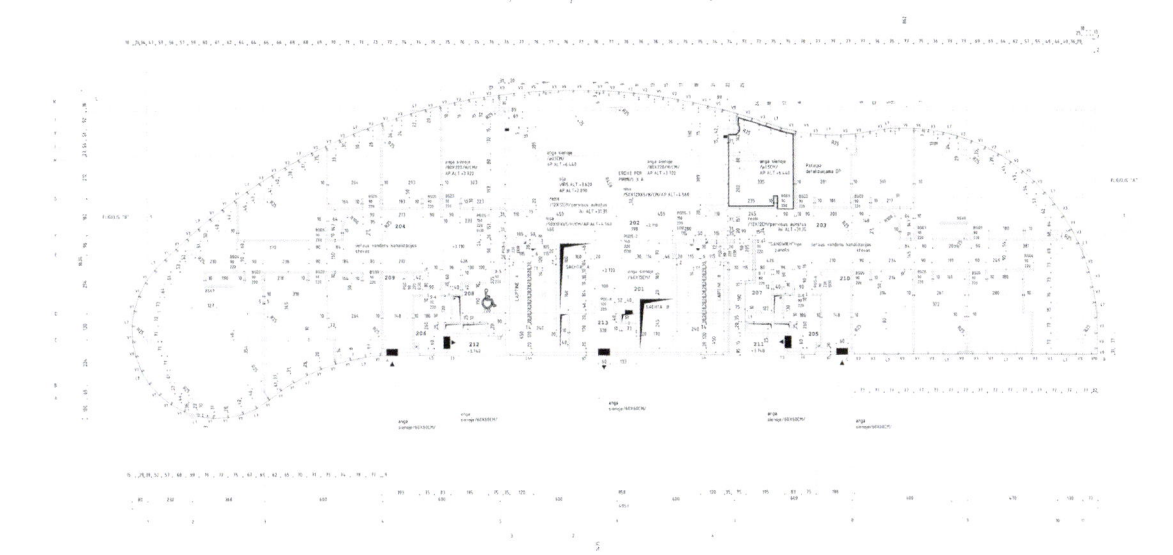

left: Elevation. right: Floor plan_Bird's-eye view, hall_Window, detail_Façade by night.
links: Ansicht. rechts. Grundriss_Vogelperspektive, Halle_Fenster, Detail_Fassade bei Nacht.

LITHUANIA_VILNIUS **MFT OFFICE**

ARCHITECTS: AUDRIUS BUČAS AND MARINA BUCIENĖ
COMPLETION: 2009_**NUMBER OF WORKPLACES:** 7
GROSS FLOOR AREA: 88 M²_**KIND OF WORKPLACES:** OPEN-PLAN
PHOTOS: RAIMONDAS URBAKAVICIUS

A long narrow corridor squeezed between the brick walls leads to the compact main office area. MFT focuses on invention, but also engages in manufacturing and installation. The main idea was to capture and reflect the whole process, i.e. manufacturing, thinking and creating. Technological elements were used to show the process and the image of constant motion, which is best portrayed by the conveyer. Thus all interior elements, including partitions and desks, can be moved by means of rails fixed to the ceiling. Convex surfaces of movable planes distort reality and present opportunities to improvise when looking for the answers to traditional questions.

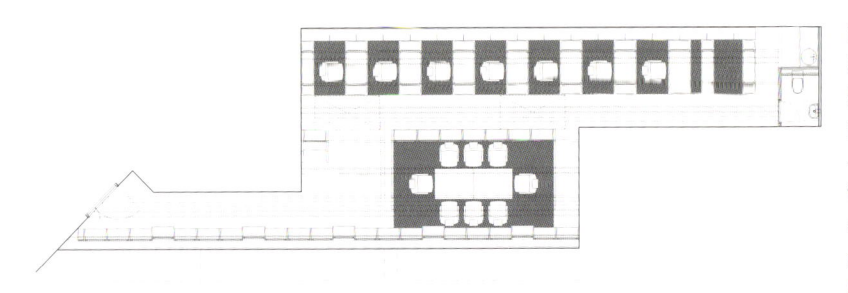

Ein langer, schmaler Korridor führt zwischen Backsteinwänden in den kompakten Bürobereich. Auch wenn sich MFT auf Innovation konzentriert, befasst sich die Firma doch auch mit Herstellung und Montage. Kernidee des Entwurfs ist, den gesamten Prozess – Überlegung, Kreativität und Produktion – darzustellen und zu reflektieren. Der prozesshafte Charakter wurde durch technische Elemente versinnbildlicht, konstante Bewegung lässt mit dem Bild eines Fließbandes dargestellt. Deshalb sind alle Elemente wie Trennwände und Schreibtische mittels Schienen an der Decke beweglich aufgehängt. Die konvexen Oberflächen brechen die Realität und stehen für die Gelegenheit zu Improvisieren, auch wenn man sich mit bekannten Fragen beschäftigt.

left: Floor plan_First step in the office area_Office view from entrance_Hanging desk. right: Meeting room_Hanging desks, when seen throug convex glass partition of meeting room_Office view from meeting room.
links: Grundriss_Eingang in den Bürobereich_Blick durch das Büro vom Eingang_Hängender Schreibtisch. rechts: Besprechungszimmer_Blick durch das gebogene Glasteil des Besprechungraums auf die hängenden Schreibtische_Blick durch das Büro vom Besprechungszimmer aus.

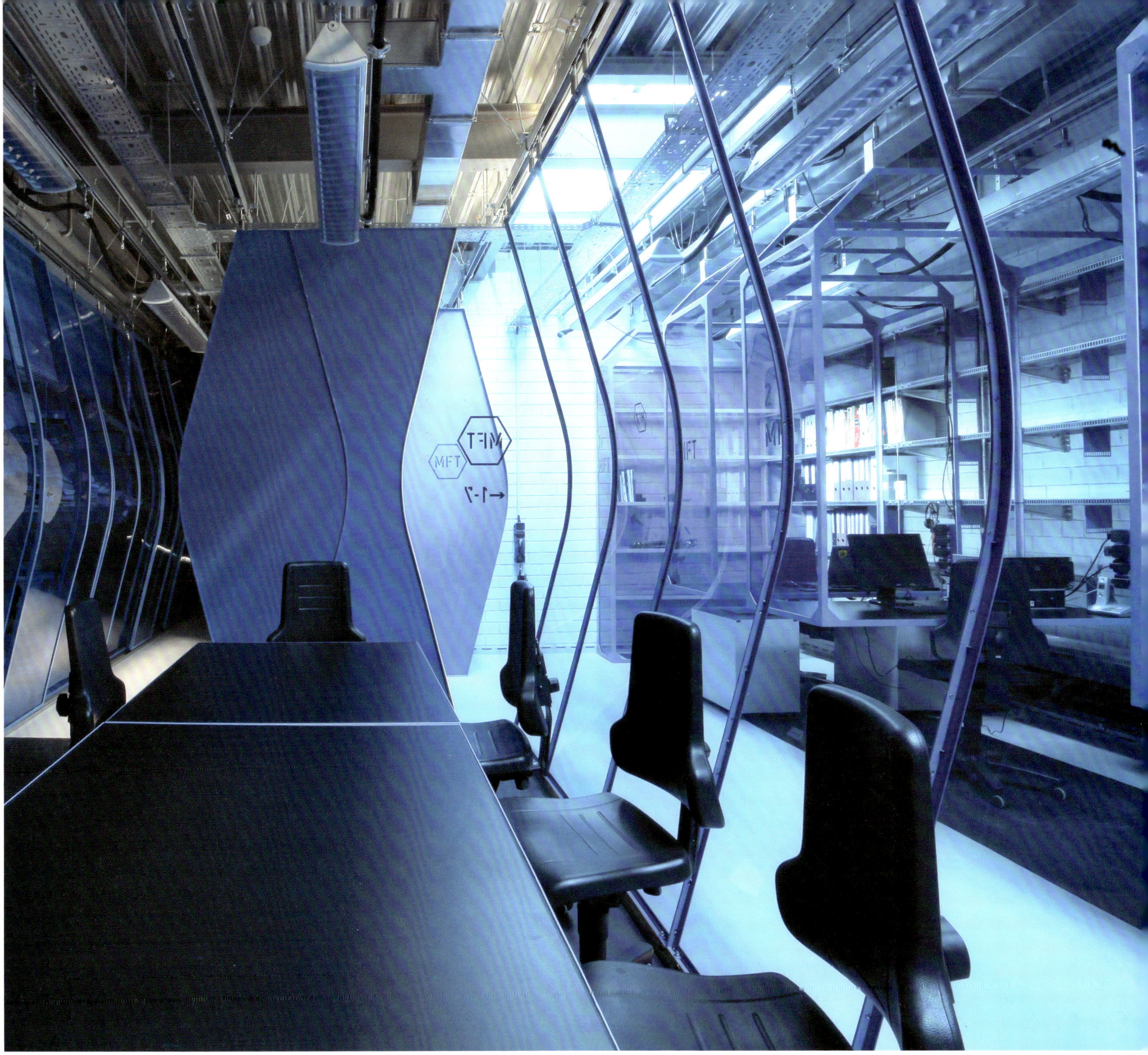
MFT
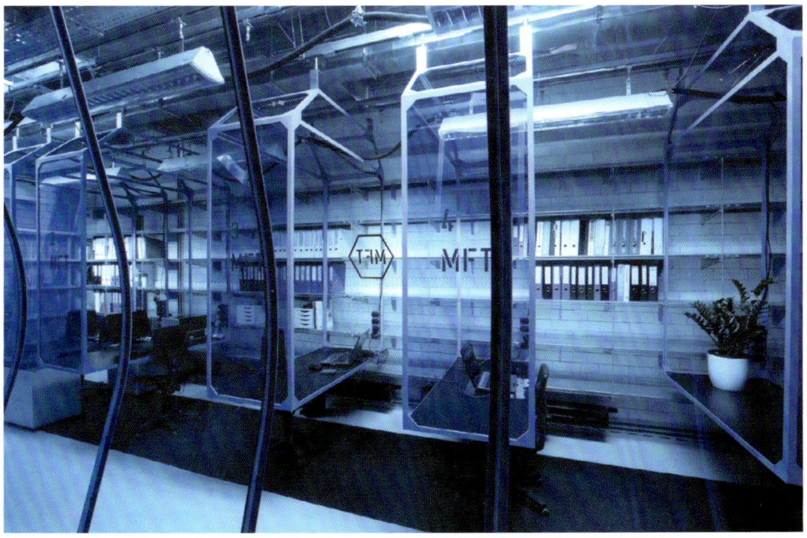
MFT
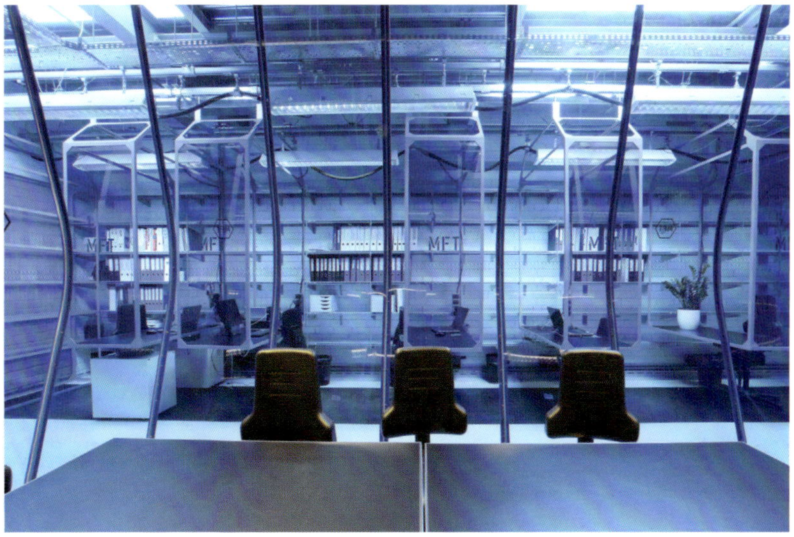
MFT

THE NETHERLANDS_ALMERE OFFICES "LA DEFENSE"

ARCHITECTS: UNSTUDIO
COMPLETION: 2004
GROSS FLOOR AREA: 70,000 M2
PHOTOS: VIVIANE SASSEN

This office appears in its urban context as a modest building volume that reflects its direct surroundings in its metallic façade finishing. The outer skin expresses uniformity and a degree of closeness of the units. Entering the inner courtyard, the building reveals its unique features. The façade adjacent to the courtyard is made of glass panels into which a multi-colored foil is integrated. Dependent on the time of the day and the angel of incidence, the façade changes from yellow to blue to red, or from purple to green and back again. Designed to be used by a number of companies, the units vary in height from five or six to three or four levels, the top level often being a duplex.

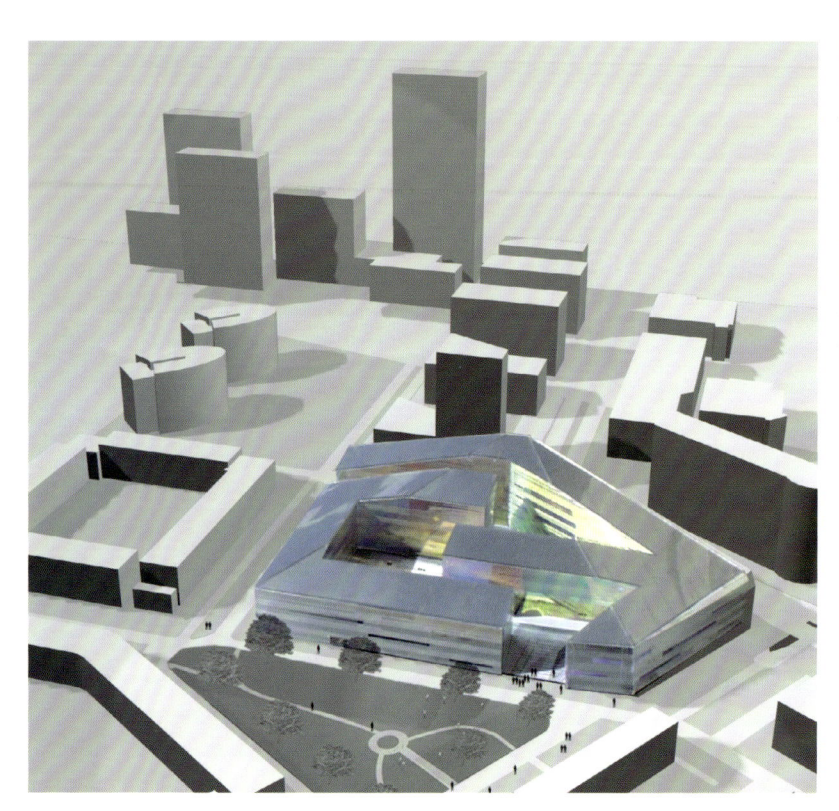

Das Bürogebäude integriert sich mit seiner metallisch glänzenden Fassade, in der sich die Umgebung spiegelt, in den städtischen Kontext. Mit dieser Außenhaut ist es einerseits urban, grenzt jedoch andererseits die Einheiten deutlich ab. Erst im Innenhof werden die eigenen Qualitäten deutlich. Die Hoffassaden bestehen aus Glasscheiben, die eine mehrfarbige Folie einschließen und so eine von Uhrzeit und Blickwinkel abhängige Färbung von Gelb zu Blau, zu Rot, oder von Purpur zu Grün und zurück aufweisen. Die Einheiten, die vielen verschiedenen Nutzern dienen sollen, haben fünf oder sechs beziehungsweise drei oder vier Geschosse und oft eine zweigeschossige Nutzung in den Obergeschossen.

left: Situation_Aerial view_Façade. right: Color impression_Façade, detail_Impression.
links: Lageplan_Luftaufnahme_Fassade. rechts: Farbimpression_Fassadendetail_Impression.

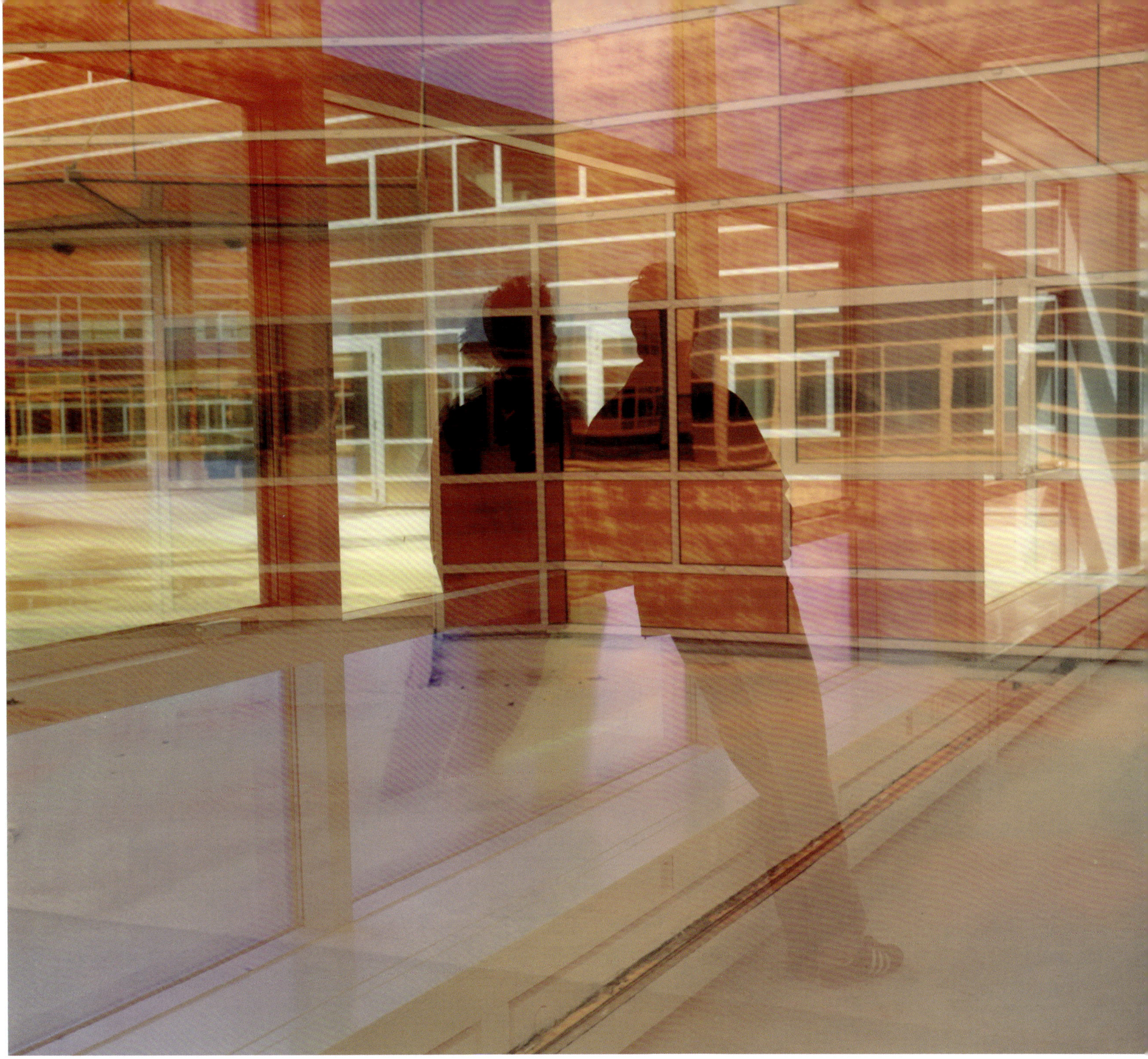
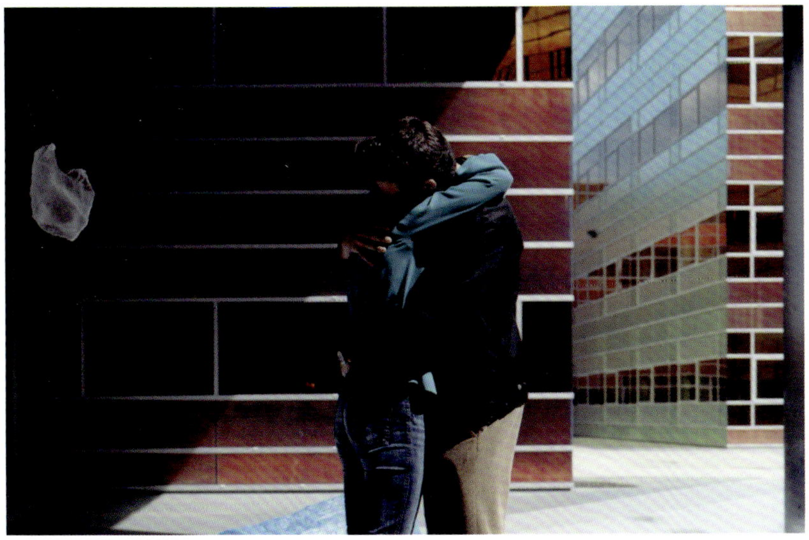
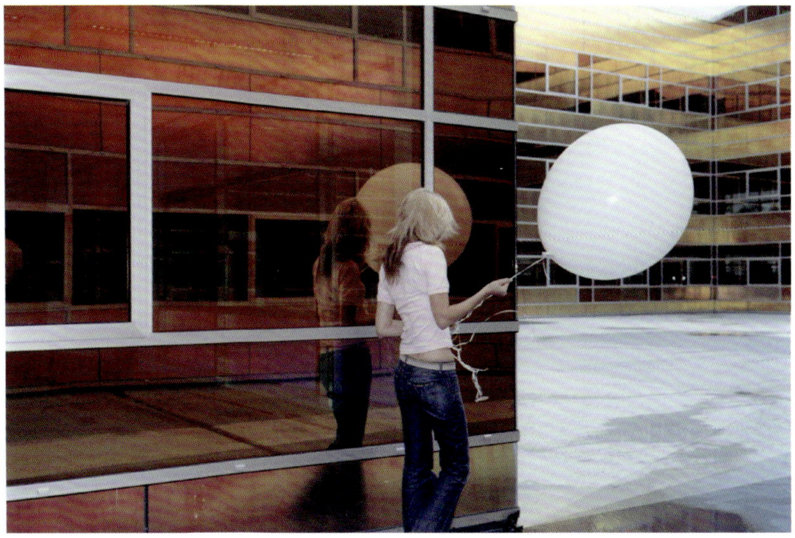

THE NETHERLANDS_AMSTERDAM ERICK VAN EGERAAT OFFICE TOWER

ARCHITECTS: ERICK VAN EGERAAT
COMPLETION: 2009 **NUMBER OF WORKPLACES:** 800
GROSS FLOOR AREA: 33,500 M² **COMMON AREA:** RESTAURANT, AUDITORIUM, CONFERENCE ROOMS, LIBRARY, FOYER, KNOW-HOW-ZONES **KIND OF WORKPLACES:** CELLULAR, TEAM
PHOTOS: CHRISTIAN RICHTERS

The office tower is part of the Zuid-As 'High-Rise' development south of Amsterdam based on an urban concept developed by De Architecten Cie. This consists of a vertical layered structure with the anatomical analogy of legs, torso and head. The tower challenges this by creating an explicit tactile and emotional presence rising out of the stacked block structure. Both an innovative composition of shifted volumes and a transformation from light to heavy materialization, it creates an expressive landmark which appears different from every angle. The lower part of the building is transparent, the upper part is characterized by a natural stone pattern and both are connected by a combination of transparent and printed glass elements and aluminum panels.

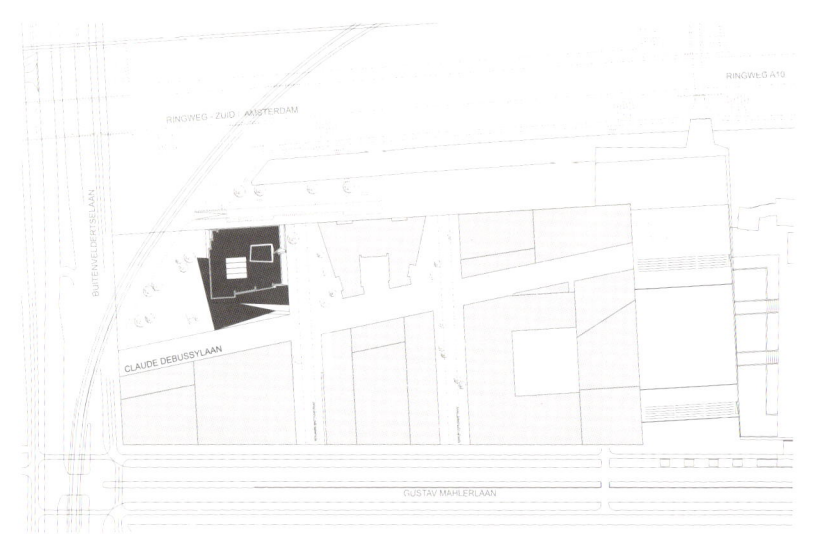

Das Büro ist Teil des Zuid-As Hochhaus-Entwicklungsgebietes auf Basis eines Plans von De Architecten Cie. Dieser sieht eine vertikale Teilung des Bauvolumens entsprechend der anatomischen Analogie Beine, Torso, Kopf vor. Der Turm stellt sich dieser Herausforderung, indem er die gestapelte Struktur in taktile und emotionale Erlebnisse auflöst. Die innovative Komposition verdrehter Volumina und die Verwandlung vom Leichten zum Schweren lassen ein von jeder Blickrichtung anders erscheinendes Wahrzeichen entstehen. Der untere Teil des Baues ist transparent, der Kopf hingegen durch ein Muster aus Naturstein schwer erscheinend und beide Teile werden durch einen Rumpf aus transparenten wie bedrucktem Glas und Aluminiumplatten verbunden.

left: Site plan_Exterior_Atrium_Corridor. right: Lobby_Staircase_Entrance_Office.
links: Lageplan_Außenansicht_Atrium_Flur. rechts: Lobby_Treppe_Eingang_Büro.

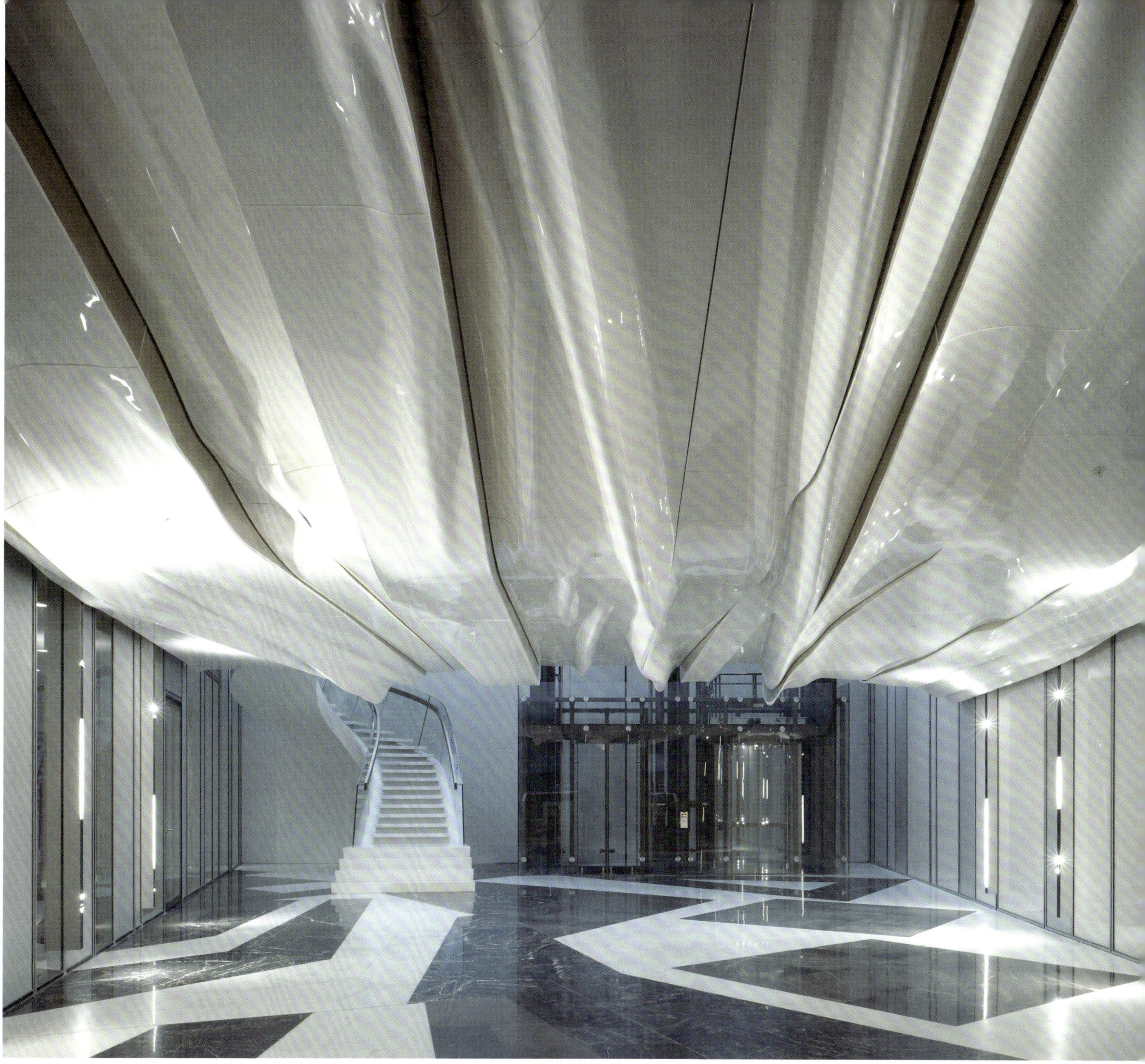
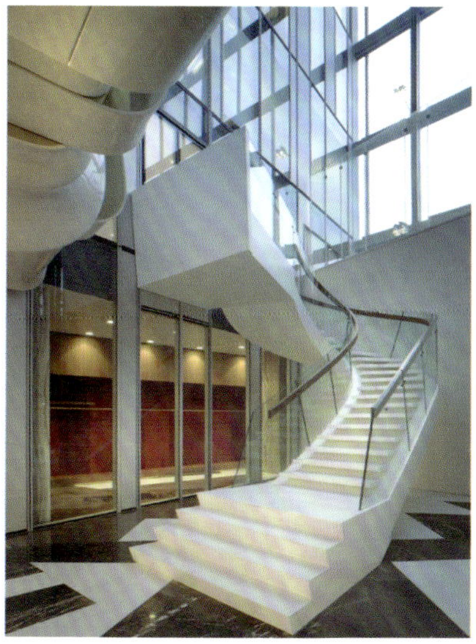
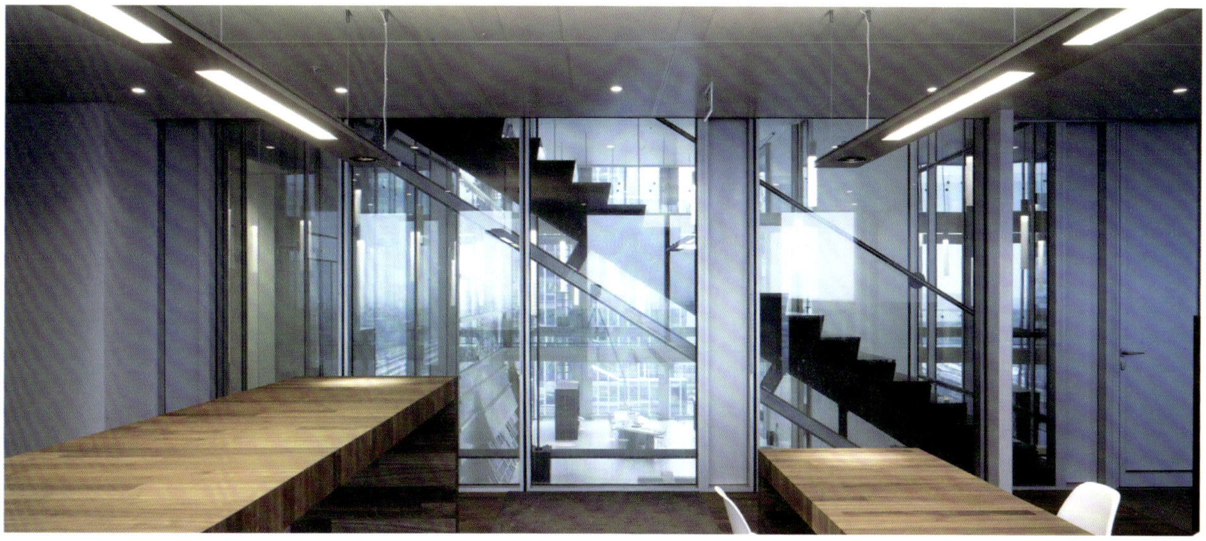

THE NETHERLANDS_AMSTERDAM POST PANIC AMSTERDAM

ARCHITECTS: MAURICE MENTJENS
WALL-GRAPHICS: POST PANIC
COMPLETION: 2009_**NUMBER OF WORKPLACES:** 40
GROSS FLOOR AREA: 565 M²_**KIND OF WORKPLACES:** COMBINATION, OPEN-PLAN, TEAM, NON-TERRITORIAL, DESKSHARING_**PHOTOS:** ARJEN SCHMITZ

The biggest priority of this project was functionality. On the one hand, separate areas to house Post Panic's different departments and facilities were required, while on the other the feel of an open space was to be preserved. Post Panic wanted to create an environment within which it could work for clients, feel inspired and pursue its own internal projects. The space had not only to reflect the company's personality and creative attitude but also provide a functioning work environment and inspirational space. Mentjens' conceptual approach guarantees that the different atmospheres come together as one world. This dynamic, inviting environment surely offers Post Panic all the required room to play.

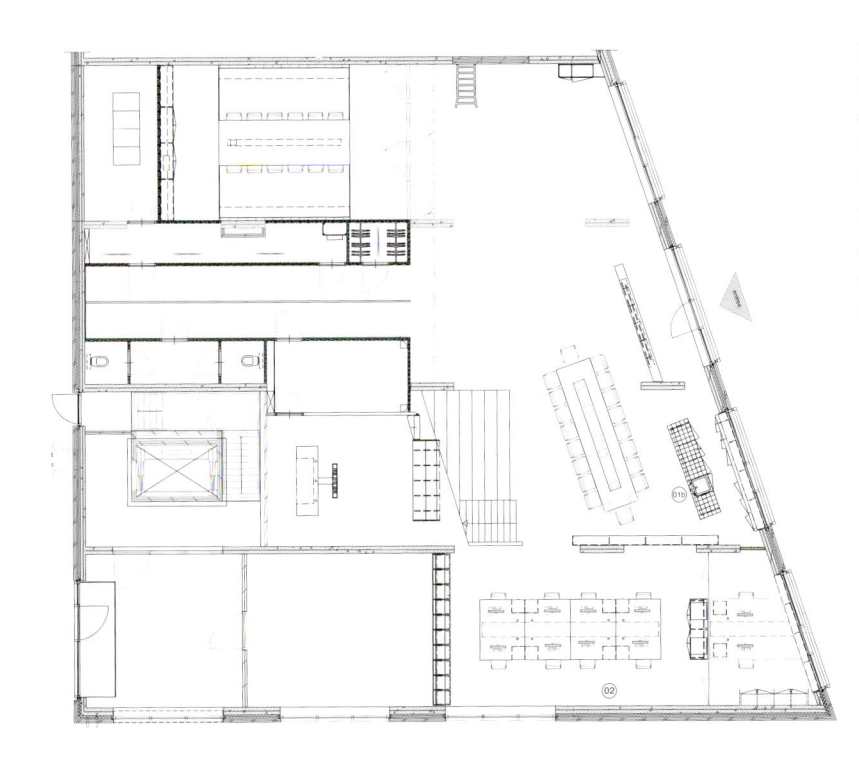

Hauptanliegen des Ausbaus, der unterschiedliche Räume und Einrichtungen in verschiedene Bereiche unterbrachte, gleichzeitig aber den Charakter eines Großraumbüros bewahrte, war die Schaffung von Funktionalität. Post Panic wünschte ein Umfeld, in dem Arbeit für Kunden, Inspiration und eigene Projekte zusammenfinden konnten. Der Raum sollte nicht allein das Charakteristische und die Arbeitsweise der Firma herausstellen, sondern auch als Arbeitsumgebung und Inspirationsraum fungieren. Mentjens konzeptioneller Ansatz garantiert das Zusammenspiel der verschiedenen Bereiche. Das dynamische, einladende Umfeld gibt Post Panic den benötigten Spielraum.

left: Ground floor plan_Entrance, bar, kitchen and café_Production area. right: Waiting area for customers.
links: Grundriss Erdgeschoss_Eingang, Bar, Küche und Cafeteria_Produktionsbereich. rechts: Wartezone für Besucher.

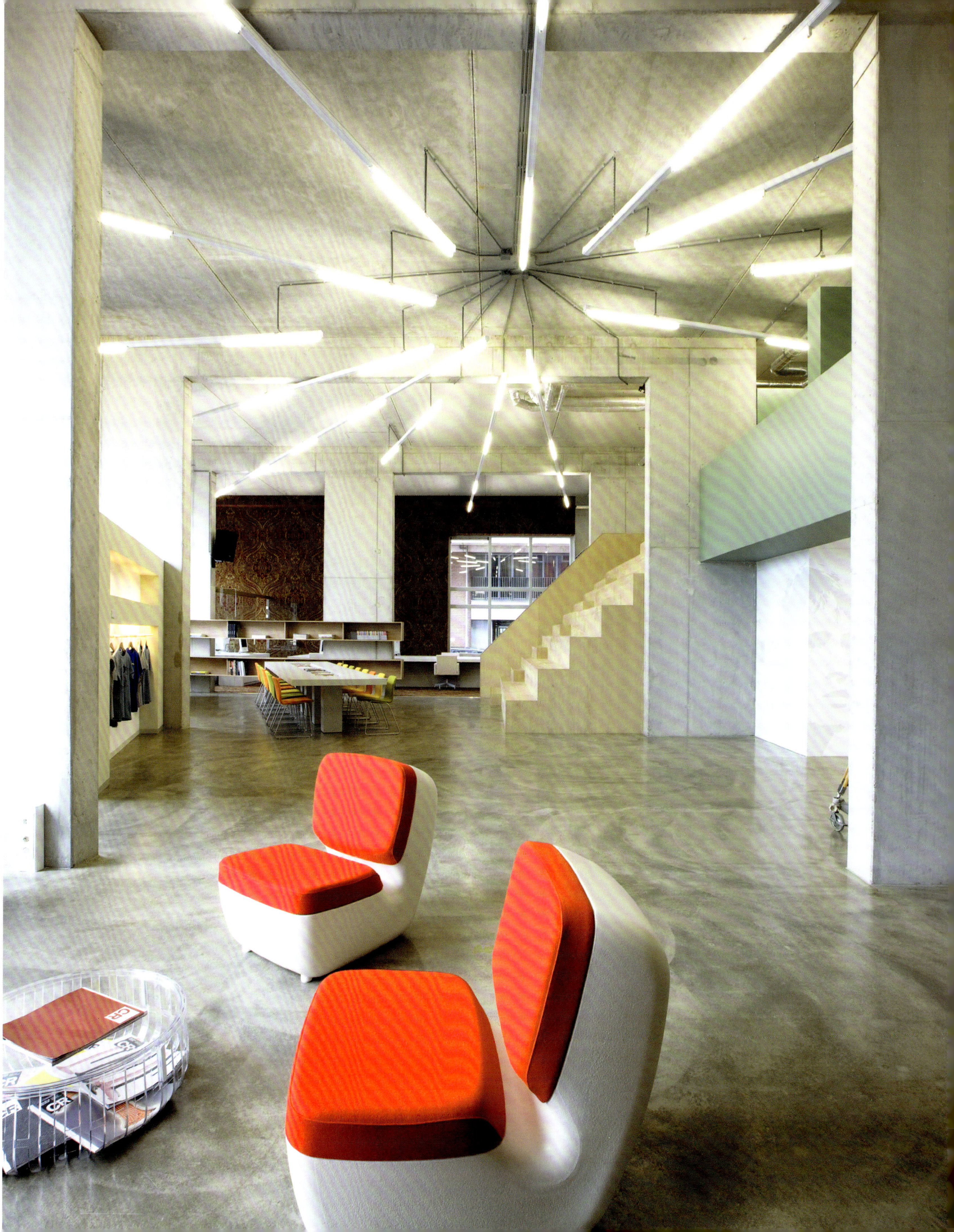

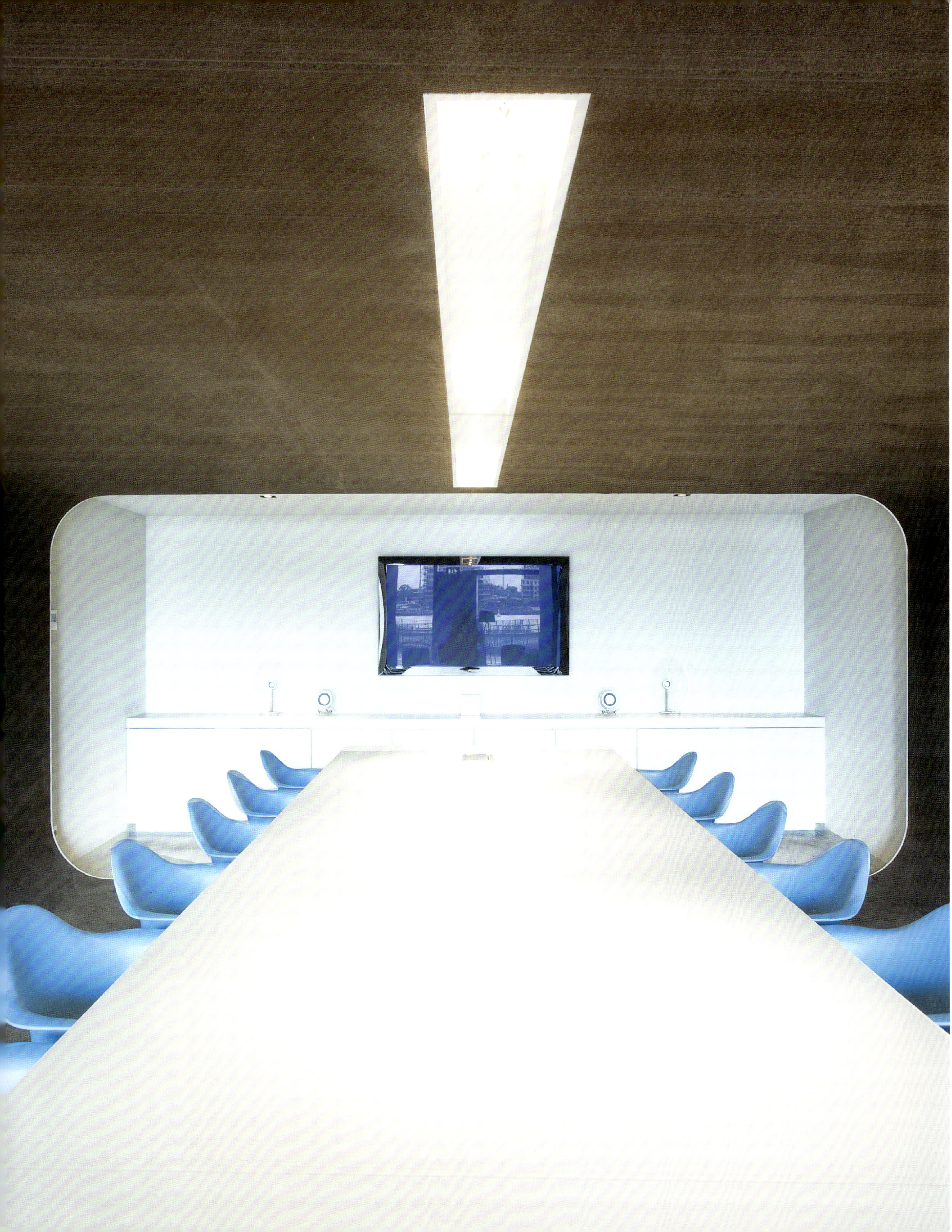

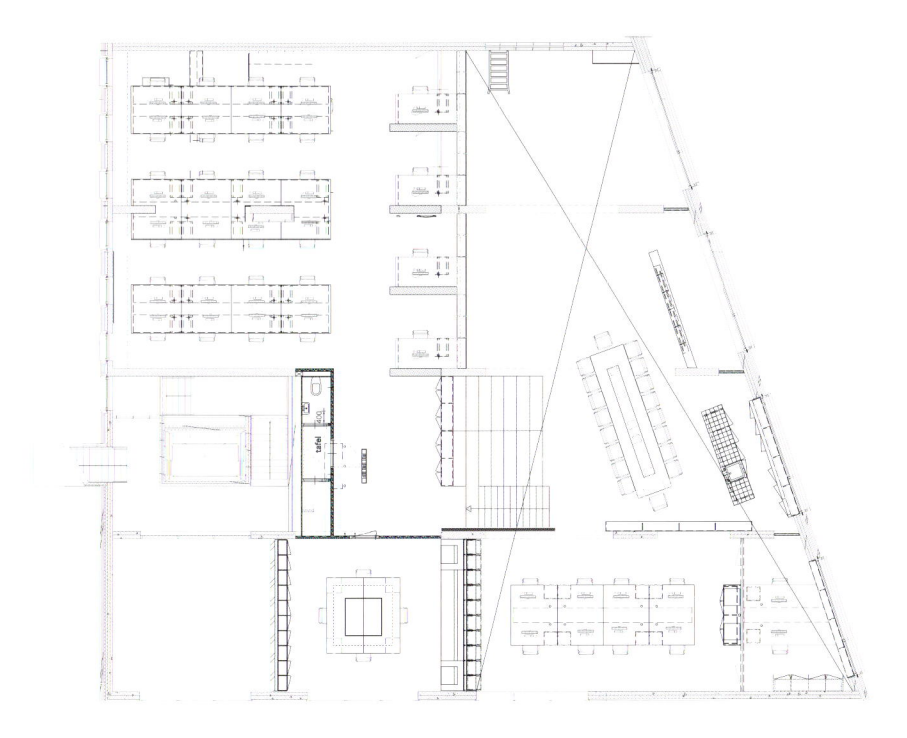

left: Meeting room. right: First floor plan_Directors office_Grandstand_ Meeting room.
links: Besprechungszimmer. rechts: Grundriss Obergeschoss_Büro der Direktoren_Tribüne mit Sitzstufen_Besprechungszimmer.

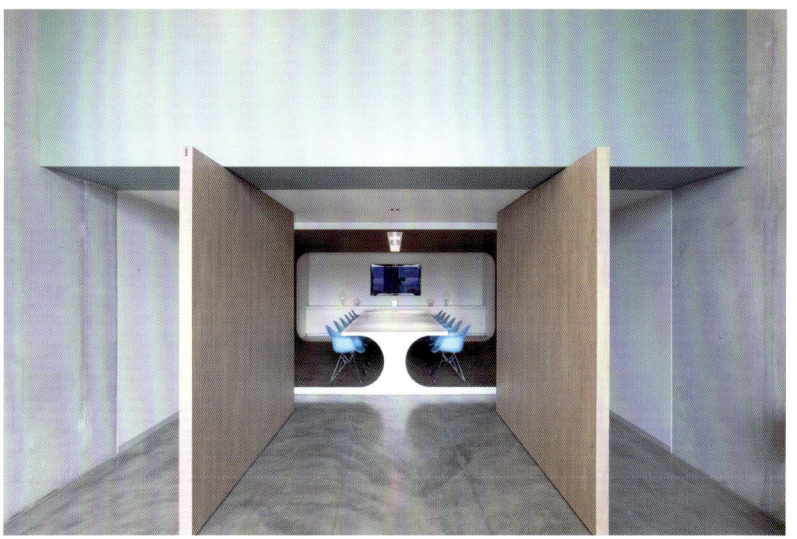

THE NETHERLANDS_AMSTERDAM ATRADIUS HEADQUARTERS

ARCHITECTS: VAN DEN OEVER, ZAAIJER & PARTNERS ARCHITECTEN_**COMPLETION:** 2008_**NUMBER OF WORKPLACES:** 600_**GROSS FLOOR AREA:** 14,159 M² **COMMON AREA:** RESTAURANT, CONFERENCE ROOMS **KIND OF WORKPLACES:** CELLULAR, OPEN-PLAN **PHOTOS:** LUUK KRAMER, AMSTERDAM (306, 307 A., B. R.), ALLARD VAN DER HOEK, AMSTERDAM (307 B. L.)

With its dynamic sculptural design, the new insurance bank head office is a conspicuous eye-catcher. An innovative office concept that is immediately observable from the outside was developed especially for this building to encourage communication and human contact. 'Space to meet one another' was the theme on which the spatial organization of the requirement plan was based. Areas in which employees of different departments can meet one another in an informal atmosphere were created by arranging eleven voids across the building in the shape of green atria. These atria, which differ in shape and height, are intended to serve as municipal parks, connected by stairs, or tree-lined squares.

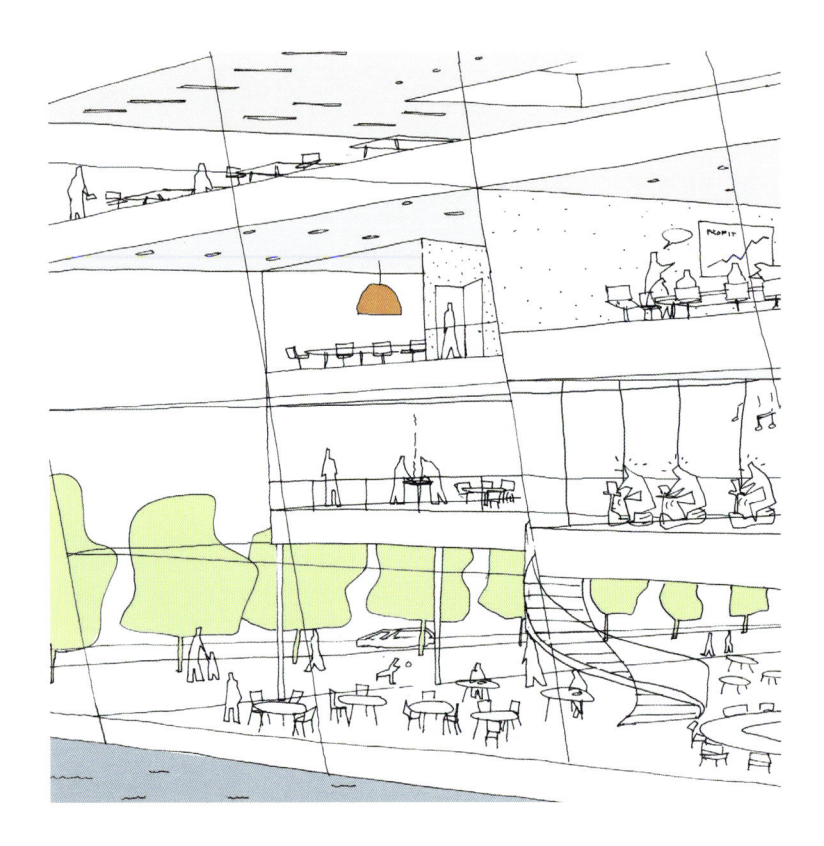

Mit seinem dynamischen Design ist der neue Hauptsitz der Versicherung ein auffälliger Hingucker. Ein innovatives Bürokonzept, das man schon von außen erkennen kann, wurde speziell für dieses Gebäude entwickelt, um die Kommunikation und den Kontakt zwischen den Menschen zu fördern. „Raum um sich zu treffen" ist das Thema, auf dem die räumliche Organisation des Anforderungsplans basiert. Es wurden Bereiche entworfen, in welchen die Angestellten verschiedener Abteilungen sich in einer ungezwungenen Atmosphäre treffen können, indem im Bauvolumen verteilt, elf Hohlräume als grüne Atrien angelegt wurden. Diese Innenhöfe von unterschiedlicher Form und Höhe fungieren als über Treppen miteinander verbundene Stadtparks oder als von Bäumen gesäumte Plätze.

left: Competition sketch_South view_View from courtyard. right: North central staircase_Central atrium_Restaurant.
links: Skizze Wettbewerb_Südansicht_Blick vom Hof. rechts: Nördliches zentrales Treppenhaus_ Zentrales Atrium_Restaurant.

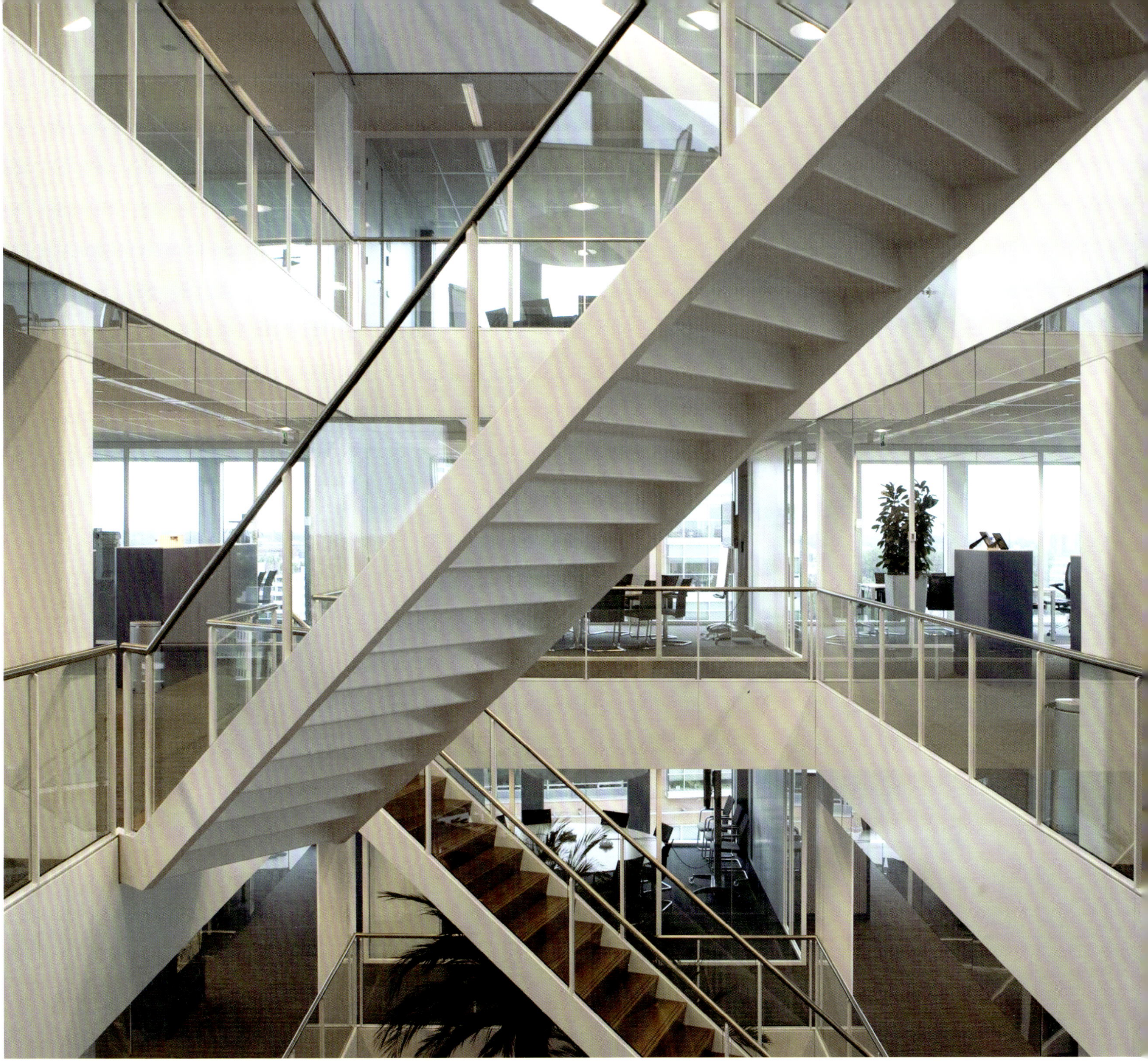
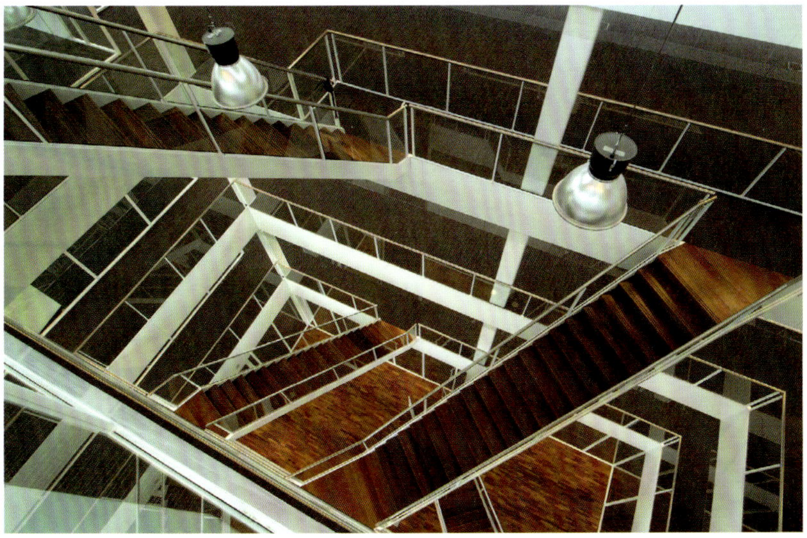
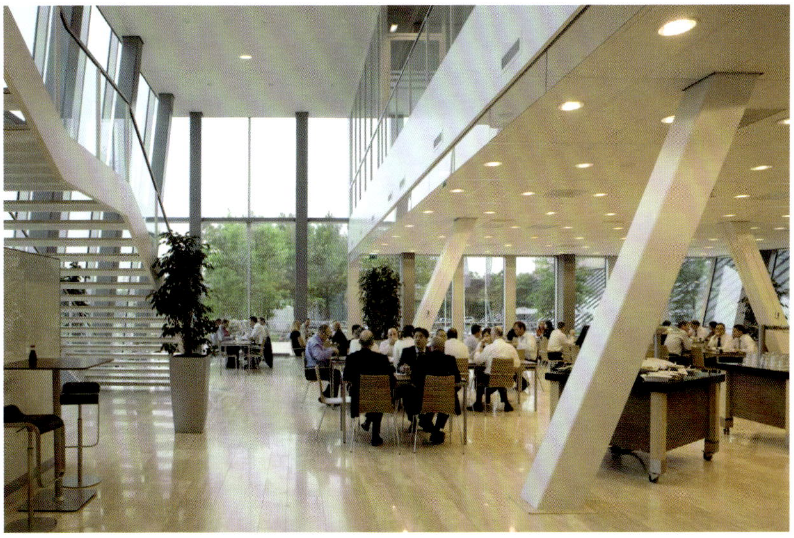

THE NETHERLANDS_AMSTERDAM **KRAANSPOOR**

ARCHITECTS: OTH ONTWERPGROEP TRUDE HOOYKAAS
STRUCTURAL ENGINEER: ARONSOHN RAADGEVENDE INGENIEURS_**COMPLETION:** 2007_**ORIGINAL BUILDING:** J.D. POSTMA, 1952_**NUMBER OF WORKSPACES:** 12 UNITS
GROSS FLOOR AREA: 12,500 M²_**COMMON AREA:** STAIRWELL, LIFT, LOBBIES_**KIND OF WORKPLACES:** VARIOUS, DEPENDING RENTER
PHOTOS: CHRISTIAAN DE BRUIJNE, KOOG A/D ZAAN (308, 309, 311 A. R.), ROB HOEKSTRA, KALMTHOUT, BELGIUM (310, 311 B. R.), FOTOSTUDIO FDW - FEDDE DE WEERT, ST. MAARTENSBURG (311 L.)

The light-weight office building was built on top of a concrete crane dock in Amsterdam's old harbor. The new construction with 270 meters of length offers a phenomenal expansive view of the river IJ and the old city center of Amsterdam. Fully respecting its foundation, the building is lifted by slender steel columns three meters above the dock. To help minimize the weight, a light-weight steel structure in combination with a thin floor system was chosen for the new development, reducing the total building weight nearly by half. Ecological claims are fulfilled by a double-glazed climate glass façade across a concrete core used for the infrastructure and floor, as well as hydrothermal heating and cooling.

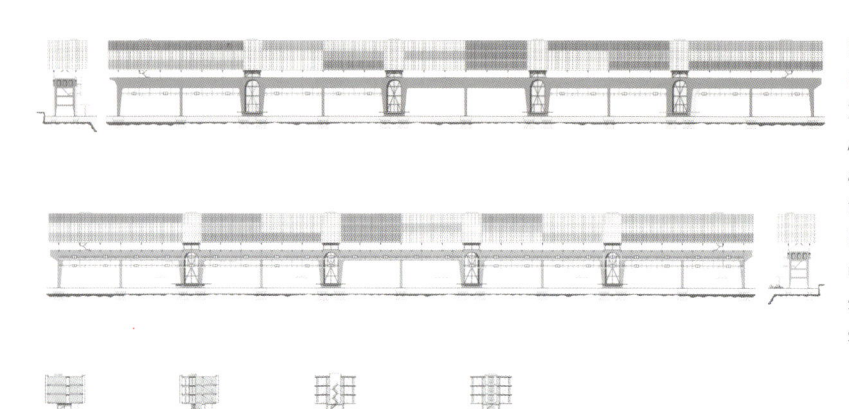

Das Bürogebäude in Leichtbauweise steht auf einer Schienenbrücke eines Kranes im alten Hafen Amsterdams. Der Neubau mit einer Länge von 270 Metern bietet fantastische Ausblicke über das IJ und die alte Innenstadt Amsterdams. Auf schlanken drei Meter langen Stahlpfeilern von dem Viadukt abgelöst, versucht der Neubau seinen Unterbau nicht zu sehr zu beeinträchtigen. Die Leichtbauweise einer Stahlkonstruktion mit einem dünnen Systemboden reduziert das Gewicht des Gebäude verglichen mit üblicher Bauweise um nahezu die Hälfte. Ökologische Ansprüche wurden mittels einer zweischaligen Klima-Glasfassade, einer Betonteilaktivierung in dem Infra+ Boden, sowie hydrothermalen Heizung und Kühlung erfüllt.

left: Elevations and sections_Exterior elevation from waterside_Exterior of stairwell, with dock. right: Exterior of stairwell and entrance.
links: Ansichten und Schnitte_Außenansicht von der Wasserseite_ Außenansicht von Treppenhaus und Dock. rechts: Treppenhaus mit Eingang.

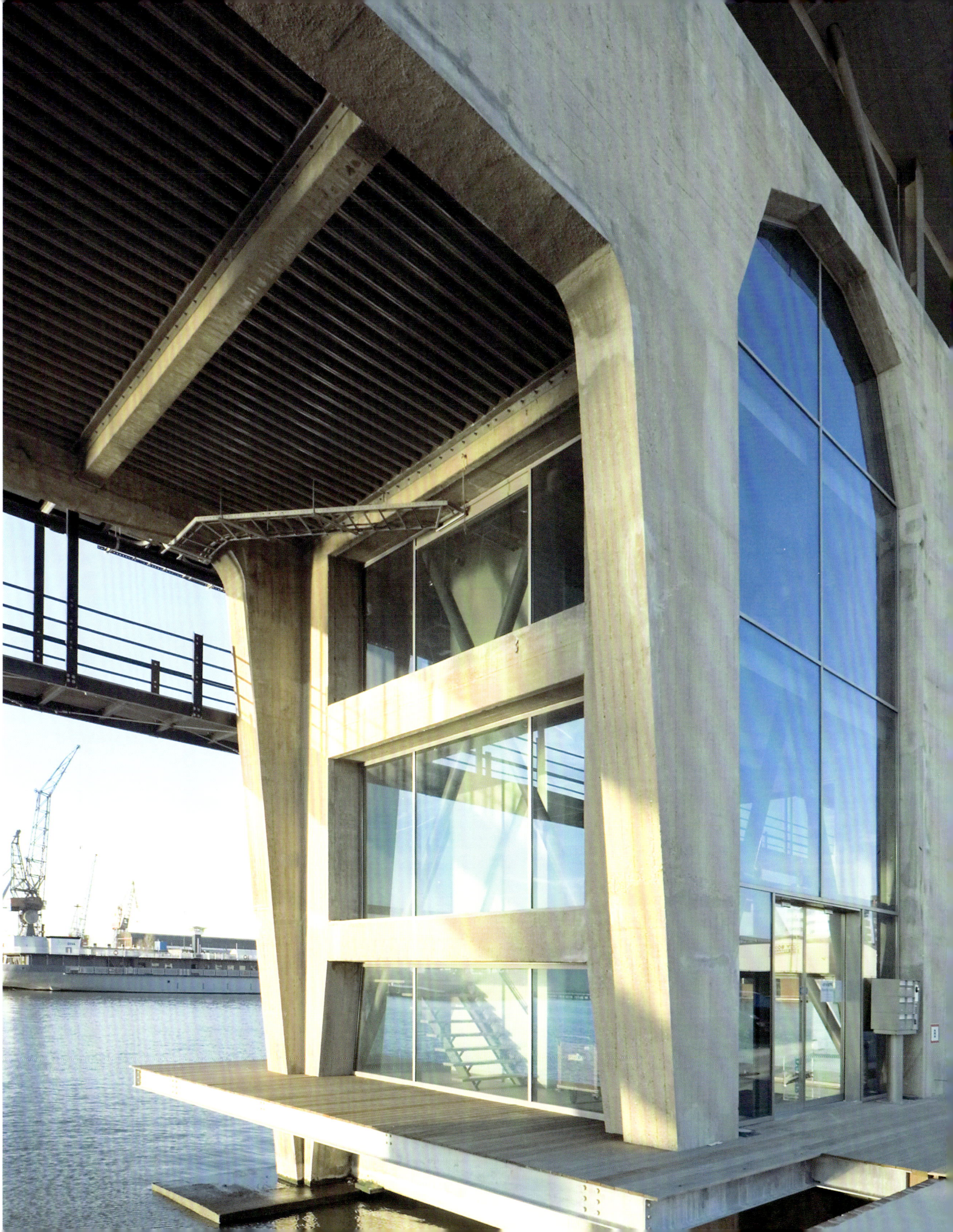

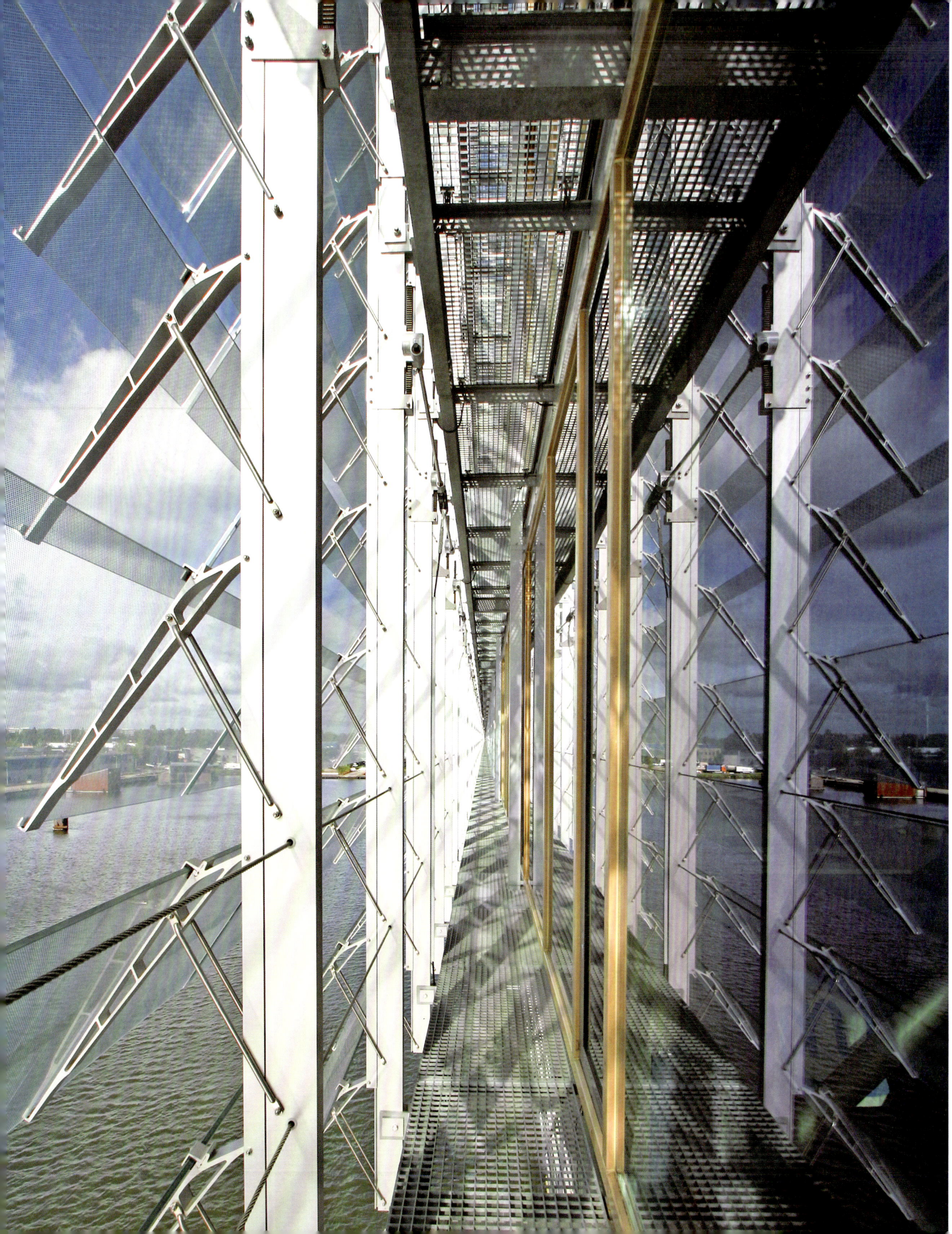

left: View between double façade. right: Sketch by Julian Wolse_City view from interior_Louver façade_Office_Common meeting room by stairwell.
links: Blick in die Doppelfassade. rechts: Skizze von Julian Wolse_Innenraum mit Blick auf die Stadt_Fassade, Verschattung_Büro_Besprechungsraum beim Treppenhaus.

THE NETHERLANDS_AMSTERDAM **MAHLER 4 OFFICE TOWER**

ARCHITECTS: RAFAEL VIÑOLY ARCHITECTS PC
COMPLETION: 2005_**GROSS FLOOR AREA:** 160,000 M²
COMMON AREA: CONFERENCE ROOMS, STAIRCASE, LOBBY
KIND OF WORKPLACES: CELLULAR, TEAM
PHOTOS: RAOUL SUERMONDT

The mixed-use development in Amsterdam's Zuid-As district between the city center and Schiphol Airport mandated a specific zoning envelope for each building, resulting in the traditional base, shaft, and crown structure of high-rise buildings, with an angled layout to yield a more dynamic urban composition. The firm's design sought to reinvent and unify this tripartite building structure through the use of an exterior stair and vertical aluminum mullions. The exterior fire escape enlivening the façades provides a fair-weather alternative to the two elevator cores and creates exterior spaces that office workers can use as informal gathering spaces, or that can be converted into small gardens and outdoor plazas.

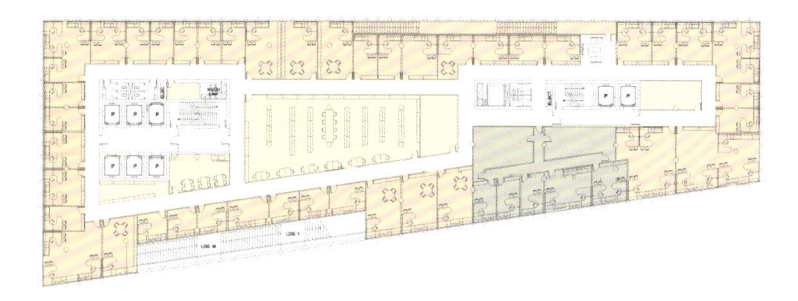

Das Mehrzweckgebäude im Amsterdamer Zuid-As-Gebiet zwischen der Innenstadt und dem Flughafen Schiphol, wo ein zonierte Aufbau der Hochhäuser in Basis, Schaft und Krone gefordert war, wurde abgewinkelt um so eine dynamischere Komposition im Stadtraum zu erreichen. Durch eine außenliegende Treppe und vertikales Aluminiumstabwerk versucht der Entwurf, die Dreiteilung neu zu erfinden und zu überwinden. Die außenliegende Feuertreppe belebt die Fassaden und bietet bei schönem Wetter eine Alternative zu den zwei Aufzugskernen. Zudem werden den Angestellten so Freiflächen, die als informelle Treffpunkte dienen und als kleine Gärten oder Plätze angelegt werden können, geboten.

left: Typical floor plan_Lobby_External stairs. right: Exterior by night_Corner with stairs_Entrance.
links: Typischer Grundriss_Lobby_Außentreppe. rechts: Nachtansicht_Gebäudeecke mit Treppen_Eingang.

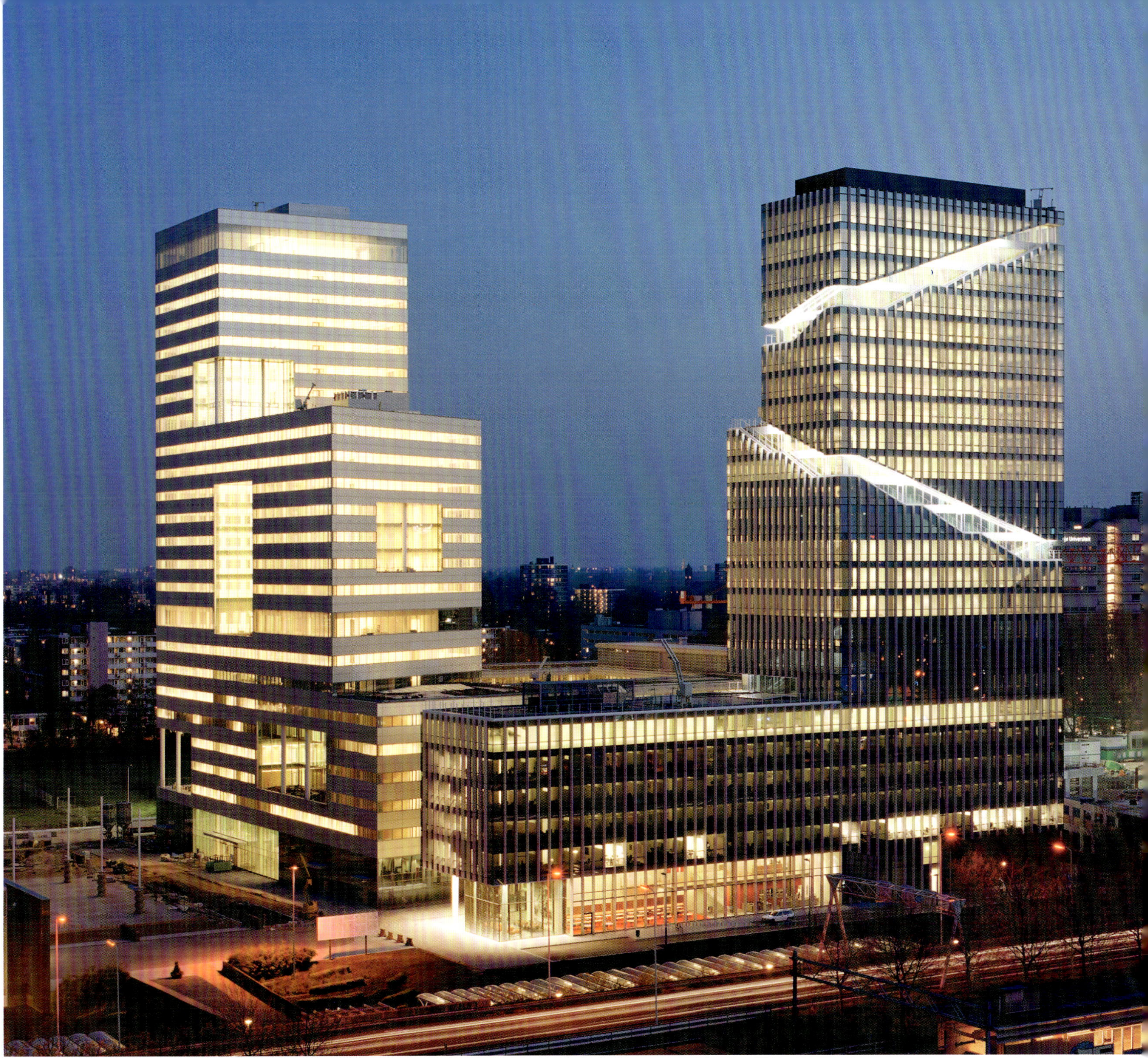

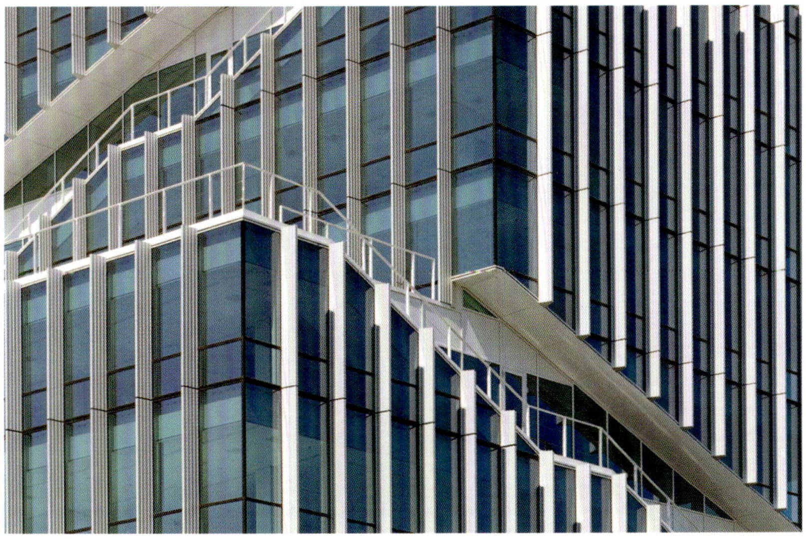

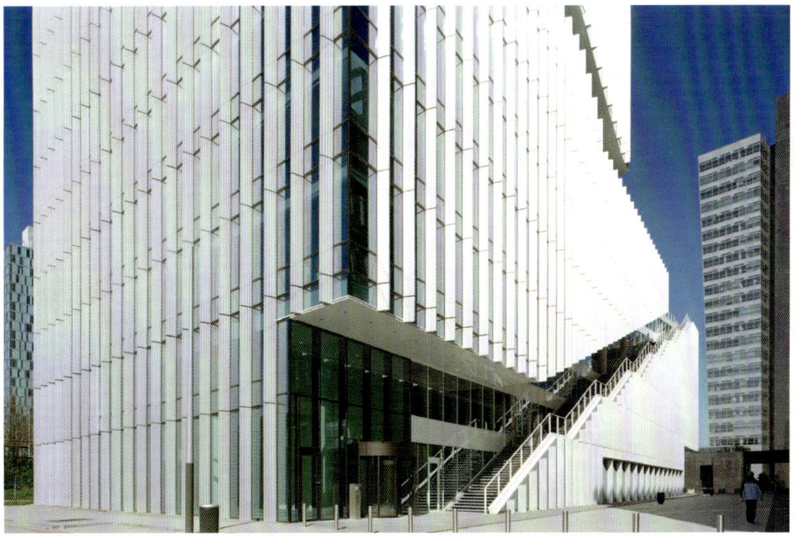

THE NETHERLANDS_BILTHOVEN **DIFRAX HEADOFFICE**

ARCHITECTS: SMITS + RAMAEKERS INTERIOR ARCHITECTS
COMPLETION: 2008_**NUMBER OF WORKPLACES:** 44
GROSS FLOOR AREA: 1,200 M²_**COMMON AREA:** LOUNGE, SHOW-MEETING, WAR ROOM_**KIND OF WORKPLACES:** CELLULAR, OPEN-PLAN, LOUNGE WORKSPACE_**PHOTOS:** HANS GERRITSEN

Difrax, an international player in the field of baby products, wanted a radical makeover of the interior design of its headoffice. The architects created office workstations, designed a showroom adjoining a meeting room, a 'battle room', a lounge, and a new entry to the 1,200-square-meter building. The resulting interior conveys a sense of warmth and protection, with great attention to lighting. According to the client's wishes, "private living" elements were transformed into office functionality. Almost all pieces of furniture were custom-made to furnish an interior that completely accommodates the needs of the client.

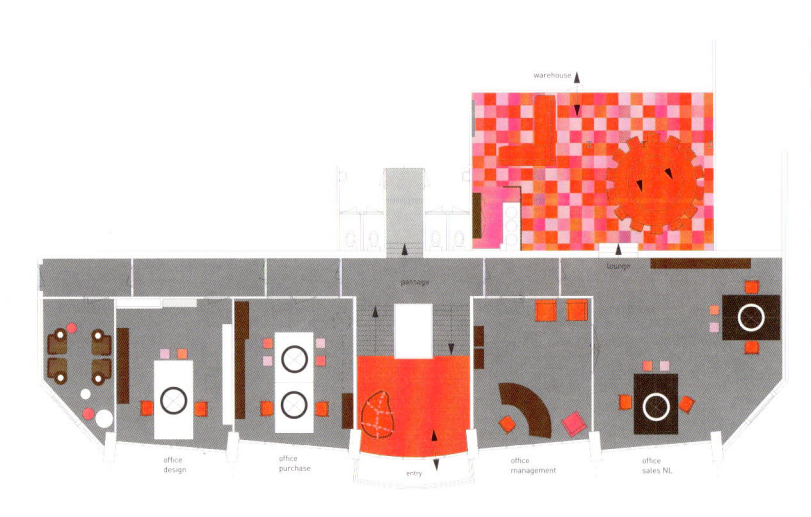

Difrax, international mit Babyprodukten handelnd, wünschte eine radikale Innenraumgestaltung seiner Hauptverwaltung. Die Architekten schufen Büroarbeitsplätze, einen Ausstellungsraum mit angrenzendem Sitzungszimmer, einen War Room sowie eine Lounge und überarbeiteten die Eingangssituation des 1200 Quadratmeter-Gebäudes. Das entschlossen gestaltete Interieur hinterlasst einen warmen und schützenden Eindruck. Der Belichtung wurde besondere Aufmerksamkeit zuteil. Dem Geschäftsfeld des Auftraggebers entsprechend, wandelten die Gestalter Motive des „Privatlebens" in funktionalen Büroraum um. Nahezu die gesamte Möblierung wurde individuell gefertigt, so dass die Bedürfnisse des Klienten bestmöglich befriedigt werden konnten.

left: Floor plan_Lounge with large round table and turn plateau _War room. right: Workstations_ Conference table surrounded by showroom cabinets_Semicircular couch for informal discussion.
links: Grundriss_Lounge mit rundem Besprechungstisch und drehbarem Aufsatz_War room. rechts: Arbeitsplätze_Konferenztisch umgeben von Präsentationsvitrinen_Halbrunde Couch für informelle Gespräche.

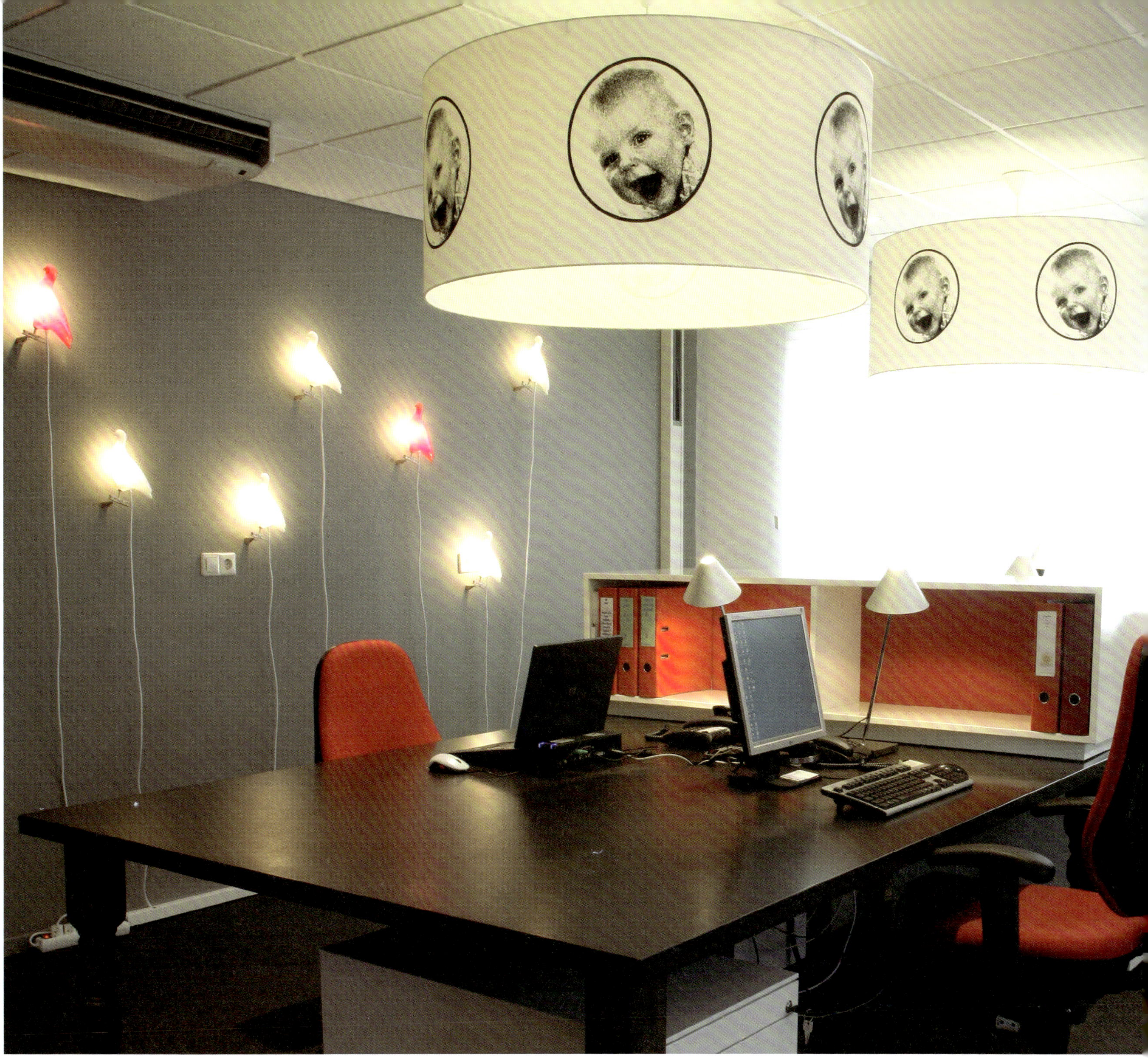

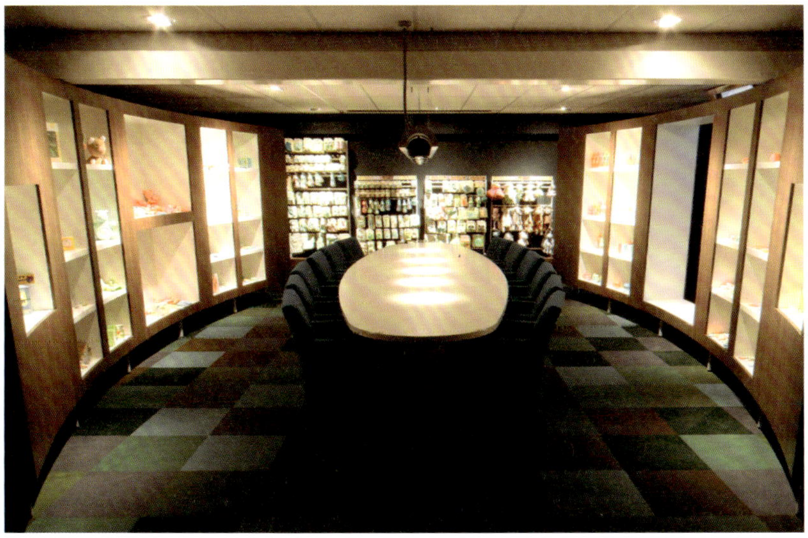

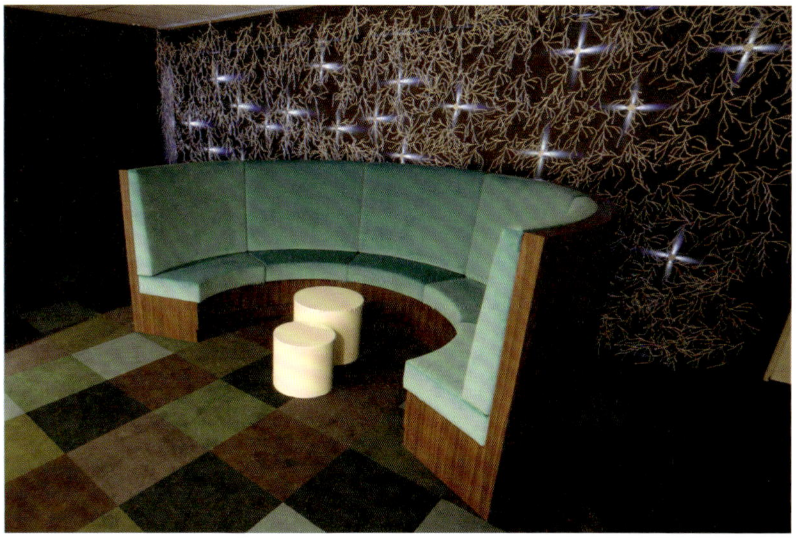

THE NETHERLANDS_DUIVENDRECHT **RECYCLED OFFICE**

ARCHITECTS: I29 INTERIOR ARCHITECTS
COMPLETION: 2009_**NUMBER OF WORKPLACES:** 15
GROSS FLOOR AREA: 400 M²_**COMMON AREA:** STAFF, LUNCH, CONFERENCE_**KIND OF WORKPLACES:** OPEN-PLAN
PHOTOS: COURTESY OF THE ARCHITECTS

Since the advertising agency Gummo wanted to rent the space only for two years, i29 convinced them to adopt the concept "reduce, reuse, recycle". They developed a theme that reflects Gummo's personality and design philosophy – simple and uncomplicated, yet stylish with a twist of humor. Everything in the office conforms to the new in-house style of white and grey. They used second-hand furniture and whatever was left over from the old office and spray-painted everything with polyurea hot spray – an environmentally friendly paint – to conform with the new color scheme and give a new soul to the old furniture. The new office is a perfect case study of a smart way to fill a temporary space stylishly and at minimal cost.

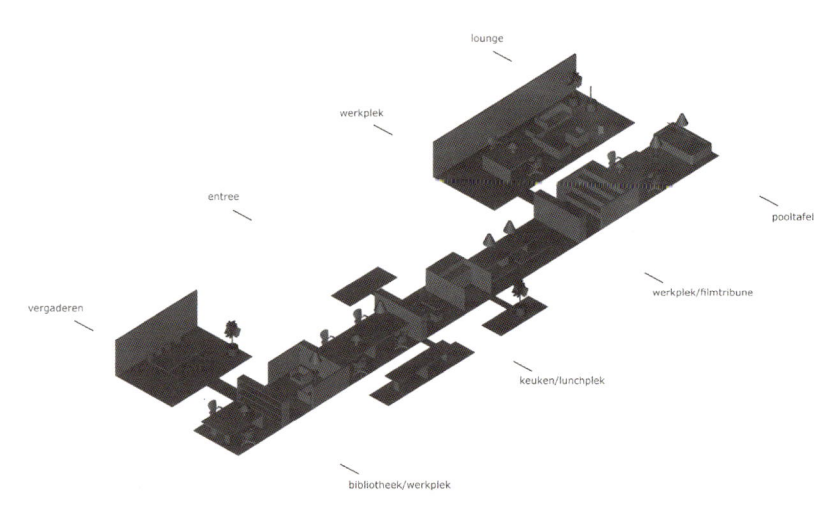

Da die Werbeagentur Gummo die Räumlichkeiten nur für zwei Jahre mieten wollte, überzeugte i29 sie von dem Konzept „sparen, wiederverwerten, wiederaufarbeiten". Die daraus entwickelte Gestaltung spiegelt Gummos Persönlichkeit und Designphilosophie wider – einfach und unkompliziert, zugleich stil- und humorvoll. Alles im Büro entspricht dem neuen Hausstil in Weiß und Grau. Möbel aus zweiter Hand und aus den alten Büros wurden verwendet und mit umweltfreundlichem Polyurethan-Spray spritzlackiert, um sie ans neue Farbschema anzupassen und ihnen neues Leben einzuhauchen. Das neue Büro ist ein gutes Beispiel dafür, wie ein Raum vorübergehend und auf geschickte Art stilvoll und kostengünstig eingerichtet werden kann.

left: Structure model_Lounge_Conference area_Pool table. right: Office_Internal library_Old furniture was spray painted with polyurea Hotspray.
links: Strukturmodell_Lounge_Konferenzbereich_Pool-Billard. rechts: Büro_Firmeneigene Bibliothek_Alte Möbel, spritzlackiert mit Polyurethan-Spray.

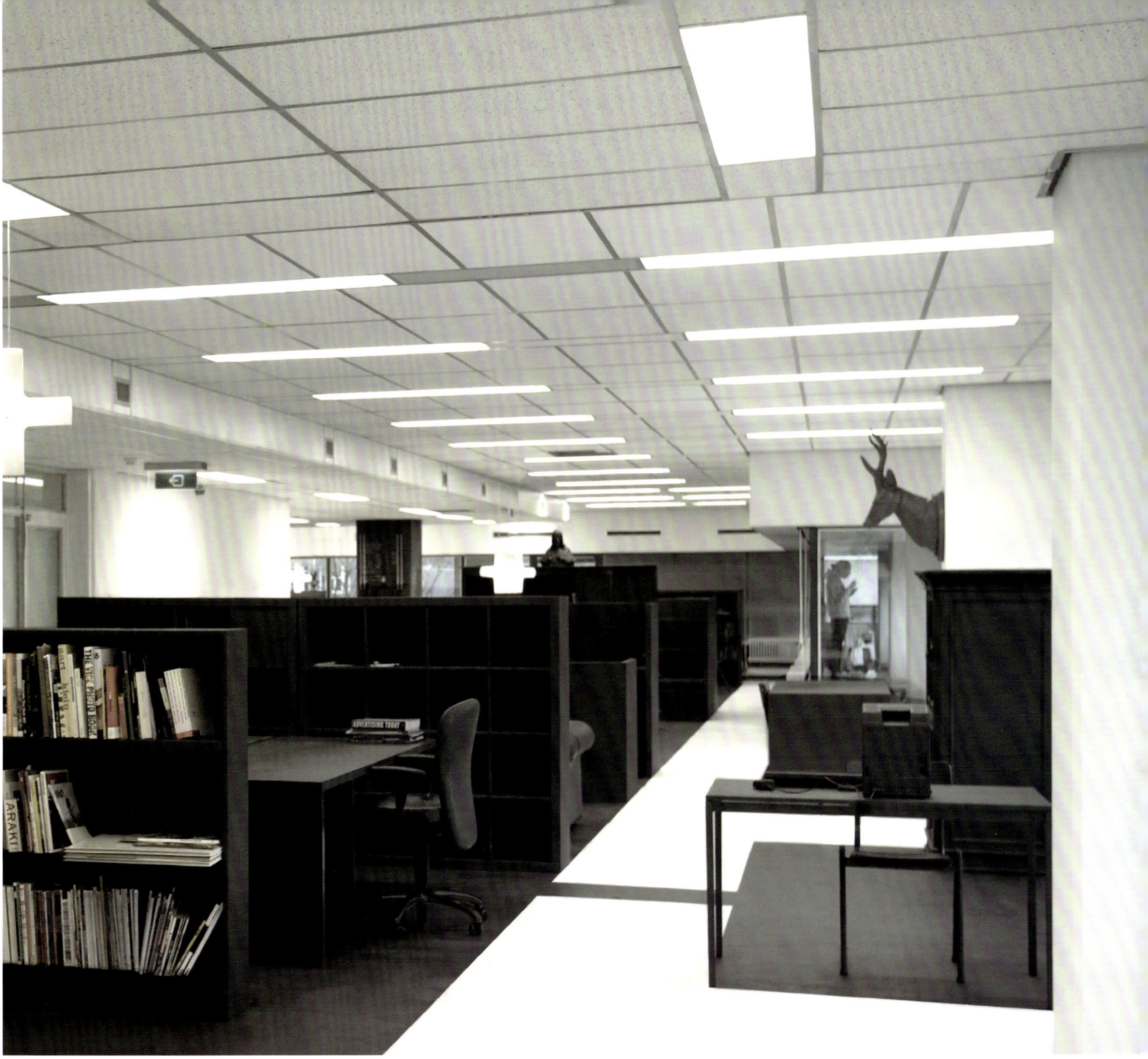
ADVERTISING TODAY
ARAKI

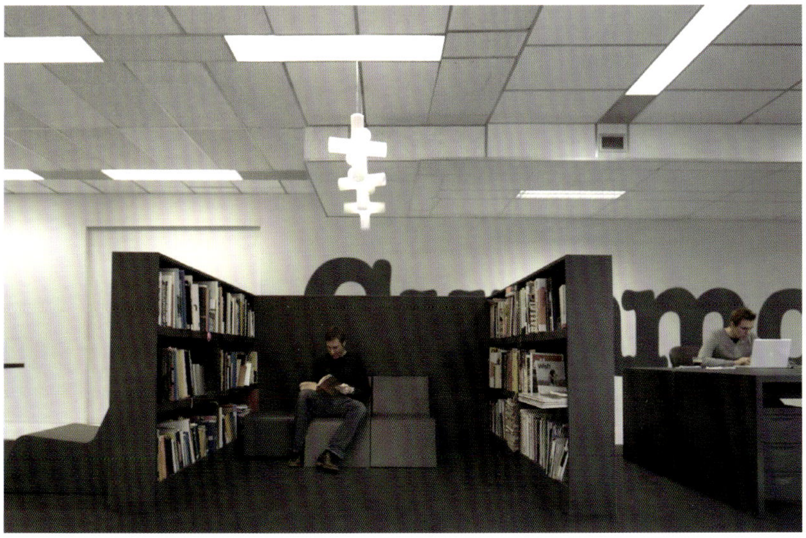

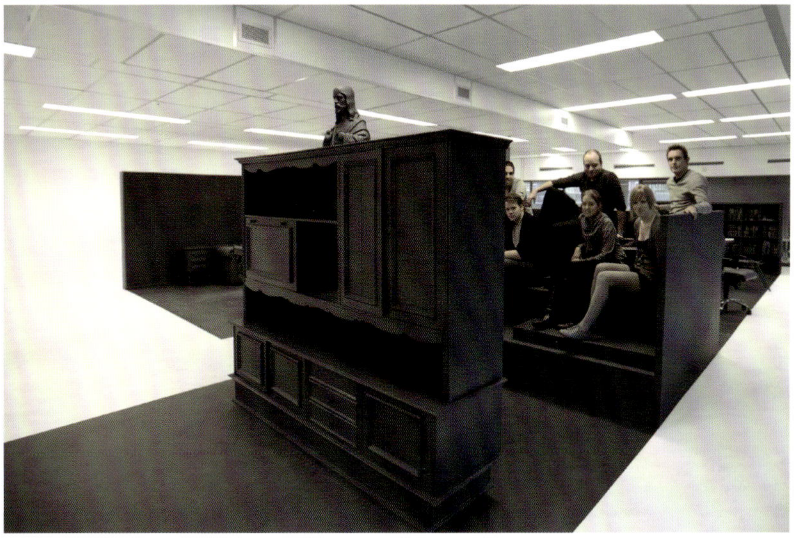

THE NETHERLANDS_EINDHOVEN CARDBOARD OFFICE FOR SCHERPONTWERP

ARCHITECTS: RO&AD ARCHITECTEN
COMPLETION: 2006_**NUMBER OF WORKPLACES:** 12
GROSS FLOOR AREA: 200 M²_**COMMON AREA:** LIBRARY, MEETING ROOM_**KIND OF WORKPLACES:** OPEN-PLAN
PHOTOS: JÖRGEN CARIS, TROUW, ANITA HUISMAN (319 A.)

The Graphic design office Scherpontwerp and publisher De Boekenmakers rented an uninspiring, very standard and poorly laid out office space. It was transformed by defining the maximum rectangular space in the office and filling the rest of the space with piled up cardboard. In the newly-created open area a long low table of piled up cardboard was placed and the borders of the open space were designed to resemble façades round a park or square, defining the open space. Behind the façades, different functions are located, like working spaces, desks, meeting spaces and cupboards cut out of honeycomb cardboard. The office is rented for five years, so recyclable and less permanent material was used for the design, reducing costs to 30 percent of the expenses.

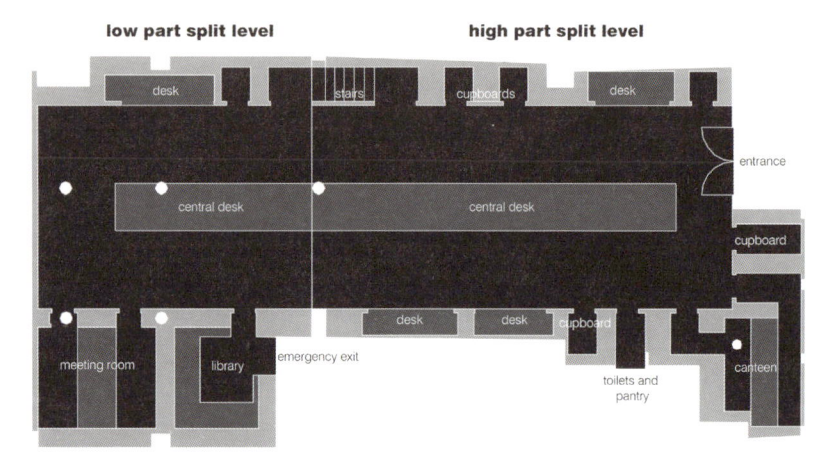

Das Graphikatelier Scherpontwerp und der Verlag De Boekenmakers hatten herkömmlichen Büroraum gemietet, der langweilige und schlecht organisiert war. Er wurde transformiert, indem zunächst der maximale rechteckige Raum gesucht und durch das Aufstapeln von Karton abgetrennt wurde. Seine Mitte nimmt eine langer niedriger Tisch aus Karton ein, die Ränder des Raumes werden von Fassaden analog zur Umbauung einer Freifläche oder eines Parks definiert. Die Fassaden verbergen verschiedene Funktionsbereiche, wie Arbeitsplätze, Versammlungsräume und Schränke aus Wabenkarton. Das Büro ist für nur fünf Jahre gemietet, und so erschien das recycelbare und wenig dauerhafte Material, das die Kosten der Büroausstattung auf 30 Prozent reduzierte, angemessen.

left: Floor plan_Workstation_"Façades" made of cardboard. right: Table in the center_View through the room_Library.
links: Grundriss_Arbeitsplatz_"Fassaden" aus Karton. rechts: Zentraler Tisch_Blick durch den Raum_Bibliothek.

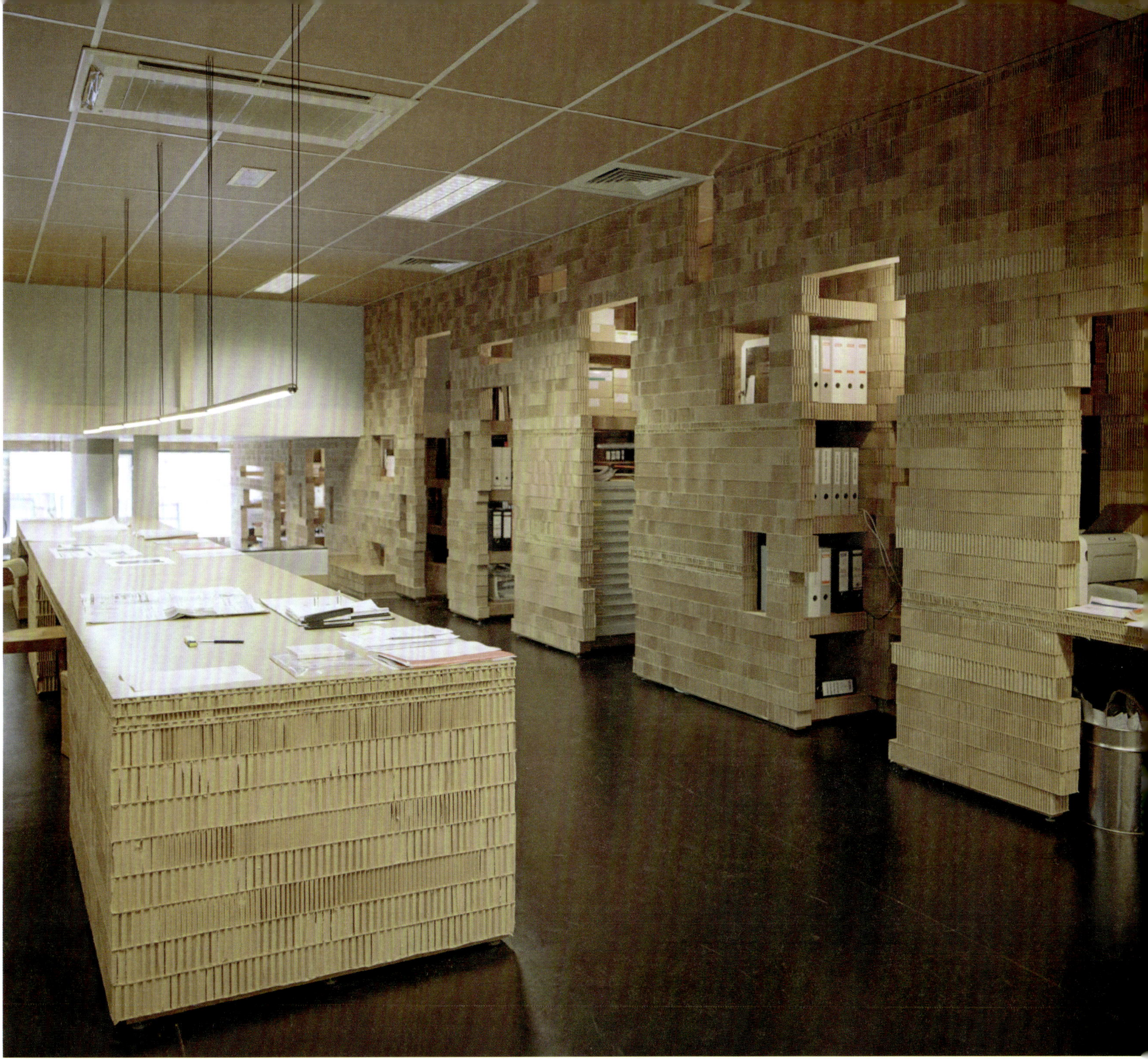

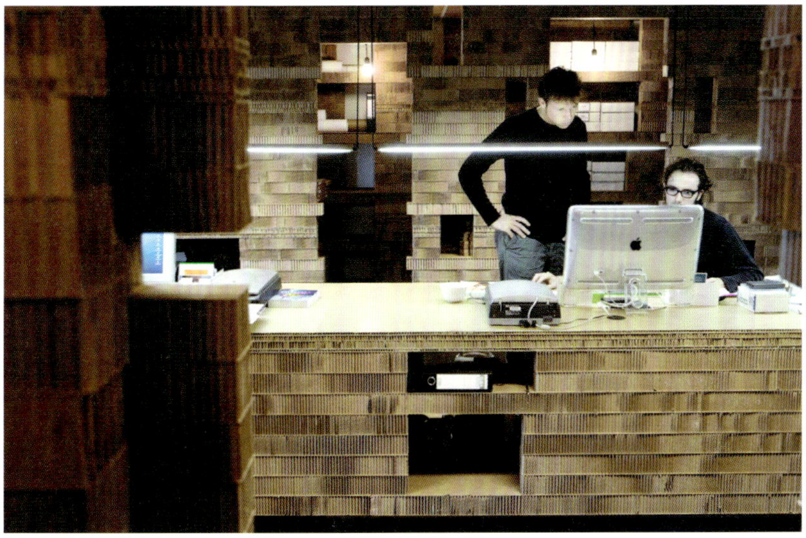

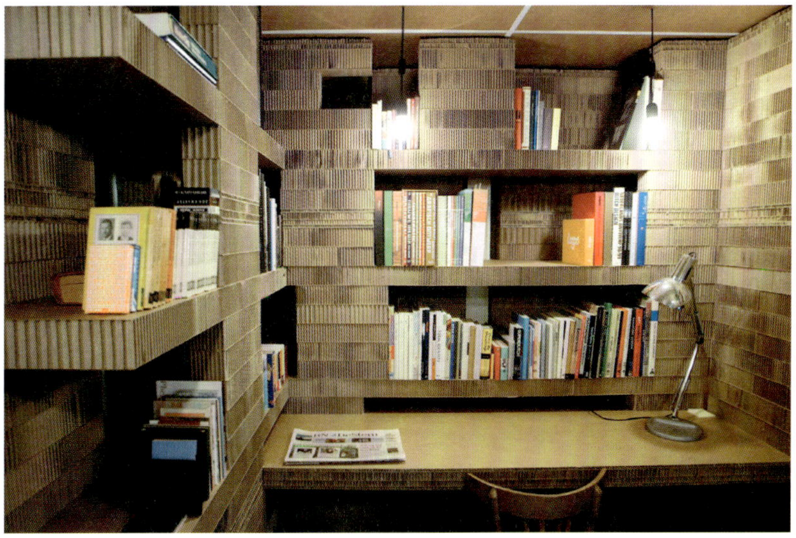

THE NETHERLANDS_GROENLO **NEDAP GROENLO**

ARCHITECTS: BARTIJN ARCHITECTEN_**COMPLETION:** 2008
NUMBER OF WORKPLACES: 450_**GROSS FLOOR AREA:** 8,000 M²
COMMON AREA: MEETING ROOM, RESTAURANT, ENTRANCE HALL_**KIND OF WORKPLACES:** COMBINATION, OPEN-PLAN, TEAM_**PHOTOS:** KIM ZWARTS

Ruud Bartijn was commissioned in the early 1990s to create new offices for Nedap that was to reflect the changing outlook of the company's management. The existing production facility received a facelift and new spaces, terraces, sky bridges and an entry forecourt were created. Freestanding columns in the forecourt represent rudimentary traces of the earlier factory. Thus, the company has grown into an entire office park in which the different market groups can operate from their own premises. Sunscreens, which are spaced away from the eaves, appear to connect the different buildings; separate yet attached, characterizing Nedap's new home in Groenlo.

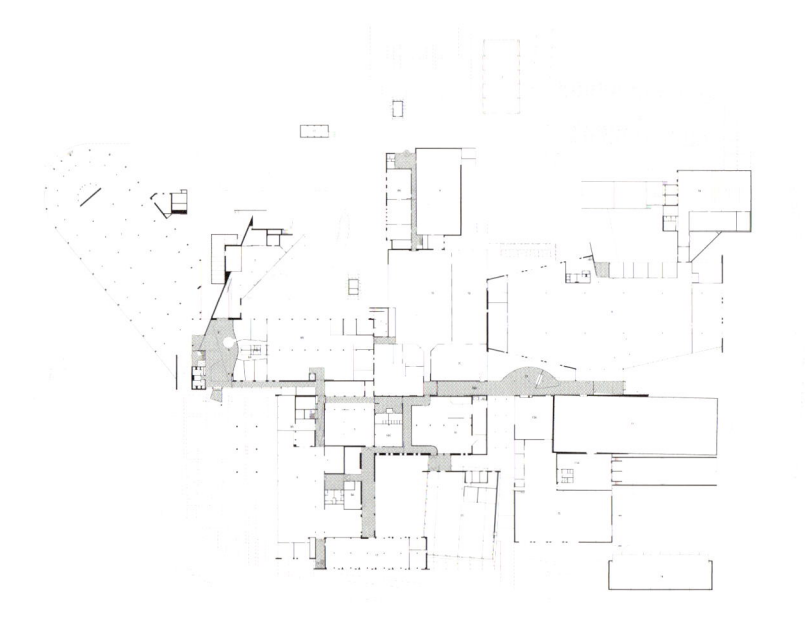

Ruud Bartijn bekam zu Beginn der 1990er Jahre den Auftrag, eine neue Niederlassung für Nedap zu kreieren, die die veränderte Zukunftsperspektive der Geschäftsleitung wiederspiegeln sollte. Die vorhandenen Fertigungsstätten wurden aktualisiert und durch neue Räume, Terrassen, Brücken sowie einem neuen Vorhof erweitert. Freistehende Rundpfeiler im Vorhof sind rudimentäre Spuren der vorherigen Fabrik. Aus der Firma erwuchs ein ganzer Büropark, in dem unterschiedliche Firmen vom jeweils eigenen Gelände aus agieren können. Für das Projekt charakteristische große, horizontale Sonnenblenden auf Trauhöhe scheinen die verschiedenen Gebäude zu verbinden.

left: Ground floor plan_Exterior view_Exterior view backyard. right: Exterior view in the early evening.
links: Grundriss Erdgeschoss_Außenansicht_Außenansicht Rückseite. rechts: Außenansicht am frühen Abend.

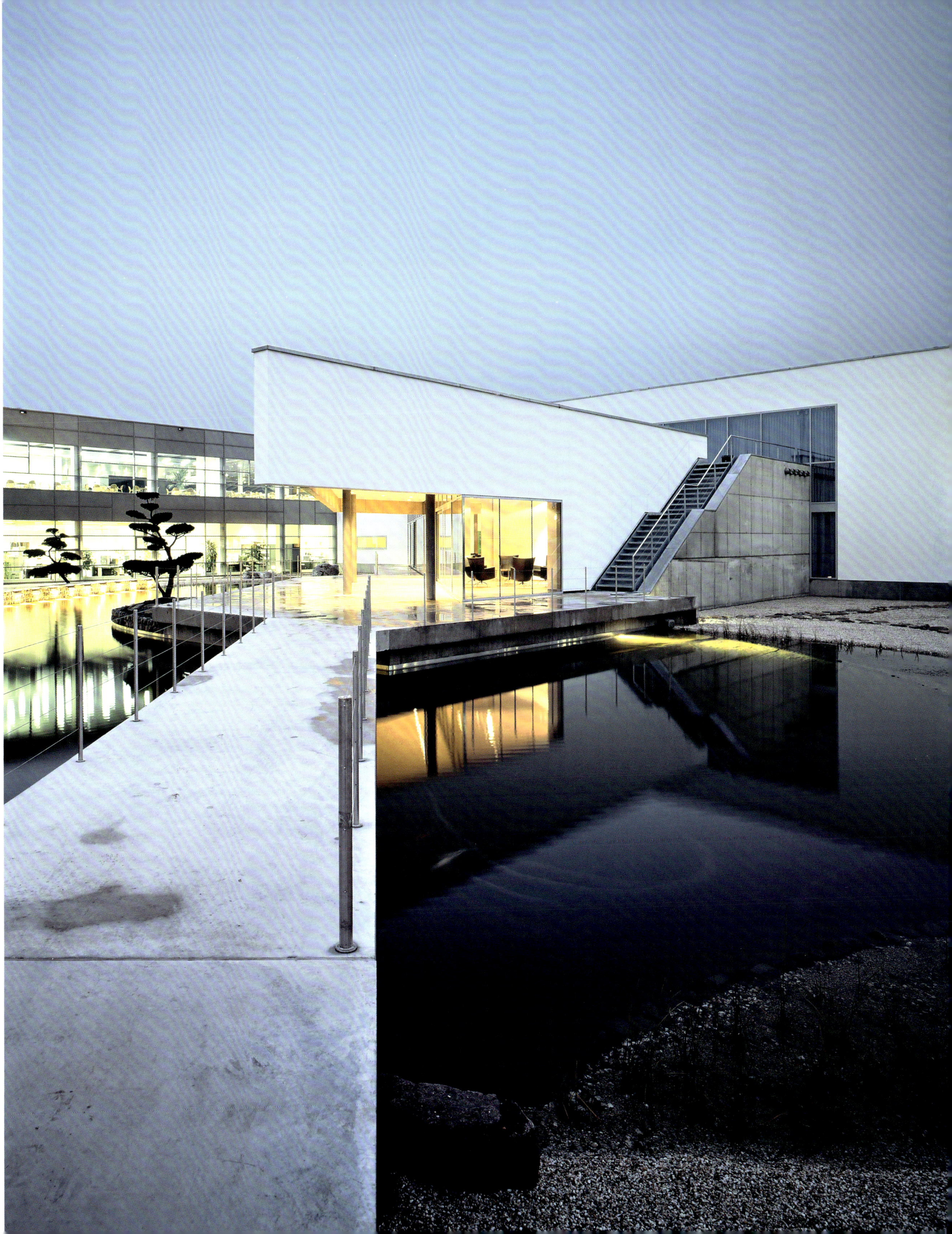

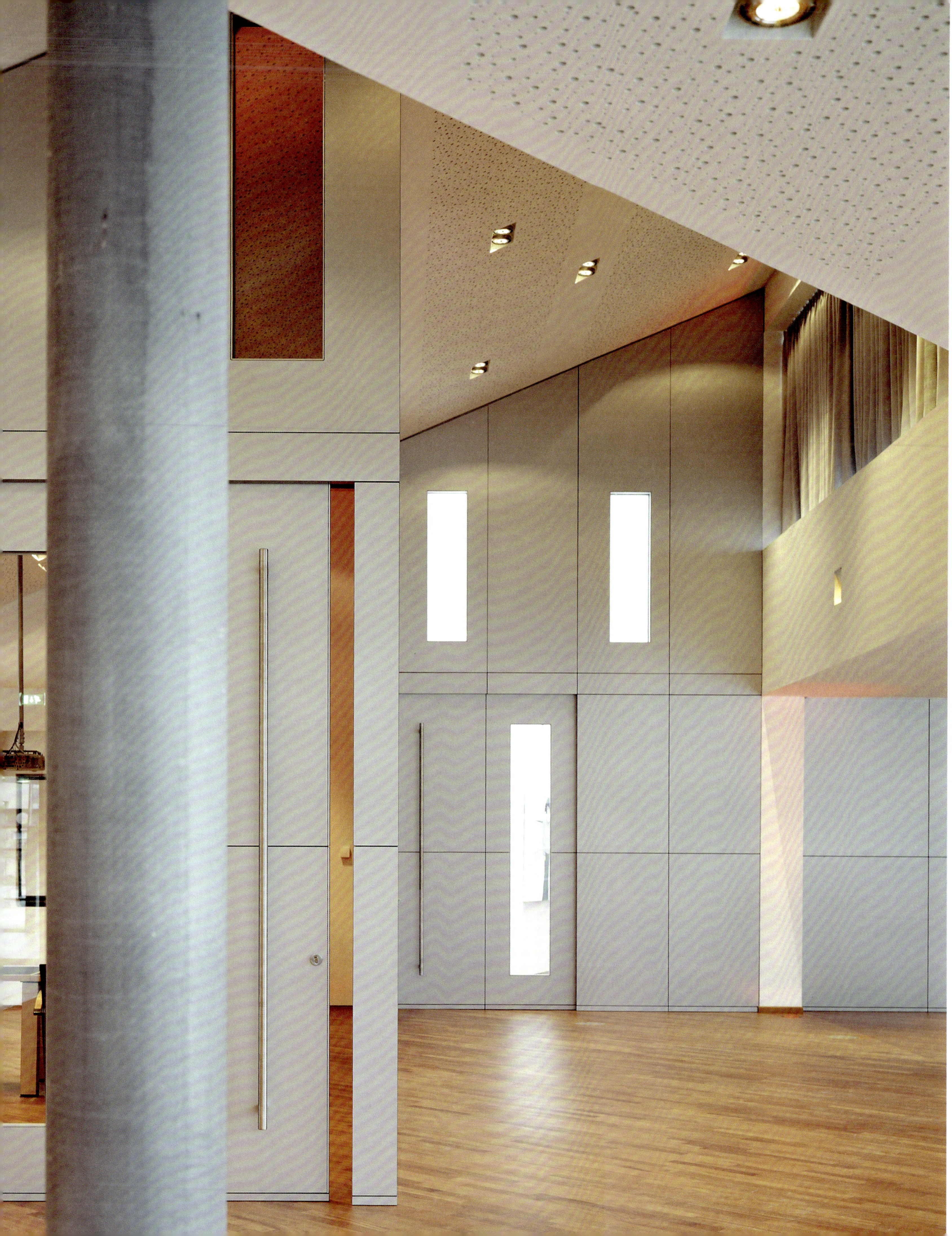

left: Interior view. right: Plan_Inner courtyard_Flexible workplaces_Office cell.
links: Innenansicht. rechts: Plan_Innenhof_Flexible Arbeitsplätze_Einzelbüros.

THE NETHERLANDS_HENDRIK-IDO-AMBACHT VISSER GROEN

ARCHITECTS: NINE OAKS / BEN HUYGEN_**COMPLETION:** 2004
NUMBER OF WORKPLACES: 10_**GROSS FLOOR AREA:** 270 M²
COMMON AREA: DESIGN STUDIO AND OFFICES
KIND OF WORKPLACES: COMBINATION
PHOTOS: COURTESY OF THE ARCHITECTS

This office of Visser Groen BV, a gardening company, is situated in a greenhouse environment. The design seems to adjust itself to its context. The typical form of a greenhouse was chosen for this building and other features of greenhouses were used as well. The working areas on the top floor have roof lights through which light pours in. In addition, white walls, floors and furnishings provide bright workplaces. The front façade resembles a greenhouse consisting of mere glass panels joined together without much detail. These huge windows offer a good connection between the inside and the outside. The side walls are covered with wooden slats to match the natural surroundings.

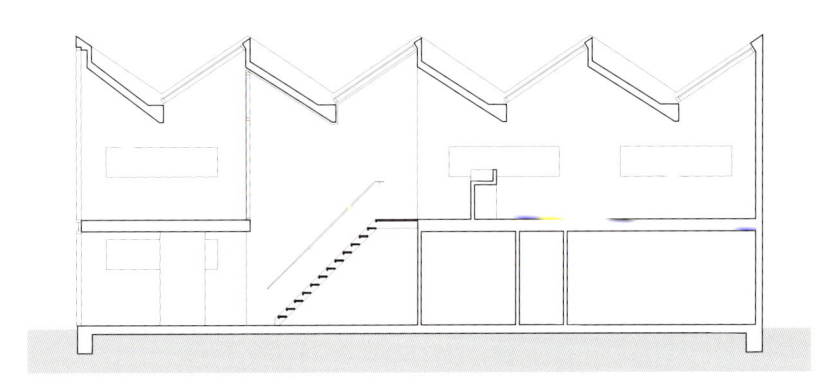

Dieses Bürogebäude für den Gartenbaubetrieb Visser Groen BV liegt inmitten von Gewächshäusern. Der Entwurf passt sich dieser Umgebung an: Für das Gebäude wurde die typische Gewächshausform gewählt und es bestehen auch weitere Ähnlichkeiten zu Gewächshäusern. Dachfenster im obersten Stockwerk, durch die viel Licht einfällt, sowie weiße Wände, Böden und Einrichtung sorgen für helle Arbeitsplätze. Die vordere Fassade ist entsprechend eines schlichten Gewächshauses gestaltet, das aus ohne großen Aufwand zusammengefügten Glasscheiben besteht. Die großen Scheiben ermöglichen eine gute Verbindung zwischen drinnen und draußen. Die Seitenwände hingegen sind mit Holzlatten verkleidet, um sich der natürlichen Umgebung anzupassen.

left: Section_Interior view_Rooflights for light-flooded office rooms. right: General view_Front façade, detail_Side wall, detail.
links: Schnitt_Innenansicht_Oberlichter für lichtdurchflutete Büroräume. rechts: Gesamtansicht_ Frontfassade_Seitenwand, Detail.

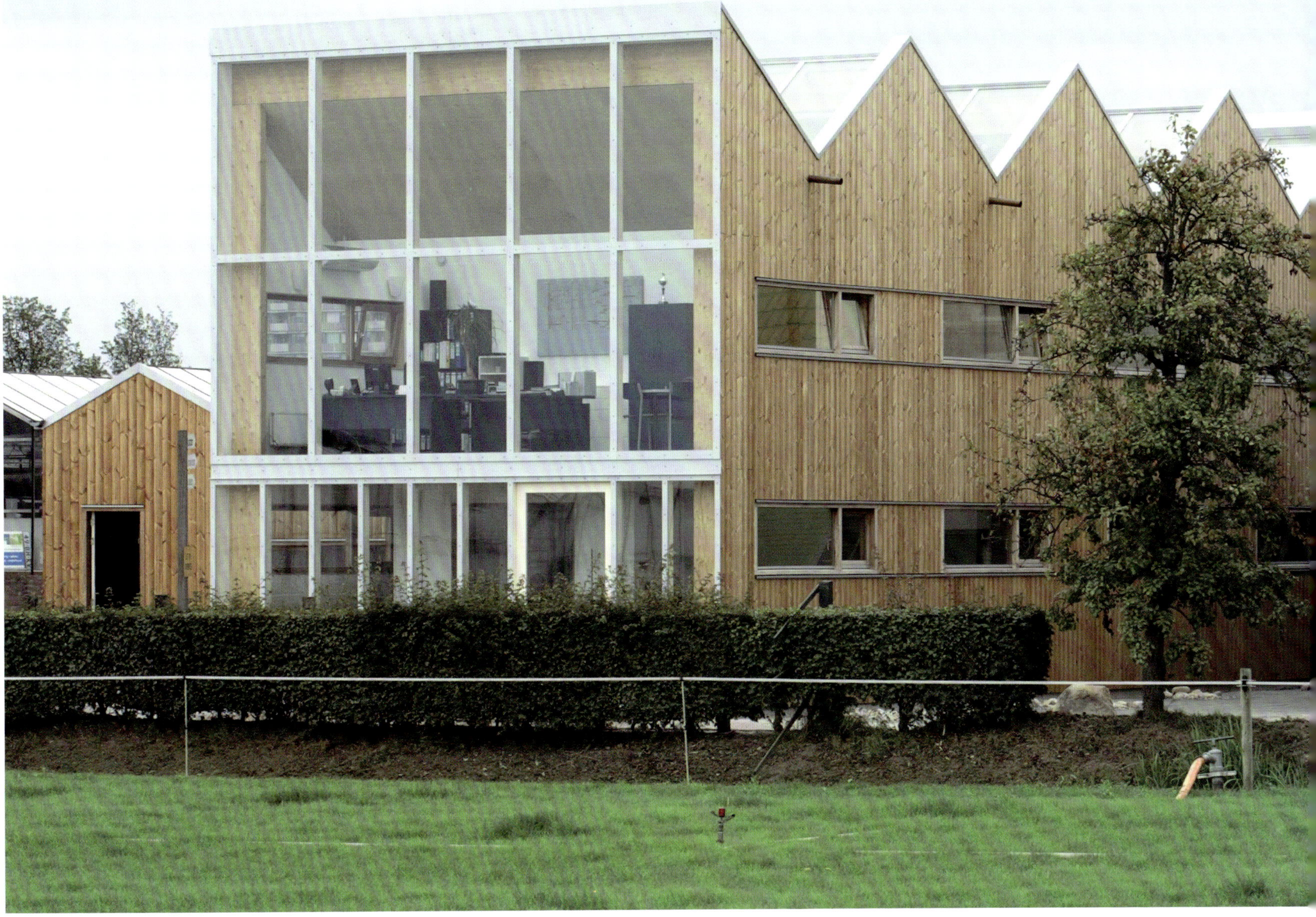
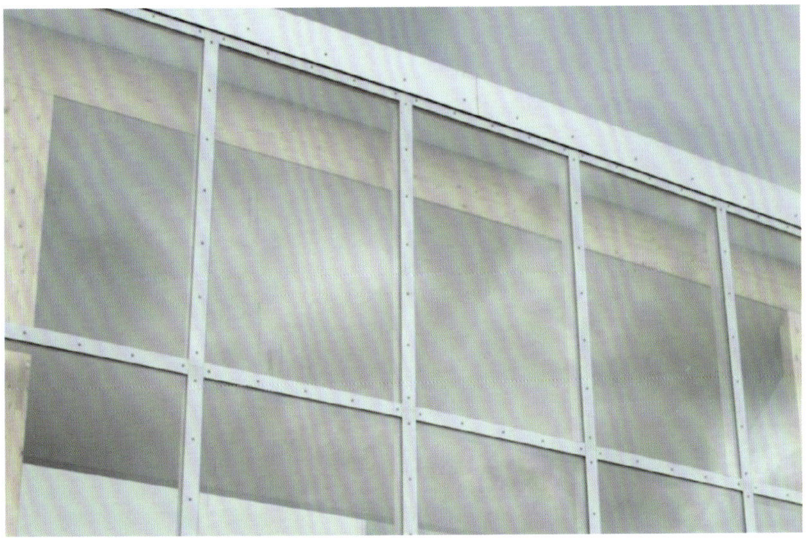
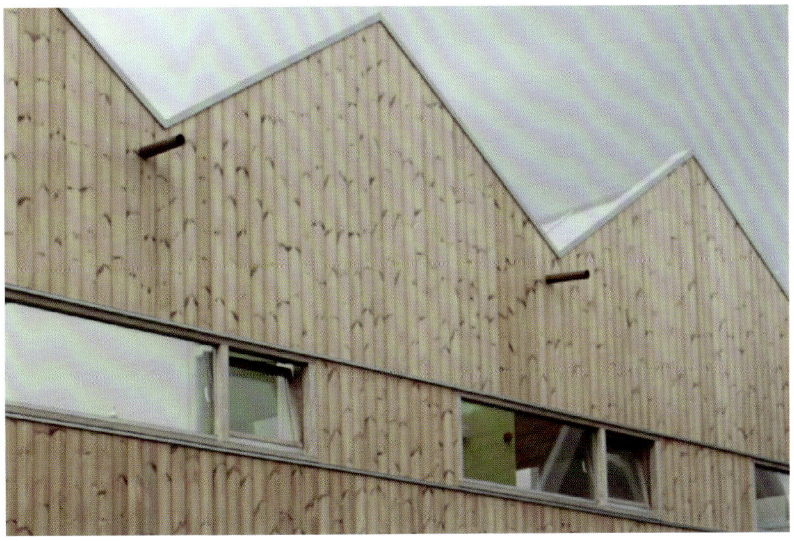

THE NETHERLANDS_ROTTERDAM **OFFICE BRAINPARK III**

ARCHITECTS: BROEKBAKEMA
COMPLETION: 2009_**NUMBER OF WORKPLACES:** 78
GROSS FLOOR AREA: 3,000 M²_**COMMON AREA:** MEETING ROOMS, ENTRANCE HALL, RESTAURANT, TERRACE,
KIND OF WORKPLACES: CELLULAR, TEAM, DESKSHARING, LOUNGE WORKSPACE_**PHOTOS:** MENNO EMMINK, DELFT

The investor together with the tenant, a law firm, decided to establish a sustainable building on the office premises Brainpark III. It is one of six office villas of four floors each at the edge of Brainpark III that constitute the transition between the high rise buildings of the area and the Fascinatio residential area. The buildings show the typical office building modernist style, yet the variations in the understated details express a villa-style individualism. Large windows dominate the façade. Their offset arrangement and the positioning of some windows at an angle promote transparency throughout the building. The all-round façade has been provided with a few modifying accents near the entrance to the terrace and occasional jutties.

Investor und Nutzer – eine Anwaltskanzlei – entschieden, in dem Büroareal Brainpark III ein nachhaltiges Gebäude zu errichten. Es ist eines von sechs Bürovillen zu je vier Stockwerken am Rand von Brainpark III, die den Übergang zwischen der hohen Bebauung des Areals und dem Wohngebiet Fascinatio herstellen. Die Volumen folgen dem für Bürobau typischen Modernismus, die Variation in den zurückhaltenden Detailformulierungen zeugt jedoch von villenartigem Individualismus. Große Fenster dominieren die Fassade, ihre versetzte Anordnung sowie die Lage einiger Fenster über Eck fördern die Alleinsichtigkeit. Die umlaufende Fassade erfährt beim Eingang der Terrasse und als Erker einige wenige akzentuierende Modifikationen.

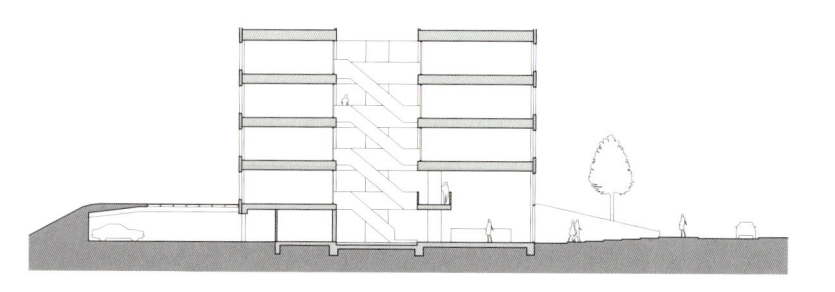

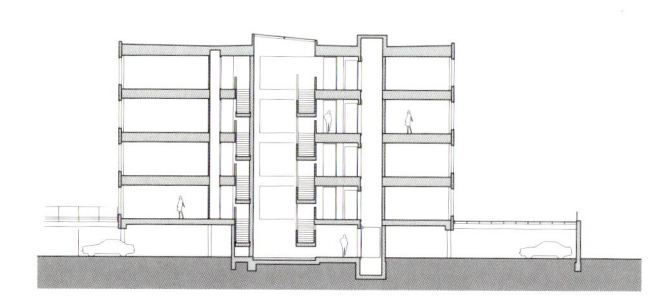

left: Sections_Exterior_Parking-lot. right: Reception_ Office_ Heart of the building.
links: Schnitte_Außenansicht_Tiefgarage. rechts: Empfang_Büro_Zentrales Atrium.

EVERSHEDS FAASEN

THE NETHERLANDS_ROTTERDAM SABIC EUROPE HEAD OFFICE

ARCHITECTS: GROUP A_**INTERIOR ARCHITECTS:** GROUP A WITH VELDHOEN + COMPANY_**COMPLETION:** 2005 **NUMBER OF WORKPLACES:** 540_**GROSS FLOOR AREA:** 10,500 M²_**COMMON AREA:** RESTAURANT, LIBRARY, BREAK-OUT SPACE_**KIND OF WORKPLACES:** OPEN-PLAN, COCKPIT, TEAM, CUBICAL, DESK-SHARING, BUSINESS CLUB, LOUNGE WORKSPACE **PHOTOS:** CHRISTIAN RICHTERS

Sabic Europe is one of the world's leading petrochemical companies. For their new European head office, they commissioned GROUP A to design an eye-catching building which would enhance the company's identity and reflect its values: renewability, transparency and approachability. These values have also been translated into a clear interior concept to which innovative working theories have been applied. All individual personalized workplaces have been replaced by working zones comprising both individual and open offices, meeting areas, concentration areas and quiet spaces. Architecture, interior and landscape were approached as a single unit to improve the building's surroundings and internal organization.

Sabic Europe ist eines der führenden petrochemischen Unternehmen weltweit. Für ihren neuen europäischen Hauptsitz wurde GROUP A beauftragt, ein auffälliges Gebäude zu entwerfen, welches die Firmenidentität betont und ihre Werte spiegelt: Erneuerung, Transparenz und Zugänglichkeit. Diese Werte wurden unter Anwendung innovativer Arbeitstheorien auch auf das Innenkonzept übertragen. Alle persönlichen Arbeitsplätze wurden durch Arbeitsbereiche ersetzt, die sowohl individuelle als auch offene Büros, Versammlungs- und Konzentrationsbereiche sowie Ruheräume umfassen. Architektur, Interieur und Landschaft wurden als Einheit betrachtet, um die Umgebung des Gebäudes und die innere Organisation zu optimalisieren.

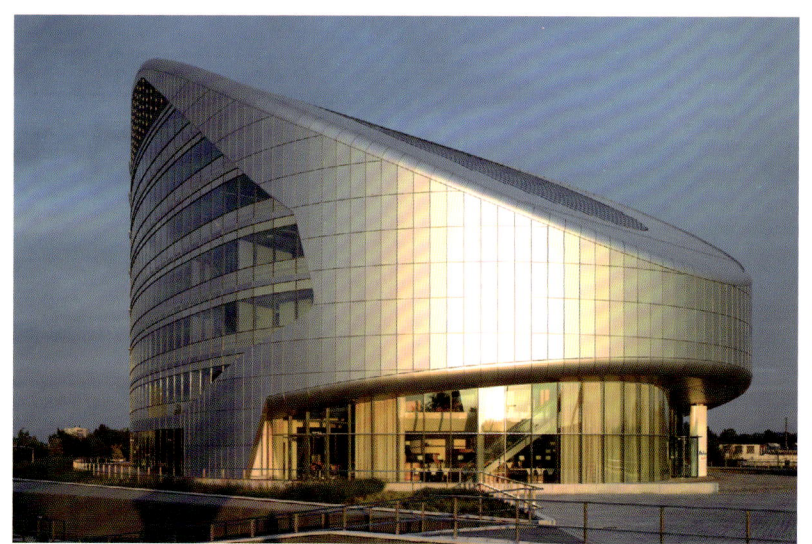

left: Sketch_Exterior elevation_Night view. right: Detail, façade.
links: Skizze_Außenansicht_Nachtaufnahme. rechts: Detail, Fassade.

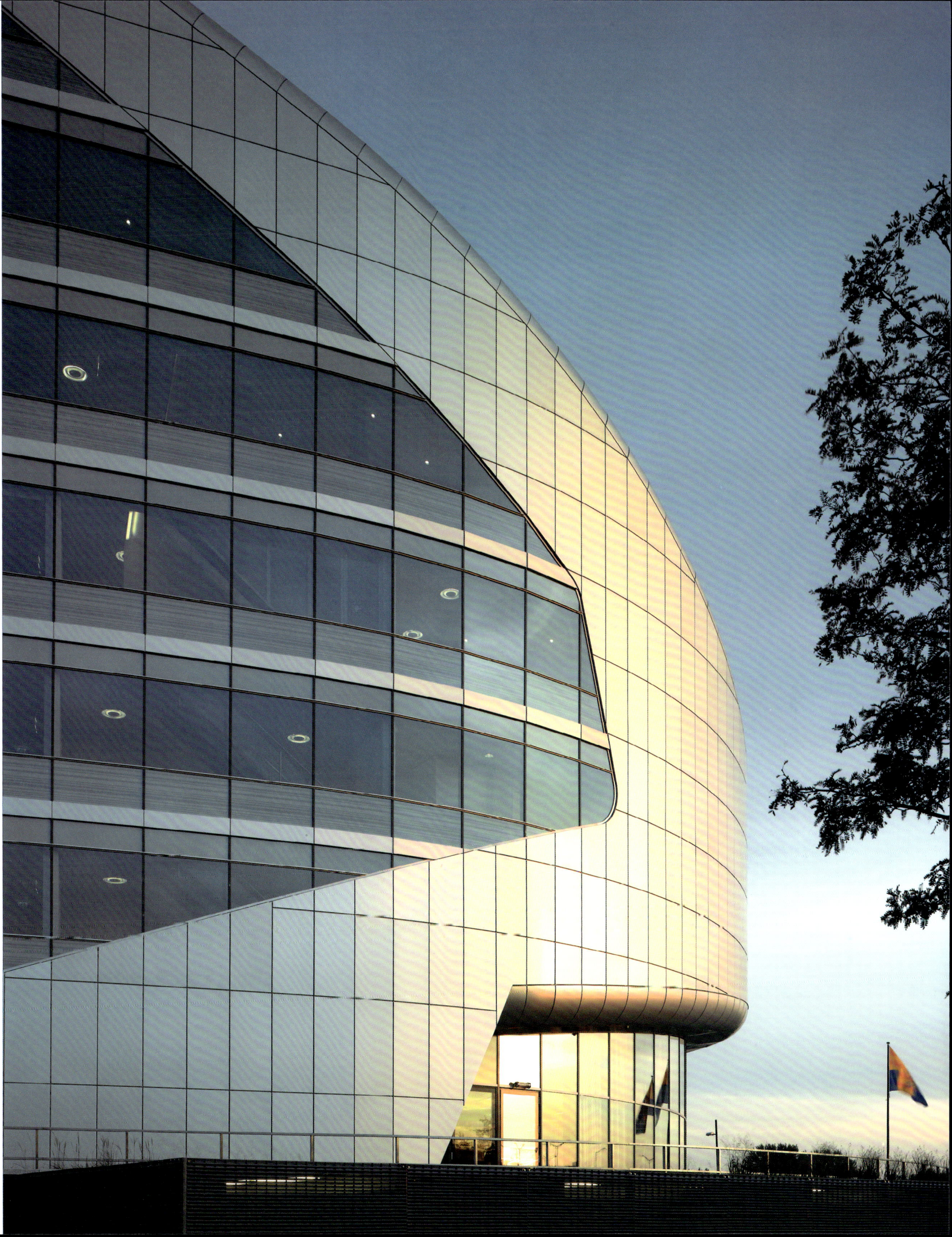

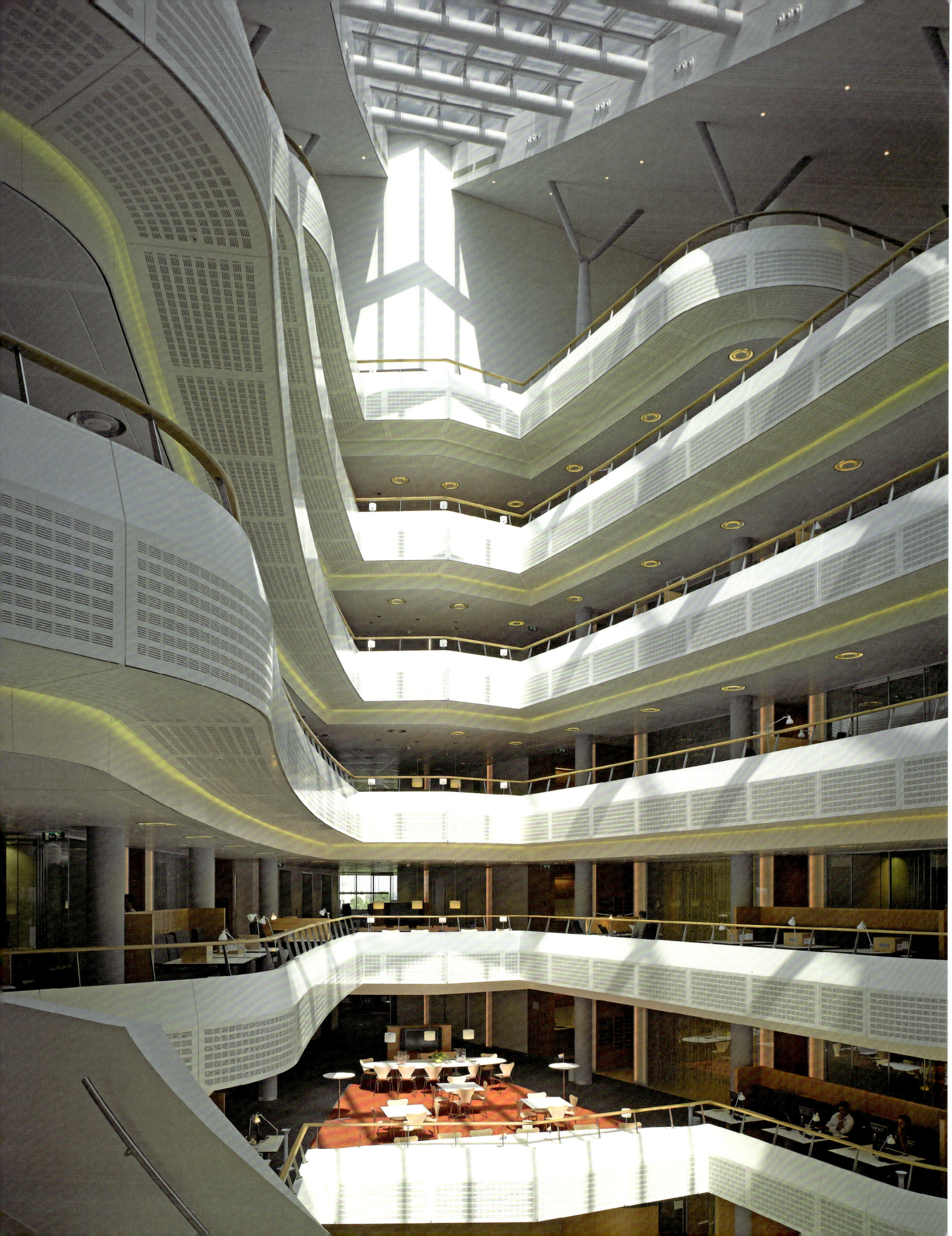

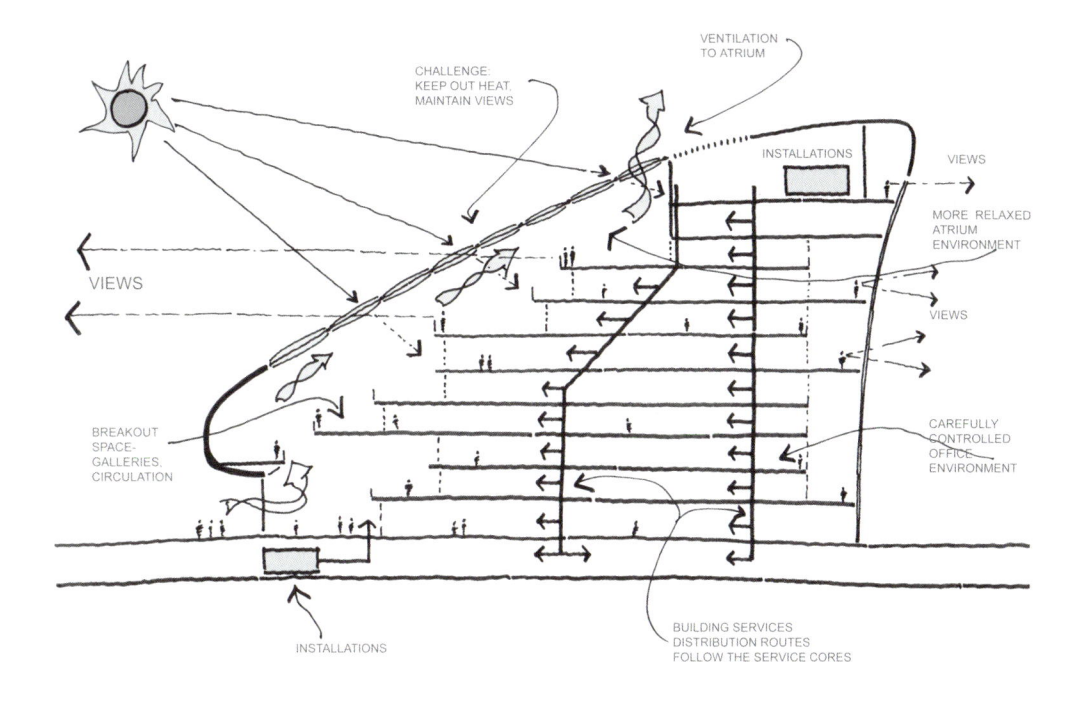

left: Office floors surrounding atrium. right: Overall concept_Window in atrium_Entrance with multi-functional desk_Business lounge_Meeting area.
links: Die Büroetagen umschließen das Atrium. rechts: Gesamtkonzept_Fenster im Atrium_Eingang mit Multifunktionstisch_Business lounge_Besprechungszone.

THE NETHERLANDS_ROTTERDAM **CABALLERO FABRIEK**

ARCHITECTS: GROUP A_**INTERIOR ARCHITECTS:** GROUP A WITH ZOOTZ INTERIOR STYLING_**COMPLETION:** 2008
NUMBER OF WORKPLACES: 500_**GROSS FLOOR AREA:** 14,500 M²
COMMON AREA: TERRACE, CAFÉ, EVENTS HALL
KIND OF WORKPLACES: OPEN-PLAN, LOUNGE WORKSPACE, START-UP CLUSTER_**PHOTOS:** SCAGLIOLA, BRAKKEE

The former tobacco factory has been transformed into a lively work environment with offices for companies from the culture, IT and media sectors. The leading theme of the design is cross-fertilization. The interior seeks to stimulate interaction amongst the tenants and between tenants and visitors. The industrial building remained intact while new functions stand out by their different designs. A new broad corridor including a meeting area, functions as the backbone of the building; with common areas for tenants as well as visitors all located on this corridor. Because of its lively character, the Caballero Fabriek is able to attract a wide audience, giving a strong new impulse to its surroundings.

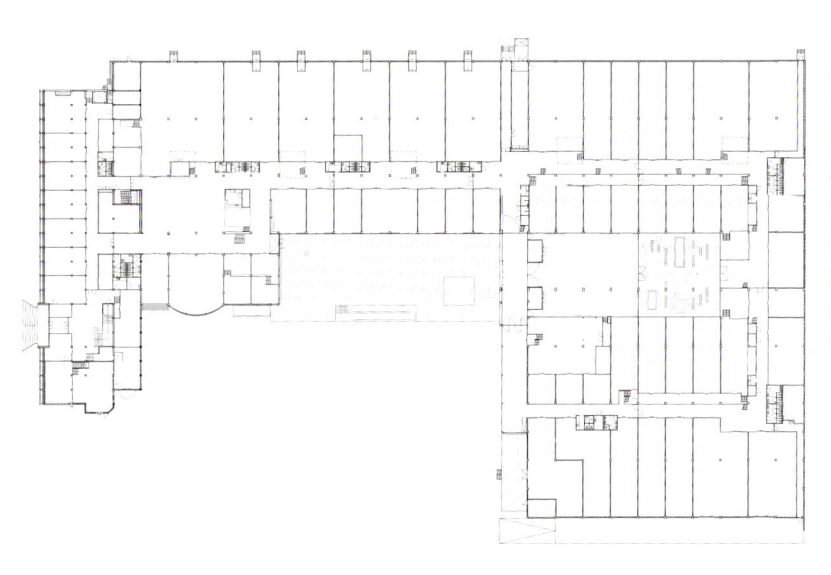

Die ehemalige Tabakfabrik wurde zu einem lebhaften Arbeitsbereich mit Firmenbüros in den Bereichen Kultur, IT und Medien umgestaltet. Das Hauptmotiv des Designs ist gegenseitiger Austausch. Das Interieur versucht die Interaktion zwischen den Inhabern und Besuchern zu fördern. Das Industriegebäude bleibt intakt, während neue Funktionen aufgrund ihres Designs hervorstechen. Ein neuer, breiter Flur einschließlich Meeting-Bereich stellt den Hauptstrang des Gebäudes dar, auf dem sich alle Gemeinschaftsräume für Inhaber sowie Besucher befinden. Aufgrund ihres lebhaften Charakters spricht die Caballero Fabriek ein breites Publikum an und gibt ihrer Umgebung einen neuen starken Impuls.

left: Ground floor plan_General elevation_Communal terrace. right: Conference "box" and corridor_Door between corridors_Entrance and Lunch café.
links: Grundriss Erdgeschoss_Totale_Öffentliche Terrasse. rechts: Besprechungs-„Box" und Flur_Tür zwischen den Fluren_Eingang und Cafeteria.

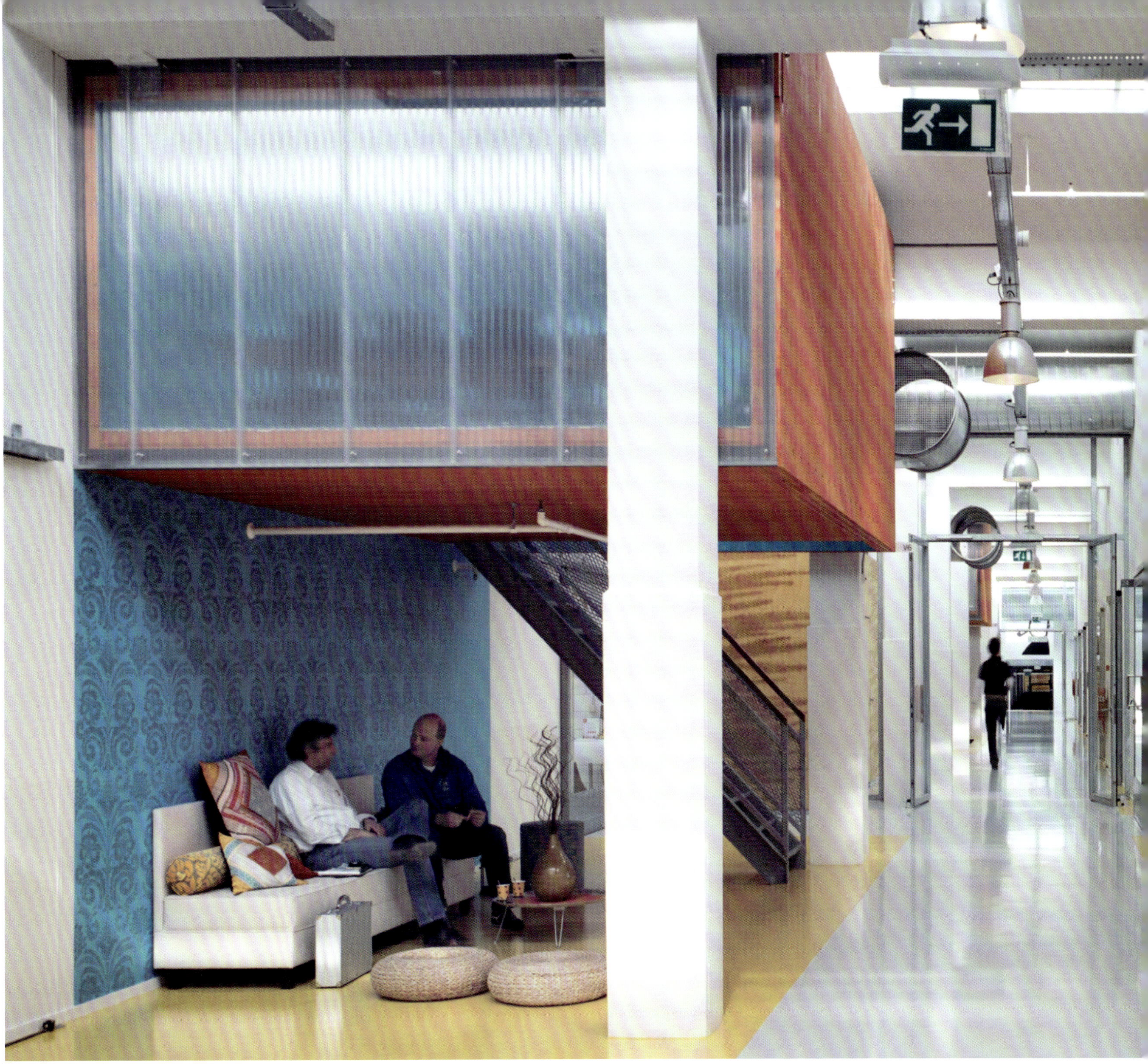

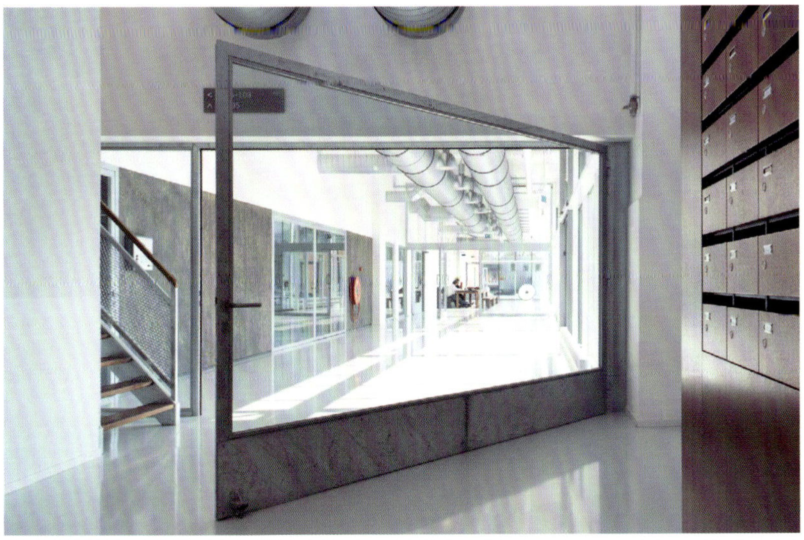

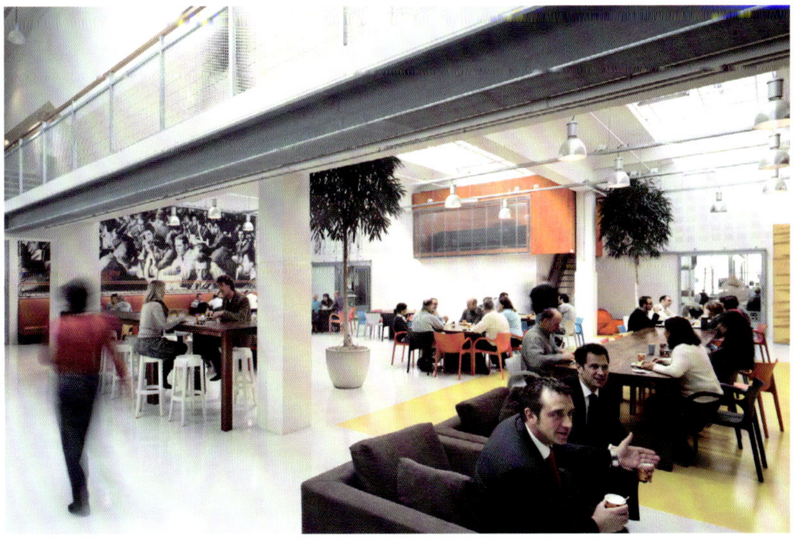

THE NETHERLANDS_ROTTERDAM DEBRUG / DEKADE UNILEVER ROTTERDAM

ARCHITECTS: JHK ARCHITECTEN_**URBAN DESIGN:** WEST 8 URBAN DESIGN & LANDSCAPE ARCHITECTURE
COMPLETION: 2007_**NUMBER OF WORKPLACES:** 800
GROSS FLOOR AREA: 34,250 M²_**COMMON AREAS:** KITCHENS
KIND OF WORKPLACES: CELLULAR, COMBINATION, OPEN-PLAN, COCKPIT, TEAM, DESKSHARING, BUSINESS CLUB, NON-TERRITORIAL, LOUNG WORKSPACE
PHOTOS: PALLADIUM PHOTODESIGN, COLOGNE

The lowest floor of the new building is 25 meters above the quay, spanning the old factory complex. The main entrance is located between the classical 19th century building and the deKade office. The elevator and staircase to the floors are in the inner court. The offices offer a breathtaking view of the city center. Atriums and patios allow light to enter the building. The vacant spaces are strategically located to ensure adequate illumination in the central zone. Transparency is visible on the outer façade and contributes to give the entire building a communicative character. deBrug therefore adequately responds to the need for a dynamic office organization in which consultations can be held in an informal atmosphere.

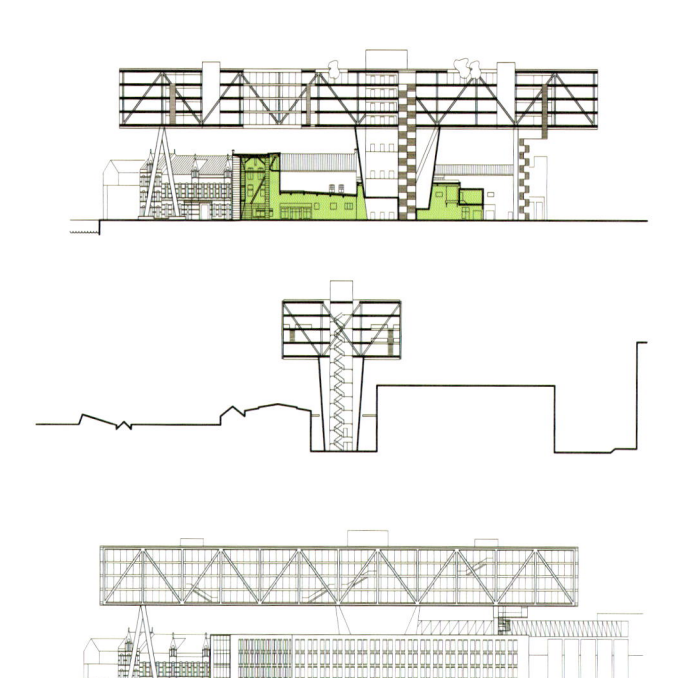

Die niedrigste Ebene, die sich über den derzeitigen Fabrikkomplex erstreckt, liegt 25 Meter über dem Kai. Der Haupteingang befindet sich zwischen dem klassischen Gebäude aus dem 19. Jahrhundert und dem Büro deKade. Aufzug und Treppenhaus zu den Stockwerken liegen im Innenhof. Die Büros bieten einen atemberaubenden Blick auf die Innenstadt. Strategisch angeordnete Innenhöfe gewährleisten eine ausreichende Beleuchtung im Zentrum zdes Volumens. Die Transparenz der Außenfassade trägt zum kommunikativen Charakter des Gebäudes bei. deBrug geht angemessen auf den Bedarf einer dynamischen Büroorganisation ein, sodass Konferenzen in zwangloser Atmosphäre gehalten werden können.

left: Sections and elevation_Front façade of deBrug and deKade_Street view from the Nassaukade at sunset. right: Main entrance on quay.
links: Schnitte und Ansicht_Vorderansicht deBrug und deKade_Straßenansicht von der Nassaukade in der Abenddämmerung. rechts: Haupteingang vom Kai.

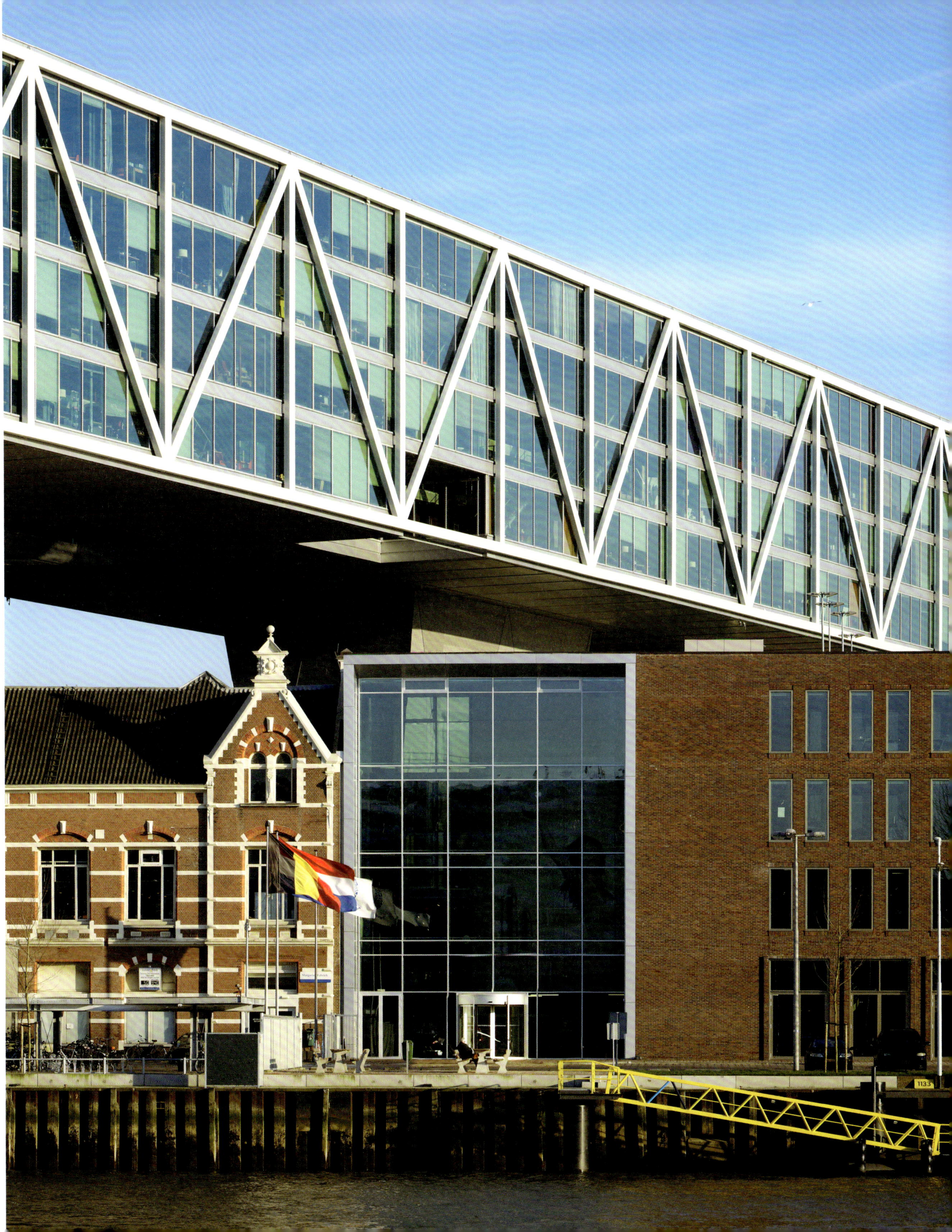
1133

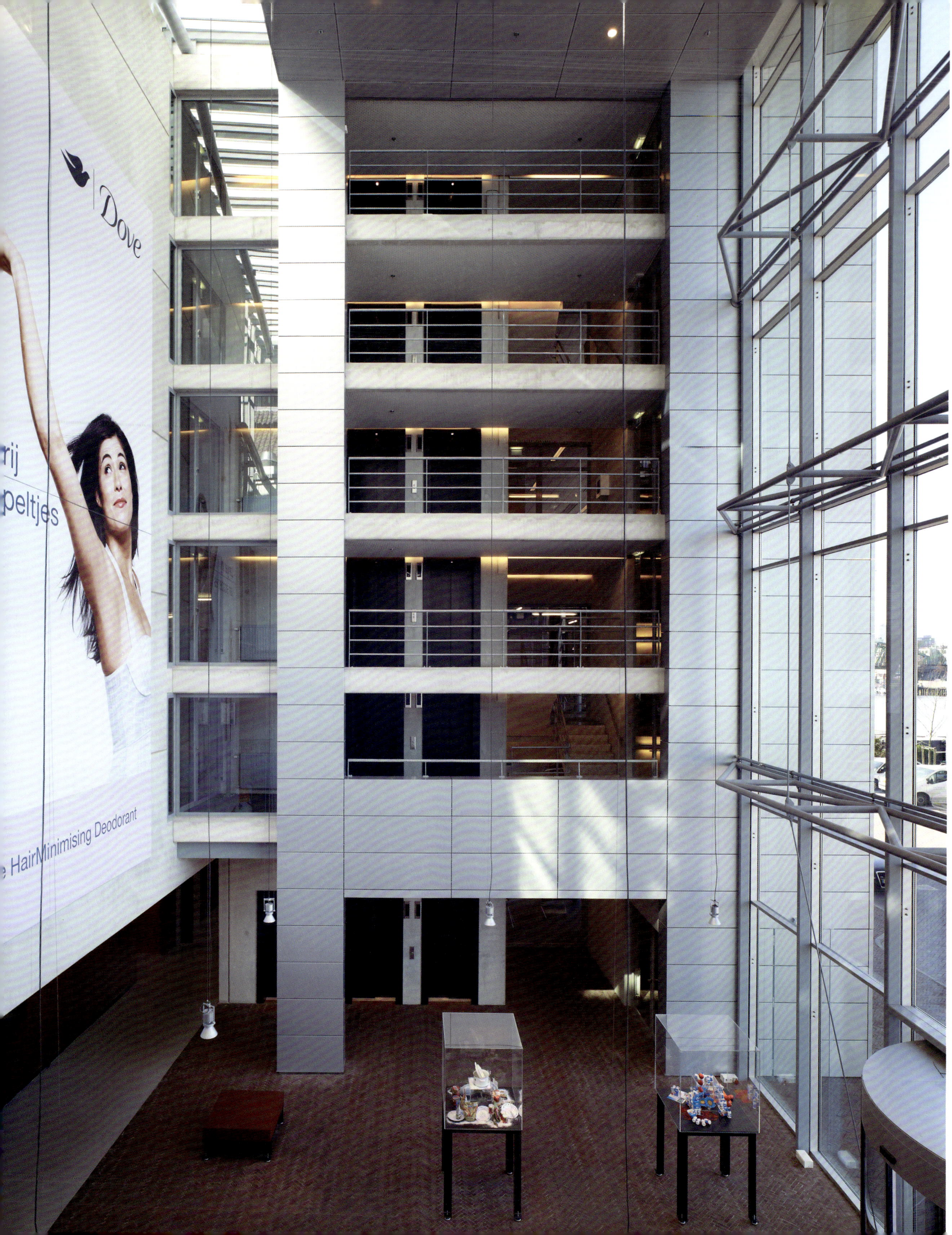
Dove
rij
peltjes
HairMinimising Deodorant

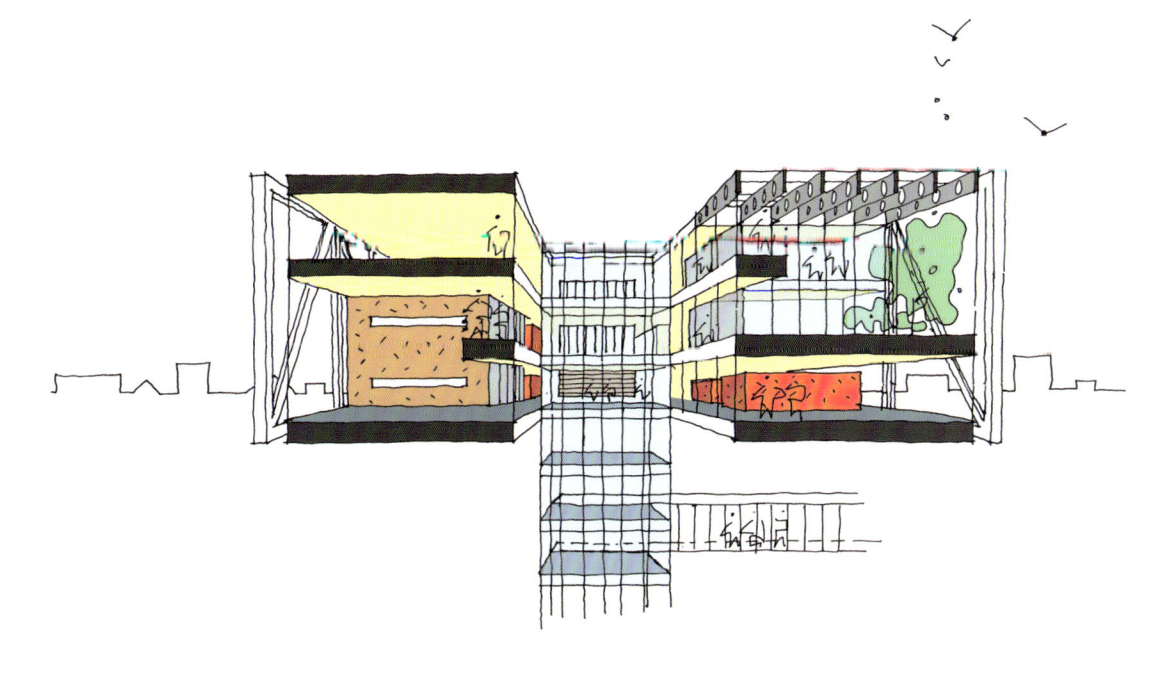

left: Interior of main entrance. right: Concept sketch_Main entrance night view_Atrium.
links: Innenansicht Haupteingang. rechts: Konzeptskizze_Haupteingang abends_Atrium.

THE NETHERLANDS_SCHEVENINGEN OFFICE VAN DER ZWAN & ZN.

ARCHITECTS: MEYER EN VAN SCHOOTEN ARCHITECTEN
LIGHTING SCULPTURE: SCABETTI_**COMPLETION:** 2009
NUMBER OF WORKPLACES: 20_**GROSS FLOOR AREA:** 2,000 M²
COMMON AREA: CONFERENCE ROOMS, BAR
KIND OF WORK-PLACES: OPEN-PLAN, BOARD ROOM
PHOTOS: JEROEN MUSCH, HANS MORREN (341 R.)

The fishing company Van der Zwan established itself on a peninsula across the harbor entrance of Scheveningen. The 360-degree orientation demanded by the location, the light glass box placed on a concrete base with sturdy concrete V-columns, the balcony on the south façade, and the stalwart image desired by the company all came together in the image of a navigating bridge. The west side is by far the most spectacular with its view of the open sea and the sunset at the end of a working day. High quality materials were chosen for durability and sustainability in the extreme sea side conditions. The building accommodates offices, conference facilities, bar and warehouse, plus fish inspection rooms and logistics.

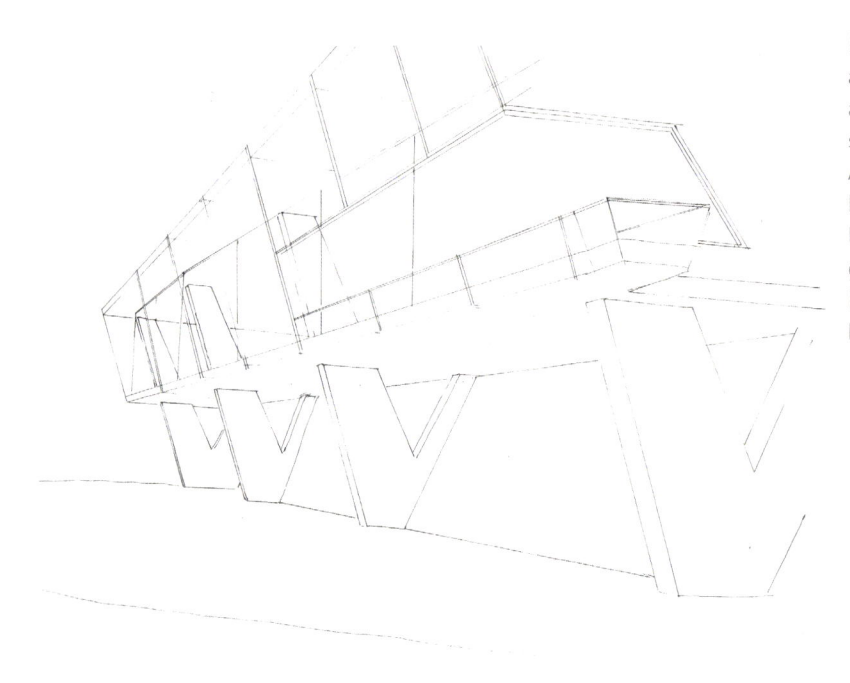

Das Fischereiunternehmen Van der Zwan siedelte sich auf einer Halbinsel an, die der Hafeneinfahrt Schevenings gegenüberliegt. Die freie Lage, die allseitige Gestaltung verlangte, der leichte Glaskasten auf Betonunterbau mit stämmigen V-förmigen Pfeilern, der Balkon der Südfassade und das vom Auftraggeber gewünschte robuste Image fanden im Bild der Steuermannsbrücke zusammen. Die Westseite, mit Blick auf das Meer und feierabendlichen Sonnenuntergängen, ist am spektakulärsten. Hochwertige Materialien gewähren im extremen Meeresklima Haltbarkeit und Nachhaltigkeit. Im Inneren finden sich Büros, Konferenzräume, eine Bar sowie Lager mit Warenkontrollräumen und Räumen für Logistik.

left: Conceptual sketch façade and construction_View from balcony on south-west façade towards the harbor entrance_Interior main office spaces. right: Exterior view from seaside.
links: Konzeptskizze, Fassade und Konstruktion_Blick vom Balkon auf der Südwestfassade zum Hafeneingang_Hauptbürobereich. rechts: Außenansicht Meerseite.

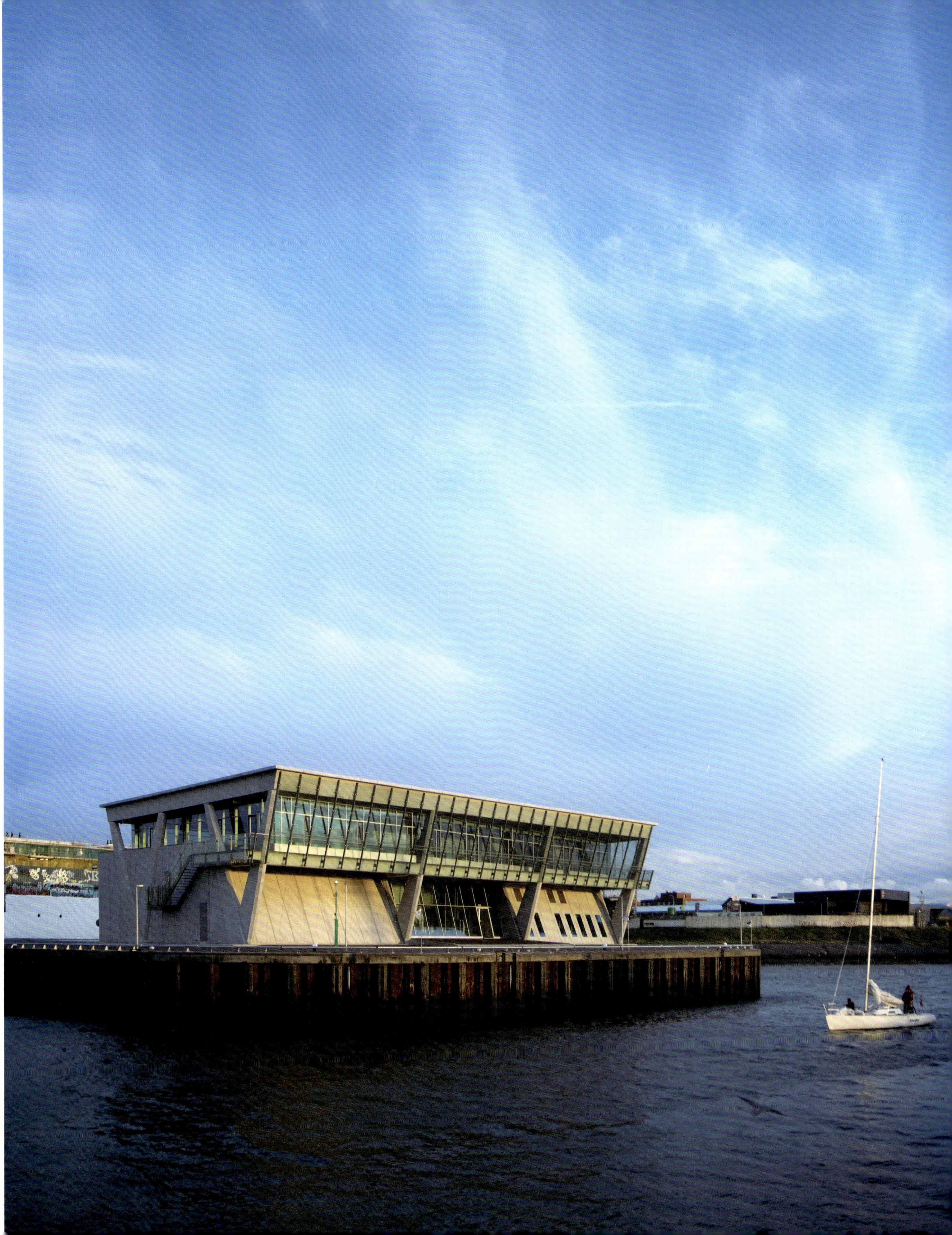

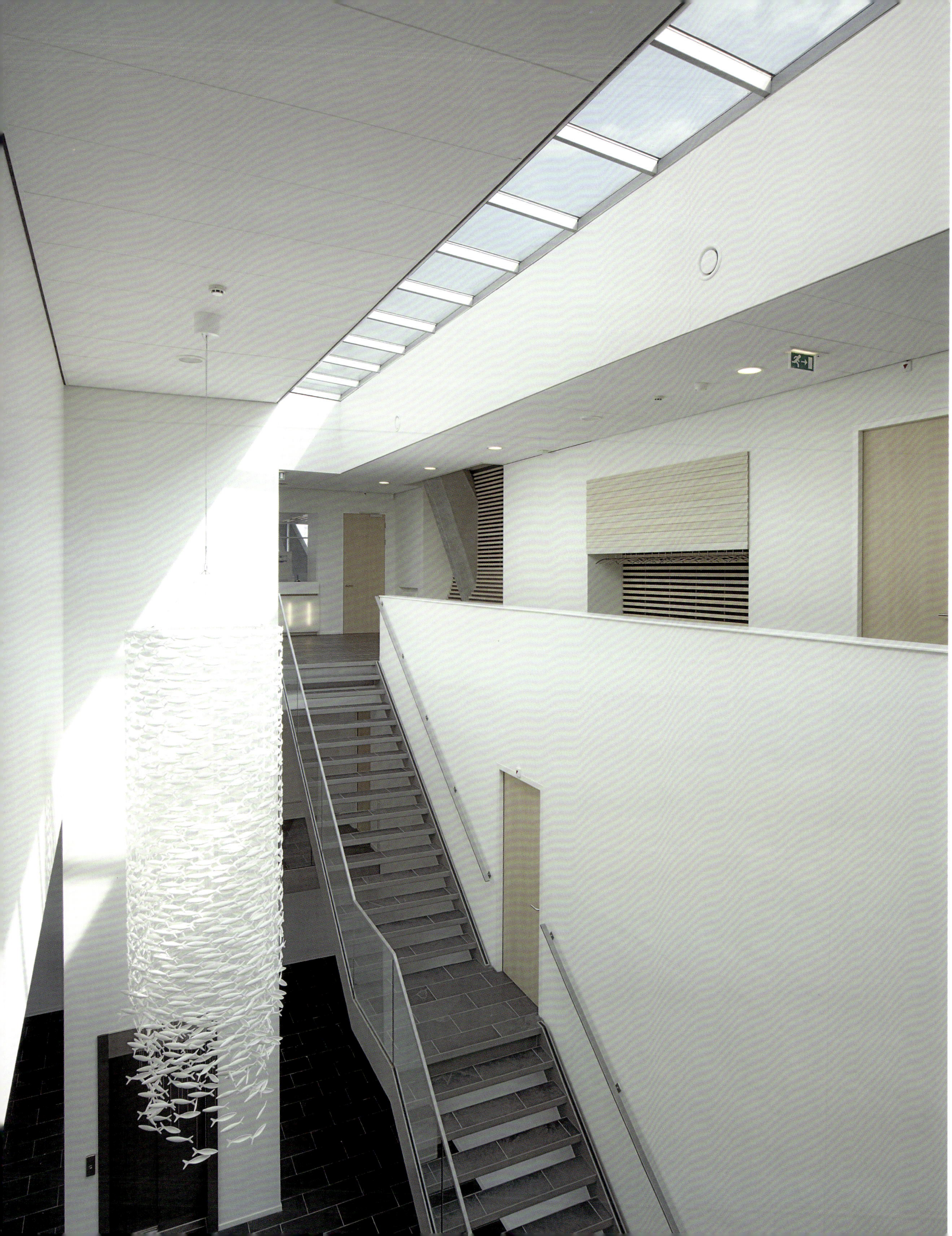

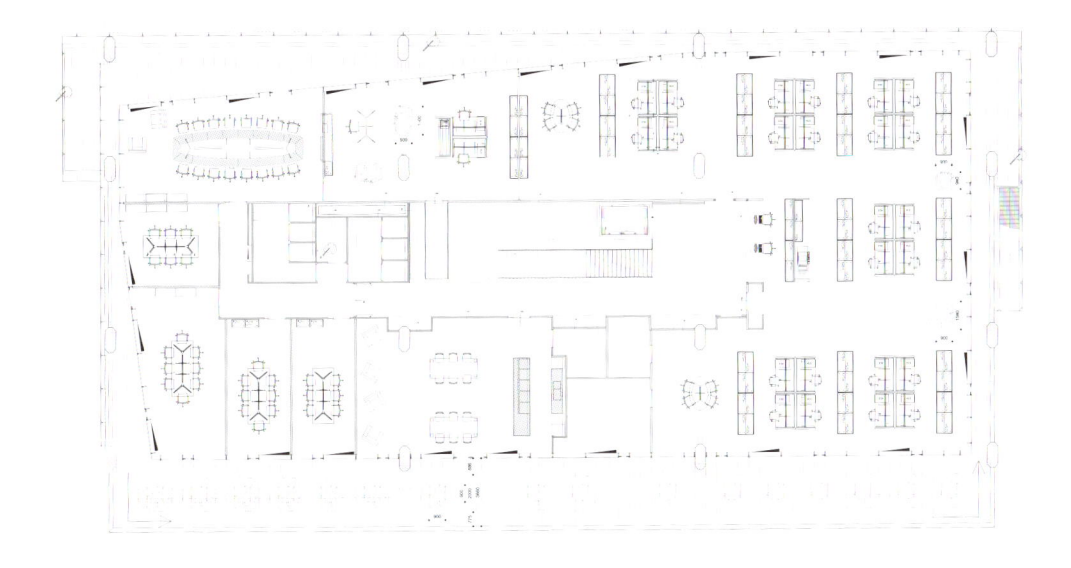

left: Main entrance hall with view on lighting sculpture by Scabetti. right: Second floor plan, office level_Front with view on double skin façade to protect against extrem weather conditions_Board room_Reception area on second floor.

links: Haupteingang mit Blick auf die Lichtskulptur von Scabetti. rechts: Grundriss, zweites Obergeschoss, Büroebene Vorderansicht mit Blick auf die zweischichtige Fassade, die auch extremsten Wetterbedinungen trotzt_Sitzungsraum_Empfangsbreich im zweiten Obergeschoss.

THE NETHERLANDS_SCHIEDAM **DE KUYPER ROYAL DISTILLERS**

ARCHITECTS: BROEKBAKEMA**_LIGHTING BAR AND MEDIA TECHNIQUES:** DEP**_FURNITURE COCKTAILBAR:** ZOINK! **COMPLETION:** 2007**_NUMBER OF WORKPLACES:** 11 **GROSS FLOOR AREA:** 1,579 M²**_COMMON AREA:** BAR**_KIND OF WORKPLACES:** OPEN-PLAN**_PHOTOS:** ROB 'T HART, ROTTERDAM

The new arrangement for the reception area of the office was designed to appeal to contemporary tastes – the world of chic cocktail bars frequented by a young, successful, dynamic, international, trend-setting and sophisticated clientele. The visit is also an instructive experience, where people can get acquainted with the distillery's history and sample the latest products through sight and taste. Visitors follow a route along a thirty-meter display cabinet through the old distillery with copper stills and wooden vats in an atmosphere of history and craftsmanship. Finally, visitors find themselves back in the reception area, which has metamorphosed into a completely different space – the Future Spirits Bar.

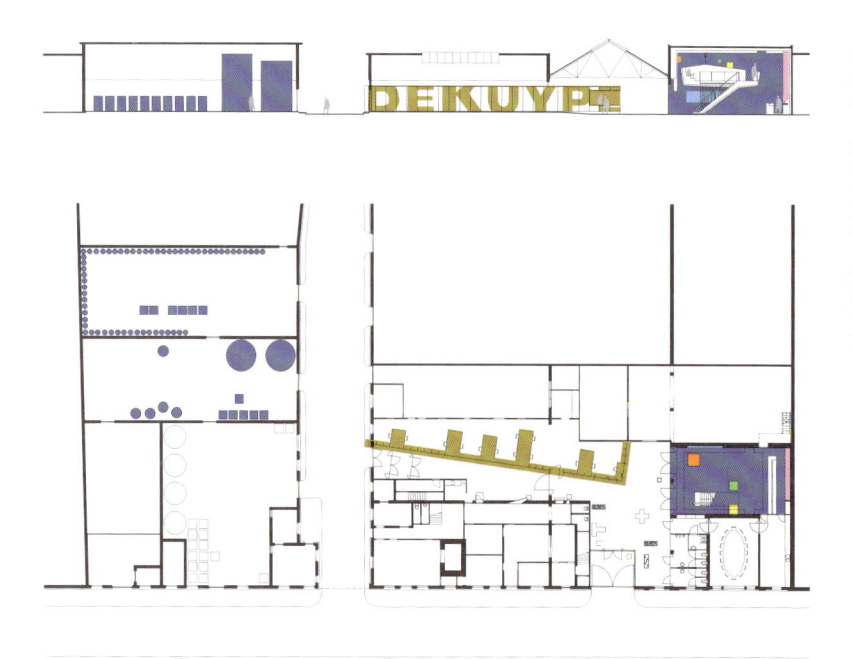

Die Neugestaltung des Empfangsbereichs des Büros sollte modernem Geschmack entsprechen – der Welt der schicken Cocktailbars, die von einem jungen, erfolgreichen, dynamischen, internationalen, zukunftsweisenden und kultivierten Publikum besucht werden. Der Besuch soll ein lehrreiches Erlebnis sein, in dem man die Geschichte der Destillerie kennen lernt und die neuesten Produkte probiert. Die Besucher folgen einem Weg entlang einer 30 Meter langen Vitrine und durch die alte Destillerie mit kupfernen Destillierapparaten und Holzfässern, eine Atmosphäre von Geschichte und Handwerkskunst. Schließlich gelangen sie zurück in den Empfangsbereich, der sich in einen völlig anderen Raum verwandelt hat – die Future Spirits Bar.

left: Section and floor plan_Future Spirits Bar_Meeting room. right: Office_Showcase_Entrance hall with reception.
links: Schnitt und Grundriss_Future Spirits Bar_Besprechungszimmer. rechts: Büro_Schaufenster_Eingangshalle mit Empfang.

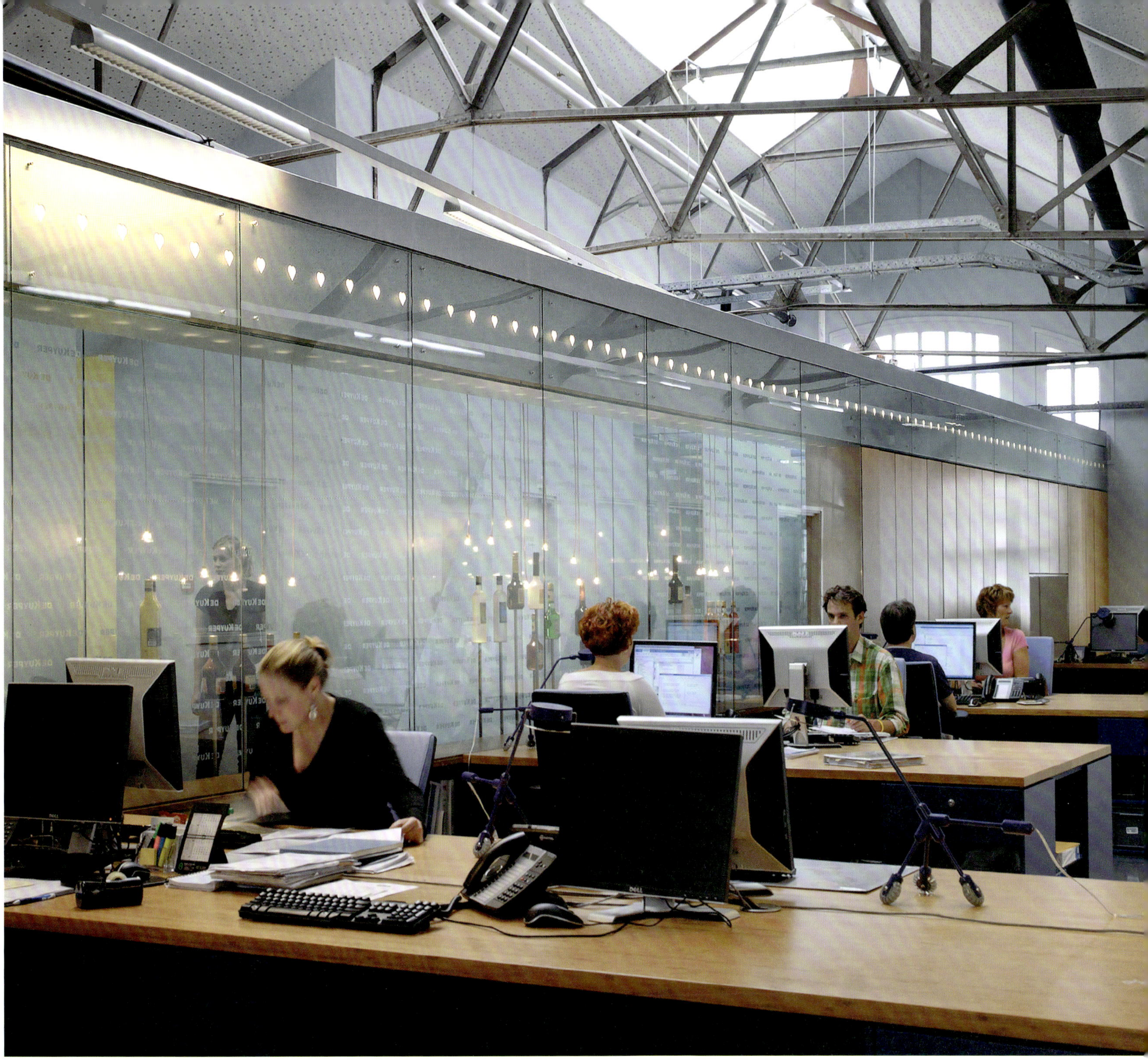
DE KUYPER

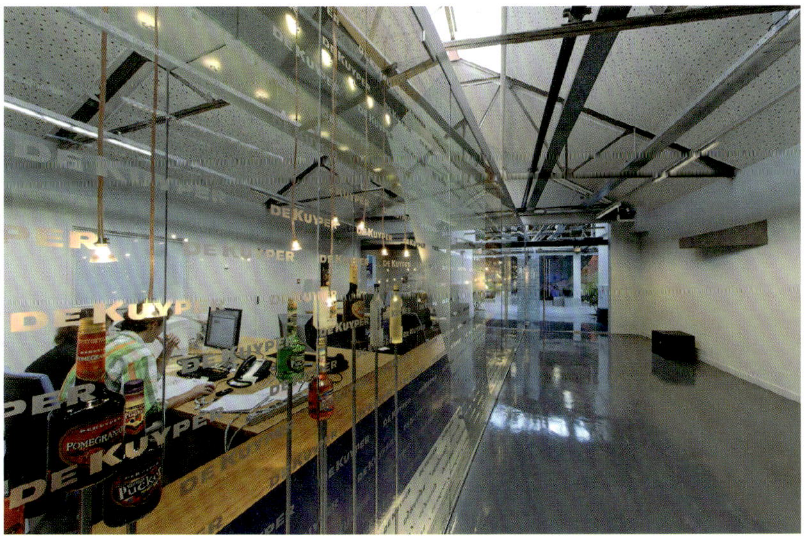
DE KUYPER

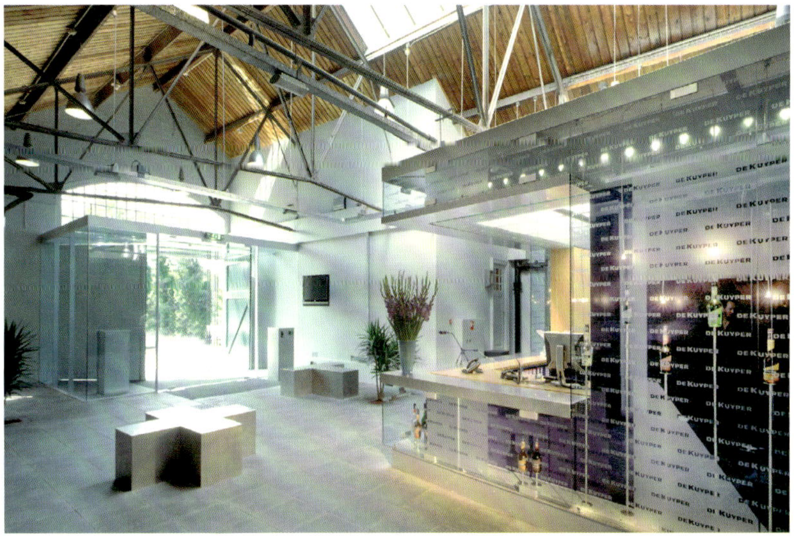
DE KUYPER

THE NETHERLANDS_SCHIPHOL **THE OUTLOOK**

ARCHITECTS: CEPEZED ARCHITECTS
COMPLETION: 2008_**NUMBER OF WORKPLACES:** 3,200
GROSS FLOOR AREA: 64,000 M²_**COMMON AREA:** COFFEE BAR, COMPANY RESTAURANT_**KIND OF WORKPLACES:** CELLULAR, COMBINATION, OPEN-PLAN, DESKSHARING, BUSINESS CLUB, NON-TERRITORIAL, LOUNGE WORKSPACE_**PHOTOS:** FAS KEUZENKAMP (344 B. L., 345), LUUK KRAMER (344 B. R.), HAROLD PEREIRA (346, 347)

The modern office complex offers an open and light ambience, considerable free height at each story, and extra-wide office bays with a minimum amount of columns. The project contains more than 38,000 square meters of office space, which is in part occupied by the Dutch head office of Microsoft. The main structure consists of a series of alternately interlocking longer and shorter office bays. Two subterranean layers and the plinth of the building contain the car parks with 850 parking places. The office floors are linked by large voids and representative staircases. The flexible and efficient layout makes it possible to respond rapidly to the individual layout wishes of diverse tenants.

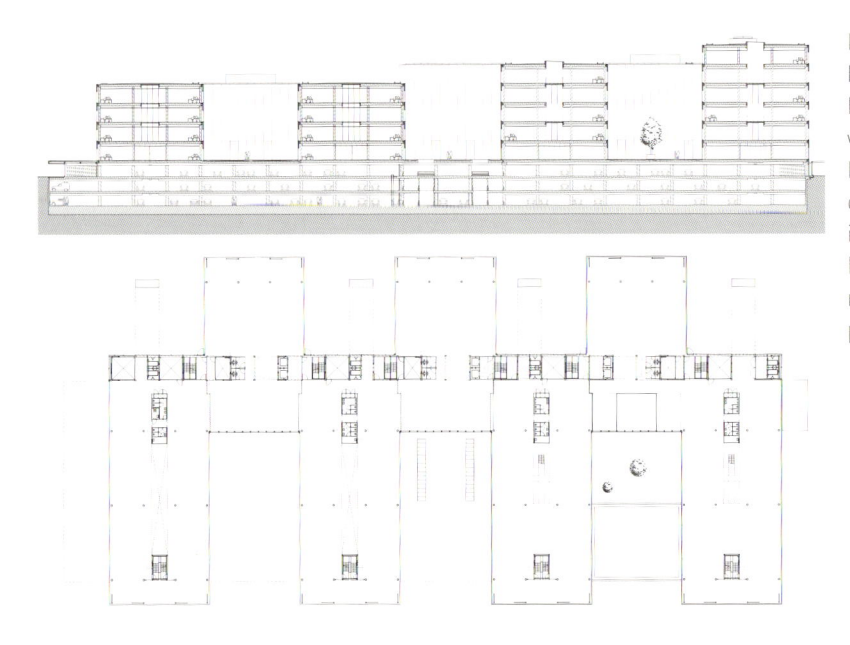

Der moderne Bürokomplex bietet eine offene und helle Atmosphäre, markante hohe Stockwerke und weite Büroräume mit wenigen Säulen. Das Projekt erstreckt sich über mehr als 38.000 Quadratmeter Büroraum und wird zum Teil von der holländischen Microsoft-Hauptverwaltung genutzt. Die Hauptstruktur besteht aus einer Reihe von abwechselnd ineinander greifenden längeren und kürzeren Büroräumen. In zwei unterirdischen Ebenen und im Sockel des Gebäudes befindet sich das Parkhaus mit 850 Stellplätzen. Die Büroebenen sind durch repräsentative Treppenaufgänge und große Leerräume verbunden. Der flexible und effiziente Aufbau ermöglicht eine rasche Anpassung an die individuellen räumlichen Wünsche der verschiedenen Nutzer.

left: Section and floor plan_Night view_View through two levels. right: Night view.
links: Schnitt und Grundriss_Nachtansicht_Blick durch zwei Stockwerke. rechts: Nachtansicht.

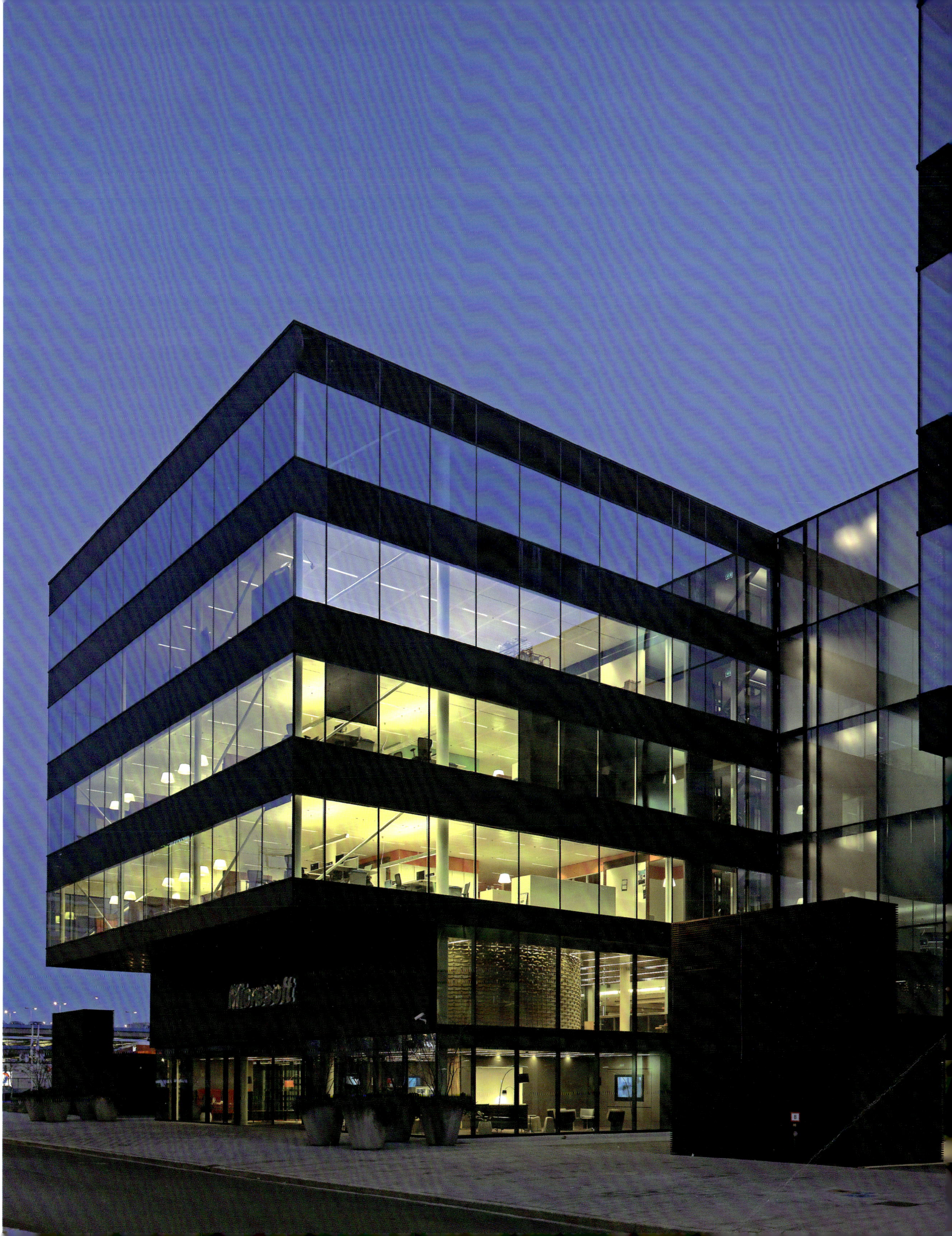
Microsoft

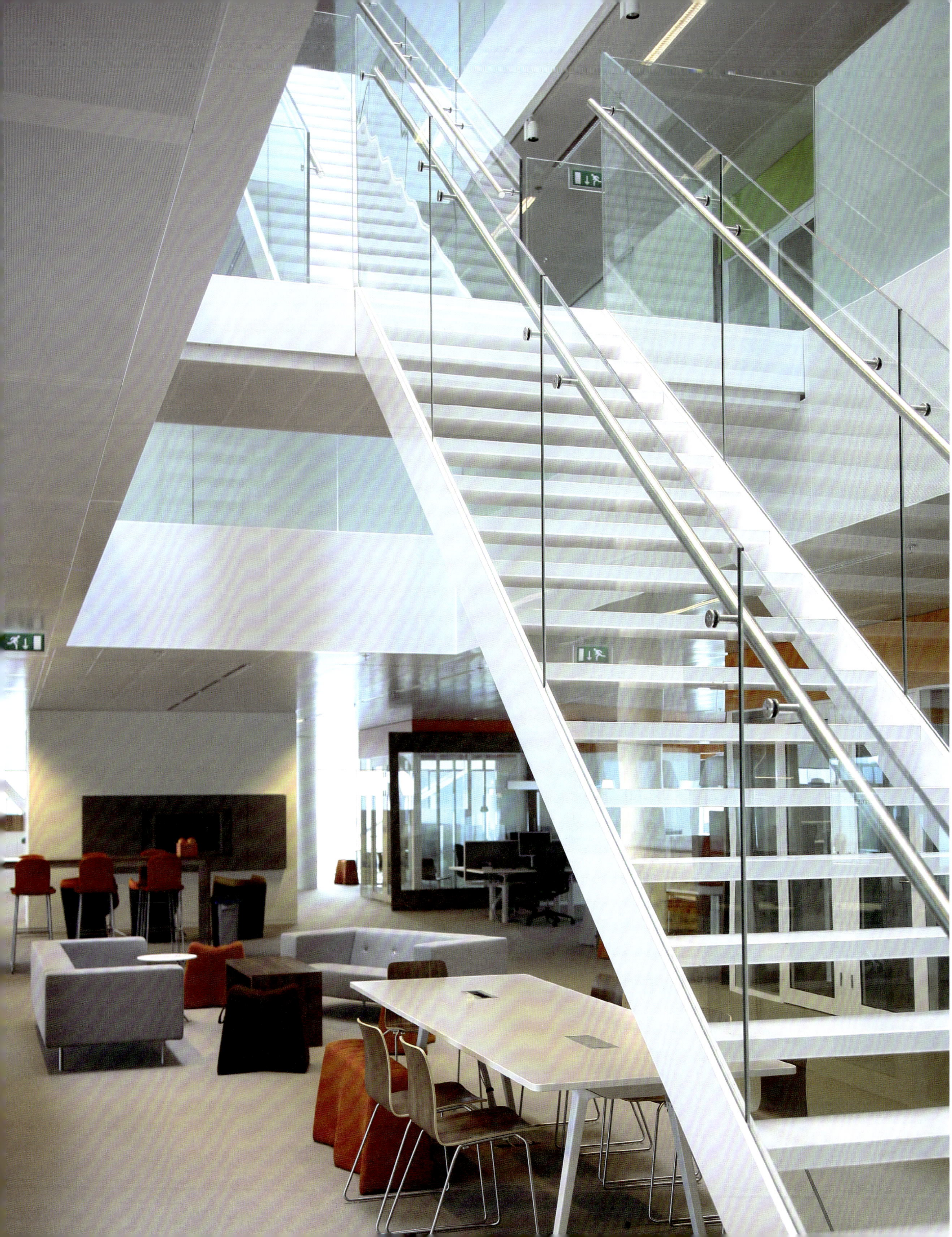

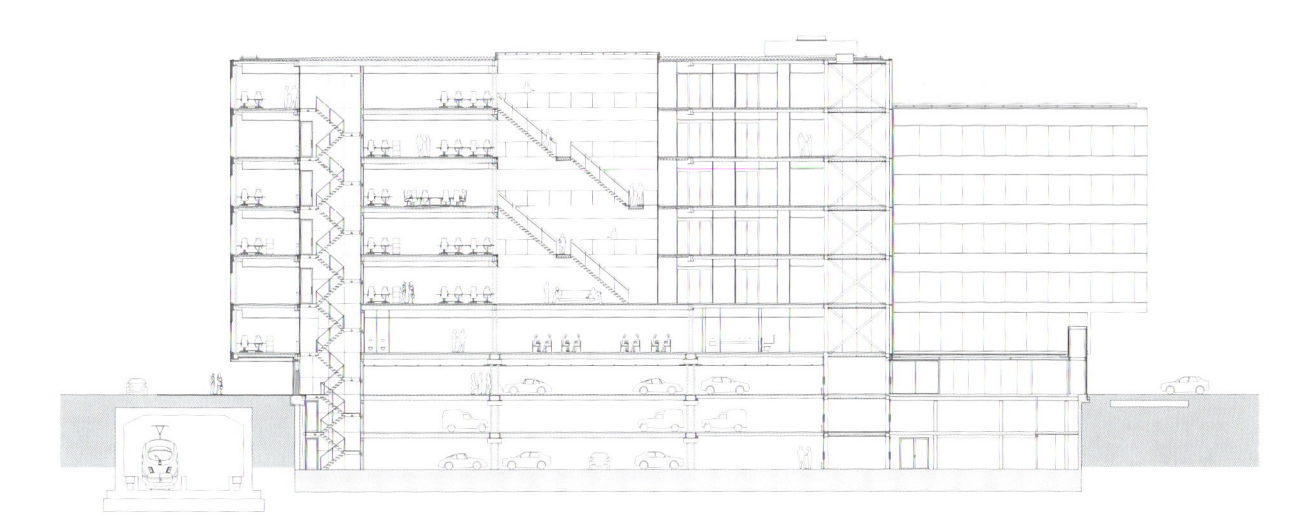

left: Community area. right: Section_Ongoing cascade stairs_Lounge area with large glass façade_Flexible workplaces.
links: Gemeinschaftsbereich. rechts: Schnitt_Treppenhaus_Lounge mit riesiger Glasfassade_Flexibler Arbeitsplatz.

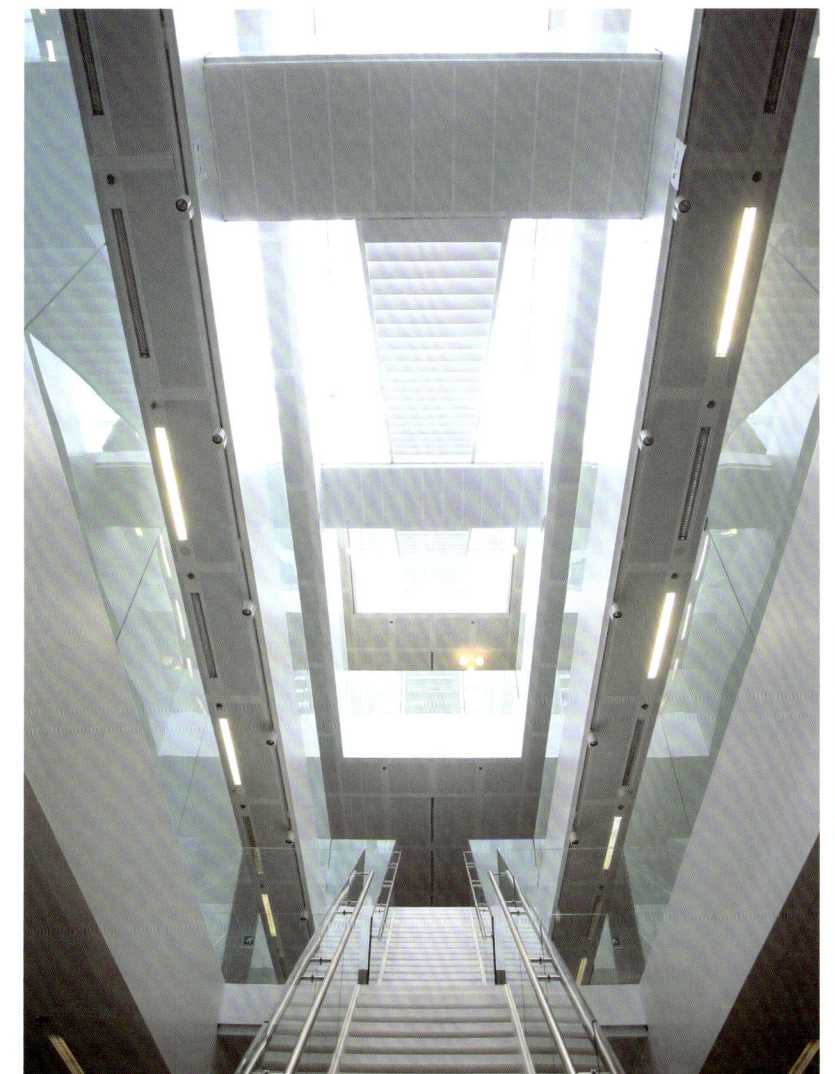

THE NETHERLANDS_UTRECHT **OFFICE KROPMAN**

ARCHITECTS: BROEKBAKEMA
COMPLETION: 2003_**NUMBER OF WORKPLACES:** 210
GROSS FLOOR AREA: 5,300 M²_**COMMON AREA:** RESTAURANT, MEETING ROOMS_**KIND OF WORKPLACES:** COMBINATION, OPEN-PLAN, DESKSHARING
PHOTOS: BASTIAAN INGENHOUSZ, DORDRECHT (348 L., 350, 351 R.), LUUK KRAMER, AMSTERDAM (348 R., 351 L.), MENNO EMMINK, DELFT (349)

The atrium that runs down all four floors becomes the light and spacious center of the building, creating a pleasant atmosphere. The glass inner walls not only enable visual contact between the office area and the center of the building, they also constitute an attractive sound barrier. By situating the sanitary, logistic and technical provisions at the far sides, the office areas on both sides of the long-drawn atrium remain as empty as possible. The division of the floors can be adapted to new requirements, ensuring that the flexible building will stay in service for a long period of time. Sustainable energy sources and an easy to maintain façade ensure that the new Kropman premises are built for the future.

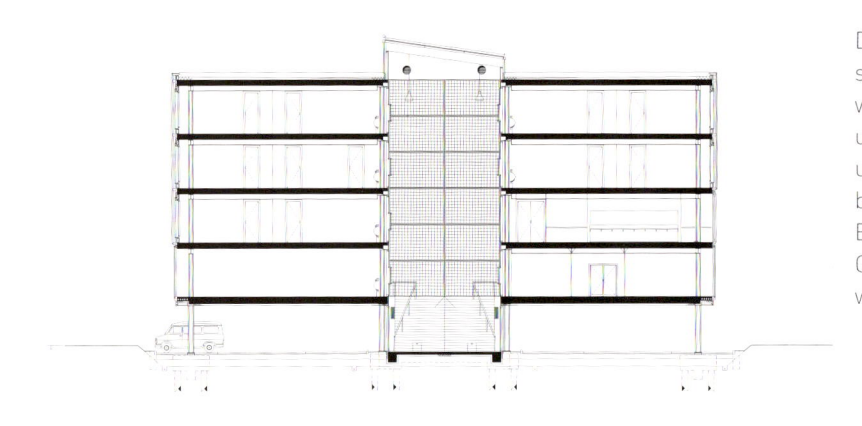

Der sich durch alle vier Stockwerke ziehende Innenhof mit angenehmer Atmosphäre ist das helle und geräumige Zentrum des Gebäudes. Die Glasinnenwände ermöglichen Blickkontakt zwischen Bürobereich und Gebäudezentrum und fungieren als Lärmschutz. Durch die Unterbringung sanitärer, logistischer und technischer Einrichtungen am anderen Ende bleiben die Bürobereiche auf beiden Seiten des langen Innenhofs so leer wie möglich. Die Aufteilung der Ebenen kann an neue Anforderungen angepasst werden, sodass das flexible Gebäude lange genutzt werden kann. Nachhaltige Energiequellen und eine wartungsfreundliche Fassade gewährleisten die Zukunft des Gebäudes.

left: Section_Entrance and reception_Cafeteria. right: Exterior view at night.
links: Schnitt_Eingang und Empfang_Cafeteria. rechts: Außenansicht bei Nacht.

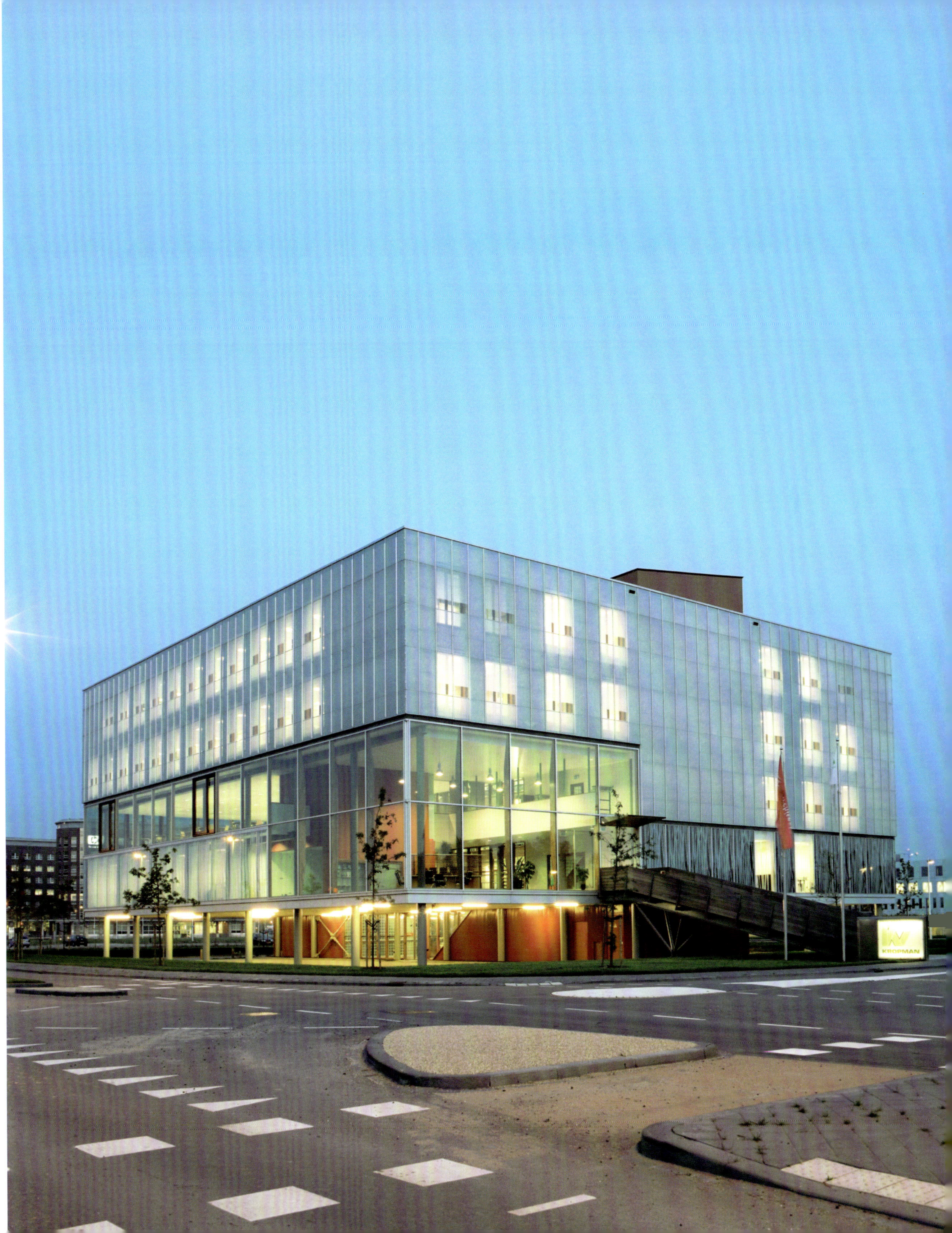
KROPMAN

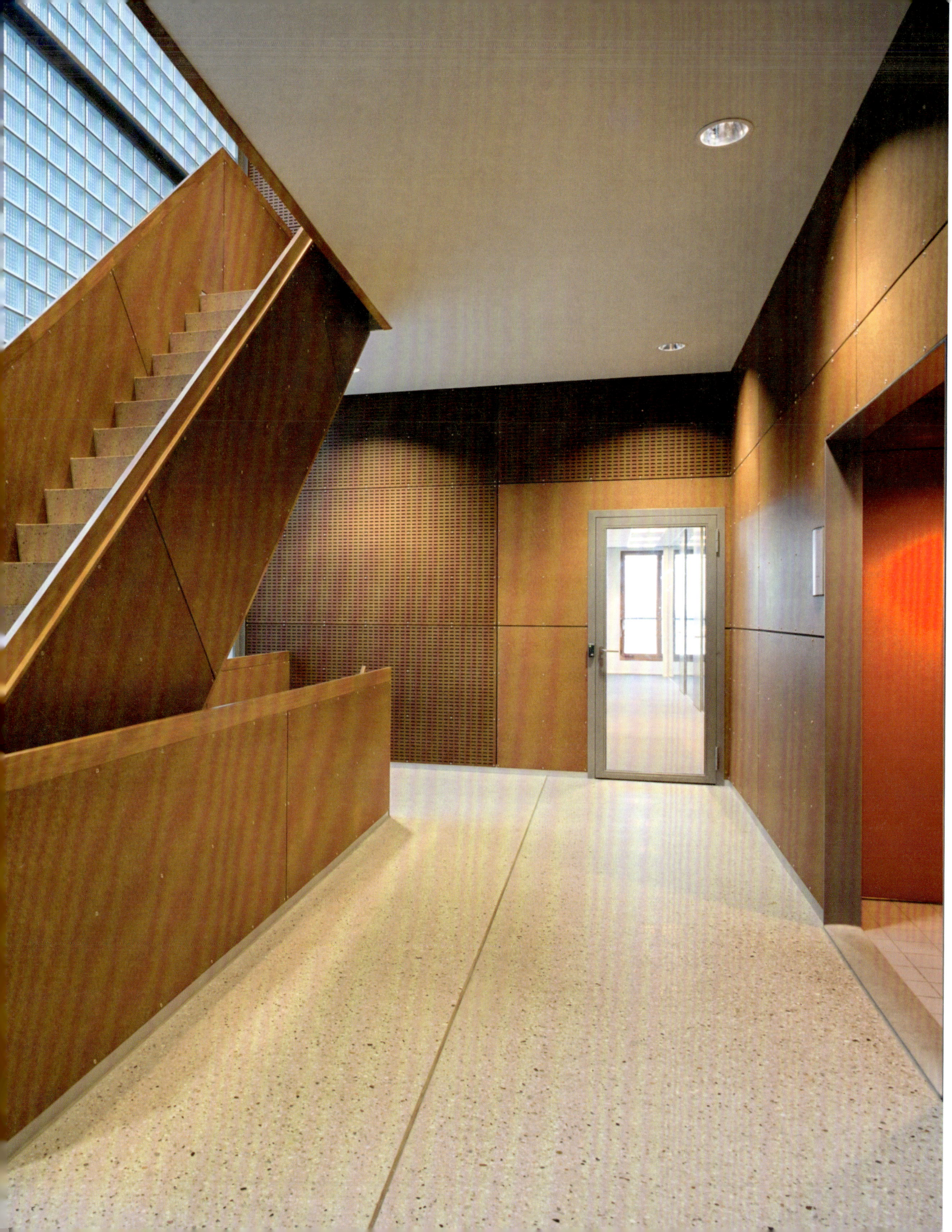

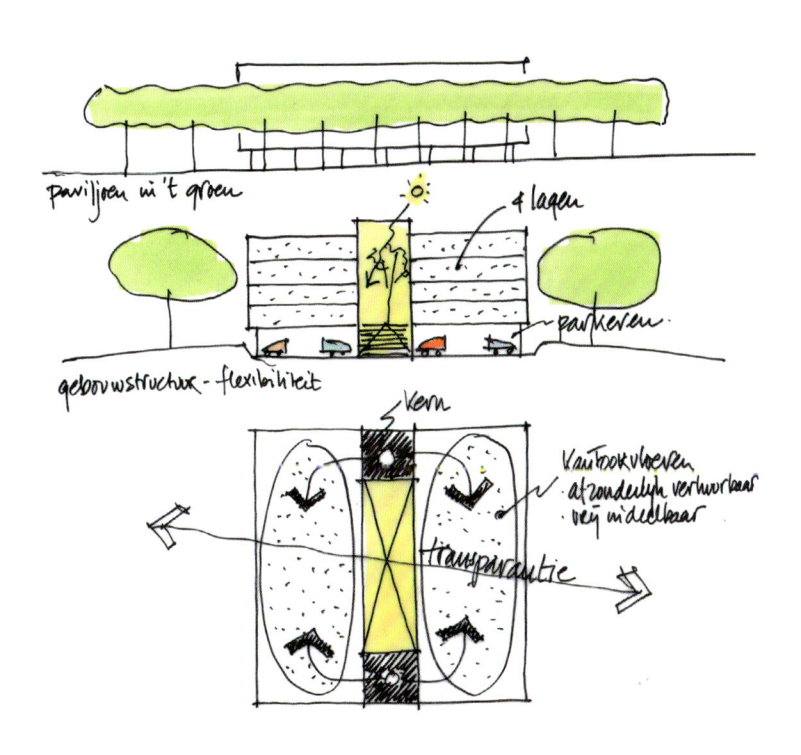

left: Stairway. right: Sketch_Office_Greened and light atrium_View from atrium to offices.
links: Treppenhaus. rechts: Skizze_Büro_Begrüntes und helles Atrium_Blick vom Atrium zu den Büros.

THE NETHERLANDS_UTRECHT **WESTRAVEN**

ARCHITECTS: CEPEZED ARCHITECTS
COMPLETION: 2007_**NUMBER OF WORKPLACES:** 2,000
GROSS FLOOR AREA: 53,000 M²_**COMMON AREA:** FUTURE CENTER, COMPANY RESTAURANT
KIND OF WORKPLACES: CELLULAR, COMBINATION, NON-TERRITORIAL, BUSINESS CLUB, OPEN-PLAN, DESKSHARING, LOUNGE_**PHOTOS:** JANNES LINDERS

The existing high-rise construction has been completely renovated and reorganized and an elongated four-story building has been realized around the foot of the tower, both for the offices of the Ministry of Public Works. Façades made entirely of glass and voids in the floors dominate the spatial structure of the high-rise block. Atriums, conservatories and inner gardens in the low-rise part stimulate spatial awareness, and also support orientation. Many of the working areas have been designed as flexible work stations, making it possible to work at various places in the building. Much attention has been devoted to implementing a perfect equilibrium between low energy consumption and an optimum working climate.

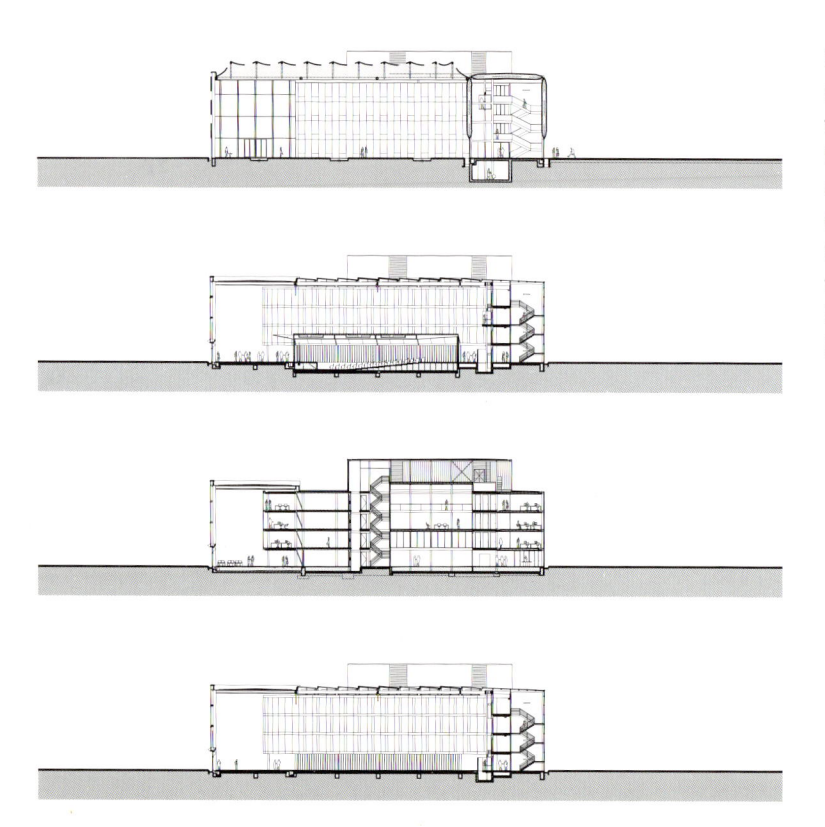

Das bestehende Hochhaus wurde vollständig renoviert und umstrukturiert und an seinem Fuß um ein langes Gebäude mit vier Stockwerken ergänzt. Beiden werden vom Ministerium für öffentliche Arbeiten genutzt. Gänzlich aus Glas bestehende Fassaden und Hohlräume in den Böden geben dem Raumerlebnis des Hochhauses einen starken Impuls. Innenhöfe, Winter- und Innengärten des niedrigen Bauteils stimulieren das Raumbewusstsein und tragen zur Orientierung bei. Viele der Arbeitsplätze wurden als flexible Arbeitsstationen entworfen, die es ermöglichen, an verschiedenen Stellen im Gebäude zu arbeiten. Besondere Aufmerksamkeit wurde auf das Gleichgewicht zwischen niedrigem Energieverbrauch und einem optimalen Arbeitsklima gelegt.

left: Cross sections_General elevation_View through window. right: Worm's-eye view atrium roof.
links: Querschnitte_Gesamtansicht_Blick durch die Fensterfront. rechts:Froschperspektive Atriumdach.

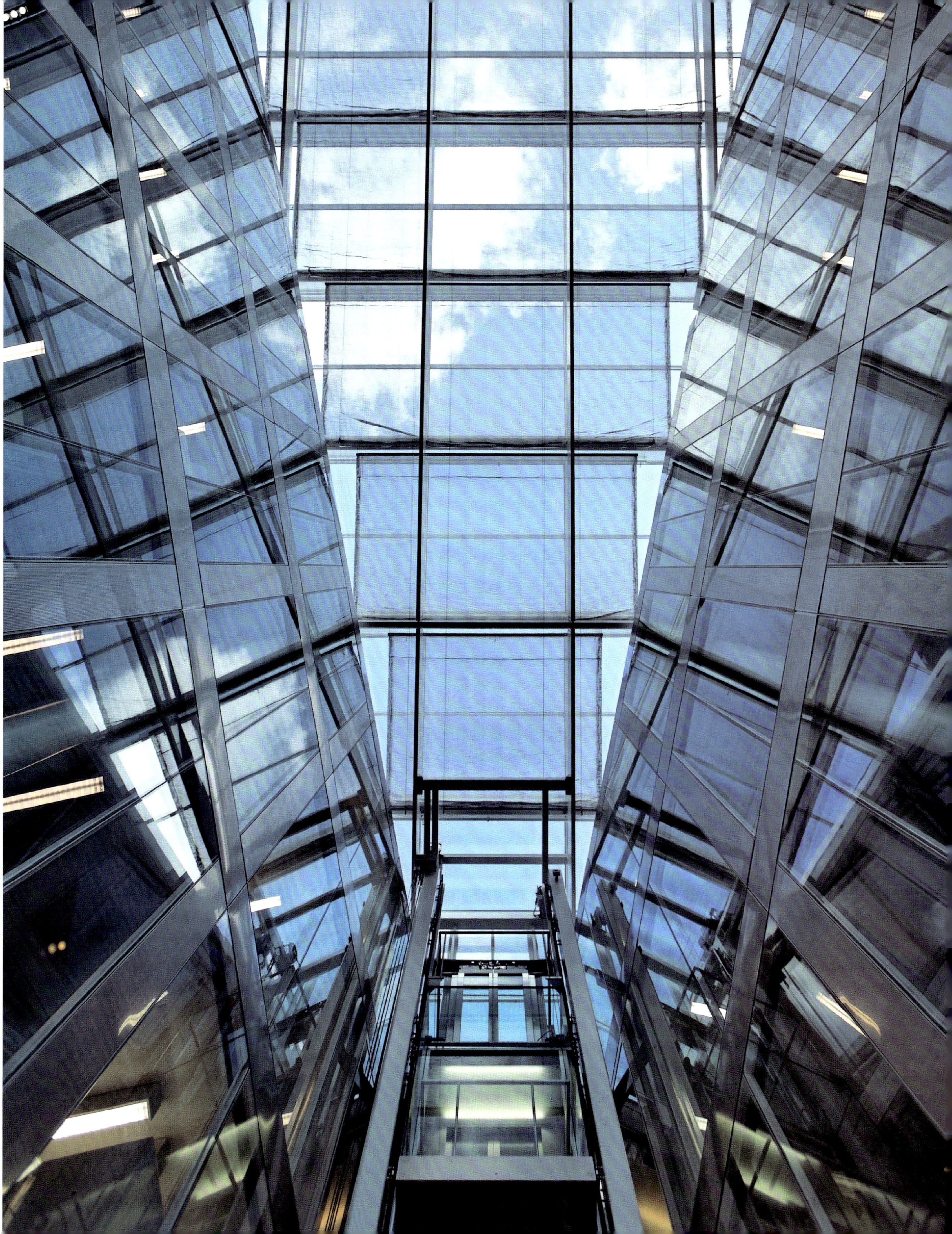

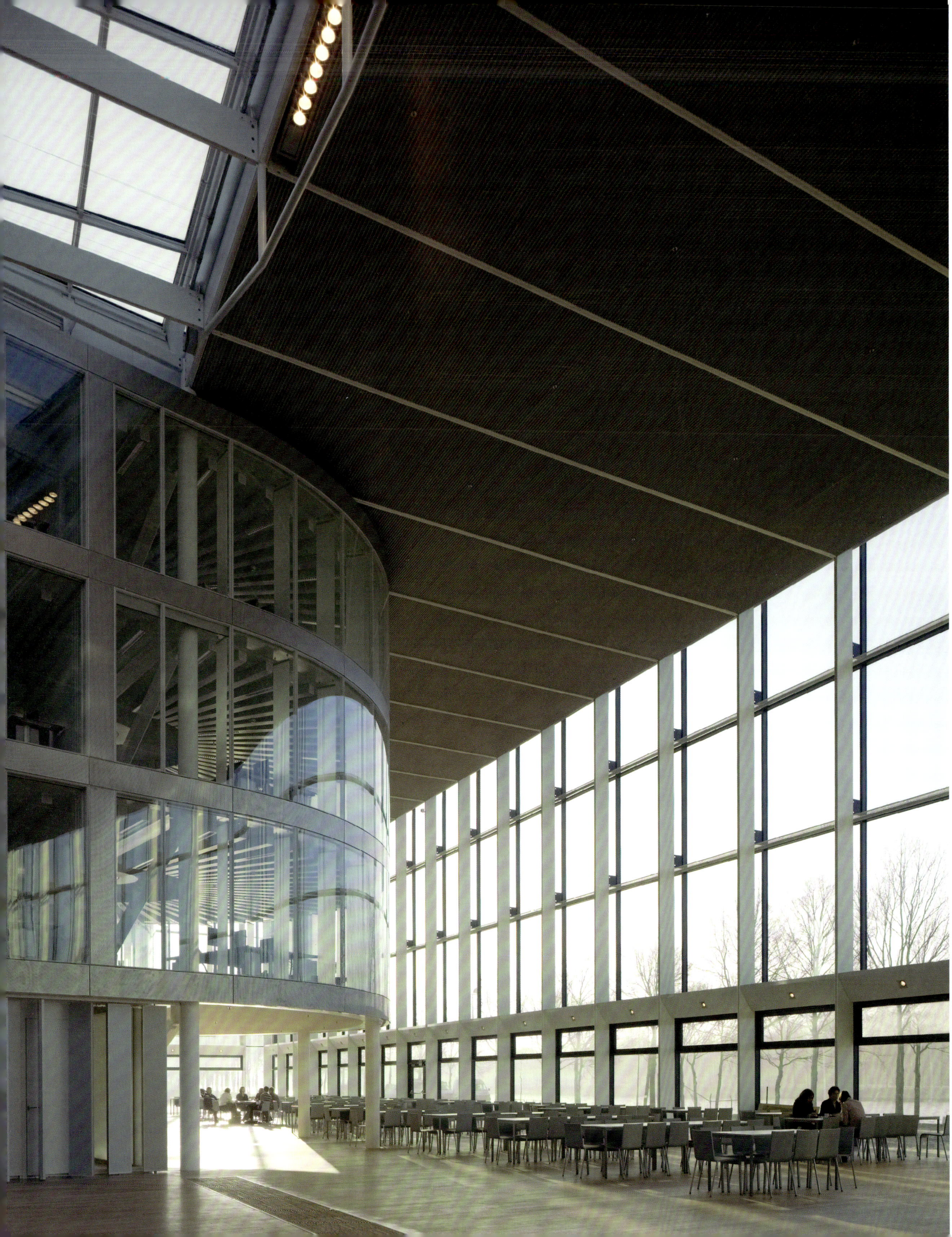

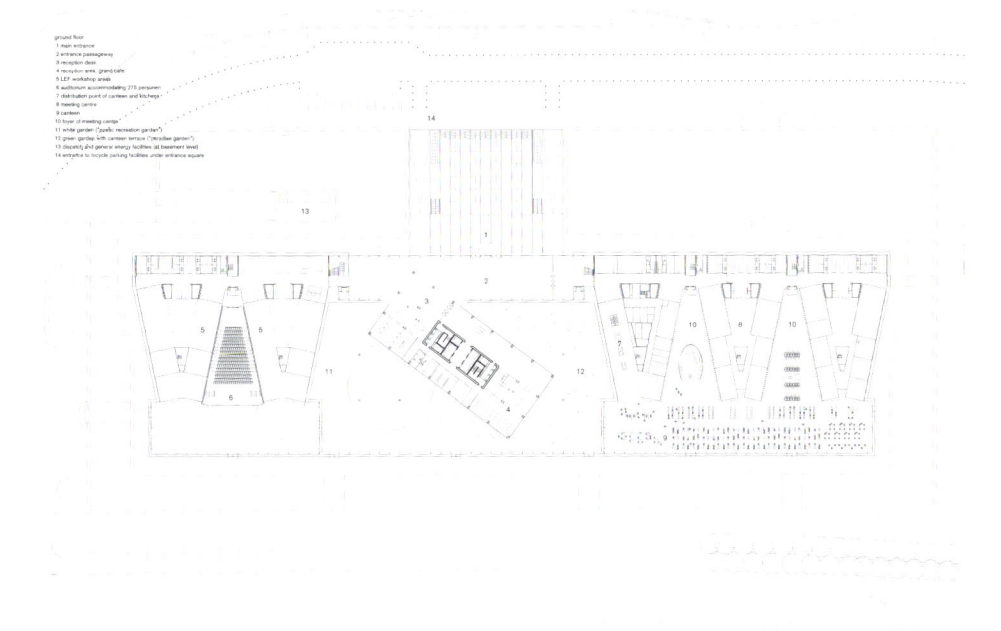

left: Conservatory of the low-rise. right: Ground floor plan_Low-rise office_View from the elevator_High-rise textile second skin.
links: Wintergarten des niedrigen Gebäudekomplexes. rechts: Grundriss Erdgeschoss_Büro_Blick aus dem Aufzug_Die textile Außenhaut des Hochhauses.

THE NETHERLANDS_UTRECHT PARKING AND OFFICES DE COPE UTRECHT

ARCHITECTS: JHK ARCHITECTEN **_COMPLETION:** 2008
NUMBER OF WORKPLACES: 180 **GROSS FLOOR AREA:** 3,000 M²
COMMON AREA: CONFERENCE ROOMS, KITCHEN
KIND OF WORKPLACES: CELLULAR**_PHOTOS:** PALLADIUM PHOTODESIGN, COLOGNE, SANDER COPIER, UTRECHT (359 L.)

The project combines public parking and office spaces in one building. The design consists of two abstract units, connected by a crossway. The parking garage functions separately from the office spaces on the three top floors, which are currently occupied by a business center. As the façade is built around both the parking decks and the office-floors, there is no way to visually distinguish between the different functions. The façade consists of inward curved panels with a golden metallic look. The gradual changes in the perforations and the jumping panels create the impression of a woven structure. Form, color, and detail provide the building with a different look depending on weather and light.

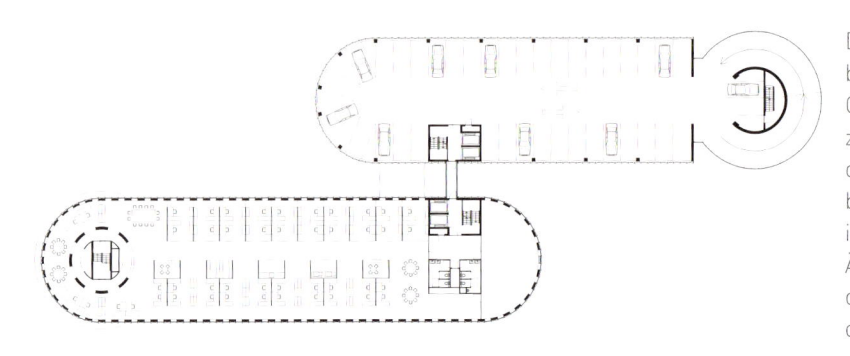

Das Projekt kombiniert öffentliches Parken und Büroräume in einem Gebäude. Das Design besteht aus zwei abstrakten Volumen, die durch einen Quergang verbunden sind. Das Parkhaus befindet sich unterhalb eines Bürozentrums mit drei Stockwerken. Dort wo die Fassade um das Parkhaus und die Büroebenen herum gebaut wurde, kann optisch nicht zwischen den beiden Funktionen unterschieden werden. Die Außenhülle besteht aus nach innen gekrümmten Platten mit goldmetallischer Optik. Die allmählichen Änderungen in der Perforation und die herausstehenden Platten schaffen den Eindruck einer Webstruktur. Form, Farbe und Detail lassen das Gebäude je nach Wetter und Licht unterschiedlich aussehen.

left: Example of office floor with upper parking level _Crossway between buiding volumes _Close up façade from interior parking floor. right: North-west façade.
links: Beispiel eines Grundrisses von Bürofläche und Parkdeck_Verbindungsbrücke zwischen den beiden Gebäuden_Nahaufnahme der Fassade vom Parkdeck aus. rechts: Nordwestfassade.

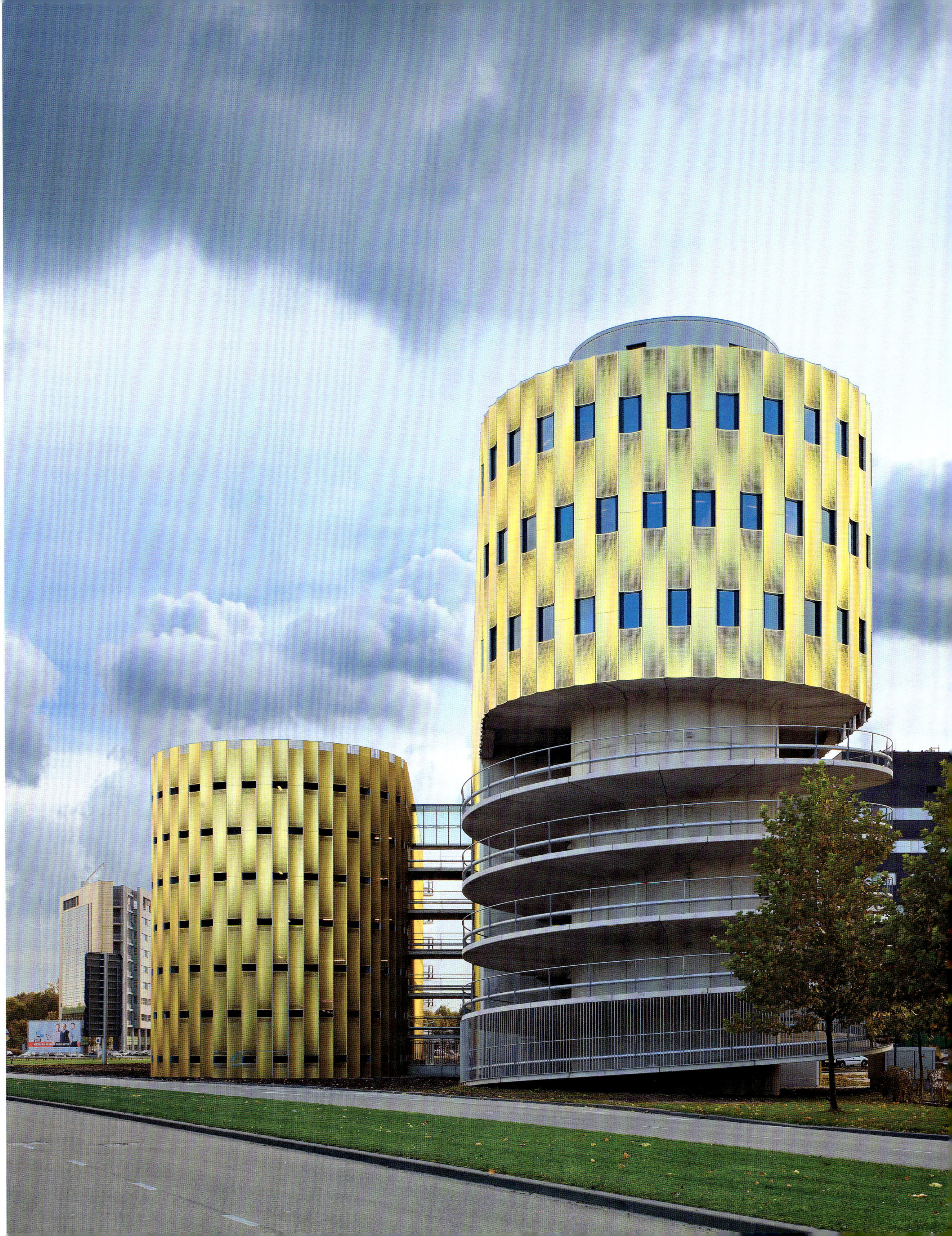

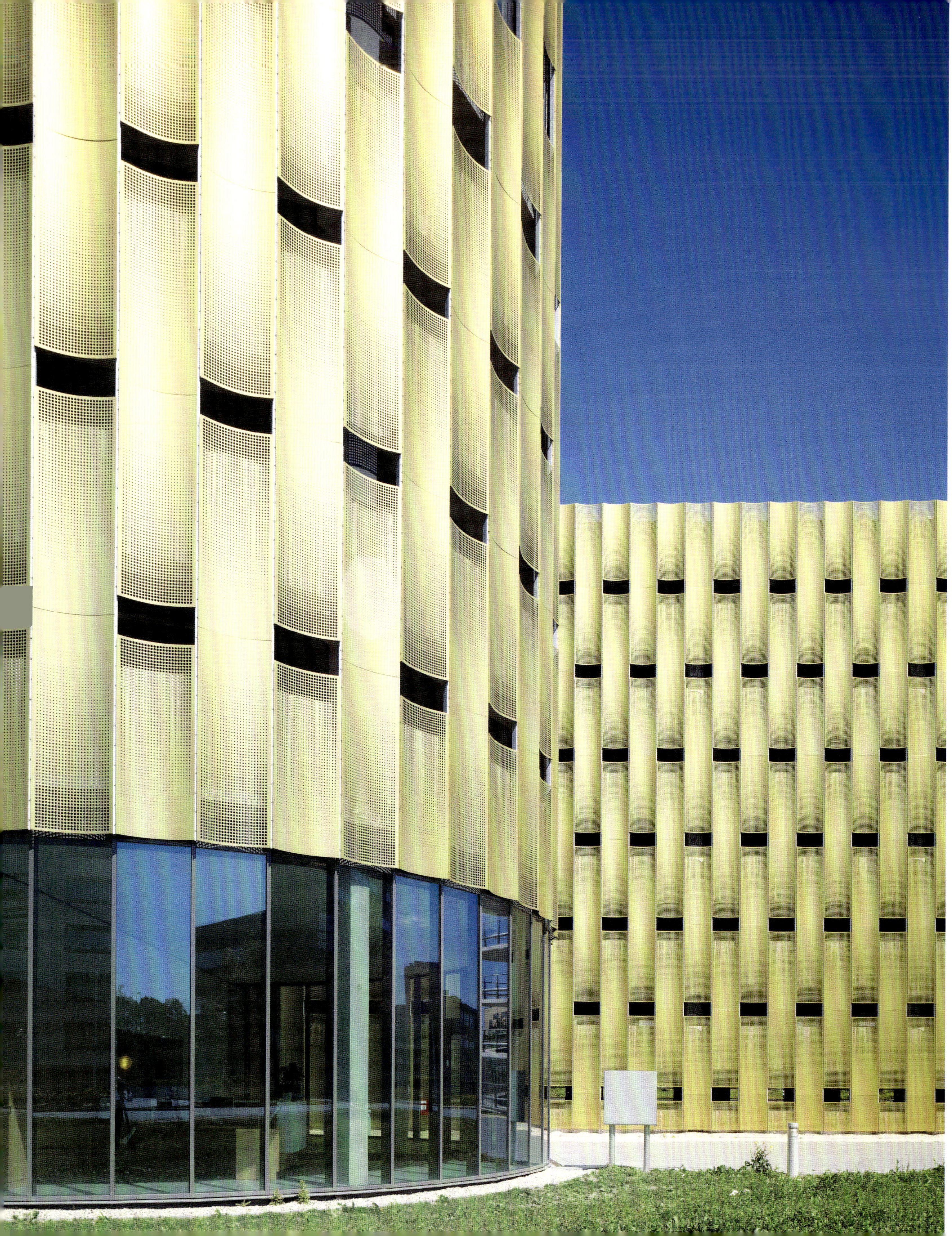

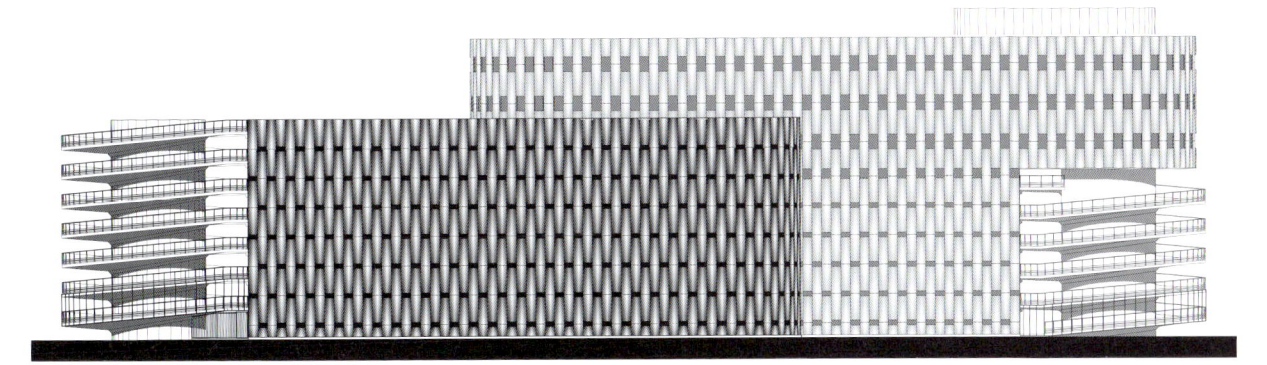

left: Main entrance to offices. right: Elevation_Close-up spiral and façade_Interior elevation, office floor_Lobby.
links: Haupteingang zum Bürogebäude. rechts: Ansicht_Nahaufnahme Spirale und Fassade_Innenansicht Büroebene_Lobby.

NORWAY_OSLO DNB NOR HEADQUARTERS

ARCHITECTS: MVRDV_**COMPLETION:** 2012
NUMBER OF WORKPLACES: 2,000
GROSS FLOOR AREA: 36,500 M²
COMMON AREA: CANTEEN, LOUNGE
PHOTOS: COURTESY OF THE ARCHITECTS

The international Norwegian financial institution DnB NOR decided to accommodate its twenty office locations currently dispersed across the city in three buildings. MVRDV was commissioned as architect for the central building and co-responsible for the concourse. The pixilated design adapts to the urban context and combines efficient and flexible internal organization, based on small-scale working entities, with a variety of specific communal spaces, a sheltered public passage, and respect for urban visual connections. The structure is conceived as a steel 'rack' which permits adaptation to the flexible nature of the organization and reflects its social and democratic character.

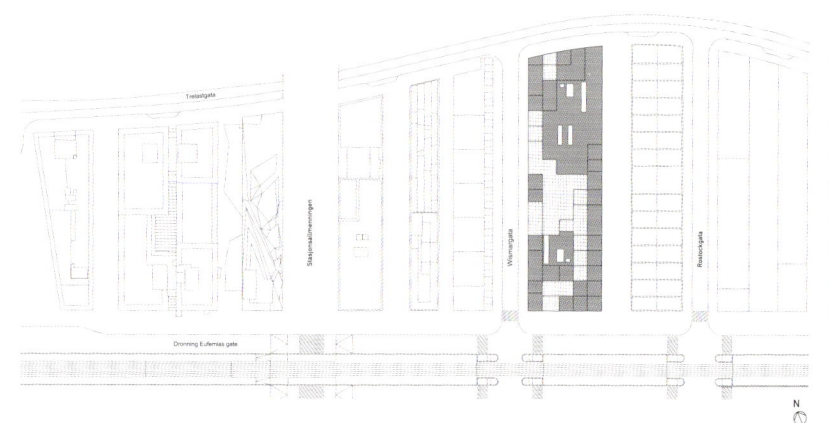

Der international agierende norwegische Finanzdienstleister DnB NOR wollte seine zwanzig über die Stadt verteilten Standorte in drei Bauten zusammenziehen. MVRDV bekam den Auftrag für den mittleren Bau und war mitverantwortlich für die Gesamtanlage. Das gepixelte Erscheinungsbild greift den städtischen Kontext auf, bietet eine geschützte Passage, respektiert städtische Ansichten und verbindet eine ebenso effiziente wie flexible interne Organisation, die auf kleine Arbeitsbereiche und vielfältige Gemeinschaftsflächen, beruht. Baulich liegt die Struktur eines Stahlgestells zugrunde, das eine flexible, der Firma entsprechende Abwandlung erlaubt und deren sozialen und demokratischen Charakter spiegelt.

left: Masterplan_South-west view_South-east view. right: West passage_East façade_South-west view.
links: Masterplan_Südwestansicht_Südostansicht. rechts: Westpassage_Ostfassade_Südwestansicht.

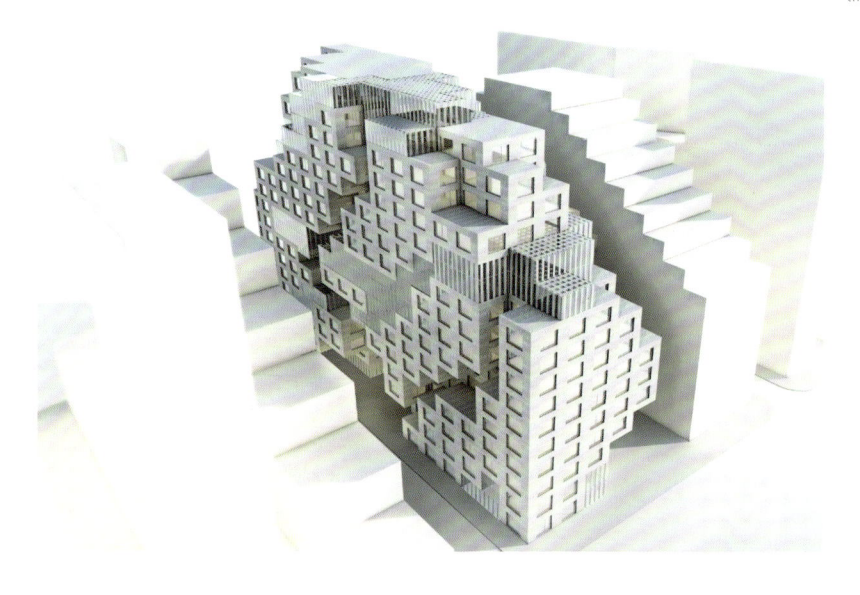

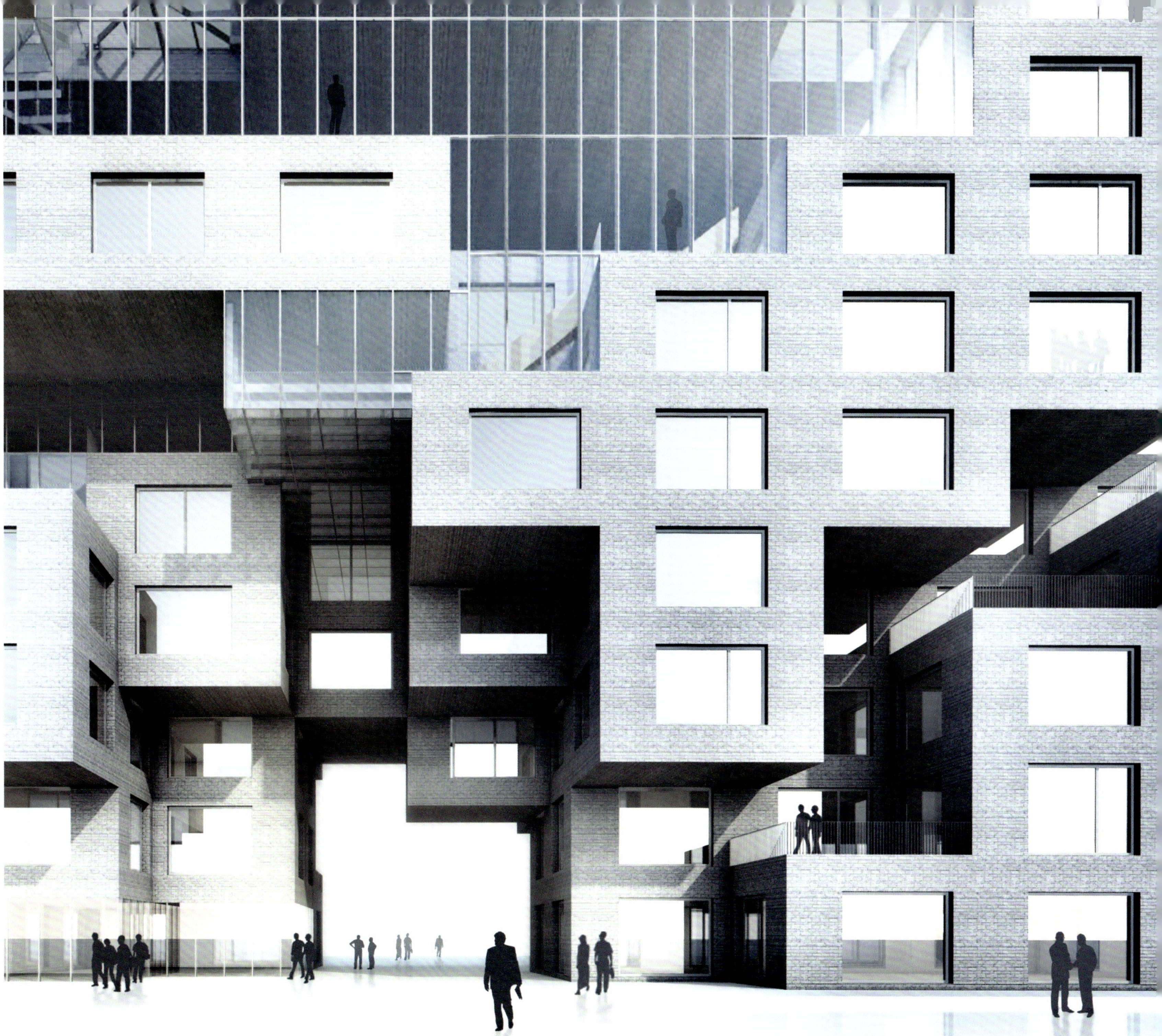
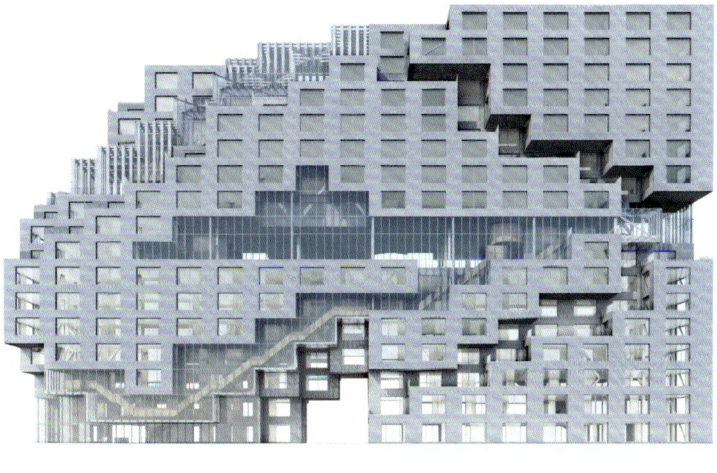
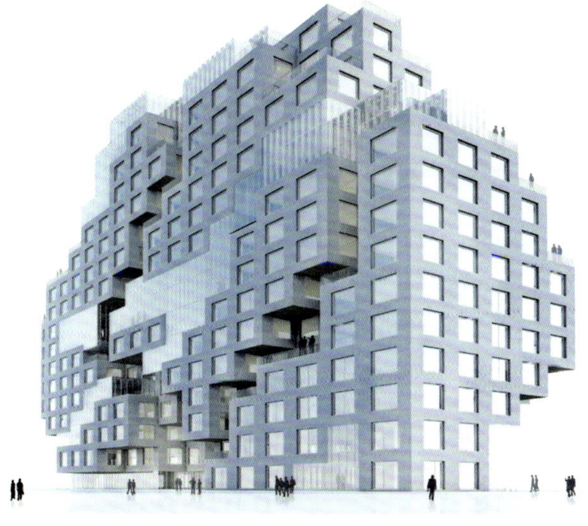

NORWAY_OSLO **URBAN ENERGY**

ARCHITECTS: TRANSFORM WITH BSAA ARCHITECTS AND ENGINEER LEMMING & ERIKSSON
COMPLETION: ONGOING_**NUMBER OF WORKPLACES:** 1,000_
GROSS FLOOR AREA: 21,500 M²_**COMMON AREA:** ATRIUM
KIND OF WORKPLACES: CELLULAR, OPEN-PLAN
PHOTOS: COURTESY OF THE ARCHITECTS

The building was designed by cutting away 50 percent of its maximum volume to introduce sufficient daylight to all 15 floors and to provide a maximum number of penthouse offices while allowing the remaining space at ground level to be landscaped for public use. The large atrium functions as a public accessible park and the cathedral-like space will be the iconographic image of a link between energy efficiency, the city, and modern office space. Large atriums placed at the perimeter of the building function as stacks for natural ventilation while a double façade reduces energy consumption during cold temperatures. The building is organized around three infrastructural legs – providing access and flexibility to the building.

Das Volumen des Baus entstand durch das Entfernen der Hälfte des maximal möglichen Bauvolumens, um allen 15 Geschossen ausreichend Tageslicht zu geben, die Büroflächen im Obergeschoss zu maximieren und auf dem Bodenniveau Freiflächen für Landschaftsgestaltung zu gewinnen. Ein großes Atrium dient als öffentlich zugänglicher Park und der kathedralartige Raum ist als Ikone der Verbindung von Energieeffizienz, Stadt und modernem Büroraum konzipiert. Große Atrien am Rand des Baues dienen der natürlichen Belüftung als Schornsteine und die doppelte Fassade reduziert den Energieverbrauch an kälteren Tagen. Drei Kerne mit der Infrastruktur geben Zugang zum Gebäude und gewährleisten dessen Flexibilität.

left: Situation and section_Exterior by night. right: Entrance_Interior view_Perspective_Plaza.
links: Lageplan und Schnitt_Nachtansicht. rechts: Eingang_Innenansicht_Perspektive_Plaza.

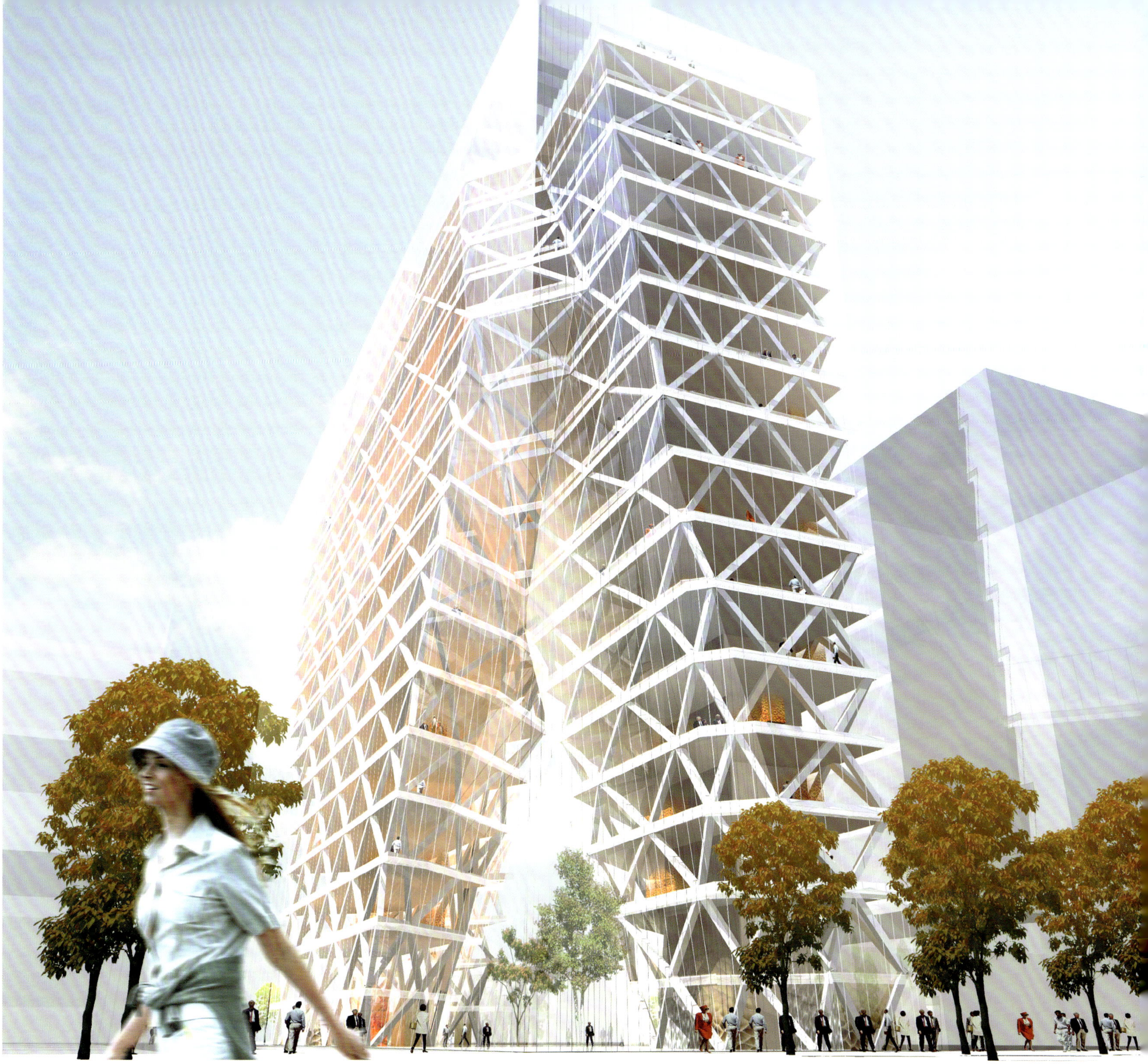
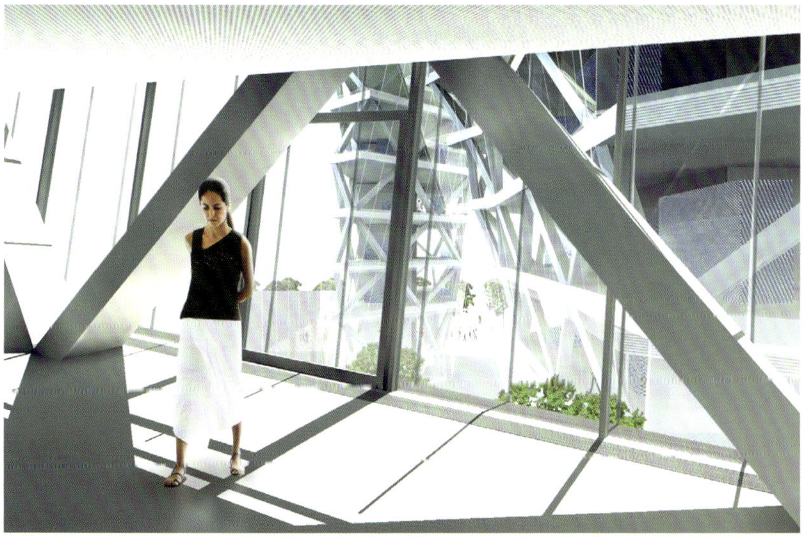
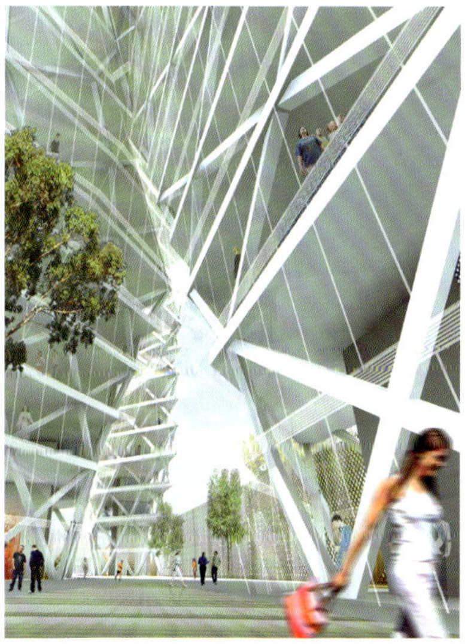
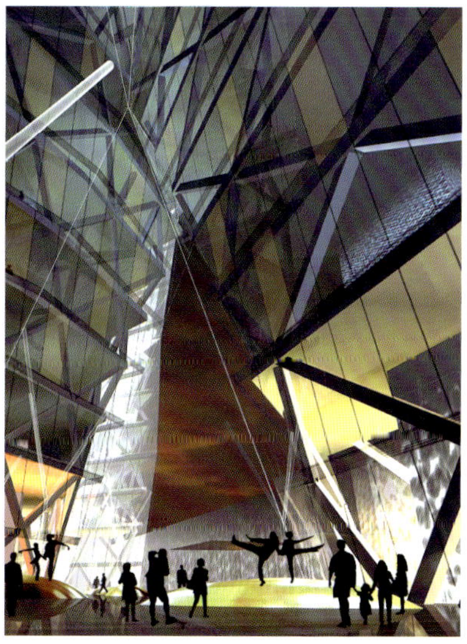

SLOVENIA_LJUBLJANA CITY MUNICIPALITY

ARCHITECTS: OFIS ARHITEKTI
COMPLETION: 2015_**NUMBER OF WORKPLACES:** 700
GROSS FLOOR AREA: 60,000 M²_**COMMON AREA:** KITCHENETTE, MEETING ROOMS, AUDITORIUM, DINING SPACE, LIBRARY, FITNESS, EXHIBITION SPACE, ARCHIVE_**KIND OF WORKPLACES:** COMBINATION_**PHOTOS:** COURTESY OF THE ARCHITECTS

The plan was for several departments to move to the same site but occupy different buildings. The heart of the new center is the main hall where citizens can organize all their documents. The site is just on the edge of the city center by the river and already occupied by a number of existing protected buildings. The rearrangement provided the chance to create a unique identity for a symbolic and landmark example of contemporary Ljubljana architecture based on the idea of cylindrical organization of a landmarked former garage-building. The mixture of public and restricted areas inside the building required a complex organizational structure – both inside and outside.

Der Auftraggeber wollte verschiedene Abteilungen auf einem Gelände, aber in unterschiedlichen Gebäuden konzentrieren. Die Schalterhalle, Anlaufstelle der Bürger für alle Dokumentenangelegenheiten, ist das Zentrum. Das Gebiet liegt direkt am Rand des Stadtkerns am Fluss und wird schon von einigen bestehenden, denkmalgeschützten Gebäuden besetzt. Die Umstrukturierung bot die Chance, in Ljubljana ein charakteristisches Gebiet zeitgenössischer Architektur mit einzigartiger Identität zu schaffen, wobei die Idee einer zylindrischen Organisation von einem ehemaligen Garagengebäude übernommen wurde. Die Mischung aus öffentlichem und eingeschränktem Bereich in einem Komplex verlangt eine ausgeklügelte Organisation im Inneren wie auch im Äußeren.

left: Site plan_Bird's-eye view, model_Main inner plaza. right: Night view_Inner hall_Glass façade.
links: Lageplan_Luftaufnahme, Modell_Innerer Hauptplatz. rechts: Nachtansicht_Innere Halle_Glasfassade.

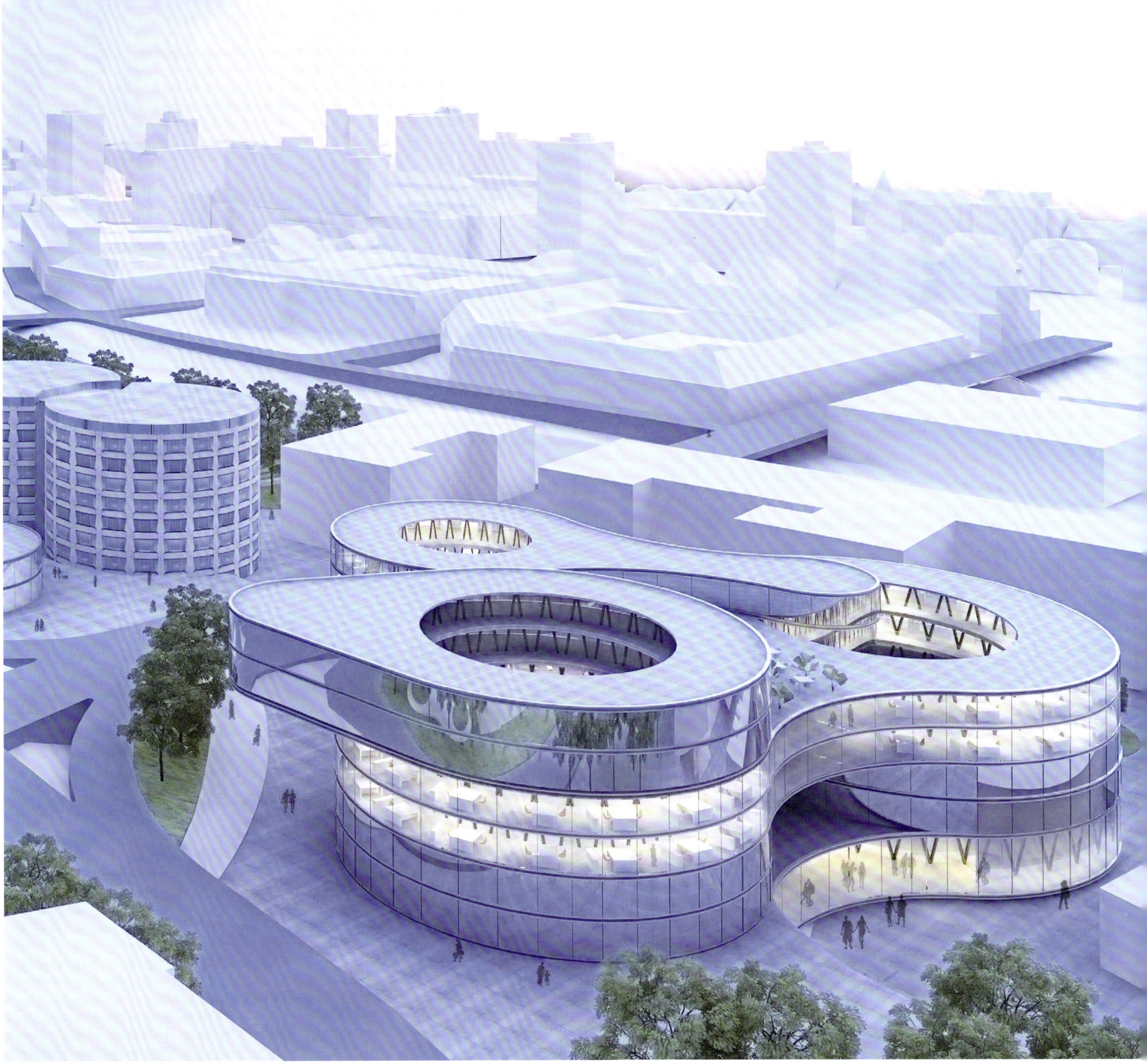

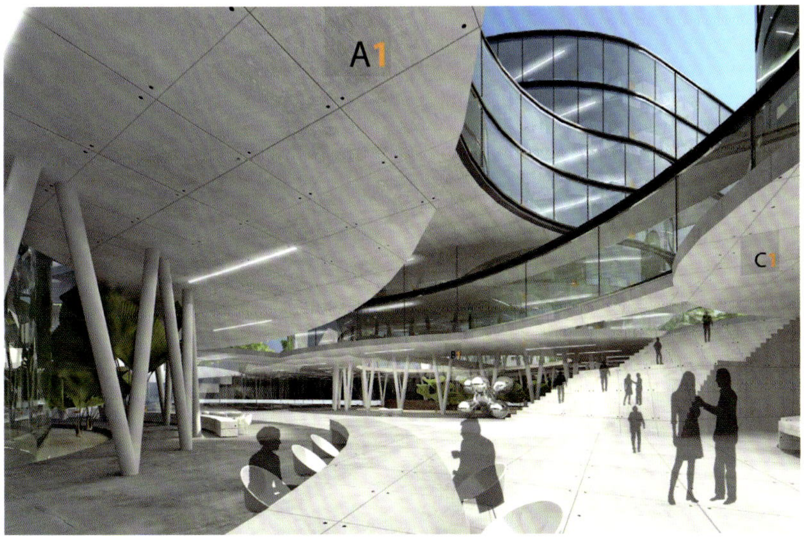
A1
C1

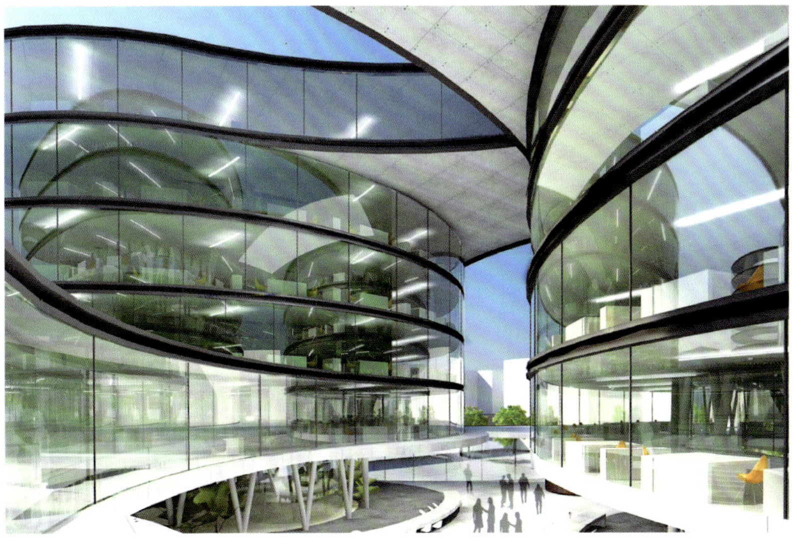

SPAIN_BARCELONA **PARCLOGISTIC ILLA-B1**

ARCHITECTS: RICARDO BOFILL TALLER DE ARQUITECTURA
COMPLETION: 2007_**NUMBER OF WORKPLACES:** 700_**GROSS FLOOR AREA:** 13,000 M²_**COMMON AREA:** MEETING ROOMS, LOBBY
KIND OF WORKPLACES: CELLULAR, OPEN-PLAN, TEAM
PHOTOS: CARLOS CASARIEGO

The brand-new building of Abertis, constituting the second phase of Barcelona's "Logistic Parc," is a 13,000-square-meter office building that accommodates on its five floors the different business areas of the company: telecommunication infrastructures, airports, parking and logistics. A central Greek-cross shape open space provides access from the lobby to the flexible working zones. The building is meant to be part of a group of three buildings with a continuous angled façade that forms an interior plaza sheltered from the highway. The interior plaza contrasts with the double glass wall, while elements of Mediterranean and Catalan architecture in red stucco are reintroduced to this patio.

Das neue Abertis-Gebäude, ein 11.000-Quadratmeter Bürohaus mit dem die zweite Ausbauphase des Parclogistic in Barcelona beginnt, beherbergt auf fünf Geschossen die verschiedenen Abteilungen der Firma: Telekommunikationsinfrastruktur, Flughafen, Parkplatz und Logistik. Ein Freiraum in Form eines griechischen Kreuzes dient als Zugang von der Lobby zu den einzelnen Arbeitsbereichen. Der Bau ist als Teil einer Dreiergruppe gedacht, die mit durchgehender, geknickter Fassade einen Innenplatz von der Autobahn abschirmen. Der Innenhof mit mediterranen und katalanischen Elementen in rotem Stuck kontrastiert mit den Doppelglasfassaden.

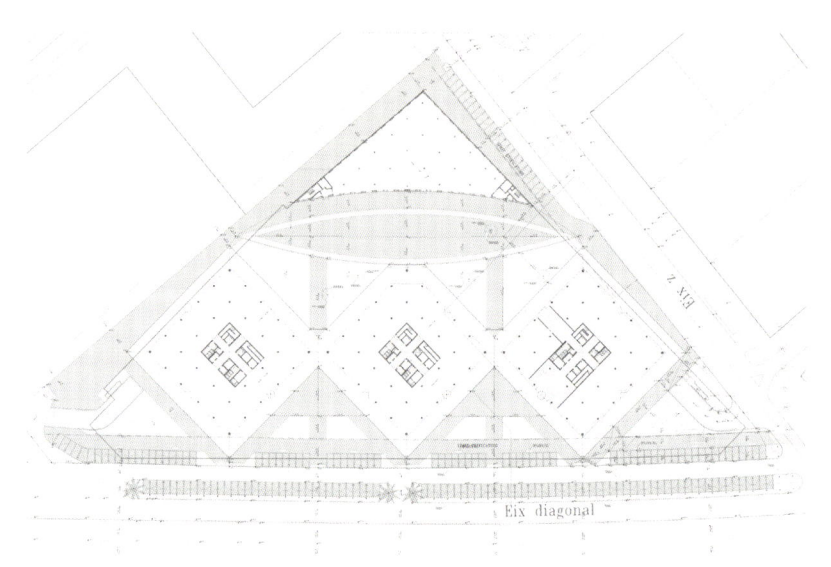

left: Site plan_Interior façade, detail_Offices corridor. right: Night view_Entrance to the offices_General view.
links: Lageplan_Innenfassade, Detail_Flur bei den Büros. rechts: Nachtansicht_Eingangsbereich zu den Büros_Gesamtansicht.

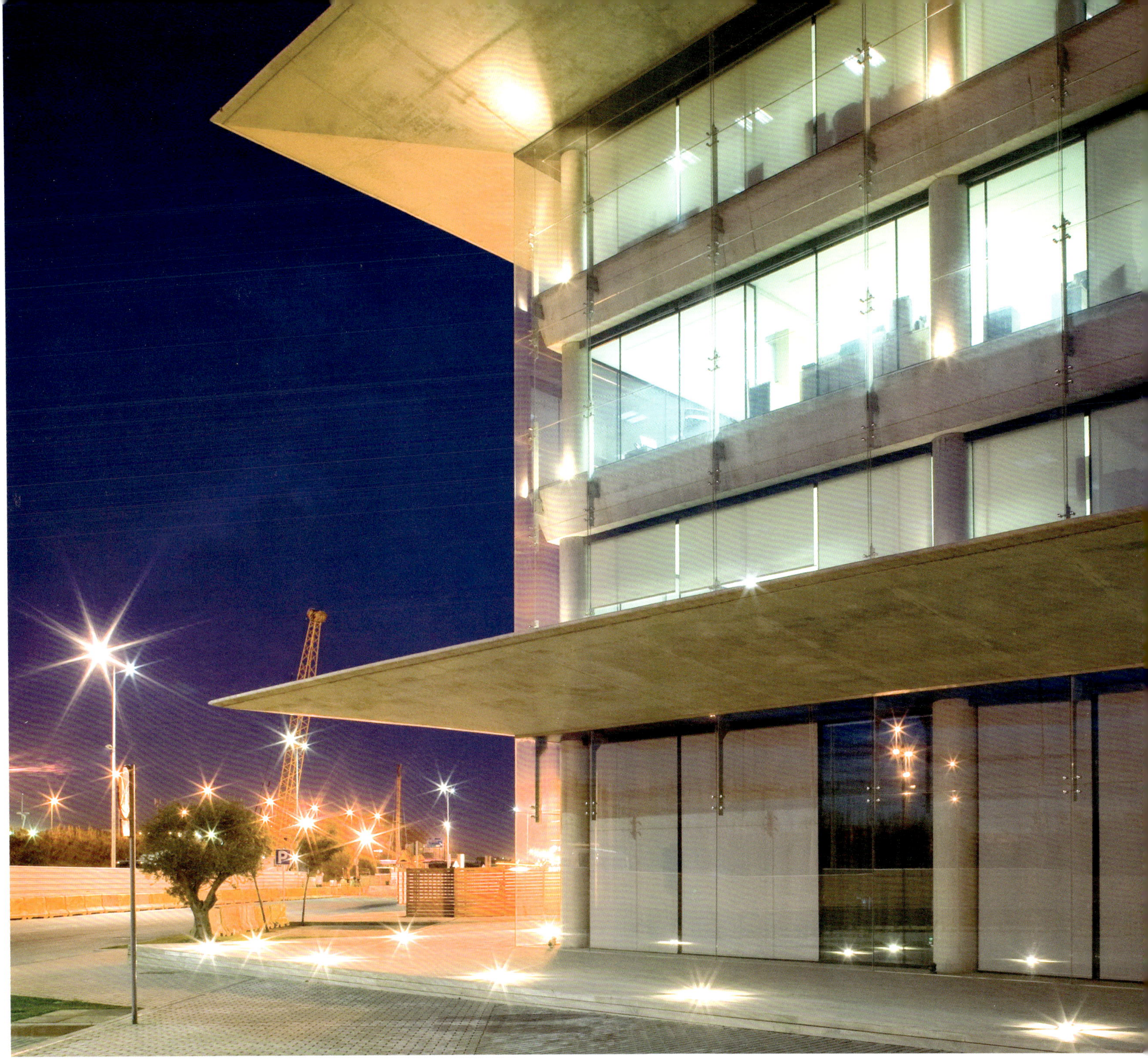

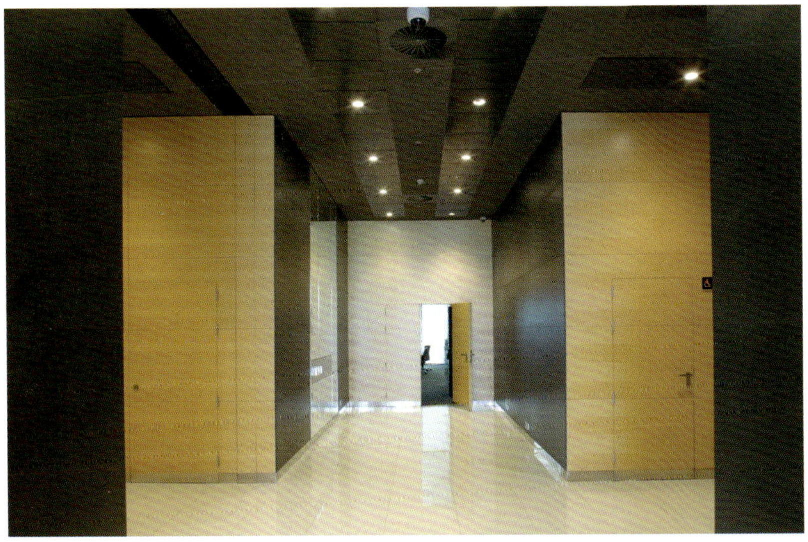

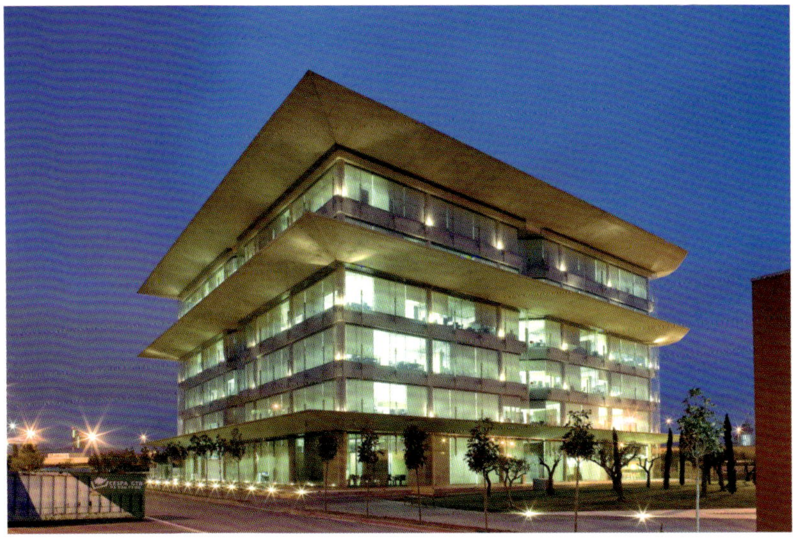

SPAIN_BARCELONA TORRE LAMINAR

ARCHITECTS: SORIANO & ASOCIADOS ARQUITECTOS
COMPLETION: 2010_**NUMBER OF WORKPLACES:** 65
GROSS FLOOR AREA: 922 M²_**COMMON AREA:** AUDIENCE, POLYVALENT ROOM, SOCIAL CENTER FOR THE NEIGHBORHOOD_**KIND OF WORKPLACES:** OPEN-PLAN
PHOTOS: COURTESY OF THE ARCHITECTS

The laminated tower explores the limits of a new kind of office buildings. It seeks answers to questions like "what is the minimum width for an office?," "what is the minimum width of a tower?," and "how long can a continuous workspace extend?." This building plays with almost impossible dimensions. A decentralized tower structure eliminates the classic opaque cores. It introduces diagonal spaces that disrupt the simple piles of slabs repeated ad infinitum. The mesh of pillars disappeared and were replaced by mixed, hybrid elements providing an overall stable instability that is resolved by a multitude of folds.

Der laminierte Turm sucht die Grenzen einer neuen Form des Bürogebäudes; eines Gebäudes, das einen Vorhang ausbildet, ein Betttuch-Turm oder eine verfestigte Fahne. Wie groß ist die minimale Tiefe eines Büros oder eines Turmbaus und wie lang kann sich ein Büroraum machen? Der Entwurf balanciert auf dem schmalen Grad zwischen Denkbarem und Unmöglichem. Trotz eindeutiger Turmstruktur umgeht der Entwurf den üblichen dunklen Kern. Er birgt diagonale Räume die einfache, endlose Abfolgen auflösen. Das Gerüst aus Pfeilerfolgen verschwindet, wird durch eine gemischte Struktur hybrider Elemente, die eine Gesamtstabilität aus in Falten aufgelösten Instabilitäten ausbilden, ersetzt.

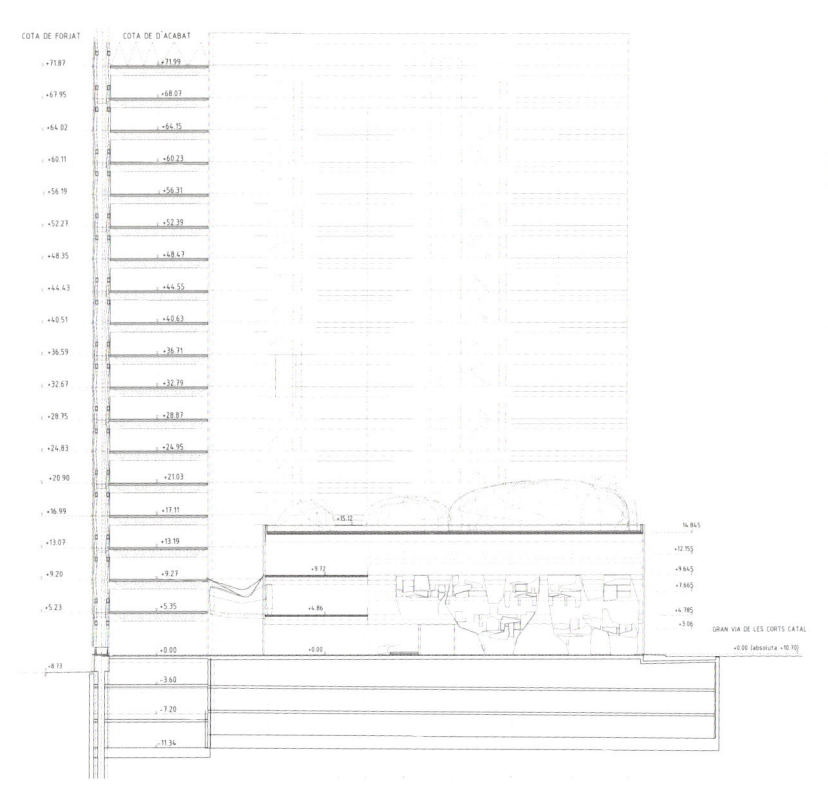

left: Section_Next to Torre Agbar_Office. right: Exterior_Tower acces_Façade, detail model.
links: Schnitt_Neben dem Torre Agbar_Büro. rechts: Außenansicht_Zugang zum Hochhaus_Fassade, Modeldetail.

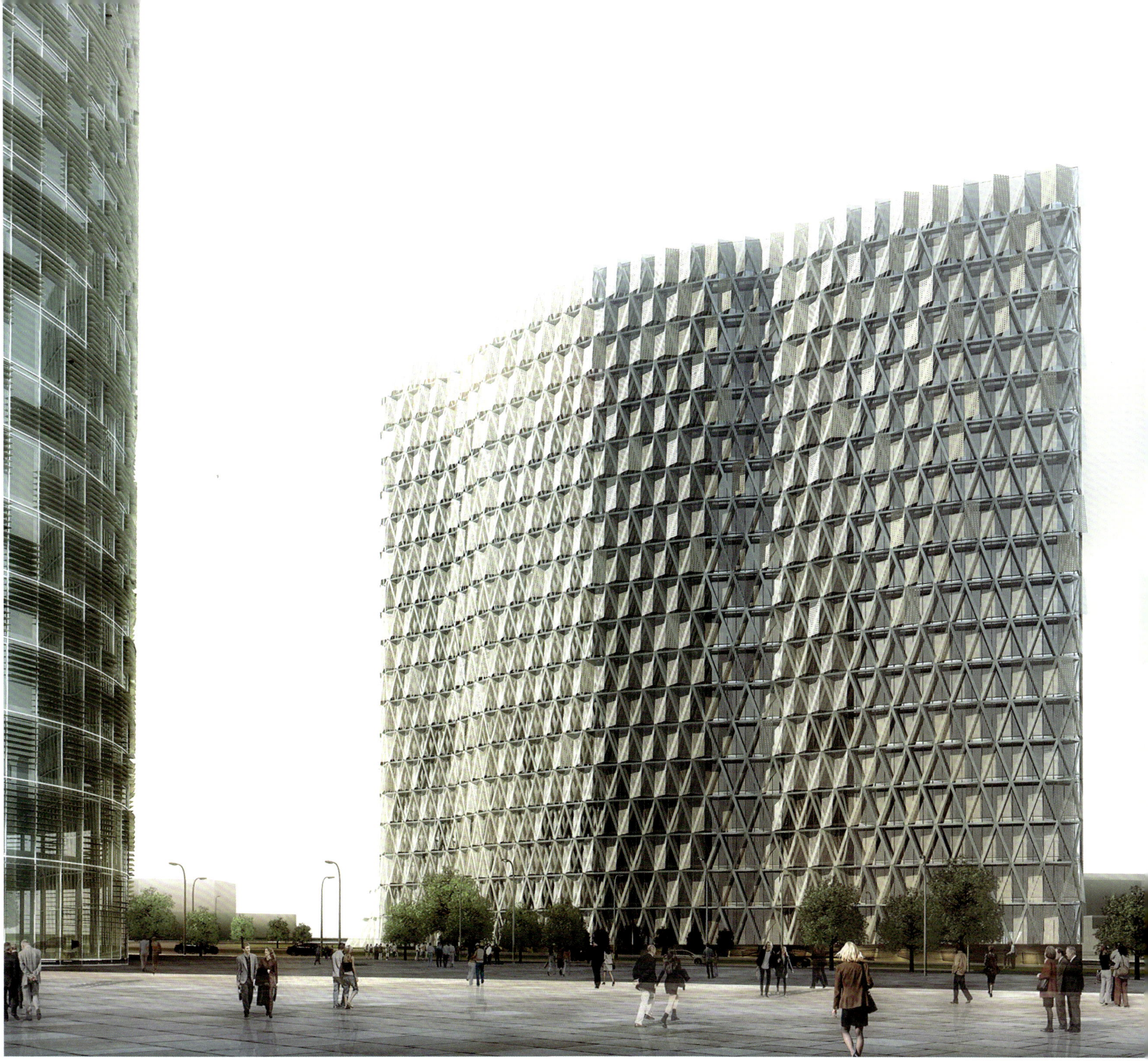

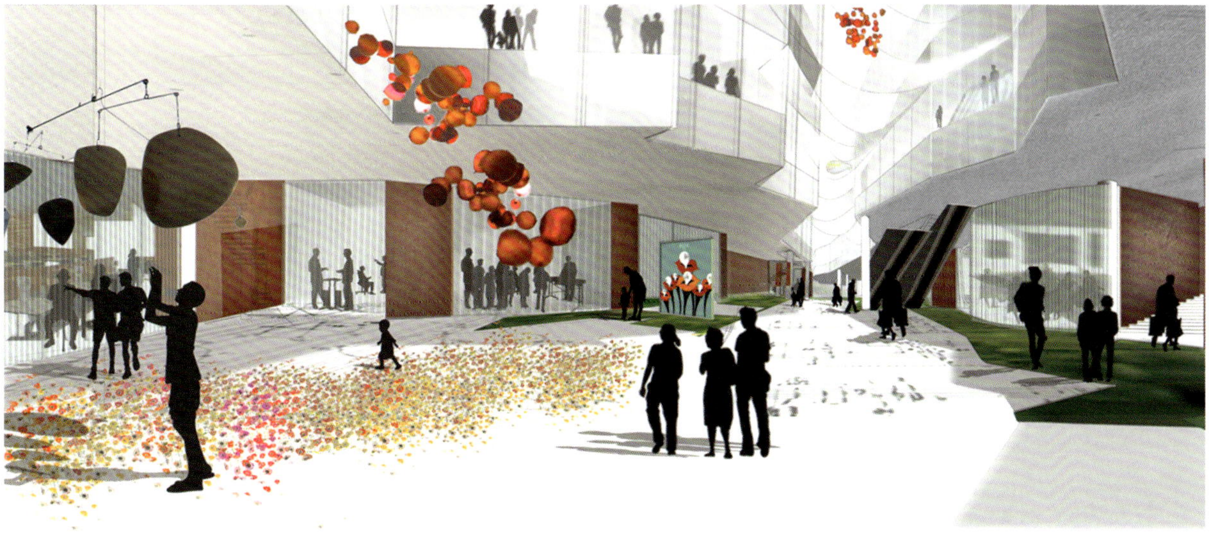

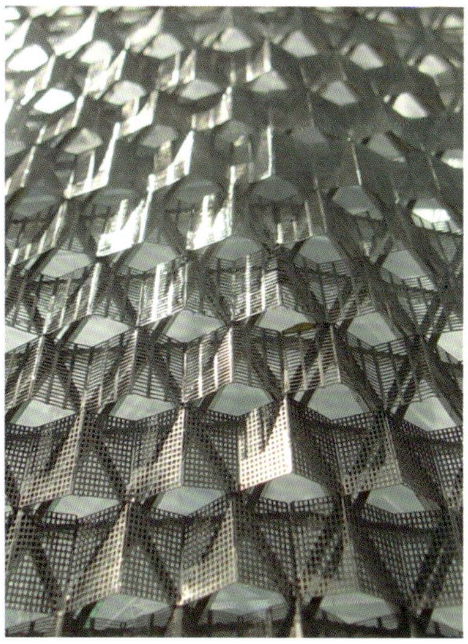

SPAIN_BARCELONA **INDRET**

INTERIOR DESIGNER: FRANCESC RIFÉ
COMPLETION: 2007_**NUMBER OF WORKPLACES:** 10
GROSS FLOOR AREA: 170 M²
KIND OF WORKPLACES: COMBINATION, COCKPIT
PHOTOS: EUGENI PONS, GIRONA

A floor of an early 20th century building in the historical center of Vilafranca del Penedès, was renovated to house the new central office of InDret. The building's principal façade had a noble look, while the other side opened to an unattractive back yard located 1.60 meters below ground level. This court was renovated as well. A great longitudinal 60 cm wall forms a structural axle, determining the location of the bathrooms for men and women. Featuring smoked glass mirrors, these bathrooms resemble cockpits, and are designed as two "suspended" boxes located below the rest of the building.

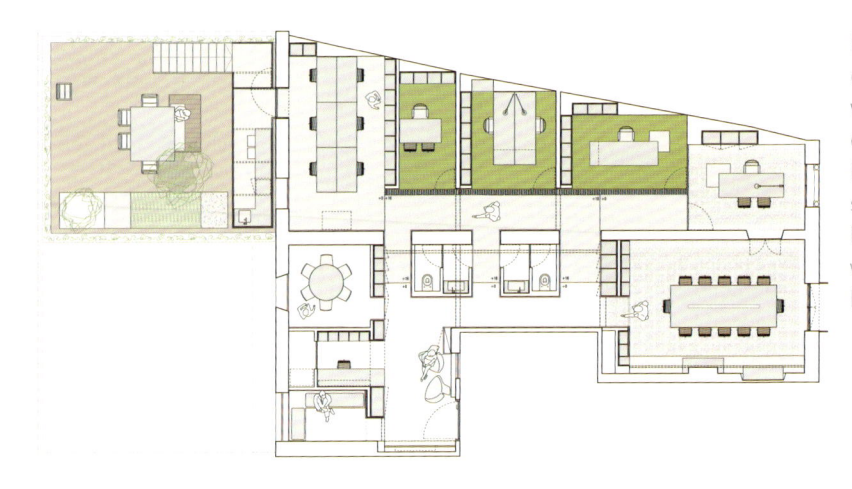

Die Hauptniederlassung von InDret in einem Geschoss eines Gebäudes aus dem frühen 20. Jahrhundert im historischen Zentrum Vilafranca del Penedès wurde renoviert. Die Hauptfassade war von eleganter Erscheinung, während die rückwärtige Fassade auf einen armseligen, 1,60 Meter tiefer liegenden Hof führte, der ebenfalls neu gestaltet wurde. Eine lange, 60 Zentimeter starke Wand teilt den Bau im Inneren der Länge nach, deshalb mussten alle Räumlichkeiten, inklusive Toiletten, entsprechend dieser Achse angeordnet werden. Sie erscheinen mit ihren Wänden aus Rauchglas als abgehängte Kästen von geringerer Höhe.

left: Floor plan_Entrance with patio_Reception desk and waiting room_Entrance and reception.
right: Conference room with old roofs and floors.
links: Grundriss_Eingang mit Innenhof_Empfangstresen und Wartebereich_Eingang und Empfang.
rechts: Konferenzraum mit alten Wänden und Fußböden.

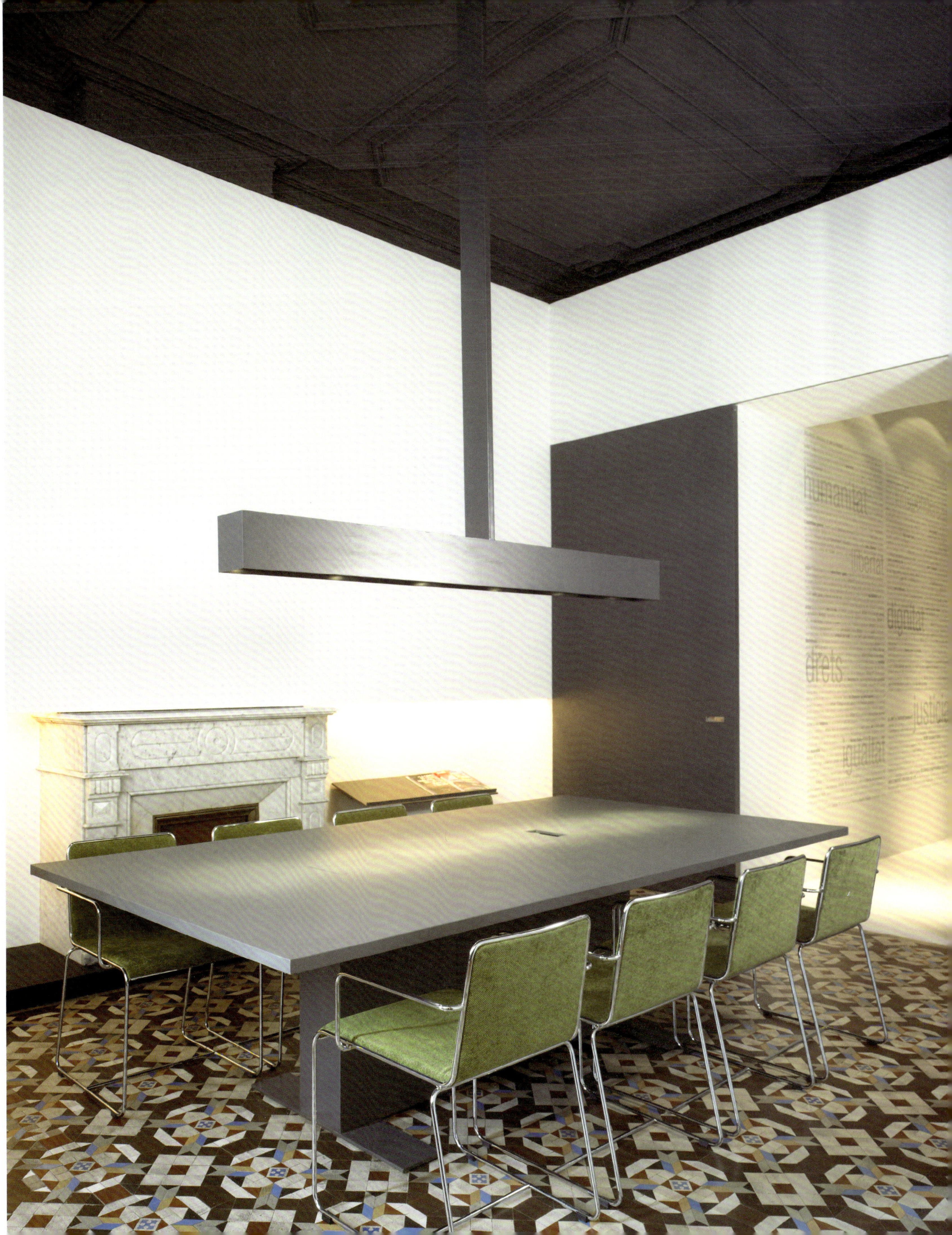
humanitat
dignitat
drets
igualtat

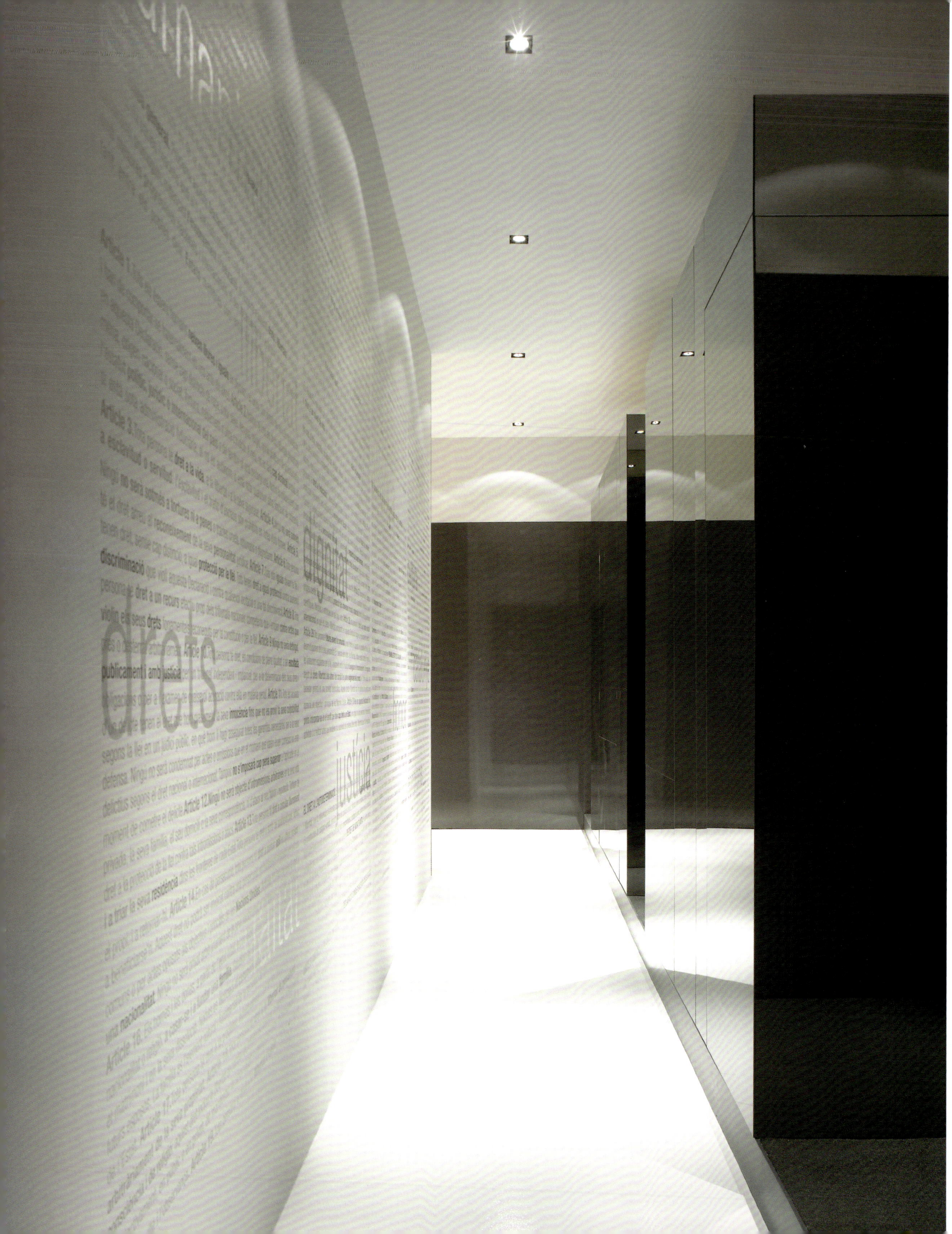

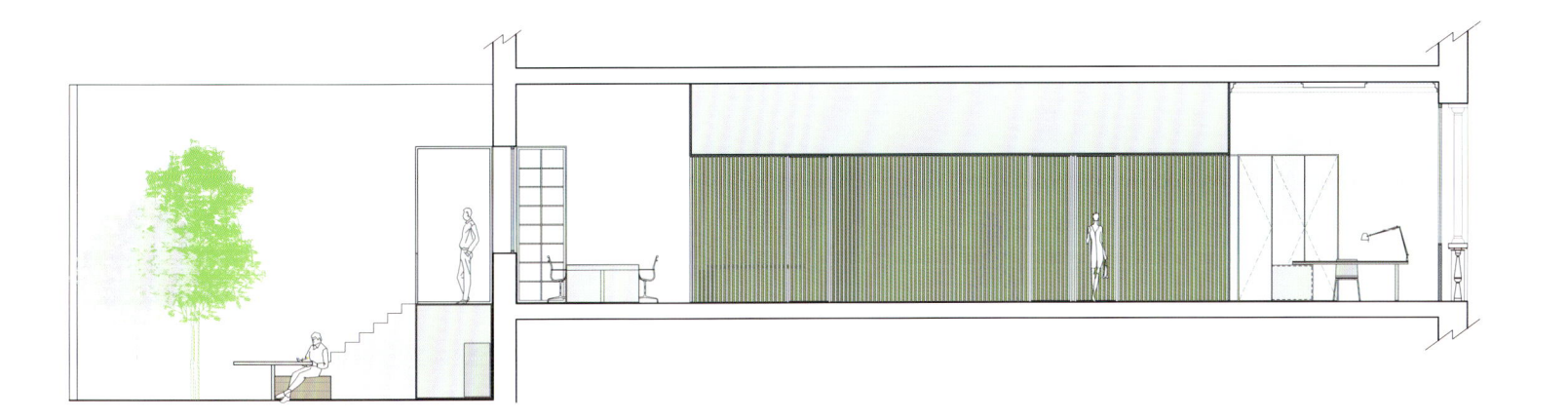

left: Texts (Universal Declaration of the Human Rights, of the Statute of Catalonia) are reflected in both rest rooms. right: Section_Office_Blinds for the offices.
links: Texte (Allgemeine Erklärung der Menschenrechte des Staates Katalonien) sind an den Wänden beider Waschräume aufgebracht. rechts: Schnitt_Büro_Sichtschutz für die Büros.

SPAIN_CÁDIZ TORRES DE HÉRCULES

ARCHITECTS: RAFAEL DE LA-HOZ CASTANYS
COMPLETION: 2009_**NUMBER OF WORKPLACES:** 1,200
GROSS FLOOR AREA: 19,600 M²_**COMMON AREA:** RESTAURANT, TRAVEL AGENCY, BANK
PHOTOS: RAFAEL DE LA-HOZ ARQUITECTOS, ROLAND HALBE (375)

The Hercules Towers, two cylindrical towers of identical volume, are located in the Bay of Gibraltar on a plot of 12,000 square meters. They are joined by a crystalline prism which houses the hallways connecting the two buildings. The 100-meter towers, which allude to the legendary "Pillars of Hercules", rise like "rigid structures" from the body of water that surrounds them. On the façade, giant letters spell out the sentence "Non plus ultra", protecting the offices from solar radiation. The circular floors are 25 meters in diameter and the vertical core houses vertical communications facilities and services, while general facilities are placed in the basement and on the roof.

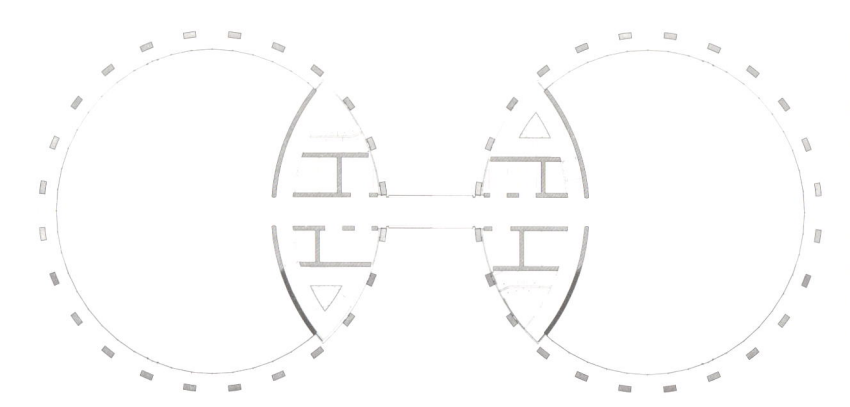

Die beiden zylindrischen, gleich großen Herkules-Türme befinden sich in der Bucht von Gibraltar auf einer Fläche von 12.000 Quadratmetern. Die Gebäude sind durch ein gläsernes Prisma verbunden, das Korridoren enthält. Die 100 Meter hohen Türme, die auf die legendären „Säulen des Herkules" anspielen, ragen wie „starre Strukturen" aus dem Wasser heraus. Passend dazu bilden die riesigen Buchstaben auf der Fassade, die die Büros vor Sonneneinstrahlung schützen, die Wörter „Non plus ultra". Die runden Ebenen haben einen Durchmesser von 25 Metern und der vertikale Kern beherbergt Kommunikation, Einrichtungen und Dienstleistungen, während allgemeine Einrichtungen im Unter- und Dachgeschoss untergebracht sind.

left: Typical floor plan_Roof terrace_Glass connection between the two towers_On a connecting bridge. right: General view.
links: Regelgeschoss_Dachterasse_Gläserne Verbindung zwischen den beiden Türmen_Auf einer Verbindungsbrücke. rechts: Gesamtansicht.

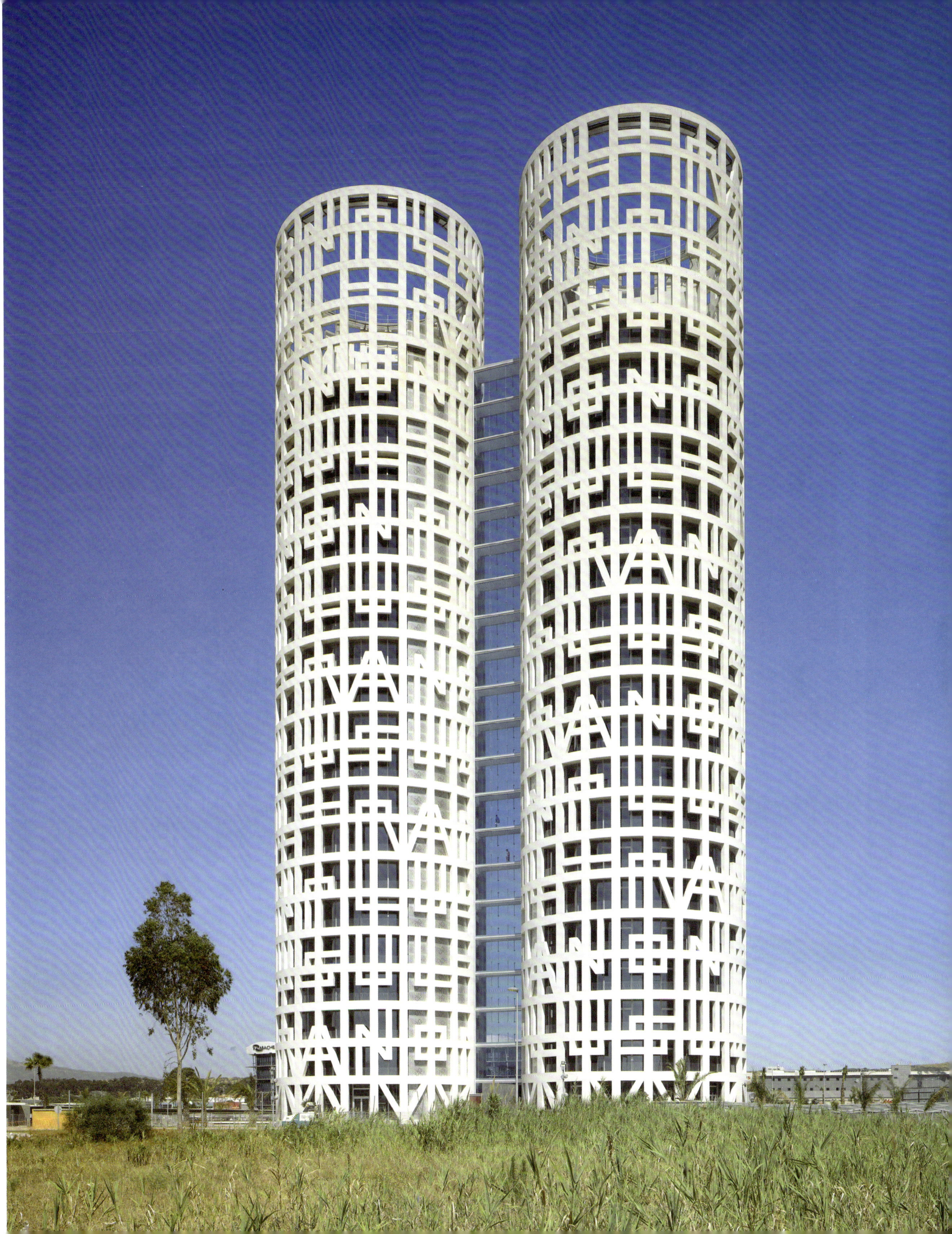

SPAIN_CEHEGÍN **THE MYSTERIOUS STORY OF THE GARDEN THAT PRODUCES WATER**

ARCHITECTS: CÓMO CREAR HISTORIAS
COMPLETION: 2011_**NUMBER OF WORKPLACES:** 30
GROSS FLOOR AREA: 580 M²_**COMMON AREA:** STORE ROOM, MEETING ROOMS_**KIND OF WORKPLACES:** COMBINATION, OPEN-PLAN, TEAM
PHOTOS: COURTESY OF THE ARCHITECTS

This office building is hidden in a garden that cleans the waste waters of the city with macrophyte beds. The envelope of the building consists of climbing plants of various colors that are irrigated by the recycled water. Steel cases interrupt this skin and frame landscape views from the windows. Behind this first envelope that protects the building from the weather, there is a second skin made of concrete linked to a steel rib structure resting in a concrete slab, the floor of the office. The inside is an open and flowing space. A fissure in the ceiling inundates this space with natural light.

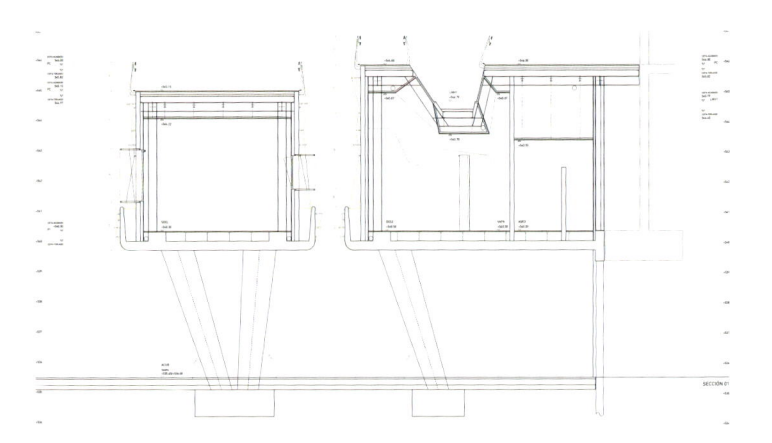

Das Bürogebäude mit Garten soll Abwasser der Stadt aufnehmen und in makrophytischen Beeten reinigen. Das Volumen ist von Kletterpflanzen wechselnder Farbe umhüllt, die von dem aufbereiteten Wasser gewässert werden. Stahlrahmen durchbrechen die Pflanzenhaut und rahmen den Fensterausblick. Hinter dieser äußeren, vor Witterungseinflüssen schützenden Haut liegt eine zweite Hülle aus Beton, die mittels Stahlstreben auf die Bodenplatte, den Betonboden des Büros, zurückbindet. Das Innere des Baus ist als offener und fließender Raum ausgebildet und durch einen Spalt in der Decke natürlich belichtet.

left: Section_Exterior, winter_Exterior, spring. right: Exterior, summer, detail, summer_Exterior, autumn.
links: Schnitt_Außenansicht Winter_Außenansicht Frühling. rechts: Außenansicht Sommer_Sommer, Detail_Außenansicht Herbst.

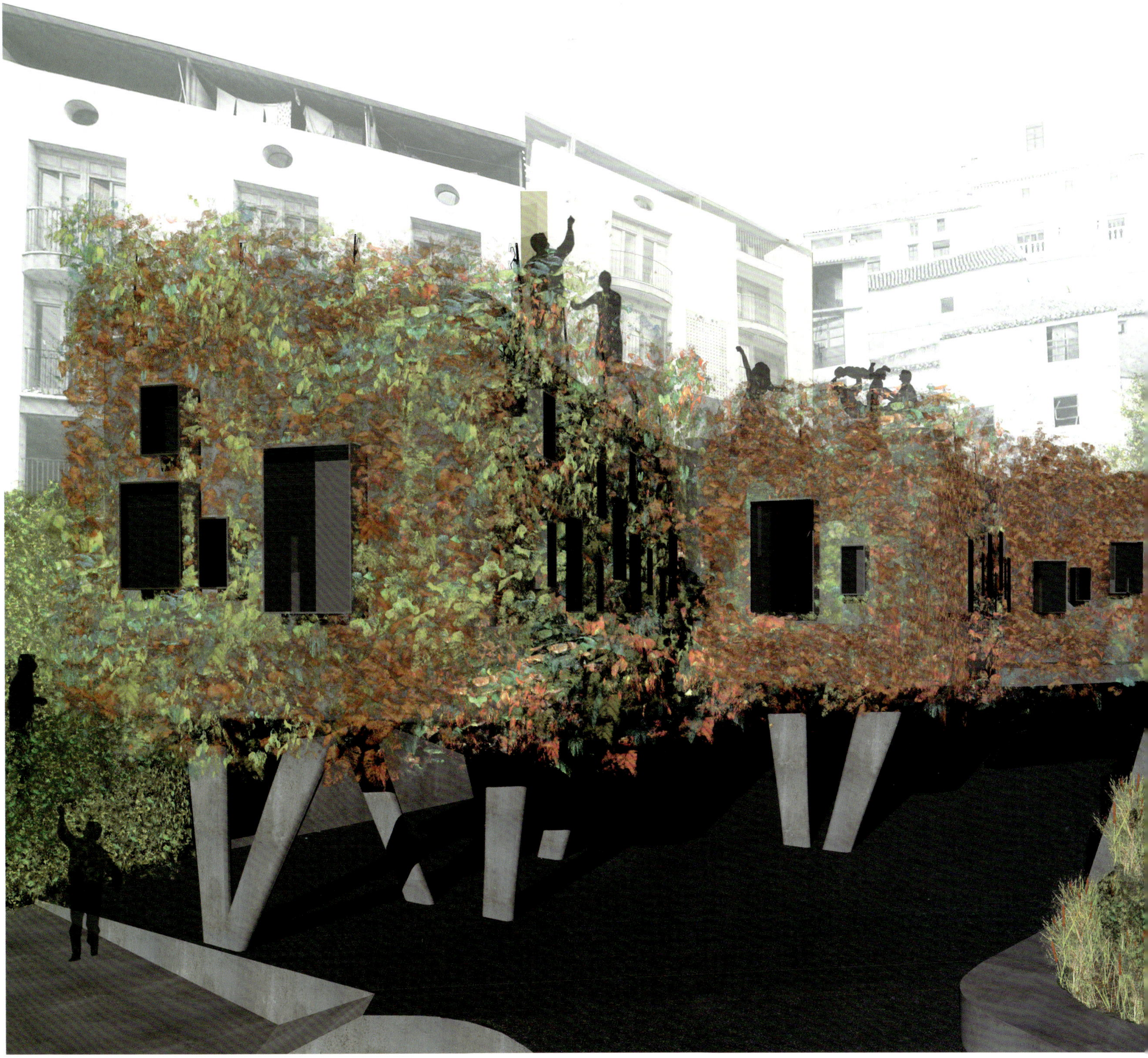
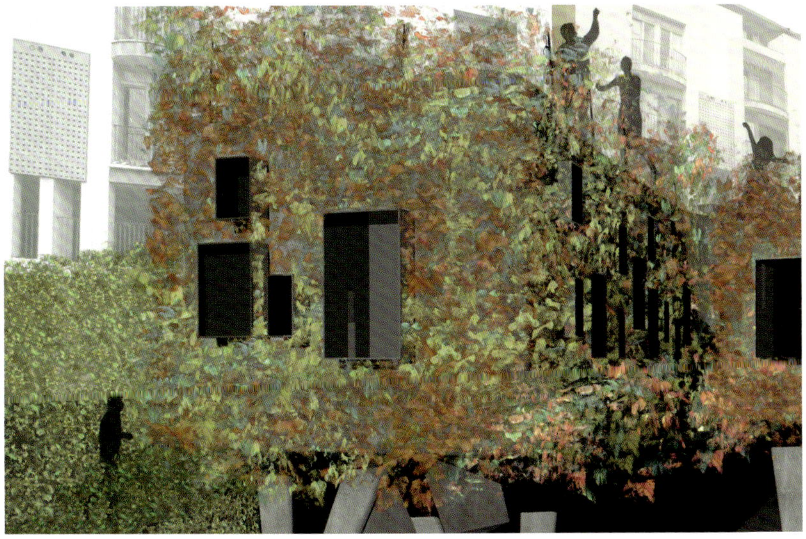
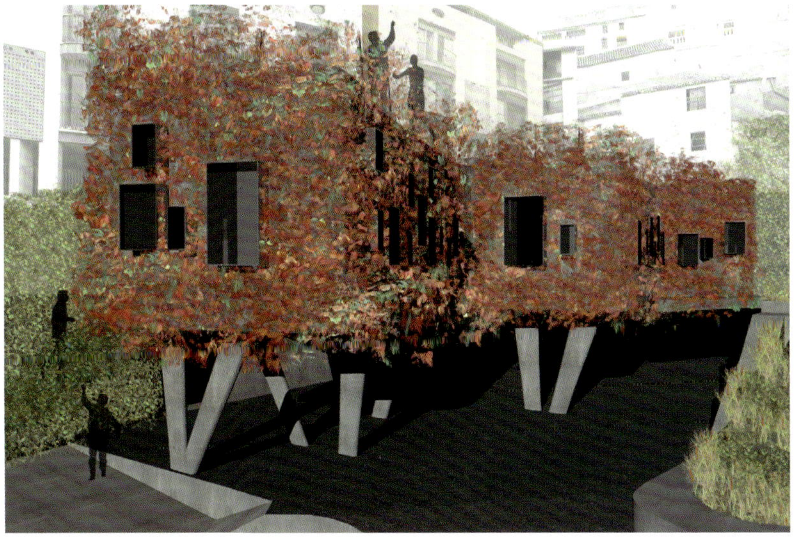

SPAIN_MADRID TELEFONICA´S DISTRICT C

ARCHITECTS: RAFAEL DE LA-HOZ CASTANYS
LANDSCAPING: LANDSCAPE ARCHITECTURE URBAN
COMPLETION: 2008_**NUMBER OF WORKPLACES:** 12,000
GROSS FLOOR AREA: 400,000 M²_**COMMON AREA:** TRAVEL AGENCY, GYM, CRÈCHE, HEALTH CENTER, RESTAURANTS, BANKS_**PHOTOS:** MIGUEL DE GUZMÁN (378, 379), JOAN ROIG (380, 381)

The new Telefónica headquarters will house all 14,000 employees of the company in one single corporate campus. All buildings are distributed around a canonical patio – the lawn of the campus – within a framework of squares set out in the corners of the premises. An environmental canopy with photovoltaic panels unites, covers, and defines the perimeter of the campus. Two different hierarchies organize the spaces: one dedicated to strictly business activities and one for employees' social and cooperative activities. Glass developed specifically for this project appears transparent from the inside and opaquely clear from the outside.

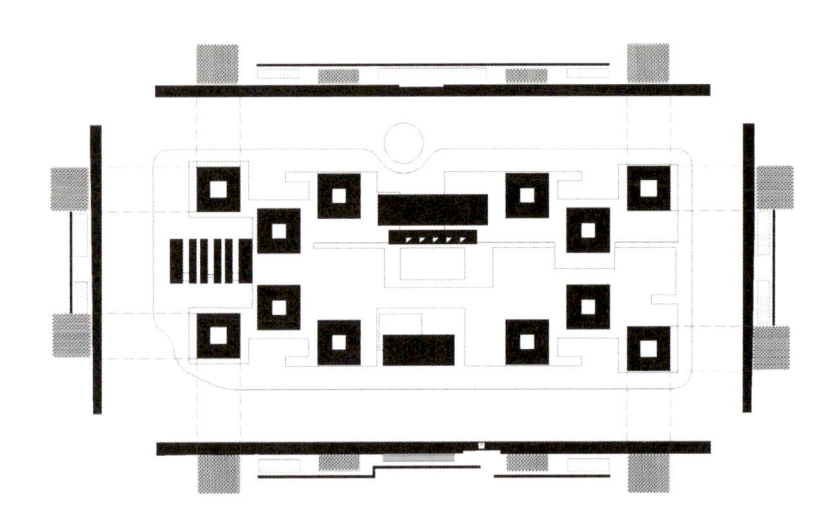

Im neuen Telefónica-Hauptsitz werden alle 14.000 Angestellten der Firma zusammengeführt. Alle Gebäude sind um einen Innenhof mit Grünfläche verteilt. Innerhalb eines Rahmens aus höheren quadratischen Gebäuden, die in den Geländeecken platziert sind, verbindet, bedeckt und begrenzt eine umweltfreundliche Überdachung mit Solaranlagen das Gelände. Die Räume werden durch zwei Hierarchien strukturiert: eine für das strenge Firmenprogramm und eine für die sozialen und kooperativen Aktivitäten der Angestellten. Das Glas, das speziell für dieses Projekt hergestellt wurde, wirkt von innen transparent und von außen undurchsichtig.

left: Site plan_General view. right: Façade.
links: Lageplan_Gesamtansicht. rechts: Fassade.

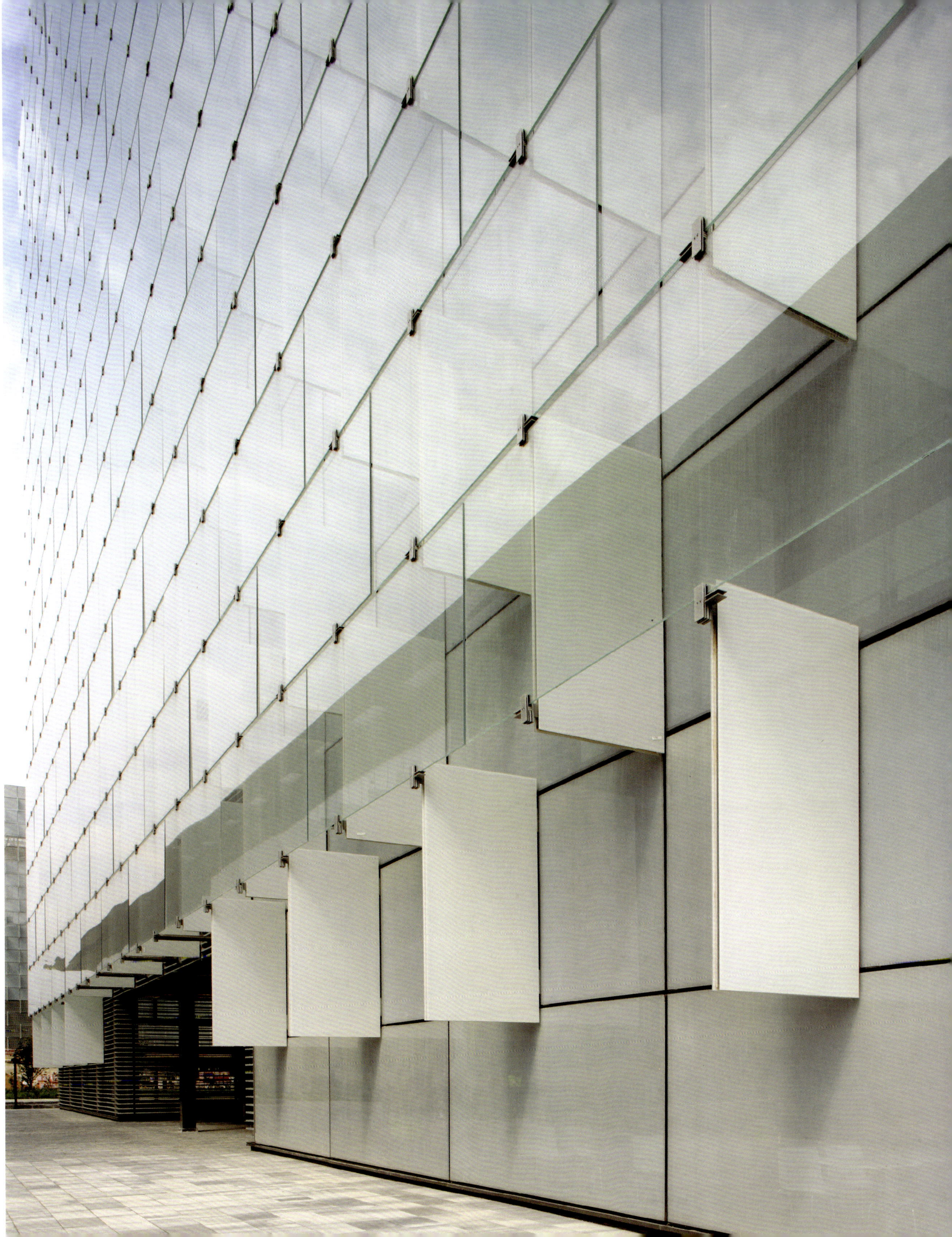

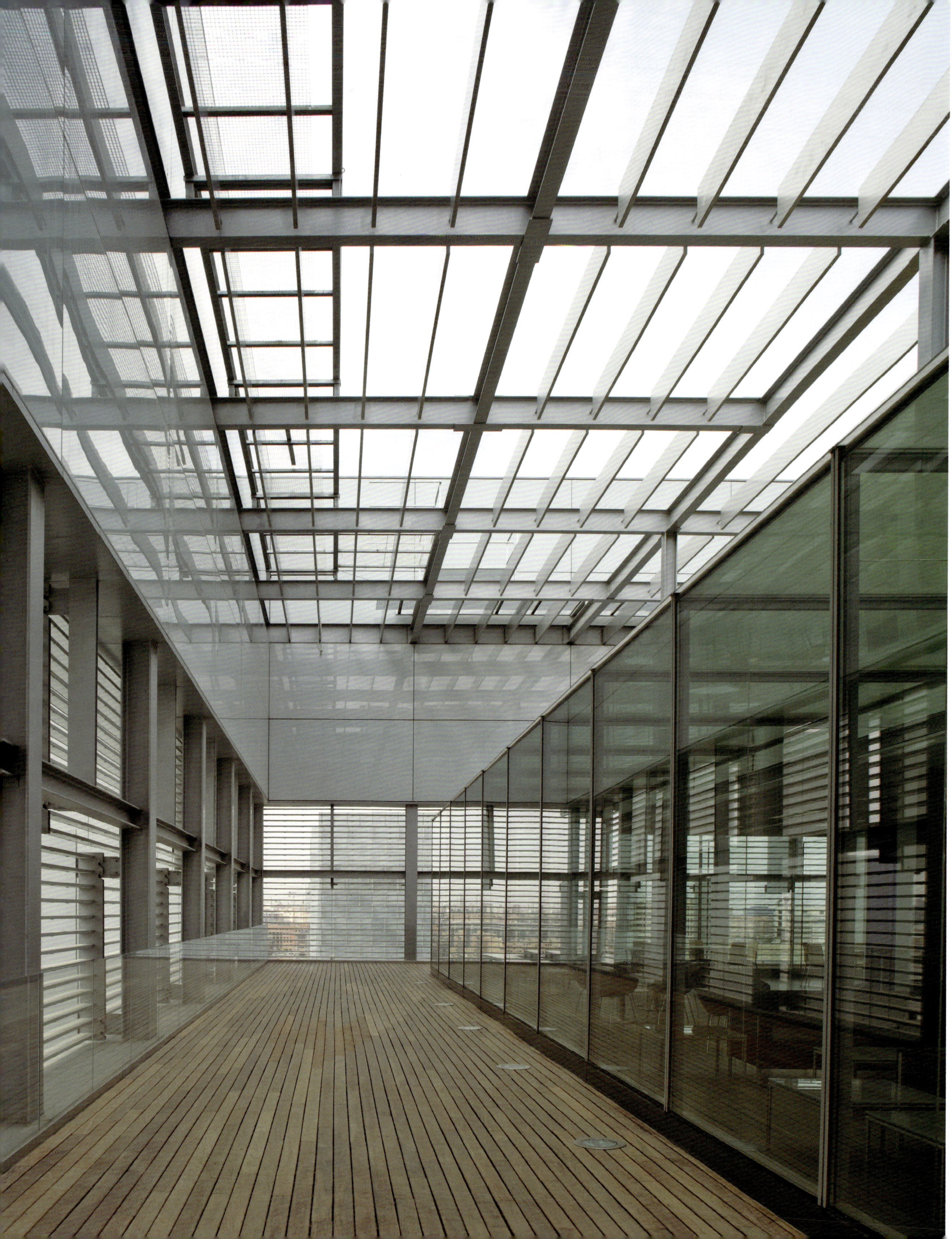

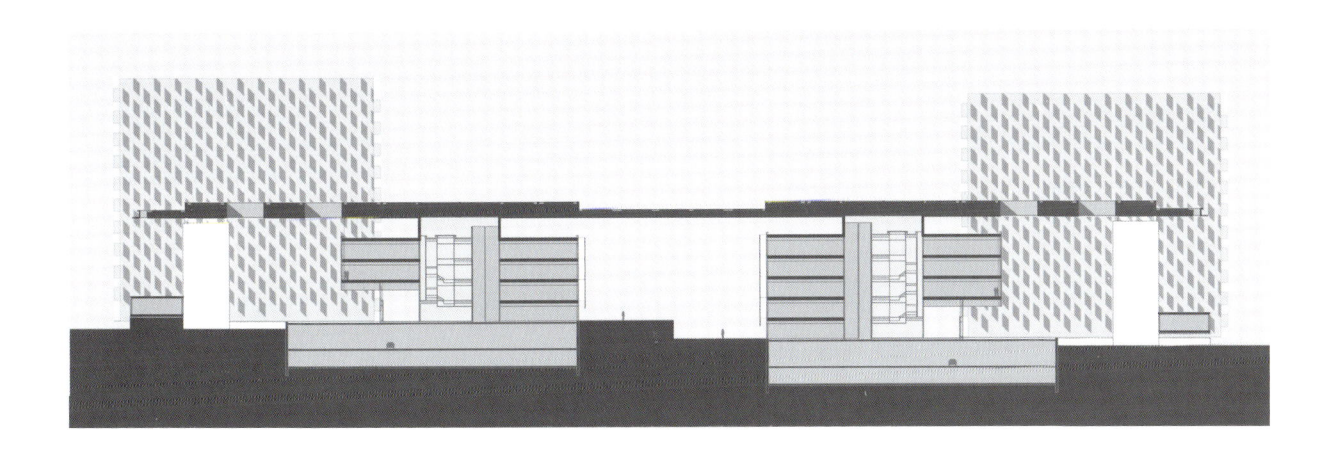

left: Interior view, office floor. right: Section_Exterior view_Landscape design_Exterior view.
links: Innenansicht, Büroebene. rechts: Schnitt_Außenansicht_Landschaftsgestaltung_Außenansicht.

SPAIN_MADRID **STUDIO IN GREEN**

ARCHITECTS: SELGASCANO – JOSE SELGAS, LUCIA CANO
COMPLETION: 2009_**NUMBER OF WORKPLACES:** 10
GROSS FLOOR AREA: 63 M²
PHOTOS: ROLAND HALBE / © ARTURIMAGES

The concept of this studio is quite simple – working under trees. For this purpose a roof that is as transparent as possible and at the same time a protection of the desk zone from direct sunlight was needed. Hence the transparent northern part is covered by sheets of 20 mm colorless Plexiglas while the southern part, where the desks are located, was closed by double sheets of uncolored fiberglass and polyester. In the first section, the view is clear and transparent. The view in the second section is translucent with the shadows of the trees projecting onto it gently. The components look as if they stem straight from a catalog, but they were actually adopted from other sectors like railway carriage construction.

Motto des Büros ist schlicht und ergreifens: Arbeiten unter Bäumen. Das Dach sollte so transparent wie möglich sein und gleichzeitig den Schreibtischbereich vor direktem Sonnenlicht schützen. Folglich wurde der nördliche Teil mit 20 Millimeter dickem, farblosem Plexiglas und der südliche Teil mit einer doppelten Schicht ungefärbtem Fiberglas und Polyester verkleidet. Im ersten Fall ist die Außensicht klar und transparent. Im letzteren ist sie lichtdurchlässig und bildet zart die Schatten der Bäume ab. Die Komponenten sehen aus, als stammten sie direkt aus einem Katalog, wurden aber aus anderen Gestaltungsbereichen wie der Konstruktion von Eisenbahnwaggons übernommen.

left: Section_Work under trees_Workplaces. right: Office in the ground_Plexiglass roof.
links: Schnitt_Arbeiten unter Bäumen_Arbeitsplätze. rechts: Büro in der Erde_Dach aus Plexoglas.

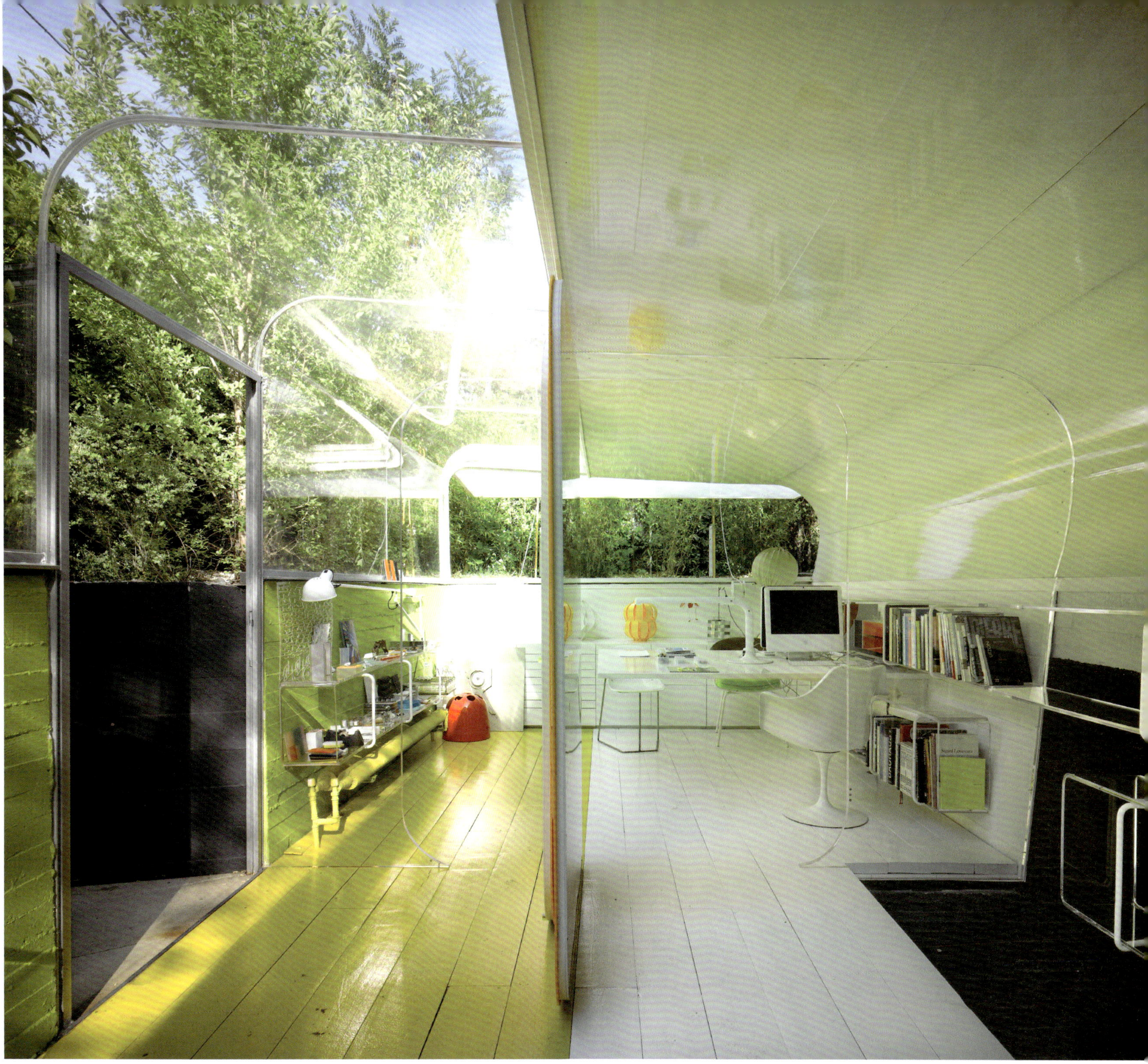

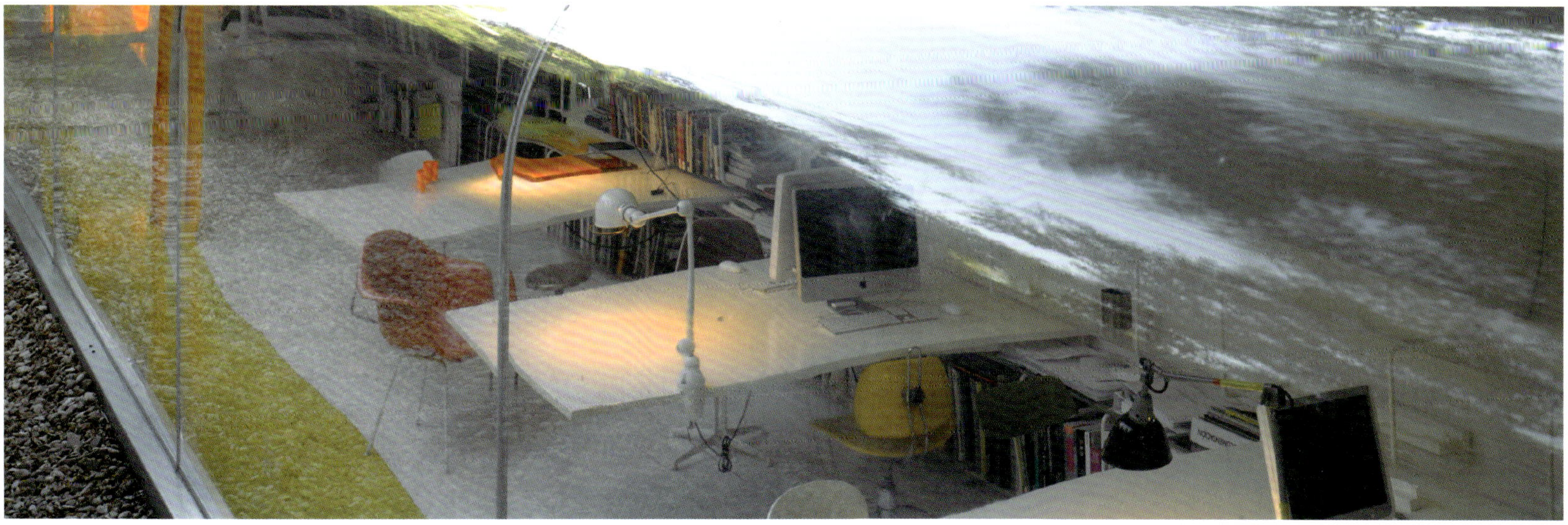

SPAIN_PINEDA DE MAR **INNOVA**

ARCHITECTS: ALCOLEA+TÁRRAGO ARQUITECTOS
COMPLETION: 2008_**NUMBER OF WORKPLACES:** 50
GROSS FLOOR AREA: 2,080 M²_**COMMON AREA:** LECTURE ROOMS
KIND OF WORKPLACES: OPEN-PLAN, DESKSHARING, BUSINESS CLUB_**PHOTOS:** SANCHEZ Y MONTORO, BARCELONA

Since the beginning of the industrial revolution, the debate around work spaces has been a constant topic in architecture. The necessity to accommodate new uses because of new activities has introduced new typologies for the discipline and cities. In this sense, it is easy to remember good examples of both buildings and cities. But administrative advances and computer technologies completely transformed the way of thinking of these spaces. This project proposes functional strips for the different areas of each floor. The entire building is a big technological black box based on the idea of neutrality, elegance and expressiveness.

Die Diskussion über Arbeitsbereiche ist seit Beginn der industriellen Revolution ein andauerndes Thema in der Architektur. Die Notwendigkeit, neue Nutzungen neuen Aktivitäten anzupassen, hat neue Typologien des Büroraums hervorgebracht und die Stadt verbessert. So ist es einfach, gelungene Beispiele von Bauwerken und von Städten aufzugreifen. Moderne Verwaltung und Computertechnologien haben jedoch die Vorstellung solcher Räume verändert. Das Projekt schlägt funktionale Streifen für die verschiedenen Programmbereiche auf jedem Stockwerk vor. Das ganze Gebäude ist eine große technologische Blackbox, die versucht, der Idee von Neutralität, Eleganz und Ausdruckskraft zu folgen.

left: First floor plan and ground floor plan_Exterior view_Box spaces. right: Terrace_Box spaces_Interior space.
links: Grundriss 1. Obergeschoss und Erdgeschoss_Außenansicht_Einzelbüros. rechts: Terrasse_Einzelbüros_Innenraum.

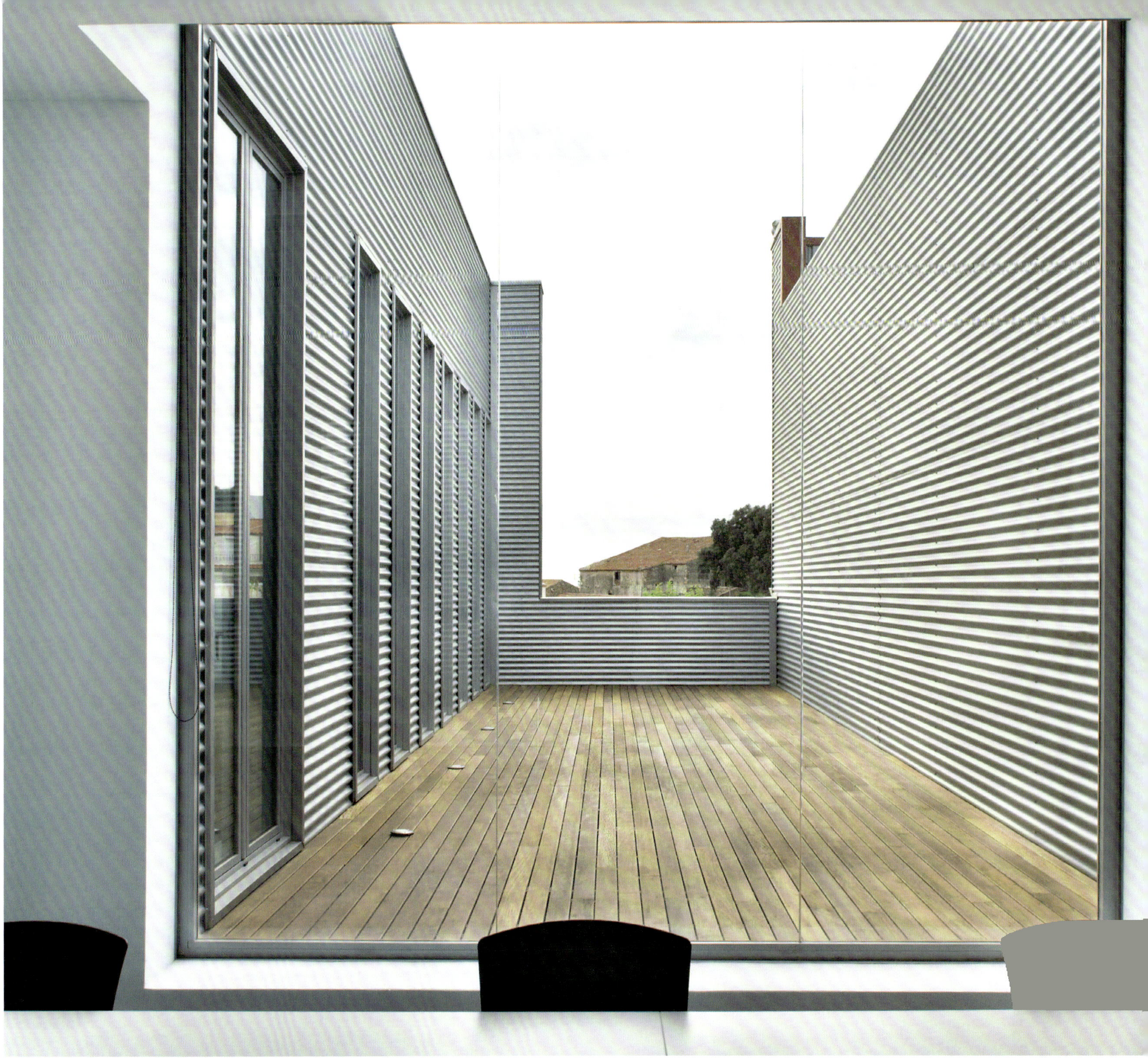
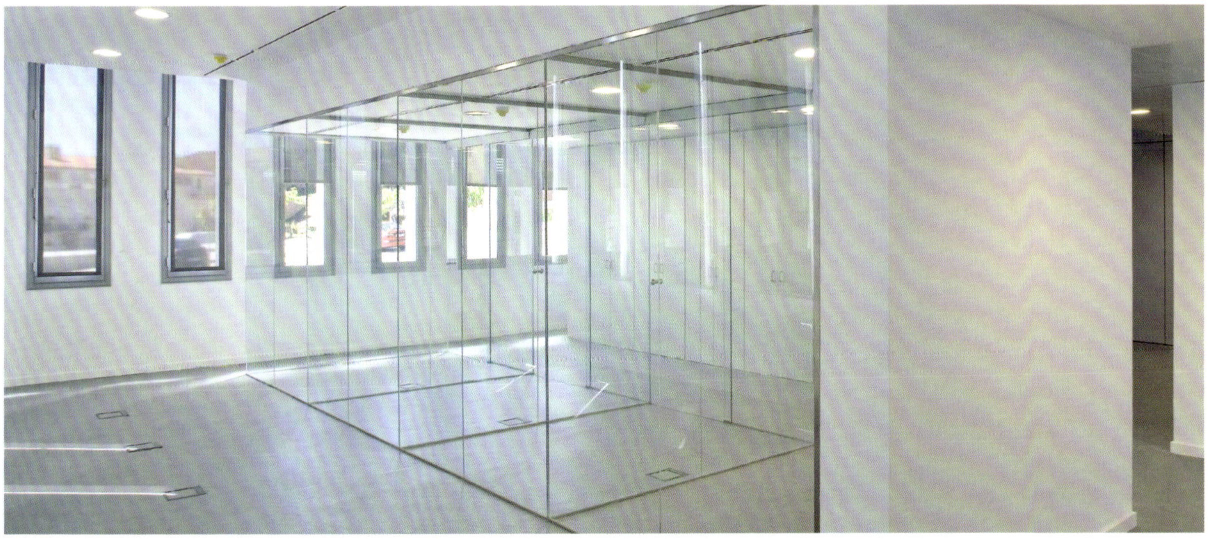
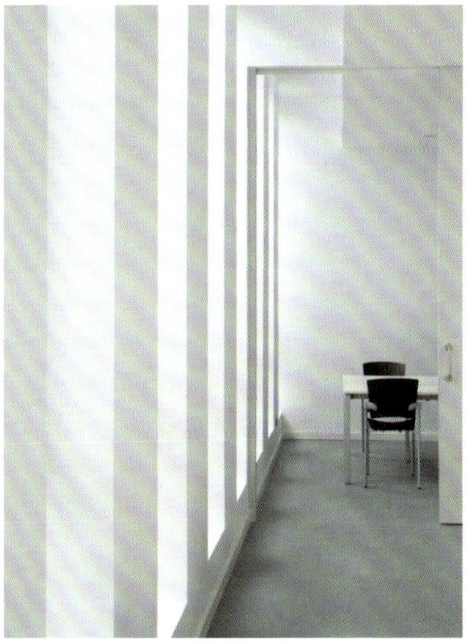

SPAIN_SANTIAGO DE COMPOSTELA SGAE CENTRAL OFFICE

ARCHITECTS: ANTÓN GARCÍA-ABRIL & ENSAMBLE STUDIO
COMPLETION: 2007_**NUMBER OF WORKPLACES:** 15
GROSS FLOOR AREA: 3,000 M²_**COMMON AREA:** PORTICOED STREET, SOCIAL CLUB, SHOP, CINEMA EXHIBITION AND CONCERT HALL_**KIND OF WORKPLACES:** OPEN-PLAN, RECORDING STUDIOS, AUDIO LABORATORIES, POST-PRODUCTION STUDIOS_**PHOTOS:** ROLAND HALBE / © ARTURIMAGES

The SGAE office is located on a site sized between a private garden and a public park from which the skyline of the historical city can be glimpsed. It completes a master plan by Arata Isozaki and defines its boundaries. The offices' design incorporates the spirit of the city developing a singular identity by interacting with its history and its contemporary language. Four functional areas (Diffusion, Formation, Public Area and Management) are distributed across four levels with access from the garden and the street. A stone wall overlooking the garden, an interior wall made of CDs, and a translucent glass wall facing the street act as filters of the different urban situations.

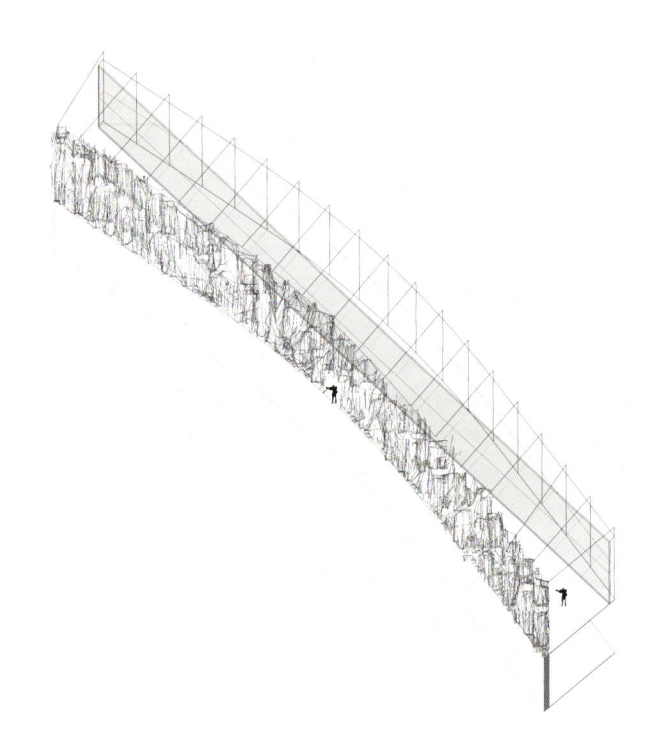

Das SGAE Büro befindet sich zwischen Privatgärten einerseits, öffentlichen Grünflächen andererseits, an einer Stelle, an der man die Silhouette der historischen Stadt sehen kann. Es vervollständigt einen Masterplan von Arata Isozaki und definiert dessen Grenze. Der Entwurf bezieht das Wesen der Stadt ein, indem er sowohl in den Dialog mit historischer als auch mit zeitgenössischer Architektursprache tritt. Vier Funktionsbereiche (Verteilung, Bildung, Öffentlichkeit und Management) sind auf vier Stockwerken mit Zugang vom Garten oder von der Straße aus verteilt. Als Filter zu den verschiedenen angrenzenden Räumen dienen eine Steinwand zum Garten, eine innenliegende Wand aus CDs und transluzentes Glas zur Straße.

left: Plan_Interior view. right: Night view_Side elevation.
links: Plan_Innenansicht. rechts: Nachtansicht_Seitenansicht.

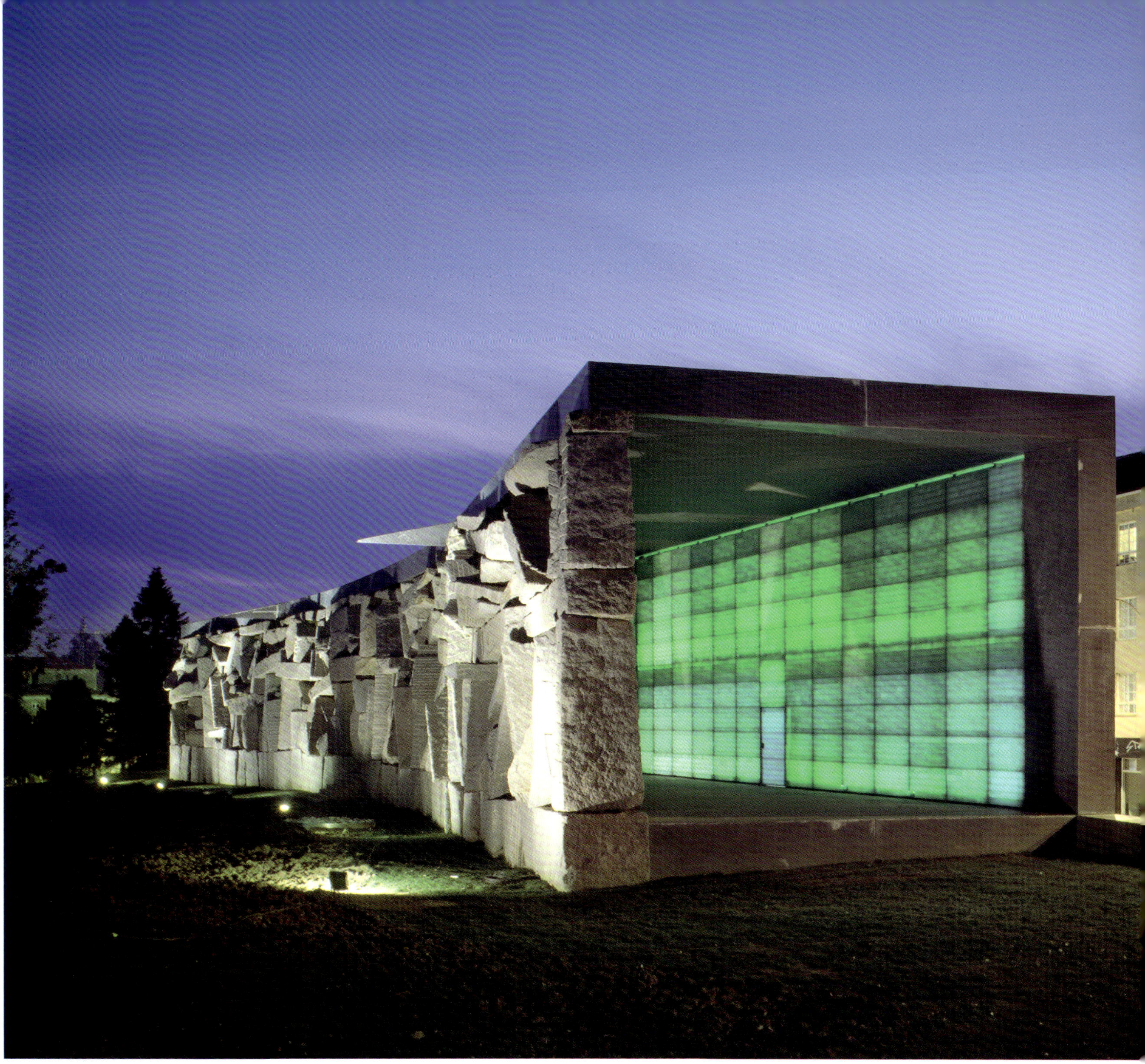

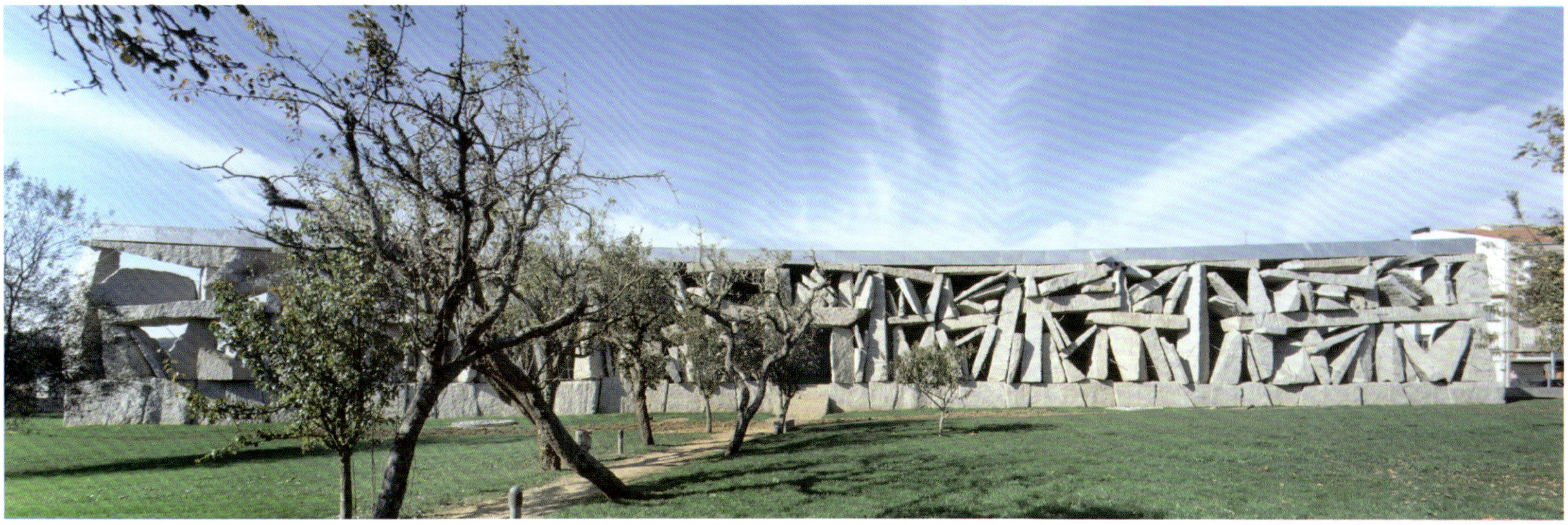

SPAIN_VIGO ARCHITECTURAL ASSOCIATION GALICIA

ARCHITECTS: IRISARRI+PIÑERA_**COMPLETION:** 2009
NUMBER OF WORKPLACES: 60_**GROSS FLOOR AREA:** 1,700 M²
COMMON AREA: EXHIBITION AREA, CAFÉ, SHOPS
KIND OF WORKPLACES: OPEN-PLAN, LOUNGE WORKSPACE
PHOTOS: OFFICE BUILDING ARCHITECTURAL ASSOCIATION GALICIA

The project aimed to maximize the building's volumetric envelope, and influence the chosen borderline conditions to highlight it as an object made independent by its abstraction. In the course of its sculpting process, ephemeral marks were left. An entire free urban void was configured in unison with the building. Together they make up part of a topography that moves from the plane to the envelope, with a full choreography of entrances and connections related to the richness of the street layout. These resolve the different levels of the place in a continuous line, linking them to the building and also to others. Organizing the vehicle traffic and creating rest areas, the project creates a uniform urban area.

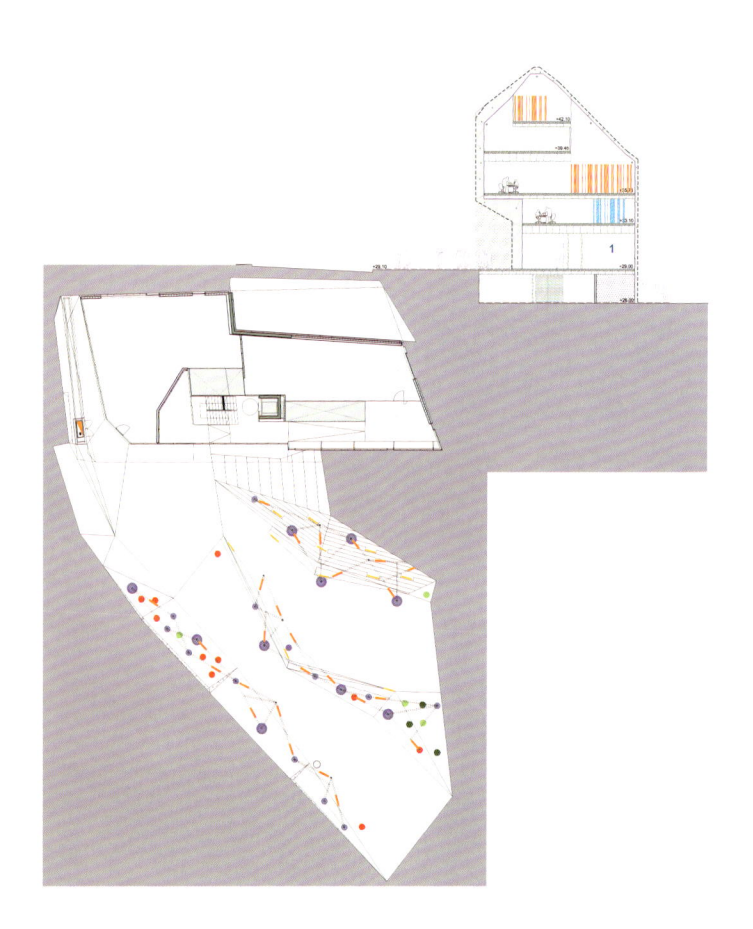

Die Maximierung der Gebäudewand und die Einwirkung auf die Grenzbedingungen sollten das Gebäude als ein durch seine Abstraktion unabhängiges Objekt hervorheben. Im Lauf des Entstehungsprozesses wurden flüchtige Spuren hinterlassen. Die gesamte innerstädtische Lücke wurde in Einklang mit dem Gebäude umgestaltet. Zusammen sind sie Teil einer Topographie, die sich von der Fläche zur Außenwand erhebt. Die Eingänge und Verbindungen sind an den Straßenverlauf angepasst. Sie lassen die verschiedenen Ebenen des Platzes ineinander übergehen, indem sie mit diesem sowie mit anderen Gebäuden verbunden sind. Dank der Organisation des Verkehrs um den Platz und der Gestaltung von Ruhebänken ergibt sich ein einzigartiges Ensemble.

left: Diagram_Bird's-eye view_Detail, façade. right: Entrance area.
links: Diagramm_Vogelperspektive_Fassadendetail. rechts: Eingangsbereich.

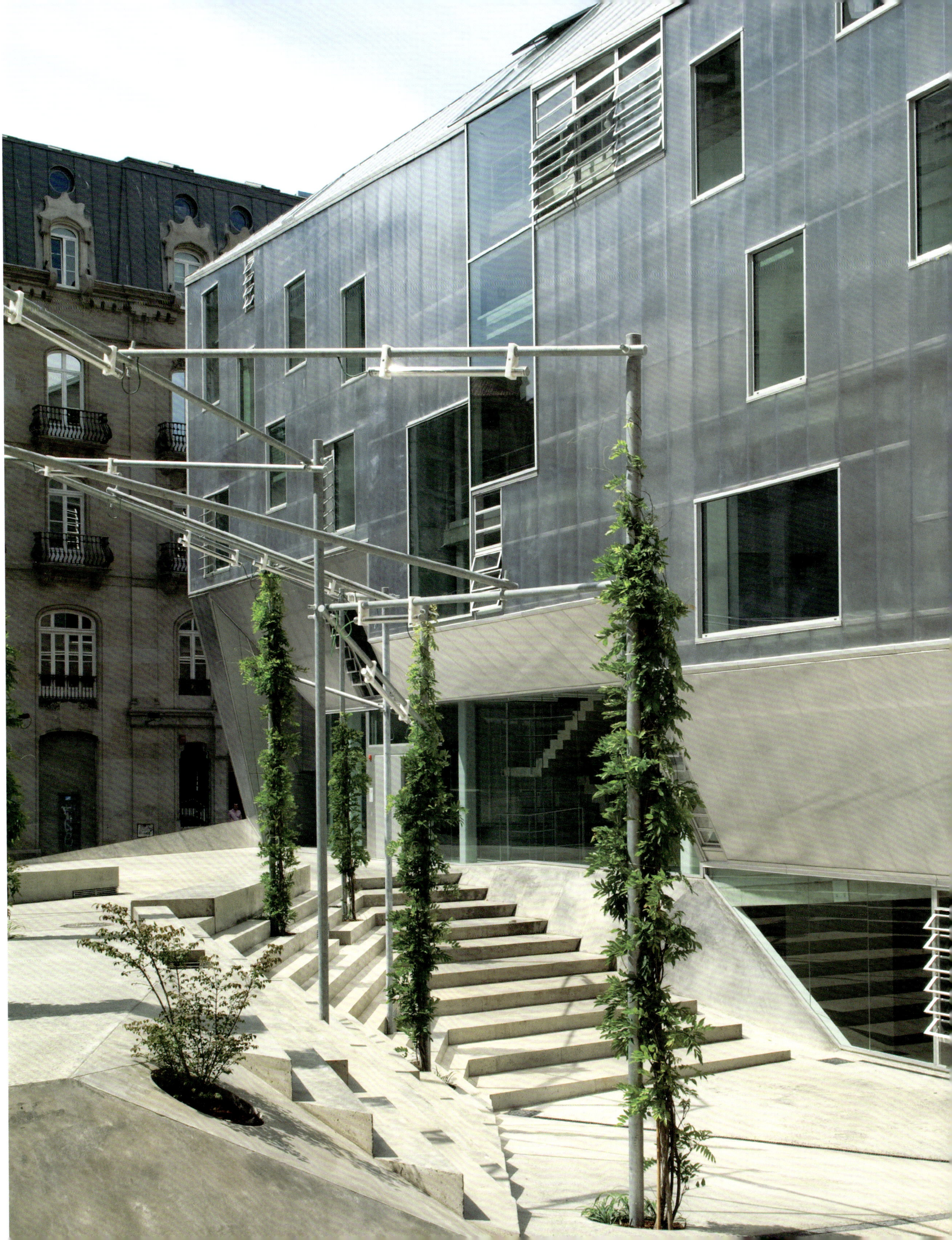

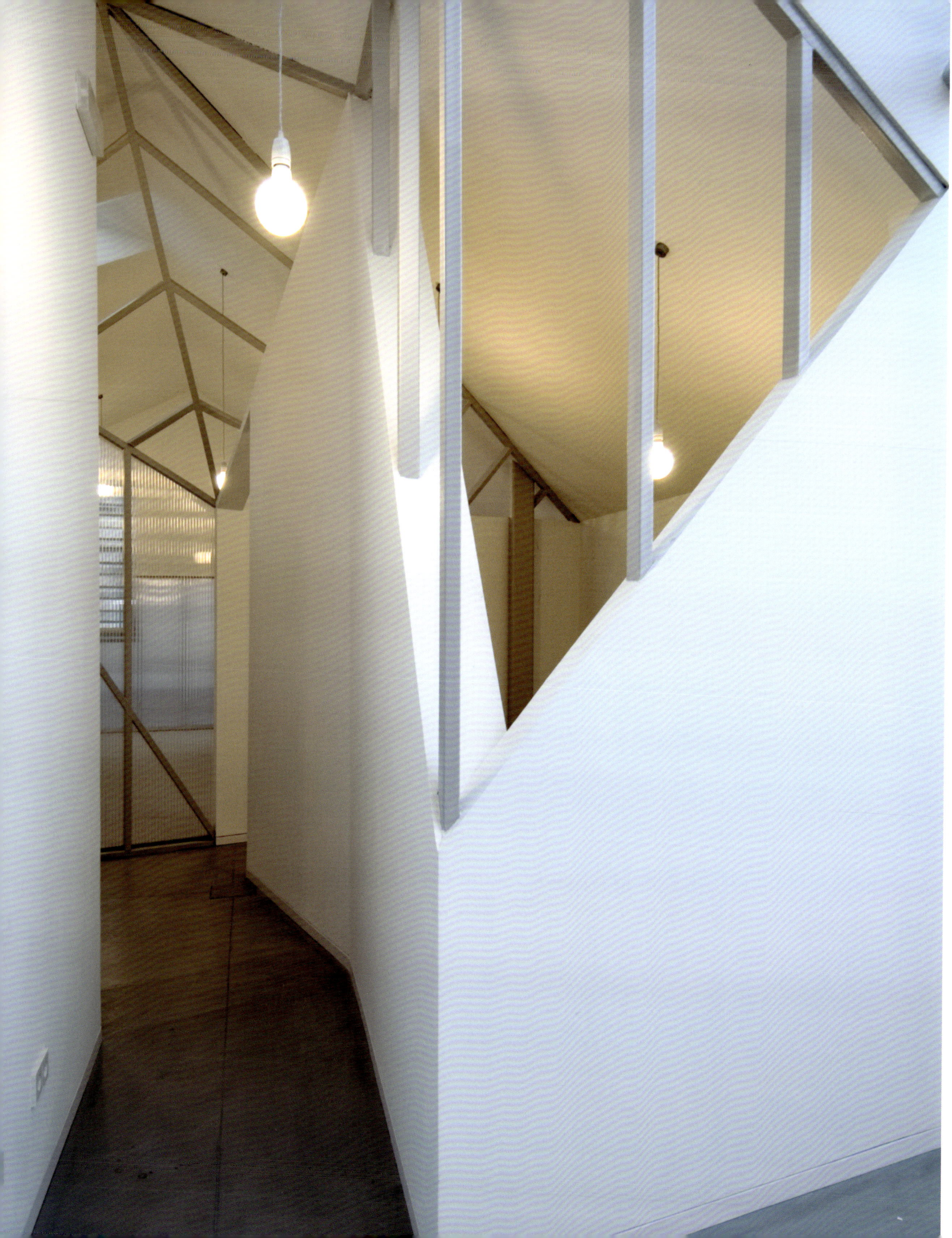

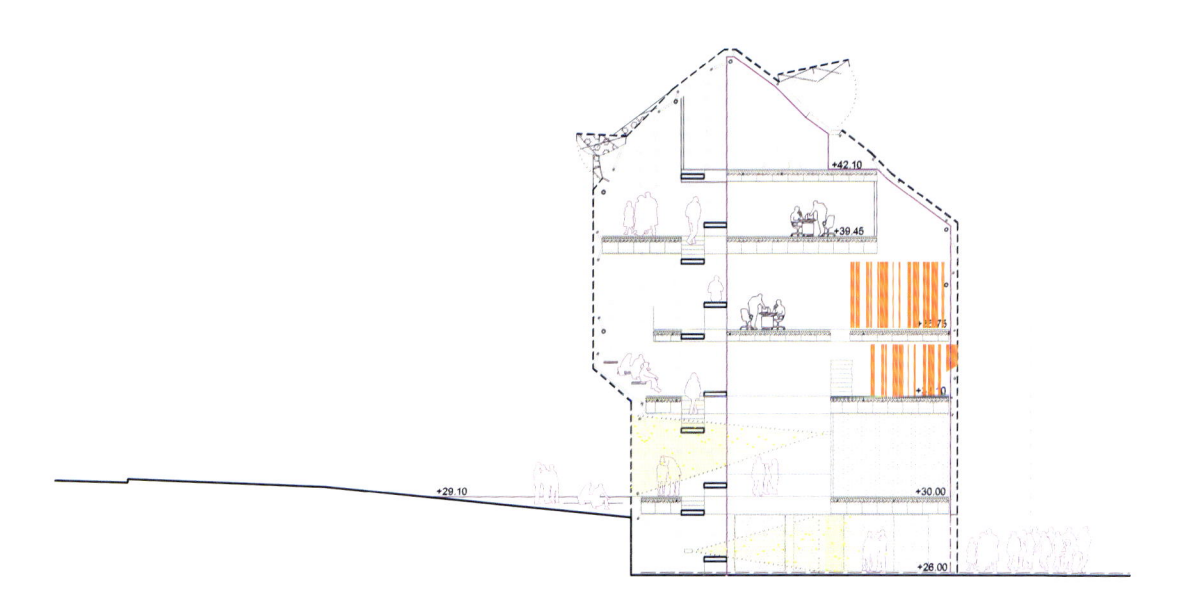

left: Interior view. right: Section_View to the stairway_Upper floor_Stairway.
links: Innenansicht. rechts: Schnitt_Blick zum Treppenhaus_Oberes Geschoss_Treppen.

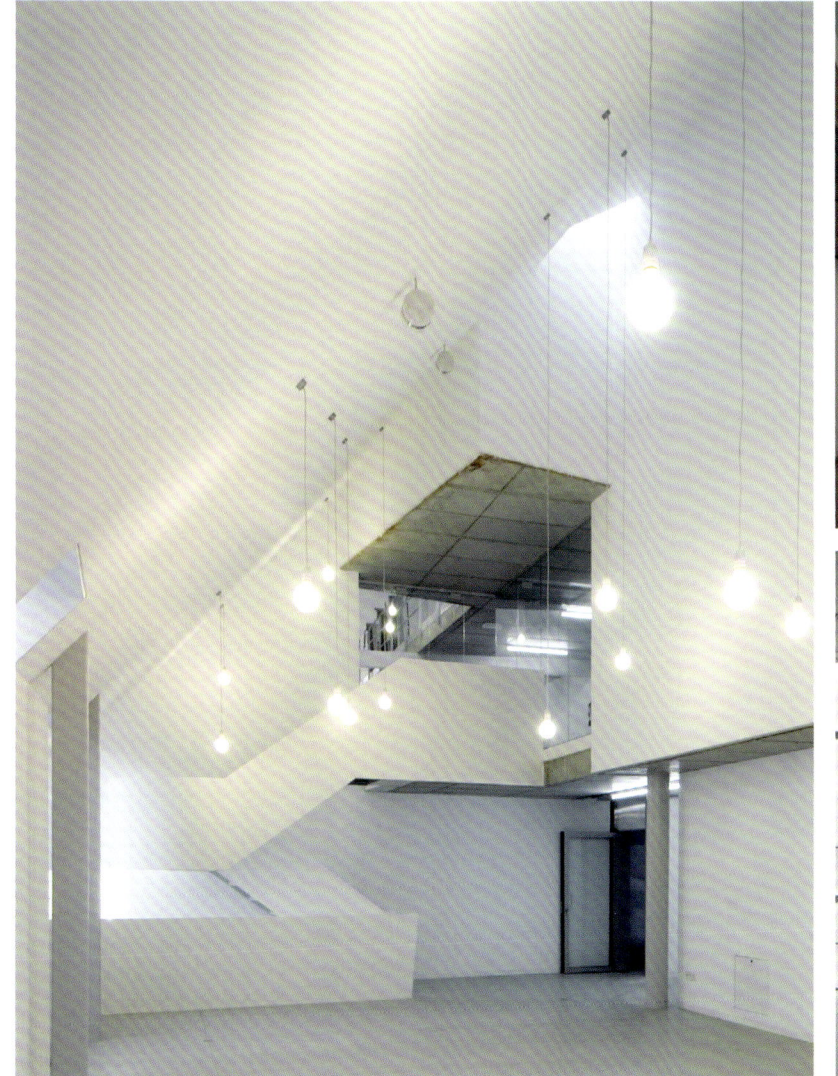

SPAIN_VITORIA-GASTEIZ **SAVINGS BANK HEADQUARTERS**

ARCHITECTS: MOZAS+AGUIRRE ARQUITECTOS / JAVIER MOZAS AND EDUARDO AGUIRRE
ARTIST: JAVIER PÉREZ, BARCELONA
COMPLETION: 2007_**NUMBER OF WORKPLACES:** 200
GROSS FLOOR AREA: 16,578 M²_**COMMON AREA:** MAIN HALL, ASSEMBLY ROOM_**KIND OF WORKPLACES:** OPEN-PLAN, BUSINESS CLUB
PHOTOS: CÉSAR SAN MILLÁN, VITORIA-GASTEIZ

The headquarters of a local savings bank reproduces the scale of the surrounding small woods, a park of the Natura 2000 networking program. The floor plan is chromosome-shaped with four arms. The structural concept is based on pairs of exterior metal supports, clad in stainless steel composite panels. One of the arms has been conceived as a 26-meter cantilever. In this case the concept changes and the pairs do not have any structural function. A double height hall located at the heart of the building has its two façades enclosed by a work of art. They have been provided with red polyurethane panels with a manually painted biological pattern. The idea is to present the building as a living organism in motion.

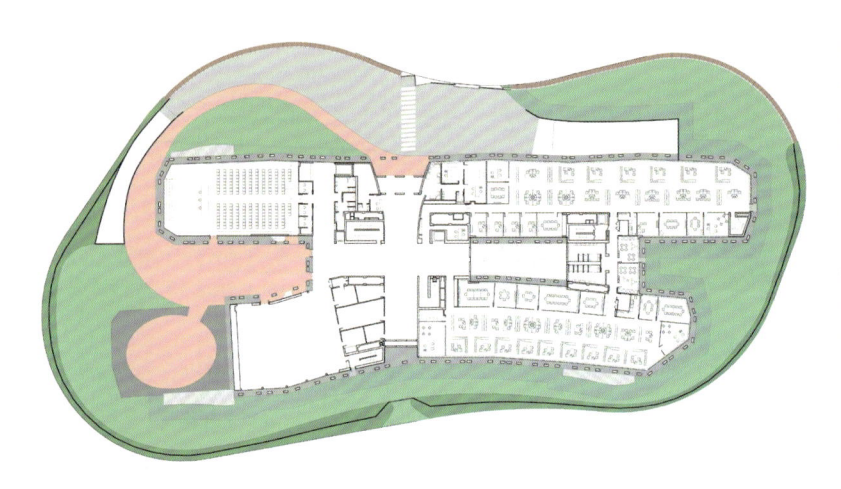

Das Hauptquartier einer lokalen Sparkasse greift die Größe der umliegenden kleinen Wälder, Teil des Natura 2000 Netzwerk-Programms auf. Der Grundriss hat mit vier Trakten die Form eines Chromosoms. Die Statik beruht auf Paaren externer Metallstützen, die mit Verbundplatten aus Edelstahl umkleidet wurden. Einer der Trakte ist als Ausleger von 26 Metern Länge ausgebildet und hier verlieren die Stützenpaare ihre Funktion. Im Zentrum des Baus liegt eine Halle doppelter Höhe, deren beide Fassaden mit einem Kunstwerk verkleidet sind. Aus roten Polyurethanplatten bestehend sind sie mit einem biologisch erscheinenden Muster handbemalt. Dahinter steckt die Idee, den Bau als sich bewegenden, lebendigen Organismus erscheinen zu lassen.

left: Ground floor plan_Workshop area_Façade, detail. right: Interior courtyard_ North façade at night.
links: Grundriss Erdgeschoss_Bereich für Workshops_Fassade, Detail. rechts: Innenhof_Nordfassade bei Nacht.

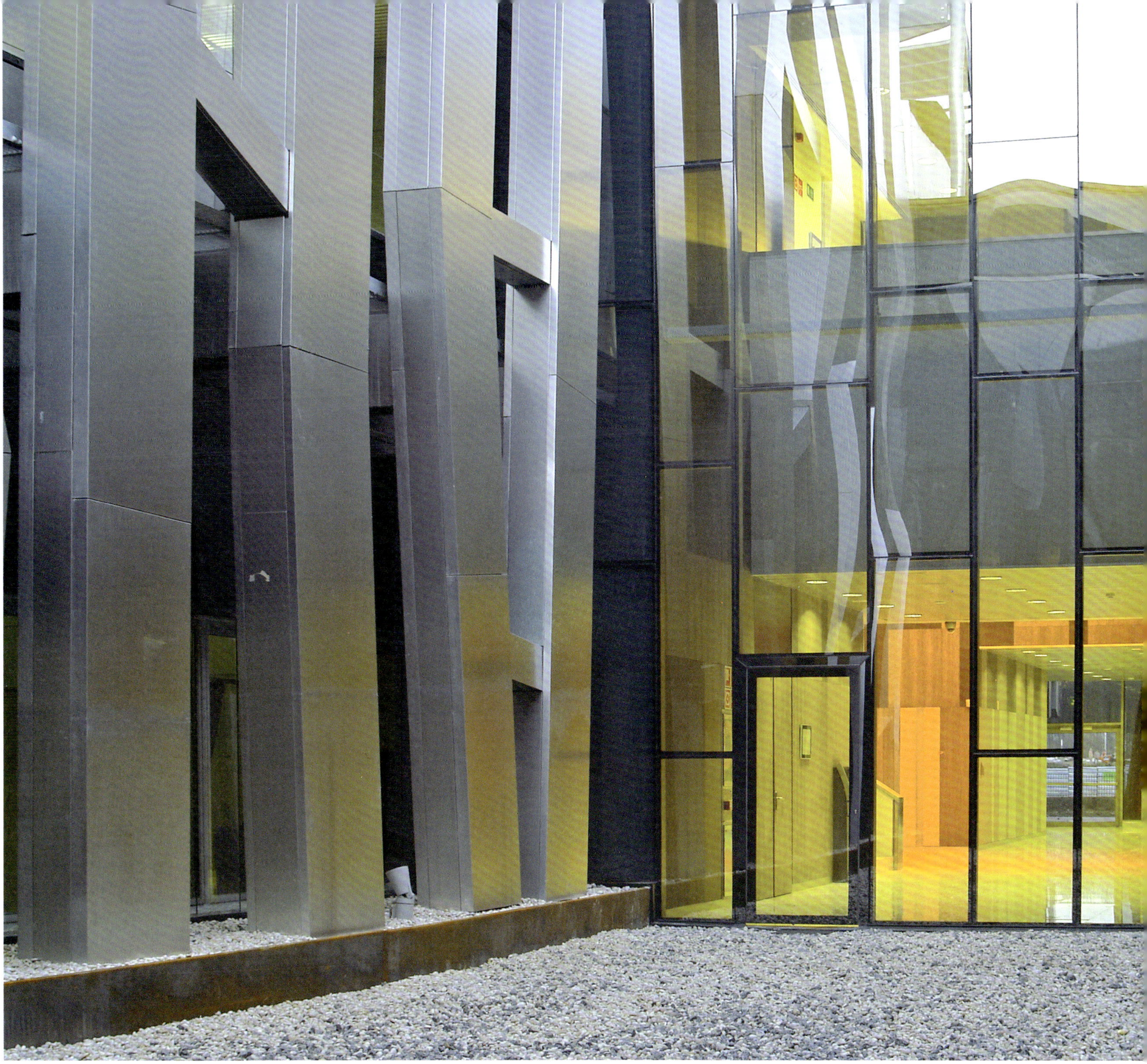

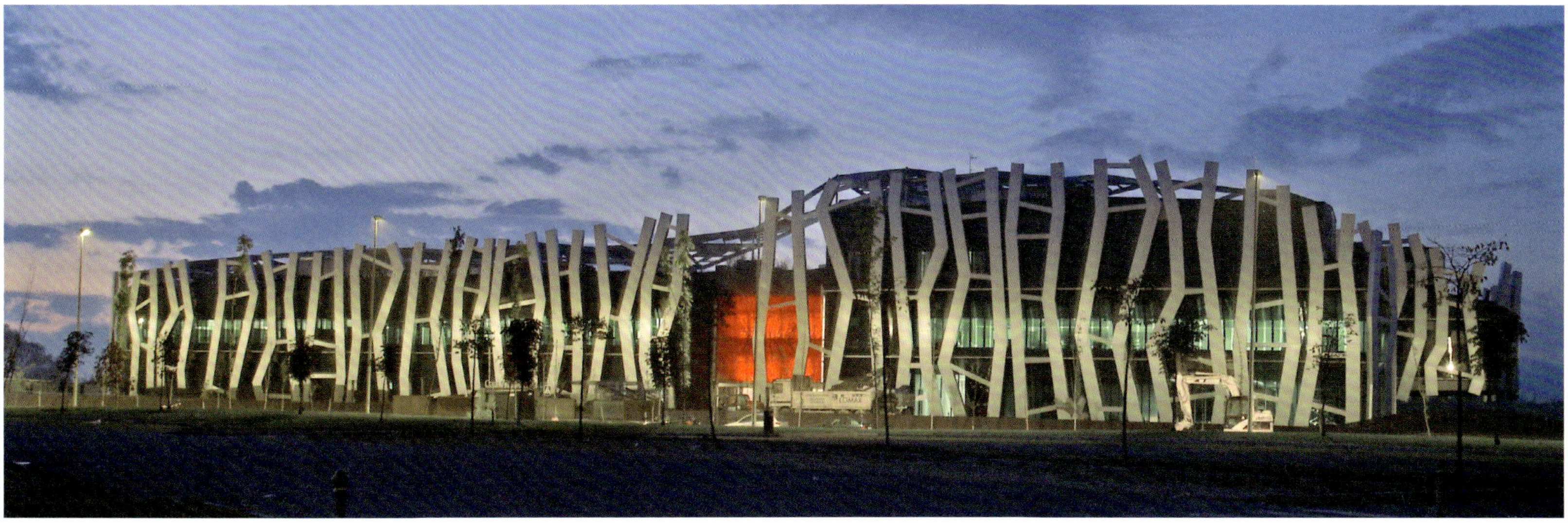

SWEDEN_STOCKHOLM PIONEN – WHITE MOUNTAIN

ARCHITECTS: ALBERT FRANCE-LANORD ARCHITECTS
COMPLETION: 2008_**NUMBER OF WORKPLACES:** 15
GROSS FLOOR AREA: 1,200 M²_**KIND OF WORKPLACES:** UNDERGROUND OPEN-PLAN_**PHOTOS:** ÅKE E:SON LINDMAN

In a former nuclear protection shelter, 30 meters beneath the granite rocks of the Vita Berg Park in Stockholm, the Internet provider found a new home for its new server halls and offices. Basically, the area is not a traditional enclosed space but is defined as an emptiness inside a mass. Starting point of the project was to treat the rock as a living organism, in which humans try to acclimate themselves by introducing the 'best' elements from above-ground: light, plants, water and technology. The client was given a strong vision from the first brief and the strong contrasts between rooms dominated by the rock with human beings as intruders and rooms where humans are in total control was only possible because of the customer's persistence.

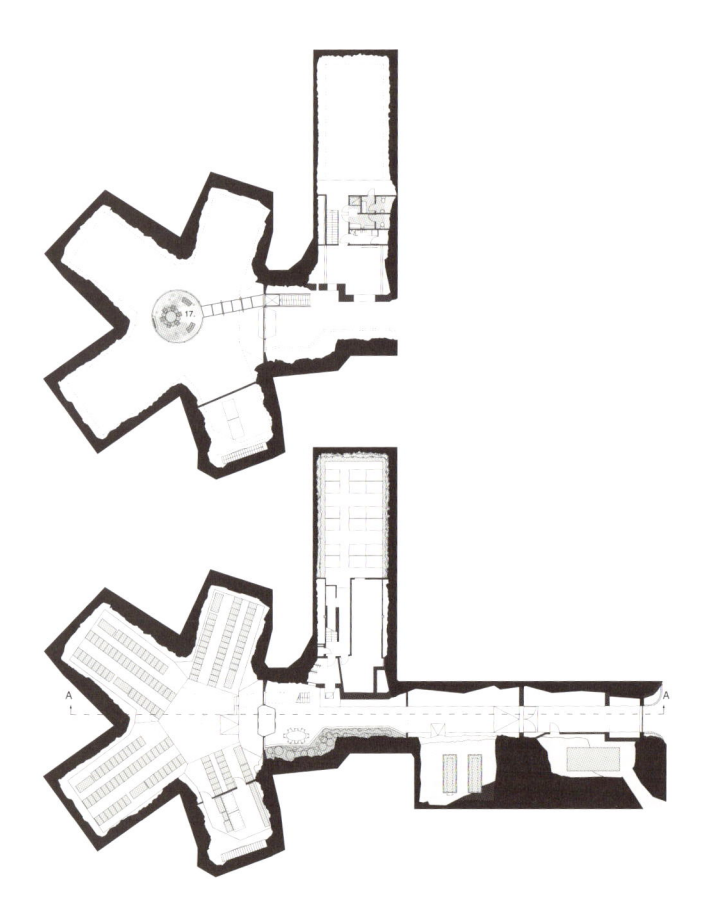

In einem Atombunker, 30 Meter tief im Granit unter dem Vita Berg Park in Stockholm, fand der Internetprovider neue Serverhallen und Büroräume. Hier ist Raum nicht länger baulich gefasstes Volumen, sondern vielmehr Leere in einer Masse. Der Entwurf nutzt den Fels als quasi lebenden Organismus, in dem sich der Mensch symbiotisch mit den besten Entwicklungen der Erde – Licht, Pflanzen, Wasser und Technik – aklimatisiert. Von Beginn an konnte der Auftraggeber sich dies gut vorstellen, und nur durch seine Ausdauer war die Realisierung von Räumen umsetzbar, in denen der Fels den Fremdkörper Mensch dominiert und im Gegensatz zu Räumen steht, in denen die Menschheit die Führung übernommen hat.

left: Floor plans_Office_Office space. right: Granite cave_ Meeting room_ In the meeting room.
links: Grundrisse_Büro_Büroraum. rechts: Höhle aus Granit_Besprechungsraum_Im Besprechungsraum.

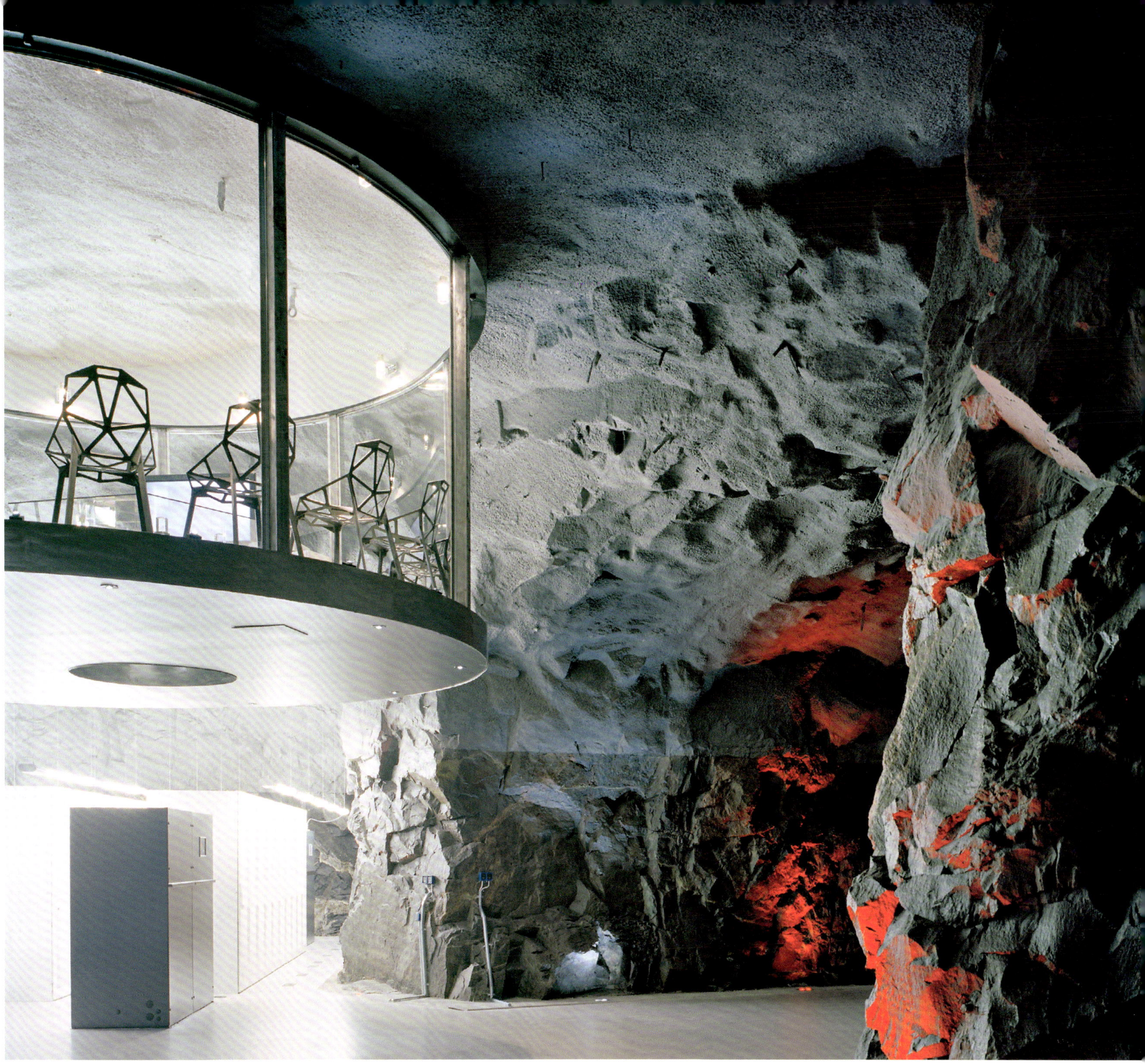

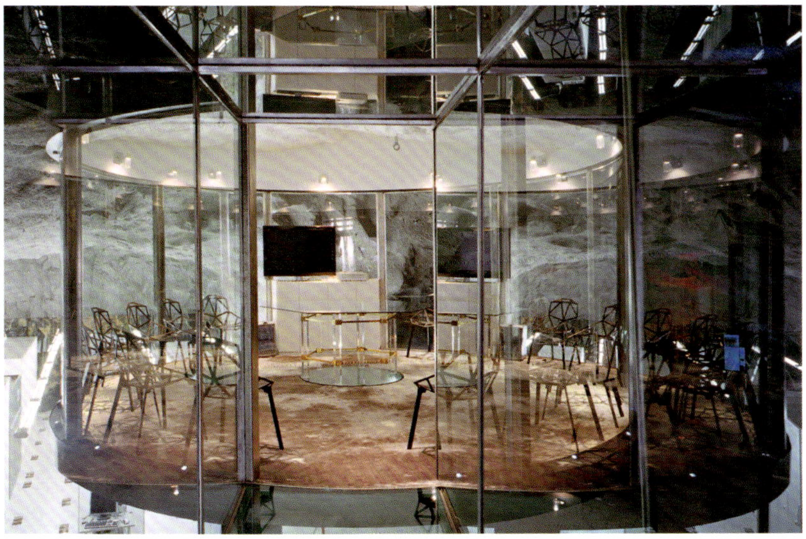

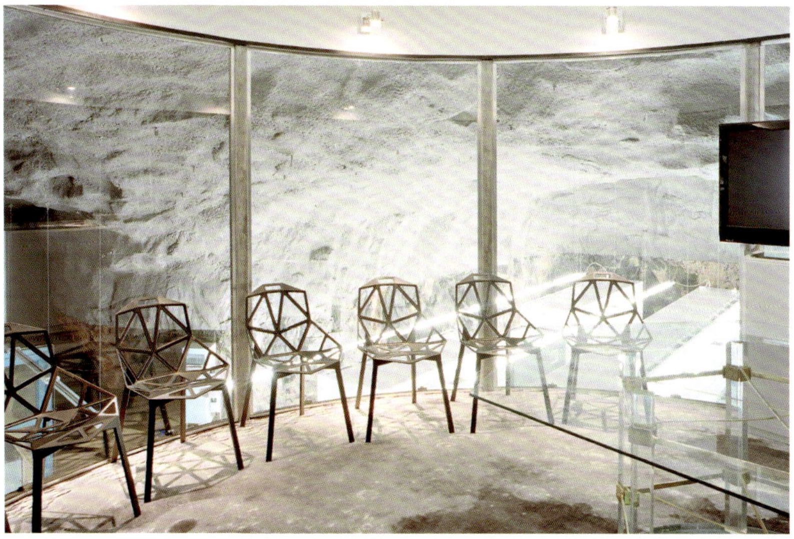

SWITZERLAND_KÜSNACHT MOBIMO VERWALTUNGS AG HEADQUARTERS

ARCHITECTS: STÜCHELI ARCHITEKTEN
COMPLETION: 2006_**NUMBER OF WORKPLACES:** 55
GROSS FLOOR AREA: 3,220 M²_**KIND OF WORKPLACES:** COMBINATION_**PHOTOS:** REINHARD ZIMMERMANN, ADLISWIL

A minimal, orange-red belt frames the complex glass structure providing it with a system and a structure. An abstract, upwards spiraling meander barely separates the interior of the building from nature. Accordingly, the interior space was also conceived as a walk along a shore, strolling on a wooden boardwalk, framed by reeds next to a lake glittering in the evening sun. The colored glass on the flexed walls results in an interplay of reflections and transparencies, with the white, abstract volume of the staircase located in the midst of this colorful landscape. The magnificent view, extensive communication space, generous room heights and a coherent color and material concept resulted in an extraordinary work environment.

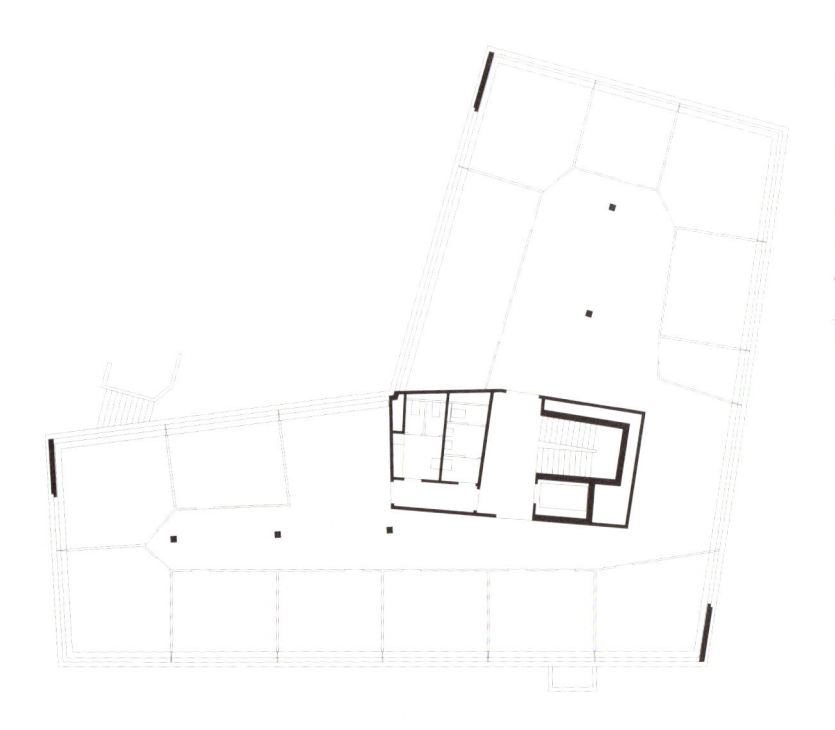

Ein minimales, orangerotes Band rahmt den komplexen Glaskörper, gibt ihm Regeln und Struktur. Ein abstrahierter, sich aufwärts windender Mäander trennt das Innenleben kaum von der Natur. Entsprechend ist auch der Innenraum als Uferspaziergang gedacht, als Wandeln auf einem hölzernen Steg, gesäumt von Schilf an einem im Abendlicht glitzernden See. Die farbigen Gläser der geknickten Korridorwände führen zu einem Spiel von Reflexionen und Transparenzen. Inmitten dieser farbig assoziierten Landschaft steht das weiße, abstrakte Volumen des Treppenhauses. Der weite Ausblick, viel Raum zur Kommunikation, die großzügige Raumhöhe und ein stimmiges Farb- und Materialkonzept erschaffen ein außerordentliches Arbeitsklima.

left: Ground floor plan_Office with colored glass partition. right: Elevation Seestrasse_Workplaces lakeside_Lobby combination offices.
links: Grundriss Erdgeschoss_Büro mit eingefärbter Glastrennwand. rechts: Ansicht Seestrasse_ Arbeitsplätze auf der Seeseite_Vorraum der Kombibüros.

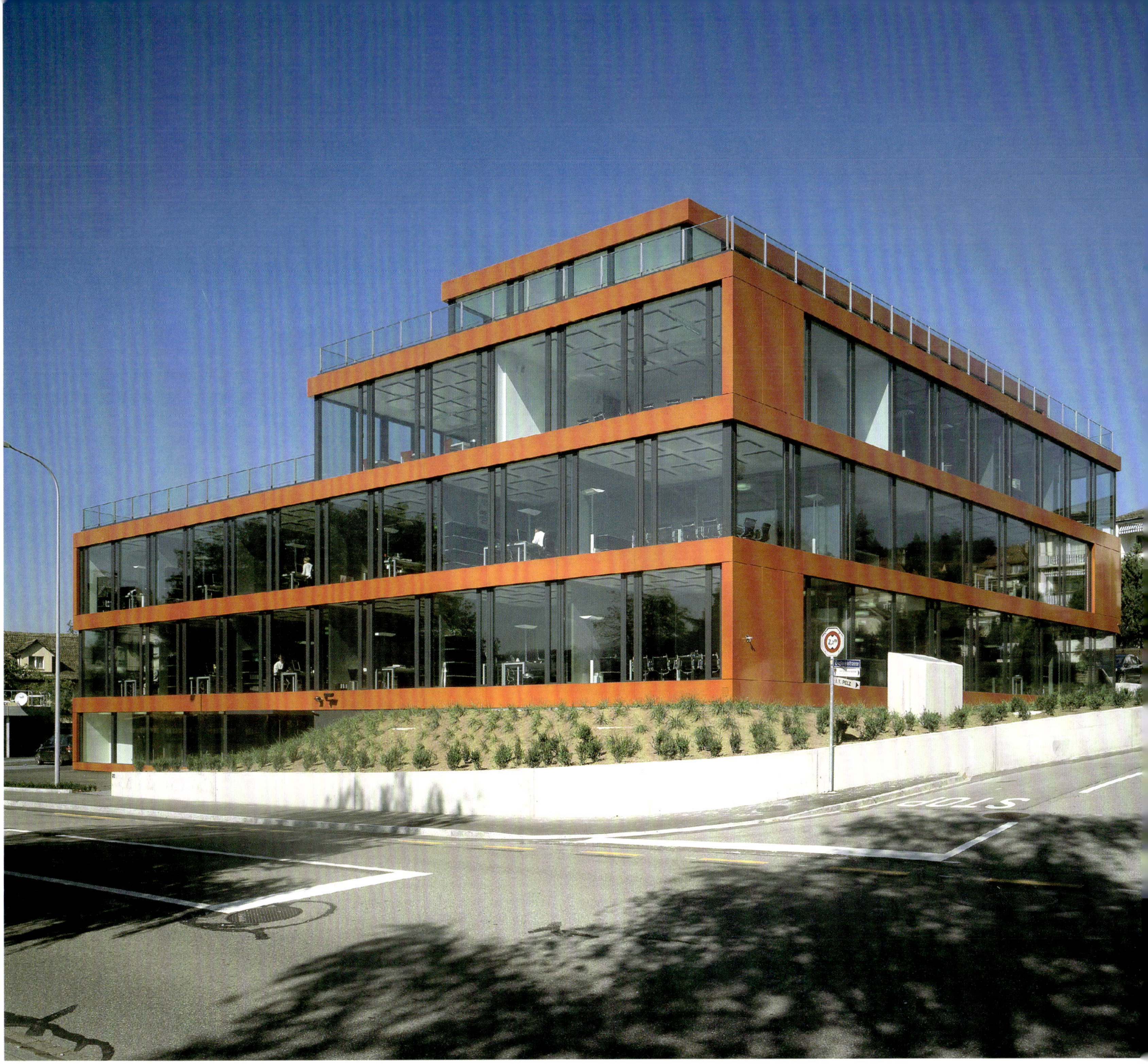
STOP

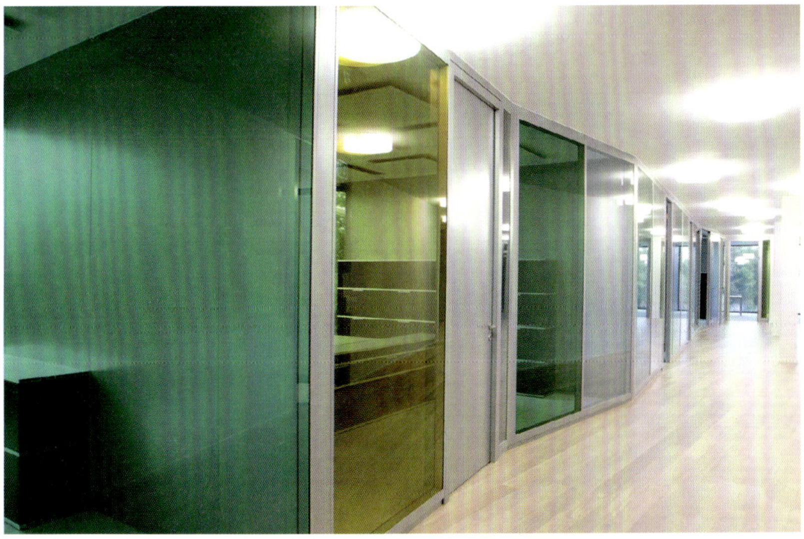

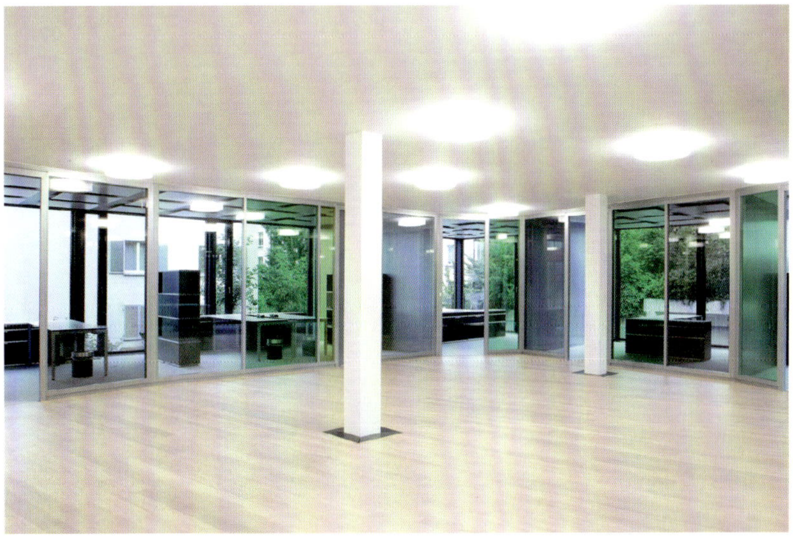

SWITZERLAND_MÜNCHENSTEIN CLARIANT SPENGLER FLEXIBLE OFFICE

ARCHITECTS: WIRTH+WIRTH ARCHITECTS
COMPLETION: 2005_**NUMBER OF WORKPLACES:** 170
GROSS FLOOR AREA: 5,550 M²_**KIND OF WORKPLACES:** CELLULAR, OPEN-PLAN, TEAM, LOUNGE WORKSPACE
PHOTOS: COURTESY OF THE ARCHITECTS

In the variation of the open space office concept selected by Clariant, each employee in the bench zone has his/her own office space near a window. In addition, the active zone offers working spaces for team activities, ad hoc meetings and discussions, while the private zone contains screened office for individual or group activities. These room dividers create the different office areas, while their sound-absorbing fabric covers improve the acoustics, and they provide illumination to the inner areas of the open space. Lounge and cafeteria zones integrated into the office landscape offer opportunities for relaxation and unimpeded communications.

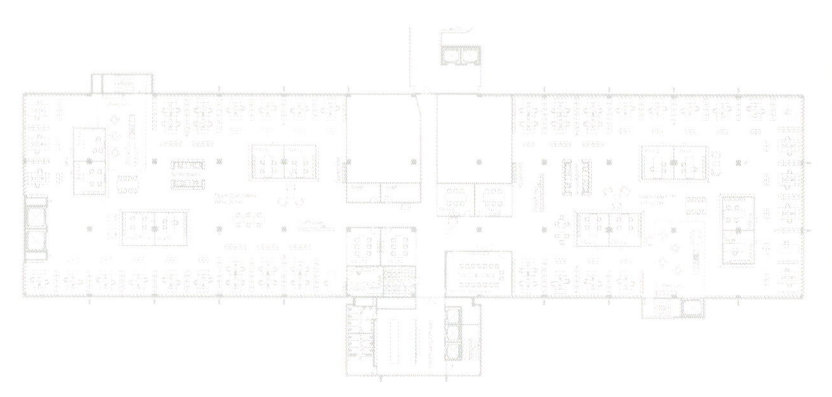

In der von Clariant gewählten Umsetzung des Open Space-Bürokonzepts hat jeder Mitarbeiter in der Bench-Zone einen eigenen Büroarbeitsplatz in Fensternähe. Zusätzlich stehen im Zwischenbereich der Active Zone freie Arbeitsplätze für Teamarbeit, Adhoc-Meetings und Diskussionen, sowie in der Private Zone abgeschirmte Einzelbüros als Einzel- oder Gruppenarbeitsplatz zur Verfügung. Als raumbildenden Elemente gliedern diese auch die Bürofläche in unterschiedliche Zonen, verbessern über ihre schallabsorbierende textilen Außenhülle die Raumakustik und beleuchten die inneren Bereiche des Open Space. In die Bürolandschaft integrierte Lounge- und Cafeteria-Zonen dienen der bewussten Entspannung und zwanglosen Kommunikation.

left: Fourth floor plan_Open-space and coffeepoint. right: Service point_Lounge workplace_Private Zone_Coffeepoint.
links: Grundriss viertes Obergeschoss_Freiraum und Café. rechts: Servicestelle_ Lounge-Arbeitsplatz_Private Zone_Café.

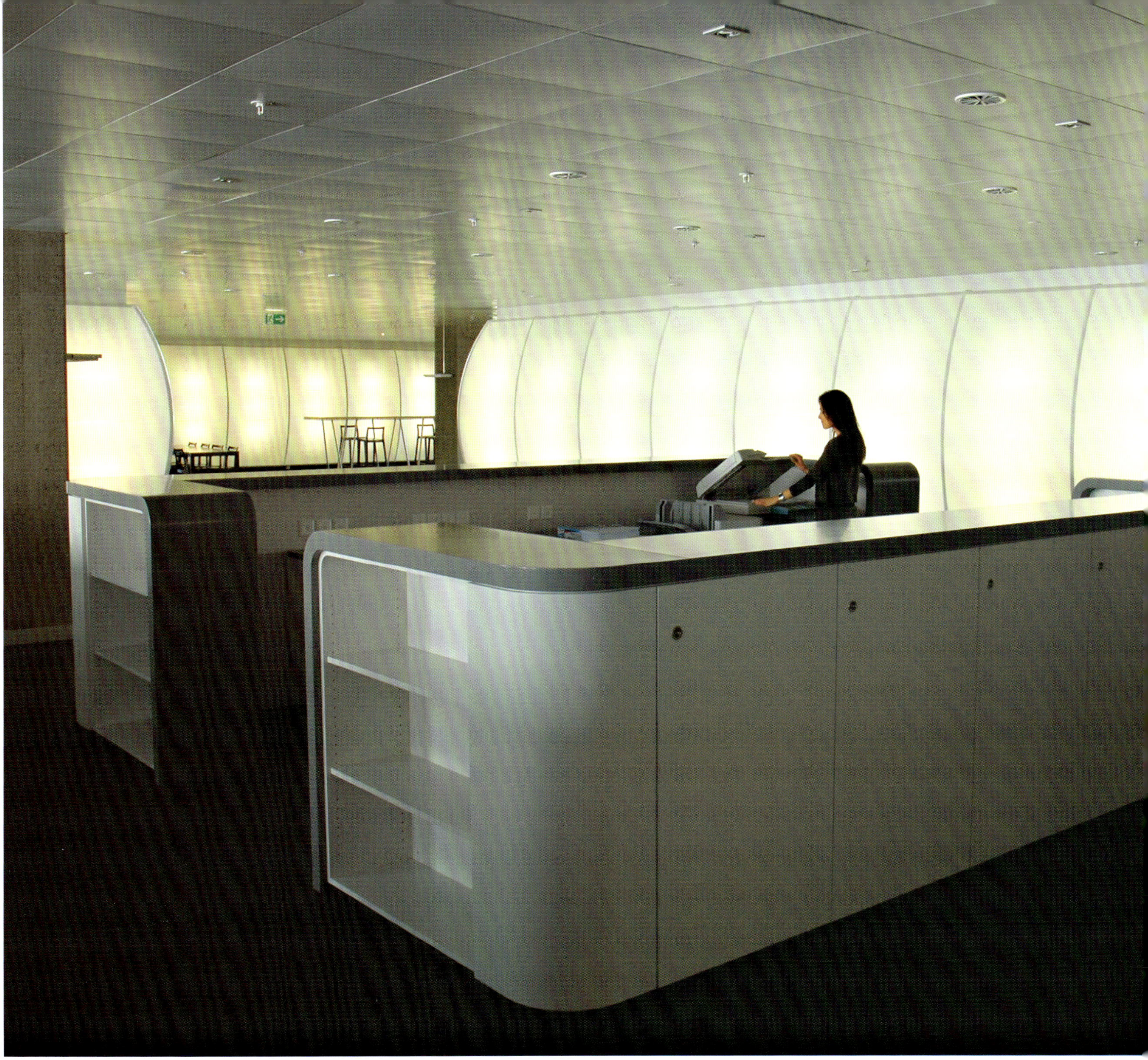

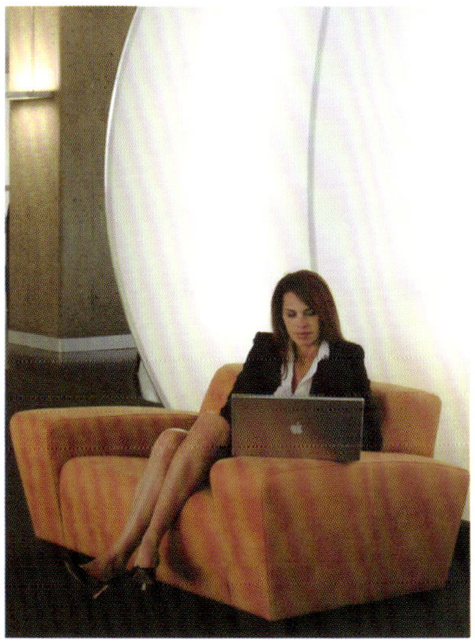

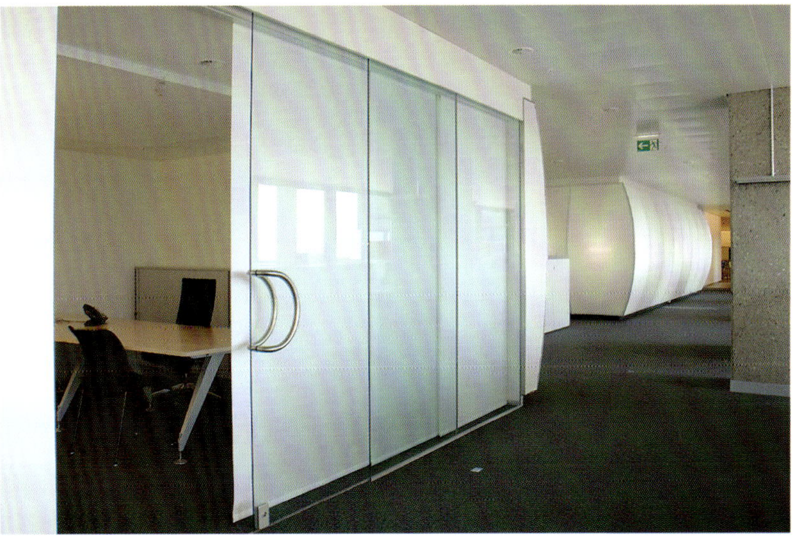

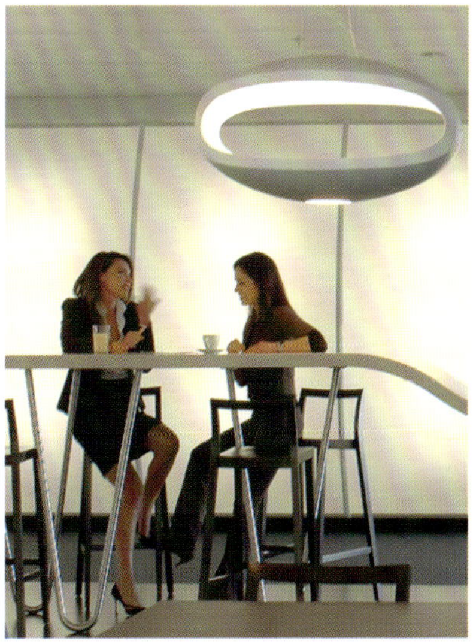

SWITZERLAND_ZURICH GOOGLE'S NEW EMEA ENGINEERING HUB

ARCHITECTS: CAMENZIND EVOLUTION_**COMPLETION:** 2008
NUMBER OF WORKPLACES: 800_**GROSS FLOOR AREA:** 12,000 M²
COMMON AREA: MEETING ROOMS, WATER LOUNGE
KIND OF WORKPLACES: CELLULAR, TEAM, LOUNGE WORKSPACE_**PHOTOS:** PETER WURMLI

The interior of the seven-floor shell and core office block reflects individuality, creativity and innovative business practice within a high-energy environment, while maintaining a small-company ambience throughout the growth of the company. The "Googlers" participated in the design process to create their own local identity, reviewing, challenging and approving the design based on research and analysis throughout the project. They decided early on that they preferred to reduce their personal net workspace area in order to gain more themed communal areas and formal and informal meeting space. The layout encourages circulation throughout the building to enhance communication between the different working groups and teams.

Das Innere des siebengeschossigen Bürogebäudes ermöglicht Individualität, Kreativität und innovative Arbeitsweise in einem hoch-technischen Umfeld, welches allen Wachstum zum Trotz das Ambiente eines kleinen Betriebes erhalten hat. Die „Googlers" waren in dem Entwurfsprozess eingebunden, schufen ihr eigenes identifikationsfähiges Umfeld und kontrollierten, hinterfragten und bestätigten den auf Untersuchungen und Analysen beruhenden Entwurf während des gesamten Prozesses. So entschieden sie schon früh, ihre eigenen Arbeitsplätze zu Gunsten thematischer Gemeinschaftsbereiche und formalen wie informellen Besprechungsräumen einzuschränken. Die Gestaltung ermuntert zur Bewegung in dem Gebäude, so dass die Kommunikation zwischen Arbeitsgruppen und Teams gefördert wird.

left: First floor plan_Offices_Workplace. right: Reception.
links: Grundriss erstes Obergeschoss_Büros_Arbeitsplatz. rechts: Empfang.

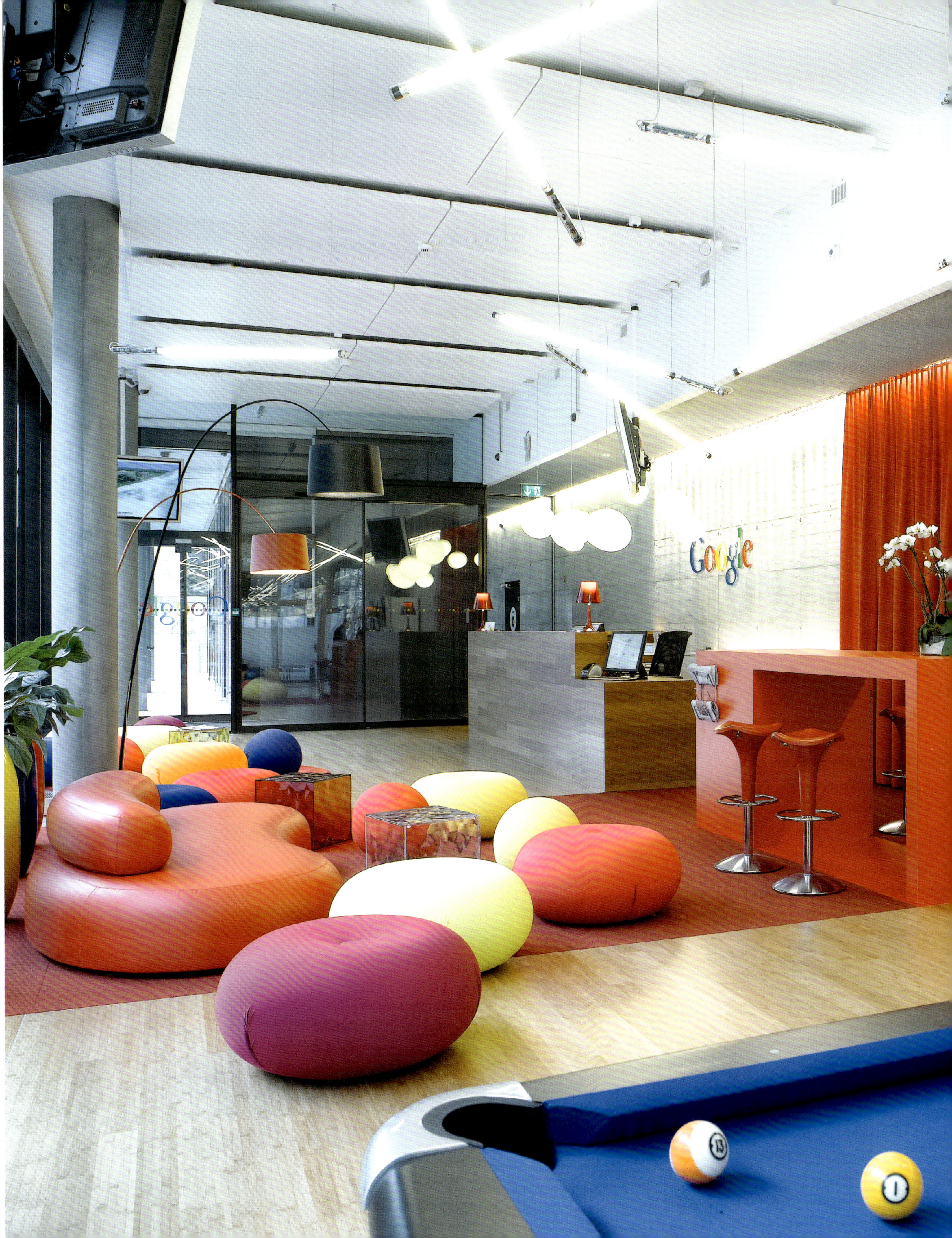
Google

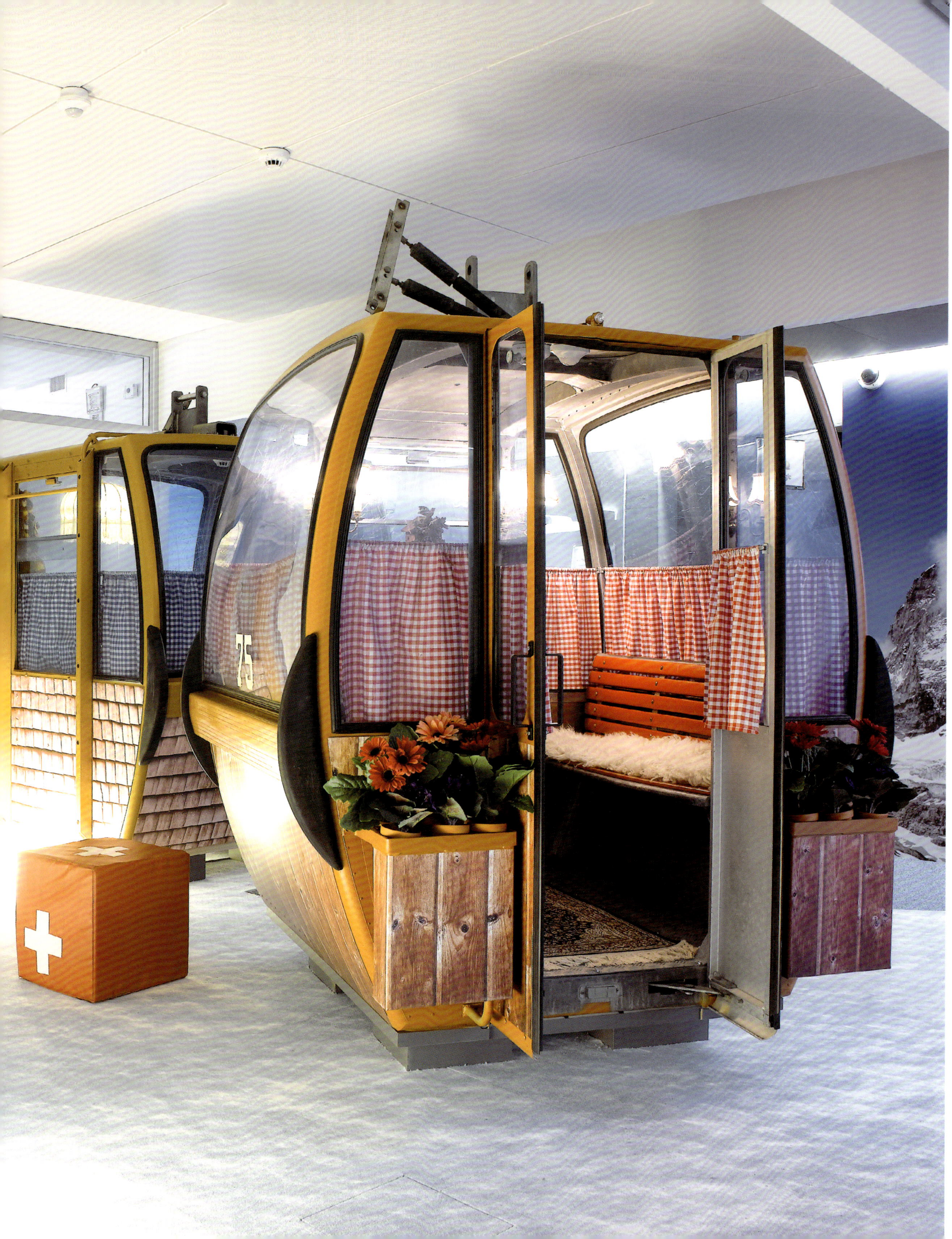
75

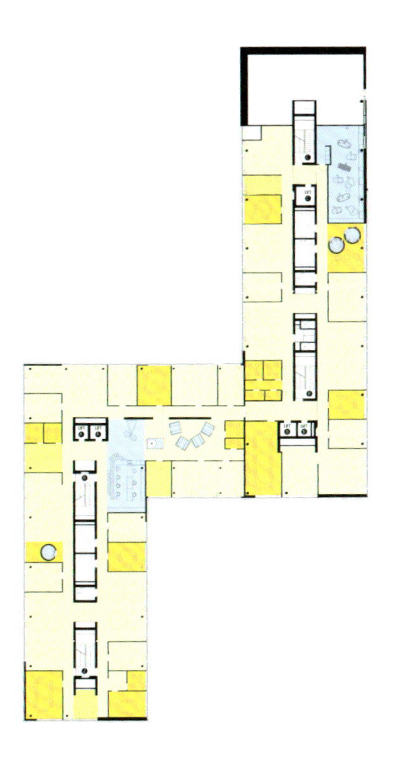

left: Meeting gondola. right: Second floor plan_Meeting egg_Informal meeting_Lounge.
links: Besprechungsgondel. rechts: Grundriss zweites Obergeschoss_Besprechungsei_Zwanglose Besprechung_Lounge.

SWITZERLAND_ZURICH COCOON – GOOGLE OFFICE HEADQUARTERS

ARCHITECTS: CAMENZIND EVOLUTION
COMPLETION: 2007_**NUMBER OF WORKPLACES:** 64_**GROSS FLOOR AREA:** 1,900 M²_**COMMON AREA:** CONFERENCE, ROOMS, CAFETRIA, LOUNGE, FITNESS AREA, ROOF TERRACE_**KIND OF WORKPLACES:** OPEN-PLAN-RAMP, TEAM_**PHOTOS:** CAMENZIND EVOLUTION, ZURICH (404, 405), FERIT KUYAS, WÄDENSWIL (406, 407)

Cocoon snugly nestles in a park-like setting in Zurich's Seefeld district. The bold stand-alone building embodies an innovative conception of interior spatial organization and interaction with the surrounding environment. In doing so, it caters for a wide variety of workplace and occupancy concepts. With its spiral massing, it may be conceived as a "communication landscape" that creates a unique spatial configuration and working environment. All spaces are arranged along a gently rising ramp, which wraps around a central, light-flooded atrium. The space planning concept dispenses with the traditional division into horizontal storys in favour of a seemingly endless sequence of elliptical floor segments.

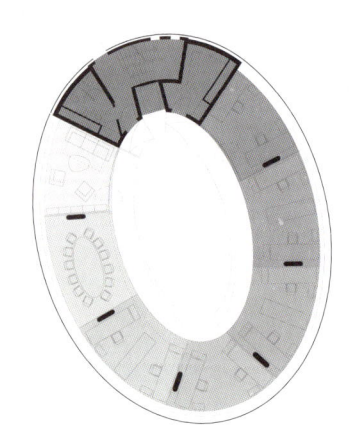

Cocoon befindet sich in einer parkartigen Umgebung im Seefeld-Bezirk von Zürich. Das frei stehende Gebäude verkörpert ein innovatives Konzept der inneren Raumorganisation und des Zusammenspiels mit der Umgebung. Es gewährleistet eine Vielfalt an Arbeitsbereichen und ein flexibeles Belegungskonzept. Das spiralförmige Kontinuum macht den Bau zu einer „Kommunikationslandschaft", die eine einzigartige räumliche Anordnung und Arbeitsumgebung schafft. Alle Räume befinden sich auf einer ansteigenden Ebene, die sich um ein zentrales, lichtdurchflutetes Atrium windet. Das Raumplanungskonzept löst sich zugunsten einer scheinbar endlosen Abfolge elliptischer Ebenen von der traditionellen Einteilung in horizontale Stockwerke.

left: Floor plan first spiral_Atrium_Spiral around the atrium_Reception desk. right: Offices on the ramp.
links: Grundriss erste Spirale_Atrium_Spirale um das Arium_Empfangstisch. rechts: Büros auf der Rampe.

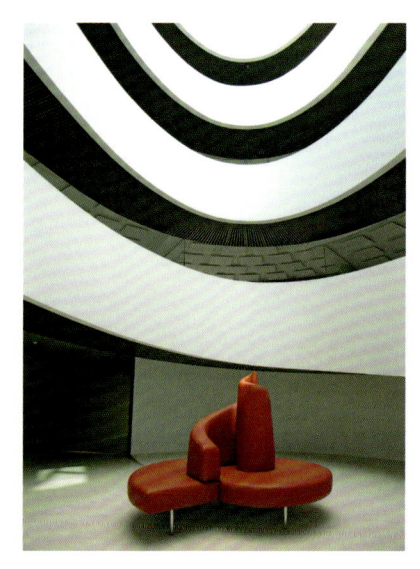

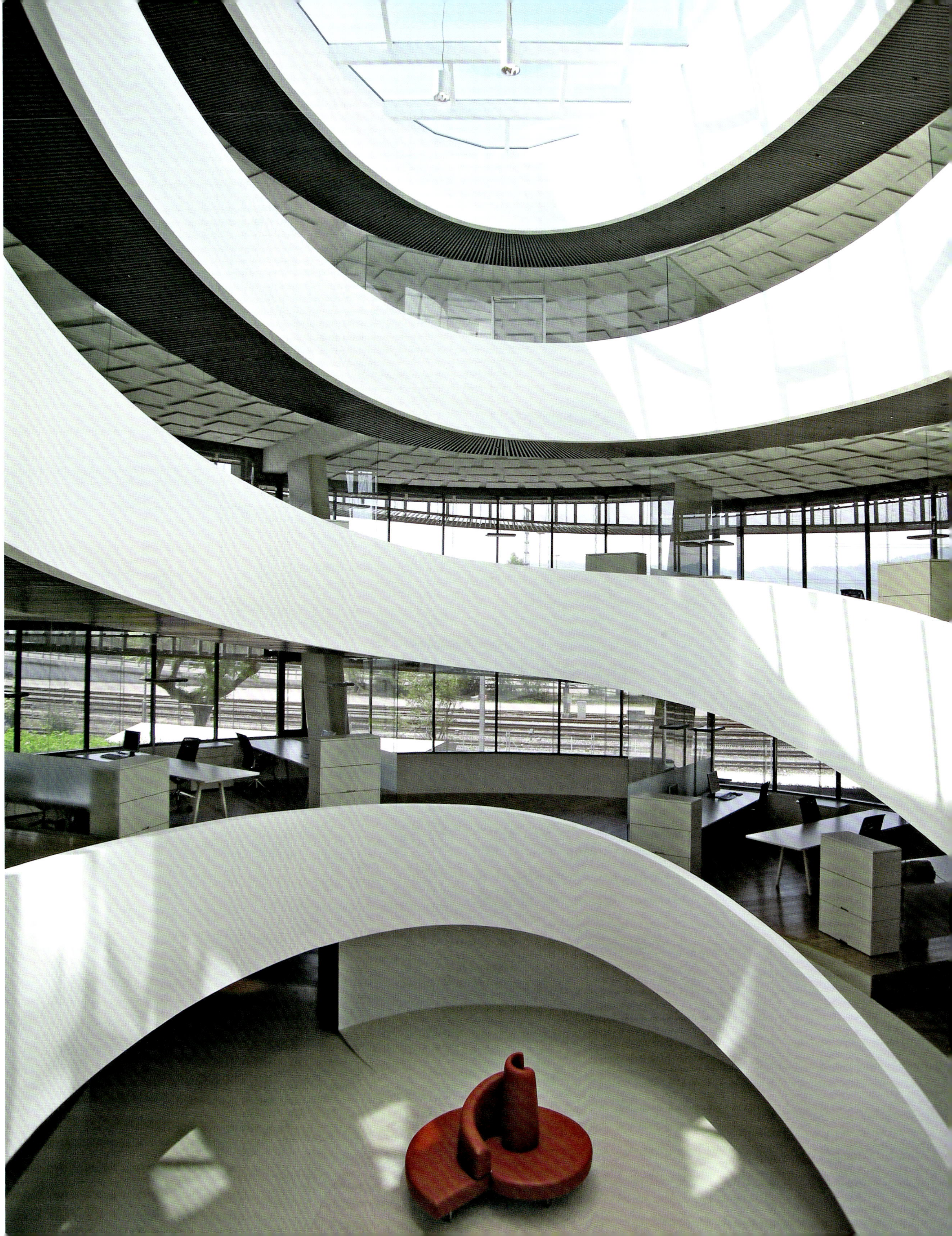

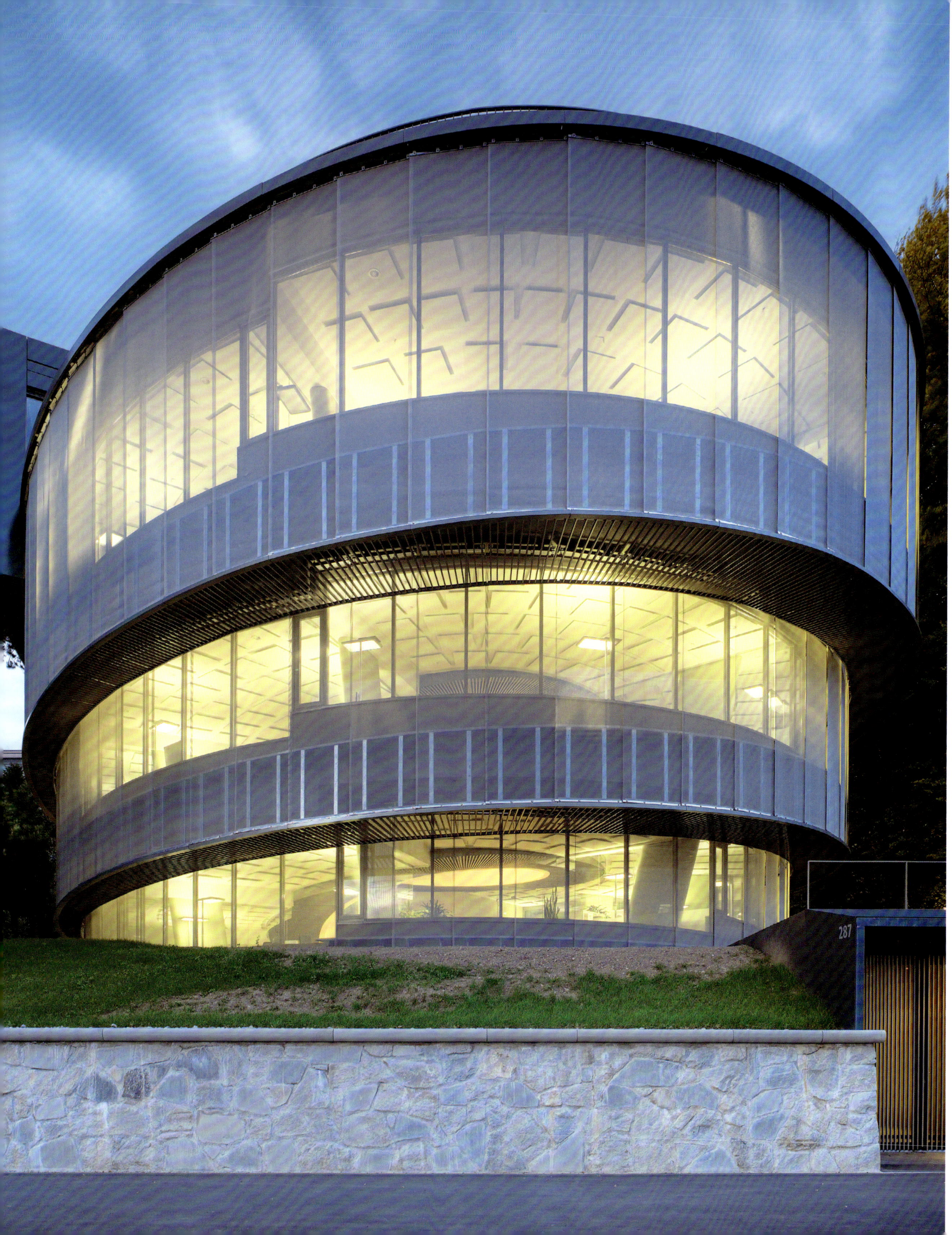
287

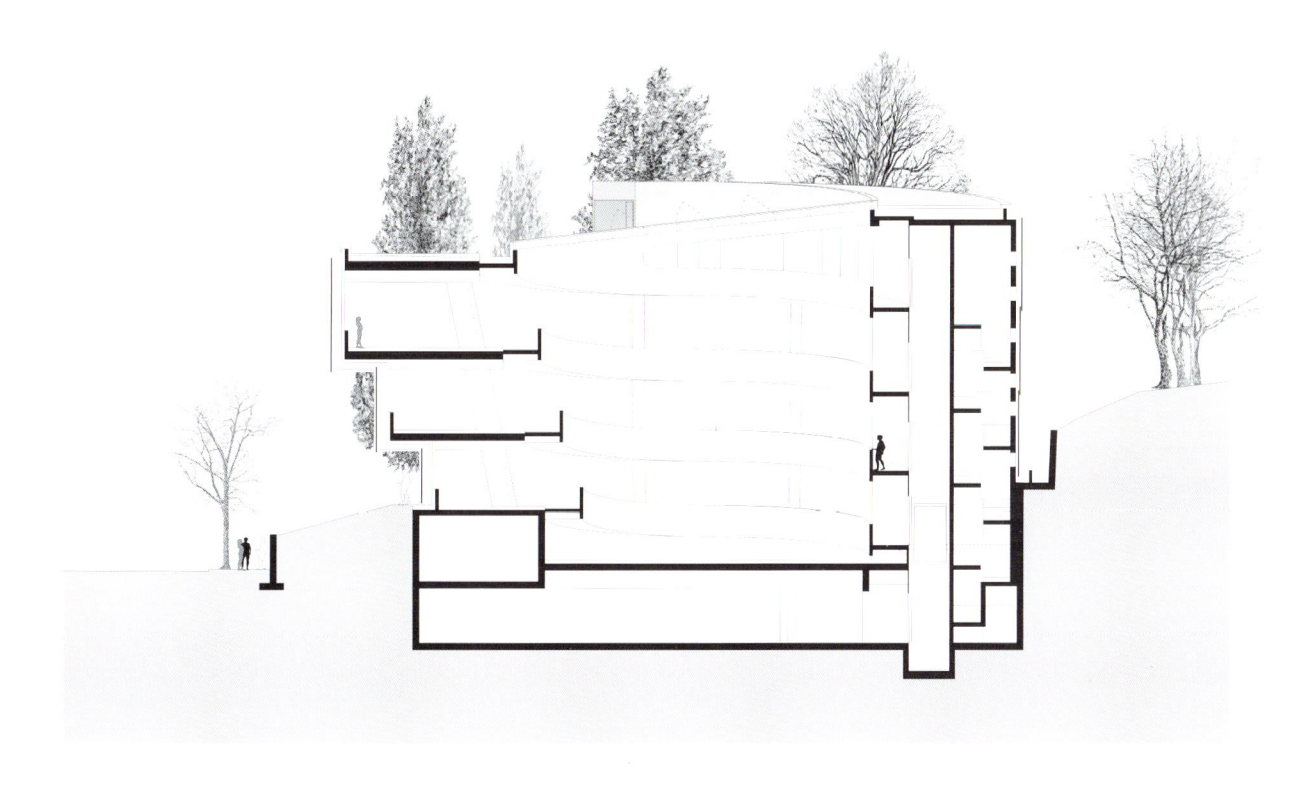

left: Exterior. right: Section_Railing_Office area_Lounge area.
links: Außenansicht. rechts: Schnitt_Geländer_Bürozone_Loungebereich.

SWITZERLAND_ZURICH **SAM HEADQUARTERS**

ARCHITECTS: ANDRES CAROSIO ARCHITEKTEN
COMPLETION: 2008_**NUMBER OF WORKPLACES:** 150
GROSS FLOOR AREA: 3,500 M²_**COMMON AREA:** "MARKETPLACE" WITH LOUNGING AREA AND TEA KITCHEN, MEETING POINTS, RELAXING ROOM, LIBRARY_**KIND OF WORKPLACES:** COMBINATION, OPEN-PLAN, TEAM, LOUNGE WORKSPACE
PHOTOS: KATRIN DERLETH / ANDRES CAROSIO ARCHITEKTEN

The upgrade of the offices of SAM, a sustainability investment specialist, particularly focused on sustainability in terms of the construction process as well as the choice of materials. Based on the concept of a "City in the City", an open office landscape was created with 150 work places distributed across various multipurpose zones just like in a city. The design concept treats interior spaces like exterior ones: conference rooms are treated as buildings, access zones as alleys, and leisure areas as public squares. The interior glass façades are graduated in their transparency according to their use. Specially developed sound-absorbing furniture helps keep the noise level low even in the open-plan offices.

Der Büroausbau für die auf Sustainability Investing (nachhaltiges Investment) spezialisierte SAM legt besonderen Wert auf Nachhaltigkeit sowohl im Bauprozess als auch in der Materialwahl. Von der Idee einer „City in the City" ausgehend wurde eine offene Bürolandschaft mit 150 Arbeitsplätzen geschaffen, die wie eine Stadt verschiedene, vielseitig nutzbare Zonen aufweist. Das gestalterische Konzept behandelt Innenräume wie Außenräume: Konferenzzimmer werden zu Bauten, Erschließungszonen zu Gassen und Aufenthaltsbereiche zu Plätzen. Die inneren farbigen Glasfassaden sind je nach Nutzung in der Transparenz abgestuft. Speziell entwickelte, Schall absorbierende Möbel helfen, den Lärmpegel auch in den Großraumbüros niedrig zu halten.

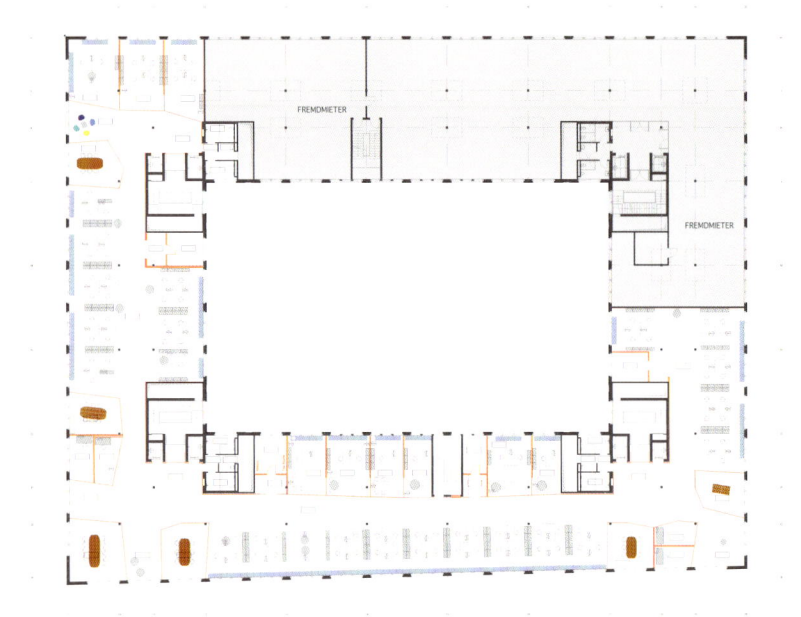

left: Floor plan fourth floor_Open-plan office_Marketplace, café. right: Conference room_Meeting areas.
links: Grundriss viertes Obergeschoss_Großraumbüro_Marktplatz, Bereich Cafeteria. rechts: Konferenzraum_Besprechungszonen.

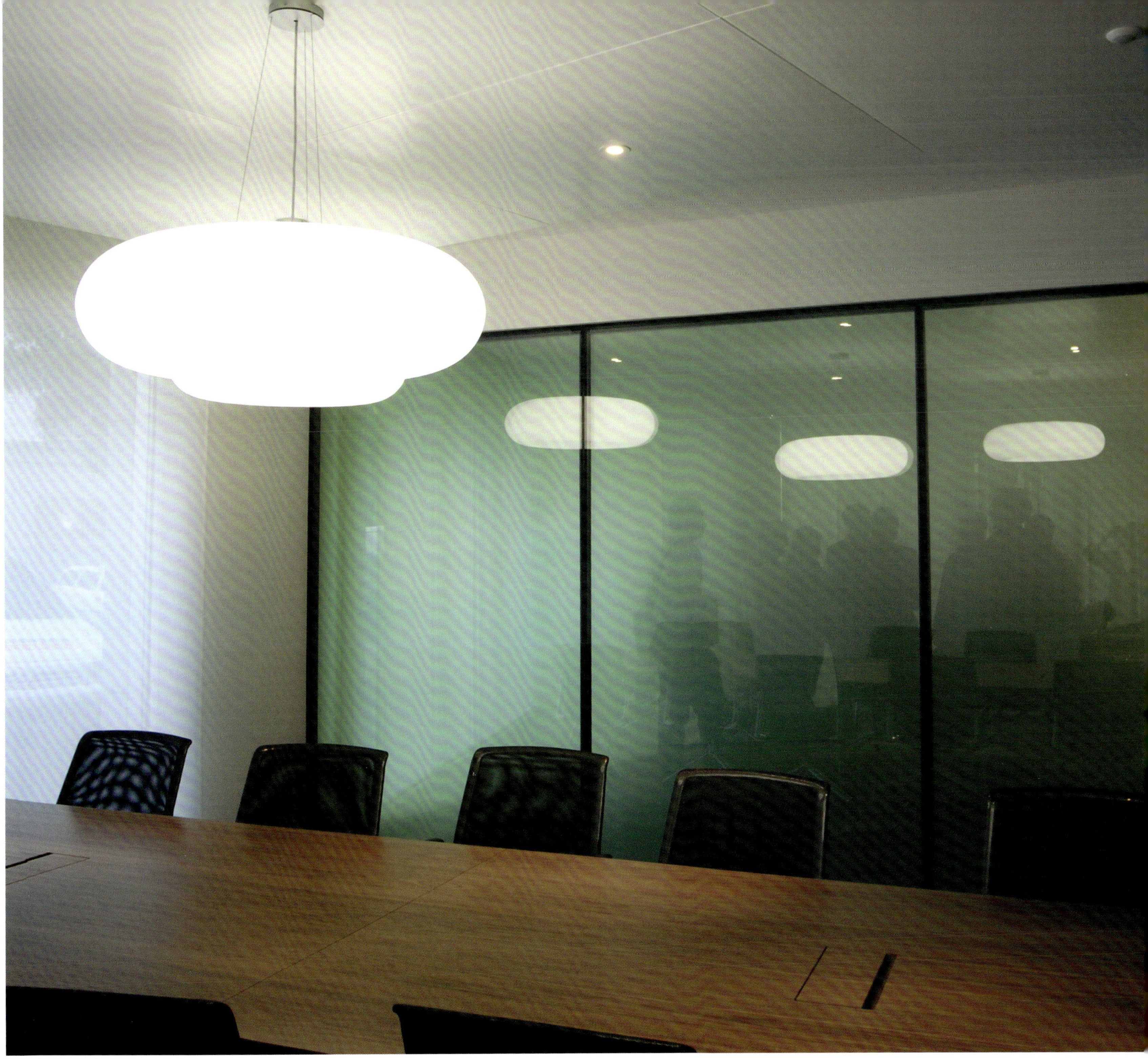

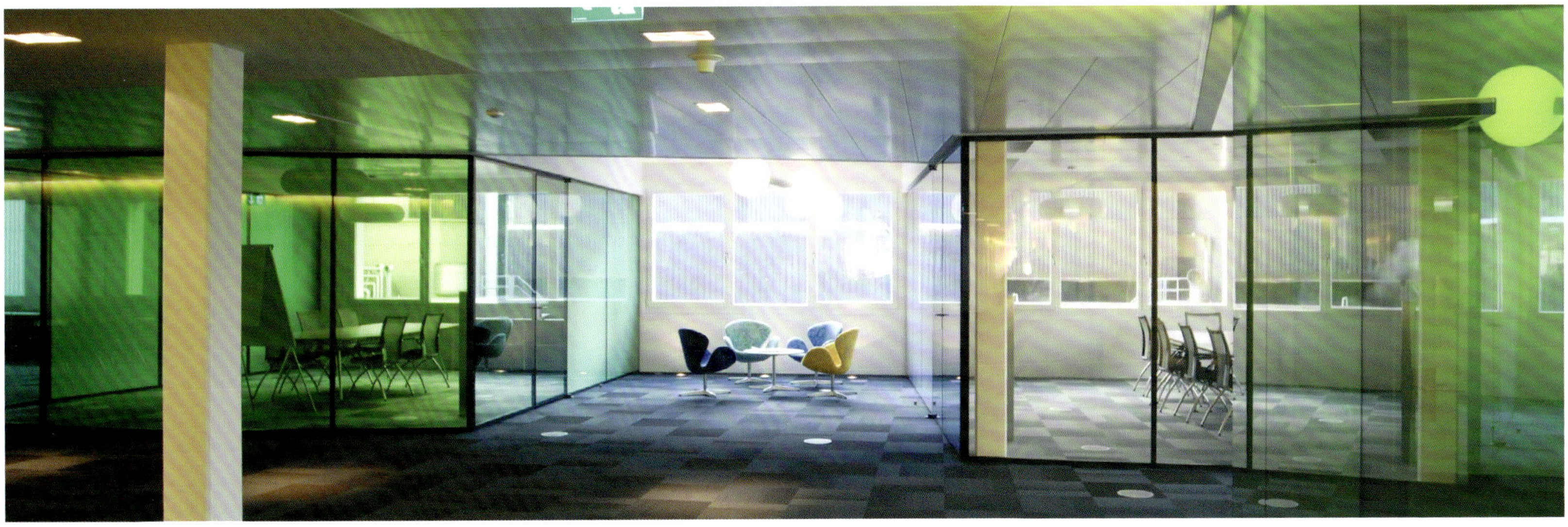

SWITZERLAND_ZURICH BANK VONTOBEL HEADQUARTERS

ARCHITECTS: STÜCHELI ARCHITEKTEN
COMPLETION: 2008_**NUMBER OF WORKPLACES:** 350
GROSS FLOOR AREA: 17,000 M²_**COMMON AREA:** CAFÉ, RESTAURANT, AUDITORIUM, CLIENT ROOMS
KIND OF WORKPLACES: OPEN-PLAN, COMBINATION
PHOTOS: REINHARD ZIMMERMANN, ADLISWIL

Within the scope of centralizing its locations, the bank chose the building constructed by Stücheli Architekten in the early 1970s as its new headquarters. The architects renewed the entire interior of the building that was already completely renovated in 1998. Specific reference images were created for the current development plan accompanied by accordingly powerful materials and colors that symbolically convey the company's values. Resembling silent winter landscapes, a noble world was created in shades of white, grey and brown. The redevelopment provided Vontobel in only eight months with top of the line offices, a restaurant with a café, as well as a luxurious customer floor with an excellent view.

Im Rahmen der Zentralisierung ihrer Standorte wählte die Bank das von Stücheli Architekten in den frühen 1970er Jahren errichtete Gebäude als ihren neuen Hauptsitz. Die Architekten erneuerten das gesamte Innenleben des bereits 1998 total sanierten Baus. Für den jetzigen Ausbau wurden spezifische Referenzbilder komponiert und eine entsprechende ausdrucksstarke Material- und Farbsprache entwickelt, welche symbolisch die Werte des Unternehmens vermittelt. In Anlehnung an stille Winterlandschaften entstand eine kontrastreiche, zurückhaltend edle Welt in Weiß-, Grau- und Brauntönen. Durch den Umbau erhielt Vontobel in nur acht Monaten modernste Büroräume, ein Restaurant mit Café sowie eine luxuriöse Kundenetage mit bester Aussicht.

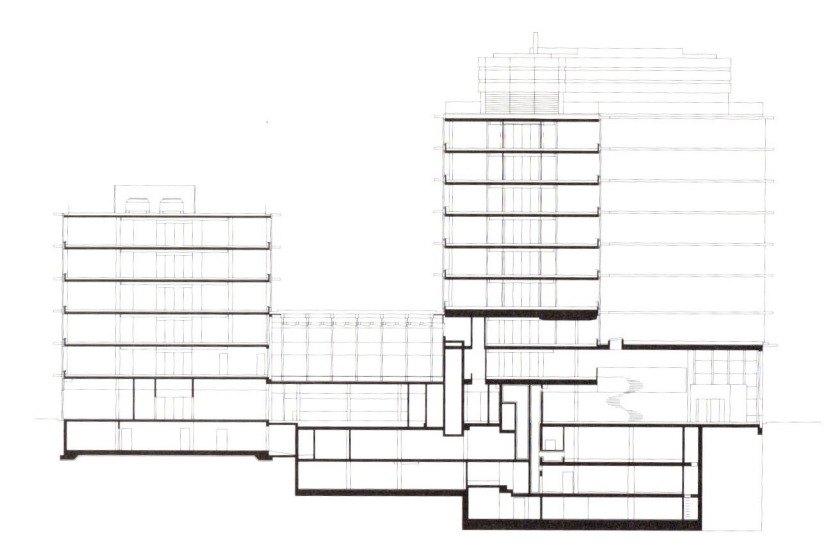

left: Section_Exterior_Meeting room for clients. right: Foyer_Restaurant_Clients area.
links: Schnitt_Außenansicht_Kundenbesprechungszimmer. rechts: Eingangshalle_Restaurant_Kundenzone.

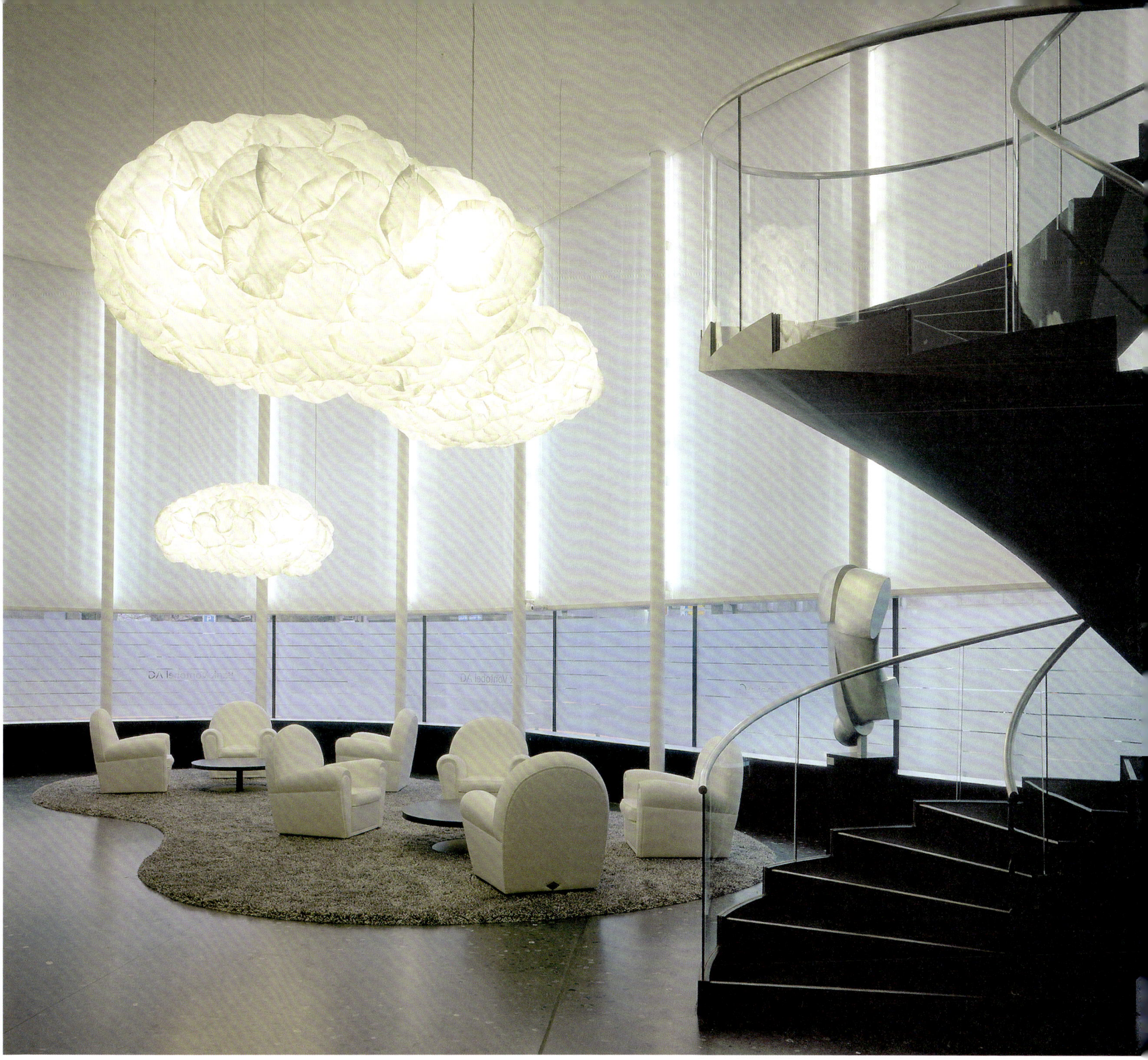

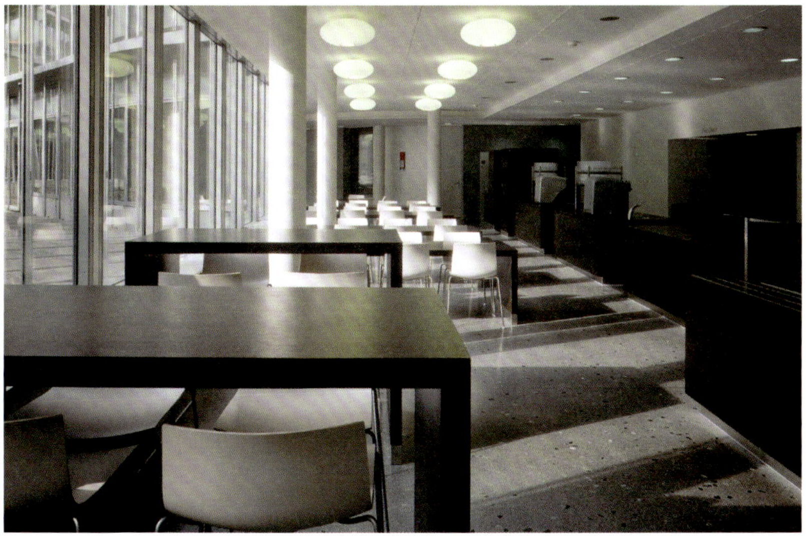

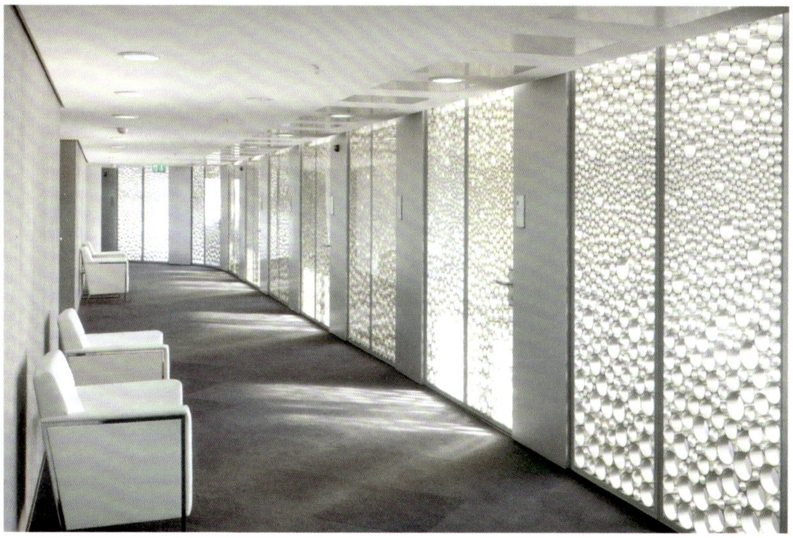

SWITZERLAND_ZURICH SUPERTANKER, ADDITION OF STORIES

ARCHITECTS: STÜCHELI ARCHITEKTEN
ORIGINAL BUILDING: 1925_**COMPLETION:** 2007
NUMBER OF WORKPLACES: 80 (ADDITION ONLY)
GROSS FLOOR AREA: 3,400 M² (ADDITION ONLY)
KIND OF WORKPLACES: OPEN-PLAN, COMBINATION
PHOTOS: REINHARD ZIMMERMANN, ADLISWIL

The added floors of the former warehouse required a design that confidently merged with the properties of the existing red brick building. A simple basic layout was created by an extension towards the street and by moving away from the row of facades on the south side to create a large terrace. The striking skin of aluminum sheet gives the light wooden construction an industrial character and visibility from a distance. The newly-established office lofts are distinguished by plenty of daylight and a unique view across the city. The added floors allowed a 25 percent increase in the building's utilization and a significant increase of its recognition value.

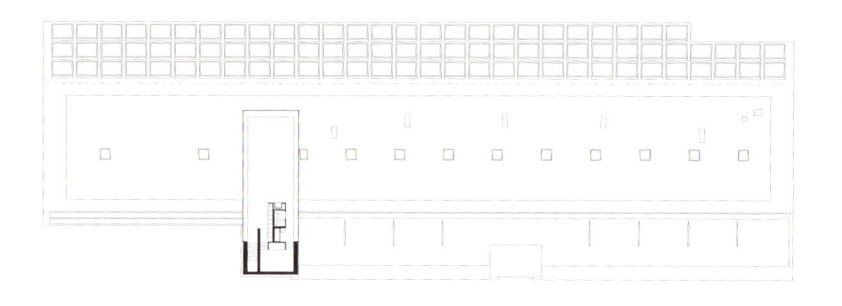

Für die Aufstockung des ehemaligen Lagerhauses galt es eine Form zu finden, die sich selbstsicher mit dem starken Charakter des bestehenden roten Backsteinbaus verbindet. Durch eine Auskragung zur Straße und das südseitige Wegrücken von der Fassadenflucht zugunsten einer großen Terrasse entstand eine einfache Grundform. Die auffällige Verkleidung aus Aluminiumblech verleiht der leichten Holzkonstruktion industriellen Charakter und macht das Gebäude weithin sichtbar. Die neu entstandenen Bürolofts zeichnen sich durch viel Tageslicht und einzigartige Sicht über die Dächer der Stadt aus. Dank der Aufstockung gelang es, die Ausnutzung des Gebäudes um 25 Prozent zu steigern und dessen Wiedererkennbarkeit markant zu erhöhen.

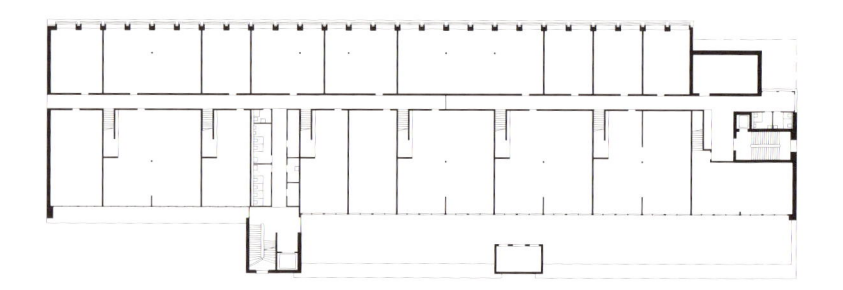

left: Floor plans fifth and sixth floor_Meeting room sixth floor_Offices sixth floor. right: Exterior_Terrace and staircase_Terrace south side.
links: Grundrisse fünftes und sechstes Obergeschoss_Besprechungszimmer sechstes Obergeschoss_Büros sechstes Obergeschoss. rechts: Außenansicht_Terrasse und Treppenhaus_Terrasse Südseite.

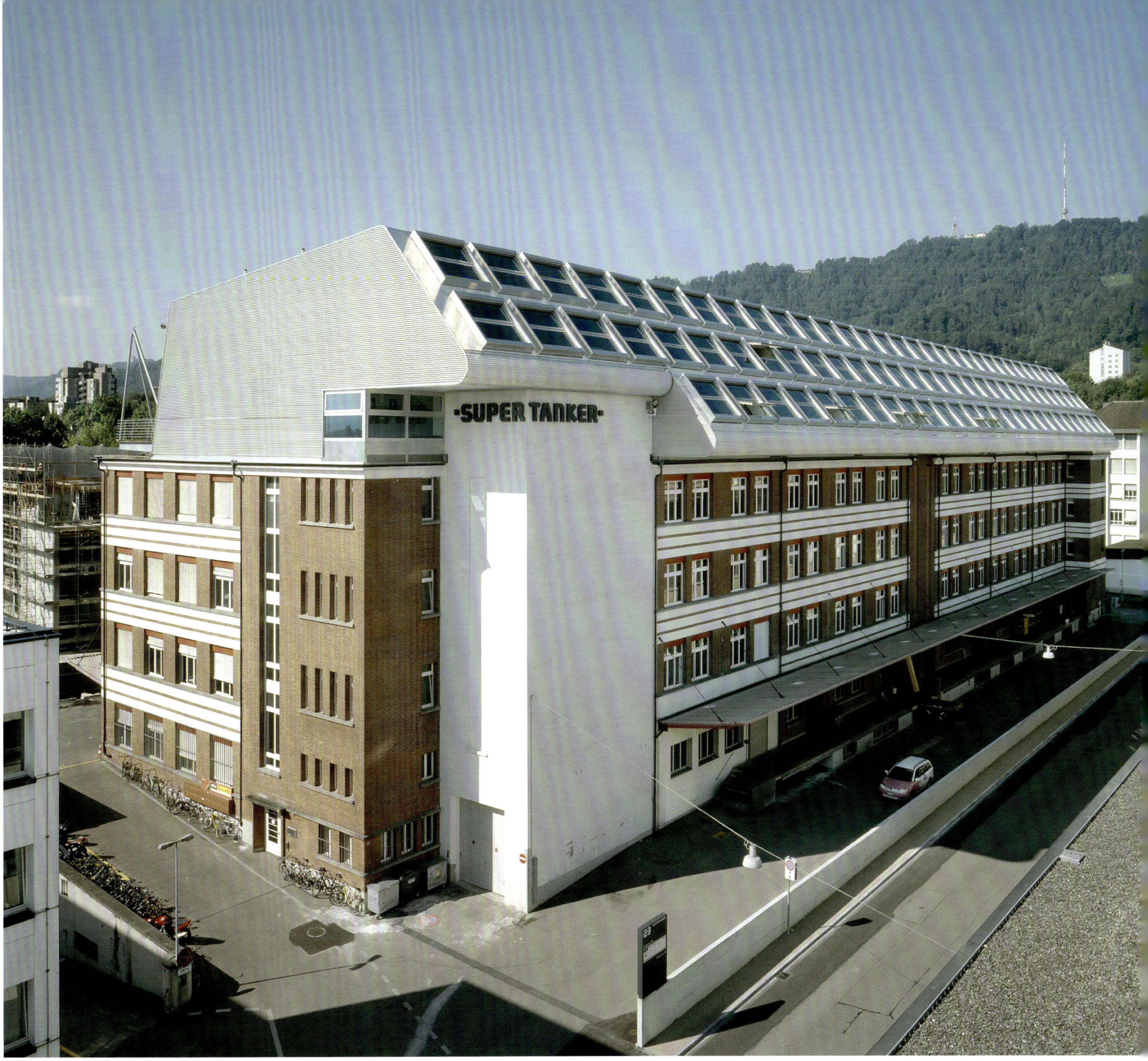
-SUPER TANKER-

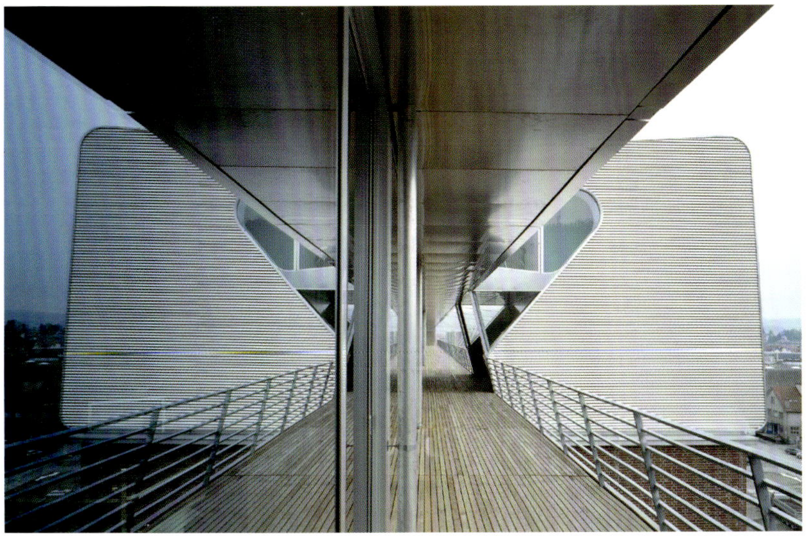

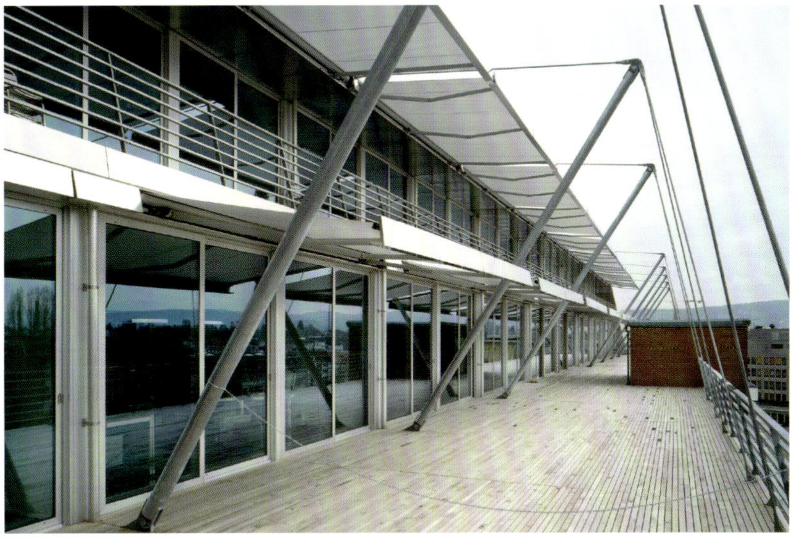

UNITED KINGDOM_LONDON THE WELLCOME TRUST HEADQUARTERS

ARCHITECTS: HOPKINS ARCHITECTS_**COMPLETION:** 2005
NUMBER OF WORKPLACES: 500_**GROSS FLOOR AREA:** 28,00 M²
COMMON AREA: MEETING ROOMS, SUITES, RESTAURANTS, BOOK STORAGE FACILITIES_**KIND OF WORKPLACES:** OPEN-PLAN_**PHOTOS:** NICK GUTTRIDGE

The new headquarters building at 215 Euston Road had to reconcile a number of different scales and textures. It consists of two blocks: a wide eight-floor block to the north, and a parallel narrower four-floor block to the south. A curved glazed roof extends across both, enveloping a generous atrium in between. On the ground floor behind the main reception area there are large formal meeting rooms, linked by an internal passage at the base of the atrium, containing the staff café, an information center and informal meeting spaces. Each floor of the northern block has five separate large flexible working floor areas. These are linked with breakout spaces and double height "mini atria" for casual interaction between team members.

Das neue Hauptquartier in der 215 Euston Road musste die unterschiedlichen Größen und Texturen der Umgebung aufgreifen. Es besteht aus einem breiten, achtgeschossigen Baukörper im Norden und einem schmaleren, viergeschossigen, parallel dazu verlaufenden im Süden. Beide sind mit einem gemeinsamen gewölbten Glasdach überfangen, das ein Atrium ausbildet. Im Erdgeschoss hinter dem Empfang befinden sich an der das Atrium durchziehenden internen Erschließungsstraße große, formale Besprechungsräume, ein Mitarbeitercafé, ein Informationszentrum und informelle Treffpunkte. Jedes Geschoss im nördlichen Block umfasst fünf große eigenständige und flexible Arbeitsbereiche, die durch nutzungsfreie Räume und Mini-Atrien doppelter Geschosshöhe als informelle Begegnungsstätte der Teams verbunden sind.

left: Section_Exterior_Café_Façade. right: Atrium.
links: Schnitt_Außenansicht_Cafeteria_Fassade. rechts: Atrium.

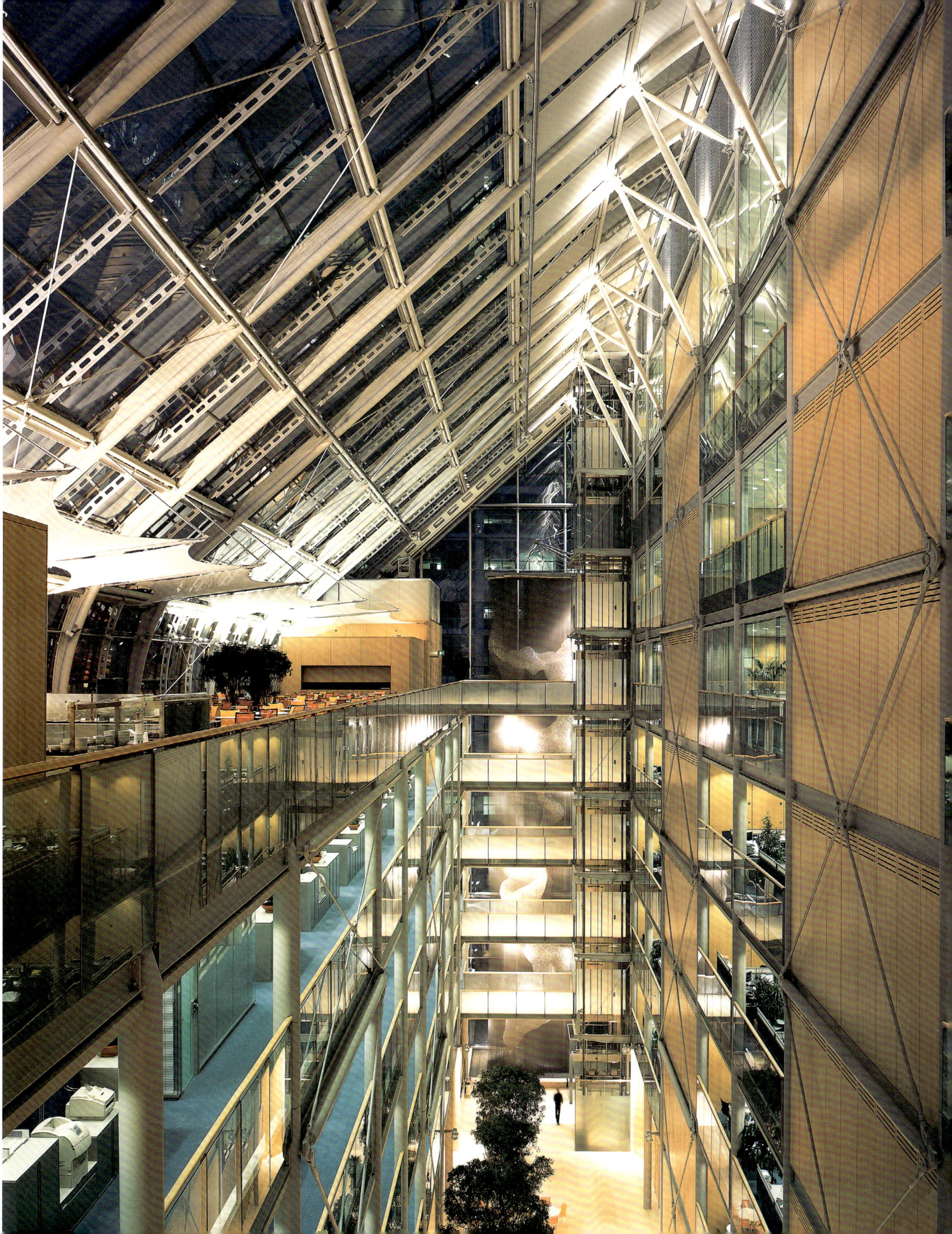

UNITED KINGDOM_LONDON **LG EUROPEAN DESIGN CENTRE**

ARCHITECTS: JUMP STUDIOS
COMPLETION: 2008_**NUMBER OF WORKPLACES:** 23
GROSS FLOOR AREA: 600 M²_**COMMON AREA:** LOUNGE, CONFERENCE ROOMS_**KIND OF WORKPLACES:** OPEN-PLAN
PHOTOS: GARETH GARDNER

The European Design Studio is one of the most important design centers of the electronic goods company and houses a team of 20 dedicated industrial and interface designers, drawn from around Europe. Relocated from Milan to London, the office intends to provide an optimum creative environment, including extensive libraries and is equipped with leading technologies to facilitate the design process. On the fifth floor of the existing building, Jump Studio provides different kinds of workplaces, along with formal as well as informal meeting areas. White dominates the layout with American walnut wood flooring and some intensive green at special locations (showcase wall, material library, prototype display, and kitchen).

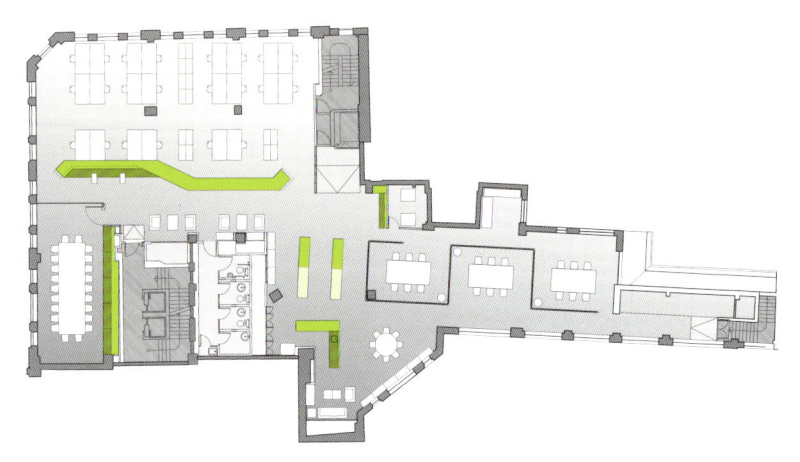

Das europäische Designatelier ist einer der wichtigsten Standorte, des Herstellers von elekronischen Kosumgütern. Hier arbeiten zwanzig Produkt- und Interfacedesigner aus ganz Europa. Das zuvor in Mailand ansässige Londoner Büro soll ein optimales Umfeld für kreative Prozesse bieten, und ist mit einer umfangreiche Bibliothek und aktuellsten Designtechnologien ausgestattet. Im vierten Obergeschoss eines älteren Gebäudes realisierte Jump Studio verschiedene Arbeitssituationen sowie formelle und informelle Besprechungsräume. Weiß dominiert das Erscheinungsbild, nur der Bodenbelag aus amerikanischem Walnussholz und ein intesives Grün in besonderen Bereichen (Schauwand, Materialbibliothek, Schaukästen für Prototypen, Küche) setzten Akzente.

left: Floor plan_Lounge area_Reception area and waiting zone. right: Meeting table and workplaces_Conference room_Detail_Lounge.
links: Grundriss_Loungebereich_Empfangsbereich und Wartezone. rechts: Besprechungstisch und Arbeitsplätze_Konferenzraum_Detail_Lounge.

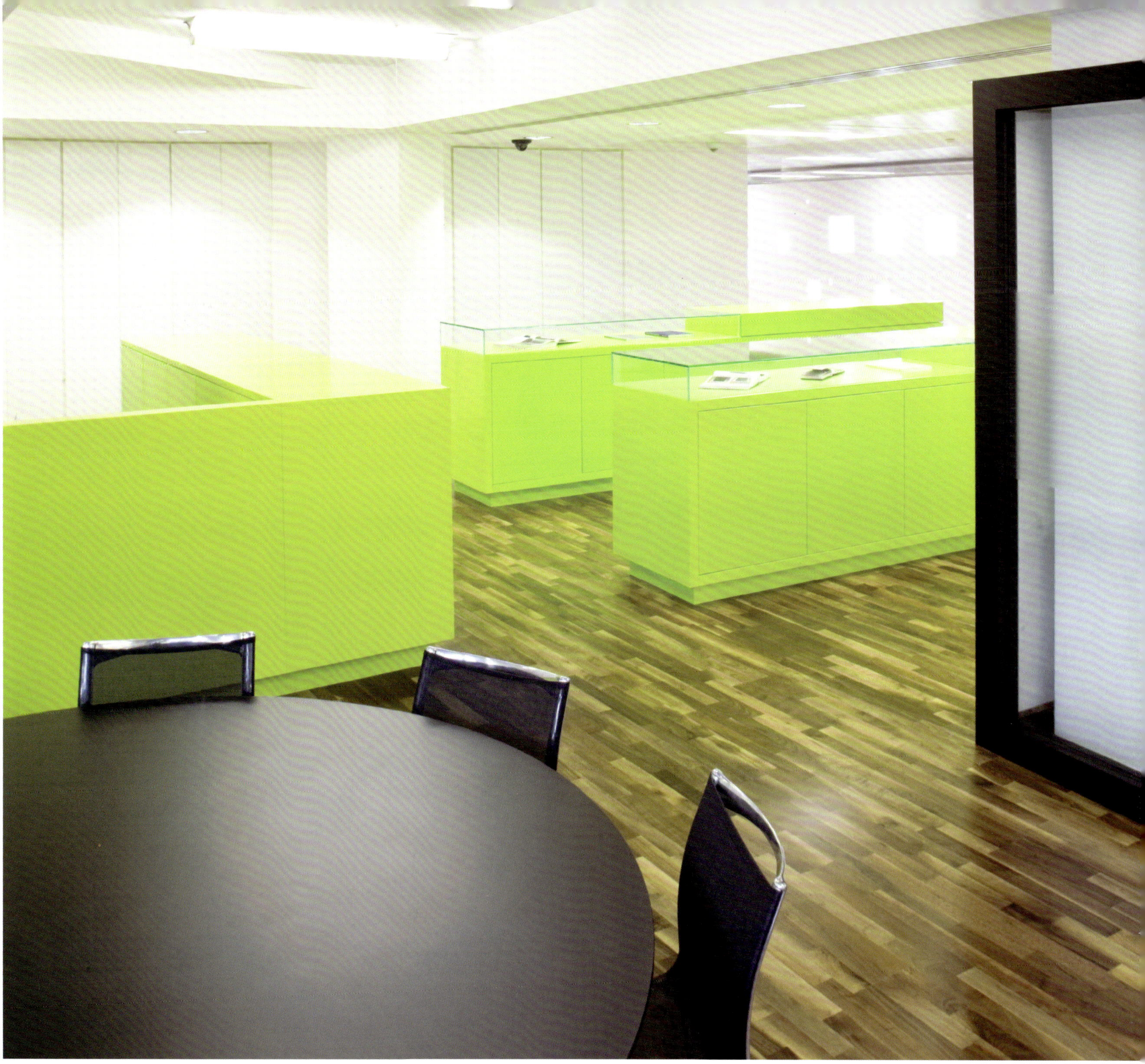
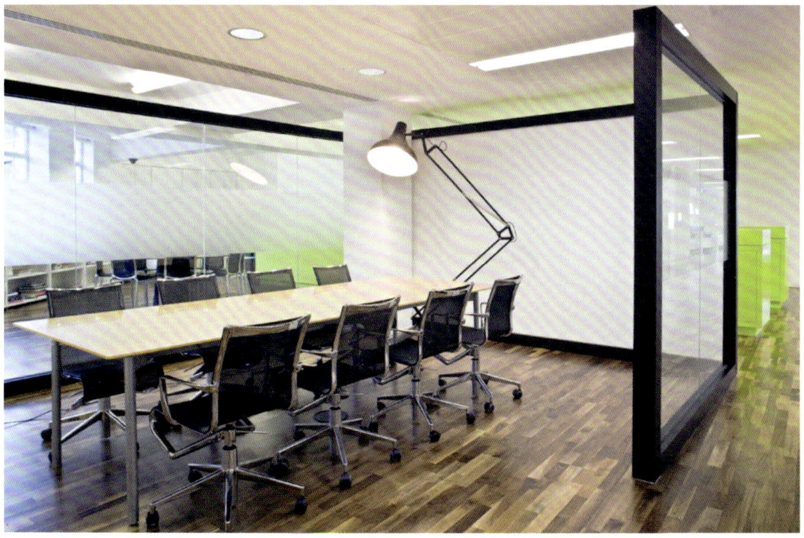
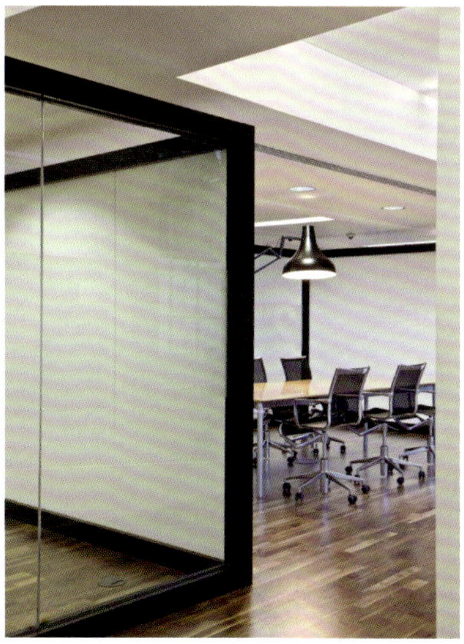
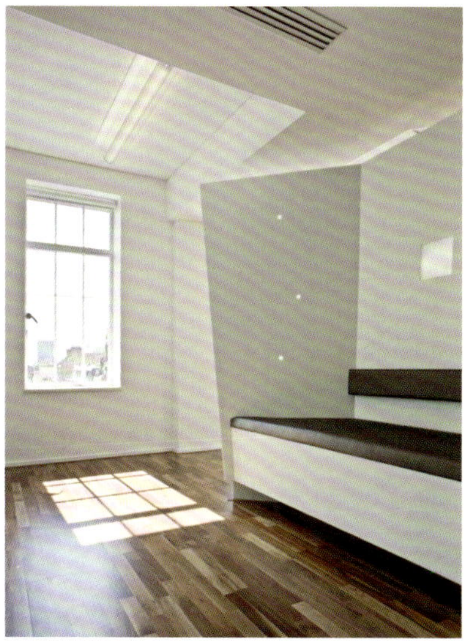

UNITED KINGDOM_LONDON **10 HILLS PLACE**

ARCHITECTS: AMANDA LEVETE ARCHITECTS
COMPLETION: 2009_**GROSS FLOOR AREA:** 1,321 M²
COMMON AREA: LOBBY_**KIND OF WORKPLACES:** OPEN-PLAN
PHOTOS: GIDON FUEHRER / © AMANDA LEVETE ARCHITECTS

Lack of daylight in the narrow streets was a key issue for the design inspired by the art work of Lucio Fontana. A slashed aluminum skin with large glazed areas facing the sky uses high quality ship hull technology for an ingenious sculptural façade assembled on-site. Self cleaning glass and hidden gutters ensure the façade remains low maintenance. The fine faceting of the aluminum strips creates complex reflections of sky and street, making the building highly visible from Oxford Street. At ground level, a glass, mesh and dichromatic film sandwich is animated with fiber optics to create a visual depth of field and a dynamic moiré pattern on an otherwise blank façade.

Mangelndes Tageslicht in den engen Gassen war das Hauptproblem bei dem von Lucio Fontanas Kunstwerken inspirierten Gebäude. Eine aufgeschlitzte Aluminiumhaut, hergestellt mit ausgefeilter Schiffsrumpftechnik und vor Ort montiert, öffnet sich mit großen Glasflächen himmelwärts als ingeniöse skulpturale Fassade. Selbstreinigendes Glas und hinter den Wölbungen verstecke Abflussrinnen garantieren geringen Unterhaltsaufwand. Eine kleinteilige Facettierung der Alminiumbänder sorgt für vielfältige Reflektionen von Straße und Himmel und garantiert einen gute Sichtbarkeit von der Oxford Street. Ein maßgeschneidertes Verbundmaterial aus Glas, Maschen und dichromatischem Film wird mit Lichtfaseroptik animiert, um Tiefe und ein dynamisches Moiré auf der Fassade zu erzeugen.

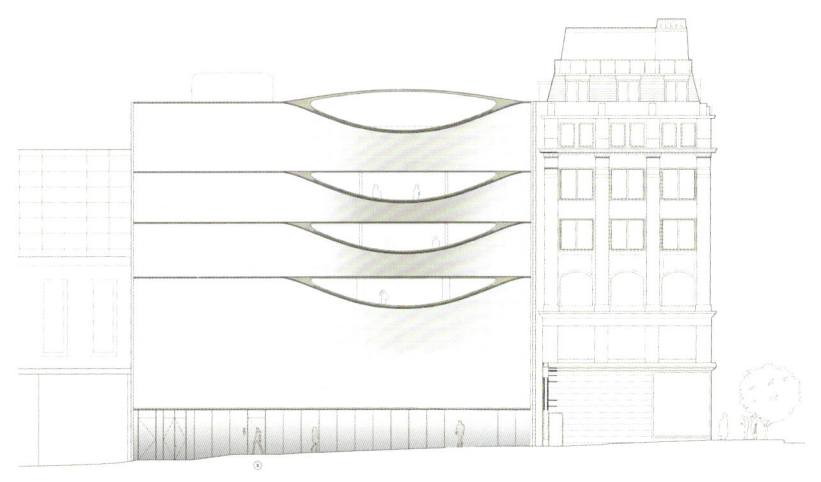

left: Elevation_Façade, detail_View from Oxford Street. right: Window_Roof terrace_Façade, detail. links: Ansicht_Fassade, Detail_Blick von der Oxford Street. rechts: Fenster_Dachterrasse_Fassade, Detail.

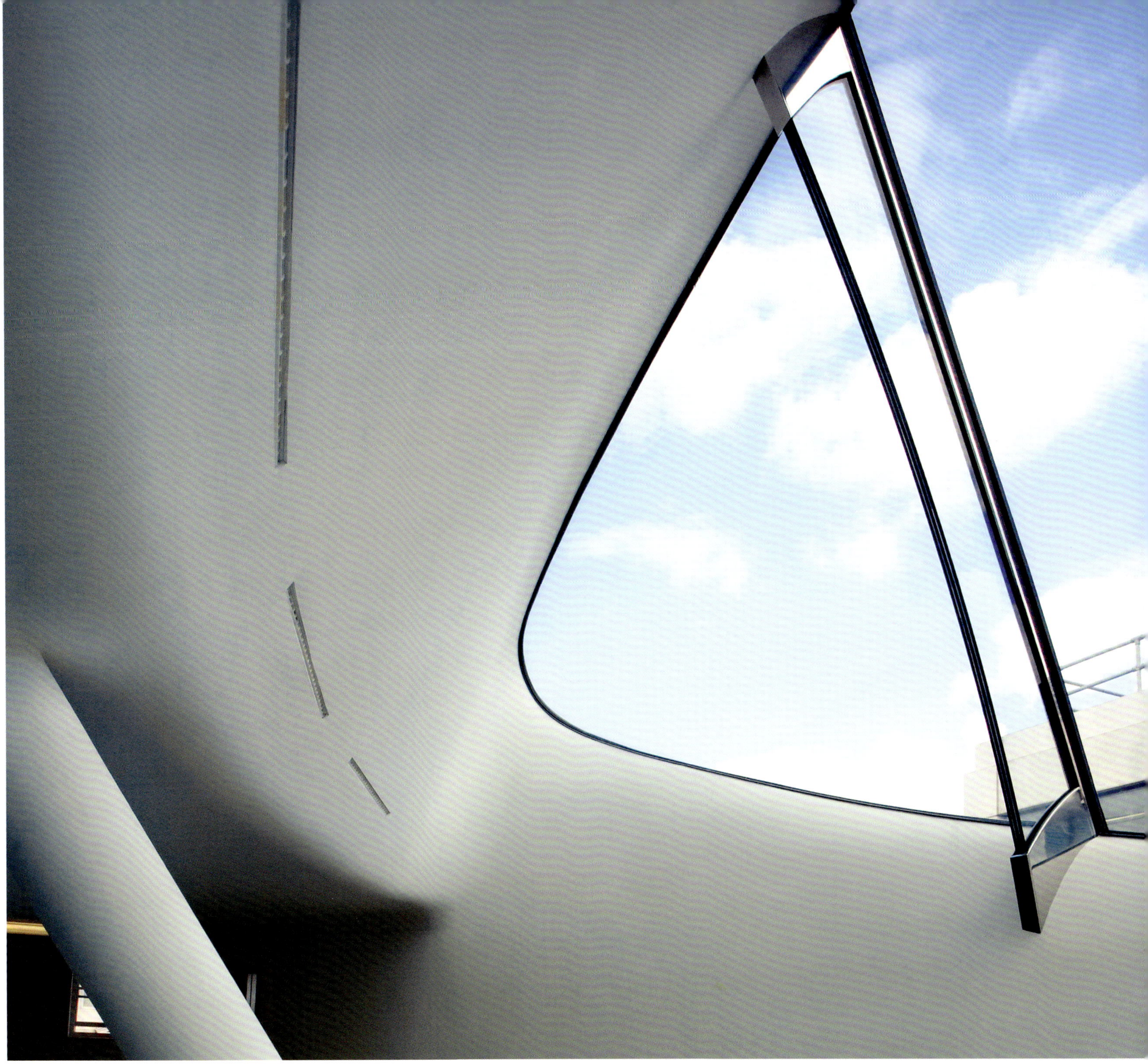
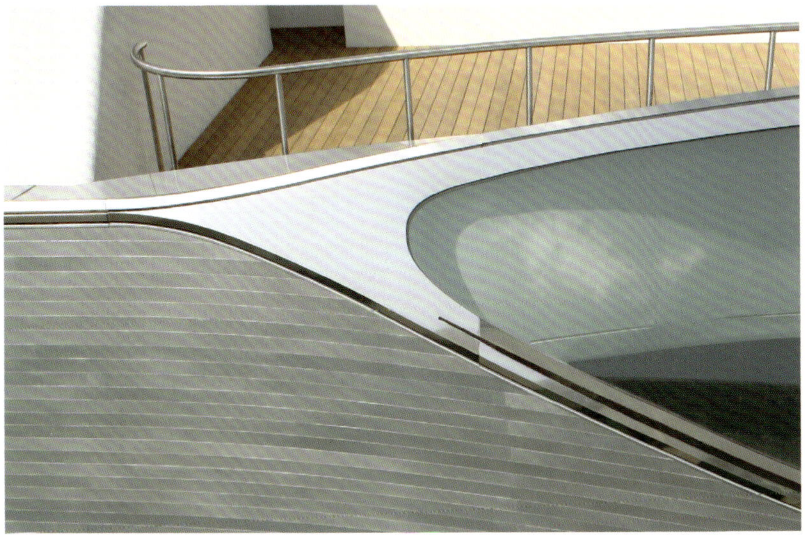
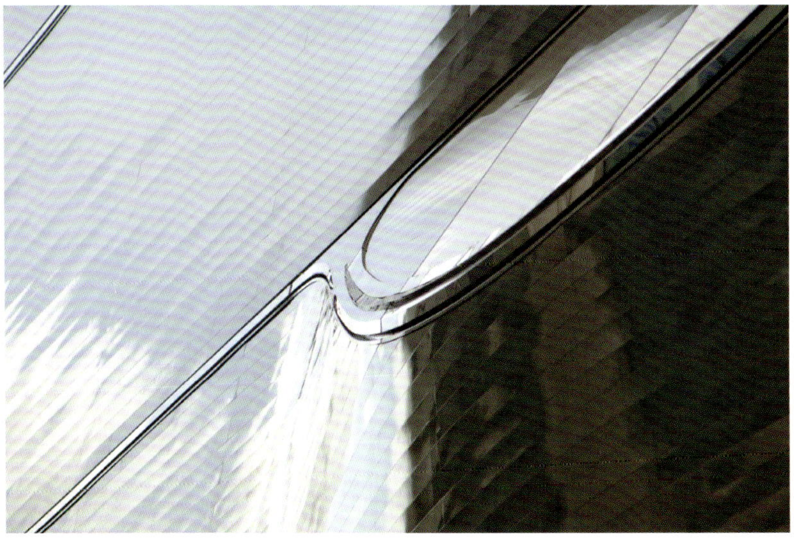

UNITED KINGDOM_LONDON **FARRINGDON BUILDINGS**

ARCHITECTS: NISSEN ADAMS
COMPLETION: 2008_**ORIGINAL BUILDING:** 1900
GROSS FLOOR AREA: 4,000 M²
COMMON AREA: ENTRANCE LOBBY
KIND OF WORKPLACES: STUDIO OFFICES
PHOTOS: DAVID LAMBERT, LONDON

Farringdon Buildings consists of a short terrace of four buildings that form an elegant city block. The aim was to create four "houses" that provide high quality studio office space with high ceilings, exposed structural elements and carefully integrated services. The area is characterized by architects, designers and media companies all seeking dramatic and unusual studio spaces in which to work. The refurbishment deliberately left the textures and unusual aspects of the original building in place and inserted a new central core to serve the studio spaces. The character of the building was preserved and the interior combines new insertions at the entrance with exposed brickwork and plastered surfaces.

Die Farringdon Buildings sind eine kurze Häuserreihe von vier Gebäuden, die einen eleganten Häuserblock bilden. Das Ziel war, vier scheinbare Einzelbauten zu errichten, die hochqualitative Büroräume mit hohen Decken, freiliegende Bauelemente und sorgfältig integrierten Service bieten. Das Viertel wird von Architekten, Designer und Medienunternehmen geprägt, die ausgefallene Büroräume suchen. Bei der Modernisierung wurden Strukturen und ungewöhnliche Aspekte des Originalgebäudes bewusst belassen und ein neuer zentraler Kern mit Raum für Büros hinzugefügt. Der Charakter des Gebäudes blieb erhalten, wobei Einbauten im Eingangsbereich mit den freiliegenden Mauerwerk und Gipsoberflächen kombiniert wurden.

left: Street elevation_Entrance area_Street elevation. right: Double height staircase at the entrance_Interior view_Interior view.
links: Straßenansicht_Eingangsbereich_Straßenansicht. rechts: Zweifache Treppenhöhe im Eingangsbereich_Innenansicht_Innenansicht.

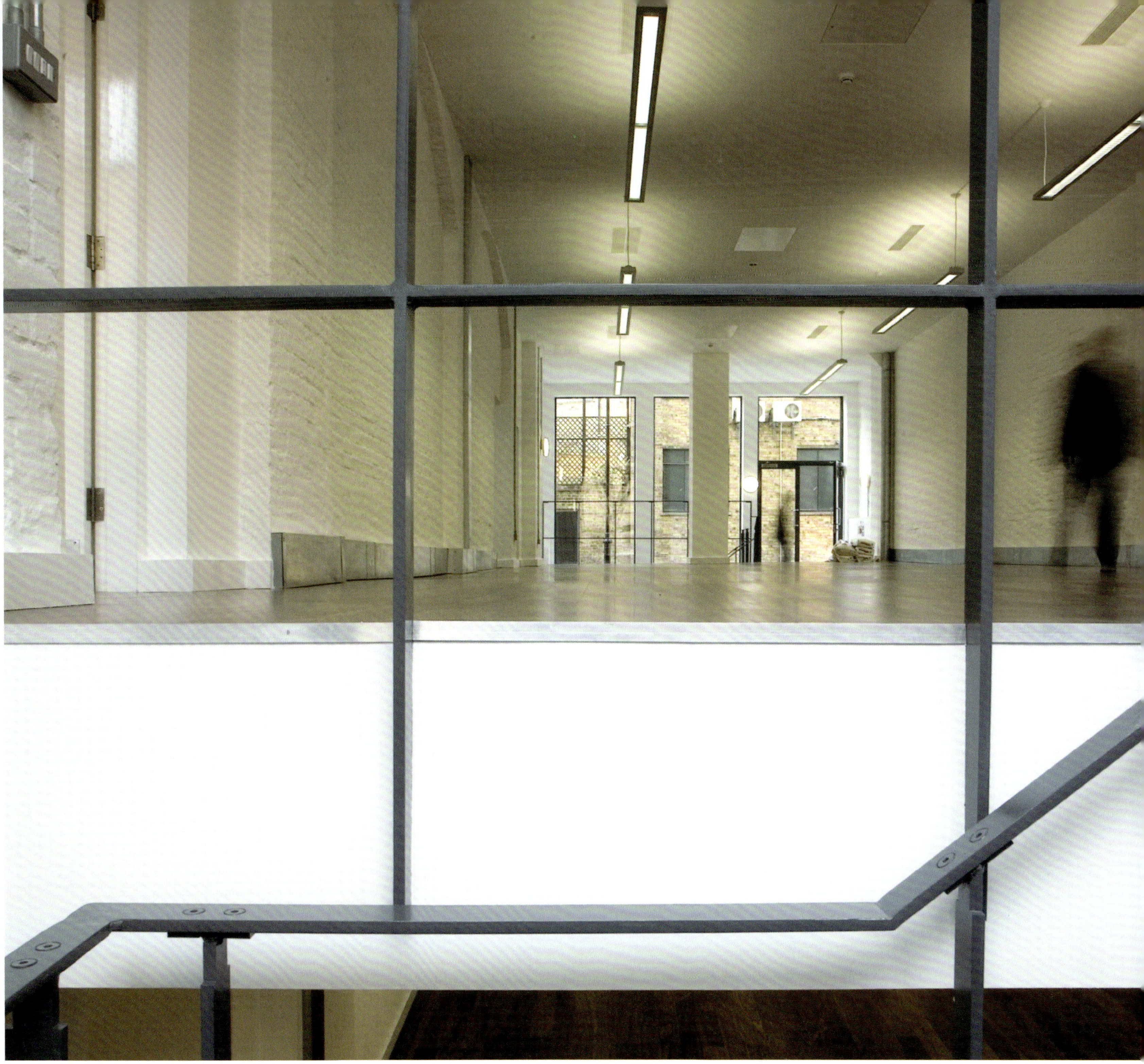

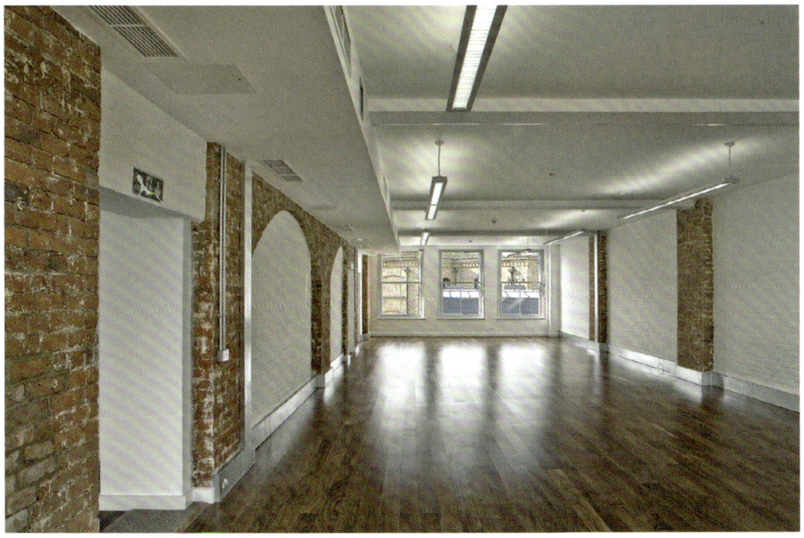

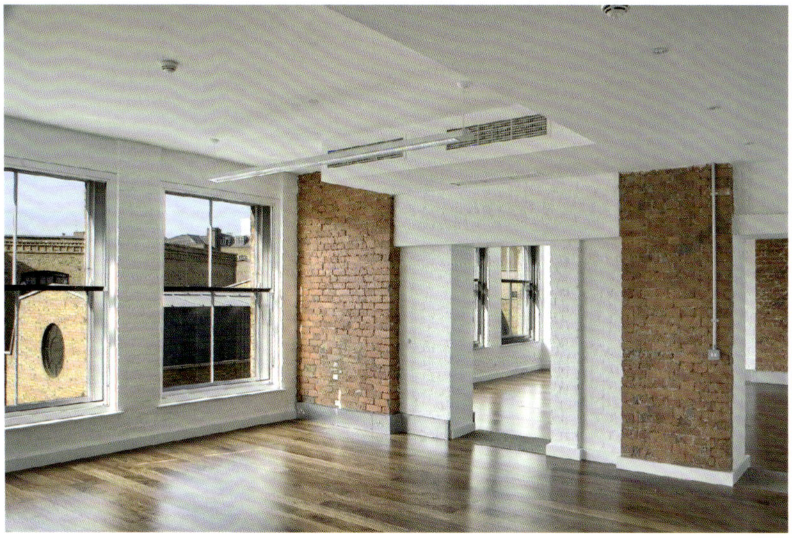

UNITED KINGDOM_LONDON **THE LONDON BRIDGE TOWER**

ARCHITECTS: RENZO PIANO BUILDING WORKSHOP WITH ADAMSON ASSOCIATES_**COMPLETION:** ONGOING
PHOTOS: HAYS DAVIDSON AND JHON MCLEAN (422 B. R., 423 B.), FRÉDÉRIC TERREAUX (423 A.), RPBW-RENZO PIANO BUILDING WORKSHOP (422 A. L., 423 B. L.)

A 70-floor mixed use tower maximizes the density in central London above one of the key commuter stations in line with urban development. Conceived like a small vertical town of 306 meters in which ten thousand people will work, the tower is a holistic response to the sustainable development of the European city. Designed like a sharp crystal pyramid, the building, inspired by church spires and top sails, is meant to introduce a light and elegant presence to the skyline. The plan is shaped by the irregular nature of the site. Each facet forms a shard, a plane of glass gently inclined inwards, rising towards the top. The corners are open and the shards do not touch, allowing the building to breathe.

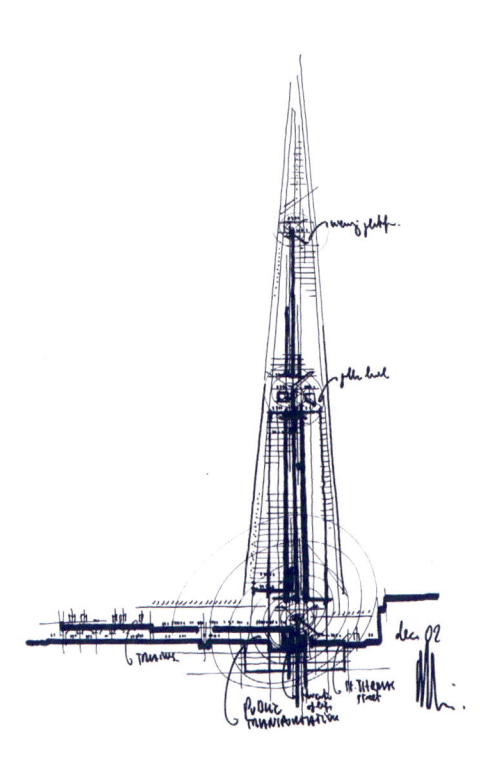

Der 70-stöckige Bau mit Funktionsmischung verdichtet oberhalb eines Pendlerbahnhofs das Zentrum Londons nach. Wie eine kleine, 306 Meter hohe, vertikale Stadt konzipiert, werden hier zehntausend Menschen arbeiten. Entsprechend des Londoner Entwicklungsplans ist der Turm eine ganzheitliche Antwort auf die Frage nach nachhaltiger Stadtentwicklung in Europa. Einer scharfkantigen, kristallinen Pyramide nachempfunden, ist das elegante, leichte Gebäude von den Kirchturmspitzen Londons und den Topsegeln auf der Themse inspiriert. Der Plan entspringt dem unregelmäßigen Baugrundstück. Jede Facette ähnelt einer Scherbe, einer leicht nach innen gebogenen Fläche, die aufwärts strebt. Die Ecken sind geöffnet und die Scherben berühren sich nicht, um dem Bau Luftigkeit zu geben.

left: Sketch_High level viewing gallery_St. Thomas street looking east. right: Low level_ Evening view from Unilever house.
links: Skizze_Oberes Stockwerk mit Blick auf die Galerie_St. Thomas street Blick nach Osten.
rechts: Untere Ebene_Abendansicht vom Unilever Haus.

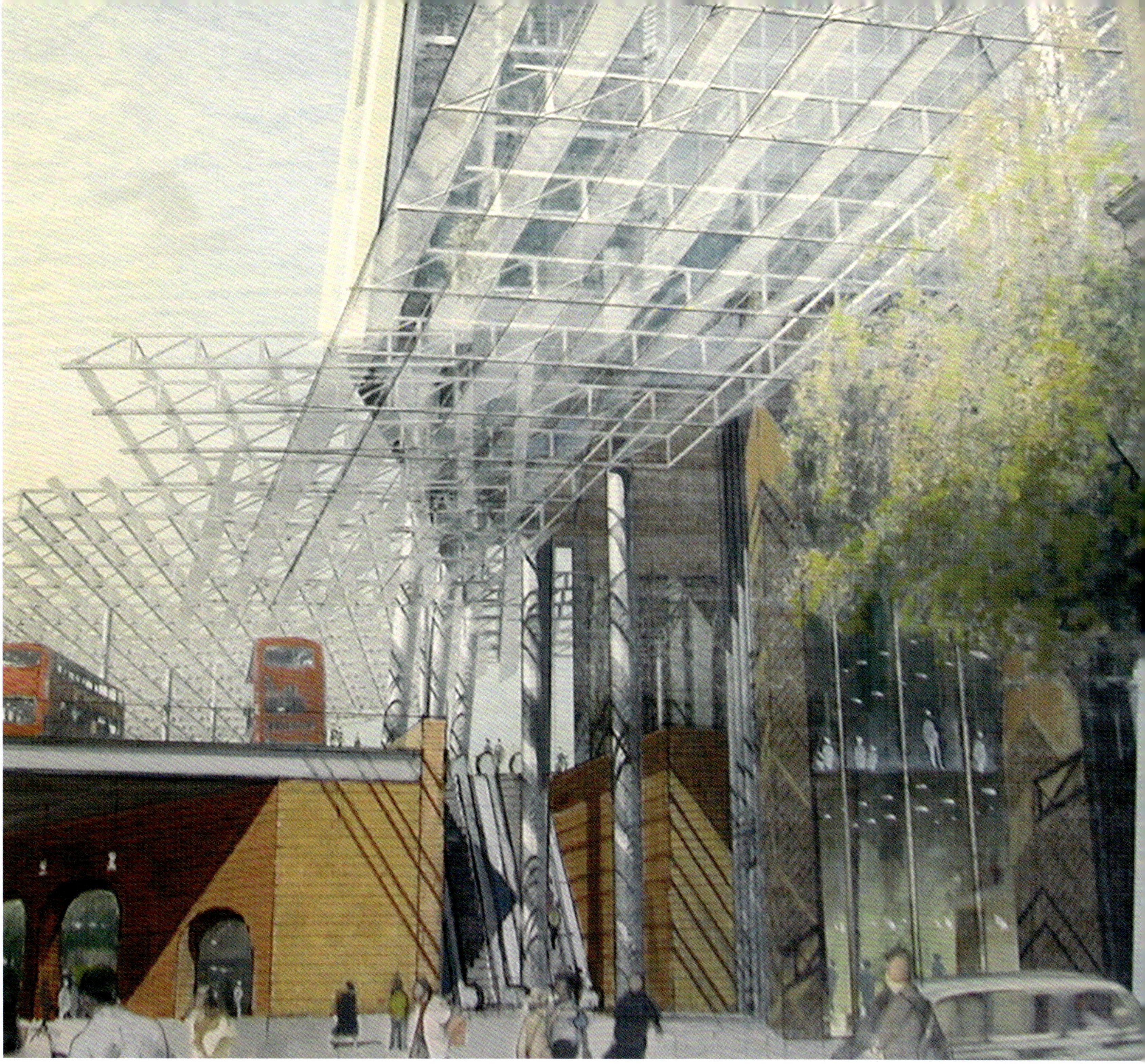

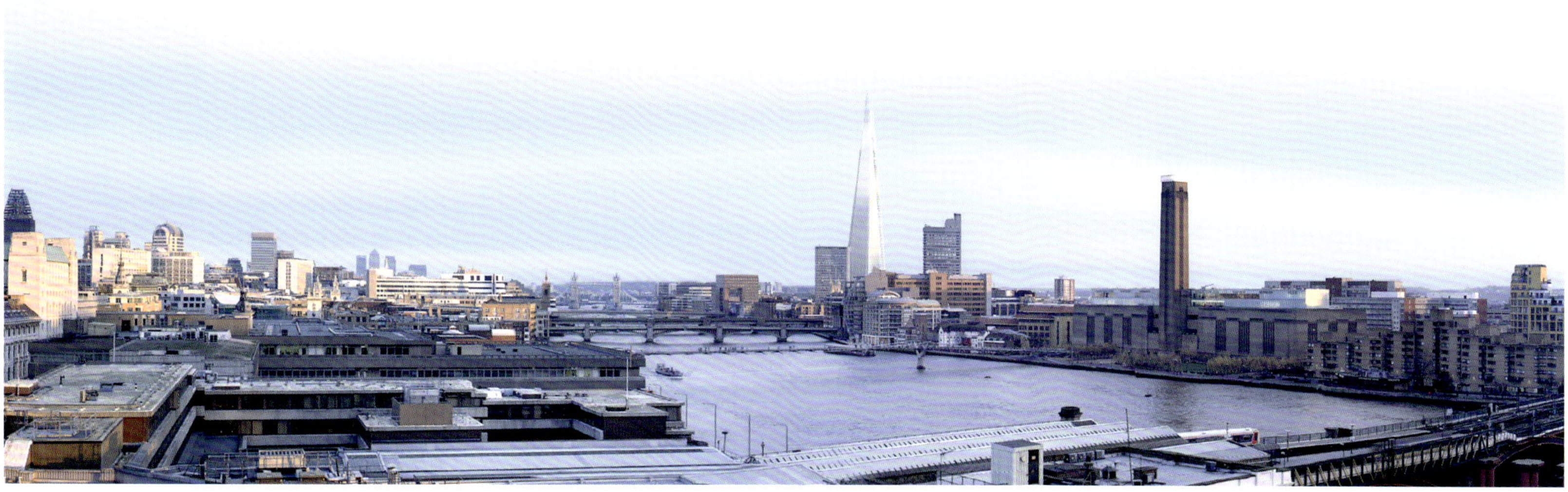

COLLECTION

north america

P LIMITED_CANADA_TORONTO (ON)_FALCON HEADQUARTERS_MEXICO_
XICO CITY_CORPORATIVO FREXPORT_MEXICO_ZAMORA MICHOACAN_3ALIT
ITAL_USA_BURBANK (CA)_111 SOUTH WACKER_USA_CHICAGO (IL)_BRAND
W SCHOOL_USA_LOS ANGELES (CA)_LARCHMONT OFFICE_USA_LOS ANGE
 (CA)_BARODA VENTURES_USA_LOS ANGELES (CA)_THE NEW YORK TIMES
LDING_USA_NEW YORK CITY (NY)_HEARST TOWER_USA_NEW YORK CIT
)_505 FIFTH AVENUE_USA_NEW YORK CITY (NY)_GSC OFFICES_USA_NEW
RK CITY (NY)_OFFICE MICHAEL NEUMANN ARCHITECTURE_USA_NEW YORK
Y (NY)_FACEBOOK HEADQUARTERS_USA_PALO ALTO (CA)_HYDRAULX_USA_
NTA MONICA (CA)_MOVING PICTURE COMPANY_USA_SANTA MONICA (CA)_
RASOTA HERALD-TRIBUNE HEADQUARTERS_USA_SARASOTA (FL)_ GRI
ITED_CANADA_TORONTO (ON)_FALCON HEADQUARTERS_MEXICO_MEXICO
Y_CORPORATIVO FREXPORT_MEXICO_ZAMORA MICHOACAN_3ALITY DIGI
_USA_BURBANK (CA)_111 SOUTH WACKER_USA_CHICAGO (IL)_BRAND
W SCHOOL_USA_LOS ANGELES (CA)_LARCHMONT OFFICE_USA_LOS ANGE
 (CA)_BARODA VENTURES_USA_LOS ANGELES (CA)_THE NEW YORK TIMES
LDING_USA_NEW YORK CITY (NY)_HEARST TOWER_USA_NEW YORK CIT
 505 FIFTH AVENUE USA NEW YORK CITY (NY) GSC OFFICES USA NEW

CANADA_TORONTO (ON) GRIP LIMITED

ARCHITECTS: JOHNSON CHOU INC.
COMPLETION: 2006_**NUMBER OF WORKPLACES:** 120
GROSS FLOOR AREA: 2,000 M²_**COMMON AREA:** MEETING AREA, LUNCH ROOM_**KIND OF WORKPLACES:** CELLULAR, OPEN-PLAN, TEAM, CUBICAL, LOUNGE WORKSPACE
PHOTOS: JOHNSON CHOU / TOM ARBAN PHOTOGRAPHY, TORONTO

The client wanted his new office to be a space that inspires and fosters creativity; a space that conveys a vivid image of a creative agency; and a space that is analogous to their own creative work, involving playfulness and wit. The challenge was how to express creativity through architecture. The solution was three-fold and began with an interpretation of the creative act: that creativity is activated by the exchange of ideas. Architecturally it was translated into the creation of a collection of formal and informal meeting spaces offering various spatial experiences and attractive paths leading to these spaces, while the notion of play was manifested in the blurring of interior and exterior elements.

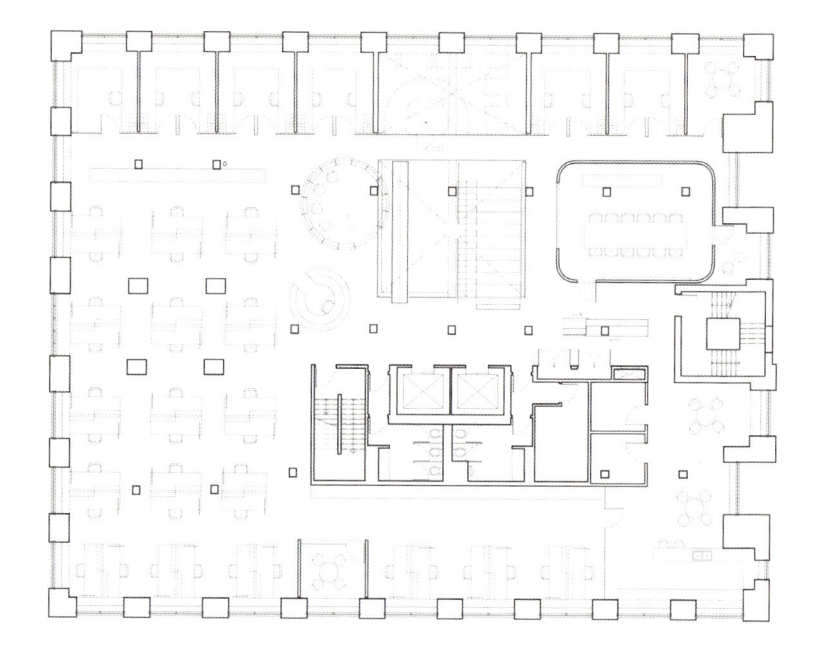

Der Bauherr hatte drei Prämissen für die Gestaltung der Büros: Der Raum sollte inspirieren und Kreativität fördern, ein einprägsames Bild einer kreativen Agentur vermitteln und analog zur eigenen Arbeit verspielt und geistreich sein. Das Problem, Kreativität im Rahmen architektonischer Möglichkeiten darzustellen wurde in drei Phasen gelöst, indem zunächst der kreative Akt als Austausch von Ideen interpretiert wurde. Dies wurde architektonisch in eine Auswahl formeller und informeller Versammlungsräume mit ganz unterschiedlichen Raumerlebnissen umgesetzt. Das Spielerische findet seinen Ausdruck in der unscharfen Anwendung von Elementen des Innen- und Außenraumes.

left: Sixth floor plan_View of entrance to "Hot Tub" meeting / presentation area_View of lunch room and "Hot Tub" beyond. right: View of reception waiting area.
links: Grundriss sechstes Obergeschoss_Blick zum Einstieg in den „Hot Tub", dem Besprechungs- und Präsentationsbereich_Essbereich, im Hintergrund der „Hot Tub". rechts: Empfangs- und Wartezone.

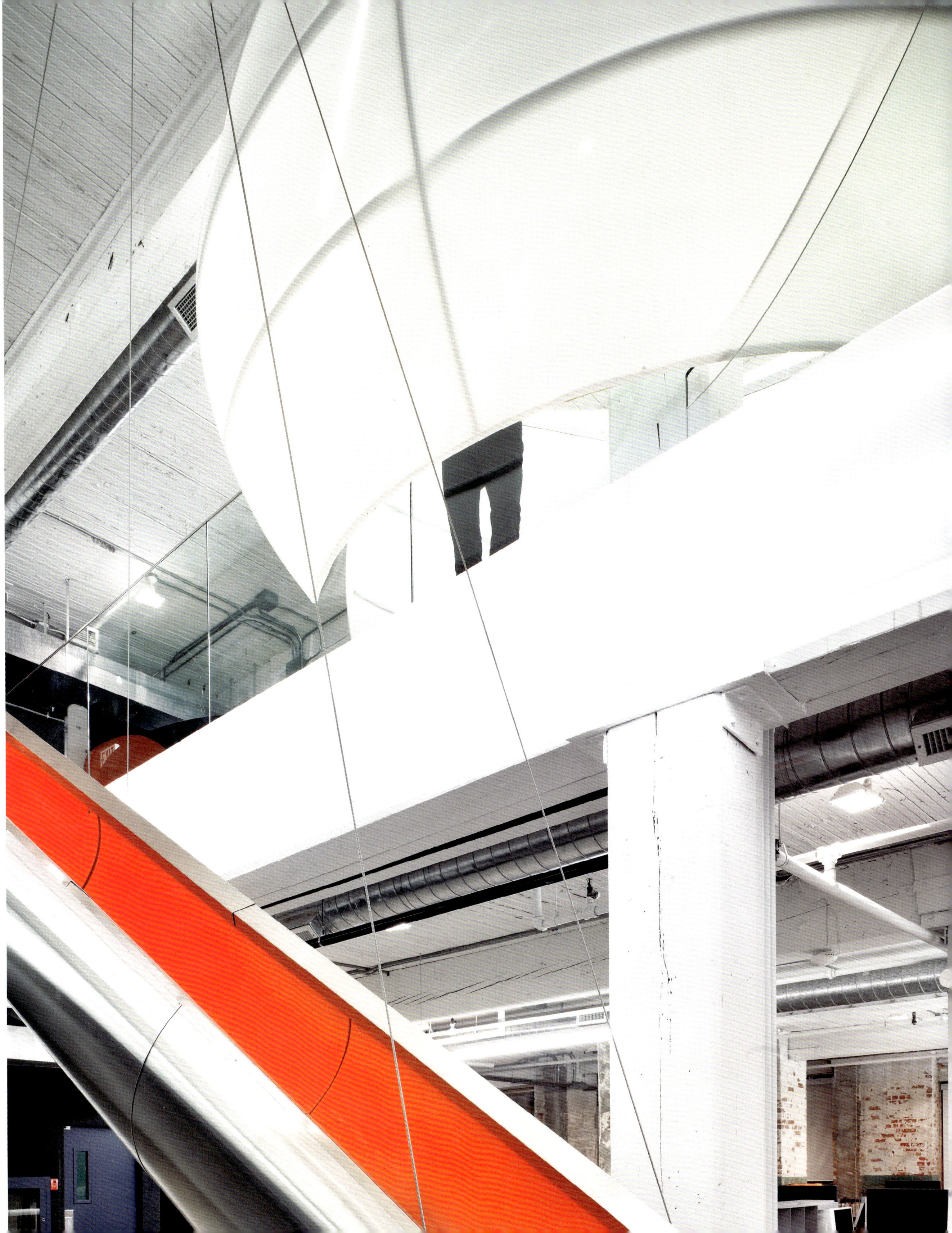

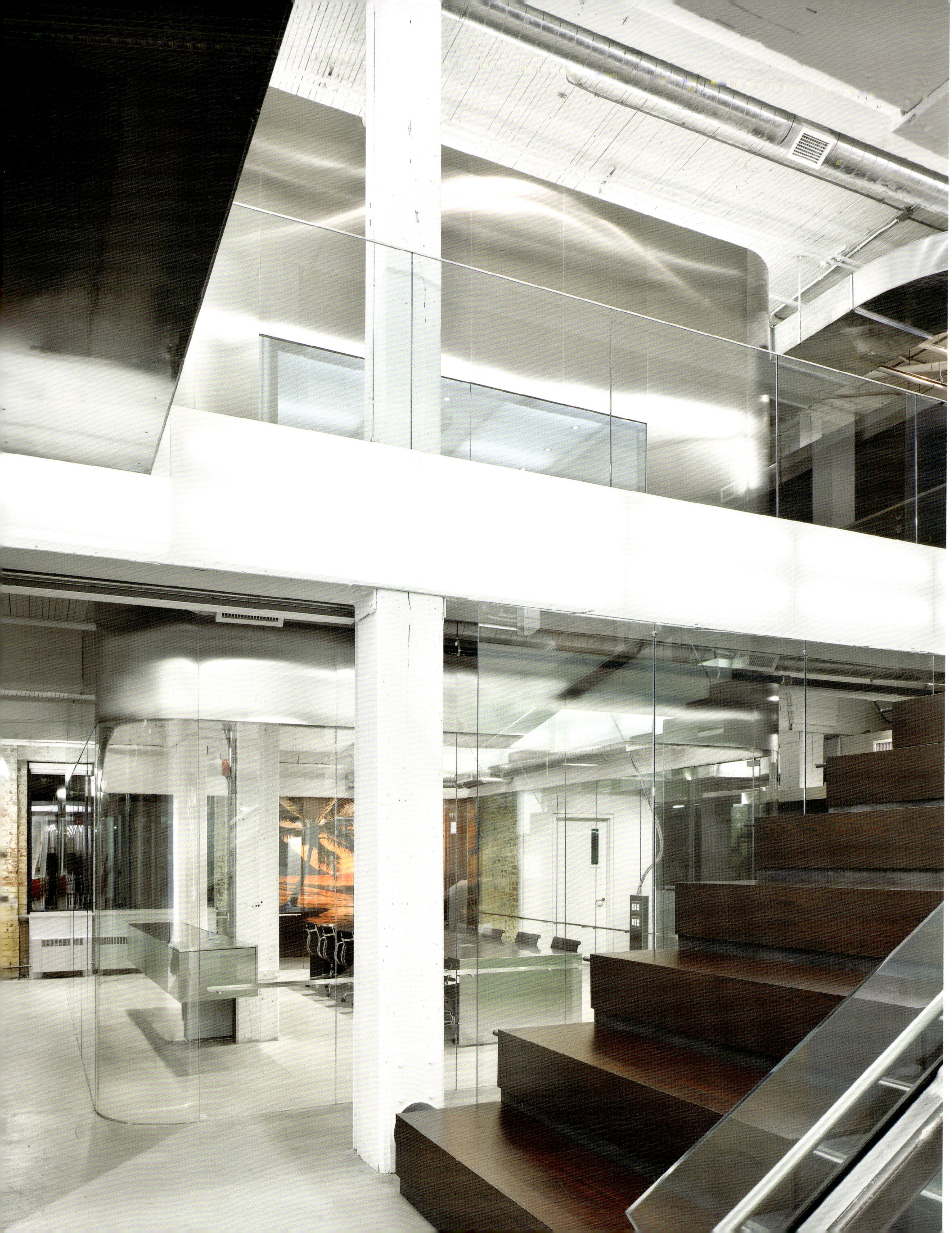

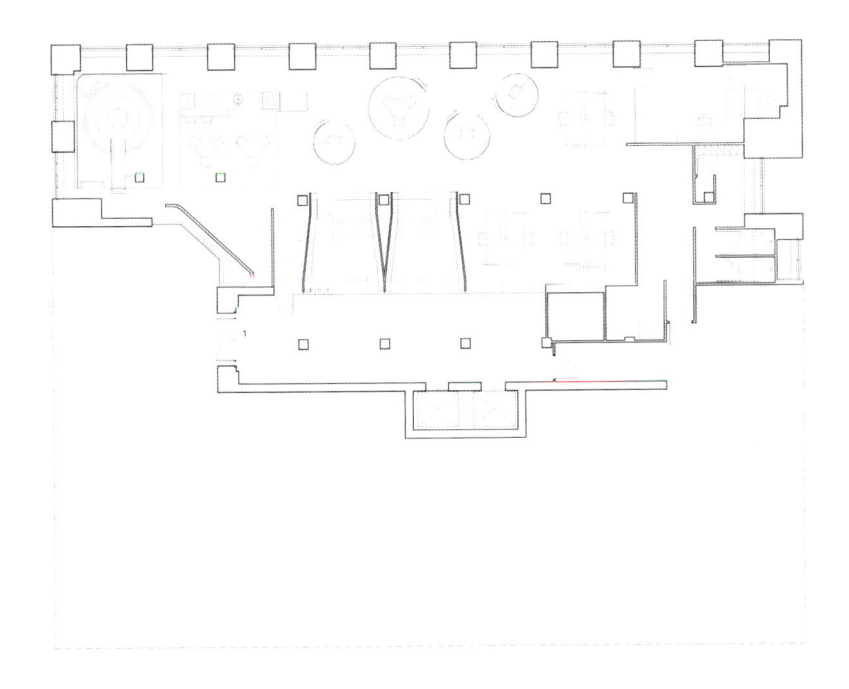

left: View of formal and creative boardrooms. right: Ground floor plan_Entrance_View at north at sixth floor atrium_View of atrium towards bleacher seating and slide.
links: Ansicht offizielle und kreative Sitzungszimmer. rechts: Grundriss Erdgeschoss_Eingang_Atrium Richtung Norden, sechstes Obergeschoss_Atrium mit heller Sitzgelegenheit und Rutsche.

MEXICO_MEXICO CITY **FALCON HEADQUARTERS**

ARCHITECTS: ROJKIND ARQUITECTOS, MICHEL ROJKIND WITH DEREK DELLEKAMP_**STRUCTURAL ENGINEER:** MONCAD, ING. JORGE CADENA_**FURNITURE:** ESRAWE STUDIO
COMPLETION: 2004_**GROSS FLOOR AREA:** 451 M²
COMMON AREA: LOUNGE_**KIND OF WORKPLACES:** OPEN-PLAN
PHOTOS: GUIDO TORRES (430, 431, 433 R.), JAIME NAVARRO (432, 433 L.)

The premise for the new headquarters was to radically change the image of the medical equipment manufacturer. The sales center would also become a work place and the ideal space to receive clients and to be presented as a business of high technology. The project was conceptualized as a crystal box floating in a garden. The building's crystal skin floats before its solid core. As lucid material, straw is encapsulated between two layers of crystal, filling the interior with orange light in contrast to the building's tones of gray. Perforations provide views beyond the gravity of traditional windows.

Grundgedanke des neuen Hauptsitzes war, ein radikal neues Bild des Herstellers medizinischer Geräte zu schaffen, in der das Verkaufzentrum zum Arbeitszentrum, zum idealen Empfangsbereich für die Kunden und zum Aushängeschild einer High-tech-Firma werden sollte. Das Projekt wurde als Kristallkasten im Garden konzipiert und mit kristallartiger Hülle über einen festen Kern realisiert. Als transluzentes Material dient Stroh zwischen Scheiben, das – im Kontrast zum grauen Innenren – gefärbtes Licht durchscheinen lässt. Die Öffnungen der Hülle ergaben sich aus dem Versuch, gezielt Ausblicke zu gewähren und die Schwere üblicher Fenster zu überwinden.

left: Ground floor plan_Exterior elevation_Detail, Façade. right: Winter garden.
links: Grundriss Erdgeschoss_Außenansicht_Detail, Fassade. rechts: Wintergarten.

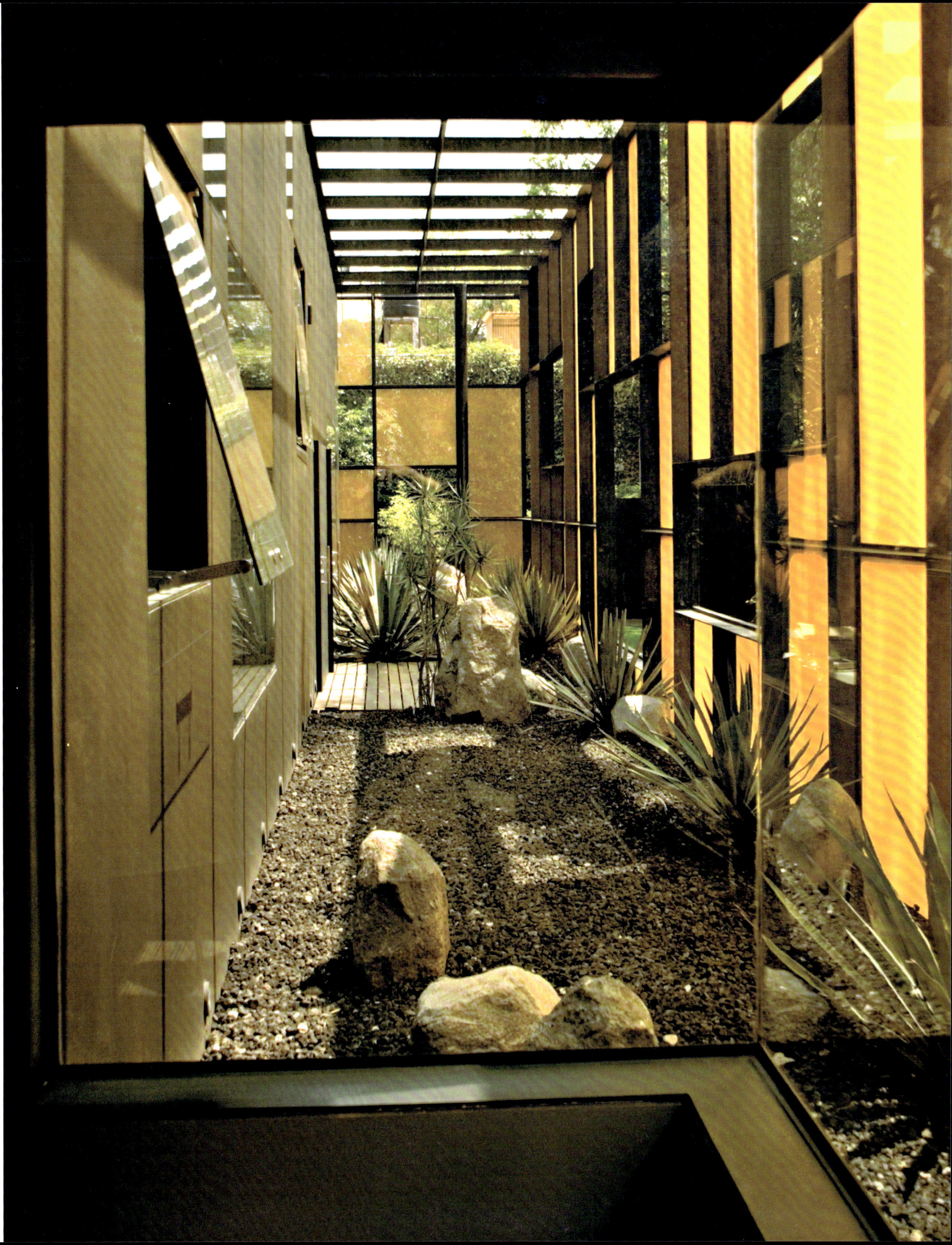

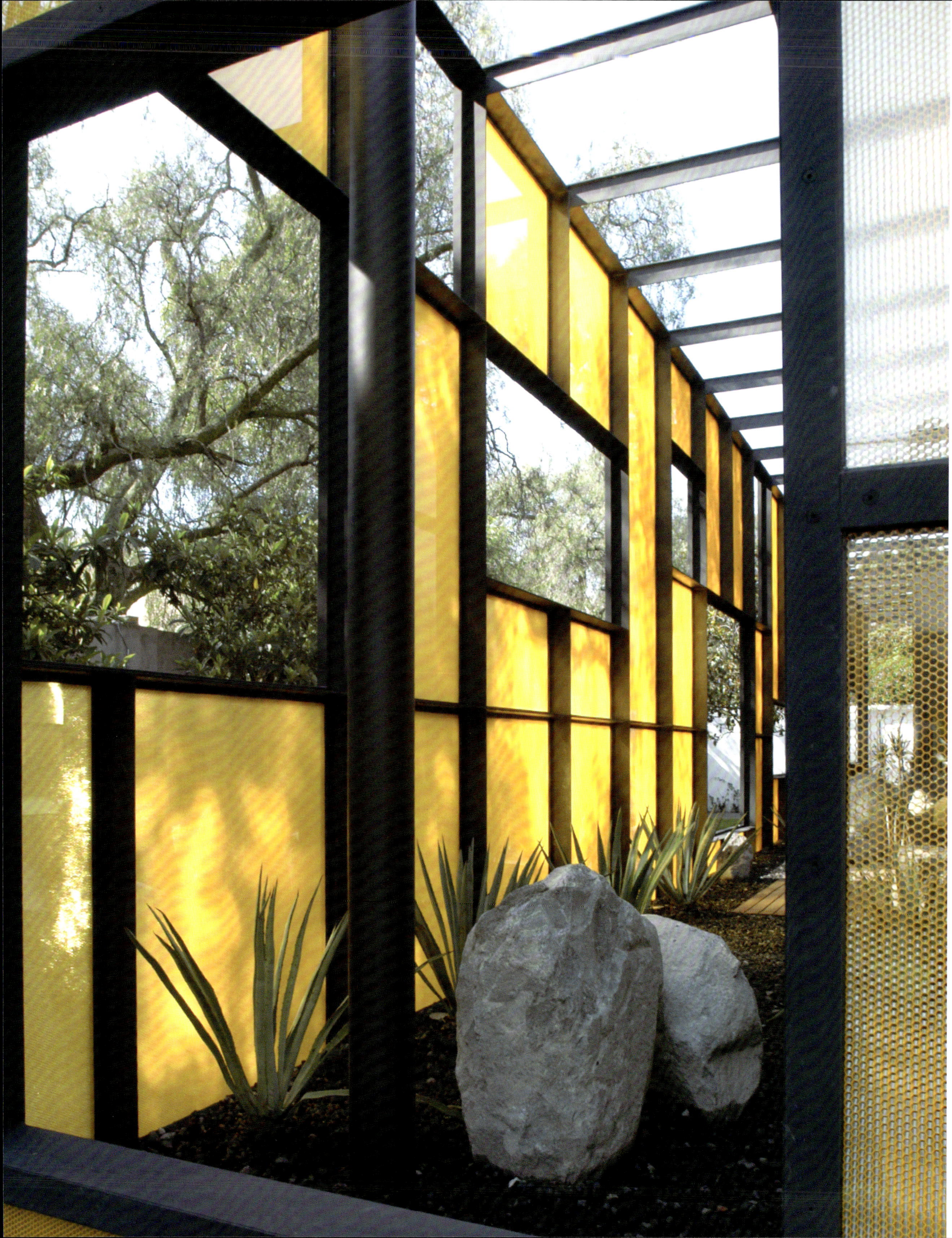

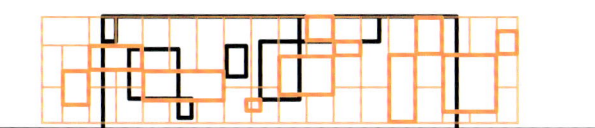

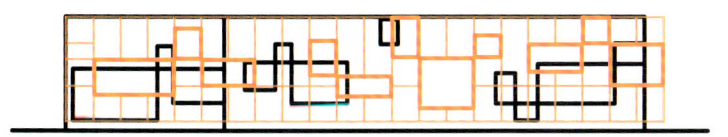

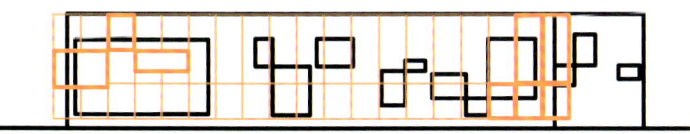

left: View through honeycomb panel to the winter garden. right: Diagram Façade_Open-plan office_Lounge area_Conference room_Detail.
links: Blick durch das waberistrukturierte Element in den Wintergarten. rechts: Diagramm Fassade_Offene Bürostruktur_Loungebereich_Konferenzraum_Detail.

MEXICO_ZAMORA MICHOACAN CORPORATIVO FREXPORT

ARCHITECTS: CC ARQUITECTOS / MANUEL CERVANTES CESPEDES_**LANDSCAPE ARCHITECTS:** HUGO SANCHEZ, TONATIUH MARTINEZ_**CONSTRUCTION:** CARLOS LOZORNIO
COMPLETION: 2007_**NUMBER OF WORKPLACES:** 40
GROSS FLOOR AREA: 1,200 M²_**KIND OF WORKPLACES:** OPEN-PLAN, TEAM, CUBICAL, LOUNGE WORKSPACE
PHOTOS: LUIS GORDOA , MEXICO

The client, a preserved food specialist, conceived the concept and idea of this building. The architects transformed it into the concept of promenades in the countryside. The gardens therefore became the focal point of the project and the input of landscapers was therefore sought. The green palette of vegetation and powerful natural stone were the elements that marked the design of the landscape, featuring all the crops (Mangoes, Strawberries, etc.) that constitute the company's production line. When walking through the passages, the owner and visitors become in direct contact with the plant life that dominates the setting.

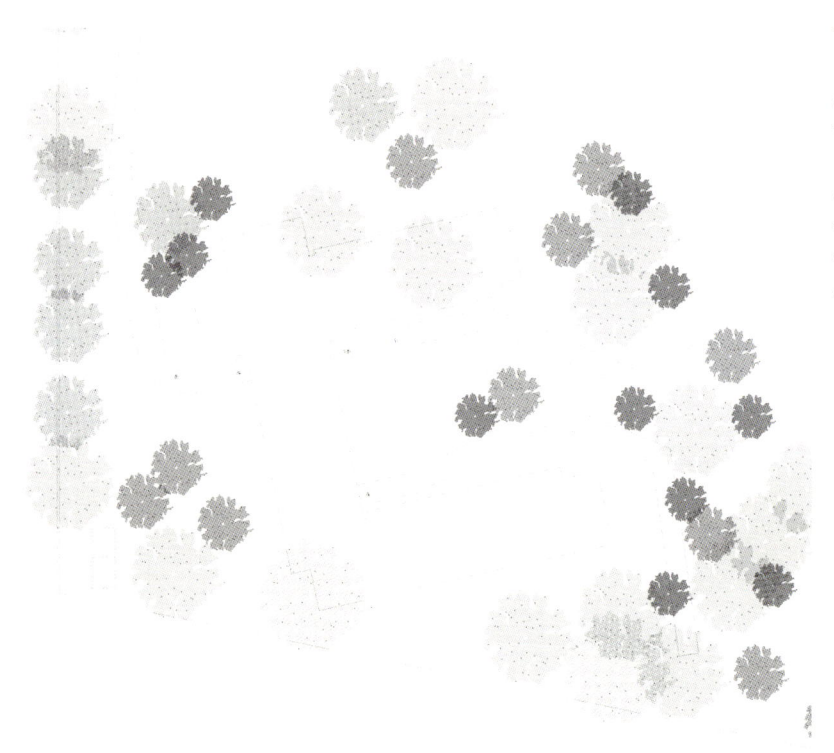

Vom Bauherrn, der mit Marmeladen, Yoghurts und Sirup handelt, stammen Konzept und Idee des Bürogebäude. Daraus, aus dem Raumprogramm und aus der Idee gestalteter Promenaden in der Landschaft entwickelten die Architekten eine Bauform. Die Gärten wurden zum Herz des Projekts, so dass die Landschaftsarchitekten als dritter Gestalter hinzukamen. Die Grünpalette und die Ausdruckskraft natürlichen Steins sowie die Kulturpflanzen, die die Firma verarbeitet (Mango, Erdbeere, usw.) charakterisierten diesen Landschaftsentwurf. So können Nutzer wie Besucher auf den Wegen direkte Erfahrung mit der die Umgebung prägenden Flora machen.

left: Site plan_General view_Main staircase. right: Administration entrance.
links: Lageplan_Gesamtansicht_Haupttreppenhaus. rechts: Eingang zum Verwaltungsgebäude.

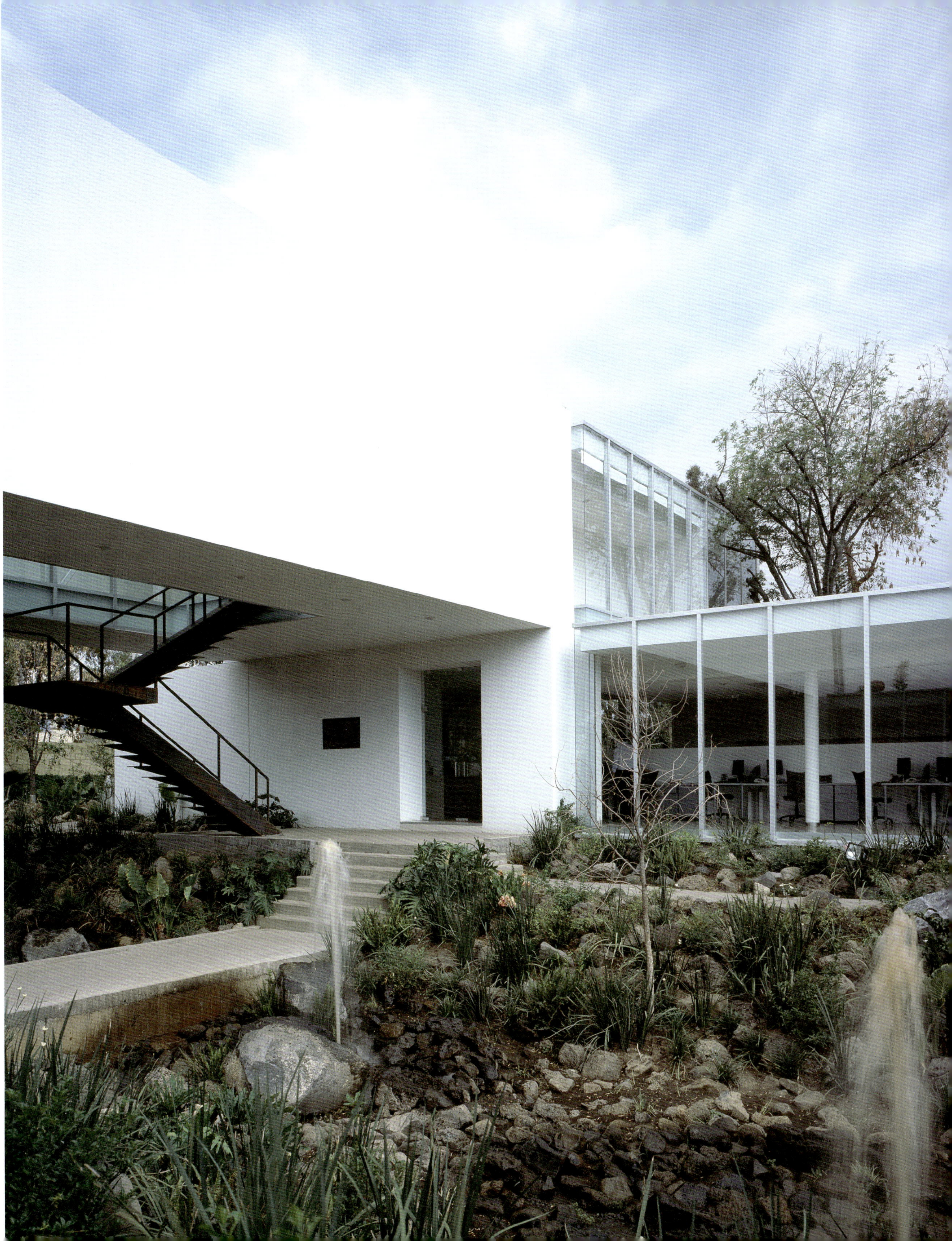

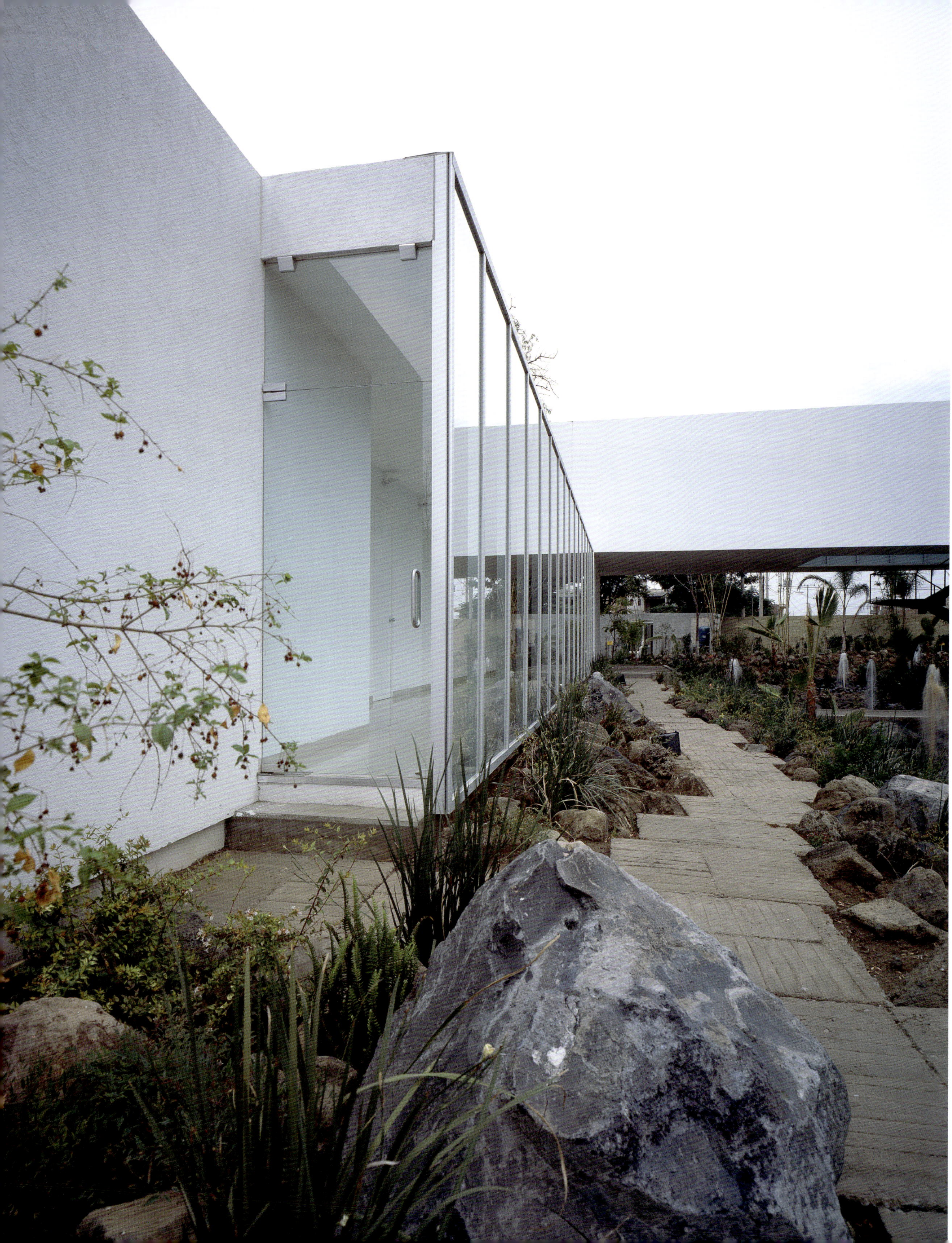

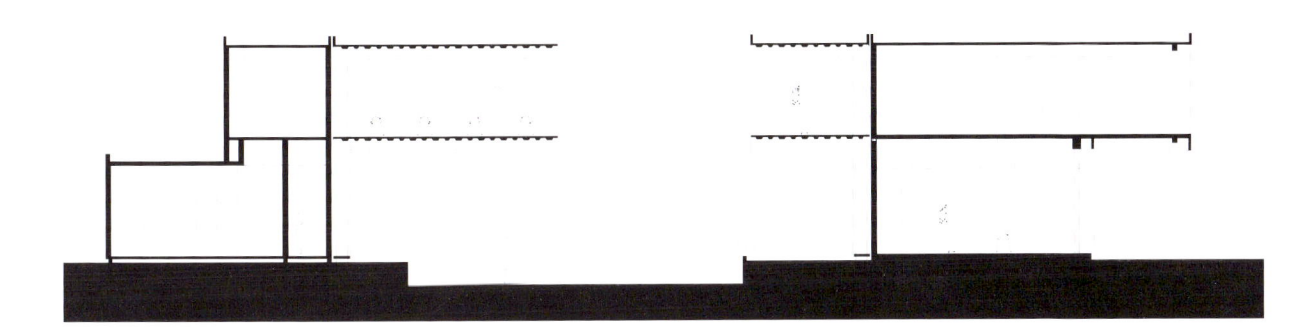

left: Visitors pathway. right: Longitudinal section_Main office cantiliver_Sales hallway 1_Visitors hallway.
links: Pfad für Besucher. rechts: Längsschnitt_Ausleger Hauptbüro_Flur Vertrieb_Flur Besucher.

USA_BURBANK (CA) **3ALITY DIGITAL**

ARCHITECTS: FUNG + BLATT ARCHITECTS, INC.
COMPLETION: 2007_**NUMBER OF WORKPLACES:** 20
GROSS FLOOR AREA: 1,860 M²_**COMMON AREA:** CONFERENCE ROOM, THEATER_**KIND OF WORKPLACES:** COMBINATION
PHOTOS: JOSH PERRIN PHOTOGRAPHY, LOS ANGELES

This film production facility inhabits two 1940s masonry warehouse bays separated by a bearing wall that provides very limited open passage space between the two areas. A dynamic work environment with administrative and technical wings was designed. It includes offices, workshops, editing rooms, an equipment cage and long sight lines for camera staging. The circular conference room became the vortex of the setting. It sits atop the central dividing wall and propels into motion a series of ripples whose trajectories penetrate and diminish the separation while establishing auxiliary spaces for informal gatherings.

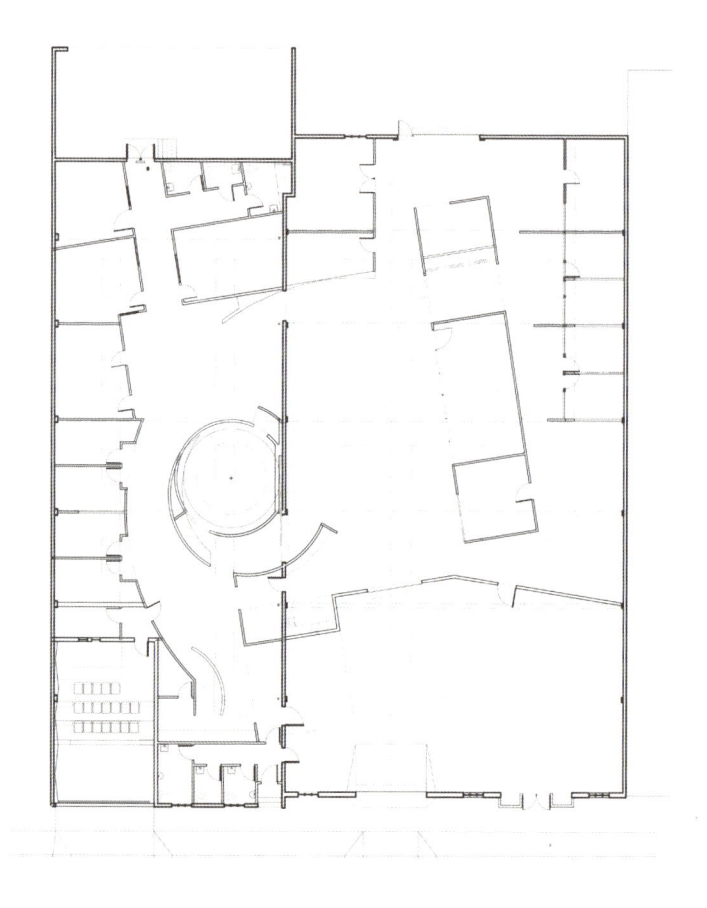

Die Räumlichkeiten des Filmherstellers befinden sich in zwei Kompartimenten eines Lagerhauses der 1940er Jahre. Diese Kompartimente sind durch eine tragende Wand voneinander getrennt, die nur begrenzte Maueröffnungen zuließ. Dennoch konnte ein dynamisches Arbeitsumfeld gestaltet werden, mit einem administrativen und technischen Trakt für Büros, Ateliers, Schneide- und Geräteräume sowie langen Fluchten für Kameraeinstellungen. Der gerundete Konferenzraum ist der Angelpunkt des Interieurs. Er erstreckt sich entlang der teilenden Wand und suggeriert eine Drehung, die den Raum gliedert und teilt, aber auch zusätzliche Plätze für informelle Treffen bereitstellt.

left: Ground floor plan_Exterior view of the conference room_Reception. right: Kitchen and lounge area_Interior view of the conference room_Fire door, dividing wall.
links: Grundriss Erdgeschoss_Außenansicht des Konferenzraums_Empfang. rechts: Küche und Lounge_Der Konferenzraum von Innen_Brandschutztür und Trennwand.

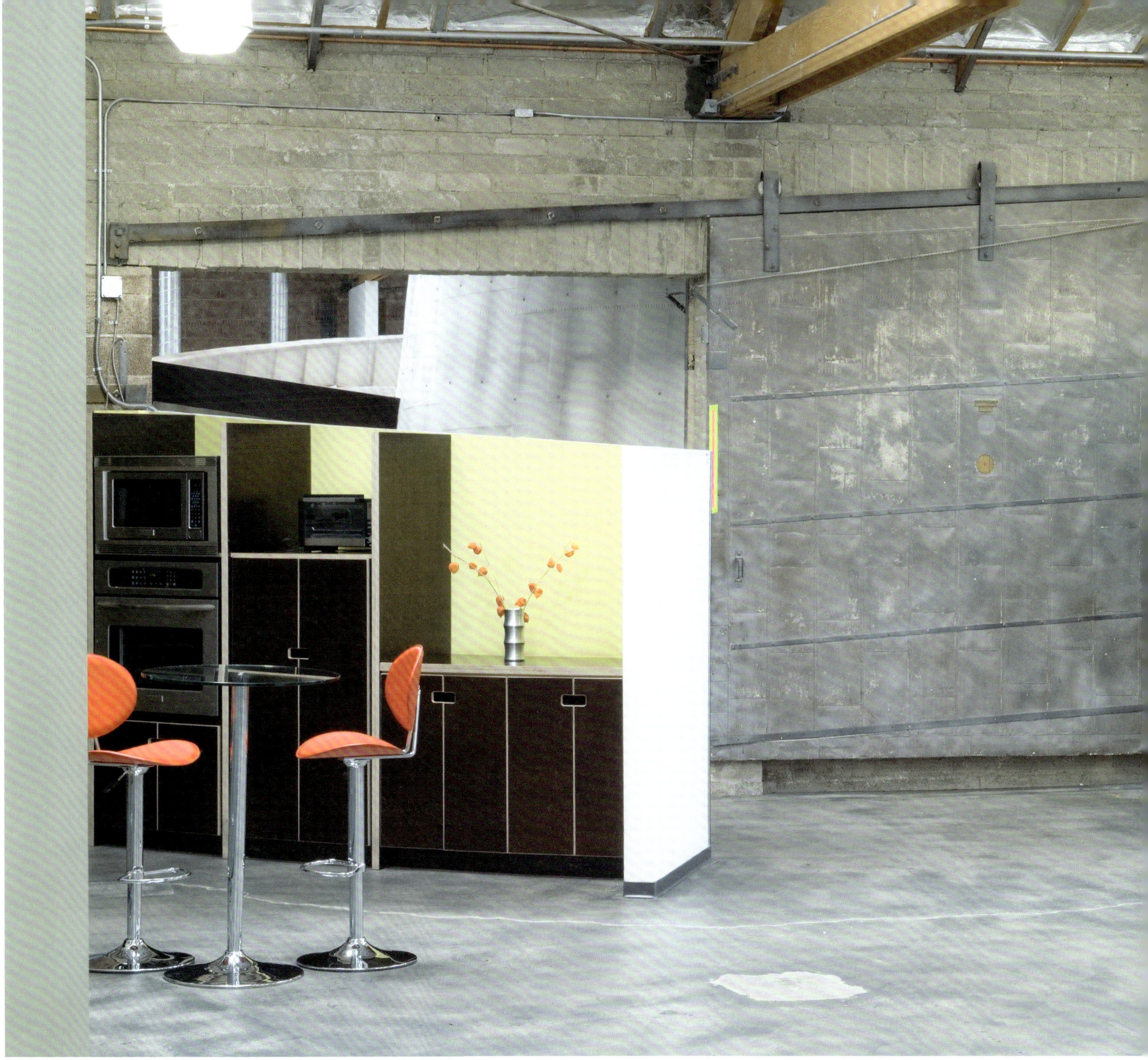

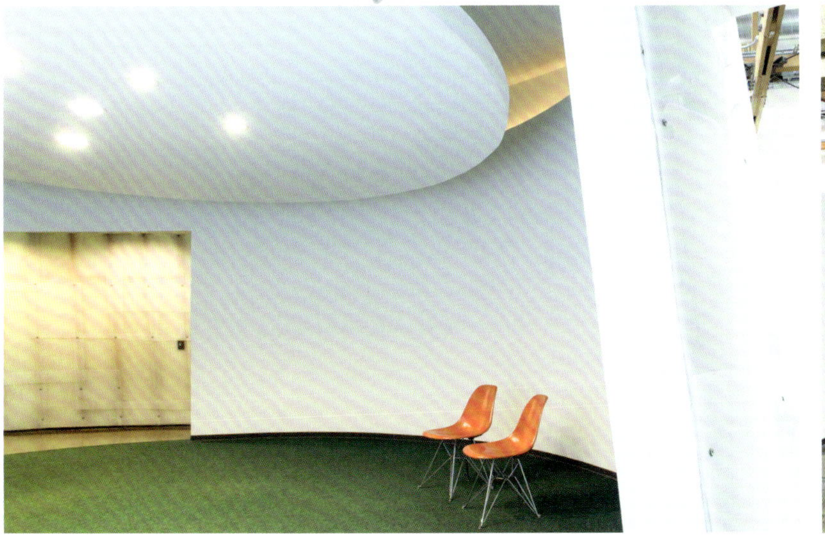

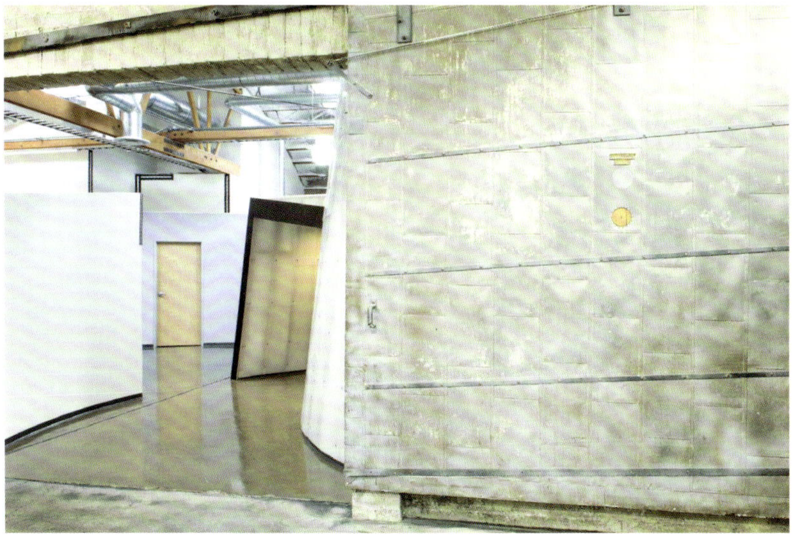

USA_CHICAGO (IL) 111 SOUTH WACKER

ARCHITECTS: GOETTSCH PARTNERS
COMPLETION: 2005_**GROSS FLOOR AREA:** 135,360 M²
KIND OF WORKPLACES: MIXED_**PHOTOS:** JAMES STEINKAMP / STEINKAMP PHOTOGRAPHY

Located in downtown Chicago, 111 South Wacker is a 53-story office building and the first-ever project certified LEED-CS Gold by the U.S. Green Building Council. Typical office floors are entirely column-free, to allow for planning efficiency and flexibility. The building's lobby is one of its more unique features, with a spiraling parking ramp that defines the space. The radial pattern of the ramp is reflected in the lobby's stepped ceiling, and this pattern is further echoed in the granite and marble floor that extends beyond the enclosure. Wrapping the lobby is a cable-supported, ultra-transparent glass wall that allows inside and outside to be perceived as a single continuous space.

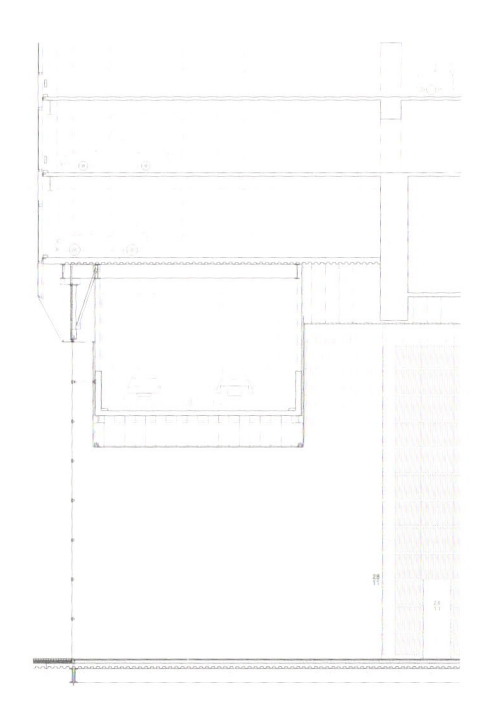

Das in der Innenstadt von Chicago stehende 111 South Wacker ist ein Bürogebäude mit 53 Stockwerken und das erste vom U.S. Green Building Council mit dem LEED-CS Gold zertifizierte Projekt. Die typischen Büroetagen ohne Säulen gewährleisten Flexibilität und Effizienz beim Planen. Eines der auffälligeren Merkmale ist das Foyer mit spiralförmiger Parkhausauffahrt. Das strahlenförmige Muster der Auffahrtsrampe spiegelt sich in der stufenförmigen Foyerdecke und findet sich auch im Granit- und Marmorboden wieder, der sich aus dem Gebäude hinaus erstreckt. Das Foyer ist von einer mit Seilen durchspannten Glaswand umgeben, welche den Innen- und Außenbereich als einen einzigen, durchgängigen Raum erscheinen lässt.

left: Lobby-cable wall section_Building base_ Lobby, detail. right: Lobby.
links: Schnitt, Foyer mit von Seilen durchspannter Glaswand_Erdgeschoss_ Lobby, Detail. rechts: Lobby.

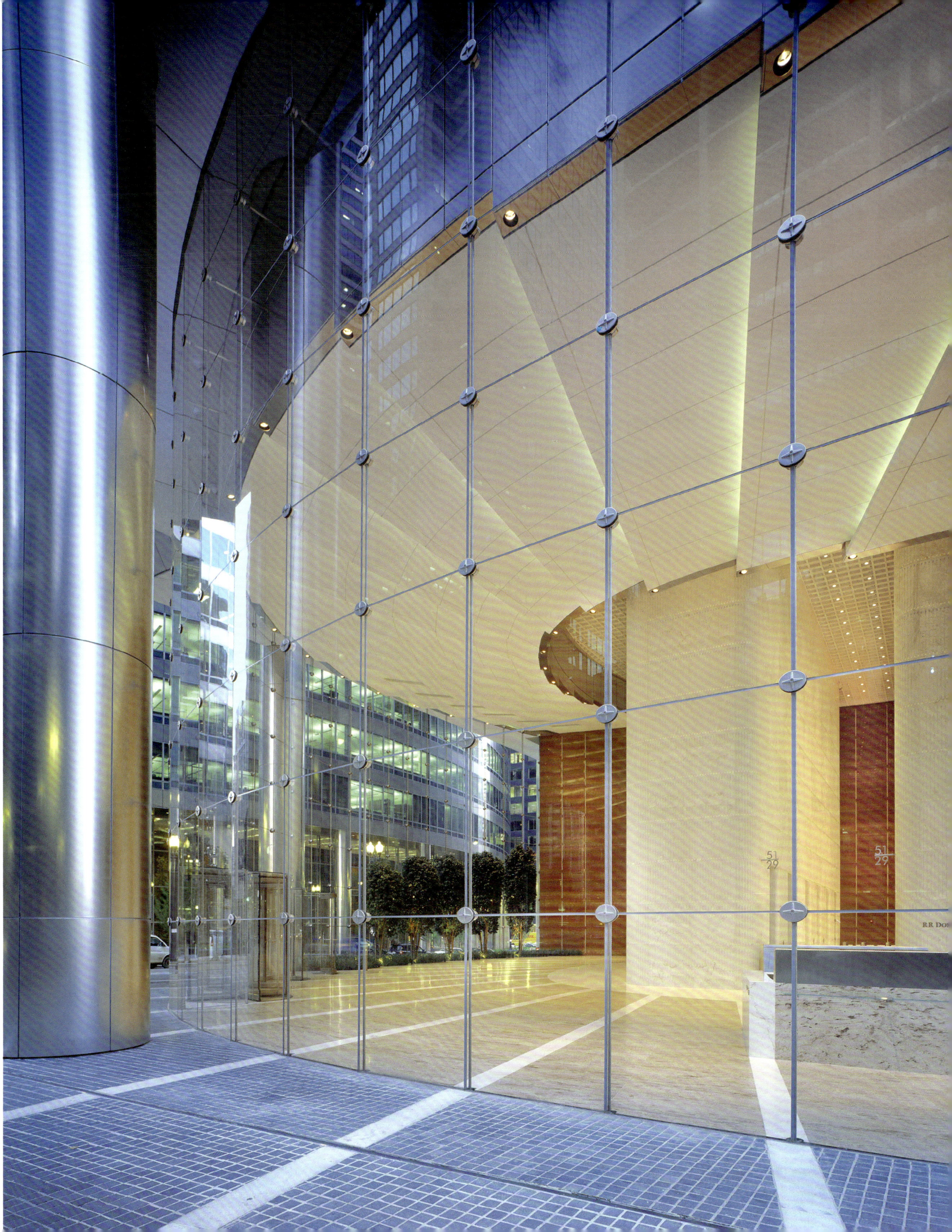

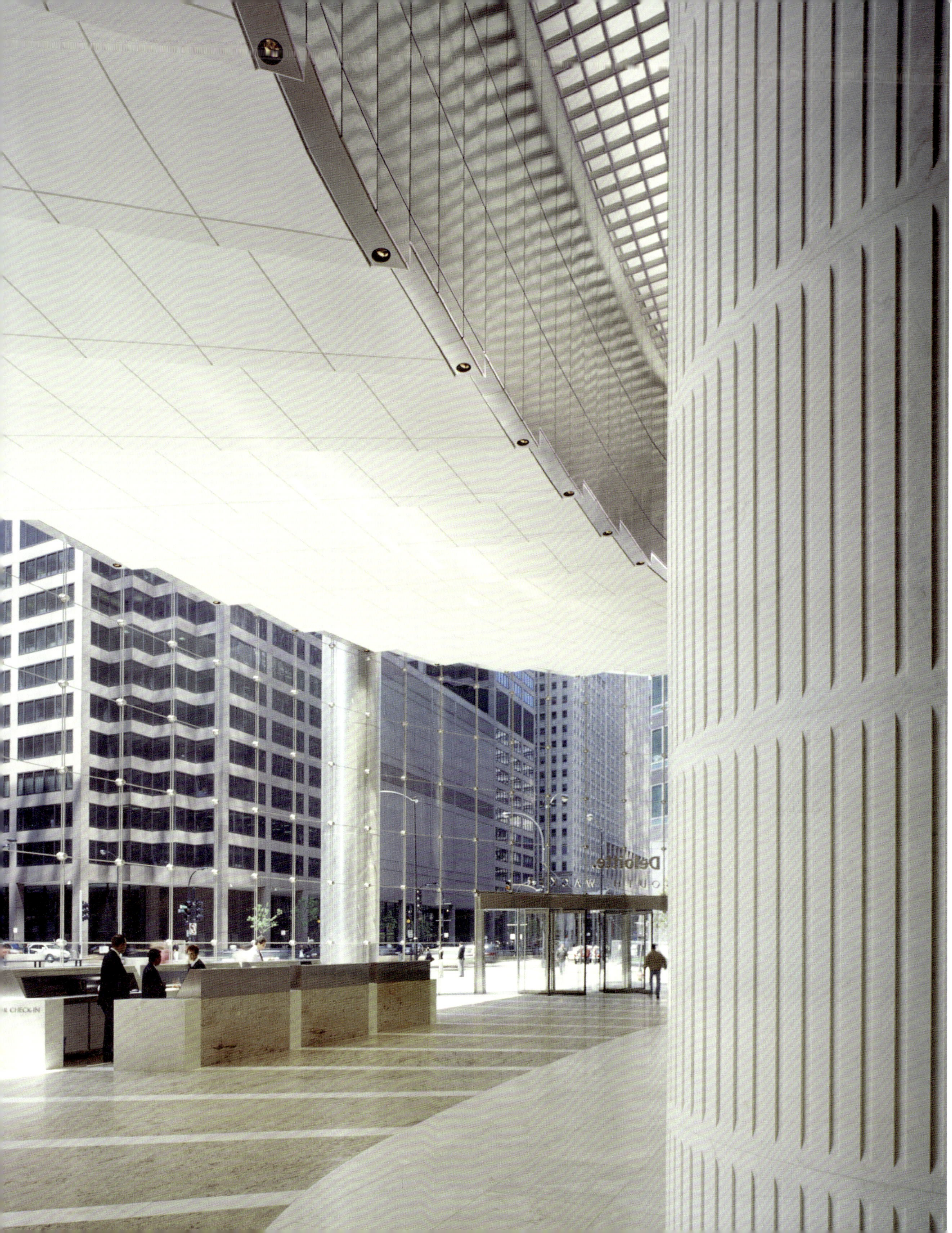
CHECK-IN

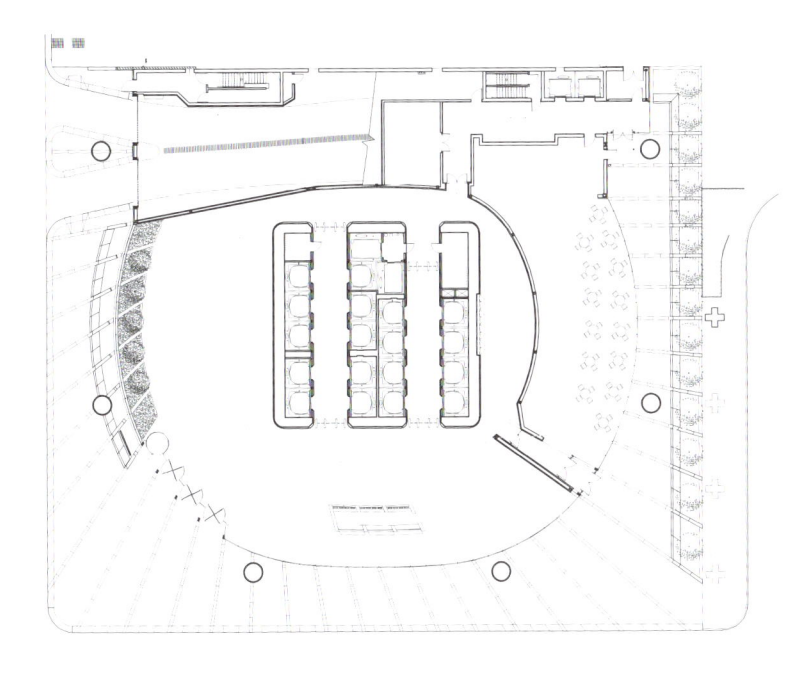

left: Lobby. right: Ground floor plan_Worm's-eye view.
links: Foyer. rechts: Grundriss Erdgeschoss_Froschperspektive.

USA_LOS ANGELES (CA) LARCHMONT OFFICE

ARCHITECTS: RIOS CLEMENTI HALE STUDIOS
COMPLETION: 2008_**NUMBER OF WORKPLACES:** 68
GROSS FLOOR AREA: 1,579 M²_**COMMON AREA:** CONFERENCE ROOMS, MODEL SHOP
KIND OF WORKPLACES: TEAM
PHOTOS: TOM BONNER, SANTA MONICA, CA

Rios Clementi Hale Studios renovated a former mini-mall for its multi-disciplined design staff and its nonhierarchical studio environment with pod work groups of 6 to 19 members. Exterior walls were replaced by window wall systems, and screened porches were created around the second-floor studio space. Exterior panels alternate between mirrored glass and expressive cut aluminum screens. Indoor "parks" are created with artificial turf in unexpected places. A display wall along the staircase exhibits photos, boards, and models of past, current, and future architectural projects of the firm. The "tree house" meeting room features floor-to-ceiling windows overlooking the street trees.

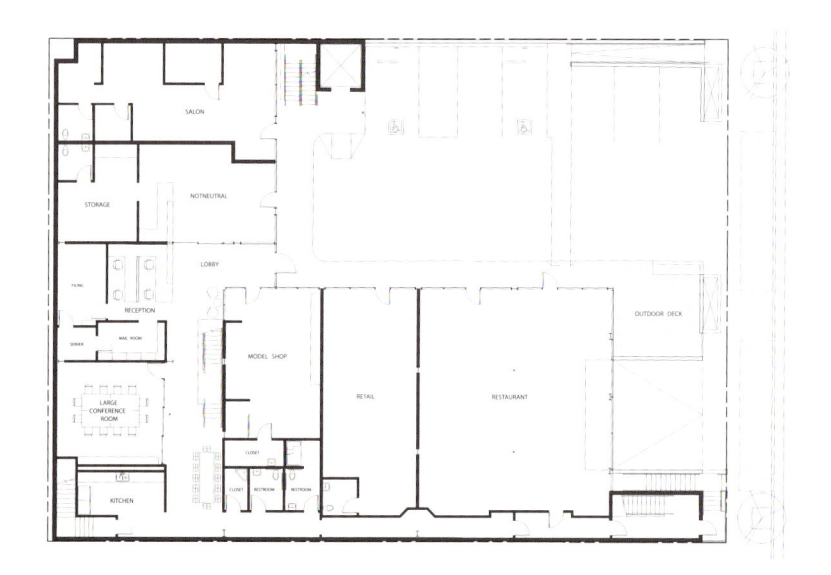

Rios Clementi Hale Studios baute eine ehemalige Mini-Mall zum Büro seines gattungsübergreifendes Designteams um. Außenwände wurden durch System-Glasfassadenelemente ersetzt und abgeschirmte Laubengänge umgeben das Atelier im Obergeschoss. Bei den außen liegenden Paneelen alternieren verspiegeltes Glas und expressive geschnittene Aluminiumplatten. Im Inneren befinden sich unerwartete Grünzonen mit künstlichem Rasen. Eine Schauwand an der Treppe zeigt Fotos, Tafeln und Modelle von vergangenen, aktuellen und künftigen Bauten der Firma. Für Pod-Arbeitsgruppen von sechs bis 19 Mitarbeitern gibt es hierarchiefreie Arbeitsplätze. Der „Baumhaus"-Konferenzraum besitzt geschosshohe Fenster mit Blick auf die Bäume der Straße.

left: First floor plan_The façade's Triton graphical panels glow at night_Façade, detail. right: "Tree house" conference room overlooking the street.
links: Grundriss Erdgeschoss_Die grafischen Elemente der Fassade leuchten bei Nacht_Fassadendetail. rechts: „Baumhaus-"Konferenzraum mit Blick auf die Straße.

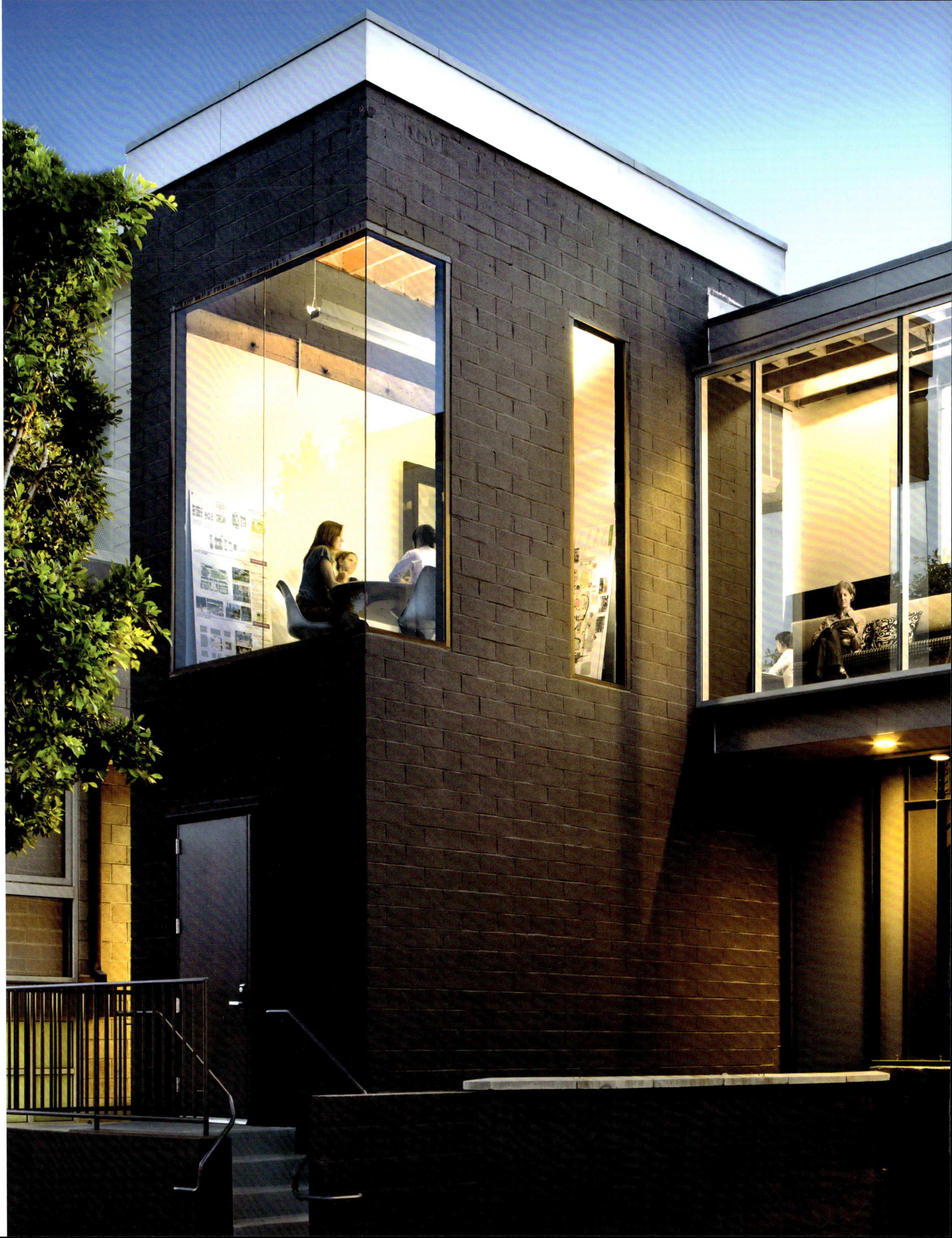

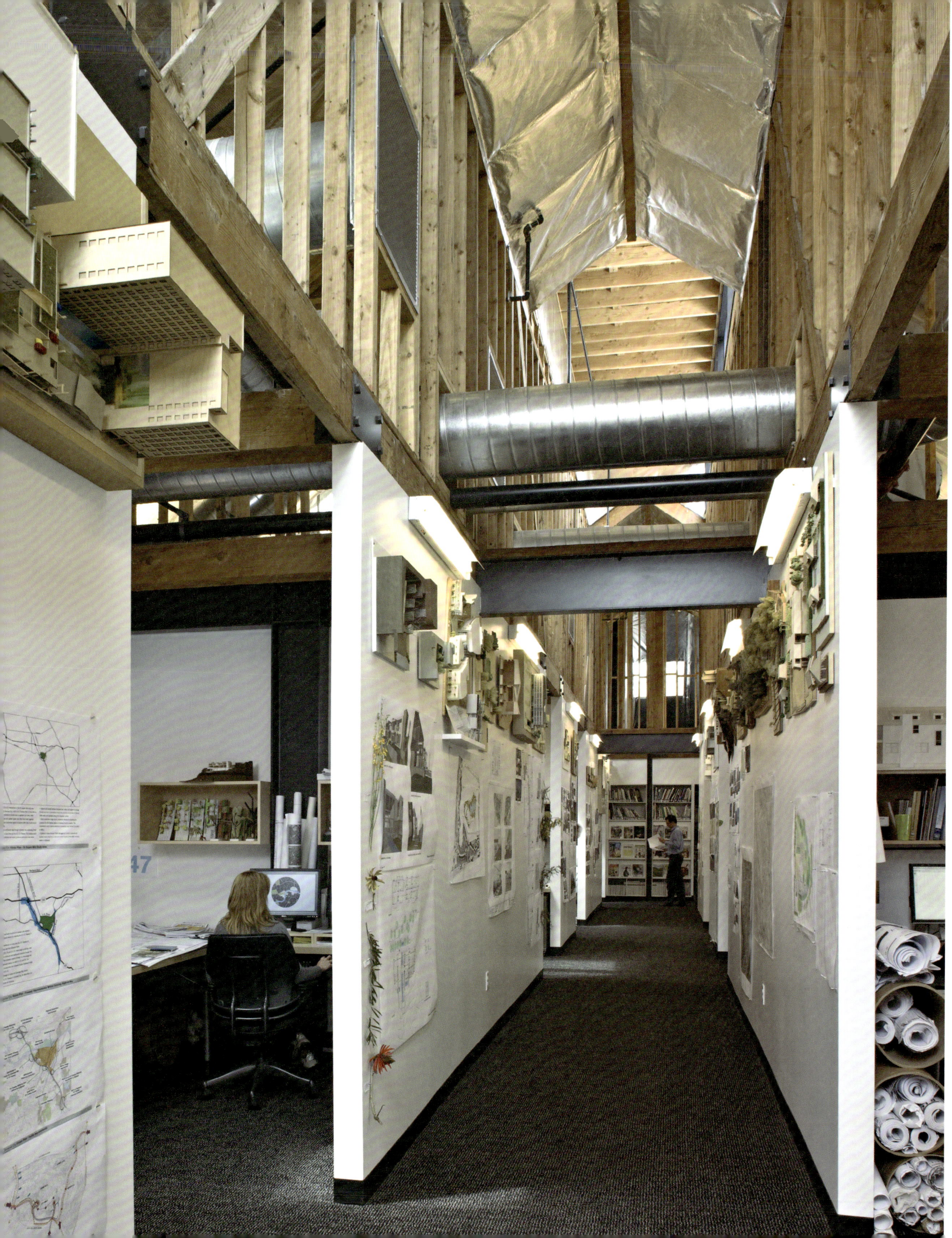
47

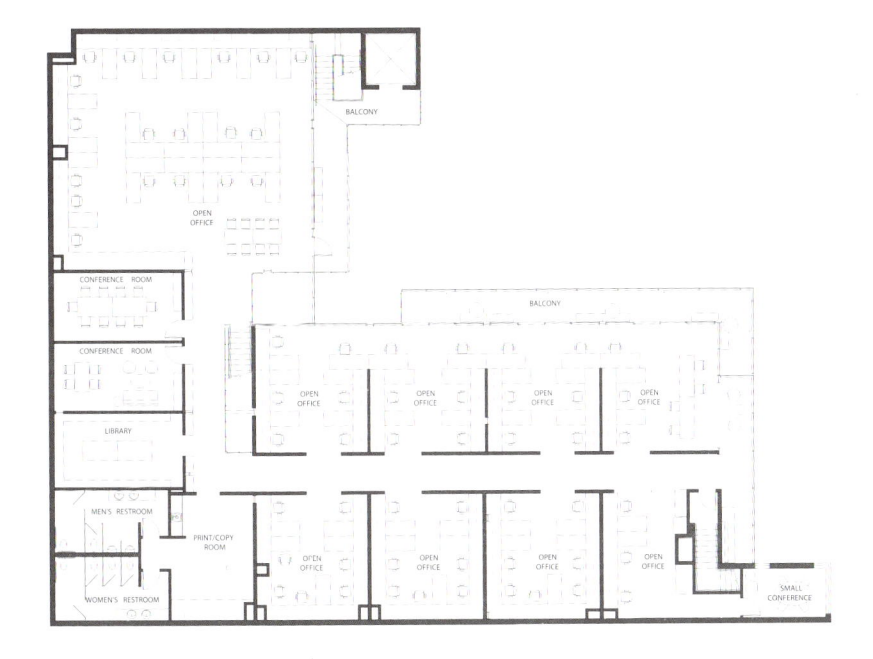

left: Work pods branch off from central corridor. right: Second floor plan_Stairs lined with projects lead to work areas_Nonhierarchical studios encourage collaboration_Work spaces face window walls with outdoor areas.

links: Die Arbeitszellen zweigen vom Hauptflur ab. rechts: Grundriss erstes Obergeschoss_Treppe zum Arbeitsbereich mit Projekten_Hierarchiefreie Büros verbessern die Zusammenarbeit_Dem Fenster zugewandter Arbeitsplatz mit Blick zum Außenbereich.

USA_LOS ANGELES (CA) **BARODA VENTURES**

ARCHITECTS: RIOS CLEMENTI HALE STUDIOS
COMPLETION: 2008_**NUMBER OF WORKPLACES:** 14
GROSS FLOOR AREA: 389 M²_**COMMON AREA:** CONFERENCE ROOMS, COURTYARDS
KIND OF WORKPLACES: CELLULAR, TEAM
PHOTOS: TOM BONNER, SANTA MONICA, CA

Rios Clementi Hale Studios adapted a surprising, yet delightful, combination of retro and contemporary styles for the renovation of the two-story Baroda Ventures office. The architects applied several themes throughout the design – classic modern furnishings with unexpected fabrics, elaborate ceiling medallions and door escutcheons, glossy surfaces, and repeated patterning at various scales – while incorporating plenty of daylight. An existing quatrefoil window design is a leitmotif throughout, seen in wallpaper and structural details. Timeless elegance was achieved by pairing traditional essentials with the latest in design to create a place of sophisticated opulence.

Eine ungewöhnliche, aber reizvolle Kombination von Retrostilen und Zeitgenössischem nutzten Rios Clementi Hale Studios zur Renovierung des zweigeschossigen Baroda Ventures Büro. Unterschiedlichste Themen – klassisch moderne Möbel mit unerwarteten Stoffen, aufwendige Decken- und Türverzierungen, glänzende Oberflächen sowie sich in verschiedener Größe wiederholende Muster – wurden in dem Entwurf mit reichlich Tageslicht verbunden. Ein bestehendes Vierpass-Fenster diente als Leitmotiv und findet sich sowohl in Tapeten als auch in Strukturelementen wieder. Zeitlose Eleganz wurde durch die Verbindung von traditionellen Elementen mit aktuellem Design in raffinierter Üppigkeit geschaffen.

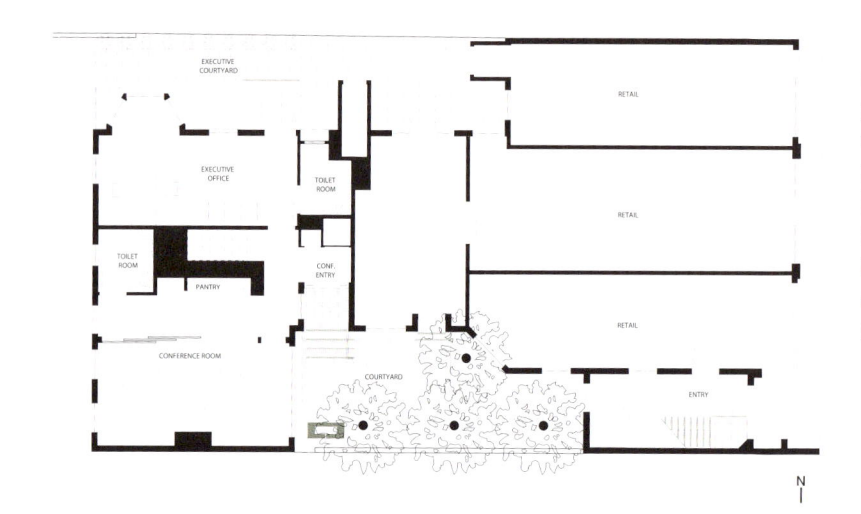

left: First floor plan_Stairs act as light well_Corridor with open offices_Ground floor courtyard greets visitors. right: Storefront system is used for interior spaces_Skylights in roof add daylight to reception area_Brass accents highlight custom table and wallcovering.
links: Grundriss Erdgeschoss_Die Treppen dienen als Lichtquelle_Flur mit offenen Büros_Der Innenhof heißt Besucher willkommen. rechts: Ladenfronten dienen als Inneneinrichtung_Oberlichter im Dach sorgen für Tageslicht im Empfangsbereich_Messingfarbene Akzente betonen den Konferenztisch und die Wandgestaltung.

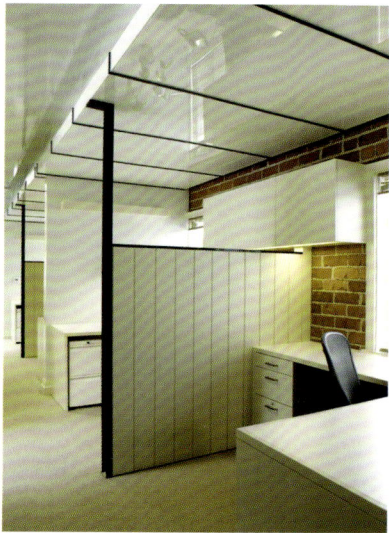

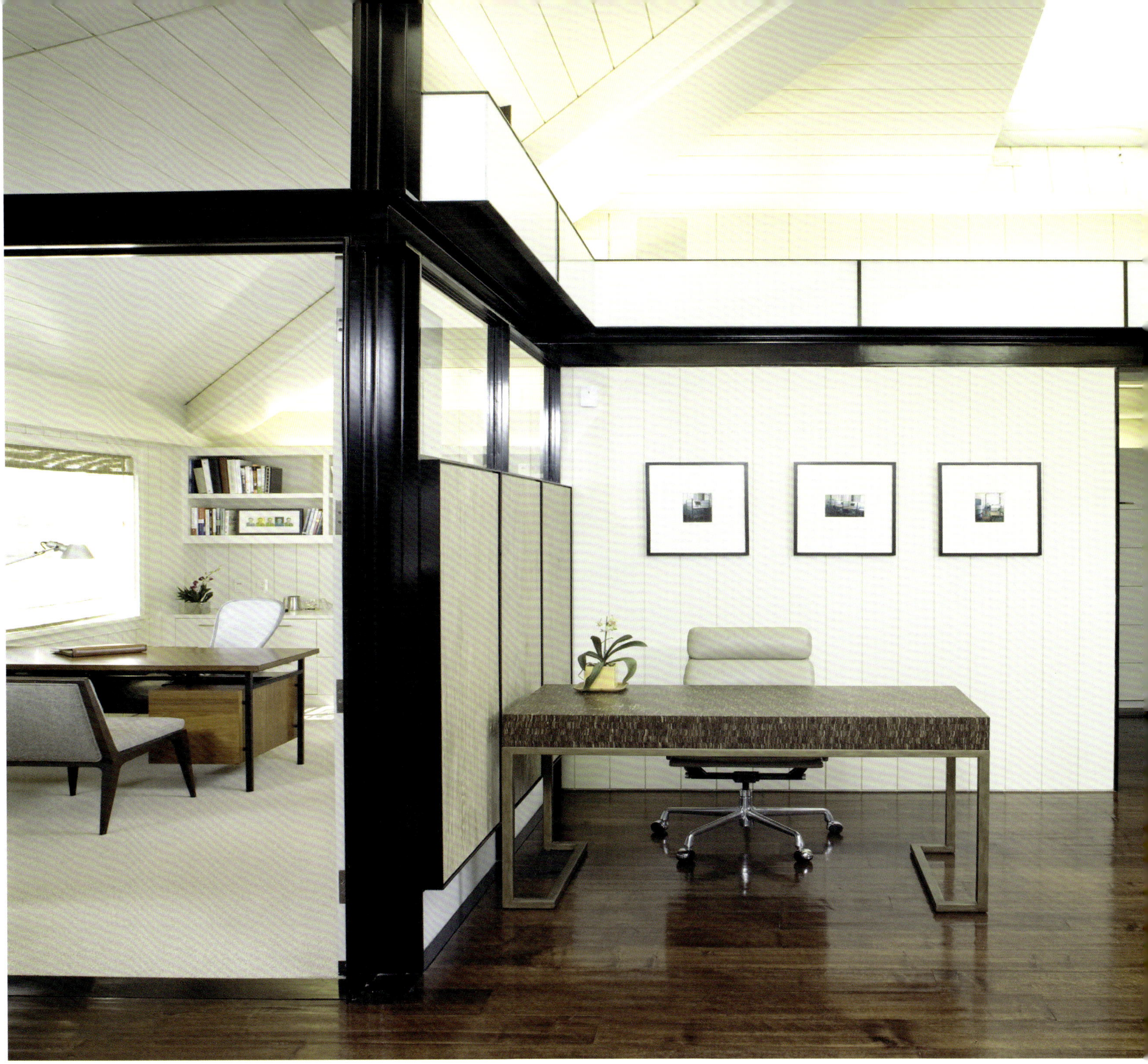

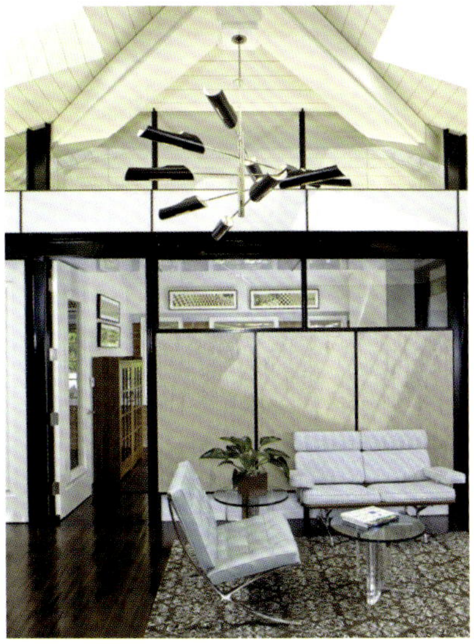

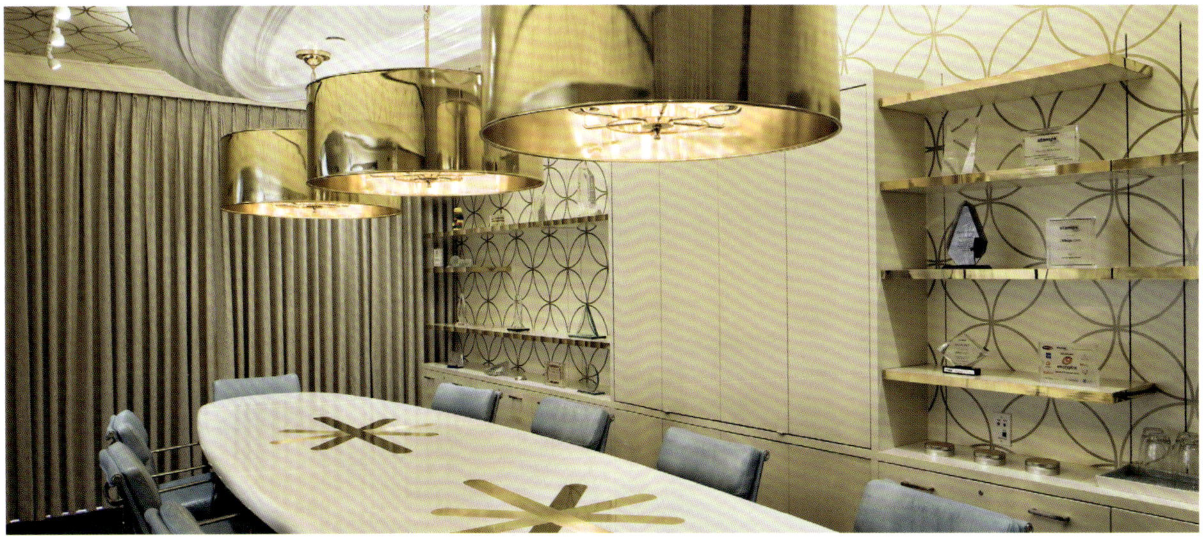

USA_LOS ANGELES (CA) **BRAND NEW SCHOOL**

ARCHITECTS: SHUBIN + DONALDSON ARCHITECTS
COMPLETION: 2005_**NUMBER OF WORKPLACES:** 50
GROSS FLOOR AREA: 975,5 M²_**COMMON AREA:** LIBRARY, CONFERENCE, LOUNGE_**KIND OF WORKPLACES:** TEAM
PHOTOS: TOM BONNER, SANTA MONICA, CA

Brand New School designs commercials for major national and international accounts. The required space had to contain open and enclosed areas to accommodate the specific functions of animators, graphic designers, art directors, and freelancers who join the company for extended periods. Like a building within a building it has two volumes: the soaring aluminum ceilings, skylights, and concrete flooring of the original shell; and the asymmetrical, but balanced, tightly-planned interior construction that houses both enclosed and open work spaces. The clean, linear organization of the assembly allows the free flow of creativity while also reflecting the precision and exactness of the company's work.

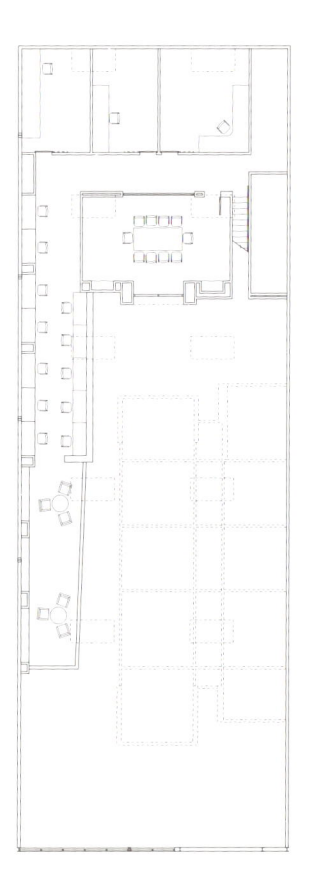

Brand New School entwirft Werbefilme für bedeutende nationale und internationale Firmen. Der Firmensitz musste deshalb sowohl offene als auch abgeschlossene Räume für die typischen Arbeiten von Trickfilmern, Grafikern, künstlerischen Leitern und Freiberuflern, die über längere Zeit hier arbeiten, bieten. Es entstand ein Gebäude im Gebäude: die hoch hinaufragende Aluminiumdecke, die Oberlichter und der Betonboden in der bestehenden Gebäudehülle sowie der asymmetrische aber ausgewogene, straff geplante Einbau, der sowohl offenen als auch geschlossenen Arbeitsraum umfasst. Die klare, lineare Organisation des Ganzen lässt der Kreativität Spielraum und zeigt zugleich die Präzision und Exaktheit der Arbeiten der Firma.

left: Mezzanine floor plan_Entry, basketball court_Mezzanine, research library. right: Work area.
links: Grundriss Zwischengeschoss_Eingang, Basketballfeld_Zwischengeschoss, Bibliothek. rechts: Arbeitsräume.

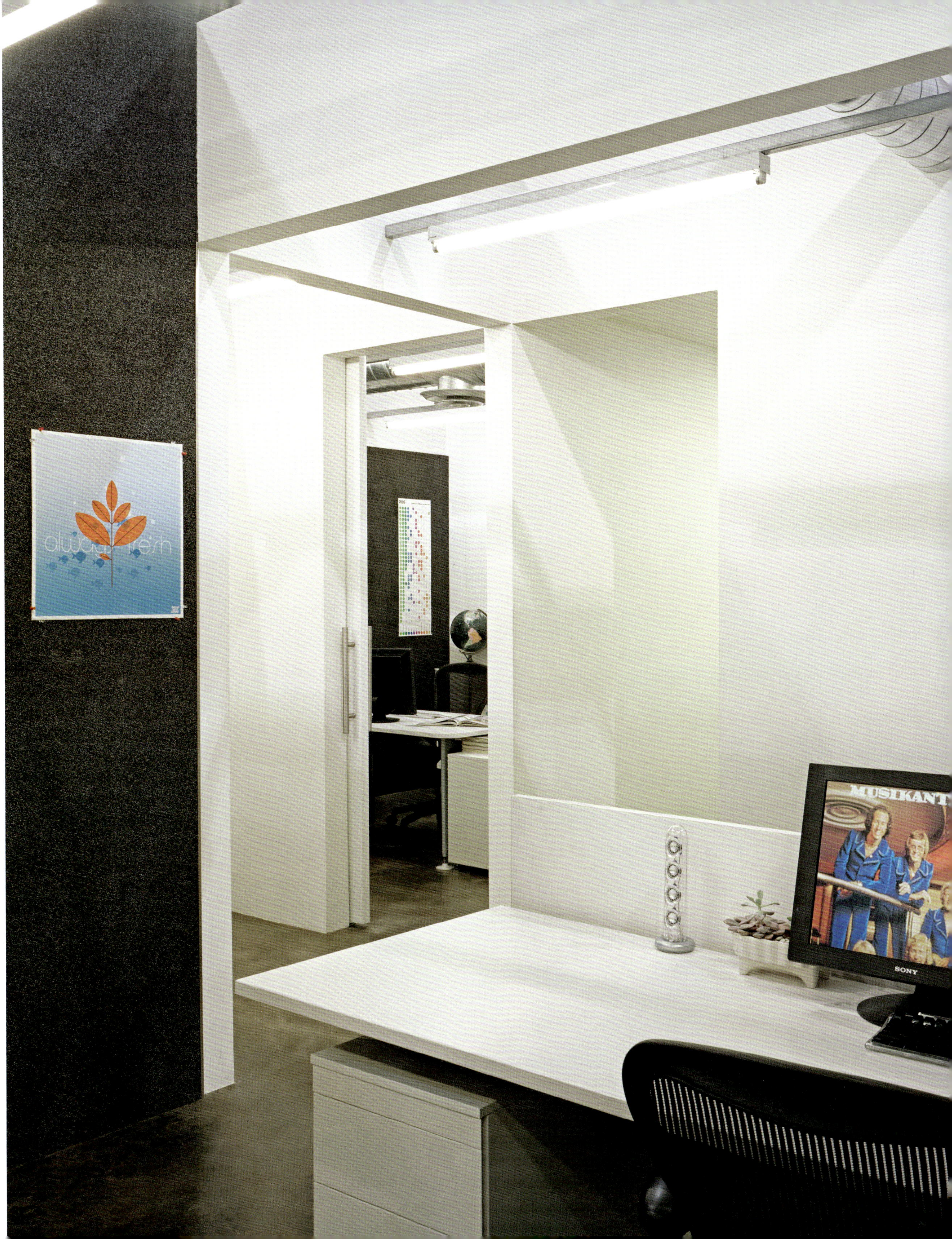
MUSIKANT
SONY

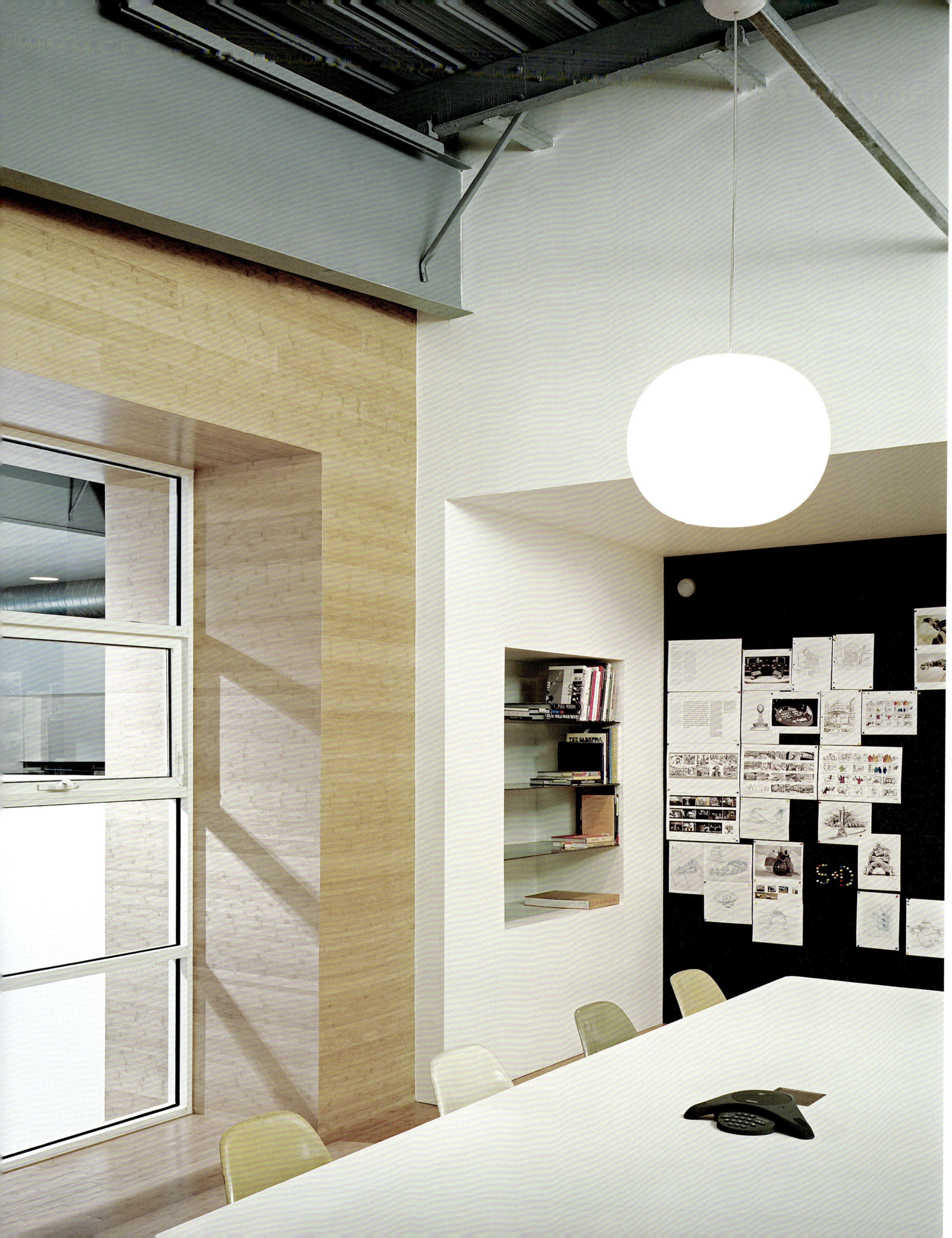

453

left: Conference room. right: First floor plan_Corridor_Kitchen, break area.
links: Konferenzraum. rechts: Grundriss, erstes Obergeschoss_Flur_Küche, Pausenbereich.

USA_NEW YORK CITY (NY) HEARST TOWER

ARCHITECTS: FOSTER + PARTNERS
COMPLETION: 2006_**ORIGINAL BUILDING:** JOSEPH URBAN AND GEORGE P. POST & SONS, 1928_**NUMBER OF WORKPLACES:** 2,200
GROSS FLOOR AREA: 79,500 M²_**COMMON AREA:** FITNESS CENTER, AUDITORIUM AND THEATER, CAFE, RESTAURANT, ATRIUM_**KIND OF WORKPLACES:** CELLULAR, OPEN-PLAN
PHOTOS: NIGEL YOUNG / FOSTER + PARTNERS

Hearst Tower revives a dream from the 1920s, when William Randolph Hearst envisaged Columbus Circle as a new media quarter in Manhattan. He commissioned a six-floor Art Deco block, anticipating that it would form the base for a tower. The forty-two-floor tower rises above the old building, linked on the outside by a skirt of glazing that presents an impression of the tower floating weightlessly above the base. The main spatial feature is a lobby that occupies the entire floor space of the old building and rises up through six floors. The building is also significant in environmental terms, using 80 percent recycled steel and designed to consume 25 per cent less energy than its conventional neighbors.

Der Hearst Tower belebt einen Traum der 1920er Jahre neu: William Randolph Hearst sah den Columbus Circle als neues Medienzentrum Manhattans. Er errichtete einen Art Déco-Bau mit sechs Stockwerken, der nur die Basis eines späteren Hochhauses bilden sollte. Jetzt erheben sich 42 Stockwerke über dem Altbau, die aufgrund der gläsernen Außenhaut fast über dem Steinbau zu schweben scheinen. Die Lobby, die die gesamte Grundfläche des Altbaus umfasst und bis zum sechsten Geschoss hinaufreicht, bietet ein großartiges Raumerlebnis. Auch ökologisch ist das Gebäude, mit zu 80 Prozent recyceltem Stahl und einem Energieverbrauch, der 25 Prozent unter dem der konventionellen Nachbarbebauung liegt, bemerkenswert.

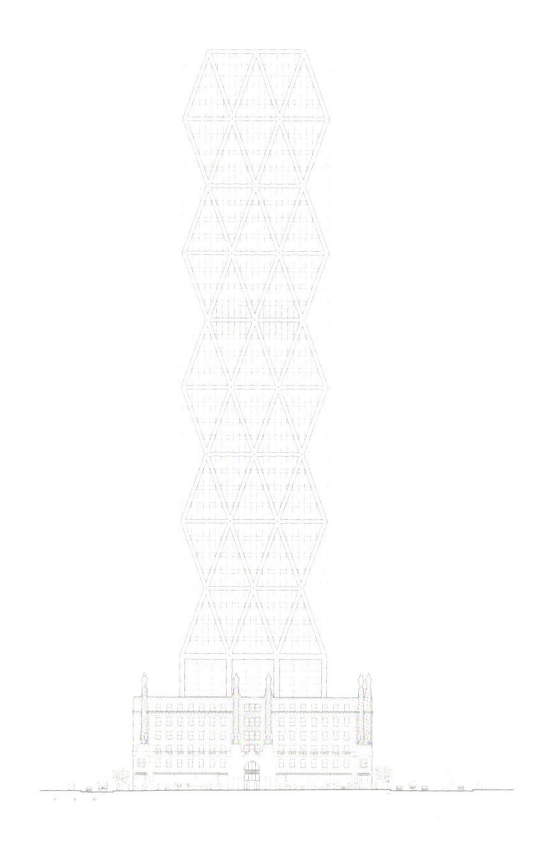

left: Elevation_Skyline. right: Façade, detail_New tower on six-story Art Deco building_View from Central Park_View along the road.
links: Ansicht_Skyline. rechts: Fassade, Detail_Neues Hochhaus über dem sechsstöckigen Art Déco-Gebäude_Blick vom Central Park_In der Straßenflucht.

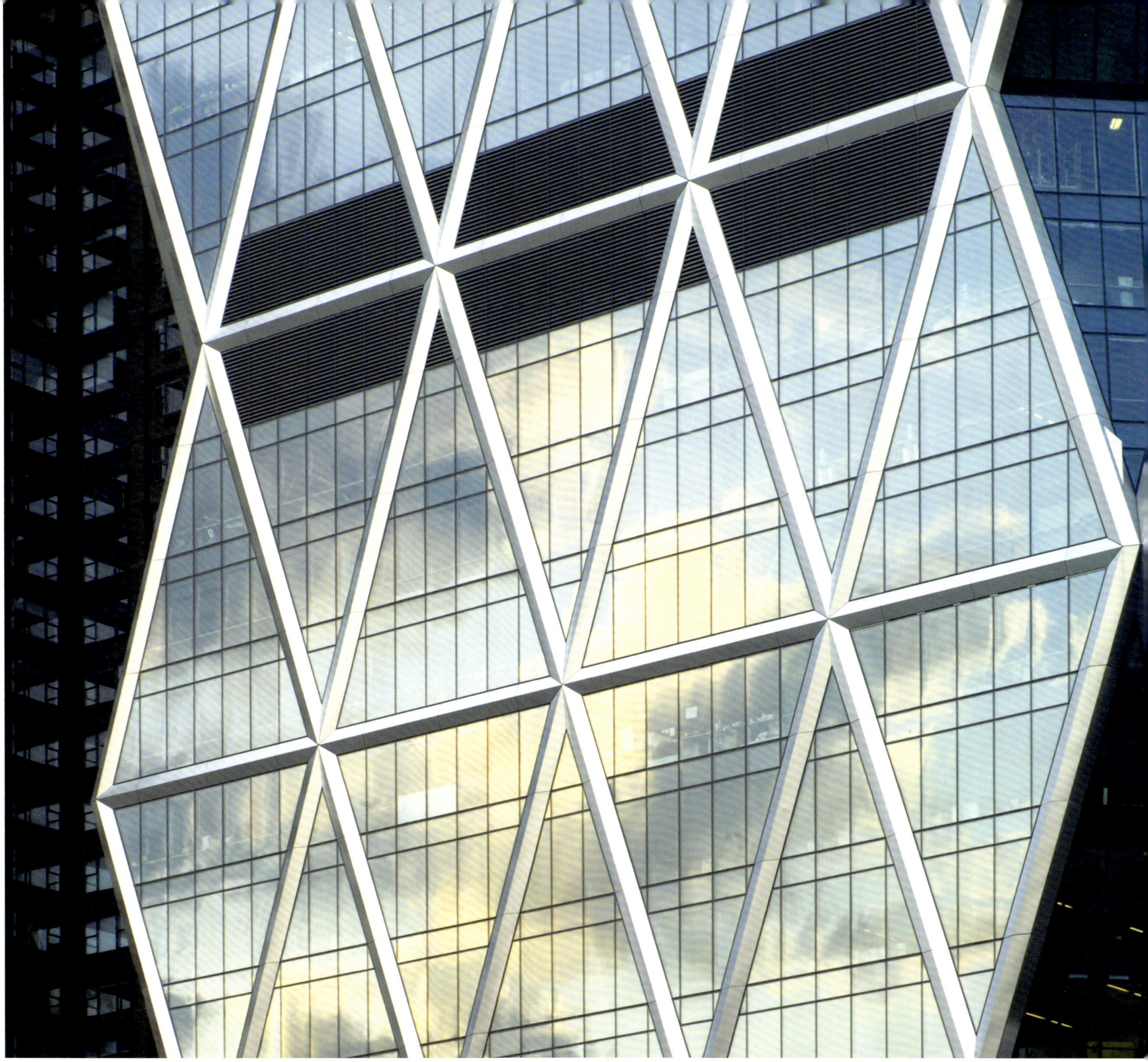
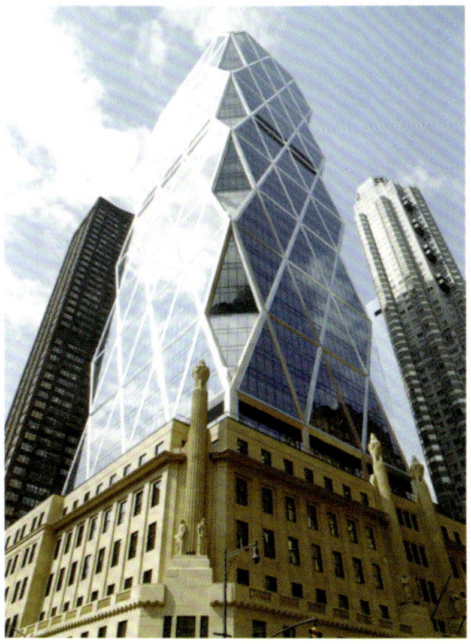
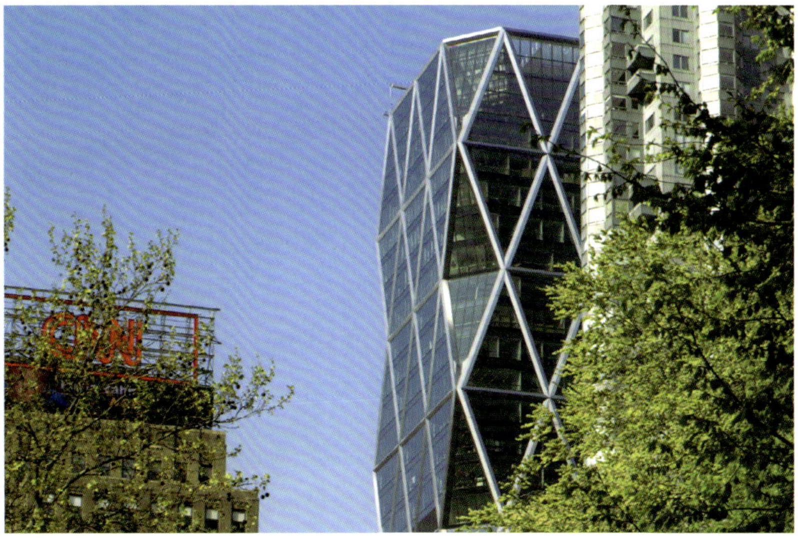
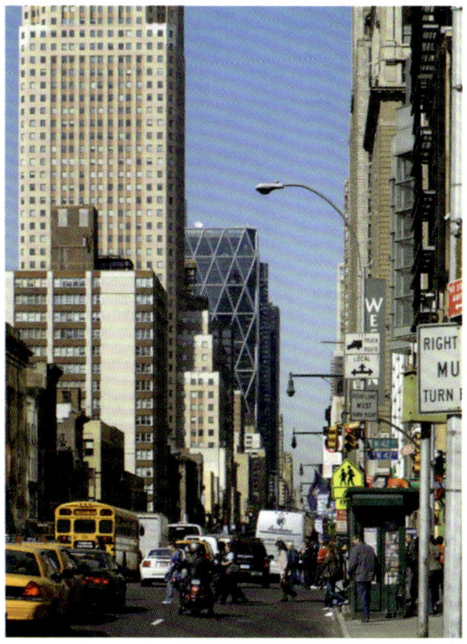

USA_NEW YORK CITY (NY) **505 FIFTH AVENUE**

ARCHITECTS: KPF – KOHN PEDERSEN FOX ASSOCIATES
COMPLETION: 2006_**GROSS FLOOR AREA:** 25,458 M²_**COMMON AREA:** LOBBY_**PHOTOS:** H. G. ESCH, WOODRUFF BROWN (458)

Unlike most office towers in the city, for which steel construction is the norm, 505 Fifth Avenue has a cast-in-place, reinforced-concrete structure that provides a level of building safety exceeding the city's building code requirements and allowing for a reduced number of columns and a cantilever above the podium. With a side-loaded core and concrete flat slab construction, the design accommodates an uninterrupted, highly transparent glass skin. The form of the building organizes its mass as a collection of pieces whose scale is related to the surrounding fabric. The entrance lobby was designed in collaboration with artist James Turrell, who turned the space into a three-dimensional light sculpture.

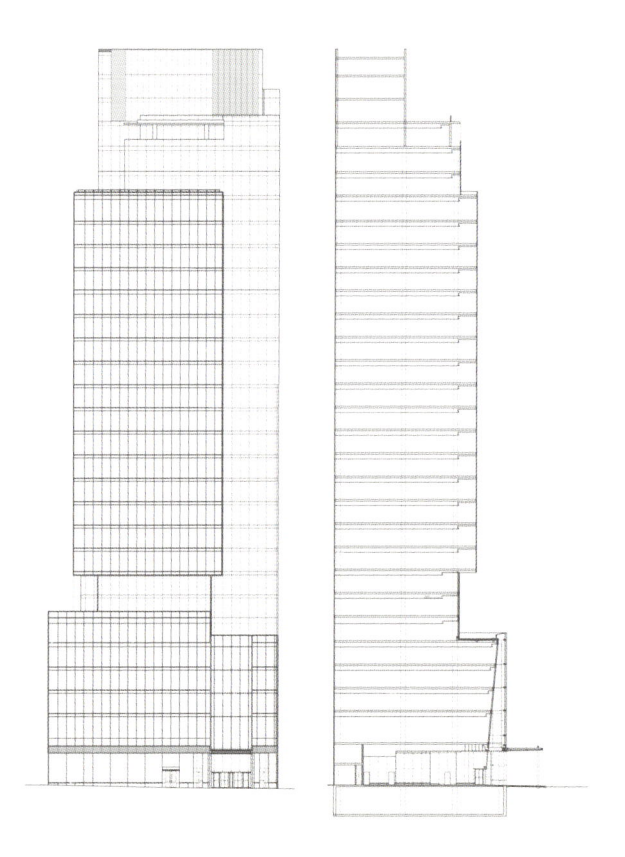

Im Gegensatz zu den meisten anderen Bürotürmen in der Stadt, die aus Stahlkonstruktionen bestehen, hat 505 Fifth Avenue eine Stahl-Ortbeton-Struktur, die bezüglich der Gebäudesicherheit die städtischen Anforderungen übersteigt, weniger Rundpfeiler benötigt und ein Auskragen des Baukörpers erlaubt. Mit einer seitlichen Lastableitung und Betonbodenplatten ermöglicht der Entwurf eine durchgehende, hochtransparente Glaswand. Die Gebäudeform gliedert das Gesamtvolumen als eine Sammlung von Teilen, die sich im Maßstab an die umliegenden Bauten anpassen. Der Eingangsbereich wurde in Zusammenarbeit mit dem Künstler James Turrell entworfen und so in eine dreidimensionale Skulptur verwandelt.

left: Section_View to the shop entrance_View from Fifth Avenue. right: Front elevation.
links: Schnitt_Blick zum Geschäftseingang_Blick von der Fifth Avenue. rechts: Vorderansicht.

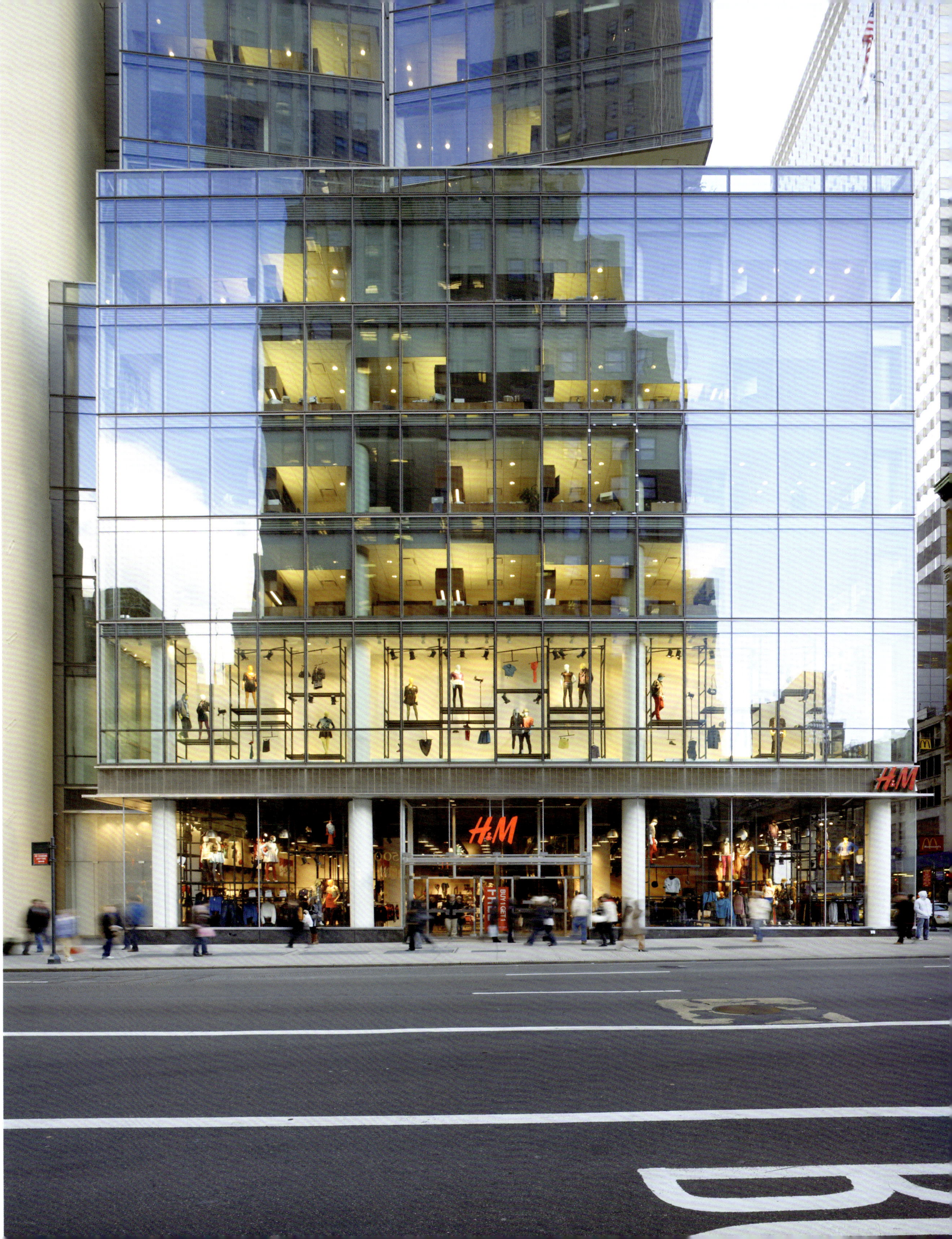
H&M
H&M

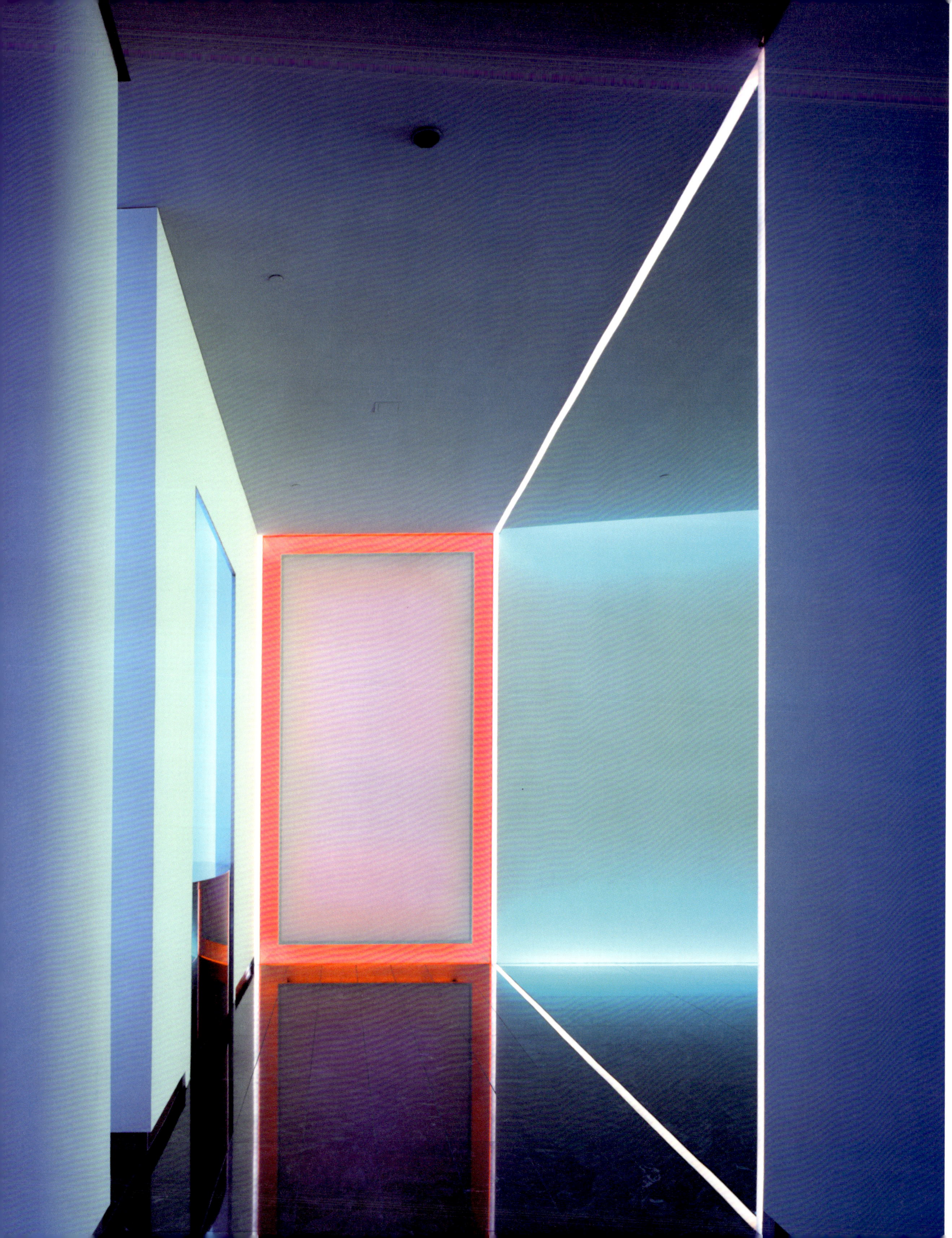

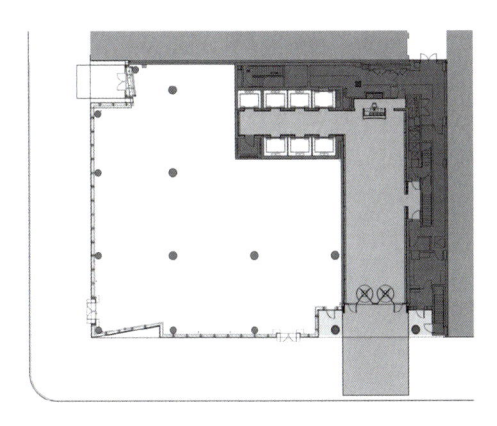

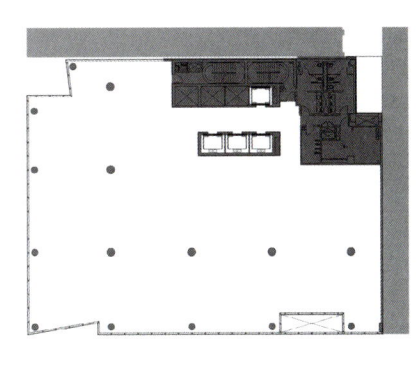

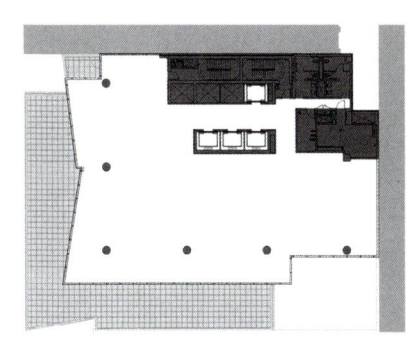

left: Lobby view. right: Floor plans_Worm's-eye view.
links: Ansicht Lobby. rechts: Grundrisse_Froschperspektive.

USA_NEW YORK CITY (NY) OFFICE MICHAEL NEUMANN ARCHITECTURE

ARCHITECTS: MICHAEL NEUMANN ARCHITECTURE, LLC
CONTRACTOR: TANGLEWOOD CONSTRUCTION
KITCHEN: DANNY DEMARCO_**LIGHTING SUPPLIER:** LIGHTING MANAGEMENT_**COMPLETION:** 2008
NUMBER OF WORKPLACES: 20_**GROSS FLOOR AREA:** 370 M²
COMMON AREA: LIBRARIES, CONFERENCE, KITCHEN
KIND OF WORKPLACES: OPEN-PLAN, TEAM, LOUNGE WORKSPACE
PHOTOS: AYLA CHRISTMA, NEW YORK CITY

The choice of the space itself was essential to the design goal of a warm, timeless, flexible, open workspace through an economic design and economic energy use. The loft offers natural lighting, a wooden floor, original brick walls, industrial windows, and exposed timber framing. The design exploits these features: wide openings and walkways provide access to daylight and ventilation, with studio desks banked against the long brick wall. "Pods" of white-stained poplar house senior staff offices and a conference room, with common areas between for team meetings. High efficiency products were used throughout: a heat pump system, metal halide/fluorescent lighting, re-used furnishings and sustainable materials like cork tile and poplar.

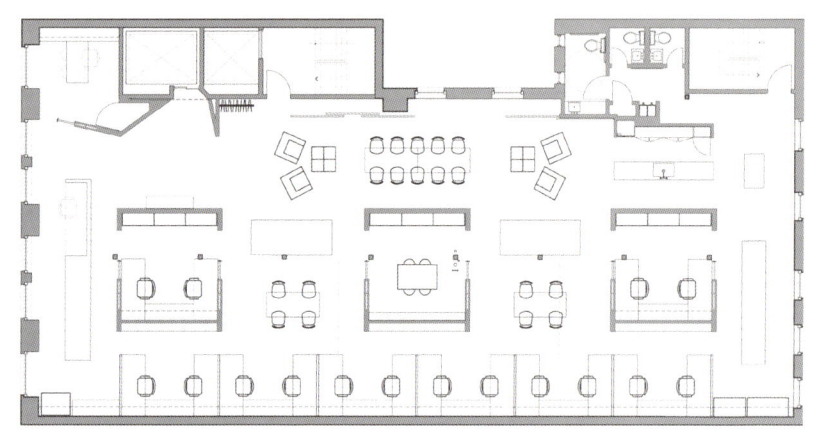

Die Ortswahl bedingte die Gestaltung des warmen, zeitlosen und offenen Arbeitsbereichs mit sparsamem Design und geringem Energieverbrauch. Das Loft verfügt über natürliches Licht, Holzböden, Sichtmauerwerk, Industriefenster und freiliegendes Fachwerk. Das Design greift diese Merkmale auf: weite Durchgänge mit Bürotischen entlang der Ziegelmauer schaffen Zugang zu Tageslicht und Belüftung. „Sockel" aus weiß gesprenkeltem Pappelholz schirmen Büros hochrangiger Mitarbeiter, Konferenzräume und dazwischen Gemeinschaftsbereiche für Team-Sitzungen ab. Es wurden durchgehend hocheffiziente Produkte benutzt: ein Wärmepumpensystem, metallene Halogenlichter/Leuchtstofflampen, wieder verwendete Einrichtung und umweltverträgliche Materialien wie Kork und Pappel.

left: Floor plan_Front work space and reception area_View between pods towards workstations.
right: View of workstations along brick wall.
links: Grundriss_Vordere Arbeitszone und Empfangsbereich. rechts: Blick auf die Arbeitsplätze entlang der Backsteinmauer.

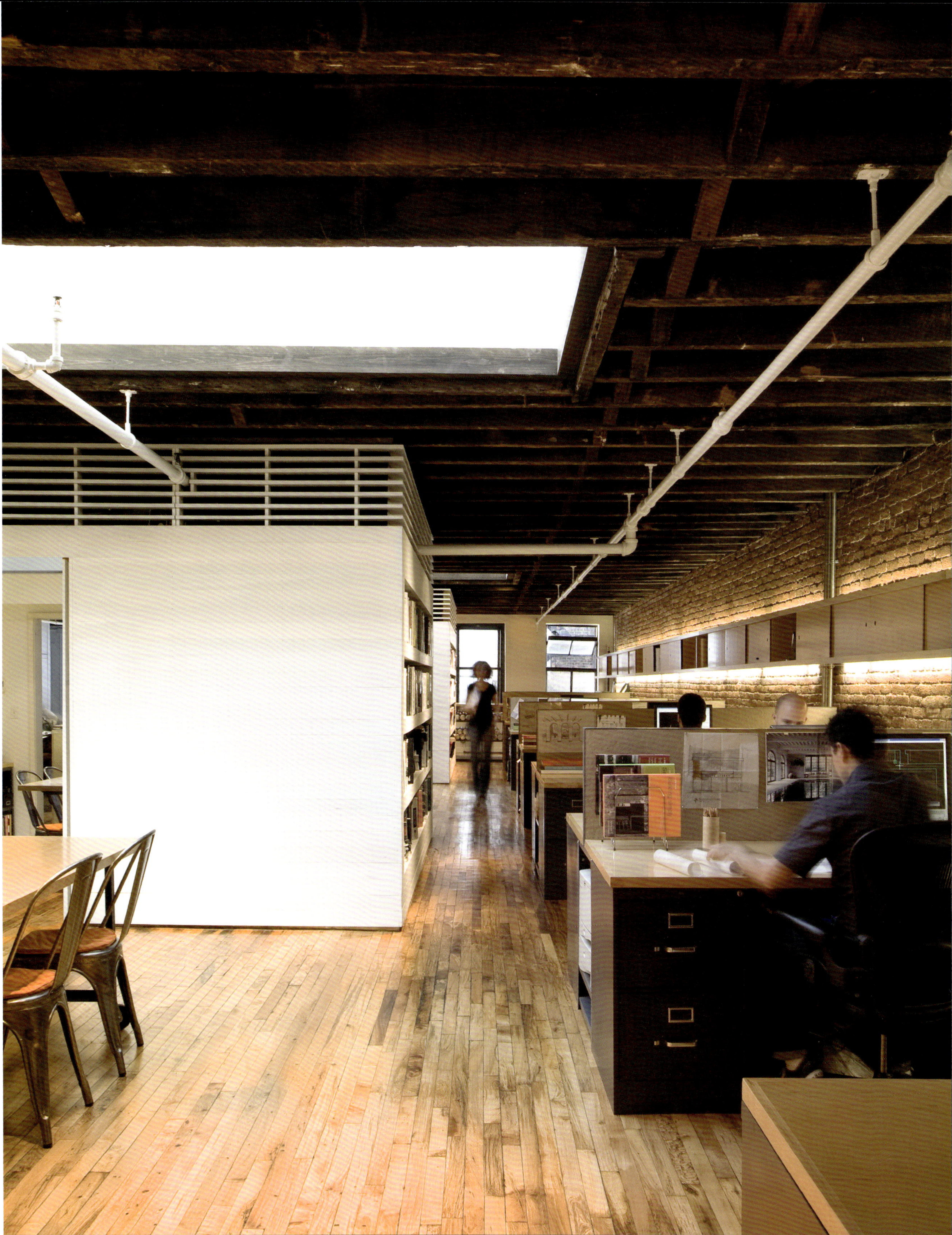

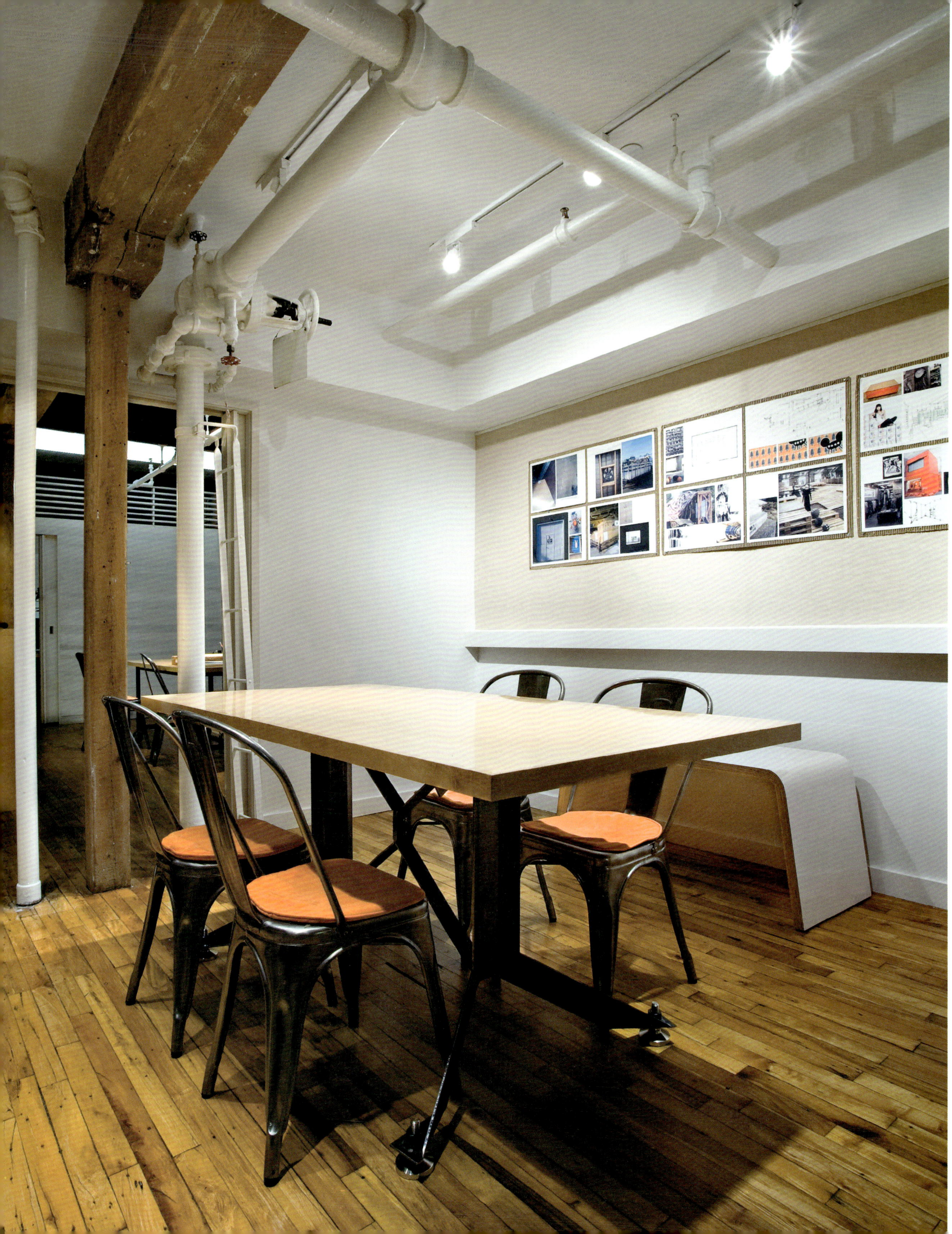

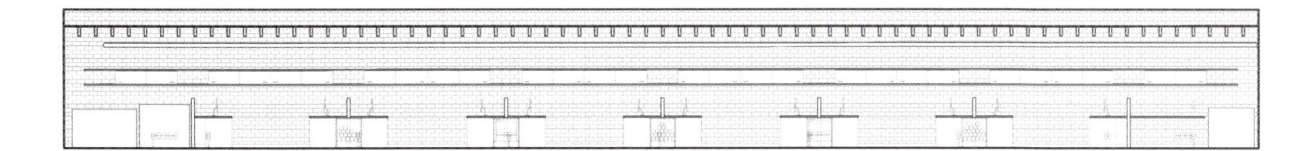

left: Conference room. right: Interior elevation_Washroom detail_View from entry area_Kitchen.
links: Konferenzraum. rechts: Innenansicht_Waschraum, Detail_Blick vom Eingangsbereich_Küche.

USA_NEW YORK CITY (NY) THE NEW YORK TIMES BUILDING

ARCHITECTS: RENZO PIANO BUILDING WORKSHOP WITH FOX & FOWLE ARCHITECTS_**COMPLETION:** 2007 **GROSS FLOOR AREA:** 1.600 000 M²_**COMMON AREA:** GROUND FLOOR GARDEN, ROOF GARDEN CONFERENCE FACILITY CAPABILITY, AUDITORIUM WITH GALLERY AND PREFUNCTION SPACE, RENOVATED ADJACENT SUBWAY ENTRANCE_**PHOTOS:** NIC LEHOUX, DROUIN SERGE (464 B. M.), RENZO PIANO BUILDING WORKSHOP (464 B. L.)

The 52-story glass and steel structure represents the values of the New York Times Company and its culture of transparency. The use of double skin curtain walls with 186,000 ceramic rods that act as a sunscreen deflecting the heat, coupled with an inner wall of floor to ceiling milky-white glass allows the building to adapt to the colors of the atmosphere. Bluish after a shower, shimmering red after a sunset. In line with the spirit of the project, the lobby of the building is very open, transparent and permeable. At ground level, a large internal garden is accessible and visible from the street, while stairs have been located on the facades. These will foster communication between departments whose movement will be visible from the outside.

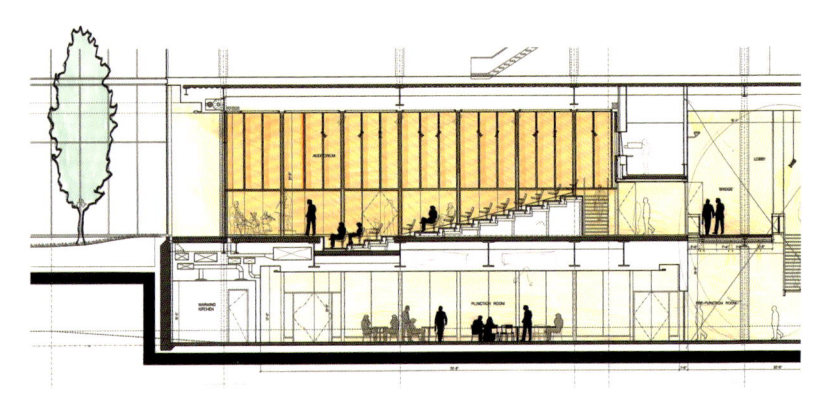

Das 52-geschossige Glas- und Stahlgebäude versinnbildlicht die Werte der New York Times Company und ihre Kultur der Transparenz. Der Einsatz einer doppelten Vorhangfassade mit 186.000 Keramikstäben, die als Sonneschutz fungieren und Hitze ableiten, sowie eine raumhohe Innenwand aus reinweißen Glas ermöglichen es dem Bau, alle Farben der Atmosphäre anzunehmen: nach einem Regen bläulich und schillernd, rot beim Sonnenuntergang. Im Geiste des Projektes ist die Lobby ganz offen, transparent und durchlässig. Ein großer innen liegender Garten im Innenhof ist von der Straße aus sichtbar und zugänglich, die Treppen in den Fassaden dienen nicht nur der abteilungsübergreifenden Begegnung, sondern machen die Bewegung im Inneren auch außen sichtbar.

left: Section_Model_Façade_View from an upper floor. right: Interior view_Entrance area with reception and ground floor garden.
links: Schnitt_Model_Fassade_Blick von einem Obergeschoss. rechts: Innenansicht_Eingangsbereich mit Empfang und Garten.

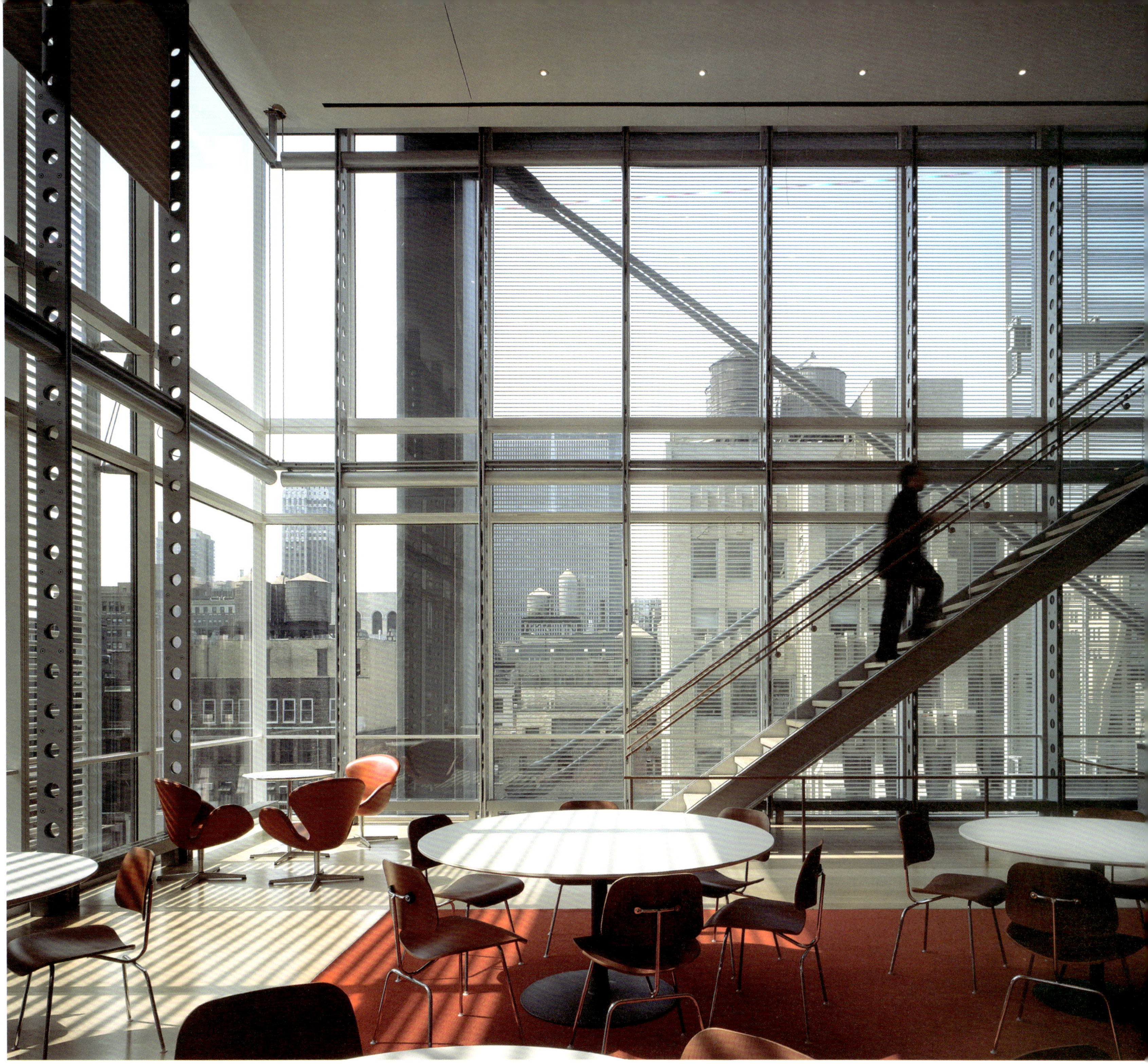

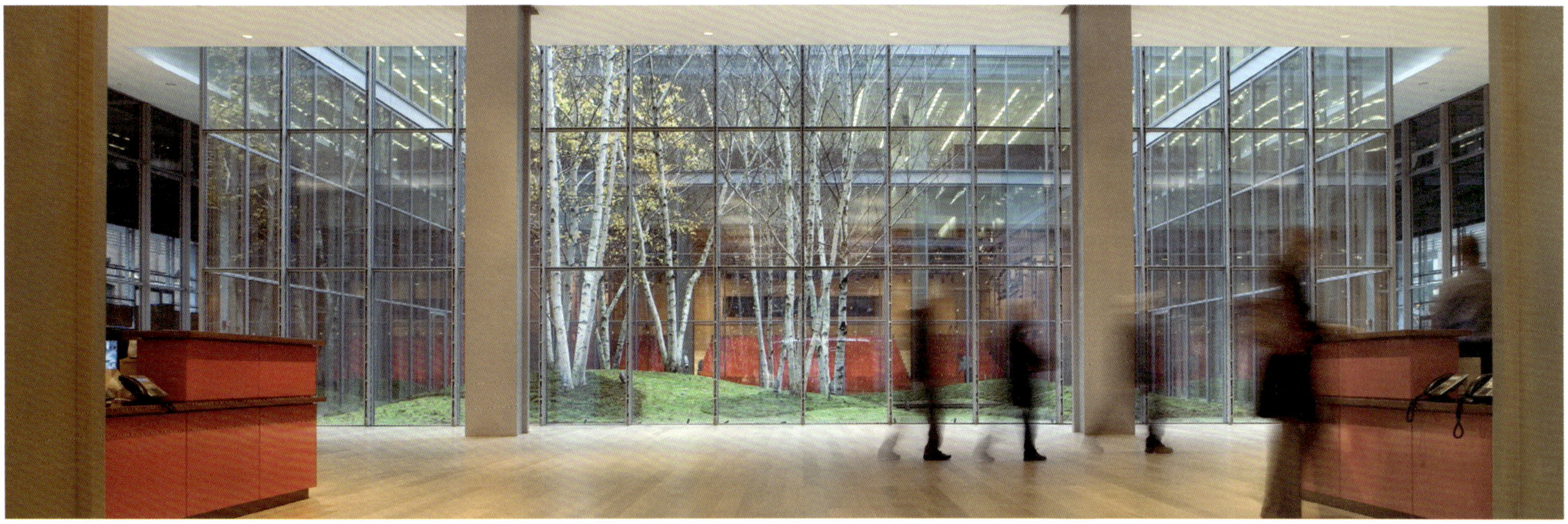

USA_NEW YORK CITY (NY) GSC OFFICES

ARCHITECTS: SKIDMORE, OWINGS & MERRILL LLP
DIGITAL MEDIA ARTIST: CORY ARCANGEL
COMPLETION: 2007_**NUMBER OF WORKPLACES:** 74
GROSS FLOOR AREA: 2,985 M²_**COMMON AREA:**
PANTRY WITH SEATING, INFORMAL CONFERENCE ROOM, TRADING DESKS, TRADING SUPPORT WORKSTATIONS, GENERAL SUPPORT WORKSTATIONS, LOUNGE
KIND OF WORKPLACES: CELLULAR, TEAM, OPEN-PLAN_**PHOTOS:** SOM / JIMMY COHRSSEN

This financial office adopted a unique approach to the corporate workplace by combining a technologically perfected work environment with the finishing of an upscale hotel and tying the design together with a large-scale work of contemporary art. The design takes full advantage of its location on two floors of an L-shaped glass office building facing Central Park. Cory Arcangel photographed Central Park, digitally manipulated the images to create a pixilated texture, and installed them in a sophisticated glass wall illuminated from behind. Caught between the digital glow of this electronic artwork and the filtered sunlight of the glass façade, the open office features custom workstations fabricated out of a natural wood material.

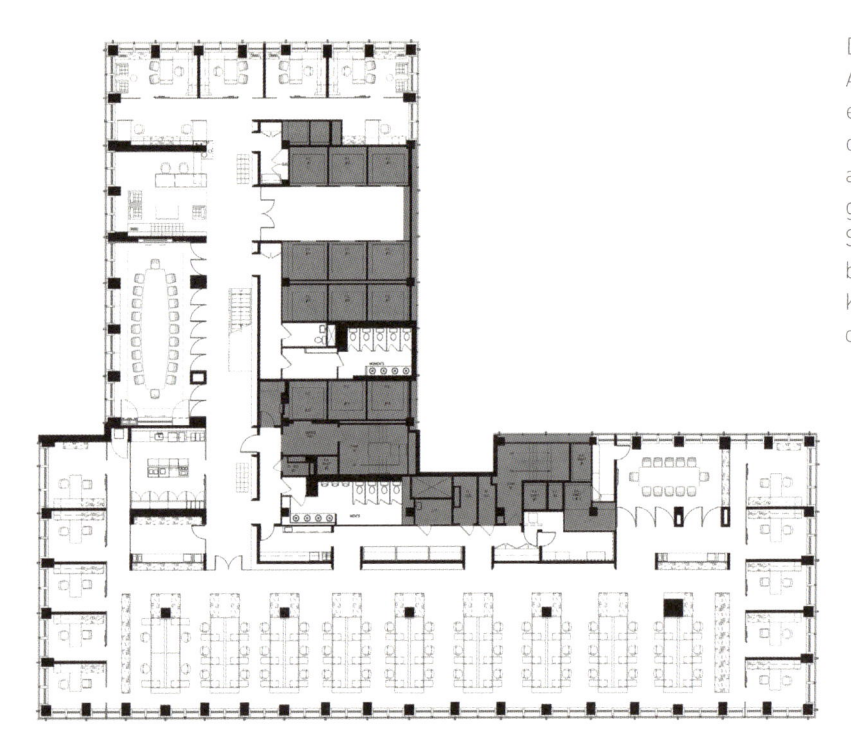

Die Kombination einer technologisch perfekten Arbeitsumgebung mit der Ausführung eines vornehmen Hotels und die Verknüpfung des Designs mit einem großflächigen Werk zeitgenössischer Kunst bringt frischen Wind in diese Finanzfirma. Das Design nutzt die Lage gegenüber des Central Parks auf zwei Ebenen als Glasbürogebäude in L-Form aus. Cory Arcangel fotografierte den Central Park, bearbeitete die Bilder digital, um eine verpixelte Struktur zu erstellen, und installierte sie auf einer eleganten, von hinten beleuchteten Glaswand. Zwischen dem digitalen Schein dieses elektronischen Kunstwerks und dem gefilterten Sonnenlicht der Glasfassade bietet das offene Büro aus natürlichem Holz maßgefertigte Arbeitsbereiche.

left: 26th floor plan_Open-plan office_Cellular office. right: Detail.
links: Grundriss, 26. Obergeschoss_Großraumbüro_Einzelbüro. rechts: Detail.

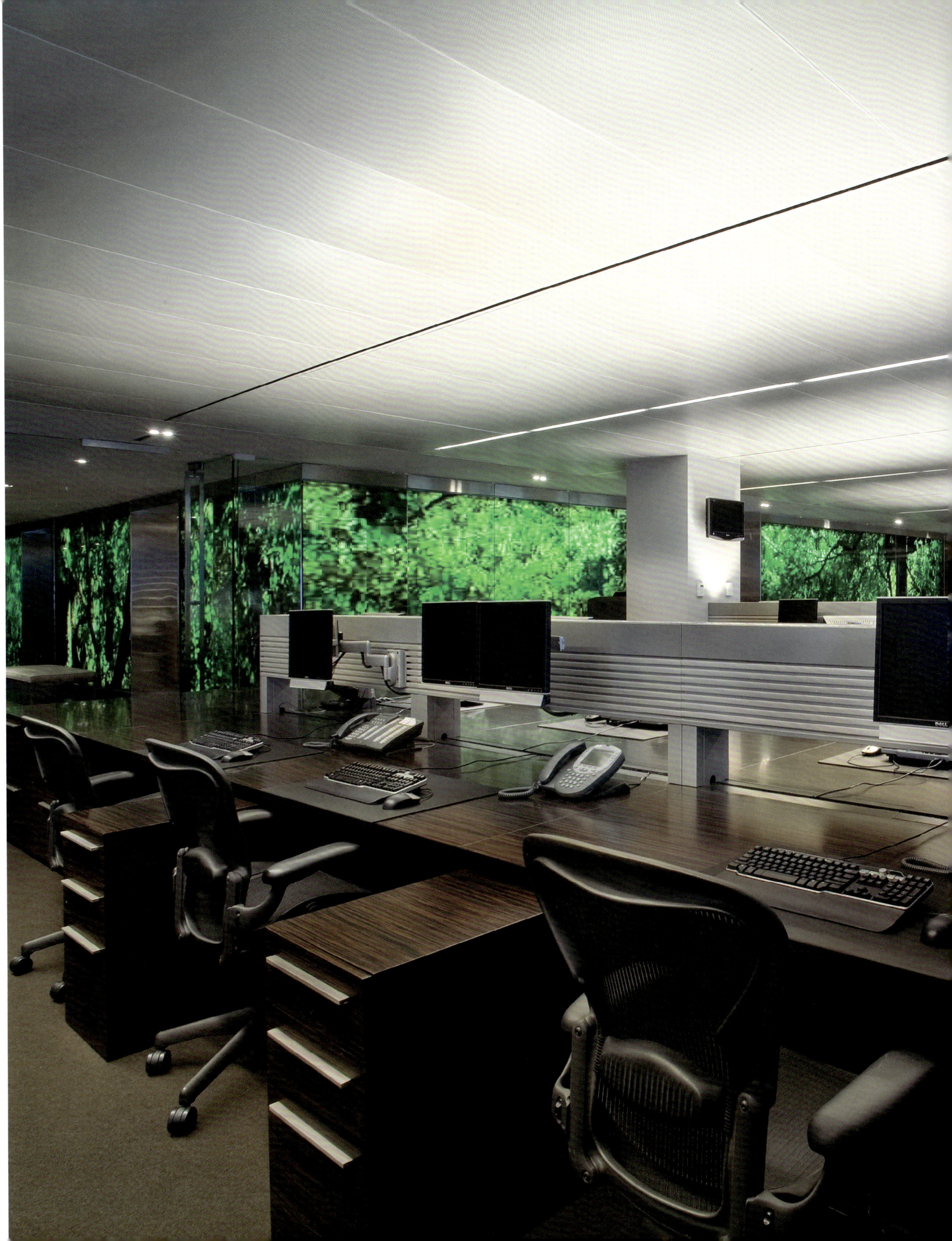

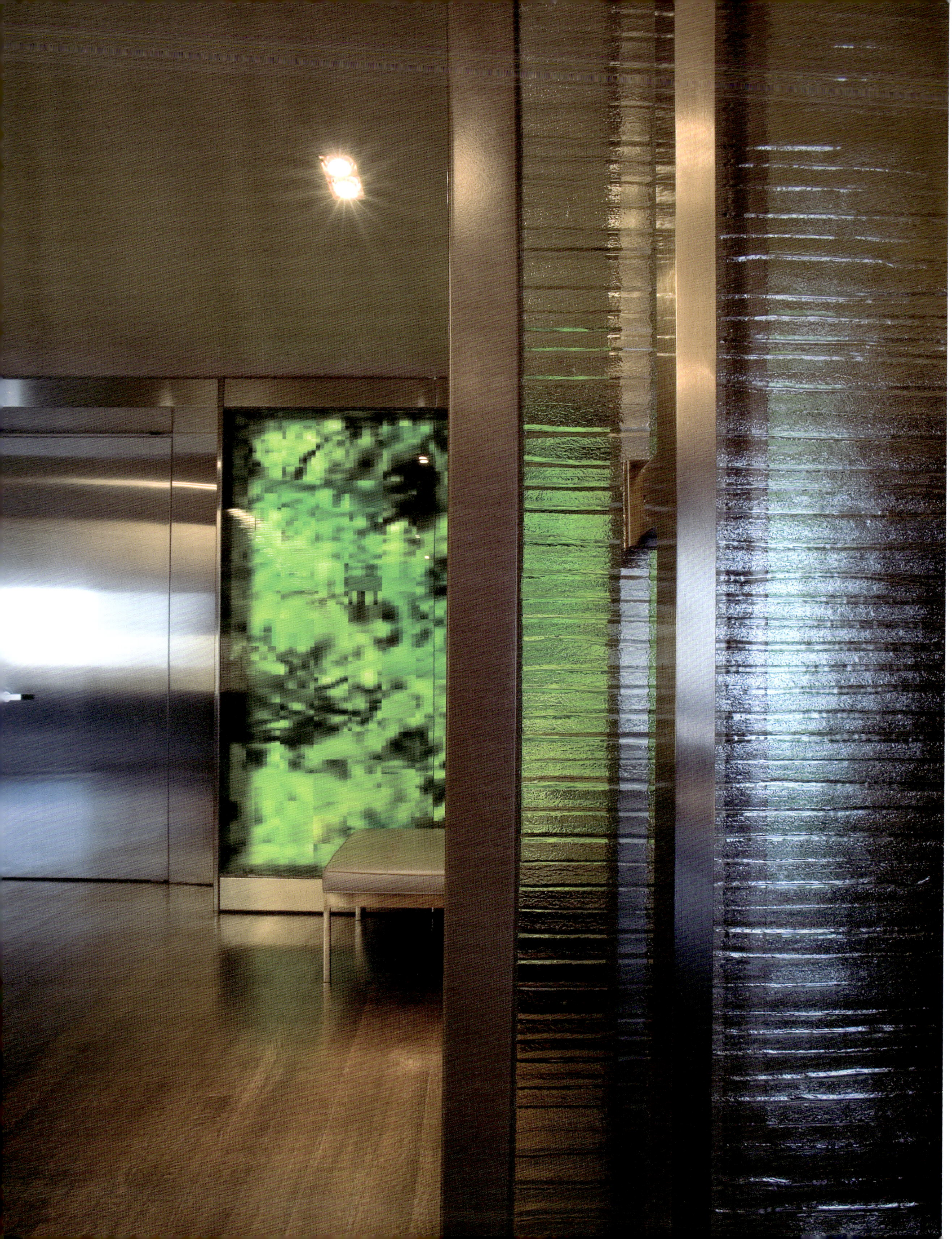

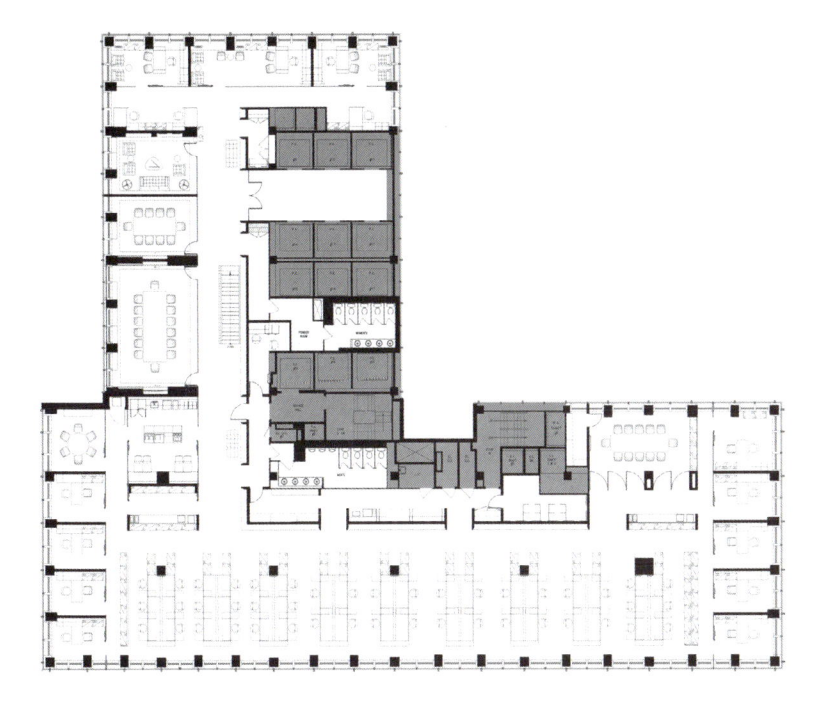

left: Detail wall structure. right: 27th floor plan_Corridor_Wrapping designed by Cory Arcangel_Reception.
links: Detail Wandstruktur. rechts: Grundriss, 27. Obergeschoss_Flur_Wandgestaltung von Cory Arcangel_Empfang.

USA_PALO ALTO (CA) FACEBOOK HEADQUARTERS

ARCHITECTS: STUDIO O+A_**COMPLETION:** 2009
NUMBER OF WORKPLACES: 800_**GROSS FLOOR AREA:** 13,935 M²
COMMON AREA: CAFETERIA, CONFERENCE ROOM, RELAXING ZONES_**KIND OF WORKPLACES:** OPEN-PLAN, TEAM, CUBICAL, DESKSHARING, LOUNGE WORKSPACE_**PHOTOS:** CÉSAR RUBIO

The new Facebook headquarters facilitates interaction and connection, reflecting the company's mission as a social networking website provider. The former laboratory facility of a high-tech manufacturer brings together more than 700 employees originally scattered throughout ten locations in and around Palo Alto. The design goal for the new facility was to maintain the history and raw aesthetic of the building and create a fun dynamic setting appropriate for the company's youthful staff. Many walls and spaces are left unfinished and employees are encouraged to write on the walls, add artwork, and move furniture as needed, allowing the building to evolve continuously.

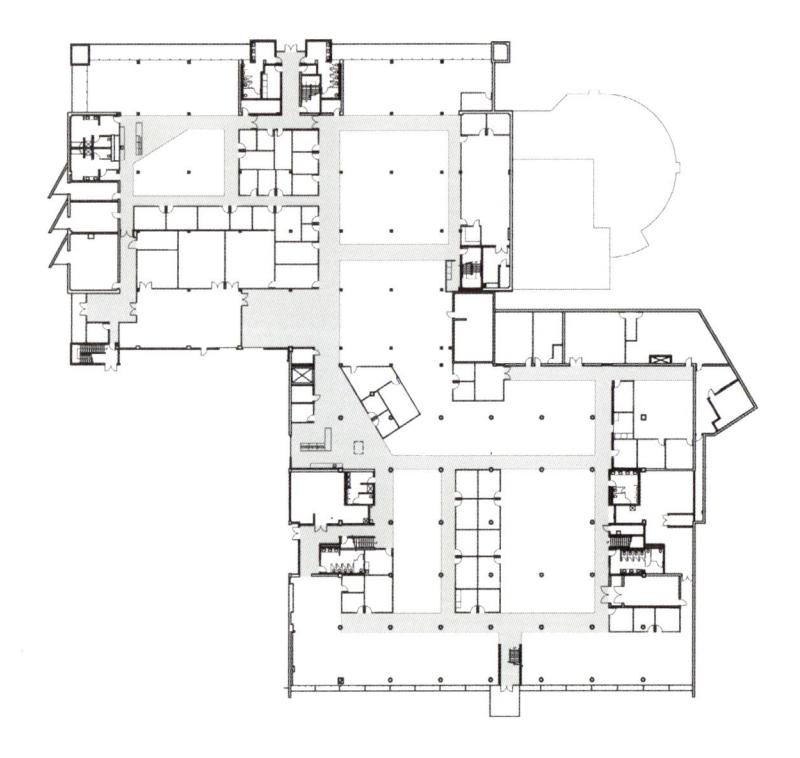

Der neue Hauptsitz von Facebook fördert – entsprechend der Aufgabe eine Anbieters eines sozialen Netzwerkes – Interaktion und Kommunikation. Das ehemalige Laborgebäude eines High-Tech Herstellers versammelt mehr als 700 Mitarbeiter, die zuvor auf zehn Arbeitsstellen in und um Palo Alto verteilt waren. Grundgedanke der Neugestaltung war, die Geschichte des Baukörpers und seine derbe Ästhetik zu erhalten, jedoch mit verspielten und dynamischen Elementen zu einem der jugendlichen Mitarbeiterstruktur entsprechenden Umfeld aufzuwerten. Zahlreiche Wände und Räume blieben unvollendet, um die Mitarbeiter zu ermutigen auf die Mauern zu kritzeln, Kunstwerke hinzuzufügen und die Möbel bedarfsgerecht zu verschieben, so dass der Bau sich stetig weiterentwickelt.

left: Ground floor plan_Second floor open office_Open office with lounge area. right: Façade.
links: Grundriss Erdgeschoss_Großraumbüro zweites Obergeschoss_Großraumbüro mit Lounge-Bereich. rechts: Fassade.

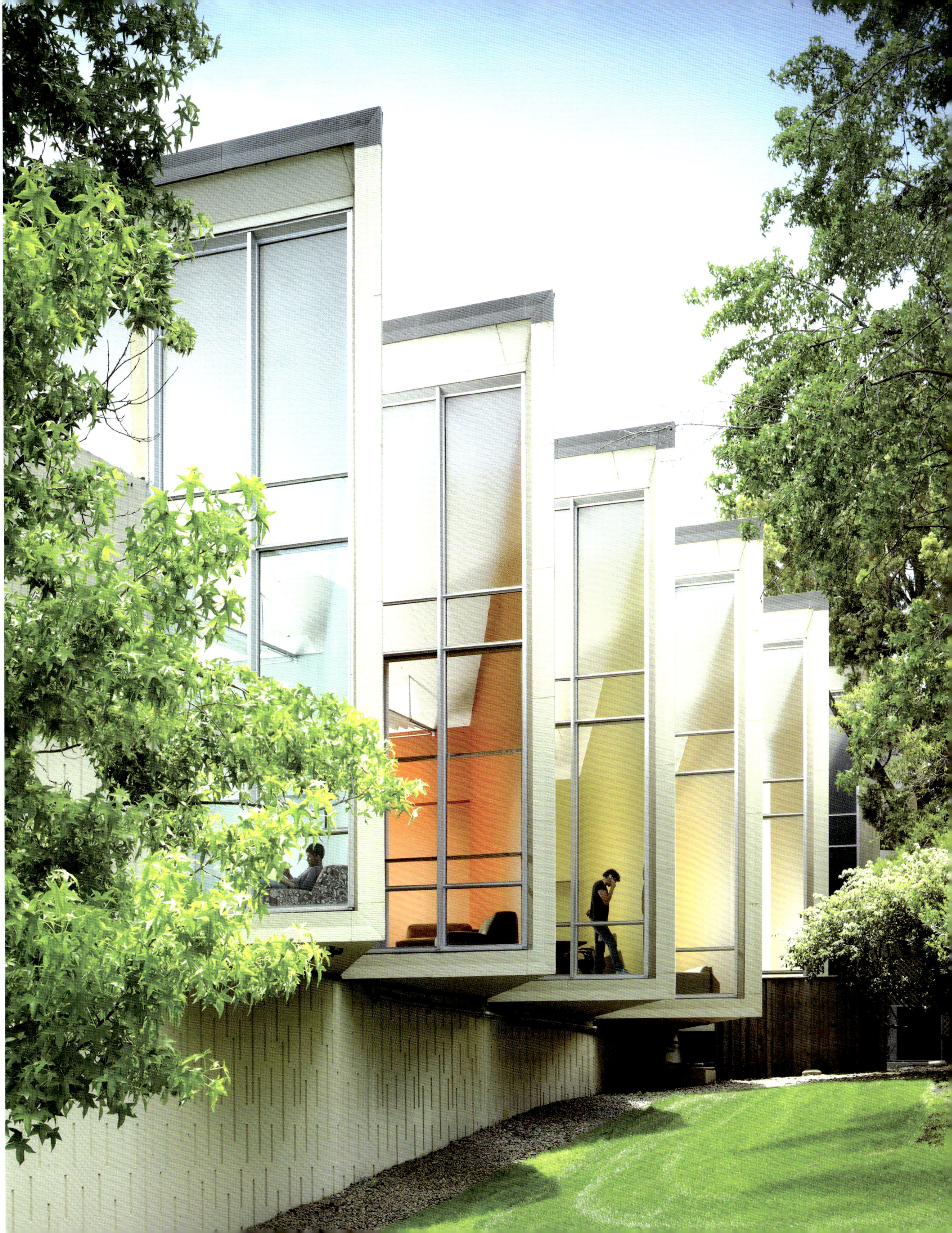

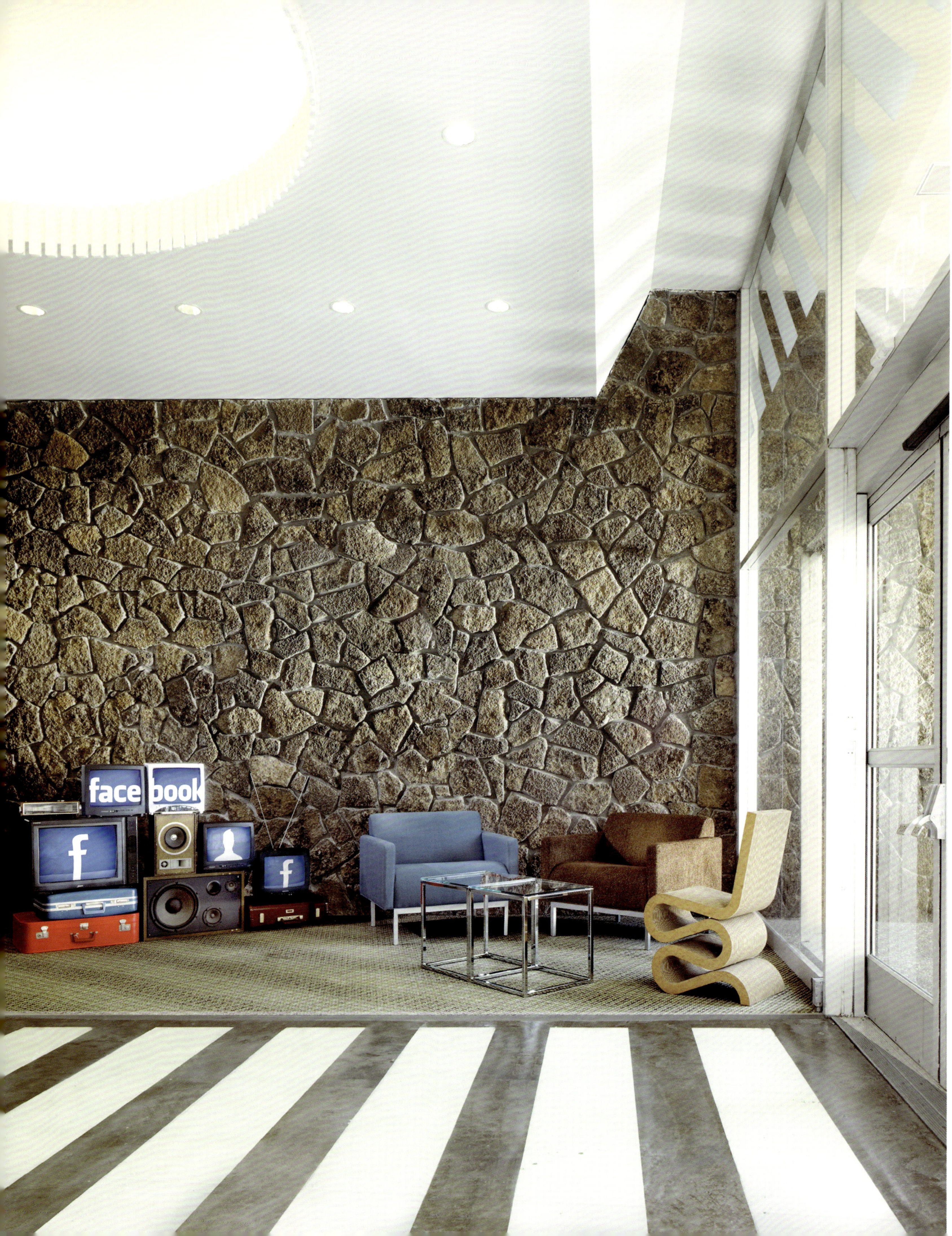
face book

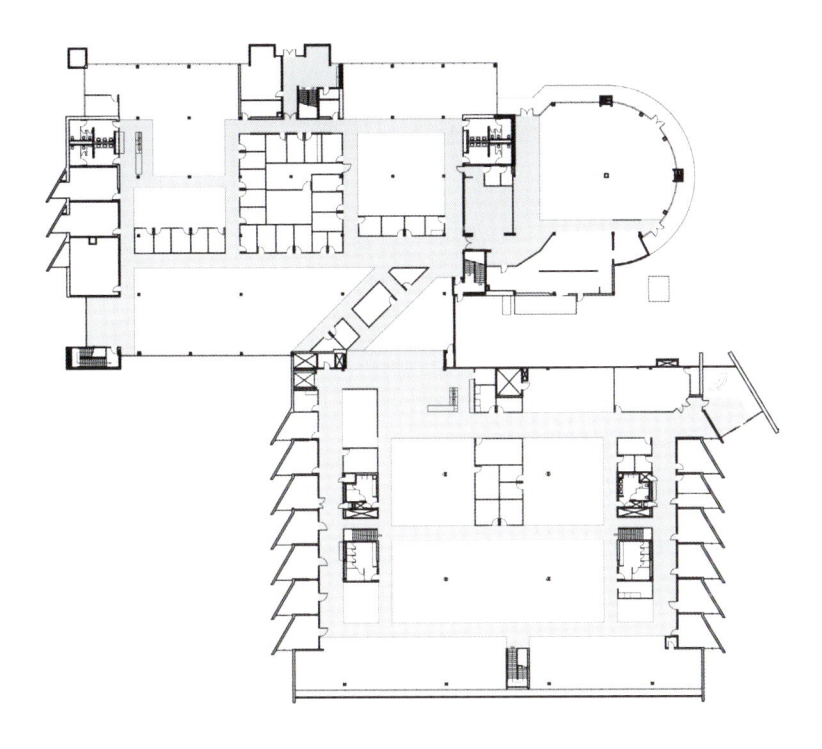

left: Lobby. right: First floor plan_Lobby_Microkitchen with view to crane table 1st floor_Loading dock / lounge area 1st floor.
links: Lobby. rechts: Grundriss 1. Obergeschoss_Lobby_Küche mit Blick auf den Kran-Tisch im 1. Obergeschoss_Lounge-Bereich im 1. Obergeschoss.

USA_SANTA MONICA (CA) HYDRAULX

ARCHITECTS: SHUBIN + DONALDSON ARCHITECTS
OTHER CREATIVES: STUDIO 440_**COMPLETION:** 2007
NUMBER OF WORKPLACES: 80_**GROSS FLOOR AREA:** 1393.5 M²
COMMON AREA: LIVING ROOM, CINEMA, KITCHEN
KIND OF WORKPLACES: DESKSHARING, LOUNGE WORKSPACE
PHOTOS: TOM BONNER, SANTA MONICA, CA

Hydraulx is a special-effects provider for the entertainment industry. The main level contains reception, a fish-bowl conference room, artists' work rooms, editing bays, private offices, and the main kitchen. The lower level has custom workstations and a double-height library. The mezzanine is home to the client lounge and the Machine Room – the brain of operations, which houses powerful computers that serve multiple sophisticated workstations. On the upper level are screening rooms, the owners' offices, kitchen, and a terrace. The architecture in many ways expresses the operation of the machine. The material truth of exposed structures and raw industrial materials defines the palette employed to create the workspace.

Hydraulx entwickelt Spezialeffekte für die Unterhaltungsindustrie. Das Hauptgeschoss ihres Büros umfasst die Rezeption, einen gläsernen Konferenzsaal, Künstlerräume, Arbeitsnischen, Privatbüros und die Hauptküche. Das untere Geschoss bietet individuelle Arbeitsplätze und eine zweigeschossige Bibliothek. Im Zwischengeschoss finden sich Kundenlounge und der Maschinenraum, die Zentrale von Hydraulx mit starken Computern, die zahlreichen, hoch spezialisierten Workstations dienen. Im Obergeschoss schließlich liegen Vorführräume, das Büro des Eigentümers, Küche und Terrasse. Die Architektur reflektiert die Tätigkeit in verschiedenster Weise. Die sichtbare Baustruktur und die unbehandelten, industriellen Materialien charakterisieren den Ausbau.

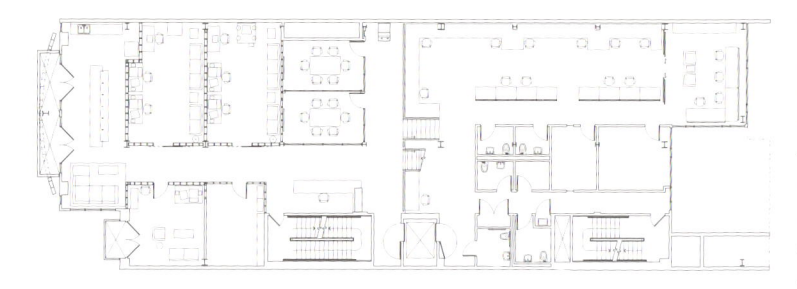

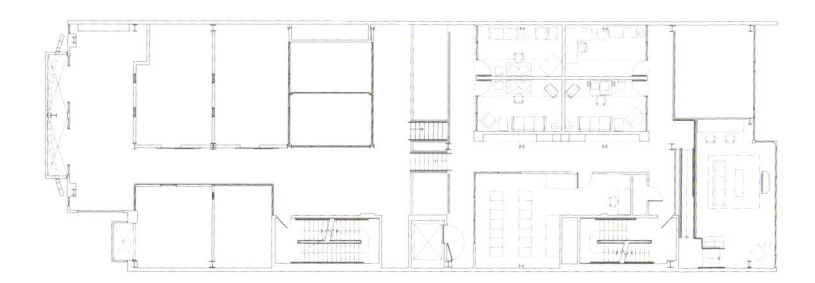

left: Floor plans_Reception, conference room_Living room. right: Work area_Workplaces_Kitchen.
links: Grundrisse_Empfang, Konferenzraum_Wohnzimmer. rechts: Arbeitsbereich_Arbeitsplätze_Küche.

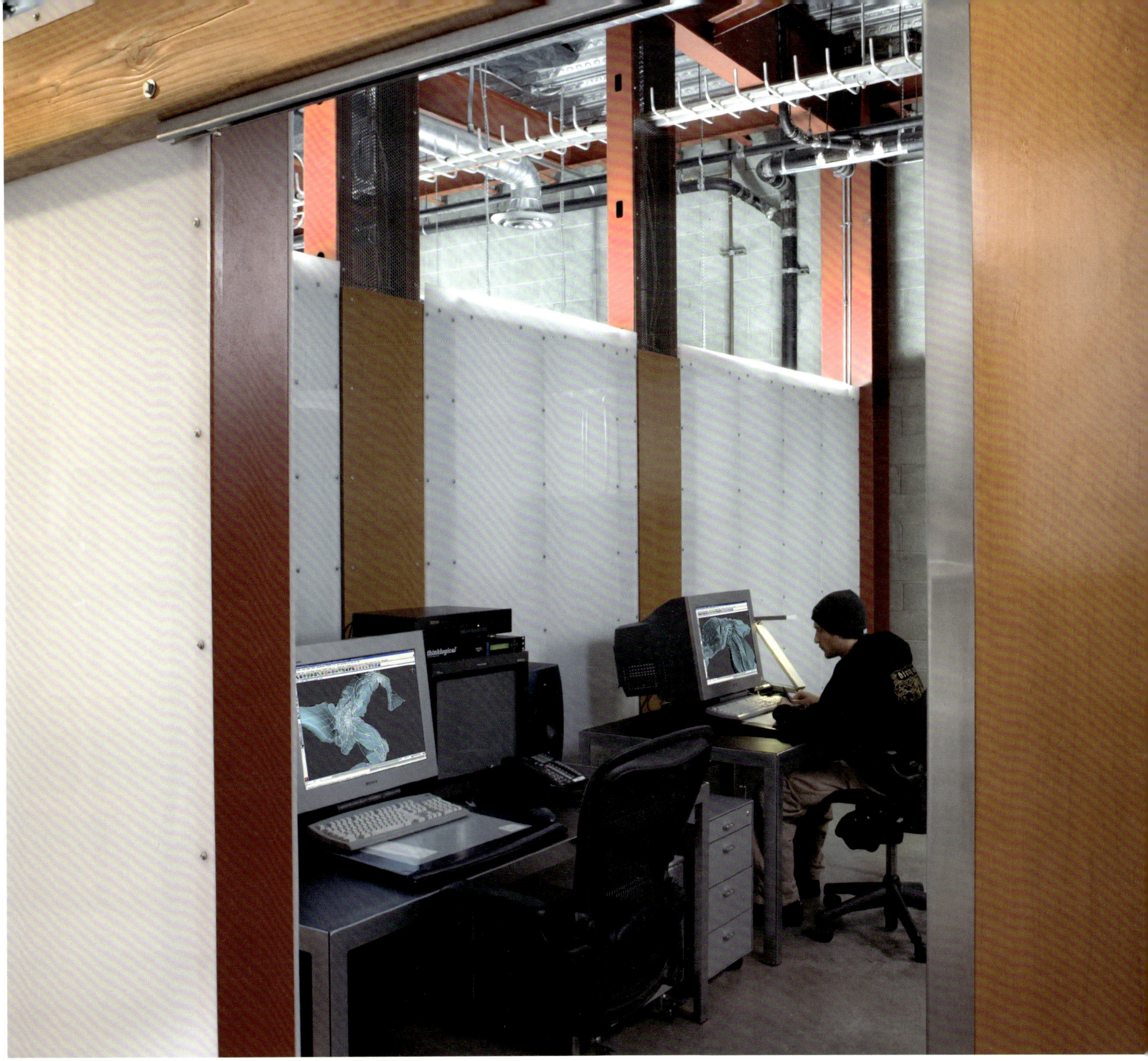
thinklogical

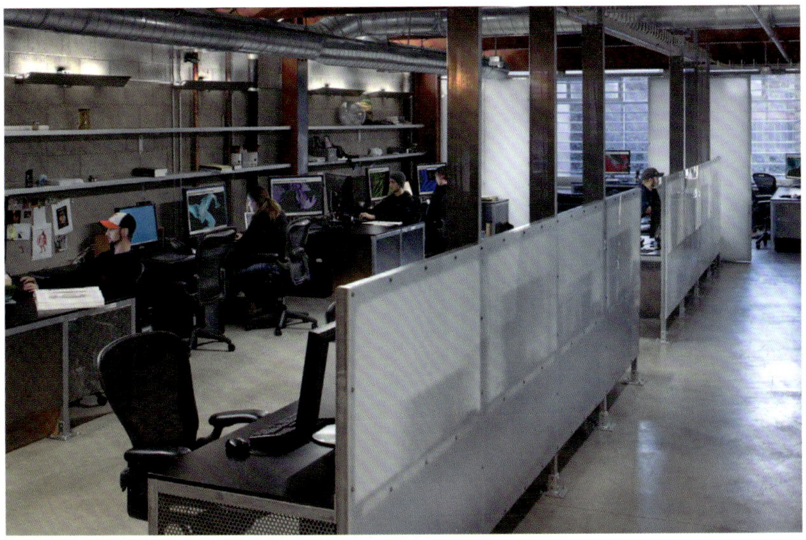

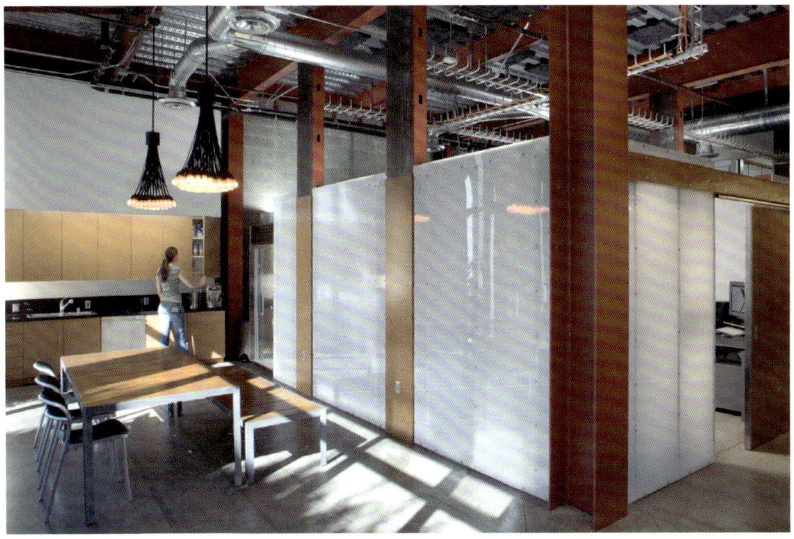

USA_SANTA MONICA (CA) MOVING PICTURE COMPANY

ARCHITECTS: PATRICK TIGHE ARCHITECTURE
COMPLETION: 2009_**NUMBER OF WORKPLACES:** 40
GROSS FLOOR AREA: 929 M²_**KIND OF WORKPLACES:** OPEN-PLAN, TEAM, POST PRODUCTION FACILITY
PHOTOS: ART GRAY

The project explores the notion of light in relation to color in reference to the company's work in the area of color manipulation in film. The developed forms and patterns were produced using studies of light, analyzing and modeling it three-dimensionally. Animation frames were chosen and layered to organize spatial qualities and create movement throughout the office environment. An organic, sinuous spine weaves its way through the suite and an attached soffit grows from the serpentine walls. Light portals pierce the organic forms and are equipped with programmable LED lighting. Patterns derived from the animated studies are emblazoned onto the laser cut walls and circumscribe the interior.

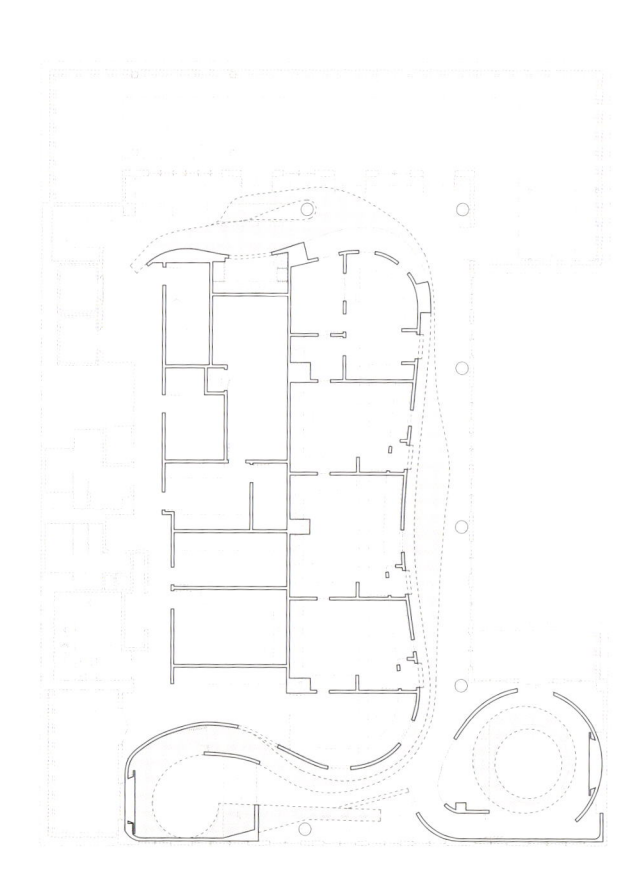

Das Projekt spielt – entsprechend der Arbeit der Firma, die Farbeinstellungen für die Filmindustrie vornimmt – mit der Verbindung von Licht und Farbe. Die hier genutzten Formen und Muster wurden mithilfe dreidimensional analysierender und modellierender Lichtstudien entwicklet. Bildschirminhalte der Animationen wurden ausgewählt und so geschichtet, dass in der Büroumgebung räumliche Qualitäten und Bewegung entstehen. Eine organische, gewundene Längswand schlängelt sich durch den Raum, bis die sich windenden Wände in die Decke übergehen. Helle Durchgänge mit programmierbaren LED-Lichtern durchbrechen die organischen Formen. Muster aus Trickfilmstudien schmücken die laser-geschnittenen Wände und grenzen das Innere ab.

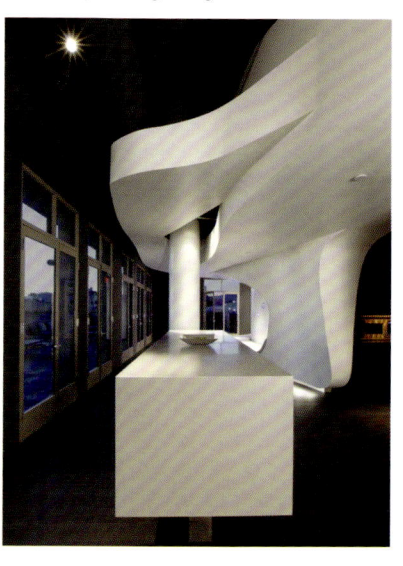

left: Ground floor plan_Stairway_Reception desk. right: Meeting lounge.
links: Grundriss_Treppenhaus_Empfangsbereich. rechts: Besprechungslounge.

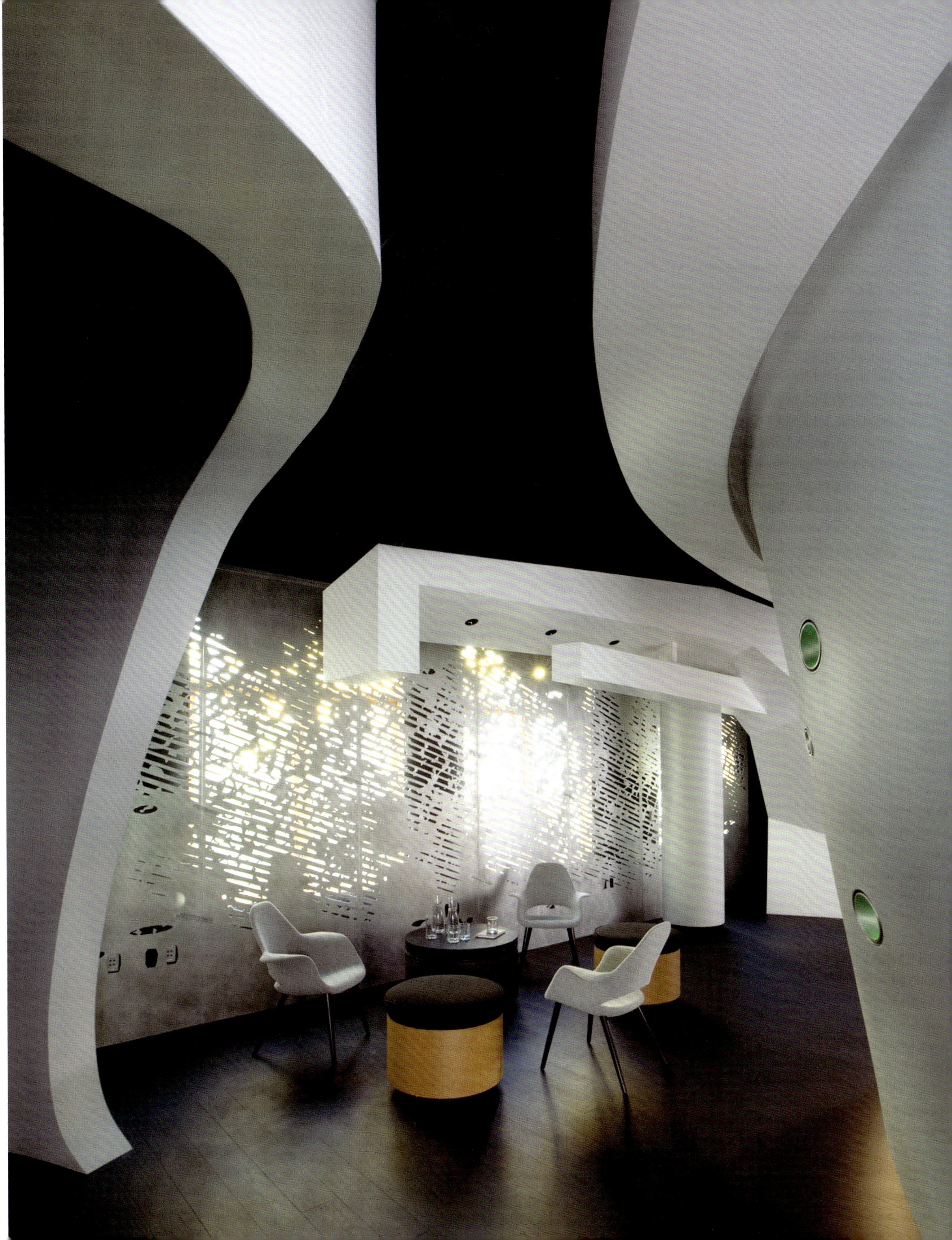

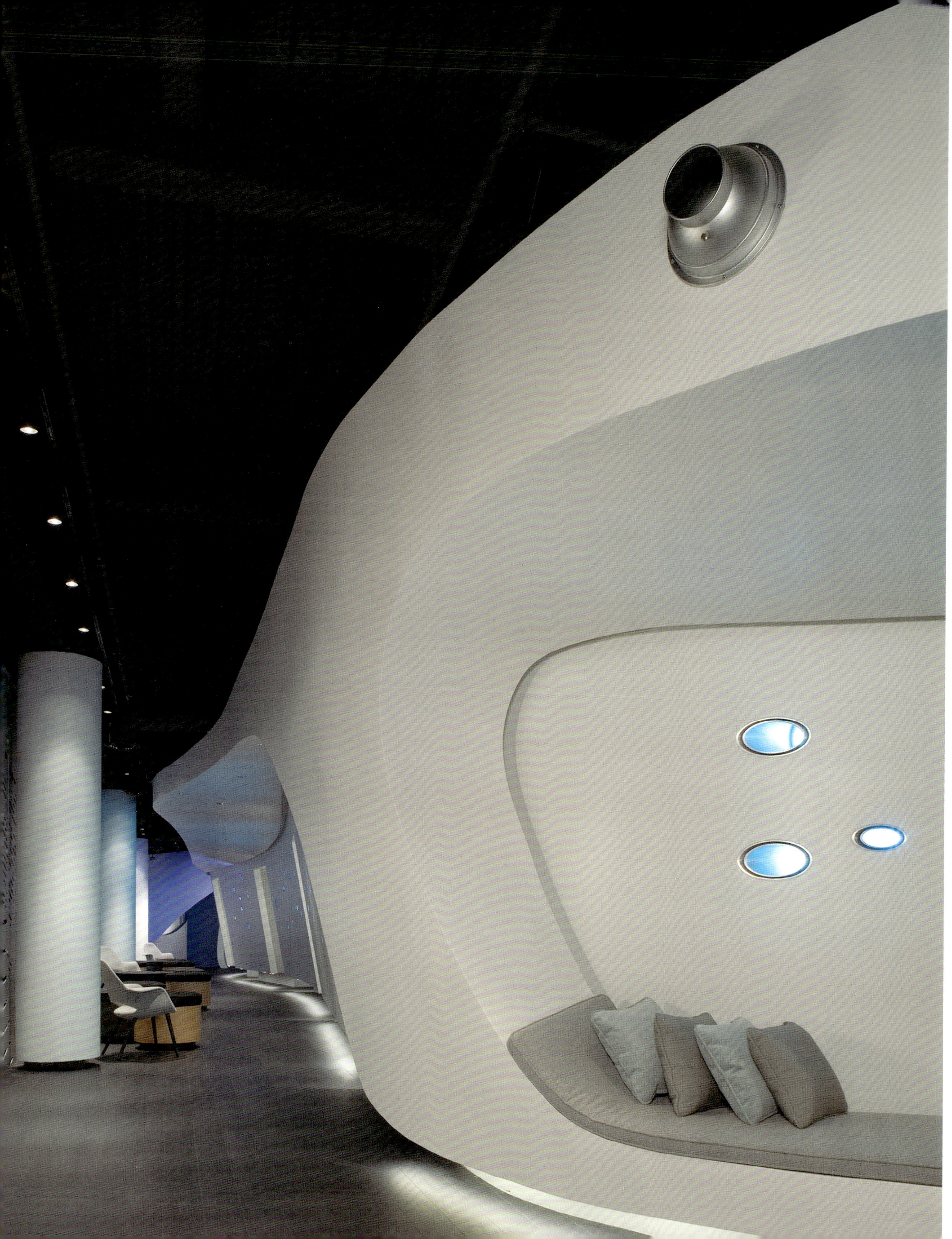

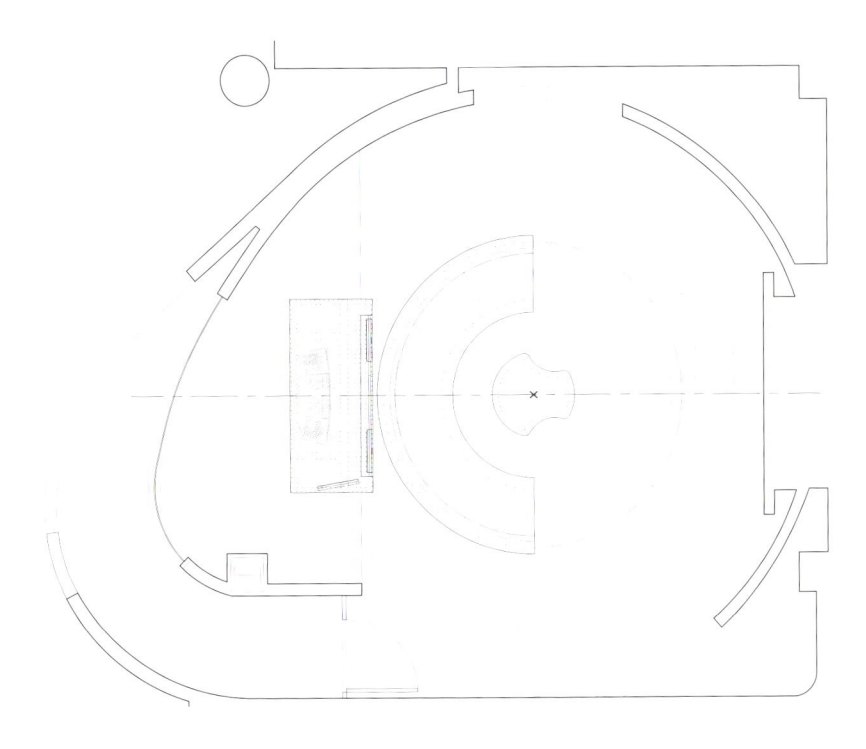

left: Workplaces and relaxing zone. right: Plan_Conference room_Projection room.
links: Arbeitsplätze und Ruhezone. rechts: Plan_Konferenzraum_Vorführraum.

USA_SARASOTA (FL) SARASOTA HERALD-TRIBUNE HEADQUARTERS

ARCHITECTS: ARQUITECTONICA
COMPLETION: 2006_**NUMBER OF WORKPLACES:** 386
GROSS FLOOR AREA: 6,620 M²_**COMMON AREA:** CAFETERIA, COVERED TERRACE_**KIND OF WORKPLACES:** OPEN-PLAN, TEAM, TELEVISION STUDIO_**PHOTOS:** NORMAN MCGRATH, NEW YORK, SARASOTA HERALD TRIBUNE, SARASOTA (480 B. M.)

The client wanted a design that would reflect the heritage of this part of the state by falling within the local architectural idiom. Modern technology was the key to accomplishing this as it allowed creation of a building that was far more weather-resistant and fuel-efficient with vast expanses of hurricane-resistant glass. To give the structure the "open airy feel" the building is placed beneath what appears to be a stand-alone roof – an undulating folded plane floating above ground on support columns. This structure becomes a giant overhang protecting the building and forming a covered plaza for the entrance lobby / exhibit space that is located within a two-story glass cube.

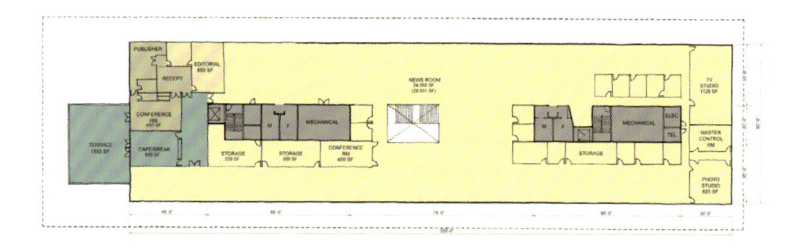

Der Kunde wünschte einen Entwurf, der durch eine lokale Architektursprache auf die Geschichte der Region anspielt. Dies wurde durch moderne Technik in einem wetterfesteren und brennstoffeffizienten Gebäude mit großen hurrikanfesten Fensterflächen erreicht. Ein großes anscheinend eigenständiges Dach auf Stützen überfängt als gefaltete Fläche den Bau und lässt ihn luftig und leicht erscheinen. Mit weitem Überstand definiert und beschützt die Struktur auch einen Freiraum vor der Lobby mit Ausstellungsraum in einem zweigeschossigen Glaskubus.

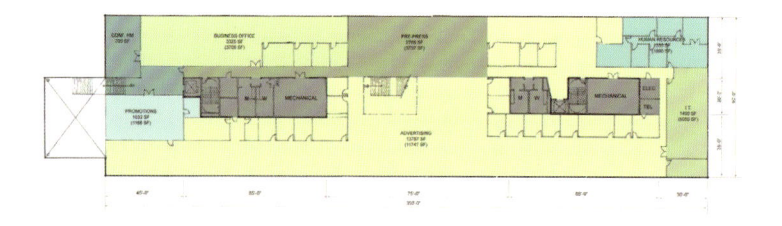

left: Floor plans_Lobby_Interior stairs_Interior stairs. right: North view of building_North-east view_Entrance area by night.
links: Grundrisse_Lobby_Innentreppen_Innentreppen. rechts: Blick von Norden_Nordostansicht_Eingangsbereich bei Nacht.

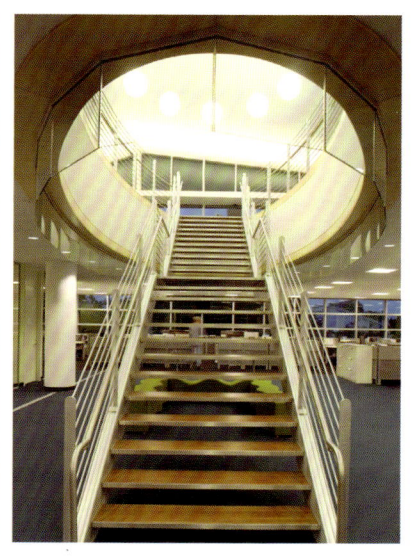

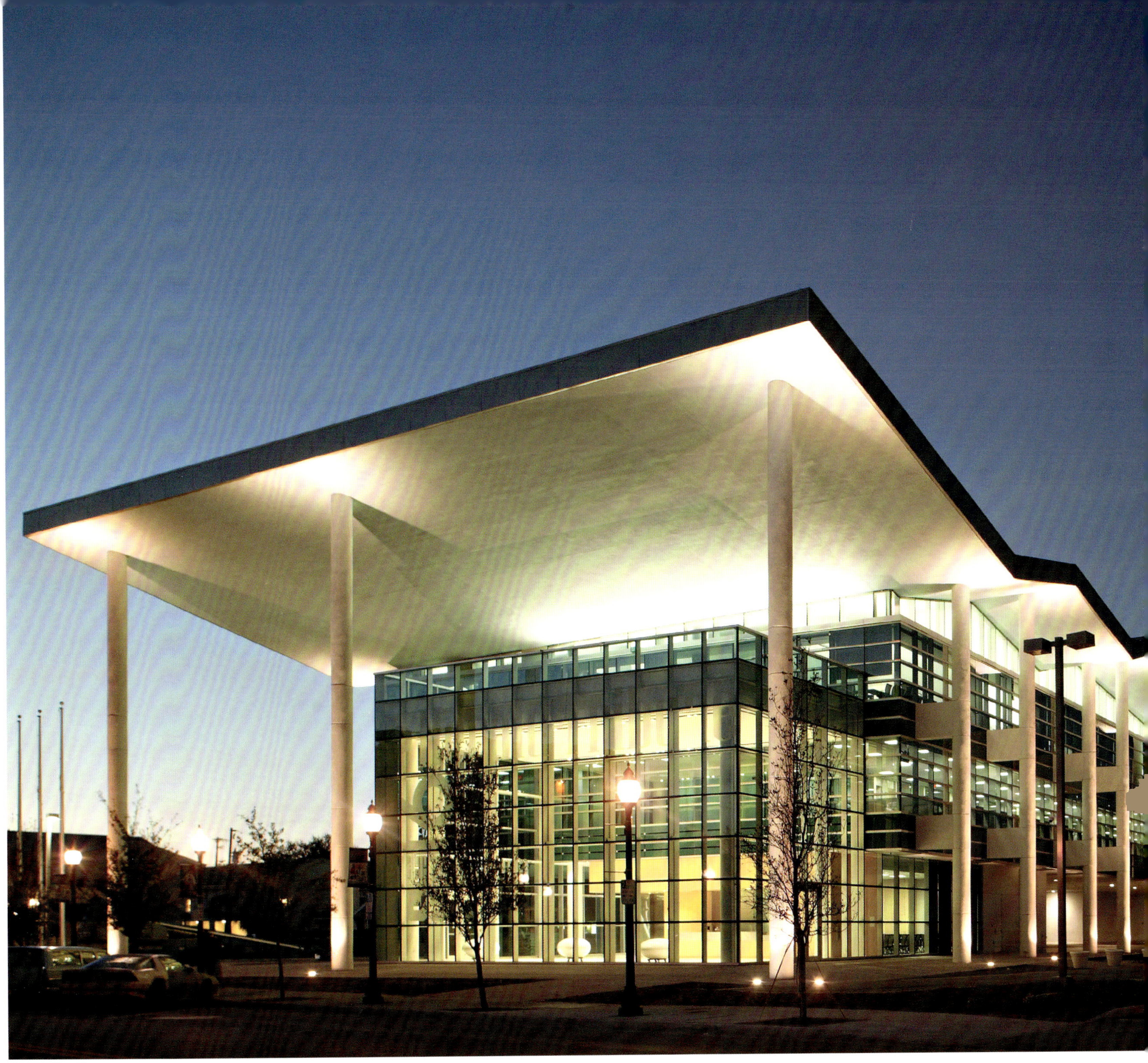

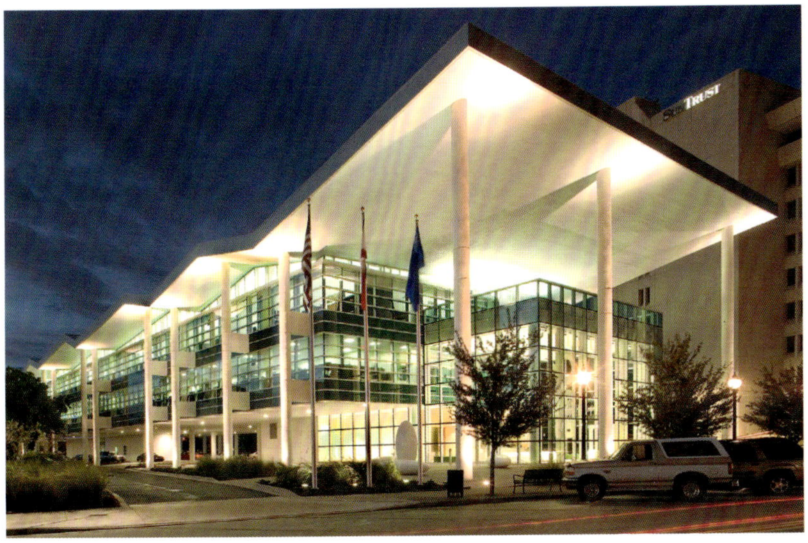

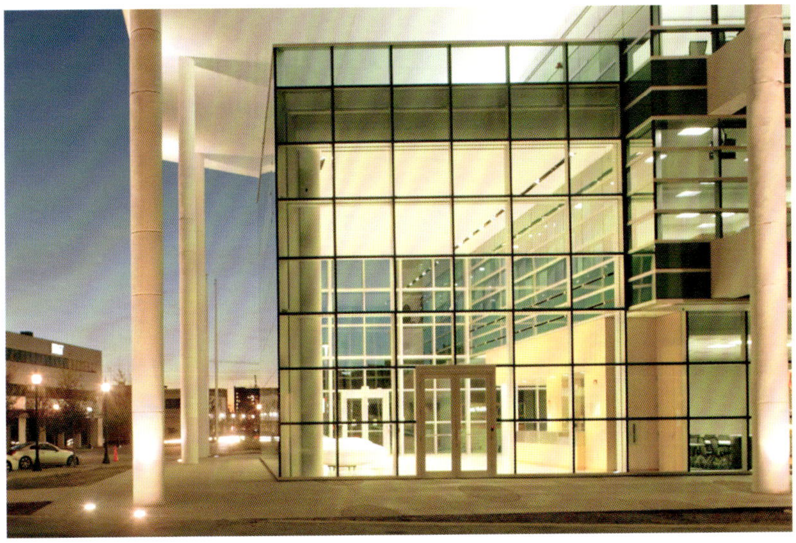

COLLECTION

south america

VAN DER LAAT & JIMÉNEZ OFFICE BUILDING_COSTA RICA_SAN JOSÉ_SOUZA, CESCON, BARRIEU E FLESCH_BRAZIL_SÃO PAULO_AGÊNCIA DE PUBLICIDADE MPM_BRAZIL_SÃO PAULO_LODUCCA AGENCY_BRAZIL_SÃO PAULO_ARCHITECTS STUDIO_BRAZIL_SÃO PAULO_ VAN DER LAAT & JIMÉNEZ OFFICE BUILDING_COSTA RICA_SAN JOSÉ_SOUZA, CESCON, BARRIEU E FLESCH_BRAZIL_SÃO PAULO_AGÊNCIA DE PUBLICIDADE MPM_BRAZIL_SÃO PAULO_LODUCCA AGENCY_BRAZIL_SÃO PAULO_ARCHITECTS STUDIO_BRAZIL_SÃO PAULO_ VAN DER LAAT & JIMÉNEZ OFFICE BUILDING_COSTA RICA_SAN JOSÉ_SOUZA, CESCON, BARRIEU E FLESCH_BRAZIL_SÃO PAULO_AGÊNCIA DE PUBLICIDADE MPM_BRAZIL_SÃO PAULO_LODUCCA AGENCY_BRAZIL_SÃO PAULO_ARCHITECTS STUDIO_BRAZIL_SÃO PAULO_ VAN DER LAAT & JIMÉNEZ OFFICE BUILDING_COSTA RICA_SAN JOSÉ_SOUZA, CESCON, BARRIEU E FLESCH

BRAZIL_SÃO PAULO **AGÊNCIA DE PUBLICIDADE MPM**

ARCHITECTS: BERNARDES + JACOBSEN ARQUITETURA
STRUCTURAL PROJECT: GRUPO DOIS ENGENHARIA DE ESTRUTURAS_**LANDSCAPE:** OFFICINA DI CASA
FURNITURE: AG / PLANCUS_**COMPLETION:** 2007
GROSS FLOOR AREA: 2,550 M²_**COMMON AREA:** MEETING ROOMS_**KIND OF WORKPLACES:** TEAM, DESKSHARING_**PHOTOS:** LEONARDO FINOTTI

The six floors of this office building are divided into pairs. On each floor there is a mezzanine level, which houses meeting rooms, administrative facilities, and corridors. The main material used for the furniture and wall coatings is wood. Wooden slats are used not only on walls, but also on the ceilings and as partitions. All these elements were designed by the architects. The dimensions of the spaces with double height are defined by the rhythmic repetition of the elements. The office spaces are isolated by the separation from the surrounding service and other establishments. This creates a special shape in relation to the side rooms and the external spaces.

Die sechs Stockwerke des Bürogebäudes wurden so aufgeteilt, dass sich auf jedem Stockwerk noch ein Zwischengeschoss befindet, welches Besprechungsräume, Verwaltungseinrichtungen und Flure beherbergt. Das Hauptmaterial, das für Möbel und Wandverkleidungen verwendet wurde, ist Holz. In gleichmäßigen Abständen angebrachte Holzlatten wurden nicht nur an den Wänden und Decken, sondern auch als Raumteiler verwendet, allesamt von den Architekten entworfen. Die Raumdimensionen mit doppelter Höhe werden von sich rhythmisch wiederholenden Elementen charakterisiert. Die Büroräume sind von den umliegenden Servicebereichen abgegrenzt, um ihnen in Bezug auf die seitlichen und außen liegenden Räume eine besondere Form zu geben.

left: Ground floor plan_Entrance area and waiting area_Bird's-eye view onto the working space.
right: Team work places on a long desk.
links: Grundriss_Eingangsbereich und Wartebereich_Vogelperspektive auf den Arbeitsbereich.
rechts: Teamarbeitsplätze an einem langen Tisch.

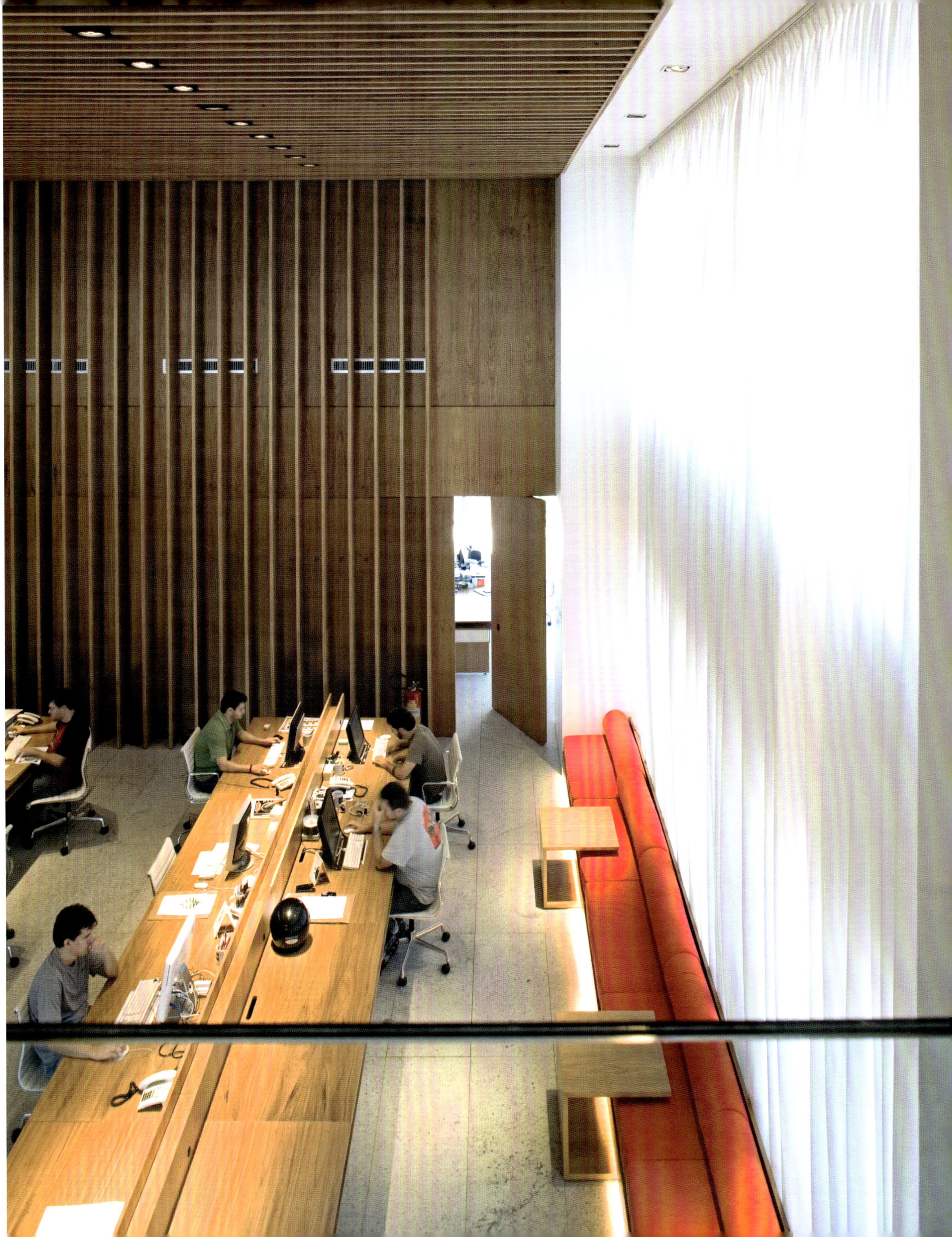

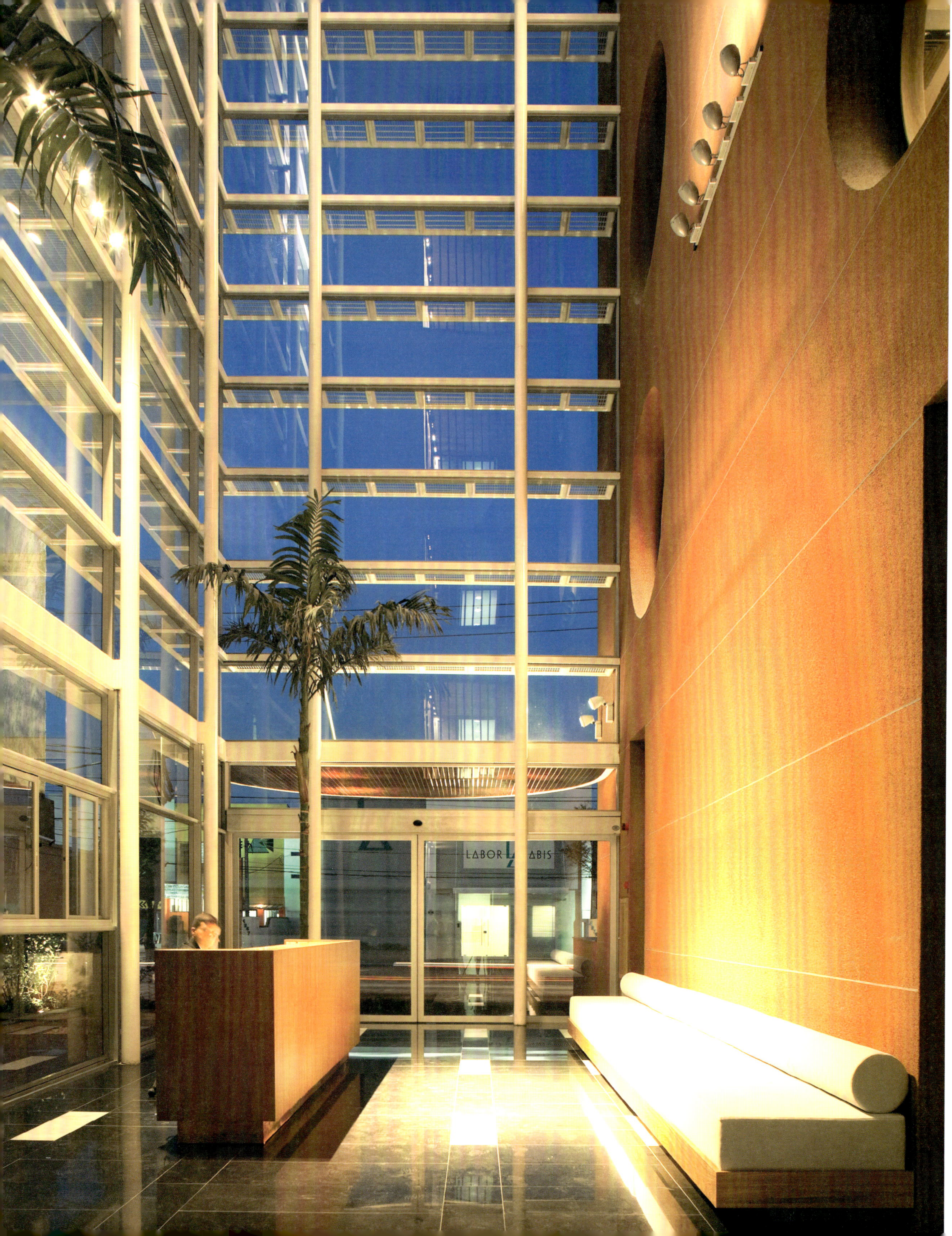
LABOR
ABIS

left: Reception. right: Elevations_Night view.
links: Empfang. rechts: Ansichten_Außenansicht bei Nacht.

BRAZIL_SÃO PAULO SOUZA, CESCON, BARRIEU E FLESCH

ARCHITECTS: RMAA / HENRIQUE REINACH AND MAURICIO MENDONÇA **OTHER CREATIVES:** SERGIO ATHIÉ AND IVO WOHNRATH_**COMPLETION:** 2007_**NUMBER OF WORKPLACES:** 15 **GROSS FLOOR AREA:** 2,400 M²_**COMMON AREA:** LIBRARY, CAFÉ AND RELAX LOUNGE_**KIND OF WORKPLACES:** CELLULAR, TEAM **PHOTOS:** PATRICIA CARDOSO, SÃO PAULO (488 B. L., 489, 491 L., B. R.), ANDRÈS OTERO, SÃO PAULO (488 B. R., 490, 491 A. R.),

The young law office Souza, Cescon Avedissian, Barrieu e Flesch occupies three floors of the E-TOWER building in Vila Olimpia. The main objectives of the interior design concept were integrating these three floors and providing the office with a daring and contemporary image. The reception and meeting rooms located in the middle floor reduce the vertical circulation and clearly present the functions of the three floors. A big opening was created across from the main entrance, visually connecting the floors and establishing a direct relationship with the outside and the city setting. The stairs and walkway guide visitors taking them on a tour close to the façade.

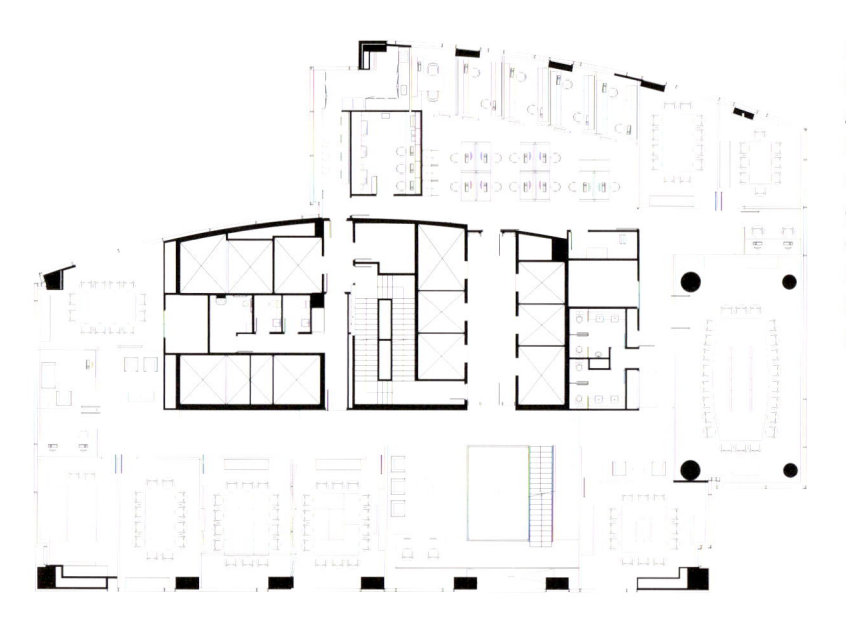

Die architektonische Innengestaltung befindet sich auf drei Geschossen im E-TOWER Gebäude in Vila Olimpia. Für das junge Anwaltsbüro Souza, Cescon Avedissian, Barrieu e Flesch waren insbesondere ein reibungsloser dieser Etagen übergreifender Ablauf sowie das Erscheinungsbild als modernes und mutiges Büro von Bedeutung. Durch die Lage der Rezeption sowie der Tagungsräume im mittleren Geschoss werden die Wege reduziert und wird eine eindeutige Raumverteilung erreicht. Dem Haupteingang gegenüber wurde eine Luftraum über die drei Geschossen geschaffen, der sie nicht nur optisch verbindet sondern zudem eine Verbindung nach draußen und zur Stadt etabliert. Die Ausrichtung der Treppen und Gänge führt den Gehenden an die Fassade.

left: 11th floor plan_Reception_Library. right: Library with stair.
links: Grundriss 11. Obergeschoss_Empfangsbereich_Bibliothek. rechts: Bibliothek mit Treppe.

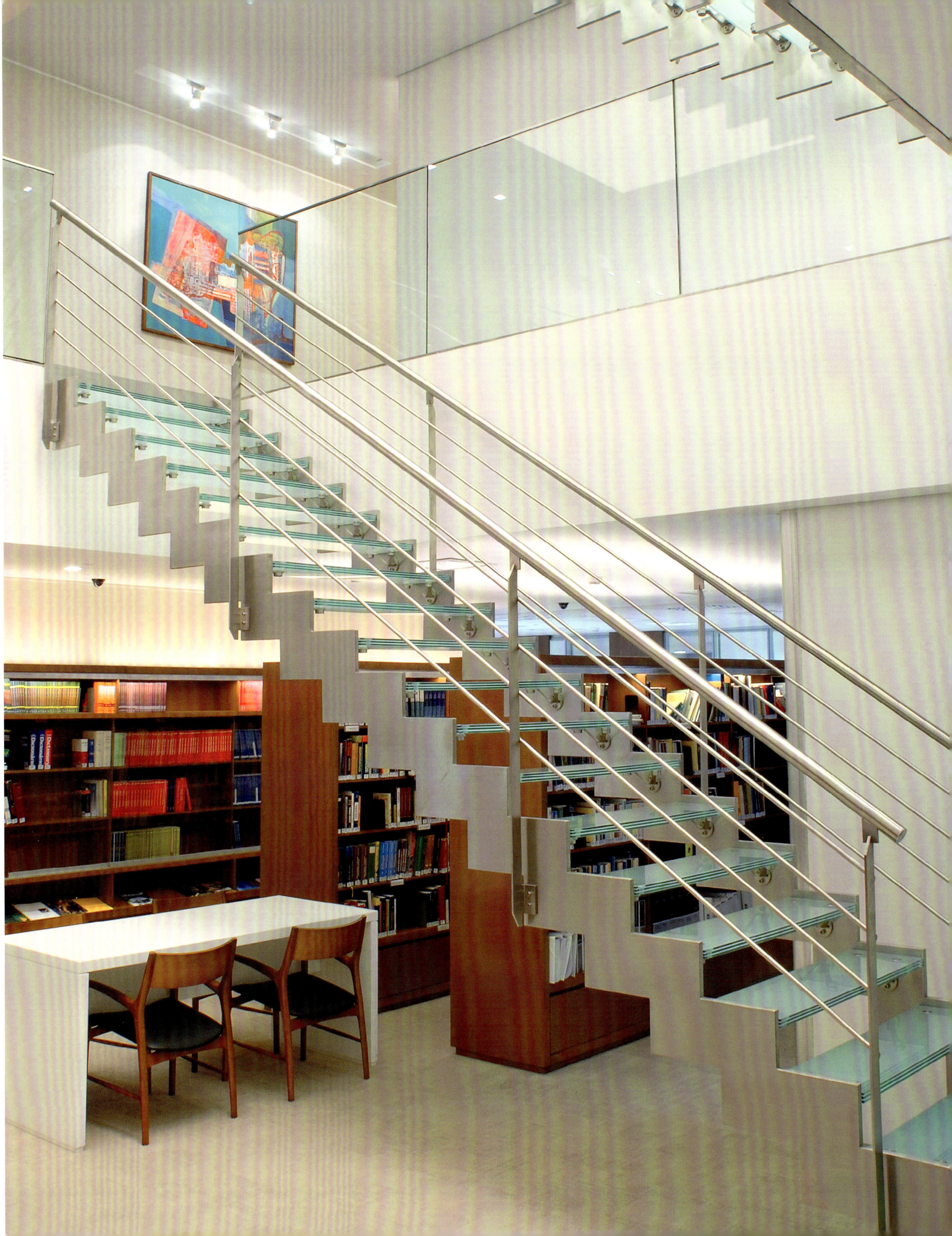

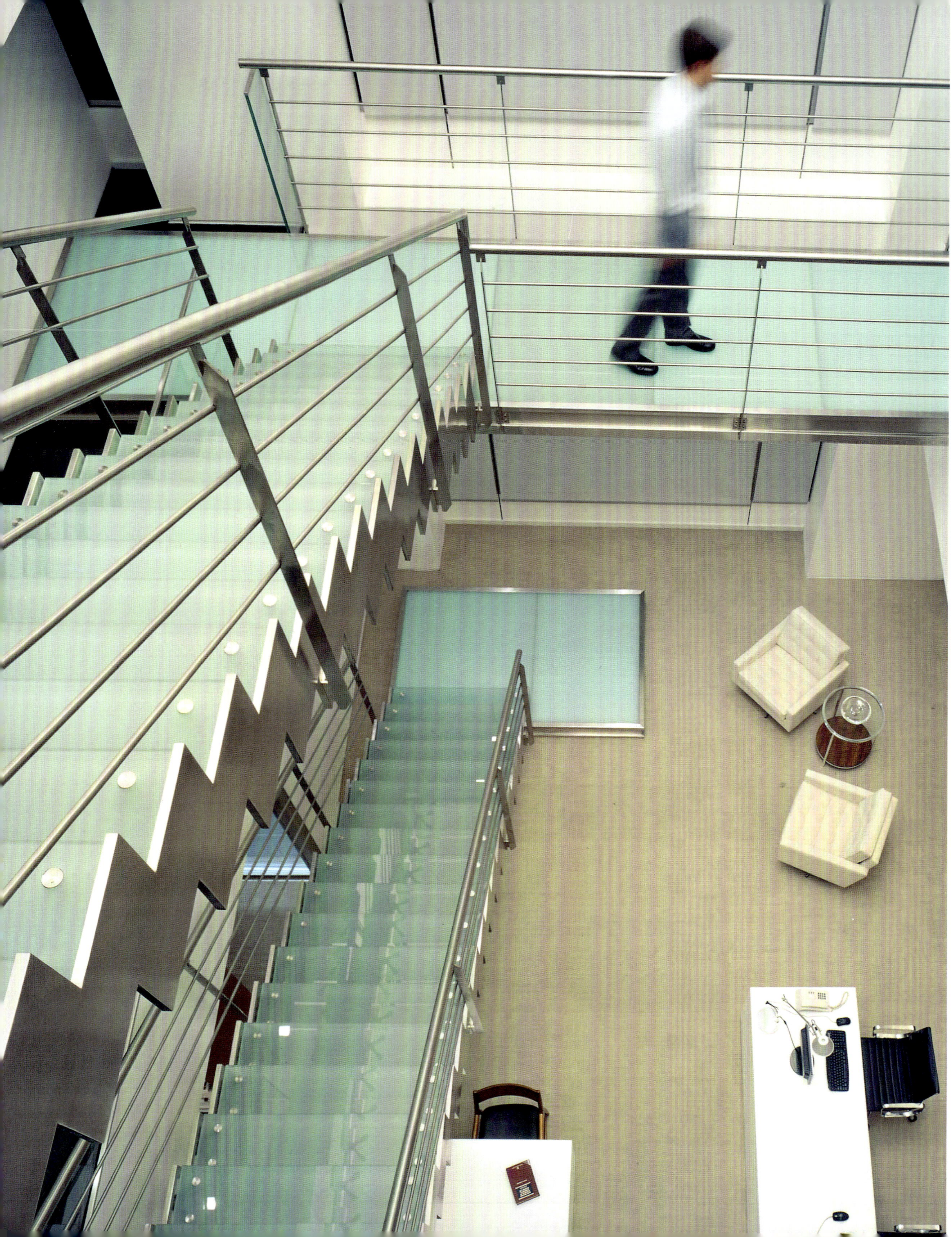

left: View downstairs. right: Sketch_Staircase_Conference room_Staircase with view to the city.
links: Blick in die Tiefe. rechts: Zeichnung_Treppe_Besprechungszimmer_Treppenhaus mit Blick über die Stadt.

BRAZIL_SÃO PAULO **LODUCCA AGENCY**

ARCHITECTS: TRIPTYQUE ARCHITECTURE
LANDSCAPE ARCHITECT: PETER WEBB
COMPLETION: 2007_**GROSS FLOOR AREA:** 1,000 M²
PHOTOS: FRAN PARENTE (492 B. L., B. R, 493), BETO CONSORTE 492 M. L., M. R)

The headquarters of the Loducca advertising agency is shielded by wide horizontally-curved cedar wood boards from the traffic and the sun. This wavy three-floor main façade contrasts with the back façade made of transparent and translucent glass elements. The entrance area is highlighted by a concrete frame that loosens up the horizontal structure. Inside also, exposed concrete dominates the open plan offices and connects the floors via a staircase that appears to have a simultaneously solidly closed and fragile balance. Light furnishings, such as a plastic igloo as a meeting area, divide the rooms.

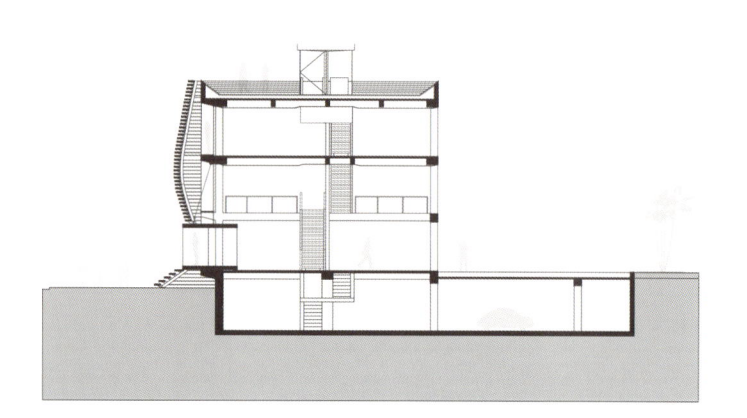

Das Hauptquartier der Werbeagentur Loducca schirmt sich mit breiten, horizontalen geschwungenen Zedernholzplanken vor dem Verkehr und der Sonneneinstrahlung ab. Diese ondulierte dreigeschossige Hauptfassade steht im Kontrast zur rückwärtigen Fassade aus transparenten und transluzenten Glaselementen. Der Eingangsbereich wird durch einen Betonrahmen betont, der die horizontale Struktur aufbricht. Auch im Inneren dominiert der nackte Beton die Großraumbüros und verbindet die Geschosse in einer Treppe, die einerseits geschlossen und massig, andererseits fragil ins Gleichgewicht gesetzt zu sein scheint. Leichte Möblierung, wie ein weißer Plastik-Iglu als Besprechungsbereich, unterteilen die Räume.

left: Section_Corner of the building_Staircase_Stair_Window. right: Façade.
links: Schnitt_Gebäudeecke_Treppenhaus_Treppe_Fenster. rechts: Fassade.

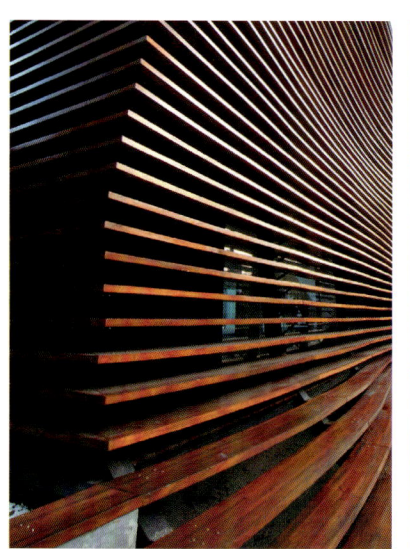

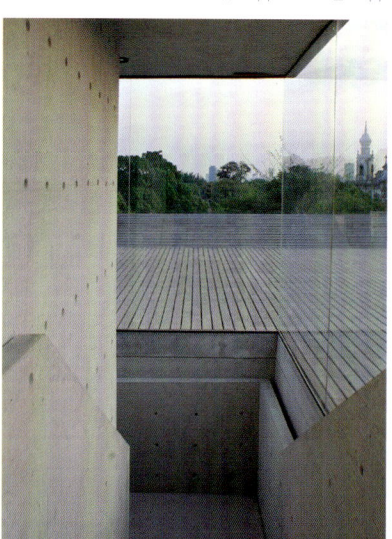

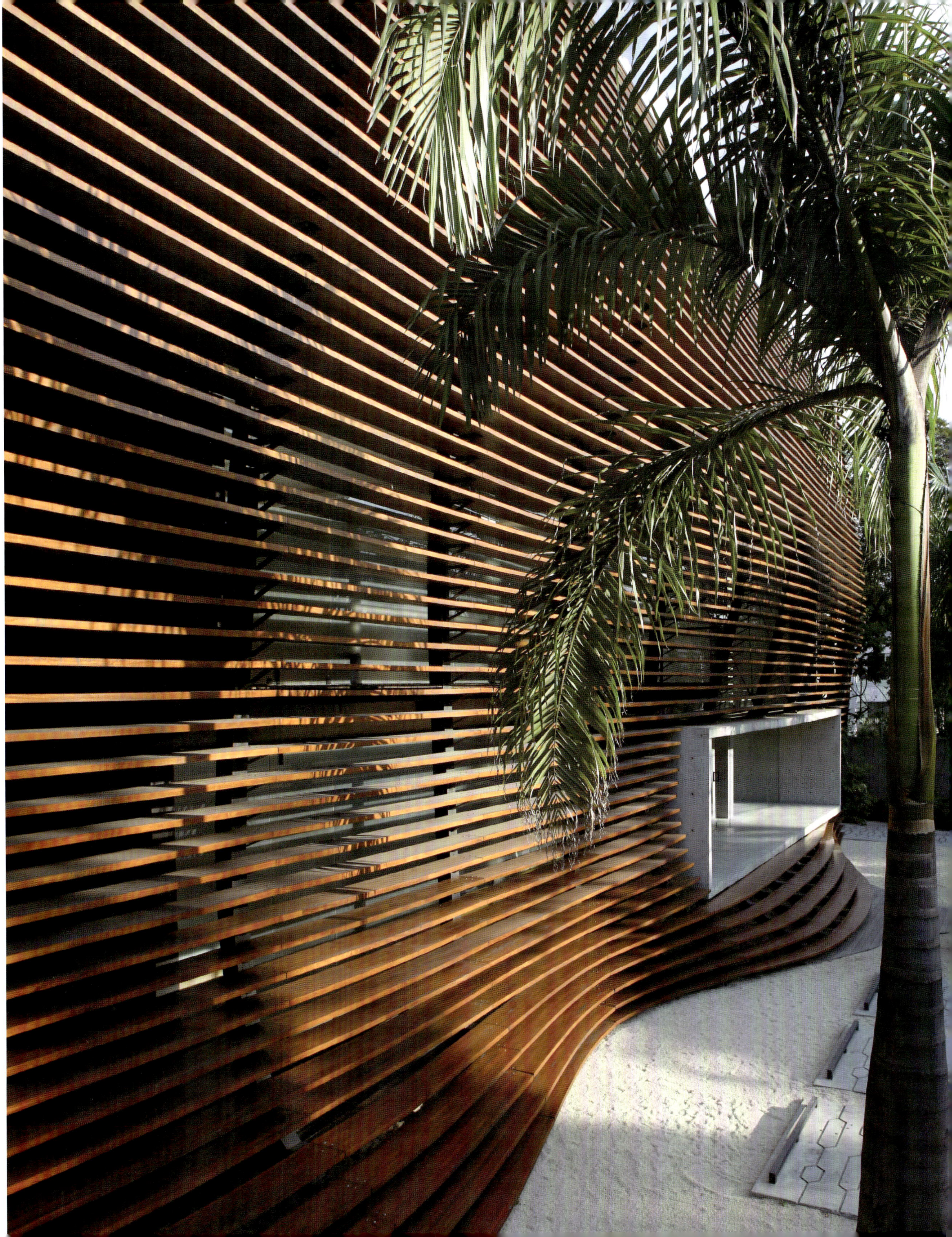

BRAZIL_SÃO PAULO ARCHITECTS STUDIO

ARCHITECTS: FREDERICO ZANELATO ARQUITETOS
COMPLETION: 2009_**NUMBER OF WORKPLACES:** 1
GROSS FLOOR AREA: 70 M²_**COMMON AREA:**
ATELIER_**KIND OF WORKPLACES:** OPEN-PLAN
PHOTOS: BEBETE VIÉGAS, SÃO PAULO

The construction site for the architecture studio is located in the middle of Serra do Itapeti near São Paulo. The natural soil profile of the irregular site and the many trees were all maintained and used as the basis of the design with simple, low cost, consistent materials. The footprint of eight by eight meters stands on four pilots. From the beginning, due to the natural environment of the area, it was decided to implement the studio with as little interference as possible, applying solutions and simple finishing with sophisticated aesthetics, demonstrating in concrete terms the concept applied to all the work produced by the studio.

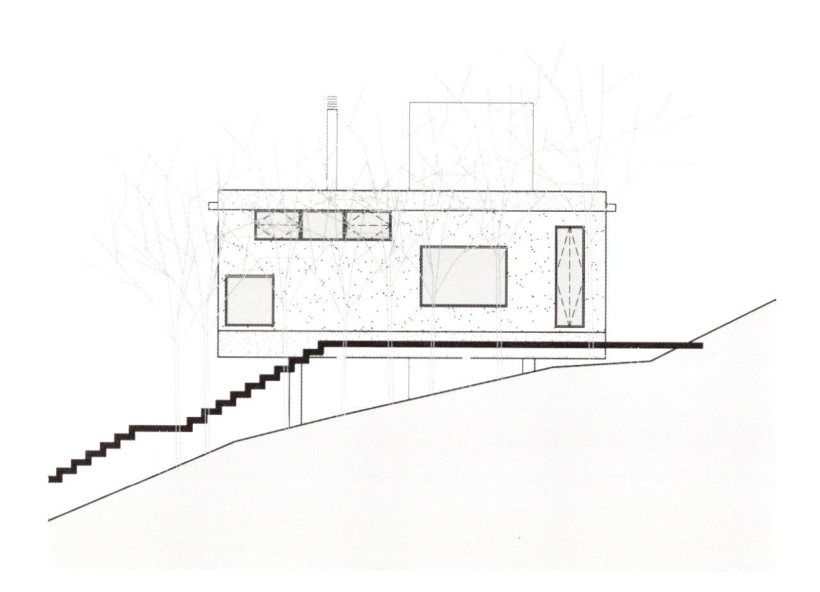

Das Baugrundstück des Architekturbüros liegt mitten in der Serra do Itapeti bei São Paulo. Das Bodenprofil des unregelmäßigen Grundstücks sowie die zahlreichen Bäume, die alle erhalten werden sollten, lagen dem Entwurf zugrunde. Einfache, preiswerte und in sich schlüssige Materialien wurden genutzt. Das Büro erhebt sich auf vier Pfeilern über einer Grundfläche von acht mal acht Metern. Ziel war die bedarfsorientierte Eingliederung des Ateliers unter möglichst geringer Störung der natürlichen Umgebung, schlichtem Erscheinungsbild aber dennoch ausgefeilter Ästhetik, um so das von dem Architekturbüro bei all seinen Bauten verfolgte Grundkonzept in einem gebauten Manifest zu demonstrieren.

left: North elevation_South elevation_Night view. right: In the middle of the nature_Workplace and conference table_View through the window.
links: Nordfassade_Südansicht_Nachtansicht. rechts: Inmitten der Natur_Arbeitsplatz und Besprechungstisch_Blick durch das Fenster.

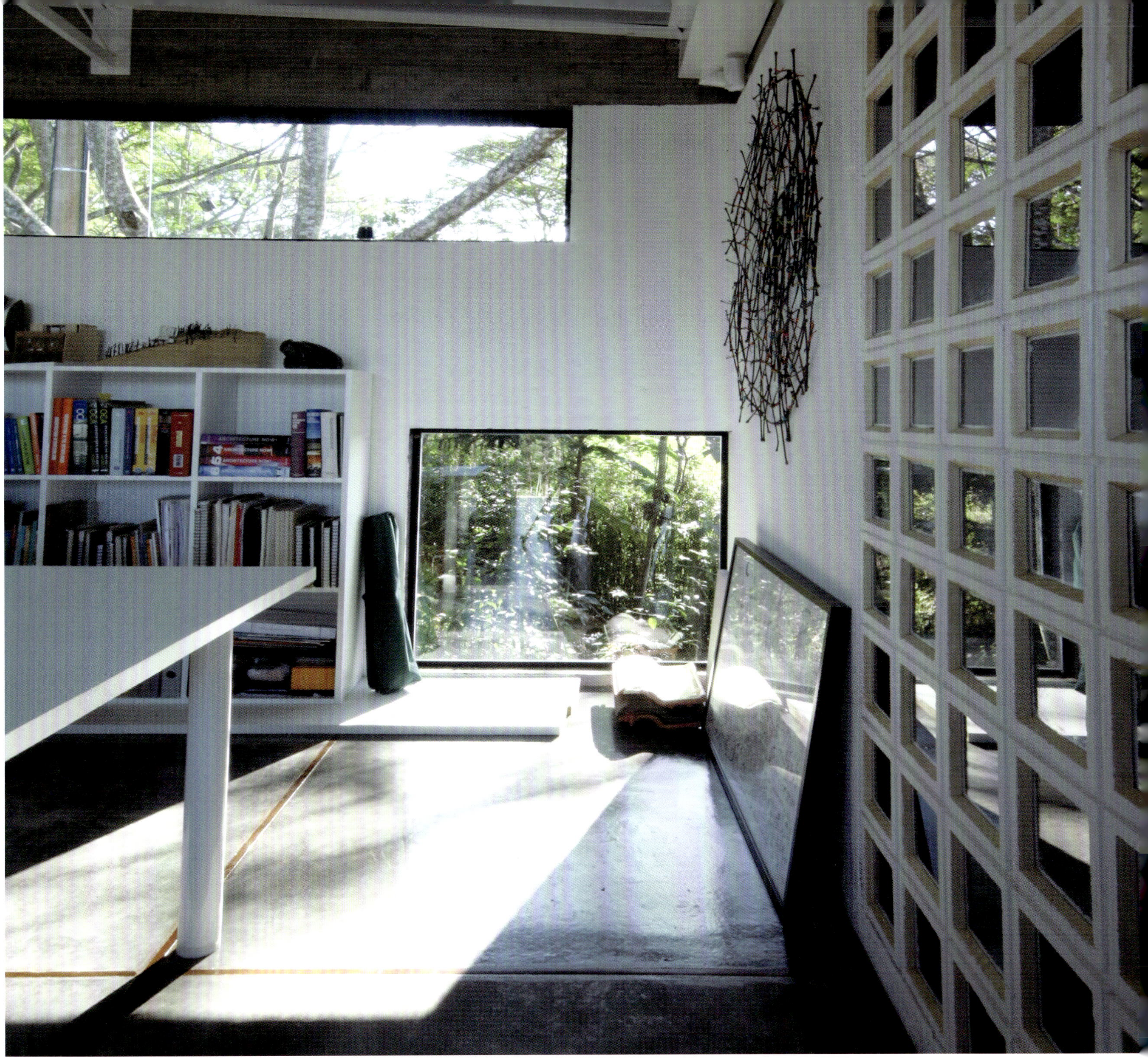

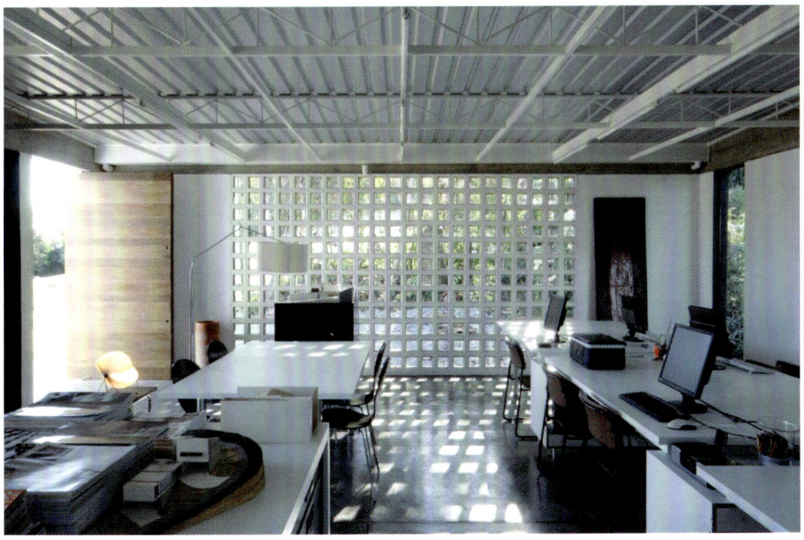

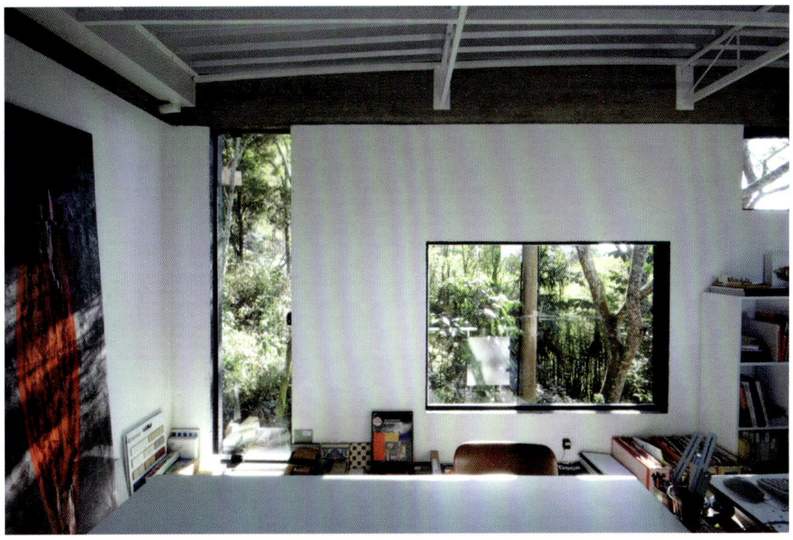

COSTA RICA_SAN JOSÉ VAN DER LAAT & JIMÉNEZ OFFICE BUILDING

ARCHITECTS: FOURNIER-ROJAS ARQUITECTOS / FORO **COMPLETION:** 2007_**NUMBER OF WORKPLACES:** 40 **GROSS FLOOR AREA:** 2,500 M²_**COMMON AREA:** CONFERENCE ROOM, STAFF DINING_**KIND OF WORKPLACES:** CELLULAR, OPEN-PLAN_**PHOTOS:** RODRIGO MONTOYA, SAN JOSÉ (496 B. L., 498, 499 L., B. R.), SYLVIA FOURNIER, SAN JOSÉ (496 B. R., 499 A. R.), ANDRÉS MONTERO, SAN JOSÉ (497)

The V&J building attempts to inject fresh ideas to the yet underdeveloped architecture and urban culture of Costa Rica. Pre-patinated copper sheathing coupled with concrete tiles with steel plate window frames and cornices provide a new material expression in a developing neighborhood. The design is suited for a tropical climate and is environmentally friendly. Thus windows are controlled perforations in the walls as opposed to large glazed surfaces, which are not suitable for the climate. The interiors offer new ideas such as a central plaza that is naturally illuminated by a large clerestory and a quarter vault, which also introduces much natural light to the interior spaces.

Das V&J Gebäude versucht die noch unterentwickelte architektonische und städtebauliche Kultur Costa Ricas mit neuen Ideen zu erweitern. Vorpatinierte Kupferverkleidung und Betonplatten sowie Stahlfenster und Gesimse setzen neue Materialakzente in dem sich verändernden Viertel. Der umweltfreundliche Entwurf reagiert auf das tropische Klima, bildet Fenster als kontrollierte Wandöffnungen und nicht als große verglaste Fläche aus. Das Innere bietet neue Ideen, wie einen natürlich beleuchteten Zentralplatz mit Lichtgaden und einer Viertelkreis Tonnenwölbung, die reichlich Licht in alle Räume scheinen lässt.

left: Main floor plan_Exterior view in the early evening_Building corner. right: View of north façade.
links: Grundriss Hauptgeschoss_Außenansicht am frühen Abend_Ecke des Gebäudes. rechts: Nordfassade.

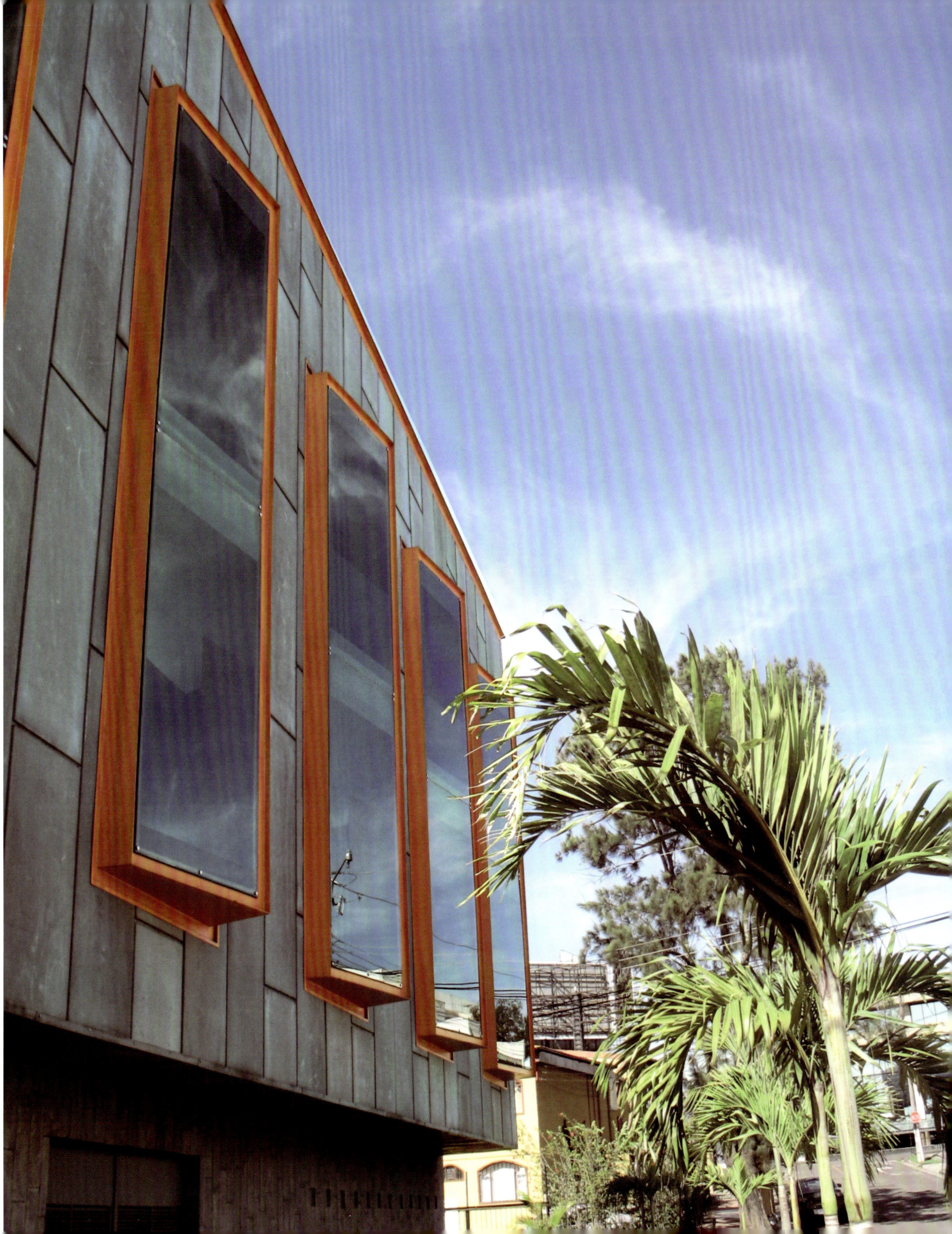

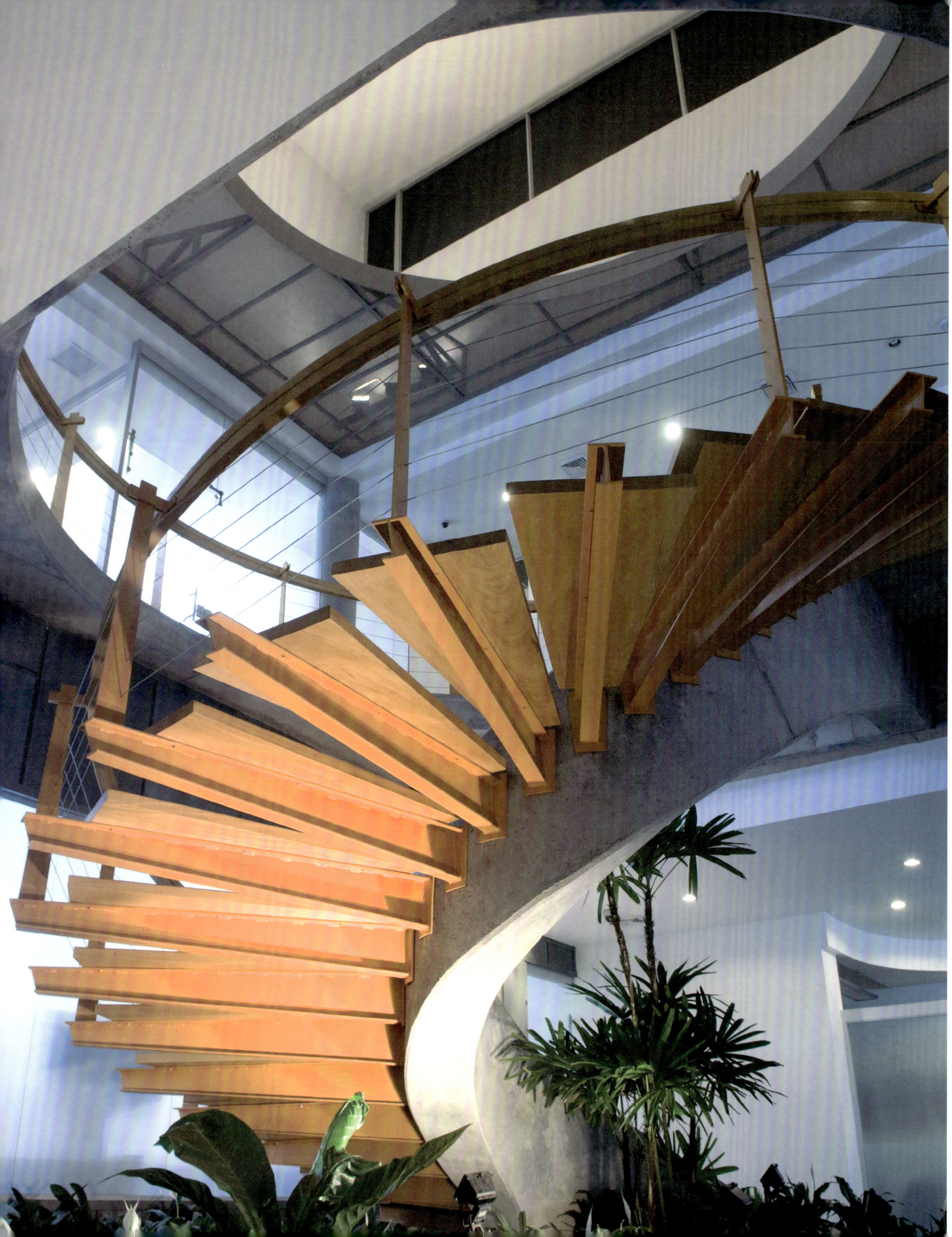

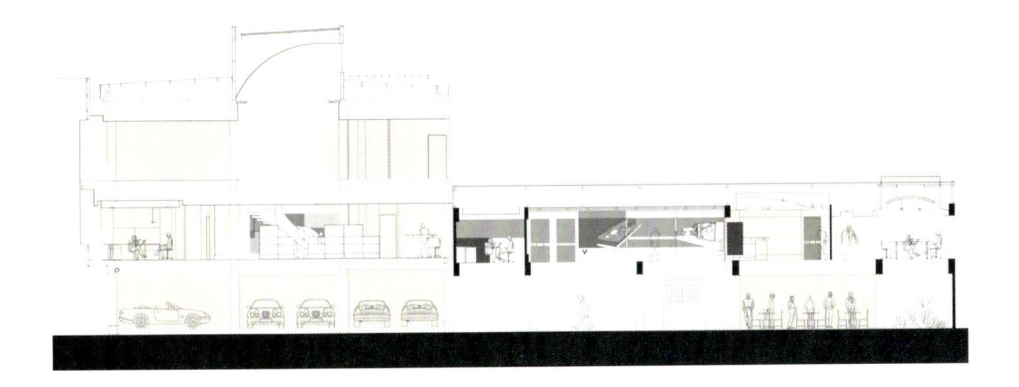

left: Central spiral stairs at atrium. right: Longitudinal section_Connecting hallway looking towards atrium_Detail of central stairs_Private office_Typical office.
links: Spiraltreppe im Atrium. rechts: Längsschnitt_Verbindender Gang Richtung Atrium_Individuelles Büro_Detail der Haupttreppe_Typisches Büro.

COLLECTION

australia

...TIONAL@DOCKLANDS_AUSTRALIA_MELBOURNE_STOCKLANDHEADOFFICE_AU...
...ALIA_SYDNEY_CHALLENGERWORKPLACE_AUSTRALIA_SYDNEY_NATIONAL@DOC...
...NDS_AUSTRALIA_MELBOURNE_STOCKLAND HEAD OFFICE_AUSTRALIA_SY...
...Y_CHALLENGER WORKPLACE_AUSTRALIA_SYDNEY_NATIONAL@DOCKLAN...
...AUSTRALIA_MELBOURNE_STOCKLANDHEADOFFICE_AUSTRALIA_SYDNEY_CH...
...ENGERWORKPLACE_AUSTRALIA_SYDNEY_NATIONAL@DOCKLANDS_AUSTRA...
...MELBOURNE_STOCKLANDHEADOFFICE_AUSTRALIA_SYDNEY_CHALENGERW...
...PLACE_AUSTRALIA_SYDNEY_NATIONAL@DOCKLANDS_AUSTRALIA_MELBOU...
...STOCKLAND HEAD OFFICE_AUSTRALIA_SYDNEY_CHALLENGER WORKP...
...E_AUSTRALIA_SYDNEY_NATIONAL@DOCKLANDS_AUSTRALIA_MELBOURNE_STOC...
...ND HEAD OFFICE_AUSTRALIA_SYDNEY_CHALLENGERWORKPLACE_AUSTRAL...
...SYDNEY_NATIONAL@DOCKLANDS_AUSTRALIA_MELBOURNE_STOCKLANDHE...
...OFFICE_AUSTRALIA_SYDNEY_CHALLENGER WORKPLACE_AUSTRALIA_SYDN...
...NATIONAL@DOCKLANDS_AUSTRALIA_MELBOURNE_STOCKLAND HEAD OFF...
...AUSTRALIA_SYDNEY_CHALLENGER WORKPLACE_AUSTRALIA_SYDNEY_N...
...ONAL@DOCKLANDS_AUSTRALIA_MELBOURNE_STOCKLAND HEAD OFFICE_AU...
...RALIA_SYDNEY_CHALLENGERWORKPLACE_AUSTRALIA_SYDNEY_NATIONAL@...
...KLANDS AUSTRALIA MELBOURNE STOCKLANDHEADOFFICE AUSTRALIA S...

AUSTRALIA_MELBOURNE NATIONAL@DOCKLANDS

ARCHITECTS: BVN ARCHITECTURE_**COMPLETION:** 2004
NUMBER OF WORKPLACES: 3.800_**GROSS FLOOR AREA:** 80,000 M²
COMMON AREA: THEATRETTE, CONFERENCE ROOMS, TRAINING ROOMS, CAFES, BREAKOUT SPACES, INDOOR PARK, NATURALLY VENTILATED WINTER GARDENS, MIXED MODE VENTILATED SUN-ROOMS, PROJECT ROOMS, OPEN AMPITHEATRE _**KIND OF WORKPLACES:** OPEN-PLAN, TEAM, NON-TERRITORIAL, LOUNGE WORKSPACE_**PHOTOS:** GOLLINGS PHOTOGRAPHY

The National Australia Bank building is based on extensive international research, both in terms of the workplace environment and state of the art sustainable architectural design. Mixed mode ventilation, workplace daylight, low energy consumption and the creation of internal landscape environments characterize the sustainable features of this building. Large open floor plates with attached service cores ensure that as corporate requirements change and flexibility is required, the building's unencumbered floor plate will suit any space needs for a very long time. It is a model of a highly flexible ground scraper building that simply required less energy to build, to run and to maintain, and that will have a longer service life.

Das Gebäude der National Australia Bank beruht auf intensiver Recherche von internationalen Bespielen sowohl im Bezug auf Arbeitsumgebung als auch zeitgemäßer nachhaltiger Architektur. Kombination aus natürlicher und mechanischer Belüftung, Tageslicht am Arbeitsplatz, niedriger Energieverbrauch und die Schaffung innenliegender Grünflächen bestimmen die Ansätze nachhaltigen Bauens, die hier realisiert wurden. Grossflächige und offene Geschosse mit festgelegten Servicekernen und frei aufteilbaren Ebenen ermöglichen Anpassungen an den Flächenbedarf und langfristige Flexibilität falls sich die Bedürfnisse des Unternehmens ändern. National@Docklands ist ein Modell eines hochflexiblen Groundscraper-Gebäudes, das weniger Energie im Bau, in der Nutzung und im Unterhalt benötigt und eine längere Nutzungsdauer gewährleistet.

left: Third level plan_Meeting room_View into the verandah "sunrooms" in front of the eastern atrium. right: Exterior_East atrium_Crystal box meeting room_Casual meeting space in the base of eastern atrium.
links: Grundriss drittes Obergeschoss_Besprechungsraum_Blick in die „Sonnenzimmer" im östlichen Atrium. rechts: Außenansicht_Östliches Atrium_Besprechungszimmer „Kristallbox"_Zwangloser Besprechungsbereich im östlichen Atrium.

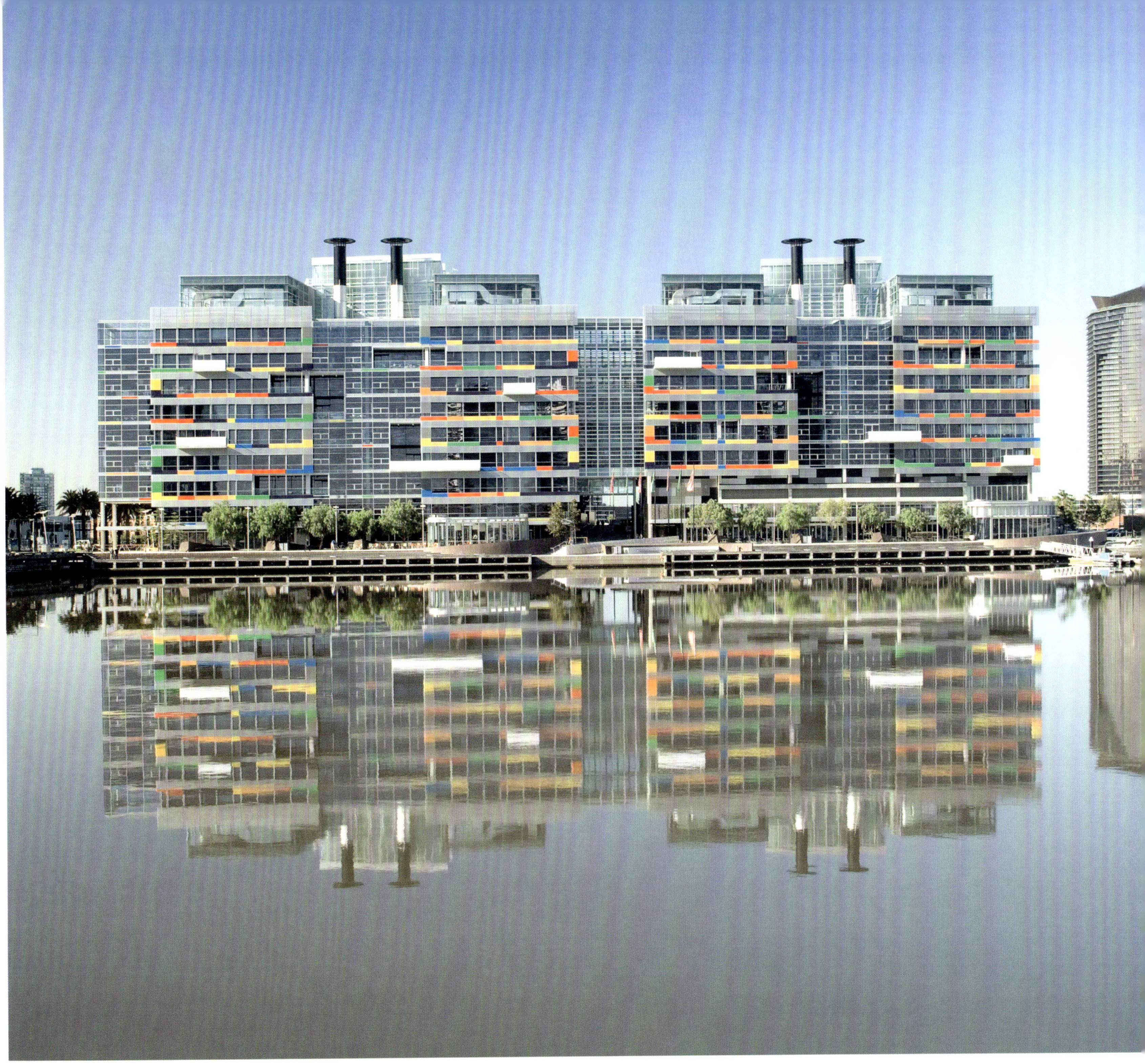
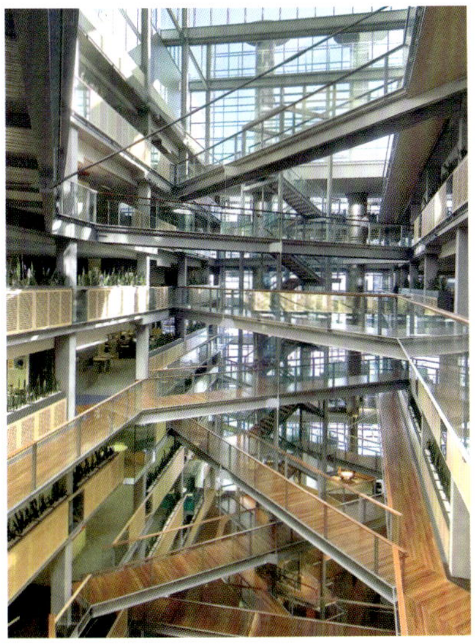
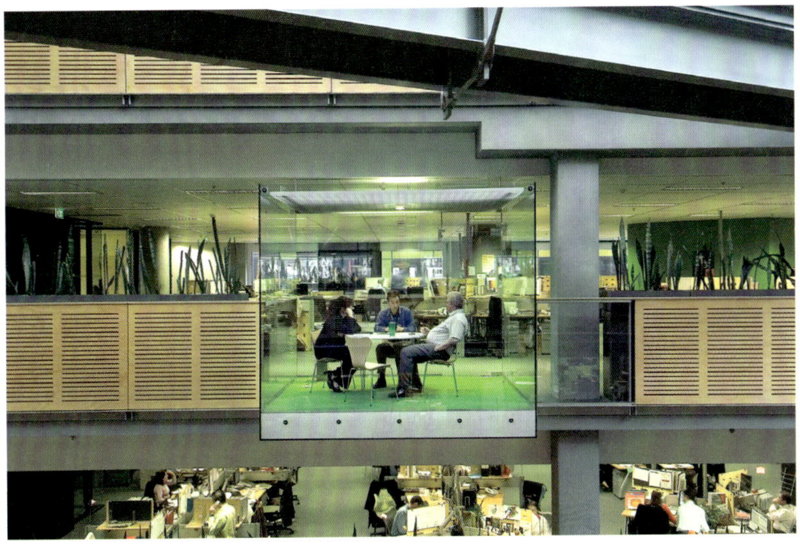
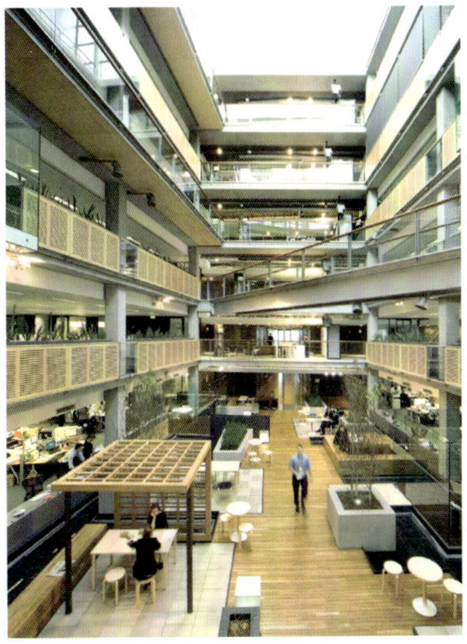

AUSTRALIA_SYDNEY **STOCKLAND HEAD OFFICE**

ARCHITECTS: BVN ARCHITECTURE
COMPLETION: 2007_**ORIGINAL BUILDING:** 1988
NUMBER OF WORKPLACES: 600_**GROSS FLOOR AREA:** 10,000 M²
COMMON AREA: STAFF CAFÉ, TRAINING AND KNOWLEDGE CENTER, CONFERENCE ROOMS, PROJECT ROOMS, BUILDING LOBBY AND RECEPTION_**KIND OF WORKPLACES:** OPEN-PLAN, TEAM, DESKSHARING, NON-TERRITORIAL, LOUNGE WORKSPACE
PHOTOS: GOLLINGS PHOTOGRAPHY

The new head office of one of Australia's largest, most diversified property groups is located in one of Stockland's existing property assets, an outdated 31 floor office tower designed and built in the 1980s. Stockland Head Office addresses the challenge of sustainability through the innovative refurbishment of eight floors of an existing building to provide a lively environment that supports wellness and activity while reducing the office's environmental footprint. Key to this is the eight-story atrium which connects all levels in a dynamic play of projecting floor planes, maximizes daylight, and improves access to views. The workplace is the first in Australia to achieve a 6-star Green Star As-Built rating.

Das neue Hauptquartier der größten und breitest gefächerten australischen Immobiliengruppe befindet sich im eigenen Anlageeigentum eines veralteten 31-stöckigen Büroturmes aus den 1980er Jahren. Stockland Head Office berücksichtigt Aspekte der Umweltverträglichkeit und Nachhaltigkeit indem es acht Stockwerke eines bestehenden Baus innovativ umgestaltet und somit ein neues lebendiges Umfeld schafft während es die Ökobilanz des Gebäudes verbessert. Der Schlüssel zu Wohlbefinden und Aktivität in dem Umbau ist das achtgeschossige Atrium, das alle Geschosse durch ein dynamisches Spiel von verspringenden Ebenen verbindet, den Tageslichteinfall maximiert und den Ausblick verbessert. Es ist die erste realisierte Arbeitsstätte Australiens, die die Einstufung 6-star Green Star As-Built erhielt.

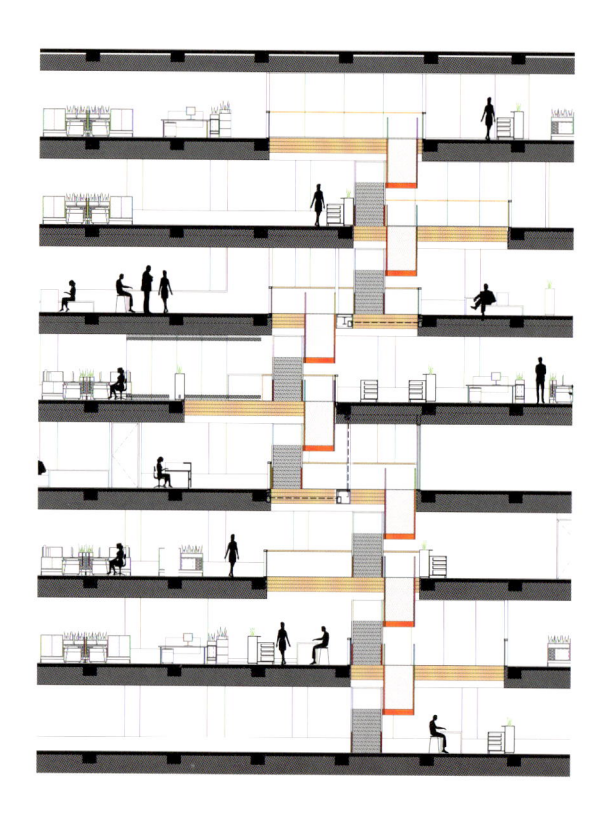

left: Section_Staircase_Atrium. right: Interior view_Meeting room_Reception area.
links: Schnitt_Treppenhaus_Atrium. rechts: Innenansicht_Besprechungsraum_Empfangsbereich.

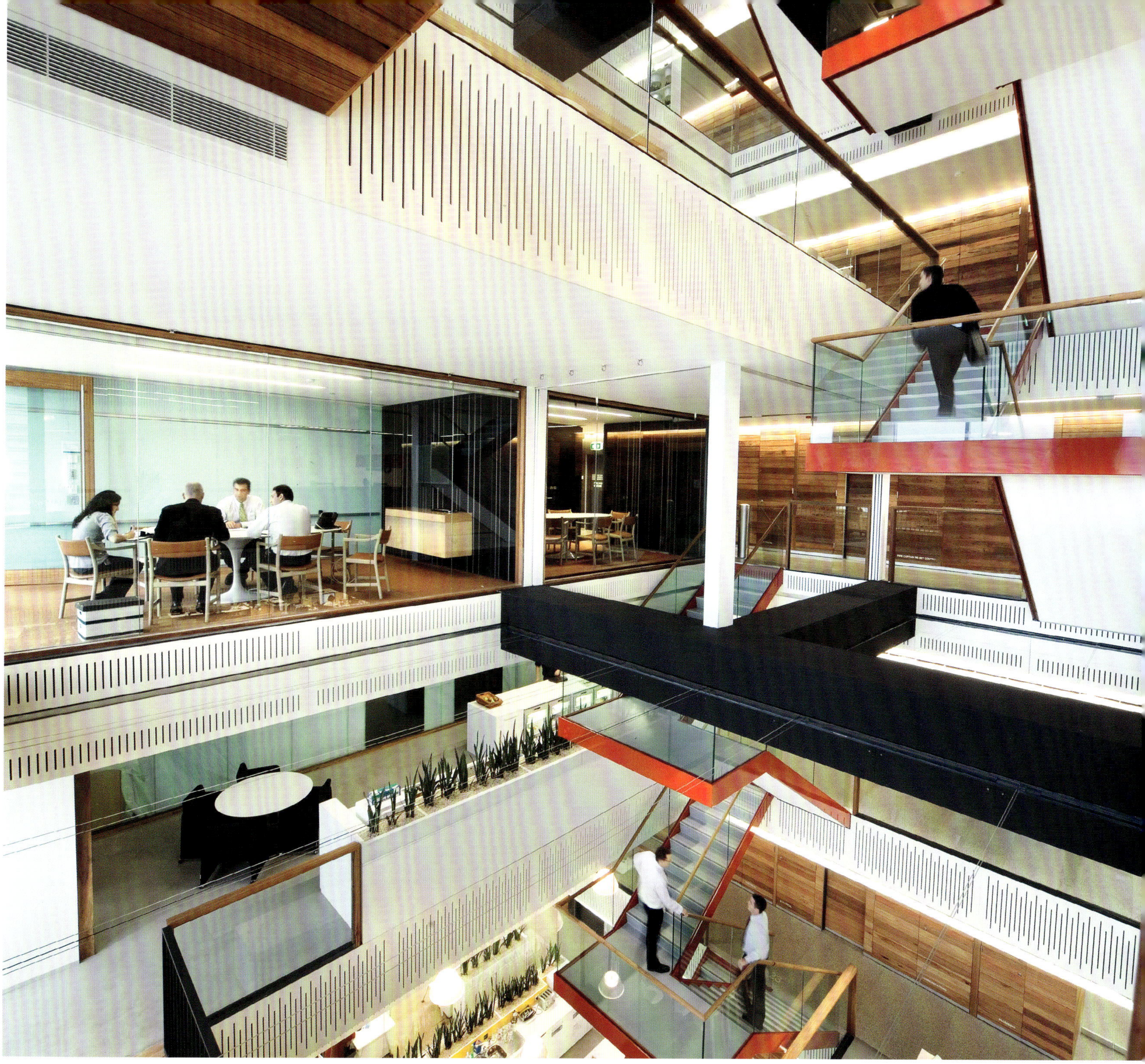

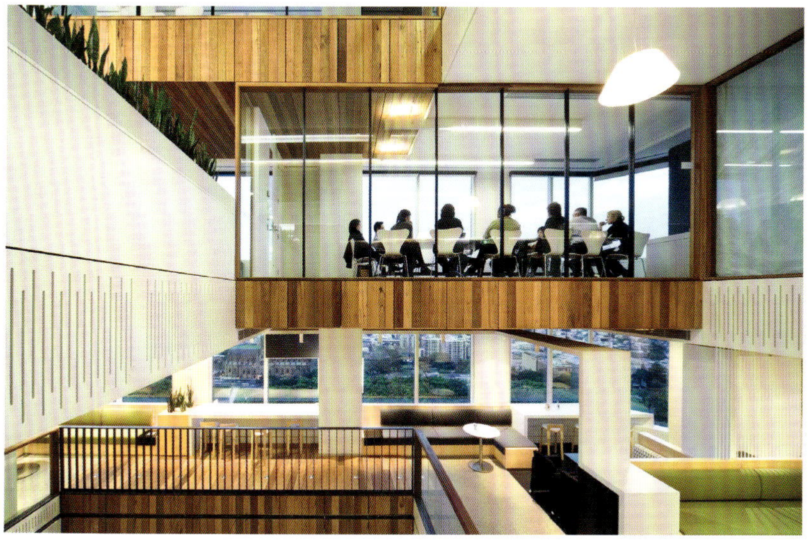

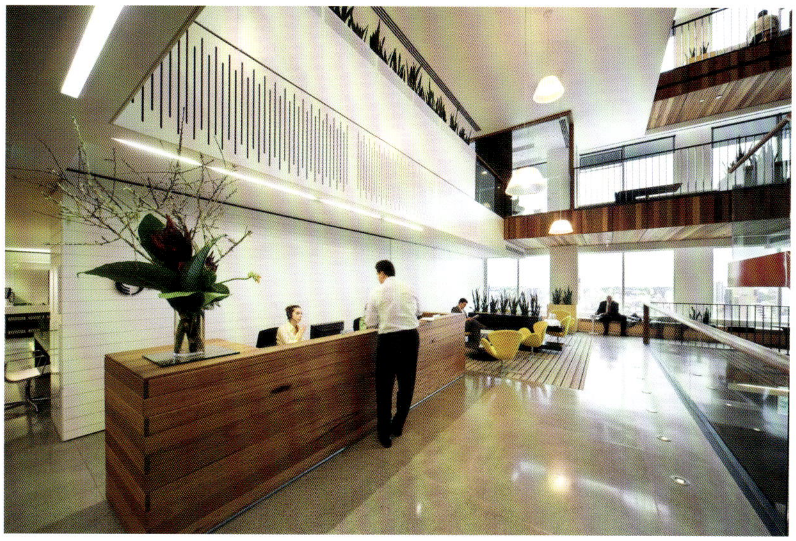

AUSTRALIA_SYDNEY **CHALLENGER WORKPLACE**

ARCHITECTS: BVN ARCHITECTURE
COMPLETION: 2008_**NUMBER OF WORKPLACES:** 620_**GROSS FLOOR AREA:** 9,750 M²_**COMMON AREA:** CAFÉ, BREAKOUT SPACE, RECREATIONAL AREAS, CONFERENCE ROOMS_**KIND OF WORKPLACES:** OPEN-PLAN, TEAM, COMBINATION, NON-TERRITORIAL, LOUNGE WORKSPACE_**PHOTOS:** GOLLINGS PHOTOGRAPHY (506, 507 B. L., B. R.), ANTHONY BROWELL (507 A., B. M.)

Challenger left a Sydney high-rise with harbor views to reinvent their workplace in a refurbished 1960s low-rise. The workplace design is inward-looking to create a new focus for the business, bringing together three separately located business units into one location and housing 600 staff over four contiguous floors. The environment provides a vast atrium, creating a centralised hub of activity that consolidates all meeting and public spaces, unified by a continuous stair. Clients experience the previously unseen energy of the business, entering the atrium via a bridge on the second floor. This project represents the design opportunities created in partnership with the client to both meet business demands and create a unique place for the people of Challenger.

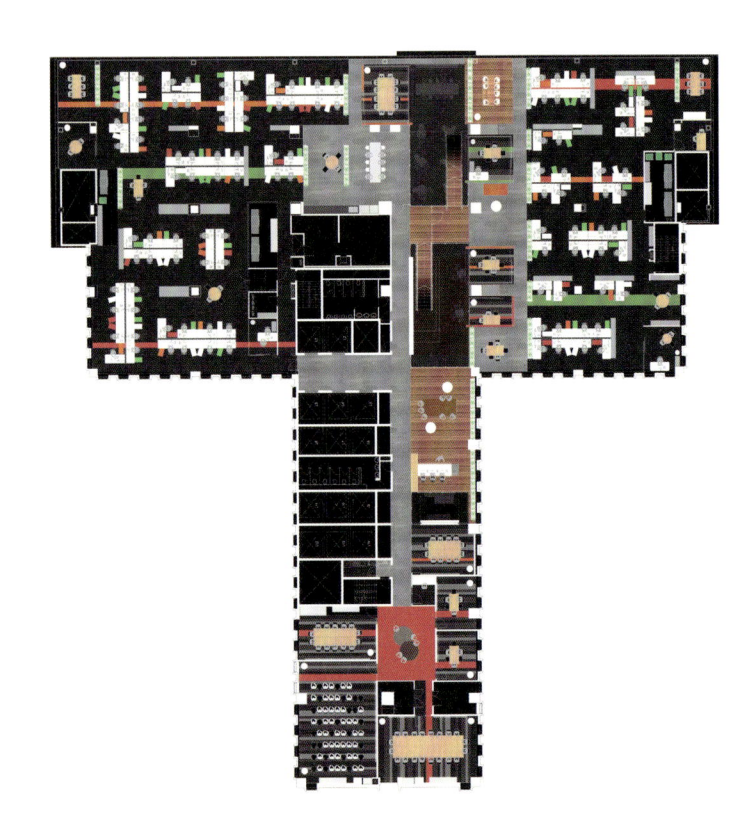

Die Firma Challenger verließ ein Hochhaus in Sydney mit Hafenblick, um sich in einem kleineren, renovierten Hochhaus der 1960er Jahre neu zu definieren. Der Entwurf ist auf das Innere ausgerichtet, um einen neuen Mittelpunkt des Unternehmens zu schaffen, der die drei eigenständigen Firmenteile und 600 Mitarbeiter auf vier zusammenhängenden Stockwerken verbindet. Ein großzügiges Atrium mit durchgehender Treppenanlage bildet den zentralen Mittelpunkt für verschiedene Aktivitäten und führt alle öffentlichen Bereiche und Konferenzräume zusammen. Wenn Kunden das Atrium über eine Brücke im zweiten Geschoss betreten, erleben sie hier unmittelbar die Dynamik des Unternehmens, die am alten Firmensitz nicht zu erkennen war. Dieses Projekt zeigt, welche Möglichkeiten in dem gemeinsamen Entwurf mit dem Bauherrn liegen - der sowohl die Erfordernisse des Unternehmens erfüllt als auch einen einzigartigen Ort für die Angestellten schafft.

left: Floor plan level 15_ Lounge space level 10_ Informal breakout space level 14. right: View from level 17_ View from reception_The long table, level 16_ Six person meeting room.
links: Grundriss 15. Etage_Loungebereich 10. Etage_Informeller Breakout-Space 14. Etage. rechts: Blick von der 17. Etage_Blick von der Rezeption_Der lange Tisch, 16. Etage_Besprechungsraum für sechs Personen.

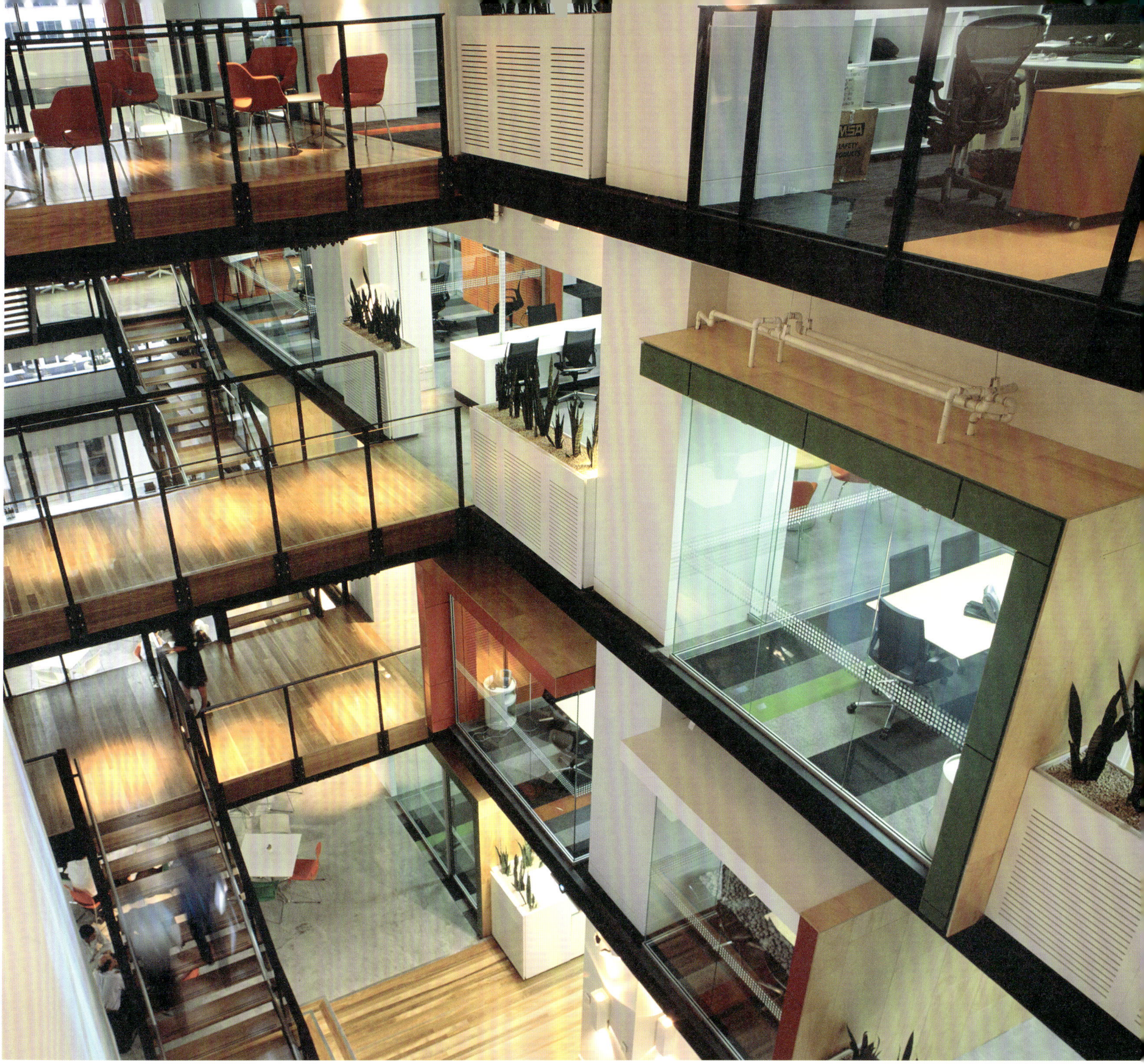

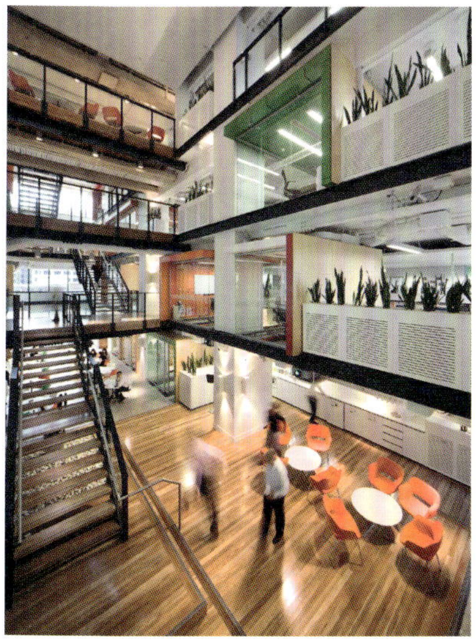

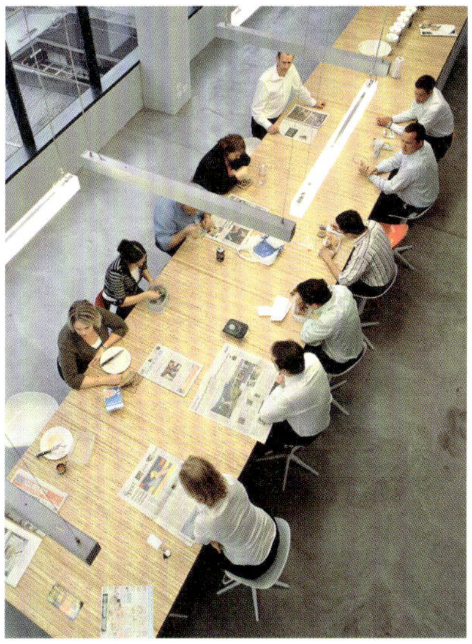

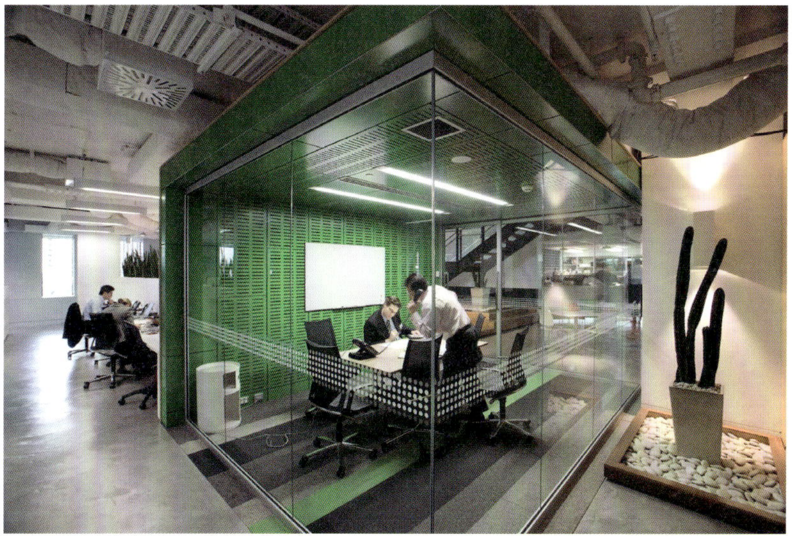

INDEX

ARCHITECTS ARCHITEKTEN

100%interior Sylvia Leydecker	www.100interior.de	256
3c+t Capolei Cavalli Architects	www.capoleicavalli.it	290
8A Architects	www.8aa.nl	22
Adamson Associates	www.adamson-associates.com	422
alcolea+tárrago arquitectos	www.alcoleatarrago.com	384
Anin · Jeromin · Fitilidis & Partner	www.ajf.de	178
Architektur Consult ZT GmbH	www.archconsult.com	46, 54
Arquitectonica	www.arquitectonica.com	12, 20, 94, 480
ASP Architekten Schneider Meyer Partner	www.asp-architekten.eu	208
ASP Schweger Assoziierte Gesamtplanung GmbH	www.schweger-architekten.eu	38
AW²	www.aw2.net	88, 100, 102
B&M architects	www.bm-ark.fi	84
Bahl + Partner Architekten BDA	www.bahl.de	156, 158
Bartijn Architecten	www.bartijn.nl	320
Bernardes + Jacobsen Arquitetura	www.bernardesjacobsen.com.br	484
beyer architekten	www.beyerarchitekten.com	240
BFGF Design Studios	www.bfgf.de	188, 192
bhss - architekten gmbh	www.bhss-architekten.com	128
Bofill, Ricardo	www.ricardobofill.com	366
Bogdan & Van Broeck Architects	www.bvbarchitects.com	58
Broekbakema	www.broekbakema.nl	326, 342, 348
BSAA architects	www.bsaa.dk	362
Bucas, Audrius		296
Bucholz McEvoy Architects, Ltd	www.bmcea.com	260, 262, 264
Buciene, Marina		296
Buro II	www.buro2.be	66
BVN Architecture	www.bvn.com.au	502, 504, 506
Camenzind Evolution	www.camenzindevolution.com	400, 404
Andres Carosio Architekten	www.carosio.ch	408
CC arquitectos / Manuel Cervantes Cespedes	www.ccarquitectos.com.mx	434
cepezed architects	www.cepezed.nl	344, 352
Johnson Chou Inc.	www.johnsonchou.com	26
Antonio Citterio and Partners	www.antoniocitterioandpartners.it	278
cma cyrus l moser l architekten	www.cma-arch.de	220
cómo crear historias	www.comocrearhistorias.com	376
Coudamy, Paul	www.paulcoudamy.com	104
Coussée&Goris Architecten	www.coussee-goris.com	42
Dal Bianco, Carlo	www.carlodalbianco.it	266
George Dasic Architects	www.dasic.com	26, 28
Dellekamp, Derek	www.dellekamparq.com	430
Despang Architekten	www.despangarchitekten.de	216
Domenig, Günther	www.domenig.at	54
Egeraat, Erick van	www.erickvanegeraat.com	300
Ensamble Studio	www.ensamble.info	386
Dietmar Feichtinger Architectes	www.feichtingerarchitectes.com	50, 90
fischerarchitekten GmbH & Co. KG	www.fischerarchitekten.de	112
Foster + Partners	www.fosterandpartners.com	454
Fournier-Rojas Arquitectos / FoRo	www.foroarq.net	496
Fox & Fowle Architects	www.fxfowle.com	464
Albert France-Lanord Architects	www.chezalbert.com	394
Fung + Blatt Architects, Inc.	www.fungandblatt.com	438
García-Abril, Antón	www.ensamble.info	386
Lars Gitz Architects	www.larsgitz.dk	72, 74, 78
Glashaus Architekten PSG	www.glashaus-architekten.de	114
Goettsch Partners	www.gpchicago.com	440
GriffnerHaus AG	www.griffner.com	258
Grimshaw Architects	www.grimshaw-architects.com	156
Group A	www.groupa.nl	328, 332
h4a Gessert + Randecker Architekten BDA	www.h4a-architekten.de	226
Hemprich Tophof Architekten	www.hemprichtophof.de	116
Henn Architekten	www.henn.com	228
Herrmann+Bosch Architekten	www.herrmann-bosch.de	212
Hopkins Architects	www.hopkins.co.uk	414
HSH Hoyer Schindele Hirschmüller	www.hsharchitektur.de	118
Huygens, Ben	www.nineoaks.eu	324
i29 interior architects	www.i29.nl	316
Irisarri + Piñera		388
JHK Architecten	www.jhk.nl	334, 356
JSC RA Studija	www.rastudija.com	292
JSWD Architekten	www.jswd-architekten.de	142, 268
Jump studios	www.jump-studios.com	416
Kaiser Schweitzer Architekten	www.kaiserschweitzerarchitekten.de	114
KBNK Architekten GmbH	www.kbnk.de	196
Klein Dytham architecture	www.klein-dytham.com	24
Kohl:Fromme Architekten	www.kohl-fromme.de	132
KPF - Kohn Pedersen Fox Associates	www.kpf.com	456
Kubalux Architekten GmbH	www.kubalux.de	144
La-Hoz Castanys, Rafael de	www.rafaeldelahoz.com	374, 378
LAN Architecture	www.lan-paris.com	110
Lava Architects	www.lav-a.eu	58
Lehanneur, Mathieu	www.mathieulehanneur.com	106
Lemming & Eriksson	www.lemming-eriksson.dk	362
Amanda Levete Architects	www.amandalevetearchitects.com	418
Maki and Associates	www.maki-and-associates.co.jp	30
Meixner Schlüter Wendt Architekten	www.meixner-schlueter-wendt.de	172, 174
Mentjens, Maurice	www.mauricementjens.com	302
merz objektbau	www.merzobjekt.de	242
META Architectuurbureau	www.meta-architectuur.be	62
Meyer en Van Schooten Architecten	www.mvsa.nl	338
Molinari Landi architects		290
C. F. Møller Architects	www.cfmoller.com	70, 76, 80
monovolume architecture + design	www.monovolume.cc	270, 274
Morphogenesis	www.morphogenesis.org	16, 18
Morphosis Architects	www.morphosis.com	96
Mozas+Aguirre arquitectos	www.mozasaguirre.com	392
MVRDV	www.mvrdv.nl	360
nendo	www.nendo.jp	32, 34
Michael Neumann Architecture, LLC	www.mnarch.com	460
Nine Oaks	www.nineoaks.eu	324
Nissen Adams	www.nissenadams.com	420
Ateliers Jean Nouvel	www.jeannouvel.com	36
nps tchoban voss Architekten BDA	www.npstv.de	38, 160
Obersteiner Architekten	www.obersteinerarchitekten.com	250
van den Oever, Zaaijer & Partners architecten	www.oz-p.nl	306
OFIS arhitekti	www.ofis-a.si	364

OTH Ontwerpgroep Trude Hooykaas	www.oth.nl	308
Ott Architekten	www.ott-arch.de	138
Palm-E Arhitektibüroo	www.palm-e.ee	82
Park Associati	www.parkassociati.com	282
PASD Feldmeier + Wrede	www.pasd.de	182, 184
Petzinka Pink Architekten	www.petzinka-pink.de	152, 164, 168
Peyker, Herfried	www.archconsult.com	46
Renzo Piano Building Workshop	www.rpbw.com	422, 464
Pink, Thomas	www.petzinka-pink.de	152, 164, 168
plajer & franz studio	www.plajer-franz.de	232
RCR Arquitectes	www.rcrarquitectes.es	42
Riehle + Partner Architekten	www.riehle-partner.de	222
Rifé, Francesc	www.rife-design.com	286, 370
Rios Clementi Hale Studios	www.rchstudios.com	444, 448
RMAA / Henrique Reinach and Mauricio Mendonça	www.rmaa.com.br	488
RO&AD architecten	www.ro-ad.org	318
Rojkind Arquitectos	www.rojkindarquitectos.com	430
Philippe Samyn and Partners	www.samynandpartners.be	60
sander.hofrichter architekten	www.a-sh.de	254
Saponaro, Filippo		288
Schweger Associated Architects GmbH	www.schweger-architects.eu	204, 234
Schweger, Peter	www.schweger-architects.eu	38, 204, 234
SEHW Architekten Hamburg	www.sehw.de	200
SelgasCano	www.selgascano.com	382
Shubin + Donaldson Architects	www.shubinanddonaldson.com	450, 474
Skidmore, Owings & Merrill LLP	www.som.com	466
Smits + Ramaekers interior architects	www.smitsenramaekers.nl	314
Soriano & Asociados arquitectos	www.federicosoriano.com	368
Splitterwerk	www.splitterwerk.at	48
Iris Steinbeck Architekten	www.irissteinbeck.de	120
Stücheli Architekten	www.stuecheli.ch	396, 410, 412
Studio o+a	www.o-plus-a.com	470
Taller de Arquitectura	www.ricardobofill.com	366
Tchoban, Sergei	www.npstv.de	38, 160
THS	www.ths.de	184
Matteo Thun & Partners	www.matteothun.com	214
Patrick Tighe Architecture	www.tighearchitecture.com	476
Transform	www.transform.dk	362
Triptyque Architecture	www.triptyque.com	492
UNStudio	www.unstudio.com	298
van den Valentyn Architektur	www.vandenvalentyn.com	134, 148
Valode & Pistre architectes	www.valode-et-pistre.com	98, 108
VBMarchitects	www.vbmarchitects.com	58
Rafael Viñoly Architects PC	www.rvapc.com	312
Viola, Marco		288
Vonbock Architekten	www.von-bock.de	124
Wagenknecht Architekten	www.wagenknecht-architekten.com	236
Wirth+Wirth Architects	www.wirth-wirth.ch	398
wma wöhr mieslinger architekten	www.wma-net.de	126
Frederico Zanelato Arquitetos	www.fredericozanelato.com	494
ZieglerBürg, Büro für Gestaltung	www.zieglerbuerg.de	246
Zucchi & Pertners	www.zucchiarchitetti.com	282

PROJECTS PROJEKTE

	3ality Digital	438	e-plus Headquarters	160
	8 Rochefoucauld	100	Facebook Headquarters	470
	10 Hills Place	418	Falcon Headquarters	430
	21 Boisseau	88	Farringdon Buildings	420
	77/32	16	Federation Complex	38
	111 South Wacker	440	Five Boats	156
	118 Elysées	102	Four Elements	
	505 Fifth Avenue	456		164
	Abspannwerk Buchhändler Weg	118	Fraunhofer Building	228
	Administrative Center Bonheiden	58	Frog Queen	48
	Advice House	80	Gelsenwasser AG, Main Administration	178
	AIG Building	26	Generali Tower	98
	Akasaka Office	34	Gennevilliers Logistics Center	90
	Architects Studio	494	Glass Box in the Columns Box	288
	Architectural Association Galicia	388	Google's new EMEA Engineering Hub	404
	Atradius Headquarters	306	Grip Limited	426
	Bank Vontobel Headquarters	410	GSC Offices	466
	Baroda Ventures	448	Hans-Sachs-Haus	182
	Benetton Group	22	Hearst Tower	454
	Binder Woodcenter	214	Hitachi Power Office	158
	BISAZZA Headquarters	266	Hugo Boss Headquarters	222
	Blaas General Partnership	270	Hydraulx	474
	BMW High Rise Premises, Revitalization	234	Ideenbotschaft	168
	BMW Office Building	232	Imtech Headquarters	242
	Bösl Medizintechnik GmbH	112	Indret	370
	Brainpark III, Office	326	Innova	384
	Brand New School	450	International Consultancy	236
	Caballero Fabriek	332	Johanniscontor	196
	Cardboard Office	104	Joker Tourism, Head Office	62
	Cardboard Office for Scherpontwerp	318	Juwi Holding Corporate Headquarters	258
	CBS Building	28	Kayac	24
	Centre "1000", Office	292	Kraanspoor	308
	Challenger Workplace	506	Krogmann Headquarters	216
	Cinetic Office Building	108	Kropman, Office	348
	City Municipality	364	La Defense, Offices	298
	Clariant Spengler Flexible Office	398	Van der Laat & Jiménez Office Building	496
	CMB Headquarters Office	290	LaboBrain	106
	Cocoon – Google Office Headquarters	400	Lamellenhaus	152
	Comm2	78	Landmark East	12
	Company Headquarters	110	Larchmont Office	444
	Constantin Höfe	142	LG European Design Centre	416
	De Cope Utrecht, Parking and Offices	356	Limerick County Council Headquarters	260
	Corporate Office for India Glycols	18	Loducca Agency	492
	Corporativo Frexport	434	London Bridge Tower, The	422
	Daimler Chrysler Marketing Office	116	Mahler 4 Office Tower	312
	De Kuyper Royal Distillers	342	Meguro Office	32
	deBrug / deKade Unilever Rotterdam	334	Meistri Office Building	82
	Deutscher Caritasverband e. V.	124	Menara Karya	20
	Difrax Head Office	314	MFT Office	296
	DnB NOR Headquarters	360	Mobimo Verwaltungs AG Headquarters	396
	Dock 2.0	172	C. F. Møller Architects Head Office	70
	Doha High Rise Office Building	36	Monastery St. Alfons	114
	Edge, The	42	Moving Picture Company	476
	Erick van Egeraat Office Tower	300	MPM, Agência de Publicidade	484
	EnBW Center Oberschwaben	126	Mutter	192
	Ermenegildo Zegna, New Headquarters	278	Mysterious Story of the Garden that Produces Water, The	376
	Euro Space Center at Libin-Transinne	60	National@Docklands	502
	Exaltis Tower	94	Navile Tre	268

NDR Radio Construction Phase 1+2	204
Nedap Groenlo	320
Michael Neumann Architecture, Office	460
New York Times Building, The	464
Ofecomes, Spanish Foreign Trade Office	286
Office Building at St. Kunibert	148
Office Building Bonn-Lengsdorf	132
Office Building Grabenstraße	46
Office Building Große Elbstraße	200
Orco Germany	120
Outlook, The	344
O-Zone, Oracle Headquarters	72
Parclogistic ILLA-B1	366
Phare Tower	96
Pionen – White Mountain	394
Portaali Business Park	84
Post Panic Amsterdam	302
Public Order Office Frankfurt	174
Q-Cells Headquarters	128
Recycled Office	316
Red Rabbit Werbeagentur GmbH	188
Rheinau Art Office	144
Roma Forum	138
Rotho Blaas Limited Company	274
Sabic Europe Head Office	328
SAM Headquarters	408
Samas	256
SAP Building Galway	262
Sarasota Herald-Tribune Headquarters	480
Savings Bank Headquarters	392
Schattdecor AG Headquarters	250
Schwarzspringer, Advertising Agency	246
SGAE Central Office	386
SILO4plus5	240
Souza, Cescon, Barrieu e Flesch	488
Statistisches Bundesamt, Renovation	254
Stockland Head Office	504
Studio in Green	382
Supertanker, Addition of Stories	412
Technology Center Munich MTZ	226
Telefonica's District C	378
THS, Administration Building	184
Tiziano 32 Headquarters	282
Torre Laminar	368
Torres de Hércules	374
TV Asahi	30
T-Center St. Marx	54
T-home Campus	134
Urban Energy	362
Vanhaerents Torhout, Office	66
VGH Warmbüchenquartier	208
Visser Groen	324
Vitus Bering Innovation Park	76
Voestalpine Stahl GmbH	50
Volksbank Karlsruhe Headquarters	212
Weißliliengasse 7	220
The Wellcome Trust Headquarters	414
Westmeath County Council Headquarters	264
Westraven	352
World Health Organisation	74
Van der Zwan & Zn., Office	338